SUBJECTS OF QUR'ÃN

ZAHID MALIK

KITAB BHAVAN
NEW DELHI-110002

Kitab Bhavan
Publishers, Distributors, Exporters & Importers
1784, Kalan Mahal, Darya Ganj
New Delhi - 1100 02 (India)

Phone : (91-11) 23277392/93, 23274686, 30906494
website : www.kitabbhavan.com
Email : nasri@vsnl.com
Fax : (91-11) 23263383

First Edition 1988
IInd Reprinted 1998
IIIrd Reprinted 2006

ISBN : 81-7151-254-2
Code No. : S00080

Published in India by :
Nusrat Ali Nasri for Kitab Bhavan
1784, Kalan Mahal, Darya Ganj
New Delhi - 1100 02 [India]

Printed in India at :
Nice Printing Press
Khureji Khas, Delhi-110051

بسم الله الرحمن الرحيم

أفلا يتدبرون القرآن

أم على قلوب أقفالها

(47:24)

Do they not then
Earnestly seek to
Understand
The Qur'an, or are
Their hearts locked up
By them?

Contents

Foreword

The publication of Mr. Zahid Malik's thematic and subject-wise compilation of the verses of the Holy Qur'an in Urdu in 1980 was acclaimed as an important contribution to Islamic scholarship and as an invaluable source of reference. The fact that despite his numerous preoccupations, Mr. Zahid Malik has been able to render this work into English is a manifestation of his deep commitment to reach a much wider readership.

The Holy Qur'an contains divine injunctions concerning the behaviour and actions of human beings and is in fact a complete code of life and is valid for all generations, times and places. That is why interpretation and explanation of the verses of the Qur'an has been one of the oldest fields of Islamic scholarship. The works of interpretation (*Tafsir*) of eminent scholars of Islam highlight and elaborate the teachings of the Qur'an. However, these works of interpretation mostly follow the order in which the verses of the Holy Book have been arranged. There was, as such, an urgent need for a thematic index which would enable easy and quick reference to the text of the different verses of the Qur'an pertaining to the same subject. The original Arabic text is accompanied by English translation based on acknowledged works of translation. He deserves a well-earned tribute for this major effort.

The book is a valuable addition to the existing works of this nature and would be of great assistance to the general readers and scholars alike.

Syed Sharifuddin Pirzada
Secretary General
Organization of Islamic Conferences

Introduction

The present book embodies an earnest effort by its learned editor, Mr. Zahid Malik, to present a comprehensive and an exhaustive survey of several themes with which the Qur'an deals. It is designed to help the writer and thinker on the character and content and meaning of the Holy Book to get at the specific passage or the verse in order that he can see it in the context of similar passages or verses spread out in the text of the Qur'an. The aim of the exercise is to view it in its totality and when seen thus, the resulting impression would tend to show that the Qur'an is free from any internal contradictions. Further such a way of looking at the various *Ayats* of the Qur'an would deepen the reader's understanding to an extent that what appeared to be controversial verses at first sight form a body of coherent, self-consistent and complete exposition of the subject-matter with which they deal. The superficial view that is often taken is that the arrangement of the various verses of the Qur'an is unscientific, in that diverse themes are dealt with in disconnected, disjointed and desultory manner. This view, in the light of modern research, is giving way to the perception that there is a serious purpose which lies at the back of the specific Quranic mode of presenting the revealed truth in a verbal form. The arrangement of verses to begin with invites and inevitably compels the reader to look at the Qur'an steadily and regard it as a whole.

Despite the fact that the Qur'an as a whole is a magnificent articulation of the revealed word of God, it becomes necessary to compile publications like the present one to supplement the conventional *tafsirs* (commentaries) of the Qur'an, to indicate the exact placement of its verses by giving copious references to the chapter and verse of the various statements contained in the Qur'an concerning a particular theme just to facilitate the task of readily having access to all it has to say on a particular subject. A great deal of effort is required to ordinarily locate a particular verse in the Qur'an. The present book makes it possible for a research student to get at all the relevant verses of the Qur'an connected with a particular topic, and wherever possible to support them by cross references to the literature on *Hadith* so that no important utterance either in the Qur'an or of the Prophet excapes notice. Sometimes, somehow, I have myself found it difficult in my own encounter with the Holy Writ to get at the particular passage or verse I have in mind but which I vaguely seem to have read before, and this involves expenditure of a great deal of time before I am able to discover precisely what I am keen to know. Meditation upon a particular theme of the Qur'an gets interrupted unless you have available some aid outside its text to enable you readily to have access to all the relevant textual material. The modern scholar is much pressed for time, if only because things are progressively happening at ever-increasing pace. As we know, the computer has already arrived on the scene and I have no doubt someone by now has analysed the Quranic themes and programmed the computer to respond to any specific question that may be addressed to it for getting copious references to the various possible answers concerning certain aspects of the Quranic topics. But be the facilities that computerisation of the Qur'an may yield, I personally think that books like *Mazamin-e-Qur'an-e-Hakim* published by the present editor will continue to be indispensable for the scholars and thinkers interested in understanding the grandeur, authority and sanctity of our sacred literature.

Mr. Zahid Malik has done well to identify the importat themes and with painstaking care has brought them in sharp focus so that diverse, relevant and pertinent *Ayats* of the Qur'an and cross references to the literature of the *Hadith* can be spotted in the shortest possible time. Judged by any standard, the quality of work that has been put into the compiling of the present reference book is superb. It is free from any lacuna or inaccuracy. Its presentation in English language will, I have no doubt, capture the attention of the worldwide scholarship and help it to probe into the variegated facets of the text of the Qur'an in order to be able to understand what it has to say on any conceivable question. There are no doubt various books which have attempted to do the same, but I think the performance of the learned editor of the present book is much more impressive, even as it is comprehensive and reliable.

I recall that when Mr. Zahid Malik published the earlier compilation in Urdu I wrote him as follows:

> "You have undertaken and completed this work as a service to the students of the Holy Qur'an, and Allah in His mercy has enabled you to have done it with remarkable success. It is your humility, coupled with the great effort you have put in, which has lent the work its real quality."

These words have now acquired even greater meaning with the compilation of this monumental work in Enlgish, and Mr. Zahid Malik's labour of love must evoke the greatest admiration of those who will benefit from its contents.

Allah Bakhsh K. Brohi
Chairman
National Hijra Council of Pakistan

Islamabad
July 8, 1987

Preface

> *"Allah raises some people to glory because they translate Quranic teachings into practice, while razes others to the ground because they flout the principles of the Qur'an."*
>
> *Umar al-Faruq.*

As most Muslims do, I begin my day with recitation of the Holy Qur'an. Though the majesty of the text and its matchless rhythm are themselves absorbing, I, as enjoined by the Book, try to seek its meaning as well. The Qur'an claims that it is a book of guidance. It is truly so. Yet I have often found it difficult to obtain the Quranic guidance on a particular problem. For instance, answer to the question of elections was not to be easily located in the Qur'an. Even teachings about matters such as morality, worship, marriage and a variety of other issues are not found in one place.

There is no doubt in my mind that the Holy Qur'an as a book of guidance, must contain injunctions on all matters, spiritual as well as temporal. Nevertheless, it is not a text book of history, philosophy or law. It is uniquely structured and, in the arrangement of its topics, it is not easy to find the matter one is looking for readily under a specific heading. It is not arranged along the customary lines. You have to read the whole book to find the jewels of guidance with which it is exquisitely studded at suitable places. A scholar or a hafiz (one who has memorised the whole of the Qur'an by heart) may locate the relevant verses easily, but for the ordinary reader it is a difficult task.

Naturally, I started looking for guide books which classified the teachings of the Qur'an according to subjects, or where the injunctions could be found alphabetically arranged. I was quite sure that such books existed. The more I looked for them the more was I amazed to find that no proper attention has been paid to this basic requirement. Concordances and indices wherein every word occurring in the Qur'an has been located are undoubtedly available. They are a praiseworthy effort. But mine was quite a different quest. I was not looking for a particular word or verse in the Qur'an. I was in fact in search of an idea or a subject. My query was what the Qur'an said on a certain topic.

Then I went round putting this question to persons who had specialised in Quranic studies. I consulted scholars of Islamiat. I discussed my predicament with men of letters and learning. More often than not they expressed the same amazement which I did: first, they would refer to certain books which they believed could answer my question, then admit their helplessness. The need for such a book was felt by all and a consensus started building up. Then finally, the moment of decision came. I resolved to take up this project myself.

It is my firm belief that the present century is the century of the revival of Islam; the re-awakening of Muslims. This is not merely a political revival. It is a total and universal re-awakening. To make it truly successful we shall have to go back to the original source of Islam, i.e. the Qur'an.

As Muslims, we believe in the unity of mankind and of the universe. This unity rests upon the truth that Allah alone is the Creator and Sustainer of this universe. In His utmost mercy He has bestowed upon man the highest dignity by choosing him as His vicegerent on earth. As a deputy of Allah, man was in constant need of instruction and guidance from Him. Revelation was the answer to his needs and craving. Hence a glorious series of revelations. Among the revealed books, we know of Taurat (Torah), Zabur (Pslams of David), Injil (the Bible) and the Holy Qur'an. The first three are found now bound together in the Bible. The Qur'an maintains a separate entity and is the final in the series.

Being the last revelation, the Qur'an must naturally contain all the basic principles and instructions man needs for the fulfilment of his destiny. It must have answers to all the questions man faces. Since it is a book for all time, it is brief, yet comprehensive; concise, yet lucid. In point of fact it is not merely a collection of prayers and wishes; it is a revolutionary mandate. History bears testimony to the fact that the Qur'an brought about an unprecedented revolution among the people of the desert of Arabia under the leadership of Prophet Muhammad (PBUH). The society that the Qur'an established set the ideals for generations to come. The mind that the Qur'an built enabled humanity to conquer nature rather than be a slave to it. It was through these teachings that an ideal society came into being in Makkah, which flowered to full bloom in Medina. All of a sudden the impact of the Qur'an began to be felt in lands near and distant as far as the Indian sub-continent, Far East Asia and the northernmost area of Europe which had been living mostly under unenlightened conditions. The light of civilization began to penetrate the enveloping gloom.

The impact continued to grow stronger, and eventually the forteenth and fifteenth centuries saw an explosion of knowledge and freedom in Europe. The origin of this massive intellectual activity certainly goes back to Islam. The European nations had eagerly followed the trail blazed by Islamic learning. No false pride or prejudice barred them from benefitting from Islamic thought. Discoveries, inventions, exploration, were the hallmark of these centuries. A new era had dawned. New vistas had opened out.

The light of the Qur'an was shining all over Europe. It closed its doors upon none. It was an open book even for those who were not Muslims. Being a revelation from the All Transcendent, it transcended all such discrimination. Its message was not limited to Muslims. It addressed itself to the whole of mankind. It guided all those who came to seek the truth. When Muslims under the impace of alien heresies drifted away from the Book, the divine light receded into distance. But now when Islam's resilience is again in evidence with a positive interest in science and technology, together with a reinvigorated faith in Islamic tradition, Muslims are recovering from the centuries-old lethargy. In this process however, Muslims have a gnawing feeling that something has gone wrong with them. They feel something is missing in their lives.

Muslims are not alone in this feeling. Mankind in general is becoming aware of the emptiness of modern life. All values of life have lost their meaning. Life has come to mean something mechanical.

There could be many reasons for this hollowness, namely over-mechanization, breakdown of human relationships, man's rupture with nature, the ever-expanding frontiers of knowledge, the frustration of the æsthetic and materialistic value system. But one thing is obvious. Modern scientific progress has left man confused.

Man, to his frustration, has now realised that the value system that had grown out of socio-economic revolution during the last centuries is no more compatible with the demands of modern times. A total reconstruction of these value systems is the fundamental need of the time.

After a lengthy stagnation, Muslims are waking up, no doubt. But things have radically changed during their period of torpor. They are a bewildered people now. They have to make up for the loss. They have to fill a number of gaps.

Looking back at the fourteen hundred years of Islam one can say without hesitation that the mainspring of Muslim thought and culture has been the Holy Qur'an. It has been, and still is, the foundation and the mainstay of Islamic life. Not only does the Qur'an re-establish man's relationship with his Creator, who is Omniscient, Merciful and Compassionate, but provides also a guidance on all the questions, whether they touch man's life in Africa or Europe. The Qur'an stimulated human interest in the studies of nature and the universe. It created an urge for knowledge; gave man dignity and self-confidence. The revolution in human outlook provided by the Qur'an had deeply engaged the attention of Muslims as well as non-Muslims. Its translation into almost all the languages of the world is, in fact, man's tribute to its eternal wisdom.

Nevertheless, during the last two centuries Muslims regrettably have not paid as much attention to the Quranic studies as they had done in the past. One notes with distress that today the minds and the hearts of the great majority of Muslims have very little rapport with the Qur'an. Today in view of the expanding frontiers of knowledge the intellectual limitations of man are becoming more and more pronounced. Amidst the glitter of material wealth and progress man's spiritual poverty is becoming painfully evident. Man's moral cravings are seeking new avenues of expression. The question poses itself: Whither humanity?

The only way out of this impasse is a restoration of man's lines of communication with his source of life – Allah Almighty. The

Qur'an holds the quintessence of Allah's commands and blessings. Muslims have mercifully not lost their contact with the Qur'an completely. The contact does exist. But the approach is not commensurate with the needs of the time. In view of the fundamental changes in socio-economic structures in world societies, and in view of the new angles of looking at things, the rapport with the Qur'an today must be total, inductive, comprehensive, liberal and consistent. The present-day problems demand a radically new approach. So the Qur'an must be studied in its entirety, not in parts. One must consult all the relevant verses on a subject, not one or two verses in isolation.

The demand for such a study is imperative. Nevertheless such a study seems to be confined only to scholars or experts in this field. Majority of people, despite their eagerness and interest, do not have enough mastery of the subject. Most often they have no time to devote to the study. They turn to the Qur'an for immediate problems and they expect ready-made answers. But no answers are readily forthcoming.

Thus there was a need for a book which could present the teachings of the Qur'an topic-wise having them synergetically organised. The idea is not new. A few attempts have been made in this direction, but they are not sufficient to meet the demands. Without intending an exhaustive survey of such works one may classify them into three categories.

First, there are books written on the pattern of dictionaries. In them, the words in the Qur'an have been arranged alphabetically. An analysis of their meaning is also given. Sometimes reference to the verse where the word is used has also been included. Examples of such studies are as follows:

1. Ahmad Shah (A Christian Scholar):
   Miftahul-Qur'an
   (Benaras/1906) in English.

2. Montgomery Watt's "Index", published together with Bell's *Introduction to the Qur'an (Islamic Survey).*

These indices, however, do not fulfil our requirements and hence do not come into our purview.

Second, books that have alphabetically arranged the words, letters and the roots mentioned in the Quranic verses. The related verses are listed under these words. Methods to refer to the Quranic verses differ widely. Some quote a part of the verse, the others refer to the surah and the number of the verse or to the number of the part (*ruku*). Examples of such studies are as follows:

1. Flugel:
   Concordantial Corani Arabicæ (Published in 1842).

2. *Mujumul-Furqan* (Ferozepur, 1907): An Urdu translation of the above.

3. Mawlavi Faqirullah:
   Mujum al-Furqan Al-Jadid (Lahore, 1331 A.H.)

4. Kazim Beg:
   Miftah Munuz al-Qur'an (Istanbul – Lahore edition, 1937).

5. Muhammad Fu'ad Abd al-Baqi:
   Al-Mu'jam al-Mufahras li Alfaz al-Qur'an al-Karim (Cairo, 1378 A.H.). Based on Flugel's work.

The fifth one is more widely used. Similarly, *Fath Al-Rahman* and *Tartib-i-Ziba* are also in common use.

This second category too does not sufficiently solve the problems of a layman. These books are helpful if one is searching for the precise location of a specific verse in the Qur'an. Since the general arrangement is not subject-wise, it may not help a person who is looking for the teachings of the Qur'an on a particular topic.

Thirdly, there are books which have arranged Quranic verses according to subjects. Here we are not referring to certain translations of the Qur'an such as those of Mohammad Marmaduke Pickthall, Abdullah Yusuf Ali and others who have added an appendix of selective subjects to their works. Following are examples:

1. Jules la Beaume:
   Le Koran Analyse.

2. Edward Montet:
   Supplement to above.

3. Muhammad Fu'ad Abd al-Baqi:
   Tafsil Ayat al-Qur'an al-Hakim. Arabic version of the above two works (Cairo, 1935).

4. Mumtaz Ali:
Tafsil Al-Bayan fi Maqasid al-Qur'an (Lahore, 1348 A.H.).

5. M. Azizud Din:
Riyazul Qur'an (Lahore, 1929).

6. M. Faris Barakat:
Al Murshid ila Ayat al-Qur'an al-Karim (Damascus, 1957).

7. M. Waheeduzzaman:
Tabwibul Qur'an (Lahore, n.d.).

8. Masum Ali Subzwari:
Index Qur'an (Karachi, n.d.).

9. Maulana Maududi:
Tafhimul Qur'an.

10. G.A. Pervez:
Tabwibul Qur'an.

Although much effort has been put in, most of these works do not precisely answer our needs. They cover very few subjects. Largely their subject lists fail to include the topics in which the modern man is interested. Moreover, they have a different focus. Some concentrate on theological and historical subjects and others on purely legal matters. Modern man faces a moral crisis. He is looking for guidance on moral issues which trouble his mind. Some of these indices are actually appendices to exegetical works. They do not make any distinction between the actual Quranic text and the matters discussed in the commentary. They are largely lists of words mentioned in the Qur'an. One of these works consists of an exhaustive index but does not give the text of the Qur'an or translation of the verse, it only gives a gist of the meaning of the verse. On the whole, almost all of these indices leave it to the reader to search for original text. They do not serve as a guide which should not only classify the subjects of the Qur'an but should also provide all the texts on those subjects for the convenience of the reader in one volume, rather than providing reference to verses at different places in the Holy Book.

Such were my conclusions after long discussions with many scholars. My preliminary studies of the problem confirmed the general inadequacy of the earlier works. Hence I thought that I should make an effort in this behalf and seek help from scholars of repute. I therefore, consulted eminent scholars like Mr. A.K. Brohi, philosopher and jurist of international repute, Justice Dr. Tanzil-ur-Rahman, then Chairman of the Council of Islamic Ideology, and Hakim Mohammad Said, Chairman, Hamdard Foundation. I must acknowledge that each one of them encouraged me and gave valuable guidance. I am also indebted to my scholar friends; Dr. Aminullah Vaseer, Dr. Hafiz Muhammad Yunus, Dr. Muhammad Khalid Musud, Mr. Zaheeruddin Barlas and Hafiz Wasi-ul-Hasan Ansari to whom I extend my sincerest thanks.

My particular thanks are due to Hafiz Wasi-ul-Hasan Ansari who was a constant help during the long period undertaken by the compilation of this volume. He has a keen sense of detail and his knowledge of the Qur'an was invaluable.

During the first stage of the planning, all the availabe material on the indices of the Qur'an was surveyed. Notes were taken and contents were analysed. A method was developed to record and sift the information already available. This stage took a few months. In the second stage, I began scanning the Qur'an. I studied each verse and prepared individual cards for the subjects covered in that particular verse. This work took me almost four years.

Excluding theological, historical and other such topics, I selected more than 800 subjects which are of immediate relevance to the needs of modern man. In order to reduce repetition and also to provide the essence of the teachings of the Qur'an, only the key verses have been given in full, along with their translation. References to all other relevant verses are given in footnotes. Cross references to relevant topics have also been given. Thus a comprehensive view of the Qur'an on a particular point can be obtained easily.

The project was indeed ambitious and its demands colossal. It was a project like computerisation of the Qur'an. It was a challenge, so in that spirit I have done what was humanly possible for me to do. I am glad that my plan has materialised. However, I lay no claim to finality. It is a modest attempt. The scope of improvement is of course not limited. By the grace of God, the book was received by scholars as a "unique and gigantic work" and a "commendable effort". The President of Pakistan, General Mohammad Zia-ul-Haq, felicitated me for the "voluminous and comprehensive research work on Holy Qur'an" noting that "the list of contents is so exhaustive and so well-arranged that one can have very easy access to the various headings of the Holy Qur'an". The national Press praised the work as a "service to the students of the Holy Qur'an" and for its "meticulously designed format that delivers the needed information quickly".

Encouraged by this response, and keeping in view the fact that a similar reference book should be printed in English also for the consumption of the English-knowing public, I undertook a similar project about three years ago. By the grace of Allah, the English edition is now in your hands. I hope that for the modern man who is craving for guidance on matters where his intellect stands confused, this book will go a long way to help him. My belief is that the Qur'an, being an eternal and universal message from God, can again rejuvenate the Muslim intellect and stimulate it once again to play the role that it played for centuries, and should again play in collaboration with the modern mind to make this planet of ours a haven of peace, prosperity and spiritual fulfilment.

I would be failing in my duty as the editor and compiler of this volume if I did not express my gratitude to Mr. A.K. Brohi for prefacing it with his beautifully written Introduction. Mr. Brohi, who passed away recently, was a great scholar and his brief essay is a book in itself.

Two other friends – if indeed they will permit me to address them as such – are Syed Sharifuddin Pirzada and retired Chief Justice Sardar Muhammad Iqbal. Only I know how much I owe to them by way of their encouragement in this most difficult but noble task.

Finally, my gratitude to Mr. Altaf Gauhar whose guidance on many points I found extremely valuable. Mr. Gauhar is a writer of world repute, not only on politics and economics but on religion as well.

Zahid Malik

LIST OF SUBJECTS

A

Subjects			Page
BEATIFIC VISION OF ALLAH			147
BEAUTY AND GRACE			148
BEAUTY OF NATURE		148	
BEDOUIN			149
BEE	See:	Honey	
BEGGARY			151
BELIEF	See:	Faith	
BELIEVERS AND DISBELIEVERS			152
BENEFICENCE			154
BEQUEATH	See:	Will	
BEQUESTS	See:	Will	
BEST COMMUNITY	See:	Muslim Nation	
BESTOWER	See:	Attributes of Allah	
BETRAYAL	See:	Deceit	
BETROTH	See:	*Nikah*	
BIBLE			155
BIGOTRY	See:	Sectarianism	
BIRDS			156
BIRTH	See:	Creation of Man	
BISHOP	See:	Clergy	

Subjects **Page**

C

Subjects			Page
CHURCHDOM	See:	Monasticism	
CIVILITY	See:	Morals	
CLAY AND MUD			173
CLEANLINESS	See:	Purification; *Wadhu*	
CLERGY			174
CLOTHES	See:	Dress	
CLOT	See:	Creation of Man	
CLOUDS			175
CODE OF LIFE	See:	Religion; *Shariah*	
COMMANDS AND PROHIBITIONS			176
COMMERCE	See:	Trade and Commerce	
COMMUNITY	See:	*Ummah*	
COMPANION OF MOSES			178
COMPANIONS OF THE CAVE	See:	Seven Sleepers	
COMPANIONS OF PROPHET MUHAMMAD (PBUH)			180
COMPASSIONATE	See:	Attributes of Allah	
COMPATIBILITY	See:	Incomparability of Qur'an	
COMPULSION IN RELIGION	See:	No Compulsion in Religion	

D

F

Subjects		Page

G

H

Subjects		Page

L

Subjects			Page
		M	
MADINAH			428
MAGIANS			428
MAGIC	See:	Sorcery	
MAHR			429
MAINTENANCE EXPENSES			431
MAKKAH			432
MALEFICENT	See:	Satan	
MALIGN	See:	Slander	
MAN			433
MAN: ALLAH'S VICEGERENT			436
MAN AND WOMAN	See:	Equality in Status of Man and Woman	
MAN'S AUGURY	See:	Scroll of Actions	
MAN'S DIGNITY	See:	Dignity of Man	
MANAT	See:	Names of Idols	
MANKIND			437
MANIFESTO	See:	Islam's Charter	

Subjects			Page
MUTUAL RELATIONS OF MUSLIMS			498

N

P

بسم الله الرحمن الرحيم

In the name of Allah, the Beneficent, the Merciful.

ABROGATION

1. Such of Our revelations as We abrogate or cause to be forgotten, we bring (in place) one better or the like thereof. Knowest thou not that Allah is Able to do all things?

2:106

2. Never sent We a messenger or a prophet before thee but when He recited (the message) Satan proposed (opposition) in respect of that which he recited thereof. But Allah abolisheth that which Satan proposeth. Then Allah establisheth His revelations. Allah is Knower, Wise;

That He may make that which the devil proposeth a temptation for those in whose hearts is a disease, and those whose hearts are hardened— Lo! the evil-doers are in open schism—

And that those who have been given knowledge may know that it is the truth from thy Lord, so that they may believe therein and their hearts may submit humbly unto Him. Lo! Allah verily is guiding those who believe unto a right path.

22:52–54

1. مَا نَنۡسَخۡ مِنۡ اٰيَةٍ اَوۡ نُنۡسِهَا نَاۡتِ بِخَيۡرٍ مِّنۡهَآ
اَوۡ مِثۡلِهَا ؕ اَلَمۡ تَعۡلَمۡ اَنَّ اللّٰهَ عَلٰى كُلِّ شَىۡءٍ قَدِيۡرٌ ﴿۱۰۶﴾

2. وَمَاۤ اَرۡسَلۡنَا مِنۡ قَبۡلِكَ مِنۡ رَّسُوۡلٍ
وَّلَا نَبِىٍّ اِلَّاۤ اِذَا تَمَنّٰٓى اَلۡقَى الشَّيۡطٰنُ
فِىۡۤ اُمۡنِيَّتِهٖ ۚ فَيَنۡسَخُ اللّٰهُ مَا يُلۡقِى
الشَّيۡطٰنُ ثُمَّ يُحۡكِمُ اللّٰهُ اٰيٰتِهٖ ؕ وَ
اللّٰهُ عَلِيۡمٌ حَكِيۡمٌ ﴿۵۲﴾
لِّيَجۡعَلَ مَا يُلۡقِى الشَّيۡطٰنُ فِتۡنَةً لِّلَّذِيۡنَ
فِىۡ قُلُوۡبِهِمۡ مَّرَضٌ وَّالۡقَاسِيَةِ قُلُوۡبُهُمۡ ؕ
وَاِنَّ الظّٰلِمِيۡنَ لَفِىۡ شِقَاقٍۢ بَعِيۡدٍ ﴿۵۳﴾
وَّلِيَعۡلَمَ الَّذِيۡنَ اُوۡتُوا الۡعِلۡمَ اَنَّهُ
الۡحَقُّ مِنۡ رَّبِّكَ فَيُؤۡمِنُوۡا بِهٖ فَتُخۡبِتَ
لَهٗ قُلُوۡبُهُمۡ ؕ وَاِنَّ اللّٰهَ لَهَادِ الَّذِيۡنَ
اٰمَنُوۡۤا اِلٰى صِرَاطٍ مُّسۡتَقِيۡمٍ ﴿۵۴﴾

ABSTINENCE

1. And of mankind is he who would sell himself, seeking the pleasure of Allah; and Allah hath compassion on (His) bondmen.

2:207

2. And if We had decreed for them: Lay down your lives or go forth from your dwellings, but few of them would have done it; though if they did what they are exhorted to do it would be better for them, and more strengthening;

And then We should bestow upon them from Our presence an immense reward,

And should guide them unto a straight path.

4:66–68

3. O ye who believe ! Shall I show you a commerce that will save you from a painful doom?

Ye should believe in Allah and His messenger, and should strive for the cause of Allah with your wealth and your lives. That is better for you, if ye did but know:

He will forgive you your sins and bring you into Gardens underneath which rivers flow, and pleasant dwellings in Gardens of Eden. That is the Supreme triumph.

And (He will give you) another blessing which ye love: help from Allah and present victory. Give good tidings (O Muhammad) to believers.

61:10–13

1. وَمِنَ النَّاسِ مَنْ يَشْرِي نَفْسَهُ ابْتِغَاءَ
مَرْضَاتِ اللَّهِ ۗ وَاللَّهُ رَءُوفٌ بِالْعِبَادِ ﴿٢٠٧﴾

2. وَلَوْ أَنَّا كَتَبْنَا عَلَيْهِمْ أَنِ اقْتُلُوا أَنْفُسَكُمْ
أَوِ اخْرُجُوا مِنْ دِيَارِكُمْ مَا فَعَلُوهُ إِلَّا قَلِيلٌ
مِنْهُمْ ۖ وَلَوْ أَنَّهُمْ فَعَلُوا مَا يُوعَظُونَ بِهِ
لَكَانَ خَيْرًا لَهُمْ وَأَشَدَّ تَثْبِيتًا ﴿٦٦﴾
وَإِذًا لَآتَيْنَاهُمْ مِنْ لَدُنَّا أَجْرًا عَظِيمًا ﴿٦٧﴾
وَلَهَدَيْنَاهُمْ صِرَاطًا مُسْتَقِيمًا ﴿٦٨﴾

3. يَا أَيُّهَا الَّذِينَ آمَنُوا هَلْ أَدُلُّكُمْ عَلَىٰ
تِجَارَةٍ تُنْجِيكُمْ مِنْ عَذَابٍ أَلِيمٍ ﴿١٠﴾
تُؤْمِنُونَ بِاللَّهِ وَرَسُولِهِ وَتُجَاهِدُونَ
فِي سَبِيلِ اللَّهِ بِأَمْوَالِكُمْ وَأَنْفُسِكُمْ ۚ
ذَٰلِكُمْ خَيْرٌ لَكُمْ إِنْ كُنْتُمْ تَعْلَمُونَ ﴿١١﴾
يَغْفِرْ لَكُمْ ذُنُوبَكُمْ وَيُدْخِلْكُمْ
جَنَّاتٍ تَجْرِي مِنْ تَحْتِهَا الْأَنْهَارُ
وَمَسَاكِنَ طَيِّبَةً فِي جَنَّاتِ عَدْنٍ ۚ
ذَٰلِكَ الْفَوْزُ الْعَظِيمُ ﴿١٢﴾
وَأُخْرَىٰ تُحِبُّونَهَا ۖ نَصْرٌ مِنَ اللَّهِ وَ
فَتْحٌ قَرِيبٌ ۗ وَبَشِّرِ الْمُؤْمِنِينَ ﴿١٣﴾

See also: Piety, Sacrifice.

ABUSE

1. Revile not those unto whom they pray beside Allah lest they wrongfully revile Allah through ignorance. Thus unto every nation have We made their deed seem fair. Then unto their Lord is their return, and He will tell them what they used to do.

6:108

2. Those who point at such of the believers as give the alms willingly and such as can find naught to give but their endeavours, and deride them— Allah (Himself) derideth them. Theirs will be a painful doom.

9:79

3. O ye who believe! Let not a folk deride a folk who may be better than they (are), nor let women (deride) women who may be better than they are; neither defame one another, nor insult one another by nicknames. Bad is the name of lewdness after faith. And whoso turneth not in repentance, such are evil doers.

49:11

4. Woe unto every slandering traducer.

104:1

1. وَلَا تَسُبُّوا الَّذِيْنَ يَدْعُوْنَ مِنْ دُوْنِ اللّٰهِ
فَيَسُبُّوا اللّٰهَ عَدْوًا بِغَيْرِ عِلْمٍ ؕ كَذٰلِكَ
زَيَّنَّا لِكُلِّ اُمَّةٍ عَمَلَهُمْ ۪ ثُمَّ اِلٰى رَبِّهِمْ
مَّرْجِعُهُمْ فَيُنَبِّئُهُمْ بِمَا كَانُوْا يَعْمَلُوْنَ ۝

2. اَلَّذِيْنَ يَلْمِزُوْنَ الْمُطَّوِّعِيْنَ مِنَ الْمُؤْمِنِيْنَ
فِي الصَّدَقٰتِ وَالَّذِيْنَ لَا يَجِدُوْنَ اِلَّا
جُهْدَهُمْ فَيَسْخَرُوْنَ مِنْهُمْ ؕ سَخِرَ اللّٰهُ
مِنْهُمْ ۫ وَلَهُمْ عَذَابٌ اَلِيْمٌ ۝٧٩

3. يٰٓاَيُّهَا الَّذِيْنَ اٰمَنُوْا لَا يَسْخَرْ قَوْمٌ
مِّنْ قَوْمٍ عَسٰٓى اَنْ يَّكُوْنُوْا خَيْرًا
مِّنْهُمْ وَلَا نِسَآءٌ مِّنْ نِّسَآءٍ عَسٰٓى
اَنْ يَّكُنَّ خَيْرًا مِّنْهُنَّ ۚ وَلَا تَلْمِزُوْٓا
اَنْفُسَكُمْ وَلَا تَنَابَزُوْا بِالْاَلْقَابِ ؕ
بِئْسَ الِاسْمُ الْفُسُوْقُ بَعْدَ الْاِيْمَانِ ۚ
وَمَنْ لَّمْ يَتُبْ فَاُولٰٓئِكَ هُمُ الظّٰلِمُوْنَ ۝١١

4. وَيْلٌ لِّكُلِّ هُمَزَةٍ لُّمَزَةِ ۝١

○

See also: Bad Habits.

ACCUMULATION OF WEALTH

1. وَالَّذِينَ يَكْنِزُونَ الذَّهَبَ وَالْفِضَّةَ
وَلَا يُنْفِقُونَهَا فِي سَبِيلِ اللَّهِ فَبَشِّرْهُمْ
بِعَذَابٍ أَلِيمٍ ﴿٣٤﴾
يَوْمَ يُحْمَىٰ عَلَيْهَا فِي نَارِ جَهَنَّمَ فَتُكْوَىٰ
بِهَا جِبَاهُهُمْ وَجُنُوبُهُمْ وَظُهُورُهُمْ
هَٰذَا مَا كَنَزْتُمْ لِأَنْفُسِكُمْ فَذُوقُوا
مَا كُنْتُمْ تَكْنِزُونَ ﴿٣٥﴾

1. They who hoard up gold and silver and spend it not in the way of Allah unto them give tidings (O Muhammad) of a painful doom:

On the Day when it will (all) be heated in the fire of hell, and their foreheads and their flanks and their backs will be branded therewith (and it will be said unto them): Here is that which ye hoarded for yourselves. Now taste of what ye used to hoard.

9:34-35

2. وَيْلٌ لِكُلِّ هُمَزَةٍ لُمَزَةٍ ﴿١﴾
الَّذِي جَمَعَ مَالًا وَعَدَّدَهُ ﴿٢﴾
يَحْسَبُ أَنَّ مَالَهُ أَخْلَدَهُ ﴿٣﴾
كَلَّا لَيُنْبَذَنَّ فِي الْحُطَمَةِ ﴿٤﴾
وَمَا أَدْرَاكَ مَا الْحُطَمَةُ ﴿٥﴾
نَارُ اللَّهِ الْمُوقَدَةُ ﴿٦﴾
الَّتِي تَطَّلِعُ عَلَى الْأَفْئِدَةِ ﴿٧﴾
إِنَّهَا عَلَيْهِمْ مُؤْصَدَةٌ ﴿٨﴾
فِي عَمَدٍ مُمَدَّدَةٍ ﴿٩﴾

2. Woe unto every slandering traducer,

Who hath gathered wealth (of this world) and arranged it:

He thinketh that his wealth will render him immortal.

Nay, but verily he will be flung to the Consuming One.

Ah, what will convey unto thee what the Consuming One is!

(It is) the fire of Allah, kindled,

Which leapeth up over the hearts (of men).

Lo! it is closed in on them

In outstretched columns.

104:1-9

See also: Miserliness.

ACTIONS

1. Think not that those who exult in what they have given, and love to be praised for what they have not done—Think not, they are in safety from the doom. A painful doom is theirs.

3:188

2. And whoso doeth good works, whether of male or female, and he (or she) is a believer, such will enter paradise and they will not be wronged the dint in a date-stone.

4:124

3. Then, as for those who believed and did good works, unto them will He pay their wages in full, adding unto them of His bounty; and as for those who were scornful and proud, them will He punish with a painful doom.

And they will not find for them, against Allah, any protecting friend or helper.

4:173–174

4. Whosoever doeth right whether male or female, and is a believer, him verify We shall quicken with good life, and We shall pay them a recompense in proportion to the best of what they used to do.

16:97

5. Say: Shall We inform you who will be the greatest losers by their works?

Those whose effort goeth astray in the life of the world, and yet they reckon that they do good work.

Those are they who disbelieve in the revelations of their Lord and in the meeting with Him. Therefor their works are vain, and on the Day of Resurrection We assign no weight to them.

18:103–105

1. لَا تَحْسَبَنَّ الَّذِيْنَ يَفْرَحُوْنَ بِمَآ اَتَوْا
وَّيُحِبُّوْنَ اَنْ يُّحْمَدُوْا بِمَا لَمْ يَفْعَلُوْا
فَلَا تَحْسَبَنَّهُمْ بِمَفَازَةٍ مِّنَ الْعَذَابِ ۚ
وَلَهُمْ عَذَابٌ اَلِيْمٌ ۝

2. وَمَنْ يَّعْمَلْ مِنَ الصّٰلِحٰتِ مِنْ ذَكَرٍ اَوْ
اُنْثٰى وَهُوَ مُؤْمِنٌ فَاُولٰٓئِكَ يَدْخُلُوْنَ
الْجَنَّةَ وَلَا يُظْلَمُوْنَ نَقِيْرًا ۝

3 فَاَمَّا الَّذِيْنَ اٰمَنُوْا وَعَمِلُوا الصّٰلِحٰتِ
فَيُوَفِّيْهِمْ اُجُوْرَهُمْ وَيَزِيْدُهُمْ مِّنْ
فَضْلِهٖ ۚ وَاَمَّا الَّذِيْنَ اسْتَنْكَفُوْا وَاسْتَكْبَرُوْا
فَيُعَذِّبُهُمْ عَذَابًا اَلِيْمًا ۙ
وَّلَا يَجِدُوْنَ لَهُمْ مِّنْ دُوْنِ اللّٰهِ وَلِيًّا وَّلَا
نَصِيْرًا ۝

4. مَنْ عَمِلَ صَالِحًا مِّنْ ذَكَرٍ اَوْ اُنْثٰى
وَهُوَ مُؤْمِنٌ فَلَنُحْيِيَنَّهٗ حَيٰوةً طَيِّبَةً
وَلَنَجْزِيَنَّهُمْ اَجْرَهُمْ بِاَحْسَنِ مَا
كَانُوْا يَعْمَلُوْنَ ۝

5. قُلْ هَلْ نُنَبِّئُكُمْ بِالْاَخْسَرِيْنَ اَعْمَالًا ۝
اَلَّذِيْنَ ضَلَّ سَعْيُهُمْ فِي الْحَيٰوةِ الدُّنْيَا
وَهُمْ يَحْسَبُوْنَ اَنَّهُمْ يُحْسِنُوْنَ صُنْعًا ۝
اُولٰٓئِكَ الَّذِيْنَ كَفَرُوْا بِاٰيٰتِ رَبِّهِمْ وَلِقَآئِهٖ
فَحَبِطَتْ اَعْمَالُهُمْ فَلَا نُقِيْمُ لَهُمْ يَوْمَ
الْقِيٰمَةِ وَزْنًا ۝

6. Whoso brigeth a good deed, he will have better than the same; while as for him who brigeth an ill deed, those who do ill deeds will be requited only what they did.

28:84

7. And as for those who believe and do good works, We shall remit from them their evil deeds and shall repay them the best that they did.

29:7

ADMONITION

1. And lo! in the cattle there is a lesson for you. We give you to drink of that which is in their bellies, from betwixt the refuse and the blood, pure milk palatable to the drinkers.

16:66

2. And lo! in the cattle there is verily a lesson for you. We give you to drink of that which is in their bellies, and many uses have ye in them, and of them do ye eat;

And on them and on the ship you are carried.

23:21–22

3. Hast thou not seen how Allah wafteth the clouds, then gathereth them, then maketh them layers, and thou seest the rain come forth from between them; He sendeth down from the heaven mountains wherein is hail, and

6. مَنْ جَآءَ بِالْحَسَنَةِ فَلَهٗ خَيْرٌ مِّنْهَا ۚ وَمَنْ
جَآءَ بِالسَّيِّئَةِ فَلَا يُجْزَى الَّذِيْنَ عَمِلُوا
السَّيِّاٰتِ اِلَّا مَا كَانُوْا يَعْمَلُوْنَ ﴿٨٤﴾

7. وَالَّذِيْنَ اٰمَنُوْا وَعَمِلُوا الصّٰلِحٰتِ لَنُكَفِّرَنَّ
عَنْهُمْ سَيِّاٰتِهِمْ وَلَنَجْزِيَنَّهُمْ اَحْسَنَ الَّذِيْ
كَانُوْا يَعْمَلُوْنَ ﴿٧﴾

○

1. وَاِنَّ لَكُمْ فِي الْاَنْعَامِ لَعِبْرَةً ۚ نُسْقِيْكُمْ
مِّمَّا فِيْ بُطُوْنِهٖ مِنْۢ بَيْنِ فَرْثٍ وَّدَمٍ
لَّبَنًا خَالِصًا سَآئِغًا لِّلشّٰرِبِيْنَ ﴿٦٦﴾

2. وَاِنَّ لَكُمْ فِي الْاَنْعَامِ لَعِبْرَةً ۚ نُسْقِيْكُمْ
مِّمَّا فِيْ بُطُوْنِهَا وَلَكُمْ فِيْهَا مَنَافِعُ
كَثِيْرَةٌ وَّمِنْهَا تَاْكُلُوْنَ ﴿٢١﴾
وَعَلَيْهَا وَعَلَى الْفُلْكِ تُحْمَلُوْنَ ﴿٢٢﴾

3. اَلَمْ تَرَ اَنَّ اللّٰهَ يُزْجِيْ سَحَابًا ثُمَّ يُؤَلِّفُ
بَيْنَهٗ ثُمَّ يَجْعَلُهٗ رُكَامًا فَتَرَى الْوَدْقَ
يَخْرُجُ مِنْ خِلٰلِهٖ ۚ وَيُنَزِّلُ مِنَ السَّمَآءِ
مِنْ جِبَالٍ فِيْهَا مِنْۢ بَرَدٍ فَيُصِيْبُ بِهٖ
مَنْ يَّشَآءُ وَيَصْرِفُهٗ عَنْ مَّنْ يَّشَآءُ ۗ
يَكَادُ سَنَا بَرْقِهٖ يَذْهَبُ بِالْاَبْصَارِ ﴿٤٣﴾
يُقَلِّبُ اللّٰهُ الَّيْلَ وَالنَّهَارَ ۗ اِنَّ فِيْ ذٰلِكَ
لَعِبْرَةً لِّاُولِي الْاَبْصَارِ ﴿٤٤﴾

smiteth therewith whom He will, and averteth it from whom He will. The flashing of His lightning all but snatcheth away the sight

Allah causeth the revolution of the day and the night. Lo! herein is indeed a lesson for those who see.

ACTIONS

Ref: 5:9; 13:29; 22:41,56; 29:9,58; 32:17; 39:35; 42:23; 48:29; 103:1-3.

Allah hath created every animal of water. Of them is (a kind) that goeth upon its belly and (a kind) that goeth upon two legs and (a kind) that goeth upon four. Allah createth what He will. Lo! Allah is Able to do all things

Verily We have sent down revelations and explained them. Allah guideth whom He will unto a straight path.

24:43-46

وَاللَّهُ خَلَقَ كُلَّ دَآبَّةٍ مِّنْ مَّآءٍ ۚ
فَمِنْهُمْ مَّنْ يَّمْشِىْ عَلٰى بَطْنِهٖ ۚ وَمِنْهُمْ
مَّنْ يَّمْشِىْ عَلٰى رِجْلَيْنِ ۚ وَمِنْهُمْ مَّنْ
يَّمْشِىْ عَلٰٓى اَرْبَعٍ ۚ يَخْلُقُ اللّٰهُ مَا يَشَآءُ ۚ
اِنَّ اللّٰهَ عَلٰى كُلِّ شَىْءٍ قَدِيْرٌ ﴿٤٥﴾
لَقَدْ اَنْزَلْنَآ اٰيٰتٍ مُّبَيِّنٰتٍ ۚ وَاللّٰهُ يَهْدِىْ
مَنْ يَّشَآءُ اِلٰى صِرَاطٍ مُّسْتَقِيْمٍ ﴿٤٦﴾

ADOPTED SON

1. Allah hath not assigned unto any man two hearts within his body, nor hath He made your wives whom ye declare (to be your mothers) your mothers, nor hath He made those whom ye claim (to be your sons) your sons. This is but a saying of your mouths. But Allah sayeth the truth and He showeth the way.

Proclaim their real parentage. That will be more equitable in the sight of Allah. And if ye know not their fathers, then (they are) your brethren in the faith, and your clients. And there is no sin for you in the mistakes that ye make unintentionally, but what your hearts purpose (that will be a sin for you) Allah is Forgiving, Merciful.

33:4-5

1. ما جعل الله لرجل من قلبين في
جوفه ۚ وما جعل ازواجكم الـئي
تظهرون منهن امهتكم ۚ وما جعل
ادعياءكم ابناءكم ۚ ذلكم قولكم
بافواهكم ۖ والله يقول الحق وهو
يهدي السبيل ①

ادعوهم لابائهم هو اقسط عند
الله ۚ فان لم تعلموا اباءهم فاخوانكم
في الدين ومواليكم ۚ وليس عليكم
جناح فيما اخطاتم به ۙ ولكن ما
تعمدت قلوبكم ۚ وكان الله
غفورا رحيما ②

ADORNMENT

1. O Children of Adam! Look to your adornment at every place of worship, and eat and drink, but be not prodigal. Lo! He loveth not the prodigals.

Say: Who hath forbidden the adornment of Allah which He hath brought forth for His bondmen, and the good things of His providing? Say: Such, on the Day of Resurrection, will be only for those who believed during the life of the world. Thus do We detail Our revelations for people who have knowledge.

7:31-32

2. Restrain thyself along with those who cry unto their Lord at morn and evening, seeking His Countenance; and let not thine eyes overlook them, desiring the pomp of the life of the world; and obey not him whose heart We have made heedless of Our remembrance, who followeth his own lust and whose case hath been abandoned.

18:28

3. Wealth and children are an ornament of life of the world. But the good deeds which endure are better in thy Lord's sight for reward, and better in respect of hope.

18:46

1. يٰبَنِيْٓ اٰدَمَ خُذُوْا زِيْنَتَكُمْ عِنْدَ كُلِّ
مَسْجِدٍ وَّ كُلُوْا وَاشْرَبُوْا وَلَا تُسْرِفُوْا ۚ
اِنَّهٗ لَا يُحِبُّ الْمُسْرِفِيْنَ ﴿٣١﴾

قُلْ مَنْ حَرَّمَ زِيْنَةَ اللّٰهِ الَّتِيْٓ اَخْرَجَ
لِعِبَادِهٖ وَالطَّيِّبٰتِ مِنَ الرِّزْقِ ۭ قُلْ هِيَ
لِلَّذِيْنَ اٰمَنُوْا فِي الْحَيٰوةِ الدُّنْيَا خَالِصَةً
يَّوْمَ الْقِيٰمَةِ ۭ كَذٰلِكَ نُفَصِّلُ الْاٰيٰتِ
لِقَوْمٍ يَّعْلَمُوْنَ ﴿٣٢﴾

2. وَاصْبِرْ نَفْسَكَ مَعَ الَّذِيْنَ يَدْعُوْنَ
رَبَّهُمْ بِالْغَدٰوةِ وَالْعَشِيِّ يُرِيْدُوْنَ
وَجْهَهٗ وَلَا تَعْدُ عَيْنٰكَ عَنْهُمْ ۚ تُرِيْدُ
زِيْنَةَ الْحَيٰوةِ الدُّنْيَا ۚ وَلَا تُطِعْ مَنْ
اَغْفَلْنَا قَلْبَهٗ عَنْ ذِكْرِنَا وَاتَّبَعَ هَوٰىهُ
وَكَانَ اَمْرُهٗ فُرُطًا ﴿٢٨﴾

3. اَلْمَالُ وَالْبَنُوْنَ زِيْنَةُ الْحَيٰوةِ الدُّنْيَا ۚ
وَالْبٰقِيٰتُ الصّٰلِحٰتُ خَيْرٌ عِنْدَ رَبِّكَ
ثَوَابًا وَّخَيْرٌ اَمَلًا ﴿٤٦﴾

4. وَالْقَوَاعِدُ مِنَ النِّسَاۗءِ الّٰتِيْ لَا يَرْجُوْنَ
نِكَاحًا فَلَيْسَ عَلَيْهِنَّ جُنَاحٌ اَنْ يَّضَعْنَ
ثِيَابَهُنَّ غَيْرَ مُتَبَرِّجٰتٍۢ بِزِيْنَةٍ ۭ وَاَنْ
يَّسْتَعْفِفْنَ خَيْرٌ لَّهُنَّ ۭ وَاللّٰهُ سَمِيْعٌ عَلِيْمٌ ﴿٦٠﴾

4. As for women past child-bearing, who have no hope of marriage, it is no sin for them if they discard their (outer) clothing in such a way as not to show adornment. But to refrain is better for them. Allah is Hearer, Knower.

24:60

Ref: 57:20. See also: Ornaments.

AGRICULTURE

1. He it is Who produceth gardens trellised and untrellised, and the date-palm and crops of divers flavour, and the olive and the pomegranate, like and unlike. Eat ye of the fruit thereof when it fruiteth and pay the due thereof upon the harvest day, and be not prodigal. Lo! Allah loveth not the prodigals.

6:141

2. And in the Earth are neighbouring tracts, vineyards and ploughed lands, and date-palms, like and unlike, which are watered with one water. And We have made some of them to excel others in fruit. Lo! herein verily are portents for people who have sense.

13:4

3. He it is Who sendeth down water from the sky, whence ye have drink, and whence are trees on which ye send your beasts to pasture.

Therewith He causeth crops to grow for you, and the olive and the date-palm and grapes and all kinds of fruit. Lo! herein is indeed a portent for people who reflect.

16:10-11

4. Will ye be left secure in that which is here before us,

In gardens and watersprings,

And tilled fields and

1. وَهُوَ الَّذِیْٓ اَنْشَاَ جَنّٰتٍ مَّعْرُوْشٰتٍ وَّغَیْرَ
مَعْرُوْشٰتٍ وَّالنَّخْلَ وَالزَّرْعَ مُخْتَلِفًا
اُكُلُهٗ وَالزَّیْتُوْنَ وَالرُّمَّانَ مُتَشَابِهًا وَّغَیْرَ
مُتَشَابِهٍ ؕ كُلُوْا مِنْ ثَمَرِهٖۤ اِذَاۤ اَثْمَرَ وَ
اٰتُوْا حَقَّهٗ یَوْمَ حَصَادِهٖ ۖ٘ وَلَا تُسْرِفُوْا ؕ
اِنَّهٗ لَا یُحِبُّ الْمُسْرِفِیْنَ ۟

2. وَفِی الْاَرْضِ قِطَعٌ مُّتَجٰوِرٰتٌ وَّجَنّٰتٌ
مِّنْ اَعْنَابٍ وَّزَرْعٌ وَّنَخِیْلٌ صِنْوَانٌ
وَّغَیْرُ صِنْوَانٍ یُّسْقٰی بِمَآءٍ وَّاحِدٍ ۫
وَنُفَضِّلُ بَعْضَهَا عَلٰی بَعْضٍ فِی الْاُكُلِ ؕ
اِنَّ فِیْ ذٰلِكَ لَاٰیٰتٍ لِّقَوْمٍ یَّعْقِلُوْنَ ۝٤

3. هُوَ الَّذِیْٓ اَنْزَلَ مِنَ السَّمَآءِ مَآءً لَّكُمْ
مِّنْهُ شَرَابٌ وَّمِنْهُ شَجَرٌ فِیْهِ تُسِیْمُوْنَ ۝١٠
یُنْۢبِتُ لَكُمْ بِهِ الزَّرْعَ وَالزَّیْتُوْنَ
وَالنَّخِیْلَ وَالْاَعْنَابَ وَمِنْ كُلِّ الثَّمَرٰتِ ؕ
اِنَّ فِیْ ذٰلِكَ لَاٰیَةً لِّقَوْمٍ یَّتَفَكَّرُوْنَ ۝١١

4. اَتُتْرَكُوْنَ فِیْ مَا هٰهُنَآ اٰمِنِیْنَ ۝١٤٦
فِیْ جَنّٰتٍ وَّعُیُوْنٍ ۝١٤٧
وَّزُرُوْعٍ وَّنَخْلٍ طَلْعُهَا هَضِیْمٌ ۝١٤٨

5. اَوَلَمْ یَرَوْا اَنَّا نَسُوْقُ الْمَآءَ اِلَی
الْاَرْضِ الْجُرُزِ فَنُخْرِجُ بِهٖ زَرْعًا
تَاْكُلُ مِنْهُ اَنْعَامُهُمْ وَاَنْفُسُهُمْ ؕ
اَفَلَا یُبْصِرُوْنَ ۝٢٧

heavy-sheathed palm-trees.

26:146-148

5. Have they not seen how We lead the water to the barren land and therewith bring forth crops whereof their cattle eat, and they themselves? Will they not then see?

32:27

6. Hast thou not seen how Allah hath sent down water from the sky and hath caused it to penetrate the earth as water-springs, and afterward thereby produceth crops of divers hues; and afterward they wither and thou seest them turn yellow; then He maketh them chaff. Lo! herein verily is a reminder for men of understanding.

39:21

6. أَلَمْ تَرَ أَنَّ اللّٰهَ أَنْزَلَ مِنَ السَّمَآءِ مَآءً
فَسَلَكَهُ يَنَابِيعَ فِي الْأَرْضِ ثُمَّ يُخْرِجُ بِهِ
زَرْعًا مُّخْتَلِفًا أَلْوَانُهُ ثُمَّ يَهِيجُ فَتَرٰىهُ
مُصْفَرًّا ثُمَّ يَجْعَلُهُ حُطَامًا ۚ إِنَّ فِي ذٰلِكَ
لَذِكْرٰى لِأُولِي الْأَلْبَابِ ﴿٢١﴾

7. Have ye seen that which ye cultivate?

Is it ye who foster it, or are We the Foster?

If We willed, We verily could make it chaff, then would ye cease not to exclaim:

56:63-65

7. أَفَرَءَيْتُمْ مَّا تَحْرُثُونَ ﴿٦٣﴾
ءَأَنْتُمْ تَزْرَعُونَهُ أَمْ نَحْنُ الزّٰرِعُونَ ﴿٦٤﴾
لَوْ نَشَآءُ لَجَعَلْنٰهُ حُطَامًا فَظَلْتُمْ
تَفَكَّهُونَ ﴿٦٥﴾

See also: Rain

ALLAH BEFRIENDS TRUE BELIEVERS

1. Knowest thou not that it is Allah unto Whom belongeth the sovereignty of the heavens and earth; and ye have not, beside Allah, any friend or helper?

2:107

2. Allah is the Protecting Friend of those who believe. He bringeth them out of darkness into light.

2:257

3. Allah knoweth best (who are) your enemies. Allah is sufficient as a Friend, and Allah is sufficient as a Helper.

4:45

4. Your friend can be only Allah; and His messenger and those who believe, who establish worship and pay the poor-due, and bow down (in prayer)

And whoso taketh Allah and His messenger and those who believe for friends (will know that), lo! the party of Allah, they are the victorious.

5:55-56

5. Warn hereby those who fear (because they know) that they will be gathered unto their Lord, for whom there is no protecting friend nor intercessor beside Him, that they may ward off (evil).

6:51

6. Lo! verily the friends of Allah are (those) on whom fear (cometh) not, nor do they grieve:

Those who believe and keep their duty (to Allah),

Theirs are good tidings in the life of the world and in the Hereafter—There is no changing the words of Allah—that is the Supreme Triumph.

10:62-64

1. أَلَمْ تَعْلَمْ أَنَّ اللّٰهَ لَهُ مُلْكُ السَّمٰوٰتِ وَالْأَرْضِ
وَمَا لَكُمْ مِّنْ دُوْنِ اللّٰهِ مِنْ وَّلِيٍّ وَّلَا نَصِيْرٍ ﴿١٠٧﴾

2. اَللّٰهُ وَلِيُّ الَّذِيْنَ اٰمَنُوْا يُخْرِجُهُمْ مِّنَ
الظُّلُمٰتِ إِلَى النُّوْرِ

3. وَاللّٰهُ اَعْلَمُ بِاَعْدَآئِكُمْ ۚ وَكَفٰى بِاللّٰهِ
وَلِيًّا ۙ وَّكَفٰى بِاللّٰهِ نَصِيْرًا ﴿٤٥﴾

4. إِنَّمَا وَلِيُّكُمُ اللّٰهُ وَرَسُوْلُهٗ وَالَّذِيْنَ
اٰمَنُوا الَّذِيْنَ يُقِيْمُوْنَ الصَّلٰوةَ وَيُؤْتُوْنَ
الزَّكٰوةَ وَهُمْ رٰكِعُوْنَ ﴿٥٥﴾
وَمَنْ يَّتَوَلَّ اللّٰهَ وَرَسُوْلَهٗ وَالَّذِيْنَ
اٰمَنُوْا فَاِنَّ حِزْبَ اللّٰهِ هُمُ الْغٰلِبُوْنَ ﴿٥٦﴾

5. وَاَنْذِرْ بِهِ الَّذِيْنَ يَخَافُوْنَ اَنْ يُّحْشَرُوْا
اِلٰى رَبِّهِمْ لَيْسَ لَهُمْ مِّنْ دُوْنِهٖ وَلِيٌّ وَّلَا
شَفِيْعٌ لَّعَلَّهُمْ يَتَّقُوْنَ ﴿٥١﴾

6. اَلَآ اِنَّ اَوْلِيَآءَ اللّٰهِ لَا خَوْفٌ عَلَيْهِمْ
وَلَا هُمْ يَحْزَنُوْنَ ﴿٦٢﴾
اَلَّذِيْنَ اٰمَنُوْا وَكَانُوْا يَتَّقُوْنَ ﴿٦٣﴾
لَهُمُ الْبُشْرٰى فِي الْحَيٰوةِ الدُّنْيَا وَفِي
الْاٰخِرَةِ ۚ لَا تَبْدِيْلَ لِكَلِمٰتِ اللّٰهِ ۚ
ذٰلِكَ هُوَ الْفَوْزُ الْعَظِيْمُ ﴿٦٤﴾

ALLAH IS NOT UNJUST

1. Allah willeth no injustice to (His) creatures.

3:108

2. The likeness of that which they spend in this life of the world is as the likeness of a biting, icy wind which smiteth the harvest of a people who have wronged themselves, and devastateth it. Allah wronged them not, but they did wrong themselves.

3:117

3. This is on account of that which your own hands have sent before (you to the judgment). Allah is no oppressor of (His) bondmen.

3:182

4. Lo! Allah wrongeth not even of the weight of an ant; and if there is a good deed, He will double it and will give (the doer) from His presence an immense reward.

4:40

5. This is because thy Lord destroyeth not the town-ships arbitrarily while their people are unconscious (of the wrong they do).

6:131

6. Lo! Allah wrongeth not mankind in aught; but mankind wrong themselves.

10:44

7. And We task not any soul beyond its scope, and with Us is a Record which

1. وَمَا اللّٰهُ يُرِيْدُ ظُلْمًا لِّلْعٰلَمِيْنَ ○

2. مَثَلُ مَا يُنْفِقُوْنَ فِيْ هٰذِهِ الْحَيٰوةِ الدُّنْيَا
كَمَثَلِ رِيْحٍ فِيْهَا صِرٌّ اَصَابَتْ حَرْثَ
قَوْمٍ ظَلَمُوْٓا اَنْفُسَهُمْ فَاَهْلَكَتْهُ وَمَا ظَلَمَهُمُ
اللّٰهُ وَلٰكِنْ اَنْفُسَهُمْ يَظْلِمُوْنَ ○

3. ذٰلِكَ بِمَا قَدَّمَتْ اَيْدِيْكُمْ وَاَنَّ اللّٰهَ
لَيْسَ بِظَلَّامٍ لِّلْعَبِيْدِ ○

4. اِنَّ اللّٰهَ لَا يَظْلِمُ مِثْقَالَ ذَرَّةٍ وَاِنْ
تَكُ حَسَنَةً يُّضٰعِفْهَا وَيُؤْتِ مِنْ لَّدُنْهُ
اَجْرًا عَظِيْمًا ○

5. ذٰلِكَ اَنْ لَّمْ يَكُنْ رَّبُّكَ مُهْلِكَ الْقُرٰى
بِظُلْمٍ وَّاَهْلُهَا غٰفِلُوْنَ ○

6. اِنَّ اللّٰهَ لَا يَظْلِمُ النَّاسَ شَيْئًا وَّلٰكِنَّ
النَّاسَ اَنْفُسَهُمْ يَظْلِمُوْنَ ○

7. وَلَا نُكَلِّفُ نَفْسًا اِلَّا وُسْعَهَا وَ
لَدَيْنَا كِتٰبٌ يَّنْطِقُ بِالْحَقِّ وَهُمْ
لَا يُظْلَمُوْنَ ○

8. وَخَلَقَ اللّٰهُ السَّمٰوٰتِ وَالْاَرْضَ بِالْحَقِّ
وَلِتُجْزٰى كُلُّ نَفْسٍ بِمَا كَسَبَتْ وَهُمْ
لَا يُظْلَمُوْنَ ○

speaketh the truth, and they will not be wronged.

23:62

8. And Allah hath created the heavens and the earth with truth, and that every soul may be repaid what it hath earned. And they will not be wronged.

45:22

9. And for all there will be ranks from what they do that He may pay them for their deeds! and they will not be wronged.

46:19

9. وَلِكُلٍّ دَرَجٰتٌ مِّمَّا عَمِلُوْا ۚ
وَلِيُوَفِّيَهُمْ اَعْمَالَهُمْ وَهُمْ لَا يُظْلَمُوْنَ ﴿١٩﴾

○

ALLAH'S BOUNTIES

1. That is because Allah never changeth the grace He hath bestowed on any people until they first change that which is in their hearts, and (that is) because Allah is Hearer, Knower.

8:53

1. ذٰلِكَ بِاَنَّ اللّٰهَ لَمْ يَكُ مُغَيِّرًا نِّعْمَةً
اَنْعَمَهَا عَلٰى قَوْمٍ حَتّٰى يُغَيِّرُوْا مَا بِاَنْفُسِهِمْ ۙ
وَاَنَّ اللّٰهَ سَمِيْعٌ عَلِيْمٌ ﴿٥٣﴾

2. And the cattle hath He created, whence ye have warm clothing and uses, and whereof ye eat;

And wherein is beauty

2. وَالْاَنْعَامَ خَلَقَهَا ۚ لَكُمْ فِيْهَا دِفْءٌ
وَّمَنَافِعُ وَمِنْهَا تَاْكُلُوْنَ ﴿٥﴾
وَلَكُمْ فِيْهَا جَمَالٌ حِيْنَ تُرِيْحُوْنَ
وَحِيْنَ تَسْرَحُوْنَ ﴿٦﴾
وَتَحْمِلُ اَثْقَالَكُمْ اِلٰى بَلَدٍ لَّمْ تَكُوْنُوْا
بٰلِغِيْهِ اِلَّا بِشِقِّ الْاَنْفُسِ ۚ اِنَّ رَبَّكُمْ
لَرَءُوْفٌ رَّحِيْمٌ ﴿٧﴾
وَّالْخَيْلَ وَالْبِغَالَ وَالْحَمِيْرَ لِتَرْكَبُوْهَا
وَزِيْنَةً ۚ وَيَخْلُقُ مَا لَا تَعْلَمُوْنَ ﴿٨﴾
وَعَلَى اللّٰهِ قَصْدُ السَّبِيْلِ وَمِنْهَا جَآئِرٌ ۚ
وَلَوْ شَآءَ لَهَدٰىكُمْ اَجْمَعِيْنَ ﴿٩﴾
هُوَ الَّذِيْٓ اَنْزَلَ مِنَ السَّمَآءِ مَآءً لَّكُمْ

ALLAH IS NOT UNJUST

Ref: 2:272,281,286; 3:25,76,117,134,148,159–160; 4:49,124; 5:13,93; 6:161; 8:61; 9:4,71,108; 10:47; 11:103; 16:32,110,128; 17:71; 18:65; 19:60; 20:112; 21:49; 36:55; 40:7; 41:46; 43:69; 49:9; 50:33; 60:8; 65:7.

See also: Principles of Allah's Justice, Responsibility for Actions, Reward.

for you, when ye bring them home, and when ye take them out to pasture.

And they bear your loads for you unto a land ye could not reach save with great trouble to yourselves. Lo! your Lord is Full of Pity, Merciful.

And horses and mules and asses (hath He created) that ye may ride them, and for ornament. And He createth that which ye know not.

And Allah's is the direction of the way, and some (roads) go not straight. And had He willed He would have led you all aright.

He it is Who sendeth down water from the sky, whence ye have drink, and whence are trees on which ye send your beasts to pasture.

Therewith He causeth crops to grow for you, and the olive and the date-palm and grapes and all kinds of fruit. Lo! herein is indeed a portent for people who reflect.

And He hath constrained the night and the day and the sun and the moon to be of service unto you, and the stars are made subservient by His command. Lo! herein indeed are portents for people who have sense.

And whatsoever He hath created for you in the earth of diverse hues, lo! therein is indeed a portent for people who take heed.

And He it is Who hath constrained the sea to be of service that ye eat fresh meat from thence, and bring forth from thence ornaments which ye wear. And thou seest the ships ploughing it that ye

مِنْهُ شَرَابٌ وَمِنْهُ شَجَرٌ فِيهِ تُسِيمُونَ (10)
يُنْبِتُ لَكُمْ بِهِ الزَّرْعَ وَالزَّيْتُونَ
وَالنَّخِيلَ وَالْأَعْنَابَ وَمِنْ كُلِّ الثَّمَرَاتِ
إِنَّ فِي ذَٰلِكَ لَآيَةً لِقَوْمٍ يَتَفَكَّرُونَ (11)
وَسَخَّرَ لَكُمُ اللَّيْلَ وَالنَّهَارَ وَالشَّمْسَ
وَالْقَمَرَ وَالنُّجُومُ مُسَخَّرَاتٌ بِأَمْرِهِ إِنَّ
فِي ذَٰلِكَ لَآيَاتٍ لِقَوْمٍ يَعْقِلُونَ (12)
وَمَا ذَرَأَ لَكُمْ فِي الْأَرْضِ مُخْتَلِفًا أَلْوَانُهُ
إِنَّ فِي ذَٰلِكَ لَآيَةً لِقَوْمٍ يَذَّكَّرُونَ (13)
وَهُوَ الَّذِي سَخَّرَ الْبَحْرَ لِتَأْكُلُوا مِنْهُ
لَحْمًا طَرِيًّا وَتَسْتَخْرِجُوا مِنْهُ حِلْيَةً
تَلْبَسُونَهَا وَتَرَى الْفُلْكَ مَوَاخِرَ فِيهِ
وَلِتَبْتَغُوا مِنْ فَضْلِهِ وَلَعَلَّكُمْ تَشْكُرُونَ (14)
وَأَلْقَىٰ فِي الْأَرْضِ رَوَاسِيَ أَنْ تَمِيدَ
بِكُمْ وَأَنْهَارًا وَسُبُلًا لَعَلَّكُمْ تَهْتَدُونَ (15)
وَعَلَامَاتٍ وَبِالنَّجْمِ هُمْ يَهْتَدُونَ (16)
أَفَمَنْ يَخْلُقُ كَمَنْ لَا يَخْلُقُ أَفَلَا
تَذَكَّرُونَ (17)
وَإِنْ تَعُدُّوا نِعْمَةَ اللَّهِ لَا تُحْصُوهَا
إِنَّ اللَّهَ لَغَفُورٌ رَحِيمٌ (18)

3. وَإِنَّ لَكُمْ فِي الْأَنْعَامِ لَعِبْرَةً نُسْقِيكُمْ
مِمَّا فِي بُطُونِهِ مِنْ بَيْنِ فَرْثٍ وَدَمٍ

(mankind) may seek of His bounty, and that haply ye may give thanks.

And He hath cast into the earth firm hills that it quake not with you, and streams and roads that ye may find a way.

And landmarks (too), and by the star they find a way.

Is He then Who createth as him who createth not? Will ye not then remember?

And if ye would count the favour of Allah ye cannot reckon it. Lo! Allah is indeed Forgiving, Merciful.

16:5-18

3. And lo! in the cattle there is a lesson for you. We give you to drink of that which is in their bellies, from betwixt the refuse and the blood, pure milk palatable to the drinkers.

And of the fruits of the date-palm, and grapes, whence ye derive strong drink and (also) good nourishment. Lo! therein is indeed a portent for people who have sense.

And thy Lord inspired the bee, saying: Choose thou habitations in the hills and in the trees and in that which they thatch;

Then eat of all fruits, and follow the ways of thy Lord, made smooth (for thee). There cometh forth from their bellies a drink diverse

لَبَنًا خَالِصًا سَآئِغًا لِّلشّٰرِبِيْنَ ﴿٦٦﴾

وَمِنْ ثَمَرٰتِ النَّخِيْلِ وَالْاَعْنَابِ
تَتَّخِذُوْنَ مِنْهُ سَكَرًا وَّرِزْقًا حَسَنًا
اِنَّ فِيْ ذٰلِكَ لَاٰيَةً لِّقَوْمٍ يَّعْقِلُوْنَ ﴿٦٧﴾

وَاَوْحٰى رَبُّكَ اِلَى النَّحْلِ اَنِ اتَّخِذِيْ
مِنَ الْجِبَالِ بُيُوْتًا وَّمِنَ الشَّجَرِ
وَمِمَّا يَعْرِشُوْنَ ﴿٦٨﴾

ثُمَّ كُلِيْ مِنْ كُلِّ الثَّمَرٰتِ فَاسْلُكِيْ
سُبُلَ رَبِّكِ ذُلُلًا يَخْرُجُ مِنْ بُطُوْنِهَا
شَرَابٌ مُّخْتَلِفٌ اَلْوَانُهٗ فِيْهِ شِفَآءٌ
لِّلنَّاسِ اِنَّ فِيْ ذٰلِكَ لَاٰيَةً لِّقَوْمٍ يَّتَفَكَّرُوْنَ ﴿٦٩﴾

4. وَاللّٰهُ جَعَلَ لَكُمْ مِّنْ اَنْفُسِكُمْ اَزْوَاجًا
وَّجَعَلَ لَكُمْ مِّنْ اَزْوَاجِكُمْ بَنِيْنَ وَحَفَدَةً
وَّرَزَقَكُمْ مِّنَ الطَّيِّبٰتِ اَفَبِالْبَاطِلِ
يُؤْمِنُوْنَ وَبِنِعْمَتِ اللّٰهِ هُمْ يَكْفُرُوْنَ ﴿٧٢﴾

5. وَاللّٰهُ اَخْرَجَكُمْ مِّنْ بُطُوْنِ اُمَّهٰتِكُمْ لَا
تَعْلَمُوْنَ شَيْئًا وَّجَعَلَ لَكُمُ السَّمْعَ وَالْاَبْصَارَ
وَالْاَفْـِٕدَةَ لَعَلَّكُمْ تَشْكُرُوْنَ ﴿٧٨﴾

اَلَمْ يَرَوْا اِلَى الطَّيْرِ مُسَخَّرٰتٍ فِيْ جَوِّ
السَّمَآءِ مَا يُمْسِكُهُنَّ اِلَّا اللّٰهُ اِنَّ فِيْ
ذٰلِكَ لَاٰيٰتٍ لِّقَوْمٍ يُّؤْمِنُوْنَ ﴿٧٩﴾

of hues, wherein is healing for mankind. Lo! herein is indeed a portent for people who reflect.

16:66-69

4. And Allah hath given you wives of your own kind, and hath given you, from your wives, sons and grandsons, and

hath made provision of good things for you. Is it then in vanity that they believe and in the grace of Allah that they disbelieve?

16:72

5. And Allah brought you forth from the wombs of your mothers knowing nothing, and gave you hearing and sight and hearts that haply ye might give thanks.

Have they not seen the birds obedient in mid-air? None holdeth them save Allah. Lo! herein, verily, are portents for a people who believe.

And Allah hath given you in your houses an abode, and hath given you (also), of the hides of cattle, tent-houses which ye find light (to carry) on the day of migration and on the day of pitching camp; and of their wool and their fur and their hair, caparison and comfort for a while:

And Allah hath given you, of that which He hath created, shelter from the sun; and hath given you places of refuge in the mountains, and hath given you coats to ward off the heat from you, and coats (of armour) to save you from your own foolhardiness. Thus doth He perfect His favours unto you, in order that ye may surrender (unto Him).

Then, if they turn away, thy duty (O Muhammad) is but plain conveyance (of the message).

They know the favour of

وَاللّٰهُ جَعَلَ لَكُمْ مِّنْ بُيُوْتِكُمْ سَكَنًا
وَّجَعَلَ لَكُمْ مِّنْ جُلُوْدِ الْاَنْعَامِ بُيُوْتًا
تَسْتَخِفُّوْنَهَا يَوْمَ ظَعْنِكُمْ وَيَوْمَ اِقَامَتِكُمْ ۙ
وَمِنْ اَصْوَافِهَا وَاَوْبَارِهَا وَاَشْعَارِهَا
اَثَاثًا وَّمَتَاعًا اِلٰى حِيْنٍ ﴿۸۰﴾
وَاللّٰهُ جَعَلَ لَكُمْ مِّمَّا خَلَقَ ظِلٰلًا وَّجَعَلَ
لَكُمْ مِّنَ الْجِبَالِ اَكْنَانًا وَّجَعَلَ لَكُمْ
سَرَابِيْلَ تَقِيْكُمُ الْحَرَّ وَسَرَابِيْلَ تَقِيْكُمْ
بَاْسَكُمْ ؕ كَذٰلِكَ يُتِمُّ نِعْمَتَهٗ عَلَيْكُمْ
لَعَلَّكُمْ تُسْلِمُوْنَ ﴿۸۱﴾
فَاِنْ تَوَلَّوْا فَاِنَّمَا عَلَيْكَ الْبَلٰغُ الْمُبِيْنُ ﴿۸۲﴾
يَعْرِفُوْنَ نِعْمَتَ اللّٰهِ ثُمَّ يُنْكِرُوْنَهَا
وَاَكْثَرُهُمُ الْكٰفِرُوْنَ ﴿۸۳﴾

6. يٰۤاَيُّهَا النَّاسُ اذْكُرُوْا نِعْمَتَ اللّٰهِ عَلَيْكُمْ ؕ
هَلْ مِنْ خَالِقٍ غَيْرُ اللّٰهِ يَرْزُقُكُمْ مِّنَ
السَّمَآءِ وَالْاَرْضِ ؕ لَاۤ اِلٰهَ اِلَّا هُوَ ۖ
فَاَنّٰى تُؤْفَكُوْنَ ﴿۳﴾

7. اَلَمْ تَرَ اَنَّ اللّٰهَ اَنْزَلَ مِنَ السَّمَآءِ مَآءً ۚ
فَاَخْرَجْنَا بِهٖ ثَمَرٰتٍ مُّخْتَلِفًا اَلْوَانُهَا ؕ
وَمِنَ الْجِبَالِ جُدَدٌ بِيْضٌ وَّحُمْرٌ
مُّخْتَلِفٌ اَلْوَانُهَا وَغَرَابِيْبُ سُوْدٌ ﴿۲۷﴾

Allah and then deny it. Most of them are ingrates.

16:78-83

6. O mankind! Remember Allah's grace toward you! Is there any creator other than Allah who provideth for you from the sky and the earth? There is no God save Him. Wither then are ye turned?

35:3

7. Hast thou not seen that Allah causeth water to fall from the sky, and We produce therewith fruit of divers hues; and among the hills are streaks white and red, of divers hues, and (others) raven-black;

And of men and beasts and cattle, in like manner, divers hues? The erudite among His bondmen fear Allah alone. Lo! Allah is Mighty, Forgiving.

35:27–28

8. We verily sent Our messengers with clear proofs, and revealed with them the Scripture and the Balance, that mankind may observe right measure; and He revealed iron, wherein is mighty power and (many) uses for mankind, and that Allah may know him who helpeth Him and His messengers, though unseen. Lo! Allah is Strong, Almighty.

57:25

9. Have We not made the earth an expanse,

And the high hills bulwarks?

And We have created you in pairs,

And have appointed your sleep for repose,

And have appointed the night as a cloak,

And have appointed the day for livelihood.

And We have built above you seven strong heavens,

وَمِنَ النَّاسِ وَالدَّوَآبِّ وَالْاَنْعَامِ
مُخْتَلِفٌ اَلْوَانُهٗ كَذٰلِكَ ۗ اِنَّمَا يَخْشَى
اللّٰهَ مِنْ عِبَادِهِ الْعُلَمٰٓؤُا ۗ اِنَّ اللّٰهَ
عَزِيْزٌ غَفُوْرٌ ﴿٢٨﴾

8. لَقَدْ اَرْسَلْنَا رُسُلَنَا بِالْبَيِّنٰتِ وَ
اَنْزَلْنَا مَعَهُمُ الْكِتٰبَ وَالْمِيْزَانَ لِيَقُوْمَ
النَّاسُ بِالْقِسْطِ ۚ وَاَنْزَلْنَا الْحَدِيْدَ
فِيْهِ بَاْسٌ شَدِيْدٌ وَّمَنَافِعُ لِلنَّاسِ
وَلِيَعْلَمَ اللّٰهُ مَنْ يَّنْصُرُهٗ وَرُسُلَهٗ
بِالْغَيْبِ ۗ اِنَّ اللّٰهَ قَوِيٌّ عَزِيْزٌ ﴿٢٥﴾

9. اَلَمْ نَجْعَلِ الْاَرْضَ مِهٰدًا ﴿٦﴾
وَّالْجِبَالَ اَوْتَادًا ﴿٧﴾
وَّخَلَقْنٰكُمْ اَزْوَاجًا ﴿٨﴾
وَّجَعَلْنَا نَوْمَكُمْ سُبَاتًا ﴿٩﴾
وَّجَعَلْنَا الَّيْلَ لِبَاسًا ﴿١٠﴾
وَّجَعَلْنَا النَّهَارَ مَعَاشًا ﴿١١﴾
وَبَنَيْنَا فَوْقَكُمْ سَبْعًا شِدَادًا ﴿١٢﴾
وَّجَعَلْنَا سِرَاجًا وَّهَّاجًا ﴿١٣﴾
وَّاَنْزَلْنَا مِنَ الْمُعْصِرٰتِ مَآءً ثَجَّاجًا ﴿١٤﴾
لِّنُخْرِجَ بِهٖ حَبًّا وَّنَبَاتًا ﴿١٥﴾
وَّجَنّٰتٍ اَلْفَافًا ﴿١٦﴾

And have appointed a dazzling lamp,

And have sent down from the rainy clouds abundant water,

Thereby to produce grain and plant,

And gardens of thick foliage.

78:6–16

10. Let man consider his food:
How We pour water in showers
Then split the earth in clefts
And cause the grain to grow therein
And grapes and green fodder
And olive-trees and palm-trees
And garden-closes of thick foliage
And fruits and grasses:
Provision for you and your cattle.
80:24–32

10. فَلْيَنظُرِ الْإِنسَانُ إِلَىٰ طَعَامِهِ (٢٤)
أَنَّا صَبَبْنَا الْمَاءَ صَبًّا (٢٥)
ثُمَّ شَقَقْنَا الْأَرْضَ شَقًّا (٢٦)
فَأَنبَتْنَا فِيهَا حَبًّا (٢٧)
وَعِنَبًا وَقَضْبًا (٢٨)
وَزَيْتُونًا وَنَخْلًا (٢٩)
وَحَدَائِقَ غُلْبًا (٣٠)
وَفَاكِهَةً وَأَبًّا (٣١)
مَّتَاعًا لَّكُمْ وَلِأَنْعَامِكُمْ (٣٢)

○

ALLAH'S CHOSEN PEOPLE

1. And do good. Lo! Allah loveth the beneficent.
2:195

2. Truly Allah loveth those who turn unto Him, and loveth those who have a care for cleanness.
2:222

3. Allah loveth the steadfast.
3:146

4. Lo! Allah loveth those who put their trust (in Him)
3:159

5. Lo! Allah loveth the equitable.
5:42

1. وَأَحْسِنُوا ۛ إِنَّ اللَّهَ يُحِبُّ الْمُحْسِنِينَ (١٩٥)

2. إِنَّ اللَّهَ يُحِبُّ التَّوَّابِينَ وَيُحِبُّ الْمُتَطَهِّرِينَ (٢٢٢)

3. وَاللَّهُ يُحِبُّ الصَّابِرِينَ ○

4. إِنَّ اللَّهَ يُحِبُّ الْمُتَوَكِّلِينَ ○

5. إِنَّ اللَّهَ يُحِبُّ الْمُقْسِطِينَ (٤٢)

ALLAH'S BOUNTIES

Ref: 2:25,40,47,122,150,211,231; 3:103,171,174; 5:3,23,114; 7:10,26; 12:6; 14:28; 16:114; 22:63,65; 23:17–22; 27:19,86; 29:67; 31:31; 32:27; 33:9; 36:33–35,41–43; 39:8,21,49; 42:32–33; 49:8; 52:29; 53:55; 54:35; 55:31, 56:63–73; 68:2; 92:19; 93:11.

6. Lo! Allah loveth those who keep their duty
9:7

7. Allah loveth the purifiers.
9:108

8. Lo! Allah loveth those who battle for His cause in ranks, as if they were a solid structure.
61:4

ALLAH'S WILL

1. The Originator of the heavens and the earth! When He decreeth a thing, He saith unto it only: Be! and it is.
2:117

2. Allah giveth without stint to whom He will.
2:212

3. Allah guideth whom He will unto a straight path.
2:213

4. Allah bestoweth His Sovereignty on whom He will. Allah is All-Embracing, All-Knowing.
2:247

5. He giveth wisdom unto whom He will, and he unto whom wisdom is given, he truly hath received abundant good. But none remember except men of understanding.
2:269

6. He it is Who fashioneth you in the wombs as pleaseth Him. There is no God save Him, the Almighty, the Wise.
3:6

6. إِنَّ اللَّهَ يُحِبُّ الْمُتَّقِينَ ﴿٧﴾

7. وَاللَّهُ يُحِبُّ الْمُطَّهِّرِينَ ﴿١٠٨﴾

8. إِنَّ اللَّهَ يُحِبُّ الَّذِينَ يُقَاتِلُونَ فِي
سَبِيلِهِ صَفًّا كَأَنَّهُم بُنْيَانٌ مَّرْصُوصٌ ﴿٤﴾

○

1. بَدِيعُ السَّمٰوٰتِ وَالْأَرْضِ ۖ وَإِذَا قَضَىٰ أَمْرًا
فَإِنَّمَا يَقُولُ لَهُ كُن فَيَكُونُ ﴿١١٧﴾

2. وَاللَّهُ يَرْزُقُ مَن يَشَاءُ بِغَيْرِ حِسَابٍ ﴿٢١٢﴾

3. وَاللَّهُ يَهْدِي مَن يَشَاءُ إِلَىٰ صِرَاطٍ
مُّسْتَقِيمٍ ﴿٢١٣﴾

4. وَاللَّهُ يُؤْتِي مُلْكَهُ مَن يَشَاءُ ۚ وَاللَّهُ
وَاسِعٌ عَلِيمٌ ﴿٢٤٧﴾

5. يُؤْتِي الْحِكْمَةَ مَن يَشَاءُ ۚ وَمَن يُؤْتَ
الْحِكْمَةَ فَقَدْ أُوتِيَ خَيْرًا كَثِيرًا ۗ وَمَا
يَذَّكَّرُ إِلَّا أُولُو الْأَلْبَابِ ﴿٢٦٩﴾

6. هُوَ الَّذِي يُصَوِّرُكُمْ فِي الْأَرْحَامِ كَيْفَ
يَشَاءُ ۚ لَا إِلَٰهَ إِلَّا هُوَ الْعَزِيزُ الْحَكِيمُ ﴿٦﴾

ALLAH'S CHOSEN PEOPLE
See also: People Whom Allah Detests.

7. Say (O Muhammad): Lo! the bounty is in Allah's hand. He bestoweth it on whom He will. Allah is All-Embracing, All-Knowing.

He selecteth for His mercy whom He will. Allah is of Infinite Bounty.

3:73–74

8. Allah would explain to you and guide you by the examples of those who were before you, and would turn to you in mercy. Allah is Knower, Wise.

And Allah would turn to you in mercy; but those who follow vain desires would have you go tremendously astray.

Allah would make the burden light for you, for man was created weak.

4:26-28

9. And whomsoever it is Allah's Will to guide, He expandeth his bosom unto the Surrender, and whomsoever it is His Will to send astray, He maketh his bosom close and narrow as if he were engaged in sheer ascent. Thus Allah layeth ignominy upon those who believe not.

6:125

10. Thy Lord is the Absolute, the Lord of Mercy. If He will, He can remove you and can cause what He will to follow after you, even as He raised you from the seed of other folk.

6:133

7. قل إن الفضل بيد الله يؤتيه
من يشاء والله واسع عليم ۝
يختص برحمته من يشاء والله
ذو الفضل العظيم ۝

8. يريد الله ليبين لكم ويهديكم سنن
الذين من قبلكم ويتوب عليكم
والله عليم حكيم ۝
والله يريد أن يتوب عليكم ويريد الذين
يتبعون الشهوات أن تميلوا ميلا عظيما ۝
يريد الله أن يخفف عنكم وخلق
الإنسان ضعيفا ۝

9. فمن يرد الله أن يهديه يشرح صدره
للإسلام ومن يرد أن يضله يجعل
صدره ضيقا حرجا كأنما يصعد في
السماء كذلك يجعل الله الرجس
على الذين لا يؤمنون ۝

10. وربك الغني ذو الرحمة إن يشأ يذهبكم
ويستخلف من بعدكم ما يشاء كما
أنشأكم من ذرية قوم آخرين ۝

11. وإن يمسسك الله بضر فلا كاشف
له إلا هو وإن يردك بخير فلا
راد لفضله يصيب به من يشاء
من عباده وهو الغفور الرحيم ۝

11. If Allah afflicteth thee with some hurt, there is none who can remove it save Him; and if He desireth good for thee, there is none who can repel His bounty. He striketh with it whom He will of His bondmen. He is the Forgiving, the Merciful.

10:107

12. Lo! thy Lord is Doer of what He will.

11:107

13. Allah effaceth what He will, and establisheth (what He will), and with Him is source of ordinance.

13:39

14. And Our word unto a thing, when We intend it, is only that We say unto it: Be! and it is.

16:40

15. Had Allah willed He could have made you (all) one nation, but He sendeth whom He will astray and guideth whom He will, and ye will indeed be asked of what ye used to do.

16:93

16, And if We willed We could withdraw that which We have revealed unto thee, then wouldst thou find no guardian for thee against Us in respect thereof.

(It is naught) save mercy from thy Lord. Lo! His kindness unto thee was ever great.

17:86–87

17. Thy Lord bringeth to pass what He willeth and choice. Glorified be Allah and Exalted above all that they associate (with Him)!

28:68

18. And if We had so willed, We could have given every soul its guidance, but the word from Me concerning evil doers took effect: that I will fill hell with the jinn and mankind

12. إِنَّ رَبَّكَ فَعَّالٌ لِّمَا يُرِيدُ

13. يَمْحُوا اللَّهُ مَا يَشَاءُ وَيُثْبِتُ ۖ وَعِندَهُ
أُمُّ الْكِتَابِ

14. إِنَّمَا قَوْلُنَا لِشَيْءٍ إِذَا أَرَدْنَاهُ أَن نَّقُولَ
لَهُ كُن فَيَكُونُ

15. وَلَوْ شَاءَ اللَّهُ لَجَعَلَكُمْ أُمَّةً وَاحِدَةً
وَلَٰكِن يُضِلُّ مَن يَشَاءُ وَيَهْدِي مَن
يَشَاءُ ۚ وَلَتُسْأَلُنَّ عَمَّا كُنتُمْ تَعْمَلُونَ

16. وَلَئِن شِئْنَا لَنَذْهَبَنَّ بِالَّذِي أَوْحَيْنَا
إِلَيْكَ ثُمَّ لَا تَجِدُ لَكَ بِهِ عَلَيْنَا وَكِيلًا
إِلَّا رَحْمَةً مِّن رَّبِّكَ ۚ إِنَّ فَضْلَهُ كَانَ
عَلَيْكَ كَبِيرًا

17. وَرَبُّكَ يَخْلُقُ مَا يَشَاءُ وَيَخْتَارُ ۗ مَا
كَانَ لَهُمُ الْخِيَرَةُ ۚ سُبْحَانَ اللَّهِ وَتَعَالَىٰ
عَمَّا يُشْرِكُونَ

18. وَلَوْ شِئْنَا لَآتَيْنَا كُلَّ نَفْسٍ هُدَاهَا
وَلَٰكِنْ حَقَّ الْقَوْلُ مِنِّي لَأَمْلَأَنَّ
جَهَنَّمَ مِنَ الْجِنَّةِ وَالنَّاسِ أَجْمَعِينَ

19. قُلْ مَن ذَا الَّذِي يَعْصِمُكُم مِّنَ اللَّهِ
إِنْ أَرَادَ بِكُمْ سُوءًا أَوْ أَرَادَ بِكُمْ
رَحْمَةً ۚ وَلَا يَجِدُونَ لَهُم مِّن دُونِ
اللَّهِ وَلِيًّا وَلَا نَصِيرًا

together.

32:13

19. Say: Who is he who can preserve you from Allah if He intendeth harm for you, or intendeth mercy for you? They will not find that they have any friend or helper other than Allah.

33:17

20. But His command, when He intendeth a thing, is only that He saith unto it: Be! and it is.

36:82

20. اِنَّمَآ اَمْرُهٗٓ اِذَآ اَرَادَ شَيْـًٔا اَنْ يَّقُوْلَ
لَهٗ كُنْ فَيَكُوْنُ ۝

21. Allah chooseth for Himself whom He will, and guideth unto Himself him who turneth (toward Him).

42:13

21. اَللّٰهُ يَجْتَبِيْٓ اِلَيْهِ مَنْ يَّشَآءُ وَيَهْدِيْٓ
اِلَيْهِ مَنْ يُّنِيْبُ ۝

22. Unto Allah belongeth the Sovereignty of the heavens and the earth. He createth what He will. He bestoweth female (offspring) upon whom He will, and bestoweth male (offspring) upon whom He will;

Or He mingleth them, males and females, and He maketh barren whom He will. Lo! He is Knower, Powerful.

42:49-50

22. لِلّٰهِ مُلْكُ السَّمٰوٰتِ وَالْاَرْضِ ؕ يَخْلُقُ
مَا يَشَآءُ ؕ يَهَبُ لِمَنْ يَّشَآءُ اِنَاثًا
وَّيَهَبُ لِمَنْ يَّشَآءُ الذُّكُوْرَ ۝

اَوْ يُزَوِّجُهُمْ ذُكْرَانًا وَّاِنَاثًا ۚ وَ
يَجْعَلُ مَنْ يَّشَآءُ عَقِيْمًا ؕ اِنَّهٗ
عَلِيْمٌ قَدِيْرٌ ۝

Ref: 2:20,90,105,142,220,251,253,255,261,272; 3:13,26,37,40,47,129,179; 4:47–48,133; 5:6,18,54; 6:39,41,73,111,137,149; 7:89,176,188; 8:6–7; 9:55,85; 10:25,49,99; 11:34,108,118; 13:31; 17:16,54; 22:14–16,18; 24:35,43–45; 25:10,51; 26:4; 28:5,56; 29:21; 30:54; 33:33; 34:9; 35:1,8,16,22; 42:8,27,29; 43:60; 47:4,30; 48:11,14; 57:21,29; 62:4; 74:31,56: 76:28,30–31; 81:29; 87:4–7.

ALMS

1. The likeness of those who spend their wealth in Allah's way is as the likeness of a grain which groweth seven ears, in every ear a hundred grains. Allah giveth increase manifold to whom He will. Allah is All-Embracing, All-Knowing.

Those who spend their wealth for the cause of Allah and afterward make not reproach and injury to follow that which they have spent; their reward is with their Lord and there shall no fear come upon them, neither shall they grieve.

A kind word with forgiveness is better than almsgiving followed by injury. Allah is Absolute, Clement.

O ye who believe! Render not vain your almsgiving by reproach and injury like him who spendeth his wealth only to be seen of men and believeth not in Allah and the Last Day. His likeness is as the likeness of a rock whereon is dust of earth; a rainstorm smiteth it, leaving it smooth and bare. They have no control of aught of that which they have gained. Allah guideth not the disbelieving folk.

And the likeness of those who spend their wealth in search of Allah's pleasure, and for the strengthening of their souls, is as the likeness of a garden on a height. The rainstorm smiteth it and it bringeth forth its fruit two-fold. And if the rainstorm smite it not, then the shower. Allah is Seer of what ye do.

2:261-265

1. مَثَلُ الَّذِينَ يُنفِقُونَ أَمْوَالَهُمْ فِي سَبِيلِ
اللَّهِ كَمَثَلِ حَبَّةٍ أَنبَتَتْ سَبْعَ سَنَابِلَ
فِي كُلِّ سُنبُلَةٍ مِّائَةُ حَبَّةٍ ۗ وَاللَّهُ
يُضَاعِفُ لِمَن يَشَاءُ ۗ وَاللَّهُ وَاسِعٌ عَلِيمٌ ﴿٢٦١﴾
الَّذِينَ يُنفِقُونَ أَمْوَالَهُمْ فِي سَبِيلِ
اللَّهِ ثُمَّ لَا يُتْبِعُونَ مَا أَنفَقُوا مَنًّا وَلَا
أَذًى ۙ لَّهُمْ أَجْرُهُمْ عِندَ رَبِّهِمْ ۚ وَلَا
خَوْفٌ عَلَيْهِمْ وَلَا هُمْ يَحْزَنُونَ ﴿٢٦٢﴾
قَوْلٌ مَّعْرُوفٌ وَمَغْفِرَةٌ خَيْرٌ مِّن صَدَقَةٍ
يَتْبَعُهَا أَذًى ۗ وَاللَّهُ غَنِيٌّ حَلِيمٌ ﴿٢٦٣﴾
يَا أَيُّهَا الَّذِينَ آمَنُوا لَا تُبْطِلُوا صَدَقَاتِكُم
بِالْمَنِّ وَالْأَذَىٰ كَالَّذِي يُنفِقُ مَالَهُ
رِئَاءَ النَّاسِ وَلَا يُؤْمِنُ بِاللَّهِ وَالْيَوْمِ
الْآخِرِ ۖ فَمَثَلُهُ كَمَثَلِ صَفْوَانٍ عَلَيْهِ
تُرَابٌ فَأَصَابَهُ وَابِلٌ فَتَرَكَهُ صَلْدًا ۖ
لَّا يَقْدِرُونَ عَلَىٰ شَيْءٍ مِّمَّا كَسَبُوا ۗ وَاللَّهُ
لَا يَهْدِي الْقَوْمَ الْكَافِرِينَ ﴿٢٦٤﴾
وَمَثَلُ الَّذِينَ يُنفِقُونَ أَمْوَالَهُمُ ابْتِغَاءَ
مَرْضَاتِ اللَّهِ وَتَثْبِيتًا مِّنْ أَنفُسِهِمْ كَمَثَلِ
جَنَّةٍ بِرَبْوَةٍ أَصَابَهَا وَابِلٌ فَآتَتْ أُكُلَهَا
ضِعْفَيْنِ فَإِن لَّمْ يُصِبْهَا وَابِلٌ فَطَلٌّ ۗ
وَاللَّهُ بِمَا تَعْمَلُونَ بَصِيرٌ ﴿٢٦٥﴾

2. If ye publish your almsgiving, it is well, but if ye hide it and give it to the poor, it will be better for you, and will atone for some of your ill-deeds. Allah is Informed of what ye do.

2:271

3. Allah hath blighted usury and made almsgiving fruitful. Allah loveth not the impious and guilty.

2:276

4. The alms are only for the poor and the needy, and those who collect them, and those whose hearts are to be reconciled, and to free the captives and the debtors, and for the cause of Allah, and (for) the wayfarers; a duty imposed by Allah. Allah is Knower, Wise.

9:60

5. Take alms of their wealth, wherewith thou mayst purify them and mayst make them grow, and pray for them. Lo! thy prayer is an assuagement for them. Allah is Hearer, Knower.

Know they not that Allah is He Who accepteth repentance from His bondmen and taketh the alms, and that Allah is He Who is the Relenting, the Merciful.

9:103-104

6. As for man, whenever his Lord trieth him by honouring him, and is gracious unto him, he saith: My Lord honoureth me.

But whenever He trieth him by straitening his means of life, he saith: My Lord despiseth me.

Nay, but ye (for your part) honour not the orphan

And urge not on the feeding of the poor,

2. إِنْ تُبْدُوا الصَّدَقَاتِ فَنِعِمَّا هِيَ ۖ وَإِنْ
تُخْفُوهَا وَتُؤْتُوهَا الْفُقَرَاءَ فَهُوَ خَيْرٌ
لَكُمْ ۚ وَيُكَفِّرُ عَنْكُمْ مِنْ سَيِّئَاتِكُمْ ۗ
وَاللَّهُ بِمَا تَعْمَلُونَ خَبِيرٌ ﴿٢٧١﴾

3. يَمْحَقُ اللَّهُ الرِّبَا وَيُرْبِي الصَّدَقَاتِ ۗ وَاللَّهُ
لَا يُحِبُّ كُلَّ كَفَّارٍ أَثِيمٍ ﴿٢٧٦﴾

4. إِنَّمَا الصَّدَقَاتُ لِلْفُقَرَاءِ وَالْمَسَاكِينِ
وَالْعَامِلِينَ عَلَيْهَا وَالْمُؤَلَّفَةِ قُلُوبُهُمْ
وَفِي الرِّقَابِ وَالْغَارِمِينَ وَفِي سَبِيلِ
اللَّهِ وَابْنِ السَّبِيلِ ۖ فَرِيضَةً مِنَ اللَّهِ ۗ
وَاللَّهُ عَلِيمٌ حَكِيمٌ ﴿٦٠﴾

5. خُذْ مِنْ أَمْوَالِهِمْ صَدَقَةً تُطَهِّرُهُمْ
وَتُزَكِّيهِمْ بِهَا وَصَلِّ عَلَيْهِمْ ۖ إِنَّ صَلَاتَكَ
سَكَنٌ لَهُمْ ۗ وَاللَّهُ سَمِيعٌ عَلِيمٌ ﴿١٠٣﴾
أَلَمْ يَعْلَمُوا أَنَّ اللَّهَ هُوَ يَقْبَلُ التَّوْبَةَ
عَنْ عِبَادِهِ وَيَأْخُذُ الصَّدَقَاتِ وَأَنَّ اللَّهَ
هُوَ التَّوَّابُ الرَّحِيمُ ﴿١٠٤﴾

6. فَأَمَّا الْإِنْسَانُ إِذَا مَا ابْتَلَاهُ رَبُّهُ
فَأَكْرَمَهُ وَنَعَّمَهُ فَيَقُولُ رَبِّي أَكْرَمَنِ ﴿١٥﴾
وَأَمَّا إِذَا مَا ابْتَلَاهُ فَقَدَرَ عَلَيْهِ
رِزْقَهُ فَيَقُولُ رَبِّي أَهَانَنِ ﴿١٦﴾
كَلَّا ۖ بَلْ لَا تُكْرِمُونَ الْيَتِيمَ ﴿١٧﴾
وَلَا تَحَاضُّونَ عَلَىٰ طَعَامِ الْمِسْكِينِ ﴿١٨﴾

And ye devour heritages with devouring greed

And love wealth with abounding love.

89:15-20

وَ تَأْكُلُوْنَ التُّرَاثَ اَكْلًا لَّمًّا ۟

وَّتُحِبُّوْنَ الْمَالَ حُبًّا جَمًّا ۟

7. Hast thou observed him who belieth religion?

That is he who repelleth the orphan?

And urgeth not the feeding of the needy.

107:1–3

7. اَرَءَيْتَ الَّذِيْ يُكَذِّبُ بِالدِّيْنِ ۟

فَذٰلِكَ الَّذِيْ يَدُعُّ الْيَتِيْمَ ۟

وَلَا يَحُضُّ عَلٰى طَعَامِ الْمِسْكِيْنِ ۟

Ref: 3:134; 8:60; 13:22; 16:75; 34:39.

See also: Charity, *Zakat*.

ANGELS

1. And when We said unto the angels: Prostrate yourselves before Adam, they fell prostrate, all save Iblis. He demurred through pride, and so became a disbeliever.

2:34

2. Say (O Muhammad, to mankind): Who is an enemy to Gabriel! For he it is who hath revealed (this Scripture) to thy heart by Allah's leave, confirming that which was (revealed) before it, and a guidance and glad tidings to believers;

Who is an enemy to Allah, and His angels and His messengers, and Gabriel and Michael! Then, lo! Allah (Himself) is an enemy to the disbelievers.

2:97–98

3. O ye who believe! Believe in Allah and His messenger and the Scripture which He hath revealed unto His messenger, and the Scripture which He revealed aforetime. Whoso disbelieveth in Allah and His angels and His scriptures and His messengers and the Last Day, he verily hath wandered far astray.

4:136

4. If thou couldst see how the angels receive those who disbelieve, smiting their faces and their backs and (saying): Taste the punishment of burning!

8:50

5. Allah chooseth from the angels messengers, and (also) from mankind. Lo! Allah is Hearer, Seer.

22:75

6. Say: The angel of death, who hath charge concerning you, will gather you, and afterward unto your Lord ye will be returned.

32:11

1. وَإِذْ قُلْنَا لِلْمَلٰٓئِكَةِ اسْجُدُوا لِاٰدَمَ فَسَجَدُوٓا إِلَّآ
إِبْلِيسَ ۖ أَبٰى وَاسْتَكْبَرَ وَكَانَ مِنَ الْكٰفِرِينَ ﴿٣٤﴾

2. قُلْ مَنْ كَانَ عَدُوًّا لِجِبْرِيلَ فَإِنَّهُۥ نَزَّلَهُۥ
عَلٰى قَلْبِكَ بِإِذْنِ اللّٰهِ مُصَدِّقًا لِمَا بَيْنَ يَدَيْهِ
وَهُدًى وَبُشْرٰى لِلْمُؤْمِنِينَ ﴿٩٧﴾
مَنْ كَانَ عَدُوًّا لِلّٰهِ وَمَلٰٓئِكَتِهِۦ وَرُسُلِهِۦ وَ
جِبْرِيلَ وَمِيكٰلَ فَإِنَّ اللّٰهَ عَدُوٌّ لِلْكٰفِرِينَ ﴿٩٨﴾

3. يٰٓأَيُّهَا الَّذِينَ اٰمَنُوٓا اٰمِنُوا بِاللّٰهِ وَرَسُولِهِۦ
وَالْكِتٰبِ الَّذِى نَزَّلَ عَلٰى رَسُولِهِۦ وَالْكِتٰبِ
الَّذِىٓ أَنْزَلَ مِنْ قَبْلُ ۚ وَمَنْ يَكْفُرْ
بِاللّٰهِ وَمَلٰٓئِكَتِهِۦ وَكُتُبِهِۦ وَرُسُلِهِۦ
وَالْيَوْمِ الْاٰخِرِ فَقَدْ ضَلَّ ضَلٰلًۢا بَعِيدًا ﴿١٣٦﴾

4. وَلَوْ تَرٰىٓ إِذْ يَتَوَفَّى الَّذِينَ كَفَرُوا ۙ الْمَلٰٓئِكَةُ
يَضْرِبُونَ وُجُوهَهُمْ وَأَدْبٰرَهُمْ ۚ وَ
ذُوقُوا عَذَابَ الْحَرِيقِ ﴿٥٠﴾

5. اَللّٰهُ يَصْطَفِى مِنَ الْمَلٰٓئِكَةِ رُسُلًا
وَّمِنَ النَّاسِ ۚ إِنَّ اللّٰهَ سَمِيعٌۢ بَصِيرٌ ﴿٧٥﴾

6. قُلْ يَتَوَفّٰىكُمْ مَلَكُ الْمَوْتِ الَّذِى
وُكِّلَ بِكُمْ ثُمَّ إِلٰى رَبِّكُمْ تُرْجَعُونَ ﴿١١﴾

7. Praise be to Allah, the Creator of the heavens and the earth, which appointeth the angels as messengers having wings two, three and four. He multiplieth in certain what He will. Lo! Allah is Able to do all things.

35:1

7. اَلْحَمْدُ لِلّٰهِ فَاطِرِ السَّمٰوٰتِ وَالْاَرْضِ
جَاعِلِ الْمَلٰٓئِكَةِ رُسُلًا اُولِیٓ اَجْنِحَةٍ
مَّثْنٰی وَثُلٰثَ وَرُبٰعَ ؕ یَزِیْدُ فِی
الْخَلْقِ مَا یَشَآءُ ؕ اِنَّ اللّٰهَ عَلٰی كُلِّ شَیْءٍ قَدِیْرٌ ﴿١﴾

8. Almost might the heavens above be rent asunder while the angels hymn the praise of their Lord and ask forgiveness for those on the earth. Lo! Allah, He is the Forgiver, the Merciful.

42:5

8. تَكَادُ السَّمٰوٰتُ یَتَفَطَّرْنَ مِنْ فَوْقِهِنَّ
وَالْمَلٰٓئِكَةُ یُسَبِّحُوْنَ بِحَمْدِ رَبِّهِمْ
وَیَسْتَغْفِرُوْنَ لِمَنْ فِی الْاَرْضِ ؕ اَلَاۤ
اِنَّ اللّٰهَ هُوَ الْغَفُوْرُ الرَّحِیْمُ ﴿٥﴾

9. When the two Receivers receive (him), seated on the right hand and on the left,
He uttereth no word but there is with him an observer ready.

50:17-18

9. اِذْ یَتَلَقَّی الْمُتَلَقِّیٰنِ عَنِ الْیَمِیْنِ وَ
عَنِ الشِّمَالِ قَعِیْدٌ ﴿١٧﴾
مَا یَلْفِظُ مِنْ قَوْلٍ اِلَّا لَدَیْهِ رَقِیْبٌ
عَتِیْدٌ ﴿١٨﴾

10. O ye who believe! Ward off from yourselves and your families a Fire whereof the fuel is men and stones, over which are set angels strong, severe, who resist not Allah in that which He commandeth them, but do that which they are commanded.

66:6

10. یٰۤاَیُّهَا الَّذِیْنَ اٰمَنُوْا قُوْۤا اَنْفُسَكُمْ
وَاَهْلِیْكُمْ نَارًا وَّقُوْدُهَا النَّاسُ
وَالْحِجَارَةُ عَلَیْهَا مَلٰٓئِكَةٌ غِلَاظٌ
شِدَادٌ لَّا یَعْصُوْنَ اللّٰهَ مَاۤ اَمَرَهُمْ
وَیَفْعَلُوْنَ مَا یُؤْمَرُوْنَ ﴿٦﴾

11. And the angels will be on the sides thereof, and eight will uphold the Throne of thy Lord that day, above them.

69:17

11. وَّالْمَلَكُ عَلٰۤی اَرْجَآئِهَا ؕ وَیَحْمِلُ
عَرْشَ رَبِّكَ فَوْقَهُمْ یَوْمَئِذٍ ثَمٰنِیَةٌ ﴿١٧﴾

12. وَمَا جَعَلْنَاۤ اَصْحٰبَ النَّارِ اِلَّا مَلٰٓئِكَةً

12. We have appointed only angels to be wardens of the Fire, and their number have We made to be

a stumbling-block for those who disbelieve; that those to whom the Scripture hath been given may have certainty, and that believers may increase in faith; and that those to whom the Scripture hath been given and believers may not doubt; and that those in whose hearts there is disease, and disblievers, may say: What meaneth Allah by this similitude? Thus Allah sendeth astray whom He will, and whom He will He guideth. None knoweth the hosts of thy Lord save Him. This is naught else than a Reminder unto mortals.

74:31

13. Lo! We revealed it on the Night of Power.

Ah, what will convey unto thee what the Night of Power is!

The Night of Power is better than a thousand months.

The angels and the Spirit descend therein, by the permission of their Lord, with all decrees.

(That night is) Peace until the rising of the dawn.

97:1–5

وَمَا جَعَلْنَا عِدَّتَهُمْ إِلَّا فِتْنَةً لِلَّذِينَ
كَفَرُوا لِيَسْتَيْقِنَ الَّذِينَ أُوتُوا
الْكِتَابَ وَيَزْدَادَ الَّذِينَ آمَنُوا إِيمَانًا
وَلَا يَرْتَابَ الَّذِينَ أُوتُوا الْكِتَابَ
وَالْمُؤْمِنُونَ وَلِيَقُولَ الَّذِينَ فِي
قُلُوبِهِمْ مَرَضٌ وَالْكَافِرُونَ مَاذَا
أَرَادَ اللَّهُ بِهَٰذَا مَثَلًا كَذَٰلِكَ يُضِلُّ
اللَّهُ مَنْ يَشَاءُ وَيَهْدِي مَنْ يَشَاءُ وَمَا
يَعْلَمُ جُنُودَ رَبِّكَ إِلَّا هُوَ وَمَا هِيَ
إِلَّا ذِكْرَىٰ لِلْبَشَرِ ﴿٣١﴾

13. إِنَّا أَنْزَلْنَاهُ فِي لَيْلَةِ الْقَدْرِ ﴿١﴾
وَمَا أَدْرَاكَ مَا لَيْلَةُ الْقَدْرِ ﴿٢﴾
لَيْلَةُ الْقَدْرِ خَيْرٌ مِنْ أَلْفِ شَهْرٍ ﴿٣﴾
تَنَزَّلُ الْمَلَائِكَةُ وَالرُّوحُ فِيهَا
بِإِذْنِ رَبِّهِمْ مِنْ كُلِّ أَمْرٍ ﴿٤﴾
سَلَامٌ هِيَ حَتَّىٰ مَطْلَعِ الْفَجْرِ ﴿٥﴾

○

Ref: 2:30–31,34,98,102,161,177,210,248,285; 3:18,39,42,45,80,87,124–125; 4:136,172; 6:8–9,50,93,111,158; 7:11; 8:9,12; 11; 12:31; 13:13,23; 15:7–8,28,30; 16:2,28,32–33,49; 17:40,61,92,95; 18:50; 20:116; 21:103; 23:24; 25:7,21–22,25; 32:11; 33:43,56; 34:40,41; 37:149–150; 38:71,73; 39:75; 41:14,30; 43:19,53,60; 47:27; 48:27; 53:27; 66:4; 70:4; 74:30–31; 78:38; 79:1–2; 89:22; 97:4;

See also: Recording Angels.

ANGER

1. And vie one with another for forgiveness from your Lord, and for a Paradise as wide as are the heavens and the earth, prepared for those who ward off (evil);

Those who spend (of that which Allah hath given them) in ease and in adversity, those who control their wrath and are forgiving toward mankind; Allah loveth the good;

3:133–134

2. And those who shun the worst of sins and indecencies and, when they are wroth, forgive.

42:37

ANIMALS

1. Beautified for mankind is love of the joys (that come) from women and offspring, and stored-up heaps of gold and silver, and horses branded (with their mark), and cattle and land. That is comfort of the life of the world. Allah! With Him is a more excellent abode.

3:14

2. O ye who believe! Fulfil your undertakings. The beast of cattle is made lawful unto you (for food) except that which is announced unto you (herein), game being unlawful when ye are on pilgrimage.

1. وَسَارِعُوٓا إِلَىٰ مَغْفِرَةٍ مِّن رَّبِّكُمْ وَجَنَّةٍ
عَرْضُهَا السَّمٰوٰتُ وَالْأَرْضُ أُعِدَّتْ لِلْمُتَّقِينَ ۝
الَّذِينَ يُنفِقُونَ فِي السَّرَّآءِ وَالضَّرَّآءِ
وَالْكٰظِمِينَ الْغَيْظَ وَالْعَافِينَ عَنِ النَّاسِ ۗ
وَاللَّهُ يُحِبُّ الْمُحْسِنِينَ ۝

2. وَالَّذِينَ يَجْتَنِبُونَ كَبٰٓئِرَ الْإِثْمِ
وَالْفَوٰحِشَ وَإِذَا مَا غَضِبُوا هُمْ
يَغْفِرُونَ ۝

1. زُيِّنَ لِلنَّاسِ حُبُّ الشَّهَوٰتِ مِنَ النِّسَآءِ
وَالْبَنِينَ وَالْقَنٰطِيرِ الْمُقَنطَرَةِ مِنَ
الذَّهَبِ وَالْفِضَّةِ وَالْخَيْلِ الْمُسَوَّمَةِ
وَالْأَنْعٰمِ وَالْحَرْثِ ۗ ذٰلِكَ مَتٰعُ
الْحَيٰوةِ الدُّنْيَا ۖ وَاللَّهُ عِندَهُ حُسْنُ الْمَـَٔابِ ۝

2. يٰٓأَيُّهَا الَّذِينَ ءَامَنُوٓا أَوْفُوا بِالْعُقُودِ ۚ أُحِلَّتْ
لَكُم بَهِيمَةُ الْأَنْعٰمِ إِلَّا مَا يُتْلَىٰ عَلَيْكُمْ
غَيْرَ مُحِلِّي الصَّيْدِ وَأَنتُمْ حُرُمٌ ۗ إِنَّ
اللَّهَ يَحْكُمُ مَا يُرِيدُ ۝

3. مَا جَعَلَ اللَّهُ مِن بَحِيرَةٍ وَلَا سَآئِبَةٍ
وَلَا وَصِيلَةٍ وَلَا حَامٍ ۙ وَلٰكِنَّ الَّذِينَ

Lo! Allah ordaineth that which pleaseth Him.

5:1

3. Allah hath not appointed anything in the nature of a *Bahirah* or a *Sai'bah* or a *Wasilah* or a *Hami*, but those

who disbelieve invent a lie against Allah. Most of them have no sense.

5:103

4. And they say: Such cattle and crops are forbidden. No-one is to eat of them save whom we will-in their make-believe-cattle whose backs are forbidden, cattle over which they mention not the name of Allah. (All that is) is a lie against Him. He will repay them for that which they invent.

And they say: That which is in the bellies of such cattle is reserved for our males and is forbidden to our wives; but if it be born dead, then they (all) may be partakers thereof. He will reward them for their attribution (of such ordinances unto Him). Lo, He is Wise, Aware.

6: 138–139

5. And the cattle hath He created, whence ye have warm clothing and uses, and whereof ye eat;

And wherein is beauty for you, when ye bring them home, and when ye take them out to pasture.

And they bear your loads for you unto a land ye could not reach save with great trouble to yourselves. Lo! your Lord is Full of Pity, Merciful.

And horses and mules and asses (hath He created) that ye may ride them, and for ornament. And He crea-

كَفَرُوا يَفْتَرُونَ عَلَى اللهِ الْكَذِبَ وَ
اَكْثَرُهُمْ لَا يَعْقِلُونَ ۝

4. وَقَالُوا هٰذِهٖ اَنْعَامٌ وَّحَرْثٌ حِجْرٌ لَّا
يَطْعَمُهَا اِلَّا مَنْ نَّشَآءُ بِزَعْمِهِمْ وَاَنْعَامٌ
حُرِّمَتْ ظُهُوْرُهَا وَاَنْعَامٌ لَّا يَذْكُرُوْنَ
اسْمَ اللهِ عَلَيْهَا افْتِرَآءً عَلَيْهِ سَيَجْزِيْهِمْ
بِمَا كَانُوْا يَفْتَرُوْنَ ۝
وَقَالُوْا مَا فِيْ بُطُوْنِ هٰذِهِ الْاَنْعَامِ خَالِصَةٌ
لِّذُكُوْرِنَا وَمُحَرَّمٌ عَلٰٓى اَزْوَاجِنَا وَاِنْ
يَّكُنْ مَّيْتَةً فَهُمْ فِيْهِ شُرَكَآءُ سَيَجْزِيْهِمْ
وَصْفَهُمْ اِنَّهٗ حَكِيْمٌ عَلِيْمٌ ۝

5. وَالْاَنْعَامَ خَلَقَهَا لَكُمْ فِيْهَا دِفْءٌ
وَّمَنَافِعُ وَمِنْهَا تَاْكُلُوْنَ ۝
وَلَكُمْ فِيْهَا جَمَالٌ حِيْنَ تُرِيْحُوْنَ
وَحِيْنَ تَسْرَحُوْنَ ۝
وَتَحْمِلُ اَثْقَالَكُمْ اِلٰى بَلَدٍ لَّمْ تَكُوْنُوْا
بٰلِغِيْهِ اِلَّا بِشِقِّ الْاَنْفُسِ اِنَّ رَبَّكُمْ
لَرَءُوْفٌ رَّحِيْمٌ ۝
وَّالْخَيْلَ وَالْبِغَالَ وَالْحَمِيْرَ لِتَرْكَبُوْهَا
وَزِيْنَةً وَيَخْلُقُ مَا لَا تَعْلَمُوْنَ ۝

6. وَاِنَّ لَكُمْ فِي الْاَنْعَامِ لَعِبْرَةً نُسْقِيْكُمْ
مِّمَّا فِيْ بُطُوْنِهٖ مِنْۢ بَيْنِ فَرْثٍ وَّدَمٍ
لَّبَنًا خَالِصًا سَآئِغًا لِّلشّٰرِبِيْنَ ۝

teth that which ye know not.

16:5-8

6. And lo! in the cattle there is a lesson for you. We give you to drink of that which is in their bellies, from betwixt the refuse and the blood, pure milk palatable to the drinkers.

16:66

7. And for every nation have We appointed a ritual, that they may mention the name of Allah over the beast of cattle that He hath given them for food and your God is One God, therefor surrender unto Him.

22:34

8. And the camels! We have appointed them among the ceremonies of Allah. Therein ye have much good. So mention the name of Allah over them when they are drawn up in lines. Then when their flanks fall (dead), eat thereof and feed the beggar and the suppliant. Thus have We made them subject unto you, that haply ye may give thanks.

22:36

9. Allah hath created every animal of water. Of them is (a kind) that goeth upon its belly and (a kind) that goeth upon two legs and (a kind) that goeth upon four. Allah createth what He will. Lo! Allah is Able to do all things.

24:45

10. Have they not seen how We have created for them of Our handiwork the cattle, so that they are their owners,

And have subdued them unto them, so that some of them they have for riding, some for food?

Benefits and (divers) drinks have they from them. Will they not then give thanks?

36:71-73

7. وَلِكُلِّ أُمَّةٍ جَعَلْنَا مَنسَكًا لِّيَذْكُرُوا
اسْمَ اللَّهِ عَلَىٰ مَا رَزَقَهُم مِّن بَهِيمَةِ
الْأَنْعَامِ ۗ فَإِلَٰهُكُمْ إِلَٰهٌ وَاحِدٌ فَلَهُ
أَسْلِمُوا ۗ

8. وَالْبُدْنَ جَعَلْنَاهَا لَكُم مِّن شَعَائِرِ اللَّهِ
لَكُمْ فِيهَا خَيْرٌ ۖ فَاذْكُرُوا اسْمَ اللَّهِ
عَلَيْهَا صَوَافَّ ۖ فَإِذَا وَجَبَتْ جُنُوبُهَا
فَكُلُوا مِنْهَا وَأَطْعِمُوا الْقَانِعَ وَالْمُعْتَرَّ ۚ
كَذَٰلِكَ سَخَّرْنَاهَا لَكُمْ لَعَلَّكُمْ تَشْكُرُونَ ﴿٣٦﴾

9. وَاللَّهُ خَلَقَ كُلَّ دَابَّةٍ مِّن مَّاءٍ ۖ
فَمِنْهُم مَّن يَمْشِي عَلَىٰ بَطْنِهِ وَمِنْهُم
مَّن يَمْشِي عَلَىٰ رِجْلَيْنِ وَمِنْهُم مَّن
يَمْشِي عَلَىٰ أَرْبَعٍ ۚ يَخْلُقُ اللَّهُ مَا يَشَاءُ ۚ
إِنَّ اللَّهَ عَلَىٰ كُلِّ شَيْءٍ قَدِيرٌ ﴿٤٥﴾

10. أَوَلَمْ يَرَوْا أَنَّا خَلَقْنَا لَهُم مِّمَّا عَمِلَتْ
أَيْدِينَا أَنْعَامًا فَهُمْ لَهَا مَالِكُونَ ﴿٧١﴾
وَذَلَّلْنَاهَا لَهُمْ فَمِنْهَا رَكُوبُهُمْ
وَمِنْهَا يَأْكُلُونَ ﴿٧٢﴾
وَلَهُمْ فِيهَا مَنَافِعُ وَمَشَارِبُ ۖ أَفَلَا
يَشْكُرُونَ ﴿٧٣﴾

Ref: 2:51,54,57,65,67,71,92–93,173,259; 4:119; 6:142–145; 7:40,73,77, 152,163, 166; 11:64,69; 12:13–14,17,43,46; 16:61,68,79–80; 18:18,22,63; 20:20,88; 21:78; 22:27; 23:21–22; 26:32,155; 27:10,18; 28:31; 29:41; 37:142; 38:23–24: 40:79–80; 43:12–13; 51:26; 54:27; 59:6; 62:5.

ANSAR

1. Lo! those who believed and left their homes and strove with their wealth and their lives for the cause of Allah, and those who took them in and helped them; these are protecting friends one of another.

8:72

2. Those who believed and left their homes and strove for the cause of Allah, and those who took them in and helped them—these are the believers in truth. For them is pardon, and a bountiful provision.

8:74

3. And the first to lead the way, of the *Muhajirin* and the *Ansar* and those who followed them in goodness — Allah is well pleased with them and they are well pleased with Him, and He hath made ready for them Gardens underneath which rivers flow, wherein they will abide for ever: That is the Supreme triumph.

9:100

4. Allah hath turned in mercy to the Prophet, and to the *Muhajirin* and the *Ansar* who followed him in the hour of hardship. After the hearts of a party of them had almost swerved aside, then turned He unto them in mercy. Lo! He is Full of Pity, Merciful for them.

9:117

1. إِنَّ الَّذِينَ آمَنُوا وَهَاجَرُوا وَجَاهَدُوا
بِأَمْوَالِهِمْ وَأَنفُسِهِمْ فِي سَبِيلِ اللَّهِ
وَالَّذِينَ آوَوا وَّنَصَرُوا أُولَٰئِكَ بَعْضُهُمْ
أَوْلِيَاءُ بَعْضٍ

2. وَالَّذِينَ آمَنُوا وَهَاجَرُوا وَجَاهَدُوا فِي
سَبِيلِ اللَّهِ وَالَّذِينَ آوَوا وَّنَصَرُوا أُولَٰئِكَ
هُمُ الْمُؤْمِنُونَ حَقًّا لَّهُم مَّغْفِرَةٌ
وَرِزْقٌ كَرِيمٌ

3. وَالسَّابِقُونَ الْأَوَّلُونَ مِنَ الْمُهَاجِرِينَ
وَالْأَنصَارِ وَالَّذِينَ اتَّبَعُوهُم بِإِحْسَانٍ
رَّضِيَ اللَّهُ عَنْهُمْ وَرَضُوا عَنْهُ وَأَعَدَّ
لَهُمْ جَنَّاتٍ تَجْرِي تَحْتَهَا الْأَنْهَارُ خَالِدِينَ
فِيهَا أَبَدًا ذَٰلِكَ الْفَوْزُ الْعَظِيمُ

4. لَّقَد تَّابَ اللَّهُ عَلَى النَّبِيِّ وَالْمُهَاجِرِينَ
وَالْأَنصَارِ الَّذِينَ اتَّبَعُوهُ فِي سَاعَةِ
الْعُسْرَةِ مِن بَعْدِ مَا كَادَ يَزِيغُ قُلُوبُ
فَرِيقٍ مِّنْهُمْ ثُمَّ تَابَ عَلَيْهِمْ إِنَّهُ بِهِمْ
رَءُوفٌ رَّحِيمٌ

5. وَالَّذِينَ تَبَوَّءُوا الدَّارَ وَالْإِيمَانَ مِن
قَبْلِهِمْ يُحِبُّونَ مَنْ هَاجَرَ إِلَيْهِمْ
وَلَا يَجِدُونَ فِي صُدُورِهِمْ حَاجَةً

5. Those who entered the city and the faith before them love those who flee unto them for refuge, and find in their breasts no need for that which hath been given them,

but prefer (the fugitives) above themselves though poverty become their lot. And whoso is saved from his own avarice–such are they who are successful.

59:9

ANT

1. And there were gathered together unto Solomon his armies of the jinn and humankind, and of the birds, and they were set in a battle order;

Till, when they reached the Valley of the Ants, an ant exclaimed: O ants! Enter your dwellings lest Solomon and his armies crush you, unperceiving.

And (Solomon) smiled, laughing at her speech, and said: My Lord, arouse me to be thankful for Thy favour wherewith Thou hast favoured me and my parents, and to do good that shall be pleasing unto Thee, and include me in (the number of) Thy righteous slaves.

27.17-19

APOSTATE

1. And they will not cease from fighting against you till they have made you renegades from your religion, if they can.

مِّمَّآ أُوتُوا وَيُؤْثِرُونَ عَلَىٰٓ أَنفُسِهِمْ
وَلَوْ كَانَ بِهِمْ خَصَاصَةٌ ۚ وَمَن يُوقَ
شُحَّ نَفْسِهِۦ فَأُولَٰٓئِكَ هُمُ الْمُفْلِحُونَ ﴿٩﴾

1. وَحُشِرَ لِسُلَيْمَٰنَ جُنُودُهُۥ مِنَ الْجِنِّ
وَالْإِنسِ وَالطَّيْرِ فَهُمْ يُوزَعُونَ ﴿١٧﴾
حَتَّىٰٓ إِذَآ أَتَوْا عَلَىٰ وَادِ النَّمْلِ قَالَتْ
نَمْلَةٌ يَٰٓأَيُّهَا النَّمْلُ ادْخُلُوا مَسَٰكِنَكُمْ
لَا يَحْطِمَنَّكُمْ سُلَيْمَٰنُ وَجُنُودُهُۥ
وَهُمْ لَا يَشْعُرُونَ ﴿١٨﴾
فَتَبَسَّمَ ضَاحِكًا مِّن قَوْلِهَا وَقَالَ
رَبِّ أَوْزِعْنِىٓ أَنْ أَشْكُرَ نِعْمَتَكَ الَّتِىٓ
أَنْعَمْتَ عَلَىَّ وَعَلَىٰ وَٰلِدَىَّ وَأَنْ أَعْمَلَ
صَٰلِحًا تَرْضَىٰهُ وَأَدْخِلْنِى بِرَحْمَتِكَ
فِى عِبَادِكَ الصَّٰلِحِينَ ﴿١٩﴾

1. وَلَا يَزَالُونَ يُقَٰتِلُونَكُمْ حَتَّىٰ يَرُدُّوكُمْ عَن
دِينِكُمْ إِنِ اسْتَطَٰعُوا ۚ وَمَن يَرْتَدِدْ مِنكُمْ
عَن دِينِهِۦ فَيَمُتْ وَهُوَ كَافِرٌ فَأُولَٰٓئِكَ حَبِطَتْ
أَعْمَٰلُهُمْ فِى الدُّنْيَا وَالْآخِرَةِ ۖ وَأُولَٰٓئِكَ
أَصْحَٰبُ النَّارِ ۖ هُمْ فِيهَا خَٰلِدُونَ ﴿٢١٧﴾

And whoso becometh a renegade and dieth in his disbelief such are they whose works have fallen both in the world and the Hereafter. Such are rightful owners of the Fire; they will abide therein.

2:217

ANSAR
See also: Migration.

2. On the day when (some) faces will be whitened and (some) faces will be blackened; and as for those whose faces have been blackened, it will be said unto them: Disbelieved ye after your (profession of) belief? Then taste the punishment for that ye disbelieved.

3:106

2. يوم تبيض وجوه وتسود وجوه فاما
الذين اسودت وجوههم اكفرتم بعد
ايمانكم فذوقوا العذاب بما كنتم تكفرون

3. Lo! those who believe, then disbelieve and then (again) believe, then disbelieve, and then increase in disbelief, Allah will never pardon them, nor will He guide them unto a way.

4:137

3. ان الذين امنوا ثم كفروا ثم امنوا ثم
كفروا ثم ازدادوا كفرا لم يكن الله
ليغفر لهم ولا ليهديهم سبيلا

4. O ye who believe! Whoso of you becometh a renegade from his religion, (Know that in his stead) Allah will bring a people whom He loveth and who love Him, humble toward believers, stern toward disbelievers, striving in the way of Allah, and fearing not the blame of any blamer. Such is the grace of Allah which He giveth unto whom He will. Allah is All-Embracing, All-Knowing.

5:54

4. يايها الذين امنوا من يرتد منكم
عن دينه فسوف يأتي الله بقوم
يحبهم ويحبونه اذلة على
المؤمنين اعزة على الكفرين
يجاهدون في سبيل الله ولا يخافون
لومة لائم ذلك فضل الله يؤتيه
من يشاء والله واسع عليم

5. Lo! those who turn back after the guidance hath been manifested unto them, Satan hath seduced them, and he giveth them the rein.

That is because they say unto those who hate what Allah hath revealed: We will obey you in some matters; and Allah knoweth their secret talk.

Then how (will it be with them) when the angels gather them, smiting their faces and their backs!

That will be because they followed that which angereth Allah, and hated that which pleaseth Him. Therefor He hath made their actions vain.

47:25–28

5. ان الذين ارتدوا على ادبارهم
من بعد ما تبين لهم الهدى
الشيطن سول لهم واملى لهم
ذلك بانهم قالوا للذين كرهوا
ما نزل الله سنطيعكم في بعض
الامر والله يعلم اسرارهم
فكيف اذا توفتهم الملئكة يضربون
وجوههم وادبارهم
ذلك بانهم اتبعوا ما اسخط الله و
كرهوا رضوانه فاحبط اعمالهم

Ref: 2:109; 3:100,177; 4:115; 5:108; 6:37,71; 16:106–107.

See also: Disbelievers and Polytheists, Renegade.

APOSTLESHIP OF MUHAMMAD (PBUH)

1. It is not (possible) for any human being unto whom Allah had given the Scripture and wisdom and the prophethood that he should afterwards have said unto mankind: Be slaves of me instead of Allah; but (what he said was): Be ye faithful servants of the Lord by virtue of your constant teaching of the Scripture and of your constant study thereof.

And he commanded you not that ye should take the angels and the prophets for lords. Would he command you to disbelieve after ye had surrendered (to Allah)?

When Allah made (His) covenant with the prophets, (He said): Behold that which I have given you of the Scripture and knowledge. And afterward there will come unto you a messenger, confirming that which ye possess. Ye shall believe in him and ye shall help him. He said: Do ye agree, and will ye take up My burden (which I lay upon you) in this (matter)? They answered: We agree. He said: Then bear ye witness. I will be a witness with you.

3:79-81

2. Muhammad is but a messenger, messengers (the like of whom) have passed away before him. Will it be that, when he dieth or is slain, ye will turn back on your heels? He who turneth back doth no hurt to Allah, and Allah will reward the

1. مَا كَانَ لِبَشَرٍ اَنْ يُّؤْتِيَهُ اللّٰهُ الْكِتٰبَ
وَالْحُكْمَ وَالنُّبُوَّةَ ثُمَّ يَقُوْلَ لِلنَّاسِ
كُوْنُوْا عِبَادًا لِّيْ مِنْ دُوْنِ اللّٰهِ وَلٰكِنْ
كُوْنُوْا رَبّٰنِيّٖنَ بِمَا كُنْتُمْ تُعَلِّمُوْنَ الْكِتٰبَ
وَبِمَا كُنْتُمْ تَدْرُسُوْنَ ○
وَلَا يَاْمُرَكُمْ اَنْ تَتَّخِذُوا الْمَلٰٓئِكَةَ وَ
النَّبِيّٖنَ اَرْبَابًا ؕ اَيَاْمُرُكُمْ بِالْكُفْرِ
بَعْدَ اِذْ اَنْتُمْ مُّسْلِمُوْنَ ○
وَاِذْ اَخَذَ اللّٰهُ مِيْثَاقَ النَّبِيّٖنَ لَمَآ
اٰتَيْتُكُمْ مِّنْ كِتٰبٍ وَّحِكْمَةٍ ثُمَّ جَآءَكُمْ
رَسُوْلٌ مُّصَدِّقٌ لِّمَا مَعَكُمْ لَتُؤْمِنُنَّ بِهٖ
وَلَتَنْصُرُنَّهٗ ؕ قَالَ ءَاَقْرَرْتُمْ وَاَخَذْتُمْ
عَلٰى ذٰلِكُمْ اِصْرِيْ ؕ قَالُوْٓا اَقْرَرْنَا ؕ قَالَ
فَاشْهَدُوْا وَاَنَا مَعَكُمْ مِّنَ الشّٰهِدِيْنَ ○

2. وَمَا مُحَمَّدٌ اِلَّا رَسُوْلٌ ۚ قَدْ خَلَتْ مِنْ
قَبْلِهِ الرُّسُلُ ؕ اَفَائِنْ مَّاتَ اَوْ قُتِلَ
انْقَلَبْتُمْ عَلٰٓى اَعْقَابِكُمْ ؕ وَمَنْ يَّنْقَلِبْ
عَلٰى عَقِبَيْهِ فَلَنْ يَّضُرَّ اللّٰهَ شَيْئًا ؕ
وَسَيَجْزِى اللّٰهُ الشّٰكِرِيْنَ ○

3. لَقَدْ مَنَّ اللّٰهُ عَلَى الْمُؤْمِنِيْنَ اِذْ بَعَثَ
فِيْهِمْ رَسُوْلًا مِّنْ اَنْفُسِهِمْ يَتْلُوْا عَلَيْهِمْ
اٰيٰتِهٖ وَيُزَكِّيْهِمْ وَيُعَلِّمُهُمُ الْكِتٰبَ
وَالْحِكْمَةَ ۚ وَاِنْ كَانُوْا مِنْ قَبْلُ
لَفِيْ ضَلٰلٍ مُّبِيْنٍ ○

thankful.

3:144

3. Allah verily hath shown grace to the believers by sending unto them a messenger of their own who reciteth unto them His revelations, and causeth them to grow, and teacheth them the Scripture and wisdom, although before (he came to them) they were in flagrant error.

3:164

4. Lo! We reveal unto thee the Scripture with the truth, that thou mayst judge between mankind by that which Allah showeth thee. And be not thou a pleader for the treacherous:

4:105

5. O Messenger! Make known that which hath been revealed unto thee from thy Lord, for if thou do it not, thou will not have conveyed His message. Allah will protect thee from mankind. Lo! Allah guideth not the disbelieving folk.

5:67

6. Say (O Muhammad): O mankind! Lo! I am the messenger of Allah to you all - (the messenger of) Him unto whom belongeth the Sovereignty of the heavens and the earth. There is no God save Him. He quickeneth and He giveth death. So believe in Allah and His messenger, the Prophet who can neither read nor write, who believeth in Allah and in His Words and follow him that haply ye may be led aright.

7:158

7. Say: I am only a mortal like you. My Lord inspireth in me that your God is only One God. And whoever hopeth for the meeting with his Lord, let him do righteous work, and make none sharer of the worship due unto his Lord.

18:110

4. إِنَّآ أَنْزَلْنَآ إِلَيْكَ الْكِتٰبَ بِالْحَقِّ
لِتَحْكُمَ بَيْنَ النَّاسِ بِمَآ أَرٰىكَ اللّٰهُ
وَلَا تَكُنْ لِّلْخَآئِنِيْنَ خَصِيْمًا

5. يٰٓأَيُّهَا الرَّسُوْلُ بَلِّغْ مَآ أُنْزِلَ إِلَيْكَ مِنْ
رَّبِّكَ وَإِنْ لَّمْ تَفْعَلْ فَمَا بَلَّغْتَ رِسَالَتَهٗ
وَاللّٰهُ يَعْصِمُكَ مِنَ النَّاسِ إِنَّ اللّٰهَ
لَا يَهْدِي الْقَوْمَ الْكٰفِرِيْنَ

6. قُلْ يٰٓأَيُّهَا النَّاسُ إِنِّيْ رَسُوْلُ اللّٰهِ إِلَيْكُمْ
جَمِيْعًا الَّذِيْ لَهٗ مُلْكُ السَّمٰوٰتِ وَالْأَرْضِ
لَآ إِلٰهَ إِلَّا هُوَ يُحْيٖ وَيُمِيْتُ فَاٰمِنُوْا
بِاللّٰهِ وَرَسُوْلِهِ النَّبِيِّ الْأُمِّيِّ الَّذِيْ يُؤْمِنُ
بِاللّٰهِ وَكَلِمٰتِهٖ وَاتَّبِعُوْهُ لَعَلَّكُمْ تَهْتَدُوْنَ

7. قُلْ إِنَّمَآ أَنَا بَشَرٌ مِّثْلُكُمْ يُوْحٰٓى إِلَيَّ
أَنَّمَآ إِلٰهُكُمْ إِلٰهٌ وَّاحِدٌ فَمَنْ كَانَ يَرْجُوْا
لِقَآءَ رَبِّهٖ فَلْيَعْمَلْ عَمَلًا صَالِحًا وَّلَا
يُشْرِكْ بِعِبَادَةِ رَبِّهٖٓ أَحَدًا

8. وَمَآ أَرْسَلْنٰكَ إِلَّا رَحْمَةً لِّلْعٰلَمِيْنَ

9. مَا كَانَ عَلَى النَّبِيِّ مِنْ حَرَجٍ فِيْمَا
فَرَضَ اللّٰهُ لَهٗ سُنَّةَ اللّٰهِ فِي الَّذِيْنَ
خَلَوْا مِنْ قَبْلُ وَكَانَ أَمْرُ اللّٰهِ
قَدَرًا مَّقْدُوْرًا

8. We sent thee not save as a mercy for the peoples.

21:107

9. There is no reproach for the Prophet in that which Allah maketh his due. That was Allah's way with those who passed away of old—and the commandment of Allah is certain destiny.

Who delivered the messages of Allah and feared Him, and feared none save Allah. Allah keepeth good account.

Muhammad is not the father of any man among you, but he is the messenger of Allah and the Seal of the Prohpets; and Allah is Aware of all things.

33:38–40

10. O Prohpet! Lo! We have sent thee as a witness and a bringer of good tidings and a warner.

And as a summoner unto Allah by His permission, and as a lamp that giveth light.

33:45-46

11. By the wise Qur'ān,

Lo! thou art of those sent

On a straight path,

A revelation of the Mighty, the Merciful,

That thou mayst warn a folk whose fathers were not warned, so they are heedless.

Already hath the word proved true of most of them, for they believe not.

36:2–7

12. And We have not taught him (Muhammad) poetry, nor is it meet for him. This is naught else than a Reminder and a Lecture making plain,

الَّذِيْنَ يُبَلِّغُوْنَ رِسٰلٰتِ اللّٰهِ وَيَخْشَوْنَهٗ
وَلَا يَخْشَوْنَ اَحَدًا اِلَّا اللّٰهَ ۗ وَكَفٰى
بِاللّٰهِ حَسِيْبًا ﴿۳۹﴾
مَا كَانَ مُحَمَّدٌ اَبَآ اَحَدٍ مِّنْ رِّجَالِكُمْ
وَلٰكِنْ رَّسُوْلَ اللّٰهِ وَخَاتَمَ النَّبِيّٖنَ ۗ
وَكَانَ اللّٰهُ بِكُلِّ شَيْءٍ عَلِيْمًا ﴿۴۰﴾

.10 يٰٓاَيُّهَا النَّبِيُّ اِنَّآ اَرْسَلْنٰكَ شَاهِدًا
وَّمُبَشِّرًا وَّنَذِيْرًا ﴿۴۵﴾
وَّدَاعِيًا اِلَى اللّٰهِ بِاِذْنِهٖ وَسِرَاجًا مُّنِيْرًا ﴿۴۶﴾

.11 وَالْقُرْاٰنِ الْحَكِيْمِ ﴿۲﴾
اِنَّكَ لَمِنَ الْمُرْسَلِيْنَ ﴿۳﴾
عَلٰى صِرَاطٍ مُّسْتَقِيْمٍ ﴿۴﴾
تَنْزِيْلَ الْعَزِيْزِ الرَّحِيْمِ ﴿۵﴾
لِتُنْذِرَ قَوْمًا مَّآ اُنْذِرَ اٰبَآؤُهُمْ
فَهُمْ غٰفِلُوْنَ ﴿۶﴾
لَقَدْ حَقَّ الْقَوْلُ عَلٰٓى اَكْثَرِهِمْ
فَهُمْ لَا يُؤْمِنُوْنَ ﴿۷﴾

.12 وَمَا عَلَّمْنٰهُ الشِّعْرَ وَمَا يَنْۢبَغِيْ لَهٗ ۗ
اِنْ هُوَ اِلَّا ذِكْرٌ وَّقُرْاٰنٌ مُّبِيْنٌ ﴿۶۹﴾
لِّيُنْذِرَ مَنْ كَانَ حَيًّا وَّيَحِقَّ الْقَوْلُ
عَلَى الْكٰفِرِيْنَ ﴿۷۰﴾

To warn whosoever liveth, and that the word may be fulfilled against the dis-believers.

36:69-70

Ref: 2:119,252; 4:79–80,106; 5:41,68; 6:14,19; 7:158; 9:128; 11:2; 13:7,30; 16:64; 17:54,105; 22:49; 25:56; 27:93; 34:28; 35:23–24; 36:30; 38:65; 42:6,48; 46:9; 48:8–9,29; 61:6; 93:1–8; 94:1–8.

See also: Manners of Prophet Muhammad (PBUH), Office of Prophethood, Revelation, *Sirah*.

AQSA MOSQUE

1. Glorified be He Who carried His servant by night from the Inviolable Place of Worship to the Far Distant Place of Worship the neighbourhood whereof We have blessed, that We might show him of Our tokens! Lo! He, only He, is the Hearer, the Seer.

17:1

A'RAF

1. And the dwellers of the Garden cry unto the dwellers of the Fire: We have found that which our Lord promised us (to be) the Truth. Have ye (too) found that which your Lord promised the Truth? They say: Yea, verily. And a crier in between them crieth: The curse of Allah is on evil—doers:

Who debar (men) from the Path of Allah and would have it crooked, and who are disbelievers in the Last Day.

Between them is a veil. And on the Heights are men who know them all by their marks. And they call unto the dwellers of the Garden: Peace be unto you! They enter it not although they hope (to enter).

And when their eyes are turned toward the dwellers of the Fire, they say: Our Lord! Place us not with the wrong—

1. سبحن الذي اسرى بعبده ليلا من
المسجد الحرام الى المسجد الاقصا
الذي بركنا حوله لنريه من ايتنا
انه هو السميع البصير ①

1. ونادى اصحب الجنة اصحب النار ان
قد وجدنا ما وعدنا ربنا حقا فهل
وجدتم ما وعد ربكم حقا قالوا نعم
فاذن مؤذن بينهم ان لعنة الله
على الظلمين ㊹
الذين يصدون عن سبيل الله ويبغونها
عوجا وهم بالاخرة كفرون ㊺
وبينهما حجاب وعلى الاعراف رجال
يعرفون كلا بسيمهم ونادوا اصحب
الجنة ان سلم عليكم لم يدخلوها
وهم يطمعون ㊻
واذا صرفت ابصارهم تلقاء اصحب النار
قالوا ربنا لا تجعلنا مع القوم الظلمين ㊼
ونادى اصحب الاعراف رجالا يعرفونهم
بسيمهم قالوا ما اغنى عنكم جمعكم
وما كنتم تستكبرون ㊽

doing folk.

And the dwellers on the Heights call unto men whom they know by their marks, (saying): What did your multitude and that in which ye took your pride avail you?

7:44—48

ASCENSION OF PROPHET MUHAMMAD (PBUH)

1. Glorified be He who carried His servant by night from the Inviolable Place of Worship to the Far Distant Place of Worship the neighbourhood whereof We have blessed, that We might show him of Our tokens! Lo! He, only He, is the Hearer, the Seer.

17:1

2. By the Star when it setteth,

Your comrade erreth not, nor is deceived;

Nor doth he speak of (his own) desire.

It is naught save an inspiration that is inspired,

Which one of mighty powers hath taught him,

One vigorous; and he grew clear to view

When he was on the uppermost horizon.

Then he drew nigh and came down

Till he was (distant) two bows' length or even nearer,

And He revealed unto His slave that which He revealed.

The heart lied not (in seeing) what it saw.

Will ye then dispute with him concerning what he seeth?

And verily he saw him yet another time

By the lote-tree of the utmost boundary,

Nigh unto which is the Garden of Abode.

When that which shroudeth did enshroud the lote-tree,

The eye turned not aside nor yet was overbold.

Verily he saw one of the greater revelations of his Lord.

53:1–18

1. سُبْحٰنَ الَّذِیْٓ اَسْرٰی بِعَبْدِهٖ لَیْلًا مِّنَ
الْمَسْجِدِ الْحَرَامِ اِلَى الْمَسْجِدِ الْاَقْصَا
الَّذِیْ بٰرَكْنَا حَوْلَهٗ لِنُرِیَهٗ مِنْ اٰیٰتِنَا
اِنَّهٗ هُوَ السَّمِیْعُ الْبَصِیْرُ ﴿١﴾

2. وَالنَّجْمِ اِذَا هَوٰی ﴿١﴾
مَا ضَلَّ صَاحِبُكُمْ وَمَا غَوٰی ﴿٢﴾
وَمَا یَنْطِقُ عَنِ الْهَوٰی ﴿٣﴾
اِنْ هُوَ اِلَّا وَحْیٌ یُّوْحٰی ﴿٤﴾
عَلَّمَهٗ شَدِیْدُ الْقُوٰی ﴿٥﴾
ذُوْ مِرَّةٍ فَاسْتَوٰی ﴿٦﴾
وَهُوَ بِالْاُفُقِ الْاَعْلٰی ﴿٧﴾
ثُمَّ دَنَا فَتَدَلّٰی ﴿٨﴾
فَكَانَ قَابَ قَوْسَیْنِ اَوْ اَدْنٰی ﴿٩﴾
فَاَوْحٰٓی اِلٰی عَبْدِهٖ مَآ اَوْحٰی ﴿١٠﴾
مَا كَذَبَ الْفُؤَادُ مَا رَاٰی ﴿١١﴾
اَفَتُمٰرُوْنَهٗ عَلٰی مَا یَرٰی ﴿١٢﴾
وَلَقَدْ رَاٰهُ نَزْلَةً اُخْرٰی ﴿١٣﴾
عِنْدَ سِدْرَةِ الْمُنْتَهٰی ﴿١٤﴾
عِنْدَهَا جَنَّةُ الْمَاْوٰی ﴿١٥﴾
اِذْ یَغْشَی السِّدْرَةَ مَا یَغْشٰی ﴿١٦﴾
مَا زَاغَ الْبَصَرُ وَمَا طَغٰی ﴿١٧﴾
لَقَدْ رَاٰی مِنْ اٰیٰتِ رَبِّهِ الْكُبْرٰی ﴿١٨﴾

ASTRONOMY

1. They ask thee, (O Muhammad), of new moons. Say: They are fixed seasons for mankind and for the pilgrimage.

2:189

2. He it is Who appointed the sun a splendour and the moon a light, and measured for her stages, that ye might know the number of the years, and the reckoning. Allah created not (all) that save in truth. He detaileth the revelations for people who have knowledge.

10:5

3. And verily in the heaven We have set mansions of the stars, and We have beautified it for beholders.

And We have guarded it from every outcast devil,

15:16-17

4. And He it is Who created the night and the day, and the sun and the moon. They float, each in an orbit.

21:33

5. And We have created above you seven paths, and We are never unmindful of creation.

23:17

6. And the sun runneth on unto a resting-place for him. That is the measuring of the Mighty, the Wise.

And for the moon We have appointed mansions till she return like an old shrivelled palm-leaf.

It is not for the sun to overtake the moon, nor doth the night outstrip the day. They float each in an orbit.

36:38—40

1. يَسْـَٔلُونَكَ عَنِ الْأَهِلَّةِ ۖ قُلْ هِيَ مَوَاقِيتُ
لِلنَّاسِ وَالْحَجِّ

2. هُوَ الَّذِي جَعَلَ الشَّمْسَ ضِيَاءً وَالْقَمَرَ
نُورًا وَقَدَّرَهُ مَنَازِلَ لِتَعْلَمُوا عَدَدَ
السِّنِينَ وَالْحِسَابَ ۚ مَا خَلَقَ اللَّهُ ذَٰلِكَ
إِلَّا بِالْحَقِّ ۚ يُفَصِّلُ الْآيَاتِ لِقَوْمٍ يَعْلَمُونَ ۝٥

3. وَلَقَدْ جَعَلْنَا فِي السَّمَاءِ بُرُوجًا وَ
زَيَّنَّاهَا لِلنَّاظِرِينَ ۝١٦
وَحَفِظْنَاهَا مِنْ كُلِّ شَيْطَانٍ رَجِيمٍ ۝١٧

4. وَهُوَ الَّذِي خَلَقَ اللَّيْلَ وَالنَّهَارَ
وَالشَّمْسَ وَالْقَمَرَ ۖ كُلٌّ فِي
فَلَكٍ يَسْبَحُونَ ۝٣٣

5. وَلَقَدْ خَلَقْنَا فَوْقَكُمْ سَبْعَ طَرَائِقَ
وَمَا كُنَّا عَنِ الْخَلْقِ غَافِلِينَ ۝١٧

6. وَالشَّمْسُ تَجْرِي لِمُسْتَقَرٍّ لَهَا ۚ
ذَٰلِكَ تَقْدِيرُ الْعَزِيزِ الْعَلِيمِ ۝٣٨
وَالْقَمَرَ قَدَّرْنَاهُ مَنَازِلَ حَتَّىٰ عَادَ
كَالْعُرْجُونِ الْقَدِيمِ ۝٣٩
لَا الشَّمْسُ يَنْبَغِي لَهَا أَنْ تُدْرِكَ
الْقَمَرَ وَلَا اللَّيْلُ سَابِقُ النَّهَارِ ۚ
وَكُلٌّ فِي فَلَكٍ يَسْبَحُونَ ۝٤٠

7. Lo! We have adorned the lowest heaven with an ornament, the planets;

With security from every froward devil.

They cannot listen to the Highest Chiefs for they are pelted from every side,

Outcast and theirs is a perpetual torment;

Save him who snatcheth a fragment, and there pursueth him a piercing flame.

37:6-10

8. Who hath created seven heavens in harmony. Thou (Muhammad) canst see no fault in the Beneficent One's creation; then look again: Canst thou see any rifts?

Then look again and yet again, thy sight will return unto thee weakened and made dim.

And verily We have beautified the world's heaven with lamps, and We have made them missiles for the devils, and for them We have prepared the doom of flame.

67:3–5

7. إِنَّا زَيَّنَّا السَّمَآءَ الدُّنْيَا بِزِينَةٍ
الْكَوَاكِبِ ۝٦
وَحِفْظًا مِّن كُلِّ شَيْطٰنٍ مَّارِدٍ ۝٧
لَا يَسَّمَّعُونَ إِلَى الْمَلَإِ الْأَعْلٰى وَيُقْذَفُونَ
مِن كُلِّ جَانِبٍ ۝٨
دُحُورًا وَّلَهُمْ عَذَابٌ وَّاصِبٌ ۝٩
إِلَّا مَنْ خَطِفَ الْخَطْفَةَ فَأَتْبَعَهُ
شِهَابٌ ثَاقِبٌ ۝١٠

8. الَّذِي خَلَقَ سَبْعَ سَمٰوٰتٍ طِبَاقًا مَا
تَرٰى فِي خَلْقِ الرَّحْمٰنِ مِن تَفٰوُتٍ
فَارْجِعِ الْبَصَرَ هَلْ تَرٰى مِن فُطُورٍ ۝٣
ثُمَّ ارْجِعِ الْبَصَرَ كَرَّتَيْنِ يَنقَلِبْ
إِلَيْكَ الْبَصَرُ خَاسِئًا وَّهُوَ حَسِيرٌ ۝٤
وَلَقَدْ زَيَّنَّا السَّمَآءَ الدُّنْيَا بِمَصَابِيحَ
وَجَعَلْنٰهَا رُجُومًا لِّلشَّيٰطِينِ وَأَعْتَدْنَا
لَهُمْ عَذَابَ السَّعِيرِ ۝٥

○

ATOM

1. O my dear son! Lo! though it be but the weight of a grain of mustard-seed, and though it be in a rock, or in the heavens, or in the earth, Allah will bring it forth. Lo! Allah is Subtle, Aware.

31:16

1. يٰبُنَيَّ إِنَّهَا إِن تَكُ مِثْقَالَ حَبَّةٍ مِّنْ
خَرْدَلٍ فَتَكُن فِي صَخْرَةٍ أَوْ فِي السَّمٰوٰتِ
أَوْ فِي الْأَرْضِ يَأْتِ بِهَا اللّٰهُ إِنَّ اللّٰهَ
لَطِيفٌ خَبِيرٌ ۝١٦

ASTRONOMY

Ref: 2:29; 16:12; 79:27–28; 86:1–3.

See also: Sky, Stars, Sun, Universe, Zodiacal Signs.

ATTRIBUTES OF ALLAH

1. Praise be to Allah, Lord of the Worlds,

The Beneficent, the Merciful.

Owner of the Day of Judgment,

1:1-3

2. And know that Allah is Aware of all things.

2:231

3. And know that Allah is Forgiving, Clement.

2:235

4. Allah! There is no God save Him, the Alive, the Eternal. Neither slumber nor sleep overtaketh Him. Unto Him belongeth whatsoever is in the heavens and whatsoever is in the earth. Who is he that intercedeth with Him save by His leave? He knoweth that which is in front of them, and that which is behind them while they encompass nothing of His knowledge save what He will. His Throne includeth the heavens and the earth, and He is never weary of preserving them. He is the Sublime, the Tremendous.

2:255

5. Allah is All-Embracing, All-Knowing.

2:261

6. Allah! There is no God save Him, the Alive, the Eternal.

3:2

7. Allah is Mighty, Able to Requite (the wrong)

3:4

8. Our Lord! Cause not our hearts to stray after Thou hast guided us, and bestow upon us mercy from Thy Presence. Lo! Thou, only Thou art the Bestower.

3:8

---

1. الْحَمْدُ لِلّٰهِ رَبِّ الْعٰلَمِيْنَ ۝
الرَّحْمٰنِ الرَّحِيْمِ ۝
مٰلِكِ يَوْمِ الدِّيْنِ ۝

2. وَاعْلَمُوْٓا اَنَّ اللّٰهَ بِكُلِّ شَيْءٍ عَلِيْمٌ ۝٢٣١

3. وَاعْلَمُوْٓا اَنَّ اللّٰهَ غَفُوْرٌ حَلِيْمٌ ۝٢٣٥

4. اَللّٰهُ لَآ اِلٰهَ اِلَّا هُوَ ۚ اَلْحَيُّ الْقَيُّوْمُ ۚ لَا تَاْخُذُهٗ
سِنَةٌ وَّلَا نَوْمٌ ۭ لَهٗ مَا فِي السَّمٰوٰتِ وَمَا
فِي الْاَرْضِ ۭ مَنْ ذَا الَّذِيْ يَشْفَعُ عِنْدَهٗٓ
اِلَّا بِاِذْنِهٖ ۭ يَعْلَمُ مَا بَيْنَ اَيْدِيْهِمْ وَمَا
خَلْفَهُمْ ۚ وَلَا يُحِيْطُوْنَ بِشَيْءٍ مِّنْ عِلْمِهٖٓ اِلَّا
بِمَا شَاۗءَ ۚ وَسِعَ كُرْسِيُّهُ السَّمٰوٰتِ وَالْاَرْضَ ۚ
وَلَا يَـــــُٔـوْدُهٗ حِفْظُهُمَا ۚ وَهُوَ الْعَلِيُّ الْعَظِيْمُ ۝٢٥٥

5. وَاللّٰهُ وَاسِعٌ عَلِيْمٌ ۝٢٦١

6. اَللّٰهُ لَآ اِلٰهَ اِلَّا هُوَ ۙ الْحَيُّ الْقَيُّوْمُ ۝

7. وَاللّٰهُ عَزِيْزٌ ذُو انْتِقَامٍ ۝

8. رَبَّنَا لَا تُزِغْ قُلُوْبَنَا بَعْدَ اِذْ ھَدَيْتَنَا
وَھَبْ لَنَا مِنْ لَّدُنْكَ رَحْمَةً ۚ اِنَّكَ
اَنْتَ الْوَھَّابُ ۝

9. Say: O Allah! Owner of Sovereignty! Thou givest sovereignty unto whom Thou wilt, and Thou withdrawest sovereignty from whom Thou wilt. Thou exaltest whom Thou wilt and Thou abasest whom Thou wilt. In Thy hand is the good. Lo! Thou art Able to do all things.

Thou causest the night to pass into the day, and Thou causest the day to pass into the night. And Thou bringest forth the living from the dead, and Thou bringest forth the dead from the living. And Thou givest sustenance to whom Thou choosest, without stint.

3:26–27

J. Allah is of Infinite Bounty.

3:74

11. Lo! Allah is Forgiving, Clement.

3:155

12. Allah's is the heritage of heavens and the earth, and Allah is Informed of what ye do.

3:180

13. Lo! Allah taketh count of all things.

4:86

14. The Originator of the heavens and the earth! How can He have a child, when there is for Him no consort, when He created all things and is Aware of all things?

Such is Allah, your Lord. There is no God save Him, the Creator of all things, so worship Him. And He taketh care of all things.

Vision comprehendeth Him not, but He comprehendeth (all) vision. He is the Subtile, the Aware.

6:101–103

9. قُلِ اللّٰهُمَّ مٰلِكَ الْمُلْكِ تُؤْتِي الْمُلْكَ
مَنْ تَشَآءُ وَتَنْزِعُ الْمُلْكَ مِمَّنْ تَشَآءُ ز وَ
تُعِزُّ مَنْ تَشَآءُ وَتُذِلُّ مَنْ تَشَآءُ ط بِيَدِكَ
الْخَيْرُ ط اِنَّكَ عَلٰى كُلِّ شَيْءٍ قَدِيْرٌ ○
تُوْلِجُ الَّيْلَ فِي النَّهَارِ وَتُوْلِجُ النَّهَارَ فِي
الَّيْلِ ز وَتُخْرِجُ الْحَيَّ مِنَ الْمَيِّتِ وَتُخْرِجُ
الْمَيِّتَ مِنَ الْحَيِّ ز وَتَرْزُقُ مَنْ تَشَآءُ
بِغَيْرِ حِسَابٍ ○

10. وَاللّٰهُ ذُو الْفَضْلِ الْعَظِيْمِ ○

11. اِنَّ اللّٰهَ غَفُوْرٌ حَلِيْمٌ ○

12. وَلِلّٰهِ مِيْرَاثُ السَّمٰوٰتِ وَالْاَرْضِ ط وَاللّٰهُ
بِمَا تَعْمَلُوْنَ خَبِيْرٌ ○

13. اِنَّ اللّٰهَ كَانَ عَلٰى كُلِّ شَيْءٍ حَسِيْبًا ﴿٨٦﴾

14. بَدِيْعُ السَّمٰوٰتِ وَالْاَرْضِ ط اَنّٰى يَكُوْنُ
لَهٗ وَلَدٌ وَّلَمْ تَكُنْ لَّهٗ صَاحِبَةٌ ط وَخَلَقَ
كُلَّ شَيْءٍ ج وَهُوَ بِكُلِّ شَيْءٍ عَلِيْمٌ ○

ذٰلِكُمُ اللّٰهُ رَبُّكُمْ ج لَآ اِلٰهَ اِلَّا هُوَ ج خَالِقُ
كُلِّ شَيْءٍ فَاعْبُدُوْهُ ج وَهُوَ عَلٰى كُلِّ
شَيْءٍ وَّكِيْلٌ ○

لَا تُدْرِكُهُ الْاَبْصَارُ ز وَهُوَ يُدْرِكُ
الْاَبْصَارَ ج وَهُوَ اللَّطِيْفُ الْخَبِيْرُ ○

15. Lo! Allah is Strong, severe in punishment.
8:52

16. And Allah is in charge of all things.
11:12

17. Lo! my Lord is Guardian over all things.
11:57

18. Lo, my Lord is Nigh, Responsive.
11:61

19. Lo! thy Lord, He is the Strong, the Mighty.
11:66

20. Say: Allah is the Creator of all things, and He is the One, the Almighty.
13:16

21. And say: Praise be to Allah, Who hath not taken unto Himself a son, and Who hath no partner in the Sovereignty, nor hath He any protecting friend through dependence. And magnify Him with all magnificence.
17:111

22. Allah prevails over all things.
18:45

23. Say: Though the sea became ink for the Words of my Lord, verily the sea would be used up before the Words of my Lord were exhausted, even though We brought the like thereof to help.
18:109

15. إِنَّ اللَّهَ قَوِيٌّ شَدِيدُ الْعِقَابِ ﴿٥٢﴾

16. وَاللَّهُ عَلَىٰ كُلِّ شَيْءٍ وَكِيلٌ ﴿١٢﴾

17. إِنَّ رَبِّي عَلَىٰ كُلِّ شَيْءٍ حَفِيظٌ ﴿٥٧﴾

18. إِنَّ رَبِّي قَرِيبٌ مُّجِيبٌ ﴿٦١﴾

19. إِنَّ رَبَّكَ هُوَ الْقَوِيُّ الْعَزِيزُ ﴿٦٦﴾

20. قُلِ اللَّهُ خَالِقُ كُلِّ شَيْءٍ وَهُوَ الْوَاحِدُ الْقَهَّارُ ﴿١٦﴾

21. وَقُلِ الْحَمْدُ لِلَّهِ الَّذِي لَمْ يَتَّخِذْ وَلَدًا وَلَمْ يَكُن لَّهُ شَرِيكٌ فِي الْمُلْكِ وَلَمْ يَكُن لَّهُ وَلِيٌّ مِّنَ الذُّلِّ وَكَبِّرْهُ تَكْبِيرًا ﴿١١١﴾

22. وَكَانَ اللَّهُ عَلَىٰ كُلِّ شَيْءٍ مُّقْتَدِرًا ﴿٤٥﴾

23. قُل لَّوْ كَانَ الْبَحْرُ مِدَادًا لِّكَلِمَاتِ رَبِّي لَنَفِدَ الْبَحْرُ قَبْلَ أَن تَنفَدَ كَلِمَاتُ رَبِّي وَلَوْ جِئْنَا بِمِثْلِهِ مَدَدًا ﴿١٠٩﴾

24. أَنَّمَا إِلَٰهُكُمْ إِلَٰهٌ وَاحِدٌ

25. فَتَعَالَى اللَّهُ الْمَلِكُ الْحَقُّ

26. إِنَّ اللَّهَ عَلَىٰ كُلِّ شَيْءٍ شَهِيدٌ ﴿١٧﴾

27. إِنَّ اللَّهَ لَعَفُوٌّ غَفُورٌ ﴿٦٠﴾

24. Your God is only One God.
18:110

25. Then Exalted be Allah, the True King!
20:114

26. Lo! Allah is Witness over all things.
22:17

27. Lo! Allah verily is Mild, Forgiving.
22:60

28. That is because Allah, He is the True, and that whereon they call instead of Him, it is the False, and because Allah, He is the High, the Great.

22:62

29. Lo! Allah is, for mankind, Full of Pity, Merciful.

22:65

30. So establish worship, pay the poor-due, and hold fast to Allah. He is your Protecting Friend. A blessed Patron and a blessed Helper!

22:78

31. Allah is the Light of the heavens and the earth. The similitude of His light is as a niche wherein is a lamp. The lamp is in a glass. The glass is as it were a shining star. (This lamp is) kindled from a blessed tree, an olive neither of the East nor of the West, whose oil would almost glow forth (of itself) though no fire touched it. Light upon light. Allah guideth unto His light whom He will. And Allah speaketh to mankind in allegories, for Allah is Knower of all things.

24:35

32. There is no God save Him. Everything will perish save His Countenance. His is the command, and unto Him ye will be brought back.

28:88

28. ذٰلِكَ بِأَنَّ اللّٰهَ هُوَ الْحَقُّ وَأَنَّ مَا
يَدْعُونَ مِنْ دُونِهِ هُوَ الْبَاطِلُ وَ
أَنَّ اللّٰهَ هُوَ الْعَلِيُّ الْكَبِيرُ ﴿٦٢﴾

29. إِنَّ اللّٰهَ بِالنَّاسِ لَرَءُوفٌ
رَّحِيمٌ ﴿٦٥﴾

30. فَأَقِيمُوا الصَّلٰوةَ وَآتُوا الزَّكٰوةَ
وَاعْتَصِمُوا بِاللّٰهِ هُوَ مَوْلٰىكُمْ فَنِعْمَ
الْمَوْلٰى وَنِعْمَ النَّصِيرُ ﴿٧٨﴾

31. اللّٰهُ نُورُ السَّمٰوٰتِ وَالْأَرْضِ مَثَلُ
نُورِهِ كَمِشْكٰوةٍ فِيهَا مِصْبَاحٌ الْمِصْبَاحُ
فِي زُجَاجَةٍ الزُّجَاجَةُ كَأَنَّهَا كَوْكَبٌ
دُرِّيٌّ يُوقَدُ مِنْ شَجَرَةٍ مُّبٰرَكَةٍ
زَيْتُونَةٍ لَّا شَرْقِيَّةٍ وَّلَا غَرْبِيَّةٍ
يَكَادُ زَيْتُهَا يُضِيءُ وَلَوْ لَمْ تَمْسَسْهُ
نَارٌ نُّورٌ عَلٰى نُورٍ يَهْدِي اللّٰهُ لِنُورِهِ
مَنْ يَّشَاءُ وَيَضْرِبُ اللّٰهُ الْأَمْثَالَ
لِلنَّاسِ وَاللّٰهُ بِكُلِّ شَيْءٍ عَلِيمٌ ﴿٣٥﴾

32. لَا إِلٰهَ إِلَّا هُوَ كُلُّ شَيْءٍ هَالِكٌ إِلَّا
وَجْهَهُ لَهُ الْحُكْمُ وَإِلَيْهِ
تُرْجَعُونَ ﴿٨٨﴾

33. فَانْظُرْ إِلٰى آثٰرِ رَحْمَتِ اللّٰهِ كَيْفَ
يُحْيِ الْأَرْضَ بَعْدَ مَوْتِهَا إِنَّ ذٰلِكَ
لَمُحْيِ الْمَوْتٰى وَهُوَ عَلٰى كُلِّ شَيْءٍ قَدِيرٌ ﴿٥٠﴾

33 Look, therefor, at the prints of Allah's mercy (in creation): how He quickeneth the earth after her death. Lo! He verily is the Quickener of the Dead, and He is Able to do all things.

30:50

34. And Allah is ever Watcher over all things.

33:52

35. He is the All-knowing Judge.

34:26

36. O mankind! Ye are the poor in your relation to Allah. And Allah! He is the Absolute, the Owner of Praise.

35:15

37. Lord of the heavens and the earth and all that is between them, the Mighty, the Pardoning.

38:66

38. The Forgiver of sin, the Accepter of repentance, the Stern in punishment, the Bountiful. There is no God save Him. Unto Him is the journeying.

40:3

39. Lo! Allah is Forgiving, Responsive.

42:23

40. And He it is Who accepteth repentance from His bondmen, and pardoneth the evil deeds, and knoweth what ye do.

And accepteth those who do good works, and giveth increase unto them of His bounty.

42:25-26

41. And He it is Who sendeth down the saving rain after they have despaired, and spreadeth out His mercy. He is the Protecting Friend, the Praiseworthy.

42:28

34. وَكَانَ اللّٰهُ عَلٰى كُلِّ شَيْءٍ رَّقِيبًا

35. وَهُوَ الْفَتَّاحُ الْعَلِيمُ

36. يٰٓأَيُّهَا النَّاسُ أَنْتُمُ الْفُقَرَآءُ إِلَى اللّٰهِ
وَاللّٰهُ هُوَ الْغَنِيُّ الْحَمِيدُ

37. رَبُّ السَّمٰوٰتِ وَالْأَرْضِ وَمَا بَيْنَهُمَا
الْعَزِيزُ الْغَفَّارُ

38. غَافِرِ الذَّنْبِ وَقَابِلِ التَّوْبِ شَدِيدِ
الْعِقَابِ ذِي الطَّوْلِ لَآ إِلٰهَ إِلَّا هُوَ
إِلَيْهِ الْمَصِيرُ

39. إِنَّ اللّٰهَ غَفُورٌ شَكُورٌ

40. وَهُوَ الَّذِي يَقْبَلُ التَّوْبَةَ عَنْ عِبَادِهِ
وَيَعْفُوا عَنِ السَّيِّاٰتِ وَيَعْلَمُ
مَا تَفْعَلُونَ
وَيَسْتَجِيبُ الَّذِينَ اٰمَنُوا وَعَمِلُوا
الصّٰلِحٰتِ وَيَزِيدُهُمْ مِّنْ فَضْلِهِ

41. وَهُوَ الَّذِي يُنَزِّلُ الْغَيْثَ مِنْ بَعْدِ
مَا قَنَطُوا وَيَنْشُرُ رَحْمَتَهُ وَهُوَ
الْوَلِيُّ الْحَمِيدُ

42. فَلِلّٰهِ الْحَمْدُ رَبِّ السَّمٰوٰتِ وَرَبِّ
الْأَرْضِ رَبِّ الْعٰلَمِينَ
وَلَهُ الْكِبْرِيَآءُ فِي السَّمٰوٰتِ وَالْأَرْضِ
وَهُوَ الْعَزِيزُ الْحَكِيمُ

42. Then praise be to Allah, Lord of the heavens and Lord of the earth, the Lord of the Worlds.

And unto Him (alone) belongeth majesty in the heavens and the earth, and He is the Mighty, the Wise.

45:36–37

43. إِنَّ اللَّهَ هُوَ الرَّزَّاقُ ذُو الْقُوَّةِ الْمَتِينُ ﴿٥٨﴾

44. تَبٰرَكَ اسْمُ رَبِّكَ ذِى الْجَلٰلِ
وَ الْإِكْرَامِ ﴿٧٨﴾

45. هُوَ الْأَوَّلُ وَ الْآخِرُ وَ الظَّاهِرُ وَ الْبَاطِنُ
وَ هُوَ بِكُلِّ شَىْءٍ عَلِيمٌ ﴿٣﴾

46. وَ اللَّهُ ذُو الْفَضْلِ الْعَظِيمِ ﴿٢٩﴾

47. إِنَّ اللَّهَ سَمِيعٌ بَصِيرٌ ﴿١﴾

48. هُوَ اللَّهُ الَّذِى لَآ إِلٰهَ إِلَّا هُوَ عٰلِمُ الْغَيْبِ
وَ الشَّهَادَةِ هُوَ الرَّحْمٰنُ الرَّحِيمُ ﴿٢٢﴾
هُوَ اللَّهُ الَّذِى لَآ إِلٰهَ إِلَّا هُوَ الْمَلِكُ
الْقُدُّوسُ السَّلٰمُ الْمُؤْمِنُ الْمُهَيْمِنُ
الْعَزِيزُ الْجَبَّارُ الْمُتَكَبِّرُ سُبْحٰنَ اللَّهِ
عَمَّا يُشْرِكُونَ ﴿٢٣﴾
هُوَ اللَّهُ الْخٰلِقُ الْبَارِئُ الْمُصَوِّرُ لَهُ
الْأَسْمَآءُ الْحُسْنٰى يُسَبِّحُ لَهُ مَا فِى
السَّمٰوٰتِ وَ الْأَرْضِ وَ هُوَ الْعَزِيزُ الْحَكِيمُ ﴿٢٤﴾

49. وَ اللَّهُ خَيْرُ الرّٰزِقِينَ ﴿١١﴾

50. يٰٓأَيُّهَا الْإِنْسٰنُ مَا غَرَّكَ بِرَبِّكَ
الْكَرِيمِ ﴿٦﴾
الَّذِى خَلَقَكَ فَسَوّٰكَ فَعَدَلَكَ ﴿٧﴾

43. Lo! Allah! He it is Who giveth livelihood, the Lord of unbreakable might.

51:58

44. Blessed be the name of thy Lord, Mighty and Glorious!

55:78

45. He is the First and the Last, and the Outward and the Inward; and He is Knower of all things.

57:3

46. And Allah is of Infinite Bounty.

57:29

47. Lo! Allah is Hearer, Knower.

58:1

48. He is Allah, than Whom there is no other God, the Knower of the Invisible and the Visible. He is the Beneficent, the Merciful.

He is Allah, than Whom there is no other God, the Sovereign Lord, the Holy One, Peace, the Keeper of Faith, the Guardian, the Majestic, the Compeller, the Superb. Glorified be Allah from all that they ascribe as partner (unto Him)!

He is Allah, the Creator, the Shaper out of naught, the Fashioner. His are the most beautiful names. All that is in the heavens and the earth glorifieth Him, and He is the Mighty, the Wise.

59:22-24

49. And Allah is the Best of providers.

62:11

50. O man! What hath made thee careless concerning thy Lord, the Bountiful,

Who created thee, then fashioned, then proportioned thee?

82:6-7

51. Lo! He it is Who produceth, then reproduceth,
And He is the Forgiving, the Loving,
Lord of the Throne of Glory,
Doer of what He will.
85:13--16

51. إِنَّهُ هُوَ يُبْدِئُ وَيُعِيدُ ۝
وَهُوَ الْغَفُورُ الْوَدُودُ ۝
ذُو الْعَرْشِ الْمَجِيدُ ۝
فَعَّالٌ لِّمَا يُرِيدُ ۝

52. Is not Allah the most conclusive of all judges.
95:8

52. أَلَيْسَ اللَّهُ بِأَحْكَمِ الْحَاكِمِينَ ۝

53. Say: He is Allah, the One!
Allah the eternally Besought of all!
He begetteth not nor was begotten,
And there is none comparable unto Him.
112:1-4

53. قُلْ هُوَ اللَّهُ أَحَدٌ ۝
اللَّهُ الصَّمَدُ ۝
لَمْ يَلِدْ وَلَمْ يُولَدْ ۝
وَلَمْ يَكُن لَّهُ كُفُوًا أَحَدٌ ۝

AUTHORITY

1. Their Prophet said unto them: Lo! Allah hath raised up Saul to be a king for you. They said: How can he have kingdom over us when we are more deserving of the kingdom than he is, since he hath not been given wealth enough? He said: Lo! Allah hath chosen him above you, and hath increased him abundantly in wisdom and stature. Allah bestoweth His Sovereignty on whom He will. Allah is All-Embracing, All-Knowing.
2:247

1. وَقَالَ لَهُمْ نَبِيُّهُمْ إِنَّ اللَّهَ قَدْ بَعَثَ لَكُمْ
طَالُوتَ مَلِكًا ۚ قَالُوا أَنَّىٰ يَكُونُ لَهُ الْمُلْكُ
عَلَيْنَا وَنَحْنُ أَحَقُّ بِالْمُلْكِ مِنْهُ وَلَمْ
يُؤْتَ سَعَةً مِّنَ الْمَالِ ۚ قَالَ إِنَّ اللَّهَ
اصْطَفَاهُ عَلَيْكُمْ وَزَادَهُ بَسْطَةً فِي الْعِلْمِ
وَالْجِسْمِ ۖ وَاللَّهُ يُؤْتِي مُلْكَهُ مَن يَشَاءُ ۚ
وَاللَّهُ وَاسِعٌ عَلِيمٌ ۝

2. Say O Allah! Owner of Sovereignty! Thou givest sovereignty unto whom Thou wilt, and Thou withdrawest sovereignty from whom Thou wilt. Thou exaltest whom Thou wilt and Thou abasest whom Thou wilt. In Thy hand is the good. Lo! Thou art Able to do all things.
3:26

2. قُلِ اللَّهُمَّ مَالِكَ الْمُلْكِ تُؤْتِي الْمُلْكَ
مَن تَشَاءُ وَتَنزِعُ الْمُلْكَ مِمَّن تَشَاءُ وَ
تُعِزُّ مَن تَشَاءُ وَتُذِلُّ مَن تَشَاءُ ۖ بِيَدِكَ
الْخَيْرُ ۖ إِنَّكَ عَلَىٰ كُلِّ شَيْءٍ قَدِيرٌ ۝

ATTRIBUTES OF ALLAH

Ref: 2:37; 11:73 24:20; 52:28; 3:155; 13:12; 17:111; 8:109; 18:110; 22:60,65: 38:66; 42:23; 45:36–37; 55:78; 57:29.

3. Those who, if We give them power in the land, establish worship and pay the poor-due and enjoin kindness and forbid iniquity. And Allah's is the sequel of events.

22:41

3. اَلَّذِيْنَ اِنْ مَّكَّنّٰهُمْ فِي الْاَرْضِ
اَقَامُوا الصَّلٰوةَ وَاٰتَوُا الزَّكٰوةَ وَاَمَرُوْا
بِالْمَعْرُوْفِ وَنَهَوْا عَنِ الْمُنْكَرِ ۭ
وَلِلّٰهِ عَاقِبَةُ الْاُمُوْرِ ۝

4. Allah hath promised such of you as believe and do good works that He will surely make them to succeed (the present rulers) in the earth even as He caused those who were before them to succeed (others) and that He will surely establish for them their religion which He hath approved for them, and will give them in exchange safety after their fear. They serve Me. They ascribe nothing as partner unto Me. Those who disbelieve henceforth, they are the miscreants.

24:55

4. وَعَدَ اللّٰهُ الَّذِيْنَ اٰمَنُوْا مِنْكُمْ وَعَمِلُوا
الصّٰلِحٰتِ لَيَسْتَخْلِفَنَّهُمْ فِي الْاَرْضِ
كَمَا اسْتَخْلَفَ الَّذِيْنَ مِنْ قَبْلِهِمْ
وَلَيُمَكِّنَنَّ لَهُمْ دِيْنَهُمُ الَّذِي ارْتَضٰى
لَهُمْ وَلَيُبَدِّلَنَّهُمْ مِّنْۢ بَعْدِ خَوْفِهِمْ
اَمْنًا ۭ يَعْبُدُوْنَنِيْ لَا يُشْرِكُوْنَ بِيْ
شَيْـــًٔا ۭ وَمَنْ كَفَرَ بَعْدَ ذٰلِكَ
فَاُولٰۗىِٕكَ هُمُ الْفٰسِقُوْنَ ۝

Ref: 4:58–61; 5:45–50; 6:6; 12:21,56; 18:84;
See also: Sovereignty of Allah.

BACKBITING

1. O ye who believe! Shun much suspicion; for lo! some suspicion is a crime. And spy not, neither back-bite one another. Would one of you love to eat the flesh of his dead brother? Ye abhor that (so abhor the other)! And keep your duty (to Allah). Lo! Allah is Relenting, Merciful.

49:12

BAD HABITS

1. (O man), follow not that whereof thou hast no knowledge. Lo! the hearing and the sight and the heart - of each of these it will be asked.

And walk not in the earth exultant. Lo! thou canst not rend the earth, nor canst thou stretch to the height of the hills.

The evil of all that is hateful in the sight of thy Lord.

17:36–38

2. Lo! they who spread the slander are a gang among you. Deem it not a bad thing for you; nay, it is good for you. Unto every man of them (will be paid) that which he hath earned of the sin; and as for him among them who had the greater share therein, his will be an awful doom.

24:11

1. يٰٓاَيُّهَا الَّذِيْنَ اٰمَنُوا اجْتَنِبُوْا كَثِيْرًا
مِّنَ الظَّنِّ اِنَّ بَعْضَ الظَّنِّ اِثْمٌ وَّلَا
تَجَسَّسُوْا وَلَا يَغْتَبْ بَّعْضُكُمْ بَعْضًا ؕ
اَيُحِبُّ اَحَدُكُمْ اَنْ يَّاْكُلَ لَحْمَ اَخِيْهِ
مَيْتًا فَكَرِهْتُمُوْهُ ؕ وَاتَّقُوا اللّٰهَ ؕ اِنَّ
اللّٰهَ تَوَّابٌ رَّحِيْمٌ ۝١٢

1. وَلَا تَقْفُ مَا لَيْسَ لَكَ بِهٖ عِلْمٌ ؕ اِنَّ
السَّمْعَ وَالْبَصَرَ وَالْفُؤَادَ كُلُّ اُولٰٓئِكَ
كَانَ عَنْهُ مَسْـُٔوْلًا ۝٣٦
وَلَا تَمْشِ فِى الْاَرْضِ مَرَحًا ۚ اِنَّكَ
لَنْ تَخْرِقَ الْاَرْضَ وَلَنْ تَبْلُغَ
الْجِبَالَ طُوْلًا ۝٣٧
كُلُّ ذٰلِكَ كَانَ سَيِّئُهٗ عِنْدَ
رَبِّكَ مَكْرُوْهًا ۝٣٨

2. اِنَّ الَّذِيْنَ جَآءُوْ بِالْاِفْكِ عُصْبَةٌ
مِّنْكُمْ ؕ لَا تَحْسَبُوْهُ شَرًّا لَّكُمْ ؕ بَلْ
هُوَ خَيْرٌ لَّكُمْ ؕ لِكُلِّ امْرِئٍ مِّنْهُمْ
مَّا اكْتَسَبَ مِنَ الْاِثْمِ ۚ وَالَّذِىْ تَوَلّٰى
كِبْرَهٗ مِنْهُمْ لَهٗ عَذَابٌ عَظِيْمٌ ۝١١

3. وَبَدَا لَهُمْ سَيِّاٰتُ مَا عَمِلُوْا وَحَاقَ
بِهِمْ مَّا كَانُوْا بِهٖ يَسْتَهْزِءُوْنَ

3. And the evils of what they did will appear unto them, and that which they used to deride will befall them.

45:33

4. O ye who believe! Let not a folk deride a folk who may be better than they (are), nor let women (deride) women who may be better than they are; neither defame one another, nor insult one another by nicknames. Bad is the name of lewdness after faith. And whoso turneth not in repentance, such are evil-doers.

O ye who believe! Shun much suspicion; for lo! some suspicion is a crime. And spy not, neither back-bite one another. Would one of you love to eat the flesh of his dead brother? Ye abhor that (so abhor the other)! And keep your duty (to Allah). Lo! Allah is Relenting, Merciful.

49:11-12

5. Woe unto every slandering traducer.

Who hath gathered wealth (of this world) and arranged it:

He thinketh that his wealth will render him immortal.

Nay, but verily he will be flung to the Consuming One.

Ah, what will convey unto thee what the Consuming One is!

(It is) the fire of Allah, kindled,

Which leapeth up over the hearts (of men).

Lo! it is closed in on them

in out-stretched columns.

104:1-9

4. يَٰٓأَيُّهَا ٱلَّذِينَ ءَامَنُوا۟ لَا يَسْخَرْ قَوْمٌ
مِّن قَوْمٍ عَسَىٰٓ أَن يَكُونُوا۟ خَيْرًا
مِّنْهُمْ وَلَا نِسَآءٌ مِّن نِّسَآءٍ عَسَىٰٓ
أَن يَكُنَّ خَيْرًا مِّنْهُنَّ ۖ وَلَا تَلْمِزُوٓا۟
أَنفُسَكُمْ وَلَا تَنَابَزُوا۟ بِٱلْأَلْقَٰبِ ۖ
بِئْسَ ٱلِٱسْمُ ٱلْفُسُوقُ بَعْدَ ٱلْإِيمَٰنِ ۚ
وَمَن لَّمْ يَتُبْ فَأُو۟لَٰٓئِكَ هُمُ ٱلظَّٰلِمُونَ ﴿١١﴾
يَٰٓأَيُّهَا ٱلَّذِينَ ءَامَنُوا۟ ٱجْتَنِبُوا۟ كَثِيرًا
مِّنَ ٱلظَّنِّ إِنَّ بَعْضَ ٱلظَّنِّ إِثْمٌ ۖ وَلَا
تَجَسَّسُوا۟ وَلَا يَغْتَب بَّعْضُكُم بَعْضًا ۚ
أَيُحِبُّ أَحَدُكُمْ أَن يَأْكُلَ لَحْمَ أَخِيهِ
مَيْتًا فَكَرِهْتُمُوهُ ۚ وَٱتَّقُوا۟ ٱللَّهَ ۚ إِنَّ
ٱللَّهَ تَوَّابٌ رَّحِيمٌ ﴿١٢﴾

5. وَيْلٌ لِّكُلِّ هُمَزَةٍ لُّمَزَةٍ ﴿١﴾
ٱلَّذِى جَمَعَ مَالًا وَعَدَّدَهُۥ ﴿٢﴾
يَحْسَبُ أَنَّ مَالَهُۥٓ أَخْلَدَهُۥ ﴿٣﴾
كَلَّا ۖ لَيُنۢبَذَنَّ فِى ٱلْحُطَمَةِ ﴿٤﴾
وَمَآ أَدْرَىٰكَ مَا ٱلْحُطَمَةُ ﴿٥﴾
نَارُ ٱللَّهِ ٱلْمُوقَدَةُ ﴿٦﴾
ٱلَّتِى تَطَّلِعُ عَلَى ٱلْأَفْـِٔدَةِ ﴿٧﴾
إِنَّهَا عَلَيْهِم مُّؤْصَدَةٌ ﴿٨﴾
فِى عَمَدٍ مُّمَدَّدَةٍ ﴿٩﴾

See also: Abuse, Back-biting, Envy Falsehood, Suspicion, Whispering.

BANISHMENT

1. Yet ye it is who slay each other and drive out a party of your people from their homes, supporting one another against them by sin and transgression—and if they came to you as captives ye would ransom them, whereas their expulsion was itself unlawful for you—Believe ye in part of the Scripture and disbelieve ye in part thereof? And what is the reward of those who do so save ignominy in the life of the world, and on the Day of Resurrection they will be consigned to the most grievous doom. For Allah is not unaware of what ye do.

2:85

2. And slay them wherever ye find them, and drive them out of the places whence they drove you out, for persecution is worse than slaughter. And fight not with them at the Inviolable Place of Worship until they first attack you there, but if they attack you (there) then slay them. Such is the reward of disbelievers.

2:191

3. And those who disbelieved said unto their messengers: Verily we will drive you out from our land, unless ye return to our religion. Then their Lord inspired them, (saying): Verily We shall destroy the wrongdoers,

1. ثُمَّ أَنْتُمْ هٰؤُلَاءِ تَقْتُلُوْنَ أَنْفُسَكُمْ وَتُخْرِجُوْنَ
فَرِيْقًا مِّنْكُمْ مِّنْ دِيَارِهِمْ تَظٰهَرُوْنَ عَلَيْهِمْ
بِالْإِثْمِ وَالْعُدْوَانِ وَإِنْ يَّأْتُوْكُمْ أُسٰرٰى
تُفٰدُوْهُمْ وَهُوَ مُحَرَّمٌ عَلَيْكُمْ إِخْرَاجُهُمْ
أَفَتُؤْمِنُوْنَ بِبَعْضِ الْكِتٰبِ وَتَكْفُرُوْنَ بِبَعْضٍ
فَمَا جَزَاءُ مَنْ يَّفْعَلُ ذٰلِكَ مِنْكُمْ إِلَّا خِزْيٌ
فِي الْحَيٰوةِ الدُّنْيَا وَيَوْمَ الْقِيٰمَةِ يُرَدُّوْنَ إِلٰى
أَشَدِّ الْعَذَابِ وَمَا اللّٰهُ بِغَافِلٍ عَمَّا تَعْمَلُوْنَ ﴿٨٥﴾

2. وَاقْتُلُوْهُمْ حَيْثُ ثَقِفْتُمُوْهُمْ وَأَخْرِجُوْهُمْ
مِّنْ حَيْثُ أَخْرَجُوْكُمْ وَالْفِتْنَةُ أَشَدُّ مِنَ
الْقَتْلِ وَلَا تُقٰتِلُوْهُمْ عِنْدَ الْمَسْجِدِ الْحَرَامِ
حَتّٰى يُقٰتِلُوْكُمْ فِيْهِ فَإِنْ قٰتَلُوْكُمْ فَاقْتُلُوْهُمْ
كَذٰلِكَ جَزَاءُ الْكٰفِرِيْنَ ﴿١٩١﴾

3. وَقَالَ الَّذِيْنَ كَفَرُوْا لِرُسُلِهِمْ لَنُخْرِجَنَّكُمْ
مِّنْ أَرْضِنَا أَوْ لَتَعُوْدُنَّ فِيْ مِلَّتِنَا
فَأَوْحٰى إِلَيْهِمْ رَبُّهُمْ لَنُهْلِكَنَّ الظّٰلِمِيْنَ ﴿١٣﴾
وَلَنُسْكِنَنَّكُمُ الْأَرْضَ مِنْ بَعْدِهِمْ
ذٰلِكَ لِمَنْ خَافَ مَقَامِيْ وَخَافَ وَعِيْدِ ﴿١٤﴾

4. أُذِنَ لِلَّذِيْنَ يُقٰتَلُوْنَ بِأَنَّهُمْ ظُلِمُوْا
وَإِنَّ اللّٰهَ عَلٰى نَصْرِهِمْ لَقَدِيْرٌ ﴿٣٩﴾

And verily We shall make you to dwell in the land after them. This is for him who feareth My Majesty and feareth My Threats.

14:13-14

4 Sanction is given unto those who fight because they have been wronged; and Allah is indeed

Ablę to give them victory:
Those who have been driven from their homes unjustly only because they said: Our Lord is Allah.

22:39-40

5. He it is Who hath caused those of the People of the Scripture who disbelieved to go forth from their homes unto the first exile. Ye deemed not that they would go forth, while they deemed that their strongholds would protect them from Allah. But Allah reached them from a place whereof they recked not, and cast terror in their hearts so that they ruined their houses with their own hands and the hands of the believers. So learn a lesson, O ye who have eyes!

And if Allah had not decreed migration for them, He verily would have punished them in this world, and theirs in the Hereafter is the punishment of the Fire.

59:2-3

6. And (it is) for the poor fugitives who have been driven out from their homes and their belongings, who seek bounty from Allah and help Allah and His messenger. They are the loyal.

59:8

الَّذِينَ أُخْرِجُوا مِن دِيَارِهِم بِغَيْرِ
حَقٍّ إِلَّا أَن يَقُولُوا رَبُّنَا اللَّهُ

5. هُوَ الَّذِي أَخْرَجَ الَّذِينَ كَفَرُوا مِنْ أَهْلِ
الْكِتَابِ مِن دِيَارِهِمْ لِأَوَّلِ الْحَشْرِ ۚ مَا
ظَنَنتُمْ أَن يَخْرُجُوا ۖ وَظَنُّوا أَنَّهُم مَّانِعَتُهُمْ
حُصُونُهُم مِّنَ اللَّهِ فَأَتَاهُمُ اللَّهُ مِنْ
حَيْثُ لَمْ يَحْتَسِبُوا ۖ وَقَذَفَ فِي
قُلُوبِهِمُ الرُّعْبَ يُخْرِبُونَ بُيُوتَهُم
بِأَيْدِيهِمْ وَأَيْدِي الْمُؤْمِنِينَ فَاعْتَبِرُوا
يَا أُولِي الْأَبْصَارِ ﴿٢﴾
وَلَوْلَا أَن كَتَبَ اللَّهُ عَلَيْهِمُ الْجَلَاءَ
لَعَذَّبَهُمْ فِي الدُّنْيَا ۖ وَلَهُمْ فِي الْآخِرَةِ
عَذَابُ النَّارِ ﴿٣﴾

6. لِلْفُقَرَاءِ الْمُهَاجِرِينَ الَّذِينَ أُخْرِجُوا
مِن دِيَارِهِمْ وَأَمْوَالِهِمْ يَبْتَغُونَ
فَضْلًا مِّنَ اللَّهِ وَرِضْوَانًا وَيَنصُرُونَ
اللَّهَ وَرَسُولَهُ ۚ أُولَٰئِكَ هُمُ الصَّادِقُونَ ﴿٨﴾

Ref: 2:246; 3:195;

BARZAKH

1. Until, when death cometh unto one of them, he saith: My Lord! Send me back,

That I may do right in that which I have left behind! But nay! It is but a word that he speaketh; and behind them is a barrier until the day when they are raised.

23:99-100

2. A dreadful doom encompassed Pharaoh's folk.

The Fire; they are exposed to it morning and evening; and on the day when the Hour upriseth (it is said): Cause Pharaoh's folk to enter the most awful doom.

40:45-46

BEATIFIC VISION OF ALLAH

1. And whoever hopeth for the meeting with his Lord, let him do righteous work, and make none sharer of the worship due unto his Lord.

18:110

2. Whoso looketh forward to the meeting with Allah (let him know that) Allah's reckoning is surely nigh, and He is the Hearer, the Knower.

29:5

3. That day will faces be resplendent,

Looking toward their Lord;

1. حَتّٰٓى اِذَا جَآءَ اَحَدَهُمُ الْمَوْتُ قَالَ
رَبِّ ارْجِعُوْنِ ﴿۹۹﴾
لَعَلِّيْٓ اَعْمَلُ صَالِحًا فِيْمَا تَرَكْتُ
كَلَّا ؕ اِنَّهَا كَلِمَةٌ هُوَ قَآئِلُهَا ؕ وَمِنْ
وَّرَآئِهِمْ بَرْزَخٌ اِلٰى يَوْمِ يُبْعَثُوْنَ ﴿۱۰۰﴾

2. وَحَاقَ بِاٰلِ فِرْعَوْنَ سُوْٓءُ الْعَذَابِ ﴿۴۵﴾
اَلنَّارُ يُعْرَضُوْنَ عَلَيْهَا غُدُوًّا وَّ
عَشِيًّا ۚ وَيَوْمَ تَقُوْمُ السَّاعَةُ ۫ اَدْخِلُوْٓا
اٰلَ فِرْعَوْنَ اَشَدَّ الْعَذَابِ ﴿۴۶﴾

1. فَمَنْ كَانَ يَرْجُوْا لِقَآءَ رَبِّهٖ فَلْيَعْمَلْ
عَمَلًا صَالِحًا وَّلَا يُشْرِكْ بِعِبَادَةِ
رَبِّهٖٓ اَحَدًا ﴿۱۱۰﴾

2. مَنْ كَانَ يَرْجُوْا لِقَآءَ اللّٰهِ فَاِنَّ اَجَلَ
اللّٰهِ لَاٰتٍ ؕ وَهُوَ السَّمِيْعُ الْعَلِيْمُ ﴿۵﴾

3. وُجُوْهٌ يَّوْمَئِذٍ نَّاضِرَةٌ ﴿۲۲﴾
اِلٰى رَبِّهَا نَاظِرَةٌ ﴿۲۳﴾
وَوُجُوْهٌ يَّوْمَئِذٍۭ بَاسِرَةٌ ﴿۲۴﴾
تَظُنُّ اَنْ يُّفْعَلَ بِهَا فَاقِرَةٌ ﴿۲۵﴾

And that day will other faces be despondent,

Thou wilt know that some great disaster is about to fall on them.

75:22-25

BARZAKH

See also: Grave.

BEAUTY AND GRACE

1. Allah it is Who appointed for you the earth for a dwelling-place and the sky for a canopy, and fashioned you and perfected your shapes, and hath provided you with good things. Such is Allah, your Lord. Then blessed be Allah, the Lord of the Worlds!

40:64

2. He created the heavens and the earth with truth, and He shaped you and made good your shapes, and unto Him is the journeying.

64:3

BEAUTY OF NATURE

1. And verily in the heaven We have set mansions of the stars, and We have beautified it for beholders.

15:16

2. Have they not then observed the sky above them, how We have constructed it and beautified it, and how there are no rifts therein!

And the earth have We spread out, and have flung firm hills therein, and have caused of every lovely kind to grow thereon,

A vision and a reminder for every penitent slave.

And We send down from the sky blessed water whereby We give growth unto gardens and the grain of crops,

And lofty date-palms with ranged clusters,

Provision (made) for men; and therewith We quicken a dead land. Even so will be the resurrection of the dead.

50:6-11

1. اَللّٰهُ الَّذِیْ جَعَلَ لَكُمُ الْاَرْضَ قَرَارًا
وَّ السَّمَآءَ بِنَآءً وَّ صَوَّرَكُمْ فَاَحْسَنَ
صُوَرَكُمْ وَ رَزَقَكُمْ مِّنَ الطَّیِّبٰتِ ذٰلِكُمُ
اللّٰهُ رَبُّكُمْ فَتَبٰرَكَ اللّٰهُ رَبُّ الْعٰلَمِیْنَ ﴿٦٤﴾

2. خَلَقَ السَّمٰوٰتِ وَ الْاَرْضَ بِالْحَقِّ
وَ صَوَّرَكُمْ فَاَحْسَنَ صُوَرَكُمْ وَ
اِلَیْهِ الْمَصِیْرُ ﴿٣﴾

1. وَ لَقَدْ جَعَلْنَا فِی السَّمَآءِ بُرُوْجًا وَّ
زَیَّنّٰهَا لِلنّٰظِرِیْنَ ﴿١٦﴾

2. اَفَلَمْ یَنْظُرُوْۤا اِلَی السَّمَآءِ فَوْقَهُمْ كَیْفَ
بَنَیْنٰهَا وَ زَیَّنّٰهَا وَ مَا لَهَا مِنْ فُرُوْجٍ ﴿٦﴾
وَ الْاَرْضَ مَدَدْنٰهَا وَ اَلْقَیْنَا فِیْهَا
رَوَاسِیَ وَ اَنْۢبَتْنَا فِیْهَا مِنْ كُلِّ
زَوْجٍۭ بَهِیْجٍ ﴿٧﴾
تَبْصِرَةً وَّ ذِكْرٰی لِكُلِّ عَبْدٍ مُّنِیْبٍ ﴿٨﴾
وَ نَزَّلْنَا مِنَ السَّمَآءِ مَآءً مُّبٰرَكًا
فَاَنْۢبَتْنَا بِهٖ جَنّٰتٍ وَّ حَبَّ الْحَصِیْدِ ﴿٩﴾
وَ النَّخْلَ بٰسِقٰتٍ لَّهَا طَلْعٌ نَّضِیْدٌ ﴿١٠﴾
رِّزْقًا لِّلْعِبَادِ وَ اَحْیَیْنَا بِهٖ بَلْدَةً مَّیْتًا
كَذٰلِكَ الْخُرُوْجُ ﴿١١﴾

BEDOUIN

1. الْأَعْرَابُ أَشَدُّ كُفْرًا وَنِفَاقًا وَأَجْدَرُ أَلَّا
يَعْلَمُوا حُدُودَ مَا أَنزَلَ اللَّهُ عَلَىٰ رَسُولِهِ
وَاللَّهُ عَلِيمٌ حَكِيمٌ ﴿٩٧﴾
وَمِنَ الْأَعْرَابِ مَن يَتَّخِذُ مَا يُنفِقُ
مَغْرَمًا وَيَتَرَبَّصُ بِكُمُ الدَّوَائِرَ عَلَيْهِمْ
دَائِرَةُ السَّوْءِ وَاللَّهُ سَمِيعٌ عَلِيمٌ ﴿٩٨﴾
وَمِنَ الْأَعْرَابِ مَن يُؤْمِنُ بِاللَّهِ وَ
الْيَوْمِ الْآخِرِ وَيَتَّخِذُ مَا يُنفِقُ قُرُبَاتٍ
عِندَ اللَّهِ وَصَلَوَاتِ الرَّسُولِ أَلَا إِنَّهَا
قُرْبَةٌ لَّهُمْ سَيُدْخِلُهُمُ اللَّهُ فِي رَحْمَتِهِ
إِنَّ اللَّهَ غَفُورٌ رَّحِيمٌ ﴿٩٩﴾

1. The wandering Arabs are more hard in disbelief and hypocrisy, and more likely to be ignorant of the limits which Allah hath revealed unto His messenger. And Allah is Knower, Wise.

And of the wandering Arabs there is he who taketh that which he expendeth (for the cause of Allah), as a loss, and awaiteth (evil) turns of fortune for you (that he may be rid of it). The evil turn of fortune will be theirs. Allah is Hearer, Knower.

And of the wandering Arabs there is he who believeth in Allah and the Last Day, and taketh that which he expendeth and also the prayers of the messenger as acceptable offerings in the sight of Allah Lo! verily it is an acceptable offering for them. Allah will bring them unto His mercy. Lo! Allah is Forgiving, Merciful.

9:97–99

2. مَا كَانَ لِأَهْلِ الْمَدِينَةِ وَمَنْ حَوْلَهُم
مِّنَ الْأَعْرَابِ أَن يَتَخَلَّفُوا عَن رَّسُولِ
اللَّهِ وَلَا يَرْغَبُوا بِأَنفُسِهِمْ عَن نَّفْسِهِ
ذَٰلِكَ بِأَنَّهُمْ لَا يُصِيبُهُمْ ظَمَأٌ وَلَا نَصَبٌ
وَلَا مَخْمَصَةٌ فِي سَبِيلِ اللَّهِ وَلَا يَطَئُونَ
مَوْطِئًا يَغِيظُ الْكُفَّارَ وَلَا يَنَالُونَ مِنْ
عَدُوٍّ نَّيْلًا إِلَّا كُتِبَ لَهُم بِهِ عَمَلٌ صَالِحٌ
إِنَّ اللَّهَ لَا يُضِيعُ أَجْرَ الْمُحْسِنِينَ ﴿١٢٠﴾
وَلَا يُنفِقُونَ نَفَقَةً صَغِيرَةً وَلَا كَبِيرَةً
وَلَا يَقْطَعُونَ وَادِيًا إِلَّا كُتِبَ لَهُمْ لِيَجْزِيَهُمُ
اللَّهُ أَحْسَنَ مَا كَانُوا يَعْمَلُونَ ﴿١٢١﴾

2. It is not for the townsfolk of Al-Madinah and for those around them of the wandering Arabs to stay behind the messenger of Allah and prefer their lives to his life. That is because neither thirst nor toil nor hunger afflicteth them in the way of Allah, nor step they any step that angereth the disbelievers, nor gain they from the enemy a gain, but a good deed is recorded for them therefor. Lo! Allah loseth not the wages of the good.

Nor spend they any spending, small or great, nor do they cross a valley, but it is recorded for them: that Allah may repay them the best of what they used to do.

9:120-121

3. Those of the wandering Arabs who were left behind will tell thee: Our possessions and our house-holds occupied us, so ask forgiveness for us! They speak with their tongues that which is not in their hearts. Say: Who can avail you aught against Allah, if He intend you hurt or intend you profit? Nay, but Allah is ever Aware of what ye do.

Nay, but ye deemed that the messenger and the believers would never return to their own folk, and that was made fairseeming in your hearts, and ye did think an evil thought, and ye were worthless folk.

And as for him who believeth not in Allah and His messenger—Lo! We have prepared a flame for disbelievers.

And Allah's is the Sovereignty of the heavens and the earth. He forgiveth whom He will, and punisheth whom He will. And Allah is ever Forgiving, Merciful.

Those who were left behind will say, when ye set forth to capture booty: Let us go with you. They fain would change the verdict of Allah. Say (unto them, O Muhammad): Ye shall not go with us. Thus hath Allah said beforehand. Then they will say: Ye are envious of us. Nay, but they

3. سَيَقُوْلُ لَكَ الْمُخَلَّفُوْنَ مِنَ الْاَعْرَابِ
شَغَلَتْنَآ اَمْوَالُنَا وَ اَهْلُوْنَا فَاسْتَغْفِرْ لَنَا
يَقُوْلُوْنَ بِاَلْسِنَتِهِمْ مَّا لَيْسَ فِيْ
قُلُوْبِهِمْ قُلْ فَمَنْ يَّمْلِكُ لَكُمْ
مِّنَ اللّٰهِ شَيْـًٔا اِنْ اَرَادَ بِكُمْ ضَرًّا
اَوْ اَرَادَ بِكُمْ نَفْعًا بَلْ كَانَ اللّٰهُ
بِمَا تَعْمَلُوْنَ خَبِيْرًا ﴿١١﴾
بَلْ ظَنَنْتُمْ اَنْ لَّنْ يَّنْقَلِبَ الرَّسُوْلُ
وَ الْمُؤْمِنُوْنَ اِلٰٓى اَهْلِيْهِمْ اَبَدًا وَّ زُيِّنَ
ذٰلِكَ فِيْ قُلُوْبِكُمْ وَظَنَنْتُمْ ظَنَّ السَّوْءِ
وَكُنْتُمْ قَوْمًا بُوْرًا ﴿١٢﴾
وَ مَنْ لَّمْ يُؤْمِنْ بِاللّٰهِ وَرَسُوْلِهٖ فَاِنَّآ
اَعْتَدْنَا لِلْكٰفِرِيْنَ سَعِيْرًا ﴿١٣﴾
وَ لِلّٰهِ مُلْكُ السَّمٰوٰتِ وَ الْاَرْضِ يَغْفِرُ
لِمَنْ يَّشَآءُ وَ يُعَذِّبُ مَنْ يَّشَآءُ وَ
كَانَ اللّٰهُ غَفُوْرًا رَّحِيْمًا ﴿١٤﴾
سَيَقُوْلُ الْمُخَلَّفُوْنَ اِذَا انْطَلَقْتُمْ اِلٰى
مَغَانِمَ لِتَاْخُذُوْهَا ذَرُوْنَا نَتَّبِعْكُمْ
يُرِيْدُوْنَ اَنْ يُّبَدِّلُوْا كَلٰمَ اللّٰهِ
قُلْ لَّنْ تَتَّبِعُوْنَا كَذٰلِكُمْ قَالَ اللّٰهُ
مِنْ قَبْلُ فَسَيَقُوْلُوْنَ بَلْ تَحْسُدُوْنَنَا
بَلْ كَانُوْا لَا يَفْقَهُوْنَ اِلَّا قَلِيْلًا ﴿١٥﴾
قُلْ لِّلْمُخَلَّفِيْنَ مِنَ الْاَعْرَابِ
سَتُدْعَوْنَ اِلٰى قَوْمٍ اُولِيْ بَاْسٍ شَدِيْدٍ

understand not, save a little.

Say unto those of the wandering Arabs who were left behind: Ye will be called against a folk of mighty prowess, to fight them until they surrender; and if ye obey, Allah will give you a fair reward; but if ye turn away as ye did turn away before, He will punish you with a painful doom.

48:11-16

4. The wandering Arabs say: We believe. Say (unto them, O Muhammad): Ye believe not, but rather say "We submit," for the faith hath not yet entered into your hearts. Yet, if ye obey Allah and His messenger, He will not withhold from you aught of (the reward of) your deeds. Lo! Allah is Forgiving, Merciful.

49:14

BEGGARY

1. A kind word with forgiveness is better than almsgiving followed by injury. Allah is Absolute, Clement.

2:263

2. (Alms are) for the poor who are straitened for the cause of Allah, who cannot travel in the land (for trade). The unthinking man accounteth them wealthy because of their restraint. Thou shalt know them by their mark: They do not beg of men with importunity. And whatsoever good thing ye spend, lo! Allah

تُقَاتِلُونَهُمْ أَوْ يُسْلِمُونَ ۖ فَإِنْ تُطِيعُوا
يُؤْتِكُمُ اللَّهُ أَجْرًا حَسَنًا ۖ وَإِنْ تَتَوَلَّوْا
كَمَا تَوَلَّيْتُمْ مِنْ قَبْلُ يُعَذِّبْكُمْ
عَذَابًا أَلِيمًا ﴿١٦﴾

4. قَالَتِ الْأَعْرَابُ آمَنَّا ۖ قُلْ لَمْ تُؤْمِنُوا
وَلَٰكِنْ قُولُوا أَسْلَمْنَا وَلَمَّا يَدْخُلِ
الْإِيمَانُ فِي قُلُوبِكُمْ ۖ وَإِنْ تُطِيعُوا
اللَّهَ وَرَسُولَهُ لَا يَلِتْكُمْ مِنْ أَعْمَالِكُمْ
شَيْئًا ۚ إِنَّ اللَّهَ غَفُورٌ رَحِيمٌ ﴿١٤﴾

1. قَوْلٌ مَعْرُوفٌ وَمَغْفِرَةٌ خَيْرٌ مِنْ صَدَقَةٍ
يَتْبَعُهَا أَذًى ۗ وَاللَّهُ غَنِيٌّ حَلِيمٌ ﴿٢٦٣﴾

2. لِلْفُقَرَاءِ الَّذِينَ أُحْصِرُوا فِي سَبِيلِ اللَّهِ لَا
يَسْتَطِيعُونَ ضَرْبًا فِي الْأَرْضِ يَحْسَبُهُمُ
الْجَاهِلُ أَغْنِيَاءَ مِنَ التَّعَفُّفِ تَعْرِفُهُمْ
بِسِيمَاهُمْ لَا يَسْأَلُونَ النَّاسَ إِلْحَافًا ۗ وَمَا
تُنْفِقُوا مِنْ خَيْرٍ فَإِنَّ اللَّهَ بِهِ عَلِيمٌ ﴿٢٧٣﴾

3. وَأَمَّا السَّائِلَ فَلَا تَنْهَرْ ﴿١٠﴾

knoweth it.

2:273

3. Therefor the beggar drive not away,

93:10

BEDOUIN

Ref: 9:90–101; 33:20; 49:14–17.

BEGGARY

Ref: 2:177,272–273; 4:6; 9:7,60; 22:28; 51:9; 59:8.

See also: Alms, Charity.

BELIEVERS AND DISBELIEVERS

1. Is one who followeth the pleasure of Allah as one who hath earned condemnation from Allah, whose habitation is the Fire, a hapless journey's end?

There are degrees (of grace and reprobation) with Allah, and Allah is Seer of what ye do.

3:162–163

2. Is he whom We have promised a fair promise which he will find (true) like him whom We suffer to enjoy awhile the comfort of the life of the world, then on the Day of Resurrection he will be of those arraigned?

28:61

3. As for those who believed and did good works, they will be made happy in a Garden.

But as for those who disbelieved and denied Our revelations, and denied the meeting of the Hereafter, such will be brought to doom.

30:15–16

4. Is he who is a believer like unto him who is an evil-liver? They are not alike.

But as for those who believe and do good works, for them are the Gardens of Retreat—a welcome (in reward) for what they used to do.

And as for those who do evil, their retreat is the Fire. Whenever they desire to issue forth from thence, they are brought back thither. Unto

1. أَفَمَنِ اتَّبَعَ رِضْوَانَ اللَّهِ كَمَنْ بَاءَ بِسَخَطٍ
مِّنَ اللَّهِ وَمَأْوٰىهُ جَهَنَّمُ ۚ وَبِئْسَ الْمَصِيرُ ○
هُمْ دَرَجٰتٌ عِنْدَ اللَّهِ ۗ وَاللَّهُ بَصِيرٌ
بِمَا يَعْمَلُونَ ○

2. أَفَمَنْ وَعَدْنٰهُ وَعْدًا حَسَنًا فَهُوَ
لَاقِيهِ كَمَنْ مَتَّعْنٰهُ مَتَاعَ الْحَيٰوةِ
الدُّنْيَا ثُمَّ هُوَ يَوْمَ الْقِيٰمَةِ مِنَ الْمُحْضَرِينَ ﴿٦١﴾

3. فَأَمَّا الَّذِينَ اٰمَنُوا وَعَمِلُوا الصّٰلِحٰتِ
فَهُمْ فِي رَوْضَةٍ يُحْبَرُونَ ﴿١٥﴾
وَأَمَّا الَّذِينَ كَفَرُوا وَكَذَّبُوا بِاٰيٰتِنَا
وَلِقَآئِ الْاٰخِرَةِ فَأُولٰٓئِكَ فِي الْعَذَابِ
مُحْضَرُونَ ﴿١٦﴾

4 أَفَمَنْ كَانَ مُؤْمِنًا كَمَنْ كَانَ فَاسِقًا ۗ
لَا يَسْتَوٗنَ ﴿١٨﴾
أَمَّا الَّذِينَ اٰمَنُوا وَعَمِلُوا الصّٰلِحٰتِ
فَلَهُمْ جَنّٰتُ الْمَأْوٰى نُزُلًا بِمَا كَانُوا
يَعْمَلُونَ ﴿١٩﴾
وَأَمَّا الَّذِينَ فَسَقُوا فَمَأْوٰىهُمُ النَّارُ ۖ
كُلَّمَآ أَرَادُوٓا أَنْ يَخْرُجُوا مِنْهَآ أُعِيدُوا
فِيهَا وَقِيلَ لَهُمْ ذُوقُوا عَذَابَ النَّارِ
الَّذِي كُنْتُمْ بِهٖ تُكَذِّبُونَ ﴿٢٠﴾

5. أَمَّنْ هُوَ قَانِتٌ اٰنَآءَ الَّيْلِ سَاجِدًا وَّ

them it is said: Taste the torment of the Fire which ye used to deny.

32:18-20

5. Is he who payeth adoration in the watches of the night, prostrate and standing,

bewaring of the Hereafter and hoping for the mercy of his Lord, (to be accounted equal with a disbeliever)? Say (unto them, O Muhammad): Are those who know equal with those who know not? But only men of understanding will pay heed.

39:9

6. Is he whose bosom Allah hath expanded for the Surrender (unto Him), so that he followeth a light from His Lord, (as he who disbelieveth)? Then woe unto those whose hearts are hardened against remembrance of Allah. Such are in plain error.

39:22

7. And the blind man and the seer are not equal, neither are those who believe and do good works (equal with) the evil-doer. Little do ye reflect!

40:58

8. Or do those who commit ill-deeds suppose that We shall make them as those who believe and do good works, the same in life and death? Bad is their judgement!

45:21

9. Not equal are the owners of the Fire and the owners of the Garden. The owners of the Garden, they are the victorious.

59:20

10. Is he who goeth groping on his face more rightly guided, or he who walketh upright on a straight road?

67:22

قَآئِمًا يَّحْذَرُ الْاٰخِرَةَ وَيَرْجُوْا رَحْمَةَ
رَبِّهٖ ؕ قُلْ هَلْ يَسْتَوِى الَّذِيْنَ
يَعْلَمُوْنَ وَالَّذِيْنَ لَا يَعْلَمُوْنَ ؕ اِنَّمَا
يَتَذَكَّرُ اُولُوا الْاَلْبَابِ ۹

6. اَفَمَنْ شَرَحَ اللّٰهُ صَدْرَهٗ لِلْاِسْلَامِ فَهُوَ
عَلٰى نُوْرٍ مِّنْ رَّبِّهٖ ؕ فَوَيْلٌ لِّلْقٰسِيَةِ
قُلُوْبُهُمْ مِّنْ ذِكْرِ اللّٰهِ ؕ اُولٰٓئِكَ
فِىْ ضَلٰلٍ مُّبِيْنٍ ۲۲

7. وَمَا يَسْتَوِى الْاَعْمٰى وَالْبَصِيْرُ ۙ۬
وَالَّذِيْنَ اٰمَنُوْا وَعَمِلُوا الصّٰلِحٰتِ وَ
لَا الْمُسِىْٓءُ ؕ قَلِيْلًا مَّا تَتَذَكَّرُوْنَ ۵۸

8. اَمْ حَسِبَ الَّذِيْنَ اجْتَرَحُوا السَّيِّاٰتِ
اَنْ نَّجْعَلَهُمْ كَالَّذِيْنَ اٰمَنُوْا وَعَمِلُوا
الصّٰلِحٰتِ ۙ سَوَآءً مَّحْيَاهُمْ وَمَمَاتُهُمْ ؕ
سَآءَ مَا يَحْكُمُوْنَ ۲۱

9. لَا يَسْتَوِىْٓ اَصْحٰبُ النَّارِ وَاَصْحٰبُ
الْجَنَّةِ ؕ اَصْحٰبُ الْجَنَّةِ هُمُ الْفَآئِزُوْنَ ۲۰

10. اَفَمَنْ يَّمْشِىْ مُكِبًّا عَلٰى وَجْهِهٖٓ اَهْدٰٓى
اَمَّنْ يَّمْشِىْ سَوِيًّا عَلٰى صِرَاطٍ مُّسْتَقِيْمٍ ۲۲

Ref: 22:19,24; 35:8; 38:28; 39:24; 41:40; 47:14–15; 68:35–36.
See also: Disbelievers and Polytheists

BENEFICENCE

1. And do good. Lo! Allah loveth the beneficent.
2:195

2. Lo! the mercy of Allah is nigh unto the good.
7:56

3. Lo! Allah loseth not the wages of the good.
9:120

4. For those who do good is the best (reward) and more (thereto). Neither dust nor ignominy cometh near their faces. Such are rightful owners of the Garden; they will abide therein.
10:26

5. Lo! Allah enjoineth justice and kindness, and giving to kinsfolk, and forbiddeth lewdness and abomination and wickedness. He exhorteth you in order that ye may take heed
16:90

6. If ye do good, ye do good for your own souls, and if ye do evil, it is for them (in like manner).
17:7

7. And unto Allah belongeth whatsoever is in the heavens and whatsoever is in the earth, that He may reward those who do evil with that which they have done, and reward those who do good

1. وَأَحْسِنُوا ۛ إِنَّ اللَّهَ يُحِبُّ الْمُحْسِنِينَ ﴿١٩٥﴾

2. إِنَّ رَحْمَتَ اللَّهِ قَرِيبٌ مِّنَ
الْمُحْسِنِينَ ﴿٥٦﴾

3. إِنَّ اللَّهَ لَا يُضِيعُ أَجْرَ الْمُحْسِنِينَ ﴿١٢٠﴾

4. لِّلَّذِينَ أَحْسَنُوا الْحُسْنَىٰ وَزِيَادَةٌ ۖ وَلَا
يَرْهَقُ وُجُوهَهُمْ قَتَرٌ وَلَا ذِلَّةٌ ۚ أُولَٰئِكَ
أَصْحَابُ الْجَنَّةِ ۖ هُمْ فِيهَا خَالِدُونَ ﴿٢٦﴾

5. إِنَّ اللَّهَ يَأْمُرُ بِالْعَدْلِ وَالْإِحْسَانِ
وَإِيتَاءِ ذِي الْقُرْبَىٰ وَيَنْهَىٰ عَنِ
الْفَحْشَاءِ وَالْمُنكَرِ وَالْبَغْيِ ۚ يَعِظُكُمْ
لَعَلَّكُمْ تَذَكَّرُونَ ﴿٩٠﴾

6. إِنْ أَحْسَنتُمْ أَحْسَنتُمْ لِأَنفُسِكُمْ ۖ وَإِنْ
أَسَأْتُمْ فَلَهَا ۚ

7. وَلِلَّهِ مَا فِي السَّمَاوَاتِ وَمَا فِي الْأَرْضِ
لِيَجْزِيَ الَّذِينَ أَسَاءُوا بِمَا عَمِلُوا
وَيَجْزِيَ الَّذِينَ أَحْسَنُوا بِالْحُسْنَى ﴿٣١﴾

8. هَلْ جَزَاءُ الْإِحْسَانِ إِلَّا الْإِحْسَانُ ﴿٦٠﴾

فَبِأَيِّ آلَاءِ رَبِّكُمَا تُكَذِّبَانِ ﴿٦١﴾

with goodness.
53 31

8. Is the reward of goodness aught save goodness?
Which is it, of the favours of your Lord, that ye deny?
55:60–61

Ref: 2:58,112,236; 3:134,148 4:125; 5:13,93; 7:161; 11:115 12:56,90; 16:128 28:14 29:69, 31:3; 33:29

BIBLE

1. He hath revealed unto thee (Muhammad) the Scripture with truth, confirming that which was (revealed) before it, even as He revealed the Torah and the Gospel.

Aforetime, for a guidance to mankind; and hath revealed the Criterion (of right and wrong).

3:3–4

2. And We caused Jesus, son of Mary, to follow in their footsteps, confirming that which was (revealed) before him in the Torah and We bestowed on him the Gospel wherein is guidance and a light, confirming that which was (revealed) before it in the Torah—a guidance and an admonition unto those who ward off (evil)..

Let the People of the Gospel judge by that which Allah hath revealed therein. Whoso judgeth not by that which Allah hath revealed, such are evil—livers.

5:46–47

3. If only the People of the Scripture would believe and ward off (evil), surely We should remit their sins from them and surely We should bring them into Gardens of Delight.

If they had observed the Torah and the Gospel and that which was revealed unto them from their Lord, they would surely have been nourished from above them and from beneath their feet.

1. نَزَّلَ عَلَيْكَ الْكِتٰبَ بِالْحَقِّ مُصَدِّقًا لِّمَا
بَيْنَ يَدَيْهِ وَاَنْزَلَ التَّوْرٰىةَ وَالْاِنْجِيْلَ ۝
مِنْ قَبْلُ هُدًى لِّلنَّاسِ وَاَنْزَلَ الْفُرْقَانَ ؕ

2. وَقَفَّيْنَا عَلٰٓى اٰثَارِهِمْ بِعِيْسَى ابْنِ
مَرْيَمَ مُصَدِّقًا لِّمَا بَيْنَ يَدَيْهِ مِنَ
التَّوْرٰىةِ ۖ وَاٰتَيْنٰهُ الْاِنْجِيْلَ فِيْهِ
هُدًى وَّنُوْرٌ ۙ وَّمُصَدِّقًا لِّمَا بَيْنَ
يَدَيْهِ مِنَ التَّوْرٰىةِ وَهُدًى وَّ
مَوْعِظَةً لِّلْمُتَّقِيْنَ ؕ ۝٤٦
وَلْيَحْكُمْ اَهْلُ الْاِنْجِيْلِ بِمَآ اَنْزَلَ
اللّٰهُ فِيْهِ ؕ وَمَنْ لَّمْ يَحْكُمْ بِمَآ اَنْزَلَ
اللّٰهُ فَاُولٰٓئِكَ هُمُ الْفٰسِقُوْنَ ۝٤٧

3. وَلَوْ اَنَّ اَهْلَ الْكِتٰبِ اٰمَنُوْا وَاتَّقَوْا لَكَفَّرْنَا
عَنْهُمْ سَيِّاٰتِهِمْ وَلَاَدْخَلْنٰهُمْ جَنّٰتِ النَّعِيْمِ ۝٦٥
وَلَوْ اَنَّهُمْ اَقَامُوا التَّوْرٰىةَ وَالْاِنْجِيْلَ
وَمَآ اُنْزِلَ اِلَيْهِمْ مِّنْ رَّبِّهِمْ لَاَكَلُوْا
مِنْ فَوْقِهِمْ وَمِنْ تَحْتِ اَرْجُلِهِمْ ؕ
مِنْهُمْ اُمَّةٌ مُّقْتَصِدَةٌ ؕ وَكَثِيْرٌ مِّنْهُمْ
سَآءَ مَا يَعْمَلُوْنَ ۝٦٦

4. قُلْ يٰٓاَهْلَ الْكِتٰبِ لَسْتُمْ عَلٰى شَيْءٍ
حَتّٰى تُقِيْمُوا التَّوْرٰىةَ وَالْاِنْجِيْلَ وَمَآ
اُنْزِلَ اِلَيْكُمْ مِّنْ رَّبِّكُمْ ؕ

Among them there are people who are moderate, but many of them are of evil conduct.

5:65–66

4. Say: O People of the Scripture! Ye have naught (of guidance) till ye observe the Torah and the Gospel and that which was revealed unto you from your Lord.

5:68

Ref: 3:3,48,65; 5:68,110; 7.157; 9:111; 48:29, 57:27

See also: Revealed Books.

BIRDS

1. And We caused the white cloud to overshadow you and sent down on you the *manna* and the *quails,* (saying): Eat of the good things where-with We have provided you

2:57

2. Then Allah sent a raven scratching up the ground, to show him how to hide his brother's naked corpse. He said: Woe unto me! Am I not able to be as this raven and so hide my brother's naked corpse! And he became repentant.

5:31

3. Have they not seen the birds obedient in mid-air? None holdeth them save Allah. Lo! herein, verily, are portents for a people who believe.

16:79

4. Hast thou not seen that Allah, He it is Whom all who are in the heavens and the earth praise, and the birds in their flight? Of each He knoweth verily the worship and the praise; and Allah is Aware of what they do.

24:41

5. And he sought among the birds and said: How is it that I see not the hoopoe, or is he among the absent?

I verily will punish him with hard punishment or I verily will slay him, or he verily shall bring me a plain excuse.

But he was not long in coming, and he said: I have found out (a thing) that thou apprehendest not, and I come unto thee from Sheba with sure tidings.

27:20-22

1. وَظَلَّلْنَا عَلَيْكُمُ الْغَمَامَ وَاَنْزَلْنَا عَلَيْكُمُ الْمَنَّ
وَالسَّلْوٰى كُلُوْا مِنْ طَيِّبٰتِ مَا رَزَقْنٰكُمْ

2. فَبَعَثَ اللّٰهُ غُرَابًا يَّبْحَثُ فِي الْاَرْضِ
لِيُرِيَهٗ كَيْفَ يُوَارِيْ سَوْءَةَ اَخِيْهِ قَالَ
يٰوَيْلَتٰٓى اَعَجَزْتُ اَنْ اَكُوْنَ مِثْلَ هٰذَا
الْغُرَابِ فَاُوَارِيَ سَوْءَةَ اَخِيْ فَاَصْبَحَ
مِنَ النّٰدِمِيْنَ ﴿٣١﴾

3. اَلَمْ يَرَوْا اِلَى الطَّيْرِ مُسَخَّرٰتٍ فِيْ جَوِّ
السَّمَآءِ مَا يُمْسِكُهُنَّ اِلَّا اللّٰهُ اِنَّ فِيْ
ذٰلِكَ لَاٰيٰتٍ لِّقَوْمٍ يُّؤْمِنُوْنَ ﴿٧٩﴾

4. اَلَمْ تَرَ اَنَّ اللّٰهَ يُسَبِّحُ لَهٗ مَنْ فِي
السَّمٰوٰتِ وَالْاَرْضِ وَالطَّيْرُ صٰٓفّٰتٍ
كُلٌّ قَدْ عَلِمَ صَلَاتَهٗ وَتَسْبِيْحَهٗ
وَاللّٰهُ عَلِيْمٌ بِمَا يَفْعَلُوْنَ ﴿٤١﴾

5. وَتَفَقَّدَ الطَّيْرَ فَقَالَ مَا لِيَ لَآ اَرَى
الْهُدْهُدَ اَمْ كَانَ مِنَ الْغَآئِبِيْنَ ﴿٢٠﴾
لَاُعَذِّبَنَّهٗ عَذَابًا شَدِيْدًا اَوْ لَاَاذْبَحَنَّهٗٓ
اَوْ لَيَاْتِيَنِّيْ بِسُلْطٰنٍ مُّبِيْنٍ ﴿٢١﴾
فَمَكَثَ غَيْرَ بَعِيْدٍ فَقَالَ اَحَطْتُّ بِمَا
لَمْ تُحِطْ بِهٖ وَجِئْتُكَ مِنْ سَبَاٍ
بِنَبَاٍ يَّقِيْنٍ ﴿٢٢﴾

6. Hast thou not seen how thy Lord dealt with the owners of the Elephant?

Did He not bring their stratagem to naught.

And send against them swarms of flying creatures,

Which pelted them with stones of baked clay,

And made them like green crops devoured (by cattle)?

105:1-5

6. أَلَمْ تَرَ كَيْفَ فَعَلَ رَبُّكَ بِأَصْحَابِ الْفِيلِ ①
أَلَمْ يَجْعَلْ كَيْدَهُمْ فِي تَضْلِيلٍ ②
وَأَرْسَلَ عَلَيْهِمْ طَيْرًا أَبَابِيلَ ③
تَرْمِيهِم بِحِجَارَةٍ مِّن سِجِّيلٍ ④
فَجَعَلَهُمْ كَعَصْفٍ مَّأْكُولٍ ⑤

BLESSING

1. Lo! the first Sanctuary appointed for mankind was that at *Bakkah*, a blessed place, a guidance to the peoples;

3:96

1. إِنَّ أَوَّلَ بَيْتٍ وُضِعَ لِلنَّاسِ لَلَّذِي بِبَكَّةَ
مُبَارَكًا وَهُدًى لِّلْعَالَمِينَ ۝

2. And this is a blessed Scripture which We have revealed, confirming that which (was revealed) before it, that thou mayst warn the Mother of Villages.

6:92

2. وَهَٰذَا كِتَابٌ أَنزَلْنَاهُ مُبَارَكٌ مُّصَدِّقُ
الَّذِي بَيْنَ يَدَيْهِ وَلِتُنذِرَ أُمَّ الْقُرَىٰ

3. And if the people of the townships had believed and kept from evil, surely We should have opened for them blessings from the sky and from the earth. But (unto every messenger) they gave the lie, and so We seized them on account of what they used to earn.

7:96

3. وَلَوْ أَنَّ أَهْلَ الْقُرَىٰ آمَنُوا وَاتَّقَوْا لَفَتَحْنَا
عَلَيْهِم بَرَكَاتٍ مِّنَ السَّمَاءِ وَالْأَرْضِ وَلَٰكِن
كَذَّبُوا فَأَخَذْنَاهُم بِمَا كَانُوا يَكْسِبُونَ ۝

BIRDS

Ref: 2:260; 3:49; 5:110; 6:38; 12:36,41; 21:79; 22:31; 24:41; 27:16–17; 34:10; 38:19; 56:21; 67:19.

4. Glorified be He Who carried His servant by night from the Inviolable Place of Worship to the Far Distant Place of Worship the neighbourhood whereof We have blessed, that We might show him of Our tokens! Lo! He, only He, is the Hearer, the Seer.

17:1

5. And say: My Lord! Cause me to land at a blessed landing-place, for Thou art Best of all who bring to land.

23:29

6. But when ye enter houses, salute one another with a greeting from Allah, blessed and sweet.

24:61

7. He placed therein firm hills rising above it, and blessed it and measured therein its sustenance in four Days, alike for (all) who ask.

41:10

8. By the Scripture that maketh plain.

Lo! We revealed it on a blessed Night—Lo! We are ever warning.

44:2-3

9. And We send down from the sky blessed water whereby

4. سُبْحٰنَ الَّذِيْٓ اَسْرٰى بِعَبْدِهٖ لَيْلًا مِّنَ
الْمَسْجِدِ الْحَرَامِ اِلَى الْمَسْجِدِ الْاَقْصَا
الَّذِيْ بٰرَكْنَا حَوْلَهٗ لِنُرِيَهٗ مِنْ اٰيٰتِنَا ۭ
اِنَّهٗ هُوَ السَّمِيْعُ الْبَصِيْرُ (1)

5. وَقُلْ رَّبِّ اَنْزِلْنِيْ مُنْزَلًا مُّبٰرَكًا
وَّاَنْتَ خَيْرُ الْمُنْزِلِيْنَ (29)

6. فَاِذَا دَخَلْتُمْ بُيُوْتًا فَسَلِّمُوْا عَلٰٓي اَنْفُسِكُمْ
تَحِيَّةً مِّنْ عِنْدِ اللّٰهِ مُبٰرَكَةً طَيِّبَةً ۭ

7. وَجَعَلَ فِيْهَا رَوَاسِيَ مِنْ فَوْقِهَا
وَبٰرَكَ فِيْهَا وَقَدَّرَ فِيْهَآ اَقْوَاتَهَا
فِيْٓ اَرْبَعَةِ اَيَّامٍ ۭ سَوَاۗءً لِّلسَّاۗىِٕلِيْنَ (10)

8. وَالْكِتٰبِ الْمُبِيْنِ (2)
اِنَّآ اَنْزَلْنٰهُ فِيْ لَيْلَةٍ مُّبٰرَكَةٍ
اِنَّا كُنَّا مُنْذِرِيْنَ (3)

9. وَنَزَّلْنَا مِنَ السَّمَاۗءِ مَاۗءً مُّبٰرَكًا
فَاَنْۢبَتْنَا بِهٖ جَنّٰتٍ وَّحَبَّ الْحَصِيْدِ (9)

We give growth unto gardens and the grain of crops,

50:9

Ref: 6:155; 21:50,81; 24:35; 28:30; 34:18; 38:29;

BOASTING OF FAVOUR

1. Those who spend their wealth for the cause of Allah and afterward make not reproach and injury to follow that which they have spent; their reward is with their Lord and there shall no fear come upon them, neither shall they grieve.

A kind word with forgiveness is better than almsgiving followed by injury. Allah is Absolute, Clement.

O ye who believe! Render not vain your alms-giving by reproach and injury like him who spendeth his wealth only to be seen of men and believeth not in Allah and the Last Day. His likeness is as the likeness of a rock whereon is dust of earth: a rainstorm smiteth it, leaving it smooth and bare. They have no control of aught of that which they have gained. Allah guideth not the disbelieving folk.

2:262-264

2. And this is the past favour wherewith thou reproachest me: that thou hast enslaved the Children of Israel.

26:22

3. They make it a favour unto thee (Muhammad) that they have surrendered (unto Him). Say: Deem not your surrender a favour unto me; nay, but Allah doth confer a favour on you, inasmuch as He hath led you to the Faith, if ye are earnest.

49:17

1. الَّذِينَ يُنفِقُونَ أَمْوَالَهُمْ فِي سَبِيلِ
اللَّهِ ثُمَّ لَا يُتْبِعُونَ مَا أَنفَقُوا مَنًّا وَلَا
أَذًى لَّهُمْ أَجْرُهُمْ عِندَ رَبِّهِمْ وَلَا
خَوْفٌ عَلَيْهِمْ وَلَا هُمْ يَحْزَنُونَ ﴿٢٦٢﴾
قَوْلٌ مَّعْرُوفٌ وَمَغْفِرَةٌ خَيْرٌ مِّن صَدَقَةٍ
يَتْبَعُهَا أَذًى ۗ وَاللَّهُ غَنِيٌّ حَلِيمٌ ﴿٢٦٣﴾
يَا أَيُّهَا الَّذِينَ آمَنُوا لَا تُبْطِلُوا صَدَقَاتِكُم
بِالْمَنِّ وَالْأَذَىٰ كَالَّذِي يُنفِقُ مَالَهُ
رِئَاءَ النَّاسِ وَلَا يُؤْمِنُ بِاللَّهِ وَالْيَوْمِ
الْآخِرِ ۖ فَمَثَلُهُ كَمَثَلِ صَفْوَانٍ عَلَيْهِ
تُرَابٌ فَأَصَابَهُ وَابِلٌ فَتَرَكَهُ صَلْدًا ۖ
لَّا يَقْدِرُونَ عَلَىٰ شَيْءٍ مِّمَّا كَسَبُوا ۗ وَاللَّهُ
لَا يَهْدِي الْقَوْمَ الْكَافِرِينَ ﴿٢٦٤﴾

2. وَتِلْكَ نِعْمَةٌ تَمُنُّهَا عَلَيَّ أَنْ عَبَّدتَّ
بَنِي إِسْرَائِيلَ ﴿٢٢﴾

3. يَمُنُّونَ عَلَيْكَ أَنْ أَسْلَمُوا ۖ قُل لَّا
تَمُنُّوا عَلَيَّ إِسْلَامَكُم ۖ بَلِ اللَّهُ يَمُنُّ
عَلَيْكُمْ أَنْ هَدَاكُمْ لِلْإِيمَانِ إِن
كُنتُمْ صَادِقِينَ ﴿١٧﴾

Ref: 74:6.

BREACH OF TRUST

1. Lo! We reveal unto thee the Scripture with the truth, that thou mayst judge, between mankind by that which Allah showeth thee. And be not thou a pleader for the treacherous;

And seek forgiveness of Allah. Lo! Allah is ever Forgiving, Merciful.

And plead not on behalf of (people) who deceive themselves. Lo! Allah loveth not one who is treacherous and sinful.

4:105–107

2. O ye who believe! Betray not Allah and His messenger, nor knowingly betray your trusts.

8:27

3. And if thou fearest treachery from any folk, then throw back to them (their treaty) fairly. Lo! Allah loveth not the treacherous.

8:58

4. Lo! Allah loveth not any treacherous ingrate.

22:38

5. He knoweth the traitor of the eyes, and that which the bosoms hide.

40:19

BRIBERY

1. And eat not up your property among yourselves in vanity, nor seek by it to gain the hearing of the judges that ye may knowingly devour a portion of the property of others wrongfully.

2:188

.1 إِنَّآ أَنزَلْنَآ إِلَيْكَ ٱلْكِتَٰبَ بِٱلْحَقِّ
لِتَحْكُمَ بَيْنَ ٱلنَّاسِ بِمَآ أَرَىٰكَ ٱللَّهُ
وَلَا تَكُن لِّلْخَآئِنِينَ خَصِيمًا ﴿١٠٥﴾
وَٱسْتَغْفِرِ ٱللَّهَ إِنَّ ٱللَّهَ كَانَ غَفُورًا رَّحِيمًا ﴿١٠٦﴾
وَلَا تُجَٰدِلْ عَنِ ٱلَّذِينَ يَخْتَانُونَ أَنفُسَهُمْ
إِنَّ ٱللَّهَ لَا يُحِبُّ مَن كَانَ خَوَّانًا أَثِيمًا ﴿١٠٧﴾

.2 يَٰٓأَيُّهَا ٱلَّذِينَ ءَامَنُوا۟ لَا تَخُونُوا۟ ٱللَّهَ وَ
ٱلرَّسُولَ وَتَخُونُوٓا۟ أَمَٰنَٰتِكُمْ وَأَنتُمْ تَعْلَمُونَ ﴿٢٧﴾

.3 وَإِمَّا تَخَافَنَّ مِن قَوْمٍ خِيَانَةً فَٱنۢبِذْ
إِلَيْهِمْ عَلَىٰ سَوَآءٍ إِنَّ ٱللَّهَ لَا يُحِبُّ ٱلْخَآئِنِينَ ﴿٥٨﴾

.4 إِنَّ ٱللَّهَ لَا يُحِبُّ كُلَّ خَوَّانٍ كَفُورٍ ﴿٣٨﴾

.5 يَعْلَمُ خَآئِنَةَ ٱلْأَعْيُنِ وَمَا تُخْفِى
ٱلصُّدُورُ ﴿١٩﴾

○

.1 وَلَا تَأْكُلُوٓا۟ أَمْوَٰلَكُم بَيْنَكُم بِٱلْبَٰطِلِ وَتُدْلُوا۟
بِهَآ إِلَى ٱلْحُكَّامِ لِتَأْكُلُوا۟ فَرِيقًا مِّنْ أَمْوَٰلِ
ٱلنَّاسِ بِٱلْإِثْمِ وَأَنتُمْ تَعْلَمُونَ ﴿١٨٨﴾

○

BREACH OF TRUST

Ref: 5:13 8:71; 12:52; 16:91-92,94.

See also: Trust

CALENDAR

1. They ask thee, (O Muhammad), of new moons. Say: They are fixed seasons for mankind and for the pilgrimage.

2:189

2. He is the Cleaver of the Daybreak, and He hath appointed the night for stillness, and the sun and the moon for reckoning. That is the measuring of the Mighty, the Wise.

6:96

3. Lo! the number of the months with Allah is twelve months by Allah's ordinance in the day that He created the heavens and the earth. Four of them are sacred; that is the right religion. So wrong not yourselves in them. And wage war on all the idolaters as they are waging war on all of you. And know that Allah is with those who keep their duty (unto Him).

Postponement (of a sacred month) is only an excess of disbelief whereby those who disbelieve are misled, they allow it one year and forbid it (another) year, that they may make up the number of the months which Allah hath hallowed, so that they allow that which Allah hath forbidden. The evil of their deeds is made fair-seeming unto them. Allah guideth not the disbelieving folk.

9:36–37

4. He it is Who appointed the sun a splendour and the moon a light, and measured for her stages, that ye might know the number of the years, and the reckoning. Allah created not (all) that save in truth. He detaileth the revelations for people who have knowledge.

10:5

1. يَسْـَٔلُونَكَ عَنِ الْأَهِلَّةِ ۖ قُلْ هِيَ مَوَاقِيتُ
لِلنَّاسِ وَالْحَجِّ ۗ

2. فَالِقُ الْإِصْبَاحِ وَجَعَلَ الَّيْلَ سَكَنًا وَالشَّمْسَ
وَالْقَمَرَ حُسْبَانًا ۚ ذَٰلِكَ تَقْدِيرُ الْعَزِيزِ الْعَلِيمِ ۝

3. إِنَّ عِدَّةَ الشُّهُورِ عِنْدَ اللَّهِ اثْنَا عَشَرَ
شَهْرًا فِي كِتَابِ اللَّهِ يَوْمَ خَلَقَ السَّمَاوَاتِ
وَالْأَرْضَ مِنْهَا أَرْبَعَةٌ حُرُمٌ ۚ ذَٰلِكَ
الدِّينُ الْقَيِّمُ ۚ فَلَا تَظْلِمُوا فِيهِنَّ
أَنْفُسَكُمْ ۚ وَقَاتِلُوا الْمُشْرِكِينَ كَافَّةً
كَمَا يُقَاتِلُونَكُمْ كَافَّةً ۚ وَاعْلَمُوا أَنَّ اللَّهَ
مَعَ الْمُتَّقِينَ ۝
إِنَّمَا النَّسِيءُ زِيَادَةٌ فِي الْكُفْرِ ۖ يُضَلُّ بِهِ
الَّذِينَ كَفَرُوا يُحِلُّونَهُ عَامًا وَيُحَرِّمُونَهُ
عَامًا لِيُوَاطِئُوا عِدَّةَ مَا حَرَّمَ اللَّهُ فَيُحِلُّوا
مَا حَرَّمَ اللَّهُ ۚ زُيِّنَ لَهُمْ سُوءُ أَعْمَالِهِمْ ۗ
وَاللَّهُ لَا يَهْدِي الْقَوْمَ الْكَافِرِينَ ۝

4. هُوَ الَّذِي جَعَلَ الشَّمْسَ ضِيَاءً وَالْقَمَرَ
نُورًا وَقَدَّرَهُ مَنَازِلَ لِتَعْلَمُوا عَدَدَ
السِّنِينَ وَالْحِسَابَ ۚ مَا خَلَقَ اللَّهُ ذَٰلِكَ
إِلَّا بِالْحَقِّ ۚ يُفَصِّلُ الْآيَاتِ لِقَوْمٍ يَعْلَمُونَ ۝

CALL FOR PRAYER

1. O ye who believe! When the call is heard for the prayer of the day of congregation, haste unto the remembrance of Allah and leave your trading. That is better for you if ye did but know.

62:9

CALUMNY

1. Who doth greater wrong than he who inventeth a lie against Allah and denieth His revelations? Lo! the wrong-doers will not be successful.

6:21

2. Who is guilty of more wrong than he who forgeth a lie against Allah, or saith: I am inspired, when he is not inspired in aught; and who saith: I will reveal the like of that which Allah hath revealed? I: thou couldst see, when the wrong-doers reach the pangs of death and the angels stretch their hands out, saying: Deliver up your souls. This day ye are awarded doom of degradation for that ye spake concerning Allah other than the truth and used to scorn His portents.

6:93

3. And speak not, concerning that which your own tongues qualify (as clean or unclean), the falsehood: "This is lawful, and this is forbidden," so that ye invent a lie against Allah. Lo! those who invent a lie against Allah will not succeed.

16:116

1. يَا أَيُّهَا الَّذِينَ آمَنُوا إِذَا نُودِيَ
لِلصَّلَاةِ مِن يَوْمِ الْجُمُعَةِ فَاسْعَوْا
إِلَىٰ ذِكْرِ اللَّهِ وَذَرُوا الْبَيْعَ ۚ ذَٰلِكُمْ
خَيْرٌ لَّكُمْ إِن كُنتُمْ تَعْلَمُونَ ⑨

1. وَمَنْ أَظْلَمُ مِمَّنِ افْتَرَىٰ عَلَى اللَّهِ كَذِبًا
أَوْ كَذَّبَ بِآيَاتِهِ ۗ إِنَّهُ لَا يُفْلِحُ الظَّالِمُونَ

2. وَمَنْ أَظْلَمُ مِمَّنِ افْتَرَىٰ عَلَى اللَّهِ كَذِبًا
أَوْ قَالَ أُوحِيَ إِلَيَّ وَلَمْ يُوحَ إِلَيْهِ شَيْءٌ
وَمَن قَالَ سَأُنزِلُ مِثْلَ مَا أَنزَلَ اللَّهُ ۗ
وَلَوْ تَرَىٰ إِذِ الظَّالِمُونَ فِي غَمَرَاتِ الْمَوْتِ
وَالْمَلَائِكَةُ بَاسِطُو أَيْدِيهِمْ أَخْرِجُوا
أَنفُسَكُمُ ۖ الْيَوْمَ تُجْزَوْنَ عَذَابَ الْهُونِ
بِمَا كُنتُمْ تَقُولُونَ عَلَى اللَّهِ غَيْرَ الْحَقِّ
وَكُنتُمْ عَنْ آيَاتِهِ تَسْتَكْبِرُونَ ○

3. وَلَا تَقُولُوا لِمَا تَصِفُ أَلْسِنَتُكُمُ الْكَذِبَ
هَٰذَا حَلَالٌ وَهَٰذَا حَرَامٌ لِّتَفْتَرُوا عَلَى
اللَّهِ الْكَذِبَ ۚ إِنَّ الَّذِينَ يَفْتَرُونَ عَلَى
اللَّهِ الْكَذِبَ لَا يُفْلِحُونَ ○

4. Or say they: He hath invented a lie concerning Allah? If Allah willed, He could have sealed thy heart (against them). And Allah will wipe out the lie and will vindicate the truth by His words. Lo! He is Aware of what is hidden in the breasts (of men).

42:24

CEASE–FIRE

1. Fight in the way of Allah against those who fight against you, but begin not hostilities. Lo! Allah loveth not aggressors.

And slay them wherever ye find them, and drive them out of the places whence they drove you out, for persecution is worse than slaughter. And fight not with them at the Inviolable Place of Worship until they first attack you there, but if they attack you (there) then slay them. Such is the reward of disbelievers.

But if they desist, then lo! Allah is Forgiving Merciful.

And fight them until persecution is no more, and religion is for Allah. But if they desist, then let there be no hostility except against wrongdoers.

2:190-193

2. Except those who seek

4. أَمْ يَقُولُونَ افْتَرَىٰ عَلَى اللَّهِ كَذِبًا
فَإِن يَشَإِ اللَّهُ يَخْتِمْ عَلَىٰ قَلْبِكَ وَ
يَمْحُ اللَّهُ الْبَاطِلَ وَيُحِقُّ الْحَقَّ بِكَلِمَتِهِ
إِنَّهُ عَلِيمٌ بِذَاتِ الصُّدُورِ ﴿٢٤﴾

○

1. وَقَاتِلُوا فِي سَبِيلِ اللَّهِ الَّذِينَ يُقَاتِلُونَكُمْ وَلَا
تَعْتَدُوا إِنَّ اللَّهَ لَا يُحِبُّ الْمُعْتَدِينَ ﴿١٩٠﴾
وَاقْتُلُوهُمْ حَيْثُ ثَقِفْتُمُوهُمْ وَأَخْرِجُوهُمْ
مِّنْ حَيْثُ أَخْرَجُوكُمْ وَالْفِتْنَةُ أَشَدُّ مِنَ
الْقَتْلِ وَلَا تُقَاتِلُوهُمْ عِندَ الْمَسْجِدِ الْحَرَامِ
حَتَّىٰ يُقَاتِلُوكُمْ فِيهِ فَإِن قَاتَلُوكُمْ فَاقْتُلُوهُمْ
كَذَٰلِكَ جَزَاءُ الْكَافِرِينَ ﴿١٩١﴾
فَإِنِ انتَهَوْا فَإِنَّ اللَّهَ غَفُورٌ رَّحِيمٌ ﴿١٩٢﴾
وَقَاتِلُوهُمْ حَتَّىٰ لَا تَكُونَ فِتْنَةٌ وَيَكُونَ
الدِّينُ لِلَّهِ فَإِنِ انتَهَوْا فَلَا عُدْوَانَ إِلَّا
عَلَى الظَّالِمِينَ ﴿١٩٣﴾

2. إِلَّا الَّذِينَ يَصِلُونَ إِلَىٰ قَوْمٍ بَيْنَكُمْ وَبَيْنَهُمْ
مِّيثَاقٌ أَوْ جَاءُوكُمْ حَصِرَتْ صُدُورُهُمْ
أَن يُقَاتِلُوكُمْ أَوْ يُقَاتِلُوا قَوْمَهُمْ وَلَوْ

refuge with a people between whom and you there is a covenant, or (those who) come unto you because their hearts forbid them to make war on you or make war on their own

---

CALUMNY

Ref: 7:37; 10:69; 11:18; 16:105; 20:61; 29:68; 61:7.

شَآءَ اللّٰهُ لَسَلَّطَهُمْ عَلَيْكُمْ فَلَقٰتَلُوْكُمْ
فَاِنِ اعْتَزَلُوْكُمْ فَلَمْ يُقَاتِلُوْكُمْ وَ اَلْقَوْا
اِلَيْكُمُ السَّلَمَ ۙ فَمَا جَعَلَ اللّٰهُ لَكُمْ
عَلَيْهِمْ سَبِيْلًا ﴿٩٠﴾

folk. Had Allah willed He could have given them power over you so that assuredly they would have fought you. So, If they hold aloof from you and wage not war against you and offer you peace, Allah alloweth you no way against them.

4:90

3\. وَ اِنْ جَنَحُوْا لِلسَّلْمِ فَاجْنَحْ لَهَا وَ تَوَكَّلْ
عَلَى اللّٰهِ ؕ اِنَّهٗ هُوَ السَّمِيْعُ الْعَلِيْمُ ﴿٦١﴾

3\. And if they incline to peace, incline thou also to it, and trust in Allah. Lo! He even He is, the Hearer, the Knower.

8:61

4\. وَ اِنْ طَآئِفَتٰنِ مِنَ الْمُؤْمِنِيْنَ اقْتَتَلُوْا
فَاَصْلِحُوْا بَيْنَهُمَا ۚ فَاِنْۢ بَغَتْ اِحْدٰىهُمَا
عَلَى الْاُخْرٰى فَقَاتِلُوا الَّتِيْ تَبْغِيْ حَتّٰى
تَفِيْٓءَ اِلٰٓى اَمْرِ اللّٰهِ ۚ فَاِنْ فَآءَتْ
فَاَصْلِحُوْا بَيْنَهُمَا بِالْعَدْلِ وَ اَقْسِطُوْا ؕ
اِنَّ اللّٰهَ يُحِبُّ الْمُقْسِطِيْنَ ﴿٩﴾
اِنَّمَا الْمُؤْمِنُوْنَ اِخْوَةٌ فَاَصْلِحُوْا بَيْنَ
اَخَوَيْكُمْ وَ اتَّقُوا اللّٰهَ لَعَلَّكُمْ تُرْحَمُوْنَ ﴿١٠﴾

4\. And if two parties of believers fall to fighting, then make peace between them. And if one party of them doth wrong to the other, fight ye that which doth wrong till it return unto the ordinance of Allah; then if it return, make peace between them justly, and act equitably Lo! Allah loveth the equitable.

The believers are naught else than brothers. Therefore make peace between your brethren and observe your duty to Allah that haply ye may obtain mercy.

49:9-10

○

See also: Peace, Prisoners of War.

CHANGES AND ALTERATIONS

1. Lo! in the creation of the heavens and the earth, and the difference of night and day, and the ships which run upon the sea with that which is of use to men, and the water which Allah sendeth down from the sky, thereby reviving the earth after its death, and dispersing all kinds of beasts therein, and (in) the ordinance of the winds, and the clouds obedient between heaven and earth: are signs (of Allah's Sovereignty) for people who have sense.

2:164

2. Lo! in the creation of the heavens and the earth and (in) the difference of night and day are tokens (of His Sovereignty) for men of understanding.

3:190

3. Lo! in the difference of day and night and all that Allah hath created in the heavens and the earth are portents, verily, for folk who ward off (evil).

10:6

4. And of His signs is the creation of the heavens and the earth, and the difference of your languages and colours. Lo! herein indeed are portents for men of knowledge.

30:22

1. إِنَّ فِي خَلْقِ السَّمٰوٰتِ وَالْأَرْضِ وَاخْتِلَافِ
اللَّيْلِ وَالنَّهَارِ وَالْفُلْكِ الَّتِي تَجْرِي فِي
الْبَحْرِ بِمَا يَنْفَعُ النَّاسَ وَمَا أَنْزَلَ اللّٰهُ
مِنَ السَّمَاءِ مِنْ مَاءٍ فَأَحْيَا بِهِ الْأَرْضَ
بَعْدَ مَوْتِهَا وَبَثَّ فِيهَا مِنْ كُلِّ دَابَّةٍ
وَتَصْرِيفِ الرِّيٰحِ وَالسَّحَابِ الْمُسَخَّرِ بَيْنَ
السَّمَاءِ وَالْأَرْضِ لَآيٰتٍ لِقَوْمٍ يَعْقِلُونَ ﴿١٦٤﴾

2. إِنَّ فِي خَلْقِ السَّمٰوٰتِ وَالْأَرْضِ وَاخْتِلَافِ
اللَّيْلِ وَالنَّهَارِ لَآيٰتٍ لِأُولِي الْأَلْبَابِ ﴿١٩٠﴾

3. إِنَّ فِي اخْتِلَافِ اللَّيْلِ وَالنَّهَارِ وَمَا خَلَقَ
اللّٰهُ فِي السَّمٰوٰتِ وَالْأَرْضِ لَآيٰتٍ
لِقَوْمٍ يَتَّقُونَ ﴿٦﴾

4. وَمِنْ آيٰتِهِ خَلْقُ السَّمٰوٰتِ وَالْأَرْضِ
وَاخْتِلَافُ أَلْسِنَتِكُمْ وَأَلْوَانِكُمْ إِنَّ
فِي ذٰلِكَ لَآيٰتٍ لِلْعٰلِمِينَ ﴿٢٢﴾

CHARITY

1. Spend your wealth for the cause of Allah, and be not cast by your own hands to ruin; and do good. Lo! Allah loveth the beneficent.

2:195

2. They ask thee, (O Muhammad), what they shall spend. Say: That which ye spend for good (must go) to parents and near kindred and orphans and the needy and the wayfarer. And whatsoever good ye do, lo! Allah is Aware of it.

2:215

3. O ye who believe! Spend of that wherewith We have provided you ere a day come when there will be no trafficking, nor friendship, nor intercession. The disbelievers, they are the wrong-doers.

2:254

4 The likeness of those who spend their wealth in Allah's way is as the likeness of a grain which groweth seven ears, in every ear a hundred grains. Allah giveth increase manifold to whom He will. Allah is All–Embracing, All–Knowing.

Those who spend their wealth for the cause of Allah and afterward make not reproach and injury to follow that which they have spent; their reward is with their Lord and there shall no fear come upon them, neither shall they grieve.

2:261-262

1. وَأَنْفِقُوا فِي سَبِيلِ اللَّهِ وَلَا تُلْقُوا بِأَيْدِيكُمْ
إِلَى التَّهْلُكَةِ ۛ وَأَحْسِنُوا ۛ إِنَّ اللَّهَ يُحِبُّ
الْمُحْسِنِينَ ﴿١٩٥﴾

2. يَسْأَلُونَكَ مَاذَا يُنْفِقُونَ ۖ قُلْ مَا أَنْفَقْتُمْ
مِنْ خَيْرٍ فَلِلْوَالِدَيْنِ وَالْأَقْرَبِينَ وَالْيَتَامَىٰ
وَالْمَسَاكِينِ وَابْنِ السَّبِيلِ ۗ وَمَا تَفْعَلُوا
مِنْ خَيْرٍ فَإِنَّ اللَّهَ بِهِ عَلِيمٌ ﴿٢١٥﴾

3. يَا أَيُّهَا الَّذِينَ آمَنُوا أَنْفِقُوا مِمَّا رَزَقْنَاكُمْ
مِنْ قَبْلِ أَنْ يَأْتِيَ يَوْمٌ لَا بَيْعٌ فِيهِ وَلَا
خُلَّةٌ وَلَا شَفَاعَةٌ ۗ وَالْكَافِرُونَ هُمُ الظَّالِمُونَ ﴿٢٥٤﴾

4. مَثَلُ الَّذِينَ يُنْفِقُونَ أَمْوَالَهُمْ فِي سَبِيلِ
اللَّهِ كَمَثَلِ حَبَّةٍ أَنْبَتَتْ سَبْعَ سَنَابِلَ
فِي كُلِّ سُنْبُلَةٍ مِائَةُ حَبَّةٍ ۗ وَاللَّهُ
يُضَاعِفُ لِمَنْ يَشَاءُ ۗ وَاللَّهُ وَاسِعٌ عَلِيمٌ ﴿٢٦١﴾
الَّذِينَ يُنْفِقُونَ أَمْوَالَهُمْ فِي سَبِيلِ
اللَّهِ ثُمَّ لَا يُتْبِعُونَ مَا أَنْفَقُوا مَنًّا وَلَا
أَذًى ۙ لَهُمْ أَجْرُهُمْ عِنْدَ رَبِّهِمْ وَلَا
خَوْفٌ عَلَيْهِمْ وَلَا هُمْ يَحْزَنُونَ ﴿٢٦٢﴾

5. وَمَثَلُ الَّذِينَ يُنْفِقُونَ أَمْوَالَهُمُ ابْتِغَاءَ
مَرْضَاتِ اللَّهِ وَتَثْبِيتًا مِنْ أَنْفُسِهِمْ كَمَثَلِ
جَنَّةٍ بِرَبْوَةٍ أَصَابَهَا وَابِلٌ فَآتَتْ أُكُلَهَا
ضِعْفَيْنِ فَإِنْ لَمْ يُصِبْهَا وَابِلٌ فَطَلٌّ ۗ
وَاللَّهُ بِمَا تَعْمَلُونَ بَصِيرٌ ﴿٢٦٥﴾

5. And the likeness of those who spend their wealth in search of Allah's pleasure, and for the strenghthening of their souls, is as the likeness of a garden on a height. The rainstorm smiteth it and it bringeth forth its fruit two-fold. And if the rainstorm smite it not, then the shower. Allah is Seer of what ye do.

2:265

6. O ye who believe! Spend of the good things which ye have earned, and of that which We bring forth from the earth for you, and seek not the bad (with intent) to spend thereof (in charity) when ye would not take it for yourselves save with disdain; and know that Allah is Absolute, Owner of Praise.

2:267

7. And whatsoever good thing ye spend, it is for yourselves, when ye spend not save in search of Allah's Countenance; and whatsoever good thing ye spend, it will be repaid to you in full, and ye will not be wronged.

2:272

8. Those who spend their wealth by night and day, by stealth and openly, verily their reward is with their Lord, and there shall no fear come upon them neither shall they grieve.

2:274

9. Ye will not attain unto piety until ye spend of that which ye love. And whatsoever ye spend, Allah is Aware thereof.

3:92

10. Lo! those who read the Scripture of Allah, and establish worship, and spend of that which We have bestowed on them secretly and openly, they look forward to imperishable gain.

That He will pay them their wages and increase them

6. يَاأَيُّهَا الَّذِينَ آمَنُوا أَنفِقُوا مِن طَيِّبَاتِ
مَا كَسَبْتُمْ وَمِمَّا أَخْرَجْنَا لَكُم مِّنَ
الْأَرْضِ وَلَا تَيَمَّمُوا الْخَبِيثَ مِنْهُ
تُنفِقُونَ وَلَسْتُم بِآخِذِيهِ إِلَّا أَن
تُغْمِضُوا فِيهِ وَاعْلَمُوا أَنَّ اللَّهَ غَنِيٌّ حَمِيدٌ

7. وَمَا تُنفِقُوا مِنْ خَيْرٍ فَلِأَنفُسِكُمْ وَ
مَا تُنفِقُونَ إِلَّا ابْتِغَاءَ وَجْهِ اللَّهِ وَمَا
تُنفِقُوا مِنْ خَيْرٍ يُوَفَّ إِلَيْكُمْ وَأَنتُمْ لَا
تُظْلَمُونَ

8. الَّذِينَ يُنفِقُونَ أَمْوَالَهُم بِاللَّيْلِ وَالنَّهَارِ سِرًّا وَ
عَلَانِيَةً فَلَهُمْ أَجْرُهُمْ عِندَ رَبِّهِمْ وَلَا خَوْفٌ
عَلَيْهِمْ وَلَا هُمْ يَحْزَنُونَ

9. لَن تَنَالُوا الْبِرَّ حَتَّىٰ تُنفِقُوا مِمَّا تُحِبُّونَ
وَمَا تُنفِقُوا مِن شَيْءٍ فَإِنَّ اللَّهَ بِهِ عَلِيمٌ

10. إِنَّ الَّذِينَ يَتْلُونَ كِتَابَ اللَّهِ وَأَقَامُوا
الصَّلَاةَ وَأَنفَقُوا مِمَّا رَزَقْنَاهُمْ سِرًّا وَ
عَلَانِيَةً يَرْجُونَ تِجَارَةً لَّن تَبُورَ
لِيُوَفِّيَهُمْ أُجُورَهُمْ وَيَزِيدَهُم مِّن
فَضْلِهِ إِنَّهُ غَفُورٌ شَكُورٌ

11. آمِنُوا بِاللَّهِ وَرَسُولِهِ وَأَنفِقُوا مِمَّا
جَعَلَكُم مُّسْتَخْلَفِينَ فِيهِ فَالَّذِينَ
آمَنُوا مِنكُمْ وَأَنفَقُوا لَهُمْ أَجْرٌ كَبِيرٌ

of His grace. Lo! He is Forgiving, Responsive.

35:29-30

11. Believe in Allah and His messenger, and spend of that whereof He hath made you trustees; and such of you as believe and spend (aright), theirs will be a great reward.

57:7

See also: Alms, *Zakat.*

CHASTE

1. وَمَن لَّمْ يَسْتَطِعْ مِنكُمْ طَوْلًا أَن يَنكِحَ
الْمُحْصَنَٰتِ الْمُؤْمِنَٰتِ فَمِن مَّا مَلَكَتْ أَيْمَٰنُكُم
مِّن فَتَيَٰتِكُمُ الْمُؤْمِنَٰتِ ۚ وَاللَّهُ أَعْلَمُ بِإِيمَٰنِكُم ۚ
بَعْضُكُم مِّنۢ بَعْضٍ ۚ فَانكِحُوهُنَّ بِإِذْنِ أَهْلِهِنَّ
وَءَاتُوهُنَّ أُجُورَهُنَّ بِالْمَعْرُوفِ مُحْصَنَٰتٍ
غَيْرَ مُسَٰفِحَٰتٍ وَلَا مُتَّخِذَٰتِ أَخْدَانٍ ۚ
فَإِذَآ أُحْصِنَّ فَإِنْ أَتَيْنَ بِفَٰحِشَةٍ فَعَلَيْهِنَّ
نِصْفُ مَا عَلَى الْمُحْصَنَٰتِ مِنَ الْعَذَابِ ۚ ذَٰلِكَ
لِمَنْ خَشِيَ الْعَنَتَ مِنكُمْ ۚ وَأَن تَصْبِرُوا۟
خَيْرٌ لَّكُمْ ۗ وَاللَّهُ غَفُورٌ رَّحِيمٌ ﴿٢٥﴾

2. الْيَوْمَ أُحِلَّ لَكُمُ الطَّيِّبَٰتُ ۖ وَطَعَامُ
الَّذِينَ أُوتُوا الْكِتَٰبَ حِلٌّ لَّكُمْ وَطَعَامُكُمْ
حِلٌّ لَّهُمْ ۖ وَالْمُحْصَنَٰتُ مِنَ الْمُؤْمِنَٰتِ
وَالْمُحْصَنَٰتُ مِنَ الَّذِينَ أُوتُوا الْكِتَٰبَ
مِن قَبْلِكُمْ إِذَآ ءَاتَيْتُمُوهُنَّ أُجُورَهُنَّ
مُحْصِنِينَ غَيْرَ مُسَٰفِحِينَ وَلَا مُتَّخِذِيٓ
أَخْدَانٍ ۗ وَمَن يَكْفُرْ بِالْإِيمَٰنِ فَقَدْ
حَبِطَ عَمَلُهُۥ وَهُوَ فِي الْءَاخِرَةِ مِنَ
الْخَٰسِرِينَ ﴿٥﴾

3. إِنَّ الَّذِينَ يَرْمُونَ الْمُحْصَنَٰتِ الْغَٰفِلَٰتِ
الْمُؤْمِنَٰتِ لُعِنُوا فِي الدُّنْيَا وَالْءَاخِرَةِ
وَلَهُمْ عَذَابٌ عَظِيمٌ ﴿٢٣﴾

1. And whoso is not able to afford to marry free, believing women, let them marry from the believing maids whom your right hands possess. Allah knoweth best (concerning) your faith. Ye (proceed) one from another; so wed them by permission of their folk, and give unto them their portions in kindness, they being honest, not debauched nor of loose conduct. And if when they are honourably married they commit lewdness they shall incur the half of the punishment (prescribed) for free women (in that case). This is for him among you who feareth to commit sin. But to have patience would be better for you. Allah is Forgiving, Merciful.

4:25

2. This day are (all) good things made lawful for you. The food of those who have received the Scripture is lawful for you, and your food is lawful for them. And so are the virtuous women of the believers and the virtuous women of those who received the Scripture before you (lawful for you) when ye give them their marriage portions and live with them in honour, not in fornication, nor taking them as secret concubines. Whoso denieth the faith, his work is vain and he will be among the losers in the Hereafter.

5:5

3. Lo! as for those who traduce virtuous, believing women (who are) careless, cursed are they in the world and the Hereafter. Theirs will be an awful doom.

24:23

CHASTITY

1. وَالَّذِينَ هُمْ لِفُرُوجِهِمْ حٰفِظُونَ ۝٥
إِلَّا عَلَىٰٓ أَزْوَاجِهِمْ أَوْ مَا مَلَكَتْ أَيْمَانُهُمْ
فَإِنَّهُمْ غَيْرُ مَلُومِينَ ۝٦

2. قُلْ لِّلْمُؤْمِنِينَ يَغُضُّوا مِنْ أَبْصَارِهِمْ
وَيَحْفَظُوا فُرُوجَهُمْ ذٰلِكَ أَزْكَىٰ لَهُمْ
إِنَّ اللّٰهَ خَبِيرٌۢ بِمَا يَصْنَعُونَ ۝٣٠
وَقُلْ لِّلْمُؤْمِنٰتِ يَغْضُضْنَ مِنْ أَبْصَارِهِنَّ
وَيَحْفَظْنَ فُرُوجَهُنَّ وَلَا يُبْدِينَ
زِينَتَهُنَّ إِلَّا مَا ظَهَرَ مِنْهَا وَلْيَضْرِبْنَ
بِخُمُرِهِنَّ عَلَىٰ جُيُوبِهِنَّ وَلَا يُبْدِينَ
زِينَتَهُنَّ إِلَّا لِبُعُولَتِهِنَّ أَوْ آبَائِهِنَّ أَوْ آبَاءِ
بُعُولَتِهِنَّ أَوْ أَبْنَائِهِنَّ أَوْ أَبْنَاءِ بُعُولَتِهِنَّ
أَوْ إِخْوَانِهِنَّ أَوْ بَنِي إِخْوَانِهِنَّ أَوْ بَنِي
أَخَوَاتِهِنَّ أَوْ نِسَائِهِنَّ أَوْ مَا مَلَكَتْ
أَيْمَانُهُنَّ أَوِ التّٰبِعِينَ غَيْرِ أُولِي الْإِرْبَةِ
مِنَ الرِّجَالِ أَوِ الطِّفْلِ الَّذِينَ لَمْ
يَظْهَرُوا عَلَىٰ عَوْرٰتِ النِّسَاءِ وَلَا يَضْرِبْنَ
بِأَرْجُلِهِنَّ لِيُعْلَمَ مَا يُخْفِينَ مِنْ زِينَتِهِنَّ
وَتُوبُوا إِلَى اللّٰهِ جَمِيعًا أَيُّهَ الْمُؤْمِنُونَ
لَعَلَّكُمْ تُفْلِحُونَ ۝٣١

3. وَلْيَسْتَعْفِفِ الَّذِينَ لَا يَجِدُونَ نِكَاحًا
حَتَّىٰ يُغْنِيَهُمُ اللّٰهُ مِنْ فَضْلِهِ وَالَّذِينَ
يَبْتَغُونَ الْكِتٰبَ مِمَّا مَلَكَتْ أَيْمَانُكُمْ
فَكَاتِبُوهُمْ إِنْ عَلِمْتُمْ فِيهِمْ خَيْرًا

1. And who guard their modesty—

Save from their wives or the (slaves) that their right hands possess, for then they are not blameworthy.

23:5-6

2. Tell the believing men to lower their gaze and be modest. That is purer for them. Lo! Allah is Aware of what they do.

And tell the believing women to lower their gaze and be modest, and to display of their adornment only that which is apparent, and to draw their veils over their bosoms, and not to reveal their adornment save to their own husbands or fathers or husbands' fathers, or their sons or their husbands' sons, or their brothers, or their brothers' sons or sisters' sons, or their women, or their slaves, or male attendants who lack vigour or children who know naught of women's nakedness. And let them not stamp their feet so as to reveal what they hide of their adornment. And turn unto Allah together, O believers, in order that ye may succeed.

24:30-31

3. And let those who cannot find a match keep chaste till Allah give them independence by His grace. And such of your slaves as seek a writing (of emancipation), write it for them if ye are aware of aught of good in them, and bestow upon them of the wealth of Allah which He hath bestowed upon you. Force not your slave-girls

to whoredom that ye may seek enjoyment of the life of the world, if they would preserve their chastity. And if one force them, then (unto them), after their compulsion, lo! Allah will be Forgiving, Merciful.

24:33

وَّ اٰتُوْهُمْ مِّنْ مَّالِ اللّٰهِ الَّذِیْٓ اٰتٰىكُمْ ؕ
وَلَا تُكْرِهُوْا فَتَیٰتِكُمْ عَلَی الْبِغَآءِ اِنْ
اَرَدْنَ تَحَصُّنًا لِّتَبْتَغُوْا عَرَضَ الْحَیٰوةِ
الدُّنْیَا ؕ وَمَنْ یُّكْرِهْهُّنَّ فَاِنَّ اللّٰهَ مِنْ
بَعْدِ اِكْرَاهِهِنَّ غَفُوْرٌ رَّحِیْمٌ ۳۳

CHILDHOOD

1. He it is Who created you from dust, then from a drop (of seed) then from a clot, then bringeth you forth as a child, then (ordaineth) that ye attain full strength and afterward that ye become old men—though some among you die before—and that ye reach an appointed term, that haply ye may understand.

40:67

1. هُوَ الَّذِیْ خَلَقَكُمْ مِّنْ تُرَابٍ ثُمَّ
مِنْ نُّطْفَةٍ ثُمَّ مِنْ عَلَقَةٍ ثُمَّ
یُخْرِجُكُمْ طِفْلًا ثُمَّ لِتَبْلُغُوْۤا اَشُدَّكُمْ
ثُمَّ لِتَكُوْنُوْا شُیُوْخًا ۚ وَمِنْكُمْ مَّنْ
یُّتَوَفّٰى مِنْ قَبْلُ وَلِتَبْلُغُوْۤا اَجَلًا
مُّسَمًّى وَّلَعَلَّكُمْ تَعْقِلُوْنَ ۶۷

CHASTITY

Ref: 4:25; 5:5; 23:7; 24:19,60; 70:29-31.

CHILDREN

1. Mothers shall suckle their children for two whole years: (that is) for those who wish to complete the suckling. The duty of feeding and clothing nursing mothers in a seemly manner is upon the father of the child. No one should be charged beyond his capa- city. A mother should not be made to suffer because of her child, nor should he to whom the child is born (be made to suffer) because of his child. And on the (father's) heir is incumbent the like of that (which was incumbent on the father). If they desire to wean the child by mutual consent and (after) consultation, it is no sin for them; and if ye wish to give your children out to nurse, it is no sin for you, provided that ye pay what is due from you in kindness. Observe your duty to Allah, and know that Allah is Seer of what ye do.

2:233

2. (On that day) neither the riches nor the progeny of those who disbelieve will aught avail them with Allah. They will be fuel for Fire.

3:10

3 They are losers who besottedly have slain their children without knowledge, and have forbidden that which Allah bestowed upon them, inventing a lie against Allah. They indeed have gone astray and are not guided.

6:140

1. والوالدات يرضعن اولادهن حولين
كاملين لمن اراد ان يتم الرضاعة
وعلى المولود له رزقهن وكسوتهن
بالمعروف لا تكلف نفس الا وسعها لا
تضار والدة بولدها ولا مولود له
بولده وعلى الوارث مثل ذلك فان
ارادا فصالا عن تراض منهما وتشاور
فلا جناح عليهما وان اردتم ان تسترضعوا
اولادكم فلا جناح عليكم اذا سلمتم ما
اتيتم بالمعروف واتقوا الله واعلموا
ان الله بما تعملون بصير ﴿٢٣٣﴾

2. ان الذين كفروا لن تغني عنهم اموالهم
ولا اولادهم من الله شيئا واولئك
هم وقود النار ﴿١٠﴾

3. قد خسر الذين قتلوا اولادهم سفها
بغير علم وحرموا ما رزقهم الله افتراء
على الله قد ضلوا وما كانوا مهتدين ﴿١٤٠﴾

4. فلا تعجبك اموالهم ولا اولادهم
انما يريد الله ليعذبهم بها في الحيوة
الدنيا وتزهق انفسهم وهم كفرون ﴿٥٥﴾

5. ولا تقتلوا اولادكم خشية املاق
نحن نرزقهم واياكم ان قتلهم
كان خطا كبيرا ﴿٣١﴾

4. So let not their riches nor their children please thee (O Muhammad). Allah thereby intendeth but to punish them in the life of the world and that their souls shall pass away while they are disbelievers.

9:55

5. Slay not your children, fearing a fall to poverty. We shall provide for them and for you. Lo! the slaying of them is great sin.

17:31

6. And it is not your wealth nor your children that will bring you near unto Us, but he who believeth and doth good (he draweth near). As for such, theirs will be twofold reward for what they did, and they will dwell secure in lofty halls.

34:37

7. Their wealth and their children will avail them naught against Allah. Such are rightful owners of the Fire; they will abide therein.

58:17

8. O ye who believe! Let not your wealth nor your children distract you from remembrance of Allah. Those who do so, they are the losers.

63:9

9. Your wealth and your children are only a temptation, whereas Allah! with Him is an immense reward.

64:15

6. وَمَآ أَمْوَالُكُمْ وَلَآ أَوْلَادُكُمْ بِالَّتِي
تُقَرِّبُكُمْ عِنْدَنَا زُلْفَىٰٓ إِلَّا مَنْ آمَنَ
وَعَمِلَ صَالِحًا فَأُولَٰٓئِكَ لَهُمْ جَزَآءُ
الضِّعْفِ بِمَا عَمِلُوا وَهُمْ فِي الْغُرُفَاتِ
آمِنُونَ ۝

7. لَنْ تُغْنِيَ عَنْهُمْ أَمْوَالُهُمْ وَلَآ أَوْلَادُهُمْ
مِّنَ اللَّهِ شَيْئًا ۚ أُولَٰٓئِكَ أَصْحَابُ النَّارِ ۚ
هُمْ فِيهَا خَالِدُونَ ۝

8. يَٰٓأَيُّهَا الَّذِينَ آمَنُوا لَا تُلْهِكُمْ أَمْوَالُكُمْ
وَلَآ أَوْلَادُكُمْ عَنْ ذِكْرِ اللَّهِ ۚ وَمَنْ
يَفْعَلْ ذَٰلِكَ فَأُولَٰٓئِكَ هُمُ الْخَاسِرُونَ ۝

9. إِنَّمَآ أَمْوَالُكُمْ وَأَوْلَادُكُمْ فِتْنَةٌ ۚ وَاللَّهُ
عِنْدَهُٓ أَجْرٌ عَظِيمٌ ۝

Ref: 3:116; 4:12, 176; 6:137, 151; 8:28; 9:69, 85; 18:46; 31:33; 57:20; 60:12; 64:15; 71:21.

See also: Childhood, Infanticide, Rights of Parents.

CLAY AND MUD

1. Lo! the likeness of Jesus with Allah is as the likeness of Adam. He created him of dust, then He said unto him: Be! and he is.

3:59

2. And if thou wonderest, then wondrous is their saying: When we are dust, are we then forsooth (to be raised) in a new creation? Such are they who disbelieve in their Lord; such have carcans on their necks; such are rightful owners of the Fire, they will abide therein.

13:5

3. Verily We created man of potter's clay of black mud altered.

15:26

4. Lo! We warn you of doom at hand, a day whereon a man will look on that which his own hands have sent before, and the disbelievers will cry. "Would that I were dust!"

78:40

1. إِنَّ مَثَلَ عِيسَىٰ عِندَ اللَّهِ كَمَثَلِ آدَمَ
خَلَقَهُ مِن تُرَابٍ ثُمَّ قَالَ لَهُ كُن
فَيَكُونُ ○

2. وَإِن تَعْجَبْ فَعَجَبٌ قَوْلُهُمْ أَإِذَا كُنَّا
تُرَابًا أَإِنَّا لَفِي خَلْقٍ جَدِيدٍ ۗ أُولَٰئِكَ
الَّذِينَ كَفَرُوا بِرَبِّهِمْ ۖ وَأُولَٰئِكَ
الْأَغْلَالُ فِي أَعْنَاقِهِمْ ۖ وَأُولَٰئِكَ أَصْحَابُ
النَّارِ ۖ هُمْ فِيهَا خَالِدُونَ ۝

3. وَلَقَدْ خَلَقْنَا الْإِنسَانَ مِن صَلْصَالٍ
مِّنْ حَمَإٍ مَّسْنُونٍ ۝

4. إِنَّا أَنذَرْنَاكُمْ عَذَابًا قَرِيبًا يَوْمَ
يَنظُرُ الْمَرْءُ مَا قَدَّمَتْ يَدَاهُ وَيَقُولُ
الْكَافِرُ يَا لَيْتَنِي كُنتُ تُرَابًا ۝

○

Ref: 15:28,33; 18:37; 23:35–37; 27:67–68; 32:7; 35:11; 37:15–17,53; 50:3.

See also: Creation of Man.

CLERGY

1. Lo! We did reveal the Torah, wherein is guidance and a light, by which the Prophets who surrendered (unto Allah) judged the Jews, and the rabbis and the priests (judged) by such of Allah's Scripture as they were bidden to observe, and thereunto were they witnesses.

5:44

2. Why do not the rabbis and the priests forbid their evil–speaking and their devouring of illicit gain? Verily evil is their handiwork.

5:63

3. They have taken as lords beside Allah their rabbis and their monks and the Messiah son of Mary, when they were bidden to worship only One God. There is no god save Him. Be He Glorified from all that they ascribe as partners (unto Him)!

9:31

4. O ye who believe! Lo! many of the (Jewish) rabbis and the (Christian) monks devour the wealth of mankind wantonly and debar (men) from the way of Allah.

9:34

1. إِنَّآ أَنزَلْنَا ٱلتَّوْرَىٰةَ فِيهَا هُدًى وَنُورٌ
يَحْكُمُ بِهَا ٱلنَّبِيُّونَ ٱلَّذِينَ أَسْلَمُوا
لِلَّذِينَ هَادُوا وَٱلرَّبَّـٰنِيُّونَ وَٱلْأَحْبَارُ
بِمَا ٱسْتُحْفِظُوا مِن كِتَـٰبِ ٱللَّهِ وَكَانُوا
عَلَيْهِ شُهَدَآءَ

2. لَوْلَا يَنْهَىٰهُمُ ٱلرَّبَّـٰنِيُّونَ وَٱلْأَحْبَارُ عَن
قَوْلِهِمُ ٱلْإِثْمَ وَأَكْلِهِمُ ٱلسُّحْتَ
لَبِئْسَ مَا كَانُوا يَصْنَعُونَ ﴿٦٣﴾

3. ٱتَّخَذُوٓا أَحْبَارَهُمْ وَرُهْبَـٰنَهُمْ أَرْبَابًا مِّن
دُونِ ٱللَّهِ وَٱلْمَسِيحَ ٱبْنَ مَرْيَمَ وَمَآ
أُمِرُوٓا إِلَّا لِيَعْبُدُوٓا إِلَـٰهًا وَٰحِدًا لَّآ إِلَـٰهَ
إِلَّا هُوَ سُبْحَـٰنَهُۥ عَمَّا يُشْرِكُونَ ﴿٣١﴾

4. يَـٰٓأَيُّهَا ٱلَّذِينَ ءَامَنُوٓا إِنَّ كَثِيرًا مِّنَ ٱلْأَحْبَارِ
وَٱلرُّهْبَانِ لَيَأْكُلُونَ أَمْوَٰلَ ٱلنَّاسِ
بِٱلْبَـٰطِلِ وَيَصُدُّونَ عَن سَبِيلِ ٱللَّهِ

CLOUDS

1. Lo! in the creation of the heavens and the earth, and the difference of night and day, and the ships which run upon the sea with that which is of use to men, and the water which Allah sendeth down from the sky, thereby reviving the earth after its death, and dispersing all kinds of beasts therein, and (in) the ordinance of the winds, and the clouds obedient between heaven and earth: are signs (of Allah's Sovereignty) for people who have sense.

2:164

2. And He it is Who sendeth the winds as tidings heralding His mercy, till, when they bear a cloud heavy (with rain), We lead it to a dead land, and then cause water to descend thereon and thereby bring forth fruits of every kind. Thus bring We forth the dead. Haply ye may remember.

7:57

3. He it is Who showeth you the lightning, a fear and a hope, and raiseth the heavy clouds.

13:12

4. Hast thou not seen how Allah wafteth the clouds, then gathereth them, then maketh them layers, and thou seest the rain come forth from between them; He sendeth down

1. إن في خلق السموت والأرض واختلاف
الليل والنهار والفلك التي تجري في
البحر بما ينفع الناس وما أنزل الله
من السماء من ماء فأحيا به الأرض
بعد موتها وبث فيها من كل دابة
وتصريف الريح والسحاب المسخر بين
السماء والأرض لآيت لقوم يعقلون (١٦٤)

2. وهو الذي يرسل الريح بشرا بين
يدي رحمته حتى إذا أقلت سحابا ثقالا
سقنه لبلد ميت فأنزلنا به الماء
فأخرجنا به من كل الثمرت كذلك
نخرج الموتى لعلكم تذكرون (٥٧)

3. هو الذي يريكم البرق خوفا وطمعا
وينشئ السحاب الثقال (١٢)

4. ألم تر أن الله يزجي سحابا ثم يؤلف
بينه ثم يجعله ركاما فترى الودق
يخرج من خلله وينزل من السماء
من جبال فيها من برد فيصيب به
من يشاء ويصرفه عن من يشاء
يكاد سنا برقه يذهب بالأبصار (٤٣)

from the heaven mountains wherein is hail, and smiteth therewith whom He will, and averteth it from whom He will. The flashing of His lightning all but snatcheth away the sight.

24:43

5. Allah is He who sendeth the winds so that they raise clouds, and spreadeth them along the sky as pleaseth Him, and causeth them to break and thou seest the rain downpouring from within them. And when He maketh it to fall on whom He will of His bondmen, lo! they rejoice;

Though before that, even before it was sent down upon them, they were in despair.

30:48-49

6. And Allah it is Who sendeth the winds and they raise a cloud; then We lead it unto a dead land and revive therewith the earth after its death. Such is the Resurrection.

35:9

COMMANDS AND PROHIBITIONS

1. And there may spring from you a nation who invite to goodness, and enjoin right conduct and forbid indecency. Such are they who are successful.

3:104

2. Ye are the best community that hath been raised up for mankind. Ye enjoin right conduct and forbid indecency; and ye believe in Allah.

3:110

5. اَللّٰهُ الَّذِىْ يُرْسِلُ الرِّيٰحَ فَتُثِيْرُ
سَحَابًا فَيَبْسُطُهٗ فِى السَّمَآءِ كَيْفَ
يَشَآءُ وَ يَجْعَلُهٗ كِسَفًا فَتَرَى الْوَدْقَ
يَخْرُجُ مِنْ خِلٰلِهٖ ۚ فَاِذَآ اَصَابَ بِهٖ
مَنْ يَّشَآءُ مِنْ عِبَادِهٖٓ اِذَا هُمْ
يَسْتَبْشِرُوْنَ ﴿٤٨﴾
وَ اِنْ كَانُوْا مِنْ قَبْلِ اَنْ يُّنَزَّلَ
عَلَيْهِمْ مِّنْ قَبْلِهٖ لَمُبْلِسِيْنَ ﴿٤٩﴾

6. وَ اللّٰهُ الَّذِىْٓ اَرْسَلَ الرِّيٰحَ فَتُثِيْرُ
سَحَابًا فَسُقْنٰهُ اِلٰى بَلَدٍ مَّيِّتٍ فَاَحْيَيْنَا
بِهِ الْاَرْضَ بَعْدَ مَوْتِهَا ۚ كَذٰلِكَ النُّشُوْرُ ﴿٩﴾

○

1. وَلْتَكُنْ مِّنْكُمْ اُمَّةٌ يَّدْعُوْنَ اِلَى الْخَيْرِ
وَ يَاْمُرُوْنَ بِالْمَعْرُوْفِ وَ يَنْهَوْنَ عَنِ
الْمُنْكَرِ ۚ وَ اُولٰٓئِكَ هُمُ الْمُفْلِحُوْنَ ○

2. كُنْتُمْ خَيْرَ اُمَّةٍ اُخْرِجَتْ لِلنَّاسِ تَاْمُرُوْنَ
بِالْمَعْرُوْفِ وَ تَنْهَوْنَ عَنِ الْمُنْكَرِ وَ تُؤْمِنُوْنَ
بِاللّٰهِ ۚ

3. خُذِ الْعَفْوَ وَ اْمُرْ بِالْعُرْفِ وَ اَعْرِضْ
عَنِ الْجٰهِلِيْنَ ﴿١٩٩﴾

3. Keep to forgiveness (O Muhammad), and enjoin kindness, and turn away from the ignorant.

7:199

CLOUDS
Ref: 2:57,210; 25:25.
See also: Rain.

4. And the believers, men and women, are protecting friends one of another; they enjoin the right and forbid the wrong, and they establish worship and they pay the poor-due, and they obey Allah and His messenger. As for these Allah will have mercy on them. Lo! Allah is Mighty, Wise.

9:71

5. Those who, if We give them power in the land, establish worship and pay the poor-due and enjoin kindness and forbid iniquity. And Allah's is the sequel of events.

22:41

6. O my dear son! Establish worship and enjoin kindness and forbid iniquity, and preserve whatever may befall thee. Lo! that is of the steadfast heart of things.

31:17

4. وَالْمُؤْمِنُونَ وَالْمُؤْمِنٰتُ بَعْضُهُمْ أَوْلِيَآءُ
بَعْضٍ يَأْمُرُونَ بِالْمَعْرُوفِ وَيَنْهَوْنَ عَنِ
الْمُنْكَرِ وَيُقِيمُونَ الصَّلٰوةَ وَيُؤْتُونَ الزَّكٰوةَ
وَيُطِيعُونَ اللّٰهَ وَرَسُولَهٗ ۭ أُولٰٓئِكَ سَيَرْحَمُهُمُ
اللّٰهُ ۭ إِنَّ اللّٰهَ عَزِيزٌ حَكِيمٌ ﴿٧١﴾

5. اَلَّذِينَ إِنْ مَّكَّنّٰهُمْ فِى الْأَرْضِ
أَقَامُوا الصَّلٰوةَ وَاٰتَوُا الزَّكٰوةَ وَأَمَرُوا
بِالْمَعْرُوفِ وَنَهَوْا عَنِ الْمُنْكَرِ ۭ
وَلِلّٰهِ عَاقِبَةُ الْأُمُورِ ﴿٤١﴾

6. يٰبُنَىَّ أَقِمِ الصَّلٰوةَ وَأْمُرْ بِالْمَعْرُوفِ
وَانْهَ عَنِ الْمُنْكَرِ وَاصْبِرْ عَلٰى مَآ
أَصَابَكَ ۭ إِنَّ ذٰلِكَ مِنْ عَزْمِ الْأُمُورِ ﴿١٧﴾

○

COMPANION OF MOSES

1. وَاِذْ قَالَ مُوْسٰى لِفَتٰىهُ لَاۤ اَبْرَحُ حَتّٰۤى
اَبْلُغَ مَجْمَعَ الْبَحْرَيْنِ اَوْ اَمْضِيَ حُقُبًا ﴿٦٠﴾
فَلَمَّا بَلَغَا مَجْمَعَ بَيْنِهِمَا نَسِيَا حُوْتَهُمَا
فَاتَّخَذَ سَبِيْلَهٗ فِي الْبَحْرِ سَرَبًا ﴿٦١﴾
فَلَمَّا جَاوَزَا قَالَ لِفَتٰىهُ اٰتِنَا غَدَآءَنَا ؗ
لَقَدْ لَقِيْنَا مِنْ سَفَرِنَا هٰذَا نَصَبًا ﴿٦٢﴾
قَالَ اَرَءَيْتَ اِذْ اَوَيْنَاۤ اِلَى الصَّخْرَةِ
فَاِنِّيْ نَسِيْتُ الْحُوْتَ ؗ وَمَاۤ اَنْسٰىنِيْهُ
اِلَّا الشَّيْطٰنُ اَنْ اَذْكُرَهٗ ۚ وَاتَّخَذَ سَبِيْلَهٗ
فِي الْبَحْرِ ۖ عَجَبًا ﴿٦٣﴾
قَالَ ذٰلِكَ مَا كُنَّا نَبْغِ ۖ فَارْتَدَّا عَلٰۤى
اٰثَارِهِمَا قَصَصًا ﴿٦٤﴾
فَوَجَدَا عَبْدًا مِّنْ عِبَادِنَاۤ اٰتَيْنٰهُ رَحْمَةً
مِّنْ عِنْدِنَا وَعَلَّمْنٰهُ مِنْ لَّدُنَّا عِلْمًا ﴿٦٥﴾
قَالَ لَهٗ مُوْسٰى هَلْ اَتَّبِعُكَ عَلٰۤى اَنْ
تُعَلِّمَنِ مِمَّا عُلِّمْتَ رُشْدًا ﴿٦٦﴾
قَالَ اِنَّكَ لَنْ تَسْتَطِيْعَ مَعِيَ صَبْرًا ﴿٦٧﴾
وَكَيْفَ تَصْبِرُ عَلٰى مَا لَمْ تُحِطْ بِهٖ خُبْرًا ﴿٦٨﴾
قَالَ سَتَجِدُنِيْۤ اِنْ شَآءَ اللّٰهُ صَابِرًا وَّلَاۤ
اَعْصِيْ لَكَ اَمْرًا ﴿٦٩﴾
قَالَ فَاِنِ اتَّبَعْتَنِيْ فَلَا تَسْـَٔلْنِيْ عَنْ
شَيْءٍ حَتّٰۤى اُحْدِثَ لَكَ مِنْهُ ذِكْرًا ﴿٧٠﴾
فَانْطَلَقَا ٚ حَتّٰۤى اِذَا رَكِبَا فِي السَّفِيْنَةِ
خَرَقَهَا ؕ قَالَ اَخَرَقْتَهَا لِتُغْرِقَ اَهْلَهَا ۚ

1. And when Moses said unto his servant: I will not give up until I reach the point where the two rivers meet, though I march on for ages.

And when they reached the point where the two met, they forgot their fish, and it took its way into the waters, being free.

And when they had gone further, he said unto his servant: Bring us our breakfast. Verily we have found fatigue in this our journey.

He said: Didst thou see, when we took refuge on the rock, and I forgot the fish—and none but Satan caused me to forget to mention it—it took its way into the waters by a marvel.

He said: This is that which we have been seeking. So they retraced their steps again.

Then found they one of Our slaves, unto whom We had given mercy from Us, and had taught him knowledge from Our presence.

Moses said unto him: May I follow thee, to the end that thou mayst teach me right conduct of that which thou hast been taught?

He said: Lo! thou canst not bear with me.

How canst thou bear with that whereof thou canst not compass any knowledge?

He said: Allah willing, thou shalt find me patient and I shall not in aught gainsay thee.

He said: Well, if thou go with me, ask me not concerning aught till I myself mention of it unto thee.

So the twain set out till, when they were in the ship, he made a hole therein. (Moses) Said: Hast thou made a hole therein to drown the folk thereof? Thou verily

لقد جئت شيئا إمرا ﴿٧١﴾
قال ألم أقل إنك لن تستطيع
معي صبرا ﴿٧٢﴾
قال لا تؤاخذني بما نسيت ولا
ترهقني من أمري عسرا ﴿٧٣﴾
فانطلقا حتى إذا لقيا غلاما فقتله
قال أقتلت نفسا زكية بغير نفس
لقد جئت شيئا نكرا ﴿٧٤﴾
قال ألم أقل لك إنك لن تستطيع
معي صبرا ﴿٧٥﴾
قال إن سألتك عن شيء بعدها
فلا تصاحبني قد بلغت من
لدني عذرا ﴿٧٦﴾
فانطلقا حتى إذا أتيا أهل قرية
استطعما أهلها فأبوا أن يضيفوهما
فوجدا فيها جدارا يريد أن ينقض
فأقامه قال لو شئت لتخذت
عليه أجرا ﴿٧٧﴾
قال هذا فراق بيني وبينك
سأنبئك بتأويل ما لم تستطع
عليه صبرا ﴿٧٨﴾
أما السفينة فكانت لمساكين
يعملون في البحر فأردت أن أعيبها
وكان وراءهم ملك يأخذ كل
سفينة غصبا ﴿٧٩﴾

hast done a dreadful thing.

He said: Did I not tell thee thou couldst not bear with me?

(Moses) said: Be not wroth with me that I forgot, and be not hard upon me for my fault.

So the twain journeyed on till, when they met a lad, he slew him. (Moses) said: What! hast thou slain an innocent soul who hath slain no man? Verily thou hast done a horrid thing.

He said: Did I not tell thee that thou couldst not bear with me?

(Moses) said: If I ask thee after this concerning aught, keep not company with me. Thou hast received an excuse from me.

So they twain journeyed on till when they came unto the folk of a certain township, they asked its folk for food, but they refused to make them guests. And they found therein a wall upon the point of falling into ruin, and he repaired it. (Moses) said: If thou hadst wished, thou couldst have taken payment for it.

He said: This is the parting between thee and me! I will announce unto thee the interpretation of that thou couldst not bear with patience.

As for the ship, it belonged to poor people working on the river, and I wished to mar it, for there was a king behind them who is taking every ship by force.

And as for the lad, his parents were believers and we feared lest he should oppress them by rebellion and disbelief.

And we intended that their Lord should change him for them for one better in purity and nearer to mercy.

And as for the wall, it belonged to two orphan boys in the city, and there was beneath it a treasure belonging to them, and their father had been righteous, and thy Lord intended that they should come to their full strength and should bring forth their treasure as a mercy from their Lord; and I did it not upon my own command. Such is the interpretation of that wherewith thou couldst not bear.

18:60–82

COMPANIONS OF PROPHET (PBUH)

1. Thus We have appointed you a middle nation, that ye may be witnesses against mankind, and that the messenger may be a witness against you, And We appointed the *qibla* which ye formerly observed only that We might know him who followeth the messenger, from him who turneth on his heels. In truth it was a hard (test) save for those whom Allah guided. But it was not Allah's purpose that your faith should be in vain, for Allah is Full of Pity, Merciful toward mankind.

2:143

2. Ye are the best community that hath been raised up for mankind. Ye enjoin right conduct and forbid indecency;

وَاَمَّا الْغُلٰمُ فَكَانَ اَبَوٰهُ مُؤْمِنَيْنِ فَخَشِيْنَآ
اَنْ يُّرْهِقَهُمَا طُغْيَانًا وَّكُفْرًا ﴿٨٠﴾
فَاَرَدْنَآ اَنْ يُّبْدِلَهُمَا رَبُّهُمَا خَيْرًا مِّنْهُ زَكٰوةً
وَّاَقْرَبَ رُحْمًا ﴿٨١﴾
وَاَمَّا الْجِدَارُ فَكَانَ لِغُلٰمَيْنِ يَتِيْمَيْنِ فِى الْمَدِيْنَةِ
وَكَانَ تَحْتَهٗ كَنْزٌ لَّهُمَا وَكَانَ اَبُوْهُمَا صَالِحًا
فَاَرَادَ رَبُّكَ اَنْ يَّبْلُغَآ اَشُدَّهُمَا وَيَسْتَخْرِجَا
كَنْزَهُمَا رَحْمَةً مِّنْ رَّبِّكَ وَمَا فَعَلْتُهٗ
عَنْ اَمْرِىْ ذٰلِكَ تَاْوِيْلُ مَا لَمْ تَسْطِعْ عَّلَيْهِ
صَبْرًا ﴿٨٢﴾

1. وَكَذٰلِكَ جَعَلْنٰكُمْ اُمَّةً وَّسَطًا لِّتَكُوْنُوْا شُهَدَآءَ
عَلَى النَّاسِ وَيَكُوْنَ الرَّسُوْلُ عَلَيْكُمْ شَهِيْدًا
وَمَا جَعَلْنَا الْقِبْلَةَ الَّتِىْ كُنْتَ عَلَيْهَآ اِلَّا لِنَعْلَمَ
مَنْ يَّتَّبِعُ الرَّسُوْلَ مِمَّنْ يَّنْقَلِبُ عَلٰى عَقِبَيْهِ
وَاِنْ كَانَتْ لَكَبِيْرَةً اِلَّا عَلَى الَّذِيْنَ
هَدَى اللّٰهُ وَمَا كَانَ اللّٰهُ لِيُضِيْعَ اِيْمَانَكُمْ
اِنَّ اللّٰهَ بِالنَّاسِ لَرَءُوْفٌ رَّحِيْمٌ ﴿١٤٣﴾

2. كُنْتُمْ خَيْرَ اُمَّةٍ اُخْرِجَتْ لِلنَّاسِ تَاْمُرُوْنَ
بِالْمَعْرُوْفِ وَتَنْهَوْنَ عَنِ الْمُنْكَرِ وَتُؤْمِنُوْنَ
بِاللّٰهِ

and ye believe in Allah.

3:110

3. Those who point at such of the believers as give the alms willingly and such as can find naught to give but their endeavours, and deride them— Allah (Himself) derideth them. Theirs will be a painful doom.

9:79

4. Not unto the weak nor unto the sick nor unto those who can find naught to spend is any fault (to be imputed though they stay at home) if they are true to Allah and His messenger. Not unto the good is there any road (of blame). Allah is Forgiving, Merciful.

Nor unto those whom, when they came to thee (asking) that thou shouldst mount them, thou didst tell: I cannot find whereon to mount you. They turned back with eyes flowing with tears, for sorrow that they could not find the means to spend.

9:91-92

5. And the first to lead the way, of the *Muhajirin* and the *Ansar*, and those who followed them in goodness—Allah is well pleased with them and they are well pleased with Him, and He hath made ready for them Gardens underneath which rivers flow, wherein they will abide for ever. That is the Supreme triumph.

9:100

6. Allah hath turned in mercy to the Prophet, and to the *Muhajirin* and the *Ansar* who followed him in the hour of hardship. After the hearts of a party of them had almost swerved aside, then turned He unto them in mercy. Lo! He is Full of Pity, Merciful for them.

3. ٱلَّذِينَ يَلْمِزُونَ ٱلْمُطَّوِّعِينَ مِنَ ٱلْمُؤْمِنِينَ
فِى ٱلصَّدَقَٰتِ وَٱلَّذِينَ لَا يَجِدُونَ إِلَّا
جُهْدَهُمْ فَيَسْخَرُونَ مِنْهُمْ سَخِرَ ٱللَّهُ
مِنْهُمْ وَلَهُمْ عَذَابٌ أَلِيمٌ ﴿٧٩﴾
4. لَيْسَ عَلَى ٱلضُّعَفَآءِ وَلَا عَلَى ٱلْمَرْضَىٰ وَلَا
عَلَى ٱلَّذِينَ لَا يَجِدُونَ مَا يُنفِقُونَ حَرَجٌ
إِذَا نَصَحُوا۟ لِلَّهِ وَرَسُولِهِۦ مَا عَلَى
ٱلْمُحْسِنِينَ مِن سَبِيلٍ وَٱللَّهُ غَفُورٌ رَّحِيمٌ ﴿٩١﴾
وَلَا عَلَى ٱلَّذِينَ إِذَا مَآ أَتَوْكَ لِتَحْمِلَهُمْ
قُلْتَ لَآ أَجِدُ مَآ أَحْمِلُكُمْ عَلَيْهِ تَوَلَّوا۟
وَّأَعْيُنُهُمْ تَفِيضُ مِنَ ٱلدَّمْعِ حَزَنًا أَلَّا
يَجِدُوا۟ مَا يُنفِقُونَ ﴿٩٢﴾
5. وَٱلسَّٰبِقُونَ ٱلْأَوَّلُونَ مِنَ ٱلْمُهَٰجِرِينَ
وَٱلْأَنصَارِ وَٱلَّذِينَ ٱتَّبَعُوهُم بِإِحْسَٰنٍ
رَّضِىَ ٱللَّهُ عَنْهُمْ وَرَضُوا۟ عَنْهُ وَأَعَدَّ
لَهُمْ جَنَّٰتٍ تَجْرِى تَحْتَهَا ٱلْأَنْهَٰرُ خَٰلِدِينَ
فِيهَآ أَبَدًا ذَٰلِكَ ٱلْفَوْزُ ٱلْعَظِيمُ ﴿١٠٠﴾
6. لَّقَد تَّابَ ٱللَّهُ عَلَى ٱلنَّبِىِّ وَٱلْمُهَٰجِرِينَ
وَٱلْأَنصَارِ ٱلَّذِينَ ٱتَّبَعُوهُ فِى سَاعَةِ
ٱلْعُسْرَةِ مِنۢ بَعْدِ مَا كَادَ يَزِيغُ قُلُوبُ
فَرِيقٍ مِّنْهُمْ ثُمَّ تَابَ عَلَيْهِمْ إِنَّهُۥ بِهِمْ
رَءُوفٌ رَّحِيمٌ ﴿١١٧﴾
وَعَلَى ٱلثَّلَٰثَةِ ٱلَّذِينَ خُلِّفُوا۟ حَتَّىٰ إِذَا
ضَاقَتْ عَلَيْهِمُ ٱلْأَرْضُ بِمَا رَحُبَتْ

And to the three also (did He turn in mercy) who were left behind, when the earth, vast as it is, was straitened for them, and their own souls were straitened for them till they bethought them that there is no refuge from Allah save toward Him.[1] Then turned He unto them in mercy that they (too) might turn (repentant unto Him). Lo! Allah! He is the Relenting, the Merciful.

9:117-118

7. And when the true believers saw the clans, they said: This is that which Allah and His messenger promised us. Allah and His messenger are true. It did but confirm them in their faith and resignation.

Of the believers are men who are true to that which they convenanted with Allah. Some of them have paid their vow by death (in battle), and some of them still are waiting; and they have not altered in the least:

33:22–23

8. Lo! those who swear allegiance unto thee (Muhammad), swear allegiance only unto Allah. The Hand of Allah is above their hands. So whosoever breaketh his oath, breaketh it only to his soul's hurt; while whosoever keepeth his convenant with Allah, on him will He bestow immense reward.

48:10

9. Allah was well pleased with the believers when they swore allegiance unto thee

وَضَاقَتْ عَلَيْهِمْ أَنفُسُهُمْ وَظَنُّوا أَن لَّا
مَلْجَأَ مِنَ اللَّهِ إِلَّا إِلَيْهِ ثُمَّ تَابَ عَلَيْهِمْ
لِيَتُوبُوا ۚ إِنَّ اللَّهَ هُوَ التَّوَّابُ الرَّحِيمُ ﴿١١٨﴾

7. وَلَمَّا رَأَى الْمُؤْمِنُونَ الْأَحْزَابَ قَالُوا
هَٰذَا مَا وَعَدَنَا اللَّهُ وَرَسُولُهُ وَصَدَقَ
اللَّهُ وَرَسُولُهُ ۚ وَمَا زَادَهُمْ إِلَّا
إِيمَانًا وَتَسْلِيمًا ﴿٢٢﴾
مِنَ الْمُؤْمِنِينَ رِجَالٌ صَدَقُوا مَا
عَاهَدُوا اللَّهَ عَلَيْهِ ۖ فَمِنْهُم مَّن قَضَىٰ
نَحْبَهُ وَمِنْهُم مَّن يَنتَظِرُ ۖ وَمَا
بَدَّلُوا تَبْدِيلًا ﴿٢٣﴾

8. إِنَّ الَّذِينَ يُبَايِعُونَكَ إِنَّمَا يُبَايِعُونَ
اللَّهَ يَدُ اللَّهِ فَوْقَ أَيْدِيهِمْ ۚ فَمَن
نَّكَثَ فَإِنَّمَا يَنكُثُ عَلَىٰ نَفْسِهِ ۖ وَمَنْ
أَوْفَىٰ بِمَا عَاهَدَ عَلَيْهُ اللَّهَ فَسَيُؤْتِيهِ
أَجْرًا عَظِيمًا ﴿١٠﴾

9. لَّقَدْ رَضِيَ اللَّهُ عَنِ الْمُؤْمِنِينَ إِذْ
يُبَايِعُونَكَ تَحْتَ الشَّجَرَةِ فَعَلِمَ مَا
فِي قُلُوبِهِمْ فَأَنزَلَ السَّكِينَةَ عَلَيْهِمْ
وَأَثَابَهُمْ فَتْحًا قَرِيبًا ﴿١٨﴾
وَمَغَانِمَ كَثِيرَةً يَأْخُذُونَهَا ۗ وَكَانَ
اللَّهُ عَزِيزًا حَكِيمًا ﴿١٩﴾

beneath the tree, and He knew what was in their hearts, and He sent down peace of re-assurance on them, and hath rewarded them with a near victory;

And much booty that they will capture.

Allah is ever Mighty, Wise

48:18-19

10. Muhammad is the messenger of Allah. And those with him are hard against the disbelievers and merciful among themselves. Thou (O Muhammad) seest them bowing and falling prostrate (in worship), seeking bounty from Allah and (His) acceptance. The mark of them is on their foreheads from traces of prostration. Such is their likeness in the *Torah* and their likeness in the *Gospel*—like as sown corn that sendeth forth its shoot and strengtheneth it and riseth firm upon its stalk, delighting the sowers that He may enrage the disbelievers with (the sight of) them. Allah hath promised, unto such of them as believe and do good works, forgiveness and immense reward.

48:29

11. And (it is) for the poor fugitives who have been driven out from their homes and their belongings, who seek bounty from Allah and help Allah and His messenger. They are the loyal.

Those who entered the city and the faith before them love those who flee unto them for refuge, and find in their breasts no need for that which hath been given them, but prefer (the refugees) above themselves though poverty become their lot. And whoso is

10. مُحَمَّدٌ رَّسُولُ اللّٰهِ ۗ وَالَّذِيْنَ مَعَهٗٓ
اَشِدَّآءُ عَلَى الْكُفَّارِ رُحَمَآءُ بَيْنَهُمْ
تَرٰىهُمْ رُكَّعًا سُجَّدًا يَّبْتَغُوْنَ فَضْلًا
مِّنَ اللّٰهِ وَرِضْوَانًا ؗ سِيْمَاهُمْ فِيْ
وُجُوْهِهِمْ مِّنْ اَثَرِ السُّجُوْدِ ۗ ذٰلِكَ
مَثَلُهُمْ فِي التَّوْرٰىةِ ۛۚ وَمَثَلُهُمْ فِي
الْاِنْجِيْلِ ۛۚ كَزَرْعٍ اَخْرَجَ شَطْـَٔهٗ
فَاٰزَرَهٗ فَاسْتَغْلَظَ فَاسْتَوٰى عَلٰى
سُوْقِهٖ يُعْجِبُ الزُّرَّاعَ لِيَغِيْظَ بِهِمُ
الْكُفَّارَ ۗ وَعَدَ اللّٰهُ الَّذِيْنَ اٰمَنُوْا
وَعَمِلُوا الصّٰلِحٰتِ مِنْهُمْ مَّغْفِرَةً
وَّاَجْرًا عَظِيْمًا ﴿٢٩﴾

11. لِلْفُقَرَآءِ الْمُهٰجِرِيْنَ الَّذِيْنَ اُخْرِجُوْا
مِنْ دِيَارِهِمْ وَاَمْوَالِهِمْ يَبْتَغُوْنَ
فَضْلًا مِّنَ اللّٰهِ وَرِضْوَانًا وَّيَنْصُرُوْنَ
اللّٰهَ وَرَسُوْلَهٗ ۗ اُولٰٓئِكَ هُمُ الصّٰدِقُوْنَ ﴿٨﴾ۚ
وَالَّذِيْنَ تَبَوَّؤُ الدَّارَ وَالْاِيْمَانَ مِنْ
قَبْلِهِمْ يُحِبُّوْنَ مَنْ هَاجَرَ اِلَيْهِمْ
وَلَا يَجِدُوْنَ فِيْ صُدُوْرِهِمْ حَاجَةً
مِّمَّآ اُوْتُوْا وَيُؤْثِرُوْنَ عَلٰٓى اَنْفُسِهِمْ
وَلَوْ كَانَ بِهِمْ خَصَاصَةٌ ۗ ۛ وَمَنْ يُّوْقَ
شُحَّ نَفْسِهٖ فَاُولٰٓئِكَ هُمُ الْمُفْلِحُوْنَ ﴿٩﴾ۚ
وَالَّذِيْنَ جَآءُوْ مِنْ بَعْدِهِمْ يَقُوْلُوْنَ
رَبَّنَا اغْفِرْ لَنَا وَلِاِخْوَانِنَا الَّذِيْنَ سَبَقُوْنَا

saved from his own avarice—such are they who are successfull.

And those who came (into the faith) after them say: Our Lord!. Forgive us and our brethern who were before us in the faith, and place not in our hearts any rancour toward those who believe. Our Lord! Thou art Full of Pity, Merciful.

59:8–10

CONCEALING TRUTH

1. Confound not truth with falsehood, nor knowingly conceal the truth.

2:42

2. And who is more unjust than he who hideth a testimony which he hath received from Allah? Allah is not unaware of what ye do.

2:140

3. Lo! those who hide the proofs and the guidance which We revealed, after we had made it clear to mankind in the Scripture: such are accursed of Allah and accursed of those who have the power to curse:

2:159

CONCEPT OF EQUALITY

1. Say: The evil and the good are not alike even though the plenty of the evil attract thee. So be mindful of your duty to Allah, O men of understanding, that ye may succeed.

5:100

2. Say (O Muhammad to the disbelievers): I say not unto you (that) I possess the treasures of Allah, nor that I have knowledge of the Unseen; and I say not unto you: Lo! I am an angel. I follow only that which is inspired in me. Say: Are

بِالْإِيمَانِ وَلَا تَجْعَلْ فِي قُلُوبِنَا غِلًّا لِّلَّذِينَ آمَنُوا رَبَّنَا إِنَّكَ رَءُوفٌ رَّحِيمٌ ﴿١٠﴾

○

1. وَلَا تَلْبِسُوا الْحَقَّ بِالْبَاطِلِ وَتَكْتُمُوا الْحَقَّ وَأَنتُمْ تَعْلَمُونَ ﴿٤٢﴾

2. وَمَنْ أَظْلَمُ مِمَّن كَتَمَ شَهَادَةً عِندَهُ مِنَ اللَّهِ ۗ وَمَا اللَّهُ بِغَافِلٍ عَمَّا تَعْمَلُونَ ﴿١٤٠﴾

3. إِنَّ الَّذِينَ يَكْتُمُونَ مَا أَنزَلْنَا مِنَ الْبَيِّنَاتِ وَالْهُدَىٰ مِن بَعْدِ مَا بَيَّنَّاهُ لِلنَّاسِ فِي الْكِتَابِ ۙ أُولَٰئِكَ يَلْعَنُهُمُ اللَّهُ وَيَلْعَنُهُمُ اللَّاعِنُونَ ﴿١٥٩﴾

○

1. قُل لَّا يَسْتَوِي الْخَبِيثُ وَالطَّيِّبُ وَلَوْ أَعْجَبَكَ كَثْرَةُ الْخَبِيثِ ۚ فَاتَّقُوا اللَّهَ يَا أُولِي الْأَلْبَابِ لَعَلَّكُمْ تُفْلِحُونَ ﴿١٠٠﴾

2. قُل لَّا أَقُولُ لَكُمْ عِندِي خَزَائِنُ اللَّهِ وَلَا أَعْلَمُ الْغَيْبَ وَلَا أَقُولُ لَكُمْ إِنِّي مَلَكٌ ۖ إِنْ أَتَّبِعُ إِلَّا مَا يُوحَىٰ إِلَيَّ ۚ قُلْ هَلْ يَسْتَوِي الْأَعْمَىٰ وَالْبَصِيرُ ۚ أَفَلَا تَتَفَكَّرُونَ ﴿٥٠﴾

3. أَفَمَن يَعْلَمُ أَنَّمَا أُنزِلَ إِلَيْكَ مِن رَّبِّكَ الْحَقُّ كَمَنْ هُوَ أَعْمَىٰ ۚ إِنَّمَا يَتَذَكَّرُ أُولُو الْأَلْبَابِ ﴿١٩﴾

the blind man and the seer equal? Will ye not then take thought?

6:50

3. Is he who knoweth that what is revealed unto thee from thy Lord is the truth like him who is blind? But only men of understanding heed;

13:19

See also: *Ansar*, Migration.

CONCEALING TRUTH

Ref: 2:146,174.

See also: Truth and Falsehood.

4. Is he who is a believer like unto him who is an evil-liver? They are not alike.

32:18

5. The blind man is not equal with the seer;

Nor is darkness (tantamount to) light;

Nor is the shadow equal with the sun's full heat;

Nor are the living equal with the dead.

35:19-22

6. Is he who payeth adoration in the watches of the night, prostrate and standing, bewaring of the Hereafter and hoping for the mercy of his Lord, (to be accounted equal with a dis-believer)? Say (unto them, O Muhammad): Are those who know equal with those who know not? But only men of understanding will pay heed.

39:9

7. And the blind man and the seer are not equal, neither are those who believe and do good works (equal with) the evil-doer. Little do ye reflect!

40:58

8. The good deed and the evil deed are not alike.

41:34

9. Or do those who commit ill-deeds suppose that We shall make them as those who believe and do good works, the same in life and death?

4. أَفَمَنْ كَانَ مُؤْمِنًا كَمَنْ كَانَ فَاسِقًا ۚ
لَا يَسْتَوُونَ ﴿١٨﴾

5. وَمَا يَسْتَوِي الْأَعْمَىٰ وَالْبَصِيرُ ﴿١٩﴾
وَلَا الظُّلُمَاتُ وَلَا النُّورُ ﴿٢٠﴾
وَلَا الظِّلُّ وَلَا الْحَرُورُ ﴿٢١﴾

وَمَا يَسْتَوِي الْأَحْيَاءُ وَلَا الْأَمْوَاتُ ۚ

6. أَمَّنْ هُوَ قَانِتٌ آنَاءَ اللَّيْلِ سَاجِدًا وَ
قَائِمًا يَحْذَرُ الْآخِرَةَ وَيَرْجُو رَحْمَةَ
رَبِّهِ ۗ قُلْ هَلْ يَسْتَوِي الَّذِينَ
يَعْلَمُونَ وَالَّذِينَ لَا يَعْلَمُونَ ۗ إِنَّمَا
يَتَذَكَّرُ أُولُو الْأَلْبَابِ ﴿٩﴾

7. وَمَا يَسْتَوِي الْأَعْمَىٰ وَالْبَصِيرُ ۙ
وَالَّذِينَ آمَنُوا وَعَمِلُوا الصَّالِحَاتِ وَ
لَا الْمُسِيءُ ۚ قَلِيلًا مَا تَتَذَكَّرُونَ ﴿٥٨﴾

8. وَلَا تَسْتَوِي الْحَسَنَةُ وَلَا السَّيِّئَةُ ۚ

9. أَمْ حَسِبَ الَّذِينَ اجْتَرَحُوا السَّيِّئَاتِ
أَنْ نَجْعَلَهُمْ كَالَّذِينَ آمَنُوا وَعَمِلُوا
الصَّالِحَاتِ سَوَاءً مَحْيَاهُمْ وَمَمَاتُهُمْ ۚ
سَاءَ مَا يَحْكُمُونَ ﴿٢١﴾

10. لَا يَسْتَوِي أَصْحَابُ النَّارِ وَأَصْحَابُ
الْجَنَّةِ ۚ أَصْحَابُ الْجَنَّةِ هُمُ الْفَائِزُونَ ﴿٢٠﴾

Bad is their judgement!

45:21

10. Not equal are the owners of the Fire and the owners of the Garden. The owners of the Gardens, they are the victorious.

59:20

CONJUGAL RIGHTS AND OBLIGATIONS

1. And they (women) have rights similar to those (of men) over them in kindness, and men are a degree above them. Allah is Mighty, Wise.

2:228

2. Unto men a fortune from that which they have earned, and unto women a fortune from that which they have earned. (Envy not one another) but ask Allah of His bounty. Lo! Allah is ever Knower of all things.

4:32

3. Men are in charge of women, because Allah hath made the one of them to excel the other, and because they spend of their property (for the support of women).

4:34

CONQUEST OF* MAKKAH

1. When Allah's succour and the triumph cometh

And thou seest mankind entering the religion of Allah in troops,

Then hymn the priases of thy Lord, and seek forgiveness of Him. Lo! He is ever ready to show mercy.

110:1–3

1. وَلَهُنَّ مِثْلُ الَّذِي عَلَيْهِنَّ بِالْمَعْرُوفِ وَلِلرِّجَالِ
عَلَيْهِنَّ دَرَجَةٌ وَاللَّهُ عَزِيزٌ حَكِيمٌ ﴿٢٢٨﴾

2. لِلرِّجَالِ نَصِيبٌ مِمَّا اكْتَسَبُوا
وَلِلنِّسَاءِ نَصِيبٌ مِمَّا اكْتَسَبْنَ وَاسْأَلُوا
اللَّهَ مِنْ فَضْلِهِ إِنَّ اللَّهَ كَانَ بِكُلِّ
شَيْءٍ عَلِيمًا ﴿٣٢﴾

3. الرِّجَالُ قَوَّامُونَ عَلَى النِّسَاءِ بِمَا فَضَّلَ
اللَّهُ بَعْضَهُمْ عَلَى بَعْضٍ وَبِمَا أَنْفَقُوا مِنْ
أَمْوَالِهِمْ

1. إِذَا جَاءَ نَصْرُ اللَّهِ وَالْفَتْحُ ﴿١﴾
وَرَأَيْتَ النَّاسَ يَدْخُلُونَ فِي
دِينِ اللَّهِ أَفْوَاجًا ﴿٢﴾
فَسَبِّحْ بِحَمْدِ رَبِّكَ وَاسْتَغْفِرْهُ
إِنَّهُ كَانَ تَوَّابًا ﴿٣﴾

CONJUGAL RIGHTS AND OBLIGATIONS
See also: Maintenance Expenses.

CONSULTATION

1. It was by the mercy of Allah that thou wast lenient with them (O Muhammad), for if thou hadst been stern and fierce of heart they would have dispersed from round about thee. So pardon them and ask forgiveness for them and consult with them upon the conduct of affairs. And when thou art resolved, then put thy trust in Allah. Lo! Allah loveth those who put their trust (in Him).

3:159

2. Now whatever ye have been given is but a passing comfort for the life of the world, and that which Allah hath is better and more lasting for those who believe and put their trust in their Lord.

And those who shun the worst of sins and indecencies and, when they are wroth, forgive.

And those who answer the call of their Lord and establish worship, and whose affairs are a matter of counsel, and who spend of what We have bestowed on them.

42:36–38

1. فَبِمَا رَحْمَةٍ مِّنَ اللّٰهِ لِنْتَ لَهُمْ وَلَوْ كُنْتَ
فَظًّا غَلِيْظَ الْقَلْبِ لَانْفَضُّوْا مِنْ حَوْلِكَ
فَاعْفُ عَنْهُمْ وَاسْتَغْفِرْ لَهُمْ وَشَاوِرْهُمْ
فِي الْاَمْرِ فَاِذَا عَزَمْتَ فَتَوَكَّلْ عَلَى اللّٰهِ
اِنَّ اللّٰهَ يُحِبُّ الْمُتَوَكِّلِيْنَ ○

2. فَمَآ اُوْتِيْتُمْ مِّنْ شَيْءٍ فَمَتَاعُ
الْحَيٰوةِ الدُّنْيَا وَمَا عِنْدَ اللّٰهِ خَيْرٌ
وَّ اَبْقٰى لِلَّذِيْنَ اٰمَنُوْا وَعَلٰى رَبِّهِمْ
يَتَوَكَّلُوْنَ ○
وَالَّذِيْنَ يَجْتَنِبُوْنَ كَبٰٓئِرَ الْاِثْمِ
وَالْفَوَاحِشَ وَاِذَا مَا غَضِبُوْا هُمْ
يَغْفِرُوْنَ ○
وَالَّذِيْنَ اسْتَجَابُوْا لِرَبِّهِمْ وَاَقَامُوا
الصَّلٰوةَ وَاَمْرُهُمْ شُوْرٰى بَيْنَهُمْ
وَمِمَّا رَزَقْنٰهُمْ يُنْفِقُوْنَ ○

○

See also: Mutual Relations of Muslims.

CORRUPTION OF SCRIPTURES

1. مِنَ الَّذِينَ هَادُوا يُحَرِّفُونَ الْكَلِمَ عَن
مَّوَاضِعِهِ وَيَقُولُونَ سَمِعْنَا وَعَصَيْنَا
وَاسْمَعْ غَيْرَ مُسْمَعٍ وَرَاعِنَا لَيًّا بِأَلْسِنَتِهِمْ
وَطَعْنًا فِي الدِّينِ وَلَوْ أَنَّهُمْ قَالُوا سَمِعْنَا
وَأَطَعْنَا وَاسْمَعْ وَانظُرْنَا لَكَانَ خَيْرًا لَّهُمْ
وَأَقْوَمَ وَلَٰكِن لَّعَنَهُمُ اللَّهُ بِكُفْرِهِمْ
فَلَا يُؤْمِنُونَ إِلَّا قَلِيلًا ﴿٤٦﴾

2. يَا أَيُّهَا الرَّسُولُ لَا يَحْزُنكَ الَّذِينَ يُسَارِعُونَ
فِي الْكُفْرِ مِنَ الَّذِينَ قَالُوا آمَنَّا بِأَفْوَاهِهِمْ
وَلَمْ تُؤْمِن قُلُوبُهُمْ ۛ وَمِنَ الَّذِينَ هَادُوا ۛ
سَمَّاعُونَ لِلْكَذِبِ سَمَّاعُونَ لِقَوْمٍ آخَرِينَ
لَمْ يَأْتُوكَ ۖ يُحَرِّفُونَ الْكَلِمَ مِن
بَعْدِ مَوَاضِعِهِ ۖ يَقُولُونَ إِنْ أُوتِيتُمْ هَٰذَا
فَخُذُوهُ وَإِن لَّمْ تُؤْتَوْهُ فَاحْذَرُوا ۚ وَمَن
يُرِدِ اللَّهُ فِتْنَتَهُ فَلَن تَمْلِكَ لَهُ مِنَ اللَّهِ
شَيْئًا ۚ أُولَٰئِكَ الَّذِينَ لَمْ يُرِدِ اللَّهُ أَن
يُطَهِّرَ قُلُوبَهُمْ ۚ لَهُمْ فِي الدُّنْيَا خِزْيٌ ۖ
وَلَهُمْ فِي الْآخِرَةِ عَذَابٌ عَظِيمٌ ﴿٤١﴾

1. Some of those who are Jews change words from their context and say: "We hear and disobey; hear thou as one who heareth not" and "Listen to us!" distorting with their tongues and slandering religion. If they had said "We hear and we obey; hear thou, and look at us" it had been better for them, and more upright. But Allah hath cursed them for their disbelief, so they believe not save a few.

4:46

2. O Messenger! Let not them grieve thee who vie one with another in the race to disbelief, of such as say with their mouths: "We believe," but their hearts believe not, and of the Jews: listeners for the sake of falsehood, listeners on behalf of other folk who come not unto thee, changing words from their context and saying: If this be given unto you, receive it, but if this be not given unto you, then beware! He whom Allah doometh unto sin, thou (by thine efforts) wilt avail him naught against Allah. Those are they for whom the Will of Allah is that He cleanse not their hearts. Theirs in the world will be ignominy, and in the Hereafter an awful doom

5:41

COURTESY TOWARD WOMEN

1. يَٰٓأَيُّهَا ٱلَّذِينَ ءَامَنُوا۟ لَا يَحِلُّ لَكُمْ أَن
تَرِثُوا۟ ٱلنِّسَآءَ كَرْهًا ۖ وَلَا تَعْضُلُوهُنَّ
لِتَذْهَبُوا۟ بِبَعْضِ مَآ ءَاتَيْتُمُوهُنَّ إِلَّآ أَن
يَأْتِينَ بِفَٰحِشَةٍ مُّبَيِّنَةٍ ۚ وَعَاشِرُوهُنَّ
بِٱلْمَعْرُوفِ ۚ فَإِن كَرِهْتُمُوهُنَّ فَعَسَىٰٓ أَن
تَكْرَهُوا۟ شَيْـًٔا وَيَجْعَلَ ٱللَّهُ فِيهِ خَيْرًا كَثِيرًا ﴿١٩﴾

1. O ye who believe! It is not lawful for you forcibly to inherit the women (of your deceased kinsmen), nor (that) ye should put constraint upon them that ye may take away a part of that which ye have given them, unless they be guilty of flagrant lewdness. But consort with them in kindness, for if ye hate them it may happen that ye hate a thing wherein Allah hath placed much good.

4:19

COVENANT

1. وَإِذْ أَخَذْنَا مِيثَٰقَ بَنِىٓ إِسْرَٰٓءِيلَ لَا تَعْبُدُونَ
إِلَّا ٱللَّهَ وَبِٱلْوَٰلِدَيْنِ إِحْسَانًا وَذِى ٱلْقُرْبَىٰ وَ
ٱلْيَتَٰمَىٰ وَٱلْمَسَٰكِينِ وَقُولُوا۟ لِلنَّاسِ حُسْنًا وَ
أَقِيمُوا۟ ٱلصَّلَوٰةَ وَءَاتُوا۟ ٱلزَّكَوٰةَ ثُمَّ تَوَلَّيْتُمْ إِلَّا
قَلِيلًا مِّنكُمْ وَأَنتُم مُّعْرِضُونَ ﴿٨٣﴾

1. And (remember) when We made a covenant with the Children of Israel, (saying): Worship none save Allah (only) and be good to parents and to kindred and to orphans and the needy, and speak kindly to mankind; and establish worship and pay the poor-due. Then, after that, ye slid back, save a few of you being averse.

2:83

2. وَإِذْ أَخَذَ ٱللَّهُ مِيثَٰقَ ٱلنَّبِيِّۦنَ لَمَآ
ءَاتَيْتُكُم مِّن كِتَٰبٍ وَحِكْمَةٍ ثُمَّ جَآءَكُمْ
رَسُولٌ مُّصَدِّقٌ لِّمَا مَعَكُمْ لَتُؤْمِنُنَّ بِهِۦ
وَلَتَنصُرُنَّهُۥ ۚ قَالَ ءَأَقْرَرْتُمْ وَأَخَذْتُمْ
عَلَىٰ ذَٰلِكُمْ إِصْرِى ۖ قَالُوٓا۟ أَقْرَرْنَا ۚ قَالَ
فَٱشْهَدُوا۟ وَأَنَا۠ مَعَكُم مِّنَ ٱلشَّٰهِدِينَ ۝

2. When Allah made (His) covenant with the Prophets, (He said): Behold that which I have given you of the Scripture and knowledge. And afterward there will come unto you a messenger, confirming that which ye possess. Ye shall believe in him and ye shall help him. He said: Do ye agree, and will ye take up My burden (which I lay upon you) in this (matter)? They answered: We agree. He said: Then bear ye witness. I will be a witness with you.

3:81

3. And because of their breaking their covenant, we have cursed them and made hard their hearts. They change words from their context and forget a part of that whereof they were admonished. Thou wilt not cease to discover treachery from all save a few of them. But bear with them and pardon them. Lo! Allah loveth the kindly.

And with those who say: "Lo! we are Christians," We made a covenant, but they forgot a part of that whereof they were admonished. Therefor We have stirred up enmity and hatred among them till the Day of Resurrection, when Allah will inform them of their handiwork.

5:13–14

4. And a generation hath succeeded them who inherited the Scriptures. They grasp the goods of this low life (as the price of evil-doing) and say: It will be forgiven us. And if there came to them (again) the offer of the like, they would accept it (and would sin again). Hath not the covenant of the Scripture been taken on their behalf that they should not speak aught concerning Allah save the truth? And they have studied that which is therein. And the abode of the Hereafter is better, for those who ward off (evil). Have ye then no sense?

7:169

3. فَبِمَا نَقْضِهِمْ مِّيثَاقَهُمْ لَعَنّٰهُمْ وَجَعَلْنَا
قُلُوبَهُمْ قٰسِيَةً يُحَرِّفُوْنَ الْكَلِمَ عَنْ
مَّوَاضِعِهٖ وَنَسُوْا حَظًّا مِّمَّا ذُكِّرُوْا بِهٖ
وَلَا تَزَالُ تَطَّلِعُ عَلٰى خَآئِنَةٍ مِّنْهُمْ اِلَّا
قَلِيْلًا مِّنْهُمْ فَاعْفُ عَنْهُمْ وَاصْفَحْ اِنَّ
اللّٰهَ يُحِبُّ الْمُحْسِنِيْنَ ﴿١٣﴾
وَمِنَ الَّذِيْنَ قَالُوْا اِنَّا نَصٰرٰى اَخَذْنَا
مِيْثَاقَهُمْ فَنَسُوْا حَظًّا مِّمَّا ذُكِّرُوْا بِهٖ
فَاَغْرَيْنَا بَيْنَهُمُ الْعَدَاوَةَ وَالْبَغْضَآءَ اِلٰى
يَوْمِ الْقِيٰمَةِ وَسَوْفَ يُنَبِّئُهُمُ اللّٰهُ
بِمَا كَانُوْا يَصْنَعُوْنَ ﴿١٤﴾

4. فَخَلَفَ مِنْۢ بَعْدِهِمْ خَلْفٌ وَّرِثُوا الْكِتٰبَ
يَاْخُذُوْنَ عَرَضَ هٰذَا الْاَدْنٰى وَيَقُوْلُوْنَ
سَيُغْفَرُ لَنَا وَاِنْ يَّاْتِهِمْ عَرَضٌ مِّثْلُهٗ
يَاْخُذُوْهُ اَلَمْ يُؤْخَذْ عَلَيْهِمْ مِّيْثَاقُ
الْكِتٰبِ اَنْ لَّا يَقُوْلُوْا عَلَى اللّٰهِ اِلَّا الْحَقَّ
وَدَرَسُوْا مَا فِيْهِ وَالدَّارُ الْاٰخِرَةُ خَيْرٌ
لِّلَّذِيْنَ يَتَّقُوْنَ اَفَلَا تَعْقِلُوْنَ ﴿١٦٩﴾

5. اِنَّ الَّذِيْنَ اٰمَنُوْا وَهَاجَرُوْا وَجٰهَدُوْا
بِاَمْوَالِهِمْ وَاَنْفُسِهِمْ فِيْ سَبِيْلِ اللّٰهِ
وَالَّذِيْنَ اٰوَوْا وَّنَصَرُوْا اُولٰٓئِكَ بَعْضُهُمْ
اَوْلِيَآءُ بَعْضٍ وَالَّذِيْنَ اٰمَنُوْا وَلَمْ يُهَاجِرُوْا

5. Lo! those who believed and left their homes and strove with their wealth and their lives for the cause of Allah, and those who took them in and helped them; these are protecting friends one of another. And those who believed but did not leave their homes, ye have

no duty to protect them till they leave their homes; but if they seek help from you in the matter of religion then it is your duty to help (them) except against a folk between whom and you there is a treaty. Allah is Seer of what ye do.

8:72

6. Such as keep the pact of Allah, and break not the covenant;

Such as unite that which Allah hath commanded should be joined, and fear their Lord, and dread a woeful reckoning;

Such as persevere in seeking their Lord's Countenance and are regular in prayer and spend of that which We bestow upon them secretly and openly, and overcome evil with good. Theirs will be the sequel of the (heavenly) Home.

Gardens of Eden which they enter, along with all who do right of their fathers and their helpmates and their seed. The angels enter unto them from every gate:

(Saying): Peace be unto you because ye persevered. Ah, passing sweet will be the sequel of the (heavenly) Home!

13:20--24

مَا لَكُمْ مِّنْ وَّلَايَتِهِمْ مِّنْ شَيْءٍ حَتّٰى
يُهَاجِرُوْا ۚ وَاِنِ اسْتَنْصَرُوْكُمْ فِي الدِّيْنِ
فَعَلَيْكُمُ النَّصْرُ اِلَّا عَلٰى قَوْمٍ بَيْنَكُمْ وَ
بَيْنَهُمْ مِّيْثَاقٌ ۗ وَ اللّٰهُ بِمَا تَعْمَلُوْنَ بَصِيْرٌ ﴿٧٢﴾

6. اَلَّذِيْنَ يُوْفُوْنَ بِعَهْدِ اللّٰهِ وَ لَا
يَنْقُضُوْنَ الْمِيْثَاقَ ﴿٢٠﴾
وَ الَّذِيْنَ يَصِلُوْنَ مَآ اَمَرَ اللّٰهُ بِهٖٓ اَنْ
يُّوْصَلَ وَ يَخْشَوْنَ رَبَّهُمْ وَ يَخَافُوْنَ
سُوْٓءَ الْحِسَابِ ﴿٢١﴾
وَ الَّذِيْنَ صَبَرُوا ابْتِغَآءَ وَجْهِ رَبِّهِمْ
وَ اَقَامُوا الصَّلٰوةَ وَ اَنْفَقُوْا مِمَّا رَزَقْنٰهُمْ
سِرًّا وَّ عَلَانِيَةً وَّ يَدْرَءُوْنَ بِالْحَسَنَةِ
السَّيِّئَةَ اُولٰٓئِكَ لَهُمْ عُقْبَى الدَّارِ ﴿٢٢﴾
جَنّٰتُ عَدْنٍ يَّدْخُلُوْنَهَا وَ مَنْ صَلَحَ
مِنْ اٰبَآئِهِمْ وَ اَزْوَاجِهِمْ وَ ذُرِّيّٰتِهِمْ
وَ الْمَلٰٓئِكَةُ يَدْخُلُوْنَ عَلَيْهِمْ مِّنْ كُلِّ بَابٍ ﴿٢٣﴾
سَلٰمٌ عَلَيْكُمْ بِمَا صَبَرْتُمْ فَنِعْمَ عُقْبَى الدَّارِ ﴿٢٤﴾

Ref: 2:63:83; 4:90:154; 5:70; 28:28;

COWARDICE

1. O ye who believe! Be not as those who disbelieved and said of their brethern who went abroad in the land or were fighting in the field: If they had been (here) with us they would not have died or been killed; that Allah may make it anguish in their hearts. Allah giveth life and causeth death, and Allah is Seer of what ye do.

3:156

2. Lo! among you there is he who loitereth; and if disaster overtook you, he would say: Allah hath been gracious unto me since I was not present with them.

4:72

3. O ye who believe! When ye meet those who disbelieve in battle, turn not your backs to them.

Whoso on that day turneth his back to them, unless manoeuvring for battle or intent to join a company, he truly hath incurred wrath from Allah, and his habitation will be hell, a hapless journey's end.

8:15–16

4. And they swear by Allah that they are in truth of you, when they are not of you, but they are folk who are afraid.

1. يَا أَيُّهَا الَّذِينَ آمَنُوا لَا تَكُونُوا كَالَّذِينَ
كَفَرُوا وَقَالُوا لِإِخْوَانِهِمْ إِذَا ضَرَبُوا فِي
الْأَرْضِ أَوْ كَانُوا غُزًّى لَوْ كَانُوا عِنْدَنَا
مَا مَاتُوا وَمَا قُتِلُوا لِيَجْعَلَ اللَّهُ ذَٰلِكَ
حَسْرَةً فِي قُلُوبِهِمْ ۗ وَاللَّهُ يُحْيِي وَيُمِيتُ
وَاللَّهُ بِمَا تَعْمَلُونَ بَصِيرٌ ۝

2. وَإِنَّ مِنْكُمْ لَمَنْ لَيُبَطِّئَنَّ فَإِنْ أَصَابَتْكُمْ
مُصِيبَةٌ قَالَ قَدْ أَنْعَمَ اللَّهُ عَلَيَّ إِذْ لَمْ
أَكُنْ مَعَهُمْ شَهِيدًا ۝

3. يَا أَيُّهَا الَّذِينَ آمَنُوا إِذَا لَقِيتُمُ الَّذِينَ
كَفَرُوا زَحْفًا فَلَا تُوَلُّوهُمُ الْأَدْبَارَ ۝

وَمَنْ يُوَلِّهِمْ يَوْمَئِذٍ دُبُرَهُ إِلَّا مُتَحَرِّفًا
لِقِتَالٍ أَوْ مُتَحَيِّزًا إِلَىٰ فِئَةٍ فَقَدْ بَاءَ بِغَضَبٍ
مِنَ اللَّهِ وَمَأْوَاهُ جَهَنَّمُ ۖ وَبِئْسَ الْمَصِيرُ ۝

4. وَيَحْلِفُونَ بِاللَّهِ إِنَّهُمْ لَمِنْكُمْ وَمَا هُمْ
مِنْكُمْ وَلَٰكِنَّهُمْ قَوْمٌ يَفْرَقُونَ ۝

لَوْ يَجِدُونَ مَلْجَأً أَوْ مَغَارَاتٍ أَوْ مُدَّخَلًا
لَوَلَّوْا إِلَيْهِ وَهُمْ يَجْمَحُونَ ۝

Had they but round a refuge, or caverns, or a place to enter, they surely had resorted thither swift as runaways.

9:56–57

Ref: 3:154–155; 4:72; 9:49;

CREATION OF MAN

1. O mankind! Be careful of your duty to your Lord Who created you from a single soul and from it created its mate and from them twain hath spread abroad a multitude of men and women.

4:1

2. He it is Who hath created you from clay, and hath decreed a term for you. A term is fixed with Him. Yet still ye doubt!

6:2

3. Verily We created man of potter's clay of black mud altered.

15:26

4. Verily We created man from a product of wet earth;

Then placed him as a drop (of seed) in a safe lodging;

Then fashioned We the drop a clot, then fashioned We the clot a little lump, then fashioned We the little lump bones, then clothed the bones with flesh, and then produced it as another creation. So blessed be Allah, the Best of Creators!

23:12–14

5. And He it is Who hath created man from water, and hath appointed for him kindred by blood and kindred by marriage; for thy Lord is ever Powerful.

25:54

1. يَٰٓأَيُّهَا النَّاسُ اتَّقُوا رَبَّكُمُ الَّذِي
خَلَقَكُم مِّن نَّفْسٍ وَّاحِدَةٍ وَّخَلَقَ مِنْهَا
زَوْجَهَا وَبَثَّ مِنْهُمَا رِجَالًا كَثِيرًا وَّنِسَآءً

2. هُوَ الَّذِي خَلَقَكُم مِّن طِينٍ ثُمَّ قَضَىٰٓ
أَجَلًا وَأَجَلٌ مُّسَمًّى عِندَهُ ثُمَّ أَنتُمْ
تَمْتَرُونَ (2)

3. وَلَقَدْ خَلَقْنَا الْإِنسَانَ مِن صَلْصَالٍ
مِّنْ حَمَإٍ مَّسْنُونٍ (26)

4. وَلَقَدْ خَلَقْنَا الْإِنسَانَ مِن سُلَٰلَةٍ
مِّن طِينٍ (12)
ثُمَّ جَعَلْنَٰهُ نُطْفَةً فِي قَرَارٍ مَّكِينٍ (13)
ثُمَّ خَلَقْنَا النُّطْفَةَ عَلَقَةً فَخَلَقْنَا
الْعَلَقَةَ مُضْغَةً فَخَلَقْنَا الْمُضْغَةَ
عِظَٰمًا فَكَسَوْنَا الْعِظَٰمَ لَحْمًا ثُمَّ
أَنشَأْنَٰهُ خَلْقًا ءَاخَرَ فَتَبَارَكَ اللَّهُ
أَحْسَنُ الْخَٰلِقِينَ (14)

5. وَهُوَ الَّذِي خَلَقَ مِنَ الْمَآءِ بَشَرًا
فَجَعَلَهُ نَسَبًا وَّصِهْرًا وَكَانَ
رَبُّكَ قَدِيرًا (54)

6. خَلَقَكُم مِّن نَّفْسٍ وَّاحِدَةٍ ثُمَّ جَعَلَ
مِنْهَا زَوْجَهَا وَأَنزَلَ لَكُم مِّنَ الْأَنْعَٰمِ
ثَمَٰنِيَةَ أَزْوَٰجٍ يَخْلُقُكُمْ فِي بُطُونِ
أُمَّهَٰتِكُمْ خَلْقًا مِّن بَعْدِ خَلْقٍ فِي
ظُلُمَٰتٍ ثَلَٰثٍ ذَٰلِكُمُ اللَّهُ رَبُّكُمْ

6. He created you from one being, then from that (being) He made its mate; and He hath provided for you of cattle eight kinds. He created you in the wombs of your mothers, creation after creation, in a threefold gloom. Such is Allah, your Lord.

39:6

7. He it is Who created you from dust, then from a drop (of seed) then from a clot, then bringeth you forth as a child, then (ordaineth) that ye attain full strength and afterward that ye become old men —though some among you die before—and that ye reach an appointed term, that haply ye may understand.

40:67

8. O mankind! Lo! We have created you male and female, and have made you nations and tribes that ye may know one another. Lo! the noblest of you, in the sight of Allah, is the best in conduct.

49:13

9. Thinketh man that he is to be left aimless?

Was he not a drop of fluid which gushed forth?

Then he became a clot; then (Allah) shaped and fashioned:

And made of him a pair, the male and female.

Is not He (Who doth so) Able to bring the dead to life?

75:36–40

10. Lo! We created man from a drop of thickened fluid to test him; so We make him hearing, knowing.

Lo! We have shown him the way, whether he be grateful or disbelieving.

76:2–3

7. هُوَ الَّذِي خَلَقَكُمْ مِّنْ تُرَابٍ ثُمَّ
مِنْ نُّطْفَةٍ ثُمَّ مِنْ عَلَقَةٍ ثُمَّ
يُخْرِجُكُمْ طِفْلًا ثُمَّ لِتَبْلُغُوا أَشُدَّكُمْ
ثُمَّ لِتَكُونُوا شُيُوخًا وَمِنْكُمْ مَّنْ
يُتَوَفّٰى مِنْ قَبْلُ وَلِتَبْلُغُوا أَجَلًا
مُّسَمًّى وَّلَعَلَّكُمْ تَعْقِلُونَ ۝

8. يٰۤاَيُّهَا النَّاسُ إِنَّا خَلَقْنٰكُمْ مِّنْ ذَكَرٍ
وَّأُنْثٰى وَجَعَلْنٰكُمْ شُعُوبًا وَّقَبَآئِلَ
لِتَعَارَفُوا إِنَّ أَكْرَمَكُمْ عِنْدَ اللهِ أَتْقٰكُمْ

9. أَيَحْسَبُ الْإِنْسَانُ أَنْ يُّتْرَكَ سُدًى ۝
أَلَمْ يَكُ نُطْفَةً مِّنْ مَّنِيٍّ يُّمْنٰى ۝
ثُمَّ كَانَ عَلَقَةً فَخَلَقَ فَسَوّٰى ۝
فَجَعَلَ مِنْهُ الزَّوْجَيْنِ الذَّكَرَ
وَالْأُنْثٰى ۝
أَلَيْسَ ذٰلِكَ بِقٰدِرٍ عَلٰٓى أَنْ يُّحْيِۦَ
الْمَوْتٰى ۝

10. إِنَّا خَلَقْنَا الْإِنْسَانَ مِنْ نُّطْفَةٍ
أَمْشَاجٍ نَّبْتَلِيهِ فَجَعَلْنٰهُ سَمِيعًا
بَصِيرًا ۝
إِنَّا هَدَيْنٰهُ السَّبِيلَ إِمَّا شَاكِرًا
وَّإِمَّا كَفُورًا ۝

11. فَلْيَنْظُرِ الْإِنْسَانُ مِمَّ خُلِقَ ۝
خُلِقَ مِنْ مَّآءٍ دَافِقٍ ۝
يَخْرُجُ مِنْ بَيْنِ الصُّلْبِ وَالتَّرَآئِبِ ۝

11. So let man consider from what he is created.

He is created from a gushing fluid.

That issued from between the loins and ribs.

86:5–7

Ref: 6:98; 30:20; 37:11; 40:64; 55:14; 77:20–23;

CREATION OF UNIVERSE

1. Lo! your Lord is Allah Who created the heavens and the earth in six Days, then mounted He the Throne. He covereth the night with the day, which is in haste to follow it, and hath made the sun and the moon and the stars subservient by His command. His verily is all creation and commandment. Blessed be Allah, the Lord of the Worlds!

7:54

2. And He it is Who created the heavens and the earth in six Days — and His Throne was upon the water—that He might try you, which of you is best in conduct.

11:7

3. Allah it is Who raised up the heavens without visible supports, then mounted the Throne, and compelled the sun and the moon to be of service, each runneth unto an appointed term; He ordereth the course; He detaileth the revelations, that haply ye may be certain of the meeting with your Lord.

And He it is Who spread out the earth and placed therein firm hills and flowing streams, and of all fruits he placed therein two spouses (male and female). He covereth the night with the day. Lo! herein verily are portents for people who take thought.

13:2–3

1. إِنَّ رَبَّكُمُ اللّٰهُ الَّذِي خَلَقَ السَّمٰوٰتِ وَ
الْأَرْضَ فِي سِتَّةِ أَيَّامٍ ثُمَّ اسْتَوٰى عَلَى
الْعَرْشِ يُغْشِي الَّيْلَ النَّهَارَ يَطْلُبُهُ
حَثِيثًا وَّالشَّمْسَ وَالْقَمَرَ وَالنُّجُوْمَ
مُسَخَّرٰتٍ بِأَمْرِهٖ أَلَا لَهُ الْخَلْقُ وَالْأَمْرُ
تَبٰرَكَ اللّٰهُ رَبُّ الْعٰلَمِيْنَ ﴿٥٤﴾

2. وَهُوَ الَّذِي خَلَقَ السَّمٰوٰتِ وَالْأَرْضَ فِي
سِتَّةِ أَيَّامٍ وَّكَانَ عَرْشُهٗ عَلَى الْمَآءِ
لِيَبْلُوَكُمْ أَيُّكُمْ أَحْسَنُ عَمَلًا

3. اللّٰهُ الَّذِي رَفَعَ السَّمٰوٰتِ بِغَيْرِ عَمَدٍ
تَرَوْنَهَا ثُمَّ اسْتَوٰى عَلَى الْعَرْشِ وَسَخَّرَ
الشَّمْسَ وَالْقَمَرَ كُلٌّ يَّجْرِي لِأَجَلٍ
مُّسَمًّى يُدَبِّرُ الْأَمْرَ يُفَصِّلُ الْاٰيٰتِ
لَعَلَّكُمْ بِلِقَآءِ رَبِّكُمْ تُوْقِنُوْنَ ﴿٢﴾
وَهُوَ الَّذِي مَدَّ الْأَرْضَ وَجَعَلَ فِيْهَا
رَوَاسِيَ وَأَنْهٰرًا وَمِنْ كُلِّ الثَّمَرٰتِ
جَعَلَ فِيْهَا زَوْجَيْنِ اثْنَيْنِ يُغْشِي الَّيْلَ
النَّهَارَ إِنَّ فِي ذٰلِكَ لَاٰيٰتٍ لِّقَوْمٍ
يَّتَفَكَّرُوْنَ ﴿٣﴾

4. وَمَا خَلَقْنَا السَّمَآءَ وَالْأَرْضَ وَمَا
بَيْنَهُمَا لٰعِبِيْنَ ﴿١٦﴾

5. وَاللّٰهُ خَلَقَ كُلَّ دَآبَّةٍ مِّنْ مَّآءٍ
فَمِنْهُمْ مَّنْ يَّمْشِي عَلٰى بَطْنِهٖ وَمِنْهُمْ

4. We created not the heaven and the earth and all that is between them in play.

21:16

5. Allah hath created every animal of water. Of them is (a kind) that goeth upon

its belly and (a kind) that goeth upon two legs and (a kind) that goeth upon four. Allah createth what He will. Lo! Allah is Able to do all things.

24:45

6. Say (O Muhammad): Travel in the land and see how He originated creation, then Allah bringeth forth the later growth. Lo! Allah is Able to do all things.

29:20

7. He it is Who produceth creation, then reproduceth it, and it is easier for Him, His is the Sublime Similitude in the heavens and in the earth. He is the Mighty, the Wise.

30:27

8. He hath created the heavens without supports that ye can see, and hath cast into the earth firm hills, so that it quake not with you; and He hath dispersed therein all kinds of beasts. And We send down water from the sky and We cause (plants) of every goodly kind to grow therein.

31:10

9. Say (O Muhammad, unto the idolaters): Disbelieve ye verily in Him Who created the earth in two Days, and ascribe ye unto Him rivals? He (and none else) is the Lord of the Worlds.

He placed therein firm hills rising above it, and blessed it and measured therein its sustenance in four Days, alike for (all) who ask.

Then turned He to the heaven when it was smoke, and said unto it and unto the earth: Come both of you, willingly or loth. They said: We come, obedient.

Then He ordained them seven heavens in two Days

مَّنْ يَّمْشِيْ عَلٰى رِجْلَيْنِ ۚ وَمِنْهُمْ مَّنْ
يَّمْشِيْ عَلٰٓى اَرْبَعٍ ۭ يَخْلُقُ اللّٰهُ مَا يَشَاۗءُ ۭ
اِنَّ اللّٰهَ عَلٰي كُلِّ شَيْءٍ قَدِيْرٌ ۝

6. قُلْ سِيْرُوْا فِي الْاَرْضِ فَانْظُرُوْا كَيْفَ
بَدَاَ الْخَلْقَ ثُمَّ اللّٰهُ يُنْشِئُ النَّشْاَةَ
الْاٰخِرَةَ ۭ اِنَّ اللّٰهَ عَلٰي كُلِّ شَيْءٍ قَدِيْرٌ ۝

7. وَهُوَ الَّذِيْ يَبْدَؤُا الْخَلْقَ ثُمَّ يُعِيْدُهٗ
وَهُوَ اَهْوَنُ عَلَيْهِ ۭ وَلَهُ الْمَثَلُ الْاَعْلٰى
فِي السَّمٰوٰتِ وَالْاَرْضِ ۚ وَهُوَ الْعَزِيْزُ
الْحَكِيْمُ ۝

8. خَلَقَ السَّمٰوٰتِ بِغَيْرِ عَمَدٍ تَرَوْنَهَا
وَاَلْقٰى فِي الْاَرْضِ رَوَاسِيَ اَنْ تَمِيْدَ
بِكُمْ وَبَثَّ فِيْهَا مِنْ كُلِّ دَاۗبَّةٍ ۭ
وَاَنْزَلْنَا مِنَ السَّمَاۗءِ مَاۗءً فَاَنْۢبَتْنَا
فِيْهَا مِنْ كُلِّ زَوْجٍ كَرِيْمٍ ۝

9. قُلْ اَىِٕنَّكُمْ لَتَكْفُرُوْنَ بِالَّذِيْ خَلَقَ
الْاَرْضَ فِيْ يَوْمَيْنِ وَتَجْعَلُوْنَ لَهٗٓ
اَنْدَادًا ۭ ذٰلِكَ رَبُّ الْعٰلَمِيْنَ ۝
وَجَعَلَ فِيْهَا رَوَاسِيَ مِنْ فَوْقِهَا
وَبٰرَكَ فِيْهَا وَقَدَّرَ فِيْهَآ اَقْوَاتَهَا
فِيْٓ اَرْبَعَةِ اَيَّامٍ ۭ سَوَاۗءً لِّلسَّاۗىِٕلِيْنَ ۝
ثُمَّ اسْتَوٰٓى اِلَى السَّمَاۗءِ وَهِيَ دُخَانٌ
فَقَالَ لَهَا وَلِلْاَرْضِ ائْتِيَا طَوْعًا اَوْ

and inspired in each heaven its mandate; and We decked the nether heaven with lamps, and rendered it inviolable. That is the measuring of the Mighty, the Knower.

41:9–12

10. We created not the heavens and the earth and all that is between them save with truth, and for a term appointed.

46:3

11. We have built the heaven with might, and We it is Who make the vast extent (thereof).

And the earth have We laid out, how gracious is the Spreader (thereof)!

And all things We have created by pairs, that haply ye may reflect.

51:47–49

12. Blessed is He in Whose hand is the Sovereignty, and He is Able to do all things:

Who hath created life and death that He may try you, which of you is best in conduct; and He is the Mighty, the Forgiving,

Who hath created seven heavens in harmony. Thou (Muhammad) canst see no fault in the Beneficent One's creation; then look again: Canst thou see any rifts?

كَرْهًا ۚ قَالَتَآ اَتَيْنَا طَآئِعِيْنَ ﴿١١﴾
فَقَضٰىهُنَّ سَبْعَ سَمٰوٰتٍ فِيْ يَوْمَيْنِ
وَاَوْحٰى فِيْ كُلِّ سَمَآءٍ اَمْرَهَا ۚ وَزَيَّنَّا
السَّمَآءَ الدُّنْيَا بِمَصَابِيْحَ ۖ وَحِفْظًا ۚ
ذٰلِكَ تَقْدِيْرُ الْعَزِيْزِ الْعَلِيْمِ ﴿١٢﴾

10. مَا خَلَقْنَا السَّمٰوٰتِ وَالْاَرْضَ وَمَا بَيْنَهُمَآ اِلَّا بِالْحَقِّ
وَاَجَلٍ مُّسَمًّى ؕ

11. وَالسَّمَآءَ بَنَيْنٰهَا بِاَيْىدٍ وَّاِنَّا
لَمُوْسِعُوْنَ ﴿٤٧﴾
وَالْاَرْضَ فَرَشْنٰهَا فَنِعْمَ الْمٰهِدُوْنَ ﴿٤٨﴾
وَمِنْ كُلِّ شَيْءٍ خَلَقْنَا زَوْجَيْنِ
لَعَلَّكُمْ تَذَكَّرُوْنَ ﴿٤٩﴾

12. تَبٰرَكَ الَّذِيْ بِيَدِهِ الْمُلْكُ ۫ وَهُوَ عَلٰى
كُلِّ شَيْءٍ قَدِيْرُ ۨ﴿١﴾
الَّذِيْ خَلَقَ الْمَوْتَ وَالْحَيٰوةَ لِيَبْلُوَكُمْ
اَيُّكُمْ اَحْسَنُ عَمَلًا ؕ وَهُوَ الْعَزِيْزُ الْغَفُوْرُ ﴿٢﴾
الَّذِيْ خَلَقَ سَبْعَ سَمٰوٰتٍ طِبَاقًا ؕ مَا
تَرٰى فِيْ خَلْقِ الرَّحْمٰنِ مِنْ تَفٰوُتٍ ؕ
فَارْجِعِ الْبَصَرَ ۙ هَلْ تَرٰى مِنْ فُطُوْرٍ ﴿٣﴾
ثُمَّ ارْجِعِ الْبَصَرَ كَرَّتَيْنِ يَنْقَلِبْ
اِلَيْكَ الْبَصَرُ خَاسِئًا وَّهُوَ حَسِيْرٌ ﴿٤﴾

Then look again and yet again, thy sight will return unto thee weakened and made dim.

67:1–4

Ref: 2:117; 5:17; 6:73,102,133,141–143; 7:57; 10:3,5–6; 13:16; 14:19–20,32 33; 15:16–23,85–86; 16:3,10–17,80–81; 20:53–55; 21:30–33; 23:78–80; 25:47-49,59–62; 28:68,73; 29:44,61–63; 30:8,11,19,48–50; 32:4, 46:4,33; 50:6–8,38; 51:56; 57:2,4; 65:12; 67:14–15; 71:14–16; 79:27–33; 87:2–5.

See also: Earth, Sky, Star, Sun, Universe.

CRIME AND PUNISHMENT

1. Humiliation from Allah and heavy punishment will smite the guilty for their scheming.

6:124

2. So if they give the lie to thee (Muhammad), say: Your Lord is a Lord of All-Embracing Mercy, but His wrath will never be withdrawn from guilty folk.

6:147

3. Who doth a greater wrong than he who inventeth a lie concerning Allah and denieth His revelations? Lo! the guilty never are successful.

10:17

4. Thou wilt see the guilty on that day linked together in chains.

Their raiment of pitch, and the Fire covering their faces.

14:49–50

5. On the Day when We shall gather the righteous unto the Beneficent, a goodly company,

And drive the guilty unto Hell, a weary herd.

19:85–86

6. Lo! whoso cometh guilty unto his Lord, verily for him is hell. There he will neither die nor live.

20:74

7. Couldst thou but see when the guilty hang their heads before their Lord, (and say): Our Lord! We have now seen and heard, so send us back; we will do right, now we are sure.

32:12

8. The guilty will be known by their marks, and will be taken by the forelocks

1. سَيُصِيبُ الَّذِينَ أَجْرَمُوا صَغَارٌ عِندَ اللَّهِ
وَعَذَابٌ شَدِيدٌ بِمَا كَانُوا يَمْكُرُونَ ○

2. فَإِن كَذَّبُوكَ فَقُل رَّبُّكُمْ ذُو رَحْمَةٍ
وَاسِعَةٍ وَلَا يُرَدُّ بَأْسُهُ عَنِ الْقَوْمِ
الْمُجْرِمِينَ ○

3. فَمَنْ أَظْلَمُ مِمَّنِ افْتَرَىٰ عَلَى اللَّهِ
كَذِبًا أَوْ كَذَّبَ بِآيَاتِهِ إِنَّهُ لَا
يُفْلِحُ الْمُجْرِمُونَ ﴿١٧﴾

4. وَتَرَى الْمُجْرِمِينَ يَوْمَئِذٍ مُّقَرَّنِينَ
فِي الْأَصْفَادِ ﴿٤٩﴾
سَرَابِيلُهُم مِّن قَطِرَانٍ وَتَغْشَىٰ
وُجُوهَهُمُ النَّارُ ﴿٥٠﴾

5. يَوْمَ نَحْشُرُ الْمُتَّقِينَ إِلَى الرَّحْمَٰنِ وَفْدًا ﴿٨٥﴾
وَنَسُوقُ الْمُجْرِمِينَ إِلَىٰ جَهَنَّمَ وِرْدًا ﴿٨٦﴾

6. إِنَّهُ مَن يَأْتِ رَبَّهُ مُجْرِمًا فَإِنَّ لَهُ
جَهَنَّمَ لَا يَمُوتُ فِيهَا وَلَا يَحْيَىٰ ﴿٧٤﴾

7. وَلَوْ تَرَىٰ إِذِ الْمُجْرِمُونَ نَاكِسُو رُءُوسِهِمْ
عِندَ رَبِّهِمْ رَبَّنَا أَبْصَرْنَا وَسَمِعْنَا
فَارْجِعْنَا نَعْمَلْ صَالِحًا إِنَّا مُوقِنُونَ ﴿١٢﴾

8. يُعْرَفُ الْمُجْرِمُونَ بِسِيمَاهُمْ فَيُؤْخَذُ
بِالنَّوَاصِي وَالْأَقْدَامِ ﴿٤١﴾

and the feet.

55:41

9. Nay but the record of the vile is in *Sijjin*—

Ah! what will convey unto thee what *Sijjin* is!—

A written record.

83:7–9

CULTURE

1. Build ye on every high place a monument for vain delight:

And seek ye out strongholds, that haply ye may last for ever!

And if ye seize by force, seize ye as tyrants?

Rather keep your duty to Allah, and obey me.

Keep your duty toward Him Who hath aided you with (the good things) that ye know.

Hath aided you with cattle and sons,

And gardens and water-springs.

Lo! I fear for you the retribution of an awful Day.

26:128–135

2. Will ye be left secure in that which is here before us,

In gardens and water-springs,

And tilled fields and heavy-sheathed palm-trees,

Though ye hew out dwe-

9. كَلَّآ إِنَّ كِتٰبَ الْفُجَّارِ لَفِىْ سِجِّيْنٍ ﴿٧﴾
وَمَآ أَدْرٰىكَ مَا سِجِّيْنٌ ﴿٨﴾
كِتٰبٌ مَّرْقُوْمٌ ﴿٩﴾

○

1. أَتَبْنُوْنَ بِكُلِّ رِيْعٍ اٰيَةً تَعْبَثُوْنَ ﴿١٢٨﴾
وَتَتَّخِذُوْنَ مَصَانِعَ لَعَلَّكُمْ تَخْلُدُوْنَ ﴿١٢٩﴾
وَإِذَا بَطَشْتُمْ بَطَشْتُمْ جَبَّارِيْنَ ﴿١٣٠﴾
فَاتَّقُوا اللّٰهَ وَأَطِيْعُوْنِ ﴿١٣١﴾
وَاتَّقُوا الَّذِىْٓ أَمَدَّكُمْ بِمَا تَعْلَمُوْنَ ﴿١٣٢﴾
أَمَدَّكُمْ بِأَنْعَامٍ وَّبَنِيْنَ ﴿١٣٣﴾
وَجَنّٰتٍ وَّعُيُوْنٍ ﴿١٣٤﴾
إِنِّىْٓ أَخَافُ عَلَيْكُمْ عَذَابَ يَوْمٍ عَظِيْمٍ ﴿١٣٥﴾

2. أَتُتْرَكُوْنَ فِىْ مَا هٰهُنَآ اٰمِنِيْنَ ﴿١٤٦﴾
فِىْ جَنّٰتٍ وَّعُيُوْنٍ ﴿١٤٧﴾
وَّزُرُوْعٍ وَّنَخْلٍ طَلْعُهَا هَضِيْمٌ ﴿١٤٨﴾
وَتَنْحِتُوْنَ مِنَ الْجِبَالِ بُيُوْتًا فٰرِهِيْنَ ﴿١٤٩﴾
فَاتَّقُوا اللّٰهَ وَأَطِيْعُوْنِ ﴿١٥٠﴾

llings in the mountains, being skilful?

Therefor keep your duty to Allah and obey me,

26:146 150

CRIME AND PUNISHMENT

Ref: 18:53; 36:59; 70:11; 82:14.

3. وَكَمْ أَهْلَكْنَا مِن قَرْيَةٍ بَطِرَتْ
مَعِيشَتَهَا ۖ فَتِلْكَ مَسَاكِنُهُمْ لَمْ
تُسْكَن مِّن بَعْدِهِمْ إِلَّا قَلِيلًا ۖ وَ
كُنَّا نَحْنُ الْوَارِثِينَ
وَمَا كَانَ رَبُّكَ مُهْلِكَ الْقُرَىٰ حَتَّىٰ
يَبْعَثَ فِي أُمِّهَا رَسُولًا يَتْلُو عَلَيْهِمْ
آيَاتِنَا ۚ وَمَا كُنَّا مُهْلِكِي الْقُرَىٰ
إِلَّا وَأَهْلُهَا ظَالِمُونَ

3. And how many a community have We destroyed that was thankless for its means of livelihood! And yonder are their dwellings, which have not been inhabited after them save a little. And We, even We, were the inheritors.

And never did thy Lord destroy the townships, till He had raised up in their mother-(town) a messenger reciting unto them Our revelations. And never did We destroy the townships unless the folk thereof were evil-doers.

28.58–59

CURE

1. يَا أَيُّهَا النَّاسُ قَدْ جَاءَتْكُم مَّوْعِظَةٌ مِّن
رَّبِّكُمْ وَشِفَاءٌ لِّمَا فِي الصُّدُورِ
وَهُدًى وَرَحْمَةٌ لِّلْمُؤْمِنِينَ

1. O mankind! There hath come unto you an exhortation from your Lord, a balm for that which is in the breasts, a guidance and a mercy for believers.

10:57

2. وَأَوْحَىٰ رَبُّكَ إِلَى النَّحْلِ أَنِ اتَّخِذِي
مِنَ الْجِبَالِ بُيُوتًا وَمِنَ الشَّجَرِ
وَمِمَّا يَعْرِشُونَ
ثُمَّ كُلِي مِن كُلِّ الثَّمَرَاتِ فَاسْلُكِي
سُبُلَ رَبِّكِ ذُلُلًا ۚ يَخْرُجُ مِن بُطُونِهَا
شَرَابٌ مُّخْتَلِفٌ أَلْوَانُهُ فِيهِ شِفَاءٌ
لِّلنَّاسِ ۗ إِنَّ فِي ذَٰلِكَ لَآيَةً لِّقَوْمٍ يَتَفَكَّرُونَ

2. And thy Lord inspired the bee, saying: Choose thou habitations in the hills and in the trees and in that which they thatch;

Then eat of all fruits, and follow the ways of thy Lord, made smooth (for thee). There cometh forth from their bellies a drink diverse of hues, wherein is healing for mankind. Lo! herein is indeed a portent for people who reflect.

16:68--69

3. وَنُنَزِّلُ مِنَ الْقُرْآنِ مَا هُوَ شِفَاءٌ وَ
رَحْمَةٌ لِّلْمُؤْمِنِينَ ۙ وَلَا يَزِيدُ الظَّالِمِينَ
إِلَّا خَسَارًا

3. And We reveal of the Qur'an that which is a healing and a mercy for believers though it increase the evil doers in naught save ruin.

17:82

CULTURE

See also: Adornment.

1. إِنَّ الَّذِينَ كَفَرُوا وَمَاتُوا وَهُمْ كُفَّارٌ أُولَٰئِكَ
عَلَيْهِمْ لَعْنَةُ اللَّهِ وَالْمَلَائِكَةِ وَالنَّاسِ أَجْمَعِينَ ﴿١٦١﴾

2. مِنَ الَّذِينَ هَادُوا يُحَرِّفُونَ الْكَلِمَ عَن
مَّوَاضِعِهِ وَيَقُولُونَ سَمِعْنَا وَعَصَيْنَا
وَاسْمَعْ غَيْرَ مُسْمَعٍ وَرَاعِنَا لَيًّا بِأَلْسِنَتِهِمْ
وَطَعْنًا فِي الدِّينِ ۚ وَلَوْ أَنَّهُمْ قَالُوا سَمِعْنَا
وَأَطَعْنَا وَاسْمَعْ وَانظُرْنَا لَكَانَ خَيْرًا لَّهُمْ
وَأَقْوَمَ وَلَٰكِن لَّعَنَهُمُ اللَّهُ بِكُفْرِهِمْ
فَلَا يُؤْمِنُونَ إِلَّا قَلِيلًا ﴿٤٦﴾

3. وَمَن يَقْتُلْ مُؤْمِنًا مُّتَعَمِّدًا فَجَزَاؤُهُ
جَهَنَّمُ خَالِدًا فِيهَا وَغَضِبَ اللَّهُ عَلَيْهِ
وَلَعَنَهُ وَأَعَدَّ لَهُ عَذَابًا عَظِيمًا ﴿٩٣﴾

4. إِن يَدْعُونَ مِن دُونِهِ إِلَّا إِنَاثًا وَإِن
يَدْعُونَ إِلَّا شَيْطَانًا مَّرِيدًا ﴿١١٧﴾
لَّعَنَهُ اللَّهُ

5. لُعِنَ الَّذِينَ كَفَرُوا مِن بَنِي إِسْرَائِيلَ
عَلَىٰ لِسَانِ دَاوُودَ وَعِيسَى ابْنِ مَرْيَمَ
ذَٰلِكَ بِمَا عَصَوا وَّكَانُوا يَعْتَدُونَ ﴿٧٨﴾

6. وَعَدَ اللَّهُ الْمُنَافِقِينَ وَالْمُنَافِقَاتِ وَالْكُفَّارَ
نَارَ جَهَنَّمَ خَالِدِينَ فِيهَا ۚ هِيَ حَسْبُهُمْ ۚ
وَلَعَنَهُمُ اللَّهُ ۖ وَلَهُمْ عَذَابٌ مُّقِيمٌ ﴿٦٨﴾

CURSE

1. Lo! those who dis-believe, and die while they are disbelievers; on them is the curse of Allah and of angels and of men combined.

2:161

2. Some of those who are Jews change words from their context and say: "We hear and disobey; hear thou as one who heareth not" and "Listen to us!" distorting with their tongues and slandering religion. If they had said: "We hear and we obey: hear thou, and look at us" it had been better for them, and more upright. But Allah hath cursed them for their disbelief, so they believe not save a few.

4:46

3. Whoso slayeth a believer of set purpose, his reward is Hell for ever. Allah is wroth against him and He hath cursed him and prepared for him an awful doom.

4:93

4. They invoke in His stead only females, they pray to none else than Satan, a rebel. Whom Allah cursed.

4:117–118

5. Those of the Children of Israel who went astray were cursed by the tongue of David, and of Jesus, son of Mary. That was because they rebelled and used to transgress.

5:78

6. Allah promiseth the hypocrites, both men and women, and the disbelievers fire of hell for their abode. It will suffice them. Allah curseth them, and theirs is the lasting torment.

9:68

7. And those who break the covenant of Allah after ratifying it, and sever that which Allah hath commanded should be joined, and make mischief in the earth: theirs is the curse and theirs the ill abode.

13:25

8. Lo! as for those who traduce virtuous, believing women (who are) careless, cursed are they in the world and the Hereafter. Theirs will be an awful doom.

24:23

9. He said: Ye have chosen idols instead of Allah. The love between you is only in the life of the world. Then on the Day of Resurrection ye will deny each other and curse each other, and your abode will be the Fire, and ye will have no helpers.

29:25

10. Lo! those who malign Allah and His messenger, Allah hath cursed them in the world and the Hereafter, and hath prepared for them the doom of the disdained.

33:57

7. وَالَّذِينَ يَنْقُضُونَ عَهْدَ اللَّهِ مِنْ بَعْدِ
مِيثَاقِهِ وَيَقْطَعُونَ مَا أَمَرَ اللَّهُ بِهِ
أَنْ يُوصَلَ وَيُفْسِدُونَ فِي الْأَرْضِ
أُولَٰئِكَ لَهُمُ اللَّعْنَةُ وَلَهُمْ سُوءُ الدَّارِ

8. إِنَّ الَّذِينَ يَرْمُونَ الْمُحْصَنَاتِ الْغَافِلَاتِ
الْمُؤْمِنَاتِ لُعِنُوا فِي الدُّنْيَا وَالْآخِرَةِ
وَلَهُمْ عَذَابٌ عَظِيمٌ

9. وَقَالَ إِنَّمَا اتَّخَذْتُمْ مِنْ دُونِ اللَّهِ
أَوْثَانًا مَوَدَّةَ بَيْنِكُمْ فِي الْحَيَاةِ الدُّنْيَا
ثُمَّ يَوْمَ الْقِيَامَةِ يَكْفُرُ بَعْضُكُمْ بِبَعْضٍ
وَيَلْعَنُ بَعْضُكُمْ بَعْضًا وَمَأْوَاكُمُ النَّارُ
وَمَا لَكُمْ مِنْ نَاصِرِينَ

10. إِنَّ الَّذِينَ يُؤْذُونَ اللَّهَ وَرَسُولَهُ
لَعَنَهُمُ اللَّهُ فِي الدُّنْيَا وَالْآخِرَةِ وَأَعَدَّ
لَهُمْ عَذَابًا مُهِينًا

Ref: 3:86–87; 4:52; 5:60; 7:44; 11:18,99; 24:7; 28:42; 33:64; 38:78; 40:52; 48:6;

DACOITY

1. The only reward of those who make war upon Allah and His messenger and strive after corruption in the land will be that they will be killed or crucified, or have their hands and feet on alternate sides cut off, or will be expelled out of the land. Such will be their degradation in the world, and in the Hereafter theirs will be an awful doom;

Save those who repent before ye overpower them. For know that Allah is Forgiving, Merciful.

5:33–34

DARKNESS

1. Allah is the Protecting Friend of those who believe. He bringeth them out of darkness into light. As for those who disbelieve, their patrons are false deities. They bring them out of light into darkness. Such are rightful owners of the Fire. They will abide therein.

2:257

2. Praise be to Allah, Who hath created the heavens and the earth, and hath appointed darkness and light. Yet those who disbelieve ascribe rivals unto their Lord.

6:1

3. Say: Who delivereth you

1. إِنَّمَا جَزٰٓؤُا الَّذِيْنَ يُحَارِبُوْنَ اللّٰهَ وَ
رَسُوْلَهٗ وَيَسْعَوْنَ فِي الْاَرْضِ فَسَادًا
اَنْ يُّقَتَّلُوْٓا اَوْ يُصَلَّبُوْٓا اَوْ تُقَطَّعَ اَيْدِيْهِمْ
وَ اَرْجُلُهُمْ مِّنْ خِلَافٍ اَوْ يُنْفَوْا مِنَ
الْاَرْضِ ؕ ذٰلِكَ لَهُمْ خِزْيٌ فِي الدُّنْيَا وَ
لَهُمْ فِي الْاٰخِرَةِ عَذَابٌ عَظِيْمٌ ﴿۳۳﴾
اِلَّا الَّذِيْنَ تَابُوْا مِنْ قَبْلِ اَنْ تَقْدِرُوْا
عَلَيْهِمْ ۚ فَاعْلَمُوْٓا اَنَّ اللّٰهَ غَفُوْرٌ رَّحِيْمٌ ﴿۳۴﴾

1. اَللّٰهُ وَلِيُّ الَّذِيْنَ اٰمَنُوْا يُخْرِجُهُمْ مِّنَ
الظُّلُمٰتِ اِلَى النُّوْرِ ۬ؕ وَالَّذِيْنَ كَفَرُوْٓا اَوْلِيٰٓـُٔهُمُ
الطَّاغُوْتُ يُخْرِجُوْنَهُمْ مِّنَ النُّوْرِ اِلَى الظُّلُمٰتِ ؕ
اُولٰٓئِكَ اَصْحٰبُ النَّارِ ۚ هُمْ فِيْهَا خٰلِدُوْنَ ﴿۲۵۷﴾

2. اَلْحَمْدُ لِلّٰهِ الَّذِيْ خَلَقَ السَّمٰوٰتِ
وَالْاَرْضَ وَجَعَلَ الظُّلُمٰتِ وَ النُّوْرَ ؕ
ثُمَّ الَّذِيْنَ كَفَرُوْا بِرَبِّهِمْ يَعْدِلُوْنَ ﴿۱﴾

3. قُلْ مَنْ يُّنَجِّيْكُمْ مِّنْ ظُلُمٰتِ الْبَرِّ
وَالْبَحْرِ تَدْعُوْنَهٗ تَضَرُّعًا وَّ خُفْيَةً ۚ لَئِنْ
اَنْجٰنَا مِنْ هٰذِهٖ لَنَكُوْنَنَّ مِنَ الشّٰكِرِيْنَ ﴿۶۳﴾

from the darkness of the land and the sea? Ye call upon Him humbly and in secret, (saying): If we are delivered from this (fear) we truly will be of the thankful.

6:63

DACOITY
See also: *Hudud.*

4. And He it is Who hath set for you the stars that ye may guide your course by them amid the darkness of the land and the sea. We have detailed Our revelations for a people who have knowledge.

6:97

5. Is he who was dead and We have raised him unto life, and set for him a light wherein he walketh among men, as him whose similitude is in utter darkness whence he cannot emerge? Thus is their conduct made fair seeming for the disbelievers.

6:122

6. Or as darkness on a vast, abysmal sea. There covereth him a wave, above which is a wave, above which is a cloud. Layer upon layer of darkness. When he holdeth out his hand he scarce can see it. And he for whom Allah hath not appointed light, for him there is no light.

24:40

4. وَهُوَ الَّذِي جَعَلَ لَكُمُ النُّجُومَ لِتَهْتَدُوا بِهَا فِي ظُلُمٰتِ الْبَرِّ وَالْبَحْرِ قَدْ فَصَّلْنَا الْاٰيٰتِ لِقَوْمٍ يَّعْلَمُوْنَ ۝

5. اَوَمَنْ كَانَ مَيْتًا فَاَحْيَيْنٰهُ وَجَعَلْنَا لَهٗ نُوْرًا يَّمْشِيْ بِهٖ فِي النَّاسِ كَمَنْ مَّثَلُهٗ فِي الظُّلُمٰتِ لَيْسَ بِخَارِجٍ مِّنْهَا كَذٰلِكَ زُيِّنَ لِلْكٰفِرِيْنَ مَا كَانُوْا يَعْمَلُوْنَ ۝

6. اَوْ كَظُلُمٰتٍ فِيْ بَحْرٍ لُّجِّيٍّ يَّغْشٰهُ مَوْجٌ مِّنْ فَوْقِهٖ مَوْجٌ مِّنْ فَوْقِهٖ سَحَابٌ ظُلُمٰتٌ بَعْضُهَا فَوْقَ بَعْضٍ اِذَآ اَخْرَجَ يَدَهٗ لَمْ يَكَدْ يَرٰىهَا وَمَنْ لَّمْ يَجْعَلِ اللّٰهُ لَهٗ نُوْرًا فَمَا لَهٗ مِنْ نُّوْرٍ ۝

See also: Light.

DAY AND NIGHT

1. Lo! in the creation of the heavens and the earth and (in) the difference of night and day are tokens (of His Sovereignty) for men of understanding.

3:190

2. He it is Who gathereth you at night and knoweth that which ye commit by the day. Then He raiseth you again to life therein, that the term appointed (for you) may be accomplished. And afterward unto Him is your return. Then He will proclaim unto you what ye used to do.

6:60

3. Lo! your Lord is Allah Who created the heavens and the earth in six Days, then mounted He the Throne. He covereth the night with the day, which is in haste to follow it, and hath made the sun and the moon and the stars subservient by His command. His verily is all creation and commandment. Blessed be Allah, the Lord of the Worlds!

7:54

4. He it is Who hath appointed for you the night that ye should rest therein and the day giving sight. Lo! herein verily are portents for a folk that heed.

10:67

5. And We appoint the night and the day two portents. Then We make dark the portent of the night, and We make the portent of the day sight-giving, that ye may seek bounty from your Lord, and that ye may know the computation of the years, and the reckoning, and everything have We expounded with a clear expounding.

17:12

1. إِنَّ فِي خَلْقِ السَّمٰوٰتِ وَالْأَرْضِ وَاخْتِلَافِ الَّيْلِ
وَالنَّهَارِ لَآيٰتٍ لِأُولِي الْأَلْبَابِ ﴿١٩٠﴾

2. وَهُوَ الَّذِي يَتَوَفّٰكُمْ بِالَّيْلِ وَيَعْلَمُ مَا
جَرَحْتُمْ بِالنَّهَارِ ثُمَّ يَبْعَثُكُمْ فِيهِ
لِيُقْضٰى أَجَلٌ مُسَمًّى ثُمَّ إِلَيْهِ مَرْجِعُكُمْ
ثُمَّ يُنَبِّئُكُمْ بِمَا كُنْتُمْ تَعْمَلُونَ ﴿٦٠﴾

3. إِنَّ رَبَّكُمُ اللّٰهُ الَّذِي خَلَقَ السَّمٰوٰتِ وَ
الْأَرْضَ فِي سِتَّةِ أَيَّامٍ ثُمَّ اسْتَوٰى عَلَى
الْعَرْشِ يُغْشِي الَّيْلَ النَّهَارَ يَطْلُبُهُ
حَثِيثًا وَالشَّمْسَ وَالْقَمَرَ وَالنُّجُومَ
مُسَخَّرٰتٍ بِأَمْرِهِ أَلَا لَهُ الْخَلْقُ وَالْأَمْرُ
تَبٰرَكَ اللّٰهُ رَبُّ الْعٰلَمِينَ ﴿٥٤﴾

4. هُوَ الَّذِي جَعَلَ لَكُمُ الَّيْلَ لِتَسْكُنُوا
فِيهِ وَالنَّهَارَ مُبْصِرًا إِنَّ فِي ذٰلِكَ
لَآيٰتٍ لِقَوْمٍ يَسْمَعُونَ ﴿٦٧﴾

5. وَجَعَلْنَا الَّيْلَ وَالنَّهَارَ آيَتَيْنِ فَمَحَوْنَا
آيَةَ الَّيْلِ وَجَعَلْنَا آيَةَ النَّهَارِ مُبْصِرَةً
لِتَبْتَغُوا فَضْلًا مِنْ رَبِّكُمْ وَلِتَعْلَمُوا عَدَدَ
السِّنِينَ وَالْحِسَابَ وَكُلَّ شَيْءٍ
فَصَّلْنٰهُ تَفْصِيلًا ﴿١٢﴾

6. يُقَلِّبُ اللّٰهُ الَّيۡلَ وَالنَّهَارَ ؕ اِنَّ فِىۡ ذٰلِكَ
لَعِبۡرَةً لِّاُولِى الۡاَبۡصَارِ ﴿۴۴﴾

7. وَهُوَ الَّذِىۡ جَعَلَ لَـكُمُ الَّيۡلَ لِبَاسًا
وَّالنَّوۡمَ سُبَاتًا وَّجَعَلَ النَّهَارَ نُشُوۡرًا ﴿۴۷﴾

8. وَهُوَ الَّذِىۡ جَعَلَ الَّيۡلَ وَالنَّهَارَ
خِلۡفَةً لِّمَنۡ اَرَادَ اَنۡ يَّذَّكَّرَ اَوۡ
اَرَادَ شُكُوۡرًا ﴿۶۲﴾

9. قُلۡ اَرَءَيۡتُمۡ اِنۡ جَعَلَ اللّٰهُ عَلَيۡكُمُ
الَّيۡلَ سَرۡمَدًا اِلٰى يَوۡمِ الۡقِيٰمَةِ مَنۡ
اِلٰـهٌ غَيۡرُ اللّٰهِ يَاۡتِيۡكُمۡ بِضِيَآءٍ ؕ
اَفَلَا تَسۡمَعُوۡنَ ﴿۷۱﴾
قُلۡ اَرَءَيۡتُمۡ اِنۡ جَعَلَ اللّٰهُ عَلَيۡكُمُ
النَّهَارَ سَرۡمَدًا اِلٰى يَوۡمِ الۡقِيٰمَةِ مَنۡ
اِلٰـهٌ غَيۡرُ اللّٰهِ يَاۡتِيۡكُمۡ بِلَيۡلٍ تَسۡكُنُوۡنَ
فِيۡهِ ؕ اَفَلَا تُبۡصِرُوۡنَ ﴿۷۲﴾
وَمِنۡ رَّحۡمَتِهٖ جَعَلَ لَـكُمُ الَّيۡلَ
وَالنَّهَارَ لِتَسۡكُنُوۡا فِيۡهِ وَلِتَبۡتَغُوۡا
مِنۡ فَضۡلِهٖ وَلَعَلَّكُمۡ تَشۡكُرُوۡنَ ﴿۷۳﴾

10. يُكَوِّرُ الَّيۡلَ عَلَى النَّهَارِ وَيُكَوِّرُ
النَّهَارَ عَلَى الَّيۡلِ وَسَخَّرَ الشَّمۡسَ
وَالۡقَمَرَ ؕ كُلٌّ يَّجۡرِىۡ لِاَجَلٍ مُّسَمًّى ؕ
اَلَا هُوَ الۡعَزِيۡزُ الۡغَفَّارُ ﴿۵﴾

6. Allah causeth the revolution of the day and the night. Lo! herein is indeed a lesson for those who see.

24:44

7. And He it is Who maketh night a covering for you, and sleep repose, and maketh day a resurrection.

25:47

8. And He it is Who hath appointed night and day in succession, for him who desireth to remember, or desireth thankfulness.

25:62

9. Say: Have ye thought, if Allah made night everlasting for you till the Day of Resurrection, who is a god beside Allah who could bring you light? Will ye not then hear?

Say: Have ye thought, if Allah made day everlasting for you till the Day of Re-surrection, who is a god beside Allah who could bring you night wherein ye rest? Will ye not then see?

Of His mercy hath He appointed for you night, and day, that therein ye may rest, and that ye may seek His bounty, and that haply ye may be thankful.

28:71–73

10. He hath created the heavens and the earth with truth. He maketh night to succeed day, and He maketh day to succeed night, and He constraineth the sun and the moon to give service, each running on for an appointed term. Is not He the Mighty, the Forgiver?

39:5

11. And have appointed your sleep for repose,

And have appointed the night as a cloak,

And have appointed the day for livelihood.

78:9–11

DAYS OF ALLAH

1. We verily sent Moses with Our revelations, saying: Bring thy people forth from darkness unto light. And remind them of the days of Allah. Lo! therein are revelations for each steadfast, thankful (heart).

14:5

2. But lo! a Day with Allah is as a thousand years of what ye reckon.

22:47

3. (Whereby) the angels and the Spirit ascend unto Him in a Day whereof the span is fifty thousand years.

70:4

11. وَّجَعَلْنَا نَوْمَكُمْ سُبَاتًا ۙ
وَّجَعَلْنَا الَّيْلَ لِبَاسًا ۙ
وَّجَعَلْنَا النَّهَارَ مَعَاشًا

○

1. وَلَقَدْ اَرْسَلْنَا مُوْسٰى بِاٰيٰتِنَآ اَنْ اَخْرِجْ
قَوْمَكَ مِنَ الظُّلُمٰتِ اِلَى النُّوْرِ ۙ
وَذَكِّرْهُمْ بِاَيّٰىمِ اللّٰهِ ؕ اِنَّ فِىْ ذٰلِكَ لَاٰيٰتٍ
لِّكُلِّ صَبَّارٍ شَكُوْرٍ

2. وَاِنَّ يَوْمًا عِنْدَ رَبِّكَ كَاَلْفِ سَنَةٍ
مِّمَّا تَعُدُّوْنَ

3. تَعْرُجُ الْمَلٰٓئِكَةُ وَالرُّوْحُ اِلَيْهِ فِىْ
يَوْمٍ كَانَ مِقْدَارُهٗ خَمْسِيْنَ اَلْفَ سَنَةٍ

○

DEATH

1. No soul can ever die except by Allah's leave and at a term appointed.

3:145

2. Wheresoever ye may be, death will overtake you, even though ye were in lofty towers.

4:78

3. He is the Omnipotent over His slaves. He sendeth guardians over you until, when death cometh unto one of you, Our messengers receive him, and they neglect not.

6:61

4. If thou couldst see, when the wrongdoers reach the pangs of death and the angels stretch their hands out, saying: Deliver up your souls. This day ye are awarded doom of degradation for that ye spake concerning Allah other than the truth, and used to scorn His portents.

Now have ye come unto Us solitary as We did create you at the first, and ye have left behind you all that We bestowed upon you, and We behold not with you those your intercessors, of whom ye claimed that they possessed a share in you. Now is the bond between you severed, and that which ye presumed hath failed you.

6:93–94

1. وَمَا كَانَ لِنَفْسٍ اَنْ تَمُوْتَ اِلَّا بِاِذْنِ اللّٰهِ
كِتٰبًا مُّؤَجَّلًا

2. اَيْنَ مَا تَكُوْنُوْا يُدْرِكْكُّمُ الْمَوْتُ وَلَوْ كُنْتُمْ
فِيْ بُرُوْجٍ مُّشَيَّدَةٍ

3. وَهُوَ الْقَاهِرُ فَوْقَ عِبَادِهٖ وَيُرْسِلُ عَلَيْكُمْ حَفَظَةً
حَتّٰٓى اِذَا جَآءَ اَحَدَكُمُ الْمَوْتُ تَوَفَّتْهُ رُسُلُنَا وَهُمْ
لَا يُفَرِّطُوْنَ ﴿٦١﴾

4. وَلَوْ تَرٰٓى اِذِ الظّٰلِمُوْنَ فِيْ غَمَرٰتِ الْمَوْتِ
وَالْمَلٰٓئِكَةُ بَاسِطُوْٓا اَيْدِيْهِمْ اَخْرِجُوْٓا
اَنْفُسَكُمْ اَلْيَوْمَ تُجْزَوْنَ عَذَابَ الْهُوْنِ
بِمَا كُنْتُمْ تَقُوْلُوْنَ عَلَى اللّٰهِ غَيْرَ الْحَقِّ
وَكُنْتُمْ عَنْ اٰيٰتِهٖ تَسْتَكْبِرُوْنَ ○

وَلَقَدْ جِئْتُمُوْنَا فُرَادٰى كَمَا خَلَقْنٰكُمْ اَوَّلَ
مَرَّةٍ وَّتَرَكْتُمْ مَّا خَوَّلْنٰكُمْ وَرَآءَ ظُهُوْرِكُمْ
وَمَا نَرٰى مَعَكُمْ شُفَعَآءَكُمُ الَّذِيْنَ زَعَمْتُمْ
اَنَّهُمْ فِيْكُمْ شُرَكٰٓؤُا لَقَدْ تَّقَطَّعَ بَيْنَكُمْ
وَضَلَّ عَنْكُمْ مَّا كُنْتُمْ تَزْعُمُوْنَ ○

5. وَلِكُلِّ اُمَّةٍ اَجَلٌ فَاِذَا جَآءَ اَجَلُهُمْ
لَا يَسْتَاْخِرُوْنَ سَاعَةً وَّلَا يَسْتَقْدِمُوْنَ ﴿٣٤﴾

6. وَمَا جَعَلْنَا لِبَشَرٍ مِّنْ قَبْلِكَ الْخُلْدَ
اَفَاۡىِٕنْ مِّتَّ فَهُمُ الْخٰلِدُوْنَ ﴿٣٤﴾

5. And every nation has its term, and when its term cometh, they cannot put it off an hour nor yet advance (it).

7:34

6. We appointed immortality for no mortal before thee. What! if thou diest, can they

be immortal?

Every soul must taste of death, and We try you with evil and with good, for ordeal. And unto Us ye will be returned.

21:34–35

7. Say: The angel of death, who hath charge concerning you, will gather you, and afterward unto your Lord ye will be returned.

32:11

8. Allah receiveth (men's) souls at the time of their death, and that (soul) which dieth not (yet) in its sleep. He keepeth that (soul) for which He hath ordained death and dismisseth the rest till an appointed term. Lo! herein verily are portents for people who take thought.

39:42

9. And the agony of death cometh in truth. (And it is said unto him): This is that which thou wast wont to shun.

50:19

10. We mete out death among you, and We are not to be outrun,

That We may transfigure you and make you what ye know not.

56:60–61

11. Say (unto them, O Muhammad): Lo! the death from which ye shrink will surely meet you, and afterward ye will be returned unto

كُلُّ نَفْسٍ ذَآئِقَةُ الْمَوْتِ وَنَبْلُوكُم
بِالشَّرِّ وَالْخَيْرِ فِتْنَةً وَإِلَيْنَا تُرْجَعُونَ ﴿٣٥﴾

7. قُلْ يَتَوَفَّاكُم مَّلَكُ الْمَوْتِ الَّذِي
وُكِّلَ بِكُمْ ثُمَّ إِلَى رَبِّكُمْ تُرْجَعُونَ ﴿١١﴾

8. اللَّهُ يَتَوَفَّى الْأَنفُسَ حِينَ مَوْتِهَا
وَالَّتِي لَمْ تَمُتْ فِي مَنَامِهَا فَيُمْسِكُ
الَّتِي قَضَى عَلَيْهَا الْمَوْتَ وَيُرْسِلُ
الْأُخْرَى إِلَى أَجَلٍ مُّسَمًّى إِنَّ فِي
ذَلِكَ لَآيَاتٍ لِّقَوْمٍ يَتَفَكَّرُونَ ﴿٤٢﴾

9. وَجَاءَتْ سَكْرَةُ الْمَوْتِ بِالْحَقِّ
ذَلِكَ مَا كُنتَ مِنْهُ تَحِيدُ ﴿١٩﴾

10. نَحْنُ قَدَّرْنَا بَيْنَكُمُ الْمَوْتَ وَمَا
نَحْنُ بِمَسْبُوقِينَ ﴿٦٠﴾
عَلَى أَن نُّبَدِّلَ أَمْثَالَكُمْ وَنُنشِئَكُمْ
فِي مَا لَا تَعْلَمُونَ ﴿٦١﴾

11. قُلْ إِنَّ الْمَوْتَ الَّذِي تَفِرُّونَ مِنْهُ
فَإِنَّهُ مُلَاقِيكُمْ ثُمَّ تُرَدُّونَ إِلَى عَالِمِ
الْغَيْبِ وَالشَّهَادَةِ فَيُنَبِّئُكُم بِمَا
كُنتُمْ تَعْمَلُونَ ﴿٨﴾

12. وَلَن يُؤَخِّرَ اللَّهُ نَفْسًا إِذَا جَاءَ أَجَلُهَا وَاللَّهُ
خَبِيرٌ بِمَا تَعْمَلُونَ ﴿١١﴾

the Knower of the Invisible and the Visible, and He will tell you what ye used to do.

62:8

12. But Allah reprieveth no soul when its term cometh, and Allah is Aware of what ye do.

63:11

Ref: 3:143,185; 10:49; 23:15,99–100; 29:57; 33:16; 39:30; 47:27; 67: 2; 71:4;

DECEIT

1. Woe unto the defrauders: Those who when they take the measure from mankind demand it full,

But if they measure unto them or weight for them, they cause them less.

83:1–3

1. وَيْلٌ لِّلْمُطَفِّفِينَ ۝
الَّذِينَ إِذَا اكْتَالُوا عَلَى النَّاسِ
يَسْتَوْفُونَ ۝
وَإِذَا كَالُوهُمْ أَو وَّزَنُوهُمْ يُخْسِرُونَ ۝

DELUGE OF NOAH

1. And it was inspired in Noah, (saying): No one of thy folk will believe save him who hath believed already. Be not distressed because of what they do.

Build the ship under Our Eyes and by Our Inspiration, and speak not unto Me on behalf of those who do wrong. Lo! they will be drowned.

And he was building the ship, and every time the chieftains of his people passed him, they made mock of him. He said: Though ye make mock of us, yet we mock at you even as ye mock;

And ye shall know to whom a punishment that will confound him cometh, and upon whom a lasting doom will fall.

(Thus it was) till, when Our commandment came to pass and the oven gushed forth water, We said: Load therein two of every kind, a pair (the male and female), and thy household, save him against whom the word hath gone forth already, and those who believe. And but a few were they who believed with him.

And he said: Embark therein! In the name of Allah be its course and its mooring. Lo! my Lord is Forgiving, Merciful.

1. وَأُوحِيَ إِلَىٰ نُوحٍ أَنَّهُ لَن يُؤْمِنَ مِن
قَوْمِكَ إِلَّا مَن قَدْ آمَنَ فَلَا تَبْتَئِسْ
بِمَا كَانُوا يَفْعَلُونَ ۝
وَاصْنَعِ الْفُلْكَ بِأَعْيُنِنَا وَوَحْيِنَا وَلَا
تُخَاطِبْنِي فِي الَّذِينَ ظَلَمُوا إِنَّهُم مُّغْرَقُونَ ۝
وَيَصْنَعُ الْفُلْكَ وَكُلَّمَا مَرَّ عَلَيْهِ مَلَأٌ
مِّن قَوْمِهِ سَخِرُوا مِنْهُ قَالَ إِن تَسْخَرُوا
مِنَّا فَإِنَّا نَسْخَرُ مِنكُمْ كَمَا تَسْخَرُونَ ۝
فَسَوْفَ تَعْلَمُونَ مَن يَأْتِيهِ عَذَابٌ
يُخْزِيهِ وَيَحِلُّ عَلَيْهِ عَذَابٌ مُّقِيمٌ ۝
حَتَّىٰ إِذَا جَاءَ أَمْرُنَا وَفَارَ التَّنُّورُ
قُلْنَا احْمِلْ فِيهَا مِن كُلٍّ زَوْجَيْنِ اثْنَيْنِ
وَأَهْلَكَ إِلَّا مَن سَبَقَ عَلَيْهِ الْقَوْلُ
وَمَنْ آمَنَ وَمَا آمَنَ مَعَهُ إِلَّا قَلِيلٌ ۝
وَقَالَ ارْكَبُوا فِيهَا بِسْمِ اللَّهِ مَجْرَاهَا
وَمُرْسَاهَا إِنَّ رَبِّي لَغَفُورٌ رَّحِيمٌ ۝

DECEIT
See also: Plotters Against Allah and His Messenger (PBUH)

And it sailed with them amid waves like mountains, and Noah cried unto his son— and he was standing aloof— O my son! Come ride with us, and be not with the disbelievers.

He said: I shall betake me to some mountain that will save me from the water. (Noah) said: This day there is none that saveth from the Commandment of Allah save him on whom He hath had mercy. And the wave came in between them, so he was among the drowned.

And it was said: O earth! Swallow thy water and, O sky! be cleared of clouds! and the water was made to subside. And the Commandment was fulfilled. And it (the ship) came to rest upon (the mount) *Al–Judi* and it was said: A far removal for wrongdoing folk!

11:36–44

2. The folk of Noah denied before them, yea, they denied Our slave and said: A madman; and he was repulsed.

So he cried unto his Lord, saying: I am vanquished, so give help.

Then opened We the gates of heaven with pouring water.

And caused the earth to gush forth springs, so that the waters met for a predestined purpose.

And We carried him upon a thing of planks and nails,

That ran (upon the waters) in Our sight, as a reward for him who was rejected.

And verily We left it as a token; but is there any that remembereth?

54:9–15

وَهِيَ تَجْرِيْ بِهِمْ فِيْ مَوْجٍ كَالْجِبَالِ
وَنَادٰى نُوْحُ ابْنَهٗ وَكَانَ فِيْ مَعْزِلٍ يّٰبُنَيَّ
ارْكَبْ مَّعَنَا وَلَا تَكُنْ مَّعَ الْكٰفِرِيْنَ ﴿٤٢﴾
قَالَ سَاٰوِيْۤ اِلٰى جَبَلٍ يَّعْصِمُنِيْ مِنَ
الْمَآءِ قَالَ لَا عَاصِمَ الْيَوْمَ مِنْ اَمْرِ
اللّٰهِ اِلَّا مَنْ رَّحِمَ وَحَالَ بَيْنَهُمَا
الْمَوْجُ فَكَانَ مِنَ الْمُغْرَقِيْنَ ﴿٤٣﴾
وَقِيْلَ يٰۤاَرْضُ ابْلَعِيْ مَآءَكِ وَيٰسَمَآءُ
اَقْلِعِيْ وَغِيْضَ الْمَآءُ وَقُضِيَ الْاَمْرُ
وَاسْتَوَتْ عَلَى الْجُوْدِيِّ وَقِيْلَ بُعْدًا
لِّلْقَوْمِ الظّٰلِمِيْنَ ﴿٤٤﴾

2. كَذَّبَتْ قَبْلَهُمْ قَوْمُ نُوْحٍ فَكَذَّبُوْا
عَبْدَنَا وَقَالُوْا مَجْنُوْنٌ وَّازْدُجِرَ ﴿٩﴾
فَدَعَا رَبَّهٗۤ اَنِّيْ مَغْلُوْبٌ فَانْتَصِرْ ﴿١٠﴾
فَفَتَحْنَاۤ اَبْوَابَ السَّمَآءِ بِمَآءٍ مُّنْهَمِرٍ ﴿١١﴾
وَّفَجَّرْنَا الْاَرْضَ عُيُوْنًا فَالْتَقَى الْمَآءُ
عَلٰۤى اَمْرٍ قَدْ قُدِرَ ﴿١٢﴾
وَحَمَلْنٰهُ عَلٰى ذَاتِ اَلْوَاحٍ وَّدُسُرٍ ﴿١٣﴾
تَجْرِيْ بِاَعْيُنِنَا جَزَآءً لِّمَنْ
كَانَ كُفِرَ ﴿١٤﴾
وَلَقَدْ تَّرَكْنٰهَاۤ اٰيَةً فَهَلْ مِنْ مُّدَّكِرٍ ﴿١٥﴾

3. اِنَّا لَمَّا طَغَا الْمَآءُ حَمَلْنٰكُمْ فِي الْجَارِيَةِ ﴿١١﴾
لِنَجْعَلَهَا لَكُمْ تَذْكِرَةً وَّتَعِيَهَاۤ اُذُنٌ
وَّاعِيَةٌ ﴿١٢﴾

3. Lo! when the waters rose, We carried you upon the ship:

That We might make it a memorial for you, and that remembering ears (that heard the story) might remember.

69:11–12

See also: Divine Punishment.

DESCRIPTION OF DOOMSDAY

1. And guard yourselves against a day when no soul will in aught avail another, nor will intercession be accepted from it, nor will compensation be received from it, nor will they be helped.

2:48

2. (On the day) when those who were followed disown those who followed (them), and they behold the doom, and all their aims collapse with them.

And those who were but followers will say: If a return were possible for us, we would disown them even as they have disowned us. Thus will Allah show them their own deeds as anguish for them, and they will not emerge from the Fire.

2:166–167

3. O ye who believe! Spend of that wherewith We have provided you ere a day come when there will be no trafficking, nor friendship, nor intercession. The disbelievers, they are the wrong-doers.

2:254

4. The weighing on that day is the true (weighing). As for those whose scale is heavy, they are the successful.

And as for those whose scale is light: those are they who lose their souls because they disbelieved Our revelations.

7:8–9

1. وَاتَّقُوا يَوْمًا لَّا تَجْزِي نَفْسٌ عَن نَّفْسٍ شَيْئًا
وَلَا يُقْبَلُ مِنْهَا شَفَاعَةٌ وَلَا يُؤْخَذُ مِنْهَا
عَدْلٌ وَلَا هُمْ يُنصَرُونَ ﴿٤٨﴾

2. إِذْ تَبَرَّأَ الَّذِينَ اتُّبِعُوا مِنَ الَّذِينَ اتَّبَعُوا
وَرَأَوُا الْعَذَابَ وَتَقَطَّعَتْ بِهِمُ الْأَسْبَابُ ﴿١٦٦﴾
وَقَالَ الَّذِينَ اتَّبَعُوا لَوْ أَنَّ لَنَا كَرَّةً فَنَتَبَرَّأَ
مِنْهُمْ كَمَا تَبَرَّءُوا مِنَّا ۗ كَذَٰلِكَ يُرِيهِمُ اللَّهُ
أَعْمَالَهُمْ حَسَرَاتٍ عَلَيْهِمْ ۖ وَمَا هُم بِخَارِجِينَ
مِنَ النَّارِ ﴿١٦٧﴾

3. يَا أَيُّهَا الَّذِينَ آمَنُوا أَنفِقُوا مِمَّا رَزَقْنَاكُم
مِّن قَبْلِ أَن يَأْتِيَ يَوْمٌ لَّا بَيْعٌ فِيهِ وَلَا
خُلَّةٌ وَلَا شَفَاعَةٌ ۗ وَالْكَافِرُونَ هُمُ الظَّالِمُونَ ﴿٢٥٤﴾

4. وَالْوَزْنُ يَوْمَئِذٍ الْحَقُّ ۚ فَمَن ثَقُلَتْ
مَوَازِينُهُ فَأُولَٰئِكَ هُمُ الْمُفْلِحُونَ ﴿٨﴾
وَمَنْ خَفَّتْ مَوَازِينُهُ فَأُولَٰئِكَ الَّذِينَ
خَسِرُوا أَنفُسَهُم بِمَا كَانُوا بِآيَاتِنَا يَظْلِمُونَ ﴿٩﴾

5. يَسْأَلُونَكَ عَنِ السَّاعَةِ أَيَّانَ مُرْسَاهَا ۖ قُلْ
إِنَّمَا عِلْمُهَا عِندَ رَبِّي ۖ لَا يُجَلِّيهَا لِوَقْتِهَا
إِلَّا هُوَ ۚ ثَقُلَتْ فِي السَّمَاوَاتِ وَالْأَرْضِ ۚ
لَا تَأْتِيكُمْ إِلَّا بَغْتَةً ۗ يَسْأَلُونَكَ كَأَنَّكَ

5. They ask thee of the (destined) Hour, when will it come to port. Say: Knowledge thereof is with my Lord only. He alone will manifest it at its proper time. It is heavy in the heavens and the earth. It cometh not to you save unawares. They question thee as if thou

couldst be well informed thereof. Say: Knowledge thereof is with Allah only, but most of mankind know not.

7:187

6. For those who disbelieve and debar (men) from the way of Allah, We add doom to doom because they wrought corruption.

And (bethink you of) the day when We raise in every nation a witness against them of their own folk, and We bring thee (Muhammad) as a witness against these. And We reveal the Scripture unto thee as an exposition of all things, and a guidance and a mercy and good tidings for those who have surrendered (to Allah).

16:88–89

7. And every man's augury have We fastened to his own neck, and We shall bring forth for him on the Day of Resurrection a book which he will find wide open.

(And it will be said unto him): Read thy book. Thy soul sufficeth as reckoner against thee this day.

17:13–14

8. And he whom Allah guideth, he is led aright; while, as for him whom He sendeth astray, for them thou wilt find no protecting friends beside Him, and We shall assemble them on the Day of Resurrection on their faces, blind, dumb and deaf; their habitation will be hell; whenever it abateth, We increase the flame for them.

That is their reward because they disbelieved Our revelations and said: When we are bones and fragments shall we, forsooth, be raised up as a new creation?

17:97–98

حفي عنها قل انما علمها عند الله
ولكن اكثر الناس لا يعلمون (١٨٧)

6. الذين كفروا وصدوا عن سبيل الله
زدنهم عذابا فوق العذاب بما كانوا
يفسدون (٨٨)
ويوم نبعث في كل امة شهيدا عليهم
من انفسهم وجئنا بك شهيدا على
هؤلاء ونزلنا عليك الكتب تبيانا
لكل شيء وهدى ورحمة وبشرى
للمسلمين (٨٩)

7. وكل انسان الزمنه طئره في عنقه
ونخرج له يوم القيمة كتبا يلقه منشورا (١٣)
اقرا كتبك كفى بنفسك اليوم
عليك حسيبا (١٤)

8. ومن يهد الله فهو المهتد ومن
يضلل فلن تجد لهم اولياء من دونه
ونحشرهم يوم القيمة على وجوههم
عميا وبكما وصما ماوىهم جهنم
كلما خبت زدنهم سعيرا (٩٧)
ذلك جزاؤهم بانهم كفروا بايتنا
وقالوا ءاذا كنا عظاما ورفاتا ءانا
لمبعوثون خلقا جديدا (٩٨)

9. On the Day when We shall gather the righteous unto the Beneficent, a goodly company.

And drive the guilty unto Hell, a weary herd.

They will have no power of intercession, save him who hath made a covenant with his Lord.

19:85–87

10. Lo! the Hour is surely coming. But I will to keep it hidden, that every soul may be rewarded for that which it striveth (to achieve).

• 20:15

11. The Day when the Trumpet is blown. On that Day We assemble the guilty white-eyed (with terror),

Murmuring among themselves: Ye have tarried but ten (days).

We are best aware of what they utter when their best in conduct say: Ye have tarried but a day.

They will ask thee of the mountains (on that day). Say: My Lord will break them into scattered dust,

And leave it as an empty plain,

Wherein thou seest neither curve nor ruggedness.

On that Day they follow the summoner who deceiveth not, and voices are hushed for the Beneficent, and thou hearest but a faint murmur.

On that Day no inter-

9. يَوْمَ نَحْشُرُ الْمُتَّقِيْنَ إِلَى الرَّحْمٰنِ وَفْدًا ﴿٨٥﴾
وَّ نَسُوْقُ الْمُجْرِمِيْنَ إِلٰى جَهَنَّمَ وِرْدًا ﴿٨٦﴾
لَا يَمْلِكُوْنَ الشَّفَاعَةَ إِلَّا مَنِ اتَّخَذَ
عِنْدَ الرَّحْمٰنِ عَهْدًا ﴿٨٧﴾

10. إِنَّ السَّاعَةَ اٰتِيَةٌ اَكَادُ اُخْفِيْهَا
لِتُجْزٰى كُلُّ نَفْسٍ بِمَا تَسْعٰى ﴿١٥﴾

11. يَّوْمَ يُنْفَخُ فِى الصُّوْرِ وَ نَحْشُرُ
الْمُجْرِمِيْنَ يَوْمَئِذٍ زُرْقًا ﴿١٠٢﴾
يَّتَخَافَتُوْنَ بَيْنَهُمْ اِنْ لَّبِثْتُمْ
اِلَّا عَشْرًا ﴿١٠٣﴾
نَحْنُ اَعْلَمُ بِمَا يَقُوْلُوْنَ اِذْ يَقُوْلُ
اَمْثَلُهُمْ طَرِيْقَةً اِنْ لَّبِثْتُمْ اِلَّا يَوْمًا ﴿١٠٤﴾
وَيَسْـَٔلُوْنَكَ عَنِ الْجِبَالِ فَقُلْ يَنْسِفُهَا
رَبِّىْ نَسْفًا ﴿١٠٥﴾
فَيَذَرُهَا قَاعًا صَفْصَفًا ﴿١٠٦﴾
لَّا تَرٰى فِيْهَا عِوَجًا وَّلَآ اَمْتًا ﴿١٠٧﴾
يَوْمَئِذٍ يَّتَّبِعُوْنَ الدَّاعِىَ لَا عِوَجَ لَهٗ
وَخَشَعَتِ الْاَصْوَاتُ لِلرَّحْمٰنِ فَلَا
تَسْمَعُ اِلَّا هَمْسًا ﴿١٠٨﴾
يَوْمَئِذٍ لَّا تَنْفَعُ الشَّفَاعَةُ اِلَّا مَنْ
اَذِنَ لَهُ الرَّحْمٰنُ وَرَضِىَ لَهٗ قَوْلًا ﴿١٠٩﴾
يَعْلَمُ مَا بَيْنَ اَيْدِيْهِمْ وَمَا خَلْفَهُمْ
وَلَا يُحِيْطُوْنَ بِهٖ عِلْمًا ﴿١١٠﴾
وَعَنَتِ الْوُجُوْهُ لِلْحَىِّ الْقَيُّوْمِ وَقَدْ

cession availeth save (that of) him unto whom the Beneficent hath given leave and whose He accepteth.

He knoweth (all) that is before them and (all) that is behind them, while they cannot compass it in knowledge.

And faces humble themselves before the Living, the Eternal. And he who beareth (a burden of) wrongdoing is indeed a failure (on that Day).

And he who hath done some good works, being a believer, he feareth not injustice nor begrudging (of his wage).

20:102–112

12. And We set a just balance for the Day of Resurrection so that no soul is wronged in aught. Though it be of the weight of a grain of mustard seed, We bring it. And We suffice for reckoners.

21:47

13. The Day when We shall roll up the heavens as a recorder rolleth up a written scroll. As We began the first creation, We shall repeat it. (It is) a promise (binding) upon Us. Lo! We are to perform it.

21:104

14. O mankind! Fear your Lord. Lo! the earthquake of the Hour (of Doom) is a tremendous thing.

On the day when ye behold it, every nursing mother will forget her nursling and every pregnant one will be delivered of her burden, and thou (Muhammad) wilt see mankind as drunken, yet they will not be drunken, but the Doom of Allah will be strong (upon them).

22:1–2

15. So withdraw from them

خَابَ مَنْ حَمَلَ ظُلْمًا ﴿١١١﴾
وَمَنْ يَعْمَلْ مِنَ الصّٰلِحٰتِ وَهُوَ
مُؤْمِنٌ فَلَا يَخٰفُ ظُلْمًا وَّلَا هَضْمًا ﴿١١٢﴾

12. وَنَضَعُ الْمَوَازِيْنَ الْقِسْطَ لِيَوْمِ الْقِيٰمَةِ
فَلَا تُظْلَمُ نَفْسٌ شَيْـًٔا ؕ وَاِنْ كَانَ
مِثْقَالَ حَبَّةٍ مِّنْ خَرْدَلٍ اَتَيْنَا بِهَا ؕ
وَكَفٰى بِنَا حٰسِبِيْنَ ﴿٤٧﴾

13. يَوْمَ نَطْوِى السَّمَآءَ كَطَىِّ السِّجِلِّ
لِلْكُتُبِ ؕ كَمَا بَدَاْنَآ اَوَّلَ خَلْقٍ
نُّعِيْدُهٗ ؕ وَعْدًا عَلَيْنَا ؕ اِنَّا كُنَّا فٰعِلِيْنَ ﴿١٠٤﴾

14. يٰۤاَيُّهَا النَّاسُ اتَّقُوْا رَبَّكُمْ ۚ اِنَّ
زَلْزَلَةَ السَّاعَةِ شَىْءٌ عَظِيْمٌ ﴿١﴾
يَوْمَ تَرَوْنَهَا تَذْهَلُ كُلُّ مُرْضِعَةٍ
عَمَّآ اَرْضَعَتْ وَتَضَعُ كُلُّ ذَاتِ حَمْلٍ
حَمْلَهَا وَتَرَى النَّاسَ سُكٰرٰى وَمَا
هُمْ بِسُكٰرٰى وَلٰكِنَّ عَذَابَ اللّٰهِ
شَدِيْدٌ ﴿٢﴾

15. فَتَوَلَّ عَنْهُمْ ۘ يَوْمَ يَدْعُ الدَّاعِ اِلٰى
شَىْءٍ نُّكُرٍ ﴿٦﴾
خُشَّعًا اَبْصَارُهُمْ يَخْرُجُوْنَ مِنَ
الْاَجْدَاثِ كَاَنَّهُمْ جَرَادٌ مُّنْتَشِرٌ ﴿٧﴾
مُّهْطِعِيْنَ اِلَى الدَّاعِ ؕ يَقُوْلُ الْكٰفِرُوْنَ
هٰذَا يَوْمٌ عَسِرٌ ﴿٨﴾

(O Muhammad) on the day when the Summoner summoneth unto a painful thing.

With downcast eyes, they come forth from the graves as they were locusts spread abroad,

Hastening toward the Summoner; the disbelievers say: This is a hard day!

54:6–8

16. Your ties of kindred and your children will avail you naught upon the Day of Resurrection. He will part you. Allah is Seer of what ye do.

60:3

17. Nay, I swear by the Day of Resurrection;

Nay, I swear by the accusing soul (that this Scripture is true).

Thinketh man that We shall not assemble his bones?

Yea, verily. We are Able to restore his very fingers!

But man would fain deny what is before him.

He asketh: When will be this Day of Resurrecttion?

But when sight is confounded

And the moon is eclipsed,

And sun and moon are united,

On that day man will cry: Whither to flee!

Alas ! No refuge!

Unto thy Lord is the recourse that day.

On that day man is told the tale of that which he hath sent before and left behind.

75:1–13

18. On the day when the first trump resoundeth.

And the second followeth it,

On that day hearts beat painfully

16. لَن تَنفَعَكُمْ أَرْحَامُكُمْ وَلَا أَوْلَادُكُمْ
يَوْمَ الْقِيَامَةِ يَفْصِلُ بَيْنَكُمْ وَاللَّهُ
بِمَا تَعْمَلُونَ بَصِيرٌ ﴿٣﴾

17. لَا أُقْسِمُ بِيَوْمِ الْقِيَامَةِ ﴿١﴾
وَلَا أُقْسِمُ بِالنَّفْسِ اللَّوَّامَةِ ﴿٢﴾
أَيَحْسَبُ الْإِنسَانُ أَلَّن نَّجْمَعَ
عِظَامَهُ ﴿٣﴾
بَلَىٰ قَادِرِينَ عَلَىٰ أَن نُّسَوِّيَ بَنَانَهُ ﴿٤﴾
بَلْ يُرِيدُ الْإِنسَانُ لِيَفْجُرَ أَمَامَهُ ﴿٥﴾
يَسْأَلُ أَيَّانَ يَوْمُ الْقِيَامَةِ ﴿٦﴾
فَإِذَا بَرِقَ الْبَصَرُ ﴿٧﴾
وَخَسَفَ الْقَمَرُ ﴿٨﴾
وَجُمِعَ الشَّمْسُ وَالْقَمَرُ ﴿٩﴾
يَقُولُ الْإِنسَانُ يَوْمَئِذٍ أَيْنَ الْمَفَرُّ ﴿١٠﴾
كَلَّا لَا وَزَرَ ﴿١١﴾
إِلَىٰ رَبِّكَ يَوْمَئِذٍ الْمُسْتَقَرُّ ﴿١٢﴾
يُنَبَّأُ الْإِنسَانُ يَوْمَئِذٍ بِمَا قَدَّمَ
وَأَخَّرَ ﴿١٣﴾

18. يَوْمَ تَرْجُفُ الرَّاجِفَةُ ﴿٦﴾
تَتْبَعُهَا الرَّادِفَةُ ﴿٧﴾
قُلُوبٌ يَوْمَئِذٍ وَاجِفَةٌ ﴿٨﴾
أَبْصَارُهَا خَاشِعَةٌ ﴿٩﴾

19. فَإِذَا جَاءَتِ الصَّاخَّةُ ﴿٣٣﴾

While eyes are downcast.

79:6–9

19. But when the Shout cometh

On the day when a man fleeth from his brother

And his mother and his father

And his wife and his children,

Every man that day will have concern enough to make him heedless (of others).

On that day faces will be bright as dawn,

Laughing, rejoicing at good news;

And other faces, on that day, with dust upon them,

Veiled in darkness,

Those are the disbelievers, the wicked.

80:33–42

20. When the sun is overthrown,

And when the stars fall,

And when the hills are moved,

And when the camels big with young are abandoned,

And when the wild beasts are herded together,

And when the seas rise,

And when souls are reunited,

And when the girl-child that was buried alive is asked

For what sin she was slain,

And when the pages are laid open,

And when the sky is torn away,

And when hell is lighted,

يَوْمَ يَفِرُّ الْمَرْءُ مِنْ أَخِيهِ ﴿٣٤﴾
وَأُمِّهِ وَأَبِيهِ ﴿٣٥﴾
وَصَاحِبَتِهِ وَبَنِيهِ ﴿٣٦﴾
لِكُلِّ امْرِئٍ مِنْهُمْ يَوْمَئِذٍ شَأْنٌ يُغْنِيهِ ﴿٣٧﴾
وُجُوهٌ يَوْمَئِذٍ مُسْفِرَةٌ ﴿٣٨﴾
ضَاحِكَةٌ مُسْتَبْشِرَةٌ ﴿٣٩﴾
وَوُجُوهٌ يَوْمَئِذٍ عَلَيْهَا غَبَرَةٌ ﴿٤٠﴾
تَرْهَقُهَا قَتَرَةٌ ﴿٤١﴾
أُولَٰئِكَ هُمُ الْكَفَرَةُ الْفَجَرَةُ ﴿٤٢﴾
20. إِذَا الشَّمْسُ كُوِّرَتْ ﴿١﴾
وَإِذَا النُّجُومُ انْكَدَرَتْ ﴿٢﴾
وَإِذَا الْجِبَالُ سُيِّرَتْ ﴿٣﴾
وَإِذَا الْعِشَارُ عُطِّلَتْ ﴿٤﴾
وَإِذَا الْوُحُوشُ حُشِرَتْ ﴿٥﴾
وَإِذَا الْبِحَارُ سُجِّرَتْ ﴿٦﴾
وَإِذَا النُّفُوسُ زُوِّجَتْ ﴿٧﴾
وَإِذَا الْمَوْءُودَةُ سُئِلَتْ ﴿٨﴾
بِأَيِّ ذَنْبٍ قُتِلَتْ ﴿٩﴾
وَإِذَا الصُّحُفُ نُشِرَتْ ﴿١٠﴾
وَإِذَا السَّمَاءُ كُشِطَتْ ﴿١١﴾
وَإِذَا الْجَحِيمُ سُعِّرَتْ ﴿١٢﴾
وَإِذَا الْجَنَّةُ أُزْلِفَتْ ﴿١٣﴾
عَلِمَتْ نَفْسٌ مَا أَحْضَرَتْ ﴿١٤﴾

And when the garden is brought nigh,

(Then) every soul will know what it hath made ready.

81:1–14

21. When Earth is shaken with her (final) earthquake

And Earth yieldeth up her burdens,

And man saith: What aileth her?

That day she will relate her chronicles,

Because thy Lord inspireth her,

That day mankind will issue forth in scattered groups to be shown their deeds.

And whoso doth good an atom's weight will see it then,

And whoso doth ill an atom's weight will see it then.

99:1–8

22. The Calamity!

What is the Calamity?

Ah, what will convey unto thee what the Calamity is!

A day wherein mankind will be as thickly–scattered moths

And the mountains will become as carded wool.

Then, as for him whose scales are heavy (with good works),

He will live a pleasant life.

But as for him whose scales are light,

The Bereft and Hungry One will be his mother.

Ah, what will convey

21. إِذَا زُلْزِلَتِ الْأَرْضُ زِلْزَالَهَا ۝١
وَأَخْرَجَتِ الْأَرْضُ أَثْقَالَهَا ۝٢
وَقَالَ الْإِنسَانُ مَا لَهَا ۝٣
يَوْمَئِذٍ تُحَدِّثُ أَخْبَارَهَا ۝٤
بِأَنَّ رَبَّكَ أَوْحَىٰ لَهَا ۝٥
يَوْمَئِذٍ يَصْدُرُ النَّاسُ أَشْتَاتًا
لِّيُرَوْا أَعْمَالَهُمْ ۝٦
فَمَن يَعْمَلْ مِثْقَالَ ذَرَّةٍ خَيْرًا
يَرَهُ ۝٧
وَمَن يَعْمَلْ مِثْقَالَ ذَرَّةٍ شَرًّا يَرَهُ ۝٨

22. الْقَارِعَةُ ۝١
مَا الْقَارِعَةُ ۝٢
وَمَا أَدْرَاكَ مَا الْقَارِعَةُ ۝٣
يَوْمَ يَكُونُ النَّاسُ كَالْفَرَاشِ
الْمَبْثُوثِ ۝٤
وَتَكُونُ الْجِبَالُ كَالْعِهْنِ الْمَنفُوشِ ۝٥
فَأَمَّا مَن ثَقُلَتْ مَوَازِينُهُ ۝٦
فَهُوَ فِي عِيشَةٍ رَّاضِيَةٍ ۝٧
وَأَمَّا مَنْ خَفَّتْ مَوَازِينُهُ ۝٨
فَأُمُّهُ هَاوِيَةٌ ۝٩
وَمَا أَدْرَاكَ مَا هِيَهْ ۝١٠
نَارٌ حَامِيَةٌ ۝١١

unto thee what she is!—

Raging Fire!

101:1–11

Ref: 2:113,281; 3:9,25,30,106–107; 4:87; 5:109,119; 6:12,22,31,51,128–130; 7:8–9; 9:105; 10:23,28,45,70; 11:102–103; 13:5; 14:21–23,31; 15:85; 16:27–29,77,111; 17:49–52,97–99; 18:47,52–53,99–101; 19:75; 20:105–112; 21:1–2,97; 22:7; 23:101; 24:24–25; 25:17–18; 27: 82–83; 28:62–67,75; 29:13; 30:12–16, 55–57; 31:33–34; 32:25; 33:63– 68; 34:3,29–30,33,42; 36:65; 37:19–21; 39:60,67–75; 40:10–11,52; 44:10–12; 46:20; 50:20–31, 41–44; 56:1–11; 64:9; 69:1–4,13–37; 70:43–44; 73:14,17–18; 78:1–5; 82:1 19; 84:1–6; 89:21–22.

See also: Life after Death, Trumpet of Israfil.

DESPAIR

1. And despair not of the Spirit of Allah. Lo! none despaireth of the Spirit of Allah save disbelieving folk.

12:87

1. وَلَا تَايْـَٔسُوْا مِنْ رَّوْحِ اللّٰهِ ۭ اِنَّهٗ لَا يَايْـَٔسُ
مِنْ رَّوْحِ اللّٰهِ اِلَّا الْقَوْمُ الْكٰفِرُوْنَ ﴿۸۷﴾

2. Those who disbelieve in the revelations of Allah and in (their) Meeting with Him, such have no hope of My mercy. For such there is a painful doom.

29:23

2. وَالَّذِيْنَ كَفَرُوْا بِاٰيٰتِ اللّٰهِ وَلِقَاۗىِٕهٖٓ
اُولٰۗىِٕكَ يَىِٕسُوْا مِنْ رَّحْمَتِيْ وَاُولٰۗىِٕكَ
لَهُمْ عَذَابٌ اَلِيْمٌ ﴿۲۳﴾

3. Say: O My slaves who have been prodigal to their own souls; Despair not of the mercy of Allah, Who forgiveth all sins. Lo! He is the Forgiving, the Merciful.

39:53

3. قُلْ يٰعِبَادِيَ الَّذِيْنَ اَسْرَفُوْا عَلٰٓي
اَنْفُسِهِمْ لَا تَقْنَطُوْا مِنْ رَّحْمَةِ اللّٰهِ ۭ
اِنَّ اللّٰهَ يَغْفِرُ الذُّنُوْبَ جَمِيْعًا ۭ اِنَّهٗ
هُوَ الْغَفُوْرُ الرَّحِيْمُ ﴿۵۳﴾

DESTINY

1. Wheresoever ye may be, death will overtake you, even though ye were in lofty towers. Yet if a happy thing befalleth them they say: This is from Allah; and if an evil thing befalleth them they say: This is of thy doing (O Muhammad). Say (unto them): All is from Allah. What is amiss with these people that they come not nigh to understand a happening?

Whatever a good befalleth thee (O man) it is from Allah, and whatever of ill befalleth thee it is from thyself.

4:78–79

1. اَيْنَ مَا تَكُوْنُوْا يُدْرِكْكُّمُ الْمَوْتُ وَلَوْ كُنْتُمْ
فِيْ بُرُوْجٍ مُّشَيَّدَةٍ ۭ وَاِنْ تُصِبْهُمْ حَسَنَةٌ
يَّقُوْلُوْا هٰذِهٖ مِنْ عِنْدِ اللّٰهِ ۚ وَاِنْ تُصِبْهُمْ
سَيِّئَةٌ يَّقُوْلُوْا هٰذِهٖ مِنْ عِنْدِكَ ۭ قُلْ كُلٌّ
مِّنْ عِنْدِ اللّٰهِ ۭ فَمَالِ هٰٓؤُلَاۗءِ الْقَوْمِ لَا
يَكَادُوْنَ يَفْقَهُوْنَ حَدِيْثًا ﴿۷۸﴾
مَآ اَصَابَكَ مِنْ حَسَنَةٍ فَمِنَ اللّٰهِ ۡ وَمَآ
اَصَابَكَ مِنْ سَيِّئَةٍ فَمِنْ نَّفْسِكَ ۭ

2. He unto Whom belongeth the Sovereignty of the heavens and the earth, He hath chosen no son nor hath He any partner in the Sovereignty. He hath created everything and hath meted out for it a measure.

25:2

3. And if We had so willed, We could have given every soul its guidance, but the word from Me concerning evildoers took effect: that I will fill hell with the jinn and mankind together.

32:13

4. Lo! We have created every thing by measure.

And Our commandment is but one (commandment), as the twinkling of an eye.

54:49–50

5. And whosoever keepeth his duty to Allah, Allah will appoint a way out for him,

And will provide for him from (a quarter) whence he hath no expectation. And whosoever putteth his trust in Allah, He will suffice him. Lo! Allah bringeth His command to pass. Allah hath set a measure for all things.

65:2–3

6. Praise the name of thy Lord the Most High,

Who createth, then disposeth:

Who measureth, then guideth;

87:1–3

2. الَّذِي لَهُ مُلْكُ السَّمٰوٰتِ وَالْاَرْضِ وَلَمْ يَتَّخِذْ وَلَدًا وَّلَمْ يَكُنْ لَّهُ شَرِيْكٌ فِي الْمُلْكِ وَخَلَقَ كُلَّ شَيْءٍ فَقَدَّرَهُ تَقْدِيْرًا ۝

3. وَلَوْ شِئْنَا لَاٰتَيْنَا كُلَّ نَفْسٍ هُدٰىهَا وَلٰكِنْ حَقَّ الْقَوْلُ مِنِّيْ لَاَمْلَـَٔنَّ جَهَنَّمَ مِنَ الْجِنَّةِ وَالنَّاسِ اَجْمَعِيْنَ ۝

4. اِنَّا كُلَّ شَيْءٍ خَلَقْنٰهُ بِقَدَرٍ ۝
وَمَآ اَمْرُنَآ اِلَّا وَاحِدَةٌ كَلَمْحٍ بِالْبَصَرِ ۝

5. وَمَنْ يَّتَّقِ اللّٰهَ يَجْعَلْ لَّهٗ مَخْرَجًا ۝ وَّيَرْزُقْهُ مِنْ حَيْثُ لَا يَحْتَسِبُ ۚ وَمَنْ يَّتَوَكَّلْ عَلَى اللّٰهِ فَهُوَ حَسْبُهٗ ۚ اِنَّ اللّٰهَ بَالِغُ اَمْرِهٖ ۚ قَدْ جَعَلَ اللّٰهُ لِكُلِّ شَيْءٍ قَدْرًا ۝

6. سَبِّحِ اسْمَ رَبِّكَ الْاَعْلَى ۝
الَّذِيْ خَلَقَ فَسَوّٰى ۝
وَالَّذِيْ قَدَّرَ فَهَدٰى ۝

○

Ref. 7:178; 10:5; 15:60; 36:28-29,38; 41:10-12; 56:60; 74:18-20; 76:16; 80:19.

See also: Responsibility for Actions.

DEVILS

1. Thus have We appointed unto every Prophet an adversary—devils of humankind and jinn who inspire in one another plausible discourse through guile. If thy Lord willed, they would not do so; so leave them alone with their devising;

6: 112

2. And eat not of that whereon Allah's name hath not been mentioned, for lo! it is abomination. Lo! the devils do inspire their minions to dispute with you. But if ye obey them, ye will be in truth idolaters.

6:121

3. Lo! We have made the devils protecting friends for those who believe not.

7:27

4. Seest thou not that We have set the devils on the disbelievers to confound them with confusion?

19:83

5. And say: My Lord! I seek refuge in Thee from suggestions of the evil ones,

And I seek refuge in Thee, my Lord, lest they be present with me,

23:97–98

6. Shall I inform you upon whom the devils descend?

They descend on every sinful, false one,

They listen eagerly, but most of them are liars.

26:221–223

1. وَكَذٰلِكَ جَعَلْنَا لِكُلِّ نَبِيٍّ عَدُوًّا شَيٰطِيْنَ
الْاِنْسِ وَالْجِنِّ يُوْحِيْ بَعْضُهُمْ اِلٰى بَعْضٍ
زُخْرُفَ الْقَوْلِ غُرُوْرًا ۚ وَلَوْ شَآءَ رَبُّكَ
مَا فَعَلُوْهُ فَذَرْهُمْ وَمَا يَفْتَرُوْنَ ○

2. وَلَا تَأْكُلُوْا مِمَّا لَمْ يُذْكَرِ اسْمُ اللّٰهِ
عَلَيْهِ وَاِنَّهٗ لَفِسْقٌ ۗ وَاِنَّ الشَّيٰطِيْنَ
لَيُوْحُوْنَ اِلٰٓى اَوْلِيٰٓئِهِمْ لِيُجَادِلُوْكُمْ ۚ
وَاِنْ اَطَعْتُمُوْهُمْ اِنَّكُمْ لَمُشْرِكُوْنَ ○

3. اِنَّا جَعَلْنَا الشَّيٰطِيْنَ اَوْلِيَآءَ لِلَّذِيْنَ لَا
يُؤْمِنُوْنَ ﴿٢٧﴾

4. اَلَمْ تَرَ اَنَّآ اَرْسَلْنَا الشَّيٰطِيْنَ عَلَى
الْكٰفِرِيْنَ تَؤُزُّهُمْ اَزًّا ﴿٨٣﴾

5. وَقُلْ رَّبِّ اَعُوْذُ بِكَ مِنْ هَمَزٰتِ
الشَّيٰطِيْنِ ﴿٩٧﴾
وَاَعُوْذُ بِكَ رَبِّ اَنْ يَّحْضُرُوْنِ ○

6. هَلْ اُنَبِّئُكُمْ عَلٰى مَنْ تَنَزَّلُ
الشَّيٰطِيْنُ ﴿٢٢١﴾
تَنَزَّلُ عَلٰى كُلِّ اَفَّاكٍ اَثِيْمٍ ﴿٢٢٢﴾
يُّلْقُوْنَ السَّمْعَ وَاَكْثَرُهُمْ كٰذِبُوْنَ ﴿٢٢٣﴾

See also: *Satan*

DHÛ'L – QARNEYN

1. They will ask thee of *Dhu'l-Qarneyn.* Say: I shall recite unto you a remembrance of him.

Lo! We made him strong in the land and gave him unto everything a road.

And he followed a road.

Till, when he reached the setting-place of the sun, he found it setting in a muddy spring, and found a people thereabout: We said: O *Dhu'l-Qarneyn!* Either punish or show them kindness.

He said: As for him who doth wrong we shall punish him, and then he will be brought back unto his Lord, Who will punish him with awful punishment!

But as for him who believeth and doth right, good will be his reward, and we shall speak unto him a mild command.

Then he followed a road.

Till, when he reached the rising–place of the sun, he found it rising on a people for whom We had appointed no shelter therefrom.

So (it was). And We knew all concerning him.

Then he followed a road.

Till, when he came bet-

1. وَيَسْـَٔلُوْنَكَ عَنْ ذِى الْقَرْنَيْنِ ؕ قُلْ
سَاَتْلُوْا عَلَيْكُمْ مِّنْهُ ذِكْرًا (٨٣)
اِنَّا مَكَّنَّا لَهٗ فِى الْاَرْضِ وَاٰتَيْنٰهُ مِنْ
كُلِّ شَىْءٍ سَبَبًا (٨٤)
فَاَتْبَعَ سَبَبًا (٨٥)
حَتّٰٓى اِذَا بَلَغَ مَغْرِبَ الشَّمْسِ وَجَدَهَا
تَغْرُبُ فِىْ عَيْنٍ حَمِئَةٍ وَّوَجَدَ عِنْدَهَا
قَوْمًا ؕ قُلْنَا يٰذَا الْقَرْنَيْنِ اِمَّآ
اَنْ تُعَذِّبَ وَاِمَّآ اَنْ تَتَّخِذَ فِيْهِمْ
حُسْنًا (٨٦)
قَالَ اَمَّا مَنْ ظَلَمَ فَسَوْفَ نُعَذِّبُهٗ
ثُمَّ يُرَدُّ اِلٰى رَبِّهٖ فَيُعَذِّبُهٗ عَذَابًا نُّكْرًا (٨٧)
وَاَمَّا مَنْ اٰمَنَ وَعَمِلَ صَالِحًا فَلَهٗ
جَزَآءَ ۨالْحُسْنٰى ۚ وَسَنَقُوْلُ لَهٗ مِنْ
اَمْرِنَا يُسْرًا ؕ (٨٨)
ثُمَّ اَتْبَعَ سَبَبًا (٨٩)
حَتّٰٓى اِذَا بَلَغَ مَطْلِعَ الشَّمْسِ وَجَدَهَا
تَطْلُعُ عَلٰى قَوْمٍ لَّمْ نَجْعَلْ لَّهُمْ مِّنْ
دُوْنِهَا سِتْرًا ۙ (٩٠)
كَذٰلِكَ ؕ وَقَدْ اَحَطْنَا بِمَا لَدَيْهِ خُبْرًا (٩١)
ثُمَّ اَتْبَعَ سَبَبًا (٩٢)
حَتّٰٓى اِذَا بَلَغَ بَيْنَ السَّدَّيْنِ وَجَدَ
مِنْ دُوْنِهِمَا قَوْمًا ۙ لَّا يَكَادُوْنَ

ween the two mountains, he found upon their hither side a folk that scarce could understand a saying.

They said: O *Dhû'l Qarneyn!* Lo! Gog and Magog are spoiling the land. So may we pay thee tribute on condition that thou set a barrier between us and them?

He said: That wherein my Lord hath established me is better (than your tribute). Do but help me with strength (of men), I will set between you and them a bank.

Give me pieces of iron – till, when he had levelled up (the gap) between the cliffs, he said: Blow!–till, when he had made it a fire, he said: Bring me molten copper to pour thereon.

And (Gog and Magog) were not able to surmount, nor could they pierce (it).

He said: This is a mercy from my Lord; but when the promise of my Lord cometh to pass, He will lay it low, for the promise of my Lord is true.

And on that day We shall let some of them surge against others, and the Trumpet will be blown. Then We shall gather them together in one gathering:

18:83–99

يَفْقَهُونَ قَوْلًا ﴿٩٣﴾
قَالُوا يٰذَا الْقَرْنَيْنِ إِنَّ يَأْجُوجَ وَمَأْجُوجَ
مُفْسِدُونَ فِي الْأَرْضِ فَهَلْ نَجْعَلُ
لَكَ خَرْجًا عَلَىٰ أَنْ تَجْعَلَ بَيْنَنَا
وَبَيْنَهُمْ سَدًّا ﴿٩٤﴾
قَالَ مَا مَكَّنِّي فِيهِ رَبِّي خَيْرٌ فَأَعِينُونِي
بِقُوَّةٍ أَجْعَلْ بَيْنَكُمْ وَبَيْنَهُمْ رَدْمًا ﴿٩٥﴾
اٰتُونِي زُبَرَ الْحَدِيدِ حَتّٰى إِذَا سَاوٰى
بَيْنَ الصَّدَفَيْنِ قَالَ انْفُخُوا حَتّٰى إِذَا
جَعَلَهُ نَارًا قَالَ اٰتُونِي أُفْرِغْ عَلَيْهِ قِطْرًا ﴿٩٦﴾
فَمَا اسْطَاعُوا أَنْ يَظْهَرُوهُ وَمَا اسْتَطَاعُوا
لَهُ نَقْبًا ﴿٩٧﴾
قَالَ هٰذَا رَحْمَةٌ مِنْ رَبِّي فَإِذَا جَاءَ
وَعْدُ رَبِّي جَعَلَهُ دَكَّاءَ وَكَانَ
وَعْدُ رَبِّي حَقًّا ﴿٩٨﴾
وَتَرَكْنَا بَعْضَهُمْ يَوْمَئِذٍ يَمُوجُ فِي بَعْضٍ
وَنُفِخَ فِي الصُّورِ فَجَمَعْنَاهُمْ جَمْعًا ﴿٩٩﴾

.DIGNITY AND DISGRACE

1. Say: O Allah! Owner of Sovereignty! Thou givest sovereignty unto whom Thou wilt, and Thou withdrawest sovereignty from whom Thou wilt. Thou exaltest whom Thou wilt and Thou abasest whom Thou wilt. In Thy hand is the good. Lo! Thou art Able to do all things.

Thou causest the night to pass into the day, and Thou causest the day to pass into the night. And Thou bringest forth the living from the dead, and Thou bringest forth the dead from the living. And Thou givest sustenance to whom Thou choosest, without stint.

3:26–27

2. Bear unto the hypocrites the tidings that for them there is a painful doom;

Those who choose disbelievers for their friends instead of believers! Do they look for power at their hands? Lo! all power appertaineth to Allah.

4:138–139

3. For those who do good is the best (reward) and more (thereto). Neither dust nor ignominy cometh near their faces. Such are rightful owners of the Garden; they will abide therein.

And those who earn ill deeds, (for them) requital of each ill deed by the like thereof; and ignominy overtaketh them–They have no protector from Allah–as if

1. قُلِ اللّٰهُمَّ مٰلِكَ الْمُلْكِ تُؤْتِى الْمُلْكَ
مَنْ تَشَآءُ وَ تَنْزِعُ الْمُلْكَ مِمَّنْ تَشَآءُ وَ
تُعِزُّ مَنْ تَشَآءُ وَ تُذِلُّ مَنْ تَشَآءُ بِيَدِكَ
الْخَيْرُ اِنَّكَ عَلٰى كُلِّ شَىْءٍ قَدِيْرٌ ○
تُوْلِجُ الَّيْلَ فِى النَّهَارِ وَ تُوْلِجُ النَّهَارَ فِى
الَّيْلِ وَ تُخْرِجُ الْحَىَّ مِنَ الْمَيِّتِ وَ تُخْرِجُ
الْمَيِّتَ مِنَ الْحَىِّ وَ تَرْزُقُ مَنْ تَشَآءُ
بِغَيْرِ حِسَابٍ ○

2. بَشِّرِ الْمُنٰفِقِيْنَ بِاَنَّ لَهُمْ عَذَابًا اَلِيْمًا ﴿۱۳۸﴾
الَّذِيْنَ يَتَّخِذُوْنَ الْكٰفِرِيْنَ اَوْلِيَآءَ مِنْ
دُوْنِ الْمُؤْمِنِيْنَ اَيَبْتَغُوْنَ عِنْدَهُمُ الْعِزَّةَ
فَاِنَّ الْعِزَّةَ لِلّٰهِ جَمِيْعًا ﴿۱۳۹﴾

3. لِلَّذِيْنَ اَحْسَنُوا الْحُسْنٰى وَ زِيَادَةٌ وَ لَا
يَرْهَقُ وُجُوْهَهُمْ قَتَرٌ وَّ لَا ذِلَّةٌ اُولٰٓئِكَ
اَصْحٰبُ الْجَنَّةِ هُمْ فِيْهَا خٰلِدُوْنَ ﴿۲۶﴾

وَ الَّذِيْنَ كَسَبُوا السَّيِّاٰتِ جَزَآءُ سَيِّئَةٍ
بِمِثْلِهَا وَ تَرْهَقُهُمْ ذِلَّةٌ مَا لَهُمْ مِّنَ
اللّٰهِ مِنْ عَاصِمٍ كَاَنَّمَآ اُغْشِيَتْ وُجُوْهُهُمْ
قِطَعًا مِّنَ الَّيْلِ مُظْلِمًا اُولٰٓئِكَ اَصْحٰبُ
النَّارِ هُمْ فِيْهَا خٰلِدُوْنَ ﴿۲۷﴾

4. مَنْ كَانَ يُرِيْدُ الْعِزَّةَ فَلِلّٰهِ الْعِزَّةُ
جَمِيْعًا اِلَيْهِ يَصْعَدُ الْكَلِمُ الطَّيِّبُ
وَ الْعَمَلُ الصَّالِحُ يَرْفَعُهٗ

their faces had been covered with a cloak of darkest night. Such are rightful owners of the Fire; they will abide therein.

10:26–27

4. Whoso desireth power (should know that) all power belongeth to Allah. Unto Him good words ascend, and the pious deed doth He exalt;

35:10

DIGNITY OF MAN

1. And (remember) when thy Lord said unto the angels: Lo! I am creating a mortal out of potter's clay of black mud altered.

So, when I have made him and have breathed into him of My spirit, do ye fall down, prostrating yourselves unto him.

So the angels fell prostrate all of them together,

Save *Iblis.*

15:28–31

2. And Allah brought you forth from the wombs of your mothers knowing nothing, and gave you hearing and sight and hearts that haply ye might give thanks.

16:78

3. Verily We have honoured the children of Adam. We carry them on the land and the sea, and have made provision of good things for them, and have preferred them above many of those whom We created with a marked preferment.

17:70

4. See ye not how Allah hath made serviceable unto you whatsoever is in heavens and whatsoever is in the earth and hath loaded you with His favours both without and within? Yet of mankind is he who disputeth concerning Allah without knowledge or guidance or a Scripture giving light.

31:20

1. وَإِذْ قَالَ رَبُّكَ لِلْمَلٰٓئِكَةِ إِنِّي خَالِقٌ
بَشَرًا مِّنْ صَلْصَالٍ مِّنْ حَمَإٍ مَّسْنُونٍ ۝
فَإِذَا سَوَّيْتُهُ وَنَفَخْتُ فِيهِ مِنْ رُّوحِي
فَقَعُوا لَهُ سٰجِدِينَ ۝
فَسَجَدَ الْمَلٰٓئِكَةُ كُلُّهُمْ أَجْمَعُونَ ۝
إِلَّآ إِبْلِيسَ

2. وَاللّٰهُ أَخْرَجَكُمْ مِّنْ بُطُونِ أُمَّهٰتِكُمْ لَا
تَعْلَمُونَ شَيْئًا وَّجَعَلَ لَكُمُ السَّمْعَ وَالْأَبْصَارَ
وَالْأَفْئِدَةَ لَعَلَّكُمْ تَشْكُرُونَ ۝

3. وَلَقَدْ كَرَّمْنَا بَنِيٓ اٰدَمَ وَحَمَلْنٰهُمْ فِي
الْبَرِّ وَالْبَحْرِ وَرَزَقْنٰهُمْ مِّنَ الطَّيِّبٰتِ
وَفَضَّلْنٰهُمْ عَلٰى كَثِيرٍ مِّمَّنْ خَلَقْنَا تَفْضِيلًا ۝

4. أَلَمْ تَرَوْا أَنَّ اللّٰهَ سَخَّرَ لَكُمْ مَّا
فِي السَّمٰوٰتِ وَمَا فِي الْأَرْضِ وَأَسْبَغَ
عَلَيْكُمْ نِعَمَهُ ظَاهِرَةً وَّبَاطِنَةً ۗ وَمِنَ
النَّاسِ مَنْ يُّجَادِلُ فِي اللّٰهِ بِغَيْرِ عِلْمٍ
وَّلَا هُدًى وَّلَا كِتٰبٍ مُّنِيرٍ ۝

5. أَوَلَمْ يَرَ الْإِنْسَانُ أَنَّا خَلَقْنٰهُ مِنْ
نُّطْفَةٍ فَإِذَا هُوَ خَصِيمٌ مُّبِينٌ ۝
وَضَرَبَ لَنَا مَثَلًا وَّنَسِيَ خَلْقَهُ ۖ
قَالَ مَنْ يُّحْيِ الْعِظَامَ وَهِيَ رَمِيمٌ ۝

5. Hath not man seen that We have created him from a drop of seed? Yet lo! he is an open opponent.

And he hath coined for Us a similitude, and hath forgotten the fact of his creation, saying: Who will revive these bones when they have rotted away?

36:77–78

6. Allah it is Who appointed for you the earth for a dwelling–place and the sky for a canopy, and fashioned you and perfected your shapes, and hath provided you with good things. Such is Allah, your Lord. Then blessed be Allah, the Lord of the Worlds!

40:64

7. Allah it is Who hath made the sea of service unto you that the ships may run thereon by His command, and that ye may seek of His bounty, and that haply ye may be thankful;

And hath made of service unto you whatsoever is in the heavens and whatsoever is in the earth; it is all from Him. Lo! herein verily are portents for people who reflect.

45:12–13

8. O mankind! Lo! We have created you male and female, and have made you nations and tribes that ye may know one another. Lo! the noblest of you, in the sight of Allah, is the best in conduct. Lo! Allah is Knower, Aware.

49:13

9. By the fig and the olive,
By Mount *Sinai,*
And by this land made safe;

Surely We created man of the best stature.

95:1–4

6. اَللّٰهُ الَّذِیْ جَعَلَ لَكُمُ الْاَرْضَ قَرَارًا
وَّ السَّمَآءَ بِنَآءً وَّ صَوَّرَكُمْ فَاَحْسَنَ
صُوَرَكُمْ وَ رَزَقَكُمْ مِّنَ الطَّيِّبٰتِ ؕ ذٰلِكُمُ
اللّٰهُ رَبُّكُمْ ۚۖ فَتَبٰرَكَ اللّٰهُ رَبُّ الْعٰلَمِيْنَ ﴿۶۴﴾

7. اَللّٰهُ الَّذِیْ سَخَّرَ لَكُمُ الْبَحْرَ لِتَجْرِیَ
الْفُلْكُ فِيْهِ بِاَمْرِهٖ وَ لِتَبْتَغُوْا مِنْ
فَضْلِهٖ وَ لَعَلَّكُمْ تَشْكُرُوْنَ ﴿۱۲﴾
وَ سَخَّرَ لَكُمْ مَّا فِی السَّمٰوٰتِ وَ مَا فِی
الْاَرْضِ جَمِيْعًا مِّنْهُ ؕ اِنَّ فِیْ ذٰلِكَ
لَاٰيٰتٍ لِّقَوْمٍ يَّتَفَكَّرُوْنَ ﴿۱۳﴾

8. يٰۤاَيُّهَا النَّاسُ اِنَّا خَلَقْنٰكُمْ مِّنْ ذَكَرٍ
وَّ اُنْثٰى وَ جَعَلْنٰكُمْ شُعُوْبًا وَّ قَبَآئِلَ
لِتَعَارَفُوْا ؕ اِنَّ اَكْرَمَكُمْ عِنْدَ اللّٰهِ اَتْقٰىكُمْ ؕ
اِنَّ اللّٰهَ عَلِيْمٌ خَبِيْرٌ ﴿۱۳﴾

9. وَ التِّيْنِ وَ الزَّيْتُوْنِ ۙ﴿۱﴾
وَ طُوْرِ سِيْنِيْنَ ۙ﴿۲﴾
وَ هٰذَا الْبَلَدِ الْاَمِيْنِ ۙ﴿۳﴾
لَقَدْ خَلَقْنَا الْاِنْسَانَ فِیْۤ اَحْسَنِ
تَقْوِيْمٍ ۙ﴿۴﴾

See also: Man: Allah's vicegerent.

DIRECTION AND DEVIATION

1. Say: Lo! the guidance of Allah (Himself) is Guid ance.

2:120

2. Say: (O Muhammad): Lo! the guidance is Allah's Guidance.

3:73

3. And whomsoever it is Allah's Will to guide, He expandeth his bosom unto the Surrender, and whomsoever it is His will to send astray, He maketh his bosom close and narrow as if he were engaged in sheer ascent. Thus Allah layeth ignominy upon those who believe not.

6:125

4. And Allah summoneth to the abode of Peace, and leadeth whom He will to a Straight path.

10:25

5. Say: O mankind! Now hath the Truth from your Lord come unto you. So whosoever is guided, is guided only for (the good of) his soul, and whosoever erreth, erreth only against it. And I am not a warder over you.

10:108

6. Whosoever goeth right, it is only for (the good of) his own soul that he goeth right, and whosoever erreth, erreth only to its hurt. No laden soul can bear another's load.

1. قُلْ إِنَّ هُدَى اللَّهِ هُوَ الْهُدَىٰ

2. قُلْ إِنَّ الْهُدَىٰ هُدَى اللَّهِ

3. فَمَنْ يُرِدِ اللَّهُ أَنْ يَهْدِيَهُ يَشْرَحْ صَدْرَهُ
لِلْإِسْلَامِ ۖ وَمَنْ يُرِدْ أَنْ يُضِلَّهُ يَجْعَلْ
صَدْرَهُ ضَيِّقًا حَرَجًا كَأَنَّمَا يَصَّعَّدُ فِي
السَّمَاءِ ۚ كَذَٰلِكَ يَجْعَلُ اللَّهُ الرِّجْسَ
عَلَى الَّذِينَ لَا يُؤْمِنُونَ ۝

4. وَاللَّهُ يَدْعُو إِلَىٰ دَارِ السَّلَامِ وَيَهْدِي
مَنْ يَشَاءُ إِلَىٰ صِرَاطٍ مُسْتَقِيمٍ ۝

5. قُلْ يَا أَيُّهَا النَّاسُ قَدْ جَاءَكُمُ الْحَقُّ
مِنْ رَبِّكُمْ ۖ فَمَنِ اهْتَدَىٰ فَإِنَّمَا
يَهْتَدِي لِنَفْسِهِ ۖ وَمَنْ ضَلَّ فَإِنَّمَا يَضِلُّ
عَلَيْهَا ۖ وَمَا أَنَا عَلَيْكُمْ بِوَكِيلٍ ۝

6. مَنِ اهْتَدَىٰ فَإِنَّمَا يَهْتَدِي لِنَفْسِهِ ۖ
وَمَنْ ضَلَّ فَإِنَّمَا يَضِلُّ عَلَيْهَا ۚ وَلَا
تَزِرُ وَازِرَةٌ وِزْرَ أُخْرَىٰ ۗ وَمَا كُنَّا
مُعَذِّبِينَ حَتَّىٰ نَبْعَثَ رَسُولًا ۝

7. مَنْ يَهْدِ اللَّهُ فَهُوَ الْمُهْتَدِ ۖ وَمَنْ يُضْلِلْ
فَلَنْ تَجِدَ لَهُ وَلِيًّا مُرْشِدًا ۝

We never punish until We have sent a messenger.

17:15

7. He whom Allah guideth, he indeed is led aright, and he whom He sendeth astray, for him thou wilt not find a guiding friend.

18:17

8. Say: As for him who is in error, the Beneficent will verily prolong his span of life until, when they behold that which they were promised, whether it be punishment (in the world), or the Hour (of Doom), they will know who is worse in position and who is weaker as an army.

Allah increaseth in right guidance those who walk aright, and the good deeds which endure are better in thy Lord's sight for reward, and better for resort.

19:75–76

9. And he for whom Allah hath not appointed light, for him there is no light.

24:40

10. Nay, but those who do wrong follow their own lusts without knowledge. Who is able to guide him whom Allah hath sent astray? For such there are no helpers.

30:29

11. He whom Allah sendeth astray, for him there is no guide.

And he whom Allah guideth, for him there can be no misleader.

39:36–37

12. He whom Allah sendeth astray, for him there is no protecting friend after Him.

42:44

13. He whom Allah sendeth astray, for him there is no road.

42:46

8. قُلْ مَنْ كَانَ فِي الضَّلٰلَةِ فَلْيَمْدُدْ لَهُ
الرَّحْمٰنُ مَدًّا ۚ حَتّٰٓى إِذَا رَأَوْا مَا
يُوعَدُونَ إِمَّا الْعَذَابَ وَإِمَّا السَّاعَةَ ۗ
فَسَيَعْلَمُونَ مَنْ هُوَ شَرٌّ مَّكَانًا
وَّأَضْعَفُ جُنْدًا ﴿٧٥﴾
وَيَزِيدُ اللّٰهُ الَّذِينَ اهْتَدَوْا هُدًى ۗ
وَالْبٰقِيٰتُ الصّٰلِحٰتُ خَيْرٌ عِنْدَ رَبِّكَ
ثَوَابًا وَّخَيْرٌ مَّرَدًّا ﴿٧٦﴾

9. وَمَنْ لَّمْ يَجْعَلِ اللّٰهُ لَهُ نُورًا فَمَا
لَهُ مِنْ نُّورٍ ﴿٤٠﴾

10. بَلِ اتَّبَعَ الَّذِينَ ظَلَمُوٓا أَهْوَآءَهُمْ
بِغَيْرِ عِلْمٍ ۚ فَمَنْ يَّهْدِي مَنْ أَضَلَّ
اللّٰهُ ۗ وَمَا لَهُمْ مِّنْ نّٰصِرِينَ ﴿٢٩﴾

11. وَمَنْ يُّضْلِلِ اللّٰهُ فَمَا لَهُ مِنْ
هَادٍ ﴿٣٦﴾
وَمَنْ يَّهْدِ اللّٰهُ فَمَا لَهُ مِنْ مُّضِلٍّ ۗ

12. وَمَنْ يُّضْلِلِ اللّٰهُ فَمَا لَهُ مِنْ وَّلِيٍّ
مِّنْ بَعْدِهٖ ۗ

13. وَمَنْ يُّضْلِلِ اللّٰهُ فَمَا لَهُ مِنْ سَبِيلٍ ﴿٤٦﴾

14. وَنَفْسٍ وَّمَا سَوّٰىهَا ﴿٧﴾
فَأَلْهَمَهَا فُجُورَهَا وَتَقْوٰىهَا ﴿٨﴾
قَدْ أَفْلَحَ مَنْ زَكّٰىهَا ﴿٩﴾

14. And a soul and Him Who perfected it

And inspired it (with conscience of) what is wrong for it and (what is) right for it.

He is indeed successful who causeth it to grow,

91:7–9

Ref: 2:10; 7:178, 186; 17:97; 18:13; 27:92; 29:6; 34:50; 39:23; 40:33, 38; 45:23; 47:17; 64:11; 76:2–3; 80:20; 90:10; 92:12.

DIRECTION OF HOLY *K'ABAH*

1. سَيَقُولُ السُّفَهَاءُ مِنَ النَّاسِ مَا وَلَّاهُمْ عَنْ
قِبْلَتِهِمُ الَّتِي كَانُوا عَلَيْهَا ۚ قُل لِّلَّهِ الْمَشْرِقُ وَ
الْمَغْرِبُ ۚ يَهْدِي مَن يَشَاءُ إِلَىٰ صِرَاطٍ مُّسْتَقِيمٍ ﴿١٤٢﴾
وَكَذَٰلِكَ جَعَلْنَاكُمْ أُمَّةً وَسَطًا لِّتَكُونُوا شُهَدَاءَ
عَلَى النَّاسِ وَيَكُونَ الرَّسُولُ عَلَيْكُمْ شَهِيدًا ۗ
وَمَا جَعَلْنَا الْقِبْلَةَ الَّتِي كُنتَ عَلَيْهَا إِلَّا لِنَعْلَمَ
مَن يَتَّبِعُ الرَّسُولَ مِمَّن يَنقَلِبُ عَلَىٰ عَقِبَيْهِ ۚ
وَإِن كَانَتْ لَكَبِيرَةً إِلَّا عَلَى الَّذِينَ
هَدَى اللَّهُ ۗ وَمَا كَانَ اللَّهُ لِيُضِيعَ إِيمَانَكُمْ ۚ
إِنَّ اللَّهَ بِالنَّاسِ لَرَءُوفٌ رَّحِيمٌ ﴿١٤٣﴾
قَدْ نَرَىٰ تَقَلُّبَ وَجْهِكَ فِي السَّمَاءِ ۖ فَلَنُوَلِّيَنَّكَ
قِبْلَةً تَرْضَاهَا ۚ فَوَلِّ وَجْهَكَ شَطْرَ الْمَسْجِدِ
الْحَرَامِ ۚ وَحَيْثُ مَا كُنتُمْ فَوَلُّوا وُجُوهَكُمْ
شَطْرَهُ ۗ وَإِنَّ الَّذِينَ أُوتُوا الْكِتَابَ لَيَعْلَمُونَ
أَنَّهُ الْحَقُّ مِن رَّبِّهِمْ ۗ وَمَا اللَّهُ بِغَافِلٍ
عَمَّا يَعْمَلُونَ ﴿١٤٤﴾
وَلَئِنْ أَتَيْتَ الَّذِينَ أُوتُوا الْكِتَابَ بِكُلِّ
آيَةٍ مَّا تَبِعُوا قِبْلَتَكَ ۚ وَمَا أَنتَ بِتَابِعٍ
قِبْلَتَهُمْ ۚ وَمَا بَعْضُهُم بِتَابِعٍ قِبْلَةَ بَعْضٍ ۚ
وَلَئِنِ اتَّبَعْتَ أَهْوَاءَهُم مِّن بَعْدِ مَا جَاءَكَ
مِنَ الْعِلْمِ ۙ إِنَّكَ إِذًا لَّمِنَ الظَّالِمِينَ ﴿١٤٥﴾

1. The foolish of the people will say: What hath turned them from the *qiblah*, which they formerly observed? Say: Unto Allah belong the East and the West. He guideth whom He will unto a straight path.

Thus We have appointed you a middle nation, that ye may be witnesses against mankind, and that the messenger may be a witness against you. And We appointed the *qiblah* which ye formerly observed only that We might know him who followeth the messenger, from him who turneth on his heels. In truth it was a hard (test) save for those whom Allah guided. But it was not Allah's purpose that your faith should be in vain, for Allah is Full of Pity, Merciful towards mankind.

We have seen the turning of thy face to heaven (for guidance, O Muhammad). And now verily We shall make thee turn (in prayer) toward a *qiblah* which is dear to thee. So turn thy face toward the Inviolable Place of Worship and ye (O Muslims), wheresoever ye may be, turn your faces (when ye pray) toward it. Lo! those who have received the Scripture know that (this Revelation) is the Truth from their Lord. And Allah is not unaware of what they do.

And even if you broughtest unto those who have received the Scripture all kinds of, portents, they would not follow thy *qiblah;* nor canst thou be a follower of their *qiblah,* nor are some of them followers of the *qiblah* of others. And if thou shouldst follow their desires after the knowledge which hath come unto thee, then surely wert thou of the evil–doers.

2:142–145

DISBELIEVERS AND POLYTHEISTS

1 إِنَّ الَّذِينَ كَفَرُوا سَوَاءٌ عَلَيْهِمْ ءَأَنذَرْتَهُمْ
أَمْ لَمْ تُنذِرْهُمْ لَا يُؤْمِنُونَ ⑥
خَتَمَ اللَّهُ عَلَىٰ قُلُوبِهِمْ وَعَلَىٰ سَمْعِهِمْ ۖ وَعَلَىٰ
أَبْصَارِهِمْ غِشَاوَةٌ ۖ وَلَهُمْ عَذَابٌ عَظِيمٌ ⑦

2. مَا يَوَدُّ الَّذِينَ كَفَرُوا مِنْ أَهْلِ الْكِتَٰبِ وَ
لَا الْمُشْرِكِينَ أَن يُنَزَّلَ عَلَيْكُم مِّنْ خَيْرٍ
مِّن رَّبِّكُمْ ۗ وَاللَّهُ يَخْتَصُّ بِرَحْمَتِهِ مَن
يَشَاءُ ۚ وَاللَّهُ ذُو الْفَضْلِ الْعَظِيمِ ⑩⑤

3. إِنَّ الَّذِينَ كَفَرُوا وَمَاتُوا وَهُمْ كُفَّارٌ أُولَٰئِكَ
عَلَيْهِمْ لَعْنَةُ اللَّهِ وَالْمَلَٰئِكَةِ وَالنَّاسِ أَجْمَعِينَ ⑯①
خَٰلِدِينَ فِيهَا ۖ لَا يُخَفَّفُ عَنْهُمُ الْعَذَابُ
وَلَا هُمْ يُنظَرُونَ ⑯②

4. إِذْ تَبَرَّأَ الَّذِينَ اتُّبِعُوا مِنَ الَّذِينَ اتَّبَعُوا
وَرَأَوُا الْعَذَابَ وَتَقَطَّعَتْ بِهِمُ الْأَسْبَابُ ⑯⑥
وَقَالَ الَّذِينَ اتَّبَعُوا لَوْ أَنَّ لَنَا كَرَّةً فَنَتَبَرَّأَ
مِنْهُمْ كَمَا تَبَرَّءُوا مِنَّا ۗ كَذَٰلِكَ يُرِيهِمُ اللَّهُ
أَعْمَٰلَهُمْ حَسَرَٰتٍ عَلَيْهِمْ ۖ وَمَا هُم بِخَٰرِجِينَ
مِنَ النَّارِ ⑯⑦

5. زُيِّنَ لِلَّذِينَ كَفَرُوا الْحَيَوٰةُ الدُّنْيَا وَ
يَسْخَرُونَ مِنَ الَّذِينَ ءَامَنُوا ۘ وَالَّذِينَ
اتَّقَوْا فَوْقَهُمْ يَوْمَ الْقِيَٰمَةِ ۗ وَاللَّهُ يَرْزُقُ
مَن يَشَاءُ بِغَيْرِ حِسَابٍ ②①②

1. As for the disbelievers, whether thou warn them or thou warn them not it is all one for them; they believĕ not.

Allah hath sealed their hearning and their hearts, and on their eyes there is a covering. Theirs will be an awful doom.

2:6–7

2. Neither those who disbelieve among the People of the Scripture nor the idolaters love that there should be sent down unto you any good thing from your Lord. But Allah chooseth for His mercy whom He will, and Allah is of Infinite Bounty.

2:105

3. Lo! those who disbelieve, and die while they are disbelievers; on them is the curse of Allah and of angels and of men combined.

They ever dwell therein. The doom will not be lightened for them, neither will they be reprieved.

2:161–162

4. (On the day) when those who were followed disown those who followed (them), and they behold the doom, and all their aims collapse with them.

And those who were but followers will say: If a return were possible for us, we would disown them even as they have disowned us. Thus will Allah show them their own deeds as anguish for them, and they will not emerge from the Fire

2:166–167

5. Beautified is the life of the world for those who disbelieve; they make a jest of the believers. But those who keep their duty to Allah will be above them on the Day of Resurrection. Allah giveth without stint to whom He will.

2:212

6. Allah is the Protecting Friend of those who believe. He bringeth them out of darkness into light. As for those who disbelieve, their patrons are false deities. They bring them out of light into darkness. Such are rightful owners of the Fire. They will abide therein.

2:257

7. (On that day) neither the riches nor the progeny of those who disbelieve will aught avail them with Allah. They will be fuel for Fire.

3:10

8. Let not their conduct grieve thee, who run easily to disbelief, for lo! they injure Allah not at all. It is Allah's Will to assign them no portion in the Hereafter, and theirs will be an awful doom.

Those who purchase disbelief at the price of faith harm Allah not at all, but theirs will be a painful doom.

And let not those who disbelieve imagine that the rein We give them bodeth good unto their souls. We only give them rein that they may grow in sinfulness. And theirs will be a shameful doom.

3:176–178

9. As for those who disbelieve, lo! if all that is in the earth were theirs, and as much again therewith, to ransom them from the doom on the day of Resurrection,

6. اَللّٰهُ وَلِيُّ الَّذِيْنَ اٰمَنُوْا يُخْرِجُهُمْ مِّنَ
الظُّلُمٰتِ اِلَى النُّوْرِ ۗ وَالَّذِيْنَ كَفَرُوْٓا اَوْلِيٰٓـئُهُمُ
الطَّاغُوْتُ يُخْرِجُوْنَهُمْ مِّنَ النُّوْرِ اِلَى الظُّلُمٰتِ ۗ
اُولٰٓئِكَ اَصْحٰبُ النَّارِ ۚ هُمْ فِيْهَا خٰلِدُوْنَ

7. اِنَّ الَّذِيْنَ كَفَرُوْا لَنْ تُغْنِيَ عَنْهُمْ اَمْوَالُهُمْ
وَلَآ اَوْلَادُهُمْ مِّنَ اللّٰهِ شَيْـًٔا ۗ وَاُولٰٓئِكَ
هُمْ وَقُوْدُ النَّارِ

8. وَلَا يَحْزُنْكَ الَّذِيْنَ يُسَارِعُوْنَ فِي الْكُفْرِ ۚ
اِنَّهُمْ لَنْ يَّضُرُّوا اللّٰهَ شَيْـًٔا ۗ يُرِيْدُ اللّٰهُ
اَلَّا يَجْعَلَ لَهُمْ حَظًّا فِي الْاٰخِرَةِ ۚ وَ
لَهُمْ عَذَابٌ عَظِيْمٌ

اِنَّ الَّذِيْنَ اشْتَرَوُا الْكُفْرَ بِالْاِيْمَانِ
لَنْ يَّضُرُّوا اللّٰهَ شَيْـًٔا ۚ وَلَهُمْ عَذَابٌ اَلِيْمٌ

وَلَا يَحْسَبَنَّ الَّذِيْنَ كَفَرُوْٓا اَنَّمَا نُمْلِيْ
لَهُمْ خَيْرٌ لِّاَنْفُسِهِمْ ۗ اِنَّمَا نُمْلِيْ لَهُمْ
لِيَزْدَادُوْٓا اِثْمًا ۚ وَلَهُمْ عَذَابٌ مُّهِيْنٌ

9. اِنَّ الَّذِيْنَ كَفَرُوْا لَوْ اَنَّ لَهُمْ مَّا فِي الْاَرْضِ
جَمِيْعًا وَّمِثْلَهٗ مَعَهٗ لِيَفْتَدُوْا بِهٖ مِنْ
عَذَابِ يَوْمِ الْقِيٰمَةِ مَا تُقُبِّلَ مِنْهُمْ ۚ
وَلَهُمْ عَذَابٌ اَلِيْمٌ

يُرِيْدُوْنَ اَنْ يَّخْرُجُوْا مِنَ النَّارِ وَمَا
هُمْ بِخٰرِجِيْنَ مِنْهَا ۡ وَلَهُمْ عَذَابٌ مُّقِيْمٌ

it would not be accepted from them. Theirs will be a painful doom.

They will wish to come forth from the Fire, but they will not come forth from it. Theirs will be a lasting doom.

5:36–37

10. Lo! they who deny Our revelations and scorn them, for them the gates of Heaven will not be opened nor will they enter the Garden until the camel goeth through the needle's eye. Thus do We requite the guilty.

7:40

11. Lo! the worst of beasts in Allah's sight are the ungrateful who will not believe;

8:55

12. O ye who believe! The idolaters only are unclean. So let them not come near the Inviolable Place of Worship after this their year. If ye fear poverty (from the loss of their merchandise) Allah shall preserve you of His bounty if He will. Lo! Allah is Knower, Wise.

9:28

13. And if thou wonderest, then wondrous is their saying: When we are dust, are we then forsooth (to be raised) in a new creation? Such are they who disbelieve in their Lord; such have carcans on their necks; such are rightful owners of the Fire, they will abide therein.

And they bid thee hasten on the evil rather than the good, when exemplary punishments have indeed occured before them. But lo! thy Lord is rich in pardon for mankind despite their wrong,

10. إِنَّ الَّذِينَ كَذَّبُوا بِآيَاتِنَا وَاسْتَكْبَرُوا
عَنْهَا لَا تُفَتَّحُ لَهُمْ أَبْوَابُ السَّمَاءِ وَلَا
يَدْخُلُونَ الْجَنَّةَ حَتَّىٰ يَلِجَ الْجَمَلُ فِي
سَمِّ الْخِيَاطِ ۚ وَكَذَٰلِكَ نَجْزِي الْمُجْرِمِينَ ﴿٤٠﴾

11. إِنَّ شَرَّ الدَّوَابِّ عِندَ اللَّهِ الَّذِينَ كَفَرُوا
فَهُمْ لَا يُؤْمِنُونَ ﴿٥٥﴾

12. يَا أَيُّهَا الَّذِينَ آمَنُوا إِنَّمَا الْمُشْرِكُونَ
نَجَسٌ فَلَا يَقْرَبُوا الْمَسْجِدَ الْحَرَامَ
بَعْدَ عَامِهِمْ هَٰذَا ۚ وَإِنْ خِفْتُمْ عَيْلَةً
فَسَوْفَ يُغْنِيكُمُ اللَّهُ مِن فَضْلِهِ إِن شَاءَ ۚ
إِنَّ اللَّهَ عَلِيمٌ حَكِيمٌ ﴿٢٨﴾

13. وَإِن تَعْجَبْ فَعَجَبٌ قَوْلُهُمْ أَإِذَا كُنَّا
تُرَابًا أَإِنَّا لَفِي خَلْقٍ جَدِيدٍ ۗ أُولَٰئِكَ
الَّذِينَ كَفَرُوا بِرَبِّهِمْ ۖ وَأُولَٰئِكَ
الْأَغْلَالُ فِي أَعْنَاقِهِمْ ۖ وَأُولَٰئِكَ أَصْحَابُ
النَّارِ ۖ هُمْ فِيهَا خَالِدُونَ ﴿٥﴾
وَيَسْتَعْجِلُونَكَ بِالسَّيِّئَةِ قَبْلَ الْحَسَنَةِ
وَقَدْ خَلَتْ مِن قَبْلِهِمُ الْمَثُلَاتُ ۗ وَإِنَّ
رَبَّكَ لَذُو مَغْفِرَةٍ لِّلنَّاسِ عَلَىٰ ظُلْمِهِمْ ۖ
وَإِنَّ رَبَّكَ لَشَدِيدُ الْعِقَابِ ﴿٦﴾
وَيَقُولُ الَّذِينَ كَفَرُوا لَوْلَا أُنزِلَ
عَلَيْهِ آيَةٌ مِّن رَّبِّهِ ۗ إِنَّمَا أَنتَ
مُنذِرٌ ۖ وَلِكُلِّ قَوْمٍ هَادٍ ﴿٧﴾

and lo! thy Lord is strong in punishment.

Those who disbelieve say: If only some portent were sent down upon him from his Lord! Thou art a warner only and for every folk is a guide.

13:5–7

14. It may be that those who disbelieve wish ardently that they were Muslims.

Let them eat and enjoy life, and let (false) hope beguile them. They will come to know!

15:2–3

15. And (bethink you of) the day when We raise up of every nation a witness, then there is no leave for disbelievers, nor are they allowed to make amends.

And when those who did wrong behold the doom, it will not be made light for them, nor will they be reprieved.

And when those who ascribed partners to Allah behold those partners of theirs, they will say: Our Lord! these are our partners unto whom we used to cry instead of Thee. But they will fling to them the saying: Lo! ye verily are liars!

And they proffer unto Allah submission on that day, and all that they used to invent hath failed them.

For those who disbelieve and debar (men) from the way of Allah, We add doom to doom because they wrought corruption.

16:84–88

16. And they say: When we are bones and fragments, shall we, forsooth, be raised up as a new creation?

Say: Be ye stones or iron;

14. رُبَمَا يَوَدُّ الَّذِينَ كَفَرُوا لَوْ كَانُوا
مُسْلِمِينَ ﴿٢﴾
ذَرْهُمْ يَأْكُلُوا وَيَتَمَتَّعُوا وَيُلْهِهِمُ
الْأَمَلُ فَسَوْفَ يَعْلَمُونَ ﴿٣﴾
15. وَيَوْمَ نَبْعَثُ مِنْ كُلِّ أُمَّةٍ شَهِيدًا ثُمَّ
لَا يُؤْذَنُ لِلَّذِينَ كَفَرُوا وَلَا هُمْ يُسْتَعْتَبُونَ ﴿٨٤﴾
وَإِذَا رَأَى الَّذِينَ ظَلَمُوا الْعَذَابَ فَلَا
يُخَفَّفُ عَنْهُمْ وَلَا هُمْ يُنْظَرُونَ ﴿٨٥﴾
وَإِذَا رَأَى الَّذِينَ أَشْرَكُوا شُرَكَاءَهُمْ
قَالُوا رَبَّنَا هَٰؤُلَاءِ شُرَكَاؤُنَا الَّذِينَ كُنَّا
نَدْعُوا مِنْ دُونِكَ ۖ فَأَلْقَوْا إِلَيْهِمُ الْقَوْلَ
إِنَّكُمْ لَكَاذِبُونَ ﴿٨٦﴾
وَأَلْقَوْا إِلَى اللَّهِ يَوْمَئِذٍ السَّلَمَ وَضَلَّ
عَنْهُمْ مَا كَانُوا يَفْتَرُونَ ﴿٨٧﴾
الَّذِينَ كَفَرُوا وَصَدُّوا عَنْ سَبِيلِ اللَّهِ
زِدْنَاهُمْ عَذَابًا فَوْقَ الْعَذَابِ بِمَا كَانُوا
يُفْسِدُونَ ﴿٨٨﴾
16. وَقَالُوا أَإِذَا كُنَّا عِظَامًا وَرُفَاتًا أَإِنَّا
لَمَبْعُوثُونَ خَلْقًا جَدِيدًا ﴿٤٩﴾
قُلْ كُونُوا حِجَارَةً أَوْ حَدِيدًا ﴿٥٠﴾
أَوْ خَلْقًا مِمَّا يَكْبُرُ فِي صُدُورِكُمْ ۚ
فَسَيَقُولُونَ مَنْ يُعِيدُنَا ۖ قُلِ الَّذِي
فَطَرَكُمْ أَوَّلَ مَرَّةٍ ۚ فَسَيُنْغِضُونَ إِلَيْكَ
رُءُوسَهُمْ وَيَقُولُونَ مَتَىٰ هُوَ ۖ قُلْ

Or some created thing that is yet greater in your thoughts! Then they will say: Who shall bring us back (to life)? Say: He Who created you at the first. Then will they shake their heads at thee, and say: When will it be? Say:

It will perhaps be soon;
17:49–51

17. Seest thou not that We have set the devils on the disbelievers to confound them with confusion?

So make no haste against them (O Muhammad). We do but number unto them a sum (of days).
19:83–84

18. As for those who disbelieve, their deeds are as a mirage in a desert. The thirsty one supposeth it to be water till he cometh unto it and findeth it naught, and findeth in the place thereof, . Allah, Who payeth him his due; and Allah is swift at reckoning:
24:39

19. Those who disbelieve say unto those who believe: Follow our way (of religion) and we verily will bear your sins (for you). They cannot bear aught of their sins. Lo! they verily are liars.

But they verily will bear their own loads and other loads beside their own, and they verily will be questioned on the Day of Resurrection concerning that which they invented.
29:12–13

20. But as for those who disbelieve, for them is fire of hell; it taketh not complete effect upon them so that they can die, nor is its torment lightened for them. Thus We

عَسٰى اَنْ يَّكُوْنَ قَرِيْبًا ﴿٥١﴾
17. اَلَمْ تَرَ اَنَّاۤ اَرْسَلْنَا الشَّيٰطِيْنَ عَلَى
الْكٰفِرِيْنَ تَؤُزُّهُمْ اَزًّا ﴿٨٣﴾
فَلَا تَعْجَلْ عَلَيْهِمْ ؕ اِنَّمَا نَعُدُّ
لَهُمْ عَدًّا ﴿٨٤﴾
18. وَالَّذِيْنَ كَفَرُوْۤا اَعْمَالُهُمْ كَسَرَابٍۭ
بِقِيْعَةٍ يَّحْسَبُهُ الظَّمْاٰنُ مَآءً ؕ حَتّٰۤى
اِذَا جَآءَهٗ لَمْ يَجِدْهُ شَيْـًٔا وَّوَجَدَ اللّٰهَ
عِنْدَهٗ فَوَفّٰىهُ حِسَابَهٗ ؕ وَاللّٰهُ
سَرِيْعُ الْحِسَابِ ﴿٣٩﴾
19. وَقَالَ الَّذِيْنَ كَفَرُوْا لِلَّذِيْنَ اٰمَنُوا
اتَّبِعُوْا سَبِيْلَنَا وَلْنَحْمِلْ خَطٰيٰكُمْ ؕ
وَمَا هُمْ بِحٰمِلِيْنَ مِنْ خَطٰيٰهُمْ مِّنْ
شَیْءٍ ؕ اِنَّهُمْ لَكٰذِبُوْنَ ﴿١٢﴾
وَلَيَحْمِلُنَّ اَثْقَالَهُمْ وَاَثْقَالًا مَّعَ
اَثْقَالِهِمْ ۫ وَلَيُسْـَٔلُنَّ يَوْمَ الْقِيٰمَةِ
عَمَّا كَانُوْا يَفْتَرُوْنَ ﴿١٣﴾
20. وَالَّذِيْنَ كَفَرُوْا لَهُمْ نَارُ جَهَنَّمَ ۚ لَا
يُقْضٰى عَلَيْهِمْ فَيَمُوْتُوْا وَلَا يُخَفَّفُ
عَنْهُمْ مِّنْ عَذَابِهَا ؕ كَذٰلِكَ
نَجْزِيْ كُلَّ كَفُوْرٍ ﴿٣٦﴾
21. وَقَالَ الَّذِيْنَ كَفَرُوْا لَا تَسْمَعُوْا لِهٰذَا الْقُرْاٰنِ
وَالْغَوْا فِيْهِ لَعَلَّكُمْ تَغْلِبُوْنَ ﴿٢٦﴾
فَلَنُذِيْقَنَّ الَّذِيْنَ كَفَرُوْا عَذَابًا شَدِيْدًا ۙ وَّ

punish every ingrate.
35:36

21. Those who disbelieve say: Heed not this Qur'ān, and drown the hearing of it; haply ye may conquer!

But verily We shall cause those who disbelieve to taste an awful doom, and verily

لَنَجْزِيَنَّهُمْ أَسْوَأَ الَّذِي كَانُوا يَعْمَلُونَ ﴿٢٧﴾
ذَٰلِكَ جَزَاءُ أَعْدَاءِ اللَّهِ النَّارُ لَهُمْ فِيهَا دَارُ
الْخُلْدِ جَزَاءً بِمَا كَانُوا بِآيَاتِنَا يَجْحَدُونَ ﴿٢٨﴾

We shall requite them the worst of what they used to do.

That is the reward of Allah's enemies: the Fire—Therein is their immortal home, payment forasmuch as they denied Our revelations.

41:26–28

DISOBEDIENCE TO ALLAH AND HIS MESSENGER (PBUH)

1. وَمَن يَعْصِ اللَّهَ وَرَسُولَهُ وَيَتَعَدَّ
حُدُودَهُ يُدْخِلْهُ نَارًا خَالِدًا فِيهَا
وَلَهُ عَذَابٌ مُّهِينٌ ﴿١٤﴾

1. And whoso disobeyeth Allah and His messenger and transgresseth His limits, He will make him enter Fire, where he will dwell for ever; his will be a shameful doom.

4:14

2. وَمَن يُشَاقِقِ الرَّسُولَ مِن بَعْدِ مَا تَبَيَّنَ
لَهُ الْهُدَىٰ وَيَتَّبِعْ غَيْرَ سَبِيلِ الْمُؤْمِنِينَ
نُوَلِّهِ مَا تَوَلَّىٰ وَنُصْلِهِ جَهَنَّمَ وَسَاءَتْ مَصِيرًا ﴿١١٥﴾

2. And whoso opposeth the messenger after the guidance (of Allah) hath been manifested unto him, and followeth other than the believer's way, We appoint for him that unto which he himself hath turned, and expose him unto hell—a hapless journey's end!

4:115

3. أَلَمْ يَعْلَمُوا أَنَّهُ مَن يُحَادِدِ اللَّهَ وَرَسُولَهُ
فَأَنَّ لَهُ نَارَ جَهَنَّمَ خَالِدًا فِيهَا ذَٰلِكَ
الْخِزْيُ الْعَظِيمُ ﴿٦٣﴾

3. Know they not that whoso opposeth Allah and His messenger, his portion verily is hell, to abide therein? That is the extreme abasement.

9:63

4. وَمَا كَانَ لِمُؤْمِنٍ وَلَا مُؤْمِنَةٍ
إِذَا قَضَى اللَّهُ وَرَسُولُهُ أَمْرًا أَن
يَكُونَ لَهُمُ الْخِيَرَةُ مِنْ أَمْرِهِمْ
وَمَن يَعْصِ اللَّهَ وَرَسُولَهُ فَقَدْ
ضَلَّ ضَلَالًا مُّبِينًا ﴿٣٦﴾

4. And it becometh not a believing man or a believing woman, when Allah and His messenger have decided an affair (for them), that they should (after that) claim any say in their affair; and whoso is rebellious to Allah and His messenger, he verily goeth astray in error manifest.

33:36

DISBELIEVERS AND POLYTHEISTS
See also: Intransigence of Disbelievers.

5. Hast thou not observed those who were forbidden conspiracy and afterward returned to that which they had been forbidden, and (now) conspire together for crime and wrongdoing and disobedience toward the messenger? And when they come unto thee they greet thee with a greeting wherewith Allah greeteth thee not, and say within themselves: Why should Allah punish us for what we say? Hell will suffice them; they will feel the heat thereof—a hapless journey's end!

O ye who believe! When ye conspire together, conspire not together for crime and wrongdoing and disobedience toward the messenger, but conspire together for righteousness and piety, and keep your duty toward Allah, unto Whom ye will be gathered.

58:8–9

5. اَلَمْ تَرَ اِلَى الَّذِيْنَ نُهُوْا عَنِ النَّجْوٰى
ثُمَّ يَعُوْدُوْنَ لِمَا نُهُوْا عَنْهُ وَيَتَنٰجَوْنَ
بِالْاِثْمِ وَالْعُدْوَانِ وَمَعْصِيَتِ الرَّسُوْلِ
وَاِذَا جَآءُوْكَ حَيَّوْكَ بِمَا لَمْ يُحَيِّكَ
بِهِ اللّٰهُ وَيَقُوْلُوْنَ فِيْٓ اَنْفُسِهِمْ لَوْلَا
يُعَذِّبُنَا اللّٰهُ بِمَا نَقُوْلُ حَسْبُهُمْ جَهَنَّمُ
يَصْلَوْنَهَا فَبِئْسَ الْمَصِيْرُ ۝

يٰٓاَيُّهَا الَّذِيْنَ اٰمَنُوْٓا اِذَا تَنَاجَيْتُمْ فَلَا
تَتَنَاجَوْا بِالْاِثْمِ وَالْعُدْوَانِ وَمَعْصِيَتِ
الرَّسُوْلِ وَتَنَاجَوْا بِالْبِرِّ وَالتَّقْوٰى
وَاتَّقُوا اللّٰهَ الَّذِيْٓ اِلَيْهِ تُحْشَرُوْنَ ۝

6. And whoso disobeyeth Allah and His messenger, lo! his is fire of hell, wherein such dwell for ever:

72:23

6. وَمَنْ يَّعْصِ اللّٰهَ وَرَسُوْلَهٗ فَاِنَّ لَهٗ
نَارَ جَهَنَّمَ خٰلِدِيْنَ فِيْهَآ اَبَدًا ۝

Ref: 8:13.21;

See also: Submission to Allah and His Messenger (PBUH)

DISPUTE OF HUSBAND AND WIFE

1. And if ye fear a breach between them twain (the man and wife), appoint an arbiter from his folk and an arbiter from her folk. If they desire amendment Allah will make them of one mind. Lo! Allah is ever Knower, Aware.

4:35

2. If a woman feareth ill-treatment from her husband, or desertion, it is no sin for them twain if they make terms of peace between themselves. Peace is better. But greed hath been made present in the minds (of men). If ye do good and keep from evil, lo! Allah is ever Informed of what ye do.

4:128

3. But if they separate, Allah will compensate each out of His abundance. Allah is ever All–Embracing, All–Knowing.

4:130

1. وَاِنْ خِفْتُمْ شِقَاقَ بَيْنِهِمَا فَابْعَثُوْا
حَكَمًا مِّنْ اَهْلِهٖ وَحَكَمًا مِّنْ اَهْلِهَا
اِنْ يُّرِيْدَآ اِصْلَاحًا يُّوَفِّقِ اللّٰهُ بَيْنَهُمَا
اِنَّ اللّٰهَ كَانَ عَلِيْمًا خَبِيْرًا ﴿٣٥﴾

2. وَاِنِ امْرَاَةٌ خَافَتْ مِنْۢ بَعْلِهَا نُشُوْزًا اَوْ
اِعْرَاضًا فَلَا جُنَاحَ عَلَيْهِمَآ اَنْ يُّصْلِحَا
بَيْنَهُمَا صُلْحًا وَالصُّلْحُ خَيْرٌ وَاُحْضِرَتِ
الْاَنْفُسُ الشُّحَّ وَاِنْ تُحْسِنُوْا وَتَتَّقُوْا فَاِنَّ
اللّٰهَ كَانَ بِمَا تَعْمَلُوْنَ خَبِيْرًا ﴿١٢٨﴾

3. وَاِنْ يَّتَفَرَّقَا يُغْنِ اللّٰهُ كُلًّا مِّنْ سَعَتِهٖ
وَكَانَ اللّٰهُ وَاسِعًا حَكِيْمًا ﴿١٣٠﴾

See also: Conjugal Rights and Obligations.

DISSENSION

1. Work not confusion in the earth after the fair ordering (thereof), and call on Him in fear and hope. Lo! the mercy of Allah is nigh unto the good.
7:56

2. Lo! Allah upholdeth not the work of mischief-makers.
10:81

3. And those who break the covenant of Allah after ratifying it, and sever that which Allah hath commanded should be joined, and make mischief in the earth: theirs is the curse and theirs the ill abode.
13:25

4. But seek the abode of the Hereafter in that which Allah hath given thee and neglect not thy portion of the world and be thou kind even as Allah hath been kind to thee, and seek not corruption in the earth; lo! Allah loveth not corrupters.
28:77

5. Corruption doth appear on land and sea because of (the evil) which men's hands have done, that He may make them taste a part of that which they have done, in order that they may return.
30:41

1. وَلَا تُفْسِدُوا فِي الْأَرْضِ بَعْدَ إِصْلَاحِهَا
وَادْعُوهُ خَوْفًا وَطَمَعًا ۚ إِنَّ رَحْمَتَ اللَّهِ
قَرِيبٌ مِّنَ الْمُحْسِنِينَ ﴿٥٦﴾

2. إِنَّ اللَّهَ لَا يُصْلِحُ عَمَلَ الْمُفْسِدِينَ ﴿٨١﴾

3. وَالَّذِينَ يَنقُضُونَ عَهْدَ اللَّهِ مِن بَعْدِ
مِيثَاقِهِ وَيَقْطَعُونَ مَا أَمَرَ اللَّهُ بِهِ
أَن يُوصَلَ وَيُفْسِدُونَ فِي الْأَرْضِ ۙ
أُولَٰئِكَ لَهُمُ اللَّعْنَةُ وَلَهُمْ سُوءُ الدَّارِ ﴿٢٥﴾

4. وَابْتَغِ فِيمَا آتَاكَ اللَّهُ الدَّارَ الْآخِرَةَ
وَلَا تَنسَ نَصِيبَكَ مِنَ الدُّنْيَا ۖ وَ
أَحْسِن كَمَا أَحْسَنَ اللَّهُ إِلَيْكَ ۖ وَلَا تَبْغِ
الْفَسَادَ فِي الْأَرْضِ ۖ إِنَّ اللَّهَ لَا
يُحِبُّ الْمُفْسِدِينَ ﴿٧٧﴾

5. ظَهَرَ الْفَسَادُ فِي الْبَرِّ وَالْبَحْرِ بِمَا
كَسَبَتْ أَيْدِي النَّاسِ لِيُذِيقَهُم
بَعْضَ الَّذِي عَمِلُوا لَعَلَّهُمْ يَرْجِعُونَ ﴿٤١﴾

Ref: 5:32; 11:85; 27:14.

DISSIMULATION

1. O ye who believe! Render not vain your alms—giving by reproach and injury like him who spendeth his wealth only to be seen of men and believeth not in Allah and the Last Day. His likeness is as the likeness of a rock whereon is dust of earth; a rainstorm smiteth it, leaving it smooth and bare. They have no control of aught of that which they have gained. Allah guideth not the disbelieving folk.

2:264

1. يٰٓاَيُّهَا الَّذِيْنَ اٰمَنُوْا لَا تُبْطِلُوْا صَدَقٰتِكُمْ
بِالْمَنِّ وَالْاَذٰى كَالَّذِيْ يُنْفِقُ مَالَهٗ
رِئَآءَ النَّاسِ وَلَا يُؤْمِنُ بِاللّٰهِ وَالْيَوْمِ
الْاٰخِرِ فَمَثَلُهٗ كَمَثَلِ صَفْوَانٍ عَلَيْهِ
تُرَابٌ فَاَصَابَهٗ وَابِلٌ فَتَرَكَهٗ صَلْدًا
لَا يَقْدِرُوْنَ عَلٰى شَيْءٍ مِّمَّا كَسَبُوْا وَاللّٰهُ
لَا يَهْدِي الْقَوْمَ الْكٰفِرِيْنَ ﴿٢٦٤﴾

2. Be not as those who came forth from their dwellings boastfully and to be seen of men, and debar (men) from the way of Allah, while Allah is surrounding all they do.

8:47

2. وَلَا تَكُوْنُوْا كَالَّذِيْنَ خَرَجُوْا مِنْ دِيَارِهِمْ
بَطَرًا وَّرِئَآءَ النَّاسِ وَيَصُدُّوْنَ عَنْ
سَبِيْلِ اللّٰهِ وَاللّٰهُ بِمَا يَعْمَلُوْنَ مُحِيْطٌ ﴿٤٧﴾

3. Ah, woe unto worshippers

Who are heedless of their prayer;

Who would be seen (at worship)

Yet refuse small kindnesses!

107:4–7

3. فَوَيْلٌ لِّلْمُصَلِّيْنَ ﴿٤﴾
الَّذِيْنَ هُمْ عَنْ صَلَاتِهِمْ سَاهُوْنَ ﴿٥﴾
الَّذِيْنَ هُمْ يُرَآءُوْنَ ﴿٦﴾
وَيَمْنَعُوْنَ الْمَاعُوْنَ ﴿٧﴾

○

See also: Hypocrites.

DIVINE FORGIVENESS

1. Allah will not take you to task for that which is unintentional in your oaths. But He will take you to task for that which your hearts have garnered. Allah is Forgiving, Clement.

2:225

2. And when those who believe in Our revelations come unto thee, say: Peace be unto you! Your Lord hath prescribed for Himself mercy, that whoso of you doth evil and repenteth afterward thereof and doth right, (for him) lo! Allah is Forgiving, Merciful.

6:54

3. Then lo! thy Lord—for those who do evil in ignorance and afterward repent and amend—lo! (for them) thy Lord is afterward indeed Forgiving, Merciful.

16:119

1. لَا يُؤَاخِذُكُمُ اللّٰهُ بِاللَّغْوِ فِيْٓ اَيْمَانِكُمْ وَلٰكِنْ
يُّؤَاخِذُكُمْ بِمَا كَسَبَتْ قُلُوْبُكُمْ وَاللّٰهُ غَفُوْرٌ حَلِيْمٌ ﴿٢٢٥﴾

2. وَ اِذَا جَآءَكَ الَّذِيْنَ يُؤْمِنُوْنَ بِاٰيٰتِنَا فَقُلْ
سَلٰمٌ عَلَيْكُمْ كَتَبَ رَبُّكُمْ عَلٰى نَفْسِهِ
الرَّحْمَةَ اَنَّهٗ مَنْ عَمِلَ مِنْكُمْ سُوْٓءًا
بِجَهَالَةٍ ثُمَّ تَابَ مِنْ بَعْدِهٖ وَاَصْلَحَ
فَاَنَّهٗ غَفُوْرٌ رَّحِيْمٌ ﴿٥٤﴾

3. ثُمَّ اِنَّ رَبَّكَ لِلَّذِيْنَ عَمِلُوا السُّوْٓءَ بِجَهَالَةٍ
ثُمَّ تَابُوْا مِنْ بَعْدِ ذٰلِكَ وَ اَصْلَحُوْٓا اِنَّ
رَبَّكَ مِنْ بَعْدِهَا لَغَفُوْرٌ رَّحِيْمٌ ﴿١١٩﴾

See also: Divine Punishment.

DIVINE PLEASURE

1. Allah saith: This is a day in which their truthfulness profiteth the truthful, for theirs are Gardens underneath which rivers flow, wherein they are secure for ever, Allah taking pleasure in them and they in Him. That is the great triumph.

5:119

2. Allah promiseth to the believers, men and women, Gardens underneath which rivers flow, wherein they will abide—blessed dwellings in Gardens of Eden. And — greater (far)! — acceptance from Allah. That is the Supreme triumph.

9:72

3. And the first to lead the way, of the *Muhajirin* and the *Ansar* and those who followed them in goodness—Allah is well pleased with them and they are well pleased with Him, and He hath made ready for them Gardens underneath which rivers flow, wherein they will abide for ever: That is the Supreme triumph.

9:100

4. (And) lo! those who believe and do good works are the best of created beings.

Their reward is with their Lord: Gardens of Eden underneath which rivers flow, wherein they dwell for ever. Allah hath pleasure in them and they have pleasure in Him. This is (in store) for him who feareth his Lord.

98:7–8

1. قَالَ اللّٰهُ هٰذَا يَوْمُ يَنْفَعُ الصّٰدِقِيْنَ
صِدْقُهُمْ ۭ لَهُمْ جَنّٰتٌ تَجْرِيْ مِنْ تَحْتِهَا
الْاَنْهٰرُ خٰلِدِيْنَ فِيْهَآ اَبَدًا ۭ رَضِيَ اللّٰهُ
عَنْهُمْ وَرَضُوْا عَنْهُ ۭ ذٰلِكَ الْفَوْزُ الْعَظِيْمُ ﴿١١٩﴾

2. وَعَدَ اللّٰهُ الْمُؤْمِنِيْنَ وَالْمُؤْمِنٰتِ جَنّٰتٍ
تَجْرِيْ مِنْ تَحْتِهَا الْاَنْهٰرُ خٰلِدِيْنَ فِيْهَا
وَمَسٰكِنَ طَيِّبَةً فِيْ جَنّٰتِ عَدْنٍ ۭ وَرِضْوَانٌ
مِّنَ اللّٰهِ اَكْبَرُ ۭ ذٰلِكَ هُوَ الْفَوْزُ الْعَظِيْمُ ﴿٧٢﴾

3. وَالسّٰبِقُوْنَ الْاَوَّلُوْنَ مِنَ الْمُهٰجِرِيْنَ
وَالْاَنْصَارِ وَالَّذِيْنَ اتَّبَعُوْهُمْ بِاِحْسَانٍ ۙ
رَّضِيَ اللّٰهُ عَنْهُمْ وَرَضُوْا عَنْهُ وَاَعَدَّ
لَهُمْ جَنّٰتٍ تَجْرِيْ تَحْتَهَا الْاَنْهٰرُ خٰلِدِيْنَ
فِيْهَآ اَبَدًا ۭ ذٰلِكَ الْفَوْزُ الْعَظِيْمُ ﴿١٠٠﴾

4. اِنَّ الَّذِيْنَ اٰمَنُوْا وَعَمِلُوا الصّٰلِحٰتِ ۙ
اُولٰۗىِٕكَ هُمْ خَيْرُ الْبَرِيَّةِ ﴿٧﴾
جَزَاۗؤُهُمْ عِنْدَ رَبِّهِمْ جَنّٰتُ عَدْنٍ
تَجْرِيْ مِنْ تَحْتِهَا الْاَنْهٰرُ خٰلِدِيْنَ
فِيْهَآ اَبَدًا ۭ رَضِيَ اللّٰهُ عَنْهُمْ وَرَضُوْا
عَنْهُ ۭ ذٰلِكَ لِمَنْ خَشِيَ رَبَّهٗ ﴿٨﴾

DIVINE PUNISHMENT

1. Say: Have ye imagined, if Allah̲ should take away your hearing and your sight and seal your hearts, who is the God who could restore it to you save Allah? See how We display the revelations unto them? Yet still they turn away.

Say: Can ye see yourselves, if the punishment of Allah come upon you unawares or openly? Would any perish save wrongdoing folk?

6:46–47

2. Say: Have ye thought: When His doom cometh unto you as a raid by night, or in the (busy) day; what is there of it that the guilty ones desire to hasten?

Is it (only) then, when it hath befallen you, that ye will believe? What! (Believe) now, when (until now) ye have been hastening it on (through disbelief)?

Then will it be said unto those who dealt unjustly: Taste the torment of eternity. Are ye requited aught save what ye used to earn?

And they ask thee to inform them (saying): Is it true? Say: Yea, by my Lord, verily it is true and ye cannot escape.

And if each soul that doth wrong had all that is in the earth, it would seek to ransom itself therewith; and they will feel remorse within them, when they see the doom. But it hath been judged between them fairly and they

قُلْ أَرَءَيْتُمْ إِنْ أَخَذَ اللَّهُ سَمْعَكُمْ وَ .1
أَبْصَارَكُمْ وَخَتَمَ عَلَىٰ قُلُوبِكُم مَّنْ إِلَٰهٌ
غَيْرُ اللَّهِ يَأْتِيكُم بِهِ ۗ انظُرْ كَيْفَ
نُصَرِّفُ الْآيَاتِ ثُمَّ هُمْ يَصْدِفُونَ ﴿٤٦﴾
قُلْ أَرَءَيْتَكُمْ إِنْ أَتَاكُمْ عَذَابُ اللَّهِ
بَغْتَةً أَوْ جَهْرَةً هَلْ يُهْلَكُ إِلَّا
الْقَوْمُ الظَّالِمُونَ ﴿٤٧﴾

قُلْ أَرَءَيْتُمْ إِنْ أَتَاكُمْ عَذَابُهُ بَيَاتًا .2
أَوْ نَهَارًا مَّاذَا يَسْتَعْجِلُ مِنْهُ الْمُجْرِمُونَ ﴿٥٠﴾
أَثُمَّ إِذَا مَا وَقَعَ آمَنتُم بِهِ ۚ آلْآنَ وَقَدْ
كُنتُم بِهِ تَسْتَعْجِلُونَ ﴿٥١﴾
ثُمَّ قِيلَ لِلَّذِينَ ظَلَمُوا ذُوقُوا عَذَابَ
الْخُلْدِ هَلْ تُجْزَوْنَ إِلَّا بِمَا كُنتُمْ تَكْسِبُونَ ﴿٥٢﴾
وَيَسْتَنۢبِـُٔونَكَ أَحَقٌّ هُوَ ۖ قُلْ إِي وَرَبِّي
إِنَّهُ لَحَقٌّ ۖ وَمَا أَنتُم بِمُعْجِزِينَ ﴿٥٣﴾
وَلَوْ أَنَّ لِكُلِّ نَفْسٍ ظَلَمَتْ مَا فِي الْأَرْضِ
لَافْتَدَتْ بِهِ ۗ وَأَسَرُّوا النَّدَامَةَ لَمَّا
رَأَوُا الْعَذَابَ ۖ وَقُضِيَ بَيْنَهُم بِالْقِسْطِ
وَهُمْ لَا يُظْلَمُونَ ﴿٥٤﴾

وَلَئِنْ أَخَّرْنَا عَنْهُمُ الْعَذَابَ إِلَىٰ أُمَّةٍ .3
مَّعْدُودَةٍ لَّيَقُولُنَّ مَا يَحْبِسُهُ ۗ أَلَا يَوْمَ
يَأْتِيهِمْ لَيْسَ مَصْرُوفًا عَنْهُمْ وَحَاقَ
بِهِم مَّا كَانُوا بِهِ يَسْتَهْزِئُونَ ﴿٨﴾

are not wronged.

10:50–54

3. And if We delay for them the doom until a reckoned time, they will surely say: What withholdeth it? Verily on the day when it cometh unto them, it cannot be averted from them, and that which they derided will surround them.

11:8

4. Even thus is the grasp of thy Lord when He graspeth the townships while they are doing wrong. Lo! His grasp is painful, very strong.
11:102

5. And warn mankind of a day when the doom will come upon them, and those who did wrong will say: Our Lord! Reprieve us for a little while. We will obey Thy call and will follow the messengers.
14:44

6. Are they who plan ill deeds then secure that Allah will not cause the earth to swallow them, or that the doom will not come on them whence they know not?

Or that He will not seize them in their going to and fro so that there be no escape for them?

Or that He will not seize them with a gradual wasting? Lo! thy Lord is indeed Full of Pity, Merciful.
16:45–47

7. And when We would destroy a township We send commandment to its folk who live at ease, and afterward they commit abomination therein, and so the Word (of doom) hath effect for it, and We annihilate it with complete annihilation.
17:16

8. There is not a township but We shall destroy it ere the Day of Resurrection, or punish it with dire punishment. That is set forth in the

4. وَكَذٰلِكَ اَخْذُ رَبِّكَ اِذَآ اَخَذَ الْقُرٰى
وَهِىَ ظَالِمَةٌ ؕ اِنَّ اَخْذَهٗۤ اَلِيْمٌ شَدِيْدٌ ﴿۱۰۲﴾

5. وَاَنْذِرِ النَّاسَ يَوْمَ يَاْتِيْهِمُ الْعَذَابُ
فَيَقُوْلُ الَّذِيْنَ ظَلَمُوْا رَبَّنَآ اَخِّرْنَآ
اِلٰٓى اَجَلٍ قَرِيْبٍ ۙ نُّجِبْ دَعْوَتَكَ وَنَتَّبِعِ
الرُّسُلَ ؕ

6. اَفَاَمِنَ الَّذِيْنَ مَكَرُوا السَّيِّاٰتِ اَنْ
يَّخْسِفَ اللّٰهُ بِهِمُ الْاَرْضَ اَوْ يَاْتِيَهُمُ
الْعَذَابُ مِنْ حَيْثُ لَا يَشْعُرُوْنَ ﴿۴۵﴾
اَوْ يَاْخُذَهُمْ فِىْ تَقَلُّبِهِمْ فَمَا هُمْ
بِمُعْجِزِيْنَ ﴿۴۶﴾

اَوْ يَاْخُذَهُمْ عَلٰى تَخَوُّفٍ ؕ فَاِنَّ رَبَّكُمْ
لَرَءُوْفٌ رَّحِيْمٌ ﴿۴۷﴾

7. وَاِذَآ اَرَدْنَآ اَنْ نُّهْلِكَ قَرْيَةً اَمَرْنَا مُتْرَ
فِيْهَا فَفَسَقُوْا فِيْهَا فَحَقَّ عَلَيْهَا الْقَوْلُ
فَدَمَّرْنٰهَا تَدْمِيْرًا ﴿۱۶﴾

8. وَاِنْ مِّنْ قَرْيَةٍ اِلَّا نَحْنُ مُهْلِكُوْهَا
قَبْلَ يَوْمِ الْقِيٰمَةِ اَوْ مُعَذِّبُوْهَا عَذَابًا
شَدِيْدًا ؕ كَانَ ذٰلِكَ فِى الْكِتٰبِ مَسْطُوْرًا ﴿۵۸﴾

9. وَيَسْتَعْجِلُوْنَكَ بِالْعَذَابِ ؕ وَلَوْلَآ اَجَلٌ
مُّسَمًّى لَّجَآءَهُمُ الْعَذَابُ ؕ وَلَيَاْتِيَنَّهُمْ
بَغْتَةً وَّهُمْ لَا يَشْعُرُوْنَ ﴿۵۳﴾
يَسْتَعْجِلُوْنَكَ بِالْعَذَابِ ؕ وَاِنَّ جَهَنَّمَ
لَمُحِيْطَةٌۢ بِالْكٰفِرِيْنَ ﴿۵۴﴾

Book (of Our decrees).
17:58

9. They bid thee hasten on the doom (of Allah). And if a term had not been appointed, the doom would assuredly have come unto them (ere now). And verily it will come upon them suddenly when they perceive not.

They bid thee hasten on the doom, when lo! hell verily will encompass the disbelievers.

On the day when the doom will overwhelm them from above them and from underneath their feet, and He will say: Taste what ye used to do!

29:53—55

يَوْمَ يَغْشٰهُمُ الْعَذَابُ مِنْ فَوْقِهِمْ
وَمِنْ تَحْتِ اَرْجُلِهِمْ وَيَقُوْلُ ذُوْقُوْا
مَا كُنْتُمْ تَعْمَلُوْنَ ۝

10. And as for those who do evil, their retreat is the Fire. Whenever they desire to issue forth from thence, they are brought back thither. Unto them it is said: Taste the torment of the Fire which ye used to deny.

And verily We make them taste the lower punishment before the greater, that haply they may return.

32:20–21

10. وَاَمَّا الَّذِيْنَ فَسَقُوْا فَمَاْوٰىهُمُ النَّارُ ؕ
كُلَّمَآ اَرَادُوْٓا اَنْ يَّخْرُجُوْا مِنْهَآ اُعِيْدُوْا
فِيْهَا وَقِيْلَ لَهُمْ ذُوْقُوْا عَذَابَ النَّارِ
الَّذِيْ كُنْتُمْ بِهٖ تُكَذِّبُوْنَ ۝
وَلَنُذِيْقَنَّهُمْ مِّنَ الْعَذَابِ الْاَدْنٰى دُوْنَ
الْعَذَابِ الْاَكْبَرِ لَعَلَّهُمْ يَرْجِعُوْنَ ۝

○

Ref: 12:107: 17:67–68; 19:75; 26:204.

See also: Divine Remission.

DIVINE REMISSION

1. And Allah inviteth unto the Garden, and unto forgiveness by His grace, and expoundeth thus His revelations to mankind that haply they may remember.

2:221

2. The devil promiseth you destitution and enjoineth on you lewdness. But Allah promiseth you forgiveness from Himself with bounty. Allah is All-Embracing, All-Knowing.

2:268

3. Allah hath promised those who believe and do good works: Theirs will be foregiveness and immense reward.

5:9

4. Lo! they who subdue their voices in the presence of the messenger of Allah, those are they whose hearts Allah hath proven unto righteousness. Theirs will be forgiveness and immense reward.

49:3

5. Lo! thy Lord is of vast mercy.

53:32

6. Know that the life of this world is only play, and idle talk, and pageantry, and boasting among you, and rivalry in respect of wealth and children as the likeness of vegetation after rain, whereof the growth is pleasing to the husbandman, but afterward it drieth up and thou seest it turning yellow, then it becometh straw. And in the Hereafter there is grievious punishment, and (also) forgiveness from Allah and His good pleasure, whereas the life of the world is but matter of illusion.

Race one with another for forgiveness from your Lord and a Garden where—of the breadth is as the breadth of the heavens and the earth.

57:20—21

1. وَاللّٰهُ يَدْعُوْٓا اِلَى الْجَنَّةِ وَالْمَغْفِرَةِ بِاِذْنِهٖ ۚ
وَيُبَيِّنُ اٰيٰتِهٖ لِلنَّاسِ لَعَلَّهُمْ
يَتَذَكَّرُوْنَ

2. اَلشَّيْطٰنُ يَعِدُكُمُ الْفَقْرَ وَيَاْمُرُكُمْ
بِالْفَحْشَاۗءِ ۚ وَاللّٰهُ يَعِدُكُمْ مَّغْفِرَةً مِّنْهُ
وَفَضْلًا ۭ وَاللّٰهُ وَاسِعٌ عَلِيْمٌ

3. وَعَدَ اللّٰهُ الَّذِيْنَ اٰمَنُوْا وَعَمِلُوا الصّٰلِحٰتِ ۙ
لَهُمْ مَّغْفِرَةٌ وَّاَجْرٌ عَظِيْمٌ

4. اِنَّ الَّذِيْنَ يَغُضُّوْنَ اَصْوَاتَهُمْ عِنْدَ
رَسُوْلِ اللّٰهِ اُولٰۗىِٕكَ الَّذِيْنَ امْتَحَنَ
اللّٰهُ قُلُوْبَهُمْ لِلتَّقْوٰى ۭ لَهُمْ مَّغْفِرَةٌ
وَّاَجْرٌ عَظِيْمٌ

5. اِنَّ رَبَّكَ وَاسِعُ الْمَغْفِرَةِ ۭ

6. اِعْلَمُوْٓا اَنَّمَا الْحَيٰوةُ الدُّنْيَا لَعِبٌ وَّ
لَهْوٌ وَّزِيْنَةٌ وَّتَفَاخُرٌۢ بَيْنَكُمْ وَ
تَكَاثُرٌ فِي الْاَمْوَالِ وَالْاَوْلَادِ ۭ كَمَثَلِ
غَيْثٍ اَعْجَبَ الْكُفَّارَ نَبَاتُهٗ ثُمَّ يَهِيْجُ
فَتَرٰىهُ مُصْفَرًّا ثُمَّ يَكُوْنُ حُطٰمًا ۭ
وَفِي الْاٰخِرَةِ عَذَابٌ شَدِيْدٌ ۙ وَّمَغْفِرَةٌ
مِّنَ اللّٰهِ وَرِضْوَانٌ ۭ وَمَا الْحَيٰوةُ
الدُّنْيَآ اِلَّا مَتَاعُ الْغُرُوْرِ ۝
سَابِقُوْٓا اِلٰى مَغْفِرَةٍ مِّنْ رَّبِّكُمْ وَجَنَّةٍ
عَرْضُهَا كَعَرْضِ السَّمَاۗءِ وَالْاَرْضِ ۙ

DIVINE WORSHIP

1. O mankind! Worship your Lord, Who hath created you and those before you so that ye may ward off (evil).

2:21

2. Lo! those who are with thy Lord are not too proud to do Him service, but they praise Him and adore Him.

7:206

3. And serve thy Lord till the Inevitable cometh unto thee.

15:99

4. Lord of the heavens and the earth and all that is between them! Therefor, worship thou Him and be thou steadfast in His service. Knowest thou one that can be named along with Him?

19:65

5. Did I not charge you, O ye sons of Adam, that ye worship not the devil—Lo! he is your open foe!—

But that ye worship Me? That was the right path.

36:60–61

6. Say (O Muhammad): Lo! I am commanded to worship Allah, making religion pure for Him (only).

And I am commanded to be the first of those who surrender (unto Him).

39:11–12

7. Lo! those who scorn My service, they will enter hell,

1 يَا أَيُّهَا النَّاسُ اعْبُدُوا رَبَّكُمُ الَّذِي خَلَقَكُمْ
وَالَّذِينَ مِنْ قَبْلِكُمْ لَعَلَّكُمْ تَتَّقُونَ ﴿٢١﴾

2. إِنَّ الَّذِينَ عِنْدَ رَبِّكَ لَا يَسْتَكْبِرُونَ
عَنْ عِبَادَتِهِ وَيُسَبِّحُونَهُ وَلَهُ يَسْجُدُونَ ﴿٢٠٦﴾

3. وَاعْبُدْ رَبَّكَ حَتّٰى يَأْتِيَكَ الْيَقِينُ ﴿٩٩﴾

4. رَبُّ السَّمٰوٰتِ وَالْأَرْضِ وَمَا بَيْنَهُمَا
فَاعْبُدْهُ وَاصْطَبِرْ لِعِبَادَتِهِ هَلْ تَعْلَمُ
لَهُ سَمِيًّا ﴿٦٥﴾

5. أَلَمْ أَعْهَدْ إِلَيْكُمْ يٰبَنِيْ اٰدَمَ أَنْ لَا
تَعْبُدُوا الشَّيْطٰنَ إِنَّهُ لَكُمْ عَدُوٌّ
مُبِينٌ ﴿٦٠﴾
وَأَنِ اعْبُدُونِي هٰذَا صِرَاطٌ مُسْتَقِيمٌ ﴿٦١﴾

6. قُلْ إِنِّي أُمِرْتُ أَنْ أَعْبُدَ اللّٰهَ مُخْلِصًا
لَهُ الدِّينَ ﴿١١﴾
وَأُمِرْتُ لِأَنْ أَكُونَ أَوَّلَ الْمُسْلِمِينَ ﴿١٢﴾

7. إِنَّ الَّذِينَ يَسْتَكْبِرُونَ عَنْ عِبَادَتِي
سَيَدْخُلُونَ جَهَنَّمَ دٰخِرِينَ ﴿٦٠﴾

8. وَمَا خَلَقْتُ الْجِنَّ وَالْإِنْسَ إِلَّا
لِيَعْبُدُونِ ﴿٥٦﴾

disgraced.

40:60

8. I created the jinn and humankind only that they might worship Me.

51:56

DIVORCE

1. Those who forswear their wives must wait four months; then, if they change their mind, lo! Allah is Forgiving, Merciful.

And if they decide upon divorce (let them remember that) Allah is Hearer, Knower.

Women who are divorced shall wait, keeping themselves apart, three (monthly) courses. And it is not lawful for them that they should conceal that which Allah hath created in their wombs if they are believers in Allah and the Last Day. And their husbands would do better to take them back in that case if they desire a reconciliation. And they (women) have rights similar to those (of men) over them in kindness, and men are a degree above them. Allah is Mighty, Wise.

Divorce must be pronounced twice and then (a women) must be retained in honour or released in kindness. And it is not lawful for you that ye take from women aught of that which ye have given them; except (in the case) when both fear that they may not be able to keep within the limits (imposed by) Allah. And if ye fear that they may not be able to keep the limits of Allah, in that case it is no sin for either of them if the woman ransom herself. These are the limits (imposed by) Allah. Transgress them not. For whoso transgresseth Allah's limits, such are wrong-doers.

1. لِلَّذِينَ يُؤْلُونَ مِن نِّسَآئِهِمْ تَرَبُّصُ أَرْبَعَةِ
أَشْهُرٍ ۖ فَإِن فَآءُو فَإِنَّ اللَّهَ غَفُورٌ رَّحِيمٌ ﴿٢٢٦﴾
وَإِنْ عَزَمُوا الطَّلَاقَ فَإِنَّ اللَّهَ سَمِيعٌ عَلِيمٌ ﴿٢٢٧﴾
وَالْمُطَلَّقَاتُ يَتَرَبَّصْنَ بِأَنفُسِهِنَّ ثَلَاثَةَ قُرُوءٍ ۚ
وَلَا يَحِلُّ لَهُنَّ أَن يَكْتُمْنَ مَا خَلَقَ اللَّهُ فِي
أَرْحَامِهِنَّ إِن كُنَّ يُؤْمِنَّ بِاللَّهِ وَالْيَوْمِ الْآخِرِ ۚ
وَبُعُولَتُهُنَّ أَحَقُّ بِرَدِّهِنَّ فِي ذَٰلِكَ إِنْ أَرَادُوا
إِصْلَاحًا ۚ وَلَهُنَّ مِثْلُ الَّذِي عَلَيْهِنَّ بِالْمَعْرُوفِ ۚ
وَلِلرِّجَالِ عَلَيْهِنَّ دَرَجَةٌ ۗ وَاللَّهُ عَزِيزٌ حَكِيمٌ ﴿٢٢٨﴾
الطَّلَاقُ مَرَّتَانِ ۖ فَإِمْسَاكٌ بِمَعْرُوفٍ أَوْ تَسْرِيحٌ
بِإِحْسَانٍ ۗ وَلَا يَحِلُّ لَكُمْ أَن تَأْخُذُوا مِمَّا
آتَيْتُمُوهُنَّ شَيْئًا إِلَّا أَن يَخَافَا أَلَّا يُقِيمَا حُدُودَ
اللَّهِ ۖ فَإِنْ خِفْتُمْ أَلَّا يُقِيمَا حُدُودَ اللَّهِ فَلَا
جُنَاحَ عَلَيْهِمَا فِيمَا افْتَدَتْ بِهِ ۗ تِلْكَ
حُدُودُ اللَّهِ فَلَا تَعْتَدُوهَا ۚ وَمَن يَتَعَدَّ
حُدُودَ اللَّهِ فَأُولَٰئِكَ هُمُ الظَّالِمُونَ ﴿٢٢٩﴾
فَإِن طَلَّقَهَا فَلَا تَحِلُّ لَهُ مِن بَعْدُ حَتَّىٰ
تَنكِحَ زَوْجًا غَيْرَهُ ۗ فَإِن طَلَّقَهَا فَلَا جُنَاحَ
عَلَيْهِمَا أَن يَتَرَاجَعَا إِن ظَنَّا أَن يُقِيمَا
حُدُودَ اللَّهِ ۗ وَتِلْكَ حُدُودُ اللَّهِ يُبَيِّنُهَا
لِقَوْمٍ يَعْلَمُونَ ﴿٢٣٠﴾
وَإِذَا طَلَّقْتُمُ النِّسَاءَ فَبَلَغْنَ أَجَلَهُنَّ
فَأَمْسِكُوهُنَّ بِمَعْرُوفٍ أَوْ سَرِّحُوهُنَّ
بِمَعْرُوفٍ ۚ وَلَا تُمْسِكُوهُنَّ ضِرَارًا لِّتَعْتَدُوا ۚ

And if he hath divorced her (the third time), then she is not lawful unto him thereafter until she hath wedded another husband. Then if he (the other husband) divorce her it is no sin for both of them that they come together again if they consider that they are able to observe the limits of Allah. These are the limits of Allah. He manifasteth them for people who have knowledge.

When ye have divorced women, and they have reached their term, then retain them in kindness or release them in kindness. Retain them not to their hurt so that ye transgress (the limits). He who doth that hath wronged his soul. Make not the revelations of Allah a laughing-stock (by your behaviour), but remember Allah's grace upon you and that which He hath revealed unto you of the Scripture and of wisdom, whereby He doth exhort you. Observe your duty to Allah and know that Allah is Aware of all things.

And when ye have divorced women and they reach their term, place not difficulties in the way of their marrying their husbands if it is agreed between them in kindness. This is an admonition for him among you who believeth in Allah and the Last Day. That is more virtuous for you, and cleaner. Allah knoweth: ye know not.

2:226—232

2. It is no sin for you if ye divorce women while yet ye have not touched them, nor appointed unto them a portion. Provide for them, the rich according to his means and the straitened according to his means, a fair provision. (This is) a bounden duty for those who do good.

If ye divorce them before ye have touched them, and ye have appointed unto them a

وَمَنْ يَفْعَلْ ذٰلِكَ فَقَدْ ظَلَمَ نَفْسَهُ ۚ وَلَا
تَتَّخِذُوٓا اٰيٰتِ اللّٰهِ هُزُوًا ۚ وَّاذْكُرُوْا نِعْمَتَ
اللّٰهِ عَلَيْكُمْ وَمَآ اَنْزَلَ عَلَيْكُمْ مِّنَ الْكِتٰبِ
وَالْحِكْمَةِ يَعِظُكُمْ بِهٖ ۚ وَاتَّقُوا اللّٰهَ وَاعْلَمُوْٓا
اَنَّ اللّٰهَ بِكُلِّ شَيْءٍ عَلِيْمٌ ﴿٢٣١﴾
وَاِذَا طَلَّقْتُمُ النِّسَآءَ فَبَلَغْنَ اَجَلَهُنَّ
فَلَا تَعْضُلُوْهُنَّ اَنْ يَّنْكِحْنَ اَزْوَاجَهُنَّ
اِذَا تَرَاضَوْا بَيْنَهُمْ بِالْمَعْرُوْفِ ۗ ذٰلِكَ يُوْعَظُ
بِهٖ مَنْ كَانَ مِنْكُمْ يُؤْمِنُ بِاللّٰهِ وَالْيَوْمِ
الْاٰخِرِ ۗ ذٰلِكُمْ اَزْكٰى لَكُمْ وَاَطْهَرُ ۗ
وَاللّٰهُ يَعْلَمُ وَاَنْتُمْ لَا تَعْلَمُوْنَ ﴿٢٣٢﴾

2. لَا جُنَاحَ عَلَيْكُمْ اِنْ طَلَّقْتُمُ النِّسَآءَ مَا لَمْ
تَمَسُّوْهُنَّ اَوْ تَفْرِضُوْا لَهُنَّ فَرِيْضَةً ۚ وَّمَتِّعُوْهُنَّ
عَلَى الْمُوْسِعِ قَدَرُهٗ وَعَلَى الْمُقْتِرِ قَدَرُهٗ ۚ مَتَاعًا
بِالْمَعْرُوْفِ ۚ حَقًّا عَلَى الْمُحْسِنِيْنَ ﴿٢٣٦﴾
وَاِنْ طَلَّقْتُمُوْهُنَّ مِنْ قَبْلِ اَنْ تَمَسُّوْهُنَّ
وَقَدْ فَرَضْتُمْ لَهُنَّ فَرِيْضَةً فَنِصْفُ مَا
فَرَضْتُمْ اِلَّآ اَنْ يَّعْفُوْنَ اَوْ يَعْفُوَا الَّذِيْ
بِيَدِهٖ عُقْدَةُ النِّكَاحِ ۚ وَاَنْ تَعْفُوْٓا
اَقْرَبُ لِلتَّقْوٰى ۚ وَلَا تَنْسَوُا الْفَضْلَ
بَيْنَكُمْ ۚ اِنَّ اللّٰهَ بِمَا تَعْمَلُوْنَ بَصِيْرٌ ﴿٢٣٧﴾

3. يٰٓاَيُّهَا الَّذِيْنَ اٰمَنُوْٓا اِذَا نَكَحْتُمُ

portion, then (pay the) half of that which ye appointed unless they (the women) agree to forgo it, or he agreeth to forgo it in whose hand is the marriage tie. To forgo is nearer to piety. And forget not kindness among yourselves. Allah is Seer of what ye do.

2:236—237

3. O ye who believe! If ye wed believing women and divorce them before ye have touched them, then there is no period that ye should reckon. But content them and release them handsomely.

33:49

4. Those who put away their wives (by saying they are as their mothers) and afterward would go back on that which they have said, (the penalty) in that case (is) the freeing of a slave before they touch one another. Unto this ye are exhorted; and Allah is Informed of what ye do.

And he who findeth not (the wherewithal), let him fast for two successive months before they touch one another; and for him who is unable to do so (the penance is) the feeding of sixty needy ones. This, that ye may put trust in Allah and His messenger. Such are the limits (imposed by Allah) and for disbelievers is a painful doom.

58:3–4

5. O Prophet! When ye (men) put away women, put them away for their (legal) period and reckon the period, and keep your duty to Allah, your Lord. Expel them not from their houses nor

الْمُؤْمِنٰتِ ثُمَّ طَلَّقْتُمُوْهُنَّ مِنْ قَبْلِ
اَنْ تَمَسُّوْهُنَّ فَمَا لَكُمْ عَلَيْهِنَّ مِنْ
عِدَّةٍ تَعْتَدُّوْنَهَا ۚ فَمَتِّعُوْهُنَّ وَ
سَرِّحُوْهُنَّ سَرَاحًا جَمِيْلًا ﴿٤٩﴾

4. وَالَّذِيْنَ يُظٰهِرُوْنَ مِنْ نِّسَآئِهِمْ ثُمَّ
يَعُوْدُوْنَ لِمَا قَالُوْا فَتَحْرِيْرُ رَقَبَةٍ
مِّنْ قَبْلِ اَنْ يَّتَمَآسَّا ۚ ذٰلِكُمْ تُوْعَظُوْنَ
بِهٖ ۚ وَاللّٰهُ بِمَا تَعْمَلُوْنَ خَبِيْرٌ ﴿٣﴾
فَمَنْ لَّمْ يَجِدْ فَصِيَامُ شَهْرَيْنِ
مُتَتَابِعَيْنِ مِنْ قَبْلِ اَنْ يَّتَمَآسَّا ۚ
فَمَنْ لَّمْ يَسْتَطِعْ فَاِطْعَامُ سِتِّيْنَ
مِسْكِيْنًا ۚ ذٰلِكَ لِتُؤْمِنُوْا بِاللّٰهِ وَ
رَسُوْلِهٖ ۚ وَتِلْكَ حُدُوْدُ اللّٰهِ ۚ وَ
لِلْكٰفِرِيْنَ عَذَابٌ اَلِيْمٌ ﴿٤﴾

5. يٰٓاَيُّهَا النَّبِيُّ اِذَا طَلَّقْتُمُ النِّسَآءَ فَطَلِّقُوْهُنَّ
لِعِدَّتِهِنَّ وَاَحْصُوا الْعِدَّةَ ۚ وَاتَّقُوا
اللّٰهَ رَبَّكُمْ ۚ لَا تُخْرِجُوْهُنَّ مِنْ
بُيُوْتِهِنَّ وَلَا يَخْرُجْنَ اِلَّآ اَنْ يَّاْتِيْنَ
بِفَاحِشَةٍ مُّبَيِّنَةٍ ۚ وَتِلْكَ حُدُوْدُ
اللّٰهِ ۚ وَمَنْ يَّتَعَدَّ حُدُوْدَ اللّٰهِ فَقَدْ
ظَلَمَ نَفْسَهٗ ۚ لَا تَدْرِيْ لَعَلَّ اللّٰهَ
يُحْدِثُ بَعْدَ ذٰلِكَ اَمْرًا ﴿١﴾
فَاِذَا بَلَغْنَ اَجَلَهُنَّ فَاَمْسِكُوْهُنَّ

let them go forth unless they commit open immorality. Such are the limits (imposed by) Allah, and whoso transgresseth Allah's limits, he verily wrongeth his soul. Thou knowest not: it may be that Allah will afterward bring some new thing to pass.

Then, when they have reached their term, take them back in kindness or part from them in kindness, and call to witness two just men among you, and keep your testimony upright for Allah. Whoso believeth in Allah and the Last Day is exhorted to act thus. And whosoever keepeth his duty to Allah, Allah will appoint a way out for him,

And will provide for him from (a quarter) whence he hath no expectation. And whosoever putteth his trust in Allah, He will suffice him. Lo! Allah bringeth His command to pass. Allah hath set a measure for all things.

And for such of your women as despair of menstruation, if ye doubt, their period (of waiting) shall be three months, along with those who have it not. And for those with child, their period shall be till they bring forth their burden. And whosoever keepeth his duty to Allah, He maketh his course easy for him.

That is the commandment of Allah which He revealeth unto you. And whoso keepeth his duty to Allah, He will remit from him his evil deeds and magnify reward for him.

Lodge them where ye dwell, according to your wealth, and harass them not so as to straiten life for them.

بِمَعْرُوفٍ أَوْ فَارِقُوهُنَّ بِمَعْرُوفٍ
وَّأَشْهِدُوا ذَوَيْ عَدْلٍ مِّنكُمْ
وَأَقِيمُوا الشَّهَادَةَ لِلَّهِ ۚ ذَٰلِكُمْ يُوعَظُ
بِهِ مَن كَانَ يُؤْمِنُ بِاللَّهِ وَالْيَوْمِ
الْآخِرِ ۚ وَمَن يَتَّقِ اللَّهَ يَجْعَل لَّهُ
مَخْرَجًا ۝

وَيَرْزُقْهُ مِنْ حَيْثُ لَا يَحْتَسِبُ ۚ
وَمَن يَتَوَكَّلْ عَلَى اللَّهِ فَهُوَ حَسْبُهُ ۚ
إِنَّ اللَّهَ بَالِغُ أَمْرِهِ ۚ قَدْ جَعَلَ
اللَّهُ لِكُلِّ شَيْءٍ قَدْرًا ۝

وَاللَّائِي يَئِسْنَ مِنَ الْمَحِيضِ مِن
نِّسَائِكُمْ إِنِ ارْتَبْتُمْ فَعِدَّتُهُنَّ ثَلَاثَةُ
أَشْهُرٍ وَاللَّائِي لَمْ يَحِضْنَ ۚ وَأُولَاتُ
الْأَحْمَالِ أَجَلُهُنَّ أَن يَضَعْنَ حَمْلَهُنَّ ۚ
وَمَن يَتَّقِ اللَّهَ يَجْعَل لَّهُ مِنْ
أَمْرِهِ يُسْرًا ۝

ذَٰلِكَ أَمْرُ اللَّهِ أَنزَلَهُ إِلَيْكُمْ ۚ وَمَن
يَتَّقِ اللَّهَ يُكَفِّرْ عَنْهُ سَيِّئَاتِهِ وَيُعْظِمْ
لَهُ أَجْرًا ۝

أَسْكِنُوهُنَّ مِنْ حَيْثُ سَكَنتُم مِّن
وُجْدِكُمْ وَلَا تُضَارُّوهُنَّ لِتُضَيِّقُوا
عَلَيْهِنَّ ۚ وَإِن كُنَّ أُولَاتِ حَمْلٍ
فَأَنفِقُوا عَلَيْهِنَّ حَتَّىٰ يَضَعْنَ حَمْلَهُنَّ ۚ
فَإِنْ أَرْضَعْنَ لَكُمْ فَآتُوهُنَّ أُجُورَهُنَّ ۖ

And if they are with child, then spend for them till they bring forth their burden. Then, if they give suck for you, give them their due payment and consult together in kindness; but if ye make difficulties for one another, then let some other woman give suck for him (the father of the child).

Let him who hath abundance spend of his abundance, and he whose provision is measured, let him spend of that which Allah hath given him. Allah asketh naught of any soul save that which He hath given it. Allah will vouchsafe, after hardship, ease.

65:1–7

وَأْتَمِرُوا بَيْنَكُمْ بِمَعْرُوفٍ ۖ وَإِنْ
تَعَاسَرْتُمْ فَسَتُرْضِعُ لَهُ أُخْرَىٰ ﴿٦﴾
لِيُنْفِقْ ذُو سَعَةٍ مِنْ سَعَتِهِ ۖ وَمَنْ
قُدِرَ عَلَيْهِ رِزْقُهُ فَلْيُنْفِقْ مِمَّا
آتَاهُ اللَّهُ ۚ لَا يُكَلِّفُ اللَّهُ نَفْسًا إِلَّا
مَا آتَاهَا ۚ سَيَجْعَلُ اللَّهُ بَعْدَ عُسْرٍ يُسْرًا ﴿٧﴾

Ref: 4:19–21, 128–130;
See also: Fosterage and Maintenance.

DIYAT

1. O ye who believe! Retaliation is prescribed for you in the matter of the murdered; the freeman for the freeman, and the slave for the slave, and the female for the female. And for him who is forgiven somewhat by his (injured) brother, prosecution according to usage and payment unto him in kindness. This is an alleviation and a mercy from your Lord. He who transgresseth after this will have a painful doom.

2:178

1. يٰٓاَيُّهَا الَّذِيْنَ اٰمَنُوْا كُتِبَ عَلَيْكُمُ الْقِصَاصُ
فِي الْقَتْلٰى ۭ اَلْحُرُّ بِالْحُرِّ وَالْعَبْدُ بِالْعَبْدِ
وَالْاُنْثٰى بِالْاُنْثٰى ۭ فَمَنْ عُفِيَ لَهٗ مِنْ اَخِيْهِ
شَيْءٌ فَاتِّبَاعٌۢ بِالْمَعْرُوْفِ وَاَدَاۗءٌ اِلَيْهِ بِاِحْسَانٍ ۭ
ذٰلِكَ تَخْفِيْفٌ مِّنْ رَّبِّكُمْ وَرَحْمَةٌ ۭ فَمَنِ
اعْتَدٰى بَعْدَ ذٰلِكَ فَلَهٗ عَذَابٌ اَلِيْمٌ ﴿١٧٨﴾

2. It is not for a believer to kill a believer unless (it be) by mistake, He who hath killed a believer by mistake must set free a believing slave and pay the blood-money to the family of the slain, unless they remit it as a charity. If he (the victim) be of a people hostile unto you, and he is a believer, then (the penance) is to set free a believing slave. And if he cometh of a folk between whom and you there is a covenant, then the blood-money must be paid unto his folk and (also) a believing slave must be set free. And whoso hath not the wherewithal must fast two consecutive months. A penance from Allah. Allah is Knower, Wise.

4:92

2. وَمَا كَانَ لِمُؤْمِنٍ اَنْ يَّقْتُلَ مُؤْمِنًا اِلَّا
خَطَـًٔا ۚ وَمَنْ قَتَلَ مُؤْمِنًا خَطَـًٔا فَتَحْرِيْرُ
رَقَبَةٍ مُّؤْمِنَةٍ وَّدِيَةٌ مُّسَلَّمَةٌ اِلٰٓى اَهْلِهٖٓ
اِلَّآ اَنْ يَّصَّدَّقُوْا ۭ فَاِنْ كَانَ مِنْ قَوْمٍ عَدُوٍّ
لَّكُمْ وَهُوَ مُؤْمِنٌ فَتَحْرِيْرُ رَقَبَةٍ مُّؤْمِنَةٍ ۭ
وَاِنْ كَانَ مِنْ قَوْمٍۢ بَيْنَكُمْ وَبَيْنَهُمْ مِّيْثَاقٌ
فَدِيَةٌ مُّسَلَّمَةٌ اِلٰٓى اَهْلِهٖ وَتَحْرِيْرُ رَقَبَةٍ
مُّؤْمِنَةٍ ۚ فَمَنْ لَّمْ يَجِدْ فَصِيَامُ شَهْرَيْنِ
مُتَتَابِعَيْنِ ۡ تَوْبَةً مِّنَ اللّٰهِ ۭ وَكَانَ اللّٰهُ
عَلِيْمًا حَكِيْمًا ﴿٩٢﴾

See also: *Qisas*

DREAM

1. When Joseph said unto his father: O my father! Lo! I saw in a dream eleven planets and the sun and the moon, I saw them prostrating themselves unto me.

He said: O my dear son! Tell not thy brethren of thy vision, lest they plot a plot against thee. Lo! Satan is for man an open foe.

Thus thy Lord will prefer thee and will teach thee the interpretation of events, and will perfect His grace upon thee and upon the family of Jacob as He perfected it upon thy forefathers, Abraham and Isaac. Lo! thy Lord is Knower, Wise.

12:4–6

2. And the king said: Lo! I saw in a dream seven fat kine which seven lean were eating, and seven green ears of corn and other (seven) dry. O notables! Expound for me my vision, if ye can interpret dreams.

They answered: Jumbled dreams! And we are not knowing in the interpretation of dreams.

And he of the two who was released, and (now) at length remembered, said: I am going to announce unto you the interpretation, therefore send me forth.

(And when he came to Joseph in the prison, he exclaimed): Joseph! O thou truthful one! Expound for us the seven fat kine which seven lean were eating and the seven green ears of corn and other (seven) dry, that I may return unto the people, so that they may know.

1. إِذْ قَالَ يُوسُفُ لِأَبِيهِ يٰٓأَبَتِ إِنِّي رَأَيْتُ
أَحَدَ عَشَرَ كَوْكَبًا وَّالشَّمْسَ وَالْقَمَرَ
رَأَيْتُهُمْ لِي سٰجِدِينَ ۝
قَالَ يٰبُنَيَّ لَا تَقْصُصْ رُءْيَاكَ عَلٰٓى
إِخْوَتِكَ فَيَكِيدُوا لَكَ كَيْدًا ۖ إِنَّ
الشَّيْطٰنَ لِلْإِنْسَانِ عَدُوٌّ مُّبِينٌ ۝
وَكَذٰلِكَ يَجْتَبِيكَ رَبُّكَ وَيُعَلِّمُكَ مِنْ
تَأْوِيلِ الْأَحَادِيثِ وَيُتِمُّ نِعْمَتَهُ عَلَيْكَ
وَعَلٰٓى اٰلِ يَعْقُوبَ كَمَآ أَتَمَّهَا عَلٰٓى أَبَوَيْكَ
مِنْ قَبْلُ إِبْرٰهِيمَ وَإِسْحٰقَ ۚ إِنَّ رَبَّكَ
عَلِيمٌ حَكِيمٌ ۝

2. وَقَالَ الْمَلِكُ إِنِّي أَرٰى سَبْعَ بَقَرٰتٍ
سِمَانٍ يَأْكُلُهُنَّ سَبْعٌ عِجَافٌ وَّسَبْعَ
سُنْبُلٰتٍ خُضْرٍ وَّأُخَرَ يٰبِسٰتٍ ۖ يٰٓأَيُّهَا
الْمَلَأُ أَفْتُونِي فِي رُءْيَايَ إِنْ كُنْتُمْ
لِلرُّءْيَا تَعْبُرُونَ ۝
قَالُوٓا أَضْغَاثُ أَحْلَامٍ ۖ وَمَا نَحْنُ
بِتَأْوِيلِ الْأَحْلَامِ بِعٰلِمِينَ ۝
وَقَالَ الَّذِي نَجَا مِنْهُمَا وَادَّكَرَ بَعْدَ
أُمَّةٍ أَنَا أُنَبِّئُكُمْ بِتَأْوِيلِهِ فَأَرْسِلُونِ ۝
يُوسُفُ أَيُّهَا الصِّدِّيقُ أَفْتِنَا فِي سَبْعِ
بَقَرٰتٍ سِمَانٍ يَأْكُلُهُنَّ سَبْعٌ عِجَافٌ
وَّسَبْعِ سُنْبُلٰتٍ خُضْرٍ وَّأُخَرَ يٰبِسٰتٍ ۙ
لَعَلِّيٓ أَرْجِعُ إِلَى النَّاسِ لَعَلَّهُمْ يَعْلَمُونَ ۝

He said: Ye shall sow seven years as usual, but that which ye reap, leave it in the ear, all save a little which ye eat.

Then after that will come seven hard years which will devour all that ye have prepared for them, save a little of that which ye have stored.

Then, after that, will come a year when the people will have plenteous crops and when they will press (wine and oil).

12:43–49

قَالَ تَزْرَعُونَ سَبْعَ سِنِينَ دَأَبًا فَمَا
حَصَدتُّمْ فَذَرُوهُ فِي سُنبُلِهِ إِلَّا قَلِيلًا
مِّمَّا تَأْكُلُونَ ﴿٤٧﴾
ثُمَّ يَأْتِي مِن بَعْدِ ذَٰلِكَ سَبْعٌ شِدَادٌ
يَأْكُلْنَ مَا قَدَّمْتُمْ لَهُنَّ إِلَّا قَلِيلًا
مِّمَّا تُحْصِنُونَ ﴿٤٨﴾
ثُمَّ يَأْتِي مِن بَعْدِ ذَٰلِكَ عَامٌ فِيهِ
يُغَاثُ النَّاسُ وَفِيهِ يَعْصِرُونَ ﴿٤٩﴾

3. And when (his son) was old enough to walk with him, (Abraham) said: O my dear son, I have seen in a dream that I must sacrifice thee. So look, what thinkest thou? He said: O my father! Do that which thou art commanded. Allah willing, thou shalt find me of the steadfast.

Then, when they had both surrendered (to Allah), and he had flung him down upon his face.

We called unto him: O Abraham!

Thou hast already fulfilled the vision. Lo! thus do We reward the good.

37:102–105

3. فَلَمَّا بَلَغَ مَعَهُ السَّعْيَ قَالَ يَا بُنَيَّ إِنِّي
أَرَىٰ فِي الْمَنَامِ أَنِّي أَذْبَحُكَ فَانظُرْ
مَاذَا تَرَىٰ ۚ قَالَ يَا أَبَتِ افْعَلْ مَا تُؤْمَرُ
سَتَجِدُنِي إِن شَاءَ اللَّهُ مِنَ الصَّابِرِينَ ﴿١٠٢﴾
فَلَمَّا أَسْلَمَا وَتَلَّهُ لِلْجَبِينِ ﴿١٠٣﴾
وَنَادَيْنَاهُ أَن يَا إِبْرَاهِيمُ ﴿١٠٤﴾
قَدْ صَدَّقْتَ الرُّؤْيَا ۚ إِنَّا كَذَٰلِكَ
نَجْزِي الْمُحْسِنِينَ ﴿١٠٥﴾

4. Allah hath fulfilled the vision for His messenger in very truth. Ye shall indeed enter the Inviolable Place of Worship, if Allah will, secure, (having your hair) shaven and cut, not fearing. But He knoweth that which ye know not, and hath given you a near victory beforehand.

48:27

4. لَّقَدْ صَدَقَ اللَّهُ رَسُولَهُ الرُّؤْيَا
بِالْحَقِّ ۖ لَتَدْخُلُنَّ الْمَسْجِدَ الْحَرَامَ
إِن شَاءَ اللَّهُ آمِنِينَ مُحَلِّقِينَ
رُءُوسَكُمْ وَمُقَصِّرِينَ لَا تَخَافُونَ ۖ
فَعَلِمَ مَا لَمْ تَعْلَمُوا فَجَعَلَ مِن دُونِ
ذَٰلِكَ فَتْحًا قَرِيبًا ﴿٢٧﴾

Ref: 12:100; 17:60;

DRESS

1. O Children of Adam! We have revealed unto you raiment to conceal your shame, and splendid vesture, but the raiment of restraint from evil, that is best. This is of the revelations of Allah, that they may remember.

O Children of Adam! Let not Satan seduce you as he caused your (first) parents to go forth from the Garden and tore off from them their robe (of innocence) that he might manifest their shame to them. Lo! he seeth you, he and his tribe, from whence ye see him not. Lo! We have made the devils protecting friends for those who believe not.

7:26–27

2. As for such, theirs will be Gardens of Eden, wherein rivers flow beneath them; therein they will be given armlets of gold and will wear green robes of finest silk and gold embroidery, reclining upon thrones therein. Blest the reward, and fair the resting-place!

18:31

3. And We taught him the art of making garments (of mail) to protect you in your daring. Are ye then thankful?

21:80

4. Lo! Allah will cause those who believe and do good works to enter Gardens underneath which rivers flow, wherein they will be allowed armlets of gold, and pearls, and their raiment therein will be silk.

22:23

1. يٰبَنِيْٓ اٰدَمَ قَدْ اَنْزَلْنَا عَلَيْكُمْ لِبَاسًا يُّوَارِيْ
سَوْاٰتِكُمْ وَرِيْشًا ۭ وَلِبَاسُ التَّقْوٰى ۙ ذٰلِكَ خَيْرٌ ۭ
ذٰلِكَ مِنْ اٰيٰتِ اللّٰهِ لَعَلَّهُمْ يَذَّكَّرُوْنَ ﴿٢٦﴾
يٰبَنِيْٓ اٰدَمَ لَا يَفْتِنَنَّكُمُ الشَّيْطٰنُ كَمَآ اَخْرَجَ
اَبَوَيْكُمْ مِّنَ الْجَنَّةِ يَنْزِعُ عَنْهُمَا لِبَاسَهُمَا
لِيُرِيَهُمَا سَوْاٰتِهِمَا ۭ اِنَّهٗ يَرٰىكُمْ هُوَ وَقَبِيْلُهٗ
مِنْ حَيْثُ لَا تَرَوْنَهُمْ ۭ اِنَّا جَعَلْنَا الشَّيٰطِيْنَ
اَوْلِيَاۗءَ لِلَّذِيْنَ لَا يُؤْمِنُوْنَ ﴿٢٧﴾

2. اُولٰۗىِٕكَ لَهُمْ جَنّٰتُ عَدْنٍ تَجْرِيْ مِنْ
تَحْتِهِمُ الْاَنْهٰرُ يُحَلَّوْنَ فِيْهَا مِنْ اَسَاوِرَ
مِنْ ذَهَبٍ وَّيَلْبَسُوْنَ ثِيَابًا خُضْرًا
مِّنْ سُنْدُسٍ وَّاِسْتَبْرَقٍ مُّتَّكِـِٕيْنَ
فِيْهَا عَلَي الْاَرَاۗىِٕكِ ۭ نِعْمَ الثَّوَابُ ۭ
وَحَسُنَتْ مُرْتَفَقًا ﴿٣١﴾

3. وَعَلَّمْنٰهُ صَنْعَةَ لَبُوْسٍ لَّكُمْ
لِتُحْصِنَكُمْ مِّنْۢ بَاْسِكُمْ ۚ فَهَلْ
اَنْتُمْ شٰكِرُوْنَ ﴿٨٠﴾

4. اِنَّ اللّٰهَ يُدْخِلُ الَّذِيْنَ اٰمَنُوْا وَ
عَمِلُوا الصّٰلِحٰتِ جَنّٰتٍ تَجْرِيْ مِنْ
تَحْتِهَا الْاَنْهٰرُ يُحَلَّوْنَ فِيْهَا مِنْ
اَسَاوِرَ مِنْ ذَهَبٍ وَّلُؤْلُؤًا ۭ وَلِبَاسُهُمْ
فِيْهَا حَرِيْرٌ ﴿٢٣﴾

EARTH

1. And He it is Who spread out the earth and placed therein firm hills and flowing streams, and of all fruits he placed therein two spouses (male and female). He covereth the night with the day. Lo! herein verily are portents for people who take thought.

And in the Earth are neighbouring tracts, vineyards and ploughed lands, and date-palms, like and unlike, which are watered with one water. And We have made some of them to excel others in fruit. Lo! herein verily are portents for people who have sense.

13:3–4

2. And the earth have We spread out, and placed therein firm hills, and caused each seemly thing to grow therein.

15:19

3. Who hath appointed the earth as a bed and hath threaded roads for you therein and hath sent down water from the sky and thereby We have brought forth divers kinds of vegetation,

(Saying): Eat ye and feed your cattle. Lo! herein verily are portents for men of thought.

Thereof We created you, and thereunto We return you, and thence We bring you forth a second time.

20:53–55

1. وَهُوَ الَّذِي مَدَّ الْأَرْضَ وَجَعَلَ فِيهَا
رَوَاسِيَ وَأَنْهَارًا ۖ وَمِنْ كُلِّ الثَّمَرَاتِ
جَعَلَ فِيهَا زَوْجَيْنِ اثْنَيْنِ ۖ يُغْشِي اللَّيْلَ
النَّهَارَ ۚ إِنَّ فِي ذَٰلِكَ لَآيَاتٍ لِقَوْمٍ
يَتَفَكَّرُونَ ﴿٣﴾
وَفِي الْأَرْضِ قِطَعٌ مُتَجَاوِرَاتٌ وَجَنَّاتٌ
مِنْ أَعْنَابٍ وَزَرْعٌ وَنَخِيلٌ صِنْوَانٌ
وَغَيْرُ صِنْوَانٍ يُسْقَىٰ بِمَاءٍ وَاحِدٍ
وَنُفَضِّلُ بَعْضَهَا عَلَىٰ بَعْضٍ فِي الْأُكُلِ ۚ
إِنَّ فِي ذَٰلِكَ لَآيَاتٍ لِقَوْمٍ يَعْقِلُونَ ﴿٤﴾

2. وَالْأَرْضَ مَدَدْنَاهَا وَأَلْقَيْنَا فِيهَا
رَوَاسِيَ وَأَنْبَتْنَا فِيهَا مِنْ كُلِّ شَيْءٍ مَوْزُونٍ ﴿١٩﴾

3. الَّذِي جَعَلَ لَكُمُ الْأَرْضَ مَهْدًا وَسَلَكَ
لَكُمْ فِيهَا سُبُلًا وَأَنْزَلَ مِنَ السَّمَاءِ مَاءً
فَأَخْرَجْنَا بِهِ أَزْوَاجًا مِنْ نَبَاتٍ شَتَّىٰ ﴿٥٣﴾
كُلُوا وَارْعَوْا أَنْعَامَكُمْ ۗ إِنَّ فِي ذَٰلِكَ
لَآيَاتٍ لِأُولِي النُّهَىٰ ﴿٥٤﴾
مِنْهَا خَلَقْنَاكُمْ وَفِيهَا نُعِيدُكُمْ وَمِنْهَا
نُخْرِجُكُمْ تَارَةً أُخْرَىٰ ﴿٥٥﴾

4. أَوَلَمْ يَرَ الَّذِينَ كَفَرُوا أَنَّ السَّمَاوَاتِ
وَالْأَرْضَ كَانَتَا رَتْقًا فَفَتَقْنَاهُمَا ۖ
وَجَعَلْنَا مِنَ الْمَاءِ كُلَّ شَيْءٍ حَيٍّ ۖ
أَفَلَا يُؤْمِنُونَ ﴿٣٠﴾

4. Have not those who disbelieve known that the heavens and the earth were of one piece, then We parted them, and We made every living thing of water. Will they not then believe?

And We have placed in the earth firm hills lest it quake with them, and We have placed therein ravines as roads that haply they may find their way.

21:30–31

وَجَعَلْنَا فِي الْأَرْضِ رَوَاسِيَ أَنْ
تَمِيدَ بِهِمْ وَجَعَلْنَا فِيهَا فِجَاجًا
سُبُلًا لَعَلَّهُمْ يَهْتَدُونَ

5. Have they not seen the earth, how much of every fruitful kind We make to grow therein?

26:7

5. أَوَلَمْ يَرَوْا إِلَى الْأَرْضِ كَمْ أَنْبَتْنَا
فِيهَا مِنْ كُلِّ زَوْجٍ كَرِيمٍ

6. Have they not seen how We lead the water to the barren land and therewith bring forth crops whereof their cattle eat, and they themselves? Will they not then see?

32:27

6. أَوَلَمْ يَرَوْا أَنَّا نَسُوقُ الْمَاءَ إِلَى
الْأَرْضِ الْجُرُزِ فَنُخْرِجُ بِهِ زَرْعًا
تَأْكُلُ مِنْهُ أَنْعَامُهُمْ وَأَنْفُسُهُمْ
أَفَلَا يُبْصِرُونَ

7. Lo! Allah graspeth the heavens and the earth that they deviate not, and if they were to deviate there is not one that could grasp them after Him. Lo! He is ever Clement, Forgiving.

35:41

7. إِنَّ اللَّهَ يُمْسِكُ السَّمَاوَاتِ وَالْأَرْضَ
أَنْ تَزُولَا وَلَئِنْ زَالَتَا إِنْ
أَمْسَكَهُمَا مِنْ أَحَدٍ مِنْ بَعْدِهِ إِنَّهُ
كَانَ حَلِيمًا غَفُورًا

8. And of His portents (is this): that thou seest the earth lowly, but when We send down water thereon it thrilleth and groweth. Lo! He Who quickeneth it is verily the Quickener of the dead. Lo! He is Able to do all things.

41:39

8. وَمِنْ آيَاتِهِ أَنَّكَ تَرَى الْأَرْضَ خَاشِعَةً
فَإِذَا أَنْزَلْنَا عَلَيْهَا الْمَاءَ اهْتَزَّتْ وَ
رَبَتْ إِنَّ الَّذِي أَحْيَاهَا لَمُحْيِي الْمَوْتَىٰ
إِنَّهُ عَلَىٰ كُلِّ شَيْءٍ قَدِيرٌ

9. And the earth hath He appointed for (His) creatures,

Wherein are fruit and sheathed palm-trees,

Husked grain and scented herb.

Which is it, of the favours of your Lord, that ye deny?

55:10–13

9. وَالْأَرْضَ وَضَعَهَا لِلْأَنَامِ
فِيهَا فَاكِهَةٌ وَالنَّخْلُ ذَاتُ الْأَكْمَامِ
وَالْحَبُّ ذُو الْعَصْفِ وَالرَّيْحَانُ
فَبِأَيِّ آلَاءِ رَبِّكُمَا تُكَذِّبَانِ

Ref: 2:22; 7:10,54; 10:3; 19:40; 27:61; 30:25; 36:36; 43:10; 50:7; 51:48; 78:6;

See also: Creation of Universe, Sky, Subjugation of Universe.

EDUCATION

1. And the believers should not all go out to fight. Of every troop of them, a party only should go forth, that they (who are left behind) may gain sound knowledge in religion, and that they may warn their folk when they return to them, so that they may beware.

9:122

2. Read: In the name of thy Lord Who createth,

Createth man from a clot.

Read: And thy Lord is the Most Bounteous,

Who teacheth by the pen,

Teacheth man that which he knew not.

96:1–5

EFFORT

1. And whoso desireth the Hereafter and striveth for it with the effort necessary, being a believer, for such, their effort findeth favour (with their Lord).

17:19

2. Say: Shall We inform you who will be the greatest losers by their works?

Those whose effort goeth astray in the life of the world, and yet they reckon that they do good work.

18:103–104

3. Then whoso doth good works and is a believer, there will be no rejection of his effort. Lo! We record (it) for him.

21:94

1. وَمَا كَانَ الْمُؤْمِنُونَ لِيَنْفِرُوا كَافَّةً فَلَوْلَا
نَفَرَ مِنْ كُلِّ فِرْقَةٍ مِّنْهُمْ طَآئِفَةٌ لِّيَتَفَقَّهُوا
فِي الدِّينِ وَلِيُنْذِرُوا قَوْمَهُمْ إِذَا رَجَعُوا
إِلَيْهِمْ لَعَلَّهُمْ يَحْذَرُونَ ﴿١٢٢﴾

2. اِقْرَاْ بِاسْمِ رَبِّكَ الَّذِي خَلَقَ ﴿١﴾
خَلَقَ الْإِنْسَانَ مِنْ عَلَقٍ ﴿٢﴾
اِقْرَاْ وَرَبُّكَ الْأَكْرَمُ ﴿٣﴾
الَّذِي عَلَّمَ بِالْقَلَمِ ﴿٤﴾
عَلَّمَ الْإِنْسَانَ مَا لَمْ يَعْلَمْ ﴿٥﴾

1. وَمَنْ أَرَادَ الْآخِرَةَ وَسَعَىٰ لَهَا سَعْيَهَا وَ
هُوَ مُؤْمِنٌ فَأُولٰٓئِكَ كَانَ سَعْيُهُمْ مَّشْكُورًا ﴿١٩﴾

2. قُلْ هَلْ نُنَبِّئُكُمْ بِالْأَخْسَرِينَ أَعْمَالًا ﴿١٠٣﴾
اَلَّذِينَ ضَلَّ سَعْيُهُمْ فِي الْحَيٰوةِ الدُّنْيَا
وَهُمْ يَحْسَبُونَ أَنَّهُمْ يُحْسِنُونَ صُنْعًا ﴿١٠٤﴾

3. فَمَنْ يَّعْمَلْ مِنَ الصّٰلِحٰتِ وَهُوَ
مُؤْمِنٌ فَلَا كُفْرَانَ لِسَعْيِهٖ
وَإِنَّا لَهٗ كٰتِبُونَ ﴿٩٤﴾

4. وَأَنْ لَّيْسَ لِلْإِنْسَانِ إِلَّا مَا سَعَىٰ ﴿٣٩﴾
وَأَنَّ سَعْيَهٗ سَوْفَ يُرٰى ﴿٤٠﴾
ثُمَّ يُجْزٰىهُ الْجَزَآءَ الْأَوْفٰى ﴿٤١﴾

4. And that man hath only that for which he maketh effort,

And that his effort will be seen.

And afterward he will be repaid for it with fullest payment;

53:39–41

EDUCATION

Ref: 2:32,145,247; 3:19,61,66; 12:76; 17:36,85; 20:114; 22:3,54; 58:11; 65:12, 67:26; 102:5.

See also: Knowledge.

EFFORT

Ref: 2:114, 205 76:22; 79:22,35; 88:9; 92:4.

ENMITY

1. O ye who believe! Be steadfast witnesses for Allah in equity, and let not hatred of any people seduce you that ye deal not justly. Deal justly, that is nearer to your duty. Observe your duty to Allah. Lo! Allah is Informed of what ye do.

5:8

2. And with those who say: "Lo! we are Christians," We made a covenant, but they forgot a part of that whereof they were admonished. Therefor We have stirred up enmity and hatred among them till the Day of Resurrection, when Allah will inform them of their handiwork.

5:14

3. The Jews say: Allah's hand is fettered. Their hands are fettered and they are accursed for saying so. Nay, but both His hands are spread out wide in bounty. He bestoweth as He will. That which hath been revealed unto thee from thy Lord is certain to increase the contumacy and disbelief of many of them, and We have cast among them enmity and hatred till the Day of Resurrection. As often as they light a fire for war, Allah extinguisheth it. Their effort is for corruption in the land, and Allah loveth not corrupters.

5:64

1. يَا أَيُّهَا الَّذِينَ آمَنُوا كُونُوا قَوَّامِينَ لِلَّهِ
شُهَدَاءَ بِالْقِسْطِ وَلَا يَجْرِمَنَّكُمْ شَنَآنُ
قَوْمٍ عَلَىٰ أَلَّا تَعْدِلُوا اعْدِلُوا هُوَ أَقْرَبُ
لِلتَّقْوَىٰ وَاتَّقُوا اللَّهَ إِنَّ اللَّهَ خَبِيرٌ بِمَا تَعْمَلُونَ ﴿٨﴾

2. وَمِنَ الَّذِينَ قَالُوا إِنَّا نَصَارَىٰ أَخَذْنَا
مِيثَاقَهُمْ فَنَسُوا حَظًّا مِمَّا ذُكِّرُوا بِهِ
فَأَغْرَيْنَا بَيْنَهُمُ الْعَدَاوَةَ وَالْبَغْضَاءَ إِلَىٰ
يَوْمِ الْقِيَامَةِ وَسَوْفَ يُنَبِّئُهُمُ اللَّهُ
بِمَا كَانُوا يَصْنَعُونَ ﴿١٤﴾

3. وَقَالَتِ الْيَهُودُ يَدُ اللَّهِ مَغْلُولَةٌ غُلَّتْ
أَيْدِيهِمْ وَلُعِنُوا بِمَا قَالُوا بَلْ يَدَاهُ
مَبْسُوطَتَانِ يُنْفِقُ كَيْفَ يَشَاءُ وَلَيَزِيدَنَّ
كَثِيرًا مِنْهُمْ مَا أُنْزِلَ إِلَيْكَ مِنْ رَبِّكَ
طُغْيَانًا وَكُفْرًا وَأَلْقَيْنَا بَيْنَهُمُ الْعَدَاوَةَ
وَالْبَغْضَاءَ إِلَىٰ يَوْمِ الْقِيَامَةِ كُلَّمَا أَوْقَدُوا
نَارًا لِلْحَرْبِ أَطْفَأَهَا اللَّهُ وَيَسْعَوْنَ فِي
الْأَرْضِ فَسَادًا وَاللَّهُ لَا يُحِبُّ الْمُفْسِدِينَ ﴿٦٤﴾

4. لَتَجِدَنَّ أَشَدَّ النَّاسِ عَدَاوَةً لِلَّذِينَ
آمَنُوا الْيَهُودَ وَالَّذِينَ أَشْرَكُوا

5. إِنَّمَا يُرِيدُ الشَّيْطَانُ أَنْ يُوقِعَ بَيْنَكُمُ الْعَدَاوَةَ
وَالْبَغْضَاءَ فِي الْخَمْرِ وَالْمَيْسِرِ وَيَصُدَّكُمْ

4. Thou wilt find the most vehement of mankind in hostility to those who believe (to be) the Jews and the idolaters.

5:82

5. Satan seeketh only to cast among you enmity and hatred

by means of strong drink and games of chance, and to turn you from remembrance of Allah and from (His) worship. Will ye then have done?

5:91

عَنْ ذِكْرِ اللّٰهِ وَعَنِ الصَّلٰوةِ فَهَلْ
اَنْتُمْ مُّنْتَهُوْنَ ○

6. The good deed and the evil deed are not alike. Repel the evil deed with one which is better, then lo! he, between whom and thee there was enmity (will become) as though he was a bosom friend.

But none is granted it save those who are steadfast, and none is granted it save the owner of great happiness.

41:34–35

6. وَلَا تَسْتَوِی الْحَسَنَةُ وَلَا السَّيِّئَةُ
اِدْفَعْ بِالَّتِیْ هِیَ اَحْسَنُ فَاِذَا الَّذِیْ
بَيْنَكَ وَبَيْنَهٗ عَدَاوَةٌ كَاَنَّهٗ وَلِیٌّ حَمِيْمٌ ۝
وَمَا يُلَقّٰهَآ اِلَّا الَّذِيْنَ صَبَرُوْا وَمَا
يُلَقّٰهَآ اِلَّا ذُوْ حَظٍّ عَظِيْمٍ ۝

7. There is a goodly pattern for you in Abraham and those with him, when they told their folk: Lo! we are guiltless of you and all that ye worship beside Allah. We have done with you. And there hath arisen between us and you hostility and hate for ever until ye believe in Allah only—

60:4

7. قَدْ كَانَتْ لَكُمْ اُسْوَةٌ حَسَنَةٌ فِیْٓ اِبْرٰهِيْمَ
وَالَّذِيْنَ مَعَهٗ اِذْ قَالُوْا لِقَوْمِهِمْ
اِنَّا بُرَءٰٓؤُا مِنْكُمْ وَمِمَّا تَعْبُدُوْنَ مِنْ
دُوْنِ اللّٰهِ كَفَرْنَا بِكُمْ وَبَدَا بَيْنَنَا وَ
بَيْنَكُمُ الْعَدَاوَةُ وَالْبَغْضَآءُ اَبَدًا حَتّٰى
تُؤْمِنُوْا بِاللّٰهِ وَحْدَهٗ

○

Ref: 2:36,85,193; 3:103; 4:29,91; 5:2,64; 6:112; 7:127,150; 8:60; 9: 83,120; 18:51; 20:39,80; 28:28; 63:4; 64:14;

ENVY

1. Many of People of the Scripture long to make you disbelievers after your belief, through envy on their own account, after the truth hath become manifest unto them. Forgive and be indulgent (toward them) until Allah give command. Lo! Allah is Able to do all things.

2:109

2. Or have they even a share in the Sovereignty? Then in that case, they would not give mankind even the speck of a date—stone.

Or are they jealous of mankind because of that which Allah of His bounty hath bestowed upon them? For We bestowed upon the house of Abraham (of old) the Scripture and Wisdom and We bestowed on them a mighty kingdom:

4:53—54

3. Say: I seek refuge in the Lord of Daybreak,

From the evil of that which He created;

From the evil of the darkness when it is intense,

And from the evil of malignant witchcraft,

And from the evil of the envier when he envieth.

113:1—5

1. وَدَّ كَثِيرٌ مِّنْ أَهْلِ الْكِتَٰبِ لَوْ يَرُدُّونَكُم مِّن
بَعْدِ إِيمَٰنِكُمْ كُفَّارًا حَسَدًا مِّنْ عِندِ أَنفُسِهِم مِّن
بَعْدِ مَا تَبَيَّنَ لَهُمُ الْحَقُّ ۖ فَاعْفُوا وَاصْفَحُوا حَتَّىٰ
يَأْتِيَ اللَّهُ بِأَمْرِهِۦٓ ۗ إِنَّ اللَّهَ عَلَىٰ كُلِّ شَيْءٍ قَدِيرٌ ۝

2. أَمْ لَهُمْ نَصِيبٌ مِّنَ الْمُلْكِ فَإِذًا لَّا يُؤْتُونَ
النَّاسَ نَقِيرًا ۝

أَمْ يَحْسُدُونَ النَّاسَ عَلَىٰ مَآ ءَاتَىٰهُمُ
اللَّهُ مِن فَضْلِهِۦ ۖ فَقَدْ ءَاتَيْنَآ ءَالَ إِبْرَٰهِيمَ
الْكِتَٰبَ وَالْحِكْمَةَ وَءَاتَيْنَٰهُم مُّلْكًا عَظِيمًا ۝

3. قُلْ أَعُوذُ بِرَبِّ الْفَلَقِ ۝
مِن شَرِّ مَا خَلَقَ ۝
وَمِن شَرِّ غَاسِقٍ إِذَا وَقَبَ ۝
وَمِن شَرِّ النَّفَّٰثَٰتِ فِي الْعُقَدِ ۝
وَمِن شَرِّ حَاسِدٍ إِذَا حَسَدَ ۝

Ref: 2:111,113; 48:15;

EQUALITY IN THE STATUS OF MAN AND WOMAN

1. And their Lord hath heard them (and He saith): Lo! I suffer not the work of any worker, male or female, to be lost. Ye proceed one from another. So those who fled and were driven forth from their homes and suffered damage for My cause, and fought and were slain, verily I shall remit their evil deeds from them and verily I shall bring them into Gardens underneath which rivers flow—A reward from Allah. And with Allah is the fairest of rewards.

3:195

2. And covet not the thing in which Allah hath made some of you excel others. Unto men a fortune from that which they have earned, and unto women a fortune from that which they have earned. (Envy not one another) but ask Allah of His bounty. Lo! Allah is ever Knower of all things.

4:32

3. And whoso doeth good works, whether of male or female, and he (or she) is a believer, such will enter paradise and they will not be wronged the dint in a date-stone.

4:124

4. Whosoever doth right, whether male or female, and is a believer, him verily We shall quicken with good life, and We shall pay them a recompense in proportion to the best of what they used to do.

16:97

1. فَاسْتَجَابَ لَهُمْ رَبُّهُمْ أَنِّي لَا أُضِيعُ عَمَلَ
عَامِلٍ مِّنكُم مِّن ذَكَرٍ أَوْ أُنثَىٰ بَعْضُكُم
مِّن بَعْضٍ فَالَّذِينَ هَاجَرُوا وَأُخْرِجُوا
مِن دِيَارِهِمْ وَأُوذُوا فِي سَبِيلِي وَقٰتَلُوا
وَقُتِلُوا لَأُكَفِّرَنَّ عَنْهُمْ سَيِّاٰتِهِمْ وَلَأُدْخِلَنَّهُمْ
جَنّٰتٍ تَجْرِي مِن تَحْتِهَا الْأَنْهٰرُ ثَوَابًا
مِّنْ عِندِ اللَّهِ وَاللَّهُ عِندَهُ حُسْنُ الثَّوَابِ

2. وَلَا تَتَمَنَّوْا مَا فَضَّلَ اللَّهُ بِهِ بَعْضَكُمْ عَلَىٰ
بَعْضٍ لِّلرِّجَالِ نَصِيبٌ مِّمَّا اكْتَسَبُوا
وَلِلنِّسَاءِ نَصِيبٌ مِّمَّا اكْتَسَبْنَ وَسْئَلُوا
اللَّهَ مِن فَضْلِهِ إِنَّ اللَّهَ كَانَ بِكُلِّ
شَيْءٍ عَلِيمًا ﴿٣٢﴾

3. وَمَن يَعْمَلْ مِنَ الصّٰلِحٰتِ مِن ذَكَرٍ أَوْ
أُنثَىٰ وَهُوَ مُؤْمِنٌ فَأُولٰئِكَ يَدْخُلُونَ
الْجَنَّةَ وَلَا يُظْلَمُونَ نَقِيرًا ﴿١٢٤﴾

4. مَنْ عَمِلَ صَالِحًا مِّن ذَكَرٍ أَوْ أُنثَىٰ
وَهُوَ مُؤْمِنٌ فَلَنُحْيِيَنَّهُ حَيٰوةً طَيِّبَةً
وَلَنَجْزِيَنَّهُمْ أَجْرَهُم بِأَحْسَنِ مَا
كَانُوا يَعْمَلُونَ ﴿٩٧﴾

5. إِنَّ الْمُسْلِمِينَ وَالْمُسْلِمٰتِ وَالْمُؤْمِنِينَ
وَالْمُؤْمِنٰتِ وَالْقٰنِتِينَ وَالْقٰنِتٰتِ وَ
الصّٰدِقِينَ وَالصّٰدِقٰتِ وَالصّٰبِرِينَ
وَالصّٰبِرٰتِ وَالْخٰشِعِينَ وَالْخٰشِعٰتِ وَ

5. Lo! men who surrender unto Allah, and women who surrender and men who believe and women who believe, and men who obey and women who obey, and men who speak the truth and women who speak the truth, and men who persevere (in righteousness) and women who persevere,

and men who are humble and women who are humble, and men who give alms and women who give alms, and men who fast and women who fast, and men who guard their modesty and women who guard (their modesty), and men who remember Allah much and women who remember—Allah hath prepared for them forgiveness and a vast reward.

33:35

EQUALITY OF ALL HUMAN BEINGS

1. O mankind! Be careful of your duty to your Lord Who created you from a single soul and from it created its mate and from them twain hath spread abroad a multitude of men and women. Be careful of your duty toward Allah in Whom ye claim (your rights) of one another, and toward the wombs (that bore you). Lo! Allah hath been a Watcher over you.

4:1

2. And He it is Who hath set for you the stars that ye may guide your course by them amid the darkness of the land and the sea. We have detailed Our revelations for a people who have knowledge.

6.97

3. O mankind! Lo! We have created you male and female,

الْمُتَصَدِّقِيْنَ وَ الْمُتَصَدِّقٰتِ وَالصَّآئِمِيْنَ
وَالصّٰٓئِمٰتِ وَ الْحٰفِظِيْنَ فُرُوْجَهُمْ
وَالْحٰفِظٰتِ وَالذّٰكِرِيْنَ اللّٰهَ كَثِيْرًا
وَّ الذّٰكِرٰتِ ۙ اَعَدَّ اللّٰهُ لَهُمْ مَّغْفِرَةً
وَّ اَجْرًا عَظِيْمًا ۝

○

1. يٰۤاَيُّهَا النَّاسُ اتَّقُوْا رَبَّكُمُ الَّذِيْ
خَلَقَكُمْ مِّنْ نَّفْسٍ وَّاحِدَةٍ وَّخَلَقَ مِنْهَا
زَوْجَهَا وَبَثَّ مِنْهُمَا رِجَالًا كَثِيْرًا وَّنِسَآءً ۚ
وَ اتَّقُوا اللّٰهَ الَّذِيْ تَسَآءَلُوْنَ بِهٖ وَالْاَرْحَامَ ؕ
اِنَّ اللّٰهَ كَانَ عَلَيْكُمْ رَقِيْبًا ۝

2. وَهُوَ الَّذِيْ جَعَلَ لَكُمُ النُّجُوْمَ لِتَهْتَدُوْا
بِهَا فِيْ ظُلُمٰتِ الْبَرِّ وَالْبَحْرِ ؕ قَدْ فَصَّلْنَا
الْاٰيٰتِ لِقَوْمٍ يَّعْلَمُوْنَ ۝

3. يٰۤاَيُّهَا النَّاسُ اِنَّا خَلَقْنٰكُمْ مِّنْ ذَكَرٍ
وَّ اُنْثٰى وَجَعَلْنٰكُمْ شُعُوْبًا وَّ قَبَآئِلَ
لِتَعَارَفُوْا ؕ اِنَّ اَكْرَمَكُمْ عِنْدَ اللّٰهِ اَتْقٰىكُمْ ؕ
اِنَّ اللّٰهَ عَلِيْمٌ خَبِيْرٌ ۝

○

and have made you nations and tribes that ye may know one another. Lo! the noblest of you, in the sight of Allah, is the best in conduct. Lo! Allah is Knower, Aware.

49:13

EQUALITY IN THE STATUS OF MAN AND WOMAN

See also: Women.

ETIQUETTES OF SOCIETY

1. O ye who believe! Enter not houses other than your own without first announcing your presence and invoking peace upon the folk thereof. That is better for you, that ye may be heedful.

24:27

2. O ye who believe! When it is said unto you, Make room in assemblies, then make room; Allah will make way for you (hereafter). And when it is said, Come up higher! go up higher; Allah will exalt those who believe among you, and those who have knowledge, to high ranks. Allah is Informed of what ye do.

58:11

ETIQUETTES OF SPEECH

1. And speak kindly to mankind;

2:83

2. Be modest in thy bearing and subdue thy voice. Lo! the harshest of all voices is the voice of the ass.

31:19

3. O ye who believe! When ye conspire together, conspire not together for crime and wrongdoing and disobedience toward the messenger, but conspire together for righteousness and piety, and keep your duty toward Allah, unto Whom ye will be gathered.

58:9

1. يٰٓاَيُّهَا الَّذِيْنَ اٰمَنُوْا لَا تَدْخُلُوْا بُيُوْتًا
غَيْرَ بُيُوْتِكُمْ حَتّٰى تَسْتَاْنِسُوْا وَتُسَلِّمُوْا
عَلٰٓى اَهْلِهَا ۭ ذٰلِكُمْ خَيْرٌ لَّكُمْ
لَعَلَّكُمْ تَذَكَّرُوْنَ ﴿٢٧﴾

2. يٰٓاَيُّهَا الَّذِيْنَ اٰمَنُوْٓا اِذَا قِيْلَ لَكُمْ
تَفَسَّحُوْا فِي الْمَجٰلِسِ فَافْسَحُوْا يَفْسَحِ
اللّٰهُ لَكُمْ ۚ وَاِذَا قِيْلَ انْشُزُوْا فَانْشُزُوْا
يَرْفَعِ اللّٰهُ الَّذِيْنَ اٰمَنُوْا مِنْكُمْ ۙ وَالَّذِيْنَ
اُوْتُوا الْعِلْمَ دَرَجٰتٍ ۭ وَاللّٰهُ بِمَا
تَعْمَلُوْنَ خَبِيْرٌ ﴿١١﴾

1. وَقُوْلُوْا لِلنَّاسِ حُسْنًا

2. وَاقْصِدْ فِيْ مَشْيِكَ وَاغْضُضْ مِنْ
صَوْتِكَ ۭ اِنَّ اَنْكَرَ الْاَصْوَاتِ
لَصَوْتُ الْحَمِيْرِ ﴿١٩﴾

3. يٰٓاَيُّهَا الَّذِيْنَ اٰمَنُوْٓا اِذَا تَنَاجَيْتُمْ فَلَا
تَتَنَاجَوْا بِالْاِثْمِ وَالْعُدْوَانِ وَمَعْصِيَتِ
الرَّسُوْلِ وَتَنَاجَوْا بِالْبِرِّ وَالتَّقْوٰى ۭ
وَاتَّقُوا اللّٰهَ الَّذِيْٓ اِلَيْهِ تُحْشَرُوْنَ ﴿٩﴾

EVIDENCE

1. And who is more unjust than he who hideth a testimony which he hath received from Allah? Allah is not unaware of what ye do.

2:140

2. Thus We have appointed you a middle nation, that ye may be witnesses against mankind, and that the messenger may be a witness against you,

2:143

3. Hide not testimony. He who hideth it, verily his heart is sinful. Allah is Aware of what ye do.

2:283

4. As for those of your women who are guilty of lewdness, call to witness four of you against them. And if they testify (to the truth of the allegation) then confine them to the houses until death take them or (until) Allah appoint for them a way (through new legislation).

4:15

5. O ye who believe! Be ye staunch in justice, witnesses for Allah, even though it be against yourselves or (your) parents or (your) kindred, whether (the case be of) a rich man or a poor man, for Allah is nearer unto both (than ye are). So follow not passion lest ye lapse (from truth) and if ye lapse or fall

1. وَمَنْ أَظْلَمُ مِمَّنْ كَتَمَ شَهَادَةً عِنْدَهُ
مِنَ اللّٰهِ ۗ وَمَا اللّٰهُ بِغَافِلٍ عَمَّا
تَعْمَلُوْنَ ۝

2. وَكَذٰلِكَ جَعَلْنٰكُمْ اُمَّةً وَّسَطًا لِّتَكُوْنُوْا شُهَدَآءَ
عَلَى النَّاسِ وَيَكُوْنَ الرَّسُوْلُ عَلَيْكُمْ شَهِيْدًا ۗ

3. وَلَا تَكْتُمُوا الشَّهَادَةَ ۗ وَمَنْ يَّكْتُمْهَا
فَاِنَّهٗۤ اٰثِمٌ قَلْبُهٗ ۗ وَاللّٰهُ بِمَا تَعْمَلُوْنَ
عَلِيْمٌ ۝

4. وَالّٰتِىْ يَاْتِيْنَ الْفَاحِشَةَ مِنْ نِّسَآئِكُمْ
فَاسْتَشْهِدُوْا عَلَيْهِنَّ اَرْبَعَةً مِّنْكُمْ ۚ فَاِنْ
شَهِدُوْا فَاَمْسِكُوْهُنَّ فِى الْبُيُوْتِ حَتّٰى
يَتَوَفّٰىهُنَّ الْمَوْتُ اَوْ يَجْعَلَ اللّٰهُ
لَهُنَّ سَبِيْلًا ۝

5. يٰۤاَيُّهَا الَّذِيْنَ اٰمَنُوْا كُوْنُوْا قَوّٰمِيْنَ بِالْقِسْطِ
شُهَدَآءَ لِلّٰهِ وَلَوْ عَلٰۤى اَنْفُسِكُمْ اَوِ الْوَالِدَيْنِ
وَالْاَقْرَبِيْنَ ۚ اِنْ يَّكُنْ غَنِيًّا اَوْ فَقِيْرًا
فَاللّٰهُ اَوْلٰى بِهِمَا ۚ فَلَا تَتَّبِعُوا الْهَوٰۤى اَنْ
تَعْدِلُوْا ۚ وَاِنْ تَلْوٗۤا اَوْ تُعْرِضُوْا فَاِنَّ اللّٰهَ
كَانَ بِمَا تَعْمَلُوْنَ خَبِيْرًا ۝

6. يٰۤاَيُّهَا الَّذِيْنَ اٰمَنُوْا كُوْنُوْا قَوّٰمِيْنَ لِلّٰهِ
شُهَدَآءَ بِالْقِسْطِ ۚ وَلَا يَجْرِمَنَّكُمْ شَنَاٰنُ

away, then lo! Allah is ever Informed of what ye do.

4:135

6. O ye who believe! Be steadfast witnesses for Allah in equity, and let not hatred of any people seduce you that ye deal not justly. Deal justly, that is nearer

to your duty. Observe your duty to Allah. Lo! Allah is Informed of what ye do.

5:8

7. O ye who believe! Let there be witnesses between you when death draweth nigh unto one of you, at the time of bequest — two witnesses, just men from among you, or two others from another tribe in case ye are compaigning in the land and the calamity of death befall you. Ye shall empanel them both after the prayer, and, if ye doubt, they shall be made to swear by Allah (saying): We will not take a bribe, even though it were (on behalf of) a near kinsman nor will we hide the testimony of Allah, for then indeed we should be of the sinful.

But then, if it is afterwards ascertained that both of them merit (the suspicion of) sin, let two others take their place of those nearly concerned, and let them swear by Allah, (saying): Verily our testimony is truer than their testimony and we have not transgressed (the bounds of duty), for then indeed we should be of the evil-doers.

Thus it is more likely that they will bear true witness or fear that after their oaths, the oaths (of others) will be taken. So be mindful of your duty (to Allah) and hearken. Allah guideth not the

قوم على ألا تعدلوا اعدلوا هو أقرب
للتقوى واتقوا الله إن الله خبير بما تعملون ٨

7. يا أيها الذين آمنوا شهادة بينكم إذا
حضر أحدكم الموت حين الوصية
اثنان ذوا عدل منكم أو آخران من
غيركم إن أنتم ضربتم في الأرض
فأصابتكم مصيبة الموت تحبسونهما
من بعد الصلوة فيقسمان بالله إن
ارتبتم لا نشتري به ثمنا ولو كان ذا
قربى ولا نكتم شهادة الله إنا إذا
لمن الآثمين ١٠٦

فإن عثر على أنهما استحقا إثما فآخران
يقومان مقامهما من الذين استحق
عليهم الأوليان فيقسمان بالله لشهادتنا
أحق من شهادتهما وما اعتدينا إنا
إذا لمن الظالمين ١٠٧

ذلك أدنى أن يأتوا بالشهادة على وجهها
أو يخافوا أن ترد أيمان بعد أيمانهم
واتقوا الله واسمعوا والله لا يهدي
القوم الفاسقين ١٠٨

8. قل كفى بالله شهيدا بيني وبينكم
إنه كان بعباده خبيرا بصيرا ٩٦

froward folk.

5:106–108

8. Say: Allah sufficeth for a witness between me and you. Lo! He is Knower, Seer of His slaves.

17:96

9. And those who accuse honourable women but bring not four witnesses, scourge them (with) eighty stripes and never (afterward) accept their testimony--They indeed are evil-doers.

24:4

10. As for those who accuse their wives but have no witnesses except themselves; let the testimony of one of them be four testimonies, (swearing) by Allah that he is of those who speak the truth.

And yet a fifth invoking the curse of Allah on him if he is of those who lie.

And it shall avert the punishment from her if she bear witness before Allah four times that the thing he saith is indeed false,

And a fifth (time) that the wrath of Allah be upon her if he speaketh truth.

24:6–9

11. Then, when they have reached their term, take them back in kindness or part from them in kindness, and call to witness two just men among you, and keep your testimony upright for Allah. Whoso believeth in Allah and the Last Day is exhorted to act thus. And whosoever keepeth his duty to Allah, Allah will appoint a way out for him,

65:2

9. وَالَّذِيْنَ يَرْمُوْنَ الْمُحْصَنٰتِ ثُمَّ لَمْ
يَاْتُوْا بِاَرْبَعَةِ شُهَدَآءَ فَاجْلِدُوْهُمْ
ثَمٰنِيْنَ جَلْدَةً وَّلَا تَقْبَلُوْا لَهُمْ
شَهَادَةً اَبَدًا ۚ وَاُولٰٓئِكَ هُمُ الْفٰسِقُوْنَ ﴿٤﴾

10. وَالَّذِيْنَ يَرْمُوْنَ اَزْوَاجَهُمْ وَلَمْ يَكُنْ
لَّهُمْ شُهَدَآءُ اِلَّآ اَنْفُسُهُمْ فَشَهَادَةُ
اَحَدِهِمْ اَرْبَعُ شَهٰدٰتٍ بِاللّٰهِ ۙ اِنَّهٗ
لَمِنَ الصّٰدِقِيْنَ ﴿٦﴾

وَالْخَامِسَةُ اَنَّ لَعْنَتَ اللّٰهِ عَلَيْهِ
اِنْ كَانَ مِنَ الْكٰذِبِيْنَ ﴿٧﴾

وَيَدْرَؤُا عَنْهَا الْعَذَابَ اَنْ تَشْهَدَ
اَرْبَعَ شَهٰدٰتٍ بِاللّٰهِ ۙ اِنَّهٗ لَمِنَ الْكٰذِبِيْنَ ﴿٨﴾

وَالْخَامِسَةَ اَنَّ غَضَبَ اللّٰهِ عَلَيْهَآ اِنْ
كَانَ مِنَ الصّٰدِقِيْنَ ﴿٩﴾

11. فَاِذَا بَلَغْنَ اَجَلَهُنَّ فَاَمْسِكُوْهُنَّ
بِمَعْرُوْفٍ اَوْ فَارِقُوْهُنَّ بِمَعْرُوْفٍ
وَّاَشْهِدُوْا ذَوَيْ عَدْلٍ مِّنْكُمْ
وَاَقِيْمُوا الشَّهَادَةَ لِلّٰهِ ۗ ذٰلِكُمْ يُوْعَظُ
بِهٖ مَنْ كَانَ يُؤْمِنُ بِاللّٰهِ وَالْيَوْمِ
الْاٰخِرِ ۗ وَمَنْ يَّتَّقِ اللّٰهَ يَجْعَلْ لَّهٗ
مَخْرَجًا ۙ ﴿٢﴾

Ref: 2:23; 3:18, 52–53, 64, 81, 99, 140; 4:33, 41, 79, 159, 166; 5:44, 83; 6:19, 130, 150; 7:37; 9:17; 10:29, 46, 61; 11:17–18; 12:26–27; 16:84; 21:56; 24:13; 28:44, 75; 29:52; 36:65; 39:69; 41:20–22; 43:19, 86; 46:8, 10; 48:8; 50:21, 37; 58:6; 70:33; 73:15; 100:7.

EVIL

1. Nay, but whosoever hath done evil and his sin surroundeth him, such are rightful owners of the Fire; they will abide therein.

2:81

2. If ye avoid the great (things) which ye are forbidden, We will remit from you your evil deeds and make you enter at a noble gate.

4:31

3. Whoso bringeth a good deed will receive tenfold the like thereof, while whoso bringeth an ill deed will be awarded but the like thereof; and they will not be wronged.

6.160

4. And those who earn ill deeds, (for them) requital of each ill deed by the like thereof; and ignominy overtaketh them—They have no protector from Allah—as if their faces had been covered with a cloak of darkest night. Such are rightful owners of the Fire; they will abide therein.

10:27

5. Establish worship at the two ends of the day and in some watches of the night. Lo! good deeds annul ill deeds. This is a reminder for the mindful.

11:114

6. Repel evil with that which is better. We are best Aware of that which they allege.

23:96

7. Whoso bringeth a good deed, he will have better than the same; while as for him who bringeth an ill-deed, those who do ill-deeds will be requited only what they did.

28:84

1. بَلٰى مَنْ كَسَبَ سَيِّئَةً وَّاَحَاطَتْ بِهٖ خَطِيْٓـئَتُهٗ
فَاُولٰٓـئِكَ اَصْحٰبُ النَّارِ ۚ هُمْ فِيْهَا خٰلِدُوْنَ

2. اِنْ تَجْتَنِبُوْا كَبَآئِرَ مَا تُنْهَوْنَ عَنْهُ نُكَفِّرْ
عَنْكُمْ سَيِّاٰتِكُمْ وَنُدْخِلْكُمْ مُّدْخَلًا كَرِيْمًا

3. مَنْ جَآءَ بِالْحَسَنَةِ فَلَهٗ عَشْرُ اَمْثَالِهَا ۚ وَ
مَنْ جَآءَ بِالسَّيِّئَةِ فَلَا يُجْزٰٓى اِلَّا مِثْلَهَا
وَهُمْ لَا يُظْلَمُوْنَ

4. وَالَّذِيْنَ كَسَبُوا السَّيِّاٰتِ جَزَآءُ سَيِّئَةٍ
بِمِثْلِهَا ۙ وَتَرْهَقُهُمْ ذِلَّةٌ ؕ مَا لَهُمْ مِّنَ
اللّٰهِ مِنْ عَاصِمٍ ۚ كَاَنَّمَآ اُغْشِيَتْ وُجُوْهُهُمْ
قِطَعًا مِّنَ الَّيْلِ مُظْلِمًا ؕ اُولٰٓـئِكَ اَصْحٰبُ
النَّارِ ۚ هُمْ فِيْهَا خٰلِدُوْنَ

5. وَاَقِمِ الصَّلٰوةَ طَرَفَيِ النَّهَارِ وَزُلَفًا
مِّنَ الَّيْلِ ؕ اِنَّ الْحَسَنٰتِ يُذْهِبْنَ
السَّيِّاٰتِ ؕ ذٰلِكَ ذِكْرٰى لِلذّٰكِرِيْنَ

6. اِدْفَعْ بِالَّتِيْ هِيَ اَحْسَنُ السَّيِّئَةَ ؕ
نَحْنُ اَعْلَمُ بِمَا يَصِفُوْنَ

7. مَنْ جَآءَ بِالْحَسَنَةِ فَلَهٗ خَيْرٌ مِّنْهَا ۚ وَمَنْ
جَآءَ بِالسَّيِّئَةِ فَلَا يُجْزَى الَّذِيْنَ عَمِلُوا
السَّيِّاٰتِ اِلَّا مَا كَانُوْا يَعْمَلُوْنَ

8. The good deed and the evil deed are not alike. Repel the evil deed with one which is better, then lo! he, between whom and thee there was enmity (will become) as though he was a bosom friend.

41:34

9. Or do those who commit ill-deeds suppose that We shall make them as those who believe and do good works, the same in life and death? Bad is their judgement!

45:21

EVIL EYE

1. And he said: O my sons! Go not in by one gate; go in by different gates. I can naught avail you as against Allah. Lo! the decision rests with Allah only. In Him do I put my trust, and in Him let all the trusting put their trust.

And when they entered in the manner which their father had enjoined, it would have naught availed them as against Allah; it was but a need of Jacob's soul which he thus satisfied; and lo! he was a lord of knowledge because We had taught him; but most of mankind know not.

12:67–68

2. And lo! those who disbelieve would fain disconcert thee with their eyes when they

8. وَلَا تَسْتَوِي الْحَسَنَةُ وَلَا السَّيِّئَةُ ۚ
ادْفَعْ بِالَّتِي هِيَ أَحْسَنُ فَإِذَا الَّذِي
بَيْنَكَ وَبَيْنَهُ عَدَاوَةٌ كَأَنَّهُ وَلِيٌّ حَمِيمٌ ﴿٣٤﴾

9. أَمْ حَسِبَ الَّذِينَ اجْتَرَحُوا السَّيِّئَاتِ
أَنْ نَجْعَلَهُمْ كَالَّذِينَ آمَنُوا وَعَمِلُوا
الصَّالِحَاتِ سَوَاءً مَحْيَاهُمْ وَمَمَاتُهُمْ ۚ
سَاءَ مَا يَحْكُمُونَ ﴿٢١﴾

1. وَقَالَ يَا بَنِيَّ لَا تَدْخُلُوا مِنْ بَابٍ وَاحِدٍ
وَادْخُلُوا مِنْ أَبْوَابٍ مُتَفَرِّقَةٍ ۖ وَمَا
أُغْنِي عَنْكُمْ مِنَ اللَّهِ مِنْ شَيْءٍ ۖ إِنِ الْحُكْمُ
إِلَّا لِلَّهِ ۖ عَلَيْهِ تَوَكَّلْتُ ۖ وَعَلَيْهِ فَلْيَتَوَكَّلِ
الْمُتَوَكِّلُونَ ﴿٦٧﴾

وَلَمَّا دَخَلُوا مِنْ حَيْثُ أَمَرَهُمْ أَبُوهُمْ
مَا كَانَ يُغْنِي عَنْهُمْ مِنَ اللَّهِ مِنْ شَيْءٍ إِلَّا
حَاجَةً فِي نَفْسِ يَعْقُوبَ قَضَاهَا ۚ وَإِنَّهُ
لَذُو عِلْمٍ لِمَا عَلَّمْنَاهُ وَلَٰكِنَّ أَكْثَرَ
النَّاسِ لَا يَعْلَمُونَ ﴿٦٨﴾

2. وَإِنْ يَكَادُ الَّذِينَ كَفَرُوا لَيُزْلِقُونَكَ
بِأَبْصَارِهِمْ لَمَّا سَمِعُوا الذِّكْرَ وَ
يَقُولُونَ إِنَّهُ لَمَجْنُونٌ ﴿٥١﴾
وَمَا هُوَ إِلَّا ذِكْرٌ لِلْعَالَمِينَ ﴿٥٢﴾

hear the Reminder, and they say: Lo! he is indeed mad;

When it is naught else than a Reminder to creation.

68:51–52

EVIL SUGGESTION

1. We verily created a man and We know what his soul whispereth to him, and We are nearer to him than his jugular vein.

50:16

2. Say: I seek refuge in the Lord of mankind,
The King of mankind,
The God of mankind,
From the evil of the sneaking whisperer,
Who whispereth in the hearts of mankind,
Of the jinn and of mankind.

114:1–6

1. وَلَقَدْ خَلَقْنَا الْإِنْسَانَ وَنَعْلَمُ مَا
تُوَسْوِسُ بِهِ نَفْسُهُ ۖ وَنَحْنُ أَقْرَبُ
إِلَيْهِ مِنْ حَبْلِ الْوَرِيدِ ﴿١٦﴾

2 قُلْ أَعُوذُ بِرَبِّ النَّاسِ ﴿١﴾
مَلِكِ النَّاسِ ﴿٢﴾
إِلَٰهِ النَّاسِ ﴿٣﴾
مِنْ شَرِّ الْوَسْوَاسِ الْخَنَّاسِ ﴿٤﴾
الَّذِي يُوَسْوِسُ فِي صُدُورِ النَّاسِ ﴿٥﴾
مِنَ الْجِنَّةِ وَالنَّاسِ ﴿٦﴾

○

EXAMPLE OF THE DISOBEDIENT

1. As for the disbelievers, whether thou warn them or thou warn them not it is all one for them; they believe not.

Allah hath sealed their hearing and their hearts, and on their eyes there is a covering. Theirs will be an awful doom.

2:6–7

2. Those who deny Our revelations are deaf and dumb in darkness. Whom Allah will, He sendeth astray, and whom He will, He placeth on a Straight path.

6:39

3. Be not as those who say, we hear, and they hear not.

Lo! the worst of beasts in Allah's sight are the deaf, the dumb, who have no sense.

Had Allah known of any good in them He would have made them hear, but had He made them hear they would have turned away, averse.

8:21–23

4. Lo! the worst of beasts in Allah's sight are the un grateful who will not believe;

8:55

5. And of them are some who listen unto thee. But canst thou make the deaf to hear even though they apprehend not?

And of them is he who

1. إِنَّ الَّذِينَ كَفَرُوا سَوَاءٌ عَلَيْهِمْ ءَأَنذَرْتَهُمْ
أَمْ لَمْ تُنذِرْهُمْ لَا يُؤْمِنُونَ ۝٦
خَتَمَ اللَّهُ عَلَىٰ قُلُوبِهِمْ وَعَلَىٰ سَمْعِهِمْ ۖ وَعَلَىٰ
أَبْصَارِهِمْ غِشَاوَةٌ ۖ وَلَهُمْ عَذَابٌ عَظِيمٌ ۝٧

2. وَالَّذِينَ كَذَّبُوا بِآيَاتِنَا صُمٌّ وَبُكْمٌ فِي
الظُّلُمَاتِ ۗ مَن يَشَإِ اللَّهُ يُضْلِلْهُ وَمَن
يَشَأْ يَجْعَلْهُ عَلَىٰ صِرَاطٍ مُّسْتَقِيمٍ ۝٣٩

3. وَلَا تَكُونُوا كَالَّذِينَ قَالُوا سَمِعْنَا
وَهُمْ لَا يَسْمَعُونَ ۝٢١
إِنَّ شَرَّ الدَّوَابِّ عِندَ اللَّهِ الصُّمُّ الْبُكْمُ
الَّذِينَ لَا يَعْقِلُونَ ۝٢٢
وَلَوْ عَلِمَ اللَّهُ فِيهِمْ خَيْرًا لَّأَسْمَعَهُمْ ۖ
وَلَوْ أَسْمَعَهُمْ لَتَوَلَّوا وَّهُم مُّعْرِضُونَ ۝٢٣

4. إِنَّ شَرَّ الدَّوَابِّ عِندَ اللَّهِ الَّذِينَ كَفَرُوا
فَهُمْ لَا يُؤْمِنُونَ ۝٥٥

5. وَمِنْهُم مَّن يَسْتَمِعُونَ إِلَيْكَ ۚ أَفَأَنتَ
تُسْمِعُ الصُّمَّ وَلَوْ كَانُوا لَا يَعْقِلُونَ ۝٤٢
وَمِنْهُم مَّن يَنظُرُ إِلَيْكَ ۚ أَفَأَنتَ
تَهْدِي الْعُمْيَ وَلَوْ كَانُوا لَا يُبْصِرُونَ ۝٤٣

6. وَمَن كَانَ فِي هَٰذِهِ أَعْمَىٰ فَهُوَ فِي
الْآخِرَةِ أَعْمَىٰ وَأَضَلُّ سَبِيلًا ۝٧٢

looketh toward thee. But canst thou guide the blind even though they see not?

10:42–43

6. Whoso is blind here will be blind in the Hereafter, and yet further from the road.

17:72

7. And who doth greater wrong than he who hath been reminded of the revelations of his Lord, yet turneth away from them and forgetteth what his hands sent forward (to the Judgement)? Lo! on their hearts We have placed coverings so that they understand not, and in their ears a deafness. And though thou call them to the guidance, in that case they can never be led aright.

18:57

8. Have they not travelled in the land, and have they hearts wherewith to feel and ears wherewith to hear? For indeed it is not the eyes that grow blind, but it is the hearts, which are within the bosoms, that grow blind.

22:46

9. Hast thou seen him who chooseth for his god his own lust? Wouldst thou then be guardian over him?

Or deemest thou that most of them hear or understand? They are but as the cattle—nay, but they are farther astray!

25:43–44

10. Lo! thou canst not make the dead to hear, nor canst thou make the deaf to hear the call when they have turned to flee;

Nor canst thou lead the blind out of their error. Thou canst make none to hear, save those who believe Our revelations and who have surrendered.

27:80–81

7. وَمَنْ أَظْلَمُ مِمَّنْ ذُكِّرَ بِآيَاتِ رَبِّهِ
فَأَعْرَضَ عَنْهَا وَنَسِيَ مَا قَدَّمَتْ يَدَاهُ
إِنَّا جَعَلْنَا عَلَىٰ قُلُوبِهِمْ أَكِنَّةً أَنْ
يَفْقَهُوهُ وَفِي آذَانِهِمْ وَقْرًا وَإِنْ تَدْعُهُمْ
إِلَى الْهُدَىٰ فَلَنْ يَهْتَدُوا إِذًا أَبَدًا ﴿٥٧﴾

8. أَفَلَمْ يَسِيرُوا فِي الْأَرْضِ فَتَكُونَ
لَهُمْ قُلُوبٌ يَعْقِلُونَ بِهَا أَوْ آذَانٌ
يَسْمَعُونَ بِهَا فَإِنَّهَا لَا تَعْمَى الْأَبْصَارُ
وَلَٰكِنْ تَعْمَى الْقُلُوبُ الَّتِي فِي الصُّدُورِ ﴿٤٦﴾

9. أَرَأَيْتَ مَنِ اتَّخَذَ إِلَٰهَهُ هَوَاهُ
أَفَأَنْتَ تَكُونُ عَلَيْهِ وَكِيلًا ﴿٤٣﴾
أَمْ تَحْسَبُ أَنَّ أَكْثَرَهُمْ يَسْمَعُونَ
أَوْ يَعْقِلُونَ إِنْ هُمْ إِلَّا كَالْأَنْعَامِ
بَلْ هُمْ أَضَلُّ سَبِيلًا ﴿٤٤﴾

10. إِنَّكَ لَا تُسْمِعُ الْمَوْتَىٰ وَلَا تُسْمِعُ الصُّمَّ
الدُّعَاءَ إِذَا وَلَّوْا مُدْبِرِينَ ﴿٨٠﴾
وَمَا أَنْتَ بِهَادِي الْعُمْيِ عَنْ ضَلَالَتِهِمْ
إِنْ تُسْمِعُ إِلَّا مَنْ يُؤْمِنُ بِآيَاتِنَا
فَهُمْ مُسْلِمُونَ ﴿٨١﴾

11. وَمَا يَسْتَوِي الْأَعْمَىٰ وَالْبَصِيرُ ﴿١٩﴾
وَلَا الظُّلُمَاتُ وَلَا النُّورُ ﴿٢٠﴾
وَلَا الظِّلُّ وَلَا الْحَرُورُ ﴿٢١﴾

11. The blind man is not equal with the seer;

Nor is darkness (tantamount to) light;

Nor is the shadow equal with the sun's full heat;

Nor are the living equal

with the dead. Lo! Allah maketh whom He will to hear. Thou canst not reach those who are in the graves.

35:19–22

وَمَا يَسْتَوِي الْأَحْيَاءُ وَلَا الْأَمْوَاتُ
إِنَّ اللَّهَ يُسْمِعُ مَنْ يَشَاءُ وَمَا أَنْتَ
بِمُسْمِعٍ مَنْ فِي الْقُبُورِ ﴿٢٢﴾

EXORCISIM

1. Nay, but when the life cometh up to the throat

And men say: Where is the wizard (who can save him now)?

And he knoweth that it is the parting;

And agony is heaped on agony;

Unto thy Lord that day will be the driving.

75:26–30

1. كَلَّا إِذَا بَلَغَتِ التَّرَاقِيَ ﴿٢٦﴾
وَقِيلَ مَنْ رَاقٍ ﴿٢٧﴾
وَظَنَّ أَنَّهُ الْفِرَاقُ ﴿٢٨﴾
وَالْتَفَّتِ السَّاقُ بِالسَّاقِ ﴿٢٩﴾
إِلَىٰ رَبِّكَ يَوْمَئِذٍ الْمَسَاقُ ﴿٣٠﴾

2. Say: I seek refuge in the Lord of Daybreak,

From the evil of that which He created.

From the evil of the darkness when it is intense.

And from the evil of malignant witchcraft,

And from the evil of the envier when he envieth.

113:1–5

2. قُلْ أَعُوذُ بِرَبِّ الْفَلَقِ ﴿١﴾
مِنْ شَرِّ مَا خَلَقَ ﴿٢﴾
وَمِنْ شَرِّ غَاسِقٍ إِذَا وَقَبَ ﴿٣﴾
وَمِنْ شَرِّ النَّفَّاثَاتِ فِي الْعُقَدِ ﴿٤﴾
وَمِنْ شَرِّ حَاسِدٍ إِذَا حَسَدَ ﴿٥﴾

EXAMPLE OF THE DISOBEDIENT

Ref: 2:18; 6:26,50,104,122; 11:24; 13:19; 21:45; 30:52–53; 31:7; 36:9; 40:58; 41:44; 43:40; 47:23–24.

EXPEDITIONS

1. And when thou settedst forth at day-break from thy house-folk to assign to the believers their positions for the battle, Allah was Hearer, Knower.

When two parties of you almost fell away, and Allah was their Protecting Friend. In Allah let believers put their trust.

Allah had already given you the victory at Badr, when ye were contemptible. So observe your duty to Allah in order that ye may be thankful.

And when thou didst say unto the believers: Is it not sufficient for you that your Lord should support you with three thousand angels sent down (to your help)?

Nay, but if ye persevere, and keep from evil, and (the enemy) attack you suddenly, your Lord will help you with five thousand angels sweeping on.

Allah ordained this only as a message of good cheer for you, and that thereby your hearts might be at rest— Victory cometh only from Allah, the Mighty, the Wise—

That He may cut off a part of those who disbelieve, or overwhelm them so that they retire, frustrated.

3:121–127

2. Allah verily made good His promise unto you when ye routed them by His leave, until (the moment) when your courage failed you, and ye disagreed about the order

1. وَإِذْ غَدَوْتَ مِنْ أَهْلِكَ تُبَوِّئُ الْمُؤْمِنِينَ
مَقَاعِدَ لِلْقِتَالِ ۗ وَاللَّهُ سَمِيعٌ عَلِيمٌ ○
إِذْ هَمَّتْ طَائِفَتَانِ مِنْكُمْ أَنْ تَفْشَلَا ۙ
وَاللَّهُ وَلِيُّهُمَا ۗ وَعَلَى اللَّهِ فَلْيَتَوَكَّلِ
الْمُؤْمِنُونَ ○
وَلَقَدْ نَصَرَكُمُ اللَّهُ بِبَدْرٍ وَأَنْتُمْ
أَذِلَّةٌ ۚ فَاتَّقُوا اللَّهَ لَعَلَّكُمْ تَشْكُرُونَ ○
إِذْ تَقُولُ لِلْمُؤْمِنِينَ أَلَنْ يَكْفِيَكُمْ أَنْ
يُمِدَّكُمْ رَبُّكُمْ بِثَلَاثَةِ آلَافٍ مِنَ الْمَلَائِكَةِ
مُنْزَلِينَ ○
بَلَىٰ ۙ إِنْ تَصْبِرُوا وَتَتَّقُوا وَيَأْتُوكُمْ مِنْ
فَوْرِهِمْ هَٰذَا يُمْدِدْكُمْ رَبُّكُمْ بِخَمْسَةِ
آلَافٍ مِنَ الْمَلَائِكَةِ مُسَوِّمِينَ ○
وَمَا جَعَلَهُ اللَّهُ إِلَّا بُشْرَىٰ لَكُمْ وَلِتَطْمَئِنَّ
قُلُوبُكُمْ بِهِ ۗ وَمَا النَّصْرُ إِلَّا مِنْ عِنْدِ
اللَّهِ الْعَزِيزِ الْحَكِيمِ ○
لِيَقْطَعَ طَرَفًا مِنَ الَّذِينَ كَفَرُوا أَوْ
يَكْبِتَهُمْ فَيَنْقَلِبُوا خَائِبِينَ ○

2. وَلَقَدْ صَدَقَكُمُ اللَّهُ وَعْدَهُ إِذْ تَحُسُّونَهُمْ
بِإِذْنِهِ ۖ حَتَّىٰ إِذَا فَشِلْتُمْ وَتَنَازَعْتُمْ فِي
الْأَمْرِ وَعَصَيْتُمْ مِنْ بَعْدِ مَا أَرَاكُمْ مَا
تُحِبُّونَ ۚ مِنْكُمْ مَنْ يُرِيدُ الدُّنْيَا وَمِنْكُمْ مَنْ
يُرِيدُ الْآخِرَةَ ۚ ثُمَّ صَرَفَكُمْ عَنْهُمْ
لِيَبْتَلِيَكُمْ ۖ وَلَقَدْ عَفَا عَنْكُمْ ۗ وَاللَّهُ ذُو

and ye disobeyed, after He had shown you that for which ye long. Some of you desired the world, and some of you desired the Hereafter. Therefore He made you flee from them, that He might try you. Yet now He hath forgiven you. Allah is the Lord of Kindness to believers.

When ye climbed (the hill) and paid no heed to anyone; while the messenger, in your rear, was calling you (to fight). Therefor He rewarded you grief for (his) grief, that (He might teach) you not to sorrow either for that which ye missed or for that which befell you. Allah is Informed of what ye do.

Then, after grief, He sent down security for you. As slumber did it overcome a party of you, while (the other) party, who were anxious on their own account, thought wrongly of Allah, the thought of ignorance. They said: Have we any part in the cause? Say (O Muhammad): The cause belongeth wholly to Allah. They hide within themselves (a thought) which they reveal not unto thee, saying; Had we had any part in the cause we should not have been slain here. Say: Even though ye had been in your houses, those appointed to be slain would have gone forth to the places where they were to lie. (All this hath been) in order that Allah might try what is in your breasts and prove what is in your hearts. Allah is Aware of what is hidden in the breasts (of men).

Lo! those of you who turned back on the day when the two hosts met, Satan alone it was who caused them to backslide, because of some of that which they have earned. Now Allah hath forgiven them. Lo! Allah is Forgiving,

فَضْلٍ عَلَى الْمُؤْمِنِينَ ○
إِذْ تُصْعِدُونَ وَلَا تَلْوُونَ عَلَىٰ أَحَدٍ وَالرَّسُولُ
يَدْعُوكُمْ فِي أُخْرَاكُمْ فَأَثَابَكُمْ غَمًّا بِغَمٍّ
لِكَيْلَا تَحْزَنُوا عَلَىٰ مَا فَاتَكُمْ وَلَا مَا أَصَابَكُمْ
وَاللَّهُ خَبِيرٌ بِمَا تَعْمَلُونَ ○

ثُمَّ أَنْزَلَ عَلَيْكُمْ مِنْ بَعْدِ الْغَمِّ أَمَنَةً
نُعَاسًا يَغْشَىٰ طَائِفَةً مِنْكُمْ وَطَائِفَةٌ قَدْ
أَهَمَّتْهُمْ أَنْفُسُهُمْ يَظُنُّونَ بِاللَّهِ غَيْرَ
الْحَقِّ ظَنَّ الْجَاهِلِيَّةِ يَقُولُونَ هَلْ لَنَا
مِنَ الْأَمْرِ مِنْ شَيْءٍ قُلْ إِنَّ الْأَمْرَ كُلَّهُ
لِلَّهِ يُخْفُونَ فِي أَنْفُسِهِمْ مَا لَا يُبْدُونَ
لَكَ يَقُولُونَ لَوْ كَانَ لَنَا مِنَ الْأَمْرِ شَيْءٌ
مَا قُتِلْنَا هَاهُنَا قُلْ لَوْ كُنْتُمْ فِي بُيُوتِكُمْ
لَبَرَزَ الَّذِينَ كُتِبَ عَلَيْهِمُ الْقَتْلُ إِلَىٰ
مَضَاجِعِهِمْ وَلِيَبْتَلِيَ اللَّهُ مَا فِي صُدُورِكُمْ
وَلِيُمَحِّصَ مَا فِي قُلُوبِكُمْ وَاللَّهُ عَلِيمٌ
بِذَاتِ الصُّدُورِ ○

إِنَّ الَّذِينَ تَوَلَّوْا مِنْكُمْ يَوْمَ الْتَقَى الْجَمْعَانِ
إِنَّمَا اسْتَزَلَّهُمُ الشَّيْطَانُ بِبَعْضِ مَا كَسَبُوا
وَلَقَدْ عَفَا اللَّهُ عَنْهُمْ إِنَّ اللَّهَ غَفُورٌ حَلِيمٌ ○

3. أَوَلَمَّا أَصَابَتْكُمْ مُصِيبَةٌ قَدْ أَصَبْتُمْ
مِثْلَيْهَا قُلْتُمْ أَنَّىٰ هَٰذَا قُلْ هُوَ مِنْ

Clement.

3:152–155

3. And was it so, when a disaster smote you, though ye had smitten (them with a disaster) twice (as great), that ye said: How is this?

Say (unto them, O Muhammad): It is from yourselves. Lo! Allah is Able to do all things.

That which befell you, on the day when the two armies met, was by permission of Allah; that He might know the true believers;

And that He might know the hypocrites.

3:165–167

4. Those unto whom men said: Lo! the people have gathered against you, therefor fear them. (The threat of danger) but increased the faith of them and they cried: Allah is Sufficient for us! Most Excellent is He in Whom we trust!

So they returned with grace and favour from Allah, and no harm touched them. They followed the good pleasure of Allah, and Allah is of Infinite Bounty.

3:173–174

5. Even as thy Lord caused thee (Muhammad) to go forth from thy home with the Truth, and lo! a party of the believers were averse (to it).

Disputing with thee of the Truth after it had been made manifest, as if they were being driven to death visible.

And when Allah promised you one of the two bands (of the enemy) that it should be yours, and ye longed that other than the armed one might be yours. And Allah willed that He should cause the Truth to triumph by His words, and cut the root of the disbelievers;

That He might cause the Truth to triumph and bring vanity to naught, however much the guilty might oppose;

When ye sought help of your Lord and He answered you (saying): I will help you with a thousand of the angels

عِنْدِ اَنْفُسِكُمْ ۭ اِنَّ اللّٰهَ عَلٰى كُلِّ
شَيْءٍ قَدِيْرٌ ○
وَمَآ اَصَابَكُمْ يَوْمَ الْتَقَى الْجَمْعٰنِ
فَبِاِذْنِ اللّٰهِ وَلِيَعْلَمَ الْمُؤْمِنِيْنَ ○
وَلِيَعْلَمَ الَّذِيْنَ نَافَقُوْا ۚ

4. اَلَّذِيْنَ قَالَ لَهُمُ النَّاسُ اِنَّ النَّاسَ
قَدْ جَمَعُوْا لَكُمْ فَاخْشَوْهُمْ فَزَادَهُمْ
اِيْمَانًا ڰ وَّقَالُوْا حَسْبُنَا اللّٰهُ وَنِعْمَ الْوَكِيْلُ ○
فَانْقَلَبُوْا بِنِعْمَةٍ مِّنَ اللّٰهِ وَفَضْلٍ لَّمْ
يَمْسَسْهُمْ سُوْۗءٌ ۙ وَّاتَّبَعُوْا رِضْوَانَ اللّٰهِ ۭ
وَاللّٰهُ ذُوْ فَضْلٍ عَظِيْمٍ ○

5. كَمَآ اَخْرَجَكَ رَبُّكَ مِنْ بَيْتِكَ بِالْحَقِّ
وَاِنَّ فَرِيْقًا مِّنَ الْمُؤْمِنِيْنَ لَكٰرِهُوْنَ ○
يُجَادِلُوْنَكَ فِي الْحَقِّ بَعْدَ مَا تَبَيَّنَ كَاَنَّمَا
يُسَاقُوْنَ اِلَى الْمَوْتِ وَهُمْ يَنْظُرُوْنَ ○
وَاِذْ يَعِدُكُمُ اللّٰهُ اِحْدَى الطَّاۗىِٕفَتَيْنِ اَنَّهَا
لَكُمْ وَتَوَدُّوْنَ اَنَّ غَيْرَ ذَاتِ الشَّوْكَةِ
تَكُوْنُ لَكُمْ وَيُرِيْدُ اللّٰهُ اَنْ يُّحِقَّ الْحَقَّ
بِكَلِمٰتِهٖ وَيَقْطَعَ دَابِرَ الْكٰفِرِيْنَ ○
لِيُحِقَّ الْحَقَّ وَيُبْطِلَ الْبَاطِلَ وَلَوْ
كَرِهَ الْمُجْرِمُوْنَ ○
اِذْ تَسْتَغِيْثُوْنَ رَبَّكُمْ فَاسْتَجَابَ لَكُمْ اَنِّىْ
مُمِدُّكُمْ بِاَلْفٍ مِّنَ الْمَلٰۗىِٕكَةِ مُرْدِفِيْنَ ○

وَمَا جَعَلَهُ اللَّهُ إِلَّا بُشْرَىٰ وَلِتَطْمَئِنَّ بِهِ
قُلُوبُكُمْ ۚ وَمَا النَّصْرُ إِلَّا مِنْ عِنْدِ اللَّهِ ۚ
إِنَّ اللَّهَ عَزِيزٌ حَكِيمٌ ﴿١٠﴾

إِذْ يُغَشِّيكُمُ النُّعَاسَ أَمَنَةً مِنْهُ وَيُنَزِّلُ
عَلَيْكُمْ مِنَ السَّمَاءِ مَاءً لِيُطَهِّرَكُمْ بِهِ
وَيُذْهِبَ عَنْكُمْ رِجْزَ الشَّيْطَانِ وَلِيَرْبِطَ
عَلَىٰ قُلُوبِكُمْ وَيُثَبِّتَ بِهِ الْأَقْدَامَ ﴿١١﴾

إِذْ يُوحِي رَبُّكَ إِلَى الْمَلَائِكَةِ أَنِّي مَعَكُمْ
فَثَبِّتُوا الَّذِينَ آمَنُوا ۚ سَأُلْقِي فِي قُلُوبِ
الَّذِينَ كَفَرُوا الرُّعْبَ فَاضْرِبُوا فَوْقَ
الْأَعْنَاقِ وَاضْرِبُوا مِنْهُمْ كُلَّ بَنَانٍ ﴿١٢﴾

ذَٰلِكَ بِأَنَّهُمْ شَاقُّوا اللَّهَ وَرَسُولَهُ ۚ وَمَنْ
يُشَاقِقِ اللَّهَ وَرَسُولَهُ فَإِنَّ اللَّهَ شَدِيدُ
الْعِقَابِ ﴿١٣﴾

6. وَاعْلَمُوا أَنَّمَا غَنِمْتُمْ مِنْ شَيْءٍ فَأَنَّ لِلَّهِ
خُمُسَهُ وَلِلرَّسُولِ وَلِذِي الْقُرْبَىٰ وَالْيَتَامَىٰ
وَالْمَسَاكِينِ وَابْنِ السَّبِيلِ إِنْ كُنْتُمْ آمَنْتُمْ
بِاللَّهِ وَمَا أَنْزَلْنَا عَلَىٰ عَبْدِنَا يَوْمَ الْفُرْقَانِ
يَوْمَ الْتَقَى الْجَمْعَانِ ۗ وَاللَّهُ عَلَىٰ كُلِّ شَيْءٍ قَدِيرٌ ﴿٤١﴾
إِذْ أَنْتُمْ بِالْعُدْوَةِ الدُّنْيَا وَهُمْ بِالْعُدْوَةِ

rank on rank.

Allah appointed it only as good tidings, and that your hearts thereby might be at rest. Victory cometh only by the help of Allah. Lo! Allah is Mighty, Wise.

When He made the slumber fall upon you as a reassurance from Him and sent down water from the sky upon you, that thereby He might purify you, and remove from you the fear of Satan, and make strong your hearts and firm (your) feet thereby.

When thy Lord inspired the angels, (saying): I am with you. So make those who believe stand firm. I will throw fear into the hearts of those who disbelieve. Then smite the necks and smite of them each finger.

That is because they opposed Allah and His messenger. Whoso opposeth Allah and His messenger, (for him) lo! Allah is severe in punishment.

8:5–13

6. And know that whatever ye take as spoils of war, lo! a fifth thereof is for Allah, and for the messenger and for the kinsman (who hath need) and orphans and the needy and the wayfarer, if ye believe in Allah and that which We revealed unto Our slave on the Day of Discrimination, the day when the two armies met. And Allah is Able to do all things.

When ye were on the near bank (of the valley) and they were on the yonder bank, and the caravan was below you (on the coast plain)

And had ye trysted to meet one another ye surely would have failed to keep the tryst, but (it happened, as it did, without the forethought of either of you) that Allah might conclude a thing that must be done; that he who perished (on that day) might perish by a clear proof (of His Sovereignty) and he who survived might survive by a clear proof (of His Sovereignty). Lo! Allah in truth is Hearer, Knower.

When Allah showed them unto thee (O Muhammad) in thy dream as few in number, and if He had shown them to thee as many, ye (Muslims) would have faltered and would have quarrelled over the affair. But Allah saved (you). Lo! He knoweth what is in the breasts (of men).

And when He made you (Muslims), when ye met (them), see them with your eyes as few, and lessened you in their eyes, (it was) that Allah might conclude a thing that must be done. Unto Allah all things are brought back.

O ye who believe! When ye meet an army, hold firm and think of Allah much, that ye may be successful.

8:41–45

القصوى والركب اسفل منكم ولو
تواعدتم لاختلفتم في الميعد ولكن
ليقضي الله امرا كان مفعولا ليهلك
من هلك عن بينة ويحيى من حي عن
بينة وان الله لسميع عليم ﴿٤٢﴾
اذ يريكهم الله في منامك قليلا ولو
اركهم كثيرا لفشلتم ولتنازعتم
في الامر ولكن الله سلم انه
عليم بذات الصدور ﴿٤٣﴾
واذ يريكموهم اذ التقيتم في اعينكم
قليلا ويقللكم في اعينهم ليقضي الله
امرا كان مفعولا والى الله ترجع الامور ﴿٤٤﴾
يايها الذين امنوا اذا لقيتم فئة فاثبتوا
واذكروا الله كثيرا لعلكم تفلحون ﴿٤٥﴾

لقد نصركم الله في مواطن كثيرة ويوم 7.
حنين اذ اعجبتكم كثرتكم فلم تغن
عنكم شيئا وضاقت عليكم الارض بما
رحبت ثم وليتم مدبرين ﴿٢٥﴾
ثم انزل الله سكينته على رسوله وعلى
المؤمنين وانزل جنودا لم تروها وعذب
الذين كفروا وذلك جزاء الكفرين ﴿٢٦﴾

يايها الذين امنوا ما لكم اذا قيل لكم 8.
انفروا في سبيل الله اثاقلتم الى الارض

7. Allah hath given you victory on many fields and on the day of *Huneyn*, when ye exulted in your multitude but it availed you naught, and the earth, vast as it is, was straitened for you; then ye turned back in flight!

Then Allah sent His peace of reassurance down upon His messenger and upon the believers, and sent down hosts ye could not see, and punished those who disbelieved. Such is the reward of disbelievers.

9:25–26

8. O ye who believe! What aileth you that when it is said unto you: Go forth in

the way of Allah, ye are bowed down to the ground with heaviness? Take ye pleasure in the life of the world rather than in the Hereafter? The comfort of the life of the world is but little than in the Hereafter.

If ye go not forth He will afflict you with a painful doom, and will choose instead of you a flok other than you. Ye cannot harm Him at all. Allah is Able to do all things.

If ye help him not, still Allah helped him when those who disbelieve drove him forth, the second of two; when they two were in the cave, when he said unto his comrade: Grieve not. Lo! Allah is with us. Then Allah caused His peace of reassurance to descend upon him and supported him with hosts ye cannot see, and made the word of those who disbelieved the nethermost, while Allah's Word it was that became the uppermost. Allah is Mighty, Wise.

Go forth, light-armed and heavy-armed, and strive with your wealth and your lives in the way of Allah! That is best for you if ye but knew.

Had it been a near adventure and an easy journey they had followed thee, but the distance seemed too far for them. Yet will they swear by Allah (saying): If we had been able we would surely have set out with you. They destroy their souls, and Allah knoweth that they verily are

أَرَضِيتُم بِالْحَيَوٰةِ الدُّنْيَا مِنَ الْآخِرَةِ
فَمَا مَتَاعُ الْحَيَوٰةِ الدُّنْيَا فِي الْآخِرَةِ
إِلَّا قَلِيلٌ ﴿٣٨﴾
إِلَّا تَنفِرُوا يُعَذِّبْكُمْ عَذَابًا أَلِيمًا
وَيَسْتَبْدِلْ قَوْمًا غَيْرَكُمْ وَلَا تَضُرُّوهُ
شَيْئًا وَاللَّهُ عَلَىٰ كُلِّ شَيْءٍ قَدِيرٌ ﴿٣٩﴾
إِلَّا تَنصُرُوهُ فَقَدْ نَصَرَهُ اللَّهُ إِذْ أَخْرَجَهُ
الَّذِينَ كَفَرُوا ثَانِيَ اثْنَيْنِ إِذْ هُمَا فِي الْغَارِ
إِذْ يَقُولُ لِصَاحِبِهِ لَا تَحْزَنْ إِنَّ اللَّهَ مَعَنَا
فَأَنزَلَ اللَّهُ سَكِينَتَهُ عَلَيْهِ وَأَيَّدَهُ بِجُنُودٍ
لَّمْ تَرَوْهَا وَجَعَلَ كَلِمَةَ الَّذِينَ كَفَرُوا
السُّفْلَىٰ وَكَلِمَةُ اللَّهِ هِيَ الْعُلْيَا وَاللَّهُ
عَزِيزٌ حَكِيمٌ ﴿٤٠﴾
انفِرُوا خِفَافًا وَثِقَالًا وَجَاهِدُوا بِأَمْوَالِكُمْ
وَأَنفُسِكُمْ فِي سَبِيلِ اللَّهِ ذَٰلِكُمْ خَيْرٌ
لَّكُمْ إِن كُنتُمْ تَعْلَمُونَ ﴿٤١﴾
لَوْ كَانَ عَرَضًا قَرِيبًا وَسَفَرًا قَاصِدًا
لَّاتَّبَعُوكَ وَلَٰكِن بَعُدَتْ عَلَيْهِمُ الشُّقَّةُ
وَسَيَحْلِفُونَ بِاللَّهِ لَوِ اسْتَطَعْنَا لَخَرَجْنَا
مَعَكُمْ يُهْلِكُونَ أَنفُسَهُمْ وَاللَّهُ يَعْلَمُ
إِنَّهُمْ لَكَٰذِبُونَ ﴿٤٢﴾
عَفَا اللَّهُ عَنكَ لِمَ أَذِنتَ لَهُمْ حَتَّىٰ يَتَبَيَّنَ
لَكَ الَّذِينَ صَدَقُوا وَتَعْلَمَ الْكَٰذِبِينَ ﴿٤٣﴾

liars.

Allah forgive thee (O Muhammad)! Wherefor didst thou grant them leave ere those who told the truth were manifest to thee and thou didst know the liars?

Those who believe in Allah and the Last Day ask no leave of thee lest they should strive with their wealth and their lives. Allah is Aware of those who keep their duty (unto Him).

They alone ask leave of thee who believe not in Allah and the Last Day, and whose hearts feel doubt, so in their doubt they waver.

And if they had wished to go forth they would assuredly have made ready some equipment, but Allah was averse to their being sent forth and held them back and (it was said unto them): Sit ye with the sedentary!

9:38–46

9. Those who were left behind rejoiced at sitting still behind the messenger of Allah, and were averse to striving with their wealth and their lives in Allah's way. And they said: Go not forth in the heat! Say: The fire of hell is more intense of heat, if they but understood.

Then let them laugh a little: they will weep much, as the reward of what they used to earn.

9:81–82

10. And those among the wandering Arabs who had an excuse came in order that permission might be granted them. And those who lied to

لَا يَسْتَأْذِنُكَ الَّذِينَ يُؤْمِنُونَ بِاللّٰهِ وَالْيَوْمِ
الْاٰخِرِ اَنْ يُّجَاهِدُوْا بِاَمْوَالِهِمْ وَاَنْفُسِهِمْ ؕ
وَاللّٰهُ عَلِيْمٌۢ بِالْمُتَّقِيْنَ ۝

اِنَّمَا يَسْتَاْذِنُكَ الَّذِيْنَ لَا يُؤْمِنُوْنَ بِاللّٰهِ
وَالْيَوْمِ الْاٰخِرِ وَارْتَابَتْ قُلُوْبُهُمْ فَهُمْ
فِيْ رَيْبِهِمْ يَتَرَدَّدُوْنَ ۝

وَلَوْ اَرَادُوا الْخُرُوْجَ لَاَعَدُّوْا لَهٗ عُدَّةً
وَّلٰكِنْ كَرِهَ اللّٰهُ انْۢبِعَاثَهُمْ فَثَبَّطَهُمْ وَقِيْلَ
اقْعُدُوْا مَعَ الْقٰعِدِيْنَ ۝

9. فَرِحَ الْمُخَلَّفُوْنَ بِمَقْعَدِهِمْ خِلٰفَ رَسُوْلِ
اللّٰهِ وَكَرِهُوْٓا اَنْ يُّجَاهِدُوْا بِاَمْوَالِهِمْ
وَاَنْفُسِهِمْ فِيْ سَبِيْلِ اللّٰهِ وَقَالُوْا لَا
تَنْفِرُوْا فِي الْحَرِّ ؕ قُلْ نَارُ جَهَنَّمَ اَشَدُّ
حَرًّا ؕ لَوْ كَانُوْا يَفْقَهُوْنَ ۝

فَلْيَضْحَكُوْا قَلِيْلًا وَّلْيَبْكُوْا كَثِيْرًا ۚ جَزَآءًۢ
بِمَا كَانُوْا يَكْسِبُوْنَ ۝

10. وَجَآءَ الْمُعَذِّرُوْنَ مِنَ الْاَعْرَابِ لِيُؤْذَنَ
لَهُمْ وَقَعَدَ الَّذِيْنَ كَذَبُوا اللّٰهَ وَرَسُوْلَهٗ ؕ
سَيُصِيْبُ الَّذِيْنَ كَفَرُوْا مِنْهُمْ عَذَابٌ اَلِيْمٌ ۝
لَيْسَ عَلَى الضُّعَفَآءِ وَلَا عَلَى الْمَرْضٰى وَلَا

Allah and His messenger sat at home. A painful doom will fall on those of them who disbelieve.

Not unto the weak nor unto the sick nor unto

those who can find naught to spend is any fault (to be imputed though they stay at home) if they are true to Allah and His messenger. Not unto the good is there any road (of blame). Allah is Forgiving, Merciful;

Nor unto those whom, when they came to thee (asking) that thou shouldst mount them, thou didst tell: I cannot find whereon to mount you. They turned back with eyes flowing with tears, for sorrow that they could not find the means to spend.

The road (of blame) is only against those who ask for leave of thee (to stay at home) when they are rich. They are content to be with the useless. Allah hath sealed their hearts so that they know not.

They will make excuse to you (Muslims) when ye return unto them. Say: Make no excuse, for we shall not believe you. Allah hath told us tidings of you. Allah and His messenger will see your conduct, and then ye will be brought back unto Him Who knoweth the Invisible as well as the Visible, and He will tell you what ye used to do.

They will swear by Allah unto you, when ye return unto them, that ye may let them be. Let them be, for lo! they are unclean, and their abode is hell as the reward for what they used to earn.

They swear unto you,

عَلَى الَّذِيْنَ لَا يَجِدُوْنَ مَا يُنْفِقُوْنَ حَرَجٌ
إِذَا نَصَحُوْا لِلّٰهِ وَرَسُوْلِهٖ ؕ مَا عَلَى
الْمُحْسِنِيْنَ مِنْ سَبِيْلٍ ؕ وَاللّٰهُ غَفُوْرٌ رَّحِيْمٌ ﴿۹۱﴾
وَّلَا عَلَى الَّذِيْنَ إِذَا مَا أَتَوْكَ لِتَحْمِلَهُمْ
قُلْتَ لَا أَجِدُ مَا أَحْمِلُكُمْ عَلَيْهِ ۪ تَوَلَّوْا
وَّأَعْيُنُهُمْ تَفِيْضُ مِنَ الدَّمْعِ حَزَنًا أَلَّا
يَجِدُوْا مَا يُنْفِقُوْنَ ﴿۹۲﴾
إِنَّمَا السَّبِيْلُ عَلَى الَّذِيْنَ يَسْتَأْذِنُوْنَكَ
وَهُمْ أَغْنِيَاءُ ۚ رَضُوْا بِأَنْ يَّكُوْنُوْا
مَعَ الْخَوَالِفِ ۙ وَطَبَعَ اللّٰهُ عَلَى قُلُوْبِهِمْ
فَهُمْ لَا يَعْلَمُوْنَ ﴿۹۳﴾
يَعْتَذِرُوْنَ إِلَيْكُمْ إِذَا رَجَعْتُمْ إِلَيْهِمْ ؕ
قُلْ لَّا تَعْتَذِرُوْا لَنْ نُّؤْمِنَ لَكُمْ قَدْ
نَبَّأَنَا اللّٰهُ مِنْ أَخْبَارِكُمْ ؕ وَسَيَرَى اللّٰهُ
عَمَلَكُمْ وَرَسُوْلُهٗ ثُمَّ تُرَدُّوْنَ إِلٰى عٰلِمِ
الْغَيْبِ وَالشَّهَادَةِ فَيُنَبِّئُكُمْ بِمَا
كُنْتُمْ تَعْمَلُوْنَ ﴿۹۴﴾
سَيَحْلِفُوْنَ بِاللّٰهِ لَكُمْ إِذَا انْقَلَبْتُمْ إِلَيْهِمْ
لِتُعْرِضُوْا عَنْهُمْ ؕ فَأَعْرِضُوْا عَنْهُمْ ؕ إِنَّهُمْ
رِجْسٌ ۫ وَّمَأْوٰىهُمْ جَهَنَّمُ ۚ جَزَاءًۢ بِمَا
كَانُوْا يَكْسِبُوْنَ ﴿۹۵﴾
يَحْلِفُوْنَ لَكُمْ لِتَرْضَوْا عَنْهُمْ ۚ فَإِنْ تَرْضَوْا
عَنْهُمْ فَإِنَّ اللّٰهَ لَا يَرْضٰى عَنِ الْقَوْمِ
الْفٰسِقِيْنَ ﴿۹۶﴾

that ye may accept them. Though ye accept them, Allah verily accepteth not wrongdoing folk.

9:90–96

11. لَقَدْ تَّابَ اللّٰهُ عَلَى النَّبِيِّ وَالْمُهٰجِرِيْنَ
وَالْأَنْصَارِ الَّذِيْنَ اتَّبَعُوْهُ فِيْ سَاعَةِ
الْعُسْرَةِ مِنْ بَعْدِ مَا كَادَ يَزِيْغُ قُلُوْبُ
فَرِيْقٍ مِّنْهُمْ ثُمَّ تَابَ عَلَيْهِمْ ۚ إِنَّهُ بِهِمْ
رَءُوْفٌ رَّحِيْمٌ ﴿١١٧﴾
وَّعَلَى الثَّلٰثَةِ الَّذِيْنَ خُلِّفُوْا ۚ حَتّٰى إِذَا
ضَاقَتْ عَلَيْهِمُ الْأَرْضُ بِمَا رَحُبَتْ
وَضَاقَتْ عَلَيْهِمْ أَنْفُسُهُمْ وَظَنُّوْا أَنْ لَّا
مَلْجَأَ مِنَ اللّٰهِ إِلَّا إِلَيْهِ ۚ ثُمَّ تَابَ عَلَيْهِمْ
لِيَتُوْبُوْا ۚ إِنَّ اللّٰهَ هُوَ التَّوَّابُ الرَّحِيْمُ ﴿١١٨﴾
يٰٓأَيُّهَا الَّذِيْنَ اٰمَنُوا اتَّقُوا اللّٰهَ وَكُوْنُوْا
مَعَ الصّٰدِقِيْنَ ﴿١١٩﴾
مَا كَانَ لِأَهْلِ الْمَدِيْنَةِ وَمَنْ حَوْلَهُمْ
مِّنَ الْأَعْرَابِ أَنْ يَّتَخَلَّفُوْا عَنْ رَّسُوْلِ
اللّٰهِ وَلَا يَرْغَبُوْا بِأَنْفُسِهِمْ عَنْ نَّفْسِهٖ ۚ
ذٰلِكَ بِأَنَّهُمْ لَا يُصِيْبُهُمْ ظَمَأٌ وَّلَا نَصَبٌ
وَّلَا مَخْمَصَةٌ فِيْ سَبِيْلِ اللّٰهِ وَلَا يَطَـُٔوْنَ
مَوْطِئًا يَّغِيْظُ الْكُفَّارَ وَلَا يَنَالُوْنَ مِنْ
عَدُوٍّ نَّيْلًا إِلَّا كُتِبَ لَهُمْ بِهٖ عَمَلٌ صَالِحٌ ۚ
إِنَّ اللّٰهَ لَا يُضِيْعُ أَجْرَ الْمُحْسِنِيْنَ ﴿١٢٠﴾
وَلَا يُنْفِقُوْنَ نَفَقَةً صَغِيْرَةً وَّلَا كَبِيْرَةً
وَّلَا يَقْطَعُوْنَ وَادِيًا إِلَّا كُتِبَ لَهُمْ لِيَجْزِيَهُمُ
اللّٰهُ أَحْسَنَ مَا كَانُوْا يَعْمَلُوْنَ ﴿١٢١﴾

11. Allah hath turned in mercy to the Prophet, and to the *Muhajirin* and the *Ansar* who followed him in the hour of hardship. After the hearts of a party of them had almost swerved aside, then turned He unto them in mercy. Lo! He is Full of Pity, Merciful for them.

And to the three also (did He turn in mercy) who were left behind, when the earth, vast as it is, was straitened for them, and their own souls were straitened for them till they bethought them that there is no refuge from Allah save toward Him. Then turned He unto them in mercy that they (too) might turn (repentant unto Him) Lo! Allah! He is the Relenting, the Merciful.

O ye who believe! Be careful of your duty to Allah, and be with the truthful.

It is not for the townsfolk of *Al-Madinah* and for those around them of the wandering Arabs to stay behind the messenger of Allah and prefer their lives to his life. That is because neither thirst nor toil nor hunger afflicteth them in the way of Allah, nor step they any step that angereth the disbelievers, nor gain they from the enemy a gain, but a good deed is recorded for them therefor. Lo! Allah loseth not the wages of the good.

Nor spend they any spending, small or great, nor do they cross a valley, but it is recorded for them: that Allah may repay them the best of what they used to do.

9:117–121

12. O ye who believe! Remember Allah's favour unto you when there came against you hosts, and We sent against them a great wind and hosts ye could not see. And Allah is ever Seer of what ye do.

When they came upon you from above you and from below you, and when eyes grew wild and hearts reached to the throats, and ye were imagining vain thoughts concerning Allah.

There were the believers sorely tried, and shaken with a mighty shock.

And, when the hypocrites, and those in whose hearts is a disease were saying: Allah and His messenger promised us naught but delusion.

And when a party of them said: O folk of *Yathrib!* There is no stand (possible) for you, therefor turn back. And certain of them (even) sought permission of the Prophet, saying: Our homes lie open (to the enemy). And they lay not open. They but wished to flee.

33:9–13

13. And Allah repulsed the disbelievers in their wrath; they gained no good. Allah averted their attack from the believers. Allah is ever Strong, Mighty.

And He brought those of the People of the Scripture

12. يَا أَيُّهَا الَّذِينَ آمَنُوا اذْكُرُوا نِعْمَةَ اللَّهِ
عَلَيْكُمْ إِذْ جَاءَتْكُمْ جُنُودٌ فَأَرْسَلْنَا
عَلَيْهِمْ رِيحًا وَجُنُودًا لَّمْ تَرَوْهَا ۚ وَ
كَانَ اللَّهُ بِمَا تَعْمَلُونَ بَصِيرًا ﴿٩﴾
إِذْ جَاءُوكُم مِّن فَوْقِكُمْ وَمِنْ أَسْفَلَ
مِنكُمْ وَإِذْ زَاغَتِ الْأَبْصَارُ وَبَلَغَتِ
الْقُلُوبُ الْحَنَاجِرَ وَتَظُنُّونَ بِاللَّهِ الظُّنُونَا
هُنَالِكَ ابْتُلِيَ الْمُؤْمِنُونَ وَزُلْزِلُوا
زِلْزَالًا شَدِيدًا ﴿١١﴾
وَإِذْ يَقُولُ الْمُنَافِقُونَ وَالَّذِينَ فِي
قُلُوبِهِم مَّرَضٌ مَّا وَعَدَنَا اللَّهُ وَ
رَسُولُهُ إِلَّا غُرُورًا ﴿١٢﴾
وَإِذْ قَالَت طَّائِفَةٌ مِّنْهُمْ يَا أَهْلَ يَثْرِبَ
لَا مُقَامَ لَكُمْ فَارْجِعُوا ۚ وَيَسْتَأْذِنُ فَرِيقٌ
مِّنْهُمُ النَّبِيَّ يَقُولُونَ إِنَّ بُيُوتَنَا عَوْرَةٌ ۛ
وَمَا هِيَ بِعَوْرَةٍ ۖ إِن يُرِيدُونَ إِلَّا فِرَارًا ﴿١٣﴾
13. وَرَدَّ اللَّهُ الَّذِينَ كَفَرُوا بِغَيْظِهِمْ لَمْ
يَنَالُوا خَيْرًا ۚ وَكَفَى اللَّهُ الْمُؤْمِنِينَ
الْقِتَالَ ۚ وَكَانَ اللَّهُ قَوِيًّا عَزِيزًا ﴿٢٥﴾
وَأَنزَلَ الَّذِينَ ظَاهَرُوهُم مِّنْ أَهْلِ
الْكِتَابِ مِن صَيَاصِيهِمْ وَقَذَفَ فِي
قُلُوبِهِمُ الرُّعْبَ فَرِيقًا تَقْتُلُونَ
وَتَأْسِرُونَ فَرِيقًا ﴿٢٦﴾

who supported them down from their strongholds, and cast panic into their hearts. Some ye slew, and ye made captive some.

33:25–26

Ref: 8:66–71; 9:47–48; 33:14–24;

EXPIATION

1. Allah will not take you to task for that which is unintentional in your oaths, but He will take you to task for the oaths which ye swear in earnest. The expiation thereof is the feeding of ten of the needy with the average of that wherewith ye feed your own folk, or the clothing of them, or the liberation of a slave, and for him who findeth not (the wherewithal to do so) then a three days' fast. This is the expiation of your oaths when ye have sworn; and keep your oaths. Thus Allah expoundeth unto you His revelations in order that ye may give thanks.

5:89

2. O ye who believe! Kill no wild game while ye are on the pilgrimage. Whoso of you killeth it of set purpose he shall pay its forfeit in the equivalent of that which he hath killed, of domestic animals, the judge to be two men among you known for justice, (the forfeit) to be brought as an offering to the *Ka'bah* or, for expiation, he shall feed poor persons, or the equivalent thereof in fasting, that he may taste the evil consequences of his deed. Allah forgiveth whatever (of this kind) may have happened in the past, but whoso relapseth, Allah will take retribution from him. Allah is Mighty, Able to Requite (the wrong).

5:95

1. لا يؤاخذكم الله باللغو في أيمانكم
ولكن يؤاخذكم بما عقدتم الأيمان
فكفارته إطعام عشرة مساكين من
أوسط ما تطعمون أهليكم أو كسوتهم
أو تحرير رقبة فمن لم يجد فصيام
ثلثة أيام ذلك كفارة أيمانكم إذا
حلفتم واحفظوا أيمانكم كذلك يبين
الله لكم آيته لعلكم تشكرون ﴿٨٩﴾

2. يأيها الذين آمنوا لا تقتلوا الصيد
وأنتم حرم ومن قتله منكم متعمدا
فجزاء مثل ما قتل من النعم يحكم
به ذوا عدل منكم هديا بلغ الكعبة
أو كفارة طعام مسكين أو عدل ذلك
صياما ليذوق وبال أمره عفا الله عما
سلف ومن عاد فينتقم الله منه
والله عزيز ذو انتقام ﴿٩٥﴾

Ref: 5:45.

FAITH

1. He who chooseth disbelief instead of faith, verily he hath gone astray from a plain road.

2:108

2. Whoso denieth the faith, his work is vain and he will be among the losers in the Hereafter.

5:5

3. On the Day when one of the portents from thy Lord cometh, its belief availeth naught a soul which theretofore believed not, nor in its belief earned good (by works). Say: Wait ye! Lo! We (too) are waiting.

6:158

4. Whoso disbelieveth in Allah after his belief—save him who is forced thereto and whose heart is still content with Faith—but whoso findeth ease in disbelief: On them is wrath from Allah. Theirs will be an awful doom.

16:106

5. Then, when they saw Our doom, they said: We believe in Allah only and reject (all) that we used to associate (with Him).

But their faith could not avail them when they saw Our doom. This is Allah's law which hath ever taken course for His bondmen. And then

1. ومن يتبدل الكفر بالإيمان فقد ضل
سواء السبيل

2. ومن يكفر بالإيمان فقد حبط
عمله وهو في الآخرة من
الخاسرين

3. يوم يأتي بعض آيات ربك لا ينفع
نفسا إيمانها لم تكن آمنت من قبل
أو كسبت في إيمانها خيرا قل انتظروا
إنا منتظرون

4. من كفر بالله من بعد إيمانه إلا من
أكره وقلبه مطمئن بالإيمان ولكن
من شرح بالكفر صدرا فعليهم
غضب من الله ولهم عذاب عظيم

5. فلما رأوا بأسنا قالوا آمنا بالله
وحده وكفرنا بما كنا به مشركين

فلم يك ينفعهم إيمانهم لما رأوا
بأسنا سنت الله التي قد خلت
في عباده وخسر هنالك الكافرون

6. ولكن الله حبب إليكم الإيمان
وزينه في قلوبكم وكره إليكم
الكفر والفسوق والعصيان أولئك

the disbelievers will be ruined.

40:84–85

6. But Allah hath endeared the faith to you and hath beautified it in your hearts, and hath made disbelief and lewdness and rebellion hateful unto you. Such are they who

are rightly guided.

(It is) a bounty and a grace from Allah; and Allah is Knower, Wise.

49:7–8

هُمُ الرّٰشِدُوْنَ ۝
فَضْلًا مِّنَ اللّٰهِ وَ نِعْمَةً ؕ وَ اللّٰهُ
عَلِيْمٌ حَكِيْمٌ ۝

7. The wandering Arabs say: We believe. Say (unto them, O Muhammad): Ye believe not, but rather say "We submit," for the faith hath not yet entered into your hearts.

49:14

7. قَالَتِ الْاَعْرَابُ اٰمَنَّا ؕ قُلْ لَّمْ تُؤْمِنُوْا
وَلٰكِنْ قُوْلُوْۤا اَسْلَمْنَا وَلَمَّا يَدْخُلِ
الْاِيْمَانُ فِيْ قُلُوْبِكُمْ ؕ

8. They make it a favour unto thee (Muhammad) that they have surrendered (unto Him). Say: Deem not your Surrender a favour unto me; nay, but Allah doth confer a favour on you, inasmuch as He hath led you to the Faith, if ye are earnest.

49:17

8. يَمُنُّوْنَ عَلَيْكَ اَنْ اَسْلَمُوْا ؕ قُلْ لَّا
تَمُنُّوْا عَلَيَّ اِسْلَامَكُمْ ۚ بَلِ اللّٰهُ يَمُنُّ
عَلَيْكُمْ اَنْ هَدٰىكُمْ لِلْاِيْمَانِ اِنْ
كُنْتُمْ صٰدِقِيْنَ ۝

9. Thou wilt not find folk who believe in Allah and the Last Day loving those who oppose Allah and His messenger, even though they be their fathers or their sons or their brethren or their clan. As for such, He hath written faith upon their hearts and hath strengthened them with a Spirit from Him, and He will bring them into Gardens underneath which rivers flow, wherein they will abide. Allah is well pleased with them, and they are well pleased with Him. They are Allah's party. Lo! is it not Allah's party who are the successful?

58:22

9. لَا تَجِدُ قَوْمًا يُّؤْمِنُوْنَ بِاللّٰهِ وَالْيَوْمِ
الْاٰخِرِ يُوَآدُّوْنَ مَنْ حَآدَّ اللّٰهَ وَرَسُوْلَهٗ
وَلَوْ كَانُوْۤا اٰبَآءَهُمْ اَوْ اَبْنَآءَهُمْ اَوْ
اِخْوَانَهُمْ اَوْ عَشِيْرَتَهُمْ ؕ اُولٰٓئِكَ كَتَبَ
فِيْ قُلُوْبِهِمُ الْاِيْمَانَ وَ اَيَّدَهُمْ
بِرُوْحٍ مِّنْهُ ؕ وَ يُدْخِلُهُمْ جَنّٰتٍ تَجْرِيْ
مِنْ تَحْتِهَا الْاَنْهٰرُ خٰلِدِيْنَ فِيْهَا ؕ
رَضِيَ اللّٰهُ عَنْهُمْ وَ رَضُوْا عَنْهُ ؕ اُولٰٓئِكَ حِزْبُ
اللّٰهِ ؕ اَلَآ اِنَّ حِزْبَ اللّٰهِ هُمُ الْمُفْلِحُوْنَ ۝

○

Ref: 2:93,177,257; 3:86,106,167,173,193: 4:25; 5:16,72; 9:23,43–44; 13:16; 39:22; 49:11; 52:21; 57:9,28; 59:9–10; 61:8; 64:8; 65:11; 66:8.

See also: *Kufr.*

FALSE ACCUSATION

1. Whoso committeth sin committeth it only against himself. Allah is ever Knower, Wise.

And whoso committeth a delinquency or crime, then throweth (the blame) thereof upon the innocent, hath burdened himself with falsehood and a flagrant crime.

4:111–112

2. And those who accuse honourable women but bring not four witnesses, scourge them (with) eighty stripes and never (afterward) accept their testimony—They indeed are evildoers—

24:4

3. As for those who accuse their wives but have no witnesses except themselves; let the testimony of one of them be four testimonies, (swearing) by Allah that he is of those who speak the truth.

24:6

4. Lo! they who spread the slander are a gang among you. Deem it not a bad thing for you; nay, it is good for you. Unto every man of them (will be paid) that which he hath earned of the sin; and as for him among them who had the greater share therein, his will be an awful doom.

1. وَمَنْ يَكْسِبْ إِثْمًا فَإِنَّمَا يَكْسِبُهُ عَلَىٰ
نَفْسِهِ ۚ وَكَانَ اللَّهُ عَلِيمًا حَكِيمًا ﴿١١١﴾
وَمَنْ يَكْسِبْ خَطِيئَةً أَوْ إِثْمًا ثُمَّ يَرْمِ
بِهِ بَرِيئًا فَقَدِ احْتَمَلَ بُهْتَانًا وَإِثْمًا مُبِينًا ﴿١١٢﴾

2. وَالَّذِينَ يَرْمُونَ الْمُحْصَنَاتِ ثُمَّ لَمْ
يَأْتُوا بِأَرْبَعَةِ شُهَدَاءَ فَاجْلِدُوهُمْ
ثَمَانِينَ جَلْدَةً وَلَا تَقْبَلُوا لَهُمْ
شَهَادَةً أَبَدًا ۚ وَأُولَٰئِكَ هُمُ الْفَاسِقُونَ ﴿٤﴾

3. وَالَّذِينَ يَرْمُونَ أَزْوَاجَهُمْ وَلَمْ يَكُنْ
لَهُمْ شُهَدَاءُ إِلَّا أَنْفُسُهُمْ فَشَهَادَةُ
أَحَدِهِمْ أَرْبَعُ شَهَادَاتٍ بِاللَّهِ ۙ إِنَّهُ
لَمِنَ الصَّادِقِينَ ﴿٦﴾

4. إِنَّ الَّذِينَ جَاءُوا بِالْإِفْكِ عُصْبَةٌ
مِنْكُمْ ۚ لَا تَحْسَبُوهُ شَرًّا لَكُمْ ۖ بَلْ
هُوَ خَيْرٌ لَكُمْ ۚ لِكُلِّ امْرِئٍ مِنْهُمْ
مَا اكْتَسَبَ مِنَ الْإِثْمِ ۚ وَالَّذِي تَوَلَّىٰ
كِبْرَهُ مِنْهُمْ لَهُ عَذَابٌ عَظِيمٌ ﴿١١﴾
لَوْلَا إِذْ سَمِعْتُمُوهُ ظَنَّ الْمُؤْمِنُونَ
وَالْمُؤْمِنَاتُ بِأَنْفُسِهِمْ خَيْرًا وَقَالُوا
هَٰذَا إِفْكٌ مُبِينٌ ﴿١٢﴾

Why did not the believers, men and women, when ye heard it, think good of their own folk, and say: It is a manifest untruth?

24:11–12

5. Lo! as for those who traduce virtuous, believing women (who are) careless, cursed are they in the world and the Hereafter. Theirs will be an awful doom.

24:23

.5 إِنَّ الَّذِينَ يَرْمُونَ الْمُحْصَنٰتِ الْغٰفِلٰتِ
الْمُؤْمِنٰتِ لُعِنُوا فِي الدُّنْيَا وَالْاٰخِرَةِ
وَلَهُمْ عَذَابٌ عَظِيمٌ

6. And those who malign believing men and believing women undeservedly, they bear the guilt of slander and manifest sin.

33:58

.6 وَالَّذِينَ يُؤْذُونَ الْمُؤْمِنِينَ وَالْمُؤْمِنٰتِ
بِغَيْرِ مَا اكْتَسَبُوا فَقَدِ احْتَمَلُوا
بُهْتَانًا وَإِثْمًا مُّبِينًا

7. O Prophet! If believing women come unto thee, taking oath of allegiance unto thee that they will ascribe no thing as partner unto Allah, and will neither steal nor commit adultery nor kill their children, nor produce any lie that they have devised between their hands and feet, nor disobey thee in what is right, then accept their allegiance and ask Allah to forgive them. Lo! Allah is Forgiving, Merciful.

60:12

.7 يٰٓاَيُّهَا النَّبِيُّ إِذَا جَآءَكَ الْمُؤْمِنٰتُ
يُبَايِعْنَكَ عَلٰٓى اَنْ لَّا يُشْرِكْنَ بِاللّٰهِ
شَيْئًا وَّلَا يَسْرِقْنَ وَلَا يَزْنِينَ
وَلَا يَقْتُلْنَ اَوْلَادَهُنَّ وَلَا يَأْتِينَ
بِبُهْتَانٍ يَّفْتَرِينَهُ بَيْنَ اَيْدِيهِنَّ
وَاَرْجُلِهِنَّ وَلَا يَعْصِينَكَ فِي
مَعْرُوفٍ فَبَايِعْهُنَّ وَاسْتَغْفِرْ لَهُنَّ
اللّٰهَ إِنَّ اللّٰهَ غَفُورٌ رَّحِيمٌ

Ref: 24:16; 25:4; 29:17; 34:43; 37:151; 46:11,28; 49:6; 68:10–16.

See also: *Ifk*, Slander.

FALSEHOOD

1. So shun the filth of idols, and shun lying speech,
22:30

2. Lo! Allah guideth not him who is a liar, an ingrate.
39:3

3. Lo! Allah guideth not one who is a prodigal, a liar.
40:28

1. فاجتنبوا الرجس من الأوثان واجتنبوا
قول الزور ﴿٣٠﴾

2. إن الله لا يهدي من هو كاذب كفار ﴿٣﴾

3. إن الله لا يهدي من هو مسرف
كذاب ﴿٢٨﴾

FAMILY AND ITS RIGHTS

1. They ask thee, (O Muhammad), what they shall spend. Say: That which ye spend for good (must go) to parents and near kindred and orphans and the needy and the wayfarer. And whatsoever good ye do, lo! Allah is Aware of it.
2:215

2. And serve Allah: And ascribe no thing as partner unto Him. (Show) kindness unto parents, and unto near kindred, and orphans, and the needy, and unto the neighbour who is a kin (unto you) and the neighbour who is not of kin, and the fellow- traveller and the wayfarer and (the slaves) whom your right hands possess. Lo! Allah loveth not such as are proud and boastful.
4:36

3. And verily We sent messengers (to mankind) before thee, and We appointed for them wives and offspring, and

1. يسئلونك ماذا ينفقون قل ما أنفقتم
من خير فللوالدين والأقربين واليتمى
والمسكين وابن السبيل وما تفعلوا
من خير فإن الله به عليم ﴿٢١٥﴾

2. واعبدوا الله ولا تشركوا به شيئا
وبالوالدين إحسانا وبذي القربى
واليتمى والمسكين والجار ذي القربى
والجار الجنب والصاحب بالجنب
وابن السبيل وما ملكت أيمانكم إن
الله لا يحب من كان مختالا فخورا ﴿٣٦﴾

3. ولقد أرسلنا رسلا من قبلك وجعلنا
لهم أزواجا وذرية وما كان لرسول
أن يأتي بآية إلا بإذن الله لكل
أجل كتاب ﴿٣٨﴾
يمحوا الله ما يشاء ويثبت وعنده
أم الكتب ﴿٣٩﴾

it was not (given) to any messenger that he should bring a portent save by Allah's leave. For everything there is a time prescribed.

Allah effaceth what He will, and establisheth (what He will), and with Him is the source of ordinance.
13:38-39

FALSEHOOD
Ref: 25:4,72; 58:2. See also: Truth.

4. وَقَضَىٰ رَبُّكَ أَلَّا تَعْبُدُوٓا۟ إِلَّآ إِيَّاهُ وَ
بِٱلْوَٰلِدَيْنِ إِحْسَٰنًا ۚ إِمَّا يَبْلُغَنَّ عِندَكَ
ٱلْكِبَرَ أَحَدُهُمَآ أَوْ كِلَاهُمَا فَلَا تَقُل لَّهُمَآ
أُفٍّ وَلَا تَنْهَرْهُمَا وَقُل لَّهُمَا قَوْلًا كَرِيمًا ﴿٢٣﴾
وَٱخْفِضْ لَهُمَا جَنَاحَ ٱلذُّلِّ مِنَ ٱلرَّحْمَةِ
وَقُل رَّبِّ ٱرْحَمْهُمَا كَمَا رَبَّيَانِى صَغِيرًا ﴿٢٤﴾
رَّبُّكُمْ أَعْلَمُ بِمَا فِى نُفُوسِكُمْ ۚ إِن تَكُونُوا۟
صَٰلِحِينَ فَإِنَّهُۥ كَانَ لِلْأَوَّٰبِينَ غَفُورًا ﴿٢٥﴾

5. وَهُوَ ٱلَّذِى خَلَقَ مِنَ ٱلْمَآءِ بَشَرًا
فَجَعَلَهُۥ نَسَبًا وَصِهْرًا ۗ وَكَانَ
رَبُّكَ قَدِيرًا ﴿٥٤﴾

6. مَّا جَعَلَ ٱللَّهُ لِرَجُلٍ مِّن قَلْبَيْنِ فِى
جَوْفِهِۦ ۚ وَمَا جَعَلَ أَزْوَٰجَكُمُ ٱلَّٰٓـِٔى
تُظَٰهِرُونَ مِنْهُنَّ أُمَّهَٰتِكُمْ ۚ وَمَا جَعَلَ
أَدْعِيَآءَكُمْ أَبْنَآءَكُمْ ۚ ذَٰلِكُمْ قَوْلُكُم
بِأَفْوَٰهِكُمْ ۖ وَٱللَّهُ يَقُولُ ٱلْحَقَّ وَهُوَ
يَهْدِى ٱلسَّبِيلَ ﴿٤﴾

ٱدْعُوهُمْ لِءَابَآئِهِمْ هُوَ أَقْسَطُ عِندَ
ٱللَّهِ ۚ فَإِن لَّمْ تَعْلَمُوٓا۟ ءَابَآءَهُمْ فَإِخْوَٰنُكُمْ
فِى ٱلدِّينِ وَمَوَٰلِيكُمْ ۚ وَلَيْسَ عَلَيْكُمْ
جُنَاحٌ فِيمَآ أَخْطَأْتُم بِهِۦ وَلَٰكِن مَّا
تَعَمَّدَتْ قُلُوبُكُمْ ۚ وَكَانَ ٱللَّهُ
غَفُورًا رَّحِيمًا ﴿٥﴾

4. Thy Lord hath decreed, that ye worship none save Him, and (that ye show) kindness to parents. If one of them or both of them attain to old age with thee, say not "Fie" unto them nor repulse them, but speak unto them a gracious word.

And lower unto them the wing of submission through mercy, and say: My Lord! Have mercy on them both as they did care for me when I was little!

Your Lord is Best Aware or what is in your minds. If ye are righteous, then lo! He was ever Forgiving unto those who turn (unto Him).

17:23—25

5. And He it is Who hath created man from water, and hath appointed for him kindred by blood and kindred by marriage; for thy Lord is ever Powerful.

25:54

6. Allah hath not assigned unto any man two hearts within his body, nor hath He made your wives whom ye declare (to be your mothers) your mothers, nor hath He made those whom ye claim (to be your sons) your sons. This is but a saying of your mouths. But Allah sayeth the truth and He showeth the way.

Proclaim their real parentage. That will be more equitable in the sight of Allah. And if ye know not their fathers, then (they are) your brethren in the faith, and your clients. And there is no sin for you in the mistakes that ye make unintentionally, but what your hearts purpose (that will be a sin for you). Allah is Forgiving, Merciful.

The Prophet is closer to the believers than their selves, and his wives are (as) their mothers. And the owners of kinship are closer one to another in the ordinance of Allah than (other) believers and the fugitives (who fled from Makkah), except that ye should do kindness to your friends. This is written in the Book (of nature).

33:4–6

7. And they who believe and whose seeds follow them in faith, We cause their seed to join them (there), and We deprive them of naught of their (life's) work. Every man is a pledge for that which he hath earned.

52:21

8. O ye who believe! Lo! among your wives and your children there are enemies for you, therefor beware of them. And if ye efface and overlook and forgive, then lo! Allah is Forgiving, Merciful.

Your wealth and your children are only a temptation, whereas Allah! with Him is an immense reward.

64:14–15

النَّبِيُّ أَوْلَىٰ بِالْمُؤْمِنِينَ مِنْ أَنفُسِهِمْ
وَأَزْوَاجُهُ أُمَّهَاتُهُمْ وَأُولُو الْأَرْحَامِ
بَعْضُهُمْ أَوْلَىٰ بِبَعْضٍ فِي كِتَابِ اللَّهِ
مِنَ الْمُؤْمِنِينَ وَالْمُهَاجِرِينَ إِلَّا أَن
تَفْعَلُوا إِلَىٰ أَوْلِيَائِكُم مَّعْرُوفًا كَانَ
ذَٰلِكَ فِي الْكِتَابِ مَسْطُورًا ۝

7. وَالَّذِينَ آمَنُوا وَاتَّبَعَتْهُمْ ذُرِّيَّتُهُم
بِإِيمَانٍ أَلْحَقْنَا بِهِمْ ذُرِّيَّتَهُمْ وَمَا
أَلَتْنَاهُم مِّنْ عَمَلِهِم مِّن شَيْءٍ كُلُّ
امْرِئٍ بِمَا كَسَبَ رَهِينٌ ۝

8. يَا أَيُّهَا الَّذِينَ آمَنُوا إِنَّ مِنْ أَزْوَاجِكُمْ
وَأَوْلَادِكُمْ عَدُوًّا لَّكُمْ فَاحْذَرُوهُمْ
وَإِن تَعْفُوا وَتَصْفَحُوا وَتَغْفِرُوا فَإِنَّ
اللَّهَ غَفُورٌ رَّحِيمٌ ۝

إِنَّمَا أَمْوَالُكُمْ وَأَوْلَادُكُمْ فِتْنَةٌ وَاللَّهُ
عِندَهُ أَجْرٌ عَظِيمٌ ۝

Ref: 6:151; 8:41,75; 13:23; 16:90; 17:26; 29:8; 31:14; 40:8; 42:23; 46:15,17. **See also**: Children, Relatives, Rights of Parents.

FASTING

1. يَاأَيُّهَا الَّذِينَ آمَنُوا كُتِبَ عَلَيْكُمُ
الصِّيَامُ كَمَا كُتِبَ عَلَى الَّذِينَ مِنْ
قَبْلِكُمْ لَعَلَّكُمْ تَتَّقُونَ ﴿١٨٣﴾
أَيَّامًا مَعْدُودَاتٍ فَمَنْ كَانَ مِنْكُمْ مَرِيضًا
أَوْ عَلَى سَفَرٍ فَعِدَّةٌ مِنْ أَيَّامٍ أُخَرَ وَعَلَى
الَّذِينَ يُطِيقُونَهُ فِدْيَةٌ طَعَامُ مِسْكِينٍ
فَمَنْ تَطَوَّعَ خَيْرًا فَهُوَ خَيْرٌ لَهُ وَأَنْ
تَصُومُوا خَيْرٌ لَكُمْ إِنْ كُنْتُمْ تَعْلَمُونَ ﴿١٨٤﴾
شَهْرُ رَمَضَانَ الَّذِي أُنْزِلَ فِيهِ الْقُرْآنُ
هُدًى لِلنَّاسِ وَبَيِّنَاتٍ مِنَ الْهُدَى وَ
الْفُرْقَانِ فَمَنْ شَهِدَ مِنْكُمُ الشَّهْرَ
فَلْيَصُمْهُ وَمَنْ كَانَ مَرِيضًا أَوْ عَلَى سَفَرٍ
فَعِدَّةٌ مِنْ أَيَّامٍ أُخَرَ يُرِيدُ اللَّهُ بِكُمُ
الْيُسْرَ وَلَا يُرِيدُ بِكُمُ الْعُسْرَ وَلِتُكْمِلُوا
الْعِدَّةَ وَلِتُكَبِّرُوا اللَّهَ عَلَى مَا هَدَاكُمْ
وَلَعَلَّكُمْ تَشْكُرُونَ ﴿١٨٥﴾
2. أُحِلَّ لَكُمْ لَيْلَةَ الصِّيَامِ الرَّفَثُ إِلَى نِسَائِكُمْ
هُنَّ لِبَاسٌ لَكُمْ وَأَنْتُمْ لِبَاسٌ لَهُنَّ عَلِمَ
اللَّهُ أَنَّكُمْ كُنْتُمْ تَخْتَانُونَ أَنْفُسَكُمْ فَتَابَ
عَلَيْكُمْ وَعَفَا عَنْكُمْ فَالْآنَ بَاشِرُوهُنَّ
وَابْتَغُوا مَا كَتَبَ اللَّهُ لَكُمْ وَكُلُوا وَاشْرَبُوا
حَتَّى يَتَبَيَّنَ لَكُمُ الْخَيْطُ الْأَبْيَضُ مِنَ الْخَيْطِ
الْأَسْوَدِ مِنَ الْفَجْرِ ثُمَّ أَتِمُّوا الصِّيَامَ إِلَى

1. O ye who believe! Fasting is prescribed for you, even as it was prescribed for those before you, that ye may ward off (evil);

(Fast) a certain number of days; and (for) him who is sick among you, or on a journey, (the same) number of other days; and for those who can afford it there is a ransom; the feeding of a man in need — But whoso doth good of his own accord, it is better for him : and that ye fast is better for you if ye did but know

The month of *Ramadhan* in which was revealed the *Qur'ān*, a guidance for mankind, and clear proofs of the guidance, and the Criterion (of right and wrong). And whosoever of you is present, let him fast the month, and whosoever of you is sick or on a journey, (let him fast the same) number of other days. Allah desireth for you ease; He desireth not hardship for you; and (He desireth) that ye should complete the period, and that ye should magnify Allah for having guided you, and that peradventure ye may be thankful.
2:183-185

2. It is made lawful for you to go in unto your wives on the night of the fast. They are raiment for you and ye are raiment for them. Allah is Aware that ye were deceiving yourselves in this respect and He hath turned in mercy toward you and relieved you. So hold intercourse with them and seek that which Allah hath ordained for you, and eat and drink until the white thread becometh distinct to you from the black thread of the dawn.

Then strictly observe the fast till nightfall and touch them not, but be at your devotions in the mosques. These are the limits imposed by Allah so approach them not. Thus Allah expoundeth His revelations to mankind that they may ward off (evil).

2:187

3. Perform the pilgrimage and the visit (to Makkah) for Allah. And if ye are prevented, then send such gifts as can be obtained with ease, and shave not your heads until the gifts have reached their destination. And whoever among you is sick or hath an ailment of the head must pay a ransom of fasting or almsgiving or offering. And if ye are in safety, then whosoever contenteth himself with the visit for the pilgrimage (shall give) such gifts as can be had with ease. And whosoever cannot find (such gifts), then a fast of three days while on the pilgrimage, and of seven when ye have returned; that is, ten in all. That is for him whose folk are not present at the Inviolable Place of Worship. Observe your duty to Allah, and know that Allah is severe in punishment.

2:196

4. It is not for a believer to kill a believer unless (it be) by mistake. He who hath killed a believer by mistake must set free a believing slave and pay the blood—money to the family of the slain. unless they

الَّيْلِ ۚ وَلَا تُبَاشِرُوْهُنَّ وَاَنْتُمْ عٰكِفُوْنَ ۙ
فِى الْمَسٰجِدِ ۗ تِلْكَ حُدُوْدُ اللّٰهِ فَلَا تَقْرَبُوْهَا ۗ
كَذٰلِكَ يُبَيِّنُ اللّٰهُ اٰيٰتِهٖ لِلنَّاسِ لَعَلَّهُمْ يَتَّقُوْنَ ﴿١٨٧﴾

3. وَاَتِمُّوا الْحَجَّ وَالْعُمْرَةَ لِلّٰهِ ۗ فَاِنْ اُحْصِرْتُمْ
فَمَا اسْتَيْسَرَ مِنَ الْهَدْيِ ۚ وَلَا تَحْلِقُوْا
رُءُوْسَكُمْ حَتّٰى يَبْلُغَ الْهَدْيُ مَحِلَّهٗ ۗ
فَمَنْ كَانَ مِنْكُمْ مَّرِيْضًا اَوْ بِهٖٓ اَذًى مِّنْ
رَّاْسِهٖ فَفِدْيَةٌ مِّنْ صِيَامٍ اَوْ صَدَقَةٍ
اَوْ نُسُكٍ ۚ فَاِذَآ اَمِنْتُمْ ۗ فَمَنْ تَمَتَّعَ بِالْعُمْرَةِ
اِلَى الْحَجِّ فَمَا اسْتَيْسَرَ مِنَ الْهَدْيِ ۚ فَمَنْ
لَّمْ يَجِدْ فَصِيَامُ ثَلٰثَةِ اَيَّامٍ فِى الْحَجِّ وَ
سَبْعَةٍ اِذَا رَجَعْتُمْ ۗ تِلْكَ عَشَرَةٌ كَامِلَةٌ ۗ
ذٰلِكَ لِمَنْ لَّمْ يَكُنْ اَهْلُهٗ حَاضِرِى الْمَسْجِدِ
الْحَرَامِ ۚ وَاتَّقُوا اللّٰهَ وَاعْلَمُوْٓا اَنَّ اللّٰهَ
شَدِيْدُ الْعِقَابِ ﴿١٩٦﴾

4. وَمَا كَانَ لِمُؤْمِنٍ اَنْ يَّقْتُلَ مُؤْمِنًا اِلَّا
خَطَـًٔا ۚ وَمَنْ قَتَلَ مُؤْمِنًا خَطَـًٔا فَتَحْرِيْرُ
رَقَبَةٍ مُّؤْمِنَةٍ وَّدِيَةٌ مُّسَلَّمَةٌ اِلٰٓى اَهْلِهٖٓ
اِلَّآ اَنْ يَّصَّدَّقُوْا ۗ فَاِنْ كَانَ مِنْ قَوْمٍ عَدُوٍّ
لَّكُمْ وَهُوَ مُؤْمِنٌ فَتَحْرِيْرُ رَقَبَةٍ مُّؤْمِنَةٍ ۗ
وَاِنْ كَانَ مِنْ قَوْمٍۢ بَيْنَكُمْ وَبَيْنَهُمْ مِّيْثَاقٌ
فَدِيَةٌ مُّسَلَّمَةٌ اِلٰٓى اَهْلِهٖ وَتَحْرِيْرُ رَقَبَةٍ
مُّؤْمِنَةٍ ۚ فَمَنْ لَّمْ يَجِدْ فَصِيَامُ شَهْرَيْنِ

remit it as a charity. If he (the victim) be of a people hostile unto you, and he is a believer, then (the penance) is to set free a believing slave. And if he cometh of a folk between whom and you there is a covenant, then the blood-money must be paid unto his folk and (also) a believing slave must be set free. And whoso hath not the wherewithal must fast two consecutive months. A penance from Allah. Allah is Knower, Wise.

4:92

5. Allah will not take you to task for that which is unintentional in your oaths, but He will take you to task for the oaths which ye swear in earnest. The expiation thereof is the feeding of ten of the needy with the average of that wherewith ye feed your own folk, or the clothing of them, or the liberation of a slave, and for him who findeth not (the wherewithal to do so) then a three days' fast. This is the expiation of your oaths when ye have sworn; and keep your oaths. Thus Allah expoundeth unto you His revelations in order that ye may give thanks.

5:89

6. O ye who believe! Kill no wild game while ye are on the pilgrimage. Whoso of you killeth it of set purpose he shall pay its forfeit in the equivalent of that which he hath killed, of domestic animals, the judge to be two men among you known for justice, (the forfeit) to be brought as an offering to the *Ka'bah*; or, for expiation, he shall feed poor persons, or the equivalent thereof in fasting, that he may taste the evil consequences of his deed. Allah forgiveth whatever (of this kind) may have happened in the past, but whoso relapseth, Allah will take retribution from him. Allah is Mighty,

مُتَتَابِعَيْنِ تَوْبَةً مِّنَ اللّٰهِ وَكَانَ اللّٰهُ
عَلِيْمًا حَكِيْمًا ﴿٩٢﴾

5. لَا يُؤَاخِذُكُمُ اللّٰهُ بِاللَّغْوِ فِيْٓ اَيْمَانِكُمْ
وَلٰكِنْ يُّؤَاخِذُكُمْ بِمَا عَقَّدْتُّمُ الْاَيْمَانَ
فَكَفَّارَتُهٗٓ اِطْعَامُ عَشَرَةِ مَسٰكِيْنَ مِنْ
اَوْسَطِ مَا تُطْعِمُوْنَ اَهْلِيْكُمْ اَوْ كِسْوَتُهُمْ
اَوْ تَحْرِيْرُ رَقَبَةٍ فَمَنْ لَّمْ يَجِدْ فَصِيَامُ
ثَلٰثَةِ اَيَّامٍ ذٰلِكَ كَفَّارَةُ اَيْمَانِكُمْ اِذَا
حَلَفْتُمْ وَاحْفَظُوْٓا اَيْمَانَكُمْ كَذٰلِكَ يُبَيِّنُ
اللّٰهُ لَكُمْ اٰيٰتِهٖ لَعَلَّكُمْ تَشْكُرُوْنَ ﴿٨٩﴾

6. يٰٓاَيُّهَا الَّذِيْنَ اٰمَنُوْا لَا تَقْتُلُوا الصَّيْدَ
وَاَنْتُمْ حُرُمٌ وَمَنْ قَتَلَهٗ مِنْكُمْ مُّتَعَمِّدًا
فَجَزَآءٌ مِّثْلُ مَا قَتَلَ مِنَ النَّعَمِ يَحْكُمُ
بِهٖ ذَوَا عَدْلٍ مِّنْكُمْ هَدْيًا بٰلِغَ الْكَعْبَةِ
اَوْ كَفَّارَةٌ طَعَامُ مَسٰكِيْنَ اَوْ عَدْلُ ذٰلِكَ
صِيَامًا لِّيَذُوْقَ وَبَالَ اَمْرِهٖ عَفَا اللّٰهُ عَمَّا
سَلَفَ وَمَنْ عَادَ فَيَنْتَقِمُ اللّٰهُ مِنْهُ
وَاللّٰهُ عَزِيْزٌ ذُو انْتِقَامٍ ﴿٩٥﴾

7. وَالَّذِيْنَ يُظٰهِرُوْنَ مِنْ نِّسَآئِهِمْ ثُمَّ
يَعُوْدُوْنَ لِمَا قَالُوْا فَتَحْرِيْرُ رَقَبَةٍ
مِّنْ قَبْلِ اَنْ يَّتَمَآسَّا ذٰلِكُمْ تُوْعَظُوْنَ
بِهٖ وَاللّٰهُ بِمَا تَعْمَلُوْنَ خَبِيْرٌ ﴿٣﴾

Able to Requite (the wrong).

5:95

7. Those who put away their wives (by saying they are as their mothers) and afterward would go back on that which they have said, (the penalty) in that case (is) the freeing of a slave before they touch one another. Unto this ye are exhorted; and Allah is Informed of what ye do.

And he who findeth not (the wherewithal), let him fast for two successive months before they touch one another; and for him who is unable to do so (the penance is) the feeding of sixty needy ones. This, that ye may put trust in Allah and His messenger. Such are the limits (imposed by Allah); and for disbelievers is a painful doom.

58:3–4

FAY

1. And that which Allah gave as spoil unto His messenger from them, ye urged not any horse or riding–camel for the sake thereof, but Allah giveth His messenger lordship over whom He will. Allah is Able to do all things.

That which Allah giveth as spoil unto His messenger from the people of the townships, it is for Allah and His messenger and for the near of kin and the orphans and the needy and the wayfarer, that it become not a commodity between the rich among you. And whatsoever the messenger giveth you, take it. And whatsoever he forbiddeth, abstain (from it). And keep your duty to Allah. Lo! Allah is stern in reprisal.

And (it is) for the poor fugitives who have been driven

فَمَنْ لَّمْ يَجِدْ فَصِيَامُ شَهْرَيْنِ
مُتَتَابِعَيْنِ مِنْ قَبْلِ اَنْ يَّتَمَآسَّا
فَمَنْ لَّمْ يَسْتَطِعْ فَاِطْعَامُ سِتِّيْنَ
مِسْكِيْنًا ذٰلِكَ لِتُؤْمِنُوْا بِاللّٰهِ وَ
رَسُوْلِهٖ وَتِلْكَ حُدُوْدُ اللّٰهِ وَ
لِلْكٰفِرِيْنَ عَذَابٌ اَلِيْمٌ ۝

○

1. وَمَآ اَفَآءَ اللّٰهُ عَلٰى رَسُوْلِهٖ مِنْهُمْ فَمَآ
اَوْجَفْتُمْ عَلَيْهِ مِنْ خَيْلٍ وَّلَا رِكَابٍ
وَّلٰكِنَّ اللّٰهَ يُسَلِّطُ رُسُلَهٗ عَلٰى مَنْ
يَّشَآءُ وَاللّٰهُ عَلٰى كُلِّ شَيْءٍ قَدِيْرٌ ۝

مَآ اَفَآءَ اللّٰهُ عَلٰى رَسُوْلِهٖ مِنْ اَهْلِ
الْقُرٰى فَلِلّٰهِ وَلِلرَّسُوْلِ وَلِذِي الْقُرْبٰى
وَالْيَتٰمٰى وَالْمَسٰكِيْنِ وَابْنِ السَّبِيْلِ
كَيْ لَا يَكُوْنَ دُوْلَةً بَيْنَ الْاَغْنِيَآءِ
مِنْكُمْ وَمَآ اٰتٰىكُمُ الرَّسُوْلُ فَخُذُوْهُ
وَمَا نَهٰىكُمْ عَنْهُ فَانْتَهُوْا وَاتَّقُوا اللّٰهَ
اِنَّ اللّٰهَ شَدِيْدُ الْعِقَابِ ۝

لِلْفُقَرَآءِ الْمُهٰجِرِيْنَ الَّذِيْنَ اُخْرِجُوْا
مِنْ دِيَارِهِمْ وَاَمْوَالِهِمْ يَبْتَغُوْنَ
فَضْلًا مِّنَ اللّٰهِ وَرِضْوَانًا وَّيَنْصُرُوْنَ
اللّٰهَ وَرَسُوْلَهٗ اُولٰٓئِكَ هُمُ الصّٰدِقُوْنَ ۝

out from their homes and their belongings, who seek bounty from Allah and help Allah and His messenger. They are the loyal.

59:6–8

FASTING
See also: *Ramadhan*
FAY
Ref: 33:50 **See also:** *Jihad.*

FEAR OF ALLAH

1. Then, even after that, your hearts were hardened and became as rocks, or worse than rocks, for hardness. For indeed there are rocks from out which rivers gush, and indeed there are rocks which split asunder so that water floweth from them. And indeed there are rocks which fall down for the fear of Allah. Allah is not unaware of what ye do.

2:74

2. O ye who believe! Allah will surely try you somewhat (in the matter) of the game which ye take with your hands and your spears, that Allah may know him who feareth Him in secret. Whoso transgresseth after this, for him there is a painful doom.

5:94

3. O Children of Adam! When messengers of your own come unto you who narrate unto you My revelations, then whosoever refraineth from evil and amendeth—there shall no fear come upon them neither shall they grieve.

7:35

4. And We verily gave Moses and Aaron the Criterion (of right and wrong) and a light and a Reminder for those who keep from evil.

Those who fear their Lord in secret and who dread the Hour (of doom).

21:48–49

1. ثُمَّ قَسَتْ قُلُوبُكُم مِّن بَعْدِ ذَٰلِكَ فَهِيَ
كَالْحِجَارَةِ أَوْ أَشَدُّ قَسْوَةً ۚ وَإِنَّ مِنَ الْحِجَارَةِ
لَمَا يَتَفَجَّرُ مِنْهُ الْأَنْهَارُ ۚ وَإِنَّ مِنْهَا لَمَا يَشَّقَّقُ
فَيَخْرُجُ مِنْهُ الْمَاءُ ۚ وَإِنَّ مِنْهَا لَمَا يَهْبِطُ مِنْ
خَشْيَةِ اللَّهِ ۗ وَمَا اللَّهُ بِغَافِلٍ عَمَّا تَعْمَلُونَ ﴿٧٤﴾

2. يَا أَيُّهَا الَّذِينَ آمَنُوا لَيَبْلُوَنَّكُمُ اللَّهُ بِشَيْءٍ
مِّنَ الصَّيْدِ تَنَالُهُ أَيْدِيكُمْ وَرِمَاحُكُمْ
لِيَعْلَمَ اللَّهُ مَن يَخَافُهُ بِالْغَيْبِ ۚ فَمَنِ
اعْتَدَىٰ بَعْدَ ذَٰلِكَ فَلَهُ عَذَابٌ أَلِيمٌ ﴿٩٤﴾

3. يَا بَنِي آدَمَ إِمَّا يَأْتِيَنَّكُمْ رُسُلٌ مِّنكُمْ
يَقُصُّونَ عَلَيْكُمْ آيَاتِي ۙ فَمَنِ اتَّقَىٰ وَأَصْلَحَ
فَلَا خَوْفٌ عَلَيْهِمْ وَلَا هُمْ يَحْزَنُونَ ﴿٣٥﴾

4. وَلَقَدْ آتَيْنَا مُوسَىٰ وَهَارُونَ الْفُرْقَانَ
وَضِيَاءً وَذِكْرًا لِّلْمُتَّقِينَ ﴿٤٨﴾
الَّذِينَ يَخْشَوْنَ رَبَّهُم بِالْغَيْبِ
وَهُم مِّنَ السَّاعَةِ مُشْفِقُونَ ﴿٤٩﴾

5. إِنَّمَا يُؤْمِنُ بِآيَاتِنَا الَّذِينَ إِذَا ذُكِّرُوا
بِهَا خَرُّوا سُجَّدًا وَسَبَّحُوا بِحَمْدِ رَبِّهِمْ
وَهُمْ لَا يَسْتَكْبِرُونَ ۩ ﴿١٥﴾
تَتَجَافَىٰ جُنُوبُهُمْ عَنِ الْمَضَاجِعِ يَدْعُونَ
رَبَّهُمْ خَوْفًا وَطَمَعًا وَمِمَّا رَزَقْنَاهُمْ
يُنفِقُونَ ﴿١٦﴾

5. Only those believe in Our revelations who, when they are reminded of them, fall down prostrate and hymn the praise of their Lord, and they are not scornful.

Who forsake their beds to cry unto their Lord in fear and hope, and spend of what We have bestowed on them.

32:15–16

6. The erudite among His bondsmen fear Allah alone. Lo! Allah is Mighty, Forgiving.
35:28

7. Thou warnest only him who followeth the Reminder and feareth the Beneficent in secret. To him bear tidings of forgiveness and a rich reward.
36:11

8. Lo! those who say: Our Lord is Allah, and thereafter walk aright, there shall no fear come upon them neither shall they grieve.
46:13

9. But for him who feareth the standing before his Lord there are two gardens.

Which is it, of the favours of your Lord, that ye deny?
55:46–47

10. If We had caused this *Qur'ān* to descend upon a mountain, thou (O Muhammad) verily hadst seen it humbled rent asunder by the fear of Allah. Such similitudes coin We for mankind that haply they may reflect.
59:21

11. Lo! those who fear their Lord in secret, theirs will be forgiveness and a great reward.
67:12

6. إِنَّمَا يَخْشَى اللَّهَ مِنْ عِبَادِهِ الْعُلَمَٰٓؤُا۟ ۗ
إِنَّ اللَّهَ عَزِيزٌ غَفُورٌ ﴿٢٨﴾

7. إِنَّمَا تُنذِرُ مَنِ اتَّبَعَ الذِّكْرَ
وَخَشِيَ الرَّحْمَٰنَ بِالْغَيْبِ ۖ فَبَشِّرْهُ
بِمَغْفِرَةٍ وَأَجْرٍ كَرِيمٍ ﴿١١﴾

8. إِنَّ الَّذِينَ قَالُوا رَبُّنَا اللَّهُ ثُمَّ
اسْتَقَامُوا فَلَا خَوْفٌ عَلَيْهِمْ
وَلَا هُمْ يَحْزَنُونَ ﴿١٣﴾

9. وَلِمَنْ خَافَ مَقَامَ رَبِّهِ جَنَّتَانِ ﴿٤٦﴾
فَبِأَيِّ آلَاءِ رَبِّكُمَا تُكَذِّبَانِ ﴿٤٧﴾

10. لَوْ أَنزَلْنَا هَٰذَا الْقُرْآنَ عَلَىٰ جَبَلٍ
لَّرَأَيْتَهُ خَاشِعًا مُّتَصَدِّعًا مِّنْ خَشْيَةِ
اللَّهِ ۚ وَتِلْكَ الْأَمْثَالُ نَضْرِبُهَا لِلنَّاسِ
لَعَلَّهُمْ يَتَفَكَّرُونَ ﴿٢١﴾

11. إِنَّ الَّذِينَ يَخْشَوْنَ رَبَّهُم بِالْغَيْبِ
لَهُم مَّغْفِرَةٌ وَأَجْرٌ كَبِيرٌ ﴿١٢﴾

12. وَأَمَّا مَنْ خَافَ مَقَامَ رَبِّهِ وَنَهَى
النَّفْسَ عَنِ الْهَوَىٰ ﴿٤٠﴾
فَإِنَّ الْجَنَّةَ هِيَ الْمَأْوَىٰ ﴿٤١﴾

12. But as for him who feared to stand before his Lord and restrained his soul from lust,

Lo! the Garden will be his home.
79:40–41

See also: Piety.

FINALITY OF PROPHETHOOD

1. And whoso seeketh as religion other than the Surrender (to Allah) it will not be accepted from him, and he will be a loser in the Hereafter.

3:85

2. This day have I perfected your religion for you and completed My favour unto you, and have chosen for you as religion AL-ISLAM.

5:3

3. Muhammad is not the father of any man among you, but he is the messenger of Allah and the Seal of the Prophets; and Allah is Aware of all things.

33:40

4. And We have not sent thee (O Muhammad) save as a bringer of good tidings and a warner unto all mankind; but most of mankind know not.

34:28

1. وَمَنْ يَبْتَغِ غَيْرَ الْإِسْلَامِ دِينًا فَلَنْ
يُقْبَلَ مِنْهُ ۚ وَهُوَ فِي الْآخِرَةِ
مِنَ الْخَاسِرِينَ ○

2. الْيَوْمَ أَكْمَلْتُ لَكُمْ دِينَكُمْ وَأَتْمَمْتُ عَلَيْكُمْ نِعْمَتِي
وَرَضِيتُ لَكُمُ الْإِسْلَامَ دِينًا

3. مَا كَانَ مُحَمَّدٌ أَبَا أَحَدٍ مِنْ رِجَالِكُمْ
وَلَٰكِنْ رَسُولَ اللَّهِ وَخَاتَمَ النَّبِيِّينَ
وَكَانَ اللَّهُ بِكُلِّ شَيْءٍ عَلِيمًا

4. وَمَا أَرْسَلْنَاكَ إِلَّا كَافَّةً لِلنَّاسِ بَشِيرًا
وَنَذِيرًا وَلَٰكِنَّ أَكْثَرَ النَّاسِ
لَا يَعْلَمُونَ

○

FIRE

1. مثلهم كمثل الذي استوقد نارا فلما
اضاءت ما حوله ذهب الله بنورهم و
تركهم في ظلمت لا يبصرون (١٧)

2. ان الذين يأكلون اموال اليتمى ظلما
انما يأكلون في بطونهم نارا
وسيصلون سعيرا (١٠)

3. والجان خلقنه من قبل من
نار السموم (٢٧)

4. قلنا ينار كوني بردا وسلما
على ابرهيم (٦٩)

5. اذ قال موسى لاهله اني انست
نارا سأتيكم منها بخبر او اتيكم
بشهاب قبس لعلكم تصطلون (٧)

6. افرءيتم النار التي تورون (٧١)
ءانتم انشأتم شجرتها ام نحن
المنشئون (٧٢)
نحن جعلنها تذكرة ومتاعا للمقوين (٧٣)
فسبح باسم ربك العظيم (٧٤)

7. لا يستوي اصحب النار واصحب
الجنة اصحب الجنة هم الفائزون (٢٠)

1. Their likeness is as the likeness of one who kindleth fire, and when it sheddeth its light around him Allah taketh away their light and leaveth them in darkness, where they cannot see.

2:17

2. Lo! Those who devour the wealth of orphans wrongfully, they do but swallow fire into their bellies, and they will be exposed to burning flame.

4:10

3. And the Jinn did We create aforetime of essential fire.

15:27

4. We said: O fire, be coolness and peace for Abraham!

21:69

5. (Remember) when Moses said unto his household: Lo! I spy afar off a fire; I will bring you tidings thence, or bring to you a borrowed flame that ye may warm yourselves.

27:7

6. Have ye observed the fire which ye strike out;

Was it ye who made the tree thereof to grow, or were We the Grower?

We, even We, appointed it a memorial and a comfort for the dwellers in the wilderness.

Therefor (O Muhammad) priase the name of thy Lord the Tremendous.

56:71–74

7. Not equal are the owners of the Fire and the owners of the Gardens. The owners of the Garden, they are the victorious.

59:20

8. But those who disbelieve and deny Our revelations, such are owners of the Fire; they will abide therein— a hapless journey's end!

64:10

9. O ye who believe! Ward off from yourselves and your families a Fire whereof the fuel is men and stones, over which are set angels strong, severe, who resist not Allah in that which He commandeth them, but do that which they are commanded.

66:6

8. وَالَّذِينَ كَفَرُوا وَكَذَّبُوا بِآيَاتِنَا أُولَٰئِكَ
أَصْحَابُ النَّارِ خَالِدِينَ فِيهَا ۖ وَبِئْسَ الْمَصِيرُ ⑩

9. يَا أَيُّهَا الَّذِينَ آمَنُوا قُوا أَنفُسَكُمْ
وَأَهْلِيكُمْ نَارًا وَقُودُهَا النَّاسُ
وَالْحِجَارَةُ عَلَيْهَا مَلَائِكَةٌ غِلَاظٌ
شِدَادٌ لَّا يَعْصُونَ اللَّهَ مَا أَمَرَهُمْ
وَيَفْعَلُونَ مَا يُؤْمَرُونَ ⑥

Ref: 2:24,80,126,167,174,175,201,221,266; 3:10,16,24,103,131,151,183, 185,192; 4:14,30,56; 5:37,64,72; 6:27,128; 7:12,38; 8:14; 9:17,35,63,68, 81,109; 10:8; 11:16–17,98,106,113; 13: 17,35; 14:30,50; 15:27; 16:62; 18:29,53,96; 20:10;21:39; 22:19,72; 23:104; 24:35,57; 27:7,90; 28:29,41; 29:24–25; 32:20; 34:42; 35:36:80; 38:27,59,61,64,76; 39:16,19; 40:41, 46–47,72; 41:19,24,28,40; 45:34; 46:20,34; 47:12,15; 51:13; 52:13–14; 54:48; 55:15,35; 57:15; 59:3,17; 66:10; 71:25; 72:23; 85:5; 87:12; 88:4; 90:20; 92:14; 98:6; 101:11; 104:6; 111:3;

See also: Hell.

FISH

1. To hunt and to eat the fish of the sea is made lawful for you, a provision for you and for seafarers; but to hunt on land is forbidden you so long as ye are on the pilgrimage. Be mindful of your duty to Allah, unto Whom ye will be gathered.

5:96

2. And He it is Who hath constrained the sea to be of service that ye eat fresh meat from thence, and bring forth from thence ornaments which ye wear. And thou seest the ships ploughing it that ye (mankind) may seek of His bounty, and that haply ye may give thanks.

16:14

3. And two seas are not alike: this, fresh, sweet, good to drink, this (other) bitter, salt. And from them both ye eat fresh meat and derive the ornament that ye wear. And thou seest the ship cleaving them with its prow that ye may seek of His bounty, and that haply ye may give thanks.

35:12

1. أُحِلَّ لَكُمْ صَيْدُ الْبَحْرِ وَطَعَامُهُ مَتَاعًا
لَّكُمْ وَلِلسَّيَّارَةِ ۖ وَحُرِّمَ عَلَيْكُمْ صَيْدُ
الْبَرِّ مَا دُمْتُمْ حُرُمًا ۗ وَاتَّقُوا اللَّهَ الَّذِي
إِلَيْهِ تُحْشَرُونَ ﴿٩٦﴾

2. وَهُوَ الَّذِي سَخَّرَ الْبَحْرَ لِتَأْكُلُوا مِنْهُ
لَحْمًا طَرِيًّا وَتَسْتَخْرِجُوا مِنْهُ حِلْيَةً
تَلْبَسُونَهَا ۖ وَتَرَى الْفُلْكَ مَوَاخِرَ فِيهِ
وَلِتَبْتَغُوا مِن فَضْلِهِ وَلَعَلَّكُمْ تَشْكُرُونَ ﴿١٤﴾

3. وَمَا يَسْتَوِي الْبَحْرَانِ هَٰذَا عَذْبٌ
فُرَاتٌ سَائِغٌ شَرَابُهُ وَهَٰذَا مِلْحٌ
أُجَاجٌ ۖ وَمِن كُلٍّ تَأْكُلُونَ لَحْمًا
طَرِيًّا وَتَسْتَخْرِجُونَ حِلْيَةً تَلْبَسُونَهَا ۖ
وَتَرَى الْفُلْكَ فِيهِ مَوَاخِرَ لِتَبْتَغُوا
مِن فَضْلِهِ وَلَعَلَّكُمْ تَشْكُرُونَ ﴿١٢﴾

Ref: 7:163; 18:61,63; 37:142; 68:48.

FLAGELLATION

1. The adulterer and the adulteress, scourge ye each one of them (with) a hundred stripes. And let not pity for the twain withhold you from obedience to Allah, if ye believe in Allah and the Last Day. And let a party of believers witness their punishment.

24:2

2. And those who accuse honourable women but bring not four witnesses, scourge them (with) eighty stripes and never (afterward) accept their testimony—They indeed are evildoers—

24:4

1. اَلزَّانِيَةُ وَالزَّانِيْ فَاجْلِدُوْا كُلَّ
وَاحِدٍ مِّنْهُمَا مِائَةَ جَلْدَةٍ ۖ وَّلَا
تَاْخُذْكُمْ بِهِمَا رَاْفَةٌ فِيْ دِيْنِ اللّٰهِ
اِنْ كُنْتُمْ تُؤْمِنُوْنَ بِاللّٰهِ وَالْيَوْمِ
الْاٰخِرِ ۚ وَلْيَشْهَدْ عَذَابَهُمَا طَآئِفَةٌ
مِّنَ الْمُؤْمِنِيْنَ ۝

2. وَالَّذِيْنَ يَرْمُوْنَ الْمُحْصَنٰتِ ثُمَّ لَمْ
يَاْتُوْا بِاَرْبَعَةِ شُهَدَآءَ فَاجْلِدُوْهُمْ
ثَمٰنِيْنَ جَلْدَةً وَّلَا تَقْبَلُوْا لَهُمْ
شَهَادَةً اَبَدًا ۚ وَاُولٰٓئِكَ هُمُ الْفٰسِقُوْنَ ۝

FOOD OF THE PEOPLE OF THE BOOK

1. This day are (all) good things made lawful for you. The food of those who have received the Scripture is lawful for you, and your food is lawful for them.

5:5

1. اَلْيَوْمَ اُحِلَّ لَكُمُ الطَّيِّبٰتُ ۗ وَطَعَامُ
الَّذِيْنَ اُوْتُوا الْكِتٰبَ حِلٌّ لَّكُمْ ۖ وَطَعَامُكُمْ
حِلٌّ لَّهُمْ

FLAGELLATION
See also: *Hudud.*

FORGIVENESS

1. And vie one with another for forgiveness from your Lord, and for a Paradise as wide as the heavens and the earth, prepared for those who ward off (evil);

Those who spend (of that which Allah hath given them) in ease and in adversity, those who control their wrath and are forgiving towards mankind; Allah loveth the good;

3:133-134

2. It was by the mercy of Allah that thou wast lenient with them (O Muhammad), for if thou hadst been stern and fierce of heart they would have dispersed from round about thee. So pardon them and ask forgiveness for them and consult with them upon the conduct of affairs.

3:159

3. If ye do good openly or keep it secret, or forgive evil, lo! Allah is ever Forgiving, Powerful.

4:149

4. Keep to forgiveness (O Muhammad), and enjoin kindness, and turn away from the ignorant.

7:199

5. If ye punish, then punish with the like of that wherewith ye were afflicted. But if ye endure patiently, verily it is better for the patient.

16:126

1. وَسَارِعُوْٓا اِلٰى مَغْفِرَةٍ مِّنْ رَّبِّكُمْ وَجَنَّةٍ
عَرْضُهَا السَّمٰوٰتُ وَالْاَرْضُ اُعِدَّتْ لِلْمُتَّقِيْنَ

اَلَّذِيْنَ يُنْفِقُوْنَ فِى السَّرَّآءِ وَالضَّرَّآءِ
وَالْكٰظِمِيْنَ الْغَيْظَ وَالْعَافِيْنَ عَنِ النَّاسِ
وَاللّٰهُ يُحِبُّ الْمُحْسِنِيْنَ

2. فَبِمَا رَحْمَةٍ مِّنَ اللّٰهِ لِنْتَ لَهُمْ وَلَوْ كُنْتَ
فَظًّا غَلِيْظَ الْقَلْبِ لَانْفَضُّوْا مِنْ حَوْلِكَ
فَاعْفُ عَنْهُمْ وَاسْتَغْفِرْ لَهُمْ وَشَاوِرْهُمْ
فِى الْاَمْرِ

3. اِنْ تُبْدُوْا خَيْرًا اَوْ تُخْفُوْهُ اَوْ تَعْفُوْا عَنْ
سُوْٓءٍ فَاِنَّ اللّٰهَ كَانَ عَفُوًّا قَدِيْرًا ﴿١٤٩﴾

4. خُذِ الْعَفْوَ وَاْمُرْ بِالْعُرْفِ وَاَعْرِضْ
عَنِ الْجٰهِلِيْنَ ﴿١٩٩﴾

5. وَاِنْ عَاقَبْتُمْ فَعَاقِبُوْا بِمِثْلِ مَا عُوْقِبْتُمْ
بِهٖ ۚ وَلَئِنْ صَبَرْتُمْ لَهُوَ خَيْرٌ لِّلصّٰبِرِيْنَ ﴿١٢٦﴾

6. وَلَا يَاْتَلِ اُولُوا الْفَضْلِ مِنْكُمْ وَالسَّعَةِ
اَنْ يُّؤْتُوْٓا اُولِى الْقُرْبٰى وَالْمَسٰكِيْنَ
وَالْمُهٰجِرِيْنَ فِىْ سَبِيْلِ اللّٰهِ ۖ وَلْيَعْفُوْا
وَلْيَصْفَحُوْا ۗ اَلَا تُحِبُّوْنَ اَنْ يَّغْفِرَ
اللّٰهُ لَكُمْ ۗ وَاللّٰهُ غَفُوْرٌ رَّحِيْمٌ ﴿٢٢﴾

6. And let not those who possess dignity and ease among you swear not to give to the near of kin and to the needy, and to fugitives for the cause of Allah. Let them forgive and show indulgence. Yearn ye not that Allah may forgive you? Allah is Forgiving, Merciful.

24:22

7. Now whatever ye have been given is but a passing comfort for the life of the world, and that which Allah hath is better and more lasting for those who believe and put their trust in their Lord.

And those who shun the worst of sins and indecencies and, when they are wroth, forgive.

42:36–37

7. فَمَآ أُوتِيتُم مِّن شَيْءٍ فَمَتَاعُ
الْحَيَوٰةِ الدُّنْيَا ۖ وَمَا عِندَ اللَّهِ خَيْرٌ
وَأَبْقَىٰ لِلَّذِينَ آمَنُوا وَعَلَىٰ رَبِّهِمْ
يَتَوَكَّلُونَ ﴿٣٦﴾
وَالَّذِينَ يَجْتَنِبُونَ كَبَائِرَ الْإِثْمِ
وَالْفَوَاحِشَ وَإِذَا مَا غَضِبُوا هُمْ
يَغْفِرُونَ ﴿٣٧﴾

8. The guerdon of an ill-deed is an ill the like thereof. But whosoever pardoneth and amendeth, his wage is the affair of Allah. Lo! He loveth not wrong-doers.

42:40

8. وَجَزَٰٓؤُا سَيِّئَةٍ سَيِّئَةٌ مِّثْلُهَا ۖ فَمَنْ
عَفَا وَأَصْلَحَ فَأَجْرُهُ عَلَى اللَّهِ ۚ إِنَّهُ
لَا يُحِبُّ الظَّٰلِمِينَ ﴿٤٠﴾

Ref: 2:52,109,187,237,286 3:134,152,155,159; 4:99,149,153; 5:13,15,95. 101; 9:43; 42:25,30,34,43; 53:32; 64:14.

FORNICATION

1. And come not near unto adultery. Lo! it is an abomination and an evil way.

17:32

2. The adulterer and the adulteress, scourge ye each one of them (with) a hundred stripes, And let not pity for the twain withhold you from obedience to Allah, if ye believe in Allah and the Last Day. And let a party of believers witness their punishment.

The adulterer shall not marry save an adulteress or an idolatress, and the adulteress none shall marry save an adulterer or an idolater. All that is forbidden unto believers.

24:2–3

3. O Prophet! If the believing women come unto thee, taking oath of allegiance unto thee that they will ascribe nothing as partner unto Allah, and will neither steal nor commit adultery nor kill their children, nor produce any lie that they have devised between their hands and feet, nor disobey thee in what is right, then accept their allegiance and ask Allah to forgive them. Lo! Allah is Forgiving, Merciful.

60:12

1. وَلَا تَقْرَبُوا الزِّنَىٰ إِنَّهُ كَانَ فَاحِشَةً
وَسَاءَ سَبِيلًا ۝

2. الزَّانِيَةُ وَالزَّانِي فَاجْلِدُوا كُلَّ
وَاحِدٍ مِّنْهُمَا مِائَةَ جَلْدَةٍ ۖ وَلَا
تَأْخُذْكُم بِهِمَا رَأْفَةٌ فِي دِينِ اللَّهِ
إِن كُنتُمْ تُؤْمِنُونَ بِاللَّهِ وَالْيَوْمِ
الْآخِرِ ۖ وَلْيَشْهَدْ عَذَابَهُمَا طَائِفَةٌ
مِّنَ الْمُؤْمِنِينَ ۝
الزَّانِي لَا يَنكِحُ إِلَّا زَانِيَةً أَوْ مُشْرِكَةً
وَالزَّانِيَةُ لَا يَنكِحُهَا إِلَّا زَانٍ أَوْ مُشْرِكٌ ۚ
وَحُرِّمَ ذَٰلِكَ عَلَى الْمُؤْمِنِينَ ۝

3. يَا أَيُّهَا النَّبِيُّ إِذَا جَاءَكَ الْمُؤْمِنَاتُ
يُبَايِعْنَكَ عَلَىٰ أَن لَّا يُشْرِكْنَ بِاللَّهِ
شَيْئًا وَلَا يَسْرِقْنَ وَلَا يَزْنِينَ
وَلَا يَقْتُلْنَ أَوْلَادَهُنَّ وَلَا يَأْتِينَ
بِبُهْتَانٍ يَفْتَرِينَهُ بَيْنَ أَيْدِيهِنَّ
وَأَرْجُلِهِنَّ وَلَا يَعْصِينَكَ فِي
مَعْرُوفٍ ۙ فَبَايِعْهُنَّ وَاسْتَغْفِرْ لَهُنَّ
اللَّهَ ۖ إِنَّ اللَّهَ غَفُورٌ رَّحِيمٌ ۝

Ref: 25:68; **See also:** *Hudud*

FOSTERAGE AND MAINTENANCE

1. وَالْوَالِدٰتُ يُرْضِعْنَ اَوْلَادَهُنَّ حَوْلَيْنِ
كَامِلَيْنِ لِمَنْ اَرَادَ اَنْ يُّتِمَّ الرَّضَاعَةَ
وَعَلَى الْمَوْلُوْدِ لَهٗ رِزْقُهُنَّ وَكِسْوَتُهُنَّ
بِالْمَعْرُوْفِ لَا تُكَلَّفُ نَفْسٌ اِلَّا وُسْعَهَا لَا
تُضَآرَّ وَالِدَةٌ بِوَلَدِهَا وَلَا مَوْلُوْدٌ لَّهٗ
بِوَلَدِهٖ وَعَلَى الْوَارِثِ مِثْلُ ذٰلِكَ فَاِنْ
اَرَادَا فِصَالًا عَنْ تَرَاضٍ مِّنْهُمَا وَتَشَاوُرٍ
فَلَا جُنَاحَ عَلَيْهِمَا وَاِنْ اَرَدْتُّمْ اَنْ تَسْتَرْضِعُوْٓا
اَوْلَادَكُمْ فَلَا جُنَاحَ عَلَيْكُمْ اِذَا سَلَّمْتُمْ مَّآ
اٰتَيْتُمْ بِالْمَعْرُوْفِ وَاتَّقُوا اللّٰهَ وَاعْلَمُوْٓا
اَنَّ اللّٰهَ بِمَا تَعْمَلُوْنَ بَصِيْرٌ ﴿٢٣٣﴾

2. وَاِنْ كُنَّ اُولَاتِ حَمْلٍ فَاَنْفِقُوْا
عَلَيْهِنَّ حَتّٰى يَضَعْنَ حَمْلَهُنَّ فَاِنْ
اَرْضَعْنَ لَكُمْ فَاٰتُوْهُنَّ اُجُوْرَهُنَّ وَ
اْتَمِرُوْا بَيْنَكُمْ بِمَعْرُوْفٍ وَاِنْ
تَعَاسَرْتُمْ فَسَتُرْضِعُ لَهٗٓ اُخْرٰى ﴿٦﴾

لِيُنْفِقْ ذُوْ سَعَةٍ مِّنْ سَعَتِهٖ وَمَنْ
قُدِرَ عَلَيْهِ رِزْقُهٗ فَلْيُنْفِقْ مِمَّآ
اٰتٰىهُ اللّٰهُ لَا يُكَلِّفُ اللّٰهُ نَفْسًا اِلَّا
مَآ اٰتٰىهَا سَيَجْعَلُ اللّٰهُ بَعْدَ عُسْرٍ يُّسْرًا ﴿٧﴾

1. Mothers shall suckle their children for two whole years; (that is) for those who wish to complete the suckling. The duty of feeding and clothing nursing mothers in a seemly manner is upon the father of the child. No one should be charged beyond his capacity. A mother should not be made to suffer because of her child, nor should he to whom the child is born (be made to suffer) because of his child. And on the (father's) heir is incumbent the like of that (which was incumbent on the father). If they desire to wean the child by mutual consent and (after) consultation, it is no sin for them; and if ye wish to give your children out to nurse, it is no sin for you, provided that ye pay what is due from you in kindness. Observe your duty to Allah, and know that Allah is Seer of what ye do.

2:233

2. And if they are with child, then spend for them till they bring forth their burden. Then, if they give suck for you, give them their due payment and consult together in kindness; but if ye make difficulties for one another, then let some other woman give suck for him (the father of the child). Let him who hath abundance spend of his abundance, and he whose provision is measured, let him spend of that which Allah hath given him. Allah asketh naught of any soul save that which He hath given it. Allah will vouchsafe, after hardship, ease.

65:6–7

See also: Divorce.

FRATERNITY

1. وَيَسْـَٔلُونَكَ عَنِ الْيَتٰمٰى قُلْ اِصْلَاحٌ لَّهُمْ خَيْرٌ
وَاِنْ تُخَالِطُوْهُمْ فَاِخْوَانُكُمْ

2. وَاعْتَصِمُوْا بِحَبْلِ اللّٰهِ جَمِيْعًا وَّلَا تَفَرَّقُوْا
وَاذْكُرُوْا نِعْمَتَ اللّٰهِ عَلَيْكُمْ اِذْ كُنْتُمْ اَعْدَآءً
فَاَلَّفَ بَيْنَ قُلُوْبِكُمْ فَاَصْبَحْتُمْ بِنِعْمَتِهٖٓ
اِخْوَانًا وَكُنْتُمْ عَلٰى شَفَا حُفْرَةٍ مِّنَ
النَّارِ فَاَنْقَذَكُمْ مِّنْهَا كَذٰلِكَ يُبَيِّنُ اللّٰهُ
لَكُمْ اٰيٰتِهٖ لَعَلَّكُمْ تَهْتَدُوْنَ ○

3. فَاِنْ تَابُوْا وَاَقَامُوا الصَّلٰوةَ وَاٰتَوُا الزَّكٰوةَ
فَاِخْوَانُكُمْ فِى الدِّيْنِ وَنُفَصِّلُ الْاٰيٰتِ
لِقَوْمٍ يَّعْلَمُوْنَ

4. اُدْعُوْهُمْ لِاٰبَآئِهِمْ هُوَ اَقْسَطُ عِنْدَ
اللّٰهِ فَاِنْ لَّمْ تَعْلَمُوْٓا اٰبَآءَهُمْ فَاِخْوَانُكُمْ
فِى الدِّيْنِ وَمَوَالِيْكُمْ

5. اِنَّمَا الْمُؤْمِنُوْنَ اِخْوَةٌ فَاَصْلِحُوْا بَيْنَ
اَخَوَيْكُمْ وَاتَّقُوا اللّٰهَ لَعَلَّكُمْ تُرْحَمُوْنَ

○

1. And they question thee concerning orphans. Say: To improve their lot is best. And if ye mingle your affairs with theirs, then (they are) your brothers.

2:220

2. And hold fast, all of you together, to the cable of Allah, and do not separate. And remember Allah's favour unto you; how ye were enemies and He made friendship between your hearts so that ye became as brothers by His grace; and (how) ye were upon the brink of an abyss of fire, and He did save you from it. Thus Allah maketh clear His revelations unto you, that haply ye may be guided.

3:103

3. But if they repent and establish worship and pay the poor-due, then are they your brethren in religion. We detail Our revelations for a people who have knowledge.

9:11

4. Proclaim their real parentage. That will be more equitable in the sight of Allah. And if ye know not their fathers, then (they are) your brethren in the faith, and your clients.

33:5

5. The believers are naught else than brothers. Therefore make peace between your brethren and observe your duty to Allah that haply ye may obtain mercy.

49:10

See also: Unity

FRIDAY CONGREGATION

1. O ye who believe! When the call is heard for the prayer of the day of congregation, haste unto the remembrance of Allah and leave your trading. That is better for you if ye did but know.

And when the prayer is ended, then disperse in the land and seek of Allah's bounty, and remember Allah much, that ye may be successful.

62:9–10

1. يٰۤاَيُّهَا الَّذِيْنَ اٰمَنُوْۤا اِذَا نُوْدِيَ
لِلصَّلٰوةِ مِنْ يَّوْمِ الْجُمُعَةِ فَاسْعَوْا
اِلٰى ذِكْرِ اللّٰهِ وَذَرُوا الْبَيْعَ ذٰلِكُمْ
خَيْرٌ لَّكُمْ اِنْ كُنْتُمْ تَعْلَمُوْنَ ۝
فَاِذَا قُضِيَتِ الصَّلٰوةُ فَانْتَشِرُوْا
فِي الْاَرْضِ وَابْتَغُوْا مِنْ فَضْلِ اللّٰهِ
وَاذْكُرُوا اللّٰهَ كَثِيْرًا لَّعَلَّكُمْ تُفْلِحُوْنَ ۝

FRIENDSHIP

1. Let not the believers take disbelievers for their friends in preference to believers. Whoso doth that hath no connection with Allah unless (it be) that ye but guard yourselves against them, taking (as it were) security. Allah biddeth you beware (only) of Himself. Unto Allah is the journeying.

3:28

1. لَا يَتَّخِذِ الْمُؤْمِنُوْنَ الْكٰفِرِيْنَ اَوْلِيَآءَ مِنْ
دُوْنِ الْمُؤْمِنِيْنَ وَمَنْ يَّفْعَلْ ذٰلِكَ فَلَيْسَ
مِنَ اللّٰهِ فِيْ شَيْءٍ اِلَّاۤ اَنْ تَتَّقُوْا مِنْهُمْ
تُقٰىةً وَيُحَذِّرُكُمُ اللّٰهُ نَفْسَهٗ وَ
اِلَى اللّٰهِ الْمَصِيْرُ ۝

2. O ye who believe! Take not for intimates others than your own folk, who would spare no pains to ruin you; they love to hamper you. Hatred is revealed by (the utterance of) their mouths, but that which their breasts hide is greater. We have made plain for you the revelations if ye will understand.

3:118

2. يٰۤاَيُّهَا الَّذِيْنَ اٰمَنُوْا لَا تَتَّخِذُوْا بِطَانَةً
مِّنْ دُوْنِكُمْ لَا يَاْلُوْنَكُمْ خَبَالًا وَدُّوْا مَا
عَنِتُّمْ قَدْ بَدَتِ الْبَغْضَآءُ مِنْ اَفْوَاهِهِمْ
وَمَا تُخْفِيْ صُدُوْرُهُمْ اَكْبَرُ قَدْ بَيَّنَّا
لَكُمُ الْاٰيٰتِ اِنْ كُنْتُمْ تَعْقِلُوْنَ ۝

3. يٰۤاَيُّهَا الَّذِيْنَ اٰمَنُوْا لَا تَتَّخِذُوا الْكٰفِرِيْنَ
اَوْلِيَآءَ مِنْ دُوْنِ الْمُؤْمِنِيْنَ اَتُرِيْدُوْنَ
اَنْ تَجْعَلُوْا لِلّٰهِ عَلَيْكُمْ سُلْطٰنًا مُّبِيْنًا ۝

3. O ye who believe! Choose not disbelievers for (your) friends in place of believers. Would ye give Allah a clear warrant against you?

4:144

4. O ye who believe! Take not the Jews and Christians for friends. They are friends one to another. He among you who taketh them for friends is (one) of them. Lo! Allah guideth not wrongdoing folk

5:51

5. Your friend can be only Allah; and His messenger and those who believe, who establish worship and pay the poor-due, and bow down (in prayer)

And whoso taketh Allah and His messenger and those who believe for friends (will know that), lo! the party of Allah, they are the victorious.

5:55–56

6. O ye who believe! Choose not for friends such of those who received the Scripture before you, and of the disbelievers, as make a jest and sport of your religion. But keep your duty to Allah if ye are true believers.

And when ye call to prayer they take it for a jest and sport. That is because they are a folk who understand not.

5:57–58

7. And the believers, men and women, are protecting friends one of another; they enjoin the right and forbid the wrong, and they establish worship and they pay the poor-due, and they obey Allah and His messenger. As

4. يٰٓاَيُّهَا الَّذِيْنَ اٰمَنُوْا لَا تَتَّخِذُوا الْيَهُوْدَ
وَالنَّصٰرٰٓى اَوْلِيَآءَ ۘ بَعْضُهُمْ اَوْلِيَآءُ
بَعْضٍ ۗ وَمَنْ يَّتَوَلَّهُمْ مِّنْكُمْ فَاِنَّهٗ مِنْهُمْ ۗ
اِنَّ اللّٰهَ لَا يَهْدِى الْقَوْمَ الظّٰلِمِيْنَ ﴿٥١﴾

5. اِنَّمَا وَلِيُّكُمُ اللّٰهُ وَرَسُوْلُهٗ وَالَّذِيْنَ
اٰمَنُوا الَّذِيْنَ يُقِيْمُوْنَ الصَّلٰوةَ وَيُؤْتُوْنَ
الزَّكٰوةَ وَهُمْ رٰكِعُوْنَ ﴿٥٥﴾

وَمَنْ يَّتَوَلَّ اللّٰهَ وَرَسُوْلَهٗ وَالَّذِيْنَ
اٰمَنُوْا فَاِنَّ حِزْبَ اللّٰهِ هُمُ الْغٰلِبُوْنَ ﴿٥٦﴾

6. يٰٓاَيُّهَا الَّذِيْنَ اٰمَنُوْا لَا تَتَّخِذُوا الَّذِيْنَ
اتَّخَذُوْا دِيْنَكُمْ هُزُوًا وَّلَعِبًا مِّنَ الَّذِيْنَ
اُوْتُوا الْكِتٰبَ مِنْ قَبْلِكُمْ وَالْكُفَّارَ
اَوْلِيَآءَ ۚ وَاتَّقُوا اللّٰهَ اِنْ كُنْتُمْ مُّؤْمِنِيْنَ ﴿٥٧﴾

وَاِذَا نَادَيْتُمْ اِلَى الصَّلٰوةِ اتَّخَذُوْهَا
هُزُوًا وَّلَعِبًا ۭ ذٰلِكَ بِاَنَّهُمْ قَوْمٌ لَّا يَعْقِلُوْنَ ﴿٥٨﴾

7. وَالْمُؤْمِنُوْنَ وَالْمُؤْمِنٰتُ بَعْضُهُمْ اَوْلِيَآءُ
بَعْضٍ ۘ يَاْمُرُوْنَ بِالْمَعْرُوْفِ وَيَنْهَوْنَ عَنِ
الْمُنْكَرِ وَيُقِيْمُوْنَ الصَّلٰوةَ وَيُؤْتُوْنَ الزَّكٰوةَ
وَيُطِيْعُوْنَ اللّٰهَ وَرَسُوْلَهٗ ۭ اُولٰۗىِٕكَ سَيَرْحَمُهُمُ
اللّٰهُ ۭ اِنَّ اللّٰهَ عَزِيْزٌ حَكِيْمٌ ﴿٧١﴾

8. اَلنَّبِيُّ اَوْلٰى بِالْمُؤْمِنِيْنَ مِنْ اَنْفُسِهِمْ
وَاَزْوَاجُهٗٓ اُمَّهٰتُهُمْ ۭ وَاُولُوا الْاَرْحَامِ

for these Allah will have mercy on them. Lo! Allah is Mighty, Wise.

9:71

8. The Prophet is closer to the believers than themselves, and his wives are (as) their mothers.

And the owners of kinship are closer one to another in the ordinance of Allah than (other) believers and the fugitives (who fled from Makkah), except that ye should do kindness to your friends. This is written in the Book (of nature).

33:6

9. O ye who believe! Choose not My enemy and your enemy for friends. Do ye give them friendship when they disbelieve in that truth which hath come unto you, driving out the messenger and you because ye believe in Allah, your Lord? If ye have come forth to strive in My way and seeking My good pleasure, (show them not friendship). Do ye show friendship unto them in secret, when I am Best Aware of what ye hide and what ye proclaim? And whosoever doth it among you, he verily hath strayed from the right way.

60:1

FULFILMENT OF PROMISE

1. And fulfil your (part of the) covenant. I shall fulfil My (part of the) covenant, and fear Me.

2:40

2. O ye who believe! Ful—

بَعْضُهُمْ أَوْلَىٰ بِبَعْضٍ فِي كِتَٰبِ اللَّهِ
مِنَ الْمُؤْمِنِينَ وَالْمُهَٰجِرِينَ إِلَّا أَن
تَفْعَلُوا إِلَىٰ أَوْلِيَائِكُم مَّعْرُوفًا كَانَ
ذَٰلِكَ فِي الْكِتَٰبِ مَسْطُورًا ۝

9. يَا أَيُّهَا الَّذِينَ آمَنُوا لَا تَتَّخِذُوا عَدُوِّي
وَعَدُوَّكُمْ أَوْلِيَاءَ تُلْقُونَ إِلَيْهِم بِالْمَوَدَّةِ
وَقَدْ كَفَرُوا بِمَا جَاءَكُم مِّنَ الْحَقِّ
يُخْرِجُونَ الرَّسُولَ وَإِيَّاكُمْ أَن تُؤْمِنُوا
بِاللَّهِ رَبِّكُمْ إِن كُنتُمْ خَرَجْتُمْ
جِهَادًا فِي سَبِيلِي وَابْتِغَاءَ مَرْضَاتِي
تُسِرُّونَ إِلَيْهِم بِالْمَوَدَّةِ وَأَنَا أَعْلَمُ
بِمَا أَخْفَيْتُمْ وَمَا أَعْلَنتُمْ وَمَن يَفْعَلْهُ
مِنكُمْ فَقَدْ ضَلَّ سَوَاءَ السَّبِيلِ ۝

1. وَأَوْفُوا بِعَهْدِي أُوفِ بِعَهْدِكُمْ وَإِيَّايَ
فَارْهَبُونِ ۝

2. يَا أَيُّهَا الَّذِينَ آمَنُوا أَوْفُوا بِالْعُقُودِ

3. وَأَوْفُوا بِالْعَهْدِ إِنَّ الْعَهْدَ كَانَ
مَسْئُولًا ۝

fil your undertak ings.

5:1

3. And keep the covenant. Lo! of the covenant it will be asked.

17:34

FRIENDSHIP
Ref: 60:7–9.
FULFILMENT OF PROMISE
Ref: 2:29,40,100,125,177; 3:76,77,183; 6:152; 7:134; 8:56; 9:1,4,7,95,111; 13:20,25; 16:91,95; 17:34; 20:115; 23:8; 33:15;23; 36:60; 48:10; 70:32.

GAMBLING

1. They question thee about strong drink and games of chance. Say: In both is great sin, and (some) utility for men; but the sin of them is greater than their usefulness.

2:219

2. O ye who believe! Strong drink and games of chance and idols and divining arrows are only an infamy of Satan's handiwork. Leave it aside in order that ye may succeed.

Satan seeketh only to cast among you enmity and hatred by means of strong drink and games of chance, and to turn you from remembrance of Allah and from (His) worship. Will ye then have done?

5:90–91

1. يَسْـَٔلُونَكَ عَنِ الْخَمْرِ وَالْمَيْسِرِ ۖ قُلْ فِيهِمَآ إِثْمٌ كَبِيرٌ وَمَنَٰفِعُ لِلنَّاسِ وَإِثْمُهُمَآ أَكْبَرُ مِن نَّفْعِهِمَا ۗ

2. يَٰٓأَيُّهَا الَّذِينَ ءَامَنُوٓا إِنَّمَا الْخَمْرُ وَالْمَيْسِرُ وَالْأَنصَابُ وَالْأَزْلَٰمُ رِجْسٌ مِّنْ عَمَلِ الشَّيْطَٰنِ فَاجْتَنِبُوهُ لَعَلَّكُمْ تُفْلِحُونَ ﴿٩٠﴾ إِنَّمَا يُرِيدُ الشَّيْطَٰنُ أَن يُوقِعَ بَيْنَكُمُ الْعَدَٰوَةَ وَالْبَغْضَآءَ فِى الْخَمْرِ وَالْمَيْسِرِ وَيَصُدَّكُمْ عَن ذِكْرِ اللَّهِ وَعَنِ الصَّلَوٰةِ ۖ فَهَلْ أَنتُم مُّنتَهُونَ ﴿٩١﴾

GARDENS

1. Is not He (best) Who created the heavens and the earth, and sendeth down for you water from the sky wherewith We cause to spring forth joyous orchards, whose trees it never hath been yours to cause to grow. Is there any God beside Allah? Nay, but they are folk who ascribe equals (unto Him)!

27:60

2. Let man consider his food:

How We pour water in showers

Then split the earth in clefts

And cause the grain to grow therein

And grapes and green fodder

And olive–trees and palm–trees

And garden–closes of thick foliage

And fruits and grasses:

Provision for you and your cattle.

80:24–32

1. أَمَّنْ خَلَقَ السَّمَٰوَٰتِ وَالْأَرْضَ وَأَنزَلَ لَكُم مِّنَ السَّمَآءِ مَآءً فَأَنۢبَتْنَا بِهِۦ حَدَآئِقَ ذَاتَ بَهْجَةٍ ۚ مَّا كَانَ لَكُمْ أَن تُنۢبِتُوا شَجَرَهَآ ۗ أَءِلَٰهٌ مَّعَ اللَّهِ ۚ بَلْ هُمْ قَوْمٌ يَعْدِلُونَ ﴿٦٠﴾

2. فَلْيَنظُرِ الْإِنسَٰنُ إِلَىٰ طَعَامِهِۦٓ ﴿٢٤﴾ أَنَّا صَبَبْنَا الْمَآءَ صَبًّا ﴿٢٥﴾ ثُمَّ شَقَقْنَا الْأَرْضَ شَقًّا ﴿٢٦﴾ فَأَنۢبَتْنَا فِيهَا حَبًّا ﴿٢٧﴾ وَعِنَبًا وَقَضْبًا ﴿٢٨﴾ وَزَيْتُونًا وَنَخْلًا ﴿٢٩﴾ وَحَدَآئِقَ غُلْبًا ﴿٣٠﴾ وَفَٰكِهَةً وَأَبًّا ﴿٣١﴾ مَّتَٰعًا لَّكُمْ وَلِأَنْعَٰمِكُمْ ﴿٣٢﴾

GAMBLING Ref: 4:29; 5:103.
GARDENS
Ref: 2:35,82,111,221,266; 3:133,142; 4:124; 5:72; 6:99; 13:4; 16:11; 7:27, 40-42,44,46,49; 9:111; 10:26; 11:23,108; 16:32.67; 23:19; 17:91; 19:60;

GENEROSITY

1. It is not righteousness that ye turn your faces to the East and the West; but righteous is he who believeth in Allah and the Last Day and the angels and the Scripture and the Prophets; and giveth his wealth, for love of Him, to kinsfolk and to orphans and the needy and the wayfarer and to those who ask, and to set slaves free; and observeth proper worship and payeth the poor-due. And those who keep their treaty when they make one, and the patient in tribulation and adversity and time of stress. Such are they who are sincere. Such are the Godfearing.

2:177

2. They ask thee, (O Muhammad), what they shall spend. Say: That which ye spend for good (must go) to parents and near kindred and orphans and the needy and the wayfarer. And whatsoever good ye do, lo! Allah is Aware of it.

2:215

3. The alms are only for the poor and the needy, and those who collect them, and those whose hearts are to be reconciled, and to free the captives and the debtors, and for the cause of Allah, and (for) the wayfarers: a duty imposed by Allah. Allah is Knower, Wise.

9:60

1. لَيْسَ الْبِرَّ اَنْ تُوَلُّوْا وُجُوْهَكُمْ قِبَلَ الْمَشْرِقِ
وَ الْمَغْرِبِ وَلٰكِنَّ الْبِرَّ مَنْ اٰمَنَ بِاللّٰهِ وَالْيَوْمِ
الْاٰخِرِ وَ الْمَلٰٓئِكَةِ وَ الْكِتٰبِ وَ النَّبِيّٖنَ ۚ وَاٰتَى
الْمَالَ عَلٰى حُبِّهٖ ذَوِى الْقُرْبٰى وَ الْيَتٰمٰى وَ
الْمَسٰكِيْنَ وَ ابْنَ السَّبِيْلِ ۙ وَ السَّآئِلِيْنَ وَفِى
الرِّقَابِ ۚ وَ اَقَامَ الصَّلٰوةَ وَ اٰتَى الزَّكٰوةَ ۚ وَ
الْمُوْفُوْنَ بِعَهْدِهِمْ اِذَا عٰهَدُوْا ۚ وَ الصّٰبِرِيْنَ
فِى الْبَاْسَآءِ وَ الضَّرَّآءِ وَحِيْنَ الْبَاْسِ ؕ اُولٰٓئِكَ
الَّذِيْنَ صَدَقُوْا ؕ وَ اُولٰٓئِكَ هُمُ الْمُتَّقُوْنَ ﴿۱۷۷﴾

2. يَسْـَٔلُوْنَكَ مَاذَا يُنْفِقُوْنَ ۬ؕ قُلْ مَآ اَنْفَقْتُمْ مِّنْ
خَيْرٍ فَلِلْوَالِدَيْنِ وَالْاَقْرَبِيْنَ وَالْيَتٰمٰى وَالْمَسٰكِيْنِ
وَابْنِ السَّبِيْلِ ؕ وَمَا تَفْعَلُوْا مِنْ خَيْرٍ فَاِنَّ اللّٰهَ بِهٖ
عَلِيْمٌ ﴿۲۱۵﴾

3. اِنَّمَا الصَّدَقٰتُ لِلْفُقَرَآءِ وَ الْمَسٰكِيْنِ
وَ الْعٰمِلِيْنَ عَلَيْهَا وَ الْمُؤَلَّفَةِ قُلُوْبُهُمْ
وَ فِى الرِّقَابِ وَ الْغٰرِمِيْنَ وَفِىْ سَبِيْلِ
اللّٰهِ وَ ابْنِ السَّبِيْلِ ؕ فَرِيْضَةً مِّنَ اللّٰهِ ؕ
وَ اللّٰهُ عَلِيْمٌ حَكِيْمٌ ﴿۶۰﴾

Ref: 2:219; 65:7.
See also: Alms.

GENIE

1. Thus have We appointed unto every Prophet an adversary—devils of humankind and jinn who inspire in one another plausible discourse through guile. If thy Lord willed, they would not do so; so leave them alone with their devising.

6:112

2. In the day when He will gather them together (He will say): O ye assembly of the jinn! Many of humankind did ye seduce. And their adherents among humankind will say: Our Lord! We enjoyed one another, but now we have arrived at the appointed term which Thou appointedst for us. He will say: Fire is your home. Abide therein for ever, save him whom Allah willeth (to deliver). Lo! thy Lord is Wise, Aware.

6:128

3. Verily We created man of potter's clay of black mud altered,

And the Jinn did We create aforetime of essential fire.

15:26–27

4. Say: Verily, though mankind and the Jinn should assemble to produce the like of this Qur'ān, They could not produce the like thereof though they were helpers one of another.

17:88

1. وَكَذٰلِكَ جَعَلْنَا لِكُلِّ نَبِيٍّ عَدُوًّا شَيٰطِيْنَ
الْاِنْسِ وَالْجِنِّ يُوْحِيْ بَعْضُهُمْ اِلٰى بَعْضٍ
زُخْرُفَ الْقَوْلِ غُرُوْرًا ۚ وَلَوْ شَآءَ رَبُّكَ
مَا فَعَلُوْهُ فَذَرْهُمْ وَمَا يَفْتَرُوْنَ ○

2. وَيَوْمَ يَحْشُرُهُمْ جَمِيْعًا ۚ يٰمَعْشَرَ الْجِنِّ
قَدِ اسْتَكْثَرْتُمْ مِّنَ الْاِنْسِ ۚ وَقَالَ اَوْلِيٰٓؤُهُمْ
مِّنَ الْاِنْسِ رَبَّنَا اسْتَمْتَعَ بَعْضُنَا بِبَعْضٍ
وَّبَلَغْنَآ اَجَلَنَا الَّذِيْٓ اَجَّلْتَ لَنَا ۚ قَالَ النَّارُ
مَثْوٰىكُمْ خٰلِدِيْنَ فِيْهَآ اِلَّا مَا شَآءَ اللّٰهُ ۗ
اِنَّ رَبَّكَ حَكِيْمٌ عَلِيْمٌ ○

3. وَلَقَدْ خَلَقْنَا الْاِنْسَانَ مِنْ صَلْصَالٍ مِّنْ حَمَاٍ
مَّسْنُوْنٍ ۚ (٢٦)
وَالْجَآنَّ خَلَقْنٰهُ مِنْ قَبْلُ مِنْ نَّارِ السَّمُوْمِ (٢٧)

4. قُلْ لَّئِنِ اجْتَمَعَتِ الْاِنْسُ وَالْجِنُّ عَلٰٓى
اَنْ يَّاْتُوْا بِمِثْلِ هٰذَا الْقُرْاٰنِ لَا يَاْتُوْنَ
بِمِثْلِهٖ وَلَوْ كَانَ بَعْضُهُمْ لِبَعْضٍ ظَهِيْرًا (٨٨)

5. قَالَ عِفْرِيْتٌ مِّنَ الْجِنِّ اَنَا اٰتِيْكَ
بِهٖ قَبْلَ اَنْ تَقُوْمَ مِنْ مَّقَامِكَ ۚ
وَاِنِّيْ عَلَيْهِ لَقَوِيٌّ اَمِيْنٌ (٣٩)

5. A stalwart of the Jinn said: I will bring it thee before thou canst rise from thy place. Lo! I verily am strong and trusty for such work.

27:39

6. And unto Soloman (We gave) the wind, whereof the morning course was a month's journey and the evening course a month's journey, and We caused the fount of copper to gush forth for him, and (We gave him) certain of the jinn who worked before him by permission of his Lord. And such of them as deviated from Our command, them We caused to taste the punishment of flaming Fire.

They made for him what he willed: synagogues and statues, basins like wells and boilers built into the ground. Give thanks, O House of David! Few of My bondmen are thankful.

And when We decreed death for him, nothing showed his death to them save a creeping creature of the earth which gnawed away his staff. And when he fell the jinn saw clearly how, if they had known the Unseen, they would not have continued in despised toil.

34:12–14

7. I created the jinn and humankind only that they might worship Me

51:56

8. O company of jinn and men, if ye have power to penetrate (all) regions of the heavens and the earth, then penetrate (them)! Ye will never penetrate them save with (Our) sanction.

55:33

6. وَلِسُلَيْمٰنَ الرِّيْحَ غُدُوُّهَا شَهْرٌ وَّ
رَوَاحُهَا شَهْرٌ ۚ وَاَسَلْنَا لَهٗ عَيْنَ
الْقِطْرِ ؕ وَمِنَ الْجِنِّ مَنْ يَّعْمَلُ بَيْنَ
يَدَيْهِ بِاِذْنِ رَبِّهٖ ؕ وَمَنْ يَّزِغْ مِنْهُمْ
عَنْ اَمْرِنَا نُذِقْهُ مِنْ عَذَابِ السَّعِيْرِ ﴿١٢﴾
يَعْمَلُوْنَ لَهٗ مَا يَشَآءُ مِنْ مَّحَارِيْبَ
وَتَمَاثِيْلَ وَجِفَانٍ كَالْجَوَابِ وَقُدُوْرٍ
رّٰسِيٰتٍ ؕ اِعْمَلُوْٓا اٰلَ دَاوٗدَ شُكْرًا ؕ
وَقَلِيْلٌ مِّنْ عِبَادِيَ الشَّكُوْرُ ﴿١٣﴾
فَلَمَّا قَضَيْنَا عَلَيْهِ الْمَوْتَ مَا دَلَّهُمْ
عَلٰى مَوْتِهٖٓ اِلَّا دَآبَّةُ الْاَرْضِ تَاْكُلُ
مِنْسَاَتَهٗ ۚ فَلَمَّا خَرَّ تَبَيَّنَتِ الْجِنُّ اَنْ
لَّوْ كَانُوْا يَعْلَمُوْنَ الْغَيْبَ مَا لَبِثُوْا
فِي الْعَذَابِ الْمُهِيْنِ ﴿١٤﴾

7. وَمَا خَلَقْتُ الْجِنَّ وَالْاِنْسَ اِلَّا
لِيَعْبُدُوْنِ ﴿٥٦﴾

8. يٰمَعْشَرَ الْجِنِّ وَالْاِنْسِ اِنِ اسْتَطَعْتُمْ
اَنْ تَنْفُذُوْا مِنْ اَقْطَارِ السَّمٰوٰتِ
وَالْاَرْضِ فَانْفُذُوْا ؕ لَا تَنْفُذُوْنَ
اِلَّا بِسُلْطٰنٍ ﴿٣٣﴾

Ref: 6:100,130; 7:38; 11:119; 23:70; 27:39; 34:46; 37:158; 38:36–38; 41:25,29; 46:18,29–32; 55:15,39,56,74; 72:1–15; 114:1–6;

GHUSL

1. O ye who believe! Draw not near unto prayer when ye are drunken, till ye know that which ye utter, nor when ye are polluted, save when journeying upon the road till ye have bathed. And if ye be ill, or on a journey, or one of you cometh from the closet, or ye have touched women, and ye find not water, then go to high clean soil and rub your faces and your hands (therewith). Lo! Allah is Benign, Forgiving.

4:43

1. يَاَيُّهَا الَّذِيْنَ اٰمَنُوْا لَا تَقْرَبُوا الصَّلٰوةَ
وَاَنْتُمْ سُكٰرٰى حَتّٰى تَعْلَمُوْا مَا تَقُوْلُوْنَ
وَلَا جُنُبًا اِلَّا عَابِرِيْ سَبِيْلٍ حَتّٰى
تَغْتَسِلُوْا ۭ وَاِنْ كُنْتُمْ مَّرْضٰٓى اَوْ عَلٰي
سَفَرٍ اَوْ جَاۗءَ اَحَدٌ مِّنْكُمْ مِّنَ الْغَاۗىِٕطِ
اَوْ لٰمَسْتُمُ النِّسَاۗءَ فَلَمْ تَجِدُوْا مَاۗءً
فَتَيَمَّمُوْا صَعِيْدًا طَيِّبًا فَامْسَحُوْا بِوُجُوْهِكُمْ
وَاَيْدِيْكُمْ ۭ اِنَّ اللّٰهَ كَانَ عَفُوًّا غَفُوْرًا ﴿٤٣﴾

GLAD TIDINGS

1. And give glad tidings (O Muhammad) unto those who believe and do good works, that theirs are Gardens underneath which rivers flow; as often as they are regaled with food of the fruit thereof, they say: This is what was given us aforetime and it is given to them in resemblance. There for them are pure companions; there for ever they abide.

2:25

1. وَبَشِّرِ الَّذِيْنَ اٰمَنُوْا وَعَمِلُوا الصّٰلِحٰتِ اَنَّ لَهُمْ
جَنّٰتٍ تَجْرِيْ مِنْ تَحْتِهَا الْاَنْهٰرُ ۭ كُلَّمَا رُزِقُوْا
مِنْهَا مِنْ ثَمَرَةٍ رِّزْقًا ۙ قَالُوْا ھٰذَا الَّذِيْ
رُزِقْنَا مِنْ قَبْلُ ۙ وَاُتُوْا بِهٖ مُتَشَابِهًا ۭ وَلَهُمْ
فِيْهَآ اَزْوَاجٌ مُّطَهَّرَةٌ ڎ وَّھُمْ فِيْهَا خٰلِدُوْنَ ﴿٢٥﴾

2. But give glad tidings to the steadfast,

Who say, when a misfortune striketh them: Lo! we are Allah's and lo! unto Him we are returning.

Such are they on whom are blessings from their Lord, and mercy. Such are the rightly guided.

2:155–157

2. وَبَشِّرِ الصّٰبِرِيْنَ ﴿١٥٥﴾
الَّذِيْنَ اِذَآ اَصَابَتْهُمْ مُّصِيْبَةٌ ۙ قَالُوْٓا اِنَّا
لِلّٰهِ وَاِنَّآ اِلَيْهِ رٰجِعُوْنَ ﴿١٥٦﴾
اُولٰۗىِٕكَ عَلَيْهِمْ صَلَوٰتٌ مِّنْ رَّبِّهِمْ وَرَحْمَةٌ ۣ
وَاُولٰۗىِٕكَ ھُمُ الْمُهْتَدُوْنَ ﴿١٥٧﴾

GHUSL
Ref: 5:6; 38:42.

3. (And remember) when the angels said: O Mary! Lo! Allah giveth thee glad tidings of a word from Him, whose name is the Messiah, Jesus, son of Mary, illustrious in the world and the Hereafter, and one of those brought near (unto Allah).

3:45

4. Those who believe and keep their duty (to Allah),

Theirs are good tidings in the life of the world and in the Hereafter—There is no changing the Words of Allah that is the Supreme Triumph.

10:63–64

5. And give good tidings (O Muhammad) to the humble,

Whose hearts fear when Allah is mentioned, and the patient of whatever may befall them, and those who establish worship and who spend of that We have bestowed on them.

22:34–35

6. And announce unto the believers the good tidings that they will have great bounty from Allah.

33:47

7. And those who put away false gods lest they should worship them and turn to Allah in repentance, for them there are glad tidings. Therefor give good tidings (O Muhammad) to My bondmen,

Who hear advice and follow the best thereof. Such are those whom Allah guideth, and such are men of understanding.

39:17–18

3. إِذْ قَالَتِ الْمَلٰٓئِكَةُ يٰمَرْيَمُ إِنَّ اللّٰهَ
يُبَشِّرُكِ بِكَلِمَةٍ مِّنْهُ ۖ اسْمُهُ الْمَسِيْحُ
عِيْسَى ابْنُ مَرْيَمَ وَجِيْهًا فِى الدُّنْيَا
وَالْاٰخِرَةِ وَمِنَ الْمُقَرَّبِيْنَ ۙ○

4. اَلَّذِيْنَ اٰمَنُوْا وَكَانُوْا يَتَّقُوْنَ ۗ (٦٣)
لَهُمُ الْبُشْرٰى فِى الْحَيٰوةِ الدُّنْيَا وَفِى
الْاٰخِرَةِ ۗ لَا تَبْدِيْلَ لِكَلِمٰتِ اللّٰهِ ۗ
ذٰلِكَ هُوَ الْفَوْزُ الْعَظِيْمُ ۗ (٦٤)

5. وَبَشِّرِ الْمُخْبِتِيْنَ ۙ (٣٤)
الَّذِيْنَ اِذَا ذُكِرَ اللّٰهُ وَجِلَتْ قُلُوْبُهُمْ
وَالصّٰبِرِيْنَ عَلٰى مَآ اَصَابَهُمْ وَالْمُقِيْمِي
الصَّلٰوةِ ۙ وَمِمَّا رَزَقْنٰهُمْ يُنْفِقُوْنَ (٣٥)

6. وَبَشِّرِ الْمُؤْمِنِيْنَ بِاَنَّ لَهُمْ مِّنَ
اللّٰهِ فَضْلًا كَبِيْرًا (٤٧)

7. وَالَّذِيْنَ اجْتَنَبُوا الطَّاغُوْتَ اَنْ يَّعْبُدُوْهَا
وَاَنَابُوْٓا اِلَى اللّٰهِ لَهُمُ الْبُشْرٰى ۚ فَبَشِّرْ عِبَادِ ۙ (١٧)

الَّذِيْنَ يَسْتَمِعُوْنَ الْقَوْلَ فَيَتَّبِعُوْنَ
اَحْسَنَهٗ ۗ اُولٰٓئِكَ الَّذِيْنَ هَدٰىهُمُ اللّٰهُ
وَاُولٰٓئِكَ هُمْ اُولُوا الْاَلْبَابِ (١٨)

8. And when Jesus son of Mary said: O Children of Israel! Lo! I am the messenger of Allah unto you, confirming that which was (revealed) before me in the Torah, and bringing good tidings of a messenger who cometh after me, whose name is the Praised One. Yet when he hath come unto them with clear proofs, they say: This is mere magic.

61:6

8. وَإِذْ قَالَ عِيسَى ابْنُ مَرْيَمَ يٰبَنِيٓ
إِسْرَآءِيلَ إِنِّي رَسُولُ اللهِ إِلَيْكُمْ
مُّصَدِّقًا لِّمَا بَيْنَ يَدَيَّ مِنَ التَّوْرٰةِ
وَمُبَشِّرًا بِرَسُولٍ يَأْتِي مِنْ بَعْدِي
اسْمُهُ أَحْمَدُ فَلَمَّا جَآءَهُمْ بِالْبَيِّنٰتِ
قَالُوا هٰذَا سِحْرٌ مُّبِينٌ ۝

GLORIFICATION OF ALLAH

1. Such as remember Allah, standing, sitting, and reclining, and consider the creation of the heavens and the earth, (and say): Our Lord! Thou createdst not this in vain. Glory be to Thee! Preserve us from doom of Fire!

3:191

1. الَّذِينَ يَذْكُرُونَ اللهَ قِيٰمًا وَّقُعُودًا وَّعَلٰى
جُنُوبِهِمْ وَيَتَفَكَّرُونَ فِي خَلْقِ السَّمٰوٰتِ
وَالْأَرْضِ رَبَّنَا مَا خَلَقْتَ هٰذَا بَاطِلًا
سُبْحٰنَكَ فَقِنَا عَذَابَ النَّارِ ۝

2. But hymn the praise of thy Lord, and be of those who make prostration (unto Him).

15:98

2. فَسَبِّحْ بِحَمْدِ رَبِّكَ وَكُنْ مِّنَ السّٰجِدِينَ ۝

3. The seven heavens and the earth and all that is therein praise Him, and there is not a thing but hymneth His praise; but ye understand not their praise, Lo! He is ever Clement, Forgiving.

17:44

3. تُسَبِّحُ لَهُ السَّمٰوٰتُ السَّبْعُ وَالْأَرْضُ
وَمَنْ فِيهِنَّ وَإِنْ مِّنْ شَيْءٍ إِلَّا يُسَبِّحُ
بِحَمْدِهِ وَلٰكِنْ لَّا تَفْقَهُونَ تَسْبِيحَهُمْ
إِنَّهُ كَانَ حَلِيمًا غَفُورًا ۝

GLAD TIDINGS

Ref: 3:39; 11:69,71,74; 15:53–55; 19:7; 22:37; 37: 100–101,112; 51:28; 61:13;

See also: Warning.

4. فَاصْبِرْ عَلَىٰ مَا يَقُولُونَ وَسَبِّحْ بِحَمْدِ
رَبِّكَ قَبْلَ طُلُوعِ الشَّمْسِ وَقَبْلَ
غُرُوبِهَا ۖ وَمِنْ آنَاءِ اللَّيْلِ فَسَبِّحْ وَ
أَطْرَافَ النَّهَارِ لَعَلَّكَ تَرْضَىٰ ﴿١٣٠﴾

5. وَذَا النُّونِ إِذ ذَّهَبَ مُغَاضِبًا فَظَنَّ أَن
لَّن نَّقْدِرَ عَلَيْهِ فَنَادَىٰ فِي الظُّلُمَاتِ
أَن لَّا إِلَٰهَ إِلَّا أَنتَ سُبْحَانَكَ إِنِّي
كُنتُ مِنَ الظَّالِمِينَ ﴿٨٧﴾

6. يَا أَيُّهَا الَّذِينَ آمَنُوا اذْكُرُوا اللَّهَ ذِكْرًا
كَثِيرًا ﴿٤١﴾
وَسَبِّحُوهُ بُكْرَةً وَأَصِيلًا ﴿٤٢﴾

7. سُبْحَانَ الَّذِي خَلَقَ الْأَزْوَاجَ كُلَّهَا
مِمَّا تُنبِتُ الْأَرْضُ وَمِنْ أَنفُسِهِمْ
وَمِمَّا لَا يَعْلَمُونَ ﴿٣٦﴾

8. فَسُبْحَانَ الَّذِي بِيَدِهِ مَلَكُوتُ كُلِّ
شَيْءٍ وَإِلَيْهِ تُرْجَعُونَ ﴿٨٣﴾

9. سُبْحَانَ رَبِّكَ رَبِّ الْعِزَّةِ عَمَّا يَصِفُونَ ﴿١٨٠﴾

10. الَّذِينَ يَحْمِلُونَ الْعَرْشَ وَمَنْ حَوْلَهُ
يُسَبِّحُونَ بِحَمْدِ رَبِّهِمْ وَيُؤْمِنُونَ
بِهِ وَيَسْتَغْفِرُونَ لِلَّذِينَ آمَنُوا

4. Therefor (O Muhammad), bear with what they say, and celebrate the praises of thy Lord ere the rising of the sun and ere the going down there-of. And glorify Him some hours of the night and at the two ends of the day, that thou mayst find acceptance.

20:130

5. And (Mention) *Dhu'n-Nun,* when he went off in anger and deemed that We had no power over him, but he cried out in the darkness, saying: There is no God save Thee. Be Thou Glorified! Lo! I have been a wrong-doer.

21:87

6. O ye who believe! Remember Allah with much remembrance,

And glorify Him early and late.

33:41-42

7. Glory be to Him Who created all the sexual pairs, of that which the earth groweth, and of themselves, and of that which they know not!

36:36

8. Therefor glory be to Him in Whose hand is the dominion over all things! Unto Him ye will be brought back.

36:83

9. Glorified be thy Lord, the Lord of Majesty, from that which they attribute (unto Him)!

37:180

10. Those who bear the Throne, and all who are round about it, hymn the praises of their Lord and believe in Him and ask forgiveness for those who believe.

40:7

11. He Who created all the pairs, and appointed for you ships and cattle whereupon ye ride.

That ye may mount upon their backs, and may remember your Lord's favour when ye mount thereon, and may say: Glorified be He Who hath subdued these unto us, and we were not capable (of subduing them);

43:12–13

11. وَالَّذِي خَلَقَ الْأَزْوَاجَ كُلَّهَا وَجَعَلَ لَكُمْ
مِّنَ الْفُلْكِ وَالْأَنْعَامِ مَا تَرْكَبُونَ ۝
لِتَسْتَوُوا عَلَىٰ ظُهُورِهِ ثُمَّ تَذْكُرُوا نِعْمَةَ
رَبِّكُمْ إِذَا اسْتَوَيْتُمْ عَلَيْهِ وَتَقُولُوا
سُبْحَانَ الَّذِي سَخَّرَ لَنَا هَٰذَا وَمَا
كُنَّا لَهُ مُقْرِنِينَ ۝

12. Therefor (O Muhammad) bear with what they say, and hymn the praise of thy Lord before the rising and before the setting of the sun;

And in the night–time hymn His praise and after the (prescribed) prostrations.

50:39–40

12. فَاصْبِرْ عَلَىٰ مَا يَقُولُونَ وَسَبِّحْ
بِحَمْدِ رَبِّكَ قَبْلَ طُلُوعِ الشَّمْسِ
وَقَبْلَ الْغُرُوبِ ۝
وَمِنَ اللَّيْلِ فَسَبِّحْهُ وَأَدْبَارَ السُّجُودِ ۝

13. All that is in the heavens and the earth glorifieth Allah; and He is the Mighty, the Wise.

57:1

13. سَبَّحَ لِلَّهِ مَا فِي السَّمَاوَاتِ وَالْأَرْضِ
وَهُوَ الْعَزِيزُ الْحَكِيمُ ۝

GOOD BEHAVIOUR

1. And (remember) when We made a covenant with the Children of Israel, (saying): Worship none save Allah (only) and be good to parents and to kindred and to orphans and the needy, and speak kindly to mankind; and establish worship and pay the poor–due. Then, after that, ye slid back, save a few of you, being averse.

2:83

1. وَإِذْ أَخَذْنَا مِيثَاقَ بَنِي إِسْرَائِيلَ لَا تَعْبُدُونَ
إِلَّا اللَّهَ وَبِالْوَالِدَيْنِ إِحْسَانًا وَذِي الْقُرْبَىٰ وَ
الْيَتَامَىٰ وَالْمَسَاكِينِ وَقُولُوا لِلنَّاسِ حُسْنًا وَ
أَقِيمُوا الصَّلَاةَ وَآتُوا الزَّكَاةَ ثُمَّ تَوَلَّيْتُمْ إِلَّا
قَلِيلًا مِّنكُمْ وَأَنتُم مُّعْرِضُونَ ۝

GLORIFICATION OF ALLAH Ref: 2:30; 4:171; 6:100; 7:143; 10:10,18; 12:108; 16:1,49; 17:1,43; 21:20; 23:91; 24:36–37,41; 25:58; 28:68; 30:17,41; 39:4,67; 40:55; 42:5; 43:82; 48:9; 52:48–49; 56:74,96; 59:1,24; 61:1; 62:1; 64:1; 68:28–29; 69:52; 76:26; 87:1.

See also: Praise to Allah, Remembrance of Allah.

2. O ye who believe! Retaliation is prescribed for you in the matter of the murdered; the freeman for the freeman, and the slave for the slave, and the female for the female. And for him who is forgiven somewhat by his (injured) brother, prosecution according to usage and payment unto him in kindness. This is an alleviation and a mercy from your Lord. He who transgresseth after this will have a painful doom.

2:178

3. When ye are greeted with a greeting, greet ye with better than it or return it. Lo! Allah taketh count of all things.

4:86

4. Call unto the way of thy Lord with wisdom and fair exhortation, and reason with them in the better way. Lo! thy Lord is Best Aware of him who strayeth from His way, and He is Best Aware of those who go aright.

16:125

5. Tell My bondmen to speak that which is kindlier. Lo! the devil soweth discord among them. Lo! the devil is for man an open foe.

17:53

6. O ye who believe! Enter not houses other

2. يا أيها الذين آمنوا كتب عليكم القصاص
في القتلى الحر بالحر والعبد بالعبد
والأنثى بالأنثى فمن عفي له من أخيه
شيء فاتباع بالمعروف وأداء إليه بإحسان
ذلك تخفيف من ربكم ورحمة فمن
اعتدى بعد ذلك فله عذاب أليم ﴿١٧٨﴾

3. وإذا حييتم بتحية فحيوا بأحسن منها
أو ردوها إن الله كان على كل شيء حسيبا ﴿٨٦﴾

4. ادع إلى سبيل ربك بالحكمة والموعظة
الحسنة وجادلهم بالتي هي أحسن إن
ربك هو أعلم بمن ضل عن سبيله
وهو أعلم بالمهتدين ﴿١٢٥﴾

5. وقل لعبادي يقولوا التي هي أحسن
إن الشيطان ينزغ بينهم إن الشيطان
كان للإنسان عدوا مبينا ﴿٥٣﴾

6. يا أيها الذين آمنوا لا تدخلوا بيوتا
غير بيوتكم حتى تستأنسوا وتسلموا
على أهلها ذلكم خير لكم
لعلكم تذكرون ﴿٢٧﴾
فإن لم تجدوا فيها أحدا فلا تدخلوها
حتى يؤذن لكم وإن قيل لكم
ارجعوا فارجعوا هو أزكى لكم

than your own without first announcing your presence and invoking peace upon the folk thereof. That is better for you, that ye may be heedful.

And if ye find no-one therein, still enter not until permission hath been given. And if it be said unto you: Go away again, then go away, for it is purer for you. Allah knoweth what ye do.

(It is) no sin for you to enter uninhabited houses wherein is comfort for you. Allah knoweth what ye proclaim and what ye hide.

Tell the believing men to lower their gaze and be modest. That is purer for them. Lo! Allah is Aware of what they do.

And tell the believing women to lower their gaze and be modest, and to display of their adornment only that which is apparent, and to draw their veils over their bosoms, and not to reveal their adornment save to their own husbands or fathers or husbands' fathers, or their sons or their husbands' sons, or their brothers, or their brothers' sons or sisters' sons, or their women, or their slaves, or male attendants who lack vigour, or children who know naught of women's nakedness. And let them not stamp their feet so as to reveal what they hide of their adornment. And turn unto Allah together, O believers, in order that ye may succeed.

24:27–31

وَاللّٰهُ بِمَا تَعْمَلُوْنَ عَلِيْمٌ ﴿٢٨﴾
لَيْسَ عَلَيْكُمْ جُنَاحٌ اَنْ تَدْخُلُوْا بُيُوْتًا
غَيْرَ مَسْكُوْنَةٍ فِيْهَا مَتَاعٌ لَّكُمْ وَاللّٰهُ
يَعْلَمُ مَا تُبْدُوْنَ وَمَا تَكْتُمُوْنَ ﴿٢٩﴾
قُلْ لِّلْمُؤْمِنِيْنَ يَغُضُّوْا مِنْ اَبْصَارِهِمْ
وَيَحْفَظُوْا فُرُوْجَهُمْ ذٰلِكَ اَزْكٰى لَهُمْ
اِنَّ اللّٰهَ خَبِيْرٌ بِمَا يَصْنَعُوْنَ ﴿٣٠﴾
وَقُلْ لِّلْمُؤْمِنٰتِ يَغْضُضْنَ مِنْ اَبْصَارِهِنَّ
وَيَحْفَظْنَ فُرُوْجَهُنَّ وَلَا يُبْدِيْنَ
زِيْنَتَهُنَّ اِلَّا مَا ظَهَرَ مِنْهَا وَلْيَضْرِبْنَ
بِخُمُرِهِنَّ عَلٰى جُيُوْبِهِنَّ وَلَا يُبْدِيْنَ
زِيْنَتَهُنَّ اِلَّا لِبُعُوْلَتِهِنَّ اَوْ اٰبَآئِهِنَّ اَوْ اٰبَآءِ
بُعُوْلَتِهِنَّ اَوْ اَبْنَآئِهِنَّ اَوْ اَبْنَآءِ بُعُوْلَتِهِنَّ
اَوْ اِخْوَانِهِنَّ اَوْ بَنِيْٓ اِخْوَانِهِنَّ اَوْ بَنِيْٓ
اَخَوٰتِهِنَّ اَوْ نِسَآئِهِنَّ اَوْ مَا مَلَكَتْ
اَيْمَانُهُنَّ اَوِ التّٰبِعِيْنَ غَيْرِ اُولِي الْاِرْبَةِ
مِنَ الرِّجَالِ اَوِ الطِّفْلِ الَّذِيْنَ لَمْ
يَظْهَرُوْا عَلٰى عَوْرٰتِ النِّسَآءِ وَلَا يَضْرِبْنَ
بِاَرْجُلِهِنَّ لِيُعْلَمَ مَا يُخْفِيْنَ مِنْ زِيْنَتِهِنَّ
وَتُوْبُوْا اِلَى اللّٰهِ جَمِيْعًا اَيُّهَ الْمُؤْمِنُوْنَ
لَعَلَّكُمْ تُفْلِحُوْنَ ۝

7. يٰۤاَيُّهَا الَّذِيْنَ اٰمَنُوْا لِيَسْتَاْذِنْكُمُ
الَّذِيْنَ مَلَكَتْ اَيْمَانُكُمْ وَالَّذِيْنَ لَمْ
يَبْلُغُوا الْحُلُمَ مِنْكُمْ ثَلٰثَ مَرّٰتٍ مِنْ

7. O ye who believe! Let your slaves, and those of you who have not come to puberty, ask leave of you at three

times (before they come into your presence); Before the prayer of dawn, and when ye lay aside your raiment for the heat of noon, and after the prayer of night. Three times of privacy for you. It is no sin for them or for you at other times, when some of you go round attendant upon others (if they come into your presence without leave). Thus Allah maketh clear the revelations for you. Allah is Knower, Wise.

And when the children among you come to puberty then let them ask leave even as those before them used to ask it. Thus Allah maketh clear His revelations for you. Allah is Knower, Wise.

As for women past child–bearing, who have no hope of marriage, it is no sin for them if they discard their (outer) clothing in such a way as not to show adornment. But to refrain is better for them. Allah is Hearer, Knower.

No blame is there upon the blind nor any blame upon the lame nor any blame upon the sick nor on yourselves if ye eat from your houses, or the houses of your fathers, or the houses of your mothers, or the houses of your broth–ers, or the houses of your sisters, or the houses of your fathers' brothers, or the hou–ses of your fathers' sisters.

قَبْلِ صَلٰوةِ الْفَجْرِ وَحِيْنَ تَضَعُوْنَ
ثِيَابَكُمْ مِّنَ الظَّهِيْرَةِ وَمِنْۢ بَعْدِ صَلٰوةِ
الْعِشَآءِ ۟ ثَلٰثُ عَوْرٰتٍ لَّكُمْ ؕ لَيْسَ
عَلَيْكُمْ وَلَا عَلَيْهِمْ جُنَاحٌۢ بَعْدَهُنَّ ؕ
طَوّٰفُوْنَ عَلَيْكُمْ بَعْضُكُمْ عَلٰى بَعْضٍ ؕ
كَذٰلِكَ يُبَيِّنُ اللّٰهُ لَكُمُ الْاٰيٰتِ ؕ
وَاللّٰهُ عَلِيْمٌ حَكِيْمٌ ﴿٥٨﴾
وَاِذَا بَلَغَ الْاَطْفَالُ مِنْكُمُ الْحُلُمَ
فَلْيَسْتَاْذِنُوْا كَمَا اسْتَاْذَنَ الَّذِيْنَ مِنْ
قَبْلِهِمْ ؕ كَذٰلِكَ يُبَيِّنُ اللّٰهُ لَكُمْ اٰيٰتِهٖ ؕ
وَاللّٰهُ عَلِيْمٌ حَكِيْمٌ ﴿٥٩﴾
وَالْقَوَاعِدُ مِنَ النِّسَآءِ الّٰتِيْ لَا يَرْجُوْنَ
نِكَاحًا فَلَيْسَ عَلَيْهِنَّ جُنَاحٌ اَنْ يَّضَعْنَ
ثِيَابَهُنَّ غَيْرَ مُتَبَرِّجٰتٍۢ بِزِيْنَةٍ ؕ وَاَنْ
يَّسْتَعْفِفْنَ خَيْرٌ لَّهُنَّ ؕ وَاللّٰهُ سَمِيْعٌ عَلِيْمٌ ﴿٦٠﴾
لَيْسَ عَلَى الْاَعْمٰى حَرَجٌ وَّلَا عَلَى الْاَعْرَجِ
حَرَجٌ وَّلَا عَلَى الْمَرِيْضِ حَرَجٌ وَّلَا عَلٰٓى
اَنْفُسِكُمْ اَنْ تَاْكُلُوْا مِنْۢ بُيُوْتِكُمْ اَوْ
بُيُوْتِ اٰبَآئِكُمْ اَوْ بُيُوْتِ اُمَّهٰتِكُمْ اَوْ
بُيُوْتِ اِخْوَانِكُمْ اَوْ بُيُوْتِ اَخَوٰتِكُمْ اَوْ
بُيُوْتِ اَعْمَامِكُمْ اَوْ بُيُوْتِ عَمّٰتِكُمْ اَوْ
بُيُوْتِ اَخْوَالِكُمْ اَوْ بُيُوْتِ خٰلٰتِكُمْ اَوْ
مَا مَلَكْتُمْ مَّفَاتِحَهٗۤ اَوْ صَدِيْقِكُمْ ؕ
لَيْسَ عَلَيْكُمْ جُنَاحٌ اَنْ تَاْكُلُوْا جَمِيْعًا

or the houses of your mothers' brothers, or the houses of your mothers' sisters, or (from that) whereof ye hold the keys, or (from the house) of a friend. No sin shall it be for you whether ye eat to–gether or apart. But when ye enter houses, salute one another with a greeting from Allah, blessed and sweet. Thus Allah maketh clear His revelations for you, that haply ye may understand.

They only are the true believers who believe in Allah and His messenger and, when they are with him on some common errand, go not away until they have asked leave of him. Lo! those who ask leave of thee, those are they who believe in Allah and His messenger. So, if they ask thy leave for some affair of theirs, give leave to whom thou wilt of them, and ask for them forgiveness of Allah. Lo! Allah is Forgiving, Merciful.

24:58–62

8. O my dear son! Establish worship and enjoin kindness and forbid iniquity, and persevere whatever may befall thee. Lo! that is of the steadfast heart of things.

Turn not thy cheek in scorn toward folk, nor walk with pertness in the land. Lo! Allah loveth not each braggart boaster.

Be modest in thy bearing and subdue thy voice. Lo! the harshest of all voices is the voice of the ass.

31:17–19

أَوْ أَشْتَاتًا ۚ فَإِذَا دَخَلْتُم بُيُوتًا فَسَلِّمُوا
عَلَىٰ أَنفُسِكُمْ تَحِيَّةً مِّنْ عِندِ اللَّهِ
مُبَارَكَةً طَيِّبَةً ۚ كَذَٰلِكَ يُبَيِّنُ اللَّهُ لَكُمُ
الْآيَاتِ لَعَلَّكُمْ تَعْقِلُونَ ﴿٦١﴾
إِنَّمَا الْمُؤْمِنُونَ الَّذِينَ آمَنُوا بِاللَّهِ
وَرَسُولِهِ وَإِذَا كَانُوا مَعَهُ عَلَىٰ أَمْرٍ
جَامِعٍ لَّمْ يَذْهَبُوا حَتَّىٰ يَسْتَأْذِنُوهُ ۚ إِنَّ
الَّذِينَ يَسْتَأْذِنُونَكَ أُولَٰئِكَ الَّذِينَ
يُؤْمِنُونَ بِاللَّهِ وَرَسُولِهِ ۚ فَإِذَا اسْتَأْذَنُوكَ
لِبَعْضِ شَأْنِهِمْ فَأْذَن لِّمَن شِئْتَ مِنْهُمْ
وَاسْتَغْفِرْ لَهُمُ اللَّهَ ۚ إِنَّ اللَّهَ غَفُورٌ رَّحِيمٌ ﴿٦٢﴾

8. يَا بُنَيَّ أَقِمِ الصَّلَاةَ وَأْمُرْ بِالْمَعْرُوفِ
وَانْهَ عَنِ الْمُنكَرِ وَاصْبِرْ عَلَىٰ مَا
أَصَابَكَ ۖ إِنَّ ذَٰلِكَ مِنْ عَزْمِ الْأُمُورِ ﴿١٧﴾
وَلَا تُصَعِّرْ خَدَّكَ لِلنَّاسِ وَلَا تَمْشِ
فِي الْأَرْضِ مَرَحًا ۖ إِنَّ اللَّهَ لَا يُحِبُّ
كُلَّ مُخْتَالٍ فَخُورٍ ﴿١٨﴾
وَاقْصِدْ فِي مَشْيِكَ وَاغْضُضْ مِن
صَوْتِكَ ۚ إِنَّ أَنكَرَ الْأَصْوَاتِ
لَصَوْتُ الْحَمِيرِ ﴿١٩﴾

GRANDEUR AND WEALTH

1. Say: O Allah! Owner of Sovereignty! Thou givest sovereignty unto whom Thou wilt, and Thou withdrawest sovereignty from whom Thou wilt. Thou exaltest whom Thou wilt and Thou abasest whom Thou wilt. In Thy hand is the good. Lo! Thou art Able to do all things.

Thou causest the night to pass into the day, and Thou causest the day to pass into the night. And Thou bringest forth the living from the dead, and Thou bringest forth the dead from the living. And Thou givest sustenance to whom Thou choosest, without stint.

3:26–27

2. Wealth and children are an ornament of life of the world. But the good deeds which endure are better in thy Lord's sight for reward, and better in respect of hope.

18:46

3. Now Korah was of Moses' folk, but he oppressed them; and We gave him so much treasure that the stores thereof would verily have been a burden for a troop of mighty men. When his own folk said unto him: Exult not; lo! Allah loveth not the exultant.

But seek the abode of the

1. قُلِ اللّٰهُمَّ مٰلِكَ الْمُلْكِ تُؤْتِي الْمُلْكَ
مَنْ تَشَآءُ وَتَنْزِعُ الْمُلْكَ مِمَّنْ تَشَآءُ وَ
تُعِزُّ مَنْ تَشَآءُ وَتُذِلُّ مَنْ تَشَآءُ بِيَدِكَ
الْخَيْرُ اِنَّكَ عَلٰى كُلِّ شَيْءٍ قَدِيْرٌ ○
تُوْلِجُ الَّيْلَ فِي النَّهَارِ وَتُوْلِجُ النَّهَارَ فِي
الَّيْلِ وَتُخْرِجُ الْحَيَّ مِنَ الْمَيِّتِ وَتُخْرِجُ
الْمَيِّتَ مِنَ الْحَيِّ وَتَرْزُقُ مَنْ تَشَآءُ
بِغَيْرِ حِسَابٍ ○

2. اَلْمَالُ وَالْبَنُوْنَ زِيْنَةُ الْحَيٰوةِ الدُّنْيَا
وَالْبٰقِيٰتُ الصّٰلِحٰتُ خَيْرٌ عِنْدَ رَبِّكَ
ثَوَابًا وَّخَيْرٌ اَمَلًا ○

3. اِنَّ قَارُوْنَ كَانَ مِنْ قَوْمِ مُوْسٰى فَبَغٰى
عَلَيْهِمْ وَاٰتَيْنٰهُ مِنَ الْكُنُوْزِ مَآ اِنَّ
مَفَاتِحَهٗ لَتَنُوْٓاُ بِالْعُصْبَةِ اُولِي الْقُوَّةِ
اِذْ قَالَ لَهٗ قَوْمُهٗ لَا تَفْرَحْ اِنَّ
اللّٰهَ لَا يُحِبُّ الْفَرِحِيْنَ ○
وَابْتَغِ فِيْمَآ اٰتٰىكَ اللّٰهُ الدَّارَ الْاٰخِرَةَ
وَلَا تَنْسَ نَصِيْبَكَ مِنَ الدُّنْيَا وَ
اَحْسِنْ كَمَآ اَحْسَنَ اللّٰهُ اِلَيْكَ وَلَا تَبْغِ
الْفَسَادَ فِي الْاَرْضِ اِنَّ اللّٰهَ لَا
يُحِبُّ الْمُفْسِدِيْنَ ○
قَالَ اِنَّمَآ اُوْتِيْتُهٗ عَلٰى عِلْمٍ عِنْدِيْ
اَوَلَمْ يَعْلَمْ اَنَّ اللّٰهَ قَدْ اَهْلَكَ مِنْ

Hereafter in that which Allah hath given thee and neglect not thy portion of the world and be thou kind even as Allah hath been kind to thee, and seek not corruption in the earth; lo! Allah loveth not corrupters.

He said: I have been given it only on account of knowledge I possess. Knew he not that Allah had destroyed already of the generations before him men who were mightier than him in strength and greater in respect of following? The guilty are not questioned of their sins.

Then went he forth before his people in his pomp. Those who were desirous of the life of the world said: Ah, would that we had the like of what hath been given unto Korah! Lo! he is lord of rare good fortune.

But those who had been given knowledge said: Woe unto you! The reward of Allah for him who believeth and doth right is better, and only the steadfast will obtain it.

So We caused the earth to swallow him and his dwelling-place. Then he had no host to help him against Allah, nor was he of those who can save themselves.

And morning found those who had coveted his place but yesterday crying: Ah, welladay! Allah enlargeth the provision for whom He will of His slaves and straiteneth it (for whom He will). If Allah had not been gracious unto us He would have caused it to swallow us (also). Ah, welladay! the

قَبْلِهٖ مِنَ الْقُرُوْنِ مَنْ هُوَ اَشَدُّ مِنْهُ
قُوَّةً وَّاَكْثَرُ جَمْعًا ۭ وَلَا يُسْـَٔلُ
عَنْ ذُنُوْبِهِمُ الْمُجْرِمُوْنَ ﴿۷۸﴾
فَخَرَجَ عَلٰى قَوْمِهٖ فِيْ زِيْنَتِهٖ ۭ قَالَ
الَّذِيْنَ يُرِيْدُوْنَ الْحَيٰوةَ الدُّنْيَا يٰلَيْتَ
لَنَا مِثْلَ مَآ اُوْتِيَ قَارُوْنُ ۙ اِنَّهٗ
لَذُوْ حَظٍّ عَظِيْمٍ ﴿۷۹﴾
وَقَالَ الَّذِيْنَ اُوْتُوا الْعِلْمَ وَيْلَكُمْ
ثَوَابُ اللّٰهِ خَيْرٌ لِّمَنْ اٰمَنَ وَعَمِلَ
صَالِحًا ۚ وَلَا يُلَقّٰىهَآ اِلَّا الصّٰبِرُوْنَ ﴿۸۰﴾
فَخَسَفْنَا بِهٖ وَبِدَارِهِ الْاَرْضَ ۣ
فَمَا كَانَ لَهٗ مِنْ فِئَةٍ يَّنْصُرُوْنَهٗ
مِنْ دُوْنِ اللّٰهِ ۤ وَمَا كَانَ مِنَ
الْمُنْتَصِرِيْنَ ﴿۸۱﴾
وَاَصْبَحَ الَّذِيْنَ تَمَنَّوْا مَكَانَهٗ
بِالْاَمْسِ يَقُوْلُوْنَ وَيْكَاَنَّ اللّٰهَ
يَبْسُطُ الرِّزْقَ لِمَنْ يَّشَاۗءُ مِنْ عِبَادِهٖ
وَيَقْدِرُ ۚ لَوْلَآ اَنْ مَّنَّ اللّٰهُ عَلَيْنَا لَخَسَفَ
بِنَا ۭ وَيْكَاَنَّهٗ لَا يُفْلِحُ الْكٰفِرُوْنَ ﴿۸۲﴾

4. وَمَآ اَرْسَلْنَا فِيْ قَرْيَةٍ مِّنْ نَّذِيْرٍ
اِلَّا قَالَ مُتْرَفُوْهَآ ۙ اِنَّا بِمَآ اُرْسِلْتُمْ
بِهٖ كٰفِرُوْنَ ﴿۳۴﴾
وَقَالُوْا نَحْنُ اَكْثَرُ اَمْوَالًا وَّاَوْلَادًا ۙ
وَّمَا نَحْنُ بِمُعَذَّبِيْنَ ﴿۳۵﴾

disbelievers never prosper.

28:76–82

4. And We sent not unto any township a warner, but its pampered ones declared: Lo! we are disbelievers in that which ye bring unto us.

And they say: We are more (than you) in wealth

and children. We are not the punished!

Say (O Muhammad): Lo! my Lord enlargeth the provision for whom He will and narroweth it (for whom He will). But most of mankind know not.

And it is not your wealth nor your children that will bring you near unto Us but he who believeth and doth good (he draweth near). As for such, theirs will be twofold reward for what they did, and they will dwell secure in lofty halls.

34:34–37

5. They it is who say: Spend not on behalf of those (who dwell) with Allah's messenger that they may disperse (and go away from you); when Allah's are the treasures of the heavens and the earth: but the hypocrites comprehend not.

They say: Surely, if we return to *Al-Madinah*, the mightier will soon drive out the weaker; when might belongeth to Allah and to His messenger and to the believers; but the hypocrites know not.

O ye who believe! Let not your wealth nor your children distract you from remembrance of Allah. Those who do so, they are the losers.

63:7–9

6. Rivalry in worldly increase distracteth you

Until ye come to the

قُلْ إِنَّ رَبِّي يَبْسُطُ الرِّزْقَ لِمَنْ
يَشَاءُ وَيَقْدِرُ وَلَٰكِنَّ أَكْثَرَ النَّاسِ
لَا يَعْلَمُونَ ﴿٣٦﴾
وَمَا أَمْوَالُكُمْ وَلَا أَوْلَادُكُمْ بِالَّتِي
تُقَرِّبُكُمْ عِنْدَنَا زُلْفَىٰ إِلَّا مَنْ آمَنَ
وَعَمِلَ صَالِحًا فَأُولَٰئِكَ لَهُمْ جَزَاءُ
الضِّعْفِ بِمَا عَمِلُوا وَهُمْ فِي الْغُرُفَاتِ
آمِنُونَ ﴿٣٧﴾

5. هُمُ الَّذِينَ يَقُولُونَ لَا تُنْفِقُوا عَلَىٰ
مَنْ عِنْدَ رَسُولِ اللَّهِ حَتَّىٰ يَنْفَضُّوا ۗ
وَلِلَّهِ خَزَائِنُ السَّمَاوَاتِ وَالْأَرْضِ
وَلَٰكِنَّ الْمُنَافِقِينَ لَا يَفْقَهُونَ ﴿٧﴾
يَقُولُونَ لَئِنْ رَجَعْنَا إِلَى الْمَدِينَةِ
لَيُخْرِجَنَّ الْأَعَزُّ مِنْهَا الْأَذَلَّ ۚ وَلِلَّهِ
الْعِزَّةُ وَلِرَسُولِهِ وَلِلْمُؤْمِنِينَ وَلَٰكِنَّ
الْمُنَافِقِينَ لَا يَعْلَمُونَ ﴿٨﴾
يَا أَيُّهَا الَّذِينَ آمَنُوا لَا تُلْهِكُمْ أَمْوَالُكُمْ
وَلَا أَوْلَادُكُمْ عَنْ ذِكْرِ اللَّهِ ۚ وَمَنْ
يَفْعَلْ ذَٰلِكَ فَأُولَٰئِكَ هُمُ الْخَاسِرُونَ ﴿٩﴾

6. أَلْهَاكُمُ التَّكَاثُرُ ﴿١﴾
حَتَّىٰ زُرْتُمُ الْمَقَابِرَ ﴿٢﴾
كَلَّا سَوْفَ تَعْلَمُونَ ﴿٣﴾
ثُمَّ كَلَّا سَوْفَ تَعْلَمُونَ ﴿٤﴾

graves.

Nay, but ye will come to know!

Nay, but ye will come to know!

Nay, would that ye knew (now) with a sure knowledge!

For ye will behold hell-fire.

Aye, ye will behold it

with sure vision.

Then on that day, ye will be asked concerning pleasure.

102:1–8

7. Woe unto every slander–ing traducer,

Who hath gathered weal–th (of this world) and arranged it.

He thinketh that his wealth will render him im–mortal.

Nay, but verily he will be flung to the Consuming One

Ah, what will convey unto thee what the Consum–ing One is!

(It is) the fire of Allah, kindled,

Which leapeth up over the hearts (of men).

Lo! it is closed in on them

In outstretched columns.

104:1–9

GRAVES

1. And because the Hour will come, there is no doubt thereof; and because Allah will raise those who are in the graves.

22:7

2. Man is (self-) destroyed: how ungrateful!

From what thing doth He create him?

From a drop of seed. He createth him and propor–tioneth him,

Then maketh the way easy for him,

Then causeth him to die, and burieth him;

كَلَّا لَوْ تَعْلَمُونَ عِلْمَ الْيَقِينِ ۝٥
لَتَرَوُنَّ الْجَحِيمَ ۝٦
ثُمَّ لَتَرَوُنَّهَا عَيْنَ الْيَقِينِ ۝٧
ثُمَّ لَتُسْأَلُنَّ يَوْمَئِذٍ عَنِ النَّعِيمِ ۝٨

7. وَيْلٌ لِّكُلِّ هُمَزَةٍ لُّمَزَةٍ ۝١
الَّذِي جَمَعَ مَالًا وَعَدَّدَهُ ۝٢
يَحْسَبُ أَنَّ مَالَهُ أَخْلَدَهُ ۝٣
كَلَّا لَيُنبَذَنَّ فِي الْحُطَمَةِ ۝٤
وَمَا أَدْرَاكَ مَا الْحُطَمَةُ ۝٥
نَارُ اللَّهِ الْمُوقَدَةُ ۝٦
الَّتِي تَطَّلِعُ عَلَى الْأَفْئِدَةِ ۝٧
إِنَّهَا عَلَيْهِم مُّؤْصَدَةٌ ۝٨
فِي عَمَدٍ مُّمَدَّدَةٍ ۝٩

○

1. وَأَنَّ السَّاعَةَ آتِيَةٌ لَّا رَيْبَ فِيهَا
وَأَنَّ اللَّهَ يَبْعَثُ مَن فِي الْقُبُورِ ۝٧

2. قُتِلَ الْإِنسَانُ مَا أَكْفَرَهُ ۝١٧
مِنْ أَيِّ شَيْءٍ خَلَقَهُ ۝١٨
مِن نُّطْفَةٍ خَلَقَهُ فَقَدَّرَهُ ۝١٩
ثُمَّ السَّبِيلَ يَسَّرَهُ ۝٢٠
ثُمَّ أَمَاتَهُ فَأَقْبَرَهُ ۝٢١
ثُمَّ إِذَا شَاءَ أَنشَرَهُ ۝٢٢

Then, when He will, He bringeth him again to life.

80:17–22

3. When the heaven is cleft asunder,

When the planets are dispersed,

When the seas are poured forth,

And the sepulchres are

GRANDEUR AND WEALTH
Ref: 8:28.

overturned,

A soul will know what it hath sent before (it) and what left behind.

82:1–5

4. Rivalry in worldly increase distracteth you

Until ye come to the graves.

102:1–2

GRAVE SINS

1. If ye avoid the great (things) which ye are forbidden, We will remit from you your evil deeds and make you enter at a noble gate.

4:31

2. And that which Allah hath is better and more lasting for those who believe and put their trust in their Lord.

And those who shun the worst of sins and indecencies and, when they are worth, forgive.

42:36–37

3. And unto Allah belongeth whatsoever is in the heavens and whatsoever is in the earth, that He may reward those who do evil with that which they have done, and reward those who do good with goodness.

Those who avoid enormities of sin and abominations, save the unwilled offences—(for them) lo! thy Lord is of vast mercy. He is Best

3. إِذَا السَّمَاءُ انْفَطَرَتْ ۝١
وَإِذَا الْكَوَاكِبُ انْتَثَرَتْ ۝٢
وَإِذَا الْبِحَارُ فُجِّرَتْ ۝٣
وَإِذَا الْقُبُورُ بُعْثِرَتْ ۝٤
عَلِمَتْ نَفْسٌ مَا قَدَّمَتْ وَأَخَّرَتْ ۝٥

4. أَلْهَاكُمُ التَّكَاثُرُ ۝١
حَتَّىٰ زُرْتُمُ الْمَقَابِرَ ۝٢

1. إِنْ تَجْتَنِبُوا كَبَائِرَ مَا تُنْهَوْنَ عَنْهُ نُكَفِّرْ
عَنْكُمْ سَيِّئَاتِكُمْ وَنُدْخِلْكُمْ مُدْخَلًا كَرِيمًا ۝٣١

2. وَمَا عِنْدَ اللَّهِ خَيْرٌ وَأَبْقَىٰ لِلَّذِينَ
آمَنُوا وَعَلَىٰ رَبِّهِمْ يَتَوَكَّلُونَ ۝٣٦
وَالَّذِينَ يَجْتَنِبُونَ كَبَائِرَ الْإِثْمِ
وَالْفَوَاحِشَ وَإِذَا مَا غَضِبُوا هُمْ
يَغْفِرُونَ ۝٣٧

3. وَلِلَّهِ مَا فِي السَّمَاوَاتِ وَمَا فِي الْأَرْضِ
لِيَجْزِيَ الَّذِينَ أَسَاءُوا بِمَا عَمِلُوا
وَيَجْزِيَ الَّذِينَ أَحْسَنُوا بِالْحُسْنَى ۝٣١
الَّذِينَ يَجْتَنِبُونَ كَبَائِرَ الْإِثْمِ
وَالْفَوَاحِشَ إِلَّا اللَّمَمَ إِنَّ رَبَّكَ
وَاسِعُ الْمَغْفِرَةِ هُوَ أَعْلَمُ بِكُمْ إِذْ
أَنْشَأَكُمْ مِنَ الْأَرْضِ وَإِذْ أَنْتُمْ أَجِنَّةٌ

Aware of you (from the time) when He created you from the earth, and when ye were hidden in the bellies of your mothers. Therefor ascribe not purity unto yourselves. He is Best Aware of him who wardeth off (evil).

53:31–32

GRAVES

See also: *Barzakh*.

GREED

1. And thou wilt find them greediest of mankind for life and (greedier) than the idolaters. (Each) one of them would like to be allowed to live a thousand years. And to live (a thousand years) would by no means remove him from the doom. Allah is Seer of what they do.

2:96

2. But greed hath been made present in the minds (of men). If ye do good and keep from evil, lo! Allah is ever Informed of what ye do.

4:128

3. Those who entered the city and the faith before them love those who flee unto them for refuge, and find in their breasts no need for that which hath been given them, but prefer (the refugees) above themselves though poverty become their lot. And whoso is saved from his own avarice—such are they who are successful.

59:9

4. So keep your duty to Allah as best ye can, and listen, and obey, and spend; that is better for your souls. And whoso is saved from his own greed, such are the successful.

64:16

فِيْ بُطُوْنِ اُمَّهٰتِكُمْ ۚ فَلَا تُزَكُّوْٓا اَنْفُسَكُمْ ؕ
هُوَ اَعْلَمُ بِمَنِ اتَّقٰى ﴿٣٢﴾

○

1. وَلَتَجِدَنَّهُمْ اَحْرَصَ النَّاسِ عَلٰى حَيٰوةٍ ۚ وَ
مِنَ الَّذِيْنَ اَشْرَكُوْا ۚ يَوَدُّ اَحَدُهُمْ لَوْ يُعَمَّرُ
اَلْفَ سَنَةٍ ۚ وَمَا هُوَ بِمُزَحْزِحِهٖ مِنَ الْعَذَابِ
اَنْ يُّعَمَّرَ ؕ وَاللّٰهُ بَصِيْرٌۢ بِمَا يَعْمَلُوْنَ ﴿٩٦﴾

2. وَاُحْضِرَتِ الْاَنْفُسُ الشُّحَّ ؕ وَاِنْ تُحْسِنُوْا
وَتَتَّقُوْا فَاِنَّ اللّٰهَ كَانَ بِمَا تَعْمَلُوْنَ
خَبِيْرًا ﴿١٢٨﴾

3. وَالَّذِيْنَ تَبَوَّؤُ الدَّارَ وَالْاِيْمَانَ مِنْ
قَبْلِهِمْ يُحِبُّوْنَ مَنْ هَاجَرَ اِلَيْهِمْ
وَلَا يَجِدُوْنَ فِيْ صُدُوْرِهِمْ حَاجَةً
مِّمَّآ اُوْتُوْا وَ يُؤْثِرُوْنَ عَلٰٓى اَنْفُسِهِمْ
وَلَوْ كَانَ بِهِمْ خَصَاصَةٌ ؕ وَمَنْ يُّوْقَ
شُحَّ نَفْسِهٖ فَاُولٰٓئِكَ هُمُ الْمُفْلِحُوْنَ ﴿٩﴾

4. فَاتَّقُوا اللّٰهَ مَا اسْتَطَعْتُمْ وَ اسْمَعُوْا
وَ اَطِيْعُوْا وَ اَنْفِقُوْا خَيْرًا لِّاَنْفُسِكُمْ ؕ
وَ مَنْ يُّوْقَ شُحَّ نَفْسِهٖ فَاُولٰٓئِكَ
هُمُ الْمُفْلِحُوْنَ ﴿١٦﴾

HABIL AND QABIL

1. وَاتْلُ عَلَيْهِمْ نَبَأَ ابْنَيْ آدَمَ بِالْحَقِّ إِذْ
قَرَّبَا قُرْبَانًا فَتُقُبِّلَ مِنْ أَحَدِهِمَا وَلَمْ
يُتَقَبَّلْ مِنَ الْآخَرِ قَالَ لَأَقْتُلَنَّكَ
قَالَ إِنَّمَا يَتَقَبَّلُ اللَّهُ مِنَ الْمُتَّقِينَ ﴿٢٧﴾

لَئِنْ بَسَطْتَ إِلَيَّ يَدَكَ لِتَقْتُلَنِي مَا أَنَا
بِبَاسِطٍ يَدِيَ إِلَيْكَ لِأَقْتُلَكَ إِنِّي أَخَافُ
اللَّهَ رَبَّ الْعَالَمِينَ ﴿٢٨﴾

إِنِّي أُرِيدُ أَنْ تَبُوءَ بِإِثْمِي وَإِثْمِكَ
فَتَكُونَ مِنْ أَصْحَابِ النَّارِ وَذَلِكَ
جَزَاءُ الظَّالِمِينَ ﴿٢٩﴾

فَطَوَّعَتْ لَهُ نَفْسُهُ قَتْلَ أَخِيهِ فَقَتَلَهُ
فَأَصْبَحَ مِنَ الْخَاسِرِينَ ﴿٣٠﴾

فَبَعَثَ اللَّهُ غُرَابًا يَبْحَثُ فِي الْأَرْضِ
لِيُرِيَهُ كَيْفَ يُوَارِي سَوْءَةَ أَخِيهِ قَالَ
يَا وَيْلَتَا أَعَجَزْتُ أَنْ أَكُونَ مِثْلَ هَذَا
الْغُرَابِ فَأُوَارِيَ سَوْءَةَ أَخِي فَأَصْبَحَ
مِنَ النَّادِمِينَ ﴿٣١﴾

1. But recite unto them with truth the tale of the two sons of Adam, how they offered each a sacrifice, and it was accepted from the one of them and it was not accepted from the other. (The one) said: I will surely kill thee. (The other) answered: Allah accepteth only from those who ward off (evil).

Even if thou stretch out thy hand against me to kill me, I shall not stretch out my hand against thee to kill thee, lo! I fear Allah, the Lord of the Worlds.

Lo! I would rather thou shouldst bear the punishment of the sin against me and thine own sin and become one of the owners of the Fire. That is the reward of evil-doers.

But (the other's) mind imposed on him the killing of his brother, so he slew him and became one of the losers.

Then Allah sent a raven scratching up the ground, to show him how to hide his brother's naked corpse. He said: Woe unto me! Am I not able to be as this raven and so hide my brother's naked corpse! And he became repentant.

5:27–31

HAJJ AND 'UMRA

1. Lo! (the mountains) *As-Safâ* and *Al-Marwah* are among the indications of Allah. It is therefore no sin for him who is on pilgrimage to the House (of God) or visiteth it, to go around them (as the pagan custom is). And he who doth good of his own accord (for him), lo! Allah is Responsive, Aware.

2:158

2. They ask thee, (O Muhammad), of new moons. Say: They are fixed seasons for mankind and for the pilgrimage. It is not righteousness that ye go to houses by the backs thereof (as do the idolaters at certain seasons), but the righteous man is he who wardeth off (evil). So go to houses by the gates thereof, and observe your duty to Allah, that ye may be successful.

2:189

3. Perform the pilgrimage and the visit (to Makkah) for Allah. And if ye are prevented, then send such gifts as can be obtained with ease, and shave not your heads until the gifts have reached their destination. And whoever among you is sick or hath an ailment of the head must pay a ransom of fasting or almsgiving or offering. And if ye are in safety, then whosoever contenteth himself with the visit for the pilgrimage (shall give) such gifts as can be had with ease. And whosoever cannot find (such gifts), then a fast of three days while on the pilgrimage, and of seven when ye have returned; that is, ten in all. That is for him whose folk are not present at the Inviolable Place of Worship. Observe your duty to Allah, and know that Allah is severe in punishment.

1. إِنَّ الصَّفَا وَالْمَرْوَةَ مِنْ شَعَآئِرِ اللّٰهِ ۚ فَمَنْ
حَجَّ الْبَيْتَ أَوِ اعْتَمَرَ فَلَا جُنَاحَ عَلَيْهِ أَنْ
يَطَّوَّفَ بِهِمَا ۗ وَمَنْ تَطَوَّعَ خَيْرًا ۙ فَإِنَّ اللّٰهَ
شَاكِرٌ عَلِيمٌ ﴿١٥٨﴾

2. يَسْئَلُونَكَ عَنِ الْأَهِلَّةِ ۗ قُلْ هِيَ مَوَاقِيتُ
لِلنَّاسِ وَالْحَجِّ ۗ وَلَيْسَ الْبِرُّ بِأَنْ تَأْتُوا
الْبُيُوتَ مِنْ ظُهُورِهَا وَلٰكِنَّ الْبِرَّ مَنِ اتَّقٰى ۚ
وَأْتُوا الْبُيُوتَ مِنْ أَبْوَابِهَا ۖ وَاتَّقُوا اللّٰهَ
لَعَلَّكُمْ تُفْلِحُونَ ﴿١٨٩﴾

3. وَأَتِمُّوا الْحَجَّ وَالْعُمْرَةَ لِلّٰهِ ۗ فَإِنْ أُحْصِرْتُمْ
فَمَا اسْتَيْسَرَ مِنَ الْهَدْيِ ۚ وَلَا تَحْلِقُوا
رُءُوسَكُمْ حَتّٰى يَبْلُغَ الْهَدْيُ مَحِلَّهُ ۗ
فَمَنْ كَانَ مِنْكُمْ مَرِيضًا أَوْ بِهِ أَذًى مِنْ
رَأْسِهِ فَفِدْيَةٌ مِنْ صِيَامٍ أَوْ صَدَقَةٍ
أَوْ نُسُكٍ ۚ فَإِذَا أَمِنْتُمْ فَمَنْ تَمَتَّعَ بِالْعُمْرَةِ
إِلَى الْحَجِّ فَمَا اسْتَيْسَرَ مِنَ الْهَدْيِ ۚ فَمَنْ
لَمْ يَجِدْ فَصِيَامُ ثَلٰثَةِ أَيَّامٍ فِي الْحَجِّ وَ
سَبْعَةٍ إِذَا رَجَعْتُمْ ۗ تِلْكَ عَشَرَةٌ كَامِلَةٌ ۗ
ذٰلِكَ لِمَنْ لَمْ يَكُنْ أَهْلُهُ حَاضِرِي الْمَسْجِدِ
الْحَرَامِ ۚ وَاتَّقُوا اللّٰهَ وَاعْلَمُوا أَنَّ اللّٰهَ
شَدِيدُ الْعِقَابِ ﴿١٩٦﴾
الْحَجُّ أَشْهُرٌ مَعْلُومٰتٌ ۚ فَمَنْ فَرَضَ فِيهِنَّ
الْحَجَّ فَلَا رَفَثَ وَلَا فُسُوقَ ۙ وَلَا جِدَالَ
فِي الْحَجِّ ۗ وَمَا تَفْعَلُوا مِنْ خَيْرٍ يَعْلَمْهُ

اللهُ ۗ وَتَزَوَّدُوا فَإِنَّ خَيْرَ الزَّادِ التَّقْوَىٰ ۚ
وَاتَّقُونِ يَا أُولِي الْأَلْبَابِ ﴿١٩٧﴾

لَيْسَ عَلَيْكُمْ جُنَاحٌ أَنْ تَبْتَغُوا فَضْلًا مِنْ
رَبِّكُمْ ۚ فَإِذَا أَفَضْتُمْ مِنْ عَرَفَاتٍ فَاذْكُرُوا اللَّهَ
عِنْدَ الْمَشْعَرِ الْحَرَامِ ۖ وَاذْكُرُوهُ كَمَا هَدَاكُمْ
وَإِنْ كُنْتُمْ مِنْ قَبْلِهِ لَمِنَ الضَّالِّينَ ﴿١٩٨﴾

ثُمَّ أَفِيضُوا مِنْ حَيْثُ أَفَاضَ النَّاسُ وَ
اسْتَغْفِرُوا اللَّهَ ۚ إِنَّ اللَّهَ غَفُورٌ رَحِيمٌ ﴿١٩٩﴾

فَإِذَا قَضَيْتُمْ مَنَاسِكَكُمْ فَاذْكُرُوا اللَّهَ
كَذِكْرِكُمْ آبَاءَكُمْ أَوْ أَشَدَّ ذِكْرًا ۗ فَمِنَ
النَّاسِ مَنْ يَقُولُ رَبَّنَا آتِنَا فِي الدُّنْيَا
وَمَا لَهُ فِي الْآخِرَةِ مِنْ خَلَاقٍ ﴿٢٠٠﴾

وَمِنْهُمْ مَنْ يَقُولُ رَبَّنَا آتِنَا فِي الدُّنْيَا حَسَنَةً
وَفِي الْآخِرَةِ حَسَنَةً وَقِنَا عَذَابَ النَّارِ ﴿٢٠١﴾

أُولَٰئِكَ لَهُمْ نَصِيبٌ مِمَّا كَسَبُوا ۚ وَاللَّهُ
سَرِيعُ الْحِسَابِ ﴿٢٠٢﴾

وَاذْكُرُوا اللَّهَ فِي أَيَّامٍ مَعْدُودَاتٍ ۚ فَمَنْ
تَعَجَّلَ فِي يَوْمَيْنِ فَلَا إِثْمَ عَلَيْهِ وَمَنْ تَأَخَّرَ
فَلَا إِثْمَ عَلَيْهِ ۚ لِمَنِ اتَّقَىٰ ۗ وَاتَّقُوا اللَّهَ
وَاعْلَمُوا أَنَّكُمْ إِلَيْهِ تُحْشَرُونَ ﴿٢٠٣﴾

The pilgrimage is (in) the well—known months, and whoever is minded to perform the pilgrimage therein (let him remember that) there is (to be) no lewdness nor abuse nor angry conversation on the pilgrimage. And whatsoever good ye do Allah knoweth it. So make provision for yourselves (hereafter); for the best provision is to ward off evil. Therefore keep your duty unto Me, O men of understanding.

It is no sin for you that ye seek the bounty of your Lord (by trading). But when ye press on in the multitude from *'Arafāt*, remember Allah by the sacred monument. Remember Him as He hath guided you, although before ye were of those astray.

Then hasten onward from the place whence the multitude hasteneth onward, and ask forgiveness of Allah. Lo! Allah is Forgiving, Merciful.

And when ye have completed your devotions, then remember Allah as ye remember your fathers or with a more lively remembrance. But of mankind is he who saith: "Our Lord! Give unto us in the world," and he hath no portion in the Hereafter.

And of them (also) is he who saith: "Our Lord! Give unto us in the world that which is good and in the Hereafter that which is good, and guard us from the doom of Fire."

For them there is in store a goodly portion out of that which they have earned. Allah is swift at reckoning.

And Remember Allah through the appointed days. Then whoso hasteneth (his departure) by two days, it is no sin for him, and whoso delayeth, it is no sin for him; that is for him who wardeth off (evil). Be careful of your duty to

Allah, and know that unto Him ye will be gathered.

2:196–203

4. Lo! the first Sanctuary appointed for mankind was that at *Bakkah* a blessed place, a guidance to the people;

Wherein are plain memorials (of Allah's guidance); the place where Abraham stood up to pray; and whosoever entereth it is safe. And pilgrimage to the House is a duty unto Allah for mankind, for him who can find a way thither. As for him who disbelieveth (let him know that) lo! Allah is Independent of (all) creatures.

3:96–97

5. And (remember) when We prepared for Abraham the place of the (holy) House, saying: Ascribe thou nothing as partner unto Me, and purify My House for those who make the round (thereof) and those who stand and those who bow and make prostration.

And proclaim unto mankind the pilgrimage. They will come unto thee on foot and on every lean camel; they will come from every deep ravine:

That they may witness things that are of benefit to them, and mention the name of Allah on appointed days over the beast of cattle that He hath bestowed upon them. Then eat thereof and feed therewith the poor, unfortunate.

Then let them make an end of their unkemptness and pay their vows and go around

4. إِنَّ أَوَّلَ بَيْتٍ وُضِعَ لِلنَّاسِ لَلَّذِي بِبَكَّةَ
مُبٰرَكًا وَّهُدًى لِّلْعٰلَمِينَ ۝
فِيهِ اٰيٰتٌۢ بَيِّنٰتٌ مَّقَامُ إِبْرٰهِيمَ ۚ وَمَنْ
دَخَلَهٗ كَانَ اٰمِنًا ۗ وَلِلّٰهِ عَلَى النَّاسِ حِجُّ
الْبَيْتِ مَنِ اسْتَطَاعَ إِلَيْهِ سَبِيلًا ۗ وَمَنْ
كَفَرَ فَإِنَّ اللّٰهَ غَنِيٌّ عَنِ الْعٰلَمِينَ ۝

5. وَإِذْ بَوَّأْنَا لِإِبْرٰهِيمَ مَكَانَ الْبَيْتِ
أَنْ لَّا تُشْرِكْ بِي شَيْئًا وَّطَهِّرْ بَيْتِيَ
لِلطَّآئِفِينَ وَالْقَآئِمِينَ وَالرُّكَّعِ السُّجُودِ ۝٢٦
وَأَذِّنْ فِي النَّاسِ بِالْحَجِّ يَأْتُوكَ رِجَالًا
وَّعَلٰى كُلِّ ضَامِرٍ يَّأْتِينَ مِنْ كُلِّ
فَجٍّ عَمِيقٍ ۝٢٧
لِّيَشْهَدُوا مَنَافِعَ لَهُمْ وَيَذْكُرُوا
اسْمَ اللّٰهِ فِي أَيَّامٍ مَّعْلُومٰتٍ عَلٰى مَا
رَزَقَهُمْ مِّنْۢ بَهِيمَةِ الْأَنْعَامِ ۚ فَكُلُوا
مِنْهَا وَأَطْعِمُوا الْبَآئِسَ الْفَقِيرَ ۝٢٨
ثُمَّ لْيَقْضُوا تَفَثَهُمْ وَلْيُوفُوا نُذُورَهُمْ
وَلْيَطَّوَّفُوا بِالْبَيْتِ الْعَتِيقِ ۝٢٩

6. لَقَدْ صَدَقَ اللّٰهُ رَسُولَهُ الرُّءْيَا
بِالْحَقِّ ۚ لَتَدْخُلُنَّ الْمَسْجِدَ الْحَرَامَ
إِنْ شَآءَ اللّٰهُ اٰمِنِينَ ۙ مُحَلِّقِينَ
رُءُوسَكُمْ وَمُقَصِّرِينَ ۙ لَا تَخَافُونَ ۚ
فَعَلِمَ مَا لَمْ تَعْلَمُوا فَجَعَلَ مِنْ دُونِ
ذٰلِكَ فَتْحًا قَرِيبًا ۝٢٧

the ancient House.

22:26–29

6. Allah hath fulfilled the vision for His messenger in very truth. Ye shall indeed enter the Inviolable Place of Worship, if Allah will, secure, (having your hair) shaven and cut, not fearing. But He knoweth that which ye know not, and hath given you a near victory beforehand.

48:27

HALAL

1. O mankind! Eat of that which is lawful and wholesome in the earth, and follow not the footsteps of the devil. Lo! he is an open enemy for you.

He enjoineth upon you only the evil and the foul, and that ye should tell concerning Allah that which ye know not.

2:168–169

2. O ye who believe! Fulfil your undertakings. The beast of cattle is made lawful unto you (for food) except that which is announced unto you (herein), game being unlawful when ye are on pilgrimage. Lo! Allah ordaineth that which pleaseth Him.

O ye who believe! Profane not Allah's monuments nor the Sacred Month nor the offerings nor the garlands, nor those repairing to the Sacred House seeking the grace and pleasure of their Lord. But when ye have left the sacred territory, then go hunting if ye will). And let not your hatred of a folk who (once) stopped your going to the Inviolable Place of Worship seduce you to transgress; but help ye one another unto righteousness and pious duty. Help not one another unto sin and transgression.

5:1–2

3. They ask thee (O Muhammad) what is made lawful for them. Say: (all)

1. يٰۤاَيُّهَا النَّاسُ كُلُوْا مِمَّا فِي الْاَرْضِ حَلٰلًا
طَيِّبًا ۖ وَّلَا تَتَّبِعُوْا خُطُوٰتِ الشَّيْطٰنِ ؕ
اِنَّهٗ لَـكُمْ عَدُوٌّ مُّبِيْنٌ ﴿۱۶۸﴾
اِنَّمَا يَاْمُرُكُمْ بِالسُّوْٓءِ وَالْفَحْشَآءِ وَاَنْ
تَقُوْلُوْا عَلَى اللّٰهِ مَا لَا تَعْلَمُوْنَ ﴿۱۶۹﴾

2. يٰۤاَيُّهَا الَّذِيْنَ اٰمَنُوْۤا اَوْفُوْا بِالْعُقُوْدِ ؕ اُحِلَّتْ
لَـكُمْ بَهِيْمَةُ الْاَنْعَامِ اِلَّا مَا يُتْلٰى عَلَيْكُمْ
غَيْرَ مُحِلِّى الصَّيْدِ وَاَنْتُمْ حُرُمٌ ؕ اِنَّ
اللّٰهَ يَحْكُمُ مَا يُرِيْدُ ﴿۱﴾
يٰۤاَيُّهَا الَّذِيْنَ اٰمَنُوْا لَا تُحِلُّوْا شَعَآئِرَ اللّٰهِ
وَلَا الشَّهْرَ الْحَـرَامَ وَلَا الْهَدْىَ وَلَا
الْقَلَۤائِدَ وَلَاۤ آٰمِّيْنَ الْبَيْتَ الْحَـرَامَ
يَبْتَغُوْنَ فَضْلًا مِّنْ رَّبِّهِمْ وَرِضْوَانًا ؕ
وَاِذَا حَلَلْتُمْ فَاصْطَادُوْا ؕ وَلَا يَجْرِمَنَّكُمْ
شَنَاٰنُ قَوْمٍ اَنْ صَدُّوْكُمْ عَنِ الْمَسْجِدِ
الْحَـرَامِ اَنْ تَعْتَدُوْا ۘ وَتَعَاوَنُوْا عَلَى الْبِرِّ
وَالتَّقْوٰى ۖ وَلَا تَعَاوَنُوْا عَلَى الْاِثْمِ وَالْعُدْوَانِ ۖ

3. يَسْـئَلُوْنَكَ مَاذَاۤ اُحِلَّ لَهُمْ ؕ قُلْ اُحِلَّ
لَـكُمُ الطَّيِّبٰتُ ۙ وَمَا عَلَّمْتُمْ مِّنَ الْجَـوَارِحِ
مُكَلِّبِيْنَ تُعَلِّمُوْنَهُنَّ مِمَّا عَلَّمَكُمُ اللّٰهُ
فَكُلُوْا مِمَّاۤ اَمْسَكْنَ عَلَيْكُمْ وَاذْكُرُوا اسْمَ
اللّٰهِ عَلَيْهِ ۖ وَاتَّقُوا اللّٰهَ ؕ اِنَّ اللّٰهَ

good things are made lawful for you. And those beasts and birds of prey which ye have trained as hounds are trained, ye teach them that which Allah taught you; so eat of that which they catch for you and mention Allah's name upon it, and observe your duty to Allah. Lo! Allah is swift to take account.

This day are (all) good things made lawful for you. The food of those who have received the Scripture is lawful for you, and your food is lawful for them. And so are the virtuous women of the believers and the virtuous women of those who received the Scripture before you (lawful for you) when ye give them their marriage portions and live with them in honour, not in fornication, nor taking them as secret concubines. Whoso denieth the faith, his work is vain and he will be among the losers in the Hereafter.

5:4–5

4. To hunt and to eat the fish of the sea is made lawful for you, a provision for you and for seafarers; but to hunt on land is forbidden you so long as ye are on the pilgrimage.

5:96

5. Eat of that over which the name of Allah hath been mentioned, if ye are believers in His revelations.

How should ye not eat of that over which the name of Allah hath been mentioned when He hath explained unto you that which is forbidden unto you, unless ye are compelled thereto. But lo! many are led astray by their own lust through ignorance. Lo! thy Lord. He is Best

سريع الحساب ④
اليوم احل لكم الطيبت ۖ وطعام
الذين اوتوا الكتب حل لكم وطعامكم
حل لهم والمحصنت من المؤمنت
والمحصنت من الذين اوتوا الكتب
من قبلكم اذا اتيتموهن اجورهن
محصنين غير مسفحين ولا متخذي
اخدان ۖ ومن يكفر بالايمان فقد
حبط عمله وهو في الاخرة من
الخسرين ⑤

احل لكم صيد البحر وطعامه متاعا 4.
لكم وللسيارة ۚ وحرم عليكم صيد
البر ما دمتم حرما ۖ

فكلوا مما ذكر اسم الله عليه ان 5.
كنتم بايته مؤمنين ○
وما لكم الا تاكلوا مما ذكر اسم الله
عليه وقد فصل لكم ما حرم عليكم الا
ما اضطررتم اليه ۖ وان كثيرا ليضلون
باهوائهم بغير علم ۖ ان ربك هو
اعلم بالمعتدين ○

يبني ادم خذوا زينتكم عند كل 6.
مسجد وكلوا واشربوا ولا تسرفوا ۚ
انه لا يحب المسرفين ○

Aware of the transgressors.

6:118–119

6. O Children of Adam! Look to your adornment at every place of worship, and eat and drink, but be not prodigal. Lo! He loveth not the prodigals.

Say: Who hath forbidden the adornment of Allah which He hath brought forth for His bondmen, and the good things of His providing? Say: Such, on the Day of Resurrection, will be only for those who believed during the life of the world. Thus do We detail Our revelations for people who have knowledge.

7:31–32

7. Now enjoy what ye have won, as lawful and good, and keep your duty to Allah. Lo! Allah is Forgiving, Merciful.

8:69

8. So eat of the lawful and good food which Allah hath provided for you, and thank the bounty of your Lord if it is Him ye serve.

16:114

9. And speak not, concerning that which your own tongues qualify (as clean or unclean), the falsehood: "This is lawful, and this is forbidden," so that ye invent a lie against Allah. Lo! those who invent a lie against Allah will not succeed.

16:116

10. The cattle are lawful unto you save that which hath been told you. So shun the filth of idols, and shun lying speech.

22:30

11. And the camels! We have appointed them among the ceremonies of Allah. Therein ye have much good. So mention the name of Allah

قُلْ مَنْ حَرَّمَ زِينَةَ اللَّهِ الَّتِي أَخْرَجَ
لِعِبَادِهِ وَالطَّيِّبَاتِ مِنَ الرِّزْقِ ۚ قُلْ هِيَ
لِلَّذِينَ آمَنُوا فِي الْحَيَاةِ الدُّنْيَا خَالِصَةً
يَوْمَ الْقِيَامَةِ ۗ كَذَٰلِكَ نُفَصِّلُ الْآيَاتِ
لِقَوْمٍ يَعْلَمُونَ ﴿٣٢﴾

7. فَكُلُوا مِمَّا غَنِمْتُمْ حَلَالًا طَيِّبًا ۚ وَاتَّقُوا
اللَّهَ ۚ إِنَّ اللَّهَ غَفُورٌ رَحِيمٌ ﴿٦٩﴾

8. فَكُلُوا مِمَّا رَزَقَكُمُ اللَّهُ حَلَالًا طَيِّبًا وَاشْكُرُوا نِعْمَتَ
اللَّهِ إِنْ كُنْتُمْ إِيَّاهُ تَعْبُدُونَ ﴿١١٤﴾

9. وَلَا تَقُولُوا لِمَا تَصِفُ أَلْسِنَتُكُمُ الْكَذِبَ
هَٰذَا حَلَالٌ وَهَٰذَا حَرَامٌ لِتَفْتَرُوا عَلَى
اللَّهِ الْكَذِبَ ۚ إِنَّ الَّذِينَ يَفْتَرُونَ عَلَى
اللَّهِ الْكَذِبَ لَا يُفْلِحُونَ ﴿١١٦﴾

10. وَأُحِلَّتْ لَكُمُ الْأَنْعَامُ إِلَّا مَا يُتْلَىٰ
عَلَيْكُمْ ۖ فَاجْتَنِبُوا الرِّجْسَ مِنَ الْأَوْثَانِ
وَاجْتَنِبُوا قَوْلَ الزُّورِ ﴿٣٠﴾

11. وَالْبُدْنَ جَعَلْنَاهَا لَكُمْ مِنْ شَعَائِرِ اللَّهِ
لَكُمْ فِيهَا خَيْرٌ ۖ فَاذْكُرُوا اسْمَ اللَّهِ
عَلَيْهَا صَوَافَّ ۖ فَإِذَا وَجَبَتْ جُنُوبُهَا
فَكُلُوا مِنْهَا وَأَطْعِمُوا الْقَانِعَ وَالْمُعْتَرَّ ۚ
كَذَٰلِكَ سَخَّرْنَاهَا لَكُمْ لَعَلَّكُمْ تَشْكُرُونَ ﴿٣٦﴾

over them when they are drawn up in lines. Then when their flanks fail (dead), eat thereof and feed the beggar and the suppliant. Thus have We made them subject unto you, that haply ye may give thanks.

22:36

12. No blame is there upon the blind nor any blame upon the lame nor any blame upon the sick nor on yourselves if ye eat from your houses, or the houses of your fathers, or the houses of your mothers, or the houses of your brothers, or the houses of your sisters, or the houses of your fathers' brothers, or the houses of your fathers' sisters, or the houses of your mothers' brothers, or the houses of your mothers' sisters, or (from that) whereof ye hold the keys, or (from the house) of a friend. No sin shall it be for you whether ye eat together or apart. But when ye enter houses, salute one another with a greeting from Allah, blessed and sweet. Thus Allah maketh clear His revelations for you, that haply ye may understand.

24:61

12. لَيْسَ عَلَى الْأَعْمٰى حَرَجٌ وَّلَا عَلَى الْأَعْرَجِ
حَرَجٌ وَّلَا عَلَى الْمَرِيْضِ حَرَجٌ وَّلَا عَلٰٓى
اَنْفُسِكُمْ اَنْ تَاْكُلُوْا مِنْ بُيُوْتِكُمْ اَوْ
بُيُوْتِ اٰبَآئِكُمْ اَوْ بُيُوْتِ اُمَّهٰتِكُمْ اَوْ
بُيُوْتِ اِخْوَانِكُمْ اَوْ بُيُوْتِ اَخَوٰتِكُمْ اَوْ
بُيُوْتِ اَعْمَامِكُمْ اَوْ بُيُوْتِ عَمّٰتِكُمْ اَوْ
بُيُوْتِ اَخْوَالِكُمْ اَوْ بُيُوْتِ خٰلٰتِكُمْ اَوْ
مَا مَلَكْتُمْ مَّفَاتِحَهٗٓ اَوْ صَدِيْقِكُمْ ؕ
لَيْسَ عَلَيْكُمْ جُنَاحٌ اَنْ تَاْكُلُوْا جَمِيْعًا
اَوْ اَشْتَاتًا ؕ فَاِذَا دَخَلْتُمْ بُيُوْتًا فَسَلِّمُوْا
عَلٰٓى اَنْفُسِكُمْ تَحِيَّةً مِّنْ عِنْدِ اللّٰهِ
مُبٰرَكَةً طَيِّبَةً ؕ كَذٰلِكَ يُبَيِّنُ اللّٰهُ لَكُمُ
الْاٰيٰتِ لَعَلَّكُمْ تَعْقِلُوْنَ ۝

Ref: 2:236; 4:24; 5:87–88; 6:119; 10:59; 33:50–51,55;
See also: *Haram*.

HARAM

1. He hath forbidden you only carrion, and blood, and swineflesh, and that which hath been immolated to (the name of) any other than Allah. But he who is driven by necessity, neither craving nor transgressing, it is no sin for him. Lo! Allah is Forgiving, Merciful.

2:173

2. Forbidden unto you (for food) are carrion and blood and swine–flesh, and that which hath been dedicated unto any other than Allah, and the strangled, and the dead through beating and the dead through falling from a height, and that which hath been killed by (the goring of) horns, and the devoured of wild beasts, saving that which ye make lawful (by the death–stroke), and that which hath been immolated unto idols. And (forbidden is it) that ye swear by the divining arrows. This is an abomination.

5:3

3. O ye who believe! For–bid not the good things which Allah hath made lawful for you, and transgress not, Lo! Allah loveth not transgressors.

5:87

4. O ye who believe! Strong drink and games of chance and idols and divining arrows are only an infamy of Satan's handiwork. Leave it aside in order that ye may succeed.

Satan seeketh only to cast among you enmity and hatred by means of strong

1. إِنَّمَا حَرَّمَ عَلَيْكُمُ الْمَيْتَةَ وَالدَّمَ وَلَحْمَ
الْخِنْزِيْرِ وَمَا أُهِلَّ بِهٖ لِغَيْرِ اللّٰهِ ۚ فَمَنِ
اضْطُرَّ غَيْرَ بَاغٍ وَّلَا عَادٍ فَلَا إِثْمَ عَلَيْهِ ۚ
إِنَّ اللّٰهَ غَفُوْرٌ رَّحِيْمٌ ﴿١٧٣﴾

2. حُرِّمَتْ عَلَيْكُمُ الْمَيْتَةُ وَالدَّمُ وَلَحْمُ الْخِنْزِيْرِ وَ
مَآ أُهِلَّ لِغَيْرِ اللّٰهِ بِهٖ وَالْمُنْخَنِقَةُ وَالْمَوْقُوْذَةُ وَ
الْمُتَرَدِّيَةُ وَالنَّطِيْحَةُ وَمَآ أَكَلَ السَّبُعُ إِلَّا مَا ذَكَّيْتُمْ
وَمَا ذُبِحَ عَلَى النُّصُبِ وَأَنْ تَسْتَقْسِمُوْا بِالْأَزْلَامِ ۚ
ذٰلِكُمْ فِسْقٌ ۗ

3. يٰٓأَيُّهَا الَّذِيْنَ اٰمَنُوْا لَا تُحَرِّمُوْا طَيِّبٰتِ مَآ
أَحَلَّ اللّٰهُ لَكُمْ وَلَا تَعْتَدُوْا ۚ إِنَّ اللّٰهَ لَا
يُحِبُّ الْمُعْتَدِيْنَ ﴿٨٧﴾

4. يٰٓأَيُّهَا الَّذِيْنَ اٰمَنُوْٓا إِنَّمَا الْخَمْرُ وَالْمَيْسِرُ
وَالْأَنْصَابُ وَالْأَزْلَامُ رِجْسٌ مِّنْ عَمَلِ
الشَّيْطٰنِ فَاجْتَنِبُوْهُ لَعَلَّكُمْ تُفْلِحُوْنَ ﴿٩٠﴾
إِنَّمَا يُرِيْدُ الشَّيْطٰنُ أَنْ يُّوْقِعَ بَيْنَكُمُ الْعَدَاوَةَ
وَالْبَغْضَآءَ فِي الْخَمْرِ وَالْمَيْسِرِ وَيَصُدَّكُمْ
عَنْ ذِكْرِ اللّٰهِ وَعَنِ الصَّلٰوةِ ۚ فَهَلْ
أَنْتُمْ مُّنْتَهُوْنَ ﴿٩١﴾

5. وَلَا تَأْكُلُوْا مِمَّا لَمْ يُذْكَرِ اسْمُ اللّٰهِ
عَلَيْهِ وَإِنَّهٗ لَفِسْقٌ ۗ وَإِنَّ الشَّيٰطِيْنَ

drink and games of chance, and to turn you from re–membrance of Allah and from (His) worship. Will ye then have done?

5:90–91

5. And eat not of that whereon Allah's name hath not been mentioned, for lo! it is abomination.

Lo! the devils do inspire their minions to dispute with you. But if ye obey then ye will be in truth as idolaters.

6:121

لَيُوحُونَ إِلَىٰ أَوْلِيَائِهِمْ لِيُجَادِلُوكُمْ ۖ
وَإِنْ أَطَعْتُمُوهُمْ إِنَّكُمْ لَمُشْرِكُونَ ○

6. Say: I find not in that which is revealed unto me aught prohibited to an eater that he eat thereof, except it be carrion, or blood poured forth, or swineflesh — for that verily is foul— or the abomination which was immolated to the name of other than Allah. But whoso is compelled (thereto), neither craving nor transgressing, (for him) Lo! thy Lord is Forgiving, Merciful.

6:145

6. قُل لَّا أَجِدُ فِي مَا أُوحِيَ إِلَيَّ مُحَرَّمًا عَلَىٰ
طَاعِمٍ يَطْعَمُهُ إِلَّا أَن يَكُونَ مَيْتَةً أَوْ
دَمًا مَّسْفُوحًا أَوْ لَحْمَ خِنزِيرٍ فَإِنَّهُ
رِجْسٌ أَوْ فِسْقًا أُهِلَّ لِغَيْرِ اللَّهِ بِهِ ۚ
فَمَنِ اضْطُرَّ غَيْرَ بَاغٍ وَلَا عَادٍ فَإِنَّ
رَبَّكَ غَفُورٌ رَّحِيمٌ ○

○

Ref: 2:217; 3:93; 5:1–3,103; 6:139–140; 7:32–33; 16:115.
See also: ***Halal***

HEART

1. As for the disbelievers, whether thou warn them or thou warn them not it is all one for them; they believe not.

Allah hath sealed their hearing and their hearts, and on their eyes there is a covering. Theirs will be an awful doom.

2:6–7

2. They only are the (true) believers whose hearts feel fear when Allah is mentioned, and when His revelations are recited unto them they increase their faith, and who trust in their Lord;

8:2

3. And know that Allah cometh in between the man and his own heart, and that He it is unto Whom ye will be gathered.

8:24

4. Who have believed and whose hearts have rest in the remembrance of Allah. Verily in the remembrance of Allah do hearts find rest!

13:28

5. And Allah brought you forth from the wombs of you mothers knowing nothing, and gave you hearing and sight and hearts that haply ye might give thanks.

16:78

6. (O man), follow not that whereof thou hast no knowledge. Lo! the hearing and the sight and the heart–of each of these it will be asked.

17:36

1. ختم الله على قلوبهم وعلى سمعهم ۗ وعلى
أبصارهم غشاوة ۖ ولهم عذاب عظيم ۝٧
إن الذين كفروا سواء عليهم ءأنذرتهم
أم لم تنذرهم لا يؤمنون ۝٦

2. إنما المؤمنون الذين إذا ذكر الله
وجلت قلوبهم وإذا تليت عليهم آياته
زادتهم إيمانا وعلى ربهم يتوكلون ۝٢

3. واعلموا أن الله يحول بين المرء و
قلبه وأنه إليه تحشرون ۝٢٤

4. الذين آمنوا وتطمئن قلوبهم بذكر
الله ۗ ألا بذكر الله تطمئن القلوب ۝٢٨

5. والله أخرجكم من بطون أمهاتكم لا
تعلمون شيئا ۙ وجعل لكم السمع والأبصار
والأفئدة ۙ لعلكم تشكرون ۝٧٨

6. ولا تقف ما ليس لك به علم ۚ إن
السمع والبصر والفؤاد كل أولئك
كان عنه مسئولا ۝٣٦

7. أفلم يسيروا في الأرض فتكون
لهم قلوب يعقلون بها أو آذان
يسمعون بها ۖ فإنها لا تعمى الأبصار
ولكن تعمى القلوب التي في الصدور ۝٤٦

7. Have they not travelled in the land, and have they hearts wherewith to feel and ears wherewith to hear? For indeed it is not the eyes that grow blind, but it is the hearts, which are within the bosoms, that grow blind.

22:46

8. مَا جَعَلَ اللّٰهُ لِرَجُلٍ مِّنْ قَلْبَيْنِ فِىْ
جَوْفِهٖ ۚ وَمَا جَعَلَ اَزْوَاجَكُمُ الّٰٓـِٔىْ
تُظٰهِرُوْنَ مِنْهُنَّ اُمَّهٰتِكُمْ ۚ وَمَا جَعَلَ
اَدْعِيَآءَكُمْ اَبْنَآءَكُمْ ؕ ذٰلِكُمْ قَوْلُكُمْ
بِاَفْوَاهِكُمْ ؕ وَاللّٰهُ يَقُوْلُ الْحَقَّ وَهُوَ
يَهْدِى السَّبِيْلَ ﴿۴﴾
اُدْعُوْهُمْ لِاٰبَآئِهِمْ هُوَ اَقْسَطُ عِنْدَ
اللّٰهِ ۚ فَاِنْ لَّمْ تَعْلَمُوْٓا اٰبَآءَهُمْ فَاِخْوَانُكُمْ
فِى الدِّيْنِ وَمَوَالِيْكُمْ ؕ وَلَيْسَ عَلَيْكُمْ
جُنَاحٌ فِيْمَآ اَخْطَاْتُمْ بِهٖ ۙ وَلٰكِنْ مَّا
تَعَمَّدَتْ قُلُوْبُكُمْ ؕ وَكَانَ اللّٰهُ
غَفُوْرًا رَّحِيْمًا ﴿۵﴾

8. Allah hath not assigned unto any man two hearts within his body, nor hath He made your wives whom ye declare (to be your mothers) your mothers, nor hath He made those whom ye claim (to be your sons) your sons. This is but a saying of your mouths. But Allah sayeth the truth and He showeth the way.

Proclaim their real parentage. That will be more equitable in the sight of Allah. And if ye know not their fathers, then (they are) your brethren in the faith, and your clients. And there is no sin for you in the mistakes that ye make unintentionally, but what your hearts purpose (that will be a sin for you). Allah is Forgiving, Merciful.

33:4–5

9. مَآ اَصَابَ مِنْ مُّصِيْبَةٍ اِلَّا بِاِذْنِ اللّٰهِ ؕ
وَمَنْ يُّؤْمِنْ بِاللّٰهِ يَهْدِ قَلْبَهٗ ؕ وَاللّٰهُ
بِكُلِّ شَىْءٍ عَلِيْمٌ ﴿۱۱﴾

9. No calamity befalleth save by Allah's leave. And whosoever believeth in Allah, He guideth his heart. And Allah is Knower of all things.

64:11

Ref: 25:32–33; 33:10.

HELL

1. Lo! Those who disbelieve Our revelations, We shall expose them to the Fire. As often as their skins are consumed We shall exchange them for fresh skins that they may taste the torment. Lo! Allah is ever Mighty, Wise.

4:56

2. He saith: Enter into the Fire among nations of the jinn and humankind who passed away before you. Every time a nation entereth, it curseth its sister (nation) till, when they have all been made to follow one another thither, the last of them saith unto the first of them: Our Lord! these led us astray, so give them double torment of the Fire. He saith: For each one there is double (torment), but ye know not.

7:38

3. Theirs will be a bed of Hell, and over them coverings (of Hell). Thus do We requite wrong–doers.

7:41

4. And the dwellers of the Fire cry out unto the dwellers of the Garden: Pour on us some water or some of that wherewith Allah hath provided you. They say: Lo! Allah hath forbidden both to disbelievers (in His guidance).

7:50

5. Already have We urged unto hell many of the jinn and humankind.

7:179

1. إِنَّ الَّذِينَ كَفَرُوا بِآيَاتِنَا سَوْفَ نُصْلِيهِمْ
نَارًا كُلَّمَا نَضِجَتْ جُلُودُهُمْ بَدَّلْنَاهُمْ
جُلُودًا غَيْرَهَا لِيَذُوقُوا الْعَذَابَ إِنَّ
اللَّهَ كَانَ عَزِيزًا حَكِيمًا ﴿٥٦﴾

2. قَالَ ادْخُلُوا فِي أُمَمٍ قَدْ خَلَتْ مِنْ
قَبْلِكُمْ مِنَ الْجِنِّ وَالْإِنْسِ فِي النَّارِ كُلَّمَا
دَخَلَتْ أُمَّةٌ لَعَنَتْ أُخْتَهَا حَتَّى إِذَا ادَّارَكُوا
فِيهَا جَمِيعًا قَالَتْ أُخْرَاهُمْ لِأُولَاهُمْ رَبَّنَا
هَؤُلَاءِ أَضَلُّونَا فَآتِهِمْ عَذَابًا ضِعْفًا مِنَ النَّارِ
قَالَ لِكُلٍّ ضِعْفٌ وَلَكِنْ لَا تَعْلَمُونَ ﴿٣٨﴾

3. لَهُمْ مِنْ جَهَنَّمَ مِهَادٌ وَمِنْ فَوْقِهِمْ
غَوَاشٍ وَكَذَلِكَ نَجْزِي الظَّالِمِينَ ﴿٤١﴾

4. وَنَادَى أَصْحَابُ النَّارِ أَصْحَابَ الْجَنَّةِ أَنْ
أَفِيضُوا عَلَيْنَا مِنَ الْمَاءِ أَوْ مِمَّا رَزَقَكُمُ
اللَّهُ قَالُوا إِنَّ اللَّهَ حَرَّمَهُمَا عَلَى الْكَافِرِينَ ﴿٥٠﴾

5. وَلَقَدْ ذَرَأْنَا لِجَهَنَّمَ كَثِيرًا مِنَ الْجِنِّ
وَالْإِنْسِ

6. وَالَّذِينَ يَكْنِزُونَ الذَّهَبَ وَالْفِضَّةَ
وَلَا يُنْفِقُونَهَا فِي سَبِيلِ اللَّهِ فَبَشِّرْهُمْ
بِعَذَابٍ أَلِيمٍ ﴿٣٤﴾
يَوْمَ يُحْمَى عَلَيْهَا فِي نَارِ جَهَنَّمَ فَتُكْوَى
بِهَا جِبَاهُهُمْ وَجُنُوبُهُمْ وَظُهُورُهُمْ
هَذَا مَا كَنَزْتُمْ لِأَنْفُسِكُمْ فَذُوقُوا
مَا كُنْتُمْ تَكْنِزُونَ ﴿٣٥﴾

6. They who hoard up gold and silver and spend it not in the way of Allah, unto them give tidings (O Muhammad) of a painful doom:

On the Day when it will (all) be heated

in the fire of hell, and their foreheads and their flanks and their backs will be branded therewith (and it will be said unto them): Here is that which ye hoarded for yourselves. Now taste of what ye used to hoard.

9:34–35

7. Those who were left behind rejoiced at sitting still behind the messenger of Allah, and were averse to striving with their wealth and their lives in Allah's way. And they said: Go not forth in the heat! Say: The fire of hell is more intense of heat, if they but understood.

9:81

8. Hell is before him, and he is made to drink a festering water,

Which he sippeth but can hardly swallow, and death cometh unto him from every side while yet he cannot die, and before him is a harsh doom.

14:16–17

9. Lo! as for My slaves, thou hast no power over any of them save such of the froward as follow thee,

And lo! for all such, hell will be the promised place:

It hath seven gates, and each gate hath an appointed portion.

15:42–44

10. And, by thy Lord, verily We shall assemble them and the devils, then We shall bring them, crouching, around hell.

Then We shall pluck out from every sect whichever of them was most stubborn in rebellion to the Beneficent.

And surely We are Best Aware of those most worthy to

7. فَرِحَ الْمُخَلَّفُوْنَ بِمَقْعَدِهِمْ خِلٰفَ رَسُوْلِ
اللّٰهِ وَكَرِهُوْٓا اَنْ يُّجَاهِدُوْا بِاَمْوَالِهِمْ
وَاَنْفُسِهِمْ فِيْ سَبِيْلِ اللّٰهِ وَقَالُوْا لَا
تَنْفِرُوْا فِي الْحَرِّ ؕ قُلْ نَارُ جَهَنَّمَ اَشَدُّ
حَرًّا ؕ لَوْ كَانُوْا يَفْقَهُوْنَ ۝

8. مِنْ وَّرَآئِهٖ جَهَنَّمُ وَيُسْقٰى مِنْ
مَّآءٍ صَدِيْدٍ ۝
يَّتَجَرَّعُهٗ وَلَا يَكَادُ يُسِيْغُهٗ وَيَاْتِيْهِ
الْمَوْتُ مِنْ كُلِّ مَكَانٍ وَّمَا هُوَ
بِمَيِّتٍ ؕ وَمِنْ وَّرَآئِهٖ عَذَابٌ غَلِيْظٌ ۝

9. اِنَّ عِبَادِيْ لَيْسَ لَكَ عَلَيْهِمْ سُلْطٰنٌ
اِلَّا مَنِ اتَّبَعَكَ مِنَ الْغٰوِيْنَ ۝
وَاِنَّ جَهَنَّمَ لَمَوْعِدُهُمْ اَجْمَعِيْنَ ۝
لَهَا سَبْعَةُ اَبْوَابٍ ؕ لِكُلِّ بَابٍ
مِّنْهُمْ جُزْءٌ مَّقْسُوْمٌ ۝

10. فَوَرَبِّكَ لَنَحْشُرَنَّهُمْ وَالشَّيٰطِيْنَ ثُمَّ
لَنُحْضِرَنَّهُمْ حَوْلَ جَهَنَّمَ جِثِيًّا ۝
ثُمَّ لَنَنْزِعَنَّ مِنْ كُلِّ شِيْعَةٍ اَيُّهُمْ اَشَدُّ
عَلَى الرَّحْمٰنِ عِتِيًّا ۝
ثُمَّ لَنَحْنُ اَعْلَمُ بِالَّذِيْنَ هُمْ اَوْلٰى
بِهَا صِلِيًّا ۝
وَاِنْ مِّنْكُمْ اِلَّا وَارِدُهَا ۚ كَانَ عَلٰى

be burned therein.

There is not one of you but shall approach it. That is a fixed ordinance of thy Lord.

Then We shall rescue those who kept from evil, and leave the evil—doers crouching there.

19:68—72

11. Lo! whoso cometh guilty unto his Lord, verily for him is hell. There he will neither die nor live.

20:74

12. Lo! ye (idolaters) and that which ye worship beside Allah are fuel of hell. There—unto ye will come.

If these had been gods they would not have come thither, but all will abide therein.

Therein wailing is their portion, and therein they hear not.

21:98—100

13. But as for those who disbelieve, garments of fire will be cut out for them; boiling fluid will be poured down on their heads.

Whereby that which is in their bellies, and their skins too, will be melted;

And for them are hooked rods of iron.

Whenever, in their anguish, they would go forth from thence they are driven back therein and (it is said unto them): Taste the doom of burning.

22:19—22

14. Then those whose scales are heavy, they are the succ—

رَبِّكَ حَتْمًا مَّقْضِيًّا ﴿٧١﴾
ثُمَّ نُنَجِّي الَّذِينَ اتَّقَوْا وَّنَذَرُ
الظّٰلِمِينَ فِيهَا جِثِيًّا ﴿٧٢﴾

11. إِنَّهُ مَنْ يَّأْتِ رَبَّهُ مُجْرِمًا فَإِنَّ لَهُ
جَهَنَّمَ ۗ لَا يَمُوتُ فِيهَا وَلَا يَحْيٰى ﴿٧٤﴾

12. إِنَّكُمْ وَمَا تَعْبُدُونَ مِنْ دُونِ اللّٰهِ
حَصَبُ جَهَنَّمَ ۗ أَنْتُمْ لَهَا وَارِدُونَ ﴿٩٨﴾
لَوْ كَانَ هٰٓؤُلَآءِ اٰلِهَةً مَّا وَرَدُوهَا ۗ
وَكُلٌّ فِيهَا خٰلِدُونَ ﴿٩٩﴾
لَهُمْ فِيهَا زَفِيرٌ وَّهُمْ فِيهَا لَا يَسْمَعُونَ ﴿١٠٠﴾

13. فَالَّذِينَ كَفَرُوا قُطِّعَتْ لَهُمْ ثِيَابٌ
مِّنْ نَّارٍ ۗ يُصَبُّ مِنْ فَوْقِ رُءُوسِهِمُ
الْحَمِيمُ ﴿١٩﴾
يُصْهَرُ بِهِ مَا فِي بُطُونِهِمْ وَالْجُلُودُ ﴿٢٠﴾
وَلَهُمْ مَّقَامِعُ مِنْ حَدِيدٍ ﴿٢١﴾
كُلَّمَا أَرَادُوا أَنْ يَّخْرُجُوا مِنْهَا مِنْ
غَمٍّ أُعِيدُوا فِيهَا ۚ وَذُوقُوا
عَذَابَ الْحَرِيقِ ﴿٢٢﴾

14. فَمَنْ ثَقُلَتْ مَوَازِينُهُ فَأُولٰٓئِكَ
هُمُ الْمُفْلِحُونَ ﴿١٠٢﴾
وَمَنْ خَفَّتْ مَوَازِينُهُ فَأُولٰٓئِكَ الَّذِينَ
خَسِرُوا أَنْفُسَهُمْ فِي جَهَنَّمَ خٰلِدُونَ ﴿١٠٣﴾
تَلْفَحُ وُجُوهَهُمُ النَّارُ وَهُمْ فِيهَا كٰلِحُونَ ﴿١٠٤﴾

essful.

And those whose scales are light are those who lose their souls, in hell abiding.

The fire burneth their faces, and they are glum therein.

23:102-104

15. Nay, but they deny the coming of) the Hour, and for those who deny (the coming of) the Hour We have prepared a flame.

When it seeth them from afar, they hear the crackling and the roar thereof.

And when they are flung into a narrow place thereof, chained together, they pray for destruction there.

Pray not that day for one destruction, but pray for many destructions!

25:11–14

16. And as for those who do evil, their retreat is the Fire. Whenever they desire to issue forth from thence, they are brought back thither. Unto them it is said: Taste the torment of the Fire. which ye used to deny.

32:20

17. But as for those who disbelieve, for them is fire of hell; it taketh not complete effect upon them so that they can die, nor is its torment lightened for them. Thus We punish every ingrate.

And they cry for help there, (saying): Our Lord! Release us; we will do right, not (the wrong) that we used to do! Did not We grant you a life long enough for him who reflected to reflect therein? And the warner came unto you. Now taste (the flavour of your deeds), for evil–doers have no helper.

35:36–37

18. And lo! for the transgre–ssors there will be an evil journey's end.

15. بَلْ كَذَّبُوا بِالسَّاعَةِ وَأَعْتَدْنَا لِمَنْ
كَذَّبَ بِالسَّاعَةِ سَعِيرًا ﴿١١﴾
إِذَا رَأَتْهُم مِّن مَّكَانٍ بَعِيدٍ سَمِعُوا لَهَا
تَغَيُّظًا وَزَفِيرًا ﴿١٢﴾
وَإِذَا أُلْقُوا مِنْهَا مَكَانًا ضَيِّقًا
مُّقَرَّنِينَ دَعَوْا هُنَالِكَ ثُبُورًا ﴿١٣﴾
لَّا تَدْعُوا الْيَوْمَ ثُبُورًا وَاحِدًا وَادْعُوا
ثُبُورًا كَثِيرًا ﴿١٤﴾

16. وَأَمَّا الَّذِينَ فَسَقُوا فَمَأْوَاهُمُ النَّارُ
كُلَّمَا أَرَادُوا أَن يَخْرُجُوا مِنْهَا أُعِيدُوا
فِيهَا وَقِيلَ لَهُمْ ذُوقُوا عَذَابَ النَّارِ
الَّذِي كُنتُم بِهِ تُكَذِّبُونَ ﴿٢٠﴾

17. وَالَّذِينَ كَفَرُوا لَهُمْ نَارُ جَهَنَّمَ لَا
يُقْضَىٰ عَلَيْهِمْ فَيَمُوتُوا وَلَا يُخَفَّفُ
عَنْهُم مِّنْ عَذَابِهَا كَذَٰلِكَ
نَجْزِي كُلَّ كَفُورٍ ﴿٣٦﴾
وَهُمْ يَصْطَرِخُونَ فِيهَا رَبَّنَا أَخْرِجْنَا
نَعْمَلْ صَالِحًا غَيْرَ الَّذِي كُنَّا نَعْمَلُ
أَوَلَمْ نُعَمِّرْكُم مَّا يَتَذَكَّرُ فِيهِ مَن
تَذَكَّرَ وَجَاءَكُمُ النَّذِيرُ فَذُوقُوا
فَمَا لِلظَّالِمِينَ مِن نَّصِيرٍ ﴿٣٧﴾

18. وَإِنَّ لِلطَّاغِينَ لَشَرَّ مَآبٍ ﴿٥٥﴾
جَهَنَّمَ يَصْلَوْنَهَا فَبِئْسَ الْمِهَادُ ﴿٥٦﴾
هَٰذَا فَلْيَذُوقُوهُ حَمِيمٌ وَغَسَّاقٌ ﴿٥٧﴾
وَآخَرُ مِن شَكْلِهِ أَزْوَاجٌ ﴿٥٨﴾

Hell, where they will burn, an evil resting place.

Here is a boiling and an ice–cold draught, so let them taste it,

And other (torment) of the kind in pairs (the two extremes)!

Here is an army rush–ing blindly with you. (Those who are already in the fire say): No word of welcome for them. Lo! they will roast at the Fire.

They say: Nay, but you (misleaders), for you there is no word of welcome. Ye prepared this for us (by your misleading). Now hapless is the plight.

They say: Our Lord! Whoever did prepare this for us, oh, give him double portion of the Fire!

And they say: What aileth us that we behold not men whom we were wont to count among the wicked!

Did we take them (wrongly) for a laughing-stock, or have our eyes missed them?

Lo! that is very truth: the wrangling of the dwellers in the Fire.

38:55–64

19. And those who disbelieve are driven unto hell in troops till, when they reach it and the gates thereof are opened, and the warders thereof say unto them: Came there not unto you messengers of your own, reciting unto you the revelations of your Lord and warning you of the meeting of this your Day? They say: Yea, verily. But the word of doom for disbelievers is fulfilled.

It is said (unto them): Enter ye the gates of hell to dwell therein. Thus hapless is the journey's end of the scorners.

39:71–72

20. Those who deny the

هٰذَا فَوْجٌ مُّقْتَحِمٌ مَّعَكُمْ ۚ لَا مَرْحَبًا
بِهِمْ ۚ إِنَّهُمْ صَالُوا النَّارِ ﴿٥٩﴾
قَالُوا بَلْ أَنتُمْ لَا مَرْحَبًا بِكُمْ ۖ أَنتُمْ
قَدَّمْتُمُوهُ لَنَا ۖ فَبِئْسَ الْقَرَارُ ﴿٦٠﴾
قَالُوا رَبَّنَا مَن قَدَّمَ لَنَا هٰذَا فَزِدْهُ
عَذَابًا ضِعْفًا فِي النَّارِ ﴿٦١﴾
وَقَالُوا مَا لَنَا لَا نَرَىٰ رِجَالًا كُنَّا
نَعُدُّهُم مِّنَ الْأَشْرَارِ ﴿٦٢﴾
أَتَّخَذْنَاهُمْ سِخْرِيًّا أَمْ زَاغَتْ
عَنْهُمُ الْأَبْصَارُ ﴿٦٣﴾
إِنَّ ذٰلِكَ لَحَقٌّ تَخَاصُمُ أَهْلِ النَّارِ ﴿٦٤﴾
19. وَسِيقَ الَّذِينَ كَفَرُوا إِلَىٰ جَهَنَّمَ زُمَرًا ۖ
حَتَّىٰ إِذَا جَاءُوهَا فُتِحَتْ أَبْوَابُهَا وَ
قَالَ لَهُمْ خَزَنَتُهَا أَلَمْ يَأْتِكُمْ رُسُلٌ
مِّنكُمْ يَتْلُونَ عَلَيْكُمْ آيَاتِ رَبِّكُمْ
وَيُنذِرُونَكُمْ لِقَاءَ يَوْمِكُمْ هٰذَا ۚ
قَالُوا بَلَىٰ وَلٰكِنْ حَقَّتْ كَلِمَةُ
الْعَذَابِ عَلَى الْكَافِرِينَ ﴿٧١﴾
قِيلَ ادْخُلُوا أَبْوَابَ جَهَنَّمَ خَالِدِينَ
فِيهَا ۖ فَبِئْسَ مَثْوَى الْمُتَكَبِّرِينَ ﴿٧٢﴾
20. الَّذِينَ كَذَّبُوا بِالْكِتَابِ وَبِمَا أَرْسَلْنَا
بِهِ رُسُلَنَا ۖ فَسَوْفَ يَعْلَمُونَ ﴿٧٠﴾
إِذِ الْأَغْلَالُ فِي أَعْنَاقِهِمْ وَالسَّلَاسِلُ
يُسْحَبُونَ ﴿٧١﴾

Scripture and that wherewith We send Our messengers. But they will come to know,

When carcans are about their necks and chains. They are dragged.

Through boiling waters, then they are thrust into the Fire.

Then it is said unto them: Where are (all) that ye used to make partners (in the Sovereignty)

Beside Allah? They say: They have failed us; but we used not to pray to anything before. Thus doth Allah send astray the disbelievers (in His guidance).

40:70–74

21. Lo! the tree of *Zaqqûm*:

The food of the sinner!

Like molten brass, it seetheth in their bellies.

As the seething of boiling water.

(And, it will be said): Take him and drag him to the midst of hell,

Then pour upon his head the torment of boiling water.

(Saying): Taste! Lo! thou wast forsooth the mighty, the noble!

Lo! this is that whereof ye used to doubt.

44:43–50

22. On the day when We say unto hell: Art thou filled? and it saith: Can there be more to come?

50:30

23. O ye who believe! Ward off from yourselves and your families a Fire whereof the fuel is men and stones, over which are set angels strong, severe, who resist not Allah in that which He commandeth them, but do that which they are commanded.

66:6

24. And for those who dis–

فِي الْحَمِيمِ ثُمَّ فِي النَّارِ يُسْجَرُونَ ﴿٧٢﴾
ثُمَّ قِيلَ لَهُمْ أَيْنَ مَا كُنتُمْ
تُشْرِكُونَ ﴿٧٣﴾
مِن دُونِ اللَّهِ قَالُوا ضَلُّوا عَنَّا بَل
لَّمْ نَكُن نَّدْعُو مِن قَبْلُ شَيْئًا
كَذَٰلِكَ يُضِلُّ اللَّهُ الْكَافِرِينَ ﴿٧٤﴾

21. إِنَّ شَجَرَتَ الزَّقُّومِ ﴿٤٣﴾
طَعَامُ الْأَثِيمِ ﴿٤٤﴾
كَالْمُهْلِ يَغْلِي فِي الْبُطُونِ ﴿٤٥﴾
كَغَلْيِ الْحَمِيمِ ﴿٤٦﴾
خُذُوهُ فَاعْتِلُوهُ إِلَىٰ سَوَاءِ الْجَحِيمِ ﴿٤٧﴾
ثُمَّ صُبُّوا فَوْقَ رَأْسِهِ مِنْ عَذَابِ الْحَمِيمِ ﴿٤٨﴾
ذُقْ إِنَّكَ أَنتَ الْعَزِيزُ الْكَرِيمُ ﴿٤٩﴾
إِنَّ هَٰذَا مَا كُنتُم بِهِ تَمْتَرُونَ ﴿٥٠﴾

22. يَوْمَ نَقُولُ لِجَهَنَّمَ هَلِ امْتَلَأْتِ
وَتَقُولُ هَلْ مِن مَّزِيدٍ ﴿٣٠﴾

23. يَا أَيُّهَا الَّذِينَ آمَنُوا قُوا أَنفُسَكُمْ وَأَهْلِيكُمْ نَارًا
وَقُودُهَا النَّاسُ وَالْحِجَارَةُ عَلَيْهَا مَلَائِكَةٌ
غِلَاظٌ شِدَادٌ لَّا يَعْصُونَ اللَّهَ مَا أَمَرَهُمْ وَ
يَفْعَلُونَ مَا يُؤْمَرُونَ ﴿٦﴾

24. وَلِلَّذِينَ كَفَرُوا بِرَبِّهِمْ عَذَابُ
جَهَنَّمَ وَبِئْسَ الْمَصِيرُ ﴿٦﴾
إِذَا أُلْقُوا فِيهَا سَمِعُوا لَهَا شَهِيقًا

believe in their Lord there is the doom of hell, a hapless journey's end!

When they are flung therein they hear its roaring as it boileth up,

As it would burst with rage. Whenever a (fresh) host is flung therein the wardens thereof ask them: Came there unto you no warner?

They say: Yea, verily, a warner came unto us; but we denied and said: Allah hath naught revealed; ye are in naught but a great error.

And they say: Had we been wont to listen or have sense, we had not been among the dwellers in the flames.

67:6–10

25. The guilty man will long to be able to ransom himself from the punishment of that day at the price of his children

And his spouse and his brother

And his kin that harboured him.

And all that are in the earth, if then it might deliver him,

But nay! for lo! it is the fire of hell

Eager to roast

It calleth him who turned and fled (from truth),

And hoarded (wealth) and withheld it.

70:11–18

26. Lo! hell lurketh in ambush,

A home for the rebellious.

They will abide therein for ages.

Therein taste they neither coolness nor (any) drink

Save boiling water and a paralysing cold:

وَّهِيَ تَفُوْرُ ۝٧
تَكَادُ تَمَيَّزُ مِنَ الْغَيْظِ ۭ كُلَّمَآ اُلْقِيَ
فِيْهَا فَوْجٌ سَاَلَهُمْ خَزَنَتُهَآ اَلَمْ
يَاْتِكُمْ نَذِيْرٌ ۝٨
قَالُوْا بَلٰى قَدْ جَاۗءَنَا نَذِيْرٌ ڏ فَكَذَّبْنَا
وَقُلْنَا مَا نَزَّلَ اللّٰهُ مِنْ شَيْءٍ ښ اِنْ
اَنْتُمْ اِلَّا فِيْ ضَلٰلٍ كَبِيْرٍ ۝٩
وَقَالُوْا لَوْ كُنَّا نَسْمَعُ اَوْ نَعْقِلُ مَا كُنَّا
فِيْٓ اَصْحٰبِ السَّعِيْرِ ۝١٠

25. يَوَدُّ الْمُجْرِمُ لَوْ يَفْتَدِيْ مِنْ عَذَابِ
يَوْمِىِٕذٍۢ بِبَنِيْهِ ۝١١
وَصَاحِبَتِهٖ وَاَخِيْهِ ۝١٢
وَفَصِيْلَتِهِ الَّتِيْ تُـــْٔوِيْهِ ۝١٣
وَمَنْ فِي الْاَرْضِ جَمِيْعًا ۙ ثُمَّ يُنْجِيْهِ ۝١٤
كَلَّا ۭ اِنَّهَا لَظٰى ۝١٥
نَزَّاعَةً لِّلشَّوٰى ۝١٦
تَدْعُوْا مَنْ اَدْبَرَ وَتَوَلّٰى ۝١٧
وَجَمَعَ فَاَوْعٰى ۝١٨

26. اِنَّ جَهَنَّمَ كَانَتْ مِرْصَادًا ۝٢١
لِّلطّٰغِيْنَ مَاٰبًا ۝٢٢
لّٰبِثِيْنَ فِيْهَآ اَحْقَابًا ۝٢٣
لَا يَذُوْقُوْنَ فِيْهَا بَرْدًا وَّلَا شَرَابًا ۝٢٤
اِلَّا حَمِيْمًا وَّغَسَّاقًا ۝٢٥
جَزَاۗءً وِّفَاقًا ۝٢٦

Reward proportioned (to their evil deeds).

78:21–26

Ref: 2:24; 3:12,116,131; 6:27; 7:38,41; 8:14,36–37; 10:27; 25:65–66; 32:13; 36:63; 39:16,24–25,47–48,60,71–72; 40:49–50; 42:44–45; 47:15; 52:11–16; 55:43–44; 70:15–18; 73:12–13; 76:4; 78:21–26; 79:36; 87:12–13; 92:14–17; 101:9–11; 102:4–7; 111:3;

See also: Paradise, *Zaqqum.*

HERESY

1. Hast thou seen him who maketh his desire his god, and Allah sendeth him astray purposely, and sealeth up his hearing and his heart, and setteth on his sight a covering? Then who will lead him after Allah (hath condemned him)? Will ye not then heed?

And they say: There is naught but our life of the world; we die and we live, and naught destroyeth us save time; when they have no knowledge whatsoever of (all) that; they do but guess.

45:23–24

HOLY MOSQUE OF *K'ABAH*

1. We have seen the turning of thy face to heaven (for guidance, O Muhammad). And now verily We shall make thee turn (in prayer) toward a *Qiblah* which is dear to thee. So turn thy face toward the Inviolable Place of Worship and ye (O Muslims), wheresoever ye may be, turn your faces (when ye pray) toward it. Lo! those who have received the Scripture know that (this Revelation) is the Truth from their Lord. And Allah is not unaware of what they do.

2:144

2. Whence-so-ever thou comest forth turn thy face toward the Inviolable Place of Worship; and wheresoever ye may be (O Muslims) turn your faces towards it (when ye pray) so that men may have no argument against you, save such of them as do injustice—Fear them not, but fear Me!—and so that I may complete My grace upon you, and that ye may be guided.

2:150

1. أَفَرَءَيْتَ مَنِ اتَّخَذَ إِلَٰهَهُ هَوَىٰهُ وَ
أَضَلَّهُ اللَّهُ عَلَىٰ عِلْمٍ وَخَتَمَ عَلَىٰ سَمْعِهِ
وَقَلْبِهِ وَجَعَلَ عَلَىٰ بَصَرِهِ غِشَٰوَةً
فَمَن يَهْدِيهِ مِنۢ بَعْدِ اللَّهِ
أَفَلَا تَذَكَّرُونَ ۝٢٣
وَقَالُوا مَا هِيَ إِلَّا حَيَاتُنَا الدُّنْيَا نَمُوتُ
وَنَحْيَا وَمَا يُهْلِكُنَا إِلَّا الدَّهْرُ وَمَا
لَهُم بِذَٰلِكَ مِنْ عِلْمٍ إِنْ هُمْ
إِلَّا يَظُنُّونَ ۝٢٤

○

1. قَدْ نَرَىٰ تَقَلُّبَ وَجْهِكَ فِي السَّمَاءِ فَلَنُوَلِّيَنَّكَ
قِبْلَةً تَرْضَىٰهَا فَوَلِّ وَجْهَكَ شَطْرَ الْمَسْجِدِ
الْحَرَامِ وَحَيْثُ مَا كُنتُمْ فَوَلُّوا وُجُوهَكُمْ
شَطْرَهُ وَإِنَّ الَّذِينَ أُوتُوا الْكِتَٰبَ لَيَعْلَمُونَ
أَنَّهُ الْحَقُّ مِن رَّبِّهِمْ وَمَا اللَّهُ بِغَٰفِلٍ
عَمَّا يَعْمَلُونَ ۝١٤٤
2. وَمِنْ حَيْثُ خَرَجْتَ فَوَلِّ وَجْهَكَ
شَطْرَ الْمَسْجِدِ الْحَرَامِ وَحَيْثُ مَا كُنتُمْ
فَوَلُّوا وُجُوهَكُمْ شَطْرَهُ لِئَلَّا يَكُونَ لِلنَّاسِ
عَلَيْكُمْ حُجَّةٌ إِلَّا الَّذِينَ ظَلَمُوا مِنْهُمْ
فَلَا تَخْشَوْهُمْ وَاخْشَوْنِي وَلِأُتِمَّ نِعْمَتِي
عَلَيْكُمْ وَلَعَلَّكُمْ تَهْتَدُونَ ۝١٥٠

3. And fight not with them at the Inviolable Place of Worship until they first attack you there, but if they attack you (there) then slay them. Such is the reward of disbelievers.

2:191

4. O ye who believe! Profane not Allah's monuments nor the Sacred Month nor the offerings nor the garlands, nor those repairing to the Sacred House, seeking the grace and pleasure of their Lord. But when ye have left the sacred terriroty, then go hunting (if ye will). And let not your hatred of a folk who (once) stopped your going to the Inviolable Place of Worship seduce you to transgress; but help ye one another unto righteousness and pious duty. Help not one another unto sin and transgression, but keep your duty to Allah. Lo! Allah is severe in punishment.

5:2

5. What (plea) have they that Allah should not punish them, when they debar (His servants) from the Inviolable Place of Worship, though they are not its fitting guardians. Its fitting guardians are those only who keep their duty to Allah. But most of them know not.

And their worship at the (holy) House is naught but whistling and hand–clapping. Therefore (it is said unto them): Taste of the doom because ye disbelieved.

8:34–35

6. Count ye the slaking of a pilgrim's thirst and tendance of

3. وَلَا تُقَاتِلُوهُمْ عِندَ الْمَسْجِدِ الْحَرَامِ حَتَّىٰ يُقَاتِلُوكُمْ فِيهِ
فَإِن قَاتَلُوكُمْ فَاقْتُلُوهُمْ كَذَٰلِكَ جَزَاءُ الْكَافِرِينَ ﴿١٩١﴾

4. يَا أَيُّهَا الَّذِينَ آمَنُوا لَا تُحِلُّوا شَعَائِرَ اللَّهِ وَلَا الشَّهْرَ
الْحَرَامَ وَلَا الْهَدْيَ وَلَا الْقَلَائِدَ وَلَا آمِّينَ الْبَيْتَ
الْحَرَامَ يَبْتَغُونَ فَضْلًا مِّن رَّبِّهِمْ وَرِضْوَانًا وَإِذَا
حَلَلْتُمْ فَاصْطَادُوا وَلَا يَجْرِمَنَّكُمْ شَنَآنُ قَوْمٍ أَن
صَدُّوكُمْ عَنِ الْمَسْجِدِ الْحَرَامِ أَن تَعْتَدُوا وَتَعَاوَنُوا
عَلَى الْبِرِّ وَالتَّقْوَىٰ وَلَا تَعَاوَنُوا عَلَى الْإِثْمِ وَالْعُدْوَانِ
وَاتَّقُوا اللَّهَ إِنَّ اللَّهَ شَدِيدُ الْعِقَابِ ﴿٢﴾

5. وَمَا لَهُمْ أَلَّا يُعَذِّبَهُمُ اللَّهُ وَهُمْ يَصُدُّونَ
عَنِ الْمَسْجِدِ الْحَرَامِ وَمَا كَانُوا أَوْلِيَاءَهُ
إِنْ أَوْلِيَاؤُهُ إِلَّا الْمُتَّقُونَ وَلَٰكِنَّ أَكْثَرَهُمْ
لَا يَعْلَمُونَ ﴿٣٤﴾

وَمَا كَانَ صَلَاتُهُمْ عِندَ الْبَيْتِ إِلَّا
مُكَاءً وَتَصْدِيَةً فَذُوقُوا الْعَذَابَ بِمَا
كُنتُمْ تَكْفُرُونَ ﴿٣٥﴾

6. أَجَعَلْتُمْ سِقَايَةَ الْحَاجِّ وَعِمَارَةَ الْمَسْجِدِ
الْحَرَامِ كَمَنْ آمَنَ بِاللَّهِ وَالْيَوْمِ الْآخِرِ
وَجَاهَدَ فِي سَبِيلِ اللَّهِ لَا يَسْتَوُونَ عِندَ
اللَّهِ وَاللَّهُ لَا يَهْدِي الْقَوْمَ الظَّالِمِينَ ﴿١٩﴾

7. يَا أَيُّهَا الَّذِينَ آمَنُوا إِنَّمَا الْمُشْرِكُونَ
نَجَسٌ فَلَا يَقْرَبُوا الْمَسْجِدَ الْحَرَامَ
بَعْدَ عَامِهِمْ هَٰذَا وَإِنْ خِفْتُمْ عَيْلَةً

the Inviolable Place of Worship as (equal to the worth of him) who believeth in Allah and the Last Day, and striveth in the way of Allah? They are not equal in the sight of Allah. Allah guideth not wrongdoing folk.

9:19

7. O ye who believe! The idolaters only are unclean. So

let them not come near the Inviolable Place of Worship after this their year. If ye fear poverty (from the loss of their merchandise) Allah shall preserve you of His bounty if He will. Lo! Allah is Knower, Wise.

9:28

8. Glorified be He Who carried His servant by night from the Inviolable Place of Worship to the Far Distant Place of Worship the neighbourhood whereof We have blessed, that We might show him of Our tokens! Lo! He, only He, is the Hearer, the Seer.

17:1

فَسَوْفَ يُغْنِيكُمُ اللّٰهُ مِنْ فَضْلِهٖۤ اِنْ شَآءَ ؕ
اِنَّ اللّٰهَ عَلِيْمٌ حَكِيْمٌ ﴿۲۸﴾

8. سُبْحٰنَ الَّذِىْۤ اَسْرٰى بِعَبْدِهٖ لَيْلًا مِّنَ
الْمَسْجِدِ الْحَرَامِ اِلَى الْمَسْجِدِ الْاَقْصَا
الَّذِىْ بٰرَكْنَا حَوْلَهٗ لِنُرِيَهٗ مِنْ اٰيٰتِنَا ؕ
اِنَّهٗ هُوَ السَّمِيْعُ الْبَصِيْرُ ﴿۱﴾

○

Ref: 2:196,217; 9:7; 22:25–29; 48:27;

HOLY SPIRIT

1. And We gave unto Jesus, son of Mary, clear proofs (of Allah's Sovereignty) and We supported him with the holy Spirit.

2:87

2. Allah knoweth best what He revealeth—they say: Lo! thou art but inventing. Most of them know not.

Say: The holy Spirit hath revealed it from thy Lord with truth, that it may con–firm (the faith of) those who believe, and as guidance and good tidings for those who have surrendered (to Allah).

16:101–102

HOMOSEXUALITY

1. And as for the two of you who are guilty thereof, punish them both. And if they repent and improve, then let them be. Lo! Allah is Relenting, Merciful.

4:16

2. And Lot! (Remember) when he said unto his folk: Will ye commit abomination such as no creature ever did before you?

Lo! ye come with lust

1. وَآتَيْنَا عِيسَى ابْنَ مَرْيَمَ الْبَيِّنَاتِ وَأَيَّدْنَاهُ
بِرُوحِ الْقُدُسِ

2. وَاللَّهُ أَعْلَمُ بِمَا يُنَزِّلُ قَالُوا إِنَّمَا
أَنْتَ مُفْتَرٍ بَلْ أَكْثَرُهُمْ لَا
يَعْلَمُونَ ﴿١٠١﴾
قُلْ نَزَّلَهُ رُوحُ الْقُدُسِ مِنْ رَبِّكَ
بِالْحَقِّ لِيُثَبِّتَ الَّذِينَ آمَنُوا وَهُدًى
وَبُشْرَى لِلْمُسْلِمِينَ ﴿١٠٢﴾

1. وَاللَّذَانِ يَأْتِيَانِهَا مِنْكُمْ فَآذُوهُمَا
فَإِنْ تَابَا وَأَصْلَحَا فَأَعْرِضُوا عَنْهُمَا
إِنَّ اللَّهَ كَانَ تَوَّابًا رَحِيمًا ﴿١٦﴾

2. وَلُوطًا إِذْ قَالَ لِقَوْمِهِ أَتَأْتُونَ الْفَاحِشَةَ
مَا سَبَقَكُمْ بِهَا مِنْ أَحَدٍ مِنَ الْعَالَمِينَ ﴿٨٠﴾
إِنَّكُمْ لَتَأْتُونَ الرِّجَالَ شَهْوَةً مِنْ دُونِ
النِّسَاءِ بَلْ أَنْتُمْ قَوْمٌ مُسْرِفُونَ ﴿٨١﴾

unto men instead of women. Nay, but ye are wanton folk.

7:80-81

HOLY SPIRIT
Ref: 2:253; 5:110; 16:2; 26:193; 40:15; 42:52; 58:22; 70:4; 78:38.
HOMOSEXUALITY
Ref: 11:77–79; 15:67–74; 21:74; 26:165–166; 27:54–55; 29:28–29,
See also: Obscenity.

HONEY

1. And thy Lord inspired the bee, saying: Choose thou habitations in the hills and in the trees and in that which they thatch;

Then eat of all fruits, and follow the ways of thy Lord, made smooth (for thee). There cometh forth from their bellies a drink diverse of hues, wherein is healing for mankind. Lo! herein is indeed a portent for people who reflect.

16:68–69

2. A similitude of the Garden which those who keep their duty (to Allah) are promised: Therein are rivers of water unpolluted, and rivers of milk whereof the flavour changeth not, and rivers of wine delicious to the drinkers, and rivers of clear-run honey; therein for them is every kind of fruit, with pardon from their Lord. (Are those who enjoy all this).

47:15

1. وَأَوْحَىٰ رَبُّكَ إِلَى النَّحْلِ أَنِ اتَّخِذِي
مِنَ الْجِبَالِ بُيُوتًا وَمِنَ الشَّجَرِ
وَمِمَّا يَعْرِشُونَ ﴿٦٨﴾
ثُمَّ كُلِي مِن كُلِّ الثَّمَرَاتِ فَاسْلُكِي
سُبُلَ رَبِّكِ ذُلُلًا ۚ يَخْرُجُ مِن بُطُونِهَا
شَرَابٌ مُّخْتَلِفٌ أَلْوَانُهُ فِيهِ شِفَاءٌ
لِّلنَّاسِ ۗ إِنَّ فِي ذَٰلِكَ لَآيَةً لِّقَوْمٍ يَتَفَكَّرُونَ ﴿٦٩﴾

2. مَّثَلُ الْجَنَّةِ الَّتِي وُعِدَ الْمُتَّقُونَ ۖ فِيهَا
أَنْهَارٌ مِّن مَّاءٍ غَيْرِ آسِنٍ وَأَنْهَارٌ
مِّن لَّبَنٍ لَّمْ يَتَغَيَّرْ طَعْمُهُ وَأَنْهَارٌ
مِّنْ خَمْرٍ لَّذَّةٍ لِّلشَّارِبِينَ ۚ
وَأَنْهَارٌ مِّنْ عَسَلٍ مُّصَفًّى ۖ وَلَهُمْ
فِيهَا مِن كُلِّ الثَّمَرَاتِ وَمَغْفِرَةٌ
مِّن رَّبِّهِمْ ۖ

HOSPITALITY

1. O ye who believe! Enter not the dwellings of the Prophet for a meal without waiting for the proper time, unless permission be granted you. But if ye are invited, enter, and, when your meal is ended, then disperse. Linger not for conversation. Lo! that would cause annoyance to the Prophet, and he would be shy of (asking) you (to go); but Allah is not shy of the truth.

33:53

2. Hath the story of Abraham's honoured guests reached thee (O Muhammad)?

When they came in unto him and said: Peace! he answered, Peace! (and thought) Folk unknown (to me).

Then he went apart unto his housefolk so that they brought a fatted calf;

And he set it before them, saying: Will ye not eat?

Then he conceived a fear of them. They said: Fear not! and gave him tidings of (the birth of) a wise son.

51:24–28

1. يَاَيُّهَا الَّذِيْنَ اٰمَنُوْا لَا تَدْخُلُوْا بُيُوْتَ
النَّبِيِّ اِلَّآ اَنْ يُّؤْذَنَ لَكُمْ اِلٰى طَعَامٍ
غَيْرَ نٰظِرِيْنَ اِنٰىهُ وَلٰكِنْ اِذَا دُعِيْتُمْ
فَادْخُلُوْا فَاِذَا طَعِمْتُمْ فَانْتَشِرُوْا وَلَا
مُسْتَاْنِسِيْنَ لِحَدِيْثٍ اِنَّ ذٰلِكُمْ كَانَ
يُؤْذِي النَّبِيَّ فَيَسْتَحْيٖ مِنْكُمْ وَاللّٰهُ
لَا يَسْتَحْيٖ مِنَ الْحَقِّ

2. هَلْ اَتٰىكَ حَدِيْثُ ضَيْفِ اِبْرٰهِيْمَ
الْمُكْرَمِيْنَ ۝
اِذْ دَخَلُوْا عَلَيْهِ فَقَالُوْا سَلٰمًا قَالَ
سَلٰمٌ قَوْمٌ مُّنْكَرُوْنَ ۝
فَرَاغَ اِلٰٓى اَهْلِهٖ فَجَآءَ بِعِجْلٍ سَمِيْنٍ ۝
فَقَرَّبَهٗٓ اِلَيْهِمْ قَالَ اَلَا تَاْكُلُوْنَ ۝
فَاَوْجَسَ مِنْهُمْ خِيْفَةً قَالُوْا لَا تَخَفْ
وَبَشَّرُوْهُ بِغُلٰمٍ عَلِيْمٍ ۝

Ref: 54:37

HOUSE

1. Lo! the first Sanctuary appointed for mankind was that at *Bakkah*, a blessed place, a guidance to the peoples,

3:96

2. And Allah hath given you in your houses an abode, and hath given you (also), of the hides of cattle, tent–houses which ye find light (to carry) on the day of migration and on the day of pitching camp; and of their wool and their fur and their hair, caparison and comfort for a while.

16:80

3. O ye who believe! Enter not houses other than your own without first announcing your presence and invoking peace upon the folk thereof. That is better for you, that ye may be heedful.

And if ye find no one therein, still enter not until permission hath been given. And if it be said unto you: Go away again, then go away, for it is purer for you. Allah knoweth what ye do.

(It is) no sin for you to enter uninhabited houses wherein is comfort for you. Allah knoweth what ye proclaim and what ye hide.

24:27–29

4. The likeness of those who choose other patrons than Allah is as the likeness of the spider when she taketh unto herself a house, and lo! the frailest of all houses is the spider's house, if they but knew.

29:41

1. اِنَّ اَوَّلَ بَيْتٍ وُّضِعَ لِلنَّاسِ لَلَّذِىْ بِبَكَّةَ
مُبٰرَكًا وَّهُدًى لِّلْعٰلَمِيْنَ ۝

2. وَاللّٰهُ جَعَلَ لَكُمْ مِّنْ بُيُوْتِكُمْ سَكَنًا
وَّجَعَلَ لَكُمْ مِّنْ جُلُوْدِ الْاَنْعَامِ بُيُوْتًا
تَسْتَخِفُّوْنَهَا يَوْمَ ظَعْنِكُمْ وَيَوْمَ اِقَامَتِكُمْ
وَمِنْ اَصْوَافِهَا وَاَوْبَارِهَا وَاَشْعَارِهَآ
اَثَاثًا وَّمَتَاعًا اِلٰى حِيْنٍ ۝

3. يٰۤاَيُّهَا الَّذِيْنَ اٰمَنُوْا لَا تَدْخُلُوْا بُيُوْتًا
غَيْرَ بُيُوْتِكُمْ حَتّٰى تَسْتَاْنِسُوْا وَتُسَلِّمُوْا
عَلٰۤى اَهْلِهَا ۗ ذٰلِكُمْ خَيْرٌ لَّكُمْ
لَعَلَّكُمْ تَذَكَّرُوْنَ ۝
فَاِنْ لَّمْ تَجِدُوْا فِيْهَاۤ اَحَدًا فَلَا تَدْخُلُوْهَا
حَتّٰى يُؤْذَنَ لَكُمْ ۚ وَاِنْ قِيْلَ لَكُمُ
ارْجِعُوْا فَارْجِعُوْا هُوَ اَزْكٰى لَكُمْ ۗ
وَاللّٰهُ بِمَا تَعْمَلُوْنَ عَلِيْمٌ ۝
لَيْسَ عَلَيْكُمْ جُنَاحٌ اَنْ تَدْخُلُوْا بُيُوْتًا
غَيْرَ مَسْكُوْنَةٍ فِيْهَا مَتَاعٌ لَّكُمْ ۗ وَاللّٰهُ
يَعْلَمُ مَا تُبْدُوْنَ وَمَا تَكْتُمُوْنَ ۝

4. مَثَلُ الَّذِيْنَ اتَّخَذُوْا مِنْ دُوْنِ اللّٰهِ
اَوْلِيَآءَ كَمَثَلِ الْعَنْكَبُوْتِ ۚ اِتَّخَذَتْ
بَيْتًا ۗ وَاِنَّ اَوْهَنَ الْبُيُوْتِ لَبَيْتُ
الْعَنْكَبُوْتِ ۘ لَوْ كَانُوْا يَعْلَمُوْنَ ۝

HUDUD

1. O ye who believe! Retaliation is prescribed for you in the matter of the murdered; the freeman for the freeman, and the slave for the slave, and the female for the female. And for him who is forgiven somewhat by his (injured) brother, prosecution according to usage and payment unto him in kindness. This is an alleviation and a mercy from your Lord. He who transgresseth after this will have a painful doom.

And there is life for you in retaliation, O men of understanding, that ye may ward off (evil).

2:178–179

2. It is not for a believer to kill a believer unless (it be) by mistake, He who hath killed a believer by mistake must set free a believing slave and pay the blood-money to the family of the slain, unless they remit it as a charity. If he (the victim) be of a people hostile unto you, and he is a believer, then (the penance) is to set free a believing slave. And if he cometh of a folk between whom and you there is a covenant, then the blood-money must be paid unto his folk and (also) a believing slave must be set free. And whoso hath not the wherewithal must fast two consecutive months. A penance from Allah. Allah is Knower, Wise.

Whoso slayeth a believer of set purpose, his reward is Hell for ever. Allah is wroth against him and He hath cursed him and prepared for him an awful doom.

4:92–93

1. يٰٓاَيُّهَا الَّذِيْنَ اٰمَنُوْا كُتِبَ عَلَيْكُمُ الْقِصَاصُ
فِي الْقَتْلٰى ۭ اَلْحُرُّ بِالْحُرِّ وَالْعَبْدُ بِالْعَبْدِ
وَالْاُنْثٰى بِالْاُنْثٰى ۭ فَمَنْ عُفِيَ لَهٗ مِنْ اَخِيْهِ
شَيْءٌ فَاتِّبَاعٌۢ بِالْمَعْرُوْفِ وَاَدَاۗءٌ اِلَيْهِ بِاِحْسَانٍ ۭ
ذٰلِكَ تَخْفِيْفٌ مِّنْ رَّبِّكُمْ وَرَحْمَةٌ ۭ فَمَنِ
اعْتَدٰى بَعْدَ ذٰلِكَ فَلَهٗ عَذَابٌ اَلِيْمٌ ﴿١٧٨﴾

وَلَكُمْ فِي الْقِصَاصِ حَيٰوةٌ يّٰٓاُولِي الْاَلْبَابِ
لَعَلَّكُمْ تَتَّقُوْنَ ﴿١٧٩﴾

2. وَمَا كَانَ لِمُؤْمِنٍ اَنْ يَّقْتُلَ مُؤْمِنًا اِلَّا
خَطَـًٔا ۚ وَمَنْ قَتَلَ مُؤْمِنًا خَطَـًٔا فَتَحْرِيْرُ
رَقَبَةٍ مُّؤْمِنَةٍ وَّدِيَةٌ مُّسَلَّمَةٌ اِلٰٓى اَهْلِهٖٓ
اِلَّآ اَنْ يَّصَّدَّقُوْا ۭ فَاِنْ كَانَ مِنْ قَوْمٍ عَدُوٍّ
لَّكُمْ وَهُوَ مُؤْمِنٌ فَتَحْرِيْرُ رَقَبَةٍ مُّؤْمِنَةٍ ۭ
وَاِنْ كَانَ مِنْ قَوْمٍۢ بَيْنَكُمْ وَبَيْنَهُمْ مِّيْثَاقٌ
فَدِيَةٌ مُّسَلَّمَةٌ اِلٰٓى اَهْلِهٖ وَتَحْرِيْرُ رَقَبَةٍ
مُّؤْمِنَةٍ ۚ فَمَنْ لَّمْ يَجِدْ فَصِيَامُ شَهْرَيْنِ
مُتَتَابِعَيْنِ ۡ تَوْبَةً مِّنَ اللّٰهِ ۭ وَكَانَ اللّٰهُ
عَلِيْمًا حَكِيْمًا ﴿٩٢﴾

وَمَنْ يَّقْتُلْ مُؤْمِنًا مُّتَعَمِّدًا فَجَزَاۗؤُهٗ
جَهَنَّمُ خٰلِدًا فِيْهَا وَغَضِبَ اللّٰهُ عَلَيْهِ
وَلَعَنَهٗ وَاَعَدَّ لَهٗ عَذَابًا عَظِيْمًا ﴿٩٣﴾

3. إِنَّمَا جَزَٰٓؤُا الَّذِينَ يُحَارِبُونَ اللَّهَ وَ
رَسُولَهُ وَيَسْعَوْنَ فِي الْأَرْضِ فَسَادًا
أَنْ يُقَتَّلُوٓا أَوْ يُصَلَّبُوٓا أَوْ تُقَطَّعَ أَيْدِيهِمْ
وَأَرْجُلُهُم مِّنْ خِلَافٍ أَوْ يُنفَوْا مِنَ
الْأَرْضِ ذَٰلِكَ لَهُمْ خِزْيٌ فِي الدُّنْيَا وَ
لَهُمْ فِي الْآخِرَةِ عَذَابٌ عَظِيمٌ ﴿٣٣﴾
إِلَّا الَّذِينَ تَابُوا مِن قَبْلِ أَن تَقْدِرُوا
عَلَيْهِمْ فَاعْلَمُوٓا أَنَّ اللَّهَ غَفُورٌ رَّحِيمٌ ﴿٣٤﴾

4. وَالسَّارِقُ وَالسَّارِقَةُ فَاقْطَعُوٓا أَيْدِيَهُمَا
جَزَآءً بِمَا كَسَبَا نَكَالًا مِّنَ اللَّهِ وَاللَّهُ
عَزِيزٌ حَكِيمٌ ﴿٣٨﴾
فَمَن تَابَ مِنْ بَعْدِ ظُلْمِهِ وَأَصْلَحَ
فَإِنَّ اللَّهَ يَتُوبُ عَلَيْهِ إِنَّ اللَّهَ غَفُورٌ رَّحِيمٌ ﴿٣٩﴾

5. وَكَتَبْنَا عَلَيْهِمْ فِيهَآ أَنَّ النَّفْسَ بِالنَّفْسِ
وَالْعَيْنَ بِالْعَيْنِ وَالْأَنفَ بِالْأَنفِ
وَالْأُذُنَ بِالْأُذُنِ وَالسِّنَّ بِالسِّنِّ
وَالْجُرُوحَ قِصَاصٌ فَمَن تَصَدَّقَ بِهِ
فَهُوَ كَفَّارَةٌ لَّهُ وَمَن لَّمْ يَحْكُم بِمَآ
أَنزَلَ اللَّهُ فَأُولَٰٓئِكَ هُمُ الظَّٰلِمُونَ ﴿٤٥﴾

6. الزَّانِيَةُ وَالزَّانِي فَاجْلِدُوا كُلَّ وَاحِدٍ مِّنْهُمَا مِائَةَ
جَلْدَةٍ وَلَا تَأْخُذْكُم بِهِمَا رَأْفَةٌ فِي دِينِ اللَّهِ إِن
كُنتُمْ تُؤْمِنُونَ بِاللَّهِ وَالْيَوْمِ الْآخِرِ وَلْيَشْهَدْ
عَذَابَهُمَا طَآئِفَةٌ مِّنَ الْمُؤْمِنِينَ ○

3. The only reward of those who make war upon Allah and His messenger and strive after corruption in the land will be that they will be killed or crucified, or have their hands and feet on alternate sides cut off, or will be expelled out of the land. Such will be their degradation in the world, and in the Hereafter theirs will be an awful doom;

Save those who repent before ye overpower them. For know that Allah is Forgiving, Merciful.

5:33–34

4. . As for the thief, both male and female, cut off their hands. It is the reward of their own deeds, an exemplary punishment from Allah. Allah is Mighty, Wise.

But whoso repenteth after his wrongdoing and amendeth, lo! Allah will relent toward him. Lo! Allah is Forgiving, Merciful.

5:38–39.

5. And We prescribed for them therein: The life for the life, and the eye for the eye, and the nose for the nose, and the ear for the ear, and the tooth for the tooth, and for wounds retaliation. But whoso forgoeth it (in the way of charity) it shall be expiation for him. Whoso judgeth not by that which Allah hath revealed: such are wrong-doers.

5:45

6. The adulterer and the adulteress, scourge ye each one of them (with) a hundred stripes, And let not pity for the twain withhold you from obedience to Allah, if ye believe in Allah and the Last Day. And let a party of believers witness their punishment.

24:2

7. And those who accuse honourable women but bring not four witnesses, scourge them (with) eighty stripes and never (afterward) accept their testimony—They indeed are evildoers—

Save those who afterward repent and make amends. (For such) lo! Allah is Forgiving, Merciful.

24:4–5

7. وَالَّذِيْنَ يَرْمُوْنَ الْمُحْصَنٰتِ ثُمَّ لَمْ يَاْتُوْا بِاَرْبَعَةِ
شُهَدَآءَ فَاجْلِدُوْهُمْ ثَمٰنِيْنَ جَلْدَةً وَّلَا
تَقْبَلُوْا لَهُمْ شَهَادَةً اَبَدًا ۚ وَاُولٰٓئِكَ هُمُ
الْفٰسِقُوْنَ ۙ﴿٤﴾

اِلَّا الَّذِيْنَ تَابُوْا مِنْۢ بَعْدِ ذٰلِكَ
وَاَصْلَحُوْا ۚ فَاِنَّ اللّٰهَ غَفُوْرٌ رَّحِيْمٌ ﴿٥﴾

Ref: 2: 187,229,230; 4: 13,14; 9: 97,112; 58: 4; 65: 1.
See also: *Qisas.*

HUMAN RIGHTS

1. Give unto orphans their wealth. Exchange not the good for the bad (in your management thereof) nor ab– sorb their wealth into your own wealth. Lo! that would be a great sin.

4:2

2. O ye who believe! Squander not your wealth among yourselves in vanity, except it be a trade by mutual consent, and kill not one another Lo! Allah is ever Merciful unto you.

And whoso doeth that through aggression and injustice, We shall cast him into Fire, and that is ever easy for Allah.

4:29–30

3. Lo! Allah commandeth you that ye restore deposits to their owners, and, if ye judge between mankind, that ye judge justly. Lo! comely is this which Alalh admonisheth you. Lo! Allah is ever Hearer, Seer.

4:58

4. So give to the kinsman his due, and to the needy, and to the wayfarer. That is best for those who seek Allah's Countenance. And such are they who are successful.

30:38

5. Lo! those who keep from evil will dwell amid gardens and watersprings,

Taking that which their Lord giveth them; for lo! aforetime thev were doers of good;

They used to sleep but little of the night,

And ere the dawning of each day would seek for– giveness.

And in their wealth the beggar and the outcast had due share.

51:15–19

1. وَاٰتُوا الْيَتٰمٰٓى اَمْوَالَهُمْ وَلَا تَتَبَدَّلُوا
الْخَبِيْثَ بِالطَّيِّبِ وَلَا تَاْكُلُوْٓا اَمْوَالَهُمْ
اِلٰٓى اَمْوَالِكُمْ اِنَّهٗ كَانَ حُوْبًا كَبِيْرًا

2. يٰٓاَيُّهَا الَّذِيْنَ اٰمَنُوْا لَا تَاْكُلُوْٓا اَمْوَالَكُمْ
بَيْنَكُمْ بِالْبَاطِلِ اِلَّآ اَنْ تَكُوْنَ تِجَارَةً
عَنْ تَرَاضٍ مِّنْكُمْ وَلَا تَقْتُلُوْٓا اَنْفُسَكُمْ
اِنَّ اللّٰهَ كَانَ بِكُمْ رَحِيْمًا
وَمَنْ يَّفْعَلْ ذٰلِكَ عُدْوَانًا وَّظُلْمًا فَسَوْفَ
نُصْلِيْهِ نَارًا وَكَانَ ذٰلِكَ عَلَى اللّٰهِ يَسِيْرًا

3. اِنَّ اللّٰهَ يَاْمُرُكُمْ اَنْ تُؤَدُّوا الْاَمٰنٰتِ اِلٰٓى
اَهْلِهَا وَاِذَا حَكَمْتُمْ بَيْنَ النَّاسِ اَنْ
تَحْكُمُوْا بِالْعَدْلِ اِنَّ اللّٰهَ نِعِمَّا يَعِظُكُمْ
بِهٖ اِنَّ اللّٰهَ كَانَ سَمِيْعًا بَصِيْرًا

4. فَاٰتِ ذَا الْقُرْبٰى حَقَّهٗ وَالْمِسْكِيْنَ
وَابْنَ السَّبِيْلِ ذٰلِكَ خَيْرٌ لِّلَّذِيْنَ
يُرِيْدُوْنَ وَجْهَ اللّٰهِ وَاُولٰٓئِكَ
هُمُ الْمُفْلِحُوْنَ

5. اِنَّ الْمُتَّقِيْنَ فِيْ جَنّٰتٍ وَّعُيُوْنٍ
اٰخِذِيْنَ مَآ اٰتٰىهُمْ رَبُّهُمْ اِنَّهُمْ
كَانُوْا قَبْلَ ذٰلِكَ مُحْسِنِيْنَ
كَانُوْا قَلِيْلًا مِّنَ الَّيْلِ مَا يَهْجَعُوْنَ
وَبِالْاَسْحَارِ هُمْ يَسْتَغْفِرُوْنَ
وَفِيْٓ اَمْوَالِهِمْ حَقٌّ لِّلسَّآئِلِ وَالْمَحْرُوْمِ

See also: Children, Orphans, Relatives, Rights of Parents, wayfarer.

HUMILITY

1. And walk not in the earth exultant. Lo! thou canst not rend the earth, nor canst thou stretch to the height of the hills.

The evil of all that is hateful in the sight of thy Lord.

17:37–38

2. The (faithful) slaves of the Beneficent are they who walk upon the earth modestly, and when the foolish ones address them answer: Peace!

25:63

3. Turn not thy cheek in scorn toward folk, nor walk with pertness in the land. Lo! Allah loveth not each braggart boaster.

Be modest in thy bearing and subdue thy voice. Lo! the harshest of all voices is the voice of the ass.

31:18–19

1. وَلَا تَمْشِ فِي الْأَرْضِ مَرَحًا ۖ إِنَّكَ لَن تَخْرِقَ الْأَرْضَ وَلَن تَبْلُغَ الْجِبَالَ طُولًا ۝
كُلُّ ذَٰلِكَ كَانَ سَيِّئُهُ عِندَ رَبِّكَ مَكْرُوهًا ۝

2. وَعِبَادُ الرَّحْمَٰنِ الَّذِينَ يَمْشُونَ عَلَى الْأَرْضِ هَوْنًا وَإِذَا خَاطَبَهُمُ الْجَاهِلُونَ قَالُوا سَلَامًا ۝

3. وَلَا تُصَعِّرْ خَدَّكَ لِلنَّاسِ وَلَا تَمْشِ فِي الْأَرْضِ مَرَحًا ۖ إِنَّ اللَّهَ لَا يُحِبُّ كُلَّ مُخْتَالٍ فَخُورٍ ۝
وَاقْصِدْ فِي مَشْيِكَ وَاغْضُضْ مِن صَوْتِكَ ۚ إِنَّ أَنكَرَ الْأَصْوَاتِ لَصَوْتُ الْحَمِيرِ ۝

See also: Pride.

HUNTING

1. They ask thee (O Muhammad) what is made lawful for them. Say: (All) good things are made lawful for you. And those beasts and birds of prey which ye have trained as hounds are trained, ye teach them that which Allah taught you; so eat of that which they catch for you and mention Allah's name upon it, and observe your duty to Allah. Lo! Allah is swift to take account.

5:4

2. To hunt and to eat the fish of the sea is made lawful for you, a provision for you and for seafarers; but to hunt on land is forbidden you so long as ye are on the pilgrimage. Be mindful of your duty to Allah, unto Whom ye will be gathered.

5:96

HYPOCRITE

1. And of mankind are some who say: We believe in Allah and the Last Day, when they believe not.

They think to beguile Allah and those who believe, and they beguile none save themselves; but they perceive not.

In their hearts is a disease, and Allah increaseth their disease. A painful doom is

1. يسئلونك ماذا أحل لهم قل أحل
لكم الطيبت وما علمتم من الجوارح
مكلبين تعلمونهن مما علمكم الله
فكلوا مما أمسكن عليكم واذكروا اسم
الله عليه واتقوا الله إن الله
سريع الحساب ﴿٤﴾

2. أحل لكم صيد البحر وطعامه متاعا
لكم وللسيارة وحرم عليكم صيد
البر ما دمتم حرما واتقوا الله الذي
إليه تحشرون ﴿٩٦﴾

○

1. ومن الناس من يقول آمنا بالله وباليوم
الآخر وما هم بمؤمنين ﴿٨﴾

يخدعون الله والذين آمنوا وما يخدعون
إلا أنفسهم وما يشعرون ﴿٩﴾

في قلوبهم مرض فزادهم الله مرضا
ولهم عذاب أليم بما كانوا يكذبون ﴿١٠﴾

وإذا قيل لهم لا تفسدوا في الأرض قالوا
إنما نحن مصلحون ﴿١١﴾

ألا إنهم هم المفسدون ولكن لا يشعرون ﴿١٢﴾

وإذا قيل لهم آمنوا كما آمن الناس قالوا
أنؤمن كما آمن السفهاء ألا إنهم هم
السفهاء ولكن لا يعلمون ﴿١٣﴾

theirs because they lie.

And when it is said unto them: Make not mischief in the earth, they say: We are peacemakers only.

Are not they indeed the mischief-makers? But they perceive not.

HUNTING
Ref: 5.1–2;

وَإِذَا لَقُوا الَّذِينَ آمَنُوا قَالُوا آمَنَّا وَإِذَا
خَلَوْا إِلَىٰ شَيَاطِينِهِمْ قَالُوا إِنَّا مَعَكُمْ إِنَّمَا
نَحْنُ مُسْتَهْزِئُونَ ﴿١٤﴾
اللَّهُ يَسْتَهْزِئُ بِهِمْ وَيَمُدُّهُمْ فِي طُغْيَانِهِمْ
يَعْمَهُونَ ﴿١٥﴾
أُولَٰئِكَ الَّذِينَ اشْتَرَوُا الضَّلَالَةَ بِالْهُدَىٰ فَمَا
رَبِحَتْ تِجَارَتُهُمْ وَمَا كَانُوا مُهْتَدِينَ ﴿١٦﴾

2. أَلَمْ تَرَ إِلَى الَّذِينَ يَزْعُمُونَ أَنَّهُمْ آمَنُوا بِمَا
أُنْزِلَ إِلَيْكَ وَمَا أُنْزِلَ مِنْ قَبْلِكَ يُرِيدُونَ
أَنْ يَتَحَاكَمُوا إِلَى الطَّاغُوتِ وَقَدْ أُمِرُوا
أَنْ يَكْفُرُوا بِهِ وَيُرِيدُ الشَّيْطَانُ أَنْ
يُضِلَّهُمْ ضَلَالًا بَعِيدًا ﴿٦٠﴾
وَإِذَا قِيلَ لَهُمْ تَعَالَوْا إِلَىٰ مَا أَنْزَلَ اللَّهُ
وَإِلَى الرَّسُولِ رَأَيْتَ الْمُنَافِقِينَ يَصُدُّونَ
عَنْكَ صُدُودًا ﴿٦١﴾
فَكَيْفَ إِذَا أَصَابَتْهُمْ مُصِيبَةٌ بِمَا قَدَّمَتْ
أَيْدِيهِمْ ثُمَّ جَاءُوكَ يَحْلِفُونَ بِاللَّهِ
إِنْ أَرَدْنَا إِلَّا إِحْسَانًا وَتَوْفِيقًا ﴿٦٢﴾
أُولَٰئِكَ الَّذِينَ يَعْلَمُ اللَّهُ مَا فِي قُلُوبِهِمْ
فَأَعْرِضْ عَنْهُمْ وَعِظْهُمْ وَقُلْ لَهُمْ فِي
أَنْفُسِهِمْ قَوْلًا بَلِيغًا ﴿٦٣﴾

3. فَمَا لَكُمْ فِي الْمُنَافِقِينَ فِئَتَيْنِ وَاللَّهُ
أَرْكَسَهُمْ بِمَا كَسَبُوا أَتُرِيدُونَ أَنْ تَهْدُوا

And when it is said unto them: Believe as the people believe, they say: Shall we believe as the foolish believe? Are not they indeed the foolish? But they know not.

And when they fall in with those who believe, they say: We believe; but when they go apart to their devils they declare: Lo! we are with you; verily we did but mock.

Allah (Himself) doth mock them, leaving them to wander blindly on in their contumacy.

These are they who purchase error at the price of guidance, so their commerce doth not prosper, neither are they guided.

2:8–16

2. Hast thou not seen those who pretend that they believe in that which is revealed unto thee and that which was revealed before thee, how they would go for judgement (in their disputes) to false deities; when they have been ordered to abjure them? Satan would mislead them far astray.

And when it is said unto them: Come unto that which Allah hath revealed and unto the messenger, thou seest the hypocrites turn from thee with aversion.

How would it be if a misfortune smote them because of that which their own hands have sent before (them)? Then would they come unto thee, swearing by Allah that they were seeking naught but harmony and kindness.

Those are they, the secrets of whose hearts Allah knoweth. So oppose them and admonish them, and address

مَنْ أَضَلَّ اللَّهُ ۖ وَمَن يُضْلِلِ اللَّهُ فَلَن
تَجِدَ لَهُ سَبِيلًا ﴿٨٨﴾

4. بَشِّرِ الْمُنَافِقِينَ بِأَنَّ لَهُمْ عَذَابًا أَلِيمًا ﴿١٣٨﴾

5. إِنَّ اللَّهَ جَامِعُ الْمُنَافِقِينَ وَالْكَافِرِينَ
فِي جَهَنَّمَ جَمِيعًا ﴿١٤٠﴾
الَّذِينَ يَتَرَبَّصُونَ بِكُمْ فَإِن كَانَ لَكُمْ
فَتْحٌ مِّنَ اللَّهِ قَالُوا أَلَمْ نَكُن مَّعَكُمْ
وَإِن كَانَ لِلْكَافِرِينَ نَصِيبٌ قَالُوا أَلَمْ
نَسْتَحْوِذْ عَلَيْكُمْ وَنَمْنَعْكُم مِّنَ الْمُؤْمِنِينَ
فَاللَّهُ يَحْكُمُ بَيْنَكُمْ يَوْمَ الْقِيَامَةِ ۗ وَلَن
يَجْعَلَ اللَّهُ لِلْكَافِرِينَ عَلَى الْمُؤْمِنِينَ سَبِيلًا ﴿١٤١﴾
إِنَّ الْمُنَافِقِينَ يُخَادِعُونَ اللَّهَ وَهُوَ خَادِعُهُمْ
وَإِذَا قَامُوا إِلَى الصَّلَاةِ قَامُوا كُسَالَىٰ
يُرَاءُونَ النَّاسَ وَلَا يَذْكُرُونَ اللَّهَ إِلَّا قَلِيلًا ﴿١٤٢﴾
مُّذَبْذَبِينَ بَيْنَ ذَٰلِكَ لَا إِلَىٰ هَٰؤُلَاءِ
وَلَا إِلَىٰ هَٰؤُلَاءِ ۚ وَمَن يُضْلِلِ اللَّهُ فَلَن
تَجِدَ لَهُ سَبِيلًا ﴿١٤٣﴾

6. إِنَّ الْمُنَافِقِينَ فِي الدَّرْكِ الْأَسْفَلِ
مِنَ النَّارِ وَلَن تَجِدَ لَهُمْ نَصِيرًا ﴿١٤٥﴾

7. الْمُنَافِقُونَ وَالْمُنَافِقَاتُ بَعْضُهُم مِّن بَعْضٍ
يَأْمُرُونَ بِالْمُنكَرِ وَيَنْهَوْنَ عَنِ الْمَعْرُوفِ
وَيَقْبِضُونَ أَيْدِيَهُمْ ۚ نَسُوا اللَّهَ فَنَسِيَهُمْ
إِنَّ الْمُنَافِقِينَ هُمُ الْفَاسِقُونَ ﴿٦٧﴾

them in plain terms about their souls.

4:60–63

3. What aileth you that ye are become two parties regarding the hypocrites, when Allah cast them back (to disbelief) because of what they earned? Seek you to guide him whom Allah hath sent astray? He whom Allah sendeth astray, for him thou (O Muhammad) canst not find a road.

4:88

4. Bear unto the hypocrites the tidings that for them there is a painful doom;

4:138

5. Lo! Allah will gather hypocrites and disbelievers, all together, into hell:

Those who wait upon occasion in regard to you and, if a victory cometh unto you from Allah, say: Are we not with you? and if the disbelievers meet with a success say: Had we not the mastery of you, and did we not protect you from the believers?– Allah will judge between you at the Day of Resurrection, and Allah will not give the disbelievers any way (of success) against the believers.

Lo! the hypocrites seek to beguile Allah, but it is Allah who beguileth them. When they stand up to wor–ship they perform it languidly and to be seen of men, and are mindful of Allah but little;

Swaying between this (and that), (belonging) neither to these nor to those. He whom Allah causeth to go astray thou (O Muhammad) .wilt not find a way for him

4:140–143

6. Lo! the hypocrites (will be) in the lowest deep of the fire, and thou wilt find not helper for them;

4:145

7. The hypocrites, both men and women proceed one from another. They enjoin the wrong and they forbid the right and they withhold their hands (from spending for the cause of Allah). They forget Allah, so He hath forgotten them. Lo! the hypocrites, they are the transgressors.

Allah promiseth the hypocrites, both men and women, and the disbelievers fire of hell for their abode. It will suffice them. Allah curseth them, and theirs is the lasting torment.

9:67–68

8. Those who point at such of the believers as give the alms willingly and such as can find naught to give but their endeavours, and deride them—Allah (Himself) derideth them. Theirs will be a painful doom.

Ask forgiveness for them (O Muhammad), or ask not forgiveness for them; though thou ask forgiveness for them seventy times, Allah will not forgive them. That is because they disbelieved in Allah and His messenger, and Allah guideth not wrongdoing folk.

9:79–80

9. If the hypocrites, and

وَعَدَ اللّٰهُ الْمُنٰفِقِيْنَ وَ الْمُنٰفِقٰتِ وَ الْكُفَّارَ
نَارَ جَهَنَّمَ خٰلِدِيْنَ فِيْهَا ۭ هِيَ حَسْبُهُمْ ۚ
وَلَعَنَهُمُ اللّٰهُ ۚ وَلَهُمْ عَذَابٌ مُّقِيْمٌ
الَّذِيْنَ يَلْمِزُوْنَ الْمُطَّوِّعِيْنَ مِنَ الْمُؤْمِنِيْنَ فِي 8.
الصَّدَقٰتِ وَالَّذِيْنَ لَا يَجِدُوْنَ اِلَّا جُهْدَهُمْ فَيَسْخَرُوْنَ
مِنْهُمْ ۭ سَخِرَ اللّٰهُ مِنْهُمْ ۡ وَلَهُمْ عَذَابٌ اَلِيْمٌ
اِسْتَغْفِرْ لَهُمْ اَوْ لَا تَسْتَغْفِرْ لَهُمْ ۭ اِنْ
تَسْتَغْفِرْ لَهُمْ سَبْعِيْنَ مَرَّةً فَلَنْ يَّغْفِرَ
اللّٰهُ لَهُمْ ۭ ذٰلِكَ بِاَنَّهُمْ كَفَرُوْا بِاللّٰهِ
وَرَسُوْلِهٖ ۭ وَاللّٰهُ لَا يَهْدِي الْقَوْمَ الْفٰسِقِيْنَ
لَئِنْ لَّمْ يَنْتَهِ الْمُنٰفِقُوْنَ وَالَّذِيْنَ 9.
فِيْ قُلُوْبِهِمْ مَّرَضٌ وَّالْمُرْجِفُوْنَ فِي
الْمَدِيْنَةِ لَنُغْرِيَنَّكَ بِهِمْ ثُمَّ لَا
يُجَاوِرُوْنَكَ فِيْهَآ اِلَّا قَلِيْلًا
مَّلْعُوْنِيْنَ ۚ اَيْنَمَا ثُقِفُوْٓا اُخِذُوْا وَقُتِّلُوْا
تَقْتِيْلًا
يَوْمَ تَرَى الْمُؤْمِنِيْنَ وَالْمُؤْمِنٰتِ 10.
يَسْعٰى نُوْرُهُمْ بَيْنَ اَيْدِيْهِمْ وَ
بِاَيْمَانِهِمْ بُشْرٰىكُمُ الْيَوْمَ جَنّٰتٌ
تَجْرِيْ مِنْ تَحْتِهَا الْاَنْهٰرُ خٰلِدِيْنَ
فِيْهَا ۭ ذٰلِكَ هُوَ الْفَوْزُ الْعَظِيْمُ
يَوْمَ يَقُوْلُ الْمُنٰفِقُوْنَ وَالْمُنٰفِقٰتُ
لِلَّذِيْنَ اٰمَنُوا انْظُرُوْنَا نَقْتَبِسْ مِنْ

those in whose hearts is a disease, and the alarmists in the city do not cease, We verily shall urge thee on against them, then they will be your neighbours in it but a little while.

Accursed, they will be seized wherever found and slain with a (fierce) slaughter.

33:60–61

10. On the day when thou (Muhammad) wilt see the believers, men and women, their light shining forth before them and on their right hands, (and wilt hear it said unto them): Glad news for you this day: Gardens underneath which rivers flow, wherein ye are immortal. That is the Supreme triumph.

On the day when the hypocritical men and the hypocritical women will say unto those who believe: Look on us that we may borrow from your light! it will be said: Go back and seek for light! Then there will separate them a wall wherein is a gate, the inner side whereof containeth mercy, while the outer side thereof is toward the doom.

They will cry unto them (saying): Were we not with you? They will say: Yea, verily but ye tempted one another, and hesitated, and doubted, and vain desires beguiled you till the ordinance of Allah came to pass; and the deceiver deceived you concerning Allah;

So this Day no ransom

نُوْرِكُمْ قِيْلَ ارْجِعُوْا وَرَآءَكُمْ
فَالْتَمِسُوْا نُوْرًا فَضُرِبَ بَيْنَهُمْ بِسُوْرٍ
لَّهٗ بَابٌ بَاطِنُهٗ فِيْهِ الرَّحْمَةُ وَظَاهِرُهٗ
مِنْ قِبَلِهِ الْعَذَابُ ﴿١٣﴾
يُنَادُوْنَهُمْ اَلَمْ نَكُنْ مَّعَكُمْ قَالُوْا بَلٰى
وَلٰكِنَّكُمْ فَتَنْتُمْ اَنْفُسَكُمْ وَتَرَبَّصْتُمْ
وَارْتَبْتُمْ وَغَرَّتْكُمُ الْاَمَانِيُّ حَتّٰى جَآءَ
اَمْرُ اللّٰهِ وَغَرَّكُمْ بِاللّٰهِ الْغَرُوْرُ ﴿١٤﴾
فَالْيَوْمَ لَا يُؤْخَذُ مِنْكُمْ فِدْيَةٌ وَّلَا
مِنَ الَّذِيْنَ كَفَرُوْا مَاْوٰىكُمُ النَّارُ
هِيَ مَوْلٰىكُمْ وَبِئْسَ الْمَصِيْرُ ﴿١٥﴾

○

can be taken from you nor from those who disbelieved. Your home is the Fire; that is your patron, and a hapless journey's end.

57:12–15

Ref: 7:138; 20:91; 21:52; 22:25; 26:71; 48:25.

See also: Dissimulation.

'IDDAH

1. When ye have divorced women, and they have reached their term, then retain them in kindness or release them in kindness. Retain them not to their hurt so that ye trans-gress (the limits). He who doth that hath wronged his soul.

2:231

2. Such of you as die and leave behind them wives, they (the wives) shall wait, keeping themselves apart, four months and ten days. And when they reach the term (prescribed for them) then there is no sin for you in aught that they may do with them-selves in decency. Allah is Informed of what ye do.

2:234

3. And do not consummate the marriage until (the term) prescribed is run. Know that Allah knoweth what is in your minds so beware of Him; and know that Allah is Forgiving, Clement

2:235

4. O ye who believe! If ye wed believing women and divorce them before ye have touched them, then there is no period that ye should reckon. But content them and release them handsomely.

33:49

1. وَإِذَا طَلَّقْتُمُ النِّسَاءَ فَبَلَغْنَ أَجَلَهُنَّ
فَأَمْسِكُوهُنَّ بِمَعْرُوفٍ أَوْ سَرِّحُوهُنَّ
بِمَعْرُوفٍ ۚ وَلَا تُمْسِكُوهُنَّ ضِرَارًا لِتَعْتَدُوا ۚ
وَمَنْ يَفْعَلْ ذَٰلِكَ فَقَدْ ظَلَمَ نَفْسَهُ ۚ

2. وَالَّذِينَ يُتَوَفَّوْنَ مِنْكُمْ وَيَذَرُونَ أَزْوَاجًا
يَتَرَبَّصْنَ بِأَنْفُسِهِنَّ أَرْبَعَةَ أَشْهُرٍ وَعَشْرًا ۖ
فَإِذَا بَلَغْنَ أَجَلَهُنَّ فَلَا جُنَاحَ عَلَيْكُمْ فِيمَا
فَعَلْنَ فِي أَنْفُسِهِنَّ بِالْمَعْرُوفِ ۗ وَاللَّهُ بِمَا
تَعْمَلُونَ خَبِيرٌ ﴿٢٣٤﴾

3. وَلَا تَعْزِمُوا عُقْدَةَ النِّكَاحِ حَتَّىٰ يَبْلُغَ الْكِتَابُ
أَجَلَهُ ۚ وَاعْلَمُوا أَنَّ اللَّهَ يَعْلَمُ مَا فِي
أَنْفُسِكُمْ فَاحْذَرُوهُ ۚ وَاعْلَمُوا أَنَّ اللَّهَ
غَفُورٌ حَلِيمٌ ﴿٢٣٥﴾

4. يَا أَيُّهَا الَّذِينَ آمَنُوا إِذَا نَكَحْتُمُ
الْمُؤْمِنَاتِ ثُمَّ طَلَّقْتُمُوهُنَّ مِنْ قَبْلِ
أَنْ تَمَسُّوهُنَّ فَمَا لَكُمْ عَلَيْهِنَّ مِنْ
عِدَّةٍ تَعْتَدُّونَهَا ۖ فَمَتِّعُوهُنَّ وَ
سَرِّحُوهُنَّ سَرَاحًا جَمِيلًا ﴿٤٩﴾

5. يَا أَيُّهَا النَّبِيُّ إِذَا طَلَّقْتُمُ النِّسَاءَ فَطَلِّقُوهُنَّ
لِعِدَّتِهِنَّ وَأَحْصُوا الْعِدَّةَ ۖ وَاتَّقُوا
اللَّهَ رَبَّكُمْ ۖ لَا تُخْرِجُوهُنَّ مِنْ
بُيُوتِهِنَّ وَلَا يَخْرُجْنَ إِلَّا أَنْ يَأْتِينَ
بِفَاحِشَةٍ مُبَيِّنَةٍ ۚ وَتِلْكَ حُدُودُ
اللَّهِ ۚ وَمَنْ يَتَعَدَّ حُدُودَ اللَّهِ فَقَدْ

5. O Prophet! When ye (men) put away women, put them away for their (legal) period and reckon the period, and keep your duty to Allah, your Lord. Expel them not from

their houses nor let them go forth unless they commit open immorality. Such are the limits (imposed by) Allah, and who—so transgresseth Allah's limits, he verily wrongeth his soul. Thou knowest not: it may be that Allah will afterward bring some new thing to pass.

Then, when they have reached their term, take them back in kindness or part from them in kindness, and call to witness two just men among you, and keep your testimony upright for Allah. Whoso believeth in Allah and the Last Day is exhorted to act thus. And whosoever keepeth his duty to Allah, Allah will appoint a way out for him,

65: 1—2

6. And for such of your women as despair of menstru—ation, if ye doubt, their period (of waiting) shall be three months, along with those who have it not. And for those with child, their period shall be till they bring forth their burden. And whosoever keepeth his duty to Allah, He maketh his course easy for him.

65:4

7. Lodge them where ye dwell, according to your wealth, and harass them not so as to straiten life for them. And if they are with child, then spend for them till they bring forth their burden. Then,

ظلم نفسه لا تدري لعل الله
يحدث بعد ذلك أمرا
فإذا بلغن أجلهن فأمسكوهن
بمعروف أو فارقوهن بمعروف
وأشهدوا ذوي عدل منكم
وأقيموا الشهادة لله ذلكم يوعظ
به من كان يؤمن بالله واليوم
الآخر ومن يتق الله يجعل له
مخرجا

6. واللائي يئسن من المحيض من
نسائكم إن ارتبتم فعدتهن ثلاثة
أشهر واللائي لم يحضن وأولات
الأحمال أجلهن أن يضعن حملهن
ومن يتق الله يجعل له من
أمره يسرا

7. أسكنوهن من حيث سكنتم من
وجدكم ولا تضاروهن لتضيقوا
عليهن وإن كن أولات حمل
فأنفقوا عليهن حتى يضعن حملهن
فإن أرضعن لكم فآتوهن أجورهن
وأتمروا بينكم بمعروف وإن
تعاسرتم فسترضع له أخرى

if they give suck for you, give them their due payment and consult together in kind—ness; but if ye make diffi—culties for one another, then let some other woman give suck for him (the father of the child).

65:6

See also: Divorce, *Mahr*

IDOLATRY

1. (Remember) When Abraham said unto his father Azar: Takest thou idols for gods? Lo! I see thee and thy folk in error manifest.

6:74

2. And when Abraham said: My Lord! Make safe this territory, and preserve me and my sons from serving idols.

My Lord! Lo! they have led many of mankind astray. But whoso followeth me, he verily is of me. And whoso disobeyeth me—Still Thou art Forgiving, Merciful.

14:35–36

3. And We verily gave Abraham of old his proper course, and We were Aware of him,

When he said unto his father and his folk: What are these images unto which ye pay devotion?

They said: We found our fathers worshippers of them.

He said: Verily ye and your fathers were in plain error.

They said: Bringest thou unto us the truth, or art thou some jester?

He said: Nay, but your Lord is the Lord of the heavens and the earth, Who created them; and I am of those who testify unto that.

And, by Allah, I shall circumvent your idols after ye have gone away and turned your backs.

Then he reduced them

1. وَإِذْ قَالَ إِبْرَاهِيمُ لِأَبِيهِ آزَرَ أَتَتَّخِذُ
أَصْنَامًا آلِهَةً ۚ إِنِّي أَرَاكَ وَقَوْمَكَ
فِي ضَلَالٍ مُبِينٍ ﴿٧٤﴾

2. وَإِذْ قَالَ إِبْرَاهِيمُ رَبِّ اجْعَلْ هَٰذَا
الْبَلَدَ آمِنًا وَاجْنُبْنِي وَبَنِيَّ أَنْ
نَعْبُدَ الْأَصْنَامَ ﴿٣٥﴾
رَبِّ إِنَّهُنَّ أَضْلَلْنَ كَثِيرًا مِنَ النَّاسِ
فَمَنْ تَبِعَنِي فَإِنَّهُ مِنِّي وَمَنْ عَصَانِي فَإِنَّكَ
غَفُورٌ رَحِيمٌ ﴿٣٦﴾

3. وَلَقَدْ آتَيْنَا إِبْرَاهِيمَ رُشْدَهُ مِنْ
قَبْلُ وَكُنَّا بِهِ عَالِمِينَ ﴿٥١﴾
إِذْ قَالَ لِأَبِيهِ وَقَوْمِهِ مَا هَٰذِهِ
التَّمَاثِيلُ الَّتِي أَنْتُمْ لَهَا عَاكِفُونَ ﴿٥٢﴾
قَالُوا وَجَدْنَا آبَاءَنَا لَهَا عَابِدِينَ ﴿٥٣﴾
قَالَ لَقَدْ كُنْتُمْ أَنْتُمْ وَآبَاؤُكُمْ
فِي ضَلَالٍ مُبِينٍ ﴿٥٤﴾
قَالُوا أَجِئْتَنَا بِالْحَقِّ أَمْ أَنْتَ مِنَ
اللَّاعِبِينَ ﴿٥٥﴾
قَالَ بَلْ رَبُّكُمْ رَبُّ السَّمَاوَاتِ
وَالْأَرْضِ الَّذِي فَطَرَهُنَّ وَأَنَا عَلَىٰ
ذَٰلِكُمْ مِنَ الشَّاهِدِينَ ﴿٥٦﴾
وَتَاللَّهِ لَأَكِيدَنَّ أَصْنَامَكُمْ بَعْدَ
أَنْ تُوَلُّوا مُدْبِرِينَ ﴿٥٧﴾
فَجَعَلَهُمْ جُذَاذًا إِلَّا كَبِيرًا لَهُمْ لَعَلَّهُمْ
إِلَيْهِ يَرْجِعُونَ ﴿٥٨﴾

to fragments, all save the chief of them, that haply they might have recourse to it.

They said: Who hath done this to our gods? Surely it must be some evil—doer.

They said: We heard a youth make mention of them, who is called Abraham.

They said: Then bring him (hither) before the people's eyes that they may testify.

They said: Is it thou who hast done this to our gods, O Abraham?

He said: But this, their chief hath done it. So question them, if they can speak.

Then gathered they apart and said: Lo! ye yourselves are the wrong–doers.

And they were utterly confounded, and they said: Well thou knowest that these speak not.

He said: Worship ye then instead of Allah that which cannot profit you at all, nor harm you?

Fie on you and all that ye worship instead of Allah!

21:51–67

4. So shun the filth of idols and shun lying speech,

Turning unto Allah (only), not ascribing partners unto Him; for whoso ascribeth partners unto Allah, it is as if he had fallen from the sky and the birds had snatched him or the wind had blown him to a far-off place.

22:30–31

قَالُوْا مَنْ فَعَلَ هٰذَا بِاٰلِهَتِنَآ
لَمِنَ الظّٰلِمِيْنَ ﴿٥٩﴾
قَالُوْا سَمِعْنَا فَتًى يَّذْكُرُهُمْ يُقَالُ
لَهٗٓ اِبْرٰهِيْمُ ﴿٦٠﴾
قَالُوْا فَاْتُوْا بِهٖ عَلٰٓى اَعْيُنِ النَّاسِ
لَعَلَّهُمْ يَشْهَدُوْنَ ﴿٦١﴾
قَالُوْٓا ءَاَنْتَ فَعَلْتَ هٰذَا بِاٰلِهَتِنَا
يٰٓاِبْرٰهِيْمُ ﴿٦٢﴾
قَالَ بَلْ فَعَلَهٗ ۖ كَبِيْرُهُمْ هٰذَا
فَسْئَلُوْهُمْ اِنْ كَانُوْا يَنْطِقُوْنَ ﴿٦٣﴾
فَرَجَعُوْٓا اِلٰٓى اَنْفُسِهِمْ فَقَالُوْٓا اِنَّكُمْ
اَنْتُمُ الظّٰلِمُوْنَ ﴿٦٤﴾
ثُمَّ نُكِسُوْا عَلٰى رُءُوْسِهِمْ ۚ لَقَدْ
عَلِمْتَ مَا هٰٓؤُلَآءِ يَنْطِقُوْنَ ﴿٦٥﴾
قَالَ اَفَتَعْبُدُوْنَ مِنْ دُوْنِ اللّٰهِ مَا لَا
يَنْفَعُكُمْ شَيْـًٔا وَّلَا يَضُرُّكُمْ ﴿٦٦﴾
اُفٍّ لَّكُمْ وَلِمَا تَعْبُدُوْنَ مِنْ دُوْنِ اللّٰهِ
4. فَاجْتَنِبُوا الرِّجْسَ مِنَ الْاَوْثَانِ وَاجْتَنِبُوْا
قَوْلَ الزُّوْرِ ﴿٣٠﴾
حُنَفَآءَ لِلّٰهِ غَيْرَ مُشْرِكِيْنَ بِهٖ ۚ وَمَنْ
يُّشْرِكْ بِاللّٰهِ فَكَاَنَّمَا خَرَّ مِنَ السَّمَآءِ
فَتَخْطَفُهُ الطَّيْرُ اَوْ تَهْوِيْ بِهِ الرِّيْحُ
فِيْ مَكَانٍ سَحِيْقٍ ﴿٣١﴾

Ref: 7:138,139; 34:13.
See also: Names of Idols, Refutation of Polytheism.

IFK

1. إِنَّ الَّذِينَ جَاءُو بِالْإِفْكِ عُصْبَةٌ
مِّنكُمْ ۚ لَا تَحْسَبُوهُ شَرًّا لَّكُم ۖ بَلْ
هُوَ خَيْرٌ لَّكُمْ ۚ لِكُلِّ امْرِئٍ مِّنْهُم
مَّا اكْتَسَبَ مِنَ الْإِثْمِ ۚ وَالَّذِي تَوَلَّىٰ
كِبْرَهُ مِنْهُمْ لَهُ عَذَابٌ عَظِيمٌ ﴿١١﴾
لَّوْلَا إِذْ سَمِعْتُمُوهُ ظَنَّ الْمُؤْمِنُونَ
وَالْمُؤْمِنَاتُ بِأَنفُسِهِمْ خَيْرًا وَقَالُوا
هَٰذَا إِفْكٌ مُّبِينٌ ﴿١٢﴾
لَّوْلَا جَاءُو عَلَيْهِ بِأَرْبَعَةِ شُهَدَاءَ ۚ
فَإِذْ لَمْ يَأْتُوا بِالشُّهَدَاءِ فَأُولَٰئِكَ
عِندَ اللَّهِ هُمُ الْكَاذِبُونَ ﴿١٣﴾
وَلَوْلَا فَضْلُ اللَّهِ عَلَيْكُمْ وَرَحْمَتُهُ
فِي الدُّنْيَا وَالْآخِرَةِ لَمَسَّكُمْ فِي مَا
أَفَضْتُمْ فِيهِ عَذَابٌ عَظِيمٌ ﴿١٤﴾
إِذْ تَلَقَّوْنَهُ بِأَلْسِنَتِكُمْ وَتَقُولُونَ
بِأَفْوَاهِكُم مَّا لَيْسَ لَكُم بِهِ عِلْمٌ
وَتَحْسَبُونَهُ هَيِّنًا وَهُوَ عِندَ اللَّهِ عَظِيمٌ ﴿١٥﴾
وَلَوْلَا إِذْ سَمِعْتُمُوهُ قُلْتُم مَّا يَكُونُ
لَنَا أَن نَّتَكَلَّمَ بِهَٰذَا سُبْحَانَكَ هَٰذَا
بُهْتَانٌ عَظِيمٌ ﴿١٦﴾
يَعِظُكُمُ اللَّهُ أَن تَعُودُوا لِمِثْلِهِ أَبَدًا
إِن كُنتُم مُّؤْمِنِينَ ﴿١٧﴾
وَيُبَيِّنُ اللَّهُ لَكُمُ الْآيَاتِ ۚ وَاللَّهُ
عَلِيمٌ حَكِيمٌ ﴿١٨﴾

1. Lo! they who spread the slander are a gang among you. Deem it not a bad thing for you; nay, it is good for you. Unto every man of them (will be paid) that which he hath earned of the sin; and as for him among them who had the greater share therein, his will be an awful doom.

Why did not the believers, men and women, when ye heard it, think good of their own folk, and say: It is a manifest untruth?

Why did they not produce four witnesses? Since they produce not witnesses, they verily are liars in the sight of Allah.

Had it not been for the grace of Allah and His mercy unto you in the world and the Hereafter, an awful doom had overtaken you for that whereof ye murmured.

When ye welcomed it with your tongues, and uttered with your mouths that whereof ye had no knowledge, ye counted it a trifle. In the sight of Allah it is very great.

Wherefor, when ye heard it, said ye not: It is not for us to speak of this. Glory be to Thee (O Allah)! This is awful calumny.

Allah admonisheth you that ye repeat not the like thereof ever, if ye are (in truth) believers.

And He expoundeth unto you the revelations. Allah is Knower, Wise.

24:11–18

See also: Slander.

IGNORANCE

1. Keep to forgiveness (O Muhammad), and enjoin kindness, and turn away from the ignorant.
7:199

2. He said: Oh Noah! Lo! he is not of thy household; lo! he is of evil conduct, so ask not of Me that whereof thou hast no knowledge. I admonish thee lest thou be among the ignorant.
11:46

3. Then lo! thy Lord—for those who do evil in ignorance and afterward repent and amend—lo! (for them) thy Lord is afterward indeed Forgiving, Merciful.
16:119

4. The (faithful) slaves of the Beneficent are they who walk upon the earth modestly, and when the foolish ones address them answer: Peace!
25:63

5. And when they hear vanity they withdraw from it and say: Unto us our works and unto you your works. Peace be unto you! We desire not the ignorant.
28:55

6. O ye who believe! If an evil-liver bring you tidings, verify it, lest ye smite some folk in ignorance and afterward repent of what ye did.
49:6

1. خُذِ الْعَفْوَ وَأْمُرْ بِالْعُرْفِ وَأَعْرِضْ
عَنِ الْجٰهِلِيْنَ ۝

2. قَالَ يٰنُوْحُ اِنَّهٗ لَيْسَ مِنْ اَهْلِكَ ۚ اِنَّهٗ
عَمَلٌ غَيْرُ صَالِحٍ ۖ فَلَا تَسْـَٔلْنِ مَا لَيْسَ
لَكَ بِهٖ عِلْمٌ ۗ اِنِّيْۤ اَعِظُكَ اَنْ تَكُوْنَ
مِنَ الْجٰهِلِيْنَ ۝

3. ثُمَّ اِنَّ رَبَّكَ لِلَّذِيْنَ عَمِلُوا السُّوْۤءَ بِجَهَالَةٍ
ثُمَّ تَابُوْا مِنْۢ بَعْدِ ذٰلِكَ وَاَصْلَحُوْۤا ۙ اِنَّ
رَبَّكَ مِنْۢ بَعْدِهَا لَغَفُوْرٌ رَّحِيْمٌ ۝

4. وَعِبَادُ الرَّحْمٰنِ الَّذِيْنَ يَمْشُوْنَ عَلَى
الْاَرْضِ هَوْنًا وَّاِذَا خَاطَبَهُمُ الْجٰهِلُوْنَ
قَالُوْا سَلٰمًا ۝

5. وَاِذَا سَمِعُوا اللَّغْوَ اَعْرَضُوْا عَنْهُ وَ
قَالُوْا لَنَاۤ اَعْمَالُنَا وَلَكُمْ اَعْمَالُكُمْ ۖ
سَلٰمٌ عَلَيْكُمْ ۖ لَا نَبْتَغِى الْجٰهِلِيْنَ ۝

6. يٰۤاَيُّهَا الَّذِيْنَ اٰمَنُوْۤا اِنْ جَاۤءَكُمْ
فَاسِقٌۢ بِنَبَاٍ فَتَبَيَّنُوْۤا اَنْ تُصِيْبُوْا
قَوْمًاۢ بِجَهَالَةٍ فَتُصْبِحُوْا عَلٰى مَا
فَعَلْتُمْ نٰدِمِيْنَ ۝

Ref: 2:67; 6:35; 25:63; 39:64; 48:26.
See also: Knowledge.

IMAM

1. And (remember) when his Lord tried Abraham with (His) commands, and he fulfilled them, He said: Lo! I have appointed thee a leader for mankind. (Abraham) said: And of my offspring (will there be leaders)? He said: My covenant includeth not wrongdoers.

2:124

2. On the day when We shall summon all men with their record, whoso is given his book in his right hand—such will read their book and they will not be wronged as shred.

Whoso is blind here will be blind in the Hereafter, and yet further from the road.

17:71–72

3. And who say: Our Lord! Vouchsafe us comfort of our wives and of our offspring, and make us patterns for (all) those who ward off (evil).

They will be awarded the high place forasmuch as they were steadfast, and they will meet therein with welcome and the word of Peace,

Abiding there for ever. Happy is it as abode and station!

25:74–76

1. وَإِذِ ابْتَلَىٰ إِبْرَاهِيمَ رَبُّهُ بِكَلِمَاتٍ فَأَتَمَّهُنَّ ۖ
قَالَ إِنِّي جَاعِلُكَ لِلنَّاسِ إِمَامًا ۖ قَالَ وَمِنْ
ذُرِّيَّتِي ۖ قَالَ لَا يَنَالُ عَهْدِي الظَّالِمِينَ ﴿١٢٤﴾

2. يَوْمَ نَدْعُو كُلَّ أُنَاسٍ بِإِمَامِهِمْ ۖ فَمَنْ
أُوتِيَ كِتَابَهُ بِيَمِينِهِ فَأُولَٰئِكَ يَقْرَءُونَ
كِتَابَهُمْ وَلَا يُظْلَمُونَ فَتِيلًا ﴿٧١﴾
وَمَنْ كَانَ فِي هَٰذِهِ أَعْمَىٰ فَهُوَ فِي
الْآخِرَةِ أَعْمَىٰ وَأَضَلُّ سَبِيلًا ﴿٧٢﴾

3. وَالَّذِينَ يَقُولُونَ رَبَّنَا هَبْ لَنَا مِنْ
أَزْوَاجِنَا وَذُرِّيَّاتِنَا قُرَّةَ أَعْيُنٍ وَاجْعَلْنَا
لِلْمُتَّقِينَ إِمَامًا ﴿٧٤﴾
أُولَٰئِكَ يُجْزَوْنَ الْغُرْفَةَ بِمَا صَبَرُوا
وَيُلَقَّوْنَ فِيهَا تَحِيَّةً وَسَلَامًا ﴿٧٥﴾
خَالِدِينَ فِيهَا ۚ حَسُنَتْ مُسْتَقَرًّا
وَمُقَامًا ﴿٧٦﴾

Ref: 9:12; 21:73; 28:4,41; 32:24.

See also: Leaders and Their Followers

INCOMPARABILITY OF QUR'ĀN

1. And if ye are in doubt concerning that which We reveal unto Our slave (Muhammad), then produce a surah of the like thereof, and call your witnesses beside Allah if ye are truthful.

And if ye do it not—and ye can never do it—then guard yourselves against the Fire prepared for disbelievers, whose fuel is of men and stones.

2:23–24

2. And this Qur'ān is not such as could ever be invented in despite of Allah; but it is a confirmation of that which was before it and an exposition of that which is decreed for mankind—There-in is no doubt—from the Lord of the Worlds.

Or say they: He hath invented it? Say: Then bring a surah like unto it, and call (for help) on all ye can be-sides Allah, if ye are truthful.

10:37–38

3. Say: Verily, though mankind and the Jinn should assemble to produce the like of this Qur'ān, they could not

1. وَإِنْ كُنْتُمْ فِي رَيْبٍ مِمَّا نَزَّلْنَا عَلَىٰ عَبْدِنَا
فَأْتُوا بِسُورَةٍ مِنْ مِثْلِهِ وَادْعُوا شُهَدَاءَكُمْ
مِنْ دُونِ اللَّهِ إِنْ كُنْتُمْ صَادِقِينَ ﴿٢٣﴾
فَإِنْ لَمْ تَفْعَلُوا وَلَنْ تَفْعَلُوا فَاتَّقُوا النَّارَ الَّتِي
وَقُودُهَا النَّاسُ وَالْحِجَارَةُ أُعِدَّتْ لِلْكَافِرِينَ ﴿٢٤﴾

2. وَمَا كَانَ هَٰذَا الْقُرْآنُ أَنْ يُفْتَرَىٰ
مِنْ دُونِ اللَّهِ وَلَٰكِنْ تَصْدِيقَ الَّذِي
بَيْنَ يَدَيْهِ وَتَفْصِيلَ الْكِتَابِ لَا رَيْبَ
فِيهِ مِنْ رَبِّ الْعَالَمِينَ ﴿٣٧﴾
أَمْ يَقُولُونَ افْتَرَاهُ ۖ قُلْ فَأْتُوا بِسُورَةٍ
مِثْلِهِ وَادْعُوا مَنِ اسْتَطَعْتُمْ مِنْ دُونِ
اللَّهِ إِنْ كُنْتُمْ صَادِقِينَ ﴿٣٨﴾

3. قُلْ لَئِنِ اجْتَمَعَتِ الْإِنْسُ وَالْجِنُّ عَلَىٰ
أَنْ يَأْتُوا بِمِثْلِ هَٰذَا الْقُرْآنِ لَا يَأْتُونَ
بِمِثْلِهِ وَلَوْ كَانَ بَعْضُهُمْ لِبَعْضٍ ظَهِيرًا ﴿٨٨﴾

O

produce the like thereof though they were helpers one of another.

17:88

· Ref. 11:13; 28:49; 52:33.

INFANTICIDE

1. And that ye slay not your children because of penury— We provide for you and for them.

6:151

2. Slay not your children, fearing a fall to poverty. We shall provide for them and for you. Lo! the slaying of them is great sin.

17:31

INGRATITUDE

1. And if We cause man to taste some mercy from Us and afterward withdraw it from him, lo! he is despairing, thankless.

And if We cause him to taste grace after some misfortune that had befallen him, he saith: The ills have gone from me. Lo! he is exultant, boastful;

11:9–10

2. And whatever of comfort ye enjoy, it is from Allah. Then, when misfortune reacheth you, unto Him ye cry for help!

And afterward, when He hath rid you of the misfortune, behold! a set of you attribute partners to their Lord,

So as to deny that which We have given them. Then enjoy life (while ye may) for ye will come to know.

16:53–55

3. And when harm toucheth

1. وَلَا تَقْتُلُوٓا أَوْلَادَكُم مِّنْ إِمْلَاقٍ ۖ نَّحْنُ
نَرْزُقُكُمْ وَإِيَّاهُمْ ۖ

2. وَلَا تَقْتُلُوٓا أَوْلَادَكُمْ خَشْيَةَ إِمْلَاقٍ ۖ
نَّحْنُ نَرْزُقُهُمْ وَإِيَّاكُمْ ۚ إِنَّ قَتْلَهُمْ
كَانَ خِطْـًٔا كَبِيرًا ﴿٣١﴾

○

1. وَلَئِنْ أَذَقْنَا الْإِنسَانَ مِنَّا رَحْمَةً ثُمَّ
نَزَعْنَاهَا مِنْهُ ۚ إِنَّهُ لَيَئُوسٌ كَفُورٌ ﴿٩﴾
وَلَئِنْ أَذَقْنَاهُ نَعْمَاءَ بَعْدَ ضَرَّاءَ مَسَّتْهُ
لَيَقُولَنَّ ذَهَبَ السَّيِّئَاتُ عَنِّي ۚ إِنَّهُ لَفَرِحٌ فَخُورٌ ﴿١٠﴾

2. وَمَا بِكُم مِّن نِّعْمَةٍ فَمِنَ اللَّهِ ۖ ثُمَّ إِذَا
مَسَّكُمُ الضُّرُّ فَإِلَيْهِ تَجْأَرُونَ ﴿٥٣﴾
ثُمَّ إِذَا كَشَفَ الضُّرَّ عَنكُمْ إِذَا فَرِيقٌ
مِّنكُم بِرَبِّهِمْ يُشْرِكُونَ ﴿٥٤﴾
لِيَكْفُرُوا بِمَا آتَيْنَاهُمْ ۚ فَتَمَتَّعُوا ۖ
فَسَوْفَ تَعْلَمُونَ ﴿٥٥﴾

3. وَإِذَا مَسَّكُمُ الضُّرُّ فِي الْبَحْرِ ضَلَّ مَن
تَدْعُونَ إِلَّا إِيَّاهُ ۖ فَلَمَّا نَجَّاكُمْ إِلَى
الْبَرِّ أَعْرَضْتُمْ ۚ وَكَانَ الْإِنسَانُ كَفُورًا ﴿٦٧﴾

you upon the sea, all unto whom ye cry (for succour) fail save Him (alone), but when He bringeth you safe to land, ye turn away, for man was ever thankless.

17:67

INFANTICIDE **Ref: 81:8–9.**

4. And when harm toucheth men they cry unto their Lord, turning to Him in repentance; then, when they have tasted of His mercy, behold! some of them attribute partners to their Lord,

So as to disbelieve in that which We have given them. (Unto such it is said): Enjoy yourselves awhile, but ye will come to know.

30:33–34

5. If ye are thankless, yet Allah is Independent of you, though He is not pleased with thanklessness for His bondmen; and if ye are thankful He is pleased therewith for you. No laden soul will bear another's load. Then unto your Lord is your return; and He will tell you what ye used to do. Lo! He knoweth what is in the breasts (of men).

And when some hurt toucheth man, he crieth unto his Lord, turning unto Him (repentant). Then, when He granteth him a boon from Him he forgetteth that for which he cried unto Him before, and setteth up rivals to Allah that he may beguile (men) from His way. Say (O Muhammad, unto such a one): Take pleasure in thy disbelief a while. Lo! thou art of the owners of the Fire.

39:7–8

4. وَإِذَا مَسَّ النَّاسَ ضُرٌّ دَعَوْا رَبَّهُمْ
مُنِيبِينَ إِلَيْهِ ثُمَّ إِذَا أَذَاقَهُمْ مِنْهُ
رَحْمَةً إِذَا فَرِيقٌ مِنْهُمْ بِرَبِّهِمْ
يُشْرِكُونَ ۝

لِيَكْفُرُوا بِمَا آتَيْنَاهُمْ فَتَمَتَّعُوا
فَسَوْفَ تَعْلَمُونَ ۝

5. إِنْ تَكْفُرُوا فَإِنَّ اللَّهَ غَنِيٌّ عَنْكُمْ وَلَا
يَرْضَىٰ لِعِبَادِهِ الْكُفْرَ وَإِنْ تَشْكُرُوا
يَرْضَهُ لَكُمْ وَلَا تَزِرُ وَازِرَةٌ وِزْرَ
أُخْرَىٰ ثُمَّ إِلَىٰ رَبِّكُمْ مَرْجِعُكُمْ فَيُنَبِّئُكُمْ
بِمَا كُنْتُمْ تَعْمَلُونَ إِنَّهُ عَلِيمٌ
بِذَاتِ الصُّدُورِ ۝

وَإِذَا مَسَّ الْإِنْسَانَ ضُرٌّ دَعَا رَبَّهُ
مُنِيبًا إِلَيْهِ ثُمَّ إِذَا خَوَّلَهُ نِعْمَةً مِنْهُ
نَسِيَ مَا كَانَ يَدْعُو إِلَيْهِ مِنْ قَبْلُ
وَجَعَلَ لِلَّهِ أَنْدَادًا لِيُضِلَّ عَنْ سَبِيلِهِ
قُلْ تَمَتَّعْ بِكُفْرِكَ قَلِيلًا إِنَّكَ مِنْ
أَصْحَابِ النَّارِ ۝

○

Ref: 10:12, 22-32; 17:83; 30:51; 31:32; 39:49-51; 41:49-51.

See also: Thankgiving.

INHERITANCE

1. Allah chargeth you concerning (the provisions for) your children: to the male the equivalent of the portion of two females, and if there be women more than two, then theirs is two-thirds of the inheritance, and if there be one (only), then the half. And to each of his parents a sixth of the inheritance, if he have a son; and if he have no son and his parents are his heirs, then to his mother appertaineth the third; and if he have brethren, then to his mother appertaineth the sixth, after any legacy he may have bequeathed, or debt (hath been paid). Your parents and your children: Ye know not which of them is nearer unto you in usefulness. It is an injunction from Allah. Lo! Allah is Knower, Wise.

And unto you belongeth a half of that which your wives leave, if they have no child; but if they have a child then unto you the fourth of that which they leave, after any legacy they may have bequeathed, or debt (they may have contracted, hath been paid). And unto them belongeth the fourth of that which ye leave if ye have no child, but if ye have a child then the eighth of that which ye leave, after any legacy ye may have bequeathed, or debt (ye may have contracted, hath been paid). And if a man or a woman have a distant heir

1. يُوصِيكُمُ اللَّهُ فِي أَوْلَادِكُمْ ۖ لِلذَّكَرِ مِثْلُ
حَظِّ الْأُنْثَيَيْنِ ۚ فَإِنْ كُنَّ نِسَاءً فَوْقَ
اثْنَتَيْنِ فَلَهُنَّ ثُلُثَا مَا تَرَكَ ۖ وَإِنْ كَانَتْ
وَاحِدَةً فَلَهَا النِّصْفُ ۚ وَلِأَبَوَيْهِ لِكُلِّ
وَاحِدٍ مِنْهُمَا السُّدُسُ مِمَّا تَرَكَ إِنْ
كَانَ لَهُ وَلَدٌ ۚ فَإِنْ لَمْ يَكُنْ لَهُ وَلَدٌ وَ
وَرِثَهُ أَبَوَاهُ فَلِأُمِّهِ الثُّلُثُ ۚ فَإِنْ كَانَ
لَهُ إِخْوَةٌ فَلِأُمِّهِ السُّدُسُ ۚ مِنْ بَعْدِ
وَصِيَّةٍ يُوصِي بِهَا أَوْ دَيْنٍ ۗ آبَاؤُكُمْ
وَأَبْنَاؤُكُمْ لَا تَدْرُونَ أَيُّهُمْ أَقْرَبُ لَكُمْ
نَفْعًا ۚ فَرِيضَةً مِنَ اللَّهِ ۗ إِنَّ اللَّهَ كَانَ
عَلِيمًا حَكِيمًا ﴿١١﴾
وَلَكُمْ نِصْفُ مَا تَرَكَ أَزْوَاجُكُمْ إِنْ
لَمْ يَكُنْ لَهُنَّ وَلَدٌ ۚ فَإِنْ كَانَ لَهُنَّ
وَلَدٌ فَلَكُمُ الرُّبُعُ مِمَّا تَرَكْنَ ۚ مِنْ بَعْدِ
وَصِيَّةٍ يُوصِينَ بِهَا أَوْ دَيْنٍ ۚ وَلَهُنَّ
الرُّبُعُ مِمَّا تَرَكْتُمْ إِنْ لَمْ يَكُنْ لَكُمْ
وَلَدٌ ۚ فَإِنْ كَانَ لَكُمْ وَلَدٌ فَلَهُنَّ الثُّمُنُ
مِمَّا تَرَكْتُمْ ۚ مِنْ بَعْدِ وَصِيَّةٍ تُوصُونَ
بِهَا أَوْ دَيْنٍ ۗ وَإِنْ كَانَ رَجُلٌ يُورَثُ
كَلَالَةً أَوِ امْرَأَةٌ وَلَهُ أَخٌ أَوْ أُخْتٌ
فَلِكُلِّ وَاحِدٍ مِنْهُمَا السُّدُسُ ۚ فَإِنْ
كَانُوا أَكْثَرَ مِنْ ذَٰلِكَ فَهُمْ شُرَكَاءُ فِي
الثُّلُثِ ۚ مِنْ بَعْدِ وَصِيَّةٍ يُوصَىٰ بِهَا أَوْ

(having left neither parent nor child), and he (or she) have a brother or a sister (only on the mother's side) then to each of them twain (the brother and the sister) the sixth, and if they be more than two, then they shall be sharers in the third, after any legacy that may have been bequeathed or debt (contracted) not injuring (the heirs by willing away more than a thid of the heritage) hath been paid. A commandment from Allah. Allah is Knower, Indulgent.

4:11–12

2. O ye who believe! It is not lawful for you forcibly to inherit the women (of your deceased kinsmen), nor (that) ye should put constraint upon them that ye may take away a part of that which ye have given them, unless they be guilty of flagrant lewdness. But consort with them in kindness, for if ye hate them it may happen that ye hate a thing wherein Allah hath placed much good.

4:19

3. And unto each We have appointed heirs of that which parents and near kindred leave; and as for those with whom your right hands have made a covenant, give them their due. Lo! Allah is ever Witness over all things.

4:33

4. They ask thee for a pronouncement, Say: Allah hath pronounced for you concerning distant kindred. If a man die childless and he have a sister, hers is half the heritage, and he would have inherited from her had she died childless. And if there be two sisters, then theirs are two–thirds of the heritage, and if they be brethren,

دَيْنٍ غَيْرَ مُضَآرٍّ ۚ وَصِيَّةً مِّنَ اللّٰهِ ؕ
وَاللّٰهُ عَلِيْمٌ حَلِيْمٌ ﴿١٢﴾

2. يٰٓاَيُّهَا الَّذِيْنَ اٰمَنُوْا لَا يَحِلُّ لَكُمْ اَنْ
تَرِثُوا النِّسَآءَ كَرْهًا ؕ وَلَا تَعْضُلُوْهُنَّ
لِتَذْهَبُوْا بِبَعْضِ مَآ اٰتَيْتُمُوْهُنَّ اِلَّآ اَنْ
يَّاْتِيْنَ بِفَاحِشَةٍ مُّبَيِّنَةٍ ۚ وَعَاشِرُوْهُنَّ
بِالْمَعْرُوْفِ ۚ فَاِنْ كَرِهْتُمُوْهُنَّ فَعَسٰٓى اَنْ
تَكْرَهُوْا شَيْـًٔا وَّيَجْعَلَ اللّٰهُ فِيْهِ خَيْرًا كَثِيْرًا ﴿١٩﴾

3. وَلِكُلٍّ جَعَلْنَا مَوَالِيَ مِمَّا تَرَكَ الْوَالِدٰنِ
وَالْاَقْرَبُوْنَ ؕ وَالَّذِيْنَ عَقَدَتْ اَيْمَانُكُمْ
فَاٰتُوْهُمْ نَصِيْبَهُمْ ؕ اِنَّ اللّٰهَ كَانَ عَلٰى
كُلِّ شَيْءٍ شَهِيْدًا ﴿٣٣﴾

4. يَسْتَفْتُوْنَكَ ؕ قُلِ اللّٰهُ يُفْتِيْكُمْ فِي الْكَلٰلَةِ ؕ
اِنِ امْرُؤٌا هَلَكَ لَيْسَ لَهٗ وَلَدٌ وَّلَهٗٓ اُخْتٌ
فَلَهَا نِصْفُ مَا تَرَكَ ۚ وَهُوَ يَرِثُهَآ اِنْ لَّمْ
يَكُنْ لَّهَا وَلَدٌ ؕ فَاِنْ كَانَتَا اثْنَتَيْنِ فَلَهُمَا
الثُّلُثٰنِ مِمَّا تَرَكَ ؕ وَاِنْ كَانُوْٓا اِخْوَةً
رِّجَالًا وَّنِسَآءً فَلِلذَّكَرِ مِثْلُ حَظِّ
الْاُنْثَيَيْنِ ؕ يُبَيِّنُ اللّٰهُ لَكُمْ اَنْ تَضِلُّوْا ؕ
وَاللّٰهُ بِكُلِّ شَيْءٍ عَلِيْمٌ ۝

men and women, unto the male is the equivalent of the share of two females. Allah expoundeth unto you, so that ye err not. Allah is Knower of all things.

4:176

Ref: 8:72; **See also: Will.**

INNOVATION

1. Then We caused Our messengers to follow in their footsteps; and We caused Jesus, son of Mary, to follow, and gave him the Gospel, and placed compassion and mercy in the hearts of those who followed him. But monasticism they invented--We ordained it not for them—only seeking Allah's pleasure, and they observed it not with right observance. So We give those of them who believe their reward, but many of them are evil-livers.

57:27

1. ثُمَّ قَفَّيْنَا عَلَىٰٓ اٰثَارِهِمْ بِرُسُلِنَا
وَقَفَّيْنَا بِعِيسَى ابْنِ مَرْيَمَ وَاٰتَيْنٰهُ
الْاِنْجِيْلَ ەۙ وَجَعَلْنَا فِىْ قُلُوْبِ
الَّذِيْنَ اتَّبَعُوْهُ رَاْفَةً وَّرَحْمَةً ؕ
وَرَهْبَانِيَّةَ ۨ ابْتَدَعُوْهَا مَا كَتَبْنٰهَا
عَلَيْهِمْ اِلَّا ابْتِغَآءَ رِضْوَانِ اللّٰهِ فَمَا
رَعَوْهَا حَقَّ رِعَايَتِهَا ۚ فَاٰتَيْنَا الَّذِيْنَ
اٰمَنُوْا مِنْهُمْ اَجْرَهُمْ ۚ وَكَثِيْرٌ
مِّنْهُمْ فٰسِقُوْنَ ۝

INTELLECTUAL

1. He giveth wisdom unto whom He will, and he unto whom wisdom is given, he truly hath received abundant good. But none remember except men of understanding.

2:269

1. يُّؤْتِى الْحِكْمَةَ مَنْ يَّشَآءُ ۚ وَمَنْ يُّؤْتَ
الْحِكْمَةَ فَقَدْ اُوْتِىَ خَيْرًا كَثِيْرًا ؕ وَمَا
يَذَّكَّرُ اِلَّآ اُولُوا الْاَلْبَابِ ۝

INTELLECTUAL
See also: Wisdom.

INTERCESSION

1. Whoso interveneth in a good cause will have the reward thereof, and whoso interveneth in an evil cause will bear the consequence thereof. Allah overseeth all things.

4:85

1. مَنْ يَشْفَعْ شَفَاعَةً حَسَنَةً يَكُنْ لَهُ نَصِيبٌ مِنْهَا ۖ وَمَنْ يَشْفَعْ شَفَاعَةً سَيِّئَةً يَكُنْ لَهُ كِفْلٌ مِنْهَا ۗ وَكَانَ اللَّهُ عَلَىٰ كُلِّ شَيْءٍ مُقِيتًا ﴿٨٥﴾

2. Or choose they intercessors other than Allah? Say: What! Even though they have power over nothing and have no intelligence?

Say: Unto Allah belongeth all intercession. His is the Sovereignty of the heavens and the earth. And afterward unto Him ye will be brought back.

39:43–44

2. أَمِ اتَّخَذُوا مِنْ دُونِ اللَّهِ شُفَعَاءَ ۚ قُلْ أَوَلَوْ كَانُوا لَا يَمْلِكُونَ شَيْئًا وَلَا يَعْقِلُونَ ﴿٤٣﴾

قُلْ لِلَّهِ الشَّفَاعَةُ جَمِيعًا ۖ لَهُ مُلْكُ السَّمَاوَاتِ وَالْأَرْضِ ۖ ثُمَّ إِلَيْهِ تُرْجَعُونَ ﴿٤٤﴾

3. And how many angels are in the heavens whose intercession availeth naught save after Allah giveth leave to whom He chooseth and accepteth!

53:26

3. وَكَمْ مِنْ مَلَكٍ فِي السَّمَاوَاتِ لَا تُغْنِي شَفَاعَتُهُمْ شَيْئًا إِلَّا مِنْ بَعْدِ أَنْ يَأْذَنَ اللَّهُ لِمَنْ يَشَاءُ وَيَرْضَىٰ ﴿٢٦﴾

Ref: 2:48,123,254,255; 6:51,70; 7:53; 10:3,18; 19:87; 20:109; 26:100; 30:13; 32:4; 36:23; 40:18; 39:43; 43:86; 74:48.

INTERNATIONAL RELATIONS

1. Except those who seek refuge with a people between whom and you there is a covenant or (those who) come unto you because their hearts forbid them to make war on you or make war on their own folk. Had Allah willed He could have given them power over you so that assuredly they would have fought you. So, if they hold aloof from you and wage not war against you and offer you peace, Allah alloweth you no way against them.

4:90

2. And if they incline to peace, incline thou also to it, and trust in Allah. Lo! He even He, is the Hearer, the Knower.

8:61

3. Excepting those of the idolaters with whom ye (Muslims) have a treaty, and who have since abated nothing of your right nor have supported anyone against you. (As for these), fulfil their treaty to them till their term. Lo! Allah loveth those who keep their duty (unto Him).

9:4

1. إلا الذين يصلون إلى قوم بينكم وبينهم
ميثاق أو جاءوكم حصرت صدورهم
أن يقاتلوكم أو يقاتلوا قومهم ولو
شاء الله لسلطهم عليكم فلقاتلوكم
فإن اعتزلوكم فلم يقاتلوكم وألقوا
إليكم السلم فما جعل الله لكم
عليهم سبيلا ۝

2. وإن جنحوا للسلم فاجنح لها وتوكل
على الله إنه هو السميع العليم ۝

3. إلا الذين عاهدتم من المشركين
ثم لم ينقصوكم شيئا ولم يظاهروا
عليكم أحدا فأتموا إليهم عهدهم إلى
مدتهم إن الله يحب المتقين ۝

4. وإن أحد من المشركين استجارك
فأجره حتى يسمع كلام الله ثم أبلغه
مأمنه ذلك بأنهم قوم لا يعلمون ۝

كيف يكون للمشركين عهد عند الله و
عند رسوله إلا الذين عاهدتم عند
المسجد الحرام فما استقاموا لكم
فاستقيموا لهم إن الله يحب المتقين ۝

4. And if anyone of the idolaters seeketh thy protection (O Muhammad), then protect him so that he may hear the Word of Allah, and afterward convey him to his place of safety. That is because they are a folk who know not.

How can there be a treaty with Allah and with His messenger for the idolaters save those with whom ye made a treaty at the Inviolable Place of Worship? So long as they are true to you, be true to them. Lo! Allah loveth those who keep their duty.

9:6–7

5. O ye who believe! If an evil–liver bring you tidings, verify it, lest ye smite some folk in ignorance and afterward repent of what ye did.

49:6

5. يَٰٓأَيُّهَا ٱلَّذِينَ ءَامَنُوٓا۟ إِن جَآءَكُمْ
فَاسِقٌۢ بِنَبَإٍ فَتَبَيَّنُوٓا۟ أَن تُصِيبُوا۟
قَوْمًۢا بِجَهَٰلَةٍ فَتُصْبِحُوا۟ عَلَىٰ مَا
فَعَلْتُمْ نَٰدِمِينَ ⑥

INTOXICATION

1. O ye who believe! Draw not near unto prayer when ye are drunken, till ye know that wnich ye utter,

4:43

1. يَٰٓأَيُّهَا ٱلَّذِينَ ءَامَنُوا۟ لَا تَقْرَبُوا۟ ٱلصَّلَوٰةَ
وَأَنتُمْ سُكَٰرَىٰ حَتَّىٰ تَعْلَمُوا۟ مَا تَقُولُونَ

2. O mankind! Fear your Lord. Lo! the earthquake of the Hour (of Doom) is a tremendous thing.

On the day when ye behold it, every nursing mother will forget her nursling and every pregnant one will be delivered of her burden, and thou (Muhammad) wilt see mankind as drunken yet they will not be drunken but the Doom of Allah will be strong (upon them).

22:1–2

2. يَٰٓأَيُّهَا ٱلنَّاسُ ٱتَّقُوا۟ رَبَّكُمْ ۚ إِنَّ
زَلْزَلَةَ ٱلسَّاعَةِ شَىْءٌ عَظِيمٌ ①
يَوْمَ تَرَوْنَهَا تَذْهَلُ كُلُّ مُرْضِعَةٍ
عَمَّآ أَرْضَعَتْ وَتَضَعُ كُلُّ ذَاتِ حَمْلٍ
حَمْلَهَا وَتَرَى ٱلنَّاسَ سُكَٰرَىٰ وَمَا
هُم بِسُكَٰرَىٰ وَلَٰكِنَّ عَذَابَ ٱللَّهِ
شَدِيدٌ ②

INTERNATIONAL RELATIONS

Ref: 2:177; 3:77; 8:56; 9:12,111; 13:20,25; 16:91,95; 17:34; 23:8; 33:15; 70:32.

INTRANSIGENCE OF DISBELIEVERS

1. The People of the Scripture ask of thee that thou shouldst cause an (actual) Book to descend upon them from heaven. They asked a greater thing of Moses aforetime, for they said: Show us Allah plainly. The storm of lightning seized them for their wickedness. Then (even after that) they chose the calf (for worship) after clear proofs (of Allah's Sovereignty) had come unto them. And We forgave them that! And We bestowed on Moses evident authority.

4:153

2. And when Our revelations are recited unto them they say: We have heard. If we wish we can speak the like of this. Lo! this is naught but fables of the men of old.

And when they said: O Allah! If this be indeed the truth from Thee, then rain down stones on us or bring on us some painful doom!

But Allah would not punish them while thou wast with them, nor will He punish them while they seek forgiveness.

What (plea) have they that Allah should not punish them, when they debar (His servants) from the Inviolable Place of Worship, though they are not its fitting guardians. Its fitting guardians are those only who keep their duty to Allah. But most of them know not.

1. يَسْـَٔلُكَ أَهْلُ الْكِتٰبِ أَنْ تُنَزِّلَ عَلَيْهِمْ
كِتٰبًا مِّنَ السَّمَآءِ فَقَدْ سَأَلُوا مُوسٰٓى أَكْبَرَ
مِنْ ذٰلِكَ فَقَالُوٓا أَرِنَا اللهَ جَهْرَةً فَأَخَذَتْهُمُ
الصّٰعِقَةُ بِظُلْمِهِمْ ۚ ثُمَّ اتَّخَذُوا الْعِجْلَ مِنْۢ
بَعْدِ مَا جَآءَتْهُمُ الْبَيِّنٰتُ فَعَفَوْنَا عَنْ
ذٰلِكَ ۚ وَاٰتَيْنَا مُوسٰى سُلْطٰنًا مُّبِيْنًا ﴿١٥٣﴾

2. وَإِذَا تُتْلٰى عَلَيْهِمْ اٰيٰتُنَا قَالُوْا قَدْ سَمِعْنَا
لَوْ نَشَآءُ لَقُلْنَا مِثْلَ هٰذَآ ۙ إِنْ هٰذَآ إِلَّآ
أَسَاطِيْرُ الْأَوَّلِيْنَ ﴿٣١﴾

وَإِذْ قَالُوا اللّٰهُمَّ إِنْ كَانَ هٰذَا هُوَ الْحَقَّ
مِنْ عِنْدِكَ فَأَمْطِرْ عَلَيْنَا حِجَارَةً مِّنَ
السَّمَآءِ أَوِ ائْتِنَا بِعَذَابٍ أَلِيْمٍ ﴿٣٢﴾

وَمَا كَانَ اللهُ لِيُعَذِّبَهُمْ وَأَنْتَ فِيْهِمْ ۚ
وَمَا كَانَ اللهُ مُعَذِّبَهُمْ وَهُمْ يَسْتَغْفِرُوْنَ ﴿٣٣﴾

وَمَا لَهُمْ أَلَّا يُعَذِّبَهُمُ اللهُ وَهُمْ يَصُدُّوْنَ
عَنِ الْمَسْجِدِ الْحَرَامِ وَمَا كَانُوٓا أَوْلِيَآءَهٗ ۚ
إِنْ أَوْلِيَآؤُهٗٓ إِلَّا الْمُتَّقُوْنَ وَلٰكِنَّ أَكْثَرَهُمْ
لَا يَعْلَمُوْنَ ﴿٣٤﴾

وَمَا كَانَ صَلَاتُهُمْ عِنْدَ الْبَيْتِ إِلَّا
مُكَآءً وَّتَصْدِيَةً ۚ فَذُوْقُوا الْعَذَابَ بِمَا
كُنْتُمْ تَكْفُرُوْنَ ﴿٣٥﴾

And their worship at the (holy) House is naught but whistling and hand–clapping. Therefore (it is said unto them): Taste of the doom because ye disbelieved

8:31–35

3. Those who disbelieve say: If only some portent were sent down upon him from his Lord! Thou art a warner only, and for every folk is a guide.

13:7

4. And they say: We will not put faith in thee till thou cause a spring to gush forth from the earth for us.

Or thou have a garden of date—palms and grapes, and cause rivers to gush forth therein abundantly;

Or thou cause the heaven to fall upon us piecemeal, as thou hast pretended, or bring Allah and the angels as a warrant;

Or thou have a house of gold; or thou ascend up into heaven, and even then we will put no faith in thine ascension till thou bring down for us a book that we can read. Say (O Muhammad): My Lord be Glorified! Am I aught save a mortal messenger!

And naught prevented mankind from believing when the guidance came unto them save that they said: Hath Allah sent a mortal as (His) messenger?

Say: If there were in the earth angels walking secure, We had sent down for them from heaven an angel as messenger.

Say: Allah sufficeth for a witness between me and you. Lo! He is Knower, Seer of His slaves.

17:90–96

3. وَيَقُولُ الَّذِينَ كَفَرُوا لَوْلَا أُنزِلَ
عَلَيْهِ آيَةٌ مِّن رَّبِّهِ ۗ إِنَّمَا أَنتَ
مُنذِرٌ ۖ وَلِكُلِّ قَوْمٍ هَادٍ ⑦

4. وَقَالُوا لَن نُّؤْمِنَ لَكَ حَتَّىٰ تَفْجُرَ لَنَا
مِنَ الْأَرْضِ يَنبُوعًا ⑨⓪
أَوْ تَكُونَ لَكَ جَنَّةٌ مِّن نَّخِيلٍ وَعِنَبٍ
فَتُفَجِّرَ الْأَنْهَارَ خِلَالَهَا تَفْجِيرًا ⑨①
أَوْ تُسْقِطَ السَّمَاءَ كَمَا زَعَمْتَ عَلَيْنَا كِسَفًا
أَوْ تَأْتِيَ بِاللَّهِ وَالْمَلَائِكَةِ قَبِيلًا ⑨②
أَوْ يَكُونَ لَكَ بَيْتٌ مِّن زُخْرُفٍ أَوْ تَرْقَىٰ
فِي السَّمَاءِ وَلَن نُّؤْمِنَ لِرُقِيِّكَ حَتَّىٰ تُنَزِّلَ
عَلَيْنَا كِتَابًا نَّقْرَؤُهُ ۗ قُلْ سُبْحَانَ رَبِّي
هَلْ كُنتُ إِلَّا بَشَرًا رَّسُولًا ⑨③
وَمَا مَنَعَ النَّاسَ أَن يُؤْمِنُوا إِذْ جَاءَهُمُ
الْهُدَىٰ إِلَّا أَن قَالُوا أَبَعَثَ اللَّهُ بَشَرًا رَّسُولًا ⑨④
قُل لَّوْ كَانَ فِي الْأَرْضِ مَلَائِكَةٌ يَمْشُونَ
مُطْمَئِنِّينَ لَنَزَّلْنَا عَلَيْهِم مِّنَ السَّمَاءِ
مَلَكًا رَّسُولًا ⑨⑤
قُلْ كَفَىٰ بِاللَّهِ شَهِيدًا بَيْنِي وَبَيْنَكُمْ ۚ
إِنَّهُ كَانَ بِعِبَادِهِ خَبِيرًا بَصِيرًا ⑨⑥

5. خُلِقَ الْإِنسَانُ مِنْ عَجَلٍ ۚ سَأُرِيكُمْ آيَاتِي فَلَا
تَسْتَعْجِلُونِ ③⑦
وَيَقُولُونَ مَتَىٰ هَٰذَا الْوَعْدُ إِن كُنتُمْ صَادِقِينَ ③⑧

5. Man is made of haste. I shall show you My portents, but ask Me not to hasten.

And they say: When will this promise (be fulfilled), if ye are truthful?

If those who disbelieved but knew the time when they will not be able to drive off the fire from their faces and from their backs, and they will not be helped!

Nay, but it will come upon them unawares so that it will stupefy them, and they will be unable to repel it, neither will they be reprieved.

21:37–40

6. We never sent before thee any messengers but lo! they verily ate food and walked in the markets. And We have appointed some of you a test for others: Will ye be stead–fast? And thy Lord is ever Seer.

And those who look not for a meeting with Us say: Why are angels not sent down unto us and (why) do we not see our Lord? Assuredly they think too highly of them–selves and are scornful with great pride.

On the day when they behold the angels, on that day there will be no good tidings for the guilty; and they will cry: A forbidding ban!

And We shall turn unto the work they did and make it scattered motes.

25:20–23

7. And they say: When (will) this promise (be ful–filled) if ye are truthful?

Say: It may be that a part of that which ye would hasten on is close behind you.

27:71–72

لَوْ يَعْلَمُ الَّذِينَ كَفَرُوا حِينَ لَا يَكُفُّونَ
عَنْ وُجُوهِهِمُ النَّارَ وَلَا عَنْ ظُهُورِهِمْ
وَلَا هُمْ يُنْصَرُونَ ۝
بَلْ تَأْتِيهِمْ بَغْتَةً فَتَبْهَتُهُمْ فَلَا
يَسْتَطِيعُونَ رَدَّهَا وَلَا هُمْ يُنْظَرُونَ ۝
6. وَمَا أَرْسَلْنَا قَبْلَكَ مِنَ الْمُرْسَلِينَ
إِلَّا إِنَّهُمْ لَيَأْكُلُونَ الطَّعَامَ وَيَمْشُونَ
فِي الْأَسْوَاقِ ۗ وَجَعَلْنَا بَعْضَكُمْ لِبَعْضٍ
فِتْنَةً أَتَصْبِرُونَ ۗ وَكَانَ رَبُّكَ بَصِيرًا ۝
وَقَالَ الَّذِينَ لَا يَرْجُونَ لِقَاءَنَا لَوْلَا
أُنْزِلَ عَلَيْنَا الْمَلَائِكَةُ أَوْ نَرَىٰ رَبَّنَا ۗ
لَقَدِ اسْتَكْبَرُوا فِي أَنْفُسِهِمْ وَعَتَوْ
عُتُوًّا كَبِيرًا ۝
يَوْمَ يَرَوْنَ الْمَلَائِكَةَ لَا بُشْرَىٰ يَوْمَئِذٍ
لِلْمُجْرِمِينَ وَيَقُولُونَ حِجْرًا مَحْجُورًا ۝
وَقَدِمْنَا إِلَىٰ مَا عَمِلُوا مِنْ عَمَلٍ
فَجَعَلْنَاهُ هَبَاءً مَنْثُورًا ۝
7. وَيَقُولُونَ مَتَىٰ هَٰذَا الْوَعْدُ إِنْ
كُنْتُمْ صَادِقِينَ ۝
قُلْ عَسَىٰ أَنْ يَكُونَ رَدِفَ لَكُمْ
بَعْضُ الَّذِي تَسْتَعْجِلُونَ ۝
8. وَقَالَ الَّذِينَ كَفَرُوا لِلَّذِينَ آمَنُوا
اتَّبِعُوا سَبِيلَنَا وَلْنَحْمِلْ خَطَايَاكُمْ
وَمَا هُمْ بِحَامِلِينَ مِنْ خَطَايَاهُمْ مِنْ

8. Those who disbelieve say unto those who believe: Fol–low our way (of religion) and we verily will bear your sins (for you). They cannot bear aught of their sins. Lo! they

verily are liars.

But they verily will bear their own loads and other loads beside their own, and they verily will be questioned on the Day of Resurrection concerning that which they invented.

29:12–13

9. They bid thee hasten on the doom (of Allah). And if a term had not been appointed, the doom would assuredly have come unto them (ere now). And verily it will come upon them suddenly when they perceive not.

They bid thee hasten on the doom, when lo! hell verily will encompass the disbelievers

On the day when the doom will overwhelm them from above them and from underneath their feet, and He will say: Taste what ye used to do!

29:53–55

10. And now that the Truth hath come unto them they say: This is mere magic, and lo! we are dis-believers therein.

And they say: If only this Qur'ān had been revealed to some great man of the two towns!

Is it they who apportion thy Lord's mercy? We have apportioned among them their livelihood in the life of the world, and raised some of

شَيْءٍ ۭ اِنَّهُمْ لَكٰذِبُوْنَ ﴿١٢﴾
وَلَيَحْمِلُنَّ اَثْقَالَهُمْ وَاَثْقَالًا مَّعَ
اَثْقَالِهِمْ ۡ وَلَيُسْـَٔلُنَّ يَوْمَ الْقِيٰمَةِ
عَمَّا كَانُوْا يَفْتَرُوْنَ ﴿١٣﴾

9. وَيَسْتَعْجِلُوْنَكَ بِالْعَذَابِ ۭ وَلَوْلَآ اَجَلٌ
مُّسَمًّى لَّجَاۗءَهُمُ الْعَذَابُ ۭ وَلَيَاْتِيَنَّهُمْ
بَغْتَةً وَّهُمْ لَا يَشْعُرُوْنَ ﴿٥٣﴾

يَسْتَعْجِلُوْنَكَ بِالْعَذَابِ ۭ وَاِنَّ جَهَنَّمَ
لَمُحِيْطَةٌ ۢ بِالْكٰفِرِيْنَ ﴿٥٤﴾

يَوْمَ يَغْشٰىهُمُ الْعَذَابُ مِنْ فَوْقِهِمْ
وَمِنْ تَحْتِ اَرْجُلِهِمْ وَيَقُوْلُ ذُوْقُوْا
مَا كُنْتُمْ تَعْمَلُوْنَ ﴿٥٥﴾

10. وَلَمَّا جَاۗءَهُمُ الْحَقُّ قَالُوْا هٰذَا سِحْرٌ
وَّاِنَّا بِهٖ كٰفِرُوْنَ ﴿٣٠﴾
وَقَالُوْا لَوْلَا نُزِّلَ هٰذَا الْقُرْاٰنُ عَلٰي
رَجُلٍ مِّنَ الْقَرْيَتَيْنِ عَظِيْمٍ ﴿٣١﴾
اَهُمْ يَقْسِمُوْنَ رَحْمَتَ رَبِّكَ ۭ نَحْنُ
قَسَمْنَا بَيْنَهُمْ مَّعِيْشَتَهُمْ فِي الْحَيٰوةِ
الدُّنْيَا وَرَفَعْنَا بَعْضَهُمْ فَوْقَ بَعْضٍ
دَرَجٰتٍ لِّيَتَّخِذَ بَعْضُهُمْ بَعْضًا سُخْرِيًّا ۭ
وَرَحْمَتُ رَبِّكَ خَيْرٌ مِّمَّا يَجْمَعُوْنَ ﴿٣٢﴾

them above others in rank that some of them may take labour from others; and the mercy of thy Lord is better than (the wealth) that they amass.

43:30–32

Ref: 2:108; 6:37; 7:203; 10:50–51; 17:59; 20:133–135; 22:48; 25:7–9; 26:204–207; 29:50; 30:58–59; 36:48–50; 37:176–179; 38:16; 42:17–18; 46:7; 67:25–26; 70:1–7; 74:52–53.

See also: Disbelievers and Polytheists.

INVOCATION

1. And when My servants question thee concerning Me, then surely I am nigh. I answer the prayer of the suppliant when he crieth unto Me. So let them hear My call and let them trust in Me, in order that they may be led aright.

2:186

2. And covet not the thing in which Allah hath made some of you excel others. Unto men a fortune from that which they have earned, and unto women a fortune from that which they have earned. (Envy not one another) but ask Allah of His bounty. Lo! Allah is ever Knower of all things.

4:32

3. Say: My Lord enjoineth justice. And set your faces, upright (toward Him) at every place of worship and call upon Him, making religion pure for Him (only). As He brought you into being, so return ye (unto Him).

7:29

4. (O mankind!) Call upon your Lord humbly and in secret. Lo! He loveth not aggressors.

Work not confusion in earth after the fair ordering (thereof), and call on Him in fear and hope. Lo! the mercy of Allah is nigh unto the good.

7:55–56

5. And do thou (O Muhammad) remember thy Lord within thyself humbly and with awe, below thy breath, at morn and evening.

1. وَإِذَا سَأَلَكَ عِبَادِي عَنِّي فَإِنِّي قَرِيبٌ أُجِيبُ
دَعْوَةَ الدَّاعِ إِذَا دَعَانِ فَلْيَسْتَجِيبُوا لِي
وَلْيُؤْمِنُوا بِي لَعَلَّهُمْ يَرْشُدُونَ ۝١٨٦

2. وَلَا تَتَمَنَّوْا مَا فَضَّلَ اللَّهُ بِهِ بَعْضَكُمْ عَلَىٰ
بَعْضٍ لِلرِّجَالِ نَصِيبٌ مِمَّا اكْتَسَبُوا
وَلِلنِّسَاءِ نَصِيبٌ مِمَّا اكْتَسَبْنَ وَاسْأَلُوا
اللَّهَ مِنْ فَضْلِهِ إِنَّ اللَّهَ كَانَ بِكُلِّ
شَيْءٍ عَلِيمًا ۝٣٢

3. قُلْ أَمَرَ رَبِّي بِالْقِسْطِ وَأَقِيمُوا وُجُوهَكُمْ
عِنْدَ كُلِّ مَسْجِدٍ وَادْعُوهُ مُخْلِصِينَ لَهُ الدِّينَ
كَمَا بَدَأَكُمْ تَعُودُونَ ۝٢٩

4. ادْعُوا رَبَّكُمْ تَضَرُّعًا وَخُفْيَةً إِنَّهُ لَا
يُحِبُّ الْمُعْتَدِينَ ۝٥٥

وَلَا تُفْسِدُوا فِي الْأَرْضِ بَعْدَ إِصْلَاحِهَا
وَادْعُوهُ خَوْفًا وَطَمَعًا إِنَّ رَحْمَتَ اللَّهِ
قَرِيبٌ مِنَ الْمُحْسِنِينَ ۝٥٦

5. وَاذْكُرْ رَبَّكَ فِي نَفْسِكَ تَضَرُّعًا وَخِيفَةً
وَدُونَ الْجَهْرِ مِنَ الْقَوْلِ بِالْغُدُوِّ
وَالْآصَالِ وَلَا تَكُنْ مِنَ الْغَافِلِينَ ۝٢٠٥

6. قُلِ ادْعُوا اللَّهَ أَوِ ادْعُوا الرَّحْمَٰنَ أَيًّا مَا
تَدْعُوا فَلَهُ الْأَسْمَاءُ الْحُسْنَىٰ وَلَا
تَجْهَرْ بِصَلَاتِكَ وَلَا تُخَافِتْ بِهَا وَابْتَغِ
بَيْنَ ذَٰلِكَ سَبِيلًا ۝١١٠

And be thou not of the neglectful.

7:205

6. Say (unto mankind): Cry unto Allah, or cry unto the Beneficent, unto whichsoever ye cry (it is the same). His are the most beautiful names. And thou (Muhammad), be not loud voiced in thy worship nor yet silent therein, but follow a way between.

17:110

Ref: 2:37; 6:52,63; 7:180; 25:77; 32:16; 35:10; 40:60 65; 52:28.
See also: **See also:** Repentance.

ISLAM

1. Lo! religion with Allah (is) The Surrender (to His Will and Guidance).

2. And whoso seeketh as religion other than the Surrender (to Allah) it will not be accepted from him, and he will be a loser in the Hereafter.

3:85

3. This day have I perfected your religion for you and completed My favour unto you, and have chosen for you as religion AL-ISLAM.

5:3

4. And whomsoever it is Allah's Will to guide, He expandeth his bosom unto the Surrender, and whomsoever it is His Will to send astray, He maketh his bosom close and narrow as if he were engaged in sheer ascent. Thus Allah layeth ignominy upon those who believe not.

6:125

5. Is he whose bosom Allah hath expanded for the Surrender (unto Him), so that he followeth a light from His Lord, (as he who disbelieveth)? Then woe unto those whose hearts are hardened against remembrance of Allah. Such are in plain error.

39:22

6. They make it a favour unto thee (Muhammad) that they have surrendered (unto Him). Say: Deem not your surrender a favour unto me; nay, but Allah doth confer a favour on you, inasmuch as He hath led you to the Faith, if ye are earnest.

49:17

1. إِنَّ الدِّينَ عِندَ اللَّهِ الْإِسْلَامُ

2. وَمَن يَبْتَغِ غَيْرَ الْإِسْلَامِ دِينًا فَلَن يُقْبَلَ مِنْهُ وَهُوَ فِي الْآخِرَةِ مِنَ الْخَاسِرِينَ

3. الْيَوْمَ أَكْمَلْتُ لَكُمْ دِينَكُمْ وَأَتْمَمْتُ عَلَيْكُمْ نِعْمَتِي وَرَضِيتُ لَكُمُ الْإِسْلَامَ دِينًا

4. فَمَن يُرِدِ اللَّهُ أَن يَهْدِيَهُ يَشْرَحْ صَدْرَهُ لِلْإِسْلَامِ وَمَن يُرِدْ أَن يُضِلَّهُ يَجْعَلْ صَدْرَهُ ضَيِّقًا حَرَجًا كَأَنَّمَا يَصَّعَّدُ فِي السَّمَاءِ كَذَٰلِكَ يَجْعَلُ اللَّهُ الرِّجْسَ عَلَى الَّذِينَ لَا يُؤْمِنُونَ

5. أَفَمَن شَرَحَ اللَّهُ صَدْرَهُ لِلْإِسْلَامِ فَهُوَ عَلَىٰ نُورٍ مِّن رَّبِّهِ فَوَيْلٌ لِّلْقَاسِيَةِ قُلُوبُهُم مِّن ذِكْرِ اللَّهِ أُولَٰئِكَ فِي ضَلَالٍ مُّبِينٍ

6. يَمُنُّونَ عَلَيْكَ أَنْ أَسْلَمُوا قُل لَّا تَمُنُّوا عَلَيَّ إِسْلَامَكُم بَلِ اللَّهُ يَمُنُّ عَلَيْكُمْ أَنْ هَدَاكُمْ لِلْإِيمَانِ إِن كُنتُمْ صَادِقِينَ

7. Is not He (best) Who answereth the wronged one when he crieth unto Him and removeth the evil, and hath made you viceroys of the earth? Is there any God beside Allah? Little do they reflect!

27:62

8. He it is Who showeth you His portents, and sendeth down for you provision from the sky. None payeth heed save him who turneth (unto Him) repentant.

Therefore (O believers) pray unto Allah, making religion pure for Him (only), however much the disbelievers be averse:

40:13–14

7. أَمَّنْ يُجِيبُ الْمُضْطَرَّ إِذَا دَعَاهُ وَيَكْشِفُ
السُّوٓءَ وَيَجْعَلُكُمْ خُلَفَآءَ الْأَرْضِ ءَإِلَٰهٌ
مَّعَ اللَّهِ قَلِيلًا مَّا تَذَكَّرُونَ ٦٢

8. هُوَ الَّذِي يُرِيكُمْ ءَايَٰتِهِۦ وَيُنَزِّلُ
لَكُم مِّنَ السَّمَآءِ رِزْقًا وَمَا يَتَذَكَّرُ
إِلَّا مَن يُنِيبُ ١٣
فَادْعُوا اللَّهَ مُخْلِصِينَ لَهُ الدِّينَ
وَلَوْ كَرِهَ الْكَافِرُونَ ١٤

Ref: 2:132,193,208,217; 3:67,83,85,102; 4:46,125; 5:3,54; 6:14; 8:39,161; 9:11,29,33,36,122; 10:22; 12:40, 101; 11:14; 48:28; 61:9; 82:14.
See also: Muslim Nation.

ISLAM'S CHARTER

1. وَقَضٰى رَبُّكَ اَلَّا تَعْبُدُوْٓا اِلَّآ اِيَّاهُ وَ
بِالْوَالِدَيْنِ اِحْسَانًا ۭ اِمَّا يَبْلُغَنَّ عِنْدَكَ
الْكِبَرَ اَحَدُهُمَآ اَوْ كِلٰهُمَا فَلَا تَقُلْ لَّهُمَآ
اُفٍّ وَّلَا تَنْهَرْهُمَا وَقُلْ لَّهُمَا قَوْلًا كَرِيْمًا ﴿۲۳﴾
وَاخْفِضْ لَهُمَا جَنَاحَ الذُّلِّ مِنَ الرَّحْمَةِ
وَقُلْ رَّبِّ ارْحَمْهُمَا كَمَا رَبَّيٰنِيْ صَغِيْرًا ﴿۲۴﴾

رَبُّكُمْ اَعْلَمُ بِمَا فِيْ نُفُوْسِكُمْ ۭ اِنْ تَكُوْنُوْا
صٰلِحِيْنَ فَاِنَّهٗ كَانَ لِلْاَوَّابِيْنَ غَفُوْرًا ﴿۲۵﴾

وَاٰتِ ذَا الْقُرْبٰى حَقَّهٗ وَالْمِسْكِيْنَ وَابْنَ
السَّبِيْلِ وَلَا تُبَذِّرْ تَبْذِيْرًا ﴿۲۶﴾
اِنَّ الْمُبَذِّرِيْنَ كَانُوْٓا اِخْوَانَ الشَّيٰطِيْنِ ۭ
وَكَانَ الشَّيْطٰنُ لِرَبِّهٖ كَفُوْرًا ﴿۲۷﴾

وَاِمَّا تُعْرِضَنَّ عَنْهُمُ ابْتِغَاۗءَ رَحْمَةٍ مِّنْ
رَّبِّكَ تَرْجُوْهَا فَقُلْ لَّهُمْ قَوْلًا مَّيْسُوْرًا ﴿۲۸﴾
وَلَا تَجْعَلْ يَدَكَ مَغْلُوْلَةً اِلٰى عُنُقِكَ
وَلَا تَبْسُطْهَا كُلَّ الْبَسْطِ فَتَقْعُدَ
مَلُوْمًا مَّحْسُوْرًا ﴿۲۹﴾
اِنَّ رَبَّكَ يَبْسُطُ الرِّزْقَ لِمَنْ يَّشَاۗءُ وَ
يَقْدِرُ ۭ اِنَّهٗ كَانَ بِعِبَادِهٖ خَبِيْرًۢا بَصِيْرًا ﴿۳۰﴾
وَلَا تَقْتُلُوْٓا اَوْلَادَكُمْ خَشْيَةَ اِمْلَاقٍ ۭ
نَحْنُ نَرْزُقُهُمْ وَاِيَّاكُمْ ۭ اِنَّ قَتْلَهُمْ
كَانَ خِطْاً كَبِيْرًا ﴿۳۱﴾

1. Thy Lord hath decreed, that ye worship none save Him, and (that ye show) kindness to parents. If one of them or both of them attain to old age with thee, say not "Fie" unto them nor repulse them, but speak unto them a gracious word.

And lower unto them the wing of submission through mercy, and say: My Lord! Have mercy on them both as they did care for me when I was little!

Your Lord is Best Aware of what is in your minds. If ye are righteous, then lo! He was ever Forgiving unto those who turn (unto Him).

Give the kinsman his due, and the needy, and the wayfarer, and squander not (thy wealth) in wantonness.

Lo! the squanderers were ever brothers of the devils, and the devil was ever an ingrate to his Lord.

But if thou turn away from them, seeking mercy from thy Lord, for which thou hopest, then speak unto them a reasonable word.

And let not thy hand be chained to thy neck nor open it with a complete opening, lest thou sit down rebuked, denuded.

Lo! thy Lord enlargeth the provision for whom He will, and straiteneth (it for whom He will) Lo, He was ever Knower, Seer of His slaves.

Slay not your children, fearing a fall to proverty. We shall provide for them and for you. Lo! the slaying of them is great sin.

وَلَا تَقْرَبُوا الزِّنَىٰٓ إِنَّهُ كَانَ فَاحِشَةً
وَسَاءَ سَبِيلًا ٣٢
وَلَا تَقْتُلُوا النَّفْسَ الَّتِي حَرَّمَ اللَّهُ إِلَّا
بِالْحَقِّ وَمَن قُتِلَ مَظْلُومًا فَقَدْ
جَعَلْنَا لِوَلِيِّهِ سُلْطَانًا فَلَا يُسْرِف فِّي
الْقَتْلِ إِنَّهُ كَانَ مَنصُورًا ٣٣
وَلَا تَقْرَبُوا مَالَ الْيَتِيمِ إِلَّا بِالَّتِي هِيَ
أَحْسَنُ حَتَّىٰ يَبْلُغَ أَشُدَّهُ وَأَوْفُوا
بِالْعَهْدِ إِنَّ الْعَهْدَ كَانَ مَسْئُولًا ٣٤
وَأَوْفُوا الْكَيْلَ إِذَا كِلْتُمْ وَزِنُوا بِالْقِسْطَاسِ
الْمُسْتَقِيمِ ذَٰلِكَ خَيْرٌ وَأَحْسَنُ تَأْوِيلًا ٣٥
وَلَا تَقْفُ مَا لَيْسَ لَكَ بِهِ عِلْمٌ إِنَّ
السَّمْعَ وَالْبَصَرَ وَالْفُؤَادَ كُلُّ أُولَٰٓئِكَ
كَانَ عَنْهُ مَسْئُولًا ٣٦
وَلَا تَمْشِ فِي الْأَرْضِ مَرَحًا إِنَّكَ
لَن تَخْرِقَ الْأَرْضَ وَلَن تَبْلُغَ
الْجِبَالَ طُولًا ٣٧
كُلُّ ذَٰلِكَ كَانَ سَيِّئُهُ عِندَ
رَبِّكَ مَكْرُوهًا ٣٨
ذَٰلِكَ مِمَّآ أَوْحَىٰٓ إِلَيْكَ رَبُّكَ مِنَ الْحِكْمَةِ
وَلَا تَجْعَلْ مَعَ اللَّهِ إِلَٰهًا آخَرَ فَتُلْقَىٰ فِي
جَهَنَّمَ مَلُومًا مَّدْحُورًا ٣٩

And come not near unto adultery. Lo! it is an abomination and an evil way.

And slay not the life which Allah hath forbidden save with right. Whoso is slain wrongfully, We have given power unto his heir, but let him not commit excess in slaying. Lo! he will be helped.

Come not near the wealth of the orphan save with that which is better till he come to strength, and keep the covenant. Lo! of the covenant it will be asked.

Fill the measure when ye measure, and weigh with a right balance; that is meet, and better in the end.

(O man), follow not that whereof thou hast no knowledge. Lo! the hearing and the sight and the heart – of each of these it will be asked.

And walk not in the earth exultant. Lo! thou canst not rend the earth, nor canst thou stretch to the height of the hills.

The evil of all that is hateful in the sight of thy Lord.

This is (part) of that wisdom wherewith thy Lord hath inspired thee (O Muhammad) And set not up with Allah any other god lest thou be cast into hell, reproved, abandoned.

17 : 23–39

See also: Islam.

I' TIKAF

1. And when We made the House (at Makkah) a resort for mankind and a sanctuary (saying): Take as your place of worship the place where Abraham stood (to pray). And We imposed a duty upon Abraham and Ishmael, (saying): Purify My House for those who go around and those who meditate therein and those who bow down and prostrate themselves (in worship).

2:125

2. And touch them (wives) not, but be at your devotions in the mosques. These are the limits imposed by Allah, so approach them not. Thus Allah expoundeth His revelations to mankind that they may ward off (evil).

2:187

1. وَإِذْ جَعَلْنَا الْبَيْتَ مَثَابَةً لِّلنَّاسِ وَأَمْنًا
وَاتَّخِذُوا مِن مَّقَامِ إِبْرٰهِيمَ مُصَلًّى وَ
عَهِدْنَا إِلَىٰ إِبْرٰهِيمَ وَإِسْمٰعِيلَ أَن طَهِّرَا
بَيْتِيَ لِلطَّائِفِينَ وَالْعٰكِفِينَ وَالرُّكَّعِ السُّجُودِ ﴿١٢٥﴾

2. وَلَا تُبَاشِرُوهُنَّ وَأَنتُمْ عٰكِفُونَ
فِي الْمَسٰجِدِ تِلْكَ حُدُودُ اللَّهِ فَلَا تَقْرَبُوهَا
كَذٰلِكَ يُبَيِّنُ اللَّهُ آيٰتِهِ لِلنَّاسِ لَعَلَّهُمْ يَتَّقُونَ ﴿١٨٧﴾

○

JEWS AND CHRISTIANS

1. And humiliation and wretchedness were stamped upon them and they were visited with wrath from Allah. That was because they disbelieved in Allah's revelations and slew the prophets wrongfully. That was for their disobedience and transgression.

2:61

2. And they say: None entereth Paradise unless he be a Jew or a Christian. These are their own desires. Say: Bring your proof (of what ye state) if ye are truthful.

2:111

3. And the Jews say the Christians follow nothing (true), and the Christians say the Jews follow nothing (true); yet both are readers of the Scripture. Even thus speak those who know not. Allah will judge between them on the Day of Resurrection concerning that wherein they differ.

2:113

4. And the Jews will not be pleased with thee, nor will the Christians, till thou follow their creed. Say: Lo! the guidance of Allah (Himself) is Guidance. And if thou shouldst follow their desires after the knowledge which hath come unto thee, then wouldst thou have from Allah no protecting friend nor helper.

2:120

5. Ignominy shall be their portion wheresoever they are found save (where they grasp) a rope from Allah and a rope from men. They have incurred anger from their Lord, and wretchedness is laid upon them. That is because they used to disbelieve the revelations of Allah, and slew the Prophets

1. وَضُرِبَتْ عَلَيْهِمُ الذِّلَّةُ وَالْمَسْكَنَةُ وَبَاءُوْ
بِغَضَبٍ مِّنَ اللّٰهِ ذٰلِكَ بِأَنَّهُمْ كَانُوْا يَكْفُرُوْنَ
بِاٰيٰتِ اللّٰهِ وَيَقْتُلُوْنَ النَّبِيّٖنَ بِغَيْرِ الْحَقِّ
ذٰلِكَ بِمَا عَصَوْا وَّكَانُوْا يَعْتَدُوْنَ ﴿٦١﴾

2. وَقَالُوْا لَنْ يَّدْخُلَ الْجَنَّةَ إِلَّا مَنْ كَانَ هُوْدًا
أَوْ نَصٰرٰى تِلْكَ أَمَانِيُّهُمْ قُلْ هَاتُوْا بُرْهَانَكُمْ
إِنْ كُنْتُمْ صٰدِقِيْنَ ﴿١١١﴾

3. وَقَالَتِ الْيَهُوْدُ لَيْسَتِ النَّصٰرٰى عَلٰى شَيْءٍ
وَّقَالَتِ النَّصٰرٰى لَيْسَتِ الْيَهُوْدُ عَلٰى شَيْءٍ
وَّهُمْ يَتْلُوْنَ الْكِتٰبَ كَذٰلِكَ قَالَ الَّذِيْنَ لَا
يَعْلَمُوْنَ مِثْلَ قَوْلِهِمْ فَاللّٰهُ يَحْكُمُ بَيْنَهُمْ
يَوْمَ الْقِيٰمَةِ فِيْمَا كَانُوْا فِيْهِ يَخْتَلِفُوْنَ ﴿١١٣﴾

4. وَلَنْ تَرْضٰى عَنْكَ الْيَهُوْدُ وَلَا النَّصٰرٰى حَتّٰى تَتَّبِعَ
مِلَّتَهُمْ قُلْ إِنَّ هُدَى اللّٰهِ هُوَ الْهُدٰى وَلَئِنِ
اتَّبَعْتَ أَهْوَاءَهُمْ بَعْدَ الَّذِيْ جَاءَكَ مِنَ
الْعِلْمِ مَا لَكَ مِنَ اللّٰهِ مِنْ وَّلِيٍّ وَّلَا نَصِيْرٍ ﴿١٢٠﴾

5. ضُرِبَتْ عَلَيْهِمُ الذِّلَّةُ أَيْنَ مَا ثُقِفُوْا إِلَّا
بِحَبْلٍ مِّنَ اللّٰهِ وَحَبْلٍ مِّنَ النَّاسِ وَبَاءُوْ
بِغَضَبٍ مِّنَ اللّٰهِ وَضُرِبَتْ عَلَيْهِمُ الْمَسْكَنَةُ
ذٰلِكَ بِأَنَّهُمْ كَانُوْا يَكْفُرُوْنَ بِاٰيٰتِ اللّٰهِ
وَيَقْتُلُوْنَ الْأَنْبِيَاءَ بِغَيْرِ حَقٍّ ذٰلِكَ
بِمَا عَصَوْا وَّكَانُوْا يَعْتَدُوْنَ ۝

wrongfully. That is because they were rebellious and used to transgress.

3:112

6. And with those who say: "Lo! we are Christians," We made a covenant, but they forgot a part of that whereof they were admonished. Therefor We have stirred up enmity and hatred among them till the Day of Resurrection, when Allah will inform them of their handiwork.

5:14

7. The Jews and Christians say: We are sons of Allah and His loved ones. Say: Why then doth He chastise you for your sins? Nay, ye are but mortals of His creating. He forgiveth whom He will, and chastiseth whom He will. Allah's is the Sovereignty of the heavens and the earth and all that is between them, and unto Him is the journeying.

5:18

8. O ye who believe! Take not the Jews and Christians for friends. They are friends one to another. He among you who taketh them for friends is (one) of them. Lo! Allah guideth not wrongdoing folk.

5:51

9. The Jews say: Allah's hand is fettered. Their hands are fettered and they are accursed for saying so, Nay, but both His hands are spread out wide in bounty. He bestoweth as He will. That which hath been revealed unto thee from thy Lord is certain to increase the contumacy and disbelief of many

6. ومن الذين قالوا إنا نصارى أخذنا
ميثاقهم فنسوا حظا مما ذكروا به
فأغرينا بينهم العداوة والبغضاء إلى
يوم القيامة وسوف ينبئهم الله
بما كانوا يصنعون ﴿١٤﴾

7. وقالت اليهود والنصارى نحن أبناء
الله وأحباؤه قل فلم يعذبكم
بذنوبكم بل أنتم بشر ممن خلق
يغفر لمن يشاء ويعذب من يشاء
ولله ملك السماوات والأرض وما
بينهما وإليه المصير ﴿١٨﴾

8. يا أيها الذين آمنوا لا تتخذوا اليهود
والنصارى أولياء بعضهم أولياء
بعض ومن يتولهم منكم فإنه منهم
إن الله لا يهدي القوم الظالمين ﴿٥١﴾

9. وقالت اليهود يد الله مغلولة غلت
أيديهم ولعنوا بما قالوا بل يداه
مبسوطتان ينفق كيف يشاء وليزيدن
كثيرا منهم ما أنزل إليك من ربك
طغيانا وكفرا وألقينا بينهم العداوة
والبغضاء إلى يوم القيامة كلما أوقدوا
نارا للحرب أطفأها الله ويسعون في
الأرض فسادا والله لا يحب المفسدين ﴿٦٤﴾

of them, and We have cast among them enmity and hatred till the Day of Resurrection. As often as they light a fire for war, Allah extinguisheth it. Their effort is for corruption in the land, and Allah loveth not corrupters.

5:64

10. Thou wilt find the most vehement of mankind in hostility to those who believe (to be) the Jews and the idolaters, and thou wilt find the nearest of them in affection to those who believe (to be) those who say: Lo! We are Christians. That is because there are among them priests and monks, and because they are not proud.
5:82

10. لَتَجِدَنَّ اَشَدَّ النَّاسِ عَدَاوَةً لِّلَّذِيْنَ
اٰمَنُوا الْيَهُوْدَ وَ الَّذِيْنَ اَشْرَكُوْا ۚ
وَلَتَجِدَنَّ اَقْرَبَهُمْ مَّوَدَّةً لِّلَّذِيْنَ
اٰمَنُوا الَّذِيْنَ قَالُوْٓا اِنَّا نَصٰرٰى ؕ ذٰلِكَ
بِاَنَّ مِنْهُمْ قِسِّيْسِيْنَ وَ رُهْبَانًا وَّ
اَنَّهُمْ لَا يَسْتَكْبِرُوْنَ ﴿۸۲﴾

See also: *Halal, Manna and Quail*, People of the Book, Sabbath, Women Permissible to Marry.

JIHAD

1. Fight in the way of Allah against those who fight agsinst you but begin not hostilities. Lo! Allah loveth not aggressors.

And slay them wherever ye find them, and drive them out of the places whence they drove you out, for persecution is worse than slaughter. And fight not with them at the Inviolable Place of Worship until they first attack you (there) then slay them. Such is the reward of disbelievers.

But if they desist, then lo! Allah is Forgiving Merciful.

And fight them until persecution is no more, and religion is for Allah. But if they desist, then let there be no hostility except against wrongdoers.

2:190–193

2. Fight in the way of Allah, and know that Allah is Hearer, Knower.

2:244

3. Those who believe do battle for the cause of Allah; and those who disbelieve do battle for the cause of idols. So fight the minions of the devil. Lo! the devil's strategy is ever weak.

4:76

4. So fight (O Muhammad) in the way of Allah— Thou art not taxed (with the responsibility for anyone) except thyself — and urge on the believers. Peradventure Allah will restrain the might of those who disbelieve. Allah is stronger in might and stronger in inflicting punishment.

4:84

1. وَقَاتِلُوا فِي سَبِيلِ اللَّهِ الَّذِينَ يُقَاتِلُونَكُمْ وَلَا
تَعْتَدُوا إِنَّ اللَّهَ لَا يُحِبُّ الْمُعْتَدِينَ ﴿١٩٠﴾

وَاقْتُلُوهُمْ حَيْثُ ثَقِفْتُمُوهُمْ وَأَخْرِجُوهُمْ
مِنْ حَيْثُ أَخْرَجُوكُمْ وَالْفِتْنَةُ أَشَدُّ مِنَ
الْقَتْلِ وَلَا تُقَاتِلُوهُمْ عِنْدَ الْمَسْجِدِ الْحَرَامِ
حَتَّى يُقَاتِلُوكُمْ فِيهِ فَإِنْ قَاتَلُوكُمْ فَاقْتُلُوهُمْ
كَذَلِكَ جَزَاءُ الْكَافِرِينَ ﴿١٩١﴾

فَإِنِ انْتَهَوْا فَإِنَّ اللَّهَ غَفُورٌ رَحِيمٌ ﴿١٩٢﴾

وَقَاتِلُوهُمْ حَتَّى لَا تَكُونَ فِتْنَةٌ وَيَكُونَ
الدِّينُ لِلَّهِ فَإِنِ انْتَهَوْا فَلَا عُدْوَانَ إِلَّا
عَلَى الظَّالِمِينَ ﴿١٩٣﴾

2. وَقَاتِلُوا فِي سَبِيلِ اللَّهِ وَاعْلَمُوا أَنَّ اللَّهَ
سَمِيعٌ عَلِيمٌ ﴿٢٤٤﴾

3. الَّذِينَ آمَنُوا يُقَاتِلُونَ فِي سَبِيلِ اللَّهِ
وَالَّذِينَ كَفَرُوا يُقَاتِلُونَ فِي سَبِيلِ
الطَّاغُوتِ فَقَاتِلُوا أَوْلِيَاءَ الشَّيْطَانِ إِنَّ
كَيْدَ الشَّيْطَانِ كَانَ ضَعِيفًا ﴿٧٦﴾

4. فَقَاتِلْ فِي سَبِيلِ اللَّهِ لَا تُكَلَّفُ إِلَّا
نَفْسَكَ وَحَرِّضِ الْمُؤْمِنِينَ عَسَى اللَّهُ أَنْ
يَكُفَّ بَأْسَ الَّذِينَ كَفَرُوا وَاللَّهُ أَشَدُّ
بَأْسًا وَأَشَدُّ تَنْكِيلًا ﴿٨٤﴾

5. Those of the believers who sit still, other than those who have a (disabling) hurt, are not on an equality with those who strive in the way of Allah with their wealth and lives. Allah hath conferred on those who strive with their wealth and lives a rank above the sedentary. Unto each Allah hath promised good, but He hath bestowed on those who strive a great reward above the sedentary;

Degrees of rank from Him, and forgiveness and mercy. Allah is ever Forgiving, Merciful.

4:95–96

6. O ye who believe! When ye meet those who disbelieve in battle, turn not your backs to them.

Whoso on that day turneth his back to them, unless manoeuvring for battle or intent to join a company, he truly hath incurred wrath from Allah, and his habitation will be hell, a hapless journey's end.

8:15–16

7. Tell those who disbelieve that if they cease (from persecution of believers) that which is past will be forgiven them; but if they return (thereto) then the example of the men of old hath already gone (before them for a warning).

And fight them until persecution is no more, and religion is all for Allah. But if they cease, then lo! Allah is Seer of what they do.

And if they turn away, then know that Allah is your Befriender – a Transcendent Patron, a Transcendent Helper!

8:38–40

5. لَا يَسْتَوِي الْقٰعِدُونَ مِنَ الْمُؤْمِنِينَ غَيْرُ
أُولِي الضَّرَرِ وَالْمُجٰهِدُونَ فِي سَبِيلِ
اللّٰهِ بِأَمْوَالِهِمْ وَأَنْفُسِهِمْ ۚ فَضَّلَ اللّٰهُ
الْمُجٰهِدِينَ بِأَمْوَالِهِمْ وَأَنْفُسِهِمْ عَلَى
الْقٰعِدِينَ دَرَجَةً ۚ وَكُلًّا وَّعَدَ اللّٰهُ
الْحُسْنٰى ۚ وَفَضَّلَ اللّٰهُ الْمُجٰهِدِينَ عَلَى
الْقٰعِدِينَ أَجْرًا عَظِيمًا ﴿٩٥﴾

دَرَجٰتٍ مِّنْهُ وَمَغْفِرَةً وَّرَحْمَةً ۚ
وَكَانَ اللّٰهُ غَفُورًا رَّحِيمًا ﴿٩٦﴾

6. يٰٓأَيُّهَا الَّذِينَ اٰمَنُوٓا إِذَا لَقِيتُمُ الَّذِينَ
كَفَرُوا زَحْفًا فَلَا تُوَلُّوهُمُ الْأَدْبَارَ ﴿١٥﴾
وَمَنْ يُّوَلِّهِمْ يَوْمَئِذٍ دُبُرَهُ إِلَّا مُتَحَرِّفًا
لِّقِتَالٍ أَوْ مُتَحَيِّزًا إِلٰى فِئَةٍ فَقَدْ بَآءَ بِغَضَبٍ
مِّنَ اللّٰهِ وَمَأْوٰىهُ جَهَنَّمُ ۚ وَبِئْسَ الْمَصِيرُ ﴿١٦﴾

7. قُلْ لِّلَّذِينَ كَفَرُوٓا إِنْ يَّنْتَهُوا يُغْفَرْ
لَهُمْ مَّا قَدْ سَلَفَ ۚ وَإِنْ يَّعُودُوا فَقَدْ
مَضَتْ سُنَّتُ الْأَوَّلِينَ ﴿٣٨﴾

وَقٰتِلُوهُمْ حَتّٰى لَا تَكُونَ فِتْنَةٌ وَّيَكُونَ
الدِّينُ كُلُّهُ لِلّٰهِ ۚ فَإِنِ انْتَهَوْا فَإِنَّ اللّٰهَ
بِمَا يَعْمَلُونَ بَصِيرٌ ﴿٣٩﴾

وَإِنْ تَوَلَّوْا فَاعْلَمُوٓا أَنَّ اللّٰهَ مَوْلٰىكُمْ ۚ
نِعْمَ الْمَوْلٰى وَنِعْمَ النَّصِيرُ ﴿٤٠﴾

8. If thou comest on them in the war, deal with them so as to strike fear in those who are behind them, that haply they may remember.

8:57

9. Make ready for them all thou canst of (armed) force and of horses tethered, that thereby ye may dismay the enemy of Allah and your enemy, and others beside them whom ye know not. Allah knoweth them. Whatsoever ye spend in the way of Allah it will be repaid to you in full, and ye will not be wronged.

And if they incline to peace, incline thou also to it, and trust in Allah. Lo! He even He, is the Hearer, the Knower.

And if they would deceive thee, then lo! Allah is Sufficient for thee.

8:60–62

10. O Prophet! Exhort the believers to fight. If there be of you twenty steadfast they shall overcome two hundred, and if there be of you a hundred (steadfast) they shall overcome a thousand of those who disbelieve, because they (the disbelievers) are a folk without intelligence.

Now hath Allah lightened your burden, for He knoweth that there is weakness in you. So if there be of you a steadfast hundred, they shall overcome two hundred, and if there be of you a

8. فَإِمَّا تَثْقَفَنَّهُمْ فِي الْحَرْبِ فَشَرِّدْ بِهِمْ
مَّنْ خَلْفَهُمْ لَعَلَّهُمْ يَذَّكَّرُونَ ۝٥٧

9. وَأَعِدُّوا لَهُمْ مَّا اسْتَطَعْتُمْ مِّنْ قُوَّةٍ
وَّمِنْ رِّبَاطِ الْخَيْلِ تُرْهِبُونَ بِهِ عَدُوَّ
اللهِ وَعَدُوَّكُمْ وَآخَرِينَ مِنْ دُونِهِمْ
لَا تَعْلَمُونَهُمْ اللهُ يَعْلَمُهُمْ وَمَا تُنْفِقُوا
مِنْ شَيْءٍ فِي سَبِيلِ اللهِ يُوَفَّ إِلَيْكُمْ
وَأَنْتُمْ لَا تُظْلَمُونَ ۝٦٠
وَإِنْ جَنَحُوا لِلسَّلْمِ فَاجْنَحْ لَهَا وَتَوَكَّلْ
عَلَى اللهِ إِنَّهُ هُوَ السَّمِيعُ الْعَلِيمُ ۝٦١
وَإِنْ يُّرِيدُوا أَنْ يَّخْدَعُوكَ فَإِنَّ حَسْبَكَ
اللهُ

10. يَا أَيُّهَا النَّبِيُّ حَرِّضِ الْمُؤْمِنِينَ عَلَى الْقِتَالِ
إِنْ يَّكُنْ مِّنْكُمْ عِشْرُونَ صَابِرُونَ يَغْلِبُوا
مِائَتَيْنِ وَإِنْ يَّكُنْ مِّنْكُمْ مِّائَةٌ يَّغْلِبُوا
أَلْفًا مِّنَ الَّذِينَ كَفَرُوا بِأَنَّهُمْ
قَوْمٌ لَّا يَفْقَهُونَ ۝٦٥
اَلْـٰٔنَ خَفَّفَ اللهُ عَنْكُمْ وَعَلِمَ أَنَّ فِيكُمْ
ضَعْفًا فَإِنْ يَّكُنْ مِّنْكُمْ مِّائَةٌ صَابِرَةٌ
يَّغْلِبُوا مِائَتَيْنِ وَإِنْ يَّكُنْ مِّنْكُمْ أَلْفٌ
يَّغْلِبُوا أَلْفَيْنِ بِإِذْنِ اللهِ وَاللهُ مَعَ الصَّابِرِينَ ۝٦٦

11. يَا أَيُّهَا الَّذِينَ آمَنُوا قَاتِلُوا الَّذِينَ يَلُونَكُمْ
مِّنَ الْكُفَّارِ وَلْيَجِدُوا فِيكُمْ غِلْظَةً

thousand (steadfast), they shall overcome two thousand by permission of Allah. Allah is with the steadfast.

8:65–66

11. O ye who believe! Fight those of the disbelievers who are near to you,

and let them find harshness in you, and know that Allah is with those who keep their duty (unto Him).

9:123

12. And strive for Allah with the endeavour which is His right. He hath chosen you and hath not laid upon you in religion any hardship;

22:78

13. And whosoever striveth, striveth only for himself, for lo! Allah is altogether Independent of (His) creatures.

29:6

14. As for those who strive in Us, We surely guide them to Our paths, and lo! Allah is with the good.

29:69

15. Now when ye meet in battle those who disbelieve, then it is smiting of the necks until, when ye have routed them, then making fast of bonds; and afterward either grace or ransom till the war lay down its brudens. That (is the ordinance). And if Allah willed He could have punished them (without you) but (thus it is ordained) that He may try some of you by means of others. And those who are slain in the way of Allah, He rendereth not their actions vain.

47:4

16. Lo! Allah loveth those who battle for His cause in

وَاعْلَمُوا أَنَّ اللَّهَ مَعَ الْمُتَّقِينَ ﴿١٢٣﴾
12. وَجَاهِدُوا فِي اللَّهِ حَقَّ جِهَادِهِ ۚ هُوَ
اجْتَبَاكُمْ وَمَا جَعَلَ عَلَيْكُمْ فِي الدِّينِ
مِنْ حَرَجٍ ۚ
13. وَمَنْ جَاهَدَ فَإِنَّمَا يُجَاهِدُ لِنَفْسِهِ ۚ
إِنَّ اللَّهَ لَغَنِيٌّ عَنِ الْعَالَمِينَ ﴿٦﴾
14. وَالَّذِينَ جَاهَدُوا فِينَا لَنَهْدِيَنَّهُمْ
سُبُلَنَا ۚ وَإِنَّ اللَّهَ لَمَعَ الْمُحْسِنِينَ ﴿٦٩﴾
15. فَإِذَا لَقِيتُمُ الَّذِينَ كَفَرُوا فَضَرْبَ
الرِّقَابِ حَتَّىٰ إِذَا أَثْخَنْتُمُوهُمْ فَشُدُّوا
الْوَثَاقَ فَإِمَّا مَنًّا بَعْدُ وَإِمَّا فِدَاءً
حَتَّىٰ تَضَعَ الْحَرْبُ أَوْزَارَهَا ۚ ذَٰلِكَ
وَلَوْ يَشَاءُ اللَّهُ لَانْتَصَرَ مِنْهُمْ وَلَٰكِنْ
لِيَبْلُوَ بَعْضَكُمْ بِبَعْضٍ ۗ وَالَّذِينَ قُتِلُوا
فِي سَبِيلِ اللَّهِ فَلَنْ يُضِلَّ أَعْمَالَهُمْ ﴿٤﴾
16. إِنَّ اللَّهَ يُحِبُّ الَّذِينَ يُقَاتِلُونَ فِي
سَبِيلِهِ صَفًّا كَأَنَّهُمْ بُنْيَانٌ مَرْصُوصٌ ﴿٤﴾
17. يَا أَيُّهَا النَّبِيُّ جَاهِدِ الْكُفَّارَ وَ
الْمُنَافِقِينَ وَاغْلُظْ عَلَيْهِمْ ۚ وَمَأْوَاهُمْ
جَهَنَّمُ ۖ وَبِئْسَ الْمَصِيرُ ﴿٩﴾

ranks. as if they were a solid structure.

61:4

17. O Prophet! Strive against the disbelievers and the hypocrites, and be stern with them. Hell will be their home, a hapless journey's end!

66:9

Ref: 2:218; 3:142; 9:73; 25:52; 47:41; 49:15.

See also: Martyrdom

JIZYA

1. Fight against such of those who have been given the Scripture as believe not in Allah nor the Last Day, and forbid not that which Allah hath forbidden by His messenger, and follow not the Religion of Truth, until they pay the tribute readily, being brought low.

9:29

1. قَاتِلُوا الَّذِيْنَ لَا يُؤْمِنُوْنَ بِاللّٰهِ وَلَا
بِالْيَوْمِ الْاٰخِرِ وَلَا يُحَرِّمُوْنَ مَا حَرَّمَ
اللّٰهُ وَرَسُوْلُهٗ وَلَا يَدِيْنُوْنَ دِيْنَ الْحَقِّ
مِنَ الَّذِيْنَ اُوْتُوا الْكِتٰبَ حَتّٰى يُعْطُوا
الْجِزْيَةَ عَنْ يَّدٍ وَّهُمْ صٰغِرُوْنَ

JOURNEY

1. (Fast) a certain number of days; and (for) him who is sick among you, or on a journey, (the same) number of other days.

2:184

1. اَيَّامًا مَّعْدُوْدٰتٍ فَمَنْ كَانَ مِنْكُمْ مَّرِيْضًا
اَوْ عَلٰى سَفَرٍ فَعِدَّةٌ مِّنْ اَيَّامٍ اُخَرَ

2. If ye be on a journey and cannot find a scribe, then a pledge in hand (shall suffice). And if one of you entrusteth to another let him who is trusted deliver up that which is entrusted to him (according to the pact between them) and let him observe his duty to Allah, his Lord. Hide not testimony. He who hideth it, verily his heart is sinful. Allah is Aware of what ye do.

2:283

2. وَاِنْ كُنْتُمْ عَلٰى سَفَرٍ وَّلَمْ تَجِدُوْا كَاتِبًا
فَرِهٰنٌ مَّقْبُوْضَةٌ فَاِنْ اَمِنَ بَعْضُكُمْ
بَعْضًا فَلْيُؤَدِّ الَّذِى اؤْتُمِنَ اَمَانَتَهٗ وَلْيَتَّقِ
اللّٰهَ رَبَّهٗ وَلَا تَكْتُمُوا الشَّهَادَةَ وَمَنْ
يَّكْتُمْهَا فَاِنَّهٗ اٰثِمٌ قَلْبُهٗ وَاللّٰهُ بِمَا
تَعْمَلُوْنَ عَلِيْمٌ

3. O ye who believe! Draw not near unto prayer when ye are drunken, till ye know that which ye utter, nor when ye are polluted, save when journeying upon the road till ye have bathed. And if ye be ill, or on a journey, or one of you cometh from the closet or ye have touched women, and ye find not water, then go to high clean soil and rub your faces and your hands (there with). Lo! Allah is Benign, Forgiving.

4:43

3 يٰۤاَيُّهَا الَّذِيْنَ اٰمَنُوْا لَا تَقْرَبُوا الصَّلٰوةَ
وَاَنْتُمْ سُكٰرٰى حَتّٰى تَعْلَمُوْا مَا تَقُوْلُوْنَ
وَلَا جُنُبًا اِلَّا عَابِرِىْ سَبِيْلٍ حَتّٰى
تَغْتَسِلُوْا وَاِنْ كُنْتُمْ مَّرْضٰۤى اَوْ عَلٰى
سَفَرٍ اَوْ جَآءَ اَحَدٌ مِّنْكُمْ مِّنَ الْغَآئِطِ
اَوْ لٰمَسْتُمُ النِّسَآءَ فَلَمْ تَجِدُوْا مَآءً
فَتَيَمَّمُوْا صَعِيْدًا طَيِّبًا فَامْسَحُوْا بِوُجُوْهِكُمْ
وَاَيْدِيْكُمْ اِنَّ اللّٰهَ كَانَ عَفُوًّا غَفُوْرًا

JOURNEY **See also:** **Wayfarer.**

JURISPRUDENCE

1. And the believers should not all go out to fight. Of every troop of them, a party only should go forth, that they (who are left behind) may gain sound knowledge in religion, and that they may warn their folk when they return to them, so that they may beware.

9:122

JUSTICE

1. Lo! Allah commandeth you that ye restore deposits to their owners, and, if ye judge between mankind, that ye judge justly. Lo! comely is this which Allah admonisheth you. Lo! Allah is ever Hearer, Seer.

4:58

2. But, nay, by thy Lord, they will not believe (in truth) until they make thee judge of what is in dispute between them and find within themselves no dislike of that which thou decidest, and submit with full submission.

4:65

3. Lo! We reveal unto thee the Scripture with the truth, that thou mayst judge, between mankind by that which Allah showeth thee. And be not thou a pleader for the treacherous;

And seek forgiveness of

1. وَمَا كَانَ الْمُؤْمِنُونَ لِيَنْفِرُوا كَافَّةً فَلَوْلَا
نَفَرَ مِنْ كُلِّ فِرْقَةٍ مِنْهُمْ طَائِفَةٌ لِيَتَفَقَّهُوا
فِي الدِّينِ وَلِيُنْذِرُوا قَوْمَهُمْ إِذَا رَجَعُوا
إِلَيْهِمْ لَعَلَّهُمْ يَحْذَرُونَ ﴿١٢٢﴾

1. إِنَّ اللَّهَ يَأْمُرُكُمْ أَنْ تُؤَدُّوا الْأَمَانَاتِ إِلَىٰ
أَهْلِهَا وَإِذَا حَكَمْتُمْ بَيْنَ النَّاسِ أَنْ
تَحْكُمُوا بِالْعَدْلِ ۚ إِنَّ اللَّهَ نِعِمَّا يَعِظُكُمْ
بِهِ ۗ إِنَّ اللَّهَ كَانَ سَمِيعًا بَصِيرًا ﴿٥٨﴾

2. فَلَا وَرَبِّكَ لَا يُؤْمِنُونَ حَتَّىٰ يُحَكِّمُوكَ
فِيمَا شَجَرَ بَيْنَهُمْ ثُمَّ لَا يَجِدُوا فِي أَنْفُسِهِمْ
حَرَجًا مِمَّا قَضَيْتَ وَيُسَلِّمُوا تَسْلِيمًا ﴿٦٥﴾

3. إِنَّا أَنْزَلْنَا إِلَيْكَ الْكِتَابَ بِالْحَقِّ
لِتَحْكُمَ بَيْنَ النَّاسِ بِمَا أَرَاكَ اللَّهُ ۚ
وَلَا تَكُنْ لِلْخَائِنِينَ خَصِيمًا ﴿١٠٥﴾
وَاسْتَغْفِرِ اللَّهَ ۖ إِنَّ اللَّهَ كَانَ غَفُورًا رَحِيمًا ﴿١٠٦﴾
وَلَا تُجَادِلْ عَنِ الَّذِينَ يَخْتَانُونَ أَنْفُسَهُمْ ۚ
إِنَّ اللَّهَ لَا يُحِبُّ مَنْ كَانَ خَوَّانًا أَثِيمًا ﴿١٠٧﴾

Allah. Lo! Allah is ever Forgiving, Merciful.

And plead not on behalf of (people) who deceive themselves. Lo! Allah loveth not one who is treacherous and sinful.

4:105–107

JURISPRUDENCE See also: Knowledge, Wisdom.
JUSTICE Ref: 24:51.

JUSTICE AND EQUITY

1. Allah tasketh not a soul beyond its scope. For it (is only) that which it hath earned, and against it (only) that which it hath deserved.

2:286

2. And if ye judge between mankind that ye judge justly. Lo! comely is this which Allah admonisheth you. Lo! Allah is ever Hearer, Seer.

O ye who believe! Obey Allah, and obey the messenger and those of you who are in authority; and if ye have a dispute concerning any matter, refer it to Allah and the messenger if ye are (in truth) believers in Allah and the Last Day. That is better and more seemly in the end.

4:58–59

3. O ye who believe! Be steadfast witnesses for Allah in equity, and let not hatred of any people seduce you that ye deal not justly. Deal justly, that is nearer to your duty. Observe your duty to Allah. Lo! Allah is Informed of what ye do.

5:8

4. And if ye give your word, do justice thereunto, even though it be (against) a kinsman; and fulfil the covenant of Allah.

6:152

5. And if two parties of believers fall to fighting, then make peace between them. And if one party of them doth wrong to the other, fight ye that which doth wrong till it return unto the ordinance of Allah; then if it return, make peace between them justly, and act equitably. Lo! Allah loveth the equitable.

49:9

1. لَا يُكَلِّفُ اللّٰهُ نَفْسًا اِلَّا وُسْعَهَا ۗ لَهَا
مَا كَسَبَتْ وَعَلَيْهَا مَا اكْتَسَبَتْ

2. وَاِذَا حَكَمْتُمْ بَيْنَ النَّاسِ اَنْ تَحْكُمُوْا
بِالْعَدْلِ ۗ اِنَّ اللّٰهَ نِعِمَّا يَعِظُكُمْ بِهٖ ۗ اِنَّ
اللّٰهَ كَانَ سَمِيْعًا بَصِيْرًا ﴿٥٨﴾
يٰاَيُّهَا الَّذِيْنَ اٰمَنُوْۤا اَطِيْعُوا اللّٰهَ وَاَطِيْعُوا
الرَّسُوْلَ وَاُولِى الْاَمْرِ مِنْكُمْ ۚ فَاِنْ
تَنَازَعْتُمْ فِيْ شَيْءٍ فَرُدُّوْهُ اِلَى اللّٰهِ وَالرَّسُوْلِ
اِنْ كُنْتُمْ تُؤْمِنُوْنَ بِاللّٰهِ وَالْيَوْمِ الْاٰخِرِ ۗ
ذٰلِكَ خَيْرٌ وَّاَحْسَنُ تَاْوِيْلًا ﴿٥٩﴾

3. يٰاَيُّهَا الَّذِيْنَ اٰمَنُوْا كُوْنُوْا قَوّٰمِيْنَ لِلّٰهِ
شُهَدَآءَ بِالْقِسْطِ ۖ وَلَا يَجْرِمَنَّكُمْ شَنَاٰنُ
قَوْمٍ عَلٰۤى اَلَّا تَعْدِلُوْا ۗ اِعْدِلُوْا ۗ هُوَ اَقْرَبُ
لِلتَّقْوٰى ۖ وَاتَّقُوا اللّٰهَ ۗ اِنَّ اللّٰهَ خَبِيْرٌۢ بِمَا تَعْمَلُوْنَ ﴿٨﴾

4. وَاِذَا قُلْتُمْ فَاعْدِلُوْا وَلَوْ كَانَ ذَا قُرْبٰى ۚ وَبِعَهْدِ
اللّٰهِ اَوْفُوْا

5. وَاِنْ طَآئِفَتٰنِ مِنَ الْمُؤْمِنِيْنَ اقْتَتَلُوْا
فَاَصْلِحُوْا بَيْنَهُمَا ۚ فَاِنْۢ بَغَتْ اِحْدٰىهُمَا
عَلَى الْاُخْرٰى فَقَاتِلُوا الَّتِيْ تَبْغِيْ حَتّٰى
تَفِيْٓءَ اِلٰۤى اَمْرِ اللّٰهِ ۚ فَاِنْ فَآءَتْ
فَاَصْلِحُوْا بَيْنَهُمَا بِالْعَدْلِ وَاَقْسِطُوْا ۗ
اِنَّ اللّٰهَ يُحِبُّ الْمُقْسِطِيْنَ ﴿٩﴾

Ref: 5:41–42; 7:29; 60:8

K'ABAH

1. And when We made the House (at Makkah) a resort for mankind and a sanctuary (saying): Take as your place of worship the place where Abraham stood (to pray). And We imposed a duty upon Abraham and Ishmael, (saying): Purify My House for those who go around and those who meditate therein and those who bow down and prostrate themselves (in worship).

2:125

2. And when Abraham and Ishmael were raising the foundations of the House (Abraham prayed): Our Lord! Accept from us (this duty). Lo! Thou, only Thou, art the Hearer, the Knower.

2:127

3. Lo! the first Sanctuary appointed for mankind was that at *Bakkah*, a blessed place, a guidance to the peoples,

Wherein are plain memorials (of Allah's guidance); the place where Abraham stood up to pray; and whosoever entereth it is safe. And pilgrimage to the House is a duty unto Allah for mankind, for him who can find a way thither. As for him who disbelieveth (let him know that) lo! Allah is Independent of (all) creatures.

3:96–97

4. Allah hath appointed the *Ka'bah*, the Sacred House, a standard for mankind, and the Sacred Month and the offerings and the garlands. That is so that ye may know that Allah knoweth whatsoever is in the heavens and whatsoever is in the earth, and that Allah

1. وَإِذْ جَعَلْنَا الْبَيْتَ مَثَابَةً لِّلنَّاسِ وَأَمْنًا ؕ
وَاتَّخِذُوا مِنْ مَّقَامِ إِبْرٰهٖمَ مُصَلًّى ؕ وَ
عَهِدْنَآ إِلٰٓى إِبْرٰهٖمَ وَإِسْمٰعِيْلَ أَنْ طَهِّرَا
بَيْتِيَ لِلطَّآئِفِيْنَ وَالْعٰكِفِيْنَ وَالرُّكَّعِ السُّجُوْدِ ﴿١٢٥﴾

2. وَإِذْ يَرْفَعُ إِبْرٰهٖمُ الْقَوَاعِدَ مِنَ الْبَيْتِ
وَإِسْمٰعِيْلُ ؕ رَبَّنَا تَقَبَّلْ مِنَّا ؕ إِنَّكَ أَنْتَ
السَّمِيْعُ الْعَلِيْمُ ﴿١٢٧﴾

3. إِنَّ أَوَّلَ بَيْتٍ وُّضِعَ لِلنَّاسِ لَلَّذِيْ بِبَكَّةَ
مُبٰرَكًا وَّهُدًى لِّلْعٰلَمِيْنَ ۚ﴿﴾

فِيْهِ اٰيٰتٌ بَيِّنٰتٌ مَّقَامُ إِبْرٰهِيْمَ ۚ وَمَنْ
دَخَلَهٗ كَانَ اٰمِنًا ؕ وَلِلّٰهِ عَلَى النَّاسِ حِجُّ
الْبَيْتِ مَنِ اسْتَطَاعَ إِلَيْهِ سَبِيْلًا ؕ وَمَنْ
كَفَرَ فَإِنَّ اللّٰهَ غَنِيٌّ عَنِ الْعٰلَمِيْنَ ﴿﴾

4. جَعَلَ اللّٰهُ الْكَعْبَةَ الْبَيْتَ الْحَرَامَ قِيٰمًا
لِّلنَّاسِ وَالشَّهْرَ الْحَرَامَ وَالْهَدْيَ
وَالْقَلَآئِدَ ؕ ذٰلِكَ لِتَعْلَمُوْٓا أَنَّ اللّٰهَ يَعْلَمُ
مَا فِي السَّمٰوٰتِ وَمَا فِي الْأَرْضِ وَأَنَّ اللّٰهَ
بِكُلِّ شَيْءٍ عَلِيْمٌ ﴿٩٧﴾

5. وَإِذْ بَوَّأْنَا لِإِبْرٰهِيْمَ مَكَانَ الْبَيْتِ
أَنْ لَّا تُشْرِكْ بِيْ شَيْئًا وَّطَهِّرْ بَيْتِيَ
لِلطَّآئِفِيْنَ وَالْقَآئِمِيْنَ وَالرُّكَّعِ السُّجُوْدِ ﴿٢٦﴾

is Knower of all things.

5:97

5. And (remember) when We prepared for Abraham the place of the (holy) House, saying: Ascribe thou no thing as partner unto Me, and purify My House for those who make the round (thereof) and those who stand and those who bow and make prostration.

22:26

See also: Makkah,

KHUL'A

1. الطَّلَاقُ مَرَّتَانِ ۖ فَإِمْسَاكٌ بِمَعْرُوفٍ أَوْ تَسْرِيحٌ
بِإِحْسَانٍ ۗ وَلَا يَحِلُّ لَكُمْ أَنْ تَأْخُذُوا مِمَّا
آتَيْتُمُوهُنَّ شَيْئًا إِلَّا أَنْ يَخَافَا أَلَّا يُقِيمَا حُدُودَ
اللَّهِ ۖ فَإِنْ خِفْتُمْ أَلَّا يُقِيمَا حُدُودَ اللَّهِ فَلَا
جُنَاحَ عَلَيْهِمَا فِيمَا افْتَدَتْ بِهِ ۗ تِلْكَ
حُدُودُ اللَّهِ فَلَا تَعْتَدُوهَا ۚ وَمَنْ يَتَعَدَّ
حُدُودَ اللَّهِ فَأُولَٰئِكَ هُمُ الظَّالِمُونَ ﴿٢٢٩﴾

2. يَا أَيُّهَا الَّذِينَ آمَنُوا لَا يَحِلُّ لَكُمْ أَنْ
تَرِثُوا النِّسَاءَ كَرْهًا ۖ وَلَا تَعْضُلُوهُنَّ
لِتَذْهَبُوا بِبَعْضِ مَا آتَيْتُمُوهُنَّ إِلَّا أَنْ
يَأْتِينَ بِفَاحِشَةٍ مُبَيِّنَةٍ ۚ وَعَاشِرُوهُنَّ
بِالْمَعْرُوفِ ۚ فَإِنْ كَرِهْتُمُوهُنَّ فَعَسَىٰ أَنْ
تَكْرَهُوا شَيْئًا وَيَجْعَلَ اللَّهُ فِيهِ خَيْرًا كَثِيرًا ﴿١٩﴾
وَإِنْ أَرَدْتُمُ اسْتِبْدَالَ زَوْجٍ مَكَانَ
زَوْجٍ وَآتَيْتُمْ إِحْدَاهُنَّ قِنْطَارًا فَلَا
تَأْخُذُوا مِنْهُ شَيْئًا ۚ أَتَأْخُذُونَهُ بُهْتَانًا
وَإِثْمًا مُبِينًا ﴿٢٠﴾
وَكَيْفَ تَأْخُذُونَهُ وَقَدْ أَفْضَىٰ بَعْضُكُمْ إِلَىٰ
بَعْضٍ وَأَخَذْنَ مِنْكُمْ مِيثَاقًا غَلِيظًا ﴿٢١﴾

3. وَإِنِ امْرَأَةٌ خَافَتْ مِنْ بَعْلِهَا نُشُوزًا أَوْ
إِعْرَاضًا فَلَا جُنَاحَ عَلَيْهِمَا أَنْ يُصْلِحَا
بَيْنَهُمَا صُلْحًا ۚ وَالصُّلْحُ خَيْرٌ ۗ وَأُحْضِرَتِ
الْأَنْفُسُ الشُّحَّ ۚ وَإِنْ تُحْسِنُوا وَتَتَّقُوا فَإِنَّ
اللَّهَ كَانَ بِمَا تَعْمَلُونَ خَبِيرًا ﴿١٢٨﴾

1. Divorce must be pronounced twice and then (a woman) must be retained in honour or released in kindness. And it is not lawful for you that ye take from women aught of that which ye have given them; except (in the case) when both fear that they may not be able to keep within the limits (imposed by) Allah. And if ye fear that they may not be able to keep the limits of Allah, in that case it is no sin for either of them if the woman ransom herself. These are the limits (imposed by) Allah. Transgress them not. For whoso transgresseth Allah's limits, such are wrong-doers.

2:229

2. O ye who believe! It is not lawful for you forcibly to inherit the women (of your deceased kinsmen), nor (that) ye should put constraint upon them that ye may take away a part of that which ye have given them, unless they be guilty of flagrant lewdness. But consort with them in kindness, for if ye hate them it may happen that ye hate a thing wherein Allah hath placed much good.

And if ye wish to exchange one wife for another and ye have given unto one of them a sum of money (however great), take nothing from it. Would ye take it by the way of calumny and open wrong?

How can ye take it (back) after one of you hath gone in unto the other, and they have taken a strong pledge from you?

4:19–21

3. If a woman feareth ill-treatment from her husband, or desertion, it is no sin for them twain if they make terms of peace between themselves. Peace is better. But greed hath been made present in the minds (of men). If ye do good and keep from evil, lo! Allah is ever Informed of what ye do.

4:128

See also: Divorce.

KNOWLEDGE

1. They will ask thee concerning the Spirit. Say: The Spirit is by command of my Lord, and of knowledge ye have been vouchsafed but little.

17:85

2. Those who have been given knowledge see that what is revealed unto thee from thy Lord is the truth and leadeth unto the Path of the Mighty, the Owner of Praise.

34:6

3. The erudite among His bondmen fear Allah alone. Lo! Allah is Mighty, Forgiving.

35:28

4. Say (unto them, O Muhammad): Are those who know equal with those who know not? But only men of understanding will pay heed.

39:9

5. O ye who believe! When it is said unto you, Make room! in assemblies, then make room; Allah will make way for you (hereafter). And when it is said, Come up higher! go up higher; Allah will exalt those who believe among you, and those who have knowledge, to high ranks. Allah is Informed of what ye do.

58:11

6. Read: In the name of thy

1. وَيَسْـَٔلُونَكَ عَنِ الرُّوحِ ۖ قُلِ الرُّوحُ مِنْ
أَمْرِ رَبِّي وَمَا أُوتِيتُم مِّنَ الْعِلْمِ
إِلَّا قَلِيلًا ﴿٨٥﴾

2. وَيَرَى الَّذِينَ أُوتُوا الْعِلْمَ الَّذِي أُنزِلَ
إِلَيْكَ مِن رَّبِّكَ هُوَ الْحَقَّ وَيَهْدِي
إِلَىٰ صِرَاطِ الْعَزِيزِ الْحَمِيدِ ﴿٦﴾

3. إِنَّمَا يَخْشَى اللَّهَ مِنْ عِبَادِهِ الْعُلَمَاءُ
إِنَّ اللَّهَ عَزِيزٌ غَفُورٌ ﴿٢٨﴾

4. قُلْ هَلْ يَسْتَوِي الَّذِينَ يَعْلَمُونَ
وَالَّذِينَ لَا يَعْلَمُونَ ۗ إِنَّمَا يَتَذَكَّرُ
أُولُوا الْأَلْبَابِ ﴿٩﴾

5. يَا أَيُّهَا الَّذِينَ آمَنُوا إِذَا قِيلَ لَكُمْ
تَفَسَّحُوا فِي الْمَجَالِسِ فَافْسَحُوا يَفْسَحِ
اللَّهُ لَكُمْ ۖ وَإِذَا قِيلَ انشُزُوا فَانشُزُوا
يَرْفَعِ اللَّهُ الَّذِينَ آمَنُوا مِنكُمْ وَالَّذِينَ
أُوتُوا الْعِلْمَ دَرَجَاتٍ ۚ وَاللَّهُ بِمَا
تَعْمَلُونَ خَبِيرٌ ﴿١١﴾

6. اقْرَأْ بِاسْمِ رَبِّكَ الَّذِي خَلَقَ ﴿١﴾
خَلَقَ الْإِنسَانَ مِنْ عَلَقٍ ﴿٢﴾
اقْرَأْ وَرَبُّكَ الْأَكْرَمُ ﴿٣﴾
الَّذِي عَلَّمَ بِالْقَلَمِ ﴿٤﴾
عَلَّمَ الْإِنسَانَ مَا لَمْ يَعْلَمْ ﴿٥﴾

Lord Who createth,

Createth man from a clot.

Read: And thy Lord is the Most Bounteous,

Who teacheth by the pen,

Teacheth man that which he knew not.

96:1–5

See also: Ignorance.

KNOWLEDGE OF HIDDEN

1. It is not (the purpose) of Allah to leave you in your present state till He shall separate the wicked from the good. And it is not (the purpose of) Allah to let you know the Unseen. But Allah chooseth of His messengers whom He will, (to receive knowledge thereof).

3:179

2. And with Him are the keys of the Invisible. None but He knoweth them. And He knoweth what is in the land and the sea. Not a leaf falleth but He knoweth it, not a grain amid the darkness of the earth, naught of wet or dry but (it is noted) in a clear record.

6:59

3. And they will say: If only a portent were sent down upon him from his Lord! Then say (O Muhammad): The Unseen belongeth to Allah. So wait! Lo, I am waiting with you.

10:20

4. And unto Allah belongeth the Unseen of the heavens and the earth, and the matter of the Hour (of Doom) is but as a twinkling of the eye, or it is nearer still. Lo! Allah is Able to do all things.

16:77

5. Say (O Muhammad): None in the heavens and the earth knoweth the Unseen save Allah; and they know not

1. مَا كَانَ اللّٰهُ لِيَذَرَ الْمُؤْمِنِيْنَ عَلٰى مَآ اَنْتُمْ
عَلَيْهِ حَتّٰى يَمِيْزَ الْخَبِيْثَ مِنَ الطَّيِّبِ ۭ وَمَا
كَانَ اللّٰهُ لِيُطْلِعَكُمْ عَلَى الْغَيْبِ وَلٰكِنَّ اللّٰهَ
يَجْتَبِىْ مِنْ رُّسُلِهٖ مَنْ يَّشَاۗءُ

2. وَعِنْدَهٗ مَفَاتِحُ الْغَيْبِ لَا يَعْلَمُهَآ اِلَّا
هُوَ ۭ وَيَعْلَمُ مَا فِي الْبَرِّ وَالْبَحْرِ ۭ وَمَا
تَسْقُطُ مِنْ وَّرَقَةٍ اِلَّا يَعْلَمُهَا وَلَا حَبَّةٍ
فِيْ ظُلُمٰتِ الْاَرْضِ وَلَا رَطْبٍ وَّلَا يَابِسٍ
اِلَّا فِيْ كِتٰبٍ مُّبِيْنٍ ﴿٥٩﴾

3. وَيَقُوْلُوْنَ لَوْلَآ اُنْزِلَ عَلَيْهِ اٰيَةٌ مِّنْ
رَّبِّهٖ ۚ فَقُلْ اِنَّمَا الْغَيْبُ لِلّٰهِ فَانْتَظِرُوْا ۚ
اِنِّىْ مَعَكُمْ مِّنَ الْمُنْتَظِرِيْنَ ﴿٢٠﴾

4. وَلِلّٰهِ غَيْبُ السَّمٰوٰتِ وَالْاَرْضِ ۭ وَمَآ
اَمْرُ السَّاعَةِ اِلَّا كَلَمْحِ الْبَصَرِ اَوْ هُوَ
اَقْرَبُ ۭ اِنَّ اللّٰهَ عَلٰى كُلِّ شَيْءٍ قَدِيْرٌ ﴿٧٧﴾

5. قُلْ لَّا يَعْلَمُ مَنْ فِي السَّمٰوٰتِ وَ
الْاَرْضِ الْغَيْبَ اِلَّا اللّٰهُ ۭ وَمَا يَشْعُرُوْنَ
اَيَّانَ يُبْعَثُوْنَ ﴿٦٥﴾

6. اِنَّ اللّٰهَ عِنْدَهٗ عِلْمُ السَّاعَةِ ۚ وَيُنَزِّلُ
الْغَيْثَ ۚ وَيَعْلَمُ مَا فِي الْاَرْحَامِ ۭ
وَمَا تَدْرِيْ نَفْسٌ مَّاذَا تَكْسِبُ غَدًا ۭ
وَمَا تَدْرِيْ نَفْسٌۢ بِاَيِّ اَرْضٍ

when they will be raised (again).

27:65

6. Lo! Allah! With Him is knowledge of the Hour. He sendeth down the rain, and knoweth that which is in the wombs. No soul knoweth what it will earn to-morrow, and no soul knoweth in what

land it will die. Lo! Allah is Knower, Aware.

31:34

تَمُوتُ ۚ إِنَّ اللَّهَ عَلِيمٌ خَبِيرٌ

7. Lo! Allah is the Knower of the Unseen of the heavens and the earth. Lo! He is Aware of the secret of (men's) breasts.

35:38

7. إِنَّ اللَّهَ عَٰلِمُ غَيْبِ السَّمَٰوَٰتِ وَالْأَرْضِ ۚ إِنَّهُ عَلِيمٌ بِذَاتِ الصُّدُورِ

8. (He is) the Knower of the Unseen, and He revealeth unto none His secret,

Save unto every messenger whom He hath chosen, and then He maketh a guard to go before him and a guard behind him.

72:26–27

8. عَٰلِمُ الْغَيْبِ فَلَا يُظْهِرُ عَلَىٰ غَيْبِهِ أَحَدًا ۝ إِلَّا مَنِ ارْتَضَىٰ مِن رَّسُولٍ فَإِنَّهُ يَسْلُكُ مِنۢ بَيْنِ يَدَيْهِ وَمِنْ خَلْفِهِ رَصَدًا

○

Ref: 6:73; 7:187; 11:123; 18:26; 32:6; 33:63; 34:48; 39:46; 49:18; 64:18; 79:42–46.

KUFR

1. He who chooseth disbelief instead of faith, verily he hath gone astray from a plain road.

2:108

2. Let not their conduct grieve thee, who run easily to disbelief, for lo! they injure Allah not at all. It is Allah's Will to assign them no portion in the Hereafter, and theirs will be an awful doom.

Those who purchase disbelief at the price of faith harm Allah not at all, but theirs will be a painful doom.

3:176–177

3. O ye who believe! Believe in Allah and His messenger and the Scripture which He hath revealed unto His messenger, and the Scripture which he revealed aforetime. Whoso disbelieveth in Allah and His angels and His scriptures and His messengers and the Last Day, he verily hath wandered far astray.

Lo! those who believe, then disbelieve and then (again) believe, then disbelieve, and then increase in disbelief, Allah will never pardon them, nor will He guide them unto a way.

4:136–137

4. O ye who believe! Choose not your fathers nor your brethren for friends if they take pleasure in disbelief

1. وَمَنْ يَتَبَدَّلِ الْكُفْرَ بِالْإِيمَانِ فَقَدْ
ضَلَّ سَوَآءَ السَّبِيلِ ۝١٠٨

2. وَلَا يَحْزُنْكَ الَّذِينَ يُسَارِعُونَ فِي الْكُفْرِ ۚ
إِنَّهُمْ لَنْ يَضُرُّوا اللّٰهَ شَيْـًٔا ۗ يُرِيدُ اللّٰهُ
أَلَّا يَجْعَلَ لَهُمْ حَظًّا فِي الْأٰخِرَةِ ۚ وَ
لَهُمْ عَذَابٌ عَظِيمٌ ۝

إِنَّ الَّذِينَ اشْتَرَوُا الْكُفْرَ بِالْإِيمَانِ
لَنْ يَضُرُّوا اللّٰهَ شَيْـًٔا ۚ وَلَهُمْ عَذَابٌ أَلِيمٌ ۝

3. يٰٓأَيُّهَا الَّذِينَ اٰمَنُوٓا اٰمِنُوا بِاللّٰهِ وَرَسُولِهٖ
وَالْكِتٰبِ الَّذِي نَزَّلَ عَلٰى رَسُولِهٖ وَالْكِتٰبِ
الَّذِيٓ أَنْزَلَ مِنْ قَبْلُ ۗ وَمَنْ يَكْفُرْ
بِاللّٰهِ وَمَلٰٓئِكَتِهٖ وَكُتُبِهٖ وَرُسُلِهٖ
وَالْيَوْمِ الْاٰخِرِ فَقَدْ ضَلَّ ضَلٰلًا ۢ بَعِيدًا ۝١٣٦

إِنَّ الَّذِينَ اٰمَنُوا ثُمَّ كَفَرُوا ثُمَّ اٰمَنُوا ثُمَّ
كَفَرُوا ثُمَّ ازْدَادُوا كُفْرًا لَمْ يَكُنِ اللّٰهُ
لِيَغْفِرَ لَهُمْ وَلَا لِيَهْدِيَهُمْ سَبِيلًا ۗ ۝١٣٧

4. يٰٓأَيُّهَا الَّذِينَ اٰمَنُوا لَا تَتَّخِذُوٓا اٰبَآءَكُمْ
وَإِخْوَانَكُمْ أَوْلِيَآءَ إِنِ اسْتَحَبُّوا الْكُفْرَ
عَلَى الْإِيمَانِ ۗ وَمَنْ يَتَوَلَّهُمْ مِنْكُمْ
فَأُولٰٓئِكَ هُمُ الظّٰلِمُونَ ۝٢٣

5. مَنْ كَفَرَ بِاللّٰهِ مِنْ بَعْدِ إِيمَانِهٖٓ إِلَّا مَنْ
أُكْرِهَ وَقَلْبُهُ مُطْمَئِنٌّ ۢ بِالْإِيمَانِ وَلٰكِنْ

rather than faith. Whoso of you taketh them for friends, such are wrong–doers.

9:23

5. Whoso disbelieveth in Allah after his belief–save him who is forced thereto and whose heart is still

content with Faith—but who-so findeth ease in disbelief: On them is wrath from Allah. Theirs will be an awful doom.

16:106

6. If ye are thankless, yet Allah is Independent of you, though He is not pleased with thanklessness for His bond-men; and if ye are thankful He is pleased therewith for you. No laden soul will bear another's load. Then unto your Lord is your return; and He will tell you what ye used to do. Lo! He knoweth what is in the breasts (of men)

And when some hurt toucheth man, he crieth unto his Lord, turning unto Him (repentant). Then, when He granteth him a boon from Him he forgetteth that for which he cried unto Him before, and setteth up rivals to Allah that he may beguile (men) from His way. Say (O Muhammad, unto such a one): Take pleasure in thy disbelief a while. Lo! thou art of the owners of the Fire.

39:7–8

مَّنْ شَرَحَ بِالْكُفْرِ صَدْرًا فَعَلَيْهِمْ
غَضَبٌ مِّنَ اللّٰهِ ۚ وَلَهُمْ عَذَابٌ عَظِيمٌ ۝

6. اِنْ تَكْفُرُوْا فَاِنَّ اللّٰهَ غَنِيٌّ عَنْكُمْ ۟ وَلَا
يَرْضٰى لِعِبَادِهِ الْكُفْرَ ۚ وَ اِنْ تَشْكُرُوْا
يَرْضَهُ لَكُمْ ؕ وَلَا تَزِرُ وَازِرَةٌ وِّزْرَ
اُخْرٰى ؕ ثُمَّ اِلٰى رَبِّكُمْ مَّرْجِعُكُمْ فَيُنَبِّئُكُمْ
بِمَا كُنْتُمْ تَعْمَلُوْنَ ؕ اِنَّهٗ عَلِيْمٌۢ
بِذَاتِ الصُّدُوْرِ ۝
وَاِذَا مَسَّ الْاِنْسَانَ ضُرٌّ دَعَا رَبَّهٗ
مُنِيْبًا اِلَيْهِ ثُمَّ اِذَا خَوَّلَهٗ نِعْمَةً مِّنْهُ
نَسِيَ مَا كَانَ يَدْعُوْۤا اِلَيْهِ مِنْ قَبْلُ
وَجَعَلَ لِلّٰهِ اَنْدَادًا لِّيُضِلَّ عَنْ سَبِيْلِهٖ ؕ
قُلْ تَمَتَّعْ بِكُفْرِكَ قَلِيْلًا ۖ اِنَّكَ مِنْ
اَصْحٰبِ النَّارِ ۝

See also: Faith.

LAILAT AL-QADR

1. Lo! We revealed it on a blessed Night—Lo! We are ever warning—

Whereupon every wise command is made clear.

As a command from Our presence—Lo! We are ever sending—

A mercy from thy Lord.

44:3–6

2. Lo! We revealed it on the Night of Power.

Ah, what will convey unto thee what the Night of Power is!

The Night of Power is better than a thousand months.

The angels and the Spirit descend therein, by the permission of their Lord, with all decrees.

(That night is) Peace until the rising of the dawn.

97:1–5

1. إِنَّآ أَنزَلْنَٰهُ فِى لَيْلَةٍ مُّبَٰرَكَةٍ
إِنَّا كُنَّا مُنذِرِينَ ﴿٣﴾
فِيهَا يُفْرَقُ كُلُّ أَمْرٍ حَكِيمٍ ﴿٤﴾
أَمْرًا مِّنْ عِندِنَآ ۚ إِنَّا كُنَّا مُرْسِلِينَ ﴿٥﴾
رَحْمَةً مِّن رَّبِّكَ

2. إِنَّآ أَنزَلْنَٰهُ فِى لَيْلَةِ ٱلْقَدْرِ ﴿١﴾
وَمَآ أَدْرَىٰكَ مَا لَيْلَةُ ٱلْقَدْرِ ﴿٢﴾
لَيْلَةُ ٱلْقَدْرِ خَيْرٌ مِّنْ أَلْفِ شَهْرٍ ﴿٣﴾
تَنَزَّلُ ٱلْمَلَٰٓئِكَةُ وَٱلرُّوحُ فِيهَا
بِإِذْنِ رَبِّهِم مِّن كُلِّ أَمْرٍ ﴿٤﴾
سَلَٰمٌ هِىَ حَتَّىٰ مَطْلَعِ ٱلْفَجْرِ ﴿٥﴾

LAUH-I-MAHFUZ

1. Allah effaceth what He will, and establisheth (what He will), and with Him is source of ordinance.
13:39

2. And every thing they did is in the Scriptures,
And every small and great thing is recorded.
54:52–53.

3. Naught of disaster befalleth in the earth or in yourselves but it is in a Book before We bring into being. Lo! that is easy for Allah.
57:22

4. Everything have We recorded in a Book.
78:29

5. Nay, but it is a Glorious Qur'ān
On a guarded tablet.
85:21–22

1. يَمْحُوا اللّٰهُ مَا يَشَآءُ وَيُثْبِتُ ۖ وَعِنْدَهٗ
أُمُّ الْكِتٰبِ ۝

2. وَكُلُّ شَيْءٍ فَعَلُوْهُ فِي الزُّبُرِ ۝
وَكُلُّ صَغِيْرٍ وَّكَبِيْرٍ مُّسْتَطَرٌ ۝

3. مَآ أَصَابَ مِنْ مُّصِيْبَةٍ فِي الْأَرْضِ
وَلَا فِيْٓ أَنْفُسِكُمْ إِلَّا فِيْ كِتٰبٍ مِّنْ قَبْلِ
أَنْ نَّبْرَاَهَا ۚ إِنَّ ذٰلِكَ عَلَى اللّٰهِ يَسِيْرٌ ۝

4. وَكُلَّ شَيْءٍ أَحْصَيْنٰهُ كِتٰبًا ۝

5. بَلْ هُوَ قُرْاٰنٌ مَّجِيْدٌ ۝
فِيْ لَوْحٍ مَّحْفُوْظٍ ۝

LEADERS AND THEIR FOLLOWERS

1. (On the day) when those who were followed disown those who followed (them), and they behold the doom, and all their aims collapse with them.

And those who were but followers will say: If a return were possible for us, we would disown them even as they have disowned us. Thus will Allah show them their own deeds as anguish for them, and they will not emerge from the Fire.

2:166–167

2. They all come forth unto their Lord. Then those who were despised say unto those who were scornful: We were unto you a following, can ye then avert from us aught of Allah's doom? They say: Had Allah guided us, we should have guided you. Whether we rage or patiently endure is (now) all one for us; we have no place of refuge.

14:21

3. On the Day when their faces are turned over in the Fire, they say: Oh, would that we had obeyed Allah and had obeyed His messenger!

And they say: Our Lord! Lo! we obeyed our princes and great men, and they misled us from the Way:

Our Lord! Oh, give them double torment and curse

1. إِذْ تَبَرَّأَ الَّذِينَ اتُّبِعُوا مِنَ الَّذِينَ اتَّبَعُوا
وَرَأَوُا الْعَذَابَ وَتَقَطَّعَتْ بِهِمُ الْأَسْبَابُ ﴿١٦٦﴾
وَقَالَ الَّذِينَ اتَّبَعُوا لَوْ أَنَّ لَنَا كَرَّةً فَنَتَبَرَّأَ
مِنْهُمْ كَمَا تَبَرَّءُوا مِنَّا ۗ كَذَٰلِكَ يُرِيهِمُ اللَّهُ
أَعْمَالَهُمْ حَسَرَاتٍ عَلَيْهِمْ ۖ وَمَا هُمْ بِخَارِجِينَ
مِنَ النَّارِ ﴿١٦٧﴾

2. وَبَرَزُوا لِلَّهِ جَمِيعًا فَقَالَ الضُّعَفَاءُ
لِلَّذِينَ اسْتَكْبَرُوا إِنَّا كُنَّا لَكُمْ تَبَعًا فَهَلْ
أَنْتُمْ مُغْنُونَ عَنَّا مِنْ عَذَابِ اللَّهِ مِنْ
شَيْءٍ ۚ قَالُوا لَوْ هَدَانَا اللَّهُ لَهَدَيْنَاكُمْ ۖ
سَوَاءٌ عَلَيْنَا أَجَزِعْنَا أَمْ صَبَرْنَا مَا
لَنَا مِنْ مَحِيصٍ ﴿٢١﴾

3. يَوْمَ تُقَلَّبُ وُجُوهُهُمْ فِي النَّارِ يَقُولُونَ
يَا لَيْتَنَا أَطَعْنَا اللَّهَ وَأَطَعْنَا الرَّسُولَا ﴿٦٦﴾

وَقَالُوا رَبَّنَا إِنَّا أَطَعْنَا سَادَتَنَا وَكُبَرَاءَنَا
فَأَضَلُّونَا السَّبِيلَا ﴿٦٧﴾

رَبَّنَا آتِهِمْ ضِعْفَيْنِ مِنَ الْعَذَابِ
وَالْعَنْهُمْ لَعْنًا كَبِيرًا ﴿٦٨﴾

4. قَالَ الَّذِينَ اسْتَكْبَرُوا لِلَّذِينَ اسْتُضْعِفُوا
أَنَحْنُ صَدَدْنَاكُمْ عَنِ الْهُدَىٰ بَعْدَ إِذْ
جَاءَكُمْ ۖ بَلْ كُنْتُمْ مُجْرِمِينَ ﴿٣٢﴾

وَقَالَ الَّذِينَ اسْتُضْعِفُوا لِلَّذِينَ اسْتَكْبَرُوا
بَلْ مَكْرُ اللَّيْلِ وَالنَّهَارِ إِذْ تَأْمُرُونَنَا أَنْ

them with a mighty curse!

33:66–68

4. And those who were proud say unto those who were despised: Did we drive you away from the guidance after it had come unto you? Nay, but ye were guilty.

Those who were despised say unto those who were

proud: Nay but (it was your) scheming night and day, when ye commanded us to disbelieve in Allah and set up rivals unto Him. And they are filled with remorse when they behold the doom.

34:32–33

5. And when they wrangle in the Fire, the weak say unto those who were proud: Lo! we were a following unto you: will ye therefor rid us of a portion of the Fire?

Those who were proud say: Lo! we are all (together) herein. Lo! Allah hath judged between (His) slaves.

40:47–48

تَكْفُرَ بِاللّٰهِ وَنَجْعَلَ لَهٗۤ اَنْدَادًا ۭ وَاَسَرُّوا
النَّدَامَةَ لَمَّا رَاَوُا الْعَذَابَ ۭ

5. وَاِذْ يَتَحَاۤجُّوْنَ فِي النَّارِ فَيَقُوْلُ الضُّعَفٰۗؤُا
لِلَّذِيْنَ اسْتَكْبَرُوْۤا اِنَّا كُنَّا لَكُمْ تَبَعًا فَهَلْ
اَنْتُمْ مُّغْنُوْنَ عَنَّا نَصِيْبًا مِّنَ النَّارِ ﴿٤٧﴾

قَالَ الَّذِيْنَ اسْتَكْبَرُوْۤا اِنَّا كُلٌّ فِيْهَاۤ ۙ
اِنَّ اللّٰهَ قَدْ حَكَمَ بَيْنَ الْعِبَادِ ﴿٤٨﴾

See also: ***Imam.***

LEADERS OF DISBELIEVERS

1. And when they went into the field against Goliath and his hosts they said: Our Lord! Bestow on us endurance, make our foothold sure, and give us help against the disbelieving folk.

So they routed them by Allah's leave and David slew Goliath; and Allah gave him the kingdom and wisdom, and taught him of that which He willeth. And if Allah had not repelled some men by others the earth would have been corrupted. But Allah is a Lord of Kindness to (His) creatures.

2:250–251

2. (Remember) when Abraham said unto his father Azar; Takest thou idols for gods? Lo! I see thee and thy folk in error manifest.

6:74

3. But none trusted Moses, save some scions of his people, (and they were) in fear of Pharaoh and their chiefs, that he would persecute them. Lo! Pharaoh was verily a tyrant in the land, and lo! he verily was of the wanton.

10:83

4. And Moses said: Our Lord! Lo! Thou hast given Pharaoh and his chiefs splendour and riches in the life of the world, Our Lord! that they may lead men

1. وَلَمَّا بَرَزُوا لِجَالُوتَ وَجُنُودِهِ قَالُوا رَبَّنَا
أَفْرِغْ عَلَيْنَا صَبْرًا وَثَبِّتْ أَقْدَامَنَا وَ
انْصُرْنَا عَلَى الْقَوْمِ الْكٰفِرِينَ ﴿٢٥٠﴾
فَهَزَمُوهُمْ بِإِذْنِ اللّٰهِ وَقَتَلَ دَاوٗدُ جَالُوتَ
وَآتٰىهُ اللّٰهُ الْمُلْكَ وَالْحِكْمَةَ وَعَلَّمَهٗ مِمَّا
يَشَاءُ وَلَوْلَا دَفْعُ اللّٰهِ النَّاسَ بَعْضَهُمْ
بِبَعْضٍ لَّفَسَدَتِ الْأَرْضُ وَلٰكِنَّ اللّٰهَ
ذُو فَضْلٍ عَلَى الْعٰلَمِينَ ﴿٢٥١﴾

2. وَإِذْ قَالَ إِبْرٰهِيمُ لِأَبِيهِ آزَرَ أَتَتَّخِذُ
أَصْنَامًا آلِهَةً إِنِّي أَرٰىكَ وَقَوْمَكَ
فِي ضَلٰلٍ مُّبِينٍ ﴿٧٤﴾

3. فَمَا آمَنَ لِمُوسٰى إِلَّا ذُرِّيَّةٌ مِّنْ قَوْمِهِ
عَلٰى خَوْفٍ مِّنْ فِرْعَوْنَ وَمَلَائِهِمْ أَنْ
يَّفْتِنَهُمْ وَإِنَّ فِرْعَوْنَ لَعَالٍ فِي الْأَرْضِ
وَإِنَّهٗ لَمِنَ الْمُسْرِفِينَ ﴿٨٣﴾

4. وَقَالَ مُوسٰى رَبَّنَا إِنَّكَ آتَيْتَ فِرْعَوْنَ
وَمَلَأَهٗ زِينَةً وَّأَمْوَالًا فِي الْحَيٰوةِ الدُّنْيَا
رَبَّنَا لِيُضِلُّوا عَنْ سَبِيلِكَ رَبَّنَا اطْمِسْ
عَلٰى أَمْوَالِهِمْ وَاشْدُدْ عَلٰى قُلُوبِهِمْ فَلَا
يُؤْمِنُوا حَتّٰى يَرَوُا الْعَذَابَ الْأَلِيمَ ﴿٨٨﴾
قَالَ قَدْ أُجِيبَتْ دَّعْوَتُكُمَا فَاسْتَقِيمَا وَلَا

astray from Thy Way. Our Lord! Destroy their riches and harden their hearts so that they believe not till they see the painful doom.

He said: Your prayer is heard. Do ye twain keep to the Straight path, and follow not the road of those who have no knowledge.

And We brought the Children of Israel across the sea, and Pharaoh with his hosts pursued them in rebellion and transgression, till, when the (fate of) drowning overtook him, he exclaimed: I believe that there is no God save Him in Whom the Children of Israel believe, and I am of those who surrender (unto Him).

What! Now! When hitherto thou hast rebelled and been of the wrong-doers?

But this day We save thee in thy body that thou mayest be a portent for those after thee. Lo! most of mankind are heedless of Our portents.

10:88–92

5. And Pharaoh said: O chiefs! I know not that ye have a god other than me, so kindle for me (a fire), O Haman, to bake the mud; and set up for me a lofty tower in order that I may survey the God of Moses; and lo! I deem him of the liars.

And he and his hosts were haughty in the land without right, and deemed that they would never be brought back to Us.

Therefor We seized him and his hosts, and abandoned them unto the sea. Behold the nature of the consequence for evil–doers!

And We made them

تَتَّبِعَآنِّ سَبِيلَ الَّذِينَ لَا يَعْلَمُونَ ٨٩
وَجٰوَزْنَا بِبَنِىٓ إِسْرَآءِيلَ الْبَحْرَ فَأَتْبَعَهُمْ
فِرْعَوْنُ وَجُنُودُهُۥ بَغْيًا وَعَدْوًا ۖ حَتّٰىٓ إِذَآ
أَدْرَكَهُ الْغَرَقُ قَالَ ءَامَنتُ أَنَّهُۥ لَآ إِلٰهَ
إِلَّا الَّذِىٓ ءَامَنَتْ بِهِۦ بَنُوٓا إِسْرَآءِيلَ وَأَنَا۠
مِنَ الْمُسْلِمِينَ ٩٠

ءَآلْـٰٔنَ وَقَدْ عَصَيْتَ قَبْلُ وَكُنتَ
مِنَ الْمُفْسِدِينَ ٩١

فَالْيَوْمَ نُنَجِّيكَ بِبَدَنِكَ لِتَكُونَ لِمَنْ
خَلْفَكَ ءَايَةً ۚ وَإِنَّ كَثِيرًا مِّنَ النَّاسِ
عَنْ ءَايٰتِنَا لَغٰفِلُونَ ٩٢

5. وَقَالَ فِرْعَوْنُ يٰٓأَيُّهَا الْمَلَأُ مَا
عَلِمْتُ لَكُم مِّنْ إِلٰهٍ غَيْرِى فَأَوْقِدْ
لِى يٰهٰمٰنُ عَلَى الطِّينِ فَاجْعَل لِّى صَرْحًا
لَّعَلِّىٓ أَطَّلِعُ إِلٰىٓ إِلٰهِ مُوسٰى وَإِنِّى
لَأَظُنُّهُۥ مِنَ الْكٰذِبِينَ ٣٨
وَاسْتَكْبَرَ هُوَ وَجُنُودُهُۥ فِى الْأَرْضِ
بِغَيْرِ الْحَقِّ وَظَنُّوٓا أَنَّهُمْ إِلَيْنَا
لَا يُرْجَعُونَ ٣٩
فَأَخَذْنٰهُ وَجُنُودَهُۥ فَنَبَذْنٰهُمْ فِى الْيَمِّ ۖ
فَانظُرْ كَيْفَ كَانَ عٰقِبَةُ الظّٰلِمِينَ ٤٠
وَجَعَلْنٰهُمْ أَئِمَّةً يَدْعُونَ إِلَى النَّارِ ۖ
وَيَوْمَ الْقِيٰمَةِ لَا يُنصَرُونَ ٤١

patterns that invite unto the Fire, and on the Day of Re–surrection they will not be helped.

28:38–41

6. Now Korah was of Moses' folk, but he oppressed them; and We gave him so much treasure that the stores thereof would verily have been a burden for a troop of mighty men. When his own folk said unto him: Exult not; lo! Allah loveth not the exultant.

But seek the abode of the Hereafter in that which Allah hath given thee and neglect not thy portion of the world and be thou kind even as Allah hath been kind to thee, and seek not corruption in the earth; lo! Allah loveth not corrupters.

He said: I have been given it only on account of knowledge I possess. Knew he not that Allah had destroyed already of the generations before him men who were mightier than him in strength and greater in respect of following? The guilty are not questioned of their sins.

Then went he forth before his people in his pomp. Those who were desirous of the life of the world said: Ah! would that we had the like of what hath been given unto Korah! Lo! he is lord of rare good fortune.

But those who had been given knowledge said: Woe unto you! The reward of Allah for him who believeth and doth right is better, and only the steadfast will obtain it.

6. إِنَّ قَارُونَ كَانَ مِنْ قَوْمِ مُوسٰى فَبَغٰى
عَلَيْهِمْ وَاٰتَيْنٰهُ مِنَ الْكُنُوْزِ مَآ إِنَّ
مَفَاتِحَهٗ لَتَنُوْٓاُ بِالْعُصْبَةِ أُولِي الْقُوَّةِ
إِذْ قَالَ لَهٗ قَوْمُهٗ لَا تَفْرَحْ إِنَّ
اللّٰهَ لَا يُحِبُّ الْفَرِحِيْنَ (٧٦)
وَابْتَغِ فِيْمَآ اٰتٰىكَ اللّٰهُ الدَّارَ الْاٰخِرَةَ
وَلَا تَنْسَ نَصِيْبَكَ مِنَ الدُّنْيَا وَ
أَحْسِنْ كَمَآ أَحْسَنَ اللّٰهُ إِلَيْكَ وَلَا تَبْغِ
الْفَسَادَ فِي الْأَرْضِ إِنَّ اللّٰهَ لَا
يُحِبُّ الْمُفْسِدِيْنَ (٧٧)
قَالَ إِنَّمَآ أُوْتِيْتُهٗ عَلٰى عِلْمٍ عِنْدِيْ
أَوَلَمْ يَعْلَمْ أَنَّ اللّٰهَ قَدْ أَهْلَكَ مِنْ
قَبْلِهٖ مِنَ الْقُرُوْنِ مَنْ هُوَ أَشَدُّ مِنْهُ
قُوَّةً وَّأَكْثَرُ جَمْعًا وَلَا يُسْئَلُ
عَنْ ذُنُوْبِهِمُ الْمُجْرِمُوْنَ (٧٨)
فَخَرَجَ عَلٰى قَوْمِهٖ فِيْ زِيْنَتِهٖ قَالَ
الَّذِيْنَ يُرِيْدُوْنَ الْحَيٰوةَ الدُّنْيَا يٰلَيْتَ
لَنَا مِثْلَ مَآ أُوْتِيَ قَارُوْنُ إِنَّهٗ
لَذُوْ حَظٍّ عَظِيْمٍ (٧٩)
وَقَالَ الَّذِيْنَ أُوْتُوا الْعِلْمَ وَيْلَكُمْ
ثَوَابُ اللّٰهِ خَيْرٌ لِّمَنْ اٰمَنَ وَعَمِلَ
صَالِحًا وَلَا يُلَقّٰهَآ إِلَّا الصّٰبِرُوْنَ (٨٠)
فَخَسَفْنَا بِهٖ وَبِدَارِهِ الْأَرْضَ
فَمَا كَانَ لَهٗ مِنْ فِئَةٍ يَّنْصُرُوْنَهٗ

So We caused the earth to swallow him and his dwelling-place. Then he had no host to help him against Allah, nor was he of those who can save themselves.

And morning found those

who had coveted his place but yesterday crying: Ah, welladay! Allah enlargeth the provision for whom He will of His slaves and straiteneth it (for whom He will). If Allah had not been gracious unto us He would have caused it to swallow us (also). Ah, welladay! the disbelievers never prosper.

28:76–82

7. The power of *Abu Lahab* will perish, and he will perish.

His wealth and gains will not exempt him.

He will be plunged in flaming Fire,

And his wife, the wood–carrier,

Will have upon her neck a halter of palm–fibre.

111:1–5

مِنْ دُوْنِ اللّٰهِ ۗ وَمَا كَانَ مِنَ
الْمُنْتَصِرِيْنَ ﴿٨١﴾
وَاَصْبَحَ الَّذِيْنَ تَمَنَّوْا مَكَانَهٗ
بِالْاَمْسِ يَقُوْلُوْنَ وَيْكَاَنَّ اللّٰهَ
يَبْسُطُ الرِّزْقَ لِمَنْ يَّشَآءُ مِنْ عِبَادِهٖ
وَيَقْدِرُ ۚ لَوْلَآ اَنْ مَّنَّ اللّٰهُ عَلَيْنَا لَخَسَفَ
بِنَا ۭ وَيْكَاَنَّهٗ لَا يُفْلِحُ الْكٰفِرُوْنَ ﴿٨٢﴾

7. تَبَّتْ يَدَآ اَبِيْ لَهَبٍ وَّتَبَّ ﴿١﴾
مَآ اَغْنٰى عَنْهُ مَالُهٗ وَمَا كَسَبَ ﴿٢﴾
سَيَصْلٰى نَارًا ذَاتَ لَهَبٍ ﴿٣﴾
وَّامْرَاَتُهٗ ۭ حَمَّالَةَ الْحَطَبِ ﴿٤﴾
فِيْ جِيْدِهَا حَبْلٌ مِّنْ مَّسَدٍ ﴿٥﴾

LI'AN

1. As for those who accuse their wives but have no witnesses except themselves; let the testimony of one of them be four testimonies, (swearing) by Allah that he is of those who speak the truth.

And yet a fifth invoking the curse of Allah on him if he is of those who lie.

And it shall avert the punishment from her if she bear witness before Allah four times that the thing he saith is indeed false,

And a fifth (time) that the wrath of Allah be upon her if he speaketh truth.

And had it not been for the grace of Allah and His mercy unto you, and that Allah is Clement, Wise, (ye had been undone).

24:6–10

1. وَالَّذِينَ يَرْمُونَ أَزْوَاجَهُمْ وَلَمْ يَكُن
لَّهُمْ شُهَدَاءُ إِلَّا أَنفُسُهُمْ فَشَهَادَةُ
أَحَدِهِمْ أَرْبَعُ شَهَادَاتٍ بِاللَّهِ إِنَّهُ
لَمِنَ الصَّادِقِينَ ﴿٦﴾
وَالْخَامِسَةُ أَنَّ لَعْنَتَ اللَّهِ عَلَيْهِ
إِن كَانَ مِنَ الْكَاذِبِينَ ﴿٧﴾
وَيَدْرَؤُا عَنْهَا الْعَذَابَ أَن تَشْهَدَ
أَرْبَعَ شَهَادَاتٍ بِاللَّهِ إِنَّهُ لَمِنَ الْكَاذِبِينَ ﴿٨﴾
وَالْخَامِسَةَ أَنَّ غَضَبَ اللَّهِ عَلَيْهَا إِن
كَانَ مِنَ الصَّادِقِينَ ﴿٩﴾
وَلَوْلَا فَضْلُ اللَّهِ عَلَيْكُمْ وَرَحْمَتُهُ
وَأَنَّ اللَّهَ تَوَّابٌ حَكِيمٌ ﴿١٠﴾

LI'AN

See also: Disputes of Husband and Wife.

LIFE AFTER DEATH

1. أَلَمْ تَرَ إِلَى الَّذِي حَاجَّ إِبْرَٰهِيمَ فِي رَبِّهِ أَنْ
آتَاهُ اللَّهُ الْمُلْكَ إِذْ قَالَ إِبْرَٰهِيمُ رَبِّيَ الَّذِي
يُحْيِي وَيُمِيتُ قَالَ أَنَا أُحْيِي وَأُمِيتُ قَالَ
إِبْرَٰهِيمُ فَإِنَّ اللَّهَ يَأْتِي بِالشَّمْسِ مِنَ الْمَشْرِقِ
فَأْتِ بِهَا مِنَ الْمَغْرِبِ فَبُهِتَ الَّذِي كَفَرَ
وَاللَّهُ لَا يَهْدِي الْقَوْمَ الظَّٰلِمِينَ ﴿٢٥٨﴾
أَوْ كَالَّذِي مَرَّ عَلَىٰ قَرْيَةٍ وَهِيَ خَاوِيَةٌ
عَلَىٰ عُرُوشِهَا قَالَ أَنَّىٰ يُحْيِي هَٰذِهِ اللَّهُ
بَعْدَ مَوْتِهَا فَأَمَاتَهُ اللَّهُ مِائَةَ عَامٍ
ثُمَّ بَعَثَهُ قَالَ كَمْ لَبِثْتَ قَالَ لَبِثْتُ
يَوْمًا أَوْ بَعْضَ يَوْمٍ قَالَ بَلْ لَبِثْتَ مِائَةَ
عَامٍ فَانْظُرْ إِلَىٰ طَعَامِكَ وَشَرَابِكَ لَمْ
يَتَسَنَّهْ وَانْظُرْ إِلَىٰ حِمَارِكَ وَلِنَجْعَلَكَ
آيَةً لِلنَّاسِ وَانْظُرْ إِلَى الْعِظَامِ كَيْفَ
نُنْشِزُهَا ثُمَّ نَكْسُوهَا لَحْمًا فَلَمَّا تَبَيَّنَ لَهُ
قَالَ أَعْلَمُ أَنَّ اللَّهَ عَلَىٰ كُلِّ شَيْءٍ قَدِيرٌ ﴿٢٥٩﴾
وَإِذْ قَالَ إِبْرَٰهِيمُ رَبِّ أَرِنِي كَيْفَ تُحْيِي
الْمَوْتَىٰ قَالَ أَوَلَمْ تُؤْمِنْ قَالَ بَلَىٰ وَلَٰكِنْ
لِيَطْمَئِنَّ قَلْبِي قَالَ فَخُذْ أَرْبَعَةً مِنَ الطَّيْرِ
فَصُرْهُنَّ إِلَيْكَ ثُمَّ اجْعَلْ عَلَىٰ كُلِّ جَبَلٍ
مِنْهُنَّ جُزْءًا ثُمَّ ادْعُهُنَّ يَأْتِينَكَ سَعْيًا
وَاعْلَمْ أَنَّ اللَّهَ عَزِيزٌ حَكِيمٌ ﴿٢٦٠﴾

2. وَقَالُوا أَإِذَا كُنَّا عِظَامًا وَرُفَاتًا أَإِنَّا
لَمَبْعُوثُونَ خَلْقًا جَدِيدًا ﴿٤٩﴾

1. Bethink thee of him who had an argument with Abraham about his Lord, because Allah had given him the kingdom; how, when Abraham said: My Lord is He who giveth life and causeth death, he answered: I give life and cause death. Abraham said: Lo! Allah causeth the sun to rise in the East, so do thou cause it to come up from the West. Thus was the disbeliever abashed. And Allah guideth not wrong-doing folk.

Or (bethink thee of) the like of him who passing by a township which had fallen into utter ruin, exclaimed: How shall Allah give this township life after its death? And Allah made him die a hundred years, then brought him back to life. He said: How long hast thou tarried? (The man) said: I have tarried a day or part of a day. (He) said: Nay but thou hast tarried for a hundred years. Just look at thy food and drink which have not rotted! Look at thine ass! And, that We may make thee a token unto mankind, look at the bones, how We adjust them and then cover them with flesh! And when (the matter) became clear unto him, he said: I know now that Allah is Able to do all things.

And when Abraham said (unto his Lord): My Lord! Show me how Thou givest life to the dead, He said: Dost thou not believe? Abraham said: Yea, but (I ask) in order that my heart may be at ease. (His Lord) said: Take four of the birds and cause them to incline unto thee, then place a part of them on each hill, then call them, they will come to thee in haste. And know

that Allah is Mighty, Wise.
2:258–260

2. And they say: When we are bones and fragments, shall we, forsooth, be raised up as a new creation?

Say: Be ye stones or iron;

Or some created thing that is yet greater in your thoughts! Then they will say: Who shall bring us back (to life)? Say: He Who created you at the first. Then will they shake their heads at thee, and say: When will it be? Say: It will perhaps be soon;

A day when He will call you and ye will answer with His praise, and ye will think that ye have tarried but a little while.

17:49–52

3. O mankind! If ye are in doubt concerning the Resurrection, then lo! We have created you from dust, then from a drop of seed, then from a clot, then from a little lump of flesh shapely and shapeless, that We may make (it) clear for you. And We cause what We will to remain in the wombs for an appointed time, and afterward We bring you forth as infants, then (give you growth) that ye attain your full strength. And among you there is he who dieth (young), and among you there is he who is brought back to the most abject time of life, so that, after knowledge, he knoweth naught. And thou (Muhammad) seest the earth barren, but when We send down water thereon, it doth thrill and swell and put forth every lovely kind (of growth).

That is because Allah, He is the Truth and because He quickeneth the dead, and because He is Able to do all things;

22:5–6

قُلْ كُونُوا حِجَارَةً اَوْ حَدِيدًا ﴿٥٠﴾

اَوْ خَلْقًا مِّمَّا يَكْبُرُ فِي صُدُوْرِكُمْ
فَسَيَقُوْلُوْنَ مَنْ يُّعِيْدُنَا ۚ قُلِ الَّذِيْ
فَطَرَكُمْ اَوَّلَ مَرَّةٍ ۚ فَسَيُنْغِضُوْنَ اِلَيْكَ
رُءُوْسَهُمْ وَيَقُوْلُوْنَ مَتٰى هُوَ ۚ قُلْ
عَسٰٓى اَنْ يَّكُوْنَ قَرِيْبًا ﴿٥١﴾

يَوْمَ يَدْعُوْكُمْ فَتَسْتَجِيْبُوْنَ بِحَمْدِهٖ
وَتَظُنُّوْنَ اِنْ لَّبِثْتُمْ اِلَّا قَلِيْلًا ﴿٥٢﴾

3. يٰٓاَيُّهَا النَّاسُ اِنْ كُنْتُمْ فِيْ رَيْبٍ مِّنَ
الْبَعْثِ فَاِنَّا خَلَقْنٰكُمْ مِّنْ تُرَابٍ ثُمَّ
مِنْ نُّطْفَةٍ ثُمَّ مِنْ عَلَقَةٍ ثُمَّ مِنْ
مُّضْغَةٍ مُّخَلَّقَةٍ وَّغَيْرِ مُخَلَّقَةٍ
لِّنُبَيِّنَ لَكُمْ ۚ وَنُقِرُّ فِي الْاَرْحَامِ مَا
نَشَآءُ اِلٰٓى اَجَلٍ مُّسَمًّى ثُمَّ نُخْرِجُكُمْ
طِفْلًا ثُمَّ لِتَبْلُغُوْٓا اَشُدَّكُمْ ۚ وَمِنْكُمْ
مَّنْ يُّتَوَفّٰى وَمِنْكُمْ مَّنْ يُّرَدُّ اِلٰٓى اَرْذَلِ
الْعُمُرِ لِكَيْلَا يَعْلَمَ مِنْۢ بَعْدِ عِلْمٍ شَيْـًٔا ۚ
وَتَرَى الْاَرْضَ هَامِدَةً فَاِذَآ اَنْزَلْنَا
عَلَيْهَا الْمَآءَ اهْتَزَّتْ وَرَبَتْ وَاَنْۢبَتَتْ
مِنْ كُلِّ زَوْجٍۢ بَهِيْجٍ ﴿٥﴾

ذٰلِكَ بِاَنَّ اللّٰهَ هُوَ الْحَقُّ وَاَنَّهٗ يُحْيِ
الْمَوْتٰى وَاَنَّهٗ عَلٰى كُلِّ شَيْءٍ قَدِيْرٌ ﴿٦﴾

4. And Allah it is Who sendeth the winds and they raise a cloud; then We lead it unto a dead land and revive therewith the earth after its death. Such is the Resurrection.

35:9

5. And the Trumpet is blown and lo! from the graves they hie unto their Lord,

Crying: Woe upon us! Who hath raised us from our place of sleep? This is that which the Beneficent did promise, and the messengers spoke truth:

36:51-52

6. Those who disbelieve assert that they will not be raised again.. Say (unto them, O Muhammad): Yea, verily, by my Lord! ye will be raised again and then ye will be informed of what ye did; and that is easy for Allah.

64:7

7. Thinketh man that We shall not assemble his bones?

Yea, verily. We are Able to restore his very fingers!

75:3-4

4. وَاللّٰهُ الَّذِىٓ اَرْسَلَ الرِّيٰحَ فَتُثِيْرُ
سَحَابًا فَسُقْنٰهُ اِلٰى بَلَدٍ مَّيِّتٍ فَاَحْيَيْنَا
بِهِ الْاَرْضَ بَعْدَ مَوْتِهَا ۚ كَذٰلِكَ النُّشُوْرُ ۝

5. وَنُفِخَ فِى الصُّوْرِ فَاِذَا هُمْ مِّنَ الْاَجْدَاثِ
اِلٰى رَبِّهِمْ يَنْسِلُوْنَ ۝
قَالُوْا يٰوَيْلَنَا مَنْۢ بَعَثَنَا مِنْ مَّرْقَدِنَا ۜ
هٰذَا مَا وَعَدَ الرَّحْمٰنُ وَصَدَقَ
الْمُرْسَلُوْنَ ۝

6. زَعَمَ الَّذِيْنَ كَفَرُوْٓا اَنْ لَّنْ يُّبْعَثُوْا ۗ
قُلْ بَلٰى وَرَبِّىْ لَتُبْعَثُنَّ ثُمَّ لَتُنَبَّؤُنَّ
بِمَا عَمِلْتُمْ ۗ وَذٰلِكَ عَلَى اللّٰهِ يَسِيْرٌ ۝

7. اَيَحْسَبُ الْاِنْسَانُ اَلَّنْ نَّجْمَعَ
عِظَامَهٗ ۝
بَلٰى قٰدِرِيْنَ عَلٰٓى اَنْ نُّسَوِّيَ بَنَانَهٗ ۝

○

Ref: 6:36; 17:97; 20:55; 23:16,82; 30:25,56; 37:16; 58:6; 100:9.

See also: Death.

LIGHT

1. Allah is the Protecting Friend of those who believe. He bringeth them out of darkness into light. As for those who disbelieve, their patrons are false deities. They bring them out of light into darkness. Such are rightful owners of the Fire. They will abide therein.

2:257

2. O mankind! Now hath a proof from your Lord come unto you, and We have sent down unto you a clear light;

4:174

3. Fain would they put out the light of Allah with their mouths, but Allah disdaineth (aught) save that He shall perfect His light, however much the disbelievers are averse.

9:32

4. (This is) a Scripture which We have revealed unto thee (Muhammad) that thereby thou mayst bring forth mankind from darkness unto light, by the permission of their Lord, unto the path of the Mighty, the Owner of Praise,

14:1

5. Allah is the Light of the heavens and the earth. The similitude of His light is as a niche wherein is a lamp. The

1. اللّٰهُ وَلِيُّ الَّذِينَ آمَنُوا يُخْرِجُهُم مِّنَ
الظُّلُمٰتِ إِلَى النُّورِ ۖ وَالَّذِينَ كَفَرُوا أَوْلِيَاؤُهُمُ
الطَّاغُوتُ يُخْرِجُونَهُم مِّنَ النُّورِ إِلَى الظُّلُمٰتِ ۗ
أُولٰئِكَ أَصْحٰبُ النَّارِ ۖ هُمْ فِيهَا خٰلِدُونَ

2. يٰأَيُّهَا النَّاسُ قَدْ جَاءَكُم بُرْهَانٌ مِّن
رَّبِّكُمْ وَأَنزَلْنَا إِلَيْكُمْ نُورًا مُّبِينًا

3. يُرِيدُونَ أَن يُطْفِئُوا نُورَ اللّٰهِ بِأَفْوٰهِهِمْ
وَيَأْبَى اللّٰهُ إِلَّا أَن يُتِمَّ نُورَهُ وَلَوْ
كَرِهَ الْكٰفِرُونَ

4. كِتٰبٌ أَنزَلْنٰهُ إِلَيْكَ لِتُخْرِجَ النَّاسَ
مِنَ الظُّلُمٰتِ إِلَى النُّورِ ۙ بِإِذْنِ رَبِّهِمْ
إِلٰى صِرَاطِ الْعَزِيزِ الْحَمِيدِ

5. اللّٰهُ نُورُ السَّمٰوٰتِ وَالْأَرْضِ ۚ مَثَلُ
نُورِهِ كَمِشْكٰوةٍ فِيهَا مِصْبَاحٌ ۖ الْمِصْبَاحُ
فِي زُجَاجَةٍ ۖ الزُّجَاجَةُ كَأَنَّهَا كَوْكَبٌ
دُرِّيٌّ يُوقَدُ مِن شَجَرَةٍ مُّبٰرَكَةٍ
زَيْتُونَةٍ لَّا شَرْقِيَّةٍ وَلَا غَرْبِيَّةٍ
يَكَادُ زَيْتُهَا يُضِيءُ وَلَوْ لَمْ تَمْسَسْهُ
نَارٌ ۚ نُّورٌ عَلٰى نُورٍ ۗ يَهْدِي اللّٰهُ لِنُورِهِ
مَن يَشَاءُ ۚ وَيَضْرِبُ اللّٰهُ الْأَمْثَالَ
لِلنَّاسِ ۗ وَاللّٰهُ بِكُلِّ شَيْءٍ عَلِيمٌ

lamp is in a glass. The glass is as it were a shining star. (This lamp is) kindled from a blessed tree, an olive neither of the East nor of the West, whose oil would almost glow forth (of itself) though no fire touched it. Light upon light,

Allah guideth unto His light whom He will. And Allah speaketh to mankind in allegories, for Allah is Knower of all things.

24:35

6. أَفَمَنْ شَرَحَ اللّٰهُ صَدْرَهٗ لِلْإِسْلَامِ فَهُوَ
عَلٰى نُوْرٍ مِّنْ رَّبِّهٖ ۚ فَوَيْلٌ لِّلْقٰسِيَةِ
قُلُوْبُهُمْ مِّنْ ذِكْرِ اللّٰهِ ۚ أُولٰٓئِكَ
فِيْ ضَلٰلٍ مُّبِيْنٍ ﴿٢٢﴾

6. Is he whose bosom Allah hath expanded for the Surrender (unto Him), so that he followeth a light from His Lord, (as he who disbelieveth)? Then woe unto those whose hearts are hardened against remembrance of Allah. Such are in plain error.

39:22

7. يٰٓأَيُّهَا الَّذِيْنَ اٰمَنُوْا تُوْبُوْٓا إِلَى اللّٰهِ
تَوْبَةً نَّصُوْحًا ۚ عَسٰى رَبُّكُمْ أَنْ
يُّكَفِّرَ عَنْكُمْ سَيِّاٰتِكُمْ وَيُدْخِلَكُمْ
جَنّٰتٍ تَجْرِيْ مِنْ تَحْتِهَا الْأَنْهٰرُ
يَوْمَ لَا يُخْزِي اللّٰهُ النَّبِيَّ وَالَّذِيْنَ
اٰمَنُوْا مَعَهٗ ۚ نُوْرُهُمْ يَسْعٰى بَيْنَ
أَيْدِيْهِمْ وَبِأَيْمَانِهِمْ يَقُوْلُوْنَ
رَبَّنَآ أَتْمِمْ لَنَا نُوْرَنَا وَاغْفِرْ لَنَا ۚ
إِنَّكَ عَلٰى كُلِّ شَيْءٍ قَدِيْرٌ ﴿٨﴾

7. O ye who believe! Turn unto Allah in sincere repentance! It may be that your Lord will remit from you your evil deeds and bring you unto Gardens underneath which rivers flow, on the day when Allah will not abase the Prophet and those who believe with him. Their light will run before them and on their right hands: they will say: Our Lord! Perfect our light for us, and forgive us! Lo! Thou art Able to do all things.

66:8

Ref: 2:17; 5:15–16,44,46; 6:1,91,122; 7:157; 10:5; 13:16; 14:5; 24:40; 33:43; 35:20; 39:69; 42:52; 57:9,12–13,19,28; 61:8; 64:8; 65:11; 71:16.
See also:, Darkness.

LIGHTNING

1. Or like a rainstorm from the sky, wherein is darkness, thunder and the flash of lightning. They thrust their fingers in their ears by reason of the thunder-claps, for fear of death. Allah encompasseth the disbelievers (in His guidance).

The lightning almost snatcheth away their sight from them. As often as it flasheth forth for them they walk therein, and when it darkeneth against them they stand still. If Allah willed, He could destroy their hearing and their sight. Lo! Allah is Able to do all things.

2:19–20

2. And when ye said: O Moses! We will not believe in thee till we see Allah plainly; and even while ye gazed the lightning seized you.

2:55

3. He it is Who showeth you the lightning, a fear and a hope, and raiseth the heavy clouds.

The thunder hymneth His praise and (so do) the angels for awe of Him. He launcheth the thunder-bolts and smiteth with them whom He will while they dispute (in doubt) concerning Allah, and He is mighty in wrath.

13:12–13

1. أَوْ كَصَيِّبٍ مِّنَ السَّمَآءِ فِيهِ ظُلُمٰتٌ وَّرَعْدٌ
وَّبَرْقٌ ۚ يَجْعَلُونَ أَصَابِعَهُمْ فِيٓ أٰذَانِهِمْ مِّنَ
الصَّوَاعِقِ حَذَرَ الْمَوْتِ ۗ وَاللّٰهُ مُحِيطٌۢ بِالْكٰفِرِينَ ﴿١٩﴾

يَكَادُ الْبَرْقُ يَخْطَفُ أَبْصَارَهُمْ ۖ كُلَّمَآ أَضَآءَ لَهُمْ مَّشَوْا
فِيهِ ۙ وَإِذَآ أَظْلَمَ عَلَيْهِمْ قَامُوا ۗ وَلَوْ شَآءَ اللّٰهُ لَذَهَبَ
بِسَمْعِهِمْ وَأَبْصَارِهِمْ ۗ إِنَّ اللّٰهَ عَلٰى كُلِّ شَيْءٍ قَدِيرٌ ﴿٢٠﴾

2. وَإِذْ قُلْتُمْ يٰمُوسٰى لَنْ نُّؤْمِنَ لَكَ حَتّٰى نَرَى اللّٰهَ
جَهْرَةً فَأَخَذَتْكُمُ الصّٰعِقَةُ وَأَنْتُمْ تَنْظُرُونَ ﴿٥٥﴾

3. هُوَ الَّذِي يُرِيكُمُ الْبَرْقَ خَوْفًا وَّطَمَعًا
وَّيُنْشِئُ السَّحَابَ الثِّقَالَ ﴿١٢﴾ ۚ

وَيُسَبِّحُ الرَّعْدُ بِحَمْدِهٖ وَالْمَلٰٓئِكَةُ
مِنْ خِيفَتِهٖ ۚ وَيُرْسِلُ الصَّوَاعِقَ فَيُصِيبُ
بِهَا مَنْ يَّشَآءُ وَهُمْ يُجَادِلُونَ فِي اللّٰهِ ۚ
وَهُوَ شَدِيدُ الْمِحَالِ ﴿١٣﴾ ۗ

Ref: 4:153; 24:43; 30:24; 41:13; 51:44; 75:7.

LOAN

1. Who is it that will lend unto Allah a goodly loan, that He may give it increase manifold? Allah straiteneth and enlargeth. Unto Him ye will return.

2:245

2. O ye who believe! When ye contract a debt for a fixed term, record it in writing. Let a scribe record it in writing between you in (terms of) equity. No scribe should refuse to write as Allah hath taught him, so let him write, and let him who incurreth the debt dictate, and let him observe his duty to Allah his Lord, and diminish naught thereof. But if he who oweth the debt is of low understanding, or weak, or unable himself to dictate, then let the guardian of his interests dictate in (terms of) equity. And call to witness, from among your men, two witnesses. And if two men be not (at hand) then a man and two women, of such as ye approve as witnesses, so that if the one erreth (through forgetfulness) the other will remember. And the witnesses must not refuse when they are summoned. Be not averse to writing down (the contract) whether it be small or great, with (record of) the term thereof. That is more equitable in the sight of Allah and more sure for testimony, and the best way of avoiding doubt between you; save only in the case when it is actual merchandise which ye transfer among yourselves from hand to hand. In that case it is no sin for you if ye write it not. And have witnesses when ye sell one to another,

1. مَنْ ذَا الَّذِيْ يُقْرِضُ اللّٰهَ قَرْضًا حَسَنًا
فَيُضٰعِفَهٗ لَهٗٓ اَضْعَافًا كَثِيْرَةً ؕ وَاللّٰهُ
يَقْبِضُ وَيَبْصُۜطُ ۪ وَاِلَيْهِ تُرْجَعُوْنَ ﴿۲۴۵﴾

2. يٰٓاَيُّهَا الَّذِيْنَ اٰمَنُوْٓا اِذَا تَدَايَنْتُمْ بِدَيْنٍ
اِلٰٓى اَجَلٍ مُّسَمًّى فَاكْتُبُوْهُ ؕ وَلْيَكْتُبْ
بَّيْنَكُمْ كَاتِبٌۢ بِالْعَدْلِ ۪ وَلَا يَاْبَ كَاتِبٌ
اَنْ يَّكْتُبَ كَمَا عَلَّمَهُ اللّٰهُ فَلْيَكْتُبْ ۚ وَلْيُمْلِلِ
الَّذِيْ عَلَيْهِ الْحَقُّ وَلْيَتَّقِ اللّٰهَ رَبَّهٗ وَلَا
يَبْخَسْ مِنْهُ شَيْــًٔا ؕ فَاِنْ كَانَ الَّذِيْ عَلَيْهِ
الْحَقُّ سَفِيْهًا اَوْ ضَعِيْفًا اَوْ لَا يَسْتَطِيْعُ اَنْ
يُّمِلَّ هُوَ فَلْيُمْلِلْ وَلِيُّهٗ بِالْعَدْلِ ؕ
وَاسْتَشْهِدُوْا شَهِيْدَيْنِ مِنْ رِّجَالِكُمْ ۚ
فَاِنْ لَّمْ يَكُوْنَا رَجُلَيْنِ فَرَجُلٌ وَّامْرَاَتٰنِ
مِمَّنْ تَرْضَوْنَ مِنَ الشُّهَدَآءِ اَنْ تَضِلَّ
اِحْدٰىهُمَا فَتُذَكِّرَ اِحْدٰىهُمَا الْاُخْرٰى ؕ
وَلَا يَاْبَ الشُّهَدَآءُ اِذَا مَا دُعُوْا ؕ وَلَا
تَسْــَٔمُوْٓا اَنْ تَكْتُبُوْهُ صَغِيْرًا اَوْ كَبِيْرًا اِلٰٓى
اَجَلِهٖ ؕ ذٰلِكُمْ اَقْسَطُ عِنْدَ اللّٰهِ وَاَقْوَمُ لِلشَّهَادَةِ
وَاَدْنٰٓى اَلَّا تَرْتَابُوْٓا اِلَّآ اَنْ تَكُوْنَ تِجَارَةً
حَاضِرَةً تُدِيْرُوْنَهَا بَيْنَكُمْ فَلَيْسَ عَلَيْكُمْ
جُنَاحٌ اَلَّا تَكْتُبُوْهَا ؕ وَاَشْهِدُوْٓا اِذَا تَبَايَعْتُمْ ۪
وَلَا يُضَآرَّ كَاتِبٌ وَّلَا شَهِيْدٌ ؕ وَاِنْ
تَفْعَلُوْا فَاِنَّهٗ فُسُوْقٌۢ بِكُمْ ؕ وَاتَّقُوا اللّٰهَ ؕ

and let no harm be done to scribe or witness. If ye do (harm to them) lo! it is a sin in you. Observe your duty to Allah. Allah is teaching you. And Allah is Knower of all things.

If ye be on a journey and cannot find a scribe, then a pledge in hand (shall suffice). And if one of you entrusteth to another let him who is trusted deliver up that which is entrusted to him (according to the pact between them) and let him observe his duty to Allah, his Lord. Hide not testimony. He who hideth it, verily his heart is sinful. Allah is Aware of what ye do.
2:282–283

3. Allah chargeth you concerning (the provisions for) your children: to the male the equivalent of the portion of two females, and if there be women more than two, then theirs is two–thirds of the inheritance, and if there be one (only), then the half. And to his parents a sixth of the inheritance, if he have a son; and if he have no son and his parents are his heirs, then to his mother appertaineth the third; and if he have brethren, then to his mother appertaineth the sixth, after any legacy he may have bequeathed, or debt (hath been paid). Your parents or your children: Ye know not which of them is nearer unto you in usefulness. It is an

وَيُعَلِّمُكُمُ اللّٰهُ ۗ وَاللّٰهُ بِكُلِّ شَيْءٍ عَلِيْمٌ ﴿٢٨٢﴾
وَاِنْ كُنْتُمْ عَلٰى سَفَرٍ وَّلَمْ تَجِدُوْا كَاتِبًا
فَرِهٰنٌ مَّقْبُوْضَةٌ ۗ فَاِنْ اَمِنَ بَعْضُكُمْ
بَعْضًا فَلْيُؤَدِّ الَّذِى اؤْتُمِنَ اَمَانَتَهٗ وَلْيَتَّقِ
اللّٰهَ رَبَّهٗ ۗ وَلَا تَكْتُمُوا الشَّهَادَةَ ۗ وَمَنْ
يَّكْتُمْهَا فَاِنَّهٗۤ اٰثِمٌ قَلْبُهٗ ۗ وَاللّٰهُ بِمَا
تَعْمَلُوْنَ عَلِيْمٌ ﴿٢٨٣﴾

3. يُوْصِيْكُمُ اللّٰهُ فِىْۤ اَوْلَادِكُمْ لِلذَّكَرِ مِثْلُ
حَظِّ الْاُنْثَيَيْنِ ۚ فَاِنْ كُنَّ نِسَآءً فَوْقَ
اثْنَتَيْنِ فَلَهُنَّ ثُلُثَا مَا تَرَكَ ۚ وَاِنْ كَانَتْ
وَاحِدَةً فَلَهَا النِّصْفُ ۗ وَلِاَبَوَيْهِ لِكُلِّ
وَاحِدٍ مِّنْهُمَا السُّدُسُ مِمَّا تَرَكَ اِنْ
كَانَ لَهٗ وَلَدٌ ۚ فَاِنْ لَّمْ يَكُنْ لَّهٗ وَلَدٌ وَّ
وَرِثَهٗۤ اَبَوٰهُ فَلِاُمِّهِ الثُّلُثُ ۚ فَاِنْ كَانَ
لَهٗۤ اِخْوَةٌ فَلِاُمِّهِ السُّدُسُ مِنْۢ بَعْدِ
وَصِيَّةٍ يُّوْصِىْ بِهَاۤ اَوْ دَيْنٍ ۗ اٰبَآؤُكُمْ
وَاَبْنَآؤُكُمْ لَا تَدْرُوْنَ اَيُّهُمْ اَقْرَبُ لَكُمْ
نَفْعًا ۗ فَرِيْضَةً مِّنَ اللّٰهِ ۗ اِنَّ اللّٰهَ كَانَ
عَلِيْمًا حَكِيْمًا ﴿١١﴾

4. اِنْ تُقْرِضُوا اللّٰهَ قَرْضًا حَسَنًا يُّضٰعِفْهُ
لَكُمْ وَيَغْفِرْ لَكُمْ ۗ وَاللّٰهُ شَكُوْرٌ حَلِيْمٌ ﴿١٧﴾

injunction from Allah. Lo! Allah is Knower, Wise.
4:11

4. If ye lend unto Allah a goodly loan, He will double it for you and will forgive you, for Allah is Responsive, Clement,
64:17

See also: Pledge.

LOVE FOR ALLAH

1. Yet of mankind are some who take unto themselves (objects of worship which they set as) rivals to Allah, loving them with a love like (that which is the due) of Allah (only)—Those who believe are stauncher in their love for Allah—Oh, that those who do evil had but known, (on the day) when they behold the doom that power belongeth wholly to Allah, and that Allah is severe in punishment!

2:165

2. Say, (O Muhammad, to mankind); If ye love Allah, follow me; Allah will love you and forgive you your sins. Allah is Forgiving, Merciful.

3:31

3. Say: If your fathers, and your sons, and your brethren, and your wives, and your tribe, and the wealth ye have acquired, and merchandise for which ye fear that there will be no sale, and dwellings ye desire are dearer to you than Allah and His messenger and striving in His way: then wait till Allah bringeth His command to pass. Allah guideth not wrongdoing folk.

9:24

4. And feed with food the needy wretch, the orphan and the prisoner. for love of Him,

1. وَمِنَ النَّاسِ مَنْ يَتَّخِذُ مِنْ دُوْنِ اللّٰهِ
اَنْدَادًا يُّحِبُّوْنَهُمْ كَحُبِّ اللّٰهِ ؕ وَ الَّذِيْنَ
اٰمَنُوْٓا اَشَدُّ حُبًّا لِّلّٰهِ ؕ وَلَوْ يَرَى الَّذِيْنَ
ظَلَمُوْٓا اِذْ يَرَوْنَ الْعَذَابَ ۙ اَنَّ الْقُوَّةَ لِلّٰهِ
جَمِيْعًا ۙ وَّ اَنَّ اللّٰهَ شَدِيْدُ الْعَذَابِ ﴿۱۶۵﴾

2. قُلْ اِنْ كُنْتُمْ تُحِبُّوْنَ اللّٰهَ فَاتَّبِعُوْنِيْ
يُحْبِبْكُمُ اللّٰهُ وَ يَغْفِرْ لَكُمْ ذُنُوْبَكُمْ ؕ
وَاللّٰهُ غَفُوْرٌ رَّحِيْمٌ ○

3. قُلْ اِنْ كَانَ اٰبَآؤُكُمْ وَ اَبْنَآؤُكُمْ وَ اِخْوَانُكُمْ
وَ اَزْوَاجُكُمْ وَ عَشِيْرَتُكُمْ وَ اَمْوَالُ ۨ اقْتَرَفْتُمُوْهَا
وَتِجَارَةٌ تَخْشَوْنَ كَسَادَهَا وَمَسٰكِنُ تَرْضَوْنَهَآ
اَحَبَّ اِلَيْكُمْ مِّنَ اللّٰهِ وَ رَسُوْلِهٖ وَجِهَادٍ فِيْ
سَبِيْلِهٖ فَتَرَبَّصُوْا حَتّٰى يَاْتِيَ اللّٰهُ بِاَمْرِهٖ ؕ
وَ اللّٰهُ لَا يَهْدِى الْقَوْمَ الْفٰسِقِيْنَ ﴿۲۴﴾

4. وَ يُطْعِمُوْنَ الطَّعَامَ عَلٰى حُبِّهٖ مِسْكِيْنًا
وَّ يَتِيْمًا وَّ اَسِيْرًا ﴿۸﴾
اِنَّمَا نُطْعِمُكُمْ لِوَجْهِ اللّٰهِ لَا نُرِيْدُ
مِنْكُمْ جَزَآءً وَّ لَا شُكُوْرًا ﴿۹﴾
اِنَّا نَخَافُ مِنْ رَّبِّنَا يَوْمًا عَبُوْسًا
قَمْطَرِيْرًا ﴿۱۰﴾

(Saying): We feed you for the sake of Allah only. We wish for no reward nor thanks from you;

Lo! we fear from our Lord a day of frowning and of fate.

76:8–10

Ref: 2:177; 3:31;

See also: Submission to Allah and His Messenger (PBUH).

LUQMĀN

1. And verily We gave Luqman wisdom, saying: Give thanks unto Allah; and whosoever giveth thanks, he giveth thanks for (the good of) his soul. And whosoever refuseth—Lo! Allah is Absolute, Owner of Praise.

And (remember) when Luqman said unto his son, when he was exhorting him: O my dear son! Ascribe no partners unto Allah. Lo! to ascribe partners (unto Him) is a tremendous wrong—

31:12–13

1. وَلَقَدْ اٰتَيْنَا لُقْمٰنَ الْحِكْمَةَ اَنِ اشْكُرْ
لِلّٰهِ ؕ وَمَنْ يَّشْكُرْ فَاِنَّمَا يَشْكُرُ لِنَفْسِهٖ ۚ
وَمَنْ كَفَرَ فَاِنَّ اللّٰهَ غَنِيٌّ حَمِيْدٌ ۝

وَاِذْ قَالَ لُقْمٰنُ لِابْنِهٖ وَهُوَ يَعِظُهٗ
يٰبُنَيَّ لَا تُشْرِكْ بِاللّٰهِ ؕ اِنَّ الشِّرْكَ
لَظُلْمٌ عَظِيْمٌ ۝١٣

○

MADINAH

1. And among those around you of the wandering Arabs there are hypocrites, and among the townspeople of Al–Madinah (there are some who) persist in hypocrisy whom thou (O Muhammad) knowest not. We, We know them, and We shall chastise them twice; then they will be relegated to a painful doom.

9:101

1. وَمِمَّنْ حَوْلَكُمْ مِّنَ الْاَعْرَابِ مُنٰفِقُوْنَ
وَمِنْ اَهْلِ الْمَدِيْنَةِ مَرَدُوْا عَلَى
النِّفَاقِ لَا تَعْلَمُهُمْ نَحْنُ نَعْلَمُهُمْ
سَنُعَذِّبُهُمْ مَّرَّتَيْنِ ثُمَّ يُرَدُّوْنَ اِلٰى
عَذَابٍ عَظِيْمٍ ﴿١٠١﴾

2. And when a party of them said: O folk of Yathrib! There is no stand (possible) for you, therefor turn back. And certain of them (even) sought permission of the Prophet, saying: Our homes lie open (to the enemy). And they lay not open. They but wished to flee.

33:13

2. وَاِذْ قَالَتْ طَّآىِٕفَةٌ مِّنْهُمْ يٰٓاَهْلَ يَثْرِبَ
لَا مُقَامَ لَكُمْ فَارْجِعُوْا ۚ وَيَسْتَاْذِنُ فَرِيْقٌ
مِّنْهُمُ النَّبِيَّ يَقُوْلُوْنَ اِنَّ بُيُوْتَنَا عَوْرَةٌ ۚ
وَمَا هِيَ بِعَوْرَةٍ ۚ اِنْ يُّرِيْدُوْنَ اِلَّا فِرَارًا ﴿١٣﴾

○

MAGIANS

1. Lo! those who believe (this Revelation), and those who are Jews, and the Saba–eans and the Christians and the Magians and the idolaters– Lo! Allah will decide between them on the Day of Resurrec–tion. Lo! Allah is Witness over all things.

22:17

1. اِنَّ الَّذِيْنَ اٰمَنُوْا وَالَّذِيْنَ هَادُوْا
وَالصّٰبِـِٕيْنَ وَالنَّصٰرٰى وَالْمَجُوْسَ وَالَّذِيْنَ
اَشْرَكُوْٓا ۖ اِنَّ اللّٰهَ يَفْصِلُ بَيْنَهُمْ يَوْمَ الْقِيٰمَةِ ۭ
اِنَّ اللّٰهَ عَلٰى كُلِّ شَيْءٍ شَهِيْدٌ ﴿١٧﴾

○

MADINAH **Ref: 9:120; 33:60; 36:20; 63:8.**

MAHR

1. And give unto the women, (whom ye marry) free gift of their marriage portions; but if they of their own accord remit unto you a part thereof, then ye are welcome to absorb it (in your wealth).

4:4

2. O ye who believe! It is not lawful for you forcibly to inherit the women (of your deceased kinsmen), nor (that) ye should put constraint upon them that ye may take away a part of that which ye have given them, unless they be guilty of flagrant lewdness. But consort with them in kindness, for if ye hate them it may happen that ye hate a thing wherein Allah hath placed much good.

And if ye wish to exchange one wife for another and ye have given unto one of them a sum of money (however great), take nothing from it. Would ye take it by the way of calumny and open wrong?

How can ye take it (back) after one of you hath gone in unto the other, and they have taken a strong pledge from you?

4:19-21

3. And those of whom ye seek content (by marrying them), give unto them their portions as a duty. And there is no sin for you in what ye do by mutual agreement after the duty (hath been done). Lo!

1. وَاٰتُوا النِّسَآءَ صَدُقٰتِهِنَّ نِحْلَةً ۚ فَاِنْ طِبْنَ لَكُمْ عَنْ شَيْءٍ مِّنْهُ نَفْسًا فَكُلُوْهُ هَنِيْٓـًٔا مَّرِيْٓـًٔا ﴿٤﴾

2. يٰٓاَيُّهَا الَّذِيْنَ اٰمَنُوْا لَا يَحِلُّ لَكُمْ اَنْ تَرِثُوا النِّسَآءَ كَرْهًا ۭ وَلَا تَعْضُلُوْهُنَّ لِتَذْهَبُوْا بِبَعْضِ مَآ اٰتَيْتُمُوْهُنَّ اِلَّآ اَنْ يَّاْتِيْنَ بِفَاحِشَةٍ مُّبَيِّنَةٍ ۚ وَعَاشِرُوْهُنَّ بِالْمَعْرُوْفِ ۚ فَاِنْ كَرِهْتُمُوْهُنَّ فَعَسٰٓى اَنْ تَكْرَهُوْا شَيْـًٔـا وَّيَجْعَلَ اللّٰهُ فِيْهِ خَيْرًا كَثِيْرًا ﴿١٩﴾

وَاِنْ اَرَدْتُّمُ اسْتِبْدَالَ زَوْجٍ مَّكَانَ زَوْجٍ ۙ وَّاٰتَيْتُمْ اِحْدٰىهُنَّ قِنْطَارًا فَلَا تَاْخُذُوْا مِنْهُ شَيْـًٔـا ۭ اَتَاْخُذُوْنَهٗ بُهْتَانًا وَّاِثْمًا مُّبِيْنًا ﴿٢٠﴾

وَكَيْفَ تَاْخُذُوْنَهٗ وَقَدْ اَفْضٰى بَعْضُكُمْ اِلٰى بَعْضٍ وَّاَخَذْنَ مِنْكُمْ مِّيْثَاقًا غَلِيْظًا ﴿٢١﴾

3. فَمَا اسْتَمْتَعْتُمْ بِهٖ مِنْهُنَّ فَاٰتُوْهُنَّ اُجُوْرَهُنَّ فَرِيْضَةً ۭ وَلَا جُنَاحَ عَلَيْكُمْ فِيْمَا تَرٰضَيْتُمْ بِهٖ مِنْۢ بَعْدِ الْفَرِيْضَةِ ۭ اِنَّ اللّٰهَ كَانَ عَلِيْمًا حَكِيْمًا ﴿٢٤﴾

4. قَدْ عَلِمْنَا مَا فَرَضْنَا عَلَيْهِمْ فِيْٓ اَزْوَاجِهِمْ وَمَا مَلَكَتْ اَيْمَانُهُمْ لِكَيْلَا يَكُوْنَ عَلَيْكَ حَرَجٌ ۭ وَكَانَ اللّٰهُ غَفُوْرًا رَّحِيْمًا ﴿٥﴾

Allah is ever Knower, Wise.

4:24

4. We are Aware of that which We enjoined upon them concerning their wives and those whom their right hands possess — that thou mayst be free from blame, for Allah is ever Forgiving, Merciful.

33:50

5. And it is no sin for you to marry such women when ye have given them their dues. And hold not to the ties of disbelieving women; and ask for (the return of) that which ye have spent; and let them (the disbelievers) ask for that which they have spent. That is the judgment of Allah. He judgeth between you. Allah is Knower, Wise.

And if any of your wives have gone from you unto the disbelievers and, afterward ye have your turn (of triumph), then give unto those whose wives have gone the like of that which they have spent, and keep your duty to Allah in Whom ye are believers.

60:10–11

5. وَلَا جُنَاحَ عَلَيْكُمْ أَنْ تَنْكِحُوهُنَّ إِذَا
آتَيْتُمُوهُنَّ أُجُورَهُنَّ ۚ وَلَا تُمْسِكُوا بِعِصَمِ
الْكَوَافِرِ وَسْئَلُوا مَا أَنْفَقْتُمْ وَلْيَسْئَلُوا مَا
أَنْفَقُوا ۚ ذَٰلِكُمْ حُكْمُ اللَّهِ ۖ يَحْكُمُ بَيْنَكُمْ ۚ
وَاللَّهُ عَلِيمٌ حَكِيمٌ ﴿١٠﴾
وَإِنْ فَاتَكُمْ شَيْءٌ مِنْ أَزْوَاجِكُمْ إِلَى
الْكُفَّارِ فَعَاقَبْتُمْ فَآتُوا الَّذِينَ ذَهَبَتْ
أَزْوَاجُهُمْ مِثْلَ مَا أَنْفَقُوا ۚ وَاتَّقُوا
اللَّهَ الَّذِي أَنْتُمْ بِهِ مُؤْمِنُونَ ﴿١١﴾

Ref. 4:25,34. 5:5.

See also: **Conjugal Rights and Obligations,** ***Nikah***

MAINTENANCE EXPENSES

1. Lodge them where ye dwell, according to your wealth, and harass them not so as to straiten life for them. And if they are with child, then spend for them till they bring forth their burden. Then, if they give suck for you, give them their due payment and consult together in kindness; but if ye make difficulties for one another, then let some other woman give suck for him (the father of the child).

Let him who hath abundance spend of his abundance, and he whose provision is measured, let him spend of that which Allah hath given him. Allah asketh naught of any soul save that which He hath given it. Allah will vouchsafe, after hardship, ease.

65:6–7

1. أَسْكِنُوهُنَّ مِنْ حَيْثُ سَكَنْتُمْ مِّنْ
وُّجْدِكُمْ وَلَا تُضَآرُّوهُنَّ لِتُضَيِّقُوا
عَلَيْهِنَّ ۚ وَإِنْ كُنَّ أُولَاتِ حَمْلٍ
فَأَنْفِقُوا عَلَيْهِنَّ حَتّٰى يَضَعْنَ حَمْلَهُنَّ ۚ
فَإِنْ أَرْضَعْنَ لَكُمْ فَاٰتُوهُنَّ أُجُورَهُنَّ ۚ
وَأْتَمِرُوا بَيْنَكُمْ بِمَعْرُوفٍ ۚ وَإِنْ
تَعَاسَرْتُمْ فَسَتُرْضِعُ لَهٗٓ أُخْرٰى ۞

لِيُنْفِقْ ذُو سَعَةٍ مِّنْ سَعَتِهٖ ۚ وَمَنْ
قُدِرَ عَلَيْهِ رِزْقُهٗ فَلْيُنْفِقْ مِمَّآ
اٰتٰىهُ اللّٰهُ ۚ لَا يُكَلِّفُ اللّٰهُ نَفْسًا إِلَّا
مَآ اٰتٰىهَا ۚ سَيَجْعَلُ اللّٰهُ بَعْدَ عُسْرٍ يُّسْرًا ۞

See also: Conjugal Rights and Obligations.

MAKKAH

1. Lo! the first Sanctuary appointed for mankind was that at *Bakkah*, a blessed place, a guidance to the peoples,
Wherein are, plain memorials (of Allah's guidance); the place where Abraham stood up to pray; and whosoever entereth it is safe. And pilgrimage to the House is a duty unto Allah for mankind, for him who can find a way thither. As for him who disbelieveth (let him know that) lo! Allah is Independent of (all) creatures.

3:96–97

2. And thus We have inspired in thee a Lecture in Arabic, that thou mayest warn the mother–town and those around it, and mayest warn of a day of assembling whereof there is no doubt.

42:7

3. And He it is Who hath withheld men's hands from you, and hath withheld your hands from them, in the valley of Makkah after He had made you victors over them. Allah is Seer of what ye do.

48:24

1. إِنَّ أَوَّلَ بَيْتٍ وُضِعَ لِلنَّاسِ لَلَّذِي بِبَكَّةَ
مُبٰرَكًا وَّهُدًى لِّلْعٰلَمِينَ ۝
فِيهِ اٰيٰتٌۢ بَيِّنٰتٌ مَّقَامُ إِبْرٰهِيمَ ۚ وَمَنْ
دَخَلَهٗ كَانَ اٰمِنًا ۗ وَلِلّٰهِ عَلَى النَّاسِ حِجُّ
الْبَيْتِ مَنِ اسْتَطَاعَ إِلَيْهِ سَبِيلًا ۗ وَمَنْ
كَفَرَ فَإِنَّ اللّٰهَ غَنِيٌّ عَنِ الْعٰلَمِينَ ۝

2. وَكَذٰلِكَ أَوْحَيْنَآ إِلَيْكَ قُرْاٰنًا عَرَبِيًّا
لِّتُنْذِرَ أُمَّ الْقُرٰى وَمَنْ حَوْلَهَا وَتُنْذِرَ
يَوْمَ الْجَمْعِ لَا رَيْبَ فِيهِ ۚ

3. وَهُوَ الَّذِي كَفَّ أَيْدِيَهُمْ عَنْكُمْ وَ
أَيْدِيَكُمْ عَنْهُمْ بِبَطْنِ مَكَّةَ مِنْۢ
بَعْدِ أَنْ أَظْفَرَكُمْ عَلَيْهِمْ ۚ وَكَانَ
اللّٰهُ بِمَا تَعْمَلُونَ بَصِيرًا ۝

Ref: 2:125-127; 5:97; 6:92; 22:26.

MAN

1. Allah would make the burden light for you, for man was created weak.

4:28

2. And if misfortune touch a man he crieth unto Us, (while reclining) on his side, or sitting or standing, but when We have relieved him of the misfortune he goeth his way as though he had not cried unto Us because of a misfortune that afflicted him. Thus is what they do made (seeming) fair unto the prodigal.

10:12

3. And if We cause man to taste some mercy from Us and afterward withdraw it from him, lo! he is despairing, thankless.

11:9

4. And He giveth you of all ye ask of Him, and if ye would count the bounty of Allah ye cannot reckon it. Lo! man is verily a wrong-doer, an ingrate.

14:34

5. Man prayeth for evil as he prayeth for good; for man was ever hasty.

17:11

6. And when We make life pleasant unto man, he turneth away and is averse; and when ill toucheth him he is in despair.

17:83

7. Say (unto them): If ye

1. يُرِيدُ اللَّهُ أَنْ يُخَفِّفَ عَنْكُمْ ۚ وَخُلِقَ
الْإِنْسَانُ ضَعِيفًا ﴿٢٨﴾

2. وَإِذَا مَسَّ الْإِنْسَانَ الضُّرُّ دَعَانَا
لِجَنْبِهِ أَوْ قَاعِدًا أَوْ قَائِمًا فَلَمَّا كَشَفْنَا
عَنْهُ ضُرَّهُ مَرَّ كَأَنْ لَمْ يَدْعُنَا إِلَىٰ ضُرٍّ
مَسَّهُ ۚ كَذَٰلِكَ زُيِّنَ لِلْمُسْرِفِينَ مَا
كَانُوا يَعْمَلُونَ ﴿١٢﴾

3. وَلَئِنْ أَذَقْنَا الْإِنْسَانَ مِنَّا رَحْمَةً ثُمَّ
نَزَعْنَاهَا مِنْهُ ۚ إِنَّهُ لَيَئُوسٌ كَفُورٌ ﴿٩﴾

4. وَآتَاكُمْ مِنْ كُلِّ مَا سَأَلْتُمُوهُ ۚ وَإِنْ
تَعُدُّوا نِعْمَتَ اللَّهِ لَا تُحْصُوهَا ۗ إِنَّ الْإِنْسَانَ
لَظَلُومٌ كَفَّارٌ ﴿٣٤﴾

5. وَيَدْعُ الْإِنْسَانُ بِالشَّرِّ دُعَاءَهُ بِالْخَيْرِ
وَكَانَ الْإِنْسَانُ عَجُولًا ﴿١١﴾

6. وَإِذَا أَنْعَمْنَا عَلَى الْإِنْسَانِ أَعْرَضَ وَنَا
بِجَانِبِهِ ۖ وَإِذَا مَسَّهُ الشَّرُّ كَانَ يَئُوسًا ﴿٨٣﴾

7. قُلْ لَوْ أَنْتُمْ تَمْلِكُونَ خَزَائِنَ رَحْمَةِ
رَبِّي إِذًا لَأَمْسَكْتُمْ خَشْيَةَ الْإِنْفَاقِ ۚ
وَكَانَ الْإِنْسَانُ قَتُورًا ﴿١٠٠﴾

8. وَلَقَدْ صَرَّفْنَا فِي هَٰذَا الْقُرْآنِ لِلنَّاسِ
مِنْ كُلِّ مَثَلٍ ۚ وَكَانَ الْإِنْسَانُ أَكْثَرَ
شَيْءٍ جَدَلًا ﴿٥٤﴾

possessed the treasures of the mercy of my Lord, ye would surely hold them back for fear of spending, for man was ever grudging.

17:100

8. And verily We have displayed for mankind in this Qur'ān all manner of similitudes, but man is more than anything contentious.

18:54

9. Now when hurt toucheth a man he crieth unto Us, and afterward when We have granted him a boon from Us, he saith: Only by force of knowledge I obtained it. Nay, but it is a test. But most of them know not.

39:49

10. We verily created a man and We know what his soul whispereth to him, and We are nearer to him than his jugular vein.

50:16

11. Or shall man have what he coveteth?

But unto Allah belongeth the after (life), and the former.

53:24–25

12. And that man hath only that for which he maketh effort,

53:39

13. Lo! man was created anxious.

70:19

14. Thinketh man that We shall not assemble his bones?

Yea, verily. We are Able to restore his very fingers!

But man would fain deny what is before him.

75:3–5

15. Hath there come upon man (ever) any period of time in which he was a thing un–

9. فَاِذَا مَسَّ الْاِنْسَانَ ضُرٌّ دَعَانَا
ثُمَّ اِذَا خَوَّلْنٰهُ نِعْمَةً مِّنَّا قَالَ
اِنَّمَآ اُوْتِيْتُهٗ عَلٰى عِلْمٍ بَلْ هِىَ فِتْنَةٌ
وَّلٰكِنَّ اَكْثَرَهُمْ لَا يَعْلَمُوْنَ ۝

10. وَلَقَدْ خَلَقْنَا الْاِنْسَانَ وَنَعْلَمُ مَا
تُوَسْوِسُ بِهٖ نَفْسُهٗ وَنَحْنُ اَقْرَبُ
اِلَيْهِ مِنْ حَبْلِ الْوَرِيْدِ ۝

11. اَمْ لِلْاِنْسَانِ مَا تَمَنّٰى ۝
فَلِلّٰهِ الْاٰخِرَةُ وَالْاُوْلٰى ۝

12. وَاَنْ لَّيْسَ لِلْاِنْسَانِ اِلَّا مَا سَعٰى ۝

13. اِنَّ الْاِنْسَانَ خُلِقَ هَلُوْعًا ۝

14. اَيَحْسَبُ الْاِنْسَانُ اَلَّنْ نَّجْمَعَ
عِظَامَهٗ ۝
بَلٰى قٰدِرِيْنَ عَلٰٓى اَنْ نُّسَوِّىَ بَنَانَهٗ ۝
بَلْ يُرِيْدُ الْاِنْسَانُ لِيَفْجُرَ اَمَامَهٗ ۝

15. هَلْ اَتٰى عَلَى الْاِنْسَانِ حِيْنٌ مِّنَ
الدَّهْرِ لَمْ يَكُنْ شَيْـًٔا مَّذْكُوْرًا ۝
اِنَّا خَلَقْنَا الْاِنْسَانَ مِنْ نُّطْفَةٍ
اَمْشَاجٍ نَّبْتَلِيْهِ فَجَعَلْنٰهُ سَمِيْعًا
بَصِيْرًا ۝
اِنَّا هَدَيْنٰهُ السَّبِيْلَ اِمَّا شَاكِرًا

remembered?

Lo! We create man from a drop of thickened fluid to test him; so We make him hearing, knowing.

Lo! We have shown him the way, whether he be grateful

or disbelieving.

76:1–3

16. O man! what hath made thee careless concerning thy Lord, the Bountiful,

Who created thee, then fashioned, then proportioned thee?

Into whatsoever form He will, He casteth thee.

82:6–8

17. We verily have created man in an atmosphere.

90:4

18. Surely We created man of the best stature.

95:4

19. Teacheth man that which he knew not,

Nay, but verily man is rebellious

That he thinketh himself independent!

Lo! unto thy Lord is the return.

96:5–8

20. Lo! man is an ingrate unto his Lord

And lo! he is a witness unto that;

And lo! in the love of wealth he is violent.

100:6–8

21. By the declining day,

Lo! man is in a state of loss,

Save those who believe

وَّ اِمَّا كَفُوْرًا

16. يٰٓاَيُّهَا الْاِنْسَانُ مَا غَرَّكَ بِرَبِّكَ الْكَرِيْمِ

الَّذِيْ خَلَقَكَ فَسَوّٰىكَ فَعَدَلَكَ

فِيْٓ اَيِّ صُوْرَةٍ مَّا شَآءَ رَكَّبَكَ

17. لَقَدْ خَلَقْنَا الْاِنْسَانَ فِيْ كَبَدٍ

18. لَقَدْ خَلَقْنَا الْاِنْسَانَ فِيْٓ اَحْسَنِ تَقْوِيْمٍ

19. عَلَّمَ الْاِنْسَانَ مَا لَمْ يَعْلَمْ

كَلَّآ اِنَّ الْاِنْسَانَ لَيَطْغٰىٓ

اَنْ رَّاٰهُ اسْتَغْنٰى

اِنَّ اِلٰى رَبِّكَ الرُّجْعٰى

20. اِنَّ الْاِنْسَانَ لِرَبِّهٖ لَكَنُوْدٌ

وَاِنَّهٗ عَلٰى ذٰلِكَ لَشَهِيْدٌ

وَاِنَّهٗ لِحُبِّ الْخَيْرِ لَشَدِيْدٌ

21. وَالْعَصْرِ

اِنَّ الْاِنْسَانَ لَفِيْ خُسْرٍ

اِلَّا الَّذِيْنَ اٰمَنُوْا وَعَمِلُوا الصّٰلِحٰتِ

وَتَوَاصَوْا بِالْحَقِّ ۙ وَتَوَاصَوْا بِالصَّبْرِ

and do good works, and exhort one another to truth and exhort one another to endurance.

103:1–3

Ref: 12:5; 17:53,67; 19:66–67; 21:37; 22:66; 25:29; 31:14; 32:7–8; 36:77; 39:8; 41:49; 42:48; 43:15; 46:15; 55:14; 75:10–11; 79:35; 80:24–32; 86:5–7; 89:15–20,23; 96:2; 99:1–3.

See also: Creation of Man, Dignity of Man, Man: Allah's vicegerent, Mankind.

MAN: ALLAH'S VICEGERENT

1. وَإِذْ قَالَ رَبُّكَ لِلْمَلٰٓئِكَةِ إِنِّي جَاعِلٌ فِي الْأَرْضِ
خَلِيفَةً ۖ قَالُوٓا أَتَجْعَلُ فِيهَا مَن يُفْسِدُ فِيهَا
وَيَسْفِكُ الدِّمَآءَ ۚ وَنَحْنُ نُسَبِّحُ بِحَمْدِكَ وَ
نُقَدِّسُ لَكَ ۖ قَالَ إِنِّيٓ أَعْلَمُ مَا لَا تَعْلَمُونَ ﴿٣٠﴾

2. وَهُوَ الَّذِي جَعَلَكُمْ خَلٰٓئِفَ الْأَرْضِ وَرَفَعَ
بَعْضَكُمْ فَوْقَ بَعْضٍ دَرَجٰتٍ لِّيَبْلُوَكُمْ
فِي مَآ ءَاتٰكُمْ ۗ إِنَّ رَبَّكَ سَرِيعُ الْعِقَابِ
وَإِنَّهُۥ لَغَفُورٌ رَّحِيمٌ ﴿١٦٥﴾

3. وَعَدَ اللّٰهُ الَّذِينَ ءَامَنُوا مِنكُمْ وَعَمِلُوا
الصّٰلِحٰتِ لَيَسْتَخْلِفَنَّهُمْ فِي الْأَرْضِ
كَمَا اسْتَخْلَفَ الَّذِينَ مِن قَبْلِهِمْ
وَلَيُمَكِّنَنَّ لَهُمْ دِينَهُمُ الَّذِي ارْتَضٰى
لَهُمْ وَلَيُبَدِّلَنَّهُم مِّنۢ بَعْدِ خَوْفِهِمْ
أَمْنًا ۚ يَعْبُدُونَنِي لَا يُشْرِكُونَ بِي
شَيْـًٔا ۚ وَمَن كَفَرَ بَعْدَ ذٰلِكَ
فَأُولٰٓئِكَ هُمُ الْفٰسِقُونَ ﴿٥٥﴾

4. أَمَّن يُجِيبُ الْمُضْطَرَّ إِذَا دَعَاهُ وَيَكْشِفُ
السُّوٓءَ وَيَجْعَلُكُمْ خُلَفَآءَ الْأَرْضِ ۗ أَءِلٰهٌ
مَّعَ اللّٰهِ ۚ قَلِيلًا مَّا تَذَكَّرُونَ ﴿٦٢﴾

1. And when thy Lord said unto the angels: Lo! I am about to place a viceroy in the earth, they said: Wilt Thou place therein one who will do harm therein and will shed blood, while we, we hymn Thy praise and sanctify Thee? He said: Surely I know that which ye know not.

2:30

2. He it is Who hath placed you as viceroys of the earth and hath exalted some of you in rank above others, that He may try you by (the test of) that which He hath given you. Lo! Thy Lord is swift in prosecution, and lo! He verily is Forgiving, Merciful.

6:165

3. Allah hath promised such of you as believe and do good works that He will surely make them to succeed (the present rulers) in the earth even as He caused those who were before them to succeed (others); and that He will surely establish for them their religion which He hath approved for them, and will give them in exchange safety after their fear. They serve Me. They ascribe nothing as partner unto Me. Those who disbelieve henceforth, they are the miscreants.

24:55

4. Is not He (best) Who answereth the wronged one when he crieth unto Him and removeth the evil, and hath made you viceroys of the earth? Is there any God beside Allah? Little do they reflect!

27:62

Ref: 7:69,74,169; 10:14,73; 33:72; 35:39; 38:26; 43:60.

See also: Dignity of Man.

MANKIND

1. فَلَمَّا سَمِعَتْ بِمَكْرِهِنَّ أَرْسَلَتْ إِلَيْهِنَّ
وَأَعْتَدَتْ لَهُنَّ مُتَّكَأً وَآتَتْ كُلَّ
وَاحِدَةٍ مِّنْهُنَّ سِكِّينًا وَقَالَتِ اخْرُجْ
عَلَيْهِنَّ فَلَمَّا رَأَيْنَهُ أَكْبَرْنَهُ وَقَطَّعْنَ
أَيْدِيَهُنَّ وَقُلْنَ حَاشَ لِلَّهِ مَا هَٰذَا
بَشَرًا إِنْ هَٰذَا إِلَّا مَلَكٌ كَرِيمٌ ﴿٣١﴾

2. وَإِذْ قَالَ رَبُّكَ لِلْمَلَائِكَةِ إِنِّي خَالِقٌ
بَشَرًا مِّن صَلْصَالٍ مِّنْ حَمَإٍ مَّسْنُونٍ ﴿٢٨﴾
فَإِذَا سَوَّيْتُهُ وَنَفَخْتُ فِيهِ مِن رُّوحِي
فَقَعُوا لَهُ سَاجِدِينَ ﴿٢٩﴾

3. قُلْ سُبْحَانَ رَبِّي هَلْ كُنتُ إِلَّا بَشَرًا
رَّسُولًا ﴿٩٣﴾
وَمَا مَنَعَ النَّاسَ أَن يُؤْمِنُوا إِذْ جَاءَهُمُ
الْهُدَىٰ إِلَّا أَن قَالُوا أَبَعَثَ اللَّهُ بَشَرًا رَّسُولًا ﴿٩٤﴾

4. قُلْ إِنَّمَا أَنَا بَشَرٌ مِّثْلُكُمْ يُوحَىٰ إِلَيَّ
أَنَّمَا إِلَٰهُكُمْ إِلَٰهٌ وَاحِدٌ فَمَن كَانَ يَرْجُو
لِقَاءَ رَبِّهِ فَلْيَعْمَلْ عَمَلًا صَالِحًا وَلَا
يُشْرِكْ بِعِبَادَةِ رَبِّهِ أَحَدًا ﴿١١٠﴾

5. وَهُوَ الَّذِي خَلَقَ مِنَ الْمَاءِ بَشَرًا
فَجَعَلَهُ نَسَبًا وَصِهْرًا وَكَانَ
رَبُّكَ قَدِيرًا ﴿٥٤﴾

1. And when she heard of their sly talk, she sent for them and prepared for them a cushioned couch (to lie on at the feast) and gave to every one of them a knife and said (to Joseph): Come out unto them! And when they saw him they exalted him and cut their hands, exclaiming: Allah Blameless! This is not a human being. This is no other than some gracious angel!

12:31

2. And (remember) when thy Lord said unto the angels: Lo! I am creating a mortal out of potter's clay of black mud altered.

So, when I have made him and have breathed into him of My spirit, do ye fall down, prostrating yourselves unto him.

15:28–29

3. Say (O Muhammad): My Lord be Glorified! Am I aught save a mortal messenger?

And naught prevented mankind from believing when the guidance came unto them save that they said: Hath Allah sent a mortal as (His) messenger?

17:93–94

4. Say I am only a mortal like you. My Lord inspireth in me that your God is only One God. And whoever hopeth for the meeting with his Lord, let him do righteous work, and make none sharer of the worship due unto his Lord.

18:110

5. And He it is Who hath created man from water, and hath appointed for him kindred by blood and kindred by marriage; for thy Lord is ever Powerful.

25:54

Ref: 3:47; 5:18; 6:91; 14:10–11; 16–103; 19:17; 21–3; 23:24; 33–34,47; 26:154,186; 30:20; 36:15; 41:6; 42:51; 64:6; 74:25,29,31,36.

See also: Creation of Man.

MANNA AND QUAILS

1. O Children of Israel! We delivered you from your enemy, and We made a cove-nant with you on the holy mountain's side, and sent down on you the *manna* and the *quails.*

(Saying): Eat of the good things wherewith We have provided you, and transgress not in respect thereof lest My wrath come upon you and he on whom My wrath cometh, he is lost indeed.

20:80–81

1. يَٰبَنِيٓ إِسۡرَٰٓءِيلَ قَدۡ أَنجَيۡنَٰكُم مِّنۡ
عَدُوِّكُمۡ وَوَٰعَدۡنَٰكُمۡ جَانِبَ ٱلطُّورِ ٱلۡأَيۡمَنَ
وَنَزَّلۡنَا عَلَيۡكُمُ ٱلۡمَنَّ وَٱلسَّلۡوَىٰ ٨٠

كُلُواْ مِن طَيِّبَٰتِ مَا رَزَقۡنَٰكُمۡ وَلَا
تَطۡغَوۡاْ فِيهِ فَيَحِلَّ عَلَيۡكُمۡ غَضَبِيۖ
وَمَن يَحۡلِلۡ عَلَيۡهِ غَضَبِي فَقَدۡ هَوَىٰ ٨١

Ref: 2:57.

MANNERS OF THE PROPHET (PBUH)

1. It was by the mercy of Allah that thou wast lenient with them (O Muhammad), for if thou hadst been stern and fierce of heart they would have dispersed from round about thee. So pardon them and ask forgiveness for them and consult with them upon the conduct of affairs. And when thou art resolved, then put thy trust in Allah. Lo! Allah loveth those who put their trust (in Him).

3:159

2. There hath come unto you a messenger, (one) of yourselves, unto whom aught that ye are overburdened is grievous, full of concern for you, for the believers full of pity, merciful.

Now, if they turn away (O Muhammad) say: Allah sufficeth me. There is no God save Him. In Him have I put my trust, and He is Lord of the Tremendous Throne.

9:128–129

3. We sent thee not save as a mercy for the peoples.

21:107

4. And lower thy wing (in kindness) unto those believers who follow thee.

26:215

5. By the pen and that which they write (therewith),

Thou art not, for thy Lord's favour unto thee, a madman.

And lo! thine verily will be a reward unfailing.

And lo! thou art of a tremendous nature.

68:1–4

1. فَبِمَا رَحْمَةٍ مِّنَ اللّٰهِ لِنْتَ لَهُمْ ۚ وَلَوْ كُنْتَ
فَظًّا غَلِيْظَ الْقَلْبِ لَانْفَضُّوْا مِنْ حَوْلِكَ ۖ
فَاعْفُ عَنْهُمْ وَاسْتَغْفِرْ لَهُمْ وَشَاوِرْهُمْ
فِي الْاَمْرِ ۚ فَاِذَا عَزَمْتَ فَتَوَكَّلْ عَلَى اللّٰهِ ۗ
اِنَّ اللّٰهَ يُحِبُّ الْمُتَوَكِّلِيْنَ ○

2. لَقَدْ جَآءَكُمْ رَسُوْلٌ مِّنْ اَنْفُسِكُمْ عَزِيْزٌ
عَلَيْهِ مَا عَنِتُّمْ حَرِيْصٌ عَلَيْكُمْ
بِالْمُؤْمِنِيْنَ رَءُوْفٌ رَّحِيْمٌ ﴿١٢٨﴾
فَاِنْ تَوَلَّوْا فَقُلْ حَسْبِيَ اللّٰهُ ۖ لَآ اِلٰهَ
اِلَّا هُوَ ۗ عَلَيْهِ تَوَكَّلْتُ وَهُوَ رَبُّ
الْعَرْشِ الْعَظِيْمِ ﴿١٢٩﴾

3. وَمَآ اَرْسَلْنٰكَ اِلَّا رَحْمَةً لِّلْعٰلَمِيْنَ ﴿١٠٧﴾

4. وَاخْفِضْ جَنَاحَكَ لِمَنِ اتَّبَعَكَ مِنَ
الْمُؤْمِنِيْنَ ○

5. وَالْقَلَمِ وَمَا يَسْطُرُوْنَ ﴿١﴾
مَآ اَنْتَ بِنِعْمَةِ رَبِّكَ بِمَجْنُوْنٍ ﴿٢﴾
وَاِنَّ لَكَ لَاَجْرًا غَيْرَ مَمْنُوْنٍ ﴿٣﴾
وَاِنَّكَ لَعَلٰى خُلُقٍ عَظِيْمٍ ﴿٤﴾

See also: Apostleship of Muhammad (PBUH)

MARKETING

1. Those who swallow usury cannot rise up save as he ariseth whom the devil hath prostrated by (his) touch. That is because they say: Trade is just like usury; where–as Allah permitteth trading and forbiddeth usury. He un–to whom an admonition from his Lord cometh and (he) refraineth (in obedience thereto), he shall keep (the profits of) that which is past, and his affair (henceforth) is with Allah. As for him who returneth (to usuary)–Such are rightful owners of the Fire. They will abide there–in.

2:275

2. And have witnesses when ye sell one to another, and let no harm be done to scribe or witness. If ye do (harm to them) lo! it is a sin in you. Observe your duty to Allah. Allah is teaching you. And Allah is Knower of all things.

2:282

3. Tell My bondmen who believe to establish worship and spend of that which We have given them, secretly and publicly, before a day cometh wherein there will be neither traffick nor befriending.

14:31

4. O ye who believe! When the call is heard for the prayer of the day of congregation, haste unto remembrance of Allah and leave your trad–ing. That is better for you if ye did but know.

62:9

1. الَّذِيْنَ يَأْكُلُوْنَ الرِّبٰوا لَا يَقُوْمُوْنَ اِلَّا كَمَا
يَقُوْمُ الَّذِيْ يَتَخَبَّطُهُ الشَّيْطٰنُ مِنَ الْمَسِّ
ذٰلِكَ بِاَنَّهُمْ قَالُوْٓا اِنَّمَا الْبَيْعُ مِثْلُ الرِّبٰوا
وَاَحَلَّ اللّٰهُ الْبَيْعَ وَحَرَّمَ الرِّبٰوا فَمَنْ
جَآءَهٗ مَوْعِظَةٌ مِّنْ رَّبِّهٖ فَانْتَهٰى فَلَهٗ
مَا سَلَفَ وَاَمْرُهٗٓ اِلَى اللّٰهِ وَمَنْ عَادَ فَاُولٰٓئِكَ
اَصْحٰبُ النَّارِ هُمْ فِيْهَا خٰلِدُوْنَ ﴿٢٧٥﴾

2. وَاَشْهِدُوْٓا اِذَا تَبَايَعْتُمْ وَلَا يُضَآرَّ كَاتِبٌ
وَّلَا شَهِيْدٌ وَاِنْ تَفْعَلُوْا فَاِنَّهٗ فُسُوْقٌ
بِكُمْ وَاتَّقُوا اللّٰهَ وَيُعَلِّمُكُمُ اللّٰهُ وَاللّٰهُ
بِكُلِّ شَيْءٍ عَلِيْمٌ ﴿٢٨٢﴾

3. قُلْ لِّعِبَادِيَ الَّذِيْنَ اٰمَنُوْا يُقِيْمُوا الصَّلٰوةَ
وَيُنْفِقُوْا مِمَّا رَزَقْنٰهُمْ سِرًّا وَّعَلَانِيَةً
مِّنْ قَبْلِ اَنْ يَّاْتِيَ يَوْمٌ لَّا بَيْعٌ فِيْهِ
وَلَا خِلٰلٌ ﴿٣١﴾

4. يٰٓاَيُّهَا الَّذِيْنَ اٰمَنُوْٓا اِذَا نُوْدِيَ
لِلصَّلٰوةِ مِنْ يَّوْمِ الْجُمُعَةِ فَاسْعَوْا
اِلٰى ذِكْرِ اللّٰهِ وَذَرُوا الْبَيْعَ ذٰلِكُمْ
خَيْرٌ لَّكُمْ اِنْ كُنْتُمْ تَعْلَمُوْنَ ﴿٩﴾

○

Ref: 2: 16,254,276; 4: 29,161: 9: 24: 24: 37; 35: 29; 61: 10.
See also: Interest.

MARTYRDOM

1. And call not those who are slain in the way of Allah "dead." Nay, they are living, only ye perceive not.

2:154

2. And what though ye be slain in Allah's way or die therein? Surely pardon from Allah and mercy are better than all that they amass.

What though ye be slain or die, when unto Allah ye are gathered?

3:157–158

3. Think not of those, who are slain in the way of Allah, as dead. Nay, they are living. With their Lord they have provision:

Jubilant (are they) because of that which Allah hath bestowed upon them of His bounty, rejoicing for the sake of those who have not joined them but are left behind: that there shall no fear come upon them neither shall they grieve.

They rejoice because of favour from Allah and kindness, and that Allah wasteth not the wage of the believers.

3:169–171

4. So those who fled and were driven forth from their homes and suffered damage for My cause, and fought and were slain, verily I shall remit their evil deeds from them and verily I shall bring them into

1. ولا تقولوا لمن يقتل في سبيل الله
اموات بل احياء ولكن لا تشعرون ﴿١٥٤﴾

2. ولئن قتلتم في سبيل الله او متم
لمغفرة من الله ورحمة خير مما
يجمعون ○
ولئن متم او قتلتم لالى الله تحشرون ○

3. ولا تحسبن الذين قتلوا في سبيل الله
امواتا بل احياء عند ربهم يرزقون ○

فرحين بما اتهم الله من فضله
ويستبشرون بالذين لم يلحقوا
بهم من خلفهم الا خوف عليهم
ولا هم يحزنون ○

يستبشرون بنعمة من الله وفضل
وان الله لا يضيع اجر المؤمنين ○

4. فالذين هاجروا و اخرجوا
من ديارهم و اوذوا في سبيلي وقتلوا
وقتلوا لاكفرن عنهم سياتهم ولادخلنهم
جنت تجري من تحتها الانهر ثوابا
من عند الله والله عنده حسن الثواب ○

5. ومن يطع الله والرسول فاولئك مع
الذين انعم الله عليهم من النبين

Gardens underneath which rivers flow—A reward from Allah. And with Allah is the fairest of rewards.

3:195

5. Whoso obeyeth Allah and the messenger, they are with

those unto whom Allah hath shown favour, of the Prophets and the saints and the martyrs and the righteous. The best of company are they!

4:69

6. Let those fight in the way of Allah who sell the life of this world for the others. Whoso fighteth in the way of Allah, be he slain or be he victorious, on him We shall bestow a vast reward.

4:74

7. Lo! Allah hath bought from the believers their lives and their wealth because the Garden will be theirs; they shall fight in the way of Allah and shall slay and be slain. It is a promise which is binding on Him in the Torah and the Gospel and the Qur'ān. Who fulfilleth His covenant better than Allah? Rejoice then in your bargain that ye have made, for that is the Supreme triumph.

9:111

8. And those who are slain in the way of Allah, He rendereth not their actions vain.

He will guide them and improve their state,

And bring them in unto the Garden which He hath made known to them.

47:4–6

9. And those who believe in Allah and His messengers, they are the loyal; and the martyrs are with their Lord; they have their reward and their light;

57:19

وَ الصِّدِّيقِينَ وَ الشُّهَدَآءِ وَ الصّٰلِحِينَ
وَحَسُنَ اُولٰٓئِكَ رَفِيقًا ﴿٦٩﴾
فَلْيُقَاتِلْ فِي سَبِيلِ اللّٰهِ الَّذِينَ يَشْرُونَ .6
الْحَيٰوةَ الدُّنْيَا بِالْاٰخِرَةِ ؕ وَمَنْ يُّقَاتِلْ
فِي سَبِيلِ اللّٰهِ فَيُقْتَلْ اَوْ يَغْلِبْ فَسَوْفَ
نُؤْتِيهِ اَجْرًا عَظِيمًا ﴿٧٤﴾
اِنَّ اللّٰهَ اشْتَرٰى مِنَ الْمُؤْمِنِينَ اَنْفُسَهُمْ .7
وَ اَمْوَالَهُمْ بِاَنَّ لَهُمُ الْجَنَّةَ ؕ يُقَاتِلُونَ
فِي سَبِيلِ اللّٰهِ فَيَقْتُلُونَ وَ يُقْتَلُونَ وَعْدًا
عَلَيْهِ حَقًّا فِي التَّوْرٰىةِ وَ الْاِنْجِيلِ وَ
الْقُرْاٰنِ ؕ وَ مَنْ اَوْفٰى بِعَهْدِهٖ مِنَ اللّٰهِ
فَاسْتَبْشِرُوا بِبَيْعِكُمُ الَّذِي بَايَعْتُمْ بِهٖ ؕ
وَ ذٰلِكَ هُوَ الْفَوْزُ الْعَظِيمُ ﴿١١١﴾
وَالَّذِينَ قُتِلُوا فِي سَبِيلِ اللّٰهِ فَلَنْ يُّضِلَّ اَعْمَالَهُمْ ﴿٤﴾ .8
سَيَهْدِيهِمْ وَ يُصْلِحُ بَالَهُمْ ﴿٥﴾
وَ يُدْخِلُهُمُ الْجَنَّةَ عَرَّفَهَا لَهُمْ ﴿٦﴾
وَ الَّذِينَ اٰمَنُوا بِاللّٰهِ وَ رُسُلِهٖٓ اُولٰٓئِكَ .9
هُمُ الصِّدِّيقُونَ ۖ وَ الشُّهَدَآءُ عِنْدَ
رَبِّهِمْ ؕ لَهُمْ اَجْرُهُمْ وَ نُوْرُهُمْ ؕ

See also: *Jihad*

MARY

1. (Remember) when the wife of 'Imrān said: My Lord! I have vowed unto Thee that which is in my belly as a con-secrated (offering). Accept it from me. Lo! Thou, only Thou, art the Hearer, the Knower!

And when she was de-livered she said: My Lord! Lo! I am delivered of a fe-male—Allah knew best of what she was delivered— the male is not as the female; and lo! I have named her Mary, and lo! I crave Thy protection for her and for her offspring from Satan the outcast.

And her Lord accepted her with full acceptance and vouchsafed to her a goodly growth; and make Zachariah her guardian. Whenever Zach-ariah went into the sanctuary where she was, he found that she had food. He said: O Mary! Whence cometh unto thee this (food)? She answered: It is from Allah. Allah giveth without stint to whom He will.

3:35–37

2. And when the angels said: O Mary! Lo! Allah hath chosen thee and made thee pure, and hath preferred thee above (all) the women of creation.

O Mary! Be obedient to thy Lord, prostrate thyself and bow with those who bow

1. إِذْ قَالَتِ امْرَاَتُ عِمْرٰنَ رَبِّ اِنِّيْ نَذَرْتُ
لَكَ مَا فِيْ بَطْنِيْ مُحَرَّرًا فَتَقَبَّلْ مِنِّيْ اِنَّكَ
اَنْتَ السَّمِيْعُ الْعَلِيْمُ ○
فَلَمَّا وَضَعَتْهَا قَالَتْ رَبِّ اِنِّيْ وَضَعْتُهَآ
اُنْثٰى وَاللّٰهُ اَعْلَمُ بِمَا وَضَعَتْ وَلَيْسَ
الذَّكَرُ كَالْاُنْثٰى وَاِنِّيْ سَمَّيْتُهَا مَرْيَمَ
وَاِنِّيْٓ اُعِيْذُهَا بِكَ وَذُرِّيَّتَهَا مِنَ
الشَّيْطٰنِ الرَّجِيْمِ ○
فَتَقَبَّلَهَا رَبُّهَا بِقَبُوْلٍ حَسَنٍ وَّاَنْۢبَتَهَا
نَبَاتًا حَسَنًا وَّكَفَّلَهَا زَكَرِيَّا كُلَّمَا دَخَلَ
عَلَيْهَا زَكَرِيَّا الْمِحْرَابَ وَجَدَ عِنْدَهَا رِزْقًا
قَالَ يٰمَرْيَمُ اَنّٰى لَكِ هٰذَا قَالَتْ هُوَ
مِنْ عِنْدِ اللّٰهِ اِنَّ اللّٰهَ يَرْزُقُ مَنْ
يَّشَآءُ بِغَيْرِ حِسَابٍ ○

2. وَاِذْ قَالَتِ الْمَلٰٓئِكَةُ يٰمَرْيَمُ اِنَّ اللّٰهَ
اصْطَفٰكِ وَطَهَّرَكِ وَاصْطَفٰكِ عَلٰى
نِسَآءِ الْعٰلَمِيْنَ ○
يٰمَرْيَمُ اقْنُتِيْ لِرَبِّكِ وَاسْجُدِيْ وَ
ارْكَعِيْ مَعَ الرّٰكِعِيْنَ ○

3. وَاذْكُرْ فِي الْكِتٰبِ مَرْيَمَ اِذِ انْتَبَذَتْ
مِنْ اَهْلِهَا مَكَانًا شَرْقِيًّا ○
فَاتَّخَذَتْ مِنْ دُوْنِهِمْ حِجَابًا فَاَرْسَلْنَآ
اِلَيْهَا رُوْحَنَا فَتَمَثَّلَ لَهَا بَشَرًا سَوِيًّا ○

(in worship).

3:42–43

3. And make mention of Mary in the Scripture, when she had withdrawn from her people to a chamber looking East.

And had chosen seclusion from them. Then We sent unto her Our Spirit and it assumed for her the likeness of a perfect man.

She said: Lo! I seek refuge in the Beneficent One from thee, if thou art God–fearing.

He said: I am only a messenger of thy Lord, that I may bestow on thee a fault–less son.

She said: How can I have a son when no mortal hath touched me, neither have I been unchaste?

He said: So (it will be). Thy Lord saith: It is easy for Me. And (it will be) that We may make of him a reve–lation for mankind and a mercy from Us, and it is a thing ordained.

And she conceived him, and she withdrew with him to a far place.

And the pangs of child–birth drove her unto the trunk of the palm-tree. She said: Oh, would that I had died ere this and had become a thing of naught, forgotten!

Then (one) cried unto her from below her, saying: Grieve not! Thy Lord hath placed a rivulet beneath thee.

And shake the trunk of the palm–tree toward thee, thou wilt cause ripe dates to fall upon thee.

So eat and drink and be consoled. And if thou meet–est any mortal, say: Lo! I have vowed a fast unto the Beneficent, and may not speak

قَالَتْ اِنِّيْٓ اَعُوْذُ بِالرَّحْمٰنِ مِنْكَ اِنْ
كُنْتَ تَقِيًّا ﴿۱۸﴾
قَالَ اِنَّمَآ اَنَا رَسُوْلُ رَبِّكِ ۖ لِاَهَبَ
لَكِ غُلٰمًا زَكِيًّا ﴿۱۹﴾
قَالَتْ اَنّٰى يَكُوْنُ لِيْ غُلٰمٌ وَّلَمْ يَمْسَسْنِيْ
بَشَرٌ وَّلَمْ اَكُ بَغِيًّا ﴿۲۰﴾
قَالَ كَذٰلِكِ ۚ قَالَ رَبُّكِ هُوَ عَلَيَّ هَيِّنٌ ۚ
وَلِنَجْعَلَهٗٓ اٰيَةً لِّلنَّاسِ وَرَحْمَةً مِّنَّا ۚ
وَكَانَ اَمْرًا مَّقْضِيًّا ﴿۲۱﴾
فَحَمَلَتْهُ فَانْتَبَذَتْ بِهٖ مَكَانًا قَصِيًّا ﴿۲۲﴾
فَاَجَآءَهَا الْمَخَاضُ اِلٰى جِذْعِ النَّخْلَةِ ۚ
قَالَتْ يٰلَيْتَنِيْ مِتُّ قَبْلَ هٰذَا وَكُنْتُ
نَسْيًا مَّنْسِيًّا ﴿۲۳﴾
فَنَادٰىهَا مِنْ تَحْتِهَآ اَلَّا تَحْزَنِيْ قَدْ
جَعَلَ رَبُّكِ تَحْتَكِ سَرِيًّا ﴿۲۴﴾
وَهُزِّيْٓ اِلَيْكِ بِجِذْعِ النَّخْلَةِ تُسٰقِطْ
عَلَيْكِ رُطَبًا جَنِيًّا ﴿۲۵﴾
فَكُلِيْ وَاشْرَبِيْ وَقَرِّيْ عَيْنًا ۚ فَاِمَّا
تَرَيِنَّ مِنَ الْبَشَرِ اَحَدًا ۙ فَقُوْلِيْٓ اِنِّيْ
نَذَرْتُ لِلرَّحْمٰنِ صَوْمًا فَلَنْ اُكَلِّمَ
الْيَوْمَ اِنْسِيًّا ﴿۲۶﴾
فَاَتَتْ بِهٖ قَوْمَهَا تَحْمِلُهٗ ۗ قَالُوْا يٰمَرْيَمُ
لَقَدْ جِئْتِ شَيْـًٔا فَرِيًّا ﴿۲۷﴾
يٰٓاُخْتَ هٰرُوْنَ مَا كَانَ اَبُوْكِ امْرَاَ

this day to any mortal.

Then she brought him to her own folk, carrying him. They said: O Mary! Thou hast come with an amazing thing.

Oh sister of Aaron! Thy father was not a wicked man nor was thy mother a harlot.

Then she pointed to him.

They said: How can we talk to one who is in the cradle, a young boy?

He spake: Lo! I am the slave of Allah. He hath given me the Scripture and hath appointed me a Prophet,

And hath made me blessed wheresoever I may be, and hath enjoined upon me prayer and almsgiving so long as I remain alive.

And (hath made me) dutiful toward her who bore me, and hath not made me arrogant, unblest.

Peace on me the day I was born, and the day I die, and the day I shall be raised alive!

19: 16—33

سَوْءٍ وَّ مَا كَانَتْ اُمُّكِ بَغِيًّا ﴿٢٨﴾

فَاَشَارَتْ اِلَيْهِ ۗ قَالُوْا كَيْفَ نُكَلِّمُ
مَنْ كَانَ فِى الْمَهْدِ صَبِيًّا ﴿٢٩﴾

قَالَ اِنِّىْ عَبْدُ اللّٰهِ ۗ اٰتٰنِىَ الْكِتٰبَ
وَ جَعَلَنِىْ نَبِيًّا ﴿٣٠﴾

وَّ جَعَلَنِىْ مُبٰرَكًا اَيْنَ مَا كُنْتُ ۖ وَ
اَوْصٰنِىْ بِالصَّلٰوةِ وَالزَّكٰوةِ مَا دُمْتُ حَيًّا ﴿٣١﴾

وَّ بَرًّا ۢ بِوَالِدَتِىْ ۫ وَ لَمْ يَجْعَلْنِىْ
جَبَّارًا شَقِيًّا ﴿٣٢﴾

وَ السَّلٰمُ عَلَىَّ يَوْمَ وُلِدْتُّ وَ يَوْمَ
اَمُوْتُ وَ يَوْمَ اُبْعَثُ حَيًّا ﴿٣٣﴾

MASTERS OF THE DITCH

1. (Self) destroyed were the owners of the ditch

Of the fuel—fed fire,

When they sat by it,

And were themselves the witness of what they did to the believers.

They had naught against them save that they believed in Allah, the Mighty, the Owner of Praise,

Him unto Whom belongeth the Sovereignty of the heavens and the earth; and Allah is of all things the Witness.

85:4—9

1. قُتِلَ اَصْحٰبُ الْاُخْدُوْدِ ﴿٤﴾
النَّارِ ذَاتِ الْوَقُوْدِ ﴿٥﴾
اِذْ هُمْ عَلَيْهَا قُعُوْدٌ ﴿٦﴾
وَّ هُمْ عَلٰى مَا يَفْعَلُوْنَ بِالْمُؤْمِنِيْنَ
شُهُوْدٌ ﴿٧﴾

وَ مَا نَقَمُوْا مِنْهُمْ اِلَّاۤ اَنْ يُّؤْمِنُوْا
بِاللّٰهِ الْعَزِيْزِ الْحَمِيْدِ ﴿٨﴾
الَّذِىْ لَهٗ مُلْكُ السَّمٰوٰتِ وَ الْاَرْضِ ؕ
وَ اللّٰهُ عَلٰى كُلِّ شَىْءٍ شَهِيْدٌ ﴿٩﴾

MARY

See also: Messiah.

MEDITATION AND DELIBERATION

1. Lo! in the creation of the heavens and the earth and (in) the difference of night and day are tokens (of His Sovereignty) for men of understanding,

Such as remember Allah, standing, sitting, and reclining, and consider the creation of the heavens and the earth, (and say): Our Lord! Thou createdst not this in vain. Glory be to Thee! Preserve us from doom of Fire!

3:190–191

2. And He it is Who spread out the earth and placed therein firm hills and flowing streams, and of all fruits He placed therein two spouses (male and female). He covereth the night with the day. Lo! herein verily are portents for people who take thought.

13:3

3; He it is Who sendeth down water from the sky, whence ye have drink, and whence are trees on which ye send your beasts to pasture.

Therewith He causeth crops to grow for you, and the olive and the date-palm and grapes and all kinds of fruit. Lo! herein is indeed a portent for people who reflect.

16:10–11

4. We have revealed unto thee the Remembrance that thou mayst explain to mankind that which hath been revealed for them, and that haply they may reflect.

16:44

5. Have they not pondered upon themselves? Allah created not the heavens and the earth, and that which is between them, save with truth and for a destined end. But truly, many of mankind are disbelievers in the meeting with their Lord.

30:8

1. إِنَّ فِي خَلْقِ السَّمٰوٰتِ وَالْأَرْضِ وَاخْتِلَافِ
اللَّيْلِ وَالنَّهَارِ لَآيٰتٍ لِّأُولِي الْأَلْبَابِ ۝
الَّذِينَ يَذْكُرُونَ اللّٰهَ قِيٰمًا وَّقُعُودًا وَّعَلٰى
جُنُوبِهِمْ وَيَتَفَكَّرُونَ فِي خَلْقِ السَّمٰوٰتِ
وَالْأَرْضِ رَبَّنَا مَا خَلَقْتَ هٰذَا بَاطِلًا
سُبْحٰنَكَ فَقِنَا عَذَابَ النَّارِ ۝

2. وَهُوَ الَّذِي مَدَّ الْأَرْضَ وَجَعَلَ فِيهَا
رَوَاسِيَ وَأَنْهٰرًا وَمِنْ كُلِّ الثَّمَرٰتِ
جَعَلَ فِيهَا زَوْجَيْنِ اثْنَيْنِ يُغْشِي الَّيْلَ
النَّهَارَ إِنَّ فِي ذٰلِكَ لَآيٰتٍ لِّقَوْمٍ
يَتَفَكَّرُونَ ۝

3. هُوَ الَّذِي أَنْزَلَ مِنَ السَّمَاءِ مَاءً لَّكُمْ مِّنْهُ شَرَابٌ
وَّمِنْهُ شَجَرٌ فِيهِ تُسِيمُونَ ۝
يُنْبِتُ لَكُمْ بِهِ الزَّرْعَ وَالزَّيْتُونَ وَالنَّخِيلَ وَالْأَعْنَابَ
وَمِنْ كُلِّ الثَّمَرٰتِ إِنَّ فِي ذٰلِكَ لَآيَةً لِّقَوْمٍ
يَتَفَكَّرُونَ ۝

4. وَأَنْزَلْنَا إِلَيْكَ الذِّكْرَ لِتُبَيِّنَ لِلنَّاسِ مَا
نُزِّلَ إِلَيْهِمْ وَلَعَلَّهُمْ يَتَفَكَّرُونَ ۝

5. أَوَلَمْ يَتَفَكَّرُوا فِي أَنْفُسِهِمْ مَا خَلَقَ
اللّٰهُ السَّمٰوٰتِ وَالْأَرْضَ وَمَا بَيْنَهُمَا
إِلَّا بِالْحَقِّ وَأَجَلٍ مُّسَمًّى وَإِنَّ
كَثِيرًا مِّنَ النَّاسِ بِلِقَآئِ رَبِّهِمْ لَكٰفِرُونَ ۝

6. If we had caused this Qur'ān to descend upon a mountain, thou (O Muham–mad) verily hadst seen it humbled rent asunder by the fear of Allah. Such similitudes coin We for mankind that haply they may reflect.

59:21

6. لَوْ اَنْزَلْنَا هٰذَا الْقُرْاٰنَ عَلٰى جَبَلٍ
لَّرَاَيْتَهٗ خَاشِعًا مُّتَصَدِّعًا مِّنْ خَشْيَةِ
اللّٰهِ ۭ وَتِلْكَ الْاَمْثَالُ نَضْرِبُهَا لِلنَّاسِ
لَعَلَّهُمْ يَتَفَكَّرُوْنَ ۝

MEMBERS OF PROPHET'S FAMILY

1. And whosoever of you is submissive unto Allah and His messenger and doth right, We shall give her reward twice over, and We have prepared for her a rich pro–vision.

O ye wives of the Pro–phet! Ye are not like any other women. If ye keep your duty (to Allah), then be not soft of speech, lest he in whose heart is a disease aspire (to you), but utter customary speech.

And stay in your houses. Bedizen not yourselves with the bedizenment of the Time of Ignorance. Be regular in prayer, and pay the poor–due, and obey Allah and His messenger. Allah's wish is but to remove uncleanness far from you, O Folk of the House–hold, and cleanse you with a thorough cleansing.

And bear in mind that which is recited in your houses of the revelations of Allah and wisdom. Lo! Allah is Subtile, Aware.

33:31–34

1. وَمَنْ يَّقْنُتْ مِنْكُنَّ لِلّٰهِ وَرَسُوْلِهٖ وَ
تَعْمَلْ صَالِحًا نُّؤْتِهَآ اَجْرَهَا مَرَّتَيْنِ ۙ
وَاَعْتَدْنَا لَهَا رِزْقًا كَرِيْمًا ۝٣١
يٰنِسَآءَ النَّبِيِّ لَسْتُنَّ كَاَحَدٍ مِّنَ
النِّسَآءِ اِنِ اتَّقَيْتُنَّ فَلَا تَخْضَعْنَ
بِالْقَوْلِ فَيَطْمَعَ الَّذِيْ فِيْ قَلْبِهٖ
مَرَضٌ وَّقُلْنَ قَوْلًا مَّعْرُوْفًا ۝٣٢
وَقَرْنَ فِيْ بُيُوْتِكُنَّ وَلَا تَبَرَّجْنَ
تَبَرُّجَ الْجَاهِلِيَّةِ الْاُوْلٰى وَاَقِمْنَ الصَّلٰوةَ
وَاٰتِيْنَ الزَّكٰوةَ وَاَطِعْنَ اللّٰهَ وَرَسُوْلَهٗ ۭ
اِنَّمَا يُرِيْدُ اللّٰهُ لِيُذْهِبَ عَنْكُمُ
الرِّجْسَ اَهْلَ الْبَيْتِ وَيُطَهِّرَكُمْ تَطْهِيْرًا ۝٣٣
وَاذْكُرْنَ مَا يُتْلٰى فِيْ بُيُوْتِكُنَّ مِنْ
اٰيٰتِ اللّٰهِ وَالْحِكْمَةِ ۭ اِنَّ اللّٰهَ كَانَ
لَطِيْفًا خَبِيْرًا ۝٣٤

MEDITATION AND DELIBERATION
Ref: 10:24; 39:42; 45:13.

.MEN OF RIGHTEOUSNESS

1. وَأَصْحَٰبُ ٱلْيَمِينِ مَآ أَصْحَٰبُ
ٱلْيَمِينِ
فِى سِدْرٍ مَّخْضُودٍ
وَطَلْحٍ مَّنضُودٍ
وَظِلٍّ مَّمْدُودٍ
وَمَآءٍ مَّسْكُوبٍ
وَفَٰكِهَةٍ كَثِيرَةٍ
لَّا مَقْطُوعَةٍ وَلَا مَمْنُوعَةٍ
وَفُرُشٍ مَّرْفُوعَةٍ
إِنَّآ أَنشَأْنَٰهُنَّ إِنشَآءً
فَجَعَلْنَٰهُنَّ أَبْكَارًا
عُرُبًا أَتْرَابًا
لِّأَصْحَٰبِ ٱلْيَمِينِ
ثُلَّةٌ مِّنَ ٱلْأَوَّلِينَ
وَثُلَّةٌ مِّنَ ٱلْءَاخِرِينَ
وَأَصْحَٰبُ ٱلشِّمَالِ مَآ أَصْحَٰبُ
ٱلشِّمَالِ
فِى سَمُومٍ وَحَمِيمٍ
وَظِلٍّ مِّن يَحْمُومٍ
لَّا بَارِدٍ وَلَا كَرِيمٍ
إِنَّهُمْ كَانُوا۟ قَبْلَ ذَٰلِكَ مُتْرَفِينَ
وَكَانُوا۟ يُصِرُّونَ عَلَى ٱلْحِنثِ ٱلْعَظِيمِ

2. وَأَمَّا مَنْ أُوتِىَ كِتَٰبَهُۥ بِشِمَالِهِۦ فَيَقُولُ
يَٰلَيْتَنِى لَمْ أُوتَ كِتَٰبِيَهْ
وَلَمْ أَدْرِ مَا حِسَابِيَهْ
يَٰلَيْتَهَا كَانَتِ ٱلْقَاضِيَةَ

1. And those on the right hand; what of those on the right hand?

Among thornless lote-trees

And clustered plantains,

And spreading shade,

And water gushing,

And fruit in plenty

Neither out of reach nor yet forbidden,

And raised couches;

Lo! We have created them a (new) creation

And made them virgins,

Lovers, friends,

For those on the right hand;

A multitude of those of old

And a multitude of those of later time.

And those on the left hand: What of those on the left hand?

In scorching wind and scalding water

And shadow of black smoke,

Neither cool nor refreshing.

Lo! heretofore they were effete with luxury

And used to persist in the awful sin.

56:27–46

2. But as for him who is given his record in his left hand, he will say: Oh, would that I had not been given my book!

And knew not what my reckoning!

Oh, would that it had been death!

My wealth hath not availed me,

My power hath gone from me.

(It will be said): Take him and fetter him

And then expose him to hell-fire

And then insert him in a chain whereof the length is seventy cubits.

Lo! he used not to believe in Allah the Tremendous,

And urged not on the feeding of the wretched:

Therefor hath he no lover here this day:

Nor any food save filth

Which none but sinners eat.

69:25–37

3. Every soul is a pledge for its own deeds;

Save those who will stand on the right hand.

In gardens they will ask one another

Concerning the guilty:

What hath brought you to this burning?

They will answer: We were not of those who prayed

Nor did we feed the wretched.

We used to wade (in vain dispute) with (all) waders,

And we used to deny the Day of Judgment,

Till the Inevitable came unto us.

The mediation of no mediators will avail them then.

74:38–48

مَآ أَغْنَىٰ عَنِّى مَالِيَهْ ﴿28﴾
هَلَكَ عَنِّى سُلْطَٰنِيَهْ ﴿29﴾
خُذُوهُ فَغُلُّوهُ ﴿30﴾
ثُمَّ ٱلْجَحِيمَ صَلُّوهُ ﴿31﴾
ثُمَّ فِى سِلْسِلَةٍ ذَرْعُهَا سَبْعُونَ
ذِرَاعًا فَٱسْلُكُوهُ ﴿32﴾
إِنَّهُۥ كَانَ لَا يُؤْمِنُ بِٱللَّهِ ٱلْعَظِيمِ ﴿33﴾
وَلَا يَحُضُّ عَلَىٰ طَعَامِ ٱلْمِسْكِينِ ﴿34﴾
فَلَيْسَ لَهُ ٱلْيَوْمَ هَٰهُنَا حَمِيمٌ ﴿35﴾
وَلَا طَعَامٌ إِلَّا مِنْ غِسْلِينٍ ﴿36﴾
لَّا يَأْكُلُهُۥٓ إِلَّا ٱلْخَٰطِـُٔونَ ﴿37﴾

3. كُلُّ نَفْسٍۭ بِمَا كَسَبَتْ رَهِينَةٌ ﴿38﴾
إِلَّآ أَصْحَٰبَ ٱلْيَمِينِ ﴿39﴾
فِى جَنَّٰتٍ يَتَسَآءَلُونَ ﴿40﴾
عَنِ ٱلْمُجْرِمِينَ ﴿41﴾
مَا سَلَكَكُمْ فِى سَقَرَ ﴿42﴾
قَالُوا۟ لَمْ نَكُ مِنَ ٱلْمُصَلِّينَ ﴿43﴾
وَلَمْ نَكُ نُطْعِمُ ٱلْمِسْكِينَ ﴿44﴾
وَكُنَّا نَخُوضُ مَعَ ٱلْخَآئِضِينَ ﴿45﴾
وَكُنَّا نُكَذِّبُ بِيَوْمِ ٱلدِّينِ ﴿46﴾
حَتَّىٰٓ أَتَىٰنَا ٱلْيَقِينُ ﴿47﴾
فَمَا تَنفَعُهُمْ شَفَٰعَةُ ٱلشَّٰفِعِينَ ﴿48﴾

Ref: 56:8-40,90-91; 90:17-20.

See also: Scroll of Actions.

MENSTRUATION

1. They question thee (O Muhammad) concerning menstruation. Say: It is an illness so let women alone at such times and go not in unto them till they are cleansed. And when they have purified themselves, then go in unto them as Allah hath enjoined upon you. Truly Allah loveth those who turn unto Him, and loveth those who have a care for cleanness.

2:222

MERCY

1. But Allah chooseth for His mercy whom He will, and Allah is of Infinite Bounty.

2:105

2. And give glad tidings to the steadfast.

Who say, when a misfortune striketh them: Lo! we are Allah's and lo! unto Him we are returning.

Such are they on whom are blessings from their Lord, and mercy. Such are the rightly guided.

2:155–157

3. Our Lord! Cause not our hearts to stray after Thou hast guided us, and bestow upon us mercy from Thy Presence. Lo! Thou, only Thou art the Bestower.

3:8

4. And when those who believe in Our revelations come unto thee, say: Peace be unto you! Your Lord hath prescribed for Himself mercy, that whoso of you doth evil through ignorance and repenteth afterward thereof and doth right, (for him) lo! He is Forgiving, Merciful.

6:54

1. وَيَسْـَٔلُونَكَ عَنِ الْمَحِيضِ قُلْ هُوَ أَذًى
فَاعْتَزِلُوا النِّسَاءَ فِي الْمَحِيضِ وَلَا تَقْرَبُوهُنَّ
حَتَّىٰ يَطْهُرْنَ فَإِذَا تَطَهَّرْنَ فَأْتُوهُنَّ مِنْ
حَيْثُ أَمَرَكُمُ اللَّهُ إِنَّ اللَّهَ يُحِبُّ التَّوَّابِينَ
وَيُحِبُّ الْمُتَطَهِّرِينَ ﴿٢٢٢﴾

1. وَاللَّهُ يَخْتَصُّ بِرَحْمَتِهِ مَنْ يَشَاءُ وَاللَّهُ
ذُو الْفَضْلِ الْعَظِيمِ ﴿١٠٥﴾

2. وَبَشِّرِ الصَّابِرِينَ ﴿١٥٥﴾
الَّذِينَ إِذَا أَصَابَتْهُمْ مُصِيبَةٌ قَالُوا إِنَّا
لِلَّهِ وَإِنَّا إِلَيْهِ رَاجِعُونَ ﴿١٥٦﴾
أُولَٰئِكَ عَلَيْهِمْ صَلَوَاتٌ مِنْ رَبِّهِمْ وَرَحْمَةٌ
وَأُولَٰئِكَ هُمُ الْمُهْتَدُونَ ﴿١٥٧﴾

3. رَبَّنَا لَا تُزِغْ قُلُوبَنَا بَعْدَ إِذْ هَدَيْتَنَا وَهَبْ لَنَا مِنْ
لَدُنْكَ رَحْمَةً إِنَّكَ أَنْتَ الْوَهَّابُ ﴿٨﴾

4. وَإِذَا جَاءَكَ الَّذِينَ يُؤْمِنُونَ بِآيَاتِنَا فَقُلْ
سَلَامٌ عَلَيْكُمْ كَتَبَ رَبُّكُمْ عَلَىٰ نَفْسِهِ
الرَّحْمَةَ أَنَّهُ مَنْ عَمِلَ مِنْكُمْ سُوءًا
بِجَهَالَةٍ ثُمَّ تَابَ مِنْ بَعْدِهِ وَأَصْلَحَ
فَأَنَّهُ غَفُورٌ رَحِيمٌ ﴿٥٤﴾

MENSTRUATION Ref: 65:4.

5. So if they give the lie to thee (Muhammad), say: Your Lord is a Lord of All-Embracing Mercy, and His wrath will never be withdrawn from guilty folk.

6:147

6. Work not confusion in the earth after the fair ordering (thereof), and call on Him in fear and hope. Lo! the mercy of Allah is nigh unto the good.

And He it is Who sendeth the winds as tidings heralding His mercy, till, when they bear a cloud heavy (with rain), We lead it to a dead land, and then cause water to descend thereon and thereby bring forth fruits of every kind. Thus bring We forth the dead. Haply ye may remember.

7:56–57

7. Say (unto them): If ye possessed the treasures of the mercy of my Lord, ye would surely hold them back for fear of spending, for man was ever grudging.

17:100

8. Our Lord! Give us mercy from Thy presence, and shape for us right conduct in our plight.

18:10

9. We sent thee not save as a mercy for the peoples.

21:107

10. Those who disbelieve in

5. فَإِن كَذَّبُوكَ فَقُل رَّبُّكُمْ ذُو رَحْمَةٍ
وَاسِعَةٍ وَلَا يُرَدُّ بَأْسُهُ عَنِ الْقَوْمِ
الْمُجْرِمِينَ

6. وَلَا تُفْسِدُوا فِي الْأَرْضِ بَعْدَ إِصْلَاحِهَا وَادْعُوهُ
خَوْفًا وَطَمَعًا إِنَّ رَحْمَتَ اللَّهِ قَرِيبٌ مِّنَ الْمُحْسِنِينَ
وَهُوَ الَّذِي يُرْسِلُ الرِّيَاحَ بُشْرًا بَيْنَ يَدَيْ رَحْمَتِهِ
حَتَّىٰ إِذَا أَقَلَّتْ سَحَابًا ثِقَالًا سُقْنَاهُ لِبَلَدٍ مَّيِّتٍ فَأَنزَلْنَا
بِهِ الْمَاءَ فَأَخْرَجْنَا بِهِ مِن كُلِّ الثَّمَرَاتِ كَذَٰلِكَ
نُخْرِجُ الْمَوْتَىٰ لَعَلَّكُمْ تَذَكَّرُونَ

7. قُل لَّوْ أَنتُمْ تَمْلِكُونَ خَزَائِنَ رَحْمَةِ
رَبِّي إِذًا لَّأَمْسَكْتُمْ خَشْيَةَ الْإِنفَاقِ
وَكَانَ الْإِنسَانُ قَتُورًا

8. رَبَّنَا آتِنَا مِن لَّدُنكَ رَحْمَةً وَهَيِّئْ
لَنَا مِنْ أَمْرِنَا رَشَدًا

9. وَمَا أَرْسَلْنَاكَ إِلَّا رَحْمَةً لِّلْعَالَمِينَ

10. وَالَّذِينَ كَفَرُوا بِآيَاتِ اللَّهِ وَلِقَائِهِ
أُولَٰئِكَ يَئِسُوا مِن رَّحْمَتِي وَأُولَٰئِكَ
لَهُمْ عَذَابٌ أَلِيمٌ

11. وَمِنْ آيَاتِهِ أَنْ خَلَقَ لَكُم مِّنْ أَنفُسِكُمْ
أَزْوَاجًا لِّتَسْكُنُوا إِلَيْهَا وَجَعَلَ بَيْنَكُم
مَّوَدَّةً وَرَحْمَةً إِنَّ فِي ذَٰلِكَ لَآيَاتٍ
لِّقَوْمٍ يَتَفَكَّرُونَ

the revelations of Allah and in (their) Meeting with Him, such have no hope of My mercy. For such there is a painful doom.

29:23

11. And of His signs is this: He created for you helpmates from yourselves that ye might find rest

in them, and He ordained between you love and mercy. Lo, herein indeed are portents for folk who reflect.

30:21

12. Say: O My slaves who have been prodigal to their own souls! Despair not of the Mercy of Allah, Who forgiveth all sins. Lo! He is the Forgiving, the Merciful.

39:53

13. Is it they who apportion thy Lord's mercy? We have apportioned among them their livelihood in the life of the world, and raised some of them above others in rank that some of them may take labour from others; and the mercy of thy Lord is better than (the wealth) that they amass.

12. قُلْ يٰعِبَادِيَ الَّذِيْنَ اَسْرَفُوْا عَلٰٓى
اَنْفُسِهِمْ لَا تَقْنَطُوْا مِنْ رَّحْمَةِ اللّٰهِ ؕ
اِنَّ اللّٰهَ يَغْفِرُ الذُّنُوْبَ جَمِيْعًا ؕ اِنَّهٗ
هُوَ الْغَفُوْرُ الرَّحِيْمُ ۝

13. اَهُمْ يَقْسِمُوْنَ رَحْمَتَ رَبِّكَ ؕ نَحْنُ
قَسَمْنَا بَيْنَهُمْ مَّعِيْشَتَهُمْ فِي الْحَيٰوةِ
الدُّنْيَا وَ رَفَعْنَا بَعْضَهُمْ فَوْقَ بَعْضٍ
دَرَجٰتٍ لِّيَتَّخِذَ بَعْضُهُمْ بَعْضًا سُخْرِيًّا ؕ
وَ رَحْمَتُ رَبِّكَ خَيْرٌ مِّمَّا يَجْمَعُوْنَ ۝

Ref: 2:64; 3:159; 4:83; 6:12; 10:21; 24:10,14,20–21; 30:21,33; 40:7; 57: 28.

MESSIAH

1. (And remember) when the angels said: O Mary! Lo! Allah giveth thee glad tidings of a word from Him, whose name is the Messiah, Jesus, son of Mary, illustrious in the world and the Hereafter, and one of those brought near (unto Allah).

He will speak unto mankind in his cradle and in his manhood, and he is of the righteous.

3:45–46

2. And because of their saying: We slew the Messiah Jesus son of Mary, Allah's messenger—They slew him not nor crucified, but it appeared so unto them; and lo! those who disagree concerning it are in doubt thereof; they have no knowledge thereof save pursuit of a conjecture; they slew him not for certain:

But Allah took him up unto Himself. Allah was ever Mighty, Wise.

4:157–158

3. They indeed have disbelieved who say: Lo! Allah is the Messiah, son of Mary, Say: Who then can do aught against Allah, if He had willed to destroy the Messiah son of Mary, and his mother and everyone on earth? Allah's is the Sovereignty of the heavens and the earth and all that is between them. He createth what He will.

5:17

1. إِذْ قَالَتِ الْمَلٰٓئِكَةُ يٰمَرْيَمُ إِنَّ اللّٰهَ
يُبَشِّرُكِ بِكَلِمَةٍ مِّنْهُ اسْمُهُ الْمَسِيْحُ
عِيْسَى ابْنُ مَرْيَمَ وَجِيْهًا فِي الدُّنْيَا
وَالْاٰخِرَةِ وَمِنَ الْمُقَرَّبِيْنَ ۝
وَيُكَلِّمُ النَّاسَ فِي الْمَهْدِ وَكَهْلًا
وَّمِنَ الصّٰلِحِيْنَ ۝

2. وَّقَوْلِهِمْ إِنَّا قَتَلْنَا الْمَسِيْحَ عِيْسَى ابْنَ مَرْيَمَ
رَسُوْلَ اللّٰهِ وَمَا قَتَلُوْهُ وَمَا صَلَبُوْهُ وَلٰكِنْ
شُبِّهَ لَهُمْ وَإِنَّ الَّذِيْنَ اخْتَلَفُوْا فِيْهِ
لَفِيْ شَكٍّ مِّنْهُ مَا لَهُمْ بِهٖ مِنْ عِلْمٍ
إِلَّا اتِّبَاعَ الظَّنِّ وَمَا قَتَلُوْهُ يَقِيْنًا ۝
بَلْ رَّفَعَهُ اللّٰهُ إِلَيْهِ وَكَانَ اللّٰهُ
عَزِيْزًا حَكِيْمًا ۝

3. لَقَدْ كَفَرَ الَّذِيْنَ قَالُوْا إِنَّ اللّٰهَ هُوَ
الْمَسِيْحُ ابْنُ مَرْيَمَ قُلْ فَمَنْ يَّمْلِكُ
مِنَ اللّٰهِ شَيْئًا إِنْ أَرَادَ أَنْ يُّهْلِكَ الْمَسِيْحَ
ابْنَ مَرْيَمَ وَأُمَّهٗ وَمَنْ فِي الْأَرْضِ
جَمِيْعًا وَلِلّٰهِ مُلْكُ السَّمٰوٰتِ وَالْأَرْضِ
وَمَا بَيْنَهُمَا يَخْلُقُ مَا يَشَآءُ

4. مَا الْمَسِيْحُ ابْنُ مَرْيَمَ إِلَّا رَسُوْلٌ
قَدْ خَلَتْ مِنْ قَبْلِهِ الرُّسُلُ وَأُمُّهٗ
صِدِّيْقَةٌ كَانَا يَأْكُلٰنِ الطَّعَامَ
اُنْظُرْ كَيْفَ نُبَيِّنُ لَهُمُ الْاٰيٰتِ ثُمَّ
انْظُرْ أَنّٰى يُؤْفَكُوْنَ ۝

4. The Messiah, son of Mary, was no other than a messenger, messengers (the like of whom) had passed away before him. And his mother was a saintly woman. And they both used to eat (earthly) food. See how We make the revelations clear for them, and see how they are turned away!

5:75

Ref: 2:87,253; 3:45-48; 4:156; 21:91; 23:50.

See also: Miracles of Prophets.

MIGRATION

1. Lo! those who believe and those who emigrate (to escape the persecution) and strive in the way of Allah, these have hope of Allah's mercy. Allah is Forgiving, Merciful.

2:218

2. So those who fled and were driven forth from their homes and suffered damage for My cause, and fought and were slain, verily I shall remit their evil deeds from them and verily I shall bring them into Gardens under-neath which rivers flow—A reward from Allah. And with Allah is the fairest of rewards.

3:195

3. Lo! as for those whom the angels take (in death) while they wrong themselves, (the angels) will ask: In what were ye engaged? They will say: We were oppressed in the land. (The angels) will say: Was not Allah's earth spacious that ye could have migrated therein? As for such, their habitation will be hell, an evil journey's end.

Except the feeble among men, and the women, and the children, who are unable to devise a plan and are not shown a way:

As for such, it may be that Allah will pardon them, Allah is ever Clement, Forgiving.

1. إِنَّ الَّذِينَ آمَنُوا وَالَّذِينَ هَاجَرُوا وَ
جَاهَدُوا فِي سَبِيلِ اللَّهِ أُولَٰئِكَ يَرْجُونَ
رَحْمَتَ اللَّهِ وَاللَّهُ غَفُورٌ رَحِيمٌ ﴿٢١٨﴾

2. فَالَّذِينَ هَاجَرُوا وَأُخْرِجُوا
مِنْ دِيَارِهِمْ وَأُوذُوا فِي سَبِيلِي وَقَاتَلُوا
وَقُتِلُوا لَأُكَفِّرَنَّ عَنْهُمْ سَيِّئَاتِهِمْ وَلَأُدْخِلَنَّهُمْ
جَنَّاتٍ تَجْرِي مِنْ تَحْتِهَا الْأَنْهَارُ ثَوَابًا
مِنْ عِنْدِ اللَّهِ وَاللَّهُ عِنْدَهُ حُسْنُ الثَّوَابِ ○

3. إِنَّ الَّذِينَ تَوَفَّاهُمُ الْمَلَائِكَةُ ظَالِمِي
أَنْفُسِهِمْ قَالُوا فِيمَ كُنْتُمْ قَالُوا كُنَّا
مُسْتَضْعَفِينَ فِي الْأَرْضِ قَالُوا أَلَمْ تَكُنْ
أَرْضُ اللَّهِ وَاسِعَةً فَتُهَاجِرُوا فِيهَا فَأُولَٰئِكَ
مَأْوَاهُمْ جَهَنَّمُ وَسَاءَتْ مَصِيرًا ﴿٩٧﴾

إِلَّا الْمُسْتَضْعَفِينَ مِنَ الرِّجَالِ وَالنِّسَاءِ
وَالْوِلْدَانِ لَا يَسْتَطِيعُونَ حِيلَةً وَلَا
يَهْتَدُونَ سَبِيلًا ﴿٩٨﴾

فَأُولَٰئِكَ عَسَى اللَّهُ أَنْ يَعْفُوَ عَنْهُمْ وَ
كَانَ اللَّهُ عَفُوًّا غَفُورًا ﴿٩٩﴾

وَمَنْ يُهَاجِرْ فِي سَبِيلِ اللَّهِ يَجِدْ فِي
الْأَرْضِ مُرَاغَمًا كَثِيرًا وَسَعَةً وَمَنْ
يَخْرُجْ مِنْ بَيْتِهِ مُهَاجِرًا إِلَى اللَّهِ وَرَسُولِهِ
ثُمَّ يُدْرِكْهُ الْمَوْتُ فَقَدْ وَقَعَ أَجْرُهُ عَلَى
اللَّهِ وَكَانَ اللَّهُ غَفُورًا رَحِيمًا ﴿١٠٠﴾

Whoso migrateth for the cause of Allah will find much refuge and abundance in the earth, and whoso forsaketh his home, a fugitive unto Allah and His messenger, and death overtaketh him, his reward is then incumbent on Allah.

Allah is ever Forgiving, Merciful.

4:97–100

4. Those who believed and left their homes and strove for the cause of Allah, and those who took them in and helped them—these are the believers in truth. For them is pardon, and a bountiful provision.

8:74

5. Those who believe, and have left their homes and striven with their wealth and their lives in Allah's way are of much greater worth in Allah's sight. These are they who are triumphant.

Their Lord giveth them good tidings of mercy from Him, and acceptance, and Gardens where enduring pleasure will be theirs;

There they will abide for ever. Lo! with Allah there is immense reward.

9:20–22

6. Those who fled their homes for the cause of Allah and then were slain or died, Allah verily will provide for them a good provision. Lo! Allah, He verily is Best of all who make provision.

Assuredly He will cause them to enter by an entry that they will love. Lo! Allah verily is Knower, Indulgent.

22:58–59

7. O ye who believe! When

4. وَالَّذِينَ آمَنُوا وَهَاجَرُوا وَجَاهَدُوا فِي
سَبِيلِ اللَّهِ وَالَّذِينَ آوَوا وَّنَصَرُوا أُولَٰئِكَ
هُمُ الْمُؤْمِنُونَ حَقًّا ۚ لَّهُم مَّغْفِرَةٌ
وَرِزْقٌ كَرِيمٌ ﴿٧٤﴾

5. الَّذِينَ آمَنُوا وَهَاجَرُوا وَجَاهَدُوا فِي
سَبِيلِ اللَّهِ بِأَمْوَالِهِمْ وَأَنفُسِهِمْ أَعْظَمُ
دَرَجَةً عِندَ اللَّهِ ۚ وَأُولَٰئِكَ هُمُ الْفَائِزُونَ ﴿٢٠﴾
يُبَشِّرُهُمْ رَبُّهُم بِرَحْمَةٍ مِّنْهُ وَرِضْوَانٍ
وَجَنَّاتٍ لَّهُمْ فِيهَا نَعِيمٌ مُّقِيمٌ ﴿٢١﴾
خَالِدِينَ فِيهَا أَبَدًا ۚ إِنَّ اللَّهَ عِندَهُ
أَجْرٌ عَظِيمٌ ﴿٢٢﴾

6. وَالَّذِينَ هَاجَرُوا فِي سَبِيلِ اللَّهِ ثُمَّ
قُتِلُوا أَوْ مَاتُوا لَيَرْزُقَنَّهُمُ اللَّهُ رِزْقًا
حَسَنًا ۚ وَإِنَّ اللَّهَ لَهُوَ خَيْرُ الرَّازِقِينَ ﴿٥٨﴾
لَيُدْخِلَنَّهُم مُّدْخَلًا يَرْضَوْنَهُ ۗ وَإِنَّ
اللَّهَ لَعَلِيمٌ حَلِيمٌ ﴿٥٩﴾

7. يَا أَيُّهَا الَّذِينَ آمَنُوا إِذَا جَاءَكُمُ الْمُؤْمِنَاتُ
مُهَاجِرَاتٍ فَامْتَحِنُوهُنَّ ۖ اللَّهُ أَعْلَمُ
بِإِيمَانِهِنَّ ۖ فَإِنْ عَلِمْتُمُوهُنَّ مُؤْمِنَاتٍ
فَلَا تَرْجِعُوهُنَّ إِلَى الْكُفَّارِ ۖ لَا هُنَّ
حِلٌّ لَّهُمْ وَلَا هُمْ يَحِلُّونَ لَهُنَّ ۖ وَ
آتُوهُم مَّا أَنفَقُوا ۚ وَلَا جُنَاحَ عَلَيْكُمْ

believing women come unto you as fugitives, examine them. Allah is Best Aware of their faith. Then if ye know them for true believers, send them not back unto the disbelievers. They are not lawful for the disbelievers, nor are they (the disbelievers) lawful for them. And give them (the disbelievers) that which they have spent (upon them). And it is no sin for you to marry such women when ye have given them their dues. And hold not to the ties of disbelieving women; and ask for (the return of) that which ye have spent; and let them (the disbelievers) ask for that which they have spent. That is the judgment of Allah. He judgeth between you. Allah is Knower, Wise.

And if any of your wives have gone from you unto the disbelievers and, afterward ye have your turn (of triumph), then give unto those whose wives have gone the like of that which they have spent, and keep your duty to Allah in Whom ye are believers.

60:10–11

أَنْ تَنْكِحُوهُنَّ إِذَآ اٰتَيْتُمُوهُنَّ أُجُورَهُنَّ
وَلَا تُمْسِكُوا بِعِصَمِ الْكَوَافِرِ وَسْـَٔلُوا مَآ
أَنْفَقْتُمْ وَلْيَسْـَٔلُوا مَآ أَنْفَقُوا ۚ ذٰلِكُمْ حُكْمُ
اللّٰهِ ۖ يَحْكُمُ بَيْنَكُمْ ۚ وَاللّٰهُ عَلِيمٌ حَكِيمٌ ۝
وَإِنْ فَاتَكُمْ شَيْءٌ مِّنْ أَزْوَاجِكُمْ إِلَى
الْكُفَّارِ فَعَاقَبْتُمْ فَاٰتُوا الَّذِينَ ذَهَبَتْ
أَزْوَاجُهُمْ مِّثْلَ مَآ أَنْفَقُوا ۚ وَاتَّقُوا
اللّٰهَ الَّذِيٓ أَنْتُمْ بِهٖ مُؤْمِنُونَ ﴿١١﴾

MILK

1. And lo! in the cattle there is a lesson for you. We give you to drink of that which is in their bellies, from betwixt the refuse and the blood, pure milk palatable to the drinkers.

16:66

1. وَإِنَّ لَكُمْ فِي الْأَنْعَامِ لَعِبْرَةً ۖ نُّسْقِيكُمْ
مِّمَّا فِي بُطُونِهٖ مِنْ بَيْنِ فَرْثٍ وَّدَمٍ
لَّبَنًا خَالِصًا سَآئِغًا لِّلشّٰرِبِينَ ﴿٦٦﴾

MIGRATION

Ref: 8:72–75; 9:100; 16:41; 29:56; 39:10; 59:7–10.

See also: ***Jihad.***

MINERALS

1. Beautified for mankind is love of the joys (that come) from women and offspring, and stored-up heaps of gold and silver, and horses branded (with their mark), and cattle and land. That is comfort of the life of the world. Allah! With Him is a more excellent abode.

3:14

2. They who hoard up gold and silver and spend it not in the way of Allah, unto them give tidings (O Muhammad) of a painful doom.

9:34

3. And assuredly We gave David grace from Us, (saying): O ye hills and birds, echo his psalms of praise! And We made the iron supple unto him,

Saying: Make thou long coats–of–mail and measure the links (thereof). And do ye right. Lo! I am Seer of what ye do.

And unto Solomon (We gave) the wind, whereof the morning course was a month's journey and the evening course a month's journey, and We caused the fount of copper to gush forth for him.

34:10–12

1. زُيِّنَ لِلنَّاسِ حُبُّ الشَّهَوٰتِ مِنَ النِّسَآءِ
وَالْبَنِيْنَ وَالْقَنَاطِيْرِ الْمُقَنْطَرَةِ مِنَ
الذَّهَبِ وَالْفِضَّةِ وَالْخَيْلِ الْمُسَوَّمَةِ
وَالْاَنْعَامِ وَالْحَرْثِ ؕ ذٰلِكَ مَتَاعُ
الْحَيٰوةِ الدُّنْيَا ۚ وَاللّٰهُ عِنْدَهٗ حُسْنُ الْمَاٰبِ ۝

2. وَالَّذِيْنَ يَكْنِزُوْنَ الذَّهَبَ وَالْفِضَّةَ
وَلَا يُنْفِقُوْنَهَا فِيْ سَبِيْلِ اللّٰهِ ۙ فَبَشِّرْهُمْ
بِعَذَابٍ اَلِيْمٍ ۝

3. وَلَقَدْ اٰتَيْنَا دَاوٗدَ مِنَّا فَضْلًا ؕ يٰجِبَالُ
اَوِّبِيْ مَعَهٗ وَالطَّيْرَ ۚ وَاَلَنَّا لَهُ
الْحَدِيْدَ ۝
اَنِ اعْمَلْ سٰبِغٰتٍ وَّقَدِّرْ فِي السَّرْدِ
وَاعْمَلُوْا صَالِحًا ؕ اِنِّيْ بِمَا تَعْمَلُوْنَ بَصِيْرٌ ۝
وَلِسُلَيْمٰنَ الرِّيْحَ غُدُوُّهَا شَهْرٌ وَّ
رَوَاحُهَا شَهْرٌ ۚ وَاَسَلْنَا لَهٗ عَيْنَ
الْقِطْرِ ؕ

MIRACLES OF PROPHET MUHAMMAD (PBUH)

1. الذين يتبعون الرسول النبي الامي
الذي يجدونه مكتوبا عندهم في التورىة
والانجيل يامرهم بالمعروف وينههم
عن المنكر ويحل لهم الطيبت ويحرم
عليهم الخبئث ويضع عنهم اصرهم
والاغلل التي كانت عليهم فالذين
امنوا به وعزروه ونصروه واتبعوا
النور الذي انزل معه اولئك هم
المفلحون ﴿١٥٧﴾

2. فلم تقتلوهم ولكن الله قتلهم وما
رميت اذ رميت ولكن الله رمى

3. لقد نصركم الله في مواطن كثيرة ويوم
حنين اذ اعجبتكم كثرتكم فلم تغن
عنكم شيئا وضاقت عليكم الارض بما
رحبت ثم وليتم مدبرين ﴿٢٥﴾
ثم انزل الله سكينته على رسوله وعلى
المؤمنين وانزل جنودا لم تروها وعذب
الذين كفروا وذلك جزاء الكفرين ﴿٢٦﴾

4. سبحن الذي اسرى بعبده ليلا من المسجد
الحرام الى المسجد الاقصا الذي بركنا حوله
لنريه من ايتنا انه هو السميع البصير ﴿١﴾

1. Those who follow the messenger, the Prophet who can neither read nor write, whom they will find des–cribed in the Torah and the Gospel (which are) with them. He will enjoin on them that which is right and forbid them that which is wrong. He will make lawful for them all good things and prohibit for them only the foul; and he will relieve them of their burden and the fetters that they used to wear. Then those who believe in him, and honour him, and help him, and follow the light which is sent down with him; they are the successful.

7:157

2. Ye (Muslims) slew them not, but Allah slew them. And thou (Muhammad) threwest not when thou didst throw, but Allah threw.

8:17

3. Allah hath given you victory on many fields and on the day of *Huneyn,* when ye exulted in your multitude but it availed you naught, and the earth, vast as it is, was straitened for you; then ye turned back in flight!

Then Allah sent His peace of reassurance down upon His messenger and upon the believers, and sent down hosts ye could not see, and punished those who dis–believed. Such is the reward of disbelievers.

9:25–26

4. Glorified be He Who carried His servant by night from the Inviolable Place of Worship to the Far Distant Place of Worship.the neigh–bourhood whereof We have blessed, that We might show him of Our tokens!

Lo! He, only He, is the Hearer, the Seer.

17:1

5. And they say: Why are not portents sent down upon him from his Lord? Say: Portents are with Allah only, and I am but a plain warner.

Is it not enough for them that We have sent down unto thee the Scripture which is read unto them? Lo! herein verily is mercy, and a reminder for folk who believe.

29:50–51

6. The hour drew nigh and the moon was rent in twain.

And if they behold a portent they turn away and say: Prolonged illusion.

They denied (the Truth) and followed their own lusts. Yet everything will come to a decision.

54:1–3

5. وَقَالُوا لَوْلَآ أُنْزِلَ عَلَيْهِ اٰيٰتٌ مِّنْ
رَّبِّهٖ قُلْ اِنَّمَا الْاٰيٰتُ عِنْدَ اللّٰهِ وَ
اِنَّمَآ اَنَا نَذِيْرٌ مُّبِيْنٌ ۝
اَوَلَمْ يَكْفِهِمْ اَنَّآ اَنْزَلْنَا عَلَيْكَ الْكِتٰبَ
يُتْلٰى عَلَيْهِمْ اِنَّ فِيْ ذٰلِكَ لَرَحْمَةً وَّ
ذِكْرٰى لِقَوْمٍ يُّؤْمِنُوْنَ ۝

6. اِقْتَرَبَتِ السَّاعَةُ وَانْشَقَّ الْقَمَرُ ۝
وَاِنْ يَّرَوْا اٰيَةً يُّعْرِضُوْا وَيَقُوْلُوْا
سِحْرٌ مُّسْتَمِرٌّ ۝
وَكَذَّبُوْا وَاتَّبَعُوْٓا اَهْوَآءَهُمْ وَكُلُّ
اَمْرٍ مُّسْتَقِرٌّ ۝

See also: Splitting of the Moon.

MIRACLES OF PROPHETS

1. And when ye said: O Moses! We will not believe in thee till we see Allah plainly; and even while ye gazed the lightning seized you.

Then We revived you after your extinction, that ye might give thanks.

And We caused the white cloud to overshadow you and sent down on you the manna and the quails, (saying): Eat of the good things wherewith We have provided you.

2:55–57

2. And when Moses asked for water for his people, We said: Smite with thy staff the rock. And there gushed out therefrom twelve springs (so that) each tribe knew their drinking-place.

2:60

3. And (remember, O Children of Israel), when We made a covenant with you and caused the Mount to tower above you.

2:63

4. And (remember) when ye slew a man and disagreed concerning it and Allah brought forth that which ye were hiding.

And We said: Smite him with some of it. Thus Allah bringeth the dead to life and showeth you His portents so that ye may understand.

2:72–73

5. And their Prophet said

1. وَإِذْ قُلْتُمْ يٰمُوسٰى لَنْ نُّؤْمِنَ لَكَ حَتّٰى نَرَى اللّٰهَ
جَهْرَةً فَأَخَذَتْكُمُ الصّٰعِقَةُ وَأَنْتُمْ تَنْظُرُوْنَ ﴿٥٥﴾
ثُمَّ بَعَثْنٰكُمْ مِّنْ بَعْدِ مَوْتِكُمْ لَعَلَّكُمْ تَشْكُرُوْنَ ﴿٥٦﴾
وَظَلَّلْنَا عَلَيْكُمُ الْغَمَامَ وَأَنْزَلْنَا عَلَيْكُمُ الْمَنَّ
وَالسَّلْوٰى ۖ كُلُوْا مِنْ طَيِّبٰتِ مَا رَزَقْنٰكُمْ

2. وَإِذِ اسْتَسْقٰى مُوْسٰى لِقَوْمِهٖ فَقُلْنَا اضْرِبْ
بِّعَصَاكَ الْحَجَرَ ۖ فَانْفَجَرَتْ مِنْهُ اثْنَتَا
عَشْرَةَ عَيْنًا ۖ قَدْ عَلِمَ كُلُّ أُنَاسٍ مَّشْرَبَهُمْ

3. وَإِذْ أَخَذْنَا مِيْثَاقَكُمْ وَرَفَعْنَا فَوْقَكُمُ
الطُّوْرَ ۖ

4. وَإِذْ قَتَلْتُمْ نَفْسًا فَادّٰرَءْتُمْ فِيْهَا ۖ وَاللّٰهُ مُخْرِجٌ
مَّا كُنْتُمْ تَكْتُمُوْنَ ﴿٧٢﴾
فَقُلْنَا اضْرِبُوْهُ بِبَعْضِهَا ۚ كَذٰلِكَ يُحْيِ اللّٰهُ
الْمَوْتٰى وَيُرِيْكُمْ اٰيٰتِهٖ لَعَلَّكُمْ تَعْقِلُوْنَ ﴿٧٣﴾

5. وَقَالَ لَهُمْ نَبِيُّهُمْ إِنَّ اٰيَةَ مُلْكِهٖ أَنْ يَّأْتِيَكُمُ
التَّابُوْتُ فِيْهِ سَكِيْنَةٌ مِّنْ رَّبِّكُمْ وَبَقِيَّةٌ
مِّمَّا تَرَكَ اٰلُ مُوْسٰى وَاٰلُ هٰرُوْنَ تَحْمِلُهُ
الْمَلٰٓئِكَةُ ۚ إِنَّ فِيْ ذٰلِكَ لَاٰيَةً لَّكُمْ إِنْ
كُنْتُمْ مُّؤْمِنِيْنَ ﴿٢٤٨﴾

unto them: Lo! the token of his kingdom is that there shall come unto you the ark wherein is peace of reassurance from your Lord, and a remnant of that which the house of Moses and the house of Aaron left behind, the angels bearing it. Lo! herein shall be a token for you if (in truth) ye are believers.

2:248

6. Or (bethink thee of) the like of him who, passing by a township which had fallen into utter ruin, exclaimed: How shall Allah give this township life after its death? And Allah made him die a hundred years, then brought him back to life. He said: How long hast thou tarried? (The man) said: I have tarried a day or part of a day. (He) said: Nay, but thou hast tarried for a hundred years. Just look at thy food and drink which have not rotted! Look at thine ass! And that We may make thee a token unto mankind, look at the bones, how We adjust them and then cover them with flesh! And when (the matter) became clear unto him, he said: I know now that Allah is Able to do all things.

And when Abraham said (unto his Lord): My Lord! Show me how Thou givest life to the dead, He said: Dost thou not believe? Abraham said: Yea, but (I ask) in order that my heart may be at ease. (His Lord) said: Take four of the birds and cause them to incline unto thee, then place a part of them on each hill, then call them, they will come to thee in haste. And know that Allah is Mighty, Wise.

2:259–260

7. Whenever Zachariah went into the sanctuary where she was, he found that she had

6. اَوۡ كَالَّذِیۡ مَرَّ عَلٰی قَرۡیَةٍ وَّهِیَ خَاوِیَةٌ
عَلٰی عُرُوۡشِهَا ۚ قَالَ اَنّٰی یُحۡیٖ هٰذِهِ اللّٰهُ
بَعۡدَ مَوۡتِهَا ۚ فَاَمَاتَهُ اللّٰهُ مِائَةَ عَامٍ
ثُمَّ بَعَثَهٗ ؕ قَالَ كَمۡ لَبِثۡتَ ؕ قَالَ لَبِثۡتُ
یَوۡمًا اَوۡ بَعۡضَ یَوۡمٍ ؕ قَالَ بَلۡ لَّبِثۡتَ مِائَةَ
عَامٍ فَانۡظُرۡ اِلٰی طَعَامِكَ وَشَرَابِكَ لَمۡ
یَتَسَنَّهۡ ۚ وَانۡظُرۡ اِلٰی حِمَارِكَ وَلِنَجۡعَلَكَ
اٰیَةً لِّلنَّاسِ وَانۡظُرۡ اِلَی الۡعِظَامِ كَیۡفَ
نُنۡشِزُهَا ثُمَّ نَكۡسُوۡهَا لَحۡمًا ؕ فَلَمَّا تَبَیَّنَ لَهٗ ۙ
قَالَ اَعۡلَمُ اَنَّ اللّٰهَ عَلٰی كُلِّ شَیۡءٍ قَدِیۡرٌ ﴿۲۵۹﴾
وَاِذۡ قَالَ اِبۡرٰهٖمُ رَبِّ اَرِنِیۡ كَیۡفَ تُحۡیِ
الۡمَوۡتٰی ؕ قَالَ اَوَلَمۡ تُؤۡمِنۡ ؕ قَالَ بَلٰی وَلٰكِنۡ
لِّیَطۡمَئِنَّ قَلۡبِیۡ ؕ قَالَ فَخُذۡ اَرۡبَعَةً مِّنَ الطَّیۡرِ
فَصُرۡهُنَّ اِلَیۡكَ ثُمَّ اجۡعَلۡ عَلٰی كُلِّ جَبَلٍ
مِّنۡهُنَّ جُزۡءًا ثُمَّ ادۡعُهُنَّ یَاۡتِیۡنَكَ سَعۡیًا ؕ
وَاعۡلَمۡ اَنَّ اللّٰهَ عَزِیۡزٌ حَكِیۡمٌ ﴿۲۶۰﴾

7. كُلَّمَا دَخَلَ عَلَیۡهَا زَكَرِیَّا الۡمِحۡرَابَ ۙ وَجَدَ
عِنۡدَهَا رِزۡقًا ۚ قَالَ یٰمَرۡیَمُ اَنّٰی لَكِ هٰذَا ؕ
قَالَتۡ هُوَ مِنۡ عِنۡدِ اللّٰهِ ؕ اِنَّ اللّٰهَ
یَرۡزُقُ مَنۡ یَّشَآءُ بِغَیۡرِ حِسَابٍ ○

8. اَنِّیۡۤ اَخۡلُقُ لَكُمۡ مِّنَ الطِّیۡنِ كَهَیۡـَٔةِ الطَّیۡرِ
فَاَنۡفُخُ فِیۡهِ فَیَكُوۡنُ طَیۡرًۢا بِاِذۡنِ اللّٰهِ ۚ
وَاُبۡرِئُ الۡاَكۡمَهَ وَالۡاَبۡرَصَ وَاُحۡیِ الۡمَوۡتٰی

food. He said: O Mary! Whence cometh unto thee this (food)? She answered: It is from Allah. Allah giveth without stint to whom He will.

3:37

8. Lo! I fashion for you out of clay the likeness of a bird, and I breathe into it and it is

بِإِذْنِ اللهِ وَأُنَبِّئُكُم بِمَا تَأْكُلُونَ وَمَا
تَدَّخِرُونَ فِي بُيُوتِكُمْ إِنَّ فِي ذَٰلِكَ
لَآيَةً لَّكُمْ إِن كُنتُم مُّؤْمِنِينَ ۝

9. وَقَالَ مُوسَىٰ يَا فِرْعَوْنُ إِنِّي رَسُولٌ مِّن
رَّبِّ الْعَالَمِينَ ۝
حَقِيقٌ عَلَىٰ أَن لَّا أَقُولَ عَلَى اللهِ إِلَّا الْحَقَّ
قَدْ جِئْتُكُم بِبَيِّنَةٍ مِّن رَّبِّكُمْ
فَأَرْسِلْ مَعِيَ بَنِي إِسْرَائِيلَ ۝
قَالَ إِن كُنتَ جِئْتَ بِآيَةٍ فَأْتِ بِهَا
إِن كُنتَ مِنَ الصَّادِقِينَ ۝
فَأَلْقَىٰ عَصَاهُ فَإِذَا هِيَ ثُعْبَانٌ مُّبِينٌ ۝
وَنَزَعَ يَدَهُ فَإِذَا هِيَ بَيْضَاءُ لِلنَّاظِرِينَ ۝

10. قَالُوا يَا مُوسَىٰ إِمَّا أَن تُلْقِيَ وَإِمَّا أَن
نَّكُونَ نَحْنُ الْمُلْقِينَ ۝
قَالَ أَلْقُوا فَلَمَّا أَلْقَوْا سَحَرُوا أَعْيُنَ النَّاسِ
وَاسْتَرْهَبُوهُمْ وَجَاءُوا بِسِحْرٍ عَظِيمٍ ۝
وَأَوْحَيْنَا إِلَىٰ مُوسَىٰ أَنْ أَلْقِ عَصَاكَ فَإِذَا
هِيَ تَلْقَفُ مَا يَأْفِكُونَ ۝
فَوَقَعَ الْحَقُّ وَبَطَلَ مَا كَانُوا يَعْمَلُونَ ۝
فَغُلِبُوا هُنَالِكَ وَانقَلَبُوا صَاغِرِينَ ۝
وَأُلْقِيَ السَّحَرَةُ سَاجِدِينَ ۝

a bird by Allah's leave. I heal him who was born blind, and the leper, and I raise the dead, by Allah's leave. And I announce unto you what ye eat and what ye store up in your houses. Lo! herein verily is a portent for you, if ye are to be believers.

3:49

9. Moses said: O Pharaoh! Lo! I am a messenger from the Lord of the Worlds,

Approved upon condition that I speak concerning Allah nothing but the truth. I come unto you (lords of Egypt) with a clear proof from your Lord. So let the Children of Israel go with me.

(Pharaoh) Said: If thou comest with a token, then produce it, if thou art of those who speak the truth.

Then he flung down his staff and lo! it was a serpent manifest;

And he drew forth his hand (from his bosom), and lo! it was white for the beholders.

7:104–108

10. They said: O Moses! Either throw (first) or let us be the first throwers.

He said: Throw! and when they threw they cast a spell upon the people's eyes, and overawed them, and produced a mighty spell.

And We inspired Moses (saying): Throw thy staff! And lo! it swallowed up their lying show.

Thus was the Truth vindicated and that which they were doing was made vain.

Thus were they there defeated and brought low.

And the wizards fell down prostrate:

Crying: We believe in the Lord of the Worlds:

The Lord of Moses and Aaron.

7:115–122

11. And it was inspired in Noah, (saying): No one of thy folk will believe save him who hath believed already. Be not distressed because of what they do.

Build the ship under Our eyes and by Our Inspiration, and speak not unto Me on behalf of those who do wrong. Lo! they will be drowned.

And he was building the ship, and every time the chieftains of his people passed him, they made mock of him. He said: Though ye make mock of Us, yet We mock at you even as ye mock;

And ye shall know to whom a punishment that will confound him cometh, and upon whom a lasting doom will fall.

(Thus it was) till, when Our commandment came to pass and the oven gushed forth water. We said: Load therein two of every kind, a pair (the male and female), and thy household, save him against whom the word hath gone forth already, and those who believe. And but a few were they who believed with him.

And he said: Embark therein! In the name of Allah be its course and its mooring. Lo! my Lord is Forgiving, Merciful.

And it sailed with them

قَالُوْٓا اٰمَنَّا بِرَبِّ الْعٰلَمِيْنَ ۝
رَبِّ مُوْسٰى وَهٰرُوْنَ ۝

11. وَاُوْحِيَ اِلٰى نُوْحٍ اَنَّهٗ لَنْ يُّؤْمِنَ مِنْ
قَوْمِكَ اِلَّا مَنْ قَدْ اٰمَنَ فَلَا تَبْتَىِٕسْ
بِمَا كَانُوْا يَفْعَلُوْنَ ۝
وَاصْنَعِ الْفُلْكَ بِاَعْيُنِنَا وَوَحْيِنَا وَلَا
تُخَاطِبْنِيْ فِي الَّذِيْنَ ظَلَمُوْا ۚ اِنَّهُمْ مُّغْرَقُوْنَ ۝
وَيَصْنَعُ الْفُلْكَ ۣ وَكُلَّمَا مَرَّ عَلَيْهِ مَلَاٌ
مِّنْ قَوْمِهٖ سَخِرُوْا مِنْهُ ۭ قَالَ اِنْ تَسْخَرُوْا
مِنَّا فَاِنَّا نَسْخَرُ مِنْكُمْ كَمَا تَسْخَرُوْنَ ۝
فَسَوْفَ تَعْلَمُوْنَ ۙ مَنْ يَّاْتِيْهِ عَذَابٌ
يُّخْزِيْهِ وَيَحِلُّ عَلَيْهِ عَذَابٌ مُّقِيْمٌ ۝
حَتّٰٓى اِذَا جَاۗءَ اَمْرُنَا وَفَارَ التَّنُّوْرُ ۙ
قُلْنَا احْمِلْ فِيْهَا مِنْ كُلٍّ زَوْجَيْنِ اثْنَيْنِ
وَاَهْلَكَ اِلَّا مَنْ سَبَقَ عَلَيْهِ الْقَوْلُ
وَمَنْ اٰمَنَ ۭ وَمَآ اٰمَنَ مَعَهٗٓ اِلَّا قَلِيْلٌ ۝
وَقَالَ ارْكَبُوْا فِيْهَا بِسْمِ اللّٰهِ مَجْــرٖىهَا
وَمُرْسٰىهَا ۭ اِنَّ رَبِّيْ لَغَفُوْرٌ رَّحِيْمٌ ۝
وَهِىَ تَجْرِيْ بِهِمْ فِيْ مَوْجٍ كَالْجِبَالِ

amid waves like mountains, and Noah cried unto his son — and he was standing aloof — O my son! Come ride with us, and be not with the disbelievers.

He said: I shall betake me to some mountain that will save me from the water. (Noah) said: This day there is none that saveth from the Commandment of Allah save him on whom He hath had mercy. And the wave came in between them, so he was among the drowned.

And it was said: O earth! Swallow thy water and, O sky! be cleared of clouds! and the water was made to subside. And the Command–ment was fulfilled. And it (the ship) came to rest upon (the mount) *Al-Judi* and it was said: A far removal for wrongdoing folk!

11:36–44

12. O my people! This is the camel of Allah, a token unto you, so suffer her to feed in Allah's earth and touch her not with harm lest a near torment seize you.

But they hamstrung her, and then he said: Enjoy life in your dwelling–place three days! This is a threat that will not be belied.

So, when Our comm–andment came to pass, We saved Salih, and those who believed with him, by a mercy from Us, from the ignominy of that day. Lo! thy Lord, He is the Strong, the Mighty.

And the (Awful) Cry overtook those who did wrong, so that morning found them prostrate in their dwell–ings.

As though they had not dwelt there. Lo! Thamûd disbelieved in their Lord. A far removal for Thamûd!

11:64–68

وَنَادٰى نُوحٌ ابْنَهٗ وَكَانَ فِيْ مَعْزِلٍ يّٰبُنَيَّ
ارْكَبْ مَّعَنَا وَلَا تَكُنْ مَّعَ الْكٰفِرِيْنَ ﴿٤٢﴾
قَالَ سَاٰوِيْۤ اِلٰى جَبَلٍ يَّعْصِمُنِيْ مِنَ
الْمَآءِ قَالَ لَا عَاصِمَ الْيَوْمَ مِنْ اَمْرِ
اللّٰهِ اِلَّا مَنْ رَّحِمَ وَحَالَ بَيْنَهُمَا
الْمَوْجُ فَكَانَ مِنَ الْمُغْرَقِيْنَ ﴿٤٣﴾
وَقِيْلَ يٰۤاَرْضُ ابْلَعِيْ مَآءَكِ وَيٰسَمَآءُ
اَقْلِعِيْ وَغِيْضَ الْمَآءُ وَقُضِيَ الْاَمْرُ
وَاسْتَوَتْ عَلَى الْجُوْدِيِّ وَقِيْلَ بُعْدًا
لِّلْقَوْمِ الظّٰلِمِيْنَ ﴿٤٤﴾
12. وَيٰقَوْمِ هٰذِهٖ نَاقَةُ اللّٰهِ لَكُمْ اٰيَةً
فَذَرُوْهَا تَاْكُلْ فِيْۤ اَرْضِ اللّٰهِ وَلَا
تَمَسُّوْهَا بِسُوْٓءٍ فَيَاْخُذَكُمْ عَذَابٌ قَرِيْبٌ ﴿٦٤﴾
فَعَقَرُوْهَا فَقَالَ تَمَتَّعُوْا فِيْ دَارِكُمْ ثَلٰثَةَ
اَيَّامٍ ذٰلِكَ وَعْدٌ غَيْرُ مَكْذُوْبٍ ﴿٦٥﴾
فَلَمَّا جَآءَ اَمْرُنَا نَجَّيْنَا صٰلِحًا وَّالَّذِيْنَ
اٰمَنُوْا مَعَهٗ بِرَحْمَةٍ مِّنَّا وَمِنْ خِزْيِ
يَوْمِئِذٍ اِنَّ رَبَّكَ هُوَ الْقَوِيُّ الْعَزِيْزُ ﴿٦٦﴾
وَاَخَذَ الَّذِيْنَ ظَلَمُوا الصَّيْحَةُ فَاَصْبَحُوْا
فِيْ دِيَارِهِمْ جٰثِمِيْنَ ﴿٦٧﴾
كَاَنْ لَّمْ يَغْنَوْا فِيْهَا اَلَاۤ اِنَّ ثَمُوْدَا۟ كَفَرُوْا
رَبَّهُمْ اَلَا بُعْدًا لِّثَمُوْدَ ﴿٦٨﴾
13. اِذْهَبُوْا بِقَمِيْصِيْ هٰذَا فَاَلْقُوْهُ عَلٰى وَجْهِ
اَبِيْ يَاْتِ بَصِيْرًا وَاْتُوْنِيْ بِاَهْلِكُمْ
اَجْمَعِيْنَ ﴿٩٣﴾

13. Go with this shirt of mine and lay it on my father's face, he will become (again) a seer; and come to me with all your folk.

When the caravan de–parted, their father had said: Truly I am conscious of the breath of Joseph, though ye call me dotard!

(Those around him) said: By Allah, lo! thou art in thine old aberration.

Then, when the bearer of glad tidings came, he laid it on his face and he became a seer once more. He said: Said I not unto you that I know from Allah that which ye know not?

12:93–96

14. And when Moses said unto his servant: I will not give up until I reach the point where the two rivers meet, though I march on for ages.

And when they reached the point where the two met, they forgot their fish, and it took its way into the waters, being free.

18:60–61

15. Then (one) cried unto her from below her, saying: Grieve not! Thy Lord hath placed a rivulet beneath thee.

And shake the trunk of the palm-tree toward thee, thou wilt cause ripe dates to fall upon thee.

So eat and drink and be consoled.

19:24–26

16. He spake: Lo! I am the slave of Allah. He hath given me the Scripture and hath appointed me a Prophet,

And hath made me blessed wheresoever I may be, and hath enjoined upon me prayer and almsgiving so

وَلَمَّا فَصَلَتِ الْعِيرُ قَالَ اَبُوهُمْ اِنِّيْ لَاَجِدُ
رِيْحَ يُوْسُفَ لَوْلَآ اَنْ تُفَنِّدُوْنِ ﴿٩٤﴾
قَالُوْا تَاللهِ اِنَّكَ لَفِيْ ضَلٰلِكَ الْقَدِيْمِ ﴿٩٥﴾
فَلَمَّآ اَنْ جَآءَ الْبَشِيْرُ اَلْقٰهُ عَلٰى وَجْهِهٖ
فَارْتَدَّ بَصِيْرًا ۚ قَالَ اَلَمْ اَقُلْ لَّكُمْ ۚ
اِنِّيْٓ اَعْلَمُ مِنَ اللهِ مَا لَا تَعْلَمُوْنَ ﴿٩٦﴾

14. وَاِذْ قَالَ مُوْسٰى لِفَتٰىهُ لَآ اَبْرَحُ حَتّٰٓى
اَبْلُغَ مَجْمَعَ الْبَحْرَيْنِ اَوْ اَمْضِيَ حُقُبًا ﴿٦٠﴾
فَلَمَّا بَلَغَا مَجْمَعَ بَيْنِهِمَا نَسِيَا حُوْتَهُمَا
فَاتَّخَذَ سَبِيْلَهٗ فِي الْبَحْرِ سَرَبًا ﴿٦١﴾

15. فَنَادٰىهَا مِنْ تَحْتِهَآ اَلَّا تَحْزَنِيْ قَدْ
جَعَلَ رَبُّكِ تَحْتَكِ سَرِيًّا ﴿٢٤﴾
وَهُزِّيْٓ اِلَيْكِ بِجِذْعِ النَّخْلَةِ تُسٰقِطْ
عَلَيْكِ رُطَبًا جَنِيًّا ﴿٢٥﴾
فَكُلِيْ وَاشْرَبِيْ وَقَرِّيْ عَيْنًا ۚ

16. قَالَ اِنِّيْ عَبْدُ اللهِ ۗ اٰتٰنِيَ الْكِتٰبَ
وَجَعَلَنِيْ نَبِيًّا ﴿٣٠﴾
وَّجَعَلَنِيْ مُبٰرَكًا اَيْنَ مَا كُنْتُ ۖ وَ
اَوْصٰنِيْ بِالصَّلٰوةِ وَالزَّكٰوةِ مَا دُمْتُ حَيًّا ﴿٣١﴾
وَّبَرًّا بِوَالِدَتِيْ ۡ وَلَمْ يَجْعَلْنِيْ
جَبَّارًا شَقِيًّا ﴿٣٢﴾
وَالسَّلٰمُ عَلَيَّ يَوْمَ وُلِدْتُّ وَيَوْمَ
اَمُوْتُ وَيَوْمَ اُبْعَثُ حَيًّا ﴿٣٣﴾

long as I remain alive.

And (hath made me) dutiful toward her who bore me, and hath not made me arrogant, unblest.

Peace on me the day I was born, and the day I die, and the day I shall be raised alive!

19:30–33

17. قَالَ فَمَا خَطْبُكَ يٰسَامِرِيُّ ﴿٩٥﴾
قَالَ بَصُرْتُ بِمَا لَمْ يَبْصُرُوْا بِهٖ
فَقَبَضْتُ قَبْضَةً مِّنْ اَثَرِ الرَّسُوْلِ
فَنَبَذْتُهَا وَكَذٰلِكَ سَوَّلَتْ لِيْ نَفْسِيْ ﴿٩٦﴾
قَالَ فَاذْهَبْ فَاِنَّ لَكَ فِي الْحَيٰوةِ اَنْ
تَقُوْلَ لَا مِسَاسَ وَاِنَّ لَكَ مَوْعِدًا لَّنْ
تُخْلَفَهٗ وَانْظُرْ اِلٰٓى اِلٰهِكَ الَّذِيْ ظَلْتَ
عَلَيْهِ عَاكِفًا لَنُحَرِّقَنَّهٗ ثُمَّ
لَنَنْسِفَنَّهٗ فِي الْيَمِّ نَسْفًا ﴿٩٧﴾
18. قَالُوْا حَرِّقُوْهُ وَانْصُرُوْٓا اٰلِهَتَكُمْ اِنْ
كُنْتُمْ فٰعِلِيْنَ ﴿٦٨﴾
قُلْنَا يٰنَارُ كُوْنِيْ بَرْدًا وَّسَلٰمًا
عَلٰٓى اِبْرٰهِيْمَ ﴿٦٩﴾
وَاَرَادُوْا بِهٖ كَيْدًا فَجَعَلْنٰهُمُ
الْاَخْسَرِيْنَ ﴿٧٠﴾
19. وَسَخَّرْنَا مَعَ دَاوٗدَ الْجِبَالَ
يُسَبِّحْنَ وَالطَّيْرَ وَكُنَّا فٰعِلِيْنَ ﴿٧٩﴾
20. وَلِسُلَيْمٰنَ الرِّيْحَ عَاصِفَةً تَجْرِيْ
بِاَمْرِهٖٓ اِلَى الْاَرْضِ الَّتِيْ بٰرَكْنَا فِيْهَا
وَكُنَّا بِكُلِّ شَيْءٍ عٰلِمِيْنَ ﴿٨١﴾
وَمِنَ الشَّيٰطِيْنِ مَنْ يَّغُوْصُوْنَ لَهٗ وَ
يَعْمَلُوْنَ عَمَلًا دُوْنَ ذٰلِكَ وَكُنَّا
لَهُمْ حٰفِظِيْنَ ﴿٨٢﴾
21. وَوَرِثَ سُلَيْمٰنُ دَاوٗدَ وَقَالَ يٰٓاَيُّهَا

17. (Moses) said: And what has thou to say, O Samiri?

He said: I perceived what they perceive not, so I seized a handful from the footsteps of the messenger, and then threw it in. Thus my soul commended to me.

(Moses) said: Then go! And lo! in this life it is for thee to say: Touch me not! and lo! there is for thee a tryst thou canst not break. Now look upon thy god of which thou hast remained a votary. Verily we will burn it and will scatter its dust over the sea.

20:95–97

18. They cried: Burn him and stand by your gods, if ye will be doing.

We said: O fire, be coolness and peace for Abraham!

And they wished to set a snare for him, but We made them the greater losers.

21:68–70

19. And We subdued the hills and the birds to hymn (His) praise along with David. We were the doers (thereof).

21:79

20. And unto Solomon (We subdued) the wind in its raging. If set by his command toward the land which We had blessed. And of everything We are Aware.

And of the evil ones (subdued We unto him) some who dived (for pearls) for him and did other work, and We were warders unto them.

21:81–82

21. And Solomon was David's heir. And he said: O mankind! Lo! we have been taught the language of

birds, and have been given (abundance) of all things. This surely is evident favour.

And there were gathered together unto Solomon his armies of the jinn and humankind, and of the birds, and they were set in a battle order;

Till, when they reached the Valley of the Ants, an ant exclaimed: O ants! Enter your dwellings lest Solomon and his armies crush you, unperceiving.

And (Solomon) smiled, laughing at her speech, and said: My Lord! arouse me to be thankful for Thy favour wherewith Thou hast favoured me and my parents, and to do good that shall be pleasing unto Thee, and include me in (the number of) Thy righteous slaves.

27:16–19

22. He said: O chiefs! Which of you will bring me her throne before they come unto me, surrendering?

A stalwart of the *jinn* said: I will bring it thee before thou canst rise from thy place. Lo! I verily am strong and trusty for such work.

One with whom was knowledge of the Scripture said: I will bring it thee before thy gaze returneth unto thee. And when he saw it set in his presence, (Solomon) said: This is of the bounty of my Lord, that He may try me whether I give thanks or am ungrateful.

النَّاسُ عُلِّمْنَا مَنْطِقَ الطَّيْرِ وَأُوتِينَا
مِنْ كُلِّ شَيْءٍ ۖ إِنَّ هَٰذَا لَهُوَ
الْفَضْلُ الْمُبِينُ ﴿١٦﴾
وَحُشِرَ لِسُلَيْمَانَ جُنُودُهُ مِنَ الْجِنِّ
وَالْإِنْسِ وَالطَّيْرِ فَهُمْ يُوزَعُونَ ﴿١٧﴾
حَتَّىٰ إِذَا أَتَوْا عَلَىٰ وَادِ النَّمْلِ قَالَتْ
نَمْلَةٌ يَا أَيُّهَا النَّمْلُ ادْخُلُوا مَسَاكِنَكُمْ
لَا يَحْطِمَنَّكُمْ سُلَيْمَانُ وَجُنُودُهُ
وَهُمْ لَا يَشْعُرُونَ ﴿١٨﴾
فَتَبَسَّمَ ضَاحِكًا مِنْ قَوْلِهَا وَقَالَ
رَبِّ أَوْزِعْنِي أَنْ أَشْكُرَ نِعْمَتَكَ الَّتِي
أَنْعَمْتَ عَلَيَّ وَعَلَىٰ وَالِدَيَّ وَأَنْ أَعْمَلَ
صَالِحًا تَرْضَاهُ وَأَدْخِلْنِي بِرَحْمَتِكَ
فِي عِبَادِكَ الصَّالِحِينَ ﴿١٩﴾
22. قَالَ يَا أَيُّهَا الْمَلَأُ أَيُّكُمْ يَأْتِينِي
بِعَرْشِهَا قَبْلَ أَنْ يَأْتُونِي مُسْلِمِينَ ﴿٣٨﴾
قَالَ عِفْرِيتٌ مِنَ الْجِنِّ أَنَا آتِيكَ
بِهِ قَبْلَ أَنْ تَقُومَ مِنْ مَقَامِكَ ۖ
وَإِنِّي عَلَيْهِ لَقَوِيٌّ أَمِينٌ ﴿٣٩﴾
قَالَ الَّذِي عِنْدَهُ عِلْمٌ مِنَ الْكِتَابِ أَنَا
آتِيكَ بِهِ قَبْلَ أَنْ يَرْتَدَّ إِلَيْكَ طَرْفُكَ ۚ
فَلَمَّا رَآهُ مُسْتَقِرًّا عِنْدَهُ قَالَ هَٰذَا
مِنْ فَضْلِ رَبِّي لِيَبْلُوَنِي أَأَشْكُرُ
أَمْ أَكْفُرُ ۖ وَمَنْ شَكَرَ فَإِنَّمَا يَشْكُرُ
لِنَفْسِهِ ۖ وَمَنْ كَفَرَ فَإِنَّ رَبِّي غَنِيٌّ كَرِيمٌ ﴿٤٠﴾

Whosoever giveth thanks he only giveth thanks for (the good of) his own soul: and whosoever is ungrateful (is ungrateful only to his own soul's hurt). For lo! my Lord is Absolute in Independence, Bountiful.

27:38–40

23. And We inspired the mother of Moses, saying: Suckle him and, when thou fearest for him, then cast him into the river and fear not nor grieve. Lo! We shall bring him back unto thee and shall make him (one) of Our messengers.

And the family of Pharoah took him up, that he might become for them an enemy and a sorrow. Lo! Pharaoh and Haman and their hosts were ever sinning.

And the wife of Pharaoh said: (He will be) a consolation for me and for thee. Kill him not. Peradventure he may be of use to us, or we may choose him for a son. And they perceived not.

And the heart of the mother of Moses became void, and she would have betrayed him if We had not fortified her heart, that she might be of the believers.

And she said unto his sister: Trace him. So she observed him from afar, and they perceived not,

And We had before forbidden foster-mothers for him, so she said: Shall I show you a household who will rear him for you and take care of him?

So We restored him to his mother that she might be comforted and not grieve, and that she might know that the promise of Allah is true.

28:7–13

24. And unto Soloman (We

23. وَاَوْحَيْنَآ اِلٰٓى اُمِّ مُوْسٰٓى اَنْ اَرْضِعِيْهِ ۚ
فَاِذَا خِفْتِ عَلَيْهِ فَاَلْقِيْهِ فِى الْيَمِّ
وَلَا تَخَافِىْ وَلَا تَحْزَنِىْ ۚ اِنَّا رَآدُّوْهُ
اِلَيْكِ وَجَاعِلُوْهُ مِنَ الْمُرْسَلِيْنَ ﴿۷﴾
فَالْتَقَطَهٗٓ اٰلُ فِرْعَوْنَ لِيَكُوْنَ لَهُمْ عَدُوًّا
وَّحَزَنًا ؕ اِنَّ فِرْعَوْنَ وَهَامٰنَ
وَجُنُوْدَهُمَا كَانُوْا خٰطِـِٕيْنَ ﴿۸﴾
وَقَالَتِ امْرَاَتُ فِرْعَوْنَ قُرَّتُ عَيْنٍ
لِّىْ وَلَكَ ؕ لَا تَقْتُلُوْهُ ۖ عَسٰٓى اَنْ يَّنْفَعَنَآ
اَوْ نَتَّخِذَهٗ وَلَدًا وَّهُمْ لَا يَشْعُرُوْنَ ﴿۹﴾
وَاَصْبَحَ فُؤَادُ اُمِّ مُوْسٰى فٰرِغًا ؕ اِنْ
كَادَتْ لَتُبْدِىْ بِهٖ لَوْلَآ اَنْ رَّبَطْنَا عَلٰى
قَلْبِهَا لِتَكُوْنَ مِنَ الْمُؤْمِنِيْنَ ﴿۱۰﴾
وَقَالَتْ لِاُخْتِهٖ قُصِّيْهِ ۫ فَبَصُرَتْ بِهٖ
عَنْ جُنُبٍ وَّهُمْ لَا يَشْعُرُوْنَ ﴿۱۱﴾
وَحَرَّمْنَا عَلَيْهِ الْمَرَاضِعَ مِنْ قَبْلُ
فَقَالَتْ هَلْ اَدُلُّكُمْ عَلٰٓى اَهْلِ بَيْتٍ
يَّكْفُلُوْنَهٗ لَكُمْ وَهُمْ لَهٗ نٰصِحُوْنَ ﴿۱۲﴾
فَرَدَدْنٰهُ اِلٰٓى اُمِّهٖ كَىْ تَقَرَّ عَيْنُهَا
وَلَا تَحْزَنَ وَلِتَعْلَمَ اَنَّ وَعْدَ اللّٰهِ
حَقٌّ

24. وَلِسُلَيْمٰنَ الرِّيْحَ غُدُوُّهَا شَهْرٌ وَّ
رَوَاحُهَا شَهْرٌ ۚ وَاَسَلْنَا لَهٗ عَيْنَ
الْقِطْرِ ؕ وَمِنَ الْجِنِّ مَنْ يَّعْمَلُ بَيْنَ

gave) the wind, whereof the morning course was a month's journey and the evening course a month's journey, and We caused the fount of copper to gush forth for him, and (We gave him) certain of the jinn who worked before him by permission of his Lord.

And such of them as deviated from Our command, them We caused to taste the punishment of flaming Fire.

They made for him what he willed: synagogues and statues, basins like wells and boilers built into the ground. Give thanks, O House of David! Few of My bondmen are thankful.

34:12–13

25. And lo! Jonah verily was of those sent (to warn).

When he fled unto the laden ship,

And then drew lots and was of those rejected;

And the fish swallowed him while he was blameworthy;

And had he not been one of those who glorify (Allah).

He would have tarried in its belly till the day when they are raised;

Then We cast him on a desert shore while he was sick;

And We caused a tree of gourd to grow above him;

And We sent him to a hundred thousand (folk) or more.

37:139–147

26. And remember Our bondman David, lord of might. Lo! he was ever turning in repentance (toward Allah).

Lo! We subdued the hills to hymn the praises (of their Lord) with him at nightfall and sunrise,

And the birds assembled; all were turning unto Him.

38:17–19

يَدَيْهِ بِإِذْنِ رَبِّهٖ ؕ وَمَنْ يَّزِغْ مِنْهُمْ
عَنْ اَمْرِنَا نُذِقْهُ مِنْ عَذَابِ السَّعِيْرِ ۝١٢
يَعْمَلُوْنَ لَهٗ مَا يَشَآءُ مِنْ مَّحَارِيْبَ
وَتَمَاثِيْلَ وَجِفَانٍ كَالْجَوَابِ وَقُدُوْرٍ
رّٰسِيٰتٍ ؕ اِعْمَلُوْۤا اٰلَ دَاوٗدَ شُكْرًا ؕ
وَقَلِيْلٌ مِّنْ عِبَادِيَ الشَّكُوْرُ ۝١٣

25. وَاِنَّ يُوْنُسَ لَمِنَ الْمُرْسَلِيْنَ ۝١٣٩
اِذْ اَبَقَ اِلَى الْفُلْكِ الْمَشْحُوْنِ ۝١٤٠
فَسَاهَمَ فَكَانَ مِنَ الْمُدْحَضِيْنَ ۝١٤١
فَالْتَقَمَهُ الْحُوْتُ وَهُوَ مُلِيْمٌ ۝١٤٢
فَلَوْلَاۤ اَنَّهٗ كَانَ مِنَ الْمُسَبِّحِيْنَ ۝١٤٣
لَلَبِثَ فِيْ بَطْنِهٖۤ اِلٰى يَوْمِ يُبْعَثُوْنَ ۝١٤٤
فَنَبَذْنٰهُ بِالْعَرَآءِ وَهُوَ سَقِيْمٌ ۝١٤٥
وَاَنْۢبَتْنَا عَلَيْهِ شَجَرَةً مِّنْ يَّقْطِيْنٍ ۝١٤٦
وَاَرْسَلْنٰهُ اِلٰى مِائَةِ اَلْفٍ اَوْ يَزِيْدُوْنَ ۝١٤٧

26. اِصْبِرْ عَلٰى مَا يَقُوْلُوْنَ وَاذْكُرْ عَبْدَنَا
دَاوٗدَ ذَا الْاَيْدِ ۚ اِنَّهٗۤ اَوَّابٌ ۝١٧
اِنَّا سَخَّرْنَا الْجِبَالَ مَعَهٗ يُسَبِّحْنَ
بِالْعَشِيِّ وَالْاِشْرَاقِ ۝١٨
وَالطَّيْرَ مَحْشُوْرَةً ؕ كُلٌّ لَّهٗۤ اَوَّابٌ ۝١٩

27. وَاذْكُرْ عَبْدَنَاۤ اَيُّوْبَ ۘ اِذْ نَادٰى رَبَّهٗۤ
اَنِّيْ مَسَّنِيَ الشَّيْطٰنُ بِنُصْبٍ وَّعَذَابٍ ۝٤١
اُرْكُضْ بِرِجْلِكَ ۚ هٰذَا مُغْتَسَلٌۢ
بَارِدٌ وَّشَرَابٌ ۝٤٢

27. And make mention (O Muhammad) of Our bondman Job, when he cried unto his Lord (saying): Lo! the devil doth afflict me with distress and torment.

(And it was said unto him): Strike the ground with thy foot. This (spring) is a cool bath and a refreshing drink.

And We bestowed on him (again) his household and therewith the like thereof, a mercy from Us, and a memorial for men of understanding.

38:41–43

MISERLINESS

1. And let not those who hoard up that which Allah hath bestowed upon them of His bounty think that it is better for them. Nay, it is worse for them. That which they hoard will be their collar on the Day of Resurrection. Allah's is the heritage of the heavens and the earth, and Allah is Informed of what ye do.

3:180

2. Who hoard their wealth and enjoin avarice on others, and hide that which Allah hath bestowed upon them of His bounty. For disbelievers We prepare a shameful doom,

4:37

3. But greed hath been made present in the minds (of men). If ye do good and keep from evil, lo! Allah is ever Informed of what ye do.

4:128

4. Say (unto them): If ye possessed the treasures of the mercy of my Lord, ye would surely hold them back for fear of spending, for man was ever grudging.

17:100

5. Lo! ye are those who are called to spend in the way of Allah, yet, among you there are some who

وَوَهَبْنَا لَهٗٓ اَهْلَهٗ وَمِثْلَهُمْ مَّعَهُمْ
رَحْمَةً مِّنَّا وَذِكْرٰى لِاُولِى الْاَلْبَابِ ﴿٤٣﴾

1. وَلَا يَحْسَبَنَّ الَّذِيْنَ يَبْخَلُوْنَ بِمَآ اٰتٰىهُمُ
اللّٰهُ مِنْ فَضْلِهٖ هُوَ خَيْرًا لَّهُمْ ۭ بَلْ
هُوَ شَرٌّ لَّهُمْ ۭ سَيُطَوَّقُوْنَ مَا بَخِلُوْا
بِهٖ يَوْمَ الْقِيٰمَةِ ۭ وَلِلّٰهِ مِيْرَاثُ السَّمٰوٰتِ
وَالْاَرْضِ ۭ وَاللّٰهُ بِمَا تَعْمَلُوْنَ خَبِيْرٌ ﴿١٨٠﴾

2. الَّذِيْنَ يَبْخَلُوْنَ وَيَاْمُرُوْنَ النَّاسَ
بِالْبُخْلِ وَيَكْتُمُوْنَ مَآ اٰتٰىهُمُ اللّٰهُ مِنْ
فَضْلِهٖ ۭ وَاَعْتَدْنَا لِلْكٰفِرِيْنَ عَذَابًا مُّهِيْنًا ﴿٣٧﴾

3. وَاُحْضِرَتِ الْاَنْفُسُ الشُّحَّ ۭ وَاِنْ تُحْسِنُوْا وَ
تَتَّقُوْا فَاِنَّ اللّٰهَ كَانَ بِمَا تَعْمَلُوْنَ
خَبِيْرًا ﴿١٢٨﴾

4. قُلْ لَّوْ اَنْتُمْ تَمْلِكُوْنَ خَزَاۗىِٕنَ رَحْمَةِ رَبِّيْٓ اِذًا لَّاَمْسَكْتُمْ
خَشْيَةَ الْاِنْفَاقِ ۭ وَكَانَ الْاِنْسَانُ قَتُوْرًا ﴿١٠٠﴾

5. هٰٓاَنْتُمْ هٰٓؤُلَاۗءِ تُدْعَوْنَ لِتُنْفِقُوْا
فِيْ سَبِيْلِ اللّٰهِ ۚ فَمِنْكُمْ مَّنْ يَّبْخَلُ ۚ
وَمَنْ يَّبْخَلْ فَاِنَّمَا يَبْخَلُ عَنْ
نَّفْسِهٖ ۭ وَاللّٰهُ الْغَنِيُّ وَاَنْتُمُ الْفُقَرَاۗءُ

MIRACLES OF PROPHETS
Ref: 27:16–22; 38:36–38.

hoard. And as for him who hoardeth, he hoardeth only from his soul. And Allah is the Rich, and ye are the poor. And if ye turn away He will exchange you for some other folk, and they will not be the likes of you.

47:38

6. So keep your duty to Allah as best ye can, and listen, and obey, and spend; that is better for your souls. And whoso is saved from his own greed, such are the successful.

64:16

7. But as for him who hoardeth and deemeth himself independent,

And disbelieveth in goodness,

Surely We will ease his way unto adversity.

His riches will not save him when he perisheth.

92:8–11

8. Woe unto every slandering traducer,

Who hath gathered wealth (of this world) and arranged it:

He thinketh that his wealth will render him immortal.

Nay, but verily he will be flung to the Consuming One

Ah, what will convey unto thee what the Consuming One is!

(It is) the fire of Allah,

وَإِنْ تَتَوَلَّوْا يَسْتَبْدِلْ قَوْمًا غَيْرَكُمْ
ثُمَّ لَا يَكُونُوا أَمْثَالَكُمْ ۝

6. فَاتَّقُوا اللَّهَ مَا اسْتَطَعْتُمْ وَاسْمَعُوا
وَأَطِيعُوا وَأَنْفِقُوا خَيْرًا لِأَنْفُسِكُمْ ۗ
وَمَنْ يُوقَ شُحَّ نَفْسِهِ فَأُولَٰئِكَ
هُمُ الْمُفْلِحُونَ ۝

7. وَأَمَّا مَنْ بَخِلَ وَاسْتَغْنَىٰ ۝
وَكَذَّبَ بِالْحُسْنَىٰ ۝
فَسَنُيَسِّرُهُ لِلْعُسْرَىٰ ۝
وَمَا يُغْنِي عَنْهُ مَالُهُ إِذَا تَرَدَّىٰ ۝

8. وَيْلٌ لِكُلِّ هُمَزَةٍ لُمَزَةٍ ۝
الَّذِي جَمَعَ مَالًا وَعَدَّدَهُ ۝
يَحْسَبُ أَنَّ مَالَهُ أَخْلَدَهُ ۝
كَلَّا لَيُنْبَذَنَّ فِي الْحُطَمَةِ ۝
وَمَا أَدْرَاكَ مَا الْحُطَمَةُ ۝
نَارُ اللَّهِ الْمُوقَدَةُ ۝
الَّتِي تَطَّلِعُ عَلَى الْأَفْئِدَةِ ۝
إِنَّهَا عَلَيْهِمْ مُؤْصَدَةٌ ۝
فِي عَمَدٍ مُمَدَّدَةٍ ۝

kindled,

Which leapeth up over the hearts (of men).

Lo! it is closed in on them.

In outstretched columns.

104:1–9

Ref: 9:34–35: 17:29; 25:67; 53:33–34; 57:24; 59:9; 70:15–18.

See also: Accumulation of Wealth, Moderation.

MISKIN

1. Give the kinsman his due, and the needy, and the wayfarer, and squander not (thy wealth) in wantonness.
17:26

2. But he hath not attempted the Ascent—
Ah, what will convey unto thee what the Ascent is!—
(It is) to free a slave,
And to feed in the day of hunger
An orphan near of kin,
Or some poor wretch in misery,
90:11–16

3. Hast thou observed him who belieth religion?
That is he who repelleth the orphan?
And urgeth not the feeding of the needy.
107:1–3

1. وَءَاتِ ذَا الْقُرْبَىٰ حَقَّهُ وَالْمِسْكِينَ وَابْنَ
السَّبِيلِ وَلَا تُبَذِّرْ تَبْذِيرًا ﴿٢٦﴾

2. فَلَا اقْتَحَمَ الْعَقَبَةَ ﴿١١﴾
وَمَا أَدْرَاكَ مَا الْعَقَبَةُ ﴿١٢﴾
فَكُّ رَقَبَةٍ ﴿١٣﴾
أَوْ إِطْعَامٌ فِي يَوْمٍ ذِي مَسْغَبَةٍ ﴿١٤﴾
يَتِيمًا ذَا مَقْرَبَةٍ ﴿١٥﴾
أَوْ مِسْكِينًا ذَا مَتْرَبَةٍ ﴿١٦﴾

3. أَرَأَيْتَ الَّذِي يُكَذِّبُ بِالدِّينِ ﴿١﴾
فَذَٰلِكَ الَّذِي يَدُعُّ الْيَتِيمَ ﴿٢﴾
وَلَا يَحُضُّ عَلَىٰ طَعَامِ الْمِسْكِينِ ﴿٣﴾

See also: Alms, Charity, *Zakat*.

MODERATION

1. And let not thy hand be chained to thy neck nor open it with a complete opening, lest thou sit down rebuked, denuded.

17:29

2. And thou (Muhammad), be not loud voiced in thy worship nor yet silent there-in, but follow a way between.

17:110

3. And those who, when they spend, are neither pro-digal nor grudging; and there is ever a firm station between the two.

25:67

4. Be modest in thy bearing and subdue thy voice. Lo! the harshest of all voices is the voice of the ass.

31:19

1. وَلَا تَجْعَلْ يَدَكَ مَغْلُولَةً إِلَىٰ عُنُقِكَ
وَلَا تَبْسُطْهَا كُلَّ الْبَسْطِ فَتَقْعُدَ
مَلُومًا مَّحْسُورًا ﴿٢٩﴾

2. وَلَا تَجْهَرْ بِصَلَاتِكَ وَلَا تُخَافِتْ
بِهَا وَابْتَغِ بَيْنَ ذَٰلِكَ سَبِيلًا ○

3. وَالَّذِينَ إِذَا أَنفَقُوا لَمْ يُسْرِفُوا وَلَمْ
يَقْتُرُوا وَكَانَ بَيْنَ ذَٰلِكَ قَوَامًا ﴿٦٧﴾

4. وَاقْصِدْ فِي مَشْيِكَ وَاغْضُضْ مِن
صَوْتِكَ ۚ إِنَّ أَنكَرَ الْأَصْوَاتِ
لَصَوْتُ الْحَمِيرِ ﴿١٩﴾

MONASTICISM

1. Thou wilt find the most vehement of mankind in hostility to those who believe (to be) the Jews and the idolaters, and thou wilt find the nearest of them in affection to those who believe (to be) those who say: Lo! We are Christians. That is because there are among them priests and monks, and because they are not proud.

5:82

1. لَتَجِدَنَّ أَشَدَّ النَّاسِ عَدَاوَةً لِّلَّذِينَ آمَنُوا الْيَهُودَ
وَالَّذِينَ أَشْرَكُوا ۖ وَلَتَجِدَنَّ أَقْرَبَهُم مَّوَدَّةً لِّلَّذِينَ
آمَنُوا الَّذِينَ قَالُوا إِنَّا نَصَارَىٰ ۚ ذَٰلِكَ بِأَنَّ مِنْهُمْ
قِسِّيسِينَ وَرُهْبَانًا وَأَنَّهُمْ لَا يَسْتَكْبِرُونَ ﴿٨٢﴾

2. O ye who believe! Lo! many of the (Jewish) rabbis and the (Christian) monks devour the wealth of mankind wantonly and debar (men) from the way of Allah.

9:34

2. يَا أَيُّهَا الَّذِينَ آمَنُوا إِنَّ كَثِيرًا مِّنَ الْأَحْبَارِ
وَالرُّهْبَانِ لَيَأْكُلُونَ أَمْوَالَ النَّاسِ
بِالْبَاطِلِ وَيَصُدُّونَ عَن سَبِيلِ اللَّهِ ۗ

3. Then We caused Our messengers to follow in their footsteps; and We caused Jesus, son of Mary, to follow, and gave him the Gospel, and placed compassion and mercy in the hearts of those who followed him. But monasticism they invented — We ordained it not for them—only seeking Allah's pleasure, and they observed it not with right observance. So We give those of them who believe their reward, but many of them are evil-livers.

57:27

3. ثُمَّ قَفَّيْنَا عَلَىٰ آثَارِهِم بِرُسُلِنَا
وَقَفَّيْنَا بِعِيسَى ابْنِ مَرْيَمَ وَآتَيْنَاهُ
الْإِنجِيلَ وَجَعَلْنَا فِي قُلُوبِ
الَّذِينَ اتَّبَعُوهُ رَأْفَةً وَرَحْمَةً ۚ
وَرَهْبَانِيَّةً ابْتَدَعُوهَا مَا كَتَبْنَاهَا
عَلَيْهِمْ إِلَّا ابْتِغَاءَ رِضْوَانِ اللَّهِ فَمَا
رَعَوْهَا حَقَّ رِعَايَتِهَا ۖ فَآتَيْنَا الَّذِينَ
آمَنُوا مِنْهُمْ أَجْرَهُمْ ۖ وَكَثِيرٌ
مِّنْهُمْ فَاسِقُونَ ﴿٢٧﴾

Ref: 9:31.

MONOTHEISM

1. وَإِلٰهُكُمْ إِلٰهٌ وَّاحِدٌ ۚ لَآ إِلٰهَ إِلَّا هُوَ الرَّحْمٰنُ الرَّحِيمُ ﴿١٦٣﴾

2. شَهِدَ اللّٰهُ أَنَّهُ لَآ إِلٰهَ إِلَّا هُوَ ۙ وَالْمَلٰٓئِكَةُ
وَأُولُوا الْعِلْمِ قَآئِمًا بِالْقِسْطِ ۚ لَآ إِلٰهَ إِلَّا
هُوَ الْعَزِيزُ الْحَكِيمُ ۝

3. وَلَا تَقُولُوا ثَلٰثَةٌ ۚ اِنْتَهُوا خَيْرًا لَّكُمْ ۚ إِنَّمَا
اللّٰهُ إِلٰهٌ وَّاحِدٌ ۚ سُبْحٰنَهُ أَنْ يَّكُونَ لَهُ
وَلَدٌ ۘ لَهُ مَا فِي السَّمٰوٰتِ وَمَا فِي
الْأَرْضِ ۚ وَكَفٰى بِاللّٰهِ وَكِيلًا ﴿١٧١﴾

4. لَقَدْ كَفَرَ الَّذِينَ قَالُوا إِنَّ اللّٰهَ هُوَ
الْمَسِيحُ ابْنُ مَرْيَمَ ۚ قُلْ فَمَنْ يَّمْلِكُ
مِنَ اللّٰهِ شَيْئًا إِنْ أَرَادَ أَنْ يُّهْلِكَ الْمَسِيحَ
ابْنَ مَرْيَمَ وَأُمَّهُ وَمَنْ فِي الْأَرْضِ
جَمِيعًا ۚ وَلِلّٰهِ مُلْكُ السَّمٰوٰتِ وَالْأَرْضِ
وَمَا بَيْنَهُمَا ۚ يَخْلُقُ مَا يَشَآءُ ۚ وَاللّٰهُ
عَلٰى كُلِّ شَيْءٍ قَدِيرٌ ﴿١٧﴾

5. أَئِنَّكُمْ لَتَشْهَدُونَ أَنَّ مَعَ اللّٰهِ آلِهَةً أُخْرٰى ۚ
قُلْ لَّآ أَشْهَدُ ۚ قُلْ إِنَّمَا هُوَ إِلٰهٌ وَّاحِدٌ
وَّإِنَّنِي بَرِيٓءٌ مِّمَّا تُشْرِكُونَ ﴿١٩﴾

6. وَجَعَلُوا لِلّٰهِ شُرَكَآءَ الْجِنَّ وَخَلَقَهُمْ وَ
خَرَقُوا لَهُ بَنِينَ وَبَنٰتٍ بِغَيْرِ عِلْمٍ ۚ
سُبْحٰنَهُ وَتَعٰلٰى عَمَّا يَصِفُونَ ۝

1. Your God is One God; there is no God save Him, the Beneficent, the Merciful.
2:163

2. Allah (Himself) is witness that there is no God save Him. And the angels and the men of learning (too are witness). Maintaining His creation in justice, there is no God save Him, the Almighty, the Wise.
3:18

3. And say not "Three—Cease"! (it is) better for you!—Allah is only One God. Far is it removed from His Transcendent Majesty that He should have a son. His is all that is in the heavens and all that is in the earth. And Allah is sufficient as Defender.
4:171

4. They indeed have disbelieved who say: Lo! Allah is the Messiah, son of Mary. Say: Who then can do aught against Allah, if He had willed to destroy the Messiah son of Mary, and his mother and everyone on earth? Allah's is the Sovereignty of the heavens and the earth and all that is between them. He createth what He will. And Allah is Able to do all things.
5:17

5. Do ye in sooth bear witness that there are gods beside Allah? Say: I bear no such witness. Say: He is only One God. Lo! I am innocent of that which ye associate (with Him).
6:19

6. Yet they ascribe as partners unto Him the jinn, although He did create them, and impute falsely, without knowledge, sons and daughters unto Him. Glorified be He and High Exalted above (all) that they ascribe (unto Him)!
6:100

7. اتَّخَذُوا أَحْبَارَهُمْ وَرُهْبَانَهُمْ أَرْبَابًا مِّن
دُونِ اللَّهِ وَالْمَسِيحَ ابْنَ مَرْيَمَ وَمَا
أُمِرُوا إِلَّا لِيَعْبُدُوا إِلَٰهًا وَاحِدًا لَّا إِلَٰهَ
إِلَّا هُوَ سُبْحَانَهُ عَمَّا يُشْرِكُونَ ﴿٣١﴾

8. ءَأَرْبَابٌ مُّتَفَرِّقُونَ خَيْرٌ أَمِ اللَّهُ
الْوَاحِدُ الْقَهَّارُ ﴿٣٩﴾

مَا تَعْبُدُونَ مِن دُونِهِ إِلَّا أَسْمَاءً
سَمَّيْتُمُوهَا أَنتُمْ وَآبَاؤُكُم مَّا أَنزَلَ اللَّهُ
بِهَا مِن سُلْطَانٍ إِنِ الْحُكْمُ إِلَّا لِلَّهِ أَمَرَ
أَلَّا تَعْبُدُوا إِلَّا إِيَّاهُ ذَٰلِكَ الدِّينُ الْقَيِّمُ
وَلَٰكِنَّ أَكْثَرَ النَّاسِ لَا يَعْلَمُونَ ﴿٤٠﴾

9. وَقَالَ اللَّهُ لَا تَتَّخِذُوا إِلَٰهَيْنِ اثْنَيْنِ
إِنَّمَا هُوَ إِلَٰهٌ وَاحِدٌ فَإِيَّايَ فَارْهَبُونِ ﴿٥١﴾

10. لَا تَجْعَلْ مَعَ اللَّهِ إِلَٰهًا آخَرَ فَتَقْعُدَ
مَذْمُومًا مَّخْذُولًا ﴿٢٢﴾

11. وَلَا تَجْعَلْ مَعَ اللَّهِ إِلَٰهًا آخَرَ فَتُلْقَىٰ فِي
جَهَنَّمَ مَلُومًا مَّدْحُورًا ﴿٣٩﴾

12. قُل لَّوْ كَانَ مَعَهُ آلِهَةٌ كَمَا يَقُولُونَ
إِذًا لَّابْتَغَوْا إِلَىٰ ذِي الْعَرْشِ سَبِيلًا ﴿٤٢﴾

سُبْحَانَهُ وَتَعَالَىٰ عَمَّا يَقُولُونَ عُلُوًّا كَبِيرًا ﴿٤٣﴾

7. They have taken as lords beside Allah their rabbis and their monks and the Messiah son of Mary, when they were bidden to worship only One God. There is no god save Him. Be He glorified from all that they ascribe as partners (unto Him)!

9:31

8. Are divers lords better, or Allah the One, the Almighty?

Those whom ye wor–ship beside Him are but names which ye have named, ye and your fathers. Allah hath revealed no sanction for them. The decision rests with Allah only, Who hath commanded you that ye worship none save Him. This is the Right religion, but most men know not.

12:39–40

9. Allah hath said: Choose not two gods. There is only One God. So of Me, Me only, be in awe.

16:51

10. Set not up with Allah any other god (O man) lest thou sit down reproved, forsaken.

17:22

11. And set not up with Allah any other god lest thou be cast into hell, reproved, abandoned.

17:39

12. Say (O Muhammad, to the disbelievers): If there were other gods along with Him, as they say, then had they sought a way against the Lord of the Throne.

Glorified is He, and High Exalted above what they say!

17:42–43

13. And say: Praise be to Allah, Who hath not taken unto Himself a son, and Who hath no partner in the Sovereignty, nor hath He any protecting friend through dependence. And magnify Him with all magnificence.

17:111

14. Say: I am only a mortal like you. My Lord inspireth in me that your God is only One God. And whoever hopeth for the meeting with his Lord, let him do righteous work, and make none sharer of the worship due unto his Lord.

18:110

15. Allah! There is no God save Him. His are the most beautiful names.

20:8

16. If there were therein Gods, beside Allah, then verily both (the heavens and the earth) had been disordered. Glorified be Allah, the Lord of the Throne, from all that they ascribe (unto Him)

21:22

17. Allah hath not chosen any son, nor is there any god along with Him; else would each god have assuredly championed that which he created, and some of them would assuredly have overcome others. Glorified be Allah above all that they allege!

23:91

18. Yet they choose beside Him other gods who create naught but are themselves created, and possess not hurt nor profit for themselves, and

13. وَقُلِ الْحَمْدُ لِلّٰهِ الَّذِىْ لَمْ يَتَّخِذْ وَلَدًا وَّلَمْ يَكُنْ
لَّهٗ شَرِيْكٌ فِى الْمُلْكِ وَلَمْ يَكُنْ لَّهٗ وَلِىٌّ مِّنَ الذُّلِّ
وَكَبِّرْهُ تَكْبِيْرًا ﴿١١١﴾

14. قُلْ اِنَّمَآ اَنَا بَشَرٌ مِّثْلُكُمْ يُوْحٰٓى اِلَىَّ اَنَّمَآ اِلٰهُكُمْ
اِلٰهٌ وَّاحِدٌ ۚ فَمَنْ كَانَ يَرْجُوْا لِقَآءَ رَبِّهٖ
فَلْيَعْمَلْ عَمَلًا صَالِحًا وَّلَا يُشْرِكْ بِعِبَادَةِ
رَبِّهٖٓ اَحَدًا ﴿١١٠﴾

15. اَللّٰهُ لَآ اِلٰهَ اِلَّا هُوَ ۭ لَهُ الْاَسْمَآءُ الْحُسْنٰى ﴿٨﴾

16. لَوْ كَانَ فِيْهِمَآ اٰلِهَةٌ اِلَّا اللّٰهُ لَفَسَدَتَا ۚ
فَسُبْحٰنَ اللّٰهِ رَبِّ الْعَرْشِ عَمَّا يَصِفُوْنَ ﴿٢٢﴾

17. مَا اتَّخَذَ اللّٰهُ مِنْ وَّلَدٍ وَّمَا كَانَ
مَعَهٗ مِنْ اِلٰهٍ اِذًا لَّذَهَبَ كُلُّ اِلٰهٍۢ
بِمَا خَلَقَ وَلَعَلَا بَعْضُهُمْ عَلٰى بَعْضٍ ۭ
سُبْحٰنَ اللّٰهِ عَمَّا يَصِفُوْنَ ﴿٩١﴾

18. وَاتَّخَذُوْا مِنْ دُوْنِهٖٓ اٰلِهَةً لَّا
يَخْلُقُوْنَ شَيْـًٔا وَّهُمْ يُخْلَقُوْنَ وَلَا
يَمْلِكُوْنَ لِاَنْفُسِهِمْ ضَرًّا وَّلَا نَفْعًا
وَّلَا يَمْلِكُوْنَ مَوْتًا وَّلَا حَيٰوةً وَّلَا نُشُوْرًا ﴿٣﴾

19. اَمَّنْ خَلَقَ السَّمٰوٰتِ وَالْاَرْضَ وَ
اَنْزَلَ لَكُمْ مِّنَ السَّمَآءِ مَآءً ۚ فَاَنْۢبَتْنَا بِهٖ
حَدَآئِقَ ذَاتَ بَهْجَةٍ ۚ مَا كَانَ لَكُمْ
اَنْ تُنْۢبِتُوْا شَجَرَهَا ۭ ءَاِلٰهٌ مَّعَ اللّٰهِ ۭ

possess not death nor life, nor power to raise the dead.

25:3

19. Is not He (best) Who created the heavens and the earth, and sendeth down for you water from the sky wherewith We cause to spring forth joyous orchards, whose trees it never hath been yours to cause to grow. Is there any God beside Allah? Nay, but they are folk who ascribe

equals (unto Him)!

Is not He (best) Who made the earth a fixed abode, and placed rivers in the folds thereof, and placed firm hills therein, and hath set a barrier between the two seas? Is there any God beside Allah? Nay, but most of them know not!

Is not He (best) Who answereth the wronged one when he crieth unto Him and removeth the evil, and hath made you viceroys of the earth? Is there any God beside Allah? Little do they reflect!

Is not He (best) Who guideth you in the darkness of the land and the sea, He Who sendeth the winds as heralds of His mercy? Is there any God beside Allah? High Exalted be Allah from all that they ascribe as partner (unto Him)!

Is not He (best) Who produceth creation, then reproduceth it, and Who provideth for you from the heaven and the earth? Is there any God beside Allah? Say: Bring your proof, if ye are truthful!

27:60–64

20. And cry not unto any other god along with Allah. There is no God save Him. Everything will perish save His Countenance His is the command, and unto Him ye will be brought back.

28:88

21. Say: He is Allah, the

بَلْ هُمْ قَوْمٌ يَعْدِلُونَ ۝٦٠
أَمَّنْ جَعَلَ الْأَرْضَ قَرَارًا وَجَعَلَ
خِلٰلَهَآ أَنْهٰرًا وَجَعَلَ لَهَا رَوَاسِيَ وَ
جَعَلَ بَيْنَ الْبَحْرَيْنِ حَاجِزًا ۗ ءَ إِلٰهٌ
مَّعَ اللّٰهِ ۚ بَلْ أَكْثَرُهُمْ لَا يَعْلَمُونَ ۝٦١
أَمَّنْ يُّجِيبُ الْمُضْطَرَّ إِذَا دَعَاهُ وَيَكْشِفُ
السُّوٓءَ وَيَجْعَلُكُمْ خُلَفَآءَ الْأَرْضِ ۗ ءَ إِلٰهٌ
مَّعَ اللّٰهِ ۚ قَلِيلًا مَّا تَذَكَّرُونَ ۝٦٢
أَمَّنْ يَّهْدِيكُمْ فِي ظُلُمٰتِ الْبَرِّ وَالْبَحْرِ
وَمَنْ يُّرْسِلُ الرِّيٰحَ بُشْرًا بَيْنَ يَدَيْ
رَحْمَتِهِ ۗ ءَ إِلٰهٌ مَّعَ اللّٰهِ ۚ تَعٰلَى اللّٰهُ
عَمَّا يُشْرِكُونَ ۝٦٣
أَمَّنْ يَّبْدَؤُا الْخَلْقَ ثُمَّ يُعِيدُهُ وَمَنْ
يَّرْزُقُكُمْ مِّنَ السَّمَآءِ وَالْأَرْضِ ۗ
ءَ إِلٰهٌ مَّعَ اللّٰهِ ۚ قُلْ هَاتُوا بُرْهَانَكُمْ
إِنْ كُنْتُمْ صٰدِقِينَ ۝٦٤
وَلَا تَدْعُ مَعَ اللّٰهِ إِلٰهًا أٰخَرَ ۘ لَآ إِلٰهَ 20.
إِلَّا هُوَ ۚ كُلُّ شَيْءٍ هَالِكٌ إِلَّا وَجْهَهُ ۚ
لَهُ الْحُكْمُ وَإِلَيْهِ تُرْجَعُونَ ۝٨٨
قُلْ هُوَ اللّٰهُ أَحَدٌ ۝ 21.
اللّٰهُ الصَّمَدُ ۝
لَمْ يَلِدْ ۙ وَلَمْ يُولَدْ ۝
وَلَمْ يَكُنْ لَّهُ كُفُوًا أَحَدٌ ۝

One!

Allah the eternally Besought of all!

He begetteth not nor was begotten.

And there is none comparable unto Him.

112:1–4

Ref: 2:22,116; 3:6; 4:48,87,116–117; 5:72–73,76; 6:22–23,56,80,101–102,107–108; 7:138–140,158; 9:30,129; 10:18,66,68; 12:40; 13:16,30; 16:22,57,72–73; 17:23; 18:15; 19:35–36,88,93; 20:14,98; 21:24–26, 29,108; 22:31,34; 25:2,68; 27:26,61–64; 28:68,70–72; 30–40; 35:3; 36: 23,74; 37:4,158–160; 38:65–66; 39:4,6,38; 40:3,12,16,62,65; 41:6,9; 44:8; 50:26; 51:51; 59:22–24; 64:13; 72:2–3,18,20; 73:9.

See also: Refutation fo Polytheism, Refutation of Trinity.

MONUMENTS OF ALLAH

1. Lo! (the mountains) *As-Safā* and *Al-Marwah* are among the indications of Allah. It is therefore no sin for him who is on pilgrimage to the House (of God) or visiteth it, to go around them (as the pagan custom is). And he who doth good of his own accord (for him), lo! Allah is Responsive, Aware.

2:158

2. It is no sin for you that ye seek the bounty of your Lord (by trading). But when ye press on in the multitude from *'Arafāt* remember Allah by the sacred monument. Remember Him as He hath guided you, although before ye were of those astray.

2:198

3. O ye who believe! Profane not Allah's monuments nor the Sacred Month nor the offerings nor the garlands, nor those repairing to the Sacred House, seeking the grace and pleasure of their Lord.

5:2

4. That (is the command). And whoso magnifieth the offerings consecrated to Allah, it surely is from devotion of the hearts.

22:32

5. And the camels! We have appointed them among the ceremonies of Allah. Therein ye have much good.

1. إِنَّ الصَّفَا وَالْمَرْوَةَ مِنْ شَعَآئِرِ اللّٰهِ ۚ فَمَنْ
حَجَّ الْبَيْتَ اَوِ اعْتَمَرَ فَلَا جُنَاحَ عَلَيْهِ اَنْ
يَّطَّوَّفَ بِهِمَا ۗ وَمَنْ تَطَوَّعَ خَيْرًا ۙ فَاِنَّ اللّٰهَ
شَاكِرٌ عَلِيْمٌ ۝١٥٨

2. لَيْسَ عَلَيْكُمْ جُنَاحٌ اَنْ تَبْتَغُوْا فَضْلًا مِّنْ
رَّبِّكُمْ ۗ فَاِذَآ اَفَضْتُمْ مِّنْ عَرَفٰتٍ فَاذْكُرُوا اللّٰهَ
عِنْدَ الْمَشْعَرِ الْحَرَامِ ۠ وَاذْكُرُوْهُ كَمَا هَدٰىكُمْ ۚ
وَاِنْ كُنْتُمْ مِّنْ قَبْلِهٖ لَمِنَ الضَّآلِّيْنَ ۝١٩٨

3. يٰٓاَيُّهَا الَّذِيْنَ اٰمَنُوْا لَا تُحِلُّوْا شَعَآئِرَ اللّٰهِ
وَلَا الشَّهْرَ الْحَرَامَ وَلَا الْهَدْيَ وَلَا
الْقَلَآئِدَ وَلَآ آٰمِّيْنَ الْبَيْتَ الْحَرَامَ
يَبْتَغُوْنَ فَضْلًا مِّنْ رَّبِّهِمْ وَرِضْوَانًا ۗ

4. ذٰلِكَ ۗ وَمَنْ يُّعَظِّمْ شَعَآئِرَ اللّٰهِ فَاِنَّهَا
مِنْ تَقْوَى الْقُلُوْبِ ۝٣٢

5. وَالْبُدْنَ جَعَلْنٰهَا لَكُمْ مِّنْ شَعَآئِرِ اللّٰهِ
لَكُمْ فِيْهَا خَيْرٌ ۖ فَاذْكُرُوا اسْمَ اللّٰهِ
عَلَيْهَا صَوَآفَّ ۚ فَاِذَا وَجَبَتْ جُنُوْبُهَا
فَكُلُوْا مِنْهَا وَاَطْعِمُوا الْقَانِعَ وَالْمُعْتَرَّ ۗ
كَذٰلِكَ سَخَّرْنٰهَا لَكُمْ لَعَلَّكُمْ تَشْكُرُوْنَ ۝٣٦

So mention the name of Allah over them when they are drawn up in lines. Then when their flanks fall (dead), eat thereof and feed the beggar and the suppliant. Thus have We made them subject unto you, that haply ye may give thanks.

22:36

MOON

1. فَالِقُ الْإِصْبَاحِ ۚ وَجَعَلَ الَّيْلَ سَكَنًا وَالشَّمْسَ
وَالْقَمَرَ حُسْبَانًا ۚ ذٰلِكَ تَقْدِيرُ الْعَزِيزِ الْعَلِيمِ ﴿٩٦﴾

2. إِنَّ رَبَّكُمُ اللّٰهُ الَّذِي خَلَقَ السَّمٰوٰتِ وَ
الْأَرْضَ فِي سِتَّةِ أَيَّامٍ ثُمَّ اسْتَوٰى عَلَى
الْعَرْشِ ۚ يُغْشِي الَّيْلَ النَّهَارَ يَطْلُبُهُ
حَثِيثًا ۙ وَّ الشَّمْسَ وَالْقَمَرَ وَالنُّجُومَ
مُسَخَّرٰتٍ بِأَمْرِهِ ۗ أَلَا لَهُ الْخَلْقُ وَالْأَمْرُ ۗ
تَبٰرَكَ اللّٰهُ رَبُّ الْعٰلَمِينَ ﴿٥٤﴾

3. هُوَ الَّذِي جَعَلَ الشَّمْسَ ضِيَاءً وَّ الْقَمَرَ
نُورًا وَّ قَدَّرَهُ مَنَازِلَ لِتَعْلَمُوا عَدَدَ
السِّنِينَ وَ الْحِسَابَ ۚ مَا خَلَقَ اللّٰهُ ذٰلِكَ
إِلَّا بِالْحَقِّ ۚ يُفَصِّلُ الْأٰيٰتِ لِقَوْمٍ يَعْلَمُونَ ﴿٥﴾

4. اَللّٰهُ الَّذِي رَفَعَ السَّمٰوٰتِ بِغَيْرِ عَمَدٍ
تَرَوْنَهَا ثُمَّ اسْتَوٰى عَلَى الْعَرْشِ وَسَخَّرَ
الشَّمْسَ وَالْقَمَرَ ۚ كُلٌّ يَّجْرِي لِأَجَلٍ
مُّسَمًّى ۚ يُدَبِّرُ الْأَمْرَ يُفَصِّلُ الْأٰيٰتِ
لَعَلَّكُمْ بِلِقَاءِ رَبِّكُمْ تُوقِنُونَ ﴿٢﴾

5. أَلَمْ تَرَ أَنَّ اللّٰهَ يَسْجُدُ لَهُ مَنْ فِي
السَّمٰوٰتِ وَمَنْ فِي الْأَرْضِ وَالشَّمْسُ
وَالْقَمَرُ وَالنُّجُومُ وَالْجِبَالُ وَالشَّجَرُ
وَالدَّوَابُّ وَكَثِيرٌ مِّنَ النَّاسِ ۗ

1. He is the Cleaver of the Daybreak, and He hath appointed the night for stillness, and the sun and the moon for reckoning. That is the measuring of the Mighty, the Wise.

6:96

2. Lo! your Lord is Allah Who created the heavens and the earth in six Days, then mounted He the Throne. He covereth the night with the day, which is in haste to follow it, and hath made the sun and the moon and the stars subservient by His command. His verily is all creation and commandment. Blessed be Allah, the Lord of the Worlds!

7:54

3. He it is Who appointed the sun a splendour and the moon a light, and measured for her stages, that ye might know the number of the years, and the reckoning Allah created not (all) that save in truth. He detaileth the revelations for people who have knowledge.

10:5

4. Allah it is Who raised up the heavens without visible supports, then mounted the Throne, and compelled the sun and the moon to be of service, each runneth unto an appointed term; He ordereth the course; He detaileth the revelations, that haply ye may be certain of the meeting with your Lord.

13:2

5. Hast thou not seen that unto Allah payeth adoration whosoever is in the heavens and whosoever is in the earth, and the sun, and the moon, and the stars, and the hills, and the trees, and the beasts, and many of mankind.

22:18

6. And for the moon We have appointed mansions till she return like an old shrivelled palm-leaf.

It is not for the sun to overtake the moon, nor doth the night outstrip the day. They float each in an orbit.

36:39–40

6. وَالْقَمَرَ قَدَّرْنٰهُ مَنَازِلَ حَتّٰى عَادَ كَالْعُرْجُوْنِ الْقَدِيْمِ ۝
لَا الشَّمْسُ يَنْۢبَغِيْ لَهَآ اَنْ تُدْرِكَ الْقَمَرَ وَلَا الَّيْلُ سَابِقُ النَّهَارِ ۭ وَكُلٌّ فِيْ فَلَكٍ يَّسْبَحُوْنَ ۝

Ref: 14:33; 16:12; 21:33; 25:61; 29:61; 31:29; 35:13; 36:40; 39:5; 41:37; 54:1; 55:5; 71:16; 74:32; 75:8–9; 84:18; 91:2.

See also: Calendar, Subjugation of Universe, Universe.

MORALS

1. When ye are greeted with a greeting, greet ye with a better than it or return it. Lo! Allah taketh count of all things.

4:86

2. There is no good in much of their secret conferences save (in) him who enjoineth almsgiving and kindness and peace-making among the people. Whoso doeth that seeking the good pleasure of Allah, We shall bestow on him a vast reward.

4:114

3. Allah loveth not the utterance of harsh speech save by one who hath been wronged. Allah is ever Hearer, Knower.

If ye do good openly or keep it secret, or forgive evil, lo! Allah is ever Forgiving, Powerful.

4:148–149

4. Work not confusion in the earth after the fair ordering (thereof), and call on Him in fear and hope. Lo! the mercy of Allah is nigh unto the good.

7:56

5. Strain not thine eyes toward that which We cause some wedded pairs among them to enjoy, and be not grieved on their account, and lower thy wing (in tenderness) for the believers.

15:88

6. Call unto the way of thy Lord with wisdom and fair exhortation, and reason with them in the better way. Lo! thy Lord is Best Aware of him who strayeth from His way, and He is Best Aware of those who go aright.

If ye punish, then punish with the like of that wherewith ye were afflicted. But if ye endure patiently, verily it is better for the patient.

16:125–126

1. وَإِذَا حُيِّيتُم بِتَحِيَّةٍ فَحَيُّوا بِأَحْسَنَ مِنْهَا
أَوْ رُدُّوهَا ۗ إِنَّ اللَّهَ كَانَ عَلَىٰ كُلِّ شَيْءٍ حَسِيبًا ﴿٨٦﴾

2. لَا خَيْرَ فِي كَثِيرٍ مِّن نَّجْوَاهُمْ إِلَّا مَنْ أَمَرَ
بِصَدَقَةٍ أَوْ مَعْرُوفٍ أَوْ إِصْلَاحٍ بَيْنَ النَّاسِ ۚ
وَمَن يَفْعَلْ ذَٰلِكَ ابْتِغَاءَ مَرْضَاتِ اللَّهِ
فَسَوْفَ نُؤْتِيهِ أَجْرًا عَظِيمًا ﴿١١٤﴾

3. لَا يُحِبُّ اللَّهُ الْجَهْرَ بِالسُّوءِ مِنَ الْقَوْلِ
إِلَّا مَن ظُلِمَ ۚ وَكَانَ اللَّهُ سَمِيعًا عَلِيمًا ﴿١٤٨﴾

إِن تُبْدُوا خَيْرًا أَوْ تُخْفُوهُ أَوْ تَعْفُوا عَن
سُوءٍ فَإِنَّ اللَّهَ كَانَ عَفُوًّا قَدِيرًا ﴿١٤٩﴾

4. وَلَا تُفْسِدُوا فِي الْأَرْضِ بَعْدَ إِصْلَاحِهَا
وَادْعُوهُ خَوْفًا وَطَمَعًا ۚ إِنَّ رَحْمَتَ اللَّهِ
قَرِيبٌ مِّنَ الْمُحْسِنِينَ ﴿٥٦﴾

5. لَا تَمُدَّنَّ عَيْنَيْكَ إِلَىٰ مَا مَتَّعْنَا بِهِ
أَزْوَاجًا مِّنْهُمْ وَلَا تَحْزَنْ عَلَيْهِمْ
وَاخْفِضْ جَنَاحَكَ لِلْمُؤْمِنِينَ ﴿٨٨﴾

6. ادْعُ إِلَىٰ سَبِيلِ رَبِّكَ بِالْحِكْمَةِ وَالْمَوْعِظَةِ
الْحَسَنَةِ ۖ وَجَادِلْهُم بِالَّتِي هِيَ أَحْسَنُ ۚ إِنَّ
رَبَّكَ هُوَ أَعْلَمُ بِمَن ضَلَّ عَن سَبِيلِهِ ۖ
وَهُوَ أَعْلَمُ بِالْمُهْتَدِينَ ﴿١٢٥﴾

وَإِنْ عَاقَبْتُمْ فَعَاقِبُوا بِمِثْلِ مَا عُوقِبْتُم
بِهِ ۖ وَلَئِن صَبَرْتُمْ لَهُوَ خَيْرٌ لِّلصَّابِرِينَ ﴿١٢٦﴾

7. Give the kinsman his due, and the needy, and the wayfarer, and squander not (thy wealth) in wantonness.

Lo! the squanderers were ever brothers of the devils, and the devil was ever an ingrate to his Lord.

But if thou turn away from them, seeking mercy from thy Lord, for which thou hopest, then speak unto them a reasonable word.

And let not thy hand be chained to thy neck nor open it with a complete opening, lest thou sit down rebuked, denuded.

17:26–29

8. And keep the covenant. Lo! of the convenant it will be asked.

Fill the measure when ye measure, and weigh with a right balance; that is meet, and better in the end.

(O man), follow not that whereof thou hast no knowledge. Lo! the hearing and the sight and the heart—of each of these it will be asked.

And walk not in the earth exultant. Lo! thou canst not rend the earth, nor canst thou stretch to the height of the hills.

The evil of all that is

7. وَآتِ ذَا الْقُرْبَىٰ حَقَّهُ وَالْمِسْكِينَ وَابْنَ
السَّبِيلِ وَلَا تُبَذِّرْ تَبْذِيرًا ﴿٢٦﴾
إِنَّ الْمُبَذِّرِينَ كَانُوا إِخْوَانَ الشَّيَاطِينِ ۖ
وَكَانَ الشَّيْطَانُ لِرَبِّهِ كَفُورًا ﴿٢٧﴾
وَإِمَّا تُعْرِضَنَّ عَنْهُمُ ابْتِغَاءَ رَحْمَةٍ مِّن
رَّبِّكَ تَرْجُوهَا فَقُل لَّهُمْ قَوْلًا مَّيْسُورًا ﴿٢٨﴾
وَلَا تَجْعَلْ يَدَكَ مَغْلُولَةً إِلَىٰ عُنُقِكَ
وَلَا تَبْسُطْهَا كُلَّ الْبَسْطِ فَتَقْعُدَ
مَلُومًا مَّحْسُورًا ﴿٢٩﴾

8. وَأَوْفُوا بِالْعَهْدِ ۖ إِنَّ الْعَهْدَ كَانَ
مَسْئُولًا ﴿٣٤﴾
وَأَوْفُوا الْكَيْلَ إِذَا كِلْتُمْ وَزِنُوا بِالْقِسْطَاسِ
الْمُسْتَقِيمِ ۚ ذَٰلِكَ خَيْرٌ وَأَحْسَنُ تَأْوِيلًا ﴿٣٥﴾

وَلَا تَقْفُ مَا لَيْسَ لَكَ بِهِ عِلْمٌ ۚ إِنَّ
السَّمْعَ وَالْبَصَرَ وَالْفُؤَادَ كُلُّ أُولَٰئِكَ
كَانَ عَنْهُ مَسْئُولًا ﴿٣٦﴾
وَلَا تَمْشِ فِي الْأَرْضِ مَرَحًا ۖ إِنَّكَ
لَن تَخْرِقَ الْأَرْضَ وَلَن تَبْلُغَ
الْجِبَالَ طُولًا ﴿٣٧﴾
كُلُّ ذَٰلِكَ كَانَ سَيِّئُهُ عِندَ
رَبِّكَ مَكْرُوهًا ﴿٣٨﴾

hateful in the sight of thy Lord.

17:34–38

9. Tell My bondmen to speak that which is kindlier. Lo! the devil soweth discord among them. Lo! the devil is for man an open foe.
17:53

10. So shun the filth of idols, and shun lying speech,
22:30

11. Repel evil with that which is better.
23:96

12. And let not those who possess dignity and ease among you swear not to give to the near of kin and to the needy, and to fugitives for the cause of Allah. Let them forgive and show indulgence. Yearn ye not that Allah may forgive you? Allah is Forgiving, Merciful.
24:22

13. O ye who believe! Let your slaves, and those of you who have not come to puberty, ask leave of you at three times (before they come into your presence); Before the prayer of dawn, and when ye lay aside your raiment for the heat of noon, and after the prayer of night. Three times of privacy for you. It is no sin for them or for you at other times, when some of you go round attendant upon others (if they come into your presence without leave). Thus Allah maketh clear the revelations for you. Allah is Knower, Wise.
24:58

9. وَقُلْ لِعِبَادِي يَقُولُوا الَّتِي هِيَ أَحْسَنُ ۚ
إِنَّ الشَّيْطٰنَ يَنْزَغُ بَيْنَهُمْ ۚ إِنَّ الشَّيْطٰنَ
كَانَ لِلْإِنْسَانِ عَدُوًّا مُّبِينًا ﴿٥٣﴾

10. فَاجْتَنِبُوا الرِّجْسَ مِنَ الْأَوْثٰنِ وَاجْتَنِبُوا قَوْلَ الزُّورِ ﴿٣٠﴾

11. اِدْفَعْ بِالَّتِي هِيَ أَحْسَنُ السَّيِّئَةَ ۚ

12. وَلَا يَأْتَلِ أُولُوا الْفَضْلِ مِنْكُمْ وَالسَّعَةِ
أَنْ يُّؤْتُوا أُولِي الْقُرْبٰى وَالْمَسٰكِيْنَ
وَالْمُهٰجِرِيْنَ فِي سَبِيْلِ اللّٰهِ ۖ وَلْيَعْفُوا
وَلْيَصْفَحُوا ۗ أَلَا تُحِبُّوْنَ أَنْ يَّغْفِرَ
اللّٰهُ لَكُمْ ۗ وَاللّٰهُ غَفُوْرٌ رَّحِيْمٌ ﴿٢٢﴾

13. يٰأَيُّهَا الَّذِيْنَ اٰمَنُوْا لِيَسْتَأْذِنْكُمُ
الَّذِيْنَ مَلَكَتْ أَيْمَانُكُمْ وَالَّذِيْنَ لَمْ
يَبْلُغُوا الْحُلُمَ مِنْكُمْ ثَلٰثَ مَرّٰتٍ ۚ مِنْ
قَبْلِ صَلٰوةِ الْفَجْرِ وَحِيْنَ تَضَعُوْنَ
ثِيَابَكُمْ مِّنَ الظَّهِيْرَةِ وَمِنْ بَعْدِ صَلٰوةِ
الْعِشَآءِ ۚ ثَلٰثُ عَوْرٰتٍ لَّكُمْ ۚ لَيْسَ
عَلَيْكُمْ وَلَا عَلَيْهِمْ جُنَاحٌ ۢ بَعْدَهُنَّ ۚ
طَوّٰفُوْنَ عَلَيْكُمْ بَعْضُكُمْ عَلٰى بَعْضٍ ۚ
كَذٰلِكَ يُبَيِّنُ اللّٰهُ لَكُمُ الْاٰيٰتِ ۗ
وَاللّٰهُ عَلِيْمٌ حَكِيْمٌ ﴿٥٨﴾

14. وَعِبَادُ الرَّحْمٰنِ الَّذِيْنَ يَمْشُوْنَ عَلَى الْأَرْضِ هَوْنًا

14. The (faithful) slaves of the Beneficent are they who walk upon the earth modestly and when

the foolish ones address them answer: Peace!

25:63

15. And when they hear vanity they withdraw from it and say: Unto us our works and unto you your works. Peace be unto you! We desire not the ignorant.

28:55

16. And argue not with the People of the Scripture unless it be in (a way) that is better, save with such of them as do wrong, and say: We believe in that which hath been revealed unto us and revealed unto you; our God and your God is One, and unto Him we surrender.

29:46

17. Turn not thy cheek in scorn toward folk, nor walk with pertness in the land. Lo! Allah loveth not each braggart boaster.

Be modest in thy bearing and subdue thy voice. Lo! the harshest of all voices is the voice of the ass.

31:18–19

18. And who is better in speech than him who prayeth unto his Lord and doth right and saith: Lo! I am of those who surrender (unto Him).

The good deed and the evil deed are not alike. Repel the evil deed with one which

وَإِذَا خَاطَبَهُمُ الْجَٰهِلُونَ قَالُوا سَلَٰمًا ﴿٦٣﴾

15. وَإِذَا سَمِعُوا اللَّغْوَ أَعْرَضُوا عَنْهُ وَقَالُوا لَنَا أَعْمَٰلُنَا
وَلَكُمْ أَعْمَٰلُكُمْ سَلَٰمٌ عَلَيْكُمْ لَا نَبْتَغِي الْجَٰهِلِينَ ﴿٥٥﴾

16. وَلَا تُجَٰدِلُوا أَهْلَ الْكِتَٰبِ إِلَّا بِالَّتِي
هِيَ أَحْسَنُ إِلَّا الَّذِينَ ظَلَمُوا مِنْهُمْ
وَقُولُوا آمَنَّا بِالَّذِي أُنْزِلَ إِلَيْنَا وَ
أُنْزِلَ إِلَيْكُمْ وَإِلَٰهُنَا وَإِلَٰهُكُمْ وَاحِدٌ
وَنَحْنُ لَهُ مُسْلِمُونَ ﴿٤٦﴾

17. وَلَا تُصَعِّرْ خَدَّكَ لِلنَّاسِ وَلَا تَمْشِ فِي الْأَرْضِ
مَرَحًا إِنَّ اللَّهَ لَا يُحِبُّ كُلَّ مُخْتَالٍ فَخُورٍ ﴿١٨﴾
وَاقْصِدْ فِي مَشْيِكَ وَاغْضُضْ مِنْ
صَوْتِكَ إِنَّ أَنْكَرَ الْأَصْوَاتِ
لَصَوْتُ الْحَمِيرِ ﴿١٩﴾

18. وَمَنْ أَحْسَنُ قَوْلًا مِمَّنْ دَعَا إِلَى
اللَّهِ وَعَمِلَ صَٰلِحًا وَقَالَ إِنَّنِي مِنَ
الْمُسْلِمِينَ ﴿٣٣﴾
وَلَا تَسْتَوِي الْحَسَنَةُ وَلَا السَّيِّئَةُ
ادْفَعْ بِالَّتِي هِيَ أَحْسَنُ فَإِذَا الَّذِي
بَيْنَكَ وَبَيْنَهُ عَدَٰوَةٌ كَأَنَّهُ وَلِيٌّ حَمِيمٌ ﴿٣٤﴾
وَمَا يُلَقَّىٰهَا إِلَّا الَّذِينَ صَبَرُوا وَمَا
يُلَقَّىٰهَا إِلَّا ذُو حَظٍّ عَظِيمٍ ﴿٣٥﴾
وَإِمَّا يَنْزَغَنَّكَ مِنَ الشَّيْطَٰنِ نَزْغٌ
فَاسْتَعِذْ بِاللَّهِ إِنَّهُ هُوَ السَّمِيعُ الْعَلِيمُ ﴿٣٦﴾

is better, then lo! he, between whom and thee there was enmity (will become) as though he was a bosom friend.

But none is granted it save those who are steadfast, and none is granted it save the owner of great happiness.

And if a whisper from the devil reach thee (O Muhammad) then seek refuge in Allah. Lo! He is the Hearer, the Knower.

41:33–36

19. And those who shun the worst of sins and indecencies and, when they are wroth, forgive.

And those who answer the call of their Lord and establish worship, and whose affairs are a matter of counsel, and who spend of what We have bestowed on them.

And those who, when great wrong is done to them, defend themselves.

The guerdon of an ill-deed is an ill the like thereof. But whosoever pardoneth and amendeth, his wage is the affair of Allah. Lo! He loveth not wrong-doers.

And whoso defendeth himself after he hath suffered wrong—for such, there is no way (of blame) against them.

The way (of blame) is only against those who oppress mankind, and wrongfully rebel in the earth. For such there is a painful doom.

And verily whoso is patient and forgiveth—lo! that, verily, is (of) the steadfast heart of things.

42:37–43

20. Then bear with them (O Muhammad) and say: Peace! But they will come

19. وَالَّذِيْنَ يَجْتَنِبُوْنَ كَبٰٓئِرَ الْاِثْمِ وَالْفَوَاحِشَ وَ
اِذَا مَا غَضِبُوْا هُمْ يَغْفِرُوْنَ ﴿٣٧﴾

وَالَّذِيْنَ اسْتَجَابُوْا لِرَبِّهِمْ وَاَقَامُوا
الصَّلٰوةَ وَاَمْرُهُمْ شُوْرٰى بَيْنَهُمْ
وَمِمَّا رَزَقْنٰهُمْ يُنْفِقُوْنَ ﴿٣٨﴾
وَالَّذِيْنَ اِذَآ اَصَابَهُمُ الْبَغْيُ هُمْ
يَنْتَصِرُوْنَ ﴿٣٩﴾
وَجَزٰٓؤُا سَيِّئَةٍ سَيِّئَةٌ مِّثْلُهَا فَمَنْ
عَفَا وَاَصْلَحَ فَاَجْرُهٗ عَلَى اللّٰهِ اِنَّهٗ
لَا يُحِبُّ الظّٰلِمِيْنَ ﴿٤٠﴾

وَلَمَنِ انْتَصَرَ بَعْدَ ظُلْمِهٖ فَاُولٰٓئِكَ
مَا عَلَيْهِمْ مِّنْ سَبِيْلٍ ﴿٤١﴾

اِنَّمَا السَّبِيْلُ عَلَى الَّذِيْنَ يَظْلِمُوْنَ
النَّاسَ وَيَبْغُوْنَ فِي الْاَرْضِ بِغَيْرِ
الْحَقِّ اُولٰٓئِكَ لَهُمْ عَذَابٌ اَلِيْمٌ ﴿٤٢﴾
وَلَمَنْ صَبَرَ وَغَفَرَ اِنَّ ذٰلِكَ لَمِنْ
عَزْمِ الْاُمُوْرِ ﴿٤٣﴾

20. فَاصْفَحْ عَنْهُمْ وَقُلْ سَلٰمٌ
فَسَوْفَ يَعْلَمُوْنَ ﴿٨٩﴾

21. يٰٓاَيُّهَا الَّذِيْنَ اٰمَنُوْا لَا يَسْخَرْ قَوْمٌ
مِّنْ قَوْمٍ عَسٰٓى اَنْ يَّكُوْنُوْا خَيْرًا
مِّنْهُمْ وَلَا نِسَآءٌ مِّنْ نِّسَآءٍ عَسٰٓى
اَنْ يَّكُنَّ خَيْرًا مِّنْهُنَّ وَلَا تَلْمِزُوْٓا

to know.

43:89

21. O ye who believe! Let not a folk deride a folk who may be better than they (are), nor let women (deride) women who may be

better than they are; neither defame one another, nor insult one another by nicknames. Bad is the name of lewdness after faith. And whoso turneth not in repentance such are evil—doers.

O ye who believe! Shun much suspicion; for lo! some suspicion is a crime. And spy not, neither backbite one another. Would one of you love to eat the flesh of his dead brother? Ye abhor that (so abhor the other)! And keep your duty (to Allah). Lo! Allah is Relenting, Merciful.

49:11–12

22. Those who avoid enor—mities of sin and abominat—ions, save the unwilled off—ences—(for them) lo! thy Lord is of vast mercy. He is Best Aware of you (from the time) when He created you from the earth, and when ye were hidden in the bellies of your mothers. Therefor ascribe not purity unto yourselves. He is Best Aware of him who ward—eth off (evil).

53:32

23. O ye who believe! When it is said unto you, Make room in assemblies, then make room; Allah will make way for you (hereafter). And when it is said, Come up higher, go up higher; Allah will exalt those who believe among you, and those who have know—

أَنفُسَكُمْ وَلَا تَنَابَزُوا بِالْأَلْقَابِ ۖ
بِئْسَ الِاسْمُ الْفُسُوقُ بَعْدَ الْإِيمَانِ ۚ
وَمَن لَّمْ يَتُبْ فَأُولَٰئِكَ هُمُ الظَّالِمُونَ ﴿١١﴾
يَا أَيُّهَا الَّذِينَ آمَنُوا اجْتَنِبُوا كَثِيرًا
مِّنَ الظَّنِّ إِنَّ بَعْضَ الظَّنِّ إِثْمٌ ۖ وَلَا
تَجَسَّسُوا وَلَا يَغْتَب بَّعْضُكُم بَعْضًا ۚ
أَيُحِبُّ أَحَدُكُمْ أَن يَأْكُلَ لَحْمَ أَخِيهِ
مَيْتًا فَكَرِهْتُمُوهُ ۚ وَاتَّقُوا اللَّهَ ۚ إِنَّ
اللَّهَ تَوَّابٌ رَّحِيمٌ ﴿١٢﴾

22. الَّذِينَ يَجْتَنِبُونَ كَبَائِرَ الْإِثْمِ
وَالْفَوَاحِشَ إِلَّا اللَّمَمَ ۚ إِنَّ رَبَّكَ
وَاسِعُ الْمَغْفِرَةِ ۚ هُوَ أَعْلَمُ بِكُمْ إِذْ
أَنشَأَكُم مِّنَ الْأَرْضِ وَإِذْ أَنتُمْ أَجِنَّةٌ
فِي بُطُونِ أُمَّهَاتِكُمْ ۖ فَلَا تُزَكُّوا أَنفُسَكُمْ ۖ
هُوَ أَعْلَمُ بِمَنِ اتَّقَىٰ ﴿٣٢﴾

23. يَا أَيُّهَا الَّذِينَ آمَنُوا إِذَا قِيلَ لَكُمْ
تَفَسَّحُوا فِي الْمَجَالِسِ فَافْسَحُوا يَفْسَحِ
اللَّهُ لَكُمْ ۖ وَإِذَا قِيلَ انشُزُوا فَانشُزُوا
يَرْفَعِ اللَّهُ الَّذِينَ آمَنُوا مِنكُمْ وَالَّذِينَ
أُوتُوا الْعِلْمَ دَرَجَاتٍ ۚ وَاللَّهُ بِمَا
تَعْمَلُونَ خَبِيرٌ ﴿١١﴾

24. وَإِن تَعْفُوا وَتَصْفَحُوا وَتَغْفِرُوا فَإِنَّ
اللَّهَ غَفُورٌ رَّحِيمٌ ﴿١٤﴾

ledge, to high ranks. Allah is Informed of what ye do.

58:11

24. And if ye efface and overlook and forgive, then lo! Allah is Forgiving, Merci—ful.

64:14

25. And those who keep their pledges and their covenant,

And those who stand by their testimony

And those who are attentive at their worship,

These will dwell in Gardens, honoured.

70:32–35

25. وَالَّذِينَ هُمْ لِأَمَانَاتِهِمْ وَعَهْدِهِمْ رَاعُونَ ﴿٣٢﴾
وَالَّذِينَ هُم بِشَهَادَاتِهِمْ قَائِمُونَ ﴿٣٣﴾
وَالَّذِينَ هُمْ عَلَىٰ صَلَاتِهِمْ يُحَافِظُونَ ﴿٣٤﴾
أُولَٰئِكَ فِي جَنَّاتٍ مُّكْرَمُونَ ﴿٣٥﴾

MORNING AND EVENING

1. He is the Cleaver of the Daybreak, and He hath appointed the night for stillness, and the sun and the moon for reckoning. That is the measuring of the Mighty, the Wise.

6:97

1. فَالِقُ الْإِصْبَاحِ وَجَعَلَ اللَّيْلَ سَكَنًا وَالشَّمْسَ
وَالْقَمَرَ حُسْبَانًا ذَٰلِكَ تَقْدِيرُ الْعَزِيزِ الْعَلِيمِ ﴿٩٦﴾

2. So glory be to Allah when ye enter the night and when ye enter the morning.

Unto Him be praise in the heavens and the earth! – and at the sun's decline and in the noonday.

30:17–18

2. فَسُبْحَانَ اللَّهِ حِينَ تُمْسُونَ وَحِينَ
تُصْبِحُونَ ﴿١٧﴾
وَلَهُ الْحَمْدُ فِي السَّمَاوَاتِ وَالْأَرْضِ
وَعَشِيًّا وَحِينَ تُظْهِرُونَ ﴿١٨﴾

3. O ye who believe! Remember Allah with much remembrance.

And glorify Him early and late.

33:41–42

3. يَا أَيُّهَا الَّذِينَ آمَنُوا اذْكُرُوا اللَّهَ ذِكْرًا
كَثِيرًا ﴿٤١﴾
وَسَبِّحُوهُ بُكْرَةً وَأَصِيلًا ﴿٤٢﴾

4. Nay, by the Moon

And the night when it withdraweth

And the dawn when it shineth forth,

Lo! this is one of the greatest (portents)

74:32–35

4. كَلَّا وَالْقَمَرِ ﴿٣٢﴾
وَاللَّيْلِ إِذْ أَدْبَرَ ﴿٣٣﴾
وَالصُّبْحِ إِذَا أَسْفَرَ ﴿٣٤﴾
إِنَّهَا لَإِحْدَى الْكُبَرِ ﴿٣٥﴾

MORALS

Ref: 17:31–33; 18:23–24; 20:131; 46:15; 70:32–35; 74:3–7; 79:40–41; 90:12–17; 91:9; 92: 5–7; 93:9–11; 99:7–8.

See also: Good Behaviour, Etiquettes of Society, Etiquettes of Speech.

MOSQUES

1. And who doth greater wrong than he who forbiddeth the approach to the sanctuaries of Allah lest His name should be mentioned therein, and striveth for their ruin? As for such, it was never meant that they should enter them except in fear. Theirs in the world is ignominy and theirs in the Hereafter is an awful doom.

2:114

2. Whencesoever thou comest forth turn thy face toward the Inviolable Place of Worship; and wheresoever ye may be (O Muslims) turn your faces towards it (when ye pray) so that men may have no argument against you, save such of them as do injustice— Fear them not, but fear Me!— and so that I may complete My grace upon you, and that ye may be guided.

2:150

3. Say: My Lord enjoineth justice. And set your faces, upright (toward Him) at every place of worship and call upon Him, making religion pure for Him (only). As He brought you into being, so return ye (unto Him).

7:29

4. O Children of Adam! Look to your adornment at every place of worship, and eat and drink, but be not prodigal. Lo! He loveth not the prodigals.

7:31

1. وَمَنْ أَظْلَمُ مِمَّنْ مَّنَعَ مَسٰجِدَ اللّٰهِ اَنْ يُّذْكَرَ
فِيْهَا اسْمُهٗ وَسَعٰى فِيْ خَرَابِهَا ؕ اُولٰٓئِكَ مَا كَانَ
لَهُمْ اَنْ يَّدْخُلُوْهَآ اِلَّا خَآئِفِيْنَ ؕ لَهُمْ فِى
الدُّنْيَا خِزْيٌ وَّلَهُمْ فِى الْاٰخِرَةِ عَذَابٌ عَظِيْمٌ ﴿۱۱۴﴾

2. وَمِنْ حَيْثُ خَرَجْتَ فَوَلِّ وَجْهَكَ
شَطْرَ الْمَسْجِدِ الْحَرَامِ ؕ وَحَيْثُ مَا كُنْتُمْ
فَوَلُّوْا وُجُوْهَكُمْ شَطْرَهٗ ۙ لِئَلَّا يَكُوْنَ لِلنَّاسِ
عَلَيْكُمْ حُجَّةٌ ۙ اِلَّا الَّذِيْنَ ظَلَمُوْا مِنْهُمْ
فَلَا تَخْشَوْهُمْ وَاخْشَوْنِيْ ۙ وَلِاُتِمَّ نِعْمَتِيْ
عَلَيْكُمْ وَلَعَلَّكُمْ تَهْتَدُوْنَ ﴿۱۵۰﴾

3. قُلْ اَمَرَ رَبِّيْ بِالْقِسْطِ ۙ وَاَقِيْمُوْا وُجُوْهَكُمْ
عِنْدَ كُلِّ مَسْجِدٍ وَّادْعُوْهُ مُخْلِصِيْنَ لَهُ الدِّيْنَ ؕ
كَمَا بَدَاَكُمْ تَعُوْدُوْنَ ﴿۲۹﴾

4. يٰبَنِيْٓ اٰدَمَ خُذُوْا زِيْنَتَكُمْ عِنْدَ كُلِّ
مَسْجِدٍ وَّكُلُوْا وَاشْرَبُوْا وَلَا تُسْرِفُوْا ۚ
اِنَّهٗ لَا يُحِبُّ الْمُسْرِفِيْنَ ﴿۳۱﴾

5. مَا كَانَ لِلْمُشْرِكِيْنَ اَنْ يَّعْمُرُوْا مَسٰجِدَ
اللّٰهِ شٰهِدِيْنَ عَلٰٓى اَنْفُسِهِمْ بِالْكُفْرِ ؕ اُولٰٓئِكَ
حَبِطَتْ اَعْمَالُهُمْ ۚۖ وَفِى النَّارِ هُمْ خٰلِدُوْنَ ﴿۱۷﴾
اِنَّمَا يَعْمُرُ مَسٰجِدَ اللّٰهِ مَنْ اٰمَنَ بِاللّٰهِ
وَالْيَوْمِ الْاٰخِرِ وَاَقَامَ الصَّلٰوةَ وَاٰتَى الزَّكٰوةَ
وَلَمْ يَخْشَ اِلَّا اللّٰهَ فَعَسٰٓى اُولٰٓئِكَ اَنْ يَّكُوْنُوْا
مِنَ الْمُهْتَدِيْنَ ﴿۱۸﴾

5. It is not for the idolaters to tend Allah's sanctuaries, bearing witness against themselves of disbelief. As for such, their works are vain and in the Fire they will abide.

He only shall tend Allah's sanctuaries who believeth in Allah and the Last Day and observeth proper worship and payeth the poor—due and feareth none save Allah. For such (only) is it possible that they can be of the rightly guided.

Count ye the slaking of a pilgrim's thirst and tendance of the Inviolable Place of Worship as (equal to the worth of him) who believeth in Allah and the Last Day, and striveth in the way of Allah? They are not equal in the sight of Allah. Allah guideth not wrongdoing folk.

9:17–19

6. And as for those who chose a place of worship out of opposition and disbelief, and in order to cause dissent among the believers, and as an outpost for those who warred against Allah and His messenger aforetime, they will surely swear: We purposed naught save good. Allah beareth witness that they verily are liars.

Never stand (to pray) there. A place of worship which was founded upon duty (to Allah) from the first day is more worthy that thou shouldst stand (to pray) therein, wherein are men who love to purify themselves. Allah loveth the purifiers.

9:107–108

7. Lo! those who disbelieve and bar (men) from the way of Allah and from the Inviolable Place of Worship, which We have appointed

أَجَعَلْتُمْ سِقَايَةَ الْحَاجِّ وَعِمَارَةَ الْمَسْجِدِ
الْحَرَامِ كَمَنْ آمَنَ بِاللّٰهِ وَالْيَوْمِ الْآخِرِ
وَجٰهَدَ فِيْ سَبِيْلِ اللّٰهِ ۭ لَا يَسْتَوٗنَ عِنْدَ
اللّٰهِ ۭ وَاللّٰهُ لَا يَهْدِي الْقَوْمَ الظّٰلِمِيْنَ ۝١٩

6. وَالَّذِيْنَ اتَّخَذُوْا مَسْجِدًا ضِرَارًا وَّ
كُفْرًا وَّتَفْرِيْقًا بَيْنَ الْمُؤْمِنِيْنَ وَإِرْصَادًا
لِّمَنْ حَارَبَ اللّٰهَ وَرَسُوْلَهٗ مِنْ قَبْلُ ۭ
وَلَيَحْلِفُنَّ إِنْ أَرَدْنَآ إِلَّا الْحُسْنٰى ۭ وَ
اللّٰهُ يَشْهَدُ إِنَّهُمْ لَكٰذِبُوْنَ ۝١٠٧
لَا تَقُمْ فِيْهِ أَبَدًا ۭ لَمَسْجِدٌ أُسِّسَ
عَلَى التَّقْوٰى مِنْ أَوَّلِ يَوْمٍ أَحَقُّ أَنْ
تَقُوْمَ فِيْهِ ۭ فِيْهِ رِجَالٌ يُّحِبُّوْنَ أَنْ
يَّتَطَهَّرُوْا ۭ وَاللّٰهُ يُحِبُّ الْمُطَّهِّرِيْنَ ۝١٠٨

7. إِنَّ الَّذِيْنَ كَفَرُوْا وَيَصُدُّوْنَ عَنْ سَبِيْلِ
اللّٰهِ وَالْمَسْجِدِ الْحَرَامِ الَّذِيْ جَعَلْنٰهُ
لِلنَّاسِ سَوَآءَ ۨ الْعَاكِفُ فِيْهِ وَالْبَادِ ۭ
وَمَنْ يُّرِدْ فِيْهِ بِإِلْحَادٍ بِظُلْمٍ نُّذِقْهُ
مِنْ عَذَابٍ أَلِيْمٍ ۝٢٥

for mankind together, the dwellers therein and the nomad; whosoever seeketh wrongful partiality therein, him We shall cause to taste a painful doom.

22:25

Ref: 2:187, 217; 5:2; 22:39-40; 24:36-37; 72:18.

See also: *K'abah*, *Quba* Mosque.

MOTHERS OF THE FAITHFUL

1. The Prophet is closer to the believers than their selves, and his wives are (as) their mothers. And the owners of kinship are closer one to another in the ordinance of Allah than (other) believers and the fugitives (who fled from Makkah), except that ye should do kindness to your friends. This is written in the Book (of nature).

33:6

2. O Prophet! Say unto thy wives: If ye desire the world's life and its adornment, come! I will content you and will release you with a fair release.

But if ye desire Allah and His messenger and the abode of the Hereafter, then lo! Allah hath prepared for the good among you an immense reward.

O ye wives of the Prophet! Whosoever of you committeth manifest lewdness, the punishment for her will be doubled, and that is easy for Allah.

And whosoever of you is submissive unto Allah and His messenger and doth right, We shall give her reward twice over, and We have prepared for her a rich provision.

O ye wives of the Prophet! Ye are not like any other women. If ye keep your duty (to Allah), then be not soft of speech, lest he in whose heart is a disease aspire (to you), but utter customary speech.

And stay in your houses. Bedizen not yourselves with the bedizenment of the Time of Ignorance. Be regular in prayer, and pay

1. النَّبِيُّ أَوْلَىٰ بِالْمُؤْمِنِينَ مِنْ أَنفُسِهِمْ
وَأَزْوَاجُهُ أُمَّهَاتُهُمْ وَأُولُو الْأَرْحَامِ
بَعْضُهُمْ أَوْلَىٰ بِبَعْضٍ فِي كِتَابِ اللَّهِ
مِنَ الْمُؤْمِنِينَ وَالْمُهَاجِرِينَ إِلَّا أَن
تَفْعَلُوا إِلَىٰ أَوْلِيَائِكُم مَّعْرُوفًا كَانَ
ذَٰلِكَ فِي الْكِتَابِ مَسْطُورًا ﴿٦﴾

2. يَا أَيُّهَا النَّبِيُّ قُل لِّأَزْوَاجِكَ إِن كُنتُنَّ
تُرِدْنَ الْحَيَاةَ الدُّنْيَا وَزِينَتَهَا
فَتَعَالَيْنَ أُمَتِّعْكُنَّ وَأُسَرِّحْكُنَّ
سَرَاحًا جَمِيلًا ﴿٢٨﴾
وَإِن كُنتُنَّ تُرِدْنَ اللَّهَ وَرَسُولَهُ
وَالدَّارَ الْآخِرَةَ فَإِنَّ اللَّهَ أَعَدَّ
لِلْمُحْسِنَاتِ مِنكُنَّ أَجْرًا عَظِيمًا ﴿٢٩﴾
يَا نِسَاءَ النَّبِيِّ مَن يَأْتِ مِنكُنَّ
بِفَاحِشَةٍ مُّبَيِّنَةٍ يُضَاعَفْ لَهَا الْعَذَابُ
ضِعْفَيْنِ وَكَانَ ذَٰلِكَ عَلَى اللَّهِ يَسِيرًا ﴿٣٠﴾
وَمَن يَقْنُتْ مِنكُنَّ لِلَّهِ وَرَسُولِهِ وَ
تَعْمَلْ صَالِحًا نُّؤْتِهَا أَجْرَهَا مَرَّتَيْنِ
وَأَعْتَدْنَا لَهَا رِزْقًا كَرِيمًا ﴿٣١﴾
يَا نِسَاءَ النَّبِيِّ لَسْتُنَّ كَأَحَدٍ مِّنَ
النِّسَاءِ إِنِ اتَّقَيْتُنَّ فَلَا تَخْضَعْنَ
بِالْقَوْلِ فَيَطْمَعَ الَّذِي فِي قَلْبِهِ
مَرَضٌ وَقُلْنَ قَوْلًا مَّعْرُوفًا ﴿٣٢﴾

the poor—due, and obey Allah and His messenger. Allah's wish is but to remove un—cleanness far from you, O Folk of the Household, and cleanse you with a thorough cleansing.

And bear in mind that which is recited in your houses of the revelations of Allah and wisdom. Lo! Allah is Subtile, Aware.

33:28—34

3. And when thou saidst unto him on whom Allah hath conferred favour and thou hast conferred favour: Keep thy wife to thyself, and fear Allah. And thou didst hide in thy mind that which Allah was to bring to light, and thou didst fear mankind whereas Allah had a better right that thou shouldst fear Him: So when Zeyd had performed the necessary formality (of di—vorce) from her, We gave her unto thee in marriage, so that (henceforth) there may be no sin for believers in respect of wives of their adopted sons, when the latter have performed the necessary formality (of release) from them. The commandment of Allah must be fulfilled.

33:37

4. And when ye ask of them (the wives of the Prophet) anything, ask it of them from behind a curtain. That is purer for your hearts and for their hearts. And it

وَقَرْنَ فِي بُيُوتِكُنَّ وَلَا تَبَرَّجْنَ
تَبَرُّجَ الْجَاهِلِيَّةِ الْأُولَىٰ وَأَقِمْنَ الصَّلَوٰةَ
وَآتِينَ الزَّكَوٰةَ وَأَطِعْنَ اللّٰهَ وَرَسُولَهُ
إِنَّمَا يُرِيدُ اللّٰهُ لِيُذْهِبَ عَنكُمُ
الرِّجْسَ أَهْلَ الْبَيْتِ وَيُطَهِّرَكُمْ تَطْهِيرًا ﴿٣٣﴾
وَاذْكُرْنَ مَا يُتْلَىٰ فِي بُيُوتِكُنَّ مِنْ
آيَاتِ اللّٰهِ وَالْحِكْمَةِ إِنَّ اللّٰهَ كَانَ
لَطِيفًا خَبِيرًا ﴿٣٤﴾

3. وَإِذْ تَقُولُ لِلَّذِي أَنْعَمَ اللّٰهُ عَلَيْهِ
وَأَنْعَمْتَ عَلَيْهِ أَمْسِكْ عَلَيْكَ زَوْجَكَ
وَاتَّقِ اللّٰهَ وَتُخْفِي فِي نَفْسِكَ مَا اللّٰهُ
مُبْدِيهِ وَتَخْشَى النَّاسَ وَاللّٰهُ أَحَقُّ
أَنْ تَخْشَاهُ فَلَمَّا قَضَىٰ زَيْدٌ مِنْهَا
وَطَرًا زَوَّجْنَاكَهَا لِكَيْ لَا يَكُونَ عَلَى
الْمُؤْمِنِينَ حَرَجٌ فِي أَزْوَاجِ أَدْعِيَائِهِمْ
إِذَا قَضَوْا مِنْهُنَّ وَطَرًا وَكَانَ
أَمْرُ اللّٰهِ مَفْعُولًا ﴿٣٧﴾

4. وَإِذَا سَأَلْتُمُوهُنَّ مَتَاعًا فَسْئَلُوهُنَّ مِنْ
وَرَاءِ حِجَابٍ ذَٰلِكُمْ أَطْهَرُ لِقُلُوبِكُمْ
وَقُلُوبِهِنَّ وَمَا كَانَ لَكُمْ أَنْ تُؤْذُوا
رَسُولَ اللّٰهِ وَلَا أَنْ تَنْكِحُوا أَزْوَاجَهُ
مِنْ بَعْدِهِ أَبَدًا إِنَّ ذَٰلِكُمْ كَانَ
عِنْدَ اللّٰهِ عَظِيمًا ﴿٥٣﴾

is not for you to cause anno—yance to the messenger of Allah, nor that ye should ever marry his wives after him. Lo! that in Allah's sight would be an enormity.

33:53

5. O Prophet! Tell thy wives and thy daughters and the women of the believers

to draw their cloaks close round them (when they go abroad). That will be better, so that they may be recognised and not annoyed. Allah is ever Forgiving, Merciful.
33:59

6. O Prophet! Why bannest thou that which Allah hath made lawful for thee, seeking to please thy wives? And Allah is Forgiving, Merciful.
66:1

7. When the Prophet confided a fact unto one of his wives and when she afterward divulged it and Allah apprised him thereof, he made known (to her) part thereof and passed over part. And when he told her all, she said: Who hath told thee? He said: The Knower, the Aware hath told me!

If ye twain turn unto Allah repentant, (ye have cause to do so) for your hearts desired (the ban) and if ye aid one another against him (Muhammad) then lo! Allah, even He, is his Protecting Friend, and Gabriel and the righteous among the believers; and, furthermore, the angels are his helpers.

It may happen that his Lord, if he divorce you, will give him in your stead wives better than you, submissive

5. يٰٓاَيُّهَا النَّبِيُّ قُلْ لِّاَزْوَاجِكَ وَبَنٰتِكَ
وَنِسَآءِ الْمُؤْمِنِيْنَ يُدْنِيْنَ عَلَيْهِنَّ
مِنْ جَلَابِيْبِهِنَّ ؕ ذٰلِكَ اَدْنٰٓى اَنْ
يُّعْرَفْنَ فَلَا يُؤْذَيْنَ ؕ وَكَانَ اللّٰهُ
غَفُوْرًا رَّحِيْمًا ﴿۵۹﴾

6. يٰٓاَيُّهَا النَّبِيُّ لِمَ تُحَرِّمُ مَآ اَحَلَّ
اللّٰهُ لَكَ ۚ تَبْتَغِيْ مَرْضَاتَ اَزْوَاجِكَ ؕ
وَاللّٰهُ غَفُوْرٌ رَّحِيْمٌ ﴿۱﴾

7. وَاِذْ اَسَرَّ النَّبِيُّ اِلٰى بَعْضِ اَزْوَاجِهٖ
حَدِيْثًا ۚ فَلَمَّا نَبَّاَتْ بِهٖ وَاَظْهَرَهُ
اللّٰهُ عَلَيْهِ عَرَّفَ بَعْضَهٗ وَاَعْرَضَ
عَنْۢ بَعْضٍ ۚ فَلَمَّا نَبَّاَهَا بِهٖ قَالَتْ
مَنْ اَنْۢبَاَكَ هٰذَا ؕ قَالَ نَبَّاَنِيَ
الْعَلِيْمُ الْخَبِيْرُ ﴿۳﴾

اِنْ تَتُوْبَآ اِلَى اللّٰهِ فَقَدْ صَغَتْ قُلُوْبُكُمَا ۚ
وَاِنْ تَظٰهَرَا عَلَيْهِ فَاِنَّ اللّٰهَ هُوَ مَوْلٰىهُ
وَجِبْرِيْلُ وَصَالِحُ الْمُؤْمِنِيْنَ ۚ
وَالْمَلٰٓئِكَةُ بَعْدَ ذٰلِكَ ظَهِيْرٌ ﴿۴﴾

عَسٰى رَبُّهٗٓ اِنْ طَلَّقَكُنَّ اَنْ يُّبْدِلَهٗٓ
اَزْوَاجًا خَيْرًا مِّنْكُنَّ مُسْلِمٰتٍ مُّؤْمِنٰتٍ
قٰنِتٰتٍ تٰٓئِبٰتٍ عٰبِدٰتٍ سٰٓئِحٰتٍ
ثَيِّبٰتٍ وَّاَبْكَارًا ﴿۵﴾

(to Allah), believing, pious, penitent, inclined to fasting, widows and maids.
66:3–5

Ref: 33:35–36,38,50–52,55.

See also: Members of Prophet's Family.

MOUNTAINS

1. And Allah hath given you, of that which He hath created, shelter from the sun; and hath given you places of refuge in the mountains,
16:81

2. Hast thou not seen that unto Allah payeth adoration whosoever is in the heavens and whosoever is in the earth, and the sun, and the moon, and the stars, and the hills, and the trees, and the beasts, and many of mankind.
22:18

3. And thou seest the hills thou deemest solid flying with the flight of clouds: the doing of Allah Who perfecteth all things. Lo! He is Informed of what ye do.
27:88

4. Have We not made the earth an expanse,
And the high hills bulwarks?
78:6–7

5. A day wherein mankind will be as thickly–scattered moths
And the mountains will become as carded wool.
101:4–5

1. وَاللّٰهُ جَعَلَ لَكُمْ مِّمَّا خَلَقَ ظِلٰلًا وَّجَعَلَ
لَكُمْ مِّنَ الْجِبَالِ اَكْنَانًا

2. اَلَمْ تَرَ اَنَّ اللّٰهَ يَسْجُدُ لَهٗ مَنْ فِى
السَّمٰوٰتِ وَمَنْ فِى الْاَرْضِ وَالشَّمْسُ
وَالْقَمَرُ وَالنُّجُوْمُ وَالْجِبَالُ وَالشَّجَرُ
وَالدَّوَآبُّ وَكَثِيْرٌ مِّنَ النَّاسِ ؕ

3. وَتَرَى الْجِبَالَ تَحْسَبُهَا جَامِدَةً وَّهِىَ
تَمُرُّ مَرَّ السَّحَابِ ؕ صُنْعَ اللّٰهِ الَّذِىْٓ
اَتْقَنَ كُلَّ شَىْءٍ ؕ اِنَّهٗ خَبِيْرٌۢ بِمَا تَفْعَلُوْنَ ﴿۸۸﴾

4. اَلَمْ نَجْعَلِ الْاَرْضَ مِهٰدًا ۙ﴿۶﴾
وَّالْجِبَالَ اَوْتَادًا ۙ﴿۷﴾

5. يَوْمَ يَكُوْنُ النَّاسُ كَالْفَرَاشِ
الْمَبْثُوْثِ ۙ﴿۴﴾
وَتَكُوْنُ الْجِبَالُ كَالْعِهْنِ الْمَنْفُوْشِ ؕ﴿۵﴾

Ref: 2:260; 7:74,143,171; 11:42–43; 13:31; 14:46; 15:82; 16:68; 17:37; 18:47; 19:90; 20:105; 21:79; 24:43; 26:149; 33:72; 34:10; 35:27; 38:18; 52:10; 56:5; 59:21; 69:14; 70:9; 73:14; 77:10; 78:20; 79:32; 81:3; 88:19.

See also: Names of Mountains.

MUBAHALA H

1. (This is) the truth from thy Lord (O Muhammad), so be not thou of those who waver.

And whoso disputeth with thee concerning him, after the knowledge which hath come unto thee, say (unto him): Come! We will summon our sons and your sons, and our women and your women, and ourselves and yourselves, then we will pray humbly (to our Lord) and (solemnly) invoke the curse of Allah upon those who lie.

Lo! This verily is the true narrative. There is no God save Allah and lo! Allah He verily is, is the Mighty, the Wise.

3:60–62

MURDER

1. They question thee (O Muhammad) with regard to warfare in the sacred month. Say: Warfare therein is a great (transgression), but to turn (men) from the way of Allah, and to disbelieve in Him and in the Inviolable Place of Worship, and to expel His people thence, is greater with Allah; for persecution is worse than killing.

2:217

2. It is not for a believer to kill a believer unless (it be) by mistake, He who hath killed a believer by mistake must set free a be–

1. اَلْحَقُّ مِنْ رَّبِّكَ فَلَا تَكُنْ مِّنَ الْمُمْتَرِيْنَ
فَمَنْ حَآجَّكَ فِيْهِ مِنْۢ بَعْدِ مَا جَآءَكَ
مِنَ الْعِلْمِ فَقُلْ تَعَالَوْا نَدْعُ اَبْنَآءَنَا
وَاَبْنَآءَكُمْ وَنِسَآءَنَا وَنِسَآءَكُمْ وَاَنْفُسَنَا
وَاَنْفُسَكُمْ ثُمَّ نَبْتَهِلْ فَنَجْعَلْ لَّعْنَتَ
اللّٰهِ عَلَى الْكٰذِبِيْنَ ○
اِنَّ هٰذَا لَهُوَ الْقَصَصُ الْحَقُّ ۚ وَمَا مِنْ اِلٰهٍ
اِلَّا اللّٰهُ ۗ وَاِنَّ اللّٰهَ لَهُوَ الْعَزِيْزُ الْحَكِيْمُ ○

1. يَسْـَٔلُوْنَكَ عَنِ الشَّهْرِ الْحَرَامِ قِتَالٍ فِيْهِ ۭ
قُلْ قِتَالٌ فِيْهِ كَبِيْرٌ ۭ وَصَدٌّ عَنْ سَبِيْلِ
اللّٰهِ وَكُفْرٌۢ بِهٖ وَالْمَسْجِدِ الْحَرَامِ ۤ وَاِخْرَاجُ
اَهْلِهٖ مِنْهُ اَكْبَرُ عِنْدَ اللّٰهِ ۚ وَالْفِتْنَةُ
اَكْبَرُ مِنَ الْقَتْلِ ۭ

2. وَمَا كَانَ لِمُؤْمِنٍ اَنْ يَّقْتُلَ مُؤْمِنًا اِلَّا
خَطَـًٔا ۚ وَمَنْ قَتَلَ مُؤْمِنًا خَطَـًٔا فَتَحْرِيْرُ
رَقَبَةٍ مُّؤْمِنَةٍ وَّدِيَةٌ مُّسَلَّمَةٌ اِلٰٓى اَهْلِهٖٓ
اِلَّآ اَنْ يَّصَّدَّقُوْا ۭ فَاِنْ كَانَ مِنْ قَوْمٍ عَدُوٍّ
لَّكُمْ وَهُوَ مُؤْمِنٌ فَتَحْرِيْرُ رَقَبَةٍ مُّؤْمِنَةٍ ۭ
وَاِنْ كَانَ مِنْ قَوْمٍۢ بَيْنَكُمْ وَبَيْنَهُمْ مِّيْثَاقٌ
فَدِيَةٌ مُّسَلَّمَةٌ اِلٰٓى اَهْلِهٖ وَتَحْرِيْرُ رَقَبَةٍ
مُّؤْمِنَةٍ ۚ فَمَنْ لَّمْ يَجِدْ فَصِيَامُ شَهْرَيْنِ

lieving slave and pay the blood–money to the family of the slain, unless they remit it as a charity. If he (the victim) be of a people hostile unto you, and he is a believer, then (the penance) is to set free a believing slave. And if he cometh of a folk between whom and you there is a covenant,

مُتَتَابِعَيْنِ تَوْبَةً مِّنَ اللّٰهِ ۗ وَكَانَ اللّٰهُ
عَلِيْمًا حَكِيْمًا ﴿٩٢﴾
وَمَنْ يَّقْتُلْ مُؤْمِنًا مُّتَعَمِّدًا فَجَزَآؤُهٗ
جَهَنَّمُ خٰلِدًا فِيْهَا وَغَضِبَ اللّٰهُ عَلَيْهِ
وَلَعَنَهٗ وَاَعَدَّ لَهٗ عَذَابًا عَظِيْمًا ﴿٩٣﴾

then the blood—money must be paid unto his folk and (also) a believing slave must be set free. And whoso hath not the wherewithal must fast two consecutive months. A penance from Allah. Allah is Knower, Wise.

Whoso slayeth a believer of set purpose, his reward is Hell for ever. Allah is wroth against him and He hath cursed him and prepared for him an awful doom.

4:92—93

3. كَتَبْنَا عَلٰى بَنِيْٓ اِسْرَآءِيْلَ اَنَّهٗ مَنْ قَتَلَ
نَفْسًا بِغَيْرِ نَفْسٍ اَوْ فَسَادٍ فِى الْاَرْضِ
فَكَاَنَّمَا قَتَلَ النَّاسَ جَمِيْعًا ۗ وَمَنْ
اَحْيَاهَا فَكَاَنَّمَآ اَحْيَا النَّاسَ جَمِيْعًا ۗ

3. We decreed for the Children of Israel that whosoever killeth a human being for other than man—slaughter or corruption in the earth, it shall be as if he had killed all mankind, and whoso saveth the life of one, it shall be as if he had saved the life of all mankind.

5:32

4. وَلَا تَقْتُلُوا النَّفْسَ الَّتِىْ حَرَّمَ اللّٰهُ اِلَّا
بِالْحَقِّ ۗ وَمَنْ قُتِلَ مَظْلُوْمًا فَقَدْ
جَعَلْنَا لِوَلِيِّهٖ سُلْطٰنًا فَلَا يُسْرِفْ فِّى
الْقَتْلِ ۗ اِنَّهٗ كَانَ مَنْصُوْرًا ﴿٣٣﴾

4. And slay not the life which Allah hath forbidden save with right. Whoso is slain wrongfully, We have given power unto his heir, but let him not commit excess in slaying. Lo! he will be helped.

17:33

Ref: 2:178; 4:29; 5:32-33; 25:68.

See also: Blood Money, *Hudud*, *Qisas*.

MUSLIM NATION

1. Our Lord! And make us submissive unto Thee and of our seed a nation submissive unto Thee, and show us our ways of worship, and relent toward us. Lo! Thou, only Thou, art the Relenting, the Merciful.

2:128

2. And I am commanded to be of those who surrender (unto Him).

10:72

3. And strive for Allah with the endeavour which is His right. He hath chosen you and hath not laid upon you in religion any hardship; the faith of your father Abraham (is yours). He hath named you Muslims of old time and in this (Scripture), that the messenger may be a witness against you, and that ye may be witnesses against mankind. So establish worship, pay the poor-due, and hold fast to Allah. He is your Protecting Friend. A blessed Patron and a blessed Helper!

22:78

1. رَبَّنَا وَاجْعَلْنَا مُسْلِمَيْنِ لَكَ وَمِنْ ذُرِّيَّتِنَآ
أُمَّةً مُّسْلِمَةً لَّكَ ۠ وَاَرِنَا مَنَاسِكَنَا وَتُبْ
عَلَيْنَا ۚ اِنَّكَ اَنْتَ التَّوَّابُ الرَّحِيْمُ ﴿١٢٨﴾

2. وَاُمِرْتُ اَنْ اَكُوْنَ مِنَ الْمُسْلِمِيْنَ ﴿٧٢﴾

3. وَجَاهِدُوْا فِي اللّٰهِ حَقَّ جِهَادِهٖ ؕ هُوَ
اجْتَبٰىكُمْ وَمَا جَعَلَ عَلَيْكُمْ فِي الدِّيْنِ
مِنْ حَرَجٍ ؕ مِلَّةَ اَبِيْكُمْ اِبْرٰهِيْمَ ؕ
هُوَ سَمّٰىكُمُ الْمُسْلِمِيْنَ ۙ۬ مِنْ قَبْلُ وَفِيْ
هٰذَا لِيَكُوْنَ الرَّسُوْلُ شَهِيْدًا عَلَيْكُمْ
وَتَكُوْنُوْا شُهَدَآءَ عَلَى النَّاسِ ۚۖ
فَاَقِيْمُوا الصَّلٰوةَ وَاٰتُوا الزَّكٰوةَ
وَاعْتَصِمُوْا بِاللّٰهِ ؕ هُوَ مَوْلٰىكُمْ ۚ فَنِعْمَ
الْمَوْلٰى وَنِعْمَ النَّصِيْرُ ﴿٧٨﴾

Ref: 2:133,136; 3:52,64,80,84,102; 5:114; 6:163; 7:126; 10:90; 11:14; 16:89,102; 27:31,38,42,81; 30:53; 33:35; 39:12; 41:32; 43:69.

See also: Mutual Relations of Muslims, Relations of Muslims with non-Muslims.

MUTUAL RELATIONS OF MUSLIMS

1. O ye who believe! Obey Allah, and obey the messenger and those of you who are in authority; and if ye have a dispute concerning any matter, refer it to Allah and the messenger if ye are (in truth) believers in Allah and the Last Day. That is better and more seemly in the end.

4:59

2. Whoso interveneth in a good cause will have the reward thereof, and whoso interveneth in an evil cause will bear the consequence thereof. Allah overseeth all things.

When ye are greeted with a greeting, greet ye with better than it or return it. Lo! Allah taketh count of all things.

4:85–86

3. Those who believed and left their homes and strove for the cause of Allah, and those who took them in and helped them—these are the believers in truth. For them is pardon, and a bountiful provision.

8:74

4. Muhammad is the messenger of Allah. And those with him are hard against the disbelievers and merciful among themselves. Thou (O Muhammad) seest them bowing and falling prostrate (in worship), seeking bounty from Allah and (His) acceptance.

48:29

5. And if two parties of believers fall to fighting, then make peace between them. And if one party of them doth wrong to the other, fight ye that which doth wrong till it return unto the ordinance of Allah; then if it return, make peace between them justly, and act equitably. Lo! Allah loveth the equitable.

The believers are naught else than brothers. Therefore make peace between your brethren and observe your duty to Allah that haply ye may obtain mercy.

49:9–10

1. يٰاَيُّهَا الَّذِيْنَ اٰمَنُوْا اَطِيْعُوا اللّٰهَ وَاَطِيْعُوا الرَّسُوْلَ وَ
اُولِي الْاَمْرِ مِنْكُمْ فَاِنْ تَنَازَعْتُمْ فِيْ شَيْءٍ فَرُدُّوْهُ اِلَى
اللّٰهِ وَالرَّسُوْلِ اِنْ كُنْتُمْ تُؤْمِنُوْنَ بِاللّٰهِ وَالْيَوْمِ
الْاٰخِرِ ذٰلِكَ خَيْرٌ وَّاَحْسَنُ تَاْوِيْلًا ﴿۵۹﴾

2. مَنْ يَّشْفَعْ شَفَاعَةً حَسَنَةً يَّكُنْ لَّهٗ نَصِيْبٌ
مِّنْهَا وَمَنْ يَّشْفَعْ شَفَاعَةً سَيِّئَةً يَّكُنْ لَّهٗ
كِفْلٌ مِّنْهَا وَكَانَ اللّٰهُ عَلٰى كُلِّ شَيْءٍ مُّقِيْتًا ﴿۸۵﴾
وَاِذَا حُيِّيْتُمْ بِتَحِيَّةٍ فَحَيُّوْا بِاَحْسَنَ مِنْهَا
اَوْ رُدُّوْهَا اِنَّ اللّٰهَ كَانَ عَلٰى كُلِّ شَيْءٍ حَسِيْبًا ﴿۸۶﴾

3. وَالَّذِيْنَ اٰمَنُوْا وَهَاجَرُوْا وَجٰهَدُوْا فِيْ سَبِيْلِ اللّٰهِ وَ
الَّذِيْنَ اٰوَوْا وَّنَصَرُوْا اُولٰٓئِكَ هُمُ الْمُؤْمِنُوْنَ حَقًّا
لَهُمْ مَّغْفِرَةٌ وَّرِزْقٌ كَرِيْمٌ ﴿۷۴﴾

4. مُحَمَّدٌ رَّسُوْلُ اللّٰهِ وَالَّذِيْنَ مَعَهٗٓ
اَشِدَّآءُ عَلَى الْكُفَّارِ رُحَمَآءُ بَيْنَهُمْ
تَرٰىهُمْ رُكَّعًا سُجَّدًا يَّبْتَغُوْنَ فَضْلًا
مِّنَ اللّٰهِ وَرِضْوَانًا

5. وَاِنْ طَآئِفَتٰنِ مِنَ الْمُؤْمِنِيْنَ اقْتَتَلُوْا فَاَصْلِحُوْا
بَيْنَهُمَا فَاِنْۢ بَغَتْ اِحْدٰىهُمَا عَلَى الْاُخْرٰى فَقَاتِلُوا
الَّتِيْ تَبْغِيْ حَتّٰى تَفِيْٓءَ اِلٰٓى اَمْرِ اللّٰهِ فَاِنْ فَآءَتْ
فَاَصْلِحُوْا بَيْنَهُمَا بِالْعَدْلِ وَاَقْسِطُوْا اِنَّ اللّٰهَ
يُحِبُّ الْمُقْسِطِيْنَ ﴿۹﴾
اِنَّمَا الْمُؤْمِنُوْنَ اِخْوَةٌ فَاَصْلِحُوْا بَيْنَ اَخَوَيْكُمْ
وَاتَّقُوا اللّٰهَ لَعَلَّكُمْ تُرْحَمُوْنَ ﴿۱۰﴾

Ref: 4:93; 5:54; 8:1,45-46,72; 49:12; 59:10

NAMES OF FRUITS

1. And He it is Who sendeth down water from the sky, and therewith We bring forth buds of every kind; We bring forth the green blade from which We bring forth the thick–clustered grain; and from the date–palm, from the pollen thereof, spring pendant bunches; and (We bring forth) gardens of grapes, and the olive and the pomegranate, alike and unlike. Look upon the fruit thereof, when they bear fruit, and upon its ripening. Lo! herein verily are portents for a people who believe.

6:99

2. And He it is Who produceth gardens trellised and untrellised, and the date–palm, and crops of divers flavour, and the olive and the pomegranate, like and unlike. Eat ye of the fruit thereof when it fruiteth, and pay the due thereof upon the harvest day, and be not prodigal. Lo! Allah loveth not the prodigals.

6:141

3. And of the fruits of the date–palm, and grapes, whence ye derive strong drink and (also) good nourishment. Lo! therein is indeed a portent for people who have sense.

16:67

4. And lofty date–palms

1. وَهُوَ الَّذِيْٓ اَنْزَلَ مِنَ السَّمَآءِ مَآءً ۚ فَاَخْرَجْنَا
بِهٖ نَبَاتَ كُلِّ شَيْءٍ فَاَخْرَجْنَا مِنْهُ خَضِرًا
نُّخْرِجُ مِنْهُ حَبًّا مُّتَرَاكِبًا ۚ وَمِنَ النَّخْلِ
مِنْ طَلْعِهَا قِنْوَانٌ دَانِيَةٌ وَّجَنّٰتٍ مِّنْ
اَعْنَابٍ وَّالزَّيْتُوْنَ وَالرُّمَّانَ مُشْتَبِهًا
وَّغَيْرَ مُتَشَابِهٍ ؕ اُنْظُرُوْٓا اِلٰى ثَمَرِهٖٓ اِذَآ اَثْمَرَ
وَيَنْعِهٖ ؕ اِنَّ فِيْ ذٰلِكُمْ لَاٰيٰتٍ لِّقَوْمٍ يُّؤْمِنُوْنَ ○

2. وَهُوَ الَّذِيْٓ اَنْشَاَ جَنّٰتٍ مَّعْرُوْشٰتٍ وَّغَيْرَ
مَعْرُوْشٰتٍ وَّالنَّخْلَ وَالزَّرْعَ مُخْتَلِفًا
اُكُلُهٗ وَالزَّيْتُوْنَ وَالرُّمَّانَ مُتَشَابِهًا وَّغَيْرَ
مُتَشَابِهٍ ؕ كُلُوْا مِنْ ثَمَرِهٖٓ اِذَآ اَثْمَرَ وَ
اٰتُوْا حَقَّهٗ يَوْمَ حَصَادِهٖ ۖ وَلَا تُسْرِفُوْا ؕ
اِنَّهٗ لَا يُحِبُّ الْمُسْرِفِيْنَ ○

3. وَمِنْ ثَمَرٰتِ النَّخِيْلِ وَالْاَعْنَابِ
تَتَّخِذُوْنَ مِنْهُ سَكَرًا وَّرِزْقًا حَسَنًا ؕ
اِنَّ فِيْ ذٰلِكَ لَاٰيَةً لِّقَوْمٍ يَّعْقِلُوْنَ ﴿٦٧﴾

4. وَالنَّخْلَ بٰسِقٰتٍ لَّهَا طَلْعٌ نَّضِيْدٌ ﴿١٠﴾
رِّزْقًا لِّلْعِبَادِ ۙ

5. وَالتِّيْنِ وَالزَّيْتُوْنِ ○
وَطُوْرِ سِيْنِيْنَ ○
وَهٰذَا الْبَلَدِ الْاَمِيْنِ ○

with ranged clusters,
Provision (made) for men:

50:10–11

5. By the fig and the olive,
By Mount Sinai,
And by this land made safe;

95:1–3

References.
DATES: 2:266; 6:99,141; 13:4; 16:11,67; 17:91; 18:32; 19:23,25; 23:19; 26:148; 36:34; 55:11; 80:29. **GRAPES:** 2:266; 6:99; 13:4; 16:11; 18:32; 23:19; 36:34; 80:28. **OLIVES:** 6:141; 16:11; 23:20; 24:35; 80:29; 95:1. **POMEGRANTES:** 6:99,55:68.

NAMES OF IDOLS

1. Have ye thought upon *Al-Lat* and *Al-'Uzza*.

And *Manat*, the third, the other?

Are yours the males and His the females?

That indeed were an unfair division!

53:19–22

2. Noah said: My Lord! Lo! they have disobeyed me and followed one whose wealth and children increase him in naught save ruin;

And they have plotted a mighty plot,

And they have said: Forsake not your gods. For–sake not *Wadd*, nor *Suw'a*, nor *Yaghûth* and *Ya'ûq* and *Nasr*.

And they have led many astray, and Thou increasest the wrong–doers in naught save error.

71:21–24

NAMES OF MOUNTAINS

1. Lo! (the mountains) *As-Safã* and *Al-Marwah* are among the indications of Allah. It is therefore no sin for him who is on pilgrimage to the House (of God) or visiteth it, to go around them (as the pagan custom is). And he who doth good of his own accord (for him), lo! Allah is Responsive, Aware.

2:158

2. And it was said: O earth! Swallow thy water and, O sky! be cleared of clouds! and the water was made to subside. And the Commandment was fulfilled. And it (the ship) came to rest upon (the mount) *Al-Judi* and it was said: A far removal for wrong doing folk!

11:44

3. And a tree that springeth forth from Mount *Sinai* that groweth oil and relish for the eaters.

23:20

1. أَفَرَءَيْتُمُ اللَّٰتَ وَالْعُزَّىٰ ﴿١٩﴾
وَمَنَوٰةَ الثَّالِثَةَ الْأُخْرَىٰ ﴿٢٠﴾
أَلَكُمُ الذَّكَرُ وَلَهُ الْأُنثَىٰ ﴿٢١﴾
تِلْكَ إِذًا قِسْمَةٌ ضِيزَىٰ ﴿٢٢﴾

2. قَالَ نُوحٌ رَّبِّ إِنَّهُمْ عَصَوْنِي وَاتَّبَعُوا
مَن لَّمْ يَزِدْهُ مَالُهُ وَوَلَدُهُ إِلَّا خَسَارًا ﴿٢١﴾
وَمَكَرُوا مَكْرًا كُبَّارًا ﴿٢٢﴾
وَقَالُوا لَا تَذَرُنَّ آلِهَتَكُمْ وَلَا
تَذَرُنَّ وَدًّا وَلَا سُوَاعًا وَلَا يَغُوثَ
وَيَعُوقَ وَنَسْرًا ﴿٢٣﴾
وَقَدْ أَضَلُّوا كَثِيرًا وَلَا تَزِدِ
الظَّالِمِينَ إِلَّا ضَلَالًا ﴿٢٤﴾

○

1. إِنَّ الصَّفَا وَالْمَرْوَةَ مِن شَعَائِرِ اللَّهِ فَمَنْ
حَجَّ الْبَيْتَ أَوِ اعْتَمَرَ فَلَا جُنَاحَ عَلَيْهِ أَن
يَطَّوَّفَ بِهِمَا وَمَن تَطَوَّعَ خَيْرًا فَإِنَّ اللَّهَ
شَاكِرٌ عَلِيمٌ ﴿١٥٨﴾

2. وَقِيلَ يَا أَرْضُ ابْلَعِي مَاءَكِ وَيَا سَمَاءُ
أَقْلِعِي وَغِيضَ الْمَاءُ وَقُضِيَ الْأَمْرُ
وَاسْتَوَتْ عَلَى الْجُودِيِّ وَقِيلَ بُعْدًا
لِّلْقَوْمِ الظَّالِمِينَ ﴿٤٤﴾

3. وَشَجَرَةً تَخْرُجُ مِن طُورِ سَيْنَاءَ تَنبُتُ
بِالدُّهْنِ وَصِبْغٍ لِّلْآكِلِينَ ﴿٢٠﴾

NAMES OF MOUNTAINS

Ref: 2:93; 4:154; 11:44; 19:52; 20:80; 28:29,46; 52:1; 95:2.

NAMES OF PROPHETS

1. And He taught Adam all the names, then showed them to the angels, saying: Inform Me of the names of these, if ye are truthful.

They said: Be glorified! We have no knowledge saving that which Thou hast taught us. Lo! Thou, only Thou, art the Knower, the Wise.

He said: O Adam! Inform them of their names, and when he had informed them of their names, He said: Did I not tell you that I know the secret of the heavens and the earth? And I know that which ye disclose and which ye hide.

2:31–33

2. Then Adam received from his Lord words (of revelation), and He relented toward him. Lo! He is the Relenting, the Merciful.

2:37

3. Then Zachariah prayed unto his Lord and said: My Lord! Bestow upon me of Thy bounty goodly offspring. Lo! Thou art the Hearer of Prayer.

And the angels called to him as he stood praying in the sanctuary: Allah giveth thee glad tidings of (a son whose name is) John (who cometh) to confirm a word from Allah, lordly, chaste, a Prophet of the righteous.

3:38–39

4. The Messiah, Jesus son of

1. وَعَلَّمَ آدَمَ الْأَسْمَاءَ كُلَّهَا ثُمَّ عَرَضَهُمْ عَلَى الْمَلَائِكَةِ
فَقَالَ أَنْبِئُونِي بِأَسْمَاءِ هَٰؤُلَاءِ إِنْ كُنْتُمْ صَادِقِينَ ﴿٣١﴾
قَالُوا سُبْحَانَكَ لَا عِلْمَ لَنَا إِلَّا مَا عَلَّمْتَنَا ۖ إِنَّكَ
أَنْتَ الْعَلِيمُ الْحَكِيمُ ﴿٣٢﴾
قَالَ يَا آدَمُ أَنْبِئْهُمْ بِأَسْمَائِهِمْ ۖ فَلَمَّا أَنْبَأَهُمْ
بِأَسْمَائِهِمْ قَالَ أَلَمْ أَقُلْ لَكُمْ إِنِّي أَعْلَمُ غَيْبَ
السَّمَاوَاتِ وَالْأَرْضِ وَأَعْلَمُ مَا تُبْدُونَ وَمَا
كُنْتُمْ تَكْتُمُونَ ﴿٣٣﴾

2. فَتَلَقَّىٰ آدَمُ مِنْ رَبِّهِ كَلِمَاتٍ فَتَابَ عَلَيْهِ ۚ
إِنَّهُ هُوَ التَّوَّابُ الرَّحِيمُ ﴿٣٧﴾

3. هُنَالِكَ دَعَا زَكَرِيَّا رَبَّهُ ۖ قَالَ رَبِّ هَبْ
لِي مِنْ لَدُنْكَ ذُرِّيَّةً طَيِّبَةً ۖ إِنَّكَ
سَمِيعُ الدُّعَاءِ ○

فَنَادَتْهُ الْمَلَائِكَةُ وَهُوَ قَائِمٌ يُصَلِّي فِي
الْمِحْرَابِ أَنَّ اللَّهَ يُبَشِّرُكَ بِيَحْيَىٰ مُصَدِّقًا
بِكَلِمَةٍ مِنَ اللَّهِ وَسَيِّدًا وَحَصُورًا وَنَبِيًّا
مِنَ الصَّالِحِينَ ○

4. إِنَّمَا الْمَسِيحُ عِيسَى ابْنُ مَرْيَمَ رَسُولُ
اللَّهِ وَكَلِمَتُهُ أَلْقَاهَا إِلَىٰ مَرْيَمَ وَرُوحٌ
مِنْهُ ۖ فَآمِنُوا بِاللَّهِ وَرُسُلِهِ

5. وَإِسْمَاعِيلَ وَالْيَسَعَ وَيُونُسَ وَلُوطًا ۚ وَ
كُلًّا فَضَّلْنَا عَلَى الْعَالَمِينَ ○

Mary, was only a messenger of Allah, and His word which He conveyed unto Mary, and a spirit from Him. So believe in Allah and His messengers.

4:171

5. And Ishmael and Elisha and Jonah and Lot, Each one of them did We prefer above

(Our) creatures.

With some of their fore-fathers and their offspring and their brethren; and We chose them and guided them unto a Straight path.

6:86–87

6. And unto (the tribe of) 'Aad (We sent) their brother, Hud. He said: O my people! Serve Allah. Ye have no other God save Him. Will ye not ward off (evil)?

7:65

7. And to (the tribe of) Thamûd (We sent) their brother Salih He said: O my people! Serve Allah. Ye have no other God save Him. A wonder from your Lord hath come unto you. Lo! this is the camel of Allah, a token unto you; so let her feed in Allah's earth, and touch her not with hurt lest painful torment seize you.

7:73

8. And unto Midian (We sent) their brother, Shuéyb. He said: O my people! Serve Allah. Ye have no other God save Him. Lo! a clear proof hath come unto you from your Lord; so give full measure and full weight and wrong not mankind in their goods, and work not confusion in the earth after the fair ordering thereof. That will be better for you, if ye are believers.

7:85

9. And the Jews say: Ezra

وَمِنْ آبَائِهِمْ وَذُرِّيَّاتِهِمْ وَإِخْوَانِهِمْ
وَاجْتَبَيْنَاهُمْ وَهَدَيْنَاهُمْ إِلَىٰ صِرَاطٍ مُسْتَقِيمٍ ○

6. وَإِلَىٰ عَادٍ أَخَاهُمْ هُودًا قَالَ يَا قَوْمِ اعْبُدُوا
اللَّهَ مَا لَكُمْ مِنْ إِلَٰهٍ غَيْرُهُ أَفَلَا تَتَّقُونَ ○

7. وَإِلَىٰ ثَمُودَ أَخَاهُمْ صَالِحًا قَالَ يَا قَوْمِ
اعْبُدُوا اللَّهَ مَا لَكُمْ مِنْ إِلَٰهٍ غَيْرُهُ قَدْ
جَاءَتْكُمْ بَيِّنَةٌ مِنْ رَبِّكُمْ هَٰذِهِ نَاقَةُ
اللَّهِ لَكُمْ آيَةً فَذَرُوهَا تَأْكُلْ فِي أَرْضِ
اللَّهِ وَلَا تَمَسُّوهَا بِسُوءٍ فَيَأْخُذَكُمْ عَذَابٌ أَلِيمٌ ○

8. وَإِلَىٰ مَدْيَنَ أَخَاهُمْ شُعَيْبًا قَالَ يَا قَوْمِ
اعْبُدُوا اللَّهَ مَا لَكُمْ مِنْ إِلَٰهٍ غَيْرُهُ
قَدْ جَاءَتْكُمْ بَيِّنَةٌ مِنْ رَبِّكُمْ
فَأَوْفُوا الْكَيْلَ وَالْمِيزَانَ وَلَا تَبْخَسُوا
النَّاسَ أَشْيَاءَهُمْ وَلَا تُفْسِدُوا فِي الْأَرْضِ
بَعْدَ إِصْلَاحِهَا ذَٰلِكُمْ خَيْرٌ لَكُمْ إِنْ
كُنْتُمْ مُؤْمِنِينَ ○

9. وَقَالَتِ الْيَهُودُ عُزَيْرٌ ابْنُ اللَّهِ وَقَالَتِ
النَّصَارَى الْمَسِيحُ ابْنُ اللَّهِ ذَٰلِكَ قَوْلُهُمْ
بِأَفْوَاهِهِمْ يُضَاهِئُونَ قَوْلَ الَّذِينَ كَفَرُوا
مِنْ قَبْلُ قَاتَلَهُمُ اللَّهُ أَنَّىٰ يُؤْفَكُونَ ○

is the son of Allah and the Christians say: The Messiah is the son of Allah. That is their saying with their mouths. They imitate the saying of those who disbelieved of old. Allah (Himself) fighteth against them. How perverse are they!

9:30

10. We verily sent Moses with Our revelations, saying: Bring thy people forth from darkness unto light. And remind them of the days of Allah. Lo! therein are revelations for each steadfast, thankful (heart).

14:5

11. And thy Lord is Best Aware of all who are in the heavens and the earth. And We preferred some of the Prophets above others, and unto David We gave the Psalms.

17:55

12. A mention of the mercy of thy Lord unto His servant, Zachariah.

When he cried unto his Lord a cry in secret,

Saying: My Lord! Lo! the bones of me wax feeble and my head is shining with grey hair, and I have never been unblest in prayer to Thee, my Lord.

Lo! I fear my kinsfolk after me, since my wife is barren. Oh, give me from Thy presence a successor!

Who shall inherit of me and inherit (also) of the house of Jacob. And make him, my Lord, acceptable (unto Thee).

19:2–6

13. And make mention (O Muhammad) in the Scripture of Abraham. Lo! he was a saint, a Prophet.

19:41

10. وَلَقَدْ اَرْسَلْنَا مُوْسٰى بِاٰيٰتِنَآ اَنْ اَخْرِجْ
قَوْمَكَ مِنَ الظُّلُمٰتِ اِلَى النُّوْرِ ۙ
وَذَكِّرْهُمْ بِاَيّٰىمِ اللّٰهِ ؕ اِنَّ فِيْ ذٰلِكَ لَاٰيٰتٍ
لِّكُلِّ صَبَّارٍ شَكُوْرٍ ۝٥

11. وَرَبُّكَ اَعْلَمُ بِمَنْ فِي السَّمٰوٰتِ
وَالْاَرْضِ ؕ وَلَقَدْ فَضَّلْنَا بَعْضَ النَّبِيّٖنَ
عَلٰى بَعْضٍ وَّاٰتَيْنَا دَاوٗدَ زَبُوْرًا ۝٥٥

12. ذِكْرُ رَحْمَتِ رَبِّكَ عَبْدَهٗ زَكَرِيَّا ۝٢
اِذْ نَادٰى رَبَّهٗ نِدَآءً خَفِيًّا ۝٣
قَالَ رَبِّ اِنِّيْ وَهَنَ الْعَظْمُ مِنِّيْ وَ
اشْتَعَلَ الرَّاْسُ شَيْبًا وَّلَمْ اَكُنْۢ
بِدُعَآئِكَ رَبِّ شَقِيًّا ۝٤
وَاِنِّيْ خِفْتُ الْمَوَالِيَ مِنْ وَّرَآءِيْ وَكَانَتِ
امْرَاَتِيْ عَاقِرًا فَهَبْ لِيْ مِنْ لَّدُنْكَ وَلِيًّا ۝٥
يَّرِثُنِيْ وَيَرِثُ مِنْ اٰلِ يَعْقُوْبَ ۖ وَاجْعَلْهُ
رَبِّ رَضِيًّا ۝٦

13. وَاذْكُرْ فِي الْكِتٰبِ اِبْرٰهِيْمَ ؕ
اِنَّهٗ كَانَ صِدِّيْقًا نَّبِيًّا ۝٤١

14. وَوَهَبْنَا لَهٗ مِنْ رَّحْمَتِنَآ اَخَاهُ هٰرُوْنَ
نَبِيًّا ۝٥٣

15. وَاذْكُرْ فِي الْكِتٰبِ اِسْمٰعِيْلَ ۫ اِنَّهٗ كَانَ
صَادِقَ الْوَعْدِ وَكَانَ رَسُوْلًا نَّبِيًّا ۝٥٤

14. And We bestowed upon him of Our mercy his brother Aaron, a Prophet (likewise).

19:53

15. And make mention in the Scripture of Ishmael. Lo! he was a keeper of his promise,

and he was a messenger (of Allah), a Prophet.

He enjoined upon his people worship and alms-giving, and was acceptable in the sight of his Lord.

19:54–55

16. And make mention in the Scripture of Idris. Lo! he was a saint, a Prophet;

And We raised him to high station.

19:56–57

17. And We verily sent Noah unto his folk, and he said: O my people! Serve Allah. Ye have no other god save Him. Will ye not ward off (evil)?

23:23

18. The folk of Lot denied the messengers (of Allah).

When their brother Lot said unto them: Will ye not ward off (evil)?

Lo! I am a faithful messenger unto you,

So keep your duty to Allah and obey me.

26:160–163

19. And Solomon was David's heir. And he said: O mankind! Lo! We have been taught the language of birds, and have been given (abundance) of all things. This surely is evident favour.

And there were gathered together unto Solomon his armies of the jinn and humankind, and of the birds, and

وَكَانَ يَأْمُرُ أَهْلَهُ بِالصَّلٰوةِ وَالزَّكٰوةِ
وَكَانَ عِنْدَ رَبِّهٖ مَرْضِيًّا ﴿٥٥﴾
16. وَاذْكُرْ فِي الْكِتٰبِ إِدْرِيسَ إِنَّهٗ
كَانَ صِدِّيقًا نَّبِيًّا ﴿٥٦﴾
وَّرَفَعْنٰهُ مَكَانًا عَلِيًّا ﴿٥٧﴾
17. وَلَقَدْ أَرْسَلْنَا نُوحًا إِلٰى قَوْمِهٖ فَقَالَ
يٰقَوْمِ اعْبُدُوا اللّٰهَ مَا لَكُمْ مِّنْ إِلٰهٍ
غَيْرُهٗ أَفَلَا تَتَّقُوْنَ ﴿٢٣﴾
18. كَذَّبَتْ قَوْمُ لُوْطِ الْمُرْسَلِيْنَ ﴿١٦٠﴾
إِذْ قَالَ لَهُمْ أَخُوْهُمْ لُوْطٌ أَلَا تَتَّقُوْنَ ﴿١٦١﴾
إِنِّيْ لَكُمْ رَسُوْلٌ أَمِيْنٌ ﴿١٦٢﴾
فَاتَّقُوا اللّٰهَ وَأَطِيْعُوْنِ ﴿١٦٣﴾
19. وَوَرِثَ سُلَيْمٰنُ دَاوٗدَ وَقَالَ يٰأَيُّهَا
النَّاسُ عُلِّمْنَا مَنْطِقَ الطَّيْرِ وَأُوْتِيْنَا
مِنْ كُلِّ شَيْءٍ إِنَّ هٰذَا لَهُوَ
الْفَضْلُ الْمُبِيْنُ ﴿١٦﴾
وَحُشِرَ لِسُلَيْمٰنَ جُنُوْدُهٗ مِنَ الْجِنِّ
وَالْإِنْسِ وَالطَّيْرِ فَهُمْ يُوْزَعُوْنَ ﴿١٧﴾
20. مَا كَانَ مُحَمَّدٌ أَبَا أَحَدٍ مِّنْ رِّجَالِكُمْ
وَلٰكِنْ رَّسُوْلَ اللّٰهِ وَخَاتَمَ النَّبِيّٖنَ
وَكَانَ اللّٰهُ بِكُلِّ شَيْءٍ عَلِيْمًا ﴿٤٠﴾

they were set in a battle order;

27:16–17

20. Muhammad is not the father of any man among you, but he is the messenger of Allah and the Seal of the Prophets., and Allah is Aware of all things.

33:40

21. Peace be unto Abraham!
Thus do We reward the good.
Lo! he is one of Our believing slaves.
And We gave him tidings of the birth of Isaac, a Prophet of the righteous.
37:109–112

22. And lo! Elias was of those sent (to warn),
When he said unto his folk: Will ye not ward off (evil)?
Will ye cry unto *Ba'al* and forsake the Best of Creators,
Allah, your Lord and Lord of your forefathers?
But they denied him, so they surely will be haled forth (to the doom)
Save the single–minded slaves of Allah.
And We left for him among the later folk (the salutation):
Peace be unto Elias!
37:123–130

23. And lo! Jonah verily was of those sent (to warn).
When he fled unto the laden ship,
And then drew lots and was of those rejected;
And the fish swallowed him while he was blame–worthy;
And had he not been one of those who glorify (Allah).
He would have tarried in its belly till the day when they are raised;
37:139–144

24. And make mention (O Muhammad) of Our bondman

21. سَلٰمٌ عَلٰٓى اِبْرٰهِيْمَ (109)
كَذٰلِكَ نَجْزِى الْمُحْسِنِيْنَ (110)
اِنَّهٗ مِنْ عِبَادِنَا الْمُؤْمِنِيْنَ (111)
وَبَشَّرْنٰهُ بِاِسْحٰقَ نَبِيًّا مِّنَ الصّٰلِحِيْنَ (112)
22. وَاِنَّ اِلْيَاسَ لَمِنَ الْمُرْسَلِيْنَ (123)
اِذْ قَالَ لِقَوْمِهٖٓ اَلَا تَتَّقُوْنَ (124)
اَتَدْعُوْنَ بَعْلًا وَّتَذَرُوْنَ اَحْسَنَ
الْخَالِقِيْنَ (125)
اللّٰهَ رَبَّكُمْ وَرَبَّ اٰبَآئِكُمُ الْاَوَّلِيْنَ (126)
فَكَذَّبُوْهُ فَاِنَّهُمْ لَمُحْضَرُوْنَ (127)
اِلَّا عِبَادَ اللّٰهِ الْمُخْلَصِيْنَ (128)
وَتَرَكْنَا عَلَيْهِ فِى الْاٰخِرِيْنَ (129)
سَلٰمٌ عَلٰٓى اِلْ يَاسِيْنَ (130)
23. وَاِنَّ يُوْنُسَ لَمِنَ الْمُرْسَلِيْنَ (139)
اِذْ اَبَقَ اِلَى الْفُلْكِ الْمَشْحُوْنِ (140)
فَسَاهَمَ فَكَانَ مِنَ الْمُدْحَضِيْنَ (141)
فَالْتَقَمَهُ الْحُوْتُ وَهُوَ مُلِيْمٌ (142)
فَلَوْلَآ اَنَّهٗ كَانَ مِنَ الْمُسَبِّحِيْنَ (143)
لَلَبِثَ فِىْ بَطْنِهٖٓ اِلٰى يَوْمِ يُبْعَثُوْنَ (144)
24. وَاذْكُرْ عَبْدَنَآ اَيُّوْبَ اِذْ نَادٰى رَبَّهٗٓ
اَنِّىْ مَسَّنِىَ الشَّيْطٰنُ بِنُصْبٍ وَّعَذَابٍ (41)
اُرْكُضْ بِرِجْلِكَ هٰذَا مُغْتَسَلٌۢ
بَارِدٌ وَّشَرَابٌ (42)

Job, when he cried unto his Lord (saying): Lo! the devil doth afflict me with distress and torment.
(And it was said unto him): Strike the ground with thy foot. This (spring) is a cool bath and a refreshing drink.
And We bestowed on him (again) his household and therewith the like thereof, a

mercy from Us, and a memorial for men of understanding.

38:41–43

ووهبنا له اهله ومثلهم معهم
رحمة منا وذكرى لاولي الالباب ﴿٤٣﴾

25. And make mention of Our bondmen. Abraham, Issac and Jacob, men of parts and vision.

Lo! We purified them with a pure thought, remembrance of the Home (of the Hereafter).

Lo! in Our sight they are verily of the elect, the excellent.

And make mention of Ishmael and Elisha and *Dhu'l-Kifl*. All are of the chosen.

38:45-48

25. واذكر عبدنا ابرهيم واسحق
ويعقوب اولي الايدي والابصار ﴿٤٥﴾

انا اخلصنهم بخالصة ذكرى الدار ﴿٤٦﴾

وانهم عندنا لمن المصطفين الاخيار ﴿٤٧﴾

واذكر اسمعيل واليسع وذا الكفل
وكل من الاخيار ﴿٤٨﴾

26. And verily Joseph brought you of old clear proofs, yet ye ceased not to be in doubt concerning what he brought you till, when he died, he said: Allah will not send any messenger after him.

40:34

26. ولقد جاءكم يوسف من قبل
بالبينت فما زلتم في شك مما
جاءكم به حتى اذا هلك قلتم
لن يبعث الله من بعده رسولا

References

AARON: 2:248; 4:163; 6:84; 7:122,142; 10:75; 19:28; 20:30,70,90,92; 21:48; 23:45; 25:35; 26:13,48; 28:34; 37:114,120.

ABRAHAM: 2:124-127,130,132-133,135,140,258,260; 3:33,65,67,68,84,95, 97; 5:54,125,163; 6:74-75,83,161; 9:70,114; 11:69,74-76; 12:6,38; 14:35; 15:51; 16:120-123; 19:46,58; 21:51,60,62,69; 22:26,43,78; 26:69; 29:16, 31; 57:26; 60:4.

See also: Miracles of Prophets.

ADAM: 3:33,59; 5:27; 7:11,19; 17:61; 18:50; 20:115-117,120-121.

DAVID: 2:251; 4:163; 5:78; 6:84; 21:78-79; 27:15-16; 34:10,13; 38:17,22, 24,26,30.
See also: Miracles of Prophets.

ELIAS: 6:85.

ELISHA: 38:48.

HUD: 11:50,53,58,60,89; 26:124.

IDRIS: 21:85.

ISSAC: 2:133,136,140; 3:84; 4:163; 6:84; 11:71; 12:6,38; 14:39; 19:49; 21:72; 29:27; 37:113; 38:45.

ISHMAEL: 2:125,127,133,136; 3:84; 4:163; 6:86; 14:39; 21:85; 38:48.

JACOB: 2:132-133,136,140; 3:84; 4:163; 6:84; 11:71; 12:6,38,68; 19:6,49; 21:72; 29:27.

JESUS: 2:87,136,253; 3:45,52,55,59,84; 4:157,163; 5:46,78,110,112,114, 116; 6:85; 19:34; 33:7; 42:13; 43:63; 57:27; 61:6,14.
See also: Miracles of Prophets, Reference to Certain Women.

JOB: 4:163; 6:84; 21:83.
See also: Miracles of Prophets.

JOHN: 6:85; 19:7,12; 21:90.

JONAH: 4:163; 6:86; 10:98.
See also: Miracles of Prophets.

JOSEPH: 6:84; 12:4,7-11,17,21,29,46,51,56,58,69,76-77,80,84-85,87,89-90,94, 99.
See also: Miracles of Prophets

LOT: 6:86; 7:80; 11:70,74,77,81,89; 15:59,61; 21:74; 22:43; 26:167; 27: 54,56; 29:26,28,32-33; 37:133; 38:13; 54:33-34; 66:10.

MUHAMMAD (PBUH): 3:144; 47:2; 48:29; 61:6.
See also: Manners of Prophet Muhammad (PBUH)

MOSES: 2:51,53-55,60-61,67,87,92,108,136,246,248; 3:84; 4:153,164; 5:20, 22,24; 6:84,91,154; 7:103-104,115,117,122,127-128,131,134,138,142-144, 148,150,154-155,159-160; 10:75,77,80-81,83-84,87-88; 11:17,96,110; 14:6,8; 17:2,101; 18:60,66; 19:51; 20:9,11,17,19,36,40,49,57,61,65,67,70,77,83,86, 88,91; 21:48; 22:44; 23:45,49; 25:35; 26:10,43,48,52,61,63,65; 27:7,9-10; 28:3,7,10,15,18-20,29-31,36-38,43-44,48,76; 29:39; 32:23; 33:7,69; 37:114, 120; 40:23,26-27,37,53; 41:45; 42:13; 43:46; 46:12,30; 51:38; 53:36; 61: 5; 79:15; 87:19.
See also: Miracles of Prophets, Pharoah, Companion of Moses.

NOAH: 3:33; 4:163; 6:84; 7:59,69; 9:70; 11:25,32,36,42,45-46,48,89; 14:9; 17:3,17; 19:58; 22:42; 25:37; 26:105-106,116; 29:14; 33:7; 37:75,79; 38:12; 40:5,31; 42:13; 50:12; 51:46; 53:52; 54:9; 57:26; 66:10; 71:1,21,26.
See also: Miracles of Prophets, Deluge of Noah.

SALIH: 7:75,77,190; 11:61-62,66,89; 26:142; 27:45.
See also: Miracles of Prophets

SAUL: 38:48.
See also: Miracles of Prophets,

SOLOMON: 2:102; 4:163; 6:84; 21:78-79,81; 27:15-18,30,36,44; 34:12; 38:30,34.
See also: Miracles of Prophets, Queen of *Sheba*

SHU'EYB: 7:88,90,92; 11:84,87,91,94; 26:117; 2:36.

ZACHARIA: 3:37-38; 6:85; 19:7; 21:89.

NATIONS

1. O Children of Israel! Remember My favour wherewith I favoured you and how I preferred you to (all) creatures.

2:47

2. And such were 'Aad. They denied the revelations of their Lord and flouted His messengers and followed the command of every froward potentate.

And a curse was made to follow them in the world and on the Day of Resurrection. Lo!' 'Aad disbelieved in their Lord. A far removal for 'Aad, the folk of Hud!

11:59–60

3. Naught hindereth Us from sending portents save that the folk of old denied them. And We gave Thamud the she–camel–a clear portent–but they did wrong in respect of her. We send not portents save to warn.

17:59

4. Until, when Gog and Magog are let loose, and they hasten out of every mound.

And the True Promise draweth nigh; then behold them, staring wide (in terror), the eyes of those who disbelieve! (They say): Alas for us! We (lived) in forgetfulness of this. Ah, but we were wrong–doers!

21:96–97

1. يٰبَنِيْٓ اِسْرَآءِيْلَ اذْكُرُوْا نِعْمَتِيَ الَّتِيْٓ اَنْعَمْتُ عَلَيْكُمْ وَاَنِّيْ فَضَّلْتُكُمْ عَلَى الْعٰلَمِيْنَ ﴿٤٧﴾

2. وَتِلْكَ عَادٌ ۟ جَحَدُوْا بِاٰيٰتِ رَبِّهِمْ وَعَصَوْا رُسُلَهٗ وَاتَّبَعُوْٓا اَمْرَ كُلِّ جَبَّارٍ عَنِيْدٍ ﴿٥٩﴾ وَاُتْبِعُوْا فِيْ هٰذِهِ الدُّنْيَا لَعْنَةً وَّيَوْمَ الْقِيٰمَةِ ؕ اَلَآ اِنَّ عَادًا كَفَرُوْا رَبَّهُمْ ؕ اَلَا بُعْدًا لِّعَادٍ قَوْمِ هُوْدٍ ﴿٦٠﴾

3. وَمَا مَنَعَنَآ اَنْ نُّرْسِلَ بِالْاٰيٰتِ اِلَّآ اَنْ كَذَّبَ بِهَا الْاَوَّلُوْنَ ؕ وَاٰتَيْنَا ثَمُوْدَ النَّاقَةَ مُبْصِرَةً فَظَلَمُوْا بِهَا ؕ وَمَا نُرْسِلُ بِالْاٰيٰتِ اِلَّا تَخْوِيْفًا ﴿٥٩﴾

4. حَتّٰٓى اِذَا فُتِحَتْ يَاْجُوْجُ وَمَاْجُوْجُ وَهُمْ مِّنْ كُلِّ حَدَبٍ يَّنْسِلُوْنَ ﴿٩٦﴾ وَاقْتَرَبَ الْوَعْدُ الْحَقُّ فَاِذَا هِيَ شَاخِصَةٌ اَبْصَارُ الَّذِيْنَ كَفَرُوْا ؕ يٰوَيْلَنَا قَدْ كُنَّا فِيْ غَفْلَةٍ مِّنْ هٰذَا بَلْ كُنَّا ظٰلِمِيْنَ ﴿٩٧﴾

5. كَذَّبَ اَصْحٰبُ لْـَٔيْكَةِ الْمُرْسَلِيْنَ ﴿١٧٦﴾ اِذْ قَالَ لَهُمْ شُعَيْبٌ اَلَا تَتَّقُوْنَ ﴿١٧٧﴾

5. The dwellers in the wood (of Midian) denied the messengers (of Allah),

When Shu'eyb said unto them: Will ye not ward off (evil)?

26:176–177

6. And unto Midian We have sent Shu'eyb, their brother. He said: O my people! Serve Allah, and look forward to the Last Day, and do not evil, making mischief, in the earth.

But they denied him, and the dreadful earthquake took them, and morning found them prostrate in their dwelling—place.

29:36–37

7. And the dwellers in the wood, and the folk of *Tubb'a* every one denied their messengers, therefor My threat took effect.

50:14

8. For the taming of Qureysh

For their taming (We cause) the caravans to set forth in winter and summer.

So let them worship the Lord of this House

Who hath fed them against hunger. And hath made them safe from fear.

106:1–4

6. وَإِلَىٰ مَدْيَنَ أَخَاهُمْ شُعَيْبًا فَقَالَ
يَٰقَوْمِ اعْبُدُوا اللَّهَ وَارْجُوا الْيَوْمَ الْآخِرَ
وَلَا تَعْثَوْا فِي الْأَرْضِ مُفْسِدِينَ ۝٣٦
فَكَذَّبُوهُ فَأَخَذَتْهُمُ الرَّجْفَةُ
فَأَصْبَحُوا فِي دَارِهِمْ جَاثِمِينَ ۝٣٧

7. وَأَصْحَٰبُ الْأَيْكَةِ وَقَوْمُ تُبَّعٍ كُلٌّ
كَذَّبَ الرُّسُلَ فَحَقَّ وَعِيدِ ۝١٤

8. لِإِيلَٰفِ قُرَيْشٍ ۝١
إِۦلَٰفِهِمْ رِحْلَةَ الشِّتَآءِ وَالصَّيْفِ ۝٢
فَلْيَعْبُدُوا رَبَّ هَٰذَا الْبَيْتِ ۝٣
الَّذِىٓ أَطْعَمَهُم مِّن جُوعٍ وَءَامَنَهُم مِّنْ خَوْفٍۭ ۝٤

○

References

'AAD: 7:65,74; 9:70; 11:50,60; 14:9; 22:42; 25:38; 26:123; 29:38; 38:12; 40:31; 41:13,15; 46:21; 50:13; 51:41; 53:50; 54:18; 69:4,6; 89:6.

CHILDREN OF ISRAEL: 2:40,83,122,211,246; 3:49,93; 5:12,32,70,72,78, 110; 7:105,134,137-138; 10:90,93; 17:2,4,101,104; 19:58; 20:47,80,94; 26:17,22,59,197; 27:76; 32:23; 40:53; 43:59; 44:30; 45:16; 46:10; 61:6, 14.

GOG AND MAGOG: 18:94-98.

See also: *Dhu'l Qarneyn*

MIDIANS: 7:85; 9:70; 11:84,95; 15:78; 20:40; 28:45; 38:13; 50:14.

THAMUD: 7:73; 9:70; 11:61,68,95; 14:9; 15:80-84; 22:42; 25:38; 26:141; 27:45; 29:38; 38:13; 40:31; 41:13,17; 50:12; 51:43; 53:51; 54:23; 69:4-5; 85:18; 89:9; 91:11.

NATURE

1. So set thy purpose (O Muhammad) for religion as a man by nature upright—the nature (framed) of Allah, in which He hath created man. There is no altering (the laws of) Allah's creation. That is the right religion, but most men know not—

30:30

NEGLIGENCE

1. Already have We urged unto hell many of the jinn and humankind, having hearts wherewith they understand not, and having eyes where–with they see not, and having ears wherewith they hear not. These are as the cattle —nay, but they are worse! These are the neglectful.

7:179

2. Lo! those who expect not the meeting with Us but desire the life of the world and feel secure there–in, and those who are neglect–ful of Our revelations:

Their home will be the Fire because of what they used to earn.

10:7–8

3. Lo! most of mankind are heedless of Our portents.

10:92

4. Their reckoning draweth nigh for mankind, while they

1. فَأَقِمْ وَجْهَكَ لِلدِّيْنِ حَنِيْفًا ۚ فِطْرَتَ
اللّٰهِ الَّتِيْ فَطَرَ النَّاسَ عَلَيْهَا ۚ لَا
تَبْدِيْلَ لِخَلْقِ اللّٰهِ ۚ ذٰلِكَ الدِّيْنُ
الْقَيِّمُ ۙ وَلٰكِنَّ اَكْثَرَ النَّاسِ لَا يَعْلَمُوْنَ ۝

1. وَلَقَدْ ذَرَاْنَا لِجَهَنَّمَ كَثِيْرًا مِّنَ الْجِنِّ
وَالْاِنْسِ ۖ لَهُمْ قُلُوْبٌ لَّا يَفْقَهُوْنَ بِهَا ۙ
وَلَهُمْ اَعْيُنٌ لَّا يُبْصِرُوْنَ بِهَا ۙ وَلَهُمْ اٰذَانٌ
لَّا يَسْمَعُوْنَ بِهَا ۚ اُولٰٓئِكَ كَالْاَنْعَامِ بَلْ
هُمْ اَضَلُّ ۚ اُولٰٓئِكَ هُمُ الْغٰفِلُوْنَ ۝١٧٩

2. اِنَّ الَّذِيْنَ لَا يَرْجُوْنَ لِقَآءَنَا وَرَضُوْا
بِالْحَيٰوةِ الدُّنْيَا وَاطْمَاَنُّوْا بِهَا وَالَّذِيْنَ
هُمْ عَنْ اٰيٰتِنَا غٰفِلُوْنَ ۝٧
اُولٰٓئِكَ مَاْوٰىهُمُ النَّارُ بِمَا كَانُوْا يَكْسِبُوْنَ ۝٨

3. وَاِنَّ كَثِيْرًا مِّنَ النَّاسِ عَنْ اٰيٰتِنَا
لَغٰفِلُوْنَ ۝٩٢

4. اِقْتَرَبَ لِلنَّاسِ حِسَابُهُمْ وَهُمْ فِيْ
غَفْلَةٍ مُّعْرِضُوْنَ ۝١
مَا يَاْتِيْهِمْ مِّنْ ذِكْرٍ مِّنْ رَّبِّهِمْ مُّحْدَثٍ
اِلَّا اسْتَمَعُوْهُ وَهُمْ يَلْعَبُوْنَ ۝٢
لَاهِيَةً قُلُوْبُهُمْ

turn away in heedlessness.

Never cometh there unto them a new reminder from their Lord but they listen to it while they play,

With hearts preoccupied.

21:1–3

NEIGHBOURS

1. And serve Allah: and ascribe nothing as partner unto Him. (Show) kindness unto parents, and unto near kindred, and orphans, and the needy, and unto the neighbour who is of kin (unto you) and the neighbour who is not of kin, and the fellow–traveller and the way–farer and (the slaves) whom your right hands possess. Lo! Allah loveth not such as are proud and boastful:

4:36

NIKAH

1. Wed not idolatresses till they believe; for lo! a believing bondwoman is better than an idolatress though she please you; and give not your daughters in marriage to idolaters till they believe, for lo! a believing slave is better than an idolater though he please you. These invite unto the Fire, and Allah inviteth unto the Garden, and unto forgiveness by His grace, and expoundeth thus His revelations to mankind that haply they may remember.

2:221

2. And if ye fear that ye will not deal fairly by the orphans, marry of the women, who seem good to you, two or three or four, and if ye fear that ye cannot do justice (to so many) then one (only) or (the captives) that your right hands possess. Thus it

1. وَاعْبُدُوا اللّٰهَ وَلَا تُشْرِكُوْا بِهٖ شَيْـًٔا وَّبِالْوَالِدَيْنِ
إِحْسَانًا وَّبِذِي الْقُرْبٰى وَالْيَتٰمٰى وَالْمَسٰكِيْنِ وَالْجَارِ
ذِي الْقُرْبٰى وَالْجَارِ الْجُنُبِ وَالصَّاحِبِ بِالْجَنْۢبِ وَ
ابْنِ السَّبِيْلِ وَمَا مَلَكَتْ أَيْمَانُكُمْ إِنَّ اللّٰهَ لَا يُحِبُّ
مَنْ كَانَ مُخْتَالًا فَخُوْرًا ﴿٣٦﴾

1. وَلَا تَنْكِحُوا الْمُشْرِكٰتِ حَتّٰى يُؤْمِنَّ وَلَأَمَةٌ
مُّؤْمِنَةٌ خَيْرٌ مِّنْ مُّشْرِكَةٍ وَّلَوْ أَعْجَبَتْكُمْ
وَلَا تُنْكِحُوا الْمُشْرِكِيْنَ حَتّٰى يُؤْمِنُوْا وَلَعَبْدٌ
مُّؤْمِنٌ خَيْرٌ مِّنْ مُّشْرِكٍ وَّلَوْ أَعْجَبَكُمْ أُولٰٓئِكَ
يَدْعُوْنَ إِلَى النَّارِ وَاللّٰهُ يَدْعُوْٓا إِلَى الْجَنَّةِ
وَالْمَغْفِرَةِ بِإِذْنِهٖ وَيُبَيِّنُ أٰيٰتِهٖ لِلنَّاسِ
لَعَلَّهُمْ يَتَذَكَّرُوْنَ ﴿٢٢١﴾

2. وَإِنْ خِفْتُمْ أَلَّا تُقْسِطُوْا فِي الْيَتٰمٰى فَانْكِحُوْا
مَا طَابَ لَكُمْ مِّنَ النِّسَآءِ مَثْنٰى وَثُلٰثَ
وَرُبٰعَ فَإِنْ خِفْتُمْ أَلَّا تَعْدِلُوْا فَوَاحِدَةً
أَوْ مَا مَلَكَتْ أَيْمَانُكُمْ ذٰلِكَ أَدْنٰٓى
أَلَّا تَعُوْلُوْا ﴿٣﴾

3. وَلَا تَنْكِحُوْا مَا نَكَحَ أٰبَآؤُكُمْ مِّنَ النِّسَآءِ إِلَّا
مَا قَدْ سَلَفَ إِنَّهٗ كَانَ فَاحِشَةً
وَّمَقْتًا وَّسَآءَ سَبِيْلًا ﴿٢٢﴾

is more likely that ye will not do injustice.

4:3

3. And marry not those women whom your fathers married, except what hath already happened (of that nature) in the past. Lo! it was ever lewdness and abomination, and an evil way.

حُرِّمَتْ عَلَيْكُمْ أُمَّهٰتُكُمْ وَبَنٰتُكُمْ وَأَخَوٰتُكُمْ
وَعَمّٰتُكُمْ وَخٰلٰتُكُمْ وَبَنٰتُ الْأَخِ وَبَنٰتُ
الْأُخْتِ وَأُمَّهٰتُكُمُ الّٰتِيٓ أَرْضَعْنَكُمْ وَأَخَوٰتُكُمْ
مِّنَ الرَّضٰعَةِ وَأُمَّهٰتُ نِسَآئِكُمْ وَرَبٰٓئِبُكُمُ
الّٰتِي فِي حُجُورِكُم مِّن نِّسَآئِكُمُ الّٰتِي
دَخَلْتُم بِهِنَّ فَإِن لَّمْ تَكُونُوا دَخَلْتُم
بِهِنَّ فَلَا جُنَاحَ عَلَيْكُمْ وَحَلٰٓئِلُ
أَبْنَآئِكُمُ الَّذِينَ مِنْ أَصْلٰبِكُمْ وَأَن
تَجْمَعُوا بَيْنَ الْأُخْتَيْنِ إِلَّا مَا قَدْ سَلَفَ
إِنَّ اللَّهَ كَانَ غَفُورًا رَّحِيمًا ﴿٢٣﴾
وَالْمُحْصَنٰتُ مِنَ النِّسَآءِ إِلَّا مَا مَلَكَتْ
أَيْمٰنُكُمْ كِتٰبَ اللَّهِ عَلَيْكُمْ وَأُحِلَّ لَكُم
مَّا وَرَآءَ ذٰلِكُمْ أَن تَبْتَغُوا بِأَمْوٰلِكُم
مُّحْصِنِينَ غَيْرَ مُسٰفِحِينَ

Forbidden unto you are your mothers, and your daughters, and your sisters, and your father's sisters, and your mother's sisters, and your brother's daughters and your sister's daughters, and your foster–mothers, and your foster–sisters, and your mothers–in–law, and your step–daughters who are under your protection (born) of your women unto whom ye have gone in – but if ye have not gone in unto them, then it is no sin for you (to marry their daughters)– and the wives of your sons who (spring) from your own loins. And (it is forbidden unto you) that ye should have two sisters together, except what hath already happened (of that nature) in the past. Lo! Allah is ever Forgiving, Merciful.

And all married women (are forbidden) unto you save those (captives) whom your right hands possess. It is a decree of Allah for you. Lawful unto you are all beyond those mentioned, so that ye seek them with your wealth in honest wedlock, not debauchery.

4:22–24

4. الْيَوْمَ أُحِلَّ لَكُمُ الطَّيِّبٰتُ وَطَعَامُ
الَّذِينَ أُوتُوا الْكِتٰبَ حِلٌّ لَّكُمْ وَطَعَامُكُمْ
حِلٌّ لَّهُمْ وَالْمُحْصَنٰتُ مِنَ الْمُؤْمِنٰتِ
وَالْمُحْصَنٰتُ مِنَ الَّذِينَ أُوتُوا الْكِتٰبَ
مِن قَبْلِكُمْ إِذَآ ءَاتَيْتُمُوهُنَّ أُجُورَهُنَّ
مُحْصِنِينَ غَيْرَ مُسٰفِحِينَ وَلَا مُتَّخِذِيٓ
أَخْدَانٍ وَمَن يَكْفُرْ بِالْإِيمٰنِ فَقَدْ
حَبِطَ عَمَلُهُ وَهُوَ فِي الْآخِرَةِ مِنَ
الْخٰسِرِينَ ﴿٥﴾

4. This day are (all) good things made lawful for you. The food of those who have received the Scripture is lawful for you, and your food is lawful for them. And so are the virtuous women of the believers and the virtuous women of those who received the Scripture before you (lawful for you) when ye give them their marriage portions and live with them in honour, not in fornication, nor taking them as secret concubines. Whoso denieth the faith, his work is vain and he will be among the losers in the Hereafter.

5:5

5. The adulterer shall not marry save an adulteress or an idolatress, and the adulteress none shall marry save an adulterer or an idolater. All that is forbidden unto believers.

24:3

6. And marry such of you as are solitary and the pious of your slaves and maid servants. If they be poor, Allah will enrich them of His bounty. Allah is of ample means, Aware.

And let those who cannot find a match keep chaste till Allah give them independence by His grace.

24:32–33

.5 اَلزَّانِیْ لَا یَنْكِحُ اِلَّا زَانِیَةً اَوْ مُشْرِكَةً
وَّ الزَّانِیَةُ لَا یَنْكِحُهَاۤ اِلَّا زَانٍ اَوْ مُشْرِكٌ
وَ حُرِّمَ ذٰلِكَ عَلَى الْمُؤْمِنِیْنَ ۝

.6 وَ اَنْكِحُوا الْاَیَامٰى مِنْكُمْ وَ الصّٰلِحِیْنَ
مِنْ عِبَادِكُمْ وَ اِمَآىِٕكُمْ اِنْ یَّكُوْنُوْا
فُقَرَآءَ یُغْنِهِمُ اللّٰهُ مِنْ فَضْلِهٖ وَ اللّٰهُ
وَاسِعٌ عَلِیْمٌ ۝

وَ لْیَسْتَعْفِفِ الَّذِیْنَ لَا یَجِدُوْنَ نِكَاحًا
حَتّٰى یُغْنِیَهُمُ اللّٰهُ مِنْ فَضْلِهٖ

○

Ref: 2:102,228; 4:19,25,129-130; 24:26; 33:37; 60:10-12.

See also: Divorce, *Khul'a, Mahr*, Polygamy, Women Permissible to Marry, Women of Prohibited Degrees.

NO COMPULSION IN RELIGION

1. There is no compulsion in religion. The right direction is henceforth distinct from error. And he who rejecteth false deities and believeth in Allah hath grasped a firm handhold which will never break. Allah is Hearer, Knower.

2:256

2. And if thy Lord willed, all who are in the earth would have believed together. Wouldst thou (Muhammad) compel men until they are believers?

It is not for any soul to believe save by the permission of Allah.

10:99–100

3. Say: O mankind! Now hath the Truth from your Lord come unto you. So whosoever is guided, is guided only for (the good of) his soul, and whosoever erreth, erreth only against it. And I am not a warder over you.

10:108

4. Say: (It is) the truth from the Lord of you (all). Then whosoever will, let him believe, and whosoever will, let him disbelieve.

18:29

5. Unto this, then, summon (O Muhammad). And be thou upright as thou art command-ed, and follow not their lusts, but say: I believe in whatever

1. لَآ إِكْرَاهَ فِي الدِّينِ قَدْ تَبَيَّنَ الرُّشْدُ مِنَ
الْغَيِّ فَمَنْ يَكْفُرْ بِالطَّاغُوتِ وَيُؤْمِنْ بِاللَّهِ
فَقَدِ اسْتَمْسَكَ بِالْعُرْوَةِ الْوُثْقَىٰ لَا انْفِصَامَ
لَهَا وَاللَّهُ سَمِيعٌ عَلِيمٌ ﴿٢٥٦﴾

2. وَلَوْ شَاءَ رَبُّكَ لَآمَنَ مَنْ فِي الْأَرْضِ
كُلُّهُمْ جَمِيعًا أَفَأَنْتَ تُكْرِهُ النَّاسَ حَتَّىٰ
يَكُونُوا مُؤْمِنِينَ ﴿٩٩﴾
وَمَا كَانَ لِنَفْسٍ أَنْ تُؤْمِنَ إِلَّا بِإِذْنِ
اللَّهِ

3. قُلْ يَا أَيُّهَا النَّاسُ قَدْ جَاءَكُمُ الْحَقُّ
مِنْ رَبِّكُمْ فَمَنِ اهْتَدَىٰ فَإِنَّمَا
يَهْتَدِي لِنَفْسِهِ وَمَنْ ضَلَّ فَإِنَّمَا يَضِلُّ
عَلَيْهَا وَمَا أَنَا عَلَيْكُمْ بِوَكِيلٍ ﴿١٠٨﴾

4. وَقُلِ الْحَقُّ مِنْ رَبِّكُمْ فَمَنْ شَاءَ
فَلْيُؤْمِنْ وَمَنْ شَاءَ فَلْيَكْفُرْ

5. فَلِذَٰلِكَ فَادْعُ وَاسْتَقِمْ كَمَا أُمِرْتَ
وَلَا تَتَّبِعْ أَهْوَاءَهُمْ وَقُلْ آمَنْتُ
بِمَا أَنْزَلَ اللَّهُ مِنْ كِتَابٍ وَأُمِرْتُ
لِأَعْدِلَ بَيْنَكُمُ اللَّهُ رَبُّنَا وَرَبُّكُمْ
لَنَا أَعْمَالُنَا وَلَكُمْ أَعْمَالُكُمْ لَا حُجَّةَ
بَيْنَنَا وَبَيْنَكُمُ اللَّهُ يَجْمَعُ بَيْنَنَا
وَإِلَيْهِ الْمَصِيرُ ﴿١٥﴾

Scripture Allah hath sent down, and I am commanded to be just among you. Allah is our Lord and your Lord. Unto us our works and unto you your works; no argument between us and you. Allah will bring us together and unto Him is the journeying.

42:15

6. Lo! This is a Reminder. Let him who will, then, choose a way unto his Lord.
73:19

7. Nay, verily. Lo! this is an Admonishment.
So whosoever will, may heed.
74:54–55

8. Lo! We have shown him the way, whether he be grateful or disbelieving.
76:3

9. This is naugnt else than a reminder unto creation,
Unto whomsoever of you willeth to walk straight.
81:27–28

10. Remind them for thou art but a remembrancer,
Thou art not at all a warder over them.
88:21–22

11. Unto you your religion, and unto me my religion.
109–6

6. إِنَّ هَٰذِهِ تَذْكِرَةٌ ۖ فَمَن شَاءَ اتَّخَذَ إِلَىٰ رَبِّهِ سَبِيلًا ﴿١٩﴾

7. كَلَّا إِنَّهُ تَذْكِرَةٌ ﴿٥٤﴾
فَمَن شَاءَ ذَكَرَهُ ﴿٥٥﴾

8. إِنَّا هَدَيْنَاهُ السَّبِيلَ إِمَّا شَاكِرًا وَإِمَّا كَفُورًا ﴿٣﴾

9. إِنْ هُوَ إِلَّا ذِكْرٌ لِّلْعَالَمِينَ ﴿٢٧﴾
لِمَن شَاءَ مِنكُمْ أَن يَسْتَقِيمَ ﴿٢٨﴾

10. فَذَكِّرْ إِنَّمَا أَنتَ مُذَكِّرٌ ﴿٢١﴾
لَّسْتَ عَلَيْهِم بِمُصَيْطِرٍ ﴿٢٢﴾

11. لَكُمْ دِينُكُمْ وَلِيَ دِينِ ﴿٦﴾

Ref: 22:78.

OATH OF ALLEGIANCE

1. Lo! those who swear allegiance unto thee (Muhammad), swear allegiance only unto Allah. The Hand of Allah is above their hands. So whosoever breaketh his oath, breaketh it only to his soul's hurt; while whosoever keepeth his covenant with Allah, on him will He bestow immense reward.

48:10

2. Allah was well pleased with the believers when they swore allegiance unto thee beneath the tree, and He knew what was in their hearts, and He sent down peace of re-assurance on them, and hath rewarded them with a near victory;

48:18

3. O Prophet! If the believing women come unto thee, taking oath of allegiance unto thee that they will ascribe nothing as partner unto Allah, and will neither steal nor commit adultery nor kill their children, nor produce any lie that they have devised between their hands and feet, nor disobey thee in what is right, then accept their allegiance and ask Allah to forgive them. Lo! Allah is Forgiving, Merciful.

60:12

1. إِنَّ الَّذِينَ يُبَايِعُونَكَ إِنَّمَا يُبَايِعُونَ
اللَّهَ يَدُ اللَّهِ فَوْقَ أَيْدِيهِمْ فَمَن
نَّكَثَ فَإِنَّمَا يَنكُثُ عَلَىٰ نَفْسِهِ وَمَنْ
أَوْفَىٰ بِمَا عَاهَدَ عَلَيْهُ اللَّهَ فَسَيُؤْتِيهِ
أَجْرًا عَظِيمًا ﴿١٠﴾

2. لَقَدْ رَضِيَ اللَّهُ عَنِ الْمُؤْمِنِينَ إِذْ
يُبَايِعُونَكَ تَحْتَ الشَّجَرَةِ فَعَلِمَ مَا
فِي قُلُوبِهِمْ فَأَنزَلَ السَّكِينَةَ عَلَيْهِمْ
وَأَثَابَهُمْ فَتْحًا قَرِيبًا ﴿١٨﴾

3. يَا أَيُّهَا النَّبِيُّ إِذَا جَاءَكَ الْمُؤْمِنَاتُ
يُبَايِعْنَكَ عَلَىٰ أَن لَّا يُشْرِكْنَ بِاللَّهِ
شَيْئًا وَلَا يَسْرِقْنَ وَلَا يَزْنِينَ
وَلَا يَقْتُلْنَ أَوْلَادَهُنَّ وَلَا يَأْتِينَ
بِبُهْتَانٍ يَفْتَرِينَهُ بَيْنَ أَيْدِيهِنَّ
وَأَرْجُلِهِنَّ وَلَا يَعْصِينَكَ فِي
مَعْرُوفٍ فَبَايِعْهُنَّ وَاسْتَغْفِرْ لَهُنَّ
اللَّهَ إِنَّ اللَّهَ غَفُورٌ رَّحِيمٌ ﴿١٢﴾

OBEDIENCE TO PROPHET MUHAMMAD (PBUH)

1. Say, (O Muhammad, to mankind); If ye love Allah, follow me; Allah will love you and forgive you your sins. Allah is Forgiving, Merciful.

Say: Obey Allah and the messenger. But if they turn away, lo! Allah loveth not the disbelievers (in His guidance).

3:31–32

2. We sent no messenger save that he should be obeyed by Allah's leave. And if, when they had wronged themselves, they had but come unto thee and asked forgiveness of Allah and the messenger had asked forgiveness for them, they would have found Allah Forgiving, Merciful.

But, nay, by thy Lord, they will not believe (in truth) until they make thee judge of what is in dispute between them and find within themselves no dislike of that which thou decidest, and submit with full submission.

4:64–65

3. Say (O Muhammad): O mankind! Lo! I am the messenger of Allah to you all—(the messenger of) Him unto whom belongeth the Sovereignty of the heavens and the earth. There is no god save Him. He quickeneth and He giveth death. So believe in Allah and His messenger, the Prophet who can neither read nor write, who believeth in Allah and in His Words and follow him that haply

1. قُلْ إِنْ كُنْتُمْ تُحِبُّوْنَ اللّٰهَ فَاتَّبِعُوْنِيْ
يُحْبِبْكُمُ اللّٰهُ وَيَغْفِرْ لَكُمْ ذُنُوْبَكُمْ
وَاللّٰهُ غَفُوْرٌ رَّحِيْمٌ ○
قُلْ أَطِيْعُوا اللّٰهَ وَالرَّسُوْلَ فَإِنْ تَوَلَّوْا
فَإِنَّ اللّٰهَ لَا يُحِبُّ الْكٰفِرِيْنَ ○

2. وَمَا أَرْسَلْنَا مِنْ رَّسُوْلٍ إِلَّا لِيُطَاعَ بِإِذْنِ
اللّٰهِ وَلَوْ أَنَّهُمْ إِذْ ظَّلَمُوْا أَنْفُسَهُمْ جَاءُوْكَ
فَاسْتَغْفَرُوا اللّٰهَ وَاسْتَغْفَرَ لَهُمُ الرَّسُوْلُ
لَوَجَدُوا اللّٰهَ تَوَّابًا رَّحِيْمًا ﴿٦٤﴾
فَلَا وَرَبِّكَ لَا يُؤْمِنُوْنَ حَتّٰى يُحَكِّمُوْكَ
فِيْمَا شَجَرَ بَيْنَهُمْ ثُمَّ لَا يَجِدُوْا فِيْ أَنْفُسِهِمْ
حَرَجًا مِّمَّا قَضَيْتَ وَيُسَلِّمُوْا تَسْلِيْمًا ﴿٦٥﴾

3. قُلْ يٰأَيُّهَا النَّاسُ إِنِّيْ رَسُوْلُ اللّٰهِ إِلَيْكُمْ
جَمِيْعًا الَّذِيْ لَهٗ مُلْكُ السَّمٰوٰتِ وَالْأَرْضِ
لَا إِلٰهَ إِلَّا هُوَ يُحْيٖ وَيُمِيْتُ فَاٰمِنُوْا
بِاللّٰهِ وَرَسُوْلِهِ النَّبِيِّ الْأُمِّيِّ الَّذِيْ يُؤْمِنُ
بِاللّٰهِ وَكَلِمٰتِهٖ وَاتَّبِعُوْهُ لَعَلَّكُمْ تَهْتَدُوْنَ ﴿١٥٨﴾

4. يٰأَيُّهَا الَّذِيْنَ اٰمَنُوا اسْتَجِيْبُوْا لِلّٰهِ وَلِلرَّسُوْلِ
إِذَا دَعَاكُمْ لِمَا يُحْيِيْكُمْ وَاعْلَمُوْا أَنَّ اللّٰهَ
يَحُوْلُ بَيْنَ الْمَرْءِ وَقَلْبِهٖ وَأَنَّهٗ
إِلَيْهِ تُحْشَرُوْنَ ﴿٢٤﴾

ye may be led aright.

7:158

4. O ye who believe! Obey Allah, and the messenger when He calleth you to that which quickeneth you, and know that Allah cometh in between the man and his own heart, and that He it is unto Whom ye will be gathered.

8:24

5. The saying of (all true) believers when they appeal unto Allah and His messenger to judge between them is only that they say: We hear and we obey. And such are the successful.

He who obeyeth Allah and His messenger, and feareth Allah, and keepeth duty (unto Him): such indeed are the victorious.

24:51–52

6. Say: Obey Allah and obey the messenger. But if ye turn away, then (it is) for him (to do) only that wherewith he hath been charged, and for you (to do) only that wherewith ye have been charged. If ye obey him, ye will go aright. But the messenger hath no other charge than to convey (the message), plainly.

24:54

7. Verily in the messenger of Allah ye have a good example for him who looketh unto Allah and the Last Day, and remembereth Allah much.

33:21

8. And it becometh not a believing man or a believing woman, when Allah and His messenger have decided an affair (for them), that they should (after that) claim any say in their affair; and whoso is rebellious to Allah and His messenger, he verily goeth

5. إنما كان قول المؤمنين إذا دعوا
إلى الله ورسوله ليحكم بينهم أن
يقولوا سمعنا وأطعنا وأولئك
هم المفلحون ﴿٥١﴾

ومن يطع الله ورسوله ويخش
الله ويتقه فأولئك هم الفائزون ﴿٥٢﴾

6. قل أطيعوا الله وأطيعوا الرسول فإن
تولوا فإنما عليه ما حمل وعليكم
ما حملتم وإن تطيعوه تهتدوا وما
على الرسول إلا البلغ المبين ﴿٥٤﴾

7. لقد كان لكم في رسول الله أسوة
حسنة لمن كان يرجوا الله واليوم
الآخر وذكر الله كثيرا ﴿٢١﴾

8. وما كان لمؤمن ولا مؤمنة
إذا قضى الله ورسوله أمرا أن
يكون لهم الخيرة من أمرهم
ومن يعص الله ورسوله فقد
ضل ضلالا مبينا ﴿٣٦﴾

9. وما آتكم الرسول فخذوه وما نهكم
عنه فانتهوا واتقوا الله إن الله
شديد العقاب ﴿٧﴾

astray in error manifest.

33:36

9. And whatsoever the messenger giveth you, take it. And whatsoever he forbiddeth, abstain (from it). And keep your duty to Allah. Lo! Allah is stern in reprisal.

59:7

Ref: 3:32,132; 4:80; 7:157; 8:1,20,46; 9:71; 24:56,63; 47:33; 48:17; 58:13; 64:12. **See also:** Submission to Allah and His Messenger (PBUH).

OBEDIENCE TO THOSE IN AUTHORITY

1. O ye who believe! Obey Allah, and obey the messenger and those of you who are in authority; and if ye have a dispute concerning any matter, refer it to Allah and the messenger if ye are (in truth) believers in Allah and the Last Day. That is better and more seemly in the end.

4:59

2. They swear by Allah solemnly that, if thou order them, they will go forth. Say: Swear not; known obedience (is better). Lo! Allah is Informed of what ye do.

24:53

OBLIGATIONS TOWARDS RELATIVES

1. Those who break the covenant of Allah after ratifying it, and sever that which Allah ordered to be joined, and (who) make mischief in the earth: Those are they who are the losers.

2:27

2. Such as unite that which Allah hath commanded should be joined, and fear their Lord, and dread a woeful reckoning.

Such as persevere in seeking their Lord's Countenance and are regular in prayer and spend ot that which We bestow upon them secretly and openly, and overcome evil with good. Theirs will be the sequel of the (heavely) Home.

13:21–22

3. And those who break the covenant of Allah after ratifying it, and sever that which Allah hath commanded should be joined, and make mischief in the earth: theirs is the curse and theirs the ill abode.

13:25

1. يَٰٓأَيُّهَا ٱلَّذِينَ ءَامَنُوٓا۟ أَطِيعُوا۟ ٱللَّهَ وَأَطِيعُوا۟
ٱلرَّسُولَ وَأُو۟لِى ٱلْأَمْرِ مِنكُمْ ۖ فَإِن
تَنَٰزَعْتُمْ فِى شَىْءٍ فَرُدُّوهُ إِلَى ٱللَّهِ وَٱلرَّسُولِ
إِن كُنتُمْ تُؤْمِنُونَ بِٱللَّهِ وَٱلْيَوْمِ ٱلْءَاخِرِ ۚ
ذَٰلِكَ خَيْرٌ وَأَحْسَنُ تَأْوِيلًا

2. وَأَقْسَمُوا۟ بِٱللَّهِ جَهْدَ أَيْمَٰنِهِمْ لَئِنْ
أَمَرْتَهُمْ لَيَخْرُجُنَّ ۖ قُل لَّا تُقْسِمُوا۟ ۖ طَاعَةٌ
مَّعْرُوفَةٌ ۚ إِنَّ ٱللَّهَ خَبِيرٌۢ بِمَا تَعْمَلُونَ

1. ٱلَّذِينَ يَنقُضُونَ عَهْدَ ٱللَّهِ مِنۢ بَعْدِ مِيثَٰقِهِۦ
وَيَقْطَعُونَ مَآ أَمَرَ ٱللَّهُ بِهِۦٓ أَن يُوصَلَ وَيُفْسِدُونَ
فِى ٱلْأَرْضِ ۚ أُو۟لَٰٓئِكَ هُمُ ٱلْخَٰسِرُونَ

2. وَٱلَّذِينَ يَصِلُونَ مَآ أَمَرَ ٱللَّهُ بِهِۦٓ أَن
يُوصَلَ وَيَخْشَوْنَ رَبَّهُمْ وَيَخَافُونَ
سُوٓءَ ٱلْحِسَابِ
وَٱلَّذِينَ صَبَرُوا۟ ٱبْتِغَآءَ وَجْهِ رَبِّهِمْ
وَأَقَامُوا۟ ٱلصَّلَوٰةَ وَأَنفَقُوا۟ مِمَّا رَزَقْنَٰهُمْ
سِرًّا وَعَلَانِيَةً وَيَدْرَءُونَ بِٱلْحَسَنَةِ
ٱلسَّيِّئَةَ أُو۟لَٰٓئِكَ لَهُمْ عُقْبَى ٱلدَّارِ

3. وَٱلَّذِينَ يَنقُضُونَ عَهْدَ ٱللَّهِ مِنۢ بَعْدِ
مِيثَٰقِهِۦ وَيَقْطَعُونَ مَآ أَمَرَ ٱللَّهُ بِهِۦٓ
أَن يُوصَلَ وَيُفْسِدُونَ فِى ٱلْأَرْضِ ۙ
أُو۟لَٰٓئِكَ لَهُمُ ٱللَّعْنَةُ وَلَهُمْ سُوٓءُ ٱلدَّارِ

OBLIGATIONS TOWARDS RELATIVES

Fef. 5:20; 6:93; 13:32; 22:52; 30:47; 34:44; 37: 72; 40:70; 41:14; 43:6-7, 23,45; 57:25.

See also: Children, Relatives, Rights of Parents.

OBSCENITY

1. Lo! We have made the devils protecting friends for those who believe not.

And when they do some lewdness they say: We found our fathers doing it and Allah hath enjoined it on us. Say: Allah, verily, enjoineth not lewdness. Tell ye concerning Allah that which ye know not?

7:27–28

2. Lo! Allah enjoineth justice and kindness, and giving to kinsfolk, and forbiddeth lewdness and abomination and wickedness. He exhorteth you in order that ye may take heed.

16:90

3. Lo! those who love that slander should be spread concerning those who believe, theirs will be a painful punishment in the world and, the Hereafter. Allah knoweth. Ye know not.

24:19

1. إِنَّا جَعَلْنَا الشَّيٰطِيْنَ أَوْلِيَآءَ لِلَّذِيْنَ لَا
يُؤْمِنُوْنَ ﴿٢٧﴾
وَإِذَا فَعَلُوْا فَاحِشَةً قَالُوْا وَجَدْنَا عَلَيْهَآ
اٰبَآءَنَا وَاللّٰهُ أَمَرَنَا بِهَا ۗ قُلْ إِنَّ اللّٰهَ
لَا يَأْمُرُ بِالْفَحْشَآءِ ۗ أَتَقُوْلُوْنَ عَلَى اللّٰهِ مَا
لَا تَعْلَمُوْنَ ﴿٢٨﴾

2. إِنَّ اللّٰهَ يَأْمُرُ بِالْعَدْلِ وَالْإِحْسَانِ
وَإِيْتَآئِ ذِي الْقُرْبٰى وَيَنْهٰى عَنِ
الْفَحْشَآءِ وَالْمُنْكَرِ وَالْبَغْيِ ۚ يَعِظُكُمْ
لَعَلَّكُمْ تَذَكَّرُوْنَ ﴿٩٠﴾

3. إِنَّ الَّذِيْنَ يُحِبُّوْنَ أَنْ تَشِيْعَ الْفَاحِشَةُ
فِي الَّذِيْنَ اٰمَنُوْا لَهُمْ عَذَابٌ أَلِيْمٌ
فِي الدُّنْيَا وَالْاٰخِرَةِ ۚ وَاللّٰهُ يَعْلَمُ
وَأَنْتُمْ لَا تَعْلَمُوْنَ ﴿١٩﴾

Ref: 2:169,268; 12:24· 17:32; 24:21; 29:45.

See also: Fornication. Homosexuality.

OFFICE OF APOSTLESHIP

1. The messenger believeth in that which hath been revealed unto him from his Lord and (so do) the believers. Each one believeth in Allah and His angels and His Scriptures and His messengers – We make no distinction between any of His messengers—and they say: We hear, and we obey. (Grant us) Thy forgiveness, our Lord. Unto Thee is the journeying.

2:285

2. It is not (possible) for any human being unto whom Allah had given the Scripture and wisdom and the Prophethood that he should afterwards have said unto mankind: Be slaves of me instead of Allah; but (what he said was): Be ye faithful servants of the Lord by virtue of your constant teaching of the Scripture and of your constant study thereof.

And he commanded you not that ye should take the angels and the Prophets for lords. Would he command you to disbelieve after ye had surrendered (to Allah)?

3:79–80

3. We sent no messenger save that he should be obeyed by Allah's leave. And if, when they had wronged themselves, they had but come unto thee and asked forgiveness of Allah and the messenger had asked forgiveness for them they would have found Allah

1. آمَنَ الرَّسُولُ بِمَا أُنْزِلَ إِلَيْهِ مِنْ رَبِّهِ
وَالْمُؤْمِنُونَ ۚ كُلٌّ آمَنَ بِاللَّهِ وَمَلَائِكَتِهِ
وَكُتُبِهِ وَرُسُلِهِ لَا نُفَرِّقُ بَيْنَ أَحَدٍ
مِنْ رُسُلِهِ ۚ وَقَالُوا سَمِعْنَا وَأَطَعْنَا ۖ
غُفْرَانَكَ رَبَّنَا وَإِلَيْكَ الْمَصِيرُ

2. مَا كَانَ لِبَشَرٍ أَنْ يُؤْتِيَهُ اللَّهُ الْكِتَابَ
وَالْحُكْمَ وَالنُّبُوَّةَ ثُمَّ يَقُولَ لِلنَّاسِ
كُونُوا عِبَادًا لِي مِنْ دُونِ اللَّهِ وَلَٰكِنْ
كُونُوا رَبَّانِيِّينَ بِمَا كُنْتُمْ تُعَلِّمُونَ الْكِتَابَ
وَبِمَا كُنْتُمْ تَدْرُسُونَ
وَلَا يَأْمُرَكُمْ أَنْ تَتَّخِذُوا الْمَلَائِكَةَ وَ
النَّبِيِّينَ أَرْبَابًا ۗ أَيَأْمُرُكُمْ بِالْكُفْرِ
بَعْدَ إِذْ أَنْتُمْ مُسْلِمُونَ

3. وَمَا أَرْسَلْنَا مِنْ رَسُولٍ إِلَّا لِيُطَاعَ بِإِذْنِ
اللَّهِ ۚ وَلَوْ أَنَّهُمْ إِذْ ظَلَمُوا أَنْفُسَهُمْ جَاءُوكَ
فَاسْتَغْفَرُوا اللَّهَ وَاسْتَغْفَرَ لَهُمُ الرَّسُولُ
لَوَجَدُوا اللَّهَ تَوَّابًا رَحِيمًا

4. يَا أَيُّهَا الرَّسُولُ بَلِّغْ مَا أُنْزِلَ إِلَيْكَ مِنْ
رَبِّكَ ۖ وَإِنْ لَمْ تَفْعَلْ فَمَا بَلَّغْتَ رِسَالَتَهُ ۚ
وَاللَّهُ يَعْصِمُكَ مِنَ النَّاسِ ۗ إِنَّ اللَّهَ
لَا يَهْدِي الْقَوْمَ الْكَافِرِينَ

Forgiving, Merciful.

4:64

4. O Messenger! Make known that which hath been revealed unto thee from thy Lord, for if thou do it not, thou will not have conveyed His message. Allah will protect thee from mankind. Lo! Allah guideth not the disbelieving folk.

5:67

5. And We sent no prophet unto any township but We did afflict its folk with tribulation and adversity that haply they might grow humble.

7:94

6. And We never sent a messenger save with the language of his folk, that he might make (the Message) clear for them. Then Allah sendeth whom He will astray, and guideth whom He will. He is the Mighty, the Wise.

14:4

7. And We sent no messenger before thee but We inspired him, (saying): There is no God save Me (Allah), so worship Me.

21:25

8. We never sent before thee any messengers but lo! they verily ate food and walked in the markets. And We have appointed some of you a test for others: Will ye be steadfast? And thy Lord is ever Seer.

25:20

9. And We sent not unto any township a warner, but its pampered ones declared: Lo! we are disbelievers in that which ye have been sent.

And they say: We are more (than you) in wealth and children. We are not the punished!

34:34–35

10. And it was not (vouchsafed) to any mortal that Allah should speak to him unless (it be) by revelation or from behind a veil, or (that) He sendeth a messenger to reveal what He will by His leave. Lo! He is Exalted, Wise.

42:51

5. وَمَآ أَرْسَلْنَا فِى قَرْيَةٍ مِّن نَّبِىٍّ إِلَّآ أَخَذْنَآ
أَهْلَهَا بِٱلْبَأْسَآءِ وَٱلضَّرَّآءِ لَعَلَّهُمْ يَضَّرَّعُونَ ﴿٩٤﴾

6. وَمَآ أَرْسَلْنَا مِن رَّسُولٍ إِلَّا بِلِسَانِ قَوْمِهِۦ
لِيُبَيِّنَ لَهُمْ فَيُضِلُّ ٱللَّهُ مَن يَشَآءُ وَ
يَهْدِى مَن يَشَآءُ وَهُوَ ٱلْعَزِيزُ ٱلْحَكِيمُ ﴿٤﴾

7. وَمَآ أَرْسَلْنَا مِن قَبْلِكَ مِن رَّسُولٍ
إِلَّا نُوحِىٓ إِلَيْهِ أَنَّهُۥ لَآ إِلَٰهَ إِلَّآ
أَنَا۠ فَٱعْبُدُونِ ﴿٢٥﴾

8. وَمَآ أَرْسَلْنَا قَبْلَكَ مِنَ ٱلْمُرْسَلِينَ
إِلَّآ إِنَّهُمْ لَيَأْكُلُونَ ٱلطَّعَامَ وَيَمْشُونَ
فِى ٱلْأَسْوَاقِ وَجَعَلْنَا بَعْضَكُمْ لِبَعْضٍ
فِتْنَةً أَتَصْبِرُونَ وَكَانَ رَبُّكَ بَصِيرًا ﴿٢٠﴾

9. وَمَآ أَرْسَلْنَا فِى قَرْيَةٍ مِّن نَّذِيرٍ
إِلَّا قَالَ مُتْرَفُوهَآ إِنَّا بِمَآ أُرْسِلْتُم
بِهِۦ كَٰفِرُونَ ﴿٣٤﴾

وَقَالُوا۟ نَحْنُ أَكْثَرُ أَمْوَٰلًا وَأَوْلَٰدًا
وَمَا نَحْنُ بِمُعَذَّبِينَ ﴿٣٥﴾

10. وَمَا كَانَ لِبَشَرٍ أَن يُكَلِّمَهُ ٱللَّهُ إِلَّا
وَحْيًا أَوْ مِن وَرَآئِ حِجَابٍ أَوْ يُرْسِلَ
رَسُولًا فَيُوحِىَ بِإِذْنِهِۦ مَا يَشَآءُ إِنَّهُۥ
عَلِىٌّ حَكِيمٌ ﴿٥١﴾

Ref: 5:20; 6:93; 13:32; 22:52; 30:47; 34:44; 37:72; 40:70; 41:14; 43:6-7,23; 45; 57:25.

See also: Office of Prophethood, Revelation.

OFFICE OF PROPHETHOOD

1. Even as We have sent unto you a messenger from among you, who reciteth unto you Our revelations and causeth you to grow, and teacheth you the Scripture and wisdom, and teacheth you that which ye knew not.

2:151

2. O Messenger! Make known that which hath been revealed unto thee from thy Lord, for if thou do it not, thou will not have conveyed His message. Allah will protect thee from mankind. Lo! Allah guideth not the disbelieving folk.

5:67

3. The duty of the messenger is only to convey (the message). Allah knoweth what ye proclaim and what ye hide.

5:99

4. Those who follow the messenger, the Prophet who can neither read nor write, whom they will find described in the Torah and the Gospel (which are) with them. He will enjoin on them that which is right and forbid them that which is wrong. He will make lawful for them all good things and prohibit for them only the foul; and he will relieve them of their burden and the fetters that they used to wear. Then those who believe in him, and honour him, and help him, and follow the light which is sent down with him; they are the successful.

7:157

1. كَمَآ أَرْسَلْنَا فِيكُمْ رَسُولًا مِّنكُمْ يَتْلُوا عَلَيْكُمْ
ءَايَٰتِنَا وَيُزَكِّيكُمْ وَيُعَلِّمُكُمُ ٱلْكِتَٰبَ وَٱلْحِكْمَةَ
وَيُعَلِّمُكُم مَّا لَمْ تَكُونُوا تَعْلَمُونَ ﴿١٥١﴾

2. يَٰٓأَيُّهَا ٱلرَّسُولُ بَلِّغْ مَآ أُنزِلَ إِلَيْكَ مِن
رَّبِّكَ ۖ وَإِن لَّمْ تَفْعَلْ فَمَا بَلَّغْتَ رِسَالَتَهُ ۚ
وَٱللَّهُ يَعْصِمُكَ مِنَ ٱلنَّاسِ ۗ إِنَّ ٱللَّهَ
لَا يَهْدِى ٱلْقَوْمَ ٱلْكَٰفِرِينَ ﴿٦٧﴾

3. مَّا عَلَى ٱلرَّسُولِ إِلَّا ٱلْبَلَٰغُ ۗ وَٱللَّهُ يَعْلَمُ
مَا تُبْدُونَ وَمَا تَكْتُمُونَ ﴿٩٩﴾

4. ٱلَّذِينَ يَتَّبِعُونَ ٱلرَّسُولَ ٱلنَّبِىَّ ٱلْأُمِّىَّ
ٱلَّذِى يَجِدُونَهُۥ مَكْتُوبًا عِندَهُمْ فِى ٱلتَّوْرَىٰةِ
وَٱلْإِنجِيلِ يَأْمُرُهُم بِٱلْمَعْرُوفِ وَيَنْهَىٰهُمْ
عَنِ ٱلْمُنكَرِ وَيُحِلُّ لَهُمُ ٱلطَّيِّبَٰتِ وَيُحَرِّمُ
عَلَيْهِمُ ٱلْخَبَٰٓئِثَ وَيَضَعُ عَنْهُمْ إِصْرَهُمْ
وَٱلْأَغْلَٰلَ ٱلَّتِى كَانَتْ عَلَيْهِمْ ۚ فَٱلَّذِينَ
ءَامَنُوا بِهِۦ وَعَزَّرُوهُ وَنَصَرُوهُ وَٱتَّبَعُوا
ٱلنُّورَ ٱلَّذِىٓ أُنزِلَ مَعَهُۥٓ ۙ أُولَٰٓئِكَ هُمُ
ٱلْمُفْلِحُونَ ﴿١٥٧﴾

See also: Office of Apostleship.

OPPRESSION

1. Allah loveth not the utterance of harsh speech save by one who hath been wronged. Allah is ever Hearer, Knower.

4:148

2. And whoso defendeth himself after he hath suffered wrong—for such, there is no way (of blame) against them.

42:41

3. And lo! for those who (now) do wrong there is an evil day like unto the evil day (which came for) their likes (of old); so let them not ask Me to hasten on (that day).

51:59

1. لَا يُحِبُّ اللّٰهُ الْجَهْرَ بِالسُّوْٓءِ مِنَ الْقَوْلِ
إِلَّا مَنْ ظُلِمَ ۗ وَكَانَ اللّٰهُ سَمِيْعًا عَلِيْمًا ﴿١٤٨﴾

2. وَلَمَنِ انْتَصَرَ بَعْدَ ظُلْمِهٖ فَأُولٰٓئِكَ
مَا عَلَيْهِمْ مِّنْ سَبِيْلٍ ﴿٤١﴾

3. فَإِنَّ لِلَّذِيْنَ ظَلَمُوْا ذَنُوْبًا مِّثْلَ ذَنُوْبِ
أَصْحٰبِهِمْ فَلَا يَسْتَعْجِلُوْنِ ﴿٥٩﴾

○

See also: Justice, Justice and Equity.

ORNAMENTS

1. And He it is Who hath constrained the sea to be of service that ye eat fresh meat from thence, and bring forth from thence ornaments which ye wear.

16:14

2. Lo! Allah will cause those who believe and do good works to enter Gardens underneath which rivers flow, wherein they will be allowed armlets of gold, and pearls, and their raiment therein will be silk.

22:23

ORPHAN

1. They ask thee, (O Muhammad), what they shall spend. Say: That which ye spend for good (must go) to parents and near kindred and orphans and the needy and the wayfarer. And whatsoever good ye do, lo! Allah is Aware of it.

2:215

2. And they question thee concerning orphans. Say: To improve their lot is best. And if ye mingle your affairs with theirs, then (they are) your brothers. Allah knoweth him who spoileth from him who improveth. Had Allah willed He could have overburdened you. Allah is Mighty, Wise.

2:220

1. وَهُوَ الَّذِي سَخَّرَ الْبَحْرَ لِتَأْكُلُوا مِنْهُ
لَحْمًا طَرِيًّا وَّتَسْتَخْرِجُوا مِنْهُ حِلْيَةً
تَلْبَسُونَهَا

2. إِنَّ اللّٰهَ يُدْخِلُ الَّذِينَ آمَنُوا وَ
عَمِلُوا الصّٰلِحٰتِ جَنّٰتٍ تَجْرِي مِنْ
تَحْتِهَا الْأَنْهٰرُ يُحَلَّوْنَ فِيهَا مِنْ
أَسَاوِرَ مِنْ ذَهَبٍ وَّلُؤْلُؤًا وَلِبَاسُهُمْ
فِيهَا حَرِيرٌ ﴿٢٣﴾

﴿١﴾

1. يَسْئَلُونَكَ مَاذَا يُنْفِقُونَ قُلْ مَا أَنْفَقْتُمْ
مِنْ خَيْرٍ فَلِلْوَالِدَيْنِ وَالْأَقْرَبِينَ وَالْيَتٰمٰى
وَالْمَسٰكِينِ وَابْنِ السَّبِيلِ وَمَا تَفْعَلُوا
مِنْ خَيْرٍ فَإِنَّ اللّٰهَ بِهِ عَلِيمٌ ﴿٢١٥﴾

2. وَيَسْئَلُونَكَ عَنِ الْيَتٰمٰى قُلْ إِصْلَاحٌ لَّهُمْ خَيْرٌ
وَإِنْ تُخَالِطُوهُمْ فَإِخْوَانُكُمْ وَاللّٰهُ يَعْلَمُ الْمُفْسِدَ مِنَ
الْمُصْلِحِ وَلَوْ شَاءَ اللّٰهُ لَأَعْنَتَكُمْ إِنَّ اللّٰهَ
عَزِيزٌ حَكِيمٌ ﴿٢٢٠﴾

3. وَآتُوا الْيَتٰمٰى أَمْوَالَهُمْ وَلَا تَتَبَدَّلُوا
الْخَبِيثَ بِالطَّيِّبِ وَلَا تَأْكُلُوا أَمْوَالَهُمْ
إِلٰى أَمْوَالِكُمْ إِنَّهُ كَانَ حُوبًا كَبِيرًا ﴿٢﴾

3. Give unto orphans their wealth. Exchange not the good for the bad (in your management thereof) nor absorb their wealth into your own wealth. Lo! that would be a great sin.

4:2

ORNAMENTS

Ref: 7:148; 13:17; 22:23; 35:12,33; 76:21

See also: Adornment

4. Give not unto the foolish (what is in) your (keeping of their) wealth, which Allah hath given you to maintain; but feed and clothe them from it and speak kindly unto them.

Prove orphans till they reach the marriageable age; then, if ye find them of sound judgment, deliver over unto them their fortune; and devour it not by squandering and in haste lest they should grow up. Whoso (of the guardians) is rich, let him abstain generously (from taking of the property of orphans); and whoso is poor let him take thereof in reason (for his guardianship). And when ye deliver up their fortune unto orphans, have (the transaction) witnessed in their presence. Allah sufficeth as a Reckoner.

Unto the men (of a family) belongeth a share of that which parents and near kindred leave, and unto the women a share of that which parents and near kindred leave, whether it be little or much—a legal share.

And when kinsfolk and orphans and the needy are present at the division (of the heritage), bestow on them therefrom and speak kindly unto them.

And let those fear (in their behaviour toward orphans) who if they left behind them weak offspring would be afraid for them. So let them mind their duty to Allah and speak justly.

Lo! Those who devour the wealth of orphans wrongfully, they do but swallow fire into their bellies, and they will be exposed to burning flame.

4. وَلَا تُؤْتُوا السُّفَهَآءَ اَمْوَالَكُمُ الَّتِيْ جَعَلَ
اللّٰهُ لَكُمْ قِيٰمًا وَّارْزُقُوْهُمْ فِيْهَا وَاكْسُوْهُمْ
وَقُوْلُوْا لَهُمْ قَوْلًا مَّعْرُوْفًا (٥)
وَابْتَلُوا الْيَتٰمٰى حَتّٰٓى اِذَا بَلَغُوا النِّكَاحَ ۚ فَاِنْ
اٰنَسْتُمْ مِّنْهُمْ رُشْدًا فَادْفَعُوْٓا اِلَيْهِمْ اَمْوَالَهُمْ ۚ
وَلَا تَاْكُلُوْهَآ اِسْرَافًا وَّبِدَارًا اَنْ يَّكْبَرُوْا ۭ
وَمَنْ كَانَ غَنِيًّا فَلْيَسْتَعْفِفْ ۚ وَمَنْ كَانَ
فَقِيْرًا فَلْيَاْكُلْ بِالْمَعْرُوْفِ ۭ فَاِذَا دَفَعْتُمْ
اِلَيْهِمْ اَمْوَالَهُمْ فَاَشْهِدُوْا عَلَيْهِمْ ۭ وَكَفٰى
بِاللّٰهِ حَسِيْبًا (٦)
لِلرِّجَالِ نَصِيْبٌ مِّمَّا تَرَكَ الْوَالِدٰنِ
وَالْاَقْرَبُوْنَ ۠ وَلِلنِّسَآءِ نَصِيْبٌ مِّمَّا تَرَكَ
الْوَالِدٰنِ وَالْاَقْرَبُوْنَ مِمَّا قَلَّ مِنْهُ
اَوْ كَثُرَ ۭ نَصِيْبًا مَّفْرُوْضًا (٧)
وَاِذَا حَضَرَ الْقِسْمَةَ اُولُوا الْقُرْبٰى وَالْيَتٰمٰى
وَالْمَسٰكِيْنُ فَارْزُقُوْهُمْ مِّنْهُ وَقُوْلُوْا
لَهُمْ قَوْلًا مَّعْرُوْفًا (٨)
وَلْيَخْشَ الَّذِيْنَ لَوْ تَرَكُوْا مِنْ خَلْفِهِمْ
ذُرِّيَّةً ضِعٰفًا خَافُوْا عَلَيْهِمْ ۠ فَلْيَتَّقُوا
اللّٰهَ وَلْيَقُوْلُوْا قَوْلًا سَدِيْدًا (٩)
اِنَّ الَّذِيْنَ يَاْكُلُوْنَ اَمْوَالَ الْيَتٰمٰى ظُلْمًا
اِنَّمَا يَاْكُلُوْنَ فِيْ بُطُوْنِهِمْ نَارًا ۭ
وَسَيَصْلَوْنَ سَعِيْرًا (١٠)

4:5–10

5. They consult thee concerning women. Say: Allah giveth you decree concerning them, and the Scripture which hath been recited unto you (giveth decree), concerning female orphans and those unto whom ye give not that which is ordained for them though ye desire to marry them, and (concerning) the weak among children, and that ye should deal justly with orphans. Whatever good ye do, lo! Allah is ever Aware of it.

4:127

5. وَيَسْتَفْتُوْنَكَ فِي النِّسَاءِ ۖ قُلِ اللّٰهُ يُفْتِيْكُمْ
فِيْهِنَّ ۙ وَمَا يُتْلٰى عَلَيْكُمْ فِي الْكِتٰبِ فِيْ
يَتٰمَى النِّسَاءِ الّٰتِيْ لَا تُؤْتُوْنَهُنَّ مَا كُتِبَ
لَهُنَّ وَتَرْغَبُوْنَ اَنْ تَنْكِحُوْهُنَّ وَالْمُسْتَضْعَفِيْنَ
مِنَ الْوِلْدَانِ ۙ وَاَنْ تَقُوْمُوْا لِلْيَتٰمٰى بِالْقِسْطِ ۗ
وَمَا تَفْعَلُوْا مِنْ خَيْرٍ فَاِنَّ اللّٰهَ كَانَ بِهٖ عَلِيْمًا

6. And approach not the wealth of the orphan save with that which is better, till he reach maturity.

6:152

6. وَلَا تَقْرَبُوْا مَالَ الْيَتِيْمِ اِلَّا بِالَّتِيْ هِيَ اَحْسَنُ حَتّٰى
يَبْلُغَ اَشُدَّهٗ ۚ

7. Nay, but ye (for your part) honour not the orphan

And urge not on the feeding of the poor,

And ye devour heritages with devouring greed

And love wealth with abounding love.

89:17–20

7. كَلَّا بَلْ لَّا تُكْرِمُوْنَ الْيَتِيْمَ ۙ
وَلَا تَحٰٓضُّوْنَ عَلٰى طَعَامِ الْمِسْكِيْنِ ۙ
وَتَاْكُلُوْنَ التُّرَاثَ اَكْلًا لَّمًّا ۙ
وَّتُحِبُّوْنَ الْمَالَ حُبًّا جَمًّا ۗ

8. Therefor the orphan oppress not,

93:9

8. فَاَمَّا الْيَتِيْمَ فَلَا تَقْهَرْ ۗ

9. Hast thou observed him who belieth religion?

That is he who repelleth the orphan?

107:1–2

9. اَرَءَيْتَ الَّذِيْ يُكَذِّبُ بِالدِّيْنِ ۗ
فَذٰلِكَ الَّذِيْ يَدُعُّ الْيَتِيْمَ ۙ

Ref: 2:83,177; 4:36; 17:34; 90:11–16; 93:6,9.

PARABLES OF QUR'ĀN

1. Their likeness is as the likeness of one who kindleth fire, and when it sheddeth its light around him Allah taketh away their light and leaveth them in darkness, where they cannot see,

Deaf, dumb and blind and they return not.

Or like a rainstorm from the sky, wherein is darkness, thunder and the flash of lightning. They thrust their fingers in their ears by reason of the thunder-claps, for fear of death. Allah encompasseth the disbelievers (in His guidance)

The lightning almost snatcheth away their sight from them. As often as it flasheth forth for them they walk therein, and when it darkeneth against them they stand still. If Allah willed, He could destroy their hearing and their sight. Lo! Allah is Able to do all things.

2:17–20

2. The likeness of those who spend their wealth in Allah's way is as the likeness of a grain which groweth seven ears, in every ear a hundred grains. Allah giveth increase manifold to whom He will. Allah is All–Embracing All–Knowing.

2:261

3. O ye who believe! Render not vain your alms–

1. مَثَلُهُمْ كَمَثَلِ الَّذِي اسْتَوْقَدَ نَارًا ۚ فَلَمَّا
أَضَاءَتْ مَا حَوْلَهُ ذَهَبَ اللَّهُ بِنُورِهِمْ وَ
تَرَكَهُمْ فِي ظُلُمَاتٍ لَا يُبْصِرُونَ ﴿١٧﴾

صُمٌّ بُكْمٌ عُمْيٌ فَهُمْ لَا يَرْجِعُونَ ﴿١٨﴾

أَوْ كَصَيِّبٍ مِنَ السَّمَاءِ فِيهِ ظُلُمَاتٌ وَرَعْدٌ
وَبَرْقٌ يَجْعَلُونَ أَصَابِعَهُمْ فِي آذَانِهِمْ مِنَ
الصَّوَاعِقِ حَذَرَ الْمَوْتِ ۚ وَاللَّهُ مُحِيطٌ بِالْكَافِرِينَ ﴿١٩﴾

يَكَادُ الْبَرْقُ يَخْطَفُ أَبْصَارَهُمْ ۖ كُلَّمَا أَضَاءَ لَهُمْ مَشَوْا
فِيهِ وَإِذَا أَظْلَمَ عَلَيْهِمْ قَامُوا ۚ وَلَوْ شَاءَ اللَّهُ لَذَهَبَ
بِسَمْعِهِمْ وَأَبْصَارِهِمْ ۚ إِنَّ اللَّهَ عَلَىٰ كُلِّ شَيْءٍ قَدِيرٌ ﴿٢٠﴾

2. مَثَلُ الَّذِينَ يُنْفِقُونَ أَمْوَالَهُمْ فِي سَبِيلِ اللَّهِ كَمَثَلِ
حَبَّةٍ أَنْبَتَتْ سَبْعَ سَنَابِلَ فِي كُلِّ سُنْبُلَةٍ مِائَةُ حَبَّةٍ ۗ
وَاللَّهُ يُضَاعِفُ لِمَنْ يَشَاءُ ۗ وَاللَّهُ وَاسِعٌ
عَلِيمٌ ﴿٢٦١﴾

3. يَا أَيُّهَا الَّذِينَ آمَنُوا لَا تُبْطِلُوا صَدَقَاتِكُمْ بِالْمَنِّ وَ
الْأَذَىٰ كَالَّذِي يُنْفِقُ مَالَهُ رِئَاءَ النَّاسِ وَلَا
يُؤْمِنُ بِاللَّهِ وَالْيَوْمِ الْآخِرِ ۖ فَمَثَلُهُ كَمَثَلِ صَفْوَانٍ
عَلَيْهِ تُرَابٌ فَأَصَابَهُ وَابِلٌ فَتَرَكَهُ صَلْدًا ۖ لَا

giving by reproach and injury like him who spendeth his wealth only to be seen of men and believeth not in Allah and the Last Day. His likeness is as the likeness of a rock whereon is dust of earth; a rainstorm smiteth it, leaving it smooth and bare. They have no control of aught of that which they have gained. Allah guideth not the disbelieving folk.

And the likeness of those who spend their wealth in search of Allah's pleasure, and for the strengthening of their souls, is as the likeness of a garden on a height. The rainstorm smiteth it and it bringeth forth its fruit two-fold. And if the rainstorm smite it not, then the shower. Allah is Seer of what ye do.

Would any of you like to have a garden of palm-trees and vines, with rivers flowing underneath it, with all kinds of fruit for him therein; and old age hath stricken him and he hath feeble offspring; and a fiery whirlwind striketh it and it is (all) consumed by fire. Thus Allah maketh plain His revelations unto you, in order that ye may give thought.

2:264–266

4. The likeness of that which they spend in this life of the world is as the likeness of a biting, icy wind which smiteth the harvest of a people who have wronged themselves, and devastateth it. Allah wronged them not, but they did wrong themselves.

3:117

5. Recite unto them the tale of him to whom We gave Our revelations, but he

يَقْدِرُونَ عَلَىٰ شَيْءٍ مِّمَّا كَسَبُوا ۗ وَاللَّهُ لَا يَهْدِي
الْقَوْمَ الْكَافِرِينَ ﴿٢٦٤﴾

وَمَثَلُ الَّذِينَ يُنفِقُونَ أَمْوَالَهُمُ ابْتِغَاءَ مَرْضَاتِ
اللَّهِ وَتَثْبِيتًا مِّنْ أَنفُسِهِمْ كَمَثَلِ جَنَّةٍ بِرَبْوَةٍ
أَصَابَهَا وَابِلٌ فَآتَتْ أُكُلَهَا ضِعْفَيْنِ فَإِن لَّمْ
يُصِبْهَا وَابِلٌ فَطَلٌّ ۗ وَاللَّهُ بِمَا تَعْمَلُونَ
بَصِيرٌ ﴿٢٦٥﴾

أَيَوَدُّ أَحَدُكُمْ أَن تَكُونَ لَهُ جَنَّةٌ مِّن
نَّخِيلٍ وَأَعْنَابٍ تَجْرِي مِن تَحْتِهَا
الْأَنْهَارُ لَهُ فِيهَا مِن كُلِّ الثَّمَرَاتِ وَ
أَصَابَهُ الْكِبَرُ وَلَهُ ذُرِّيَّةٌ ضُعَفَاءُ فَأَصَابَهَا
إِعْصَارٌ فِيهِ نَارٌ فَاحْتَرَقَتْ ۗ كَذَٰلِكَ
يُبَيِّنُ اللَّهُ لَكُمُ الْآيَاتِ لَعَلَّكُمْ تَتَفَكَّرُونَ ﴿٢٦٦﴾

4. مَثَلُ مَا يُنفِقُونَ فِي هَٰذِهِ الْحَيَاةِ الدُّنْيَا
كَمَثَلِ رِيحٍ فِيهَا صِرٌّ أَصَابَتْ حَرْثَ
قَوْمٍ ظَلَمُوا أَنفُسَهُمْ فَأَهْلَكَتْهُ ۚ وَمَا ظَلَمَهُمُ
اللَّهُ وَلَٰكِنْ أَنفُسَهُمْ يَظْلِمُونَ ○

5. وَاتْلُ عَلَيْهِمْ نَبَأَ الَّذِي آتَيْنَاهُ آيَاتِنَا فَانسَلَخَ
مِنْهَا فَأَتْبَعَهُ الشَّيْطَانُ فَكَانَ مِنَ الْغَاوِينَ ﴿١٧٥﴾

وَلَوْ شِئْنَا لَرَفَعْنَاهُ بِهَا وَلَٰكِنَّهُ أَخْلَدَ
إِلَى الْأَرْضِ وَاتَّبَعَ هَوَاهُ ۚ فَمَثَلُهُ كَمَثَلِ

sloughed them off, so Satan overtook him and he became of those who are led astray.

And had We willed We could have raised him by their means, but he clung to the earth and followed his own lust. Therefor his likeness is as the likeness of a dog; if thou attackest him he panteth with his tongue out, and if thou leavest him, he panteth with his tounge out. Such is the likeness of the people who deny Our revelations. Narrate unto them the history (of the men of old), that haply they may take thought.

7:175—176

6. The similitude of the life of the world is only as water which We send down from the sky, then the earth's growth of that which men and cattle eat mingleth with it till, when the earth hath taken on her ornaments and is embellished, and her people deem that they are masters of her, Our commandment cometh by night or by day and We make it as reaped corn as if it had not flourished yesterday. Thus do We expound the revelations for people who reflect.

10:24

7. He sendeth down water from the sky, so that valleys flow according to their measure, and the flood beareth (on its surface) swelling foam—from that which they smelt in the fire in order to make ornaments and tools riseth a foam like unto it—thus Allah coineth (the similitude of) the true and the false. Then, as for the foam, it passeth away as scum upon the banks, while, as for that which is of use to man-

الْكَلْبِ ۚ إِن تَحْمِلْ عَلَيْهِ يَلْهَثْ أَوْ
تَتْرُكْهُ يَلْهَث ۚ ذَّٰلِكَ مَثَلُ الْقَوْمِ الَّذِينَ
كَذَّبُوا بِآيَاتِنَا ۚ فَاقْصُصِ الْقَصَصَ
لَعَلَّهُمْ يَتَفَكَّرُونَ

6. إِنَّمَا مَثَلُ الْحَيَوٰةِ الدُّنْيَا كَمَاءٍ أَنزَلْنَٰهُ
مِنَ السَّمَاءِ فَاخْتَلَطَ بِهِ نَبَاتُ الْأَرْضِ
مِمَّا يَأْكُلُ النَّاسُ وَالْأَنْعَامُ حَتَّىٰ
إِذَا أَخَذَتِ الْأَرْضُ زُخْرُفَهَا وَازَّيَّنَتْ
وَظَنَّ أَهْلُهَا أَنَّهُمْ قَٰدِرُونَ عَلَيْهَا أَتَىٰهَا
أَمْرُنَا لَيْلًا أَوْ نَهَارًا فَجَعَلْنَٰهَا حَصِيدًا
كَأَن لَّمْ تَغْنَ بِالْأَمْسِ ۚ كَذَٰلِكَ نُفَصِّلُ
الْآيَٰتِ لِقَوْمٍ يَتَفَكَّرُونَ (24)

7. أَنزَلَ مِنَ السَّمَاءِ مَاءً فَسَالَتْ أَوْدِيَةٌ
بِقَدَرِهَا فَاحْتَمَلَ السَّيْلُ زَبَدًا رَّابِيًا
وَمِمَّا يُوقِدُونَ عَلَيْهِ فِي النَّارِ ابْتِغَاءَ
حِلْيَةٍ أَوْ مَتَٰعٍ زَبَدٌ مِّثْلُهُ ۚ كَذَٰلِكَ
يَضْرِبُ اللَّهُ الْحَقَّ وَالْبَٰطِلَ ۚ
فَأَمَّا الزَّبَدُ فَيَذْهَبُ جُفَاءً ۖ وَأَمَّا مَا
يَنفَعُ النَّاسَ فَيَمْكُثُ فِي الْأَرْضِ ۚ
كَذَٰلِكَ يَضْرِبُ اللَّهُ الْأَمْثَالَ (17)

8. مَّثَلُ الَّذِينَ كَفَرُوا بِرَبِّهِمْ ۖ أَعْمَٰلُهُمْ
كَرَمَادٍ اشْتَدَّتْ بِهِ الرِّيحُ فِي يَوْمٍ

kind, it remaineth in the earth. Thus Allah coineth the similitudes.

13:17

8. A similitude of those who disbelieve in their Lord: Their works are as ashes which the wind bloweth hard

upon a stormy day. They have no control of aught that they have earned. That is the extreme failure.

14:18

9. Seest thou not how Allah coineth a similitude: A goodly saying, as a goodly tree, its root set firm, its branches reaching into heaven,

Giving its fruit at every season by permission of its Lord? Allah coineth the similitude for mankind in order that they may reflect.

And the similitude of a bad saying is as a bad tree, uprooted from upon the earth possessing no stability.

14:24–26

10. Allah coineth a similitude: (on the one hand) a (mere) chattel slave, who hath control of nothing, and (on the other hand) one on whom We have bestowed a fair provision from Us, and he spendeth thereof secretly and openly. Are they equal? Praise be to Allah! But most of them know not.

And Allah coineth a similitude: Two men, one of them dumb, having control of nothing, and he is a burden on his owner; withersoever he directeth him to go, he bringeth no good. Is he equal with one who enjoineth justice and followeth a straight path (of conduct)?

16:75–76

عَاصِفٍ ۖ لَا يَقْدِرُونَ مِمَّا كَسَبُوا عَلَىٰ
شَيْءٍ ۚ ذَٰلِكَ هُوَ الضَّلَالُ الْبَعِيدُ ﴿١٨﴾
9. أَلَمْ تَرَ كَيْفَ ضَرَبَ اللَّهُ مَثَلًا كَلِمَةً
طَيِّبَةً كَشَجَرَةٍ طَيِّبَةٍ أَصْلُهَا ثَابِتٌ
وَفَرْعُهَا فِي السَّمَاءِ ﴿٢٤﴾

تُؤْتِي أُكُلَهَا كُلَّ حِينٍ بِإِذْنِ رَبِّهَا ۗ وَ
يَضْرِبُ اللَّهُ الْأَمْثَالَ لِلنَّاسِ لَعَلَّهُمْ يَتَذَكَّرُونَ ﴿٢٥﴾

وَمَثَلُ كَلِمَةٍ خَبِيثَةٍ كَشَجَرَةٍ خَبِيثَةٍ اجْتُثَّتْ
مِنْ فَوْقِ الْأَرْضِ مَا لَهَا مِنْ قَرَارٍ ﴿٢٦﴾

10. ضَرَبَ اللَّهُ مَثَلًا عَبْدًا مَمْلُوكًا لَا
يَقْدِرُ عَلَىٰ شَيْءٍ وَمَنْ رَزَقْنَاهُ مِنَّا رِزْقًا
حَسَنًا فَهُوَ يُنْفِقُ مِنْهُ سِرًّا وَجَهْرًا ۖ
هَلْ يَسْتَوُونَ ۚ الْحَمْدُ لِلَّهِ ۚ بَلْ
أَكْثَرُهُمْ لَا يَعْلَمُونَ ﴿٧٥﴾

وَضَرَبَ اللَّهُ مَثَلًا رَجُلَيْنِ أَحَدُهُمَا
أَبْكَمُ لَا يَقْدِرُ عَلَىٰ شَيْءٍ وَهُوَ كَلٌّ عَلَىٰ
مَوْلَاهُ أَيْنَمَا يُوَجِّهْهُ لَا يَأْتِ بِخَيْرٍ ۖ
هَلْ يَسْتَوِي هُوَ وَمَنْ يَأْمُرُ بِالْعَدْلِ ۙ
وَهُوَ عَلَىٰ صِرَاطٍ مُسْتَقِيمٍ ﴿٧٦﴾

11. وَضَرَبَ اللَّهُ مَثَلًا قَرْيَةً كَانَتْ آمِنَةً
مُطْمَئِنَّةً يَأْتِيهَا رِزْقُهَا رَغَدًا مِنْ كُلِّ
مَكَانٍ فَكَفَرَتْ بِأَنْعُمِ اللَّهِ فَأَذَاقَهَا اللَّهُ

11. Allah coineth a similitude: a township that dwelt secure and well content, its provision coming to it in abundance from every side, but it disbelieved in Allah's favours, so Allah made it experience

the garb of dearth and fear because of what they used to do.

16:112

12. And coin for them the similitude of the life of the world as water which We send down from the sky, and the vegetation of the earth mingleth with it and then becometh dry twigs that the winds scatter. Allah is Able to do all things.

18:45

13. O mankind! A similitude is coined, so pay ye heed to it: Lo! those on whom ye call beside Allah will never create a fly though they combine together for the purpose. And if the fly took something from them, they could not rescue it from him. So weak are (both) the seeker and the sought!

22:73

14. Allah is the Light of the heavens and the earth. The similitude of His light is as a niche wherein is a lamp. The lamp is in a glass. The glass is as it were a shining star. (This lamp is) kindled from a blessed tree, an olive neither of the East nor of the West, whose oil would almost glow forth (of itself) though no fire touched it. Light upon light, Allah guideth unto His light whom He will. And Allah speaketh to mankind

لِبَاسَ الْجُوْعِ وَالْخَوْفِ بِمَا كَانُوْا يَصْنَعُوْنَ ﴿١١٢﴾

12. وَاضْرِبْ لَهُمْ مَّثَلَ الْحَيٰوةِ الدُّنْيَا كَمَآءٍ
اَنْزَلْنٰهُ مِنَ السَّمَآءِ فَاخْتَلَطَ بِهٖ نَبَاتُ
الْاَرْضِ فَاَصْبَحَ هَشِيْمًا تَذْرُوْهُ الرِّيٰحُ
وَكَانَ اللّٰهُ عَلٰى كُلِّ شَيْءٍ مُّقْتَدِرًا ﴿٤٥﴾

13. يٰاَيُّهَا النَّاسُ ضُرِبَ مَثَلٌ فَاسْتَمِعُوْا
لَهٗ اِنَّ الَّذِيْنَ تَدْعُوْنَ مِنْ
دُوْنِ اللّٰهِ لَنْ يَّخْلُقُوْا ذُبَابًا وَّلَوِ
اجْتَمَعُوْا لَهٗ وَاِنْ يَّسْلُبْهُمُ الذُّبَابُ
شَيْئًا لَّا يَسْتَنْقِذُوْهُ مِنْهُ ضَعُفَ
الطَّالِبُ وَالْمَطْلُوْبُ ﴿٧٣﴾

14. اَللّٰهُ نُوْرُ السَّمٰوٰتِ وَالْاَرْضِ مَثَلُ
نُوْرِهٖ كَمِشْكٰوةٍ فِيْهَا مِصْبَاحٌ اَلْمِصْبَاحُ
فِيْ زُجَاجَةٍ اَلزُّجَاجَةُ كَاَنَّهَا كَوْكَبٌ
دُرِّيٌّ يُّوْقَدُ مِنْ شَجَرَةٍ مُّبٰرَكَةٍ
زَيْتُوْنَةٍ لَّا شَرْقِيَّةٍ وَّلَا غَرْبِيَّةٍ
يَّكَادُ زَيْتُهَا يُضِيْٓءُ وَلَوْ لَمْ تَمْسَسْهُ
نَارٌ نُوْرٌ عَلٰى نُوْرٍ يَهْدِى اللّٰهُ لِنُوْرِهٖ
مَنْ يَّشَآءُ وَيَضْرِبُ اللّٰهُ الْاَمْثَالَ
لِلنَّاسِ وَاللّٰهُ بِكُلِّ شَيْءٍ عَلِيْمٌ ﴿٣٥﴾

15. وَالَّذِيْنَ كَفَرُوْٓا اَعْمَالُهُمْ كَسَرَابٍ
بِقِيْعَةٍ يَّحْسَبُهُ الظَّمْاٰنُ مَآءً حَتّٰٓى
اِذَا جَآءَهٗ لَمْ يَجِدْهُ شَيْئًا وَّوَجَدَ اللّٰهَ

in allegories, for Allah is Knower of all things.

24:35

15. As for those who disbelieve, their deeds are as a mirage in a desert. The thirsty one supposeth it to be

عِنْدَهٗ فَوَفّٰىهُ حِسَابَهٗ ؕ وَاللّٰهُ
سَرِيْعُ الْحِسَابِ ﴿٣٩﴾
اَوْ كَظُلُمٰتٍ فِيْ بَحْرٍ لُّجِّيٍّ يَّغْشٰىهُ مَوْجٌ
مِّنْ فَوْقِهٖ مَوْجٌ مِّنْ فَوْقِهٖ سَحَابٌ ؕ
ظُلُمٰتٌۢ بَعْضُهَا فَوْقَ بَعْضٍ ؕ اِذَآ اَخْرَجَ
يَدَهٗ لَمْ يَكَدْ يَرٰىهَا ؕ وَمَنْ لَّمْ
يَجْعَلِ اللّٰهُ لَهٗ نُوْرًا فَمَا لَهٗ مِنْ نُّوْرٍ ﴿٤٠﴾

16. مَثَلُ الَّذِيْنَ اتَّخَذُوْا مِنْ دُوْنِ اللّٰهِ
اَوْلِيَآءَ كَمَثَلِ الْعَنْكَبُوْتِ ۚ اِتَّخَذَتْ
بَيْتًا ؕ وَاِنَّ اَوْهَنَ الْبُيُوْتِ لَبَيْتُ
الْعَنْكَبُوْتِ ۘ لَوْ كَانُوْا يَعْلَمُوْنَ ﴿٤١﴾

17. مُحَمَّدٌ رَّسُوْلُ اللّٰهِ ؕ وَالَّذِيْنَ مَعَهٗ
اَشِدَّآءُ عَلَى الْكُفَّارِ رُحَمَآءُ بَيْنَهُمْ
تَرٰىهُمْ رُكَّعًا سُجَّدًا يَّبْتَغُوْنَ فَضْلًا
مِّنَ اللّٰهِ وَرِضْوَانًا ۫ سِيْمَاهُمْ فِيْ
وُجُوْهِهِمْ مِّنْ اَثَرِ السُّجُوْدِ ؕ ذٰلِكَ
مَثَلُهُمْ فِي التَّوْرٰىةِ ۛ وَمَثَلُهُمْ فِي
الْاِنْجِيْلِ ۛ كَزَرْعٍ اَخْرَجَ شَطْـَٔهٗ
فَاٰزَرَهٗ فَاسْتَغْلَظَ فَاسْتَوٰى عَلٰى
سُوْقِهٖ يُعْجِبُ الزُّرَّاعَ لِيَغِيْظَ بِهِمُ
الْكُفَّارَ ؕ وَعَدَ اللّٰهُ الَّذِيْنَ اٰمَنُوْا
وَعَمِلُوا الصّٰلِحٰتِ مِنْهُمْ مَّغْفِرَةً
وَّاَجْرًا عَظِيْمًا ﴿٢٩﴾

water till he cometh unto it and findeth it naught, and findeth, in the place thereof, Allah, Who payeth him his due; and Allah is swift at reckoning:

Or as darkness on a vast, abysmal sea. There covereth him a wave, above which is a wave, above which is a cloud. Layer upon layer of darkness. When he holdeth out his hand he scarce can see it. And he for whom Allah hath not appointed light, for him there is no light.

24:39–40

16. The likeness of those who choose other patrons than Allah is as the likeness of the spider when she taketh unto herself a house, and lo! the frailest of all houses is the spider's house, if they but knew.

29:41

17. Muhammad is the messenger of Allah. And those with him are hard against the disbelievers and merciful among themselves. Thou (O Muhammad) seest them bowing and falling prostrate (in worship), seeking bounty from Allah and (His) acceptance. The mark of them is on their foreheads from traces of prostration. Such is their likeness in the Torah and their likeness in the Gospel—like as sown corn that sendeth forth its shoot and strengtheneth it and riseth firm upon its stalk, delighting the sowers—that He may enrage the disbelievers with (the sight of) them. Allah hath promised, unto such of them as believe and do good works, forgiveness and immense reward.

48:29

18. Know that the life of this world is only play, and idle talk, and pageantry, and boasting among you, and rivalry in respect of wealth and children as the likeness of vegetation after rain, whereof the growth is pleasing to the husbandman, but afterward it drieth up and thou seest it turning yellow, then it becometh straw. And in the Hereafter there is grievous punishment, and (also) forgiveness from Allah and His good pleasure, whereas the life of the world is but matter of illusion.

57:20

18. اِعْلَمُوْٓا اَنَّمَا الْحَيٰوةُ الدُّنْيَا لَعِبٌ وَّ
لَهْوٌ وَّ زِيْنَةٌ وَّ تَفَاخُرٌۢ بَيْنَكُمْ وَ
تَكَاثُرٌ فِى الْاَمْوَالِ وَ الْاَوْلَادِ ؕ كَمَثَلِ
غَيْثٍ اَعْجَبَ الْكُفَّارَ نَبَاتُهٗ ثُمَّ يَهِيْجُ
فَتَرٰىهُ مُصْفَرًّا ثُمَّ يَكُوْنُ حُطٰمًا ؕ
وَ فِى الْاٰخِرَةِ عَذَابٌ شَدِيْدٌ ۙ وَّ مَغْفِرَةٌ
مِّنَ اللّٰهِ وَ رِضْوَانٌ ؕ وَ مَا الْحَيٰوةُ
الدُّنْيَآ اِلَّا مَتَاعُ الْغُرُوْرِ ۝

19. The likeness of those who are entrusted with the Law of Moses, yet apply it not, is as the likenss of the ass carrying books. Wretched is the likeness of folk who deny the revelations of Allah. And Allah guideth not wrong–doing folk.

62:5

19. مَثَلُ الَّذِيْنَ حُمِّلُوا التَّوْرٰىةَ ثُمَّ لَمْ
يَحْمِلُوْهَا كَمَثَلِ الْحِمَارِ يَحْمِلُ
اَسْفَارًا ؕ بِئْسَ مَثَلُ الْقَوْمِ الَّذِيْنَ
كَذَّبُوْا بِاٰيٰتِ اللّٰهِ ؕ وَ اللّٰهُ لَا يَهْدِى
الْقَوْمَ الظّٰلِمِيْنَ ۝

○

Ref: 2:26,171; 3:59; 6:122; 7:40,58; 11:24; 16:26,60,74–75,92; 17:48,89; 18:32–44,54; 25:9,33,39; 29:43; 30:27–28,58; 36:13–28,79–81; 39:27,29; 41:39; 43:17,59; 45:23; 47:3,10,15; 59:15–17,21; 63:4; 66:10–12; 67:22; 68:17–32; 74:31.

PARADISE

1. And give glad tidings (O Muhammad) unto those who believe and do good works; that theirs are Gardens underneath which rivers flow; as often as they are regaled with food of the fruit thereof, they say: This is what was given us aforetime; and it is given to them in resemblance. There for them are pure companions; there for ever they abide.

2:25

2. And vie one with another for forgiveness from your Lord, and for a Paradise as wide as are the heavens and the earth, prepared for those who ward off (evil);

3:133

3. Or deemed ye that ye would enter Paradise while yet Allah knoweth not those of you who really strive, nor knoweth those (of you) who are steadfast?

3:142

4. Lo! they who deny Our revelations and scorn them, for them the gates of Heaven will not be opened nor will they enter the Garden until the camel goeth through the needle's eye. Thus do We requite the guilty.

7:40

5. Lo! those who ward off (evil) are among Gardens and watersprings.

(And it is said unto

1. وَبَشِّرِ الَّذِينَ آمَنُوا وَعَمِلُوا الصَّالِحَاتِ أَنَّ لَهُمْ
جَنَّاتٍ تَجْرِي مِن تَحْتِهَا الْأَنْهَارُ ۖ كُلَّمَا رُزِقُوا
مِنْهَا مِن ثَمَرَةٍ رِّزْقًا ۙ قَالُوا هَٰذَا الَّذِي
رُزِقْنَا مِن قَبْلُ ۖ وَأُتُوا بِهِ مُتَشَابِهًا ۖ وَلَهُمْ
فِيهَا أَزْوَاجٌ مُّطَهَّرَةٌ ۖ وَهُمْ فِيهَا خَالِدُونَ ﴿٢٥﴾

2. وَسَارِعُوا إِلَىٰ مَغْفِرَةٍ مِّن رَّبِّكُمْ وَجَنَّةٍ
عَرْضُهَا السَّمَاوَاتُ وَالْأَرْضُ أُعِدَّتْ لِلْمُتَّقِينَ

3. أَمْ حَسِبْتُمْ أَن تَدْخُلُوا الْجَنَّةَ وَلَمَّا
يَعْلَمِ اللَّهُ الَّذِينَ جَاهَدُوا مِنكُمْ وَيَعْلَمَ
الصَّابِرِينَ

4. إِنَّ الَّذِينَ كَذَّبُوا بِآيَاتِنَا وَاسْتَكْبَرُوا
عَنْهَا لَا تُفَتَّحُ لَهُمْ أَبْوَابُ السَّمَاءِ وَلَا
يَدْخُلُونَ الْجَنَّةَ حَتَّىٰ يَلِجَ الْجَمَلُ فِي
سَمِّ الْخِيَاطِ ۚ وَكَذَٰلِكَ نَجْزِي الْمُجْرِمِينَ ﴿٤٠﴾

5. إِنَّ الْمُتَّقِينَ فِي جَنَّاتٍ وَعُيُونٍ ﴿٤٥﴾
ادْخُلُوهَا بِسَلَامٍ آمِنِينَ ﴿٤٦﴾
وَنَزَعْنَا مَا فِي صُدُورِهِم مِّنْ غِلٍّ
إِخْوَانًا عَلَىٰ سُرُرٍ مُّتَقَابِلِينَ ﴿٤٧﴾
لَا يَمَسُّهُمْ فِيهَا نَصَبٌ وَمَا هُم مِّنْهَا
بِمُخْرَجِينَ ﴿٤٨﴾

them): Enter them in peace, secure.

And We remove whatever rancour may be in their breasts. As brethren, face to face, (they rest) on couches raised.

Toil cometh not unto them there, nor will they be expelled from thence.

15:45–48

6. Lo! as for those who believe and do good works–Lo! We suffer not the reward of one whose work is goodly to be lost.

As for such, theirs will be Gardens of Eden, wherein rivers flow beneath them; therein they will be given armlets of gold and will wear green robes of finest silk and gold embroidery, reclining upon thrones therein. Blest the reward, and fair the resting–place!

18:30–31

7. Lo! those who believe and do good works, theirs are the Gardens of Paradise for welcome.

18:107

8. But for him who feareth the standing before his Lord there are two gardens.

Which is it, of the favours of your Lord, that ye deny?

Of spreading branches.

Which is it, of the favours of your Lord, that ye deny?

Wherein are two foun–tains flowing.

Which is it, of the favours of your Lord, that ye deny?

Wherein is every kind of fruit in pairs,

Which is it, of the favours of your Lord, that ye deny?

Reclining upon couches lined with silk brocade, the fruit of both the Gardens near to hand.

Which is it, of the favours of your Lord, that ye deny?

Therein are those of modest gaze, whom neither man nor jinni will have touched before them.

Which is it, of the favours of your Lord, that ye deny?

6. إِنَّ الَّذِينَ آمَنُوا وَعَمِلُوا الصَّالِحَاتِ
إِنَّا لَا نُضِيعُ أَجْرَ مَنْ أَحْسَنَ عَمَلًا ﴿٣٠﴾
أُولَٰئِكَ لَهُمْ جَنَّاتُ عَدْنٍ تَجْرِي مِنْ
تَحْتِهِمُ الْأَنْهَارُ يُحَلَّوْنَ فِيهَا مِنْ أَسَاوِرَ
مِنْ ذَهَبٍ وَيَلْبَسُونَ ثِيَابًا خُضْرًا
مِنْ سُنْدُسٍ وَإِسْتَبْرَقٍ مُتَّكِئِينَ
فِيهَا عَلَى الْأَرَائِكِ ۚ نِعْمَ الثَّوَابُ ۚ
وَحَسُنَتْ مُرْتَفَقًا ﴿٣١﴾

7. إِنَّ الَّذِينَ آمَنُوا وَعَمِلُوا الصَّالِحَاتِ كَانَتْ
لَهُمْ جَنَّاتُ الْفِرْدَوْسِ نُزُلًا ﴿١٠٧﴾

8. وَلِمَنْ خَافَ مَقَامَ رَبِّهِ جَنَّتَانِ ﴿٤٦﴾
فَبِأَيِّ آلَاءِ رَبِّكُمَا تُكَذِّبَانِ ﴿٤٧﴾
ذَوَاتَا أَفْنَانٍ ﴿٤٨﴾
فَبِأَيِّ آلَاءِ رَبِّكُمَا تُكَذِّبَانِ ﴿٤٩﴾
فِيهِمَا عَيْنَانِ تَجْرِيَانِ ﴿٥٠﴾
فَبِأَيِّ آلَاءِ رَبِّكُمَا تُكَذِّبَانِ ﴿٥١﴾
فِيهِمَا مِنْ كُلِّ فَاكِهَةٍ زَوْجَانِ ﴿٥٢﴾
فَبِأَيِّ آلَاءِ رَبِّكُمَا تُكَذِّبَانِ ﴿٥٣﴾
مُتَّكِئِينَ عَلَىٰ فُرُشٍ بَطَائِنُهَا مِنْ
إِسْتَبْرَقٍ ۚ وَجَنَى الْجَنَّتَيْنِ دَانٍ ﴿٥٤﴾
فَبِأَيِّ آلَاءِ رَبِّكُمَا تُكَذِّبَانِ ﴿٥٥﴾
فِيهِنَّ قَاصِرَاتُ الطَّرْفِ لَمْ يَطْمِثْهُنَّ
إِنْسٌ قَبْلَهُمْ وَلَا جَانٌّ ﴿٥٦﴾
فَبِأَيِّ آلَاءِ رَبِّكُمَا تُكَذِّبَانِ ﴿٥٧﴾

(In beauty) like the jacynth and the coral-stone.

Which is it, of the favours of your Lord, that ye deny?

Is the reward of good–ness aught save goodness?

Which is it, of the favours of your Lord, that ye deny?

And beside them are two other Gardens,

Which is it, of the favours of your Lord, that ye deny?

Dark green with foliage.

Which is it, of the favours of your Lord, that ye deny?

Wherein are two abun–dant springs.

Which is it, of the favours of your Lord, that ye deny?

Wherein is fruit, the date–palm and pomegranate.

Which is it, of the favours of your Lord, that ye deny?

Wherein (are found) the good and beautiful–

Which is it, of the favours of your Lord, that ye deny?–

Fair ones, close-guarded in pavilions–

Which is it, of the favours of your Lord, that ye deny?–

Whom neither man nor jinni will have touched before them–

Which is it, of the favours of your Lord, that ye deny?–

Reclining on green cushions and fair carpets.

Which is it, of the favours of your Lord, that ye deny?

Blessed be the name of thy Lord, Mighty and Glorious!

55:46–78

9. And the foremost in the

كَأَنَّهُنَّ الْيَاقُوتُ وَالْمَرْجَانُ ﴿٥٨﴾
فَبِأَيِّ آلَاءِ رَبِّكُمَا تُكَذِّبَانِ ﴿٥٩﴾
هَلْ جَزَاءُ الْإِحْسَانِ إِلَّا الْإِحْسَانُ ﴿٦٠﴾
فَبِأَيِّ آلَاءِ رَبِّكُمَا تُكَذِّبَانِ ﴿٦١﴾
وَمِنْ دُونِهِمَا جَنَّتَانِ ﴿٦٢﴾
فَبِأَيِّ آلَاءِ رَبِّكُمَا تُكَذِّبَانِ ﴿٦٣﴾
مُدْهَامَّتَانِ ﴿٦٤﴾
فَبِأَيِّ آلَاءِ رَبِّكُمَا تُكَذِّبَانِ ﴿٦٥﴾
فِيهِمَا عَيْنَانِ نَضَّاخَتَانِ ﴿٦٦﴾
فَبِأَيِّ آلَاءِ رَبِّكُمَا تُكَذِّبَانِ ﴿٦٧﴾
فِيهِمَا فَاكِهَةٌ وَنَخْلٌ وَرُمَّانٌ ﴿٦٨﴾
فَبِأَيِّ آلَاءِ رَبِّكُمَا تُكَذِّبَانِ ﴿٦٩﴾
فِيهِنَّ خَيْرَاتٌ حِسَانٌ ﴿٧٠﴾
فَبِأَيِّ آلَاءِ رَبِّكُمَا تُكَذِّبَانِ ﴿٧١﴾
حُورٌ مَقْصُورَاتٌ فِي الْخِيَامِ ﴿٧٢﴾
فَبِأَيِّ آلَاءِ رَبِّكُمَا تُكَذِّبَانِ ﴿٧٣﴾
لَمْ يَطْمِثْهُنَّ إِنْسٌ قَبْلَهُمْ وَلَا جَانٌّ ﴿٧٤﴾
فَبِأَيِّ آلَاءِ رَبِّكُمَا تُكَذِّبَانِ ﴿٧٥﴾
مُتَّكِئِينَ عَلَىٰ رَفْرَفٍ خُضْرٍ وَ
عَبْقَرِيٍّ حِسَانٍ ﴿٧٦﴾
فَبِأَيِّ آلَاءِ رَبِّكُمَا تُكَذِّبَانِ ﴿٧٧﴾
تَبَارَكَ اسْمُ رَبِّكَ ذِي الْجَلَالِ
وَالْإِكْرَامِ ﴿٧٨﴾

9. وَالسَّابِقُونَ السَّابِقُونَ ﴿١٠﴾
أُولَٰئِكَ الْمُقَرَّبُونَ ﴿١١﴾

race, the foremost in the race:

Those are they who will be brought nigh

In Gardens of delight;

A multitude of those of old

And a few of those of later time,

On lined couches,

Reclining therein face to face.

There wait on them immortal youths

With bowls and ewers and a cup from a pure spring

Wherefrom they get no aching of the head nor any madness,

And fruit that they prefer

And flesh of fowls that they desire.

And (there are) fair ones with wide, lovely eyes,

Like unto hidden pearls,

Reward for what they used to do.

There hear they no vain speaking nor recrimination

(Naught) but the saying: Peace, (and again) Peace!

And those on the right hand; what of those on the right hand?

Among thornless lote-trees

And clustered plantains,

And spreading shade,

And water gushing,

And fruit in plenty

Neither out of reach nor yet forbidden,

And raised couches;

Lo! We have created them a (new) creation

And made them virgins,

Lovers, friends,

For those on the right hand;

فِيْ جَنّٰتِ النَّعِيْمِ (١٢)
ثُلَّةٌ مِّنَ الْاَوَّلِيْنَ (١٣)
وَقَلِيْلٌ مِّنَ الْاٰخِرِيْنَ (١٤)
عَلٰى سُرُرٍ مَّوْضُوْنَةٍ (١٥)
مُّتَّكِـِٕيْنَ عَلَيْهَا مُتَقٰبِلِيْنَ (١٦)
يَطُوْفُ عَلَيْهِمْ وِلْدَانٌ مُّخَلَّدُوْنَ (١٧)
بِاَكْوَابٍ وَّاَبَارِيْقَ ۙ وَكَاْسٍ
مِّنْ مَّعِيْنٍ (١٨)
لَّا يُصَدَّعُوْنَ عَنْهَا وَلَا يُنْزِفُوْنَ (١٩)
وَفَاكِهَةٍ مِّمَّا يَتَخَيَّرُوْنَ (٢٠)
وَلَحْمِ طَيْرٍ مِّمَّا يَشْتَهُوْنَ (٢١)
وَحُوْرٌ عِيْنٌ (٢٢)
كَاَمْثَالِ اللُّؤْلُؤِ الْمَكْنُوْنِ (٢٣)
جَزَاۤءًۢ بِمَا كَانُوْا يَعْمَلُوْنَ (٢٤)
لَا يَسْمَعُوْنَ فِيْهَا لَغْوًا وَّلَا تَاْثِيْمًا (٢٥)
اِلَّا قِيْلًا سَلٰمًا سَلٰمًا (٢٦)
وَاَصْحٰبُ الْيَمِيْنِ ۙ مَآ اَصْحٰبُ
الْيَمِيْنِ (٢٧)
فِيْ سِدْرٍ مَّخْضُوْدٍ (٢٨)
وَّطَلْحٍ مَّنْضُوْدٍ (٢٩)
وَّظِلٍّ مَّمْدُوْدٍ (٣٠)
وَّمَاۤءٍ مَّسْكُوْبٍ (٣١)
وَّفَاكِهَةٍ كَثِيْرَةٍ (٣٢)
لَّا مَقْطُوْعَةٍ وَّلَا مَمْنُوْعَةٍ (٣٣)
وَّفُرُشٍ مَّرْفُوْعَةٍ (٣٤)
اِنَّآ اَنْشَاْنٰهُنَّ اِنْشَاۤءً (٣٥)

A multitude of those of old

And a multitude of those of later time.

56:10–40

Ref: 2:35,82; 3:15,185; 4:124; 7:19,22,42; 9:111; 11:23; 19:63; 25:74–76; 35:33; 40:40; 46:14; 57:21.

See also: Hell.

PEACE–MAKING

1. There is no good in much of their secret conferences save(in) him who enjoineth almsgiving and kindness and peace–making among the people. Whoso doeth that seeking the good pleasure of Allah, We shall bestow on him a vast reward.

4:114

2. And if two parties of believers fall to fighting, then make peace between them. And if one party of them doth wrong to the other, fight ye that which doth wrong till it return unto the ordinance of Allah; then if it return, make peace between them justly, and act equitably. Lo! Allah loveth the equitable.

The believers are naught else than brothers. Therefore make peace between your brethren and observe your duty to Allah that haply ye may obtain mercy.

49:9–10

فَجَعَلْنٰهُنَّ اَبْكَارًا ﴿٣٦﴾
عُرُبًا اَتْرَابًا ﴿٣٧﴾
لِّاَصْحٰبِ الْيَمِيْنِ ﴿٣٨﴾
ثُلَّةٌ مِّنَ الْاَوَّلِيْنَ ﴿٣٩﴾
وَ ثُلَّةٌ مِّنَ الْاٰخِرِيْنَ ﴿٤٠﴾

○

لَا خَيْرَ فِيْ كَثِيْرٍ مِّنْ نَّجْوٰىهُمْ اِلَّا مَنْ اَمَرَ
بِصَدَقَةٍ اَوْ مَعْرُوْفٍ اَوْ اِصْلَاحٍ بَيْنَ النَّاسِ
وَ مَنْ يَّفْعَلْ ذٰلِكَ ابْتِغَآءَ مَرْضَاتِ اللّٰهِ
فَسَوْفَ نُؤْتِيْهِ اَجْرًا عَظِيْمًا ﴿١١٤﴾

2. وَ اِنْ طَآىِٕفَتٰنِ مِنَ الْمُؤْمِنِيْنَ اقْتَتَلُوْا
فَاَصْلِحُوْا بَيْنَهُمَا ۚ فَاِنْۢ بَغَتْ اِحْدٰىهُمَا
عَلَى الْاُخْرٰى فَقَاتِلُوا الَّتِيْ تَبْغِيْ حَتّٰى
تَفِيْٓءَ اِلٰٓى اَمْرِ اللّٰهِ ۚ فَاِنْ فَآءَتْ
فَاَصْلِحُوْا بَيْنَهُمَا بِالْعَدْلِ وَ اَقْسِطُوْا
اِنَّ اللّٰهَ يُحِبُّ الْمُقْسِطِيْنَ ﴿٩﴾
اِنَّمَا الْمُؤْمِنُوْنَ اِخْوَةٌ فَاَصْلِحُوْا بَيْنَ
اَخَوَيْكُمْ وَ اتَّقُوا اللّٰهَ لَعَلَّكُمْ تُرْحَمُوْنَ ﴿١٠﴾

○

See also: Cease-fire.

PEACE AND SECURITY

1. O people of the Scripture! Now hath Our messenger come unto you, expounding unto you much of that which ye used to hide in the Scripture, and forgiving much. Now hath come unto you light from Allah and a plain Scripture:

Whereby Allah guideth him who seeketh His good pleasure unto paths of peace, He bringeth them out of darkness unto light by His decree, and guideth them unto a straight path.

5:15–16

2. How should I fear that which ye set up beside Him, when ye fear not to set up beside Allah that for which He hath revealed unto you no warrant? Which of the two factions hath more right to safety? (Answer me that) if ye have knowledge.

Those who believe and obscure not their belief by wrong-doing, theirs is safety; and they are rightly guided.

6:81–82

3. For them is the abode of peace with their Lord. He will be their Protecting Friend because of what they used to do.

6:127

4. And if they incline to peace, incline thou also to it, and trust in Allah. Lo! He even He, is the Hearer, the Knower.

8:61

1. يَاَهْلَ الْكِتٰبِ قَدْ جَاءَكُمْ رَسُوْلُنَا
يُبَيِّنُ لَكُمْ كَثِيْرًا مِّمَّا كُنْتُمْ تُخْفُوْنَ
مِنَ الْكِتٰبِ وَيَعْفُوْا عَنْ كَثِيْرٍ قَدْ جَاءَكُمْ
مِّنَ اللّٰهِ نُوْرٌ وَّكِتٰبٌ مُّبِيْنٌ ﴿١٥﴾
يَّهْدِيْ بِهِ اللّٰهُ مَنِ اتَّبَعَ رِضْوَانَهٗ
سُبُلَ السَّلٰمِ وَيُخْرِجُهُمْ مِّنَ الظُّلُمٰتِ
اِلَى النُّوْرِ بِاِذْنِهٖ وَيَهْدِيْهِمْ اِلٰى
صِرَاطٍ مُّسْتَقِيْمٍ ﴿١٦﴾

2. وَكَيْفَ اَخَافُ مَآ اَشْرَكْتُمْ وَلَا تَخَافُوْنَ
اَنَّكُمْ اَشْرَكْتُمْ بِاللّٰهِ مَا لَمْ يُنَزِّلْ بِهٖ
عَلَيْكُمْ سُلْطٰنًا فَاَيُّ الْفَرِيْقَيْنِ اَحَقُّ
بِالْاَمْنِ اِنْ كُنْتُمْ تَعْلَمُوْنَ ۝
اَلَّذِيْنَ اٰمَنُوْا وَلَمْ يَلْبِسُوْٓا اِيْمَانَهُمْ بِظُلْمٍ
اُولٰٓئِكَ لَهُمُ الْاَمْنُ وَهُمْ مُّهْتَدُوْنَ ۝

3. لَهُمْ دَارُ السَّلٰمِ عِنْدَ رَبِّهِمْ وَهُوَ
وَلِيُّهُمْ بِمَا كَانُوْا يَعْمَلُوْنَ ۝

4. وَاِنْ جَنَحُوْا لِلسَّلْمِ فَاجْنَحْ لَهَا وَتَوَكَّلْ
عَلَى اللّٰهِ اِنَّهٗ هُوَ السَّمِيْعُ الْعَلِيْمُ ۝

5. وَعَدَ اللّٰهُ الَّذِيْنَ اٰمَنُوْا مِنْكُمْ وَعَمِلُوا
الصّٰلِحٰتِ لَيَسْتَخْلِفَنَّهُمْ فِى الْاَرْضِ
كَمَا اسْتَخْلَفَ الَّذِيْنَ مِنْ قَبْلِهِمْ

5. Allah hath promised such of you as believe and do good works that He will surely make them to succeed (the present rulers) in the earth even as He caused those who were before them to succeed (others); and that He will surely establish for them

their religion which He hath approved for them, and will give them in exchange safety after their fear.

24:55

وَلَيُمَكِّنَنَّ لَهُمْ دِينَهُمُ الَّذِي ارْتَضَىٰ
لَهُمْ وَلَيُبَدِّلَنَّهُم مِّن بَعْدِ خَوْفِهِمْ
أَمْنًا

6. The (faithful) slaves of the Beneficent are they who walk upon the earth modestly, and when the foolish ones address them answer: Peace!

25:63

6. وَعِبَادُ الرَّحْمَٰنِ الَّذِينَ يَمْشُونَ عَلَى
الْأَرْضِ هَوْنًا وَإِذَا خَاطَبَهُمُ الْجَاهِلُونَ
قَالُوا سَلَامًا

PEDIGREE

1. And when the trumpet is blown there will be no kinship among them that day, nor will they ask of one another.

23:101

1. فَإِذَا نُفِخَ فِي الصُّورِ فَلَا أَنسَابَ
بَيْنَهُمْ يَوْمَئِذٍ وَلَا يَتَسَاءَلُونَ

2. And He it is Who hath created man from water, and hath appointed for him kindred by blood and kindred by marriage; for thy Lord is ever Powerful.

25:54

2. وَهُوَ الَّذِي خَلَقَ مِنَ الْمَاءِ بَشَرًا فَجَعَلَهُ نَسَبًا
وَصِهْرًا وَكَانَ رَبُّكَ قَدِيرًا

3. O mankind! Keep your duty to your Lord and fear a Day when the parent will not be able to avail the child in aught, nor the child to avail the parent. Lo! Allah's promise is the very truth. Let not the life of the world beguile you, nor let the deceiver beguile you in regard to Allah.

31:33

3. يَا أَيُّهَا النَّاسُ اتَّقُوا رَبَّكُمْ وَاخْشَوْا يَوْمًا
لَّا يَجْزِي وَالِدٌ عَن وَلَدِهِ وَلَا مَوْلُودٌ
هُوَ جَازٍ عَن وَالِدِهِ شَيْئًا إِنَّ وَعْدَ
اللَّهِ حَقٌّ فَلَا تَغُرَّنَّكُمُ الْحَيَاةُ الدُّنْيَا
وَلَا يَغُرَّنَّكُم بِاللَّهِ الْغَرُورُ

PEACE AND SECURITY

Ref: 4:94; 10:9–10; 13:24; 19:62; 20:47; 21:102; 33:44; 39:73; 47:35; 56:26

4. O mankind! Lo! We have created you male and female, and have made you nations and tribes that ye may know one another. Lo! the noblest of you, in the sight of Allah, is the best in conduct. Lo! Allah is Knower, Aware.

49:13

5. Your ties of kindred and your children will avail you naught upon the Day of Resurrection. He will part you. Allah is Seer of what ye do.

60:3

PEN

1. By the pen and that which they write (therewith),

Thou art not, for thy Lord's favour unto thee, a madman.

And lo! thine verily will be a reward unfailing.

And lo! thou art of a tremendous nature.

68:1–4

2. Read: In the name of thy Lord Who createth,

Createth man from a clot.

Read: And thy Lord is the Most Bounteous,

Who teacheth by the pen,

4. يَاَيُّهَا النَّاسُ اِنَّا خَلَقْنٰكُمْ مِّنْ ذَكَرٍ وَّاُنْثٰى
وَجَعَلْنٰكُمْ شُعُوْبًا وَّقَبَآئِلَ لِتَعَارَفُوْا ۚ اِنَّ
اَكْرَمَكُمْ عِنْدَ اللّٰهِ اَتْقٰىكُمْ ۚ اِنَّ اللّٰهَ عَلِيْمٌ
خَبِيْرٌ ﴿۱۳﴾

5. لَنْ تَنْفَعَكُمْ اَرْحَامُكُمْ وَلَآ اَوْلَادُكُمْ ۚ
يَوْمَ الْقِيٰمَةِ ۚ يَفْصِلُ بَيْنَكُمْ ۚ وَاللّٰهُ
بِمَا تَعْمَلُوْنَ بَصِيْرٌ ﴿۳﴾

1. وَالْقَلَمِ وَمَا يَسْطُرُوْنَ ﴿۱﴾
مَآ اَنْتَ بِنِعْمَةِ رَبِّكَ بِمَجْنُوْنٍ ﴿۲﴾
وَاِنَّ لَكَ لَاَجْرًا غَيْرَ مَمْنُوْنٍ ﴿۳﴾
وَاِنَّكَ لَعَلٰى خُلُقٍ عَظِيْمٍ ﴿۴﴾

2. اِقْرَاْ بِاسْمِ رَبِّكَ الَّذِيْ خَلَقَ ﴿۱﴾
خَلَقَ الْاِنْسَانَ مِنْ عَلَقٍ ﴿۲﴾
اِقْرَاْ وَرَبُّكَ الْاَكْرَمُ ﴿۳﴾
الَّذِيْ عَلَّمَ بِالْقَلَمِ ﴿۴﴾
عَلَّمَ الْاِنْسَانَ مَا لَمْ يَعْلَمْ ﴿۵﴾

Teacheth man that which he knew not,

96:1–5

PEOPLE OF THE BOOK

1. Many of the People of the Scripture long to make you disbelievers after your belief, through envy on their own account, after the truth hath become manifest unto them. Forgive and be indulgent (toward them) until Allah give command. Lo! Allah is Able to do all things.

2:109

2. Say: O People of the Scripture! Come to an agreement between us and you: that we shall worship none but Allah, and that we shall ascribe no partner unto Him, and that none of us shall take others for lords beside Allah. And if they turn away, then say: Bear witness that we are they who have surrendered (unto Him).

O People of the Scripture! Why will ye argue about Abraham, when the Torah and the Gospel were not revealed till after him? Have ye then no sense?

3:64–65

3. They are not all alike. Of the People of the Scripture there is a staunch community who recite the revelations of Allah in the night season, falling prostrate (before Him).

They believe in Allah and the Last Day, and enjoin right conduct and forbid indecency, and vie one with another in good works. These are of the righteous.

3:113–114

4. O ye unto whom the Scripture hath been given! Believe in what We have revealed confirming

1. وَدَّ كَثِيرٌ مِّنْ أَهْلِ الْكِتَٰبِ لَوْ يَرُدُّونَكُم مِّنۢ
بَعْدِ إِيمَٰنِكُمْ كُفَّارًا حَسَدًا مِّنْ عِندِ أَنفُسِهِم مِّنۢ
بَعْدِ مَا تَبَيَّنَ لَهُمُ الْحَقُّ فَاعْفُوا وَاصْفَحُوا حَتَّىٰ
يَأْتِيَ اللَّهُ بِأَمْرِهِ إِنَّ اللَّهَ عَلَىٰ كُلِّ شَيْءٍ قَدِيرٌ ﴿١٠٩﴾

2. قُلْ يَٰٓأَهْلَ الْكِتَٰبِ تَعَالَوْا إِلَىٰ كَلِمَةٍ سَوَآءٍ
بَيْنَنَا وَبَيْنَكُمْ أَلَّا نَعْبُدَ إِلَّا اللَّهَ وَلَا نُشْرِكَ
بِهِ شَيْـًٔا وَلَا يَتَّخِذَ بَعْضُنَا بَعْضًا أَرْبَابًا
مِّن دُونِ اللَّهِ فَإِن تَوَلَّوْا فَقُولُوا اشْهَدُوا
بِأَنَّا مُسْلِمُونَ ○
يَٰٓأَهْلَ الْكِتَٰبِ لِمَ تُحَآجُّونَ فِىٓ إِبْرَٰهِيمَ
وَمَآ أُنزِلَتِ التَّوْرَىٰةُ وَالْإِنجِيلُ إِلَّا مِنۢ
بَعْدِهِۦٓ أَفَلَا تَعْقِلُونَ ○

3. لَيْسُوا سَوَآءً مِّنْ أَهْلِ الْكِتَٰبِ أُمَّةٌ
قَآئِمَةٌ يَتْلُونَ ءَايَٰتِ اللَّهِ ءَانَآءَ الَّيْلِ وَهُمْ
يَسْجُدُونَ ○
يُؤْمِنُونَ بِاللَّهِ وَالْيَوْمِ الْءَاخِرِ وَيَأْمُرُونَ
بِالْمَعْرُوفِ وَيَنْهَوْنَ عَنِ الْمُنكَرِ وَيُسَٰرِعُونَ
فِى الْخَيْرَٰتِ وَأُو۟لَٰٓئِكَ مِنَ الصَّٰلِحِينَ ○

4. يَٰٓأَيُّهَا الَّذِينَ أُوتُوا الْكِتَٰبَ ءَامِنُوا بِمَا نَزَّلْنَا
مُصَدِّقًا لِّمَا مَعَكُم مِّن قَبْلِ أَن نَّطْمِسَ
وُجُوهًا فَنَرُدَّهَا عَلَىٰٓ أَدْبَارِهَآ أَوْ نَلْعَنَهُمْ
كَمَا لَعَنَّآ أَصْحَٰبَ السَّبْتِ وَكَانَ
أَمْرُ اللَّهِ مَفْعُولًا ﴿٤٧﴾

that which ye possess, before We destroy countenances so as to confound them, or curse them as We cursed the Sabbath-breakers (of old time) The commandment of Allah is always executed.

4:47

5. This day are all good things made lawful for you. The food of those who have received the Scripture is lawful for you, and your food is lawful for them. And so are the virtuous women of the believers and the virtuous women of those who received the Scripture before you (lawful for you) when ye give them their marriage portions and live with them in honour, not in fornication, nor taking them as secret concubines.

5:5

6. Say: O People of the Scripture! Ye have naught (of guidance) till ye observe the Torah and the Gospel and that which was revealed unto you from your Lord. That which is revealed unto thee (Muhammad) from thy Lord is certain to increase the contumacy and disbelief of many of them. But grieve not for the disbelieving folk.

5:68

5. الْيَوْمَ أُحِلَّ لَكُمُ الطَّيِّبَٰتُ ۖ وَطَعَامُ
الَّذِينَ أُوتُوا الْكِتَٰبَ حِلٌّ لَّكُمْ وَطَعَامُكُمْ
حِلٌّ لَّهُمْ ۖ وَالْمُحْصَنَٰتُ مِنَ الْمُؤْمِنَٰتِ
وَالْمُحْصَنَٰتُ مِنَ الَّذِينَ أُوتُوا الْكِتَٰبَ
مِن قَبْلِكُمْ إِذَا آتَيْتُمُوهُنَّ أُجُورَهُنَّ
مُحْصِنِينَ غَيْرَ مُسَٰفِحِينَ وَلَا مُتَّخِذِي
أَخْدَانٍ ۗ

6. قُلْ يَٰأَهْلَ الْكِتَٰبِ لَسْتُمْ عَلَىٰ شَيْءٍ
حَتَّىٰ تُقِيمُوا التَّوْرَىٰةَ وَالْإِنجِيلَ وَمَا
أُنزِلَ إِلَيْكُم مِّن رَّبِّكُمْ ۗ وَلَيَزِيدَنَّ
كَثِيرًا مِّنْهُم مَّا أُنزِلَ إِلَيْكَ مِن رَّبِّكَ
طُغْيَٰنًا وَكُفْرًا ۖ فَلَا تَأْسَ عَلَى
الْقَوْمِ الْكَٰفِرِينَ ﴿٦٨﴾

References

JEWS: 2:62,111,113,120,135; 3:67; 4:160; 5:18,41,51,69,82; 9:30; 22:17

CHRISTIANS: 2:62,111,113,120, 135; 3:67; 5:14,18,51,69,82; 9:30; 22:17

SABAENS: 2:62; 5:69; 22:17. **See also: Jews and Christian, Revealed Books.**

PEOPLE WHOM ALLAH DETESTS

1. Lo! Allah loveth not aggressors.

2:190

2. Lo! Allah loveth not the disbelievers (in His guidance).

3:32

3. Allah loveth not wrong-doers.

3:57

4. Lo! Allah loveth not such as are proud and boastful.

4:36

5. Lo! Allah loveth not one who is treacherous and sinful.

4:107

6. And Allah loveth not corrupters.

5:64

7. Lo! Allah loveth not transgressors.

5:87

8. And be not prodigal. Lo! Allah loveth not the prodigals.

6:141

9. Lo! Allah loveth not the treacherous.

8:58

10. Lo! He loveth not the proud.

16:23

1. إن الله لا يحب المعتدين
2. فإن الله لا يحب الكافرين
3. والله لا يحب الظالمين
4. إن الله لا يحب من كان مختالا فخورا
5. إن الله لا يحب من كان خوانا أثيما
6. والله لا يحب المفسدين
7. إن الله لا يحب المعتدين
8. ولا تسرفوا إنه لا يحب المسرفين
9. إن الله لا يحب الخائنين
10. إنه لا يحب المستكبرين
11. إن الله لا يحب كل خوان كفور
12. إن الله لا يحب الفرحين

11. Lo! Allah loveth not any treacherous ingrate.

22:38

12. Lo! Allah loveth not the exultant.

28:76

PERFUME

1. And the earth hath He appointed for (His) creatures,

Wherein are fruit and sheathed palm—trees,

Husked grain and scented herb.

Which is it, of the favours of your Lord, that ye deny?

55:10—13

1. وَالْأَرْضَ وَضَعَهَا لِلْأَنَامِ ۝
فِيهَا فَاكِهَةٌ وَالنَّخْلُ ذَاتُ الْأَكْمَامِ ۝
وَالْحَبُّ ذُو الْعَصْفِ وَالرَّيْحَانُ ۝
فَبِأَيِّ آلَاءِ رَبِّكُمَا تُكَذِّبَانِ ۝

○

PERSEVERANCE

1. O ye who believe! Seek help in steadfastness and prayer. Lo! Allah is with the steadfast.

2:153

1. يَا أَيُّهَا الَّذِينَ آمَنُوا اسْتَعِينُوا بِالصَّبْرِ وَ
الصَّلَاةِ ۚ إِنَّ اللَّهَ مَعَ الصَّابِرِينَ ۝

2. And surely We shall try you with something of fear and hunger, and loss of wealth and lives and crops; but give glad tidings to the steadfast.

2:155

2. وَلَنَبْلُوَنَّكُمْ بِشَيْءٍ مِنَ الْخَوْفِ وَالْجُوعِ
وَنَقْصٍ مِنَ الْأَمْوَالِ وَالْأَنْفُسِ وَالثَّمَرَاتِ ۗ
وَبَشِّرِ الصَّابِرِينَ ۝

3. O ye who believe! Endure, outdo all others in endurance, be ready, and observe your duty to Allah, in order that ye may succeed.

3:200

3. يَا أَيُّهَا الَّذِينَ آمَنُوا اصْبِرُوا وَصَابِرُوا
وَرَابِطُوا وَاتَّقُوا اللَّهَ لَعَلَّكُمْ تُفْلِحُونَ ۝

4. If ye punish, then punish with the like of that wherewith ye were afflicted. But if ye endure patiently, verily it is better for the patient.

Endure thou patiently (O Muhammad). Thine endurance is only by (the help of) Allah. Grieve not for them, and be not in distress because of that which they devise.

16:126—127

4. وَإِنْ عَاقَبْتُمْ فَعَاقِبُوا بِمِثْلِ مَا عُوقِبْتُمْ
بِهِ ۖ وَلَئِنْ صَبَرْتُمْ لَهُوَ خَيْرٌ لِلصَّابِرِينَ ۝

وَاصْبِرْ وَمَا صَبْرُكَ إِلَّا بِاللَّهِ ۚ وَلَا تَحْزَنْ
عَلَيْهِمْ وَلَا تَكُ فِي ضَيْقٍ مِمَّا يَمْكُرُونَ ۝

PERFUME Ref: 56:89.

5. And give good tidings (O Muhammad) to the humble,

Whose hearts fear when Allah is mentioned, and the patient of whatever may befall them, and those who establish worship and who spend of that We have bestowed on them.

22:34–35

6. O my dear son! Establish worship and enjoin kindness and forbid iniquity and persevere whatever may befall thee. Lo! that is of the steadfast heart of things.

31:17

7. The good deed and the evil deed are not alike. Repel the evil deed with one which is better, then lo! he, between whom and thee there was enmity (will become) as though he was a bosom friend.

But none is granted it save those who are steadfast, and none is granted it save the owner of great happiness.

41:34–35

.5 وَبَشِّرِ الْمُخْبِتِيْنَ ۝
الَّذِيْنَ إِذَا ذُكِرَ اللّٰهُ وَجِلَتْ قُلُوْبُهُمْ
وَالصّٰبِرِيْنَ عَلٰى مَآ أَصَابَهُمْ وَالْمُقِيْمِي
الصَّلٰوةِ وَمِمَّا رَزَقْنٰهُمْ يُنْفِقُوْنَ ۝

.6 يٰبُنَيَّ أَقِمِ الصَّلٰوةَ وَأْمُرْ بِالْمَعْرُوْفِ
وَانْهَ عَنِ الْمُنْكَرِ وَاصْبِرْ عَلٰى مَآ
أَصَابَكَ إِنَّ ذٰلِكَ مِنْ عَزْمِ الْأُمُوْرِ ۝

.7 وَلَا تَسْتَوِي الْحَسَنَةُ وَلَا السَّيِّئَةُ
اِدْفَعْ بِالَّتِيْ هِيَ أَحْسَنُ فَإِذَا الَّذِيْ
بَيْنَكَ وَبَيْنَهُ عَدَاوَةٌ كَأَنَّهُ وَلِيٌّ حَمِيْمٌ ۝
وَمَا يُلَقّٰهَآ إِلَّا الَّذِيْنَ صَبَرُوْا وَمَا
يُلَقّٰهَآ إِلَّا ذُوْ حَظٍّ عَظِيْمٍ ۝

See also: Steadfastness.

PHARAOH

1. But none trusted Moses, save some scions of his people, (and they were) in fear of Pharaoh and their chiefs, that he would persecute them. Lo! Pharaoh was verily a tyrant in the land, and lo! he verily was of the wanton.

10:83

2. And Moses said: Our Lord! Lo! Thou hast given Pharaoh and his chiefs splendour and riches in the life of the world, Our Lord! that they may lead men astray from Thy Way. Our Lord! Destroy their riches and harden their hearts so that they believe not till they see the painful doom.

10:88

3. And verily We sent Moses with Our revelations and a clear warrant,

Unto Pharaoh and his chiefs, but they did follow the command of Pharaoh, and the command of Pharaoh was no right guide.

He will go before his people on the Day of Resurrection and will lead them to the Fire for watering-place. Ah, hapless is the watering-place (whither they are) led.

A curse is made to follow them in the world and on the Day of Resurrection. Hapless is the gift (that will be) given (them).

11:96–99

1. فَمَآ اٰمَنَ لِمُوْسٰٓى اِلَّا ذُرِّيَّةٌ مِّنْ قَوْمِهٖ
عَلٰى خَوْفٍ مِّنْ فِرْعَوْنَ وَ مَلَا۟ئِهِمْ اَنْ
يَّفْتِنَهُمْ ؕ وَاِنَّ فِرْعَوْنَ لَعَالٍ فِى الْاَرْضِ ۚ
وَاِنَّهٗ لَمِنَ الْمُسْرِفِيْنَ ﴿٨٣﴾

2. وَقَالَ مُوْسٰى رَبَّنَآ اِنَّكَ اٰتَيْتَ فِرْعَوْنَ
وَمَلَاَهٗ زِيْنَةً وَّ اَمْوَالًا فِى الْحَيٰوةِ الدُّنْيَا ۙ
رَبَّنَا لِيُضِلُّوْا عَنْ سَبِيْلِكَ ۚ رَبَّنَا اطْمِسْ
عَلٰٓى اَمْوَالِهِمْ وَاشْدُدْ عَلٰى قُلُوْبِهِمْ فَلَا
يُؤْمِنُوْا حَتّٰى يَرَوُا الْعَذَابَ الْاَلِيْمَ ﴿٨٨﴾

3. وَلَقَدْ اَرْسَلْنَا مُوْسٰى بِاٰيٰتِنَا
وَسُلْطٰنٍ مُّبِيْنٍ ۙ﴿٩٦﴾

اِلٰى فِرْعَوْنَ وَمَلَا۟ئِهٖ فَاتَّبَعُوْٓا اَمْرَ
فِرْعَوْنَ ۚ وَمَآ اَمْرُ فِرْعَوْنَ بِرَشِيْدٍ ﴿٩٧﴾

يَقْدُمُ قَوْمَهٗ يَوْمَ الْقِيٰمَةِ فَاَوْرَدَهُمُ
النَّارَ ؕ وَبِئْسَ الْوِرْدُ الْمَوْرُوْدُ ﴿٩٨﴾

وَاُتْبِعُوْا فِىْ هٰذِهٖ لَعْنَةً وَّيَوْمَ الْقِيٰمَةِ ؕ
بِئْسَ الرِّفْدُ الْمَرْفُوْدُ ﴿٩٩﴾

4. تِلْكَ اٰيٰتُ الْكِتٰبِ الْمُبِيْنِ ﴿٢﴾

نَتْلُوْا عَلَيْكَ مِنْ نَّبَاِ مُوْسٰى وَفِرْعَوْنَ
بِالْحَقِّ لِقَوْمٍ يُّؤْمِنُوْنَ ﴿٣﴾

4. These are revelations of the Scripture that maketh plain.

We narrate unto thee (somewhat) of the story of Moses and Pharaoh with truth, for folk who believe.

Lo! Pharaoh exalted himself in the earth and made its people castes.

A tribe among them he oppressed, killing their sons and sparing their women. Lo! he was of those who work corruption.

And We desired to show favour unto those who were oppressed in the earth, and to make them examples and to make them the inheritors,

And to establish them in the earth, and to show Pharaoh and Hâmân and their hosts that which they feared from them.

And We inspired the mother of Moses, saying: Suckle him and, when thou fearest for him, then cast him into the river and fear not nor grieve. Lo! We shall bring him back unto thee and shall make him (one) of Our messengers.

And the family of Pharaoh took him up, that he might become for them an enemy and a sorrow. Lo! Pharaoh and Hâmân and their hosts were ever sinning.

And the wife of Pharaoh said: (He will be) a consolation for me and for thee. Kill him not. Peradventure he may be of use to us, or we may choose him for a son. And they perceived not.

28:2–9

5. And Pharaoh said: O chiefs! I know not that ye have a god other than me, so kindle for me (a fire), O

إِنَّ فِرْعَوْنَ عَلَا فِي الْأَرْضِ وَجَعَلَ
أَهْلَهَا شِيَعًا يَسْتَضْعِفُ طَائِفَةً مِّنْهُمْ
يُذَبِّحُ أَبْنَاءَهُمْ وَيَسْتَحْيِي نِسَاءَهُمْ
إِنَّهُ كَانَ مِنَ الْمُفْسِدِينَ ④
وَنُرِيدُ أَن نَّمُنَّ عَلَى الَّذِينَ اسْتُضْعِفُوا
فِي الْأَرْضِ وَنَجْعَلَهُمْ أَئِمَّةً وَنَجْعَلَهُمُ
الْوَارِثِينَ ⑤
وَنُمَكِّنَ لَهُمْ فِي الْأَرْضِ وَنُرِيَ فِرْعَوْنَ
وَهَامَانَ وَجُنُودَهُمَا مِنْهُم مَّا كَانُوا
يَحْذَرُونَ ⑥
وَأَوْحَيْنَا إِلَىٰ أُمِّ مُوسَىٰ أَنْ أَرْضِعِيهِ
فَإِذَا خِفْتِ عَلَيْهِ فَأَلْقِيهِ فِي الْيَمِّ
وَلَا تَخَافِي وَلَا تَحْزَنِي إِنَّا رَادُّوهُ
إِلَيْكِ وَجَاعِلُوهُ مِنَ الْمُرْسَلِينَ ⑦
فَالْتَقَطَهُ آلُ فِرْعَوْنَ لِيَكُونَ لَهُمْ عَدُوًّا
وَحَزَنًا إِنَّ فِرْعَوْنَ وَهَامَانَ
وَجُنُودَهُمَا كَانُوا خَاطِئِينَ ⑧

وَقَالَتِ امْرَأَتُ فِرْعَوْنَ قُرَّتُ عَيْنٍ
لِّي وَلَكَ لَا تَقْتُلُوهُ عَسَىٰ أَن يَنفَعَنَا
أَوْ نَتَّخِذَهُ وَلَدًا وَهُمْ لَا يَشْعُرُونَ ⑨

5. وَقَالَ فِرْعَوْنُ يَا أَيُّهَا الْمَلَأُ مَا
عَلِمْتُ لَكُم مِّنْ إِلَٰهٍ غَيْرِي فَأَوْقِدْ
لِي يَا هَامَانُ عَلَى الطِّينِ فَاجْعَل لِّي صَرْحًا

Hämän, to bake the mud, and set up for me a lofty tower in order that I may survey the God of Moses; and lo! I deem him of the liars.

And he and his hosts were haughty in the land without right, and deemed that they would never be brought back to Us.

Therefor We seized him and his hosts, and abandoned them unto the sea. Behold the nature of the consequence for evil–doers!

28:38–40

6. And Pharaoh said: O Haman! Build for me a tower that haply I may reach the roads–

The roads of the heavens, and may look upon the God of Moses, though verily I think him a liar. Thus was the evil that he did made fair–seeming unto Pharaoh, and he was debarred from the (right) way. The plot of Pharaoh ended but in ruin.

40:36–37

7. Hath there come unto thee the history of Moses?

How his Lord called him in the holy vale of Ṭuwa,

(Saying:) Go thou unto Pharaoh–Lo! he hath rebelled–

And say (unto him): Hast thou (will) to grow (in grace)?

Then I will guide thee to the Lord and thou shalt fear (Him).

And he showed him the tremendous token.

But he denied and disobeyed,

Then turned he away in haste,

Then gathered he and summoned

لَعَلِّيٓ اَطَّلِعُ اِلٰٓى اِلٰهِ مُوْسٰى وَاِنِّيْ
لَاَظُنُّهٗ مِنَ الْكٰذِبِيْنَ ۝
وَاسْتَكْبَرَ هُوَ وَجُنُوْدُهٗ فِى الْاَرْضِ
بِغَيْرِ الْحَقِّ وَظَنُّوْٓا اَنَّهُمْ اِلَيْنَا
لَا يُرْجَعُوْنَ ۝
فَاَخَذْنٰهُ وَجُنُوْدَهٗ فَنَبَذْنٰهُمْ فِى الْيَمِّ
فَانْظُرْ كَيْفَ كَانَ عَاقِبَةُ الظّٰلِمِيْنَ ۝

6. وَقَالَ فِرْعَوْنُ يٰهَامٰنُ ابْنِ لِيْ
صَرْحًا لَّعَلِّيْٓ اَبْلُغُ الْاَسْبَابَ ۝
اَسْبَابَ السَّمٰوٰتِ فَاَطَّلِعَ اِلٰٓى اِلٰهِ
مُوْسٰى وَاِنِّيْ لَاَظُنُّهٗ كَاذِبًا ۚ وَكَذٰلِكَ
زُيِّنَ لِفِرْعَوْنَ سُوْٓءُ عَمَلِهٖ وَصُدَّ
عَنِ السَّبِيْلِ ۚ وَمَا كَيْدُ فِرْعَوْنَ
اِلَّا فِيْ تَبَابٍ ۝

7. هَلْ اَتٰىكَ حَدِيْثُ مُوْسٰى ۝
اِذْ نَادٰىهُ رَبُّهٗ بِالْوَادِ الْمُقَدَّسِ طُوًى ۝
اِذْهَبْ اِلٰى فِرْعَوْنَ اِنَّهٗ طَغٰى ۝
فَقُلْ هَلْ لَّكَ اِلٰٓى اَنْ تَزَكّٰى ۝
وَاَهْدِيَكَ اِلٰى رَبِّكَ فَتَخْشٰى ۝
فَاَرٰىهُ الْاٰيَةَ الْكُبْرٰى ۝
فَكَذَّبَ وَعَصٰى ۝
ثُمَّ اَدْبَرَ يَسْعٰى ۝
فَحَشَرَ فَنَادٰى ۝
فَقَالَ اَنَا رَبُّكُمُ الْاَعْلٰى ۝
فَاَخَذَهُ اللّٰهُ نَكَالَ الْاٰخِرَةِ وَالْاُوْلٰى ۝
اِنَّ فِيْ ذٰلِكَ لَعِبْرَةً لِّمَنْ يَّخْشٰى ۝

And proclaimed: "I (Pharaoh) am your Lord the Highest."

So Allah seized him (and made him) an example for the after (life) and for the former.

Lo! herein is indeed a lesson for him who feareth.

79:15–26

Ref: 17:102; 20:24,60; 73:16; 85:17–18.

See also: Miracles of Prophets.

PIETY

1. It is not righteousness that ye turn your faces to the East and the West; but righteous is he who believeth in Allah and the Last Day and the angels and the Scripture and the Prophets; and giveth his wealth, for love of Him, to kinsfolk and to orphans and the needy and the wayfarer and to those who ask, and to set slaves free; and observeth proper worship and payeth the poor-due. And those who keep their treaty when they make one, and the patient in tribulation and adversity and time of stress. Such are they who are sincere. Such are the Godfearing.

2:177

2. It is not righteousness that ye go to houses by the backs thereof (as do the idolaters at certain seasons), but the righteous man is he who wardeth off (evil). So go to houses by the gates thereof, and observe your duty to Allah, that ye may be successful.

2:189

3. And whatsoever good ye do Allah knoweth it. So make provision for yourselves (hereafter); for the best provision is to ward off evil. Therefore keep your duty unto Me, O men of understanding.

2:197

4. Eat of that which Allah

1. ليس البر ان تولوا وجوهكم قبل المشرق
والمغرب ولكن البر من امن بالله واليوم
الاخر والملئكة والكتب والنبين واتى
المال على حبه ذوي القربى واليتمى و
المسكين وابن السبيل والسائلين وفي
الرقاب واقام الصلوة واتى الزكوة و
الموفون بعهدهم اذا عهدوا والصبرين
في البأساء والضراء وحين البأس اولئك
الذين صدقوا واولئك هم المتقون ﴿١٧٧﴾

2. وليس البر بان تاتوا البيوت من
ظهورها ولكن البر من اتقى واتوا البيوت
من ابوابها واتقوا الله لعلكم
تفلحون ﴿١٨٩﴾

3. وما تفعلوا من خير يعلمه الله
وتزودوا فان خير الزاد التقوى واتقون
يا ولي الالباب ﴿١٩٧﴾

4. وكلوا مما رزقكم الله حللا طيبا
واتقوا الله الذي انتم به مؤمنون ﴿٨٨﴾

5. يبني ادم قد انزلنا عليكم لباسا يواري
سواتكم وريشا ولباس التقوى ذلك خير
ذلك من ايت الله لعلهم يذكرون ﴿٢٦﴾

hath bestowed on you as food lawful and good, and keep your duty to Allah in Whom ye are believers.

5:88

5. O Children of Adam! We have revealed unto you raiment to conceal your shame, and splendid vesture,

but the raiment of restraint from evil, that is best. This is of the revelations of Allah, that they may remember.

7:26

6. He only shall tend Allah's sanctuaries who believeth in Allaḥ and the Last Day and observeth proper worship and payeth the poor–due and feareth none save Allah. For such (only) is it possible that they can be of the rightly guided.

9:18

7. A place of worship which was founded upon duty (to Allah) from the first day is more worthy that thou shouldst stand (to pray) therein, wherein are men who love to purify themselves. Allah loveth the purifiers.

Is he who founded his building upon duty to Allah and His good pleasure better, or he who founded his build–ing on the brink of a crumb–ling, overhanging precipice so that it toppled with him into the fire of hell? Allah guideth not wrongdoing folk.

9:108–109

8. And enjoin upon thy people worship and be con–stant therein. We ask not of thee a provision: We pro–vide for thee. And the sequel is for righteousness.

20:132

9. That (is the command). And whoso magnifieth the offerings consecrated to Allah,

6. اِنَّمَا يَعْمُرُ مَسٰجِدَ اللّٰهِ مَنْ اٰمَنَ بِاللّٰهِ
وَالْيَوْمِ الْاٰخِرِ وَاَقَامَ الصَّلٰوةَ وَاٰتَى الزَّكٰوةَ
وَلَمْ يَخْشَ اِلَّا اللّٰهَ فَعَسٰٓى اُولٰٓئِكَ اَنْ يَّكُوْنُوْا
مِنَ الْمُهْتَدِيْنَ ﴿١٨﴾

7. لَمَسْجِدٌ اُسِّسَ عَلَى التَّقْوٰى مِنْ اَوَّلِ
يَوْمٍ اَحَقُّ اَنْ تَقُوْمَ فِيْهِ ؕ فِيْهِ رِجَالٌ
يُّحِبُّوْنَ اَنْ يَّتَطَهَّرُوْا ؕ وَاللّٰهُ يُحِبُّ
الْمُطَّهِّرِيْنَ ﴿١٠٨﴾
اَفَمَنْ اَسَّسَ بُنْيَانَهٗ عَلٰى تَقْوٰى مِنَ
اللّٰهِ وَرِضْوَانٍ خَيْرٌ اَمْ مَّنْ اَسَّسَ بُنْيَانَهٗ
عَلٰى شَفَا جُرُفٍ هَارٍ فَانْهَارَ بِهٖ فِيْ نَارِ
جَهَنَّمَ ؕ وَاللّٰهُ لَا يَهْدِي الْقَوْمَ الظّٰلِمِيْنَ ﴿١٠٩﴾

8. وَاْمُرْ اَهْلَكَ بِالصَّلٰوةِ وَاصْطَبِرْ عَلَيْهَا ؕ
لَا نَسْـَٔلُكَ رِزْقًا ؕ نَحْنُ نَرْزُقُكَ ؕ
وَالْعَاقِبَةُ لِلتَّقْوٰى ﴿١٣٢﴾

9. ذٰلِكَ ۗ وَمَنْ يُّعَظِّمْ شَعَآئِرَ اللّٰهِ فَاِنَّهَا
مِنْ تَقْوَى الْقُلُوْبِ ﴿٣٢﴾

10. تِلْكَ الدَّارُ الْاٰخِرَةُ نَجْعَلُهَا لِلَّذِيْنَ
لَا يُرِيْدُوْنَ عُلُوًّا فِي الْاَرْضِ وَلَا
فَسَادًا ؕ وَالْعَاقِبَةُ لِلْمُتَّقِيْنَ ﴿٨٣﴾

it surely is from devotion of the hearts.

22:32

10. As for that Abode of the Hereafter We assign it unto those who seek not oppression in the earth, nor yet corrup–tion. The sequel is for those who ward off (evil)

28:83

11. Turning unto Him (only); and be careful of your duty unto Him, and establish worship, and be not of those who ascribe partners (unto Him).

30:31

12. And whoso bringeth the truth and believeth therein— Such are the dutiful.

39:33

PLAY AND IDLE SPORT

1. And forsake those who take their religion for a pastime and a jest, and whom the life of the world beguileth. Remind (mankind) hereby lest a soul be destroyed by what it earneth. It hath beside Allah no friend nor intercessor, and though it offer every compensation it will not be accepted from it. Those are they who perish by their own deserts. For them is drink of boiling water and a painful doom, because they disbelieved.

6:70

2. This life of the world is but a pastime and a game. Lo! the home of the Hereafter — that is Life, if they but knew.

29:64

3. But when they spy some merchandise or pastime they break away to it and leave thee standing. Say: That which Allah hath is better than pastime and than merchandise, and Allah is the Best of providers.

62:11

11. مُنِيبِينَ إِلَيْهِ وَاتَّقُوهُ وَأَقِيمُوا الصَّلَوٰةَ
وَلَا تَكُونُوا مِنَ الْمُشْرِكِينَ ۝٣١

12. وَالَّذِي جَاءَ بِالصِّدْقِ وَصَدَّقَ بِهِ
أُولَٰئِكَ هُمُ الْمُتَّقُونَ ۝٣٣

1. وَذَرِ الَّذِينَ اتَّخَذُوا دِينَهُمْ لَعِبًا وَلَهْوًا
وَغَرَّتْهُمُ الْحَيَوٰةُ الدُّنْيَا وَذَكِّرْ بِهِ
أَن تُبْسَلَ نَفْسٌ بِمَا كَسَبَتْ لَيْسَ لَهَا
مِن دُونِ اللَّهِ وَلِيٌّ وَلَا شَفِيعٌ وَإِن
تَعْدِلْ كُلَّ عَدْلٍ لَّا يُؤْخَذْ مِنْهَا أُولَٰئِكَ
الَّذِينَ أُبْسِلُوا بِمَا كَسَبُوا لَهُمْ شَرَابٌ
مِّنْ حَمِيمٍ وَعَذَابٌ أَلِيمٌ بِمَا
كَانُوا يَكْفُرُونَ ۝٧٠

2. وَمَا هَٰذِهِ الْحَيَوٰةُ الدُّنْيَا إِلَّا لَهْوٌ وَ
لَعِبٌ وَإِنَّ الدَّارَ الْآخِرَةَ لَهِيَ
الْحَيَوَانُ لَوْ كَانُوا يَعْلَمُونَ ۝٦٤

3. وَإِذَا رَأَوْا تِجَارَةً أَوْ لَهْوًا انفَضُّوا
إِلَيْهَا وَتَرَكُوكَ قَائِمًا قُلْ مَا عِندَ
اللَّهِ خَيْرٌ مِّنَ اللَّهْوِ وَمِنَ التِّجَارَةِ
وَاللَّهُ خَيْرُ الرَّازِقِينَ ۝١١

PIETY

Ref: 2:2–5,179–180,235,241; 5:3,7; 8:69; 22:37; 25:74; 33:35; 47:17; 48:26; 49:1,3; 58:9; 74:56; 91:8; 96:11–12.

See also: Abstinence, Fear of Allah.

PLEDGE

1. If ye be on a journey and cannot find a scribe, then a pledge in hand (shall suffice). And if one of you entrusteth to another let him who is trusted deliver up that which is entrusted to him (according to the pact between them) and let him observe his duty to Allah his Lord. Hide not testimony. He who hideth it, verily his heart is sinful. Allah is Aware of what ye do.

2:283

PLOTTERS AGAINST ALLAH AND HIS MESSENGER (PBUH)

1. And thus have We made in every city great ones of its wicked ones, that they should plot therein. They do but plot against themselves, though they perceive not.

And When a token cometh unto them, they say: We will not believe till we are given that which Allah's messengers are given. Allah knoweth best with whom to place His message. Humiliation from Allah and heavy punishment will smite the guilty for their scheming.

6:123–124

2. And when those who disbelieve plot against thee (O Muhammad) to wound thee fatally, or to kill thee

1. وَإِنْ كُنْتُمْ عَلَىٰ سَفَرٍ وَلَمْ تَجِدُوا كَاتِبًا
فَرِهٰنٌ مَقْبُوضَةٌ فَإِنْ أَمِنَ بَعْضُكُمْ
بَعْضًا فَلْيُؤَدِّ الَّذِي اؤْتُمِنَ أَمَانَتَهُ وَلْيَتَّقِ
اللَّهَ رَبَّهُ وَلَا تَكْتُمُوا الشَّهَادَةَ وَمَنْ
يَكْتُمْهَا فَإِنَّهُ آثِمٌ قَلْبُهُ وَاللَّهُ بِمَا
تَعْمَلُونَ عَلِيمٌ

1. وَكَذَٰلِكَ جَعَلْنَا فِي كُلِّ قَرْيَةٍ أَكَابِرَ
مُجْرِمِيهَا لِيَمْكُرُوا فِيهَا وَمَا يَمْكُرُونَ
إِلَّا بِأَنْفُسِهِمْ وَمَا يَشْعُرُونَ

وَإِذَا جَاءَتْهُمْ آيَةٌ قَالُوا لَنْ نُؤْمِنَ
حَتَّىٰ نُؤْتَىٰ مِثْلَ مَا أُوتِيَ رُسُلُ اللَّهِ اللَّهُ
أَعْلَمُ حَيْثُ يَجْعَلُ رِسَالَتَهُ سَيُصِيبُ
الَّذِينَ أَجْرَمُوا صَغَارٌ عِنْدَ اللَّهِ وَعَذَابٌ
شَدِيدٌ بِمَا كَانُوا يَمْكُرُونَ

2. وَإِذْ يَمْكُرُ بِكَ الَّذِينَ كَفَرُوا لِيُثْبِتُوكَ
أَوْ يَقْتُلُوكَ أَوْ يُخْرِجُوكَ وَيَمْكُرُونَ
وَيَمْكُرُ اللَّهُ وَاللَّهُ خَيْرُ الْمَاكِرِينَ

or to drive thee forth; they plot, but Allah (also) plotteth; and Allah is the best of plotters.

8:30

PLEDGE **See also: Loan.**

3. And when We cause mankind to taste of mercy after some adversity which had afflicted them, behold! they have some plot against Our revelations. Say: Allah is more swift in plotting. Lo! Our messengers write down that which ye plot.

10:21

4. Are they who plan ill deeds then secure that Allah will not cause the earth to swallow them, or that the doom will not come on them whence they know not?

16:45

5. And those who plot iniquities, theirs will be an awful doom; and the plotting of such (folk) will come to naught.

35:10

6. And they swore by Allah, their most binding oath, that if a warner came unto them they would be more tract–able than any of the nations; yet, when a warner came unto them, it aroused in them naught save repugnance,

(Shown in their) be–having arrogantly in the land and plotting evil; and the evil plot encloseth but the mer who make it. Then, can they expect aught save the treat–ment of the folk of old?

3. وَإِذَآ أَذَقْنَا النَّاسَ رَحْمَةً مِّنْ بَعْدِ ضَرَّآءَ
مَسَّتْهُمْ إِذَا لَهُمْ مَّكْرٌ فِيٓ ءَايَاتِنَا ۚ قُلِ
اللَّهُ أَسْرَعُ مَكْرًا ۚ إِنَّ رُسُلَنَا
يَكْتُبُونَ مَا تَمْكُرُونَ ﴿٢١﴾

4. أَفَأَمِنَ الَّذِينَ مَكَرُوا السَّيِّـَٔاتِ أَنْ
يَخْسِفَ اللَّهُ بِهِمُ الْأَرْضَ أَوْ يَأْتِيَهُمُ
الْعَذَابُ مِنْ حَيْثُ لَا يَشْعُرُونَ ﴿٤٥﴾

5. وَالَّذِينَ يَمْكُرُونَ السَّيِّـَٔاتِ لَهُمْ
عَذَابٌ شَدِيدٌ ۖ وَمَكْرُ أُولَٰٓئِكَ هُوَ
يَبُورُ ﴿١٠﴾

6. وَأَقْسَمُوا بِاللَّهِ جَهْدَ أَيْمَانِهِمْ لَئِنْ
جَآءَهُمْ نَذِيرٌ لَّيَكُونُنَّ أَهْدَىٰ مِنْ
إِحْدَى الْأُمَمِ ۖ فَلَمَّا جَآءَهُمْ نَذِيرٌ
مَّا زَادَهُمْ إِلَّا نُفُورًا ﴿٤٢﴾

اسْتِكْبَارًا فِي الْأَرْضِ وَمَكْرَ السَّيِّئِ ۚ
وَلَا يَحِيقُ الْمَكْرُ السَّيِّئُ إِلَّا بِأَهْلِهِ ۚ
فَهَلْ يَنْظُرُونَ إِلَّا سُنَّتَ الْأَوَّلِينَ ۚ
فَلَنْ تَجِدَ لِسُنَّتِ اللَّهِ تَبْدِيلًا ۖ
وَلَنْ تَجِدَ لِسُنَّتِ اللَّهِ تَحْوِيلًا ﴿٤٣﴾

Thou wilt not find for Allah's way of treatment any sub–stitute, nor wilt thou find for Allah's way of treatment aught of power to change.

35:42–43

See also: Deceit.

POETS

1. As for poets, the erring follow them.

Hast thou not seen how they stray in every valley,

And how they say that which they do not?

Save those who believe and do good works, and remember Allah much, and vindicate themselves after they have been wronged. Those who do wrong will come to know by what a (great) reverse they will be overturned!

26:224–227

2. And We have not taught him (Muhammad) poetry, nor is it meet for him.

36:69

3. That it is indeed the speech of an illustrious messenger.

It is not poet's speech—little is it that ye believe!

69:40–41

POLYGAMY

1. And if ye fear that ye will not deal fairly by the orphans, marry of the women, who seem good to you, two or three or four, and if ye fear that ye cannot do justice (to so many) then one (only) or (the captives) that your right hands possess. Thus it is more likely that ye will not do injustice.

4:3

2. Ye will not be able to

1. وَالشُّعَرَاءُ يَتَّبِعُهُمُ الْغَاوُونَ ﴿٢٢٤﴾
أَلَمْ تَرَ أَنَّهُمْ فِي كُلِّ وَادٍ يَهِيمُونَ ﴿٢٢٥﴾
وَأَنَّهُمْ يَقُولُونَ مَا لَا يَفْعَلُونَ ﴿٢٢٦﴾
إِلَّا الَّذِينَ آمَنُوا وَعَمِلُوا الصَّالِحَاتِ
وَذَكَرُوا اللَّهَ كَثِيرًا وَانْتَصَرُوا مِنْ
بَعْدِ مَا ظُلِمُوا ۗ وَسَيَعْلَمُ الَّذِينَ
ظَلَمُوا أَيَّ مُنْقَلَبٍ يَنْقَلِبُونَ ﴿٢٢٧﴾

2. وَمَا عَلَّمْنَاهُ الشِّعْرَ وَمَا يَنْبَغِي لَهُ ۚ
إِنْ هُوَ إِلَّا ذِكْرٌ وَقُرْآنٌ مُبِينٌ ﴿٦٩﴾

3. إِنَّهُ لَقَوْلُ رَسُولٍ كَرِيمٍ ﴿٤٠﴾
وَمَا هُوَ بِقَوْلِ شَاعِرٍ ۚ قَلِيلًا مَا تُؤْمِنُونَ ﴿٤١﴾

○

1. وَإِنْ خِفْتُمْ أَلَّا تُقْسِطُوا فِي الْيَتَامَىٰ فَانْكِحُوا
مَا طَابَ لَكُمْ مِنَ النِّسَاءِ مَثْنَىٰ وَثُلَاثَ
وَرُبَاعَ ۖ فَإِنْ خِفْتُمْ أَلَّا تَعْدِلُوا فَوَاحِدَةً
أَوْ مَا مَلَكَتْ أَيْمَانُكُمْ ۚ ذَٰلِكَ أَدْنَىٰ
أَلَّا تَعُولُوا ﴿٣﴾

2. وَلَنْ تَسْتَطِيعُوا أَنْ تَعْدِلُوا بَيْنَ النِّسَاءِ
وَلَوْ حَرَصْتُمْ ۖ فَلَا تَمِيلُوا كُلَّ الْمَيْلِ
فَتَذَرُوهَا كَالْمُعَلَّقَةِ ۚ وَإِنْ تُصْلِحُوا وَتَتَّقُوا
فَإِنَّ اللَّهَ كَانَ غَفُورًا رَحِيمًا ﴿١٢٩﴾

deal equally between (your) wives, however much ye wish (to do so). But turn not altogether away (from one), leaving her as in suspense. If ye do good and keep from evil lo! Allah is ever Forgiving, Merciful.

4:129

POLYGAMY

See also: Conjugal Rights and Obligations.

PRAISE TO ALLAH

1. Praise be to Allah, Lord of the Worlds,

1:1

2. Praise be to Allah, Who hath created the heavens and the earth, and hath appointed darkness and light. Yet those who disbelieve ascribe rivals unto their Lord.

6:1

3. The thunder hymneth His praise and (so do) the angels for awe of Him. He launcheth the thunder—bolts and smiteth with them whom He will while they dispute (in doubt) concerning Allah, and He is mighty in wrath.

13:13

4. But hymn the praise of thy Lord, and be of those who make prostration (unto Him):

And serve thy Lord till the Inevitable cometh unto thee.

15:98–99

5. The seven heavens and the earth and all that is therein praise Him, and there is not a thing but hymneth His praise; but ye understand not their praise Lo! He is ever Clement, Forgiving.

17:44

6. And say: praise be to Allah, Who hath not taken unto Himself a son, and Who hath no partner in the Sovereignty, nor hath He any protecting friend through dependence. And magnify Him

1. اَلْحَمْدُ لِلّٰهِ رَبِّ الْعٰلَمِيْنَ ۙ

2. اَلْحَمْدُ لِلّٰهِ الَّذِىْ خَلَقَ السَّمٰوٰتِ
وَ الْاَرْضَ وَجَعَلَ الظُّلُمٰتِ وَ النُّوْرَ ۬ ط
ثُمَّ الَّذِيْنَ كَفَرُوْا بِرَبِّهِمْ يَعْدِلُوْنَ ۝١

3. وَيُسَبِّحُ الرَّعْدُ بِحَمْدِهٖ وَ الْمَلٰٓئِكَةُ
مِنْ خِيْفَتِهٖ ۚ وَيُرْسِلُ الصَّوَاعِقَ فَيُصِيْبُ
بِهَا مَنْ يَّشَآءُ وَهُمْ يُجَادِلُوْنَ فِى اللّٰهِ ۚ
وَ هُوَ شَدِيْدُ الْمِحَالِ ۝١٣ ط

4. فَسَبِّحْ بِحَمْدِ رَبِّكَ وَكُنْ مِّنَ السّٰجِدِيْنَ ۝٩٨

وَاعْبُدْ رَبَّكَ حَتّٰى يَاْتِيَكَ الْيَقِيْنُ ۝٩٩

5. تُسَبِّحُ لَهُ السَّمٰوٰتُ السَّبْعُ وَ الْاَرْضُ
وَمَنْ فِيْهِنَّ ۭ وَاِنْ مِّنْ شَىْءٍ اِلَّا يُسَبِّحُ
بِحَمْدِهٖ وَلٰكِنْ لَّا تَفْقَهُوْنَ تَسْبِيْحَهُمْ ۭ
اِنَّهٗ كَانَ حَلِيْمًا غَفُوْرًا ۝٤٤

6. وَقُلِ الْحَمْدُ لِلّٰهِ الَّذِىْ لَمْ يَتَّخِذْ وَلَدًا
وَّلَمْ يَكُنْ لَّهٗ شَرِيْكٌ فِى الْمُلْكِ
وَلَمْ يَكُنْ لَّهٗ وَلِىٌّ مِّنَ الذُّلِّ
وَكَبِّرْهُ تَكْبِيْرًا ۝١١١

7. قُلِ الْحَمْدُ لِلّٰهِ وَسَلٰمٌ عَلٰى عِبَادِهِ
الَّذِيْنَ اصْطَفٰى ۭ آٰللّٰهُ خَيْرٌ اَمَّا
يُشْرِكُوْنَ ۝

with all magnificence.

17:111

7. Say (O Muhammad) Praise be to Allah, and peace be on His slaves whom He hath chosen! Is Allah best, or (all) that ye ascribe as partners (unto Him)?

27:59

8. Priase be to Allah, the Creator of the heavens and the earth, Who appointeth the angels as messengers having wings two, three and four. He multiplieth in certain what He will. Lo! Allah is Able to do all things.

35:1

9. Glorified be thy Lord, the Lord of Majesty, from that which they attribute (unto Him)!

And peace be unto those sent (to warn)!

And praise be to Allah Lord of the Worlds!

37:180–182

10. Those who bear the Throne, and all who are round about it, hymn the praises of their Lord and believe in Him and ask forgiveness for those who believe (saying): Our Lord! Thou comprehendest all things in mercy and knowledge, therefor forgive those who repent and follow Thy way. Ward off from them the punishment of hell.

40:7

11. Then have patience (O Muhammad). Lo! the promise of Allah is true. And ask forgiveness of thy sin, and hymn the praise of thy Lord at fall of night and in the early hours.

40:55

8. اَلْحَمْدُ لِلّٰهِ فَاطِرِ السَّمٰوٰتِ وَالْاَرْضِ
جَاعِلِ الْمَلٰٓئِكَةِ رُسُلًا اُولِيْٓ اَجْنِحَةٍ
مَّثْنٰى وَثُلٰثَ وَرُبٰعَ ۭ يَزِيْدُ فِي
الْخَلْقِ مَا يَشَاۗءُ ۭ اِنَّ اللّٰهَ عَلٰي كُلِّ شَيْءٍ قَدِيْرٌ ①

9. سُبْحٰنَ رَبِّكَ رَبِّ الْعِزَّةِ عَمَّا يَصِفُوْنَ ⑱
وَسَلٰمٌ عَلَى الْمُرْسَلِيْنَ ⑱
وَالْحَمْدُ لِلّٰهِ رَبِّ الْعٰلَمِيْنَ ⑱

10. اَلَّذِيْنَ يَحْمِلُوْنَ الْعَرْشَ وَمَنْ حَوْلَهٗ
يُسَبِّحُوْنَ بِحَمْدِ رَبِّهِمْ وَيُؤْمِنُوْنَ
بِهٖ وَيَسْتَغْفِرُوْنَ لِلَّذِيْنَ اٰمَنُوْا ۚ رَبَّنَا
وَسِعْتَ كُلَّ شَيْءٍ رَّحْمَةً وَّعِلْمًا فَاغْفِرْ
لِلَّذِيْنَ تَابُوْا وَاتَّبَعُوْا سَبِيْلَكَ وَقِهِمْ
عَذَابَ الْجَحِيْمِ ⑦

11. فَاصْبِرْ اِنَّ وَعْدَ اللّٰهِ حَقٌّ وَّاسْتَغْفِرْ
لِذَنْۢبِكَ وَسَبِّحْ بِحَمْدِ رَبِّكَ بِالْعَشِيِّ
وَالْاِبْكَارِ ⑤

Ref: 6:45; 7:206; 10:10; 17:1; 18:1; 24:41; 25:1,10,61; 27:93; 29:63; 30:18; 31:25; 33:41–42; 34:1; 35:34; 36:36,83; 37:159; 39:74–75; 40:65; 41:38; 42:5; 43:82–85: 45:36–37; 61:1,62:1; 64:1; 67:1; 68:29; 69:52.

See also: Glorification of Allah, Remembrance of Allah.

PREACHING

1. And there may spring from you a nation who invite to goodness, and enjoin right conduct and forbid indecency. Such are they who are successful.

3:104

2. Ye are the best community that hath been raised up for mankind. Ye enjoin right conduct and forbid indecency; and ye believe in Allah. And if the People of the Scripture had believed it had been better for them. Some of them are believers; but most of them are evil-livers.

3:110

3. Of the People of the Scripture there is a staunch community who recite the revelations of Allah in the night season, falling prostrate (before Him).

They believe in Allah and the Last Day, and enjoin right conduct and forbid indecency, and vie one with another in good works. These are of the righteous.

3:113–114

4. O Messenger! Make known that which hath been revealed unto thee from thy Lord, for if thou do it not, thou will not have conveyed His message. Allah will protect thee from mankind. Lo! Allah guideth not the disbelieving folk.

5:67

1. وَلْتَكُنْ مِّنْكُمْ أُمَّةٌ يَّدْعُوْنَ إِلَى الْخَيْرِ
وَيَأْمُرُوْنَ بِالْمَعْرُوْفِ وَيَنْهَوْنَ عَنِ
الْمُنْكَرِ وَأُولٰٓئِكَ هُمُ الْمُفْلِحُوْنَ ○

2. كُنْتُمْ خَيْرَ أُمَّةٍ أُخْرِجَتْ لِلنَّاسِ تَأْمُرُوْنَ
بِالْمَعْرُوْفِ وَتَنْهَوْنَ عَنِ الْمُنْكَرِ وَتُؤْمِنُوْنَ
بِاللّٰهِ وَلَوْ اٰمَنَ أَهْلُ الْكِتٰبِ لَكَانَ خَيْرًا لَّهُمْ
مِنْهُمُ الْمُؤْمِنُوْنَ وَأَكْثَرُهُمُ الْفٰسِقُوْنَ ○

3. مِنْ أَهْلِ الْكِتٰبِ أُمَّةٌ قَآئِمَةٌ يَّتْلُوْنَ
اٰيٰتِ اللّٰهِ اٰنَآءَ الَّيْلِ وَهُمْ يَسْجُدُوْنَ ○

يُؤْمِنُوْنَ بِاللّٰهِ وَالْيَوْمِ الْاٰخِرِ وَيَأْمُرُوْنَ
بِالْمَعْرُوْفِ وَيَنْهَوْنَ عَنِ الْمُنْكَرِ وَيُسَارِعُوْنَ
فِي الْخَيْرٰتِ وَأُولٰٓئِكَ مِنَ الصّٰلِحِيْنَ ○

4. يٰٓأَيُّهَا الرَّسُوْلُ بَلِّغْ مَآ أُنْزِلَ إِلَيْكَ مِنْ
رَّبِّكَ وَإِنْ لَّمْ تَفْعَلْ فَمَا بَلَّغْتَ رِسَالَتَهُ
وَاللّٰهُ يَعْصِمُكَ مِنَ النَّاسِ إِنَّ اللّٰهَ
لَا يَهْدِي الْقَوْمَ الْكٰفِرِيْنَ ﴿٦٧﴾

5. مَا عَلَى الرَّسُوْلِ إِلَّا الْبَلٰغُ وَاللّٰهُ يَعْلَمُ
مَا تُبْدُوْنَ وَمَا تَكْتُمُوْنَ ﴿٩٩﴾

6. وَمَآ أَرْسَلْنَا مِنْ رَّسُوْلٍ إِلَّا بِلِسَانِ قَوْمِهِ
لِيُبَيِّنَ لَهُمْ فَيُضِلُّ اللّٰهُ مَنْ يَّشَآءُ وَ

5. The duty of the messenger is only to convey (the message). Allah knoweth what ye proclaim and what ye hide.

5:99

6. And We never sent a messenger save with the language of his folk, that he might make (the Message) clear for them.

Then Allah sendeth whom He will astray, and guideth whom He will. He is the Mighty, the Wise.

14:4

7. Call unto the way of thy Lord with wisdom and fair exhortation, and reason with them in the better way. Lo! thy Lord is Best Aware of him who strayeth from His way, and He is Best Aware of those who go aright.

16:125

8. And enjoin upon thy people worship and be constant therein. We ask not of thee a provision: We provide for thee. And the sequel is for righteousness.

20:132

9. Unto each nation have We given sacred rites which they are to perform; so let them not dispute with thee of the matter, but summon thou unto thy Lord. Lo! thou indeed followest right guidance.

22:67

10. And warn thy tribe of near kindred.

26:214

11. And argue not with the People of the Scripture unless it be in (a way) that is better, save with such of them as do wrong, and say: We believe in that which hath been revealed unto us and revealed unto you: our God and your God is One, and unto Him we surrender.

29:46

يَهْدِي مَن يَشَاءُ ۚ وَهُوَ الْعَزِيزُ الْحَكِيمُ ﴿٤﴾

7. ادْعُ إِلَىٰ سَبِيلِ رَبِّكَ بِالْحِكْمَةِ وَالْمَوْعِظَةِ
الْحَسَنَةِ ۖ وَجَادِلْهُم بِالَّتِي هِيَ أَحْسَنُ ۚ إِنَّ
رَبَّكَ هُوَ أَعْلَمُ بِمَن ضَلَّ عَن سَبِيلِهِ
وَهُوَ أَعْلَمُ بِالْمُهْتَدِينَ ﴿١٢٥﴾

8. وَأْمُرْ أَهْلَكَ بِالصَّلَاةِ وَاصْطَبِرْ عَلَيْهَا ۖ
لَا نَسْأَلُكَ رِزْقًا ۖ نَّحْنُ نَرْزُقُكَ ۗ
وَالْعَاقِبَةُ لِلتَّقْوَىٰ ﴿١٣٢﴾

9. لِّكُلِّ أُمَّةٍ جَعَلْنَا مَنسَكًا هُمْ نَاسِكُوهُ ۖ
فَلَا يُنَازِعُنَّكَ فِي الْأَمْرِ ۚ وَادْعُ إِلَىٰ رَبِّكَ ۖ
إِنَّكَ لَعَلَىٰ هُدًى مُّسْتَقِيمٍ ﴿٦٧﴾

10 وَأَنذِرْ عَشِيرَتَكَ الْأَقْرَبِينَ ﴿٢١٤﴾

11. وَلَا تُجَادِلُوا أَهْلَ الْكِتَابِ إِلَّا بِالَّتِي
هِيَ أَحْسَنُ إِلَّا الَّذِينَ ظَلَمُوا مِنْهُمْ ۖ
وَقُولُوا آمَنَّا بِالَّذِي أُنزِلَ إِلَيْنَا وَ
أُنزِلَ إِلَيْكُمْ وَإِلَٰهُنَا وَإِلَٰهُكُمْ وَاحِدٌ
وَنَحْنُ لَهُ مُسْلِمُونَ ﴿٤٦﴾

12. وَمَنْ أَحْسَنُ قَوْلًا مِّمَّن دَعَا إِلَى
اللَّهِ وَعَمِلَ صَالِحًا وَقَالَ إِنَّنِي مِنَ
الْمُسْلِمِينَ ﴿٣٣﴾

12. And who is better in speech than him who prayeth unto his Lord and doth right, and saith: Lo! I am of those who surrender (unto Him).

41:33

Ref: 2:44; 3:23,153; 7:62,67,79,94,157,193; 10:41–43; 11:57; 13:40; 14:44–45,52; 16:35, 82, 18:57; 20:43–44; 21:106; 24:54; 28:56,87; 29:18,69; 33:39,46; 36:17; 40:41,43; 41:44; 42:13,48; 46:23,35; 53:30; 61:14; 64:12; 72:20–23; 79:17,19.

See also: Commands and Prohibitions.

PREDESTINATION AND FREE WILL

1. He it is Who fashioneth you in the wombs as pleaseth Him. There is no God save Him, the Almighty, the Wise.

He it is Who hath revealed unto thee (Muhammad) the Scripture wherein are clear revelations—They are the substance of the Book— and others (which are) allegorical. But those in whose hearts is doubt pursue, forsooth, that which is allegorical seeking (to cause) dissension by seeking to explain it. None knoweth its explanation save Allah. And those who are of sound instruction say: We believe therein; the whole is from our Lord; but only men of understanding really heed.

Our Lord! Cause not our hearts to stray after Thou hast guided us, and bestow upon us mercy from Thy Presence. Lo! Thou, only Thou art the Bestower.

3:6–8

2. Ye (Muslims) slew them not, but Allah slew them. And thou (Muhammad) threwest not when, thou didst throw, but Allah threw, that He might test the believers by a fair test from Him. Lo! Allah is Hearer, Knower.

8:17

3. Even if thou (O Muhammad) desirest their right guidance, still Allah assuredly will not guide him who misleadeth

هُوَ الَّذِي يُصَوِّرُكُمْ فِي الْأَرْحَامِ كَيْفَ
يَشَاءُ ۚ لَا إِلَٰهَ إِلَّا هُوَ الْعَزِيزُ الْحَكِيمُ ○

هُوَ الَّذِي أَنْزَلَ عَلَيْكَ الْكِتَابَ مِنْهُ
آيَاتٌ مُحْكَمَاتٌ هُنَّ أُمُّ الْكِتَابِ وَأُخَرُ
مُتَشَابِهَاتٌ ۖ فَأَمَّا الَّذِينَ فِي قُلُوبِهِمْ زَيْغٌ
فَيَتَّبِعُونَ مَا تَشَابَهَ مِنْهُ ابْتِغَاءَ الْفِتْنَةِ
وَابْتِغَاءَ تَأْوِيلِهِ ۗ وَمَا يَعْلَمُ تَأْوِيلَهُ إِلَّا
اللَّهُ ۗ وَالرَّاسِخُونَ فِي الْعِلْمِ يَقُولُونَ آمَنَّا
بِهِ كُلٌّ مِنْ عِنْدِ رَبِّنَا ۗ وَمَا يَذَّكَّرُ
إِلَّا أُولُو الْأَلْبَابِ ○

رَبَّنَا لَا تُزِغْ قُلُوبَنَا بَعْدَ إِذْ هَدَيْتَنَا
وَهَبْ لَنَا مِنْ لَدُنْكَ رَحْمَةً ۚ إِنَّكَ
أَنْتَ الْوَهَّابُ ○

2. فَلَمْ تَقْتُلُوهُمْ وَلَٰكِنَّ اللَّهَ قَتَلَهُمْ ۚ وَمَا
رَمَيْتَ إِذْ رَمَيْتَ وَلَٰكِنَّ اللَّهَ رَمَىٰ ۚ
وَلِيُبْلِيَ الْمُؤْمِنِينَ مِنْهُ بَلَاءً حَسَنًا ۚ
إِنَّ اللَّهَ سَمِيعٌ عَلِيمٌ ○

3. إِنْ تَحْرِصْ عَلَىٰ هُدَاهُمْ فَإِنَّ اللَّهَ لَا
يَهْدِي مَنْ يُضِلُّ ۖ وَمَا لَهُمْ مِنْ نَاصِرِينَ ○

4. وَمِنَ النَّاسِ مَنْ يُجَادِلُ فِي اللَّهِ بِغَيْرِ
عِلْمٍ وَيَتَّبِعُ كُلَّ شَيْطَانٍ مَرِيدٍ ○

Such have no helpers.

16:37

4. Among mankind is he who disputeth concerning Allah without knowledge, and followeth each froward devil;

For him it is decreed that whoso taketh him for friend, he verily will mislead him and will guide him to the punishment of the Flame.

22:3–4

كُتِبَ عَلَيْهِ اَنَّهٗ مَنْ تَوَلَّاهُ فَاَنَّهٗ
يُضِلُّهٗ وَيَهْدِيْهِ اِلٰى عَذَابِ السَّعِيْرِ ﴿٤﴾

5. And the commandment of Allah is certain destiny—

33:38

5. وَكَانَ اَمْرُاللّٰهِ قَدَرًا مَّقْدُوْرًا ﴿٣٨﴾

6. And that man hath only that for which he maketh effort.

And that his effort will be seen,

53:39–40

6. وَاَنْ لَّيْسَ لِلْاِنْسَانِ اِلَّا مَا سَعٰى ﴿٣٩﴾
وَاَنَّ سَعْيَهٗ سَوْفَ يُرٰى ﴿٤٠﴾

Ref: 2:221,253; 6:112; 13:31; 14:4; 16:116–117; 22:8–10; 31:20–22; 35:8; 36:8–9; 42:8,10,16.

See also: Destiny, Responsibility for Actions.

PRIDE

1. Lo! Allah loveth not such as are proud and boastful.
4:36

2. The Messiah will never scorn to be a slave unto Allah, nor will the favoured angels. Whoso scorneth His service and is proud, all such will He assemble unto Him;

Then, as for those who believed and did good works, unto them will He pay their wages in full, adding unto them of His bounty; and as for those who were scornful and proud, them will He punish with a painful doom

And they will not find for them, against Allah, any protecting friend or helper.
4: 172–174

3. Be not as those who came forth from their dwell–ings boastfully and to be seen of men, and debar (men) from the way of Allah, while Allah is surrounding all they do.

8:47

4. Your God is One God. But as for those who believe not in the Hereafter their hearts refuse to know, for they are proud,

Assuredly Allah knoweth that which they keep hidden and that which they proclaim. Lo! He loveth not the proud.
16:22–23

1. إِنَّ اللّٰهَ لَا يُحِبُّ مَنْ كَانَ مُخْتَالًا فَخُورًا ﴿٣٦﴾
2. لَنْ يَّسْتَنْكِفَ الْمَسِيْحُ اَنْ يَّكُوْنَ عَبْدًا
لِّلّٰهِ وَلَا الْمَلٰٓئِكَةُ الْمُقَرَّبُوْنَ ۭ وَمَنْ
يَّسْتَنْكِفْ عَنْ عِبَادَتِهٖ وَيَسْتَكْبِرْ
فَسَيَحْشُرُهُمْ اِلَيْهِ جَمِيْعًا ﴿١٧٢﴾
فَاَمَّا الَّذِيْنَ اٰمَنُوْا وَعَمِلُوا الصّٰلِحٰتِ
فَيُوَفِّيْهِمْ اُجُوْرَهُمْ وَيَزِيْدُهُمْ مِّنْ
فَضْلِهٖ ۚ وَاَمَّا الَّذِيْنَ اسْتَنْكَفُوْا وَاسْتَكْبَرُوْا
فَيُعَذِّبُهُمْ عَذَابًا اَلِيْمًا ۙ
وَّلَا يَجِدُوْنَ لَهُمْ مِّنْ دُوْنِ اللّٰهِ وَلِيًّا وَّلَا
نَصِيْرًا ﴿١٧٣﴾
3. وَلَا تَكُوْنُوْا كَالَّذِيْنَ خَرَجُوْا مِنْ دِيَارِهِمْ
بَطَرًا وَّرِئَاۤءَ النَّاسِ وَيَصُدُّوْنَ عَنْ
سَبِيْلِ اللّٰهِ ۭ وَاللّٰهُ بِمَا يَعْمَلُوْنَ مُحِيْطٌ ﴿٤٧﴾
4. اِلٰهُكُمْ اِلٰهٌ وَّاحِدٌ ۚ فَالَّذِيْنَ لَا يُؤْمِنُوْنَ
بِالْاٰخِرَةِ قُلُوْبُهُمْ مُّنْكِرَةٌ وَّهُمْ
مُّسْتَكْبِرُوْنَ ﴿٢٢﴾
لَا جَرَمَ اَنَّ اللّٰهَ يَعْلَمُ مَا يُسِرُّوْنَ وَمَا
يُعْلِنُوْنَ ۭ اِنَّهٗ لَا يُحِبُّ الْمُسْتَكْبِرِيْنَ ﴿٢٣﴾
5. فَادْخُلُوْٓا اَبْوَابَ جَهَنَّمَ خٰلِدِيْنَ فِيْهَا ۭ
فَلَبِئْسَ مَثْوَى الْمُتَكَبِّرِيْنَ ﴿٢٩﴾
6. تِلْكَ الدَّارُ الْاٰخِرَةُ نَجْعَلُهَا لِلَّذِيْنَ
لَا يُرِيْدُوْنَ عُلُوًّا فِي الْاَرْضِ وَلَا

5. So enter the gates of hell, to dwell therein for ever. Woeful indeed will be the lodging of the arrogant.
16:29

6. As for that Abode of the Hereafter We assign it unto tho-se who seek not oppression in

the earth, nor yet corruption. The sequel is for those who ward off (evil).

28:83

فَسَادًا ۚ وَالْعَاقِبَةُ لِلْمُتَّقِينَ ﴿٨٣﴾

7. Turn not thy cheek in scorn toward folk, nor walk with pertness in the land. Lo! Allah loveth not each braggart boaster.

Be modest in thy bearing and subdue thy voice. Lo! the harshest of all voices is the voice of the ass.

31:18–19

7. وَلَا تُصَعِّرْ خَدَّكَ لِلنَّاسِ وَلَا تَمْشِ فِي الْأَرْضِ مَرَحًا ۖ إِنَّ اللَّهَ لَا يُحِبُّ كُلَّ مُخْتَالٍ فَخُورٍ ﴿١٨﴾

وَاقْصِدْ فِي مَشْيِكَ وَاغْضُضْ مِن صَوْتِكَ ۚ إِنَّ أَنكَرَ الْأَصْوَاتِ لَصَوْتُ الْحَمِيرِ ﴿١٩﴾

8. Moses said: Lo! I seek refuge in my Lord and your Lord from every scorner who believeth not in a Day of Reckoning.

40:27

8. وَقَالَ مُوسَىٰ إِنِّي عُذْتُ بِرَبِّي وَرَبِّكُم مِّن كُلِّ مُتَكَبِّرٍ لَّا يُؤْمِنُ بِيَوْمِ الْحِسَابِ ﴿٢٧﴾

9. And your Lord hath said: Pray unto Me and I will hear your prayer. Lo! those who scorn My service, they will enter hell, disgraced.

40:60

9. وَقَالَ رَبُّكُمُ ادْعُونِي أَسْتَجِبْ لَكُمْ ۚ إِنَّ الَّذِينَ يَسْتَكْبِرُونَ عَنْ عِبَادَتِي سَيَدْخُلُونَ جَهَنَّمَ دَاخِرِينَ ﴿٦٠﴾

○

Ref: 4:173; 6:93; 7:88,146; 17:37; 21:19; 23:46–47; 28:76; 32:15; 35:42–43; 39:59–60; 40:27,35,75; 41:37–38; 45:31–32; 46:20; 57:23–24; 63:5; 77:48; 84:21–22.

PRINCIPLES OF ALLAH'S JUSTICE

1. Unto Allah (belongeth) whatsoever is in the heavens and whatsoever is in the earth; and whether ye make known what is in your minds or hide it, Allah will bring you to account for it. He will forgive whom He will and He will punish whom He will. Allah is Able to do all things.

2:284

2. Allah tasketh not a soul beyond its scope. For it (is only) that which it hath earned, and against it (only) that which it hath deserved.

2:286

3. Yet whoso doeth evil or wrongeth his own soul, then seeketh pardon of Allah, will find Allah Forgiving, Merciful.

Whoso committeth sin committeth it only against himself. Allah is ever Knower, Wise.

4:110–111

4. This is because thy Lord destroyeth not the townships arbitrarily while their people are unconscious (of the wrong they do).

For all there will be ranks from what they did. Thy Lord is not unaware of what they do.

Thy Lord is the Absolute, the Lord of Mercy. If He will, He can remove you and can cause what He will to follow after you, even as

.1 لِلّٰهِ مَا فِي السَّمٰوٰتِ وَمَا فِي الْأَرْضِ ۗ وَإِنْ
تُبْدُوا مَا فِي أَنْفُسِكُمْ أَوْ تُخْفُوهُ يُحَاسِبْكُمْ
بِهِ اللّٰهُ ۗ فَيَغْفِرُ لِمَنْ يَشَاءُ وَيُعَذِّبُ مَنْ
يَشَاءُ ۗ وَاللّٰهُ عَلٰى كُلِّ شَيْءٍ قَدِيرٌ ۝

.2 لَا يُكَلِّفُ اللّٰهُ نَفْسًا إِلَّا وُسْعَهَا ۗ لَهَا
مَا كَسَبَتْ وَعَلَيْهَا مَا اكْتَسَبَتْ ۗ

.3 وَمَنْ يَعْمَلْ سُوءًا أَوْ يَظْلِمْ نَفْسَهُ ثُمَّ
يَسْتَغْفِرِ اللّٰهَ يَجِدِ اللّٰهَ غَفُورًا رَحِيمًا ۝

وَمَنْ يَكْسِبْ إِثْمًا فَإِنَّمَا يَكْسِبُهُ عَلٰى
نَفْسِهِ ۗ وَكَانَ اللّٰهُ عَلِيمًا حَكِيمًا ۝

.4 ذٰلِكَ أَنْ لَمْ يَكُنْ رَبُّكَ مُهْلِكَ الْقُرٰى
بِظُلْمٍ وَأَهْلُهَا غٰفِلُونَ ۝

وَلِكُلٍّ دَرَجٰتٌ مِمَّا عَمِلُوا ۗ وَمَا رَبُّكَ
بِغٰفِلٍ عَمَّا يَعْمَلُونَ ۝

وَرَبُّكَ الْغَنِيُّ ذُو الرَّحْمَةِ ۗ إِنْ يَشَأْ يُذْهِبْكُمْ
وَيَسْتَخْلِفْ مِنْ بَعْدِكُمْ مَا يَشَاءُ كَمَا
أَنْشَأَكُمْ مِنْ ذُرِّيَّةِ قَوْمٍ آخَرِينَ ۝

.5 هَلْ يَنْظُرُونَ إِلَّا أَنْ تَأْتِيَهُمُ الْمَلٰئِكَةُ
أَوْ يَأْتِيَ أَمْرُ رَبِّكَ ۗ كَذٰلِكَ فَعَلَ الَّذِينَ
مِنْ قَبْلِهِمْ ۗ وَمَا ظَلَمَهُمُ اللّٰهُ وَلٰكِنْ

He raised you from the seed of other folk.

6:131–133

5. Await they aught save that the angels should come unto them or thy Lord's command should come to pass? Even so did those before them. Allah wronged them not, but

they did wrong themselves.

So that the evils of what they did smote them, and that which they used to mock surrounded them.

16:33–34

6. Every soul must taste of death, and We try you with evil and with good, for ordeal. And unto Us ye will be returned.

21:35

7. And no burdened soul can bear another's burden and if one heavy laden crieth for (help with) his load, naught of it will be lifted even though he (unto whom he crieth) be of kin. Thou warnest only those who fear their Lord in secret, and have established worship. He who groweth (in goodness), groweth only for himself, (he cannot by his merit redeem others). Unto Allah is the journeying.

35:18

8. And for all there will be ranks from what they do that He may pay them for their deeds! and they will not be wronged.

46:19

9. And unto Allah belonge–th whatsoever is in the heavens and whatosever is in the earth, that He may reward those who do evil with that which they have done, and reward those

كَانُوْٓا اَنْفُسَهُمْ يَظْلِمُوْنَ ﴿٣٣﴾
فَاَصَابَهُمْ سَيِّاٰتُ مَا عَمِلُوْا وَحَاقَ
بِهِمْ مَّا كَانُوْا بِهٖ يَسْتَهْزِءُوْنَ ﴿٣٤﴾

كُلُّ نَفْسٍ ذَآئِقَةُ الْمَوْتِ ۭ وَنَبْلُوْكُمْ .6
بِالشَّرِّ وَالْخَيْرِ فِتْنَةً ۭ وَاِلَيْنَا تُرْجَعُوْنَ ﴿٣٥﴾

وَلَا تَزِرُ وَازِرَةٌ وِّزْرَ اُخْرٰى ۭ وَاِنْ .7
تَدْعُ مُثْقَلَةٌ اِلٰى حِمْلِهَا لَا يُحْمَلْ مِنْهُ
شَيْءٌ وَّلَوْ كَانَ ذَا قُرْبٰى ۭ اِنَّمَا تُنْذِرُ
الَّذِيْنَ يَخْشَوْنَ رَبَّهُمْ بِالْغَيْبِ وَاَقَامُوا
الصَّلٰوةَ ۭ وَمَنْ تَزَكّٰى فَاِنَّمَا يَتَزَكّٰى
لِنَفْسِهٖ ۭ وَاِلَى اللّٰهِ الْمَصِيْرُ ﴿١٨﴾

وَلِكُلٍّ دَرَجٰتٌ مِّمَّا عَمِلُوْا ۚ .8
وَلِيُوَفِّيَهُمْ اَعْمَالَهُمْ وَهُمْ لَا يُظْلَمُوْنَ ﴿١٩﴾

وَلِلّٰهِ مَا فِي السَّمٰوٰتِ وَمَا فِي الْاَرْضِ ۙ لِيَجْزِيَ الَّذِيْنَ .9
اَسَاۗءُوْا بِمَا عَمِلُوْا وَيَجْزِيَ الَّذِيْنَ اَحْسَنُوْا بِالْحُسْنٰى ﴿٣١﴾

اَلَّا تَزِرُ وَازِرَةٌ وِّزْرَ اُخْرٰى ﴿٣٨﴾ .10

○

who do good with goodness.

53:31

10. That no laden one shall bear another's load,

53:38

Ref: 6:160; 7:29–30,18:65–82.

See also: Allah is not unjust, Responsibility for Actions, Recompense.

PRINCIPLES OF GOVERNMENT

1. It was by the mercy of Allah that thou wast lenient with them (O Muhammad), for if thou hadst been stern and fierce of heart they would have dispersed from round about thee. So pardon them and ask forgiveness for them and consult with them upon the conduct of affairs. And when thou art resolved, then put thy trust in Allah. Lo! Allah loveth those who put their trust (in Him).

3:159

2. And if ye judge between mankind that ye judge justly. Lo! comely is this which Allah admonisheth you. Lo! Allah is ever Hearer, Seer.

O ye who believe! Obey Allah, and obey the messenger and those of you who are in authority; and if ye have a dispute concerning any matter, refer it to Allah and the messenger if ye are (in truth) believers in Allah and the Last Day. That is better and more seemly in the end.

4:58–59

3. Those who, if We give them power in the land, establish worship and pay the poor-due and enjoin kindness and forbid iniquity. And Allah's is the sequel of events.

22:41

1. فَبِمَا رَحْمَةٍ مِّنَ اللّٰهِ لِنْتَ لَهُمْ وَلَوْ كُنْتَ فَظًّا
غَلِيْظَ الْقَلْبِ لَانْفَضُّوْا مِنْ حَوْلِكَ فَاعْفُ عَنْهُمْ
وَاسْتَغْفِرْ لَهُمْ وَشَاوِرْهُمْ فِي الْأَمْرِ فَإِذَا عَزَمْتَ
فَتَوَكَّلْ عَلَى اللّٰهِ إِنَّ اللّٰهَ يُحِبُّ
الْمُتَوَكِّلِيْنَ ﴿١٥٩﴾

2. وَإِذَا حَكَمْتُمْ بَيْنَ النَّاسِ أَنْ
تَحْكُمُوْا بِالْعَدْلِ إِنَّ اللّٰهَ نِعِمَّا يَعِظُكُمْ
بِهٖ إِنَّ اللّٰهَ كَانَ سَمِيْعًا بَصِيْرًا ﴿٥٨﴾

يٰٓأَيُّهَا الَّذِيْنَ اٰمَنُوْٓا أَطِيْعُوا اللّٰهَ وَأَطِيْعُوا
الرَّسُوْلَ وَأُولِي الْأَمْرِ مِنْكُمْ فَإِنْ
تَنَازَعْتُمْ فِيْ شَيْءٍ فَرُدُّوْهُ إِلَى اللّٰهِ وَالرَّسُوْلِ
إِنْ كُنْتُمْ تُؤْمِنُوْنَ بِاللّٰهِ وَالْيَوْمِ الْاٰخِرِ
ذٰلِكَ خَيْرٌ وَّأَحْسَنُ تَأْوِيْلًا ﴿٥٩﴾

3. اَلَّذِيْنَ إِنْ مَّكَّنّٰهُمْ فِي الْأَرْضِ
أَقَامُوا الصَّلٰوةَ وَاٰتَوُا الزَّكٰوةَ وَأَمَرُوْا
بِالْمَعْرُوْفِ وَنَهَوْا عَنِ الْمُنْكَرِ
وَلِلّٰهِ عَاقِبَةُ الْأُمُوْرِ ﴿٤١﴾

See also: Consultation.

PRISONERS OF WAR

1. وَإِذْ أَخَذْنَا مِيثَاقَكُمْ لَا تَسْفِكُونَ دِمَآءَكُمْ
وَلَا تُخْرِجُونَ أَنفُسَكُم مِّن دِيَارِكُمْ ثُمَّ أَقْرَرْتُمْ
وَأَنتُمْ تَشْهَدُونَ ﴿٨٤﴾

ثُمَّ أَنتُمْ هَٰٓؤُلَآءِ تَقْتُلُونَ أَنفُسَكُمْ وَتُخْرِجُونَ
فَرِيقًا مِّنكُم مِّن دِيَارِهِمْ تَظَٰهَرُونَ عَلَيْهِم
بِٱلْإِثْمِ وَٱلْعُدْوَٰنِ وَإِن يَأْتُوكُمْ أُسَٰرَىٰ
تُفَٰدُوهُمْ وَهُوَ مُحَرَّمٌ عَلَيْكُمْ إِخْرَاجُهُمْ
أَفَتُؤْمِنُونَ بِبَعْضِ ٱلْكِتَٰبِ وَتَكْفُرُونَ بِبَعْضٍ
فَمَا جَزَآءُ مَن يَفْعَلُ ذَٰلِكَ مِنكُمْ إِلَّا خِزْىٌ
فِى ٱلْحَيَوٰةِ ٱلدُّنْيَا وَيَوْمَ ٱلْقِيَٰمَةِ يُرَدُّونَ إِلَىٰٓ
أَشَدِّ ٱلْعَذَابِ وَمَا ٱللَّهُ بِغَٰفِلٍ عَمَّا تَعْمَلُونَ ﴿٨٥﴾

2. مَا كَانَ لِنَبِىٍّ أَن يَكُونَ لَهُۥٓ أَسْرَىٰ حَتَّىٰ
يُثْخِنَ فِى ٱلْأَرْضِ تُرِيدُونَ عَرَضَ
ٱلدُّنْيَا وَٱللَّهُ يُرِيدُ ٱلْءَاخِرَةَ وَٱللَّهُ
عَزِيزٌ حَكِيمٌ ﴿٦٧﴾

لَّوْلَا كِتَٰبٌ مِّنَ ٱللَّهِ سَبَقَ لَمَسَّكُمْ فِيمَآ
أَخَذْتُمْ عَذَابٌ عَظِيمٌ ﴿٦٨﴾

فَكُلُوا۟ مِمَّا غَنِمْتُمْ حَلَٰلًا طَيِّبًا وَٱتَّقُوا۟
ٱللَّهَ إِنَّ ٱللَّهَ غَفُورٌ رَّحِيمٌ ﴿٦٩﴾

يَٰٓأَيُّهَا ٱلنَّبِىُّ قُل لِّمَن فِىٓ أَيْدِيكُم مِّنَ
ٱلْأَسْرَىٰٓ إِن يَعْلَمِ ٱللَّهُ فِى قُلُوبِكُمْ خَيْرًا
يُؤْتِكُمْ خَيْرًا مِّمَّآ أُخِذَ مِنكُمْ وَيَغْفِرْ
لَكُمْ وَٱللَّهُ غَفُورٌ رَّحِيمٌ ﴿٧٠﴾

1. And when We made with you a covenant (saying): Shed not the blood of your people nor turn (a party of) your people out of your dwellings. Then ye ratified (Our covenant). and ye were witnesses (thereto).

Yet ye it is who slay each other and drive out a party of your people from their homes, supporting one another against them by sin and transgression—and if they came to you as captives ye would ransom them, whereas their expulsion was itself unlawful for you—Believe ye in part of the Scripture and disbelieve ye in part thereof? And what is the reward of those who do so save ignominy in the life of the world, and on the Day of Resurrection they will be consigned to the most grievous doom. For Allah is not unaware of what ye do.

2:84–85

2. It is not for any Prophet to have captives until he hath made slaughter in the land. Ye desire the lure of this world and Allah desireth (for you) the Hereafter, and Allah is Mighty, Wise.

Had it not been for an ordinance of Allah which had gone before, an awful doom had come upon you on account of what ye took.

Now enjoy what ye have won, as lawful and good, and keep your duty to Allah. Lo! Allah is Forgiving, Merciful.

O Prophet! Say unto those captives who are in your hands: If Allah knoweth any good in your hearts He will give you better than that which hath been taken from you, and will forgive you. Lo! Allah is Forgiving, Merciful.

And if they would betray thee, they betrayed Allah before, and He gave (thee) power over them. Allah is Knower, Wise.

8:67–71

3. Now when ye meet in battle those who disbelieve, then it is smiting of the necks until, when ye have routed them, then making fast of bonds; and afterward either grace or ransom till the war lay down its burdens. That (is the ordinance). And if Allah willed He could have punished them (without you) but (thus it is ordained) that He may try some of you by means of others. And those who are slain in the way of Allah, He rendereth not their actions vain

47:4

PSALMS OF DAVID

1. And thy Lord is Best Aware of all who are in the heavens and the earth. And We preferred some of the Prophets above others, and unto David We gave the Psalms.

17:55

2. And verily We have written in the Scripture, after the Reminder: My righteous slaves will inherit the earth

21:105

وَإِنْ يُرِيدُوا خِيَانَتَكَ فَقَدْ خَانُوا اللَّهَ
مِنْ قَبْلُ فَأَمْكَنَ مِنْهُمْ ۗ وَاللَّهُ عَلِيمٌ حَكِيمٌ ﴿٧١﴾

3. فَإِذَا لَقِيتُمُ الَّذِينَ كَفَرُوا فَضَرْبَ
الرِّقَابِ حَتَّىٰ إِذَا أَثْخَنْتُمُوهُمْ فَشُدُّوا
الْوَثَاقَ فَإِمَّا مَنًّا بَعْدُ وَإِمَّا فِدَاءً
حَتَّىٰ تَضَعَ الْحَرْبُ أَوْزَارَهَا ۚ ذَٰلِكَ ۛ
وَلَوْ يَشَاءُ اللَّهُ لَانْتَصَرَ مِنْهُمْ وَلَٰكِنْ
لِيَبْلُوَ بَعْضَكُمْ بِبَعْضٍ ۗ وَالَّذِينَ قُتِلُوا
فِي سَبِيلِ اللَّهِ فَلَنْ يُضِلَّ أَعْمَالَهُمْ ﴿٤﴾

○

1. وَرَبُّكَ أَعْلَمُ بِمَنْ فِي السَّمَاوَاتِ
وَالْأَرْضِ ۗ وَلَقَدْ فَضَّلْنَا بَعْضَ النَّبِيِّينَ
عَلَىٰ بَعْضٍ ۖ وَآتَيْنَا دَاوُودَ زَبُورًا ﴿٥٥﴾

2. وَلَقَدْ كَتَبْنَا فِي الزَّبُورِ مِنْ بَعْدِ
الذِّكْرِ أَنَّ الْأَرْضَ يَرِثُهَا عِبَادِيَ
الصَّالِحُونَ ﴿١٠٥﴾

○

PRISONERS OF WAR See aslo: Jihad

PSALMS OF DAVID

Ref: 4:163. See also: Revealed Books.

PURIFICATION

1. Truly Allah loveth those who turn unto Him, and loveth those who have a care for cleanness.

2:222

2. O ye who believe! When ye rise up for prayer, wash your faces, and your hands up to the elbows, and lightly rub your heads and (wash) your feet up to the ankles. And if ye are unclean, purify your-selves. And if ye are sick or on a journey, or one of you cometh from the closet, or ye have had contact with women, and ye find not water, then go to clean, high ground and rub your faces and your hands with some of it. Allah would not place a burden on you, but He would purify you and would perfect His grace upon you, that ye may give thanks.

5:6

3. O thou enveloped in thy cloak
Arise and warn!
Thy Lord magnify,
Thy raiment purify,
Pollution shun!

74:1–5

1. إِنَّ اللّٰهَ يُحِبُّ التَّوَّابِيْنَ وَيُحِبُّ الْمُتَطَهِّرِيْنَ ﴿٢٢٢﴾

2. يٰٓاَيُّهَا الَّذِيْنَ اٰمَنُوْٓا اِذَا قُمْتُمْ اِلَى الصَّلٰوةِ
فَاغْسِلُوْا وُجُوْهَكُمْ وَاَيْدِيَكُمْ اِلَى الْمَرَافِقِ
وَامْسَحُوْا بِرُءُوْسِكُمْ وَاَرْجُلَكُمْ اِلَى
الْكَعْبَيْنِ ۚ وَاِنْ كُنْتُمْ جُنُبًا فَاطَّهَّرُوْا ۚ وَ
اِنْ كُنْتُمْ مَّرْضٰٓى اَوْ عَلٰى سَفَرٍ اَوْ جَآءَ اَحَدٌ
مِّنْكُمْ مِّنَ الْغَآئِطِ اَوْ لٰمَسْتُمُ النِّسَآءَ فَلَمْ
تَجِدُوْا مَآءً فَتَيَمَّمُوْا صَعِيْدًا طَيِّبًا
فَامْسَحُوْا بِوُجُوْهِكُمْ وَاَيْدِيْكُمْ مِّنْهُ ۚ
مَا يُرِيْدُ اللّٰهُ لِيَجْعَلَ عَلَيْكُمْ مِّنْ حَرَجٍ
وَّلٰكِنْ يُّرِيْدُ لِيُطَهِّرَكُمْ وَلِيُتِمَّ نِعْمَتَهٗ
عَلَيْكُمْ لَعَلَّكُمْ تَشْكُرُوْنَ ﴿٦﴾

3. يٰٓاَيُّهَا الْمُدَّثِّرُ ﴿١﴾
قُمْ فَاَنْذِرْ ﴿٢﴾
وَرَبَّكَ فَكَبِّرْ ﴿٣﴾
وَثِيَابَكَ فَطَهِّرْ ﴿٤﴾
وَالرُّجْزَ فَاهْجُرْ ﴿٥﴾

Ref: 4:43; 9:108.

QISAS

1. O ye who believe! Retaliation is prescribed for you in the matter of the murdered; the freeman for the freeman, and the slave for the slave, and the female for the female. And for him who is forgiven somewhat by his (injured) brother, prosecution according to usage and payment unto him in kindness. This is an alleviation and a mercy from your Lord. He who transgresseth after this will have a painful doom.

And there is life for you in retaliation, O men of understanding, that ye may ward off (evil).

2:178–179

2. The forbidden month for the forbidden month, and forbidden things in retaliation. And one who attacketh you, attack him in like manner as he attacked you. Observe your duty to Allah, and know that Allah is with those who ward off (evil).

2:194

3. And We prescribed for them therein: The life for the life, and the eye for the eye, and the nose for the nose, and the ear for the ear, and the tooth for the tooth, and for wounds retaliation. But whoso forgoeth it (in the way of charity) it shall be expiation for him. Whoso judgeth not by that which Allah hath revealed: such are wrong-doers,

5:45

1. يَا أَيُّهَا الَّذِينَ آمَنُوا كُتِبَ عَلَيْكُمُ الْقِصَاصُ فِي الْقَتْلَى الْحُرُّ بِالْحُرِّ وَالْعَبْدُ بِالْعَبْدِ وَالْأُنْثَىٰ بِالْأُنْثَىٰ ۚ فَمَنْ عُفِيَ لَهُ مِنْ أَخِيهِ شَيْءٌ فَاتِّبَاعٌ بِالْمَعْرُوفِ وَأَدَاءٌ إِلَيْهِ بِإِحْسَانٍ ۗ ذَٰلِكَ تَخْفِيفٌ مِنْ رَبِّكُمْ وَرَحْمَةٌ ۗ فَمَنِ اعْتَدَىٰ بَعْدَ ذَٰلِكَ فَلَهُ عَذَابٌ أَلِيمٌ ﴿١٧٨﴾

وَلَكُمْ فِي الْقِصَاصِ حَيَاةٌ يَا أُولِي الْأَلْبَابِ لَعَلَّكُمْ تَتَّقُونَ ﴿١٧٩﴾

2. الشَّهْرُ الْحَرَامُ بِالشَّهْرِ الْحَرَامِ وَالْحُرُمَاتُ قِصَاصٌ ۚ فَمَنِ اعْتَدَىٰ عَلَيْكُمْ فَاعْتَدُوا عَلَيْهِ بِمِثْلِ مَا اعْتَدَىٰ عَلَيْكُمْ ۚ وَاتَّقُوا اللَّهَ وَاعْلَمُوا أَنَّ اللَّهَ مَعَ الْمُتَّقِينَ ﴿١٩٤﴾

3. وَكَتَبْنَا عَلَيْهِمْ فِيهَا أَنَّ النَّفْسَ بِالنَّفْسِ وَالْعَيْنَ بِالْعَيْنِ وَالْأَنْفَ بِالْأَنْفِ وَالْأُذُنَ بِالْأُذُنِ وَالسِّنَّ بِالسِّنِّ وَالْجُرُوحَ قِصَاصٌ ۚ فَمَنْ تَصَدَّقَ بِهِ فَهُوَ كَفَّارَةٌ لَهُ ۚ وَمَنْ لَمْ يَحْكُمْ بِمَا أَنْزَلَ اللَّهُ فَأُولَٰئِكَ هُمُ الظَّالِمُونَ ﴿٤٥﴾

Ref: 4:92–93; 22:60

See also: *Diyat, Ḥudud*.

QUALITIES OF FAITHFUL AND PIOUS

1. This is the Scripture whereof there is no doubt, a guidance unto those who ward off (evil);

Who believe in the unseen, and establish worship, and spend of that We have bestowed upon them;

And who believe in that which is revealed unto thee (Muhammad) and that which was revealed before thee, and are certain of the Hereafter.

These depend on guidance from their Lord. These are the successful.

2:2–5

2. Those who believe are stauncher in their love for Allah.

2:165

3. Those who say: Our Lord! Lo! we believe. So forgive us our sins and guard us from the punishment of Fire.

The steadfast, and the truthful, and the obedient, those who spend (and hoard not,) those who pray for pardon in the watches of the night.

3:16–17

4. And vie one with another for forgiveness from your Lord, and for a Paradise as wide as are the heavens and the earth, prepared for those who ward off (evil),

1. ذٰلِكَ الْكِتٰبُ لَا رَيْبَ ۛ فِيْهِ ۛ هُدًى لِّلْمُتَّقِيْنَ ﴿٢﴾
الَّذِيْنَ يُؤْمِنُوْنَ بِالْغَيْبِ وَيُقِيْمُوْنَ الصَّلٰوةَ
وَمِمَّا رَزَقْنٰهُمْ يُنْفِقُوْنَ ﴿٣﴾
وَالَّذِيْنَ يُؤْمِنُوْنَ بِمَآ اُنْزِلَ اِلَيْكَ وَمَآ
اُنْزِلَ مِنْ قَبْلِكَ ۚ وَبِالْاٰخِرَةِ هُمْ يُوْقِنُوْنَ ﴿٤﴾
اُولٰٓئِكَ عَلٰى هُدًى مِّنْ رَّبِّهِمْ ۗ وَاُولٰٓئِكَ
هُمُ الْمُفْلِحُوْنَ ﴿٥﴾

2. وَالَّذِيْنَ اٰمَنُوْٓا اَشَدُّ حُبًّا لِّلّٰهِ ؕ

3. اَلَّذِيْنَ يَقُوْلُوْنَ رَبَّنَآ اِنَّنَآ اٰمَنَّا فَاغْفِرْ لَنَا
ذُنُوْبَنَا وَقِنَا عَذَابَ النَّارِ ۝
اَلصّٰبِرِيْنَ وَالصّٰدِقِيْنَ وَالْقٰنِتِيْنَ وَ
الْمُنْفِقِيْنَ وَالْمُسْتَغْفِرِيْنَ بِالْاَسْحَارِ ۝

4. وَسَارِعُوْٓا اِلٰى مَغْفِرَةٍ مِّنْ رَّبِّكُمْ وَجَنَّةٍ
عَرْضُهَا السَّمٰوٰتُ وَالْاَرْضُ ۙ اُعِدَّتْ لِلْمُتَّقِيْنَ ۝
الَّذِيْنَ يُنْفِقُوْنَ فِى السَّرَّآءِ وَالضَّرَّآءِ
وَالْكٰظِمِيْنَ الْغَيْظَ وَالْعَافِيْنَ عَنِ النَّاسِ ؕ
وَاللّٰهُ يُحِبُّ الْمُحْسِنِيْنَ ۝
وَالَّذِيْنَ اِذَا فَعَلُوْا فَاحِشَةً اَوْ ظَلَمُوْٓا
اَنْفُسَهُمْ ذَكَرُوا اللّٰهَ فَاسْتَغْفَرُوْا لِذُنُوْبِهِمْ
وَمَنْ يَّغْفِرُ الذُّنُوْبَ اِلَّا اللّٰهُ وَلَمْ
يُصِرُّوْا عَلٰى مَا فَعَلُوْا وَهُمْ يَعْلَمُوْنَ ۝

5. اِنَّمَا الْمُؤْمِنُوْنَ الَّذِيْنَ اِذَا ذُكِرَ اللّٰهُ

Those who spend (of that which Allah hath given them) in ease and in adversity, those who control their wrath and are forgiving toward mankind; Allah loveth the good;

And those who when

وَجِلَتْ قُلُوبُهُمْ وَإِذَا تُلِيَتْ عَلَيْهِمْ آيَاتُهُ
زَادَتْهُمْ إِيمَانًا وَعَلَىٰ رَبِّهِمْ يَتَوَكَّلُونَ ﴿٢﴾
الَّذِينَ يُقِيمُونَ الصَّلَاةَ وَمِمَّا رَزَقْنَاهُمْ
يُنفِقُونَ ﴿٣﴾

أُولَٰئِكَ هُمُ الْمُؤْمِنُونَ حَقًّا ۚ لَّهُمْ دَرَجَاتٌ
عِندَ رَبِّهِمْ وَمَغْفِرَةٌ وَرِزْقٌ كَرِيمٌ ﴿٤﴾

6. إِنَّ اللَّهَ اشْتَرَىٰ مِنَ الْمُؤْمِنِينَ أَنفُسَهُمْ
وَأَمْوَالَهُم بِأَنَّ لَهُمُ الْجَنَّةَ ۚ يُقَاتِلُونَ
فِي سَبِيلِ اللَّهِ فَيَقْتُلُونَ وَيُقْتَلُونَ ۖ وَعْدًا
عَلَيْهِ حَقًّا فِي التَّوْرَاةِ وَالْإِنجِيلِ وَ
الْقُرْآنِ ۚ وَمَنْ أَوْفَىٰ بِعَهْدِهِ مِنَ اللَّهِ
فَاسْتَبْشِرُوا بِبَيْعِكُمُ الَّذِي بَايَعْتُم بِهِ ۚ
وَذَٰلِكَ هُوَ الْفَوْزُ الْعَظِيمُ ﴿١١١﴾

التَّائِبُونَ الْعَابِدُونَ الْحَامِدُونَ السَّائِحُونَ
الرَّاكِعُونَ السَّاجِدُونَ الْآمِرُونَ بِالْمَعْرُوفِ
وَالنَّاهُونَ عَنِ الْمُنكَرِ وَالْحَافِظُونَ
لِحُدُودِ اللَّهِ ۗ وَبَشِّرِ الْمُؤْمِنِينَ ﴿١١٢﴾

7. الَّذِينَ يُوفُونَ بِعَهْدِ اللَّهِ وَلَا
يَنقُضُونَ الْمِيثَاقَ ﴿٢٠﴾

وَالَّذِينَ يَصِلُونَ مَا أَمَرَ اللَّهُ بِهِ أَن
يُوصَلَ وَيَخْشَوْنَ رَبَّهُمْ وَيَخَافُونَ
سُوءَ الْحِسَابِ ﴿٢١﴾

they do an evil thing or wrong themselves remember Allah and implore forgiveness for their sins—Who forgiveth sins save Allah only?—and will not knowingly repeat (the wrong) they did.

3:133–135

5. They only are the (true) believers whose hearts feel fear when Allah is mentioned, and when His revelations are recited unto them they increase their faith, and who trust in their Lord,

Who establish worship and spend of that We have bestowed on them.

Those are they who are in truth believers. For them are grades (of honour) with their Lord, and pardon, and a bountiful provision.

8:2–4

6. Lo! Allah hath bought from the believers their lives and their wealth because the Garden will be theirs; they shall fight in the way of Allah and shall slay and be slain. It is a promise which is binding on Him in the Torah and the Gospel and the Qur'ān. Who fulfilleth his covenant better than Allah? Rejoice then in your bargain that ye have made, for that is the Supreme triumph.

(Triumphant) are those who turn repentant (to Allah), those who serve (Him), those who praise (Him), those who fast, those who bow down, those who fall prostrate (in worship), those who enjoin the right and who forbid the wrong and those who keep the limits (ordained) of Allah—And give glad tiding to believers!

9:111–112

7. Such as keep the pact of Allah, and break not the covenant;

Such as unite that which Allah hath commanded should be joined, and fear their Lord, and dread a woeful reckoning;

Such as persevere in seeking their Lord's Countenance and are regular in prayer and spend of that which We bestow upon them secretly and openly, and overcome evil with good. Theirs will be the sequel of the (heavenly) Home.

13:20–22

8. Those who, if We give them power in the land, establish worship and pay the poor-due and enjoin kindness and forbid iniquity. And Allah's is the sequel of events.

22:41

9. Successful indeed are the believers,

Who are humble in their prayers,

And who shun vain conversation,

And who are payers of poor-due;

And who guard their modesty—

Save from their wives or the (slaves) that their right hands possess, for then they

وَالَّذِيْنَ صَبَرُوا ابْتِغَآءَ وَجْهِ رَبِّهِمْ
وَاَقَامُوا الصَّلٰوةَ وَاَنْفَقُوْا مِمَّا رَزَقْنٰهُمْ
سِرًّا وَّعَلَانِيَةً وَّيَدْرَءُوْنَ بِالْحَسَنَةِ
السَّيِّئَةَ اُولٰٓئِكَ لَهُمْ عُقْبَى الدَّارِ ۝٢٢

8. اَلَّذِيْنَ اِنْ مَّكَّنّٰهُمْ فِى الْاَرْضِ اَقَامُوا الصَّلٰوةَ
وَاٰتَوُا الزَّكٰوةَ وَاَمَرُوْا بِالْمَعْرُوْفِ وَنَهَوْا عَنِ
الْمُنْكَرِ ۗ وَلِلّٰهِ عَاقِبَةُ الْاُمُوْرِ ۝

9. قَدْ اَفْلَحَ الْمُؤْمِنُوْنَ ۝١
الَّذِيْنَ هُمْ فِيْ صَلَاتِهِمْ خٰشِعُوْنَ ۝٢
وَالَّذِيْنَ هُمْ عَنِ اللَّغْوِ مُعْرِضُوْنَ ۝٣
وَالَّذِيْنَ هُمْ لِلزَّكٰوةِ فٰعِلُوْنَ ۝٤
وَالَّذِيْنَ هُمْ لِفُرُوْجِهِمْ حٰفِظُوْنَ ۝٥
اِلَّا عَلٰٓى اَزْوَاجِهِمْ اَوْ مَا مَلَكَتْ اَيْمَانُهُمْ فَاِنَّهُمْ
غَيْرُ مَلُوْمِيْنَ ۝٦
فَمَنِ ابْتَغٰى وَرَآءَ ذٰلِكَ فَاُولٰٓئِكَ
هُمُ الْعٰدُوْنَ ۝٧
وَالَّذِيْنَ هُمْ لِاَمٰنٰتِهِمْ وَعَهْدِهِمْ رٰعُوْنَ ۝٨
وَالَّذِيْنَ هُمْ عَلٰى صَلَوٰتِهِمْ يُحَافِظُوْنَ ۝٩
اُولٰٓئِكَ هُمُ الْوٰرِثُوْنَ ۝١٠
الَّذِيْنَ يَرِثُوْنَ الْفِرْدَوْسَ ۗ هُمْ
فِيْهَا خٰلِدُوْنَ ۝١١

are not blameworthy.

But whoso craveth beyond that, such are transgressors—

And who are shepherds of their pledge and their covenant,

And who pay heed to their prayers.

These are the heirs,

Who will inherit Paradise. There they will abide.

23:1–11

10. The (faithful) slaves of the Beneficent are they who walk upon the earth modestly, and when the foolish ones address them answer: Peace!

And who spend the night before their Lord, prostrate and standing,

And who say: Our Lord! Avert from us the doom of hell; lo! the doom thereof is anguish;

Lo! it is wretched as abode and station;

And those who, when they spend, are neither prodigal nor grudging; and there is ever a firm station between the two;

And those who cry not unto any other god along with Allah, nor take the life which Allah hath forbidden save in (course of) justice, nor commit adultery—and whoso doth this shall pay the penalty;

The doom will be doubled for him on the Day of Resurrection, and he will abide therein disdained for ever;

Save him who repenteth and believeth and doth righteous work; as for such, Allah will change their evil deeds

10. وَعِبَادُ الرَّحْمٰنِ الَّذِيْنَ يَمْشُوْنَ عَلَى الْاَرْضِ هَوْنًا
وَّاِذَا خَاطَبَهُمُ الْجٰهِلُوْنَ قَالُوْا سَلٰمًا ﴿٦٣﴾

وَالَّذِيْنَ يَبِيْتُوْنَ لِرَبِّهِمْ سُجَّدًا
وَّقِيَامًا ﴿٦٤﴾
وَالَّذِيْنَ يَقُوْلُوْنَ رَبَّنَا اصْرِفْ عَنَّا
عَذَابَ جَهَنَّمَ ۖ اِنَّ عَذَابَهَا كَانَ
غَرَامًا ﴿٦٥﴾
اِنَّهَا سَآءَتْ مُسْتَقَرًّا وَّمُقَامًا ﴿٦٦﴾

وَالَّذِيْنَ اِذَآ اَنْفَقُوْا لَمْ يُسْرِفُوْا وَلَمْ يَقْتُرُوْا وَكَانَ
بَيْنَ ذٰلِكَ قَوَامًا ﴿٦٧﴾

وَالَّذِيْنَ لَا يَدْعُوْنَ مَعَ اللّٰهِ اِلٰهًا
اٰخَرَ وَلَا يَقْتُلُوْنَ النَّفْسَ الَّتِيْ حَرَّمَ
اللّٰهُ اِلَّا بِالْحَقِّ وَلَا يَزْنُوْنَ ۚ وَمَنْ
يَّفْعَلْ ذٰلِكَ يَلْقَ اَثَامًا ﴿٦٨﴾

يُّضٰعَفْ لَهُ الْعَذَابُ يَوْمَ الْقِيٰمَةِ وَ
يَخْلُدْ فِيْهٖ مُهَانًا ﴿٦٩﴾

اِلَّا مَنْ تَابَ وَاٰمَنَ وَعَمِلَ عَمَلًا صَالِحًا
فَاُولٰٓئِكَ يُبَدِّلُ اللّٰهُ سَيِّاٰتِهِمْ حَسَنٰتٍ ۗ
وَكَانَ اللّٰهُ غَفُوْرًا رَّحِيْمًا ﴿٧٠﴾

وَمَنْ تَابَ وَعَمِلَ صَالِحًا فَاِنَّهٗ يَتُوْبُ
اِلَى اللّٰهِ مَتَابًا ﴿٧١﴾
وَالَّذِيْنَ لَا يَشْهَدُوْنَ الزُّوْرَ ۙ وَاِذَا

to good deeds. Allah is ever Forgiving, Merciful.

And whosoever repenteth and doth good, he verily repenteth toward Allah with true repentance—

And those who will not witness vanity, but when they pass near senseless play, pass by with dignity.

And those who, when they are reminded of the revelations of their Lord, fall not deaf and blind thereat.

And who say:Our Lord! Vouchsafe us comfort of our wives and of our offspring, and make us patterns for (all) those who ward off (evil).

They will be awarded the high place forasmuch as they were steadfast, and they will meet therein with welcome and the word of Peace.

Abiding there for ever. Happy is it as abode and station!

25:63–76

11. Lo! men who surrender unto Allah, and women who surrender, and men who believe, and women who believe, and men who obey and women who obey, and men who speak the truth and women who speak the truth, and men who persevere (in righteousness) and women who persevere, and men who are humble and women who are humble, and men who give alms and women who give alms, and men who fast and women who fast, and men who guard their modesty and women who guard (their modesty), and men who remember Allah much and women who remember, Allah hath prepared for them forgiveness and a vast reward.

33:35

مَرُّوا بِاللَّغْوِ مَرُّوا كِرَامًا ﴿٧٢﴾
وَالَّذِينَ إِذَا ذُكِّرُوا بِآيَاتِ رَبِّهِمْ لَمْ
يَخِرُّوا عَلَيْهَا صُمًّا وَعُمْيَانًا ﴿٧٣﴾
وَالَّذِينَ يَقُولُونَ رَبَّنَا هَبْ لَنَا مِنْ أَزْوَاجِنَا وَ
ذُرِّيَّاتِنَا قُرَّةَ أَعْيُنٍ وَاجْعَلْنَا لِلْمُتَّقِينَ إِمَامًا ﴿٧٤﴾
أُولَٰئِكَ يُجْزَوْنَ الْغُرْفَةَ بِمَا صَبَرُوا وَيُلَقَّوْنَ فِيهَا
تَحِيَّةً وَسَلَامًا ﴿٧٥﴾
خَالِدِينَ فِيهَا حَسُنَتْ مُسْتَقَرًّا وَمُقَامًا ﴿٧٦﴾

11. إِنَّ الْمُسْلِمِينَ وَالْمُسْلِمَاتِ وَالْمُؤْمِنِينَ وَالْمُؤْمِنَاتِ وَ
الْقَانِتِينَ وَالْقَانِتَاتِ وَالصَّادِقِينَ وَالصَّادِقَاتِ وَ
الصَّابِرِينَ وَالصَّابِرَاتِ وَالْخَاشِعِينَ وَالْخَاشِعَاتِ وَ
الْمُتَصَدِّقِينَ وَالْمُتَصَدِّقَاتِ وَالصَّائِمِينَ وَالصَّائِمَاتِ
وَالْحَافِظِينَ فُرُوجَهُمْ وَالْحَافِظَاتِ وَالذَّاكِرِينَ اللَّهَ
كَثِيرًا وَالذَّاكِرَاتِ أَعَدَّ اللَّهُ لَهُمْ مَغْفِرَةً وَأَجْرًا
عَظِيمًا ﴿٣٥﴾

12. فَمَا أُوتِيتُمْ مِنْ شَيْءٍ فَمَتَاعُ
الْحَيَاةِ الدُّنْيَا وَمَا عِنْدَ اللَّهِ خَيْرٌ
وَأَبْقَىٰ لِلَّذِينَ آمَنُوا وَعَلَىٰ رَبِّهِمْ
يَتَوَكَّلُونَ ﴿٣٦﴾
وَالَّذِينَ يَجْتَنِبُونَ كَبَائِرَ الْإِثْمِ
وَالْفَوَاحِشَ وَإِذَا مَا غَضِبُوا هُمْ
يَغْفِرُونَ ﴿٣٧﴾
وَالَّذِينَ اسْتَجَابُوا لِرَبِّهِمْ وَأَقَامُوا

12. Now whatever ye have been given is but a passing comfort for the life of the world, and that which Allah hath is better and more lasting for those who be–lieve and put their trust in their Lord.

And those who shun the worst of sins and indecencies and, when they are wroth, forgive.

And those who answer the call of their Lord and establish worship, and whose affairs are a matter of counsel, and who spend of what We have bestowed on them.

And those who, when great wrong is done to them, defend themselves.

42:36–39

13. Muhammad is the messenger of Allah. And those with him are hard against the disbelievers and merciful among themselves. Thou (O Muhammad) seest them bowing and falling prostrate (in worship), seeking bounty from Allah and (His) acceptance. The mark of them is on their foreheads from traces of prostration. Such is their likeness in the Torah and their likeness in the Gospel—like as sown corn that sendeth forth its shoot and strengtheneth it and riseth firm upon its stalk, delighting the sowers—that He may enrage the disbelievers with (the sight of) them. Allah hath promised, unto such of them as believe and do good works, forgiveness and immense reward.

48:29

14. Lo! those who keep from evil will dwell amid gardens and watersprings,

Taking that which their Lord giveth them;

الصَّلٰوةَ وَاَمْرُهُمْ شُوْرٰى بَيْنَهُمْ
وَمِمَّا رَزَقْنٰهُمْ يُنْفِقُوْنَ ۝٣٨
وَالَّذِيْنَ اِذَآ اَصَابَهُمُ الْبَغْيُ هُمْ
يَنْتَصِرُوْنَ ۝٣٩

13. مُحَمَّدٌ رَّسُوْلُ اللّٰهِ ۭ وَالَّذِيْنَ مَعَهٗٓ
اَشِدَّاۗءُ عَلَى الْكُفَّارِ رُحَمَاۗءُ بَيْنَهُمْ
تَرٰىهُمْ رُكَّعًا سُجَّدًا يَّبْتَغُوْنَ فَضْلًا
مِّنَ اللّٰهِ وَرِضْوَانًا ۡ سِيْمَاهُمْ فِيْ
وُجُوْهِهِمْ مِّنْ اَثَرِ السُّجُوْدِ ۭ ذٰلِكَ
مَثَلُهُمْ فِي التَّوْرٰىةِ ۚ وَمَثَلُهُمْ فِي
الْاِنْجِيْلِ ۚ كَزَرْعٍ اَخْرَجَ شَطْــَٔهٗ
فَاٰزَرَهٗ فَاسْتَغْلَظَ فَاسْتَوٰى عَلٰى
سُوْقِهٖ يُعْجِبُ الزُّرَّاعَ لِيَغِيْظَ بِهِمُ
الْكُفَّارَ ۭ وَعَدَ اللّٰهُ الَّذِيْنَ اٰمَنُوْا
وَعَمِلُوا الصّٰلِحٰتِ مِنْهُمْ مَّغْفِرَةً
وَّاَجْرًا عَظِيْمًا ۝٢٩

14. اِنَّ الْمُتَّقِيْنَ فِيْ جَنّٰتٍ وَّعُيُوْنٍ ۝١٥
اٰخِذِيْنَ مَآ اٰتٰىهُمْ رَبُّهُمْ ۭ اِنَّهُمْ
كَانُوْا قَبْلَ ذٰلِكَ مُحْسِنِيْنَ ۝١٦
كَانُوْا قَلِيْلًا مِّنَ الَّيْلِ مَا يَهْجَعُوْنَ ۝١٧
وَبِالْاَسْحَارِ هُمْ يَسْتَغْفِرُوْنَ ۝١٨
وَفِيْٓ اَمْوَالِهِمْ حَقٌّ لِّلسَّاۗىِٕلِ وَالْمَحْرُوْمِ ۝١٩

for lo! aforetime they were doers of good;

They used to sleep but little of the night,

And ere the dawning of each day would seek forgiveness.

And in their wealth the beggar and the outcast had due share.

51:15–19

Ref: 2:256,277,285; 3:110; 5:54–56; 7:181; 32:15–16; 49:15.

QUBA MOSQUE

1. لَمَسْجِدٌ أُسِّسَ عَلَى التَّقْوٰى مِنْ أَوَّلِ يَوْمٍ أَحَقُّ
أَنْ تَقُوْمَ فِيْهِ ۚ فِيْهِ رِجَالٌ يُّحِبُّوْنَ أَنْ يَّتَطَهَّرُوْا ۚ
وَاللّٰهُ يُحِبُّ الْمُطَّهِّرِيْنَ ﴿١٠٨﴾
أَفَمَنْ أَسَّسَ بُنْيَانَهٗ عَلٰى تَقْوٰى مِنَ
اللّٰهِ وَرِضْوَانٍ خَيْرٌ أَمْ مَّنْ أَسَّسَ بُنْيَانَهٗ
عَلٰى شَفَا جُرُفٍ هَارٍ فَانْهَارَ بِهٖ فِيْ نَارِ
جَهَنَّمَ ۗ وَاللّٰهُ لَا يَهْدِي الْقَوْمَ الظّٰلِمِيْنَ ﴿١٠٩﴾

1. A place of worship which was founded upon duty (to Allah) from the first day is more worthy that thou shouldst stand (to pray) therein wherein are men who love to purify themselves. Allah loveth the purifiers.

Is he who founded his building upon duty to Allah and His good pleasure better, or he who founded his building on the brink of a crumbling, overhanging precipice so that it toppled with him into the fire of hell? Allah guideth not wrongdoing folk.

9:108–109

QUEEN OF SHEBA

1. وَوَرِثَ سُلَيْمٰنُ دَاوٗدَ وَقَالَ يٰٓأَيُّهَا النَّاسُ عُلِّمْنَا
مَنْطِقَ الطَّيْرِ وَأُوْتِيْنَا مِنْ كُلِّ شَيْءٍ ۖ إِنَّ هٰذَا لَهُوَ
الْفَضْلُ الْمُبِيْنُ ﴿١٦﴾
وَحُشِرَ لِسُلَيْمٰنَ جُنُوْدُهٗ مِنَ الْجِنِّ وَالْإِنْسِ وَ
الطَّيْرِ فَهُمْ يُوْزَعُوْنَ ﴿١٧﴾
حَتّٰىٓ إِذَآ أَتَوْا عَلٰى وَادِ النَّمْلِ ۙ قَالَتْ نَمْلَةٌ يّٰٓأَيُّهَا
النَّمْلُ ادْخُلُوْا مَسٰكِنَكُمْ ۚ لَا يَحْطِمَنَّكُمْ سُلَيْمٰنُ
وَجُنُوْدُهٗ ۙ وَهُمْ لَا يَشْعُرُوْنَ ﴿١٨﴾
فَتَبَسَّمَ ضَاحِكًا مِّنْ قَوْلِهَا وَقَالَ رَبِّ أَوْزِعْنِيْٓ
أَنْ أَشْكُرَ نِعْمَتَكَ الَّتِيْٓ أَنْعَمْتَ عَلَيَّ وَعَلٰى وَالِدَيَّ
وَأَنْ أَعْمَلَ صَالِحًا تَرْضٰىهُ وَأَدْخِلْنِيْ بِرَحْمَتِكَ
فِيْ عِبَادِكَ الصّٰلِحِيْنَ ﴿١٩﴾

1. And Solomon was David's heir. And he said: O mankind! Lo! we have been taught the language of birds, and have been given (abundance) of all things. This surely is evident favour.

And there were gathered together unto Solomon his armies of the jinn and humankind, and of the birds, and they were set in a battle order;

Till, when they reached the Valley of the Ants, an ant exclaimed: O ants! Enter your dwellings lest Solomon and his armies crush you, unperceiving.

And (Solomon) smiled, laughing at her speech, and said: My Lord, arouse me to be thankful for Thy favour wherewith Thou hast favoured me and my parents, and to do

---

QUBA MOSQUE

See also: Mosques.

good that shall be pleasing unto Thee, and include me in (the number of) Thy righteous slaves.

And he sought among the birds and said: How is it that I see not the hoopoe, or is he among the absent?

I verily will punish him with hard punishment or I verily will slay him, or he verily shall bring me a plain excuse.

But he was not long in coming, and he said: I have found out (a thing) that thou apprehendest not, and I come unto thee from Sheba with sure tidings.

Lo! I found a woman ruling over them, and she hath been given (abundance) of all things, and hers is a mighty throne.

I found her and her people worshipping the sun instead of Allah; and Satan maketh their works fair-seeming unto them, and debarreth them from the way (of Truth), so that they go not aright:

So that they worship not Allah. Who bringeth forth the hidden in the heavens and the earth, and knoweth what ye hide and what ye proclaim.

Allah; there is no God save Him, the Lord of the Tremendous Throne.

(Solomon) said: We shall see whether thou speakest truth or whether thou art of the liars.

Go with this my letter and throw it down unto them; then turn away and see what

وَتَفَقَّدَ الطَّيْرَ فَقَالَ مَالِيَ لَآ أَرَى
الْهُدْهُدَ ۖ أَمْ كَانَ مِنَ الْغَآئِبِينَ ﴿٢٠﴾
لَأُعَذِّبَنَّهُ عَذَابًا شَدِيدًا أَوْ لَأَاذْبَحَنَّهُ
أَوْ لَيَأْتِيَنِّي بِسُلْطَانٍ مُّبِينٍ ﴿٢١﴾
فَمَكَثَ غَيْرَ بَعِيدٍ فَقَالَ أَحَطتُّ بِمَا
لَمْ تُحِطْ بِهِ وَجِئْتُكَ مِن سَبَإٍ
بِنَبَإٍ يَقِينٍ ﴿٢٢﴾
إِنِّي وَجَدتُّ امْرَأَةً تَمْلِكُهُمْ وَأُوتِيَتْ
مِن كُلِّ شَيْءٍ وَلَهَا عَرْشٌ عَظِيمٌ ﴿٢٣﴾
وَجَدتُّهَا وَقَوْمَهَا يَسْجُدُونَ لِلشَّمْسِ
مِن دُونِ اللَّهِ وَزَيَّنَ لَهُمُ الشَّيْطَانُ
أَعْمَالَهُمْ فَصَدَّهُمْ عَنِ السَّبِيلِ
فَهُمْ لَا يَهْتَدُونَ ﴿٢٤﴾
أَلَّا يَسْجُدُوا لِلَّهِ الَّذِي يُخْرِجُ الْخَبْءَ
فِي السَّمَاوَاتِ وَالْأَرْضِ وَيَعْلَمُ مَا
تُخْفُونَ وَمَا تُعْلِنُونَ ﴿٢٥﴾
اللَّهُ لَا إِلَٰهَ إِلَّا هُوَ رَبُّ الْعَرْشِ الْعَظِيمِ ﴿٢٦﴾
قَالَ سَنَنظُرُ أَصَدَقْتَ أَمْ كُنتَ
مِنَ الْكَاذِبِينَ ﴿٢٧﴾
اذْهَب بِّكِتَابِي هَٰذَا فَأَلْقِهْ إِلَيْهِمْ
ثُمَّ تَوَلَّ عَنْهُمْ فَانظُرْ مَاذَا يَرْجِعُونَ ﴿٢٨﴾
قَالَتْ يَا أَيُّهَا الْمَلَأُ إِنِّي أُلْقِيَ إِلَيَّ
كِتَابٌ كَرِيمٌ ﴿٢٩﴾
إِنَّهُ مِن سُلَيْمَانَ وَإِنَّهُ بِسْمِ
اللَّهِ الرَّحْمَٰنِ الرَّحِيمِ ﴿٣٠﴾

(answer) they return.

(The Queen of Sheba) said (when she received the letter): O chieftains! Lo! there hath been thrown unto me a noble letter.

Lo! it is from Solomon, and lo! it is: In the name of Allah, the Beneficent, the Merciful;

Exalt not yourselves against me, but come unto me as those who surrender.

She said: O chieftains! Pronounce for me in my case. I decide no case till ye are present with me.

They said: We are lords of might and lords of great prowess, but it is for thee to command; so consider what thou wilt command.

She said: Lo! kings, when they enter a township, ruin it and make the honour of its people shame. Thus will they do.

But lo! I am going to send a present unto them, and to see with what (answer) the messengers return.

So when (the envoy) came unto Solomon, (the king) said: What! Would ye help me with wealth? But that which Allah hath given me is better than that which He hath given you. Nay it is ye (and not I) who exult in your gift.

Return unto them. We verily shall come unto them with hosts that they cannot resist, and we shall drive them out from thence with shame, and they will be abased.

He said: O chiefs! Which of you will bring me her throne before they come unto me, surrendering?

A stalwart of the jinn said: I will bring it thee before thou canst rise from

ألا تعلوا علي وأتوني مسلمين ﴿٣١﴾
قالت يا أيها الملؤا أفتوني في أمري
ما كنت قاطعة أمرا حتى تشهدون ﴿٣٢﴾

قالوا نحن أولوا قوة وأولوا بأس شديد
والأمر إليك فانظري ماذا تأمرين ﴿٣٣﴾

قالت إن الملوك إذا دخلوا قرية
أفسدوها وجعلوا أعزة أهلها أذلة
وكذلك يفعلون ﴿٣٤﴾

وإني مرسلة إليهم بهدية فناظرة
بم يرجع المرسلون ﴿٣٥﴾

فلما جاء سليمن قال أتمدونن
بمال فما ءاتىن الله خير مما ءاتىكم
بل أنتم بهديتكم تفرحون ﴿٣٦﴾

ارجع إليهم فلنأتينهم بجنود لا
قبل لهم بها ولنخرجنهم منها
أذلة وهم صغرون ﴿٣٧﴾

قال يا أيها الملؤا أيكم يأتيني
بعرشها قبل أن يأتوني مسلمين ﴿٣٨﴾

قال عفريت من الجن أنا ءاتيك
به قبل أن تقوم من مقامك
وإني عليه لقوي أمين ﴿٣٩﴾

thy place. Lo! I verily am strong and trusty for such work.

One with whom was knowledge of the Scripture said: I will bring it thee before thy gaze returneth unto thee. And when he saw it set in his presence,(Solomon) said:This is of the bounty of my Lord, that He may try me whether I give thanks or am ungrateful. Whosoever giveth thanks he only giveth thanks for (the good of) his own soul: and whosoever is ungrateful (is ungrateful only to his own soul's hurt). For lo! my Lord is Absolute in independence, Bountiful.

He said: Disguise her throne for her that we may see whether she will go aright or be of those not rightly guided.

So, when she came, it was said (unto her): Is thy throne like this? She said: (It is) as though it were the very one. And (Solomon said:) We were given the knowledge before her and we had surrendered (to Allah).

And (all) that she was wont to worship instead of Allah hindered her, for she came of disbelieving folk.

It was said unto her: Enter the hall. And when she saw it she deemed it a pool and bared her legs. (Solomon) said: Lo! it is a hall, made smooth, of glass. She said: My Lord! Lo! I have wronged myself, and I surrender with Solomon unto Allah, the Lord of the Worlds.

27:16–44

قَالَ الَّذِيْ عِنْدَهٗ عِلْمٌ مِّنَ الْكِتٰبِ اَنَا
اٰتِيْكَ بِهٖ قَبْلَ اَنْ يَّرْتَدَّ اِلَيْكَ طَرْفُكَ
فَلَمَّا رَاٰهُ مُسْتَقِرًّا عِنْدَهٗ قَالَ هٰذَا
مِنْ فَضْلِ رَبِّيْ لِيَبْلُوَنِيْٓ ءَاَشْكُرُ
اَمْ اَكْفُرُ وَمَنْ شَكَرَ فَاِنَّمَا يَشْكُرُ
لِنَفْسِهٖ وَمَنْ كَفَرَ فَاِنَّ رَبِّيْ غَنِيٌّ كَرِيْمٌ ۝

قَالَ نَكِّرُوْا لَهَا عَرْشَهَا نَنْظُرْ اَتَهْتَدِيْٓ
اَمْ تَكُوْنُ مِنَ الَّذِيْنَ لَا يَهْتَدُوْنَ ۝

فَلَمَّا جَآءَتْ قِيْلَ اَهٰكَذَا عَرْشُكِ
قَالَتْ كَاَنَّهٗ هُوَ وَاُوْتِيْنَا الْعِلْمَ
مِنْ قَبْلِهَا وَكُنَّا مُسْلِمِيْنَ ۝

وَصَدَّهَا مَا كَانَتْ تَّعْبُدُ مِنْ دُوْنِ اللّٰهِ
اِنَّهَا كَانَتْ مِنْ قَوْمٍ كٰفِرِيْنَ ۝

قِيْلَ لَهَا ادْخُلِي الصَّرْحَ فَلَمَّا رَاَتْهُ
حَسِبَتْهُ لُجَّةً وَّكَشَفَتْ عَنْ سَاقَيْهَا
قَالَ اِنَّهٗ صَرْحٌ مُّمَرَّدٌ مِّنْ قَوَارِيْرَ
قَالَتْ رَبِّ اِنِّيْ ظَلَمْتُ نَفْسِيْ وَاَسْلَمْتُ
مَعَ سُلَيْمٰنَ لِلّٰهِ رَبِّ الْعٰلَمِيْنَ ۝

QUR'ĀN

1. This is the Scripture whereof there is no doubt, a guidance unto those who ward off (evil);

2:2

2. And if ye are in doubt concerning that which We reveal unto Our slave (Muhammad), then produce a sûrah of the like thereof, and call your witnesses beside Allah if ye are truthful.

And if ye do it not—and ye can never do it—then guard yourselves against the Fire prepared for disbelievers, whose fuel is of men and stones.

2:23—24

3. The month of *Rama<u>dh</u>an* in which was revealed the Qur'ān, a guidance for mankind,

2:185

4. Will they not then ponder on the Qur'ān? If it had been from other than Allah they would have found therein much incongruity.

4:82

5. And when the Qur'ān is recited, give ear to it and pay heed, that ye may obtain mercy.

7:204

6. And this Qur'ān is not such as could ever be invented despite of Allah; but it is a confirmation of that which was before it and an exposition of that which is decreed for mankind—Therein is no doubt—from the Lord of the Worlds.

1. ذٰلِكَ الْكِتٰبُ لَا رَيْبَ فِيْهِ هُدًى لِّلْمُتَّقِيْنَ (2)

2. وَاِنْ كُنْتُمْ فِيْ رَيْبٍ مِّمَّا نَزَّلْنَا عَلٰى عَبْدِنَا فَاْتُوْا بِسُوْرَةٍ مِّنْ مِّثْلِهٖ وَادْعُوْا شُهَدَآءَكُمْ مِّنْ دُوْنِ اللّٰهِ اِنْ كُنْتُمْ صٰدِقِيْنَ (23)

فَاِنْ لَّمْ تَفْعَلُوْا وَلَنْ تَفْعَلُوْا فَاتَّقُوا النَّارَ الَّتِيْ وَقُوْدُهَا النَّاسُ وَالْحِجَارَةُ اُعِدَّتْ لِلْكٰفِرِيْنَ (24)

3. شَهْرُ رَمَضَانَ الَّذِيْٓ اُنْزِلَ فِيْهِ الْقُرْاٰنُ هُدًى لِّلنَّاسِ

4. اَفَلَا يَتَدَبَّرُوْنَ الْقُرْاٰنَ وَلَوْ كَانَ مِنْ عِنْدِ غَيْرِ اللّٰهِ لَوَجَدُوْا فِيْهِ اخْتِلَافًا كَثِيْرًا (82)

5. وَاِذَا قُرِئَ الْقُرْاٰنُ فَاسْتَمِعُوْا لَهٗ وَاَنْصِتُوْا لَعَلَّكُمْ تُرْحَمُوْنَ (204)

6. وَمَا كَانَ هٰذَا الْقُرْاٰنُ اَنْ يُّفْتَرٰى مِنْ دُوْنِ اللّٰهِ وَلٰكِنْ تَصْدِيْقَ الَّذِيْ بَيْنَ يَدَيْهِ وَتَفْصِيْلَ الْكِتٰبِ لَا رَيْبَ فِيْهِ مِنْ رَّبِّ الْعٰلَمِيْنَ (37)

اَمْ يَقُوْلُوْنَ افْتَرٰىهُ قُلْ فَاْتُوْا بِسُوْرَةٍ مِّثْلِهٖ وَادْعُوْا مَنِ اسْتَطَعْتُمْ مِّنْ دُوْنِ اللّٰهِ اِنْ كُنْتُمْ صٰدِقِيْنَ (38)

Or say they: He hath invented it? Say: Then bring a sûrah like unto it, and call (for help) on all ye can besides Allah, if ye are truthful.

10:37–38

7. And when thou recitest the Qur'ān, seek refuge in Allah from Satan the outcast.

16:98

8. Say: Verily, though mankind and the *jinn* should assemble to produce the like of this Qur'ān, they could not produce the like thereof though they were helpers one of another.

And verily We have displayed for mankind in this Qur'ān all kinds of similitudes, but most of mankind refuse aught save disbelief.

17:88–89

9. Lo! We offered the trust unto the heavens and the earth and the hills, but they shrank from bearing it and were afraid of it. And man assumed it. Lo! he hath proved a tyrant and a fool:

33:72

10. By the wise *Qur'ān*

Lo! thou art of those sent

On a straight path,

A revelation of the Mighty, the Merciful,

That thou mayst warn a folk whose fathers were not warned, so they are heedless.

36:2–6

7. فَإِذَا قَرَأْتَ الْقُرْآنَ فَاسْتَعِذْ بِاللَّهِ
مِنَ الشَّيْطَانِ الرَّجِيمِ ﴿٩٨﴾

8. قُلْ لَئِنِ اجْتَمَعَتِ الْإِنْسُ وَالْجِنُّ عَلَىٰ
أَنْ يَأْتُوا بِمِثْلِ هَٰذَا الْقُرْآنِ لَا يَأْتُونَ
بِمِثْلِهِ وَلَوْ كَانَ بَعْضُهُمْ لِبَعْضٍ ظَهِيرًا ﴿٨٨﴾
وَلَقَدْ صَرَّفْنَا لِلنَّاسِ فِي هَٰذَا الْقُرْآنِ
مِنْ كُلِّ مَثَلٍ فَأَبَىٰ أَكْثَرُ النَّاسِ
إِلَّا كُفُورًا ﴿٨٩﴾

9. إِنَّا عَرَضْنَا الْأَمَانَةَ عَلَى السَّمَاوَاتِ
وَالْأَرْضِ وَالْجِبَالِ فَأَبَيْنَ أَنْ
يَحْمِلْنَهَا وَأَشْفَقْنَ مِنْهَا وَحَمَلَهَا
الْإِنْسَانُ ۖ إِنَّهُ كَانَ ظَلُومًا جَهُولًا ﴿٧٢﴾

10. وَالْقُرْآنِ الْحَكِيمِ ﴿٢﴾
إِنَّكَ لَمِنَ الْمُرْسَلِينَ ﴿٣﴾
عَلَىٰ صِرَاطٍ مُسْتَقِيمٍ ﴿٤﴾
تَنْزِيلَ الْعَزِيزِ الرَّحِيمِ ﴿٥﴾
لِتُنْذِرَ قَوْمًا مَا أُنْذِرَ آبَاؤُهُمْ
فَهُمْ غَافِلُونَ ﴿٦﴾

11. اللَّهُ نَزَّلَ أَحْسَنَ الْحَدِيثِ كِتَابًا
مُتَشَابِهًا مَثَانِيَ تَقْشَعِرُّ مِنْهُ جُلُودُ

11. Allah hath (now) revealed the fairest of statements, a Scripture consistent, (wherein promises of reward are) paired (with threats of punishment, whereat doth creep

the flesh of those who fear their Lord, so that their flesh and their hearts soften at Allah's reminder. Such is Allah's guidance, wherewith He guideth whom He will. And him whom Allah sendeth astray, for him there is no guide.

39:23

12. And verily We have coined for mankind in this Qur'an all kinds of similitudes, that haply they may reflect;

A Lecture in Arabic, containing no crookedness, that haply they may ward off (evil).

39:27–28

13. A revelation from the Beneficent, the Merciful.

A Scripture whereof the verses are expounded, a Lecture in Arabic for people who have knowledge.

Good tidings and a warning. But most of them turn away so that they hear not.

41:2–4

14. And if We had appointed it a Lecture in a foreign tongue they would assuredly have said: If only its verses were expounded (so that we might understand)? What! A foreign tongue and an Arab?—Say unto them (O Muhammad): For those who believe it is a guidance and a healing; and as for those who disbelieve, there is a deafness in their ears, and it is blindness for

الَّذِيْنَ يَخْشَوْنَ رَبَّهُمْ ثُمَّ تَلِيْنُ
جُلُوْدُهُمْ وَقُلُوْبُهُمْ اِلٰى ذِكْرِ اللّٰهِ
ذٰلِكَ هُدَى اللّٰهِ يَهْدِيْ بِهٖ مَنْ يَّشَآءُ
وَمَنْ يُّضْلِلِ اللّٰهُ فَمَا لَهٗ مِنْ هَادٍ ۝٢٣

12. وَلَقَدْ ضَرَبْنَا لِلنَّاسِ فِيْ هٰذَا الْقُرْاٰنِ
مِنْ كُلِّ مَثَلٍ لَّعَلَّهُمْ يَتَذَكَّرُوْنَ ۝٢٧
قُرْاٰنًا عَرَبِيًّا غَيْرَ ذِيْ عِوَجٍ لَّعَلَّهُمْ يَتَّقُوْنَ ۝٢٨

13. تَنْزِيْلٌ مِّنَ الرَّحْمٰنِ الرَّحِيْمِ ۝٢
كِتٰبٌ فُصِّلَتْ اٰيٰتُهٗ قُرْاٰنًا عَرَبِيًّا
لِّقَوْمٍ يَّعْلَمُوْنَ ۝٣
بَشِيْرًا وَّنَذِيْرًا فَاَعْرَضَ اَكْثَرُهُمْ
فَهُمْ لَا يَسْمَعُوْنَ ۝٤

14. وَلَوْ جَعَلْنٰهُ قُرْاٰنًا اَعْجَمِيًّا لَّقَالُوْا
لَوْلَا فُصِّلَتْ اٰيٰتُهٗ ءَاَعْجَمِيٌّ وَّعَرَبِيٌّ
قُلْ هُوَ لِلَّذِيْنَ اٰمَنُوْا هُدًى وَّشِفَآءٌ
وَالَّذِيْنَ لَا يُؤْمِنُوْنَ فِيْ اٰذَانِهِمْ
وَقْرٌ وَّهُوَ عَلَيْهِمْ عَمًى اُولٰٓئِكَ
يُنَادَوْنَ مِنْ مَّكَانٍ بَعِيْدٍ ۝٤٤

15. وَكَذٰلِكَ اَوْحَيْنَا اِلَيْكَ قُرْاٰنًا عَرَبِيًّا
لِّتُنْذِرَ اُمَّ الْقُرٰى وَمَنْ حَوْلَهَا وَتُنْذِرَ
يَوْمَ الْجَمْعِ لَا رَيْبَ فِيْهِ فَرِيْقٌ فِي الْجَنَّةِ

them. Such are called to from afar.

41:44

15. And thus We have inspired in thee a Lecture in Arabic, that thou mayest warn the mother—town and those around it, and mayest warn of a day of assembling whereof there is no doubt. A host will be in the

Garden, and a host of them in the Flame.

42:7

16. By the Scripture which maketh plain:

Lo! We have appointed it a Lecture in Arabic that haply ye may understand.

And lo! in the Source of Decrees, which We possess, it is indeed sublime, decisive.

43:2–4

17. Or say they: He hath invented it? Nay, but they will not believe!

Then let them produce speech the like thereof, if they are truthful.

52:33–34

18. Nay, I swear by the places of the stars–

And lo! that verily is a tremendous oath, if ye but knew–

That (this is indeed a noble Qur'ān

In a Book kept hidden

Which none toucheth save the purified,

A revelation from the Lord of the Worlds.

Is it this Statement that ye scorn,

And make denial thereof of your livelihood?

56:75–82

19. If We had caused this Qur'ān to descend upon a mountain, thou (O Muhammad) verily hadst seen it humbled rent asunder by the

وَفَرِيْقٌ فِي السَّعِيْرِ ۝

16. وَالْكِتٰبِ الْمُبِيْنِ ۝
إِنَّا جَعَلْنٰهُ قُرْءٰنًا عَرَبِيًّا لَّعَلَّكُمْ تَعْقِلُوْنَ ۝
وَإِنَّهٗ فِيْٓ أُمِّ الْكِتٰبِ لَدَيْنَا لَعَلِيٌّ حَكِيْمٌ ۝

17. أَمْ يَقُوْلُوْنَ تَقَوَّلَهٗ ۚ بَلْ لَّا يُؤْمِنُوْنَ ۝
فَلْيَأْتُوْا بِحَدِيْثٍ مِّثْلِهٖٓ إِنْ كَانُوْا
صٰدِقِيْنَ ۝

18. فَلَآ أُقْسِمُ بِمَوٰقِعِ النُّجُوْمِ ۝
وَإِنَّهٗ لَقَسَمٌ لَّوْ تَعْلَمُوْنَ عَظِيْمٌ ۝
إِنَّهٗ لَقُرْءٰنٌ كَرِيْمٌ ۝
فِيْ كِتٰبٍ مَّكْنُوْنٍ ۝
لَّا يَمَسُّهٗٓ إِلَّا الْمُطَهَّرُوْنَ ۝
تَنْزِيْلٌ مِّنْ رَّبِّ الْعٰلَمِيْنَ ۝
أَفَبِهٰذَا الْحَدِيْثِ أَنْتُمْ مُّدْهِنُوْنَ ۝
وَتَجْعَلُوْنَ رِزْقَكُمْ أَنَّكُمْ تُكَذِّبُوْنَ ۝

19. لَوْ أَنْزَلْنَا هٰذَا الْقُرْءٰنَ عَلٰى جَبَلٍ
لَّرَأَيْتَهٗ خٰشِعًا مُّتَصَدِّعًا مِّنْ خَشْيَةِ
اللّٰهِ ۚ وَتِلْكَ الْأَمْثَالُ نَضْرِبُهَا لِلنَّاسِ
لَعَلَّهُمْ يَتَفَكَّرُوْنَ ۝

20. إِنَّا نَحْنُ نَزَّلْنَا عَلَيْكَ الْقُرْءٰنَ
تَنْزِيْلًا ۝

fear of Allah. Such similitudes coin We for mankind that haply they may reflect.

59:21

20. Lo! We, even We, have revealed unto thee the Qur'ān, a revelation;

76:23

21. Nay, but it is a Glorious Qur'an
On a guarded tablet.
85:21–22

22. Lo! We revealed it on the Night of Power.
97:1

QUR'AN AND SCIENCE

1. Lo! in the creation of the heavens and the earth, and the difference of night and day, and the ships which run upon the sea with that which is of use to men, and the water which Allah sendeth down from the sky, thereby reviving the earth after its death, and dispersing all kinds of beasts therein, and (in) the ordinance of the winds, and the clouds obedient between heaven and earth: are signs of (Allah's Sovereignty) for people who have sense.
2:164

2. Lo! Allah (it is) Who splitteth the grain of corn and the date–stone (for sprouting). He bringeth forth the living from the dead, and is the bringer–forth of the dead from the living. Such is Allah. How then are ye per–verted?

He is the Cleaver of the Daybreak, and He hath app–ointed the night for stillness, and the sun and the moon for reckoning. That is the

بَلْ هُوَ قُرْآنٌ مَّجِيدٌ ۝
فِي لَوْحٍ مَّحْفُوظٍ ۝

22 إِنَّا أَنزَلْنَاهُ فِي لَيْلَةِ الْقَدْرِ ۝

1. إِنَّ فِي خَلْقِ السَّمَاوَاتِ وَالْأَرْضِ وَاخْتِلَافِ
اللَّيْلِ وَالنَّهَارِ وَالْفُلْكِ الَّتِي تَجْرِي فِي
الْبَحْرِ بِمَا يَنفَعُ النَّاسَ وَمَا أَنزَلَ اللَّهُ
مِنَ السَّمَاءِ مِن مَّاءٍ فَأَحْيَا بِهِ الْأَرْضَ
بَعْدَ مَوْتِهَا وَبَثَّ فِيهَا مِن كُلِّ دَابَّةٍ
وَتَصْرِيفِ الرِّيَاحِ وَالسَّحَابِ الْمُسَخَّرِ بَيْنَ
السَّمَاءِ وَالْأَرْضِ لَآيَاتٍ لِّقَوْمٍ يَعْقِلُونَ ۝١٦٤

2. إِنَّ اللَّهَ فَالِقُ الْحَبِّ وَالنَّوَىٰ يُخْرِجُ الْحَيَّ
مِنَ الْمَيِّتِ وَمُخْرِجُ الْمَيِّتِ مِنَ الْحَيِّ ۚ
ذَٰلِكُمُ اللَّهُ فَأَنَّىٰ تُؤْفَكُونَ ۝

فَالِقُ الْإِصْبَاحِ وَجَعَلَ اللَّيْلَ سَكَنًا وَالشَّمْسَ وَ
الْقَمَرَ حُسْبَانًا ۚ ذَٰلِكَ تَقْدِيرُ الْعَزِيزِ الْعَلِيمِ ۝٩٦

وَهُوَ الَّذِي جَعَلَ لَكُمُ النُّجُومَ لِتَهْتَدُوا
بِهَا فِي ظُلُمَاتِ الْبَرِّ وَالْبَحْرِ ۗ قَدْ فَصَّلْنَا
الْآيَاتِ لِقَوْمٍ يَعْلَمُونَ ۝

measuring of the Mighty, the Wise.

And He it is Who hath set for you the stars that ye may guide your course by them amid the darkness of the land and the sea.

QUR'ĀN

Ref: 10:15; 38:8; 44:1-4; 47:24; 53:1-5; 55:1-2; 69:38-48; 72:1-2; 80:11-16; 97:1-9.

See also: Incomparability of Qur'ān, Parābles of Qur'ān, Qur'ānic Prayers, Qur'ānic Prophesies, Qur'ān's challenge to Sceptics, Recitation of Qur'ān, Revelation.

We have detailed Our revelations for a people who have knowledge.

And He it is Who hath produced you from a single being, and (hath given you) a habitation and a repository. We have detailed Our revelations for a people who have understanding.

He it is Who sendeth down water from the sky, and therewith We bring forth buds of every kind; We bring forth the green blade from which We bring forth the thick-clustered grain; and from the date-palm, from the pollen thereof, spring pendant bunches; and (We bring forth) gardens of grapes, and the olive and the pomegranate, alike and unlike. Look upon the fruit thereof, when they bear fruit, and upon its ripening. Lo! herein verily are portents for a people who believe.

Yet they ascribe as partners unto Him the jinn, although He did create them, and impute falsely, without knowledge, sons and daughters unto Him. Glorified be He and High Exalted above (all) that they ascribe (unto Him)!

The Originator of the heavens and the earth!

6:95–101

وَهُوَ الَّذِيْٓ اَنْشَاَكُمْ مِّنْ نَّفْسٍ وَّاحِدَةٍ
فَمُسْتَقَرٌّ وَّمُسْتَوْدَعٌ قَدْ فَصَّلْنَا الْاٰيٰتِ
لِقَوْمٍ يَّفْقَهُوْنَ ○

وَهُوَ الَّذِيْٓ اَنْزَلَ مِنَ السَّمَآءِ مَآءً فَاَخْرَجْنَا
بِهٖ نَبَاتَ كُلِّ شَيْءٍ فَاَخْرَجْنَا مِنْهُ خَضِرًا
نُّخْرِجُ مِنْهُ حَبًّا مُّتَرَاكِبًا وَمِنَ النَّخْلِ
مِنْ طَلْعِهَا قِنْوَانٌ دَانِيَةٌ وَّجَنّٰتٍ مِّنْ
اَعْنَابٍ وَّالزَّيْتُوْنَ وَالرُّمَّانَ مُشْتَبِهًا
وَّغَيْرَ مُتَشَابِهٍ اُنْظُرُوْٓا اِلٰى ثَمَرِهٖٓ اِذَآ اَثْمَرَ
وَيَنْعِهٖ اِنَّ فِيْ ذٰلِكُمْ لَاٰيٰتٍ لِّقَوْمٍ يُّؤْمِنُوْنَ ○

وَجَعَلُوْا لِلّٰهِ شُرَكَآءَ الْجِنَّ وَخَلَقَهُمْ وَ
خَرَقُوْا لَهٗ بَنِيْنَ وَبَنٰتٍ بِغَيْرِ عِلْمٍ
سُبْحٰنَهٗ وَتَعٰلٰى عَمَّا يَصِفُوْنَ ○
بَدِيْعُ السَّمٰوٰتِ وَالْاَرْضِ

3. اِنَّ رَبَّكُمُ اللّٰهُ الَّذِيْ خَلَقَ السَّمٰوٰتِ وَالْاَرْضَ فِيْ
سِتَّةِ اَيَّامٍ ثُمَّ اسْتَوٰى عَلَى الْعَرْشِ يُغْشِي الَّيْلَ
النَّهَارَ يَطْلُبُهٗ حَثِيْثًا وَّالشَّمْسَ وَالْقَمَرَ وَالنُّجُوْمَ
مُسَخَّرٰتٍ بِاَمْرِهٖ اَلَا لَهُ الْخَلْقُ وَالْاَمْرُ تَبٰرَكَ
اللّٰهُ رَبُّ الْعٰلَمِيْنَ ۝٥٤

4. قُلْ هَلْ مِنْ شُرَكَآئِكُمْ مَّنْ يَّبْدَؤُا
الْخَلْقَ ثُمَّ يُعِيْدُهٗ قُلِ اللّٰهُ يَبْدَؤُا الْخَلْقَ
ثُمَّ يُعِيْدُهٗ فَاَنّٰى تُؤْفَكُوْنَ ۝٣٤

3. Lo! your Lord is Allah Who created the heavens and the earth in six Days, then mounted He the Throne. He covereth the night with the day, which is in haste to follow it, and hath made the sun and the moon and the stars subservient by His command. His verily is all creation and commandment. Blessed be Allah, the Lord of the Worlds!

7:54

4. Say: Is there of your partners (whom ye escribe unto Allah) one that produceth Creation and then reproduceth it? Say: Allah produceth Creation, then reproduceth it. How then, are ye misled!

10:34

5. Allah it is Who raised up the heavens without visible supports, then mounted the Throne, and compelled the sun and the moon to be of service, each runneth unto an appointed term; He ordereth the course; He detaileth the revelations, that haply ye may be certain of the meeting with your Lord.

And He it is Who spread out the earth and placed therein firm hills and flowing streams, and of all fruits He placed therein two spouses (male and female). He covereth the night with the day. Lo! herein verily are portents for people who take thought.

And in the Earth are neighbouring tracts, vineyards and ploughed lands, and date-palms, like and unlike, which are watered with one water. And We have made some of them to excel others in fruit. Lo! herein verily are portents for people who have sense.

13:2–4

6. Allah sendeth down water from the sky and therewith reviveth the earth after her death. Lo! herein is indeed a portent for a folk who hear.

And lo! in the cattle there is a lesson for you. We give you to drink of that which is in their bellies, from betwixt the refuse and the blood, pure milk palatable to the drinkers.

16:65–66

5. اَللّٰهُ الَّذِىْ رَفَعَ السَّمٰوٰتِ بِغَيْرِ عَمَدٍ
تَرَوْنَهَا ثُمَّ اسْتَوٰى عَلَى الْعَرْشِ وَسَخَّرَ
الشَّمْسَ وَالْقَمَرَ ؕ كُلٌّ يَّجْرِىْ لِاَجَلٍ
مُّسَمًّى ؕ يُدَبِّرُ الْاَمْرَ يُفَصِّلُ الْاٰيٰتِ
لَعَلَّكُمْ بِلِقَآءِ رَبِّكُمْ تُوْقِنُوْنَ ﴿۲﴾
وَهُوَ الَّذِىْ مَدَّ الْاَرْضَ وَجَعَلَ فِيْهَا
رَوَاسِىَ وَاَنْهٰرًا ؕ وَمِنْ كُلِّ الثَّمَرٰتِ
جَعَلَ فِيْهَا زَوْجَيْنِ اثْنَيْنِ يُغْشِى الَّيْلَ
النَّهَارَ ؕ اِنَّ فِىْ ذٰلِكَ لَاٰيٰتٍ لِّقَوْمٍ
يَّتَفَكَّرُوْنَ ﴿۳﴾
وَفِى الْاَرْضِ قِطَعٌ مُّتَجٰوِرٰتٌ وَّجَنّٰتٌ
مِّنْ اَعْنَابٍ وَّزَرْعٌ وَّنَخِيْلٌ صِنْوَانٌ
وَّغَيْرُ صِنْوَانٍ يُّسْقٰى بِمَآءٍ وَّاحِدٍ
وَنُفَضِّلُ بَعْضَهَا عَلٰى بَعْضٍ فِى الْاُكُلِ ؕ
اِنَّ فِىْ ذٰلِكَ لَاٰيٰتٍ لِّقَوْمٍ يَّعْقِلُوْنَ ﴿۴﴾
6. وَاللّٰهُ اَنْزَلَ مِنَ السَّمَآءِ مَآءً فَاَحْيَا
بِهِ الْاَرْضَ بَعْدَ مَوْتِهَا ؕ اِنَّ فِىْ ذٰلِكَ
لَاٰيَةً لِّقَوْمٍ يَّسْمَعُوْنَ ﴿۶۵﴾
وَاِنَّ لَكُمْ فِى الْاَنْعَامِ لَعِبْرَةً ؕ نُسْقِيْكُمْ
مِّمَّا فِىْ بُطُوْنِهٖ مِنْۢ بَيْنِ فَرْثٍ وَّدَمٍ
لَّبَنًا خَالِصًا سَآئِغًا لِّلشّٰرِبِيْنَ ﴿۶۶﴾

7. اَوَلَمْ يَرَ الَّذِيْنَ كَفَرُوْۤا اَنَّ السَّمٰوٰتِ
وَالْاَرْضَ كَانَتَا رَتْقًا فَفَتَقْنٰهُمَا ؕ
وَجَعَلْنَا مِنَ الْمَآءِ كُلَّ شَىْءٍ حَىٍّ ؕ

7. Have not those who disbelieve known that the heavens and the earth were of one piece, then We parted them, and We made every living thing of water? Will they not then believe?

And We have placed in the earth firm hills lest it quake with them, and We have placed therein ravines as roads that haply they may find their way.

And We have made the sky a roof withheld (from them). Yet they turn away from its portents.

And He it is Who created the night and the day, and the sun and the moon. They float, each in an orbit.

21:30–33

8. The Day when We shall roll up the heavens as a recorder rolleth up a written scroll. As We began the first creation, We shall repeat it. (It is) a promise (binding) upon Us. Lo! We are to perform it.

21:104

9. Verily We created man from a product of wet earth;

Then placed him as a drop (of seed) in a safe lodging;

Then fashioned We the drop a clot, then fashioned We the clot a little lump, then fashioned We the little lump bones, then clothed the bones with flesh, and then

أَفَلَا يُؤْمِنُونَ ﴿٣٠﴾
وَجَعَلْنَا فِي الْأَرْضِ رَوَاسِيَ أَنْ
تَمِيدَ بِهِمْ وَجَعَلْنَا فِيهَا فِجَاجًا
سُبُلًا لَعَلَّهُمْ يَهْتَدُونَ ﴿٣١﴾
وَجَعَلْنَا السَّمَاءَ سَقْفًا مَحْفُوظًا ۖ
وَهُمْ عَنْ آيَاتِهَا مُعْرِضُونَ ﴿٣٢﴾
وَهُوَ الَّذِي خَلَقَ اللَّيْلَ وَالنَّهَارَ
وَالشَّمْسَ وَالْقَمَرَ ۖ كُلٌّ فِي
فَلَكٍ يَسْبَحُونَ ﴿٣٣﴾

8. يَوْمَ نَطْوِي السَّمَاءَ كَطَيِّ السِّجِلِّ
لِلْكُتُبِ ۚ كَمَا بَدَأْنَا أَوَّلَ خَلْقٍ
نُعِيدُهُ ۚ وَعْدًا عَلَيْنَا ۚ إِنَّا كُنَّا فَاعِلِينَ ﴿١٠٤﴾

9. وَلَقَدْ خَلَقْنَا الْإِنْسَانَ مِنْ سُلَالَةٍ
مِنْ طِينٍ ﴿١٢﴾
ثُمَّ جَعَلْنَاهُ نُطْفَةً فِي قَرَارٍ مَكِينٍ ﴿١٣﴾
ثُمَّ خَلَقْنَا النُّطْفَةَ عَلَقَةً فَخَلَقْنَا
الْعَلَقَةَ مُضْغَةً فَخَلَقْنَا الْمُضْغَةَ
عِظَامًا فَكَسَوْنَا الْعِظَامَ لَحْمًا ثُمَّ
أَنْشَأْنَاهُ خَلْقًا آخَرَ ۚ فَتَبَارَكَ اللَّهُ
أَحْسَنُ الْخَالِقِينَ ﴿١٤﴾
ثُمَّ إِنَّكُمْ بَعْدَ ذَٰلِكَ لَمَيِّتُونَ ﴿١٥﴾
ثُمَّ إِنَّكُمْ يَوْمَ الْقِيَامَةِ تُبْعَثُونَ ﴿١٦﴾

produced it as another creation. So blessed be Allah, the Best of Creators!

Then lo! after that ye surely die.

Then lo! on the Day of Resurrection ye are raised (again).

And We have created above you seven paths, and We are never unmindful of creation.

And We send down from the sky water in measure, and We give it lodging in the earth, and lo! We are able to withdraw it.

Then We produce for you therewith gardens of date-palms and grapes, wherein is much fruit for you and whereof ye eat;

And a tree that springeth forth from Mount Sinai that groweth oil and relish for the eaters.

And lo! in the cattle there is verily a lesson for you. We give you to drink of that which is in their bellies, and many uses have ye in them, and of them do ye eat;

And on them and on the ship ye are carried.
23:12–22

10. Hast thou not seen how Allah wafteth the clouds, then gathereth them, then maketh them layers, and thou seest the rain come forth from between them; He sendeth down from the heaven mountains wherein is hail, and smiteth therewith whom He will, and averteth it from whom He will. The flashing of His lightning all but snatcheth away the sight.

Allah causeth the re-

وَلَقَدْ خَلَقْنَا فَوْقَكُمْ سَبْعَ طَرَآئِقَ ۖ
وَمَا كُنَّا عَنِ الْخَلْقِ غٰفِلِيْنَ ﴿١٧﴾
وَاَنْزَلْنَا مِنَ السَّمَآءِ مَآءً بِقَدَرٍ
فَاَسْكَنّٰهُ فِی الْاَرْضِ ۖ وَاِنَّا عَلٰى
ذَهَابٍ بِهٖ لَقٰدِرُوْنَ ﴿١٨﴾
فَاَنْشَاْنَا لَكُمْ بِهٖ جَنّٰتٍ مِّنْ نَّخِيْلٍ
وَّاَعْنَابٍ ۘ لَكُمْ فِيْهَا فَوَاكِهُ كَثِيْرَةٌ
وَّمِنْهَا تَاْكُلُوْنَ ﴿١٩﴾
وَشَجَرَةً تَخْرُجُ مِنْ طُوْرِ سَيْنَآءَ تَنْبُتُ
بِالدُّهْنِ وَصِبْغٍ لِّلْاٰكِلِيْنَ ﴿٢٠﴾
وَاِنَّ لَكُمْ فِی الْاَنْعَامِ لَعِبْرَةً ۚ نُسْقِيْكُمْ
مِّمَّا فِیْ بُطُوْنِهَا وَلَكُمْ فِيْهَا مَنَافِعُ
كَثِيْرَةٌ وَّمِنْهَا تَاْكُلُوْنَ ﴿٢١﴾
وَعَلَيْهَا وَعَلَى الْفُلْكِ تُحْمَلُوْنَ ﴿٢٢﴾
10. اَلَمْ تَرَ اَنَّ اللّٰهَ يُزْجِیْ سَحَابًا ثُمَّ يُؤَلِّفُ
بَيْنَهٗ ثُمَّ يَجْعَلُهٗ رُكَامًا فَتَرَى الْوَدْقَ
يَخْرُجُ مِنْ خِلٰلِهٖ ۚ وَيُنَزِّلُ مِنَ السَّمَآءِ
مِنْ جِبَالٍ فِيْهَا مِنْ بَرَدٍ فَيُصِيْبُ بِهٖ
مَنْ يَّشَآءُ وَيَصْرِفُهٗ عَنْ مَّنْ يَّشَآءُ ۭ
يَكَادُ سَنَا بَرْقِهٖ يَذْهَبُ بِالْاَبْصَارِ ﴿٤٣﴾
يُقَلِّبُ اللّٰهُ الَّيْلَ وَالنَّهَارَ ۭ اِنَّ فِیْ ذٰلِكَ
لَعِبْرَةً لِّاُولِی الْاَبْصَارِ ﴿٤٤﴾
وَاللّٰهُ خَلَقَ كُلَّ دَآبَّةٍ مِّنْ مَّآءٍ ۚ فَمِنْهُمْ مَّنْ يَّمْشِیْ

volution of the day and the night. Lo! herein is indeed a lesson for those who see.

Allah hath created every animal of water. Of them is (a kind) that goeth upon its belly and (a kind) that goeth upon two legs and (a kind) that goeth upon four. Allah createth what He will. Lo! Allah is Able to do all things.

24:43–45

11. Have they not seen the earth, how much of every fruitful kind We make to grow therein?

Lo! herein is indeed a portent; yet most of them are not believers.

26:7–8

12. And thou seest the hills thou deemest solid flying with the flight of clouds: the doing of Allah Who perfecteth all things. Lo! He is Informed of what ye do.

27:88

13. See they not how Allah produceth creation, then reproduceth it? Lo! for Allah that is easy.

Say (O Muhammad): Travel in the land and see how He originated creation, then Allah bringeth forth the later growth. Lo! Allah is Able to do all things.

29:19–20

14. Glory be to Him Who created all the sexual pairs, of that which the earth groweth, and of themselves, and of that which they know not!

A token unto them is night. We strip it of the day,

عَلٰى بَطْنِهٖ وَمِنْهُمْ مَّنْ يَّمْشِىْ عَلٰى رِجْلَيْنِ وَمِنْهُمْ
مَّنْ يَّمْشِىْ عَلٰٓى اَرْبَعٍ يَخْلُقُ اللّٰهُ مَا يَشَآءُ اِنَّ
اللّٰهَ عَلٰى كُلِّ شَىْءٍ قَدِيْرٌ ﴿٤٥﴾

11. اَوَلَمْ يَرَوْا اِلَى الْاَرْضِ كَمْ اَنْۢبَتْنَا
فِيْهَا مِنْ كُلِّ زَوْجٍ كَرِيْمٍ ﴿٧﴾
اِنَّ فِىْ ذٰلِكَ لَاٰيَةً وَمَا كَانَ
اَكْثَرُهُمْ مُّؤْمِنِيْنَ ﴿٨﴾

12. وَتَرَى الْجِبَالَ تَحْسَبُهَا جَامِدَةً وَّهِىَ
تَمُرُّ مَرَّ السَّحَابِ صُنْعَ اللّٰهِ الَّذِىْٓ
اَتْقَنَ كُلَّ شَىْءٍ اِنَّهٗ خَبِيْرٌۢ بِمَا تَفْعَلُوْنَ ﴿٨٨﴾

13. اَوَلَمْ يَرَوْا كَيْفَ يُبْدِئُ اللّٰهُ الْخَلْقَ
ثُمَّ يُعِيْدُهٗ اِنَّ ذٰلِكَ عَلَى اللّٰهِ يَسِيْرٌ ﴿١٩﴾
قُلْ سِيْرُوْا فِى الْاَرْضِ فَانْظُرُوْا كَيْفَ
بَدَاَ الْخَلْقَ ثُمَّ اللّٰهُ يُنْشِئُ النَّشْاَةَ
الْاٰخِرَةَ اِنَّ اللّٰهَ عَلٰى كُلِّ شَىْءٍ قَدِيْرٌ ﴿٢٠﴾

14. سُبْحٰنَ الَّذِىْ خَلَقَ الْاَزْوَاجَ كُلَّهَا
مِمَّا تُنْۢبِتُ الْاَرْضُ وَمِنْ اَنْفُسِهِمْ
وَمِمَّا لَا يَعْلَمُوْنَ ﴿٣٦﴾
وَاٰيَةٌ لَّهُمُ الَّيْلُ نَسْلَخُ مِنْهُ النَّهَارَ
فَاِذَا هُمْ مُّظْلِمُوْنَ ﴿٣٧﴾
وَالشَّمْسُ تَجْرِىْ لِمُسْتَقَرٍّ لَّهَا
ذٰلِكَ تَقْدِيْرُ الْعَزِيْزِ الْعَلِيْمِ ﴿٣٨﴾
وَالْقَمَرَ قَدَّرْنٰهُ مَنَازِلَ حَتّٰى عَادَ كَالْعُرْجُوْنِ
الْقَدِيْمِ ﴿٣٩﴾

and lo! they are in darkness:

And the sun runneth on unto a resting-place for him. That is the measuring of the Mighty, the Wise.

And for the moon We have appointed mansions till she return like an old shrivelled palm-leaf.

It is not for the sun to overtake the moon, nor doth the night outstrip the day. They float each in an orbit.

36:36–40

15. Say (O Muhammad, unto the idolaters): Disbelieve ye verily in Him Who created the earth in two Days, and ascribe ye unto Him rivals? He (and none else) is the Lord of the Worlds.

He placed therein firm hills rising above it, and blessed it and measured therein its sustenance in four Days, alike for (all) who ask.

Then turned He to the heaven when it was smoke, and said unto it and unto the earth: Come both of you, willingly or loth. They said: We come, obedient.

Then He ordained them seven heavens in two Days and inspired in each heaven its mandate; and We decked the nether heaven with lamps, and rendered it inviolable. That is the measuring of the Mighty, the Knower.

41:9–12

16. We shall show them Our portents on the horizons and within themselves until it will be manifest unto them that it is the Truth. Doth not thy Lord suffice, since He is Witness over all things?

41:53

17. We have built the heaven

لَا الشَّمْسُ يَنْۢبَغِيْ لَهَآ اَنْ تُدْرِكَ الْقَمَرَ وَلَا
الَّيْلُ سَابِقُ النَّهَارِ ۭ وَكُلٌّ فِيْ فَلَكٍ يَّسْبَحُوْنَ ۝٤٠

15. قُلْ اَىِٕنَّكُمْ لَتَكْفُرُوْنَ بِالَّذِيْ خَلَقَ
الْاَرْضَ فِيْ يَوْمَيْنِ وَتَجْعَلُوْنَ لَهٗٓ
اَنْدَادًا ۭ ذٰلِكَ رَبُّ الْعٰلَمِيْنَ ۝٩

وَجَعَلَ فِيْهَا رَوَاسِيَ مِنْ فَوْقِهَا
وَبٰرَكَ فِيْهَا وَقَدَّرَ فِيْهَآ اَقْوَاتَهَا
فِيْٓ اَرْبَعَةِ اَيَّامٍ ۭ سَوَاۗءً لِّلسَّاۗىِٕلِيْنَ ۝١٠

ثُمَّ اسْتَوٰٓى اِلَى السَّمَاۗءِ وَهِيَ دُخَانٌ
فَقَالَ لَهَا وَلِلْاَرْضِ ائْتِيَا طَوْعًا اَوْ
كَرْهًا ۭ قَالَتَآ اَتَيْنَا طَاۗىِٕعِيْنَ ۝١١

فَقَضٰىهُنَّ سَبْعَ سَمٰوٰتٍ فِيْ يَوْمَيْنِ
وَاَوْحٰى فِيْ كُلِّ سَمَاۗءٍ اَمْرَهَا ۭ وَزَيَّنَّا
السَّمَاۗءَ الدُّنْيَا بِمَصَابِيْحَ ڰ وَحِفْظًا ۭ
ذٰلِكَ تَقْدِيْرُ الْعَزِيْزِ الْعَلِيْمِ ۝١٢

16. سَنُرِيْهِمْ اٰيٰتِنَا فِي الْاٰفَاقِ وَفِيْٓ اَنْفُسِهِمْ
حَتّٰى يَتَبَيَّنَ لَهُمْ اَنَّهُ الْحَقُّ ۭ اَوَلَمْ
يَكْفِ بِرَبِّكَ اَنَّهٗ عَلٰي كُلِّ شَيْءٍ شَهِيْدٌ ۝٥٣

17. وَالسَّمَاۗءَ بَنَيْنٰهَا بِاَيْىدٍ وَّاِنَّا
لَمُوْسِعُوْنَ ۝٤٧
وَالْاَرْضَ فَرَشْنٰهَا فَنِعْمَ الْمٰهِدُوْنَ ۝٤٨
وَمِنْ كُلِّ شَيْءٍ خَلَقْنَا زَوْجَيْنِ

with might, and We it is Who make the vast extent (thereof).

And the earth have We laid out, how gracious was the Spreader (thereof)!

And all things We have created by pairs, that haply ye

may reflect.

51:47–49

18. And when the trumpet shall sound one blast

And the earth with the mountains shall be lifted up and crushed with one crash,

Then, on that day, will the Event befall.

And the heaven will split asunder, for that day it will be frail.

69:13–16

19. What aileth you that ye hope not toward Allah for dignity

When He created you by (divers) stages?

See ye not how Allah hath created seven heavens in harmony,

And hath made the moon a light therein, and made the sun a lamp?

And Allah hath caused you to grow as a growth from the earth,

And afterward He maketh you return thereto, and He will bring you forth again, a (new) forthbringing.

And Allah hath made the earth a wide expanse for you

That ye may tread the valley–ways thereof.

71:13–20

20. But when sight is confounded

And the moon is eclipsed,

And sun and moon are united,

لَعَلَّكُمْ تَذَكَّرُوْنَ ﴿٤٩﴾

18. فَاِذَا نُفِخَ فِی الصُّوْرِ نَفْخَةٌ وَّاحِدَةٌ ﴿١٣﴾
وَّحُمِلَتِ الْاَرْضُ وَالْجِبَالُ فَدُكَّتَا
دَكَّةً وَّاحِدَةً ﴿١٤﴾
فَيَوْمَئِذٍ وَّقَعَتِ الْوَاقِعَةُ ﴿١٥﴾
وَانْشَقَّتِ السَّمَآءُ فَهِیَ يَوْمَئِذٍ وَّاهِيَةٌ ﴿١٦﴾

19. مَا لَكُمْ لَا تَرْجُوْنَ لِلّٰهِ وَقَارًا ﴿١٣﴾
وَقَدْ خَلَقَكُمْ اَطْوَارًا ﴿١٤﴾
اَلَمْ تَرَوْا كَيْفَ خَلَقَ اللّٰهُ سَبْعَ
سَمٰوٰتٍ طِبَاقًا ﴿١٥﴾
وَّجَعَلَ الْقَمَرَ فِيْهِنَّ نُوْرًا وَّجَعَلَ
الشَّمْسَ سِرَاجًا ﴿١٦﴾
وَاللّٰهُ اَنْۢبَتَكُمْ مِّنَ الْاَرْضِ نَبَاتًا ﴿١٧﴾
ثُمَّ يُعِيْدُكُمْ فِيْهَا وَيُخْرِجُكُمْ اِخْرَاجًا ﴿١٨﴾
وَاللّٰهُ جَعَلَ لَكُمُ الْاَرْضَ بِسَاطًا ﴿١٩﴾
لِّتَسْلُكُوْا مِنْهَا سُبُلًا فِجَاجًا ﴿٢٠﴾

20. فَاِذَا بَرِقَ الْبَصَرُ ﴿٧﴾
وَخَسَفَ الْقَمَرُ ﴿٨﴾
وَجُمِعَ الشَّمْسُ وَالْقَمَرُ ﴿٩﴾
يَقُوْلُ الْاِنْسَانُ يَوْمَئِذٍ اَيْنَ الْمَفَرُّ ﴿١٠﴾
كَلَّا لَا وَزَرَ ﴿١١﴾
اِلٰى رَبِّكَ يَوْمَئِذِ ۨالْمُسْتَقَرُّ ﴿١٢﴾
يُنَبَّؤُا الْاِنْسَانُ يَوْمَئِذٍۢ بِمَا قَدَّمَ
وَاَخَّرَ ﴿١٣﴾

On that day man will cry: Whither to flee!

Alas! No refuge!

Unto thy Lord is the recourse that day.

On that day man is told the tale of that which he hath sent before and left behind.

75:7–13

21. When the heaven is cleft asunder,

When the planets are dispersed,

When the seas are poured forth,

And the sepulchres are overturned,

A soul will know what it hath sent before (it) and what left behind.

82:1–5

22. So let man consider from what he is created.

He is created from a gushing fluid.

That issued from be–tween the loins and ribs.

86:5–7

21. إِذَا السَّمَآءُ انْفَطَرَتْ ۝١

وَإِذَا الْكَوَاكِبُ انْتَثَرَتْ ۝٢

وَإِذَا الْبِحَارُ فُجِّرَتْ ۝٣

وَإِذَا الْقُبُوْرُ بُعْثِرَتْ ۝٤

عَلِمَتْ نَفْسٌ مَّا قَدَّمَتْ وَأَخَّرَتْ ۝٥

22. فَلْيَنْظُرِ الْإِنْسَانُ مِمَّ خُلِقَ ۝٥

خُلِقَ مِنْ مَّآءٍ دَافِقٍ ۝٦

يَّخْرُجُ مِنْ بَيْنِ الصُّلْبِ وَالتَّرَآئِبِ ۝٧

See also: Creation of Man, Creation of Universe.

QUR'ĀN'S CHALLENGE TO SCEPTICS

1. And if ye are in doubt concerning that which We reveal unto Our slave (Muhammad), then produce a sûrah of the like thereof, and call your witnesses beside Allah if ye are truthful.

And if ye do it not— and ye can never do it— then guard yourselves against the Fire prepared for disbelievers, whose fuel is of men and stones.

2:23–24

2. And this Qur'an is not such as could ever be invented despite of Allah; but it is a confirmation of that which was before it and an exposition of that which is decreed for mankind—Therein is no doubt—from the Lord of the Worlds.

Or say they: He hath invented it? Say: Then bring a sûrah like unto it, and call (for help) on all ye can besides Allah, if ye are truthful.

10:37–38

3. Or they say: He hath invented it. Say: Then bring ten sûrahs, the like thereof, invented, and call on everyone ye can beside Allah, if ye are truthful!

11:13

4. Say: Verily, though mankind and the jinn, should assemble to produce the like of this Qur'ān they could not produce the like thereof though they were helpers one of another.

17:88

5. Or say they: He hath invented it? Nay, but they will not believe!

Then let them produce speech the like thereof, if they are truthful.

52:33–34

1. وَإِنْ كُنْتُمْ فِي رَيْبٍ مِّمَّا نَزَّلْنَا عَلَىٰ عَبْدِنَا
فَأْتُوا بِسُورَةٍ مِّنْ مِّثْلِهِ وَادْعُوا شُهَدَآءَكُمْ
مِّنْ دُونِ اللّٰهِ إِنْ كُنْتُمْ صٰدِقِينَ ﴿٢٣﴾
فَإِنْ لَّمْ تَفْعَلُوا وَلَنْ تَفْعَلُوا فَاتَّقُوا النَّارَ الَّتِي
وَقُودُهَا النَّاسُ وَالْحِجَارَةُ أُعِدَّتْ لِلْكٰفِرِينَ ﴿٢٤﴾

2. وَمَا كَانَ هٰذَا الْقُرْاٰنُ أَنْ يُّفْتَرٰى مِنْ دُونِ اللّٰهِ
وَلٰكِنْ تَصْدِيقَ الَّذِي بَيْنَ يَدَيْهِ وَتَفْصِيلَ الْكِتٰبِ
لَا رَيْبَ فِيهِ مِنْ رَّبِّ الْعٰلَمِينَ ﴿٣٧﴾
أَمْ يَقُولُونَ افْتَرٰىهُ قُلْ فَأْتُوا بِسُورَةٍ مِّثْلِهِ
وَادْعُوا مَنِ اسْتَطَعْتُمْ مِّنْ دُونِ اللّٰهِ إِنْ كُنْتُمْ
صٰدِقِينَ ﴿٣٨﴾

3. أَمْ يَقُولُونَ افْتَرٰىهُ قُلْ فَأْتُوا بِعَشْرِ
سُوَرٍ مِّثْلِهِ مُفْتَرَيٰتٍ وَّادْعُوا مَنِ
اسْتَطَعْتُمْ مِّنْ دُونِ اللّٰهِ إِنْ كُنْتُمْ
صٰدِقِينَ ﴿١٣﴾

4. قُلْ لَّئِنِ اجْتَمَعَتِ الْإِنْسُ وَالْجِنُّ عَلٰى أَنْ يَّأْتُوا
بِمِثْلِ هٰذَا الْقُرْاٰنِ لَا يَأْتُونَ بِمِثْلِهِ وَلَوْ كَانَ
بَعْضُهُمْ لِبَعْضٍ ظَهِيرًا ﴿٨٨﴾

5. أَمْ يَقُولُونَ تَقَوَّلَهُ بَلْ لَّا يُؤْمِنُونَ ﴿٣٣﴾
فَلْيَأْتُوا بِحَدِيثٍ مِّثْلِهِ إِنْ كَانُوا
صٰدِقِينَ ﴿٣٤﴾

See also: Incomparability of Qur'ān

QUR'ĀNIC PRAYERS

1. Thee (alone) we worship; Thee (alone) we ask for help.

Show us the straight path,

The path of those whom Thou hast favoured;

Not (the path) of those who earn Thine anger nor of those who go astray.

1:4–7

2. Our Lord! And make us submissive unto Thee and of our seed a nation submissive unto Thee, and show us our ways of worship, and relent toward us. Lo! Thou, only Thou, art the Relenting, the Merciful.

2:128

3. Our Lord! Condemn us not if we forget, or miss the mark! Our Lord! Lay not on us such a burden as Thou didst lay on those before us! Our Lord! Impose not on us that which we have not the strength to bear! Pardon us, absolve us and have mercy on us, Thou, our Protector, and give us victory over the disbelieving folk.

2:286

4. Our Lord! Cause not our hearts to stray after Thou hast guided us, and bestow upon us mercy from Thy Presence. Lo! Thou, only Thou art the Bestower.

Our Lord! it is Thou Who gatherest mankind together to a Day of which there is no doubt. Lo! Allah faileth not to keep the tryst

3:8–9

1. إِيَّاكَ نَعْبُدُ وَإِيَّاكَ نَسْتَعِينُ ۝
اِهْدِنَا الصِّرَاطَ الْمُسْتَقِيمَ ۝
صِرَاطَ الَّذِينَ أَنْعَمْتَ عَلَيْهِمْ غَيْرِ
الْمَغْضُوبِ عَلَيْهِمْ وَلَا الضَّالِّينَ ۝

2. رَبَّنَا وَاجْعَلْنَا مُسْلِمَيْنِ لَكَ وَمِنْ ذُرِّيَّتِنَا
أُمَّةً مُسْلِمَةً لَكَ وَأَرِنَا مَنَاسِكَنَا وَتُبْ
عَلَيْنَا إِنَّكَ أَنْتَ التَّوَّابُ الرَّحِيمُ ۝١٢٨

3. رَبَّنَا لَا تُؤَاخِذْنَا إِنْ نَسِينَا أَوْ أَخْطَأْنَا رَبَّنَا وَلَا
تَحْمِلْ عَلَيْنَا إِصْرًا كَمَا حَمَلْتَهُ عَلَى الَّذِينَ مِنْ
قَبْلِنَا رَبَّنَا وَلَا تُحَمِّلْنَا مَا لَا طَاقَةَ لَنَا بِهِ وَ
اعْفُ عَنَّا وَاغْفِرْ لَنَا وَارْحَمْنَا أَنْتَ مَوْلَانَا
فَانْصُرْنَا عَلَى الْقَوْمِ الْكَافِرِينَ ۝٢٨٦

4. رَبَّنَا لَا تُزِغْ قُلُوبَنَا بَعْدَ إِذْ هَدَيْتَنَا وَهَبْ لَنَا مِنْ
لَدُنْكَ رَحْمَةً إِنَّكَ أَنْتَ الْوَهَّابُ ۝٨
رَبَّنَا إِنَّكَ جَامِعُ النَّاسِ لِيَوْمٍ لَا رَيْبَ
فِيهِ إِنَّ اللَّهَ لَا يُخْلِفُ الْمِيعَادَ ۝

5. قُلِ اللَّهُمَّ مَالِكَ الْمُلْكِ تُؤْتِي الْمُلْكَ
مَنْ تَشَاءُ وَتَنْزِعُ الْمُلْكَ مِمَّنْ تَشَاءُ وَ
تُعِزُّ مَنْ تَشَاءُ وَتُذِلُّ مَنْ تَشَاءُ بِيَدِكَ
الْخَيْرُ إِنَّكَ عَلَىٰ كُلِّ شَيْءٍ قَدِيرٌ ۝

5. Say: O Allah! Owner of Sovereignty! Thou givest sovereignty unto whom Thou wilt, and Thou withdrawest sovereignty from whom Thou wilt. Thou exaltest whom Thou wilt and Thou abasest whom Thou wilt. In Thy hand is the good. Lo! Thou art Able to do all things.

Thou causest the night to pass into the day, and Thou causet the day to pass into the night. And Thou bringest forth the living from the dead, and Thou bringest forth the dead from the living. And Thou givest sustenance to whom Thou choosest, without stint.

3:26–27

6. Our Lord! Forgive us for our sins and wasted efforts, make our foot-hold sure, and give us victory over the disbelieving folk.

3:147

7. Such as remember Allah, standing, sitting, and reclining, and consider the creation of the heavens and the earth, (and say): Our Lord! Thou createdst not this in vain. Glory be to Thee! Preserve us from doom of Fire!

Our Lord! Whom Thou causest to enter the Fire: him indeed Thou hast confounded. For evil–doers there will be no helpers.

Our Lord! Lo! We have heard a crier calling unto Faith: "Believe ye in your Lord!" So we believed. Our Lord! Therefor forgive us our sins, and remit from us our evil deeds, and make us die the death of the righteous!

Our Lord! And give us that which Thou hast promised to us by Thy messengers. Confound us not upon the Day of Resurrection. Lo! Thou breakest not the tryst.

3:191–194

تُولِجُ الَّيْلَ فِي النَّهَارِ وَ تُولِجُ النَّهَارَ فِي
الَّيْلِ وَ تُخْرِجُ الْحَيَّ مِنَ الْمَيِّتِ وَ تُخْرِجُ
الْمَيِّتَ مِنَ الْحَيِّ وَ تَرْزُقُ مَنْ تَشَآءُ
بِغَيْرِ حِسَابٍ ○

6. رَبَّنَا اغْفِرْ لَنَا ذُنُوبَنَا وَ إِسْرَافَنَا فِي
أَمْرِنَا وَ ثَبِّتْ أَقْدَامَنَا وَ انْصُرْنَا
عَلَى الْقَوْمِ الْكٰفِرِينَ ○

7. الَّذِينَ يَذْكُرُونَ اللّٰهَ قِيٰمًا وَ قُعُودًا وَ عَلٰى
جُنُوبِهِمْ وَ يَتَفَكَّرُونَ فِي خَلْقِ السَّمٰوٰتِ
وَ الْأَرْضِ رَبَّنَا مَا خَلَقْتَ هٰذَا بَاطِلًا
سُبْحٰنَكَ فَقِنَا عَذَابَ النَّارِ ○
رَبَّنَآ إِنَّكَ مَنْ تُدْخِلِ النَّارَ فَقَدْ
أَخْزَيْتَهُ وَ مَا لِلظّٰلِمِينَ مِنْ أَنْصَارٍ ○
رَبَّنَآ إِنَّنَا سَمِعْنَا مُنَادِيًا يُّنَادِي لِلْإِيمَانِ
أَنْ آمِنُوا بِرَبِّكُمْ فَآمَنَّا رَبَّنَا فَاغْفِرْ لَنَا
ذُنُوبَنَا وَ كَفِّرْ عَنَّا سَيِّاٰتِنَا وَ تَوَفَّنَا مَعَ الْأَبْرَارِ ○
رَبَّنَا وَ آتِنَا مَا وَعَدْتَّنَا عَلٰى رُسُلِكَ وَ لَا
تُخْزِنَا يَوْمَ الْقِيٰمَةِ إِنَّكَ لَا تُخْلِفُ الْمِيعَادَ ○

8. رَبِّ اجْعَلْنِي مُقِيمَ الصَّلٰوةِ وَ مِنْ
ذُرِّيَّتِي رَبَّنَا وَ تَقَبَّلْ دُعَآءِ ○
رَبَّنَا اغْفِرْ لِي وَ لِوَالِدَيَّ وَ لِلْمُؤْمِنِينَ
يَوْمَ يَقُومُ الْحِسَابُ ○

8. My Lord! Make me to establish proper worship, and some of my posterity (also); our Lord! and accept the prayer.

Our Lord! Forgive me and my parents and believers on the day when the account is cast.

14:40–41

9. And say: My Lord! Cause me to come in with a firm incoming and to go out with a firm outgoing. And give me from Thy presence a sustaining Power.

17:80

10. My Lord! Relieve my mind.

And ease my task for me;

And loose a knot from my tongue,

That, they may understand my saying,

Appoint for me a henchman from my folk,

20:25–29

11. My Lord! Increase me in knowledge.

20:114

12. And say: My Lord! Cause me to land at a blessed landing place, for Thou art Best of all who bring to land.

23:29

13. And say: My Lord! I seek refuge in Thee from suggestions of the evil ones,

And I seek refuge in Thee, my Lord, lest they be present with me,

23:97–98

14. And Say: My Lord! Forgive and have mercy, for Thou art Best of all who show mercy!

23:118

15. Our Lord! Make us not a prey for those who disbelieve, and forgive us, our Lord! Lo! Thou, only Thou, art the Mighty, the Wise.

60:5

16. My Lord! Forgive me and my parents and him who entereth my house believing, and believing men and believing women, and increase not the wrong–doers in aught save ruin.

71:28

9. وَقُل رَّبِّ أَدْخِلْنِي مُدْخَلَ صِدْقٍ وَأَخْرِجْنِي مُخْرَجَ
صِدْقٍ وَاجْعَل لِّي مِن لَّدُنكَ سُلْطَانًا نَّصِيرًا ﴿٨٠﴾

10. قَالَ رَبِّ اشْرَحْ لِي صَدْرِي ﴿٢٥﴾
وَيَسِّرْ لِي أَمْرِي ﴿٢٦﴾
وَاحْلُلْ عُقْدَةً مِّن لِّسَانِي ﴿٢٧﴾
يَفْقَهُوا قَوْلِي ﴿٢٨﴾
وَاجْعَل لِّي وَزِيرًا مِّنْ أَهْلِي ﴿٢٩﴾

11. رَّبِّ زِدْنِي عِلْمًا ﴿١١٤﴾

12. وَقُل رَّبِّ أَنزِلْنِي مُنزَلًا مُّبَارَكًا
وَأَنتَ خَيْرُ الْمُنزِلِينَ ﴿٢٩﴾

13. وَقُل رَّبِّ أَعُوذُ بِكَ مِنْ هَمَزَاتِ
الشَّيَاطِينِ ﴿٩٧﴾
وَأَعُوذُ بِكَ رَبِّ أَن يَحْضُرُونِ ○

14. وَقُل رَّبِّ اغْفِرْ وَارْحَمْ وَأَنتَ
خَيْرُ الرَّاحِمِينَ ﴿١١٨﴾

15. رَبَّنَا لَا تَجْعَلْنَا فِتْنَةً لِّلَّذِينَ كَفَرُوا
وَاغْفِرْ لَنَا رَبَّنَا إِنَّكَ أَنتَ الْعَزِيزُ
الْحَكِيمُ ﴿٥﴾

16. رَّبِّ اغْفِرْ لِي وَلِوَالِدَيَّ وَلِمَن
دَخَلَ بَيْتِيَ مُؤْمِنًا وَلِلْمُؤْمِنِينَ
وَالْمُؤْمِنَاتِ وَلَا تَزِدِ الظَّالِمِينَ إِلَّا تَبَارًا ﴿٢٨﴾

17. Say: I seek refuge in the Lord of Day break,
From the evil of that which He created;
From the evil of the darkness when it is intense,
And from the evil of malignant witchcraft,
And from the evil of the envier when he envieth.
113:1–5

17. قُلْ اَعُوْذُ بِرَبِّ الْفَلَقِ ۝١
مِنْ شَرِّ مَا خَلَقَ ۝٢
وَمِنْ شَرِّ غَاسِقٍ اِذَا وَقَبَ ۝٣
وَمِنْ شَرِّ النَّفّٰثٰتِ فِى الْعُقَدِ ۝٤
وَمِنْ شَرِّ حَاسِدٍ اِذَا حَسَدَ ۝٥

18. Say: I seek refuge in the Lord of mankind,
The King of mankind,
The God of mankind,
From the evil of the sneaking whisperer,
Who whispereth in the hearts of mankind,
Of the jinn and of mankind.
114:1–6

18. قُلْ اَعُوْذُ بِرَبِّ النَّاسِ ۝١
مَلِكِ النَّاسِ ۝٢
اِلٰهِ النَّاسِ ۝٣
مِنْ شَرِّ الْوَسْوَاسِ الْخَنَّاسِ ۝٤
الَّذِىْ يُوَسْوِسُ فِىْ صُدُوْرِ النَّاسِ ۝٥
مِنَ الْجِنَّةِ وَالنَّاسِ ۝٦

○

Ref: 2:129,250,285; 3:16,38,53,173; 4:75; 7:23,47,89,126,151,155–156; 10:85–86,88; 11:47; 12:101; 14:38; 17:24; 18:10; 19:4–6; 21:83,87–89; 23:93–94,118; 25:74; 26:83–89; 27:19; 28:16,21–22,24; 40:7–8; 46:15; 59:10; 60:4; 66:8,11.

QUR'ĀNIC PROPHECIES

1. He it is Who hath sent His messenger with the guidance and the Religion of Truth, that He may cause it to prevail over all religions, however much the idolaters may be averse.

9:33

2. And those who became fugitives for the cause of Allah after they had been oppressed, We verily shall give them goodly lodging in the world, and surely the reward of the Hereafter is greater, if they but knew;

16:41

3. Allah hath promised such of you as believe and do good works that He will surely make them to succeed (the present rulers) in the earth even as He caused those who were before them to succeed (others); and that He will surely establish for them their religion which He hath approved for them, and will give them in exchange safety after their fear. They serve Me. They ascribe nothing as partner unto Me. Those who disbelieve henceforth, they are the miscreants.

24:55

4. Lo! He Who hath given thee the Qurān for a law will surely bring thee home again. Say: My Lord is Best Aware of him who bringeth guidance and him who is in error manifest.

28:85

5. The Romans have been defeated.

In the nearer land, and

1. هُوَ الَّذِيٓ اَرْسَلَ رَسُوْلَهٗ بِالْهُدٰى وَ
دِيْنِ الْحَقِّ لِيُظْهِرَهٗ عَلَى الدِّيْنِ كُلِّهٖ ۙ
وَلَوْ كَرِهَ الْمُشْرِكُوْنَ ﴿۳۳﴾

2. وَالَّذِيْنَ هَاجَرُوْا فِي اللّٰهِ مِنْۢ بَعْدِ
مَا ظُلِمُوْا لَنُبَوِّئَنَّهُمْ فِي الدُّنْيَا حَسَنَةً ؕ
وَلَاَجْرُ الْاٰخِرَةِ اَكْبَرُ ۘ لَوْ كَانُوْا يَعْلَمُوْنَ ﴿۴۱﴾

3. وَعَدَ اللّٰهُ الَّذِيْنَ اٰمَنُوْا مِنْكُمْ وَعَمِلُوا
الصّٰلِحٰتِ لَيَسْتَخْلِفَنَّهُمْ فِي الْاَرْضِ
كَمَا اسْتَخْلَفَ الَّذِيْنَ مِنْ قَبْلِهِمْ ۪
وَلَيُمَكِّنَنَّ لَهُمْ دِيْنَهُمُ الَّذِي ارْتَضٰى
لَهُمْ وَلَيُبَدِّلَنَّهُمْ مِّنْۢ بَعْدِ خَوْفِهِمْ
اَمْنًا ؕ يَعْبُدُوْنَنِيْ لَا يُشْرِكُوْنَ بِيْ
شَيْئًا ؕ وَمَنْ كَفَرَ بَعْدَ ذٰلِكَ
فَاُولٰٓئِكَ هُمُ الْفٰسِقُوْنَ ﴿۵۵﴾

4. اِنَّ الَّذِيْ فَرَضَ عَلَيْكَ الْقُرْاٰنَ
لَرَآدُّكَ اِلٰى مَعَادٍ ؕ قُلْ رَّبِّيْٓ اَعْلَمُ
مَنْ جَآءَ بِالْهُدٰى وَمَنْ هُوَ فِيْ
ضَلٰلٍ مُّبِيْنٍ ﴿۸۵﴾

5. غُلِبَتِ الرُّوْمُ ۙ﴿۲﴾
فِيْٓ اَدْنَى الْاَرْضِ وَهُمْ مِّنْۢ بَعْدِ
غَلَبِهِمْ سَيَغْلِبُوْنَ ۙ﴿۳﴾
فِيْ بِضْعِ سِنِيْنَ ؕ لِلّٰهِ الْاَمْرُ مِنْ
قَبْلُ وَمِنْۢ بَعْدُ ؕ وَيَوْمَئِذٍ يَّفْرَحُ
الْمُؤْمِنُوْنَ ۙ﴿۴﴾

they, after their defeat will be victorious.

Within ten years– Allah's is the command in the former case and in the latter–and in that the believers will rejoice.

In Allah's help to victory He helpeth to victory whom He will. He is the Mighty, the Merciful.

It is a promise of Allah.

Allah faileth not His promise, but most of mankind know not.

30:2-6

6. Allah hath fulfilled the vision for His messenger in very truth. Ye shall indeed enter the Inviolable Place of Worship, if Allah will, secure, (having your hair) shaven and cut, not fearing. But He knoweth that which ye know not, and hath given you a near victory beforehand.

48:27

7. Are your disbelievers better than those, or have ye some immunity in the Scriptures?

Or say they: We are a host victorious?

The hosts will all be routed and will turn and flee.

54:43–45

بِنَصْرِ اللّٰهِ ؕ يَنْصُرُ مَنْ يَّشَآءُ ؕ وَهُوَ
الْعَزِيْزُ الرَّحِيْمُ ۝٥
وَعْدَ اللّٰهِ ؕ لَا يُخْلِفُ اللّٰهُ وَعْدَهٗ وَلٰكِنَّ
اَكْثَرَ النَّاسِ لَا يَعْلَمُوْنَ ۝٦

6. لَقَدْ صَدَقَ اللّٰهُ رَسُوْلَهُ الرُّءْيَا
بِالْحَقِّ ۚ لَتَدْخُلُنَّ الْمَسْجِدَ الْحَرَامَ
اِنْ شَآءَ اللّٰهُ اٰمِنِيْنَ ۙ مُحَلِّقِيْنَ
رُءُوْسَكُمْ وَمُقَصِّرِيْنَ ۙ لَا تَخَافُوْنَ ؕ
فَعَلِمَ مَا لَمْ تَعْلَمُوْا فَجَعَلَ مِنْ دُوْنِ
ذٰلِكَ فَتْحًا قَرِيْبًا ۝٢٧

7. اَكُفَّارُكُمْ خَيْرٌ مِّنْ اُولٰٓئِكُمْ اَمْ
لَكُمْ بَرَآءَةٌ فِى الزُّبُرِ ۝٤٣
اَمْ يَقُوْلُوْنَ نَحْنُ جَمِيْعٌ مُّنْتَصِرٌ ۝٤٤
سَيُهْزَمُ الْجَمْعُ وَيُوَلُّوْنَ الدُّبُرَ ۝٤٥

○

RAIN

1. And the water which Allah sendeth down from the sky, thereby reviving the earth after its death.

2:164

1. وَمَآ أَنْزَلَ اللّٰهُ مِنَ السَّمَآءِ مِنْ مَّآءٍ
فَأَحْيَا بِهِ الْأَرْضَ بَعْدَ مَوْتِهَا

2. He sendeth down water from the sky, so that valleys flow according to their measure, and the flood beareth (on its surface) swelling foam—from that which they smelt in the fire in order to make ornaments and tools riseth a foam like unto it—thus Allah coineth (the similitude of) the true and the false. Then, as for the foam, it passeth away as scum upon the banks, while, as for that which is of use to mankind, it remaineth in the earth. Thus Allah coineth the similitudes.

13:17

2. أَنْزَلَ مِنَ السَّمَآءِ مَآءً فَسَالَتْ أَوْدِيَةٌۢ
بِقَدَرِهَا فَاحْتَمَلَ السَّيْلُ زَبَدًا رَّابِيًا ۚ
وَمِمَّا يُوقِدُونَ عَلَيْهِ فِي النَّارِ ابْتِغَآءَ
حِلْيَةٍ أَوْ مَتَاعٍ زَبَدٌ مِّثْلُهُ ۚ كَذٰلِكَ
يَضْرِبُ اللّٰهُ الْحَقَّ وَالْبَاطِلَ ۚ
فَأَمَّا الزَّبَدُ فَيَذْهَبُ جُفَآءً ۚ وَأَمَّا مَا
يَنْفَعُ النَّاسَ فَيَمْكُثُ فِي الْأَرْضِ ۚ
كَذٰلِكَ يَضْرِبُ اللّٰهُ الْأَمْثَالَ ۝١٧

3. And He it is Who sendeth down the saving rain after they have despaired, and spreadeth out His mercy. He is the Protecting Friend, the Praise-worthy.

42:28

3. وَهُوَ الَّذِي يُنَزِّلُ الْغَيْثَ مِنْ بَعْدِ
مَا قَنَطُوا وَيَنْشُرُ رَحْمَتَهُ ۚ وَهُوَ
الْوَلِيُّ الْحَمِيدُ ۝٢٨

○

RAMADHAN

1. The month of *Ramadhan* in which was revealed the *Qur'ān*, a guidance for mankind, and clear proofs of the guidance, and the Criterion (of right and wrong). And whosoever of you is present, let him fast the month.

2:185

1. شَهْرُ رَمَضَانَ الَّذِي أُنْزِلَ فِيهِ الْقُرْآنُ
هُدًى لِّلنَّاسِ وَبَيِّنٰتٍ مِّنَ الْهُدٰى وَ
الْفُرْقَانِ ۚ فَمَنْ شَهِدَ مِنْكُمُ الشَّهْرَ
فَلْيَصُمْهُ

RAIN

Ref: 2:22,164; 6:99; 7:50,84; 8:11; 13:17; 14:32; 15:22; 16:10,65; 20:53; 22:5,63; 23:18; 25:48; 27:60; 30:24; 31:10; 32:27; 35:27; 50:9.

See also: Agriculture, Clouds.

RAMADHAN

Ref: 2:44,113,129,151,252; 3:58,101,108,113; 8:31; 10:15, 61; 13:30; 19:58; 22:72; 23:66; 27:92; 28:3,45,59; 29:48; 31:7; 39:71; 45:6,8; 62:2; 65:11; 98:2.

RECITATION OF QUR'ĀN

1. Those unto whom We have given the Scripture, who read it with the right reading, those believe in it. And whoso disbelieveth in it, those are they who are the losers.

2:121

2. Allah verily hath shown grace to the believers by sending unto them a messenger of their own who reciteth unto them His revelations, and causeth them to grow, and teacheth them the Scripture and wisdom, although before (he came to them) they were in flagrant error.

3:164

3. And when the Qur'an is recited, give ear to it and pay heed, that ye may obtain mercy.

7:204

4. They only are the (true) believers whose hearts feel fear when Allah is mentioned, and when the revelations of Allah are recited unto them they increase their faith, and who trust in their Lord;

8:2

5. And when thou recitest the Qur'ān, seek refuge in Allah from Satan the outcast.

16:98

6. Lo! those who read the Scripture of Allah, and establish worship, and spend of that which We have bestowed on them secretly and openly, they look forward to imperishable gain.

That He will pay them their wages and increase them of His grace. Lo! He is Forgiving, Responsive.

35:29–30

1. اَلَّذِيْنَ اٰتَيْنٰهُمُ الْكِتٰبَ يَتْلُوْنَهٗ حَقَّ تِلَاوَتِهٖ
اُولٰٓئِكَ يُؤْمِنُوْنَ بِهٖ ؕ وَمَنْ يَّكْفُرْ بِهٖ فَاُولٰٓئِكَ
هُمُ الْخٰسِرُوْنَ ﴿۱۲۱﴾

2. لَقَدْ مَنَّ اللّٰهُ عَلَى الْمُؤْمِنِيْنَ اِذْ بَعَثَ فِيْهِمْ رَسُوْلًا
مِّنْ اَنْفُسِهِمْ يَتْلُوْا عَلَيْهِمْ اٰيٰتِهٖ وَيُزَكِّيْهِمْ وَ
يُعَلِّمُهُمُ الْكِتٰبَ وَالْحِكْمَةَ ۚ وَاِنْ كَانُوْا مِنْ قَبْلُ
لَفِيْ ضَلٰلٍ مُّبِيْنٍ ﴿۱۶۴﴾

3 وَاِذَا قُرِئَ الْقُرْاٰنُ فَاسْتَمِعُوْا لَهٗ وَ
اَنْصِتُوْا لَعَلَّكُمْ تُرْحَمُوْنَ ﴿۲۰۴﴾

4. اِنَّمَا الْمُؤْمِنُوْنَ الَّذِيْنَ اِذَا ذُكِرَ اللّٰهُ
وَجِلَتْ قُلُوْبُهُمْ وَاِذَا تُلِيَتْ عَلَيْهِمْ اٰيٰتُهٗ
زَادَتْهُمْ اِيْمَانًا وَّعَلٰى رَبِّهِمْ يَتَوَكَّلُوْنَ ﴿۲﴾

5. فَاِذَا قَرَاْتَ الْقُرْاٰنَ فَاسْتَعِذْ بِاللّٰهِ
مِنَ الشَّيْطٰنِ الرَّجِيْمِ ﴿۹۸﴾

6. اِنَّ الَّذِيْنَ يَتْلُوْنَ كِتٰبَ اللّٰهِ وَاَقَامُوا
الصَّلٰوةَ وَاَنْفَقُوْا مِمَّا رَزَقْنٰهُمْ سِرًّا وَّ
عَلَانِيَةً يَّرْجُوْنَ تِجَارَةً لَّنْ تَبُوْرَ ﴿۲۹﴾
لِيُوَفِّيَهُمْ اُجُوْرَهُمْ وَيَزِيْدَهُمْ مِّنْ
فَضْلِهٖ ؕ اِنَّهٗ غَفُوْرٌ شَكُوْرٌ ﴿۳۰﴾

RECOMPENSE

1. Whosoever desireth the reward of the world, We bestow on him thereof; and whoso desireth the reward of the Hereafter, We bestow on him thereof, We shall reward the thankful.

3: 145

2. Whoso desireth the reward of the world, (let him know that) with Allah is the reward of the world and the Hereafter. Allah is ever Hearer, Seer.

4:134

3. Wealth and children are an ornament of life of the world. But the good deeds which endure are better in thy Lord's sight for reward, and better in respect of hope.

18:46

1. وَمَنْ يُّرِدْ ثَوَابَ الدُّنْيَا نُؤْتِهٖ مِنْهَا ۚ وَمَنْ
يُّرِدْ ثَوَابَ الْاٰخِرَةِ نُؤْتِهٖ مِنْهَا ۚ وَ
سَنَجْزِى الشّٰكِرِيْنَ ○

2. مَنْ كَانَ يُرِيْدُ ثَوَابَ الدُّنْيَا فَعِنْدَ اللّٰهِ
ثَوَابُ الدُّنْيَا وَ الْاٰخِرَةِ ۚ وَ كَانَ اللّٰهُ
سَمِيْعًا بَصِيْرًا

3. اَلْمَالُ وَالْبَنُوْنَ زِيْنَةُ الْحَيٰوةِ الدُّنْيَا ۚ
وَالْبٰقِيٰتُ الصّٰلِحٰتُ خَيْرٌ عِنْدَ رَبِّكَ
ثَوَابًا وَّ خَيْرٌ اَمَلًا

○

Ref: 3: 148, 195; 4: 134; 18: 31, 44, 46; 28: 80.
See also: Sin.

RECORDING ANGELS

1. He is the Omnipotent over His slaves. He sendeth guardians over you until, when death cometh unto one of you, Our messengers receive him, and they neglect not.

6:61

2. Or deem they that We cannot hear their secret thoughts and private confidences? Nay, but Our envoys, present with them, do record.

43:80

3. We verily created a man and We know what his soul whispereth to him, and We are nearer to him than his jugular vein.

When the two Receivers receive (him), seated on the right hand and on the left,

He uttereth no word but there is with him an observer ready.

50:16–18

4. Lo! there are above you guardians,

Generous and recording,

Who know (all) that ye do.

82:10–12

5. By the heaven and the Morning Star

—Ah, what will tell thee what the Morning Star is!

—The piercing Star!

No human soul but hath a guardian over it.

86:1–4

1. وَهُوَ الْقَاهِرُ فَوْقَ عِبَادِهِ وَيُرْسِلُ عَلَيْكُمْ
حَفَظَةً حَتَّى إِذَا جَاءَ أَحَدَكُمُ الْمَوْتُ
تَوَفَّتْهُ رُسُلُنَا وَهُمْ لَا يُفَرِّطُونَ ﴿٦١﴾

2. أَمْ يَحْسَبُونَ أَنَّا لَا نَسْمَعُ سِرَّهُمْ
وَنَجْوَاهُمْ بَلَى وَرُسُلُنَا لَدَيْهِمْ يَكْتُبُونَ ﴿٨٠﴾

3. وَلَقَدْ خَلَقْنَا الْإِنْسَانَ وَنَعْلَمُ مَا
تُوَسْوِسُ بِهِ نَفْسُهُ وَنَحْنُ أَقْرَبُ
إِلَيْهِ مِنْ حَبْلِ الْوَرِيدِ ﴿١٦﴾
إِذْ يَتَلَقَّى الْمُتَلَقِّيَانِ عَنِ الْيَمِينِ وَ
عَنِ الشِّمَالِ قَعِيدٌ ﴿١٧﴾
مَا يَلْفِظُ مِنْ قَوْلٍ إِلَّا لَدَيْهِ رَقِيبٌ
عَتِيدٌ ﴿١٨﴾

4. وَإِنَّ عَلَيْكُمْ لَحَافِظِينَ ﴿١٠﴾
كِرَامًا كَاتِبِينَ ﴿١١﴾
يَعْلَمُونَ مَا تَفْعَلُونَ ﴿١٢﴾

5. وَالسَّمَاءِ وَالطَّارِقِ ﴿١﴾
وَمَا أَدْرَاكَ مَا الطَّارِقُ ﴿٢﴾
النَّجْمُ الثَّاقِبُ ﴿٣﴾
إِنْ كُلُّ نَفْسٍ لَمَّا عَلَيْهَا حَافِظٌ ﴿٤﴾

Ref: 10:21; 13:11.

See also: Angels, Scroll of Actions.

REFERENCE TO CERTAIN WOMEN

1. (Remember) when the wife of 'Imrān said: My Lord! I have vowed unto Thee that which is in my belly as a consecrated (offering). Accept it from me. Lo! Thou, only Thou, art the Hearer, the Knower!

And when she was delivered she said: My Lord! Lo! I am delivered of a female—Allah knew best of what she was delivered— the male is not as the female; and lo! I have named her Mary, and lo! I crave Thy protection for her and for her offspring from Satan the outcast.

3:35–36

2. Allah citeth an example for those who disbelieve: the wife of Noah and the wife of Lot, who were under two of Our righteous slaves yet betrayed them so that they (the husbands) availed them naught against Allah and it was said (unto them): Enter the Fire along with those who enter.

And Allah citeth an example for those who believe: the wife of Pharaoh when she said: My Lord! Build for me a home with thee in the Garden, and deliver me from Pharaoh and his work, and deliver me from evildoing folk;

1. اِذْ قَالَتِ امْرَاَتُ عِمْرٰنَ رَبِّ اِنِّيْ نَذَرْتُ
لَكَ مَا فِيْ بَطْنِيْ مُحَرَّرًا فَتَقَبَّلْ مِنِّيْ ۚ اِنَّكَ
اَنْتَ السَّمِيْعُ الْعَلِيْمُ ○
فَلَمَّا وَضَعَتْهَا قَالَتْ رَبِّ اِنِّيْ وَضَعْتُهَآ
اُنْثٰى ۗ وَاللّٰهُ اَعْلَمُ بِمَا وَضَعَتْ ۗ وَلَيْسَ
الذَّكَرُ كَالْاُنْثٰى ۚ وَاِنِّيْ سَمَّيْتُهَا مَرْيَمَ
وَاِنِّيْٓ اُعِيْذُهَا بِكَ وَذُرِّيَّتَهَا مِنَ
الشَّيْطٰنِ الرَّجِيْمِ ○

2. ضَرَبَ اللّٰهُ مَثَلًا لِّلَّذِيْنَ كَفَرُوا
امْرَاَتَ نُوْحٍ وَّامْرَاَتَ لُوْطٍ ۭ كَانَتَا
تَحْتَ عَبْدَيْنِ مِنْ عِبَادِنَا صَالِحَيْنِ
فَخَانَتٰهُمَا فَلَمْ يُغْنِيَا عَنْهُمَا مِنَ اللّٰهِ
شَيْـًٔا وَّقِيْلَ ادْخُلَا النَّارَ مَعَ الدّٰخِلِيْنَ ⑩
وَضَرَبَ اللّٰهُ مَثَلًا لِّلَّذِيْنَ اٰمَنُوا امْرَاَتَ
فِرْعَوْنَ ۘ اِذْ قَالَتْ رَبِّ ابْنِ لِيْ عِنْدَكَ
بَيْتًا فِي الْجَنَّةِ وَنَجِّنِيْ مِنْ فِرْعَوْنَ
وَعَمَلِهٖ وَنَجِّنِيْ مِنَ الْقَوْمِ الظّٰلِمِيْنَ ⑪
وَمَرْيَمَ ابْنَتَ عِمْرٰنَ الَّتِيْٓ اَحْصَنَتْ
فَرْجَهَا فَنَفَخْنَا فِيْهِ مِنْ رُّوْحِنَا
وَصَدَّقَتْ بِكَلِمٰتِ رَبِّهَا وَكُتُبِهٖ
وَكَانَتْ مِنَ الْقٰنِتِيْنَ ⑫

○

And Mary, daughter of 'Imran, whose body was chaste, therefor We breathed therein something of Our Spirit, And she put faith in the words of her Lord and His scriptures, and was of the obedient.

66: 10–12

Ref: 3:37,43,45; 4:156,171; 5:110,112, 114,116, 7:83; 11:71,81; 12:21,30,51; 15:60; 19:5,16-29; 27:23-44,57; 28:9,29,32; 51:29; 111:4.

See also: Women.

REFUTATON OF POLYTHEISM

1. They who are idolaters will say: Had Allah willed, we had not ascribed (unto Him) partners neither had our fathers, nor had we forbidden aught. Thus did those who were before them give the lie (to Allah's messengers) till they tasted of the fear of Us. Say: Have ye any knowledge that ye can adduce for us? Lo! ye follow naught but an opinion. Lo! ye do but guess.
6:148

2. They worship beside Allah that which neither hurteth them nor profiteth them, and they say: These are our intercessors with Allah. Say: Would ye inform Allah of (something) that He knoweth not in the heavens or in the earth? Praised be He and High Exalted above all that ye associate (with Him)!
10:18

3. On the Day when We gather them all together, then We say unto those who ascribed partners (unto Us): Stand back, ye and your (pretended) partners (of Allah)! And We separate them, the one from the other, and their (pretended) partners say: It was not us ye worshipped.

Allah sufficeth as a witness between us and you, that we were unaware of your worship.
10:28–29

4. And they have chosen

1. سَيَقُولُ الَّذِينَ أَشْرَكُوا لَوْ شَاءَ اللَّهُ مَا
أَشْرَكْنَا وَلَا آبَاؤُنَا وَلَا حَرَّمْنَا مِن شَيْءٍ
كَذَٰلِكَ كَذَّبَ الَّذِينَ مِن قَبْلِهِمْ حَتَّىٰ
ذَاقُوا بَأْسَنَا قُلْ هَلْ عِندَكُم مِّنْ عِلْمٍ
فَتُخْرِجُوهُ لَنَا إِن تَتَّبِعُونَ إِلَّا الظَّنَّ وَ
إِنْ أَنتُمْ إِلَّا تَخْرُصُونَ ﴿١٤٨﴾

2. وَيَعْبُدُونَ مِن دُونِ اللَّهِ مَا لَا يَضُرُّهُمْ
وَلَا يَنفَعُهُمْ وَيَقُولُونَ هَٰؤُلَاءِ شُفَعَاؤُنَا
عِندَ اللَّهِ قُلْ أَتُنَبِّئُونَ اللَّهَ بِمَا لَا يَعْلَمُ
فِي السَّمَاوَاتِ وَلَا فِي الْأَرْضِ سُبْحَانَهُ
وَتَعَالَىٰ عَمَّا يُشْرِكُونَ ﴿١٨﴾

3. وَيَوْمَ نَحْشُرُهُمْ جَمِيعًا ثُمَّ نَقُولُ لِلَّذِينَ أَشْرَكُوا
مَكَانَكُمْ أَنتُمْ وَشُرَكَاؤُكُمْ فَزَيَّلْنَا بَيْنَهُمْ وَقَالَ
شُرَكَاؤُهُم مَّا كُنتُمْ إِيَّانَا تَعْبُدُونَ ﴿٢٨﴾
فَكَفَىٰ بِاللَّهِ شَهِيدًا بَيْنَنَا وَبَيْنَكُمْ إِن كُنَّا عَنْ
عِبَادَتِكُمْ لَغَافِلِينَ ﴿٢٩﴾

4. وَاتَّخَذُوا مِن دُونِ اللَّهِ آلِهَةً لِّيَكُونُوا
لَهُمْ عِزًّا ﴿٨١﴾
كَلَّا ۚ سَيَكْفُرُونَ بِعِبَادَتِهِمْ وَيَكُونُونَ
عَلَيْهِمْ ضِدًّا ﴿٨٢﴾

5. وَقَالُوا اتَّخَذَ الرَّحْمَٰنُ وَلَدًا ﴿٨٨﴾
لَّقَدْ جِئْتُمْ شَيْئًا إِدًّا ﴿٨٩﴾
تَكَادُ السَّمَاوَاتُ يَتَفَطَّرْنَ مِنْهُ وَتَنشَقُّ
الْأَرْضُ وَتَخِرُّ الْجِبَالُ هَدًّا ﴿٩٠﴾

(other) gods beside Allah that they may be a power for them.

Nay, but they will deny their worship of them, and become opponents unto them.
19:81–82

5. And they say: The Beneficent hath taken unto Himself a son.

Assuredly ye utter a disastrous thing,

Whereby almost the heavens are torn, and the earth is split asunder and the mountains fall in ruins,

That ye ascribe unto the Beneficent a son,

When it is not meet for (the Majesty of) the Beneficent that He should choose a son.

There is none in the heavens and the earth but cometh unto the Beneficent as a slave.

19:88–93

6. And set not any other god along with Allah; lo! I am a plain warner unto you from Him.

51:51

7. Have ye thought upon Al-Lat and Al-'Uzza

And Manat the third the other?

Are yours the males and His the females?

That indeed were an unfair division!

They are but names which ye have named, ye and your fathers, for which Allah hath revealed no warrant. They follow but a guess and that which (they) themselves desire. And now the guidance from their Lord hath come unto them.

53:19–23

8. Say: Have ye thought: If (all) your water were to disappear into the earth, who then could bring you gushing water?

67:30

أَنْ دَعَوْا لِلرَّحْمَٰنِ وَلَدًا ﴿٩١﴾
وَمَا يَنبَغِي لِلرَّحْمَٰنِ أَن يَتَّخِذَ وَلَدًا ﴿٩٢﴾
إِن كُلُّ مَن فِي السَّمَاوَاتِ وَالْأَرْضِ
إِلَّا آتِي الرَّحْمَٰنِ عَبْدًا ﴿٩٣﴾

6. وَلَا تَجْعَلُوا مَعَ اللَّهِ إِلَٰهًا آخَرَ
إِنِّي لَكُم مِّنْهُ نَذِيرٌ مُّبِينٌ ﴿٥١﴾

7. أَفَرَأَيْتُمُ اللَّاتَ وَالْعُزَّىٰ ﴿١٩﴾
وَمَنَاةَ الثَّالِثَةَ الْأُخْرَىٰ ﴿٢٠﴾
أَلَكُمُ الذَّكَرُ وَلَهُ الْأُنثَىٰ ﴿٢١﴾
تِلْكَ إِذًا قِسْمَةٌ ضِيزَىٰ ﴿٢٢﴾
إِنْ هِيَ إِلَّا أَسْمَاءٌ سَمَّيْتُمُوهَا أَنتُمْ
وَآبَاؤُكُم مَّا أَنزَلَ اللَّهُ بِهَا مِن
سُلْطَانٍ إِن يَتَّبِعُونَ إِلَّا الظَّنَّ وَمَا
تَهْوَى الْأَنفُسُ وَلَقَدْ جَاءَهُم مِّن
رَّبِّهِمُ الْهُدَىٰ ﴿٢٣﴾

8. قُلْ أَرَأَيْتُمْ إِنْ أَصْبَحَ مَاؤُكُمْ غَوْرًا
فَمَن يَأْتِيكُم بِمَاءٍ مَّعِينٍ ﴿٣٠﴾

9. قُلْ يَا أَيُّهَا الْكَافِرُونَ ﴿١﴾
لَا أَعْبُدُ مَا تَعْبُدُونَ ﴿٢﴾
وَلَا أَنتُمْ عَابِدُونَ مَا أَعْبُدُ ﴿٣﴾
وَلَا أَنَا عَابِدٌ مَّا عَبَدتُّمْ ﴿٤﴾
وَلَا أَنتُمْ عَابِدُونَ مَا أَعْبُدُ ﴿٥﴾
لَكُمْ دِينُكُمْ وَلِيَ دِينِ ﴿٦﴾

9. Say: O disbelievers!

I worship not that which ye worship;

Nor worship ye that which I worship.

And I shall not worship that which ye worship.

Nor will ye worship that which I worship.

Unto you your religion, and unto me my religion.

109:1–6

Ref: 16:35; 22:73. See also: Monotheism

REFUTATION OF TRINITY

1. O People of the Scripture! Do not exaggerate in your religion nor utter aught concerning Allah save the truth. The Messiah, Jesus son of Mary, was only a messenger of Allah, and His word which He conveyed unto Mary, and a spirit from Him. So believe in Allah and His messengers, and say not "Three—Cease"! (it is) better for you!—Allah is only One God. Far is it removed from His Transcedent Majesty that He should have a son. His is all that is in the heavens and all that is in the earth. And Allah is sufficient as Defender.

The Messiah will never scorn to be a slave unto Allah, nor will the favoured angels. Whoso scorneth His service and is proud, all such will He assemble unto Him;

Then, as for those who believed and did good works, unto them will He pay their wages in full, adding unto them of His bounty; and as for those who were scornful and proud, them will He punish with a painful doom and they will not find for them, against Allah, any protecting friend or helper.

4: 171—173

2. They surely disbelieve who say: Lo! Allah is the

1. يٰاَهْلَ الْكِتٰبِ لَا تَغْلُوْا فِيْ دِيْنِكُمْ وَلَا تَقُوْلُوْا عَلَى
اللّٰهِ اِلَّا الْحَقَّ ۗ اِنَّمَا الْمَسِيْحُ عِيْسَى ابْنُ مَرْيَمَ رَسُوْلُ
اللّٰهِ وَكَلِمَتُهٗ ۚ اَلْقٰىهَآ اِلٰى مَرْيَمَ وَرُوْحٌ مِّنْهُ ۖ فَاٰمِنُوْا
بِاللّٰهِ وَرُسُلِهٖ ۚ وَلَا تَقُوْلُوْا ثَلٰثَةٌ ۗ اِنْتَهُوْا خَيْرًا
لَّكُمْ ۗ اِنَّمَا اللّٰهُ اِلٰهٌ وَّاحِدٌ ۗ سُبْحٰنَهٗٓ اَنْ يَّكُوْنَ لَهٗ
وَلَدٌ ۘ لَهٗ مَا فِى السَّمٰوٰتِ وَمَا فِى الْاَرْضِ ۗ وَكَفٰى
بِاللّٰهِ وَكِيْلًا ﴿١٧١﴾
لَنْ يَّسْتَنْكِفَ الْمَسِيْحُ اَنْ يَّكُوْنَ عَبْدًا
لِّلّٰهِ وَلَا الْمَلٰۤىِٕكَةُ الْمُقَرَّبُوْنَ ۗ وَمَنْ
يَّسْتَنْكِفْ عَنْ عِبَادَتِهٖ وَيَسْتَكْبِرْ
فَسَيَحْشُرُهُمْ اِلَيْهِ جَمِيْعًا ﴿١٧٢﴾
فَاَمَّا الَّذِيْنَ اٰمَنُوْا وَعَمِلُوا الصّٰلِحٰتِ فَيُوَفِّيْهِمْ
اُجُوْرَهُمْ وَيَزِيْدُهُمْ مِّنْ فَضْلِهٖ ۚ وَاَمَّا الَّذِيْنَ اسْتَنْكَفُوْا
وَاسْتَكْبَرُوْا فَيُعَذِّبُهُمْ عَذَابًا اَلِيْمًا ۙ وَّلَا يَجِدُوْنَ
لَهُمْ مِّنْ دُوْنِ اللّٰهِ وَلِيًّا وَّلَا نَصِيْرًا ﴿١٧٣﴾

2. لَقَدْ كَفَرَ الَّذِيْنَ قَالُوْٓا اِنَّ اللّٰهَ هُوَ
الْمَسِيْحُ ابْنُ مَرْيَمَ ۗ وَقَالَ الْمَسِيْحُ
يٰبَنِيْٓ اِسْرَاۤءِيْلَ اعْبُدُوا اللّٰهَ رَبِّيْ وَ
رَبَّكُمْ ۗ اِنَّهٗ مَنْ يُّشْرِكْ بِاللّٰهِ فَقَدْ
حَرَّمَ اللّٰهُ عَلَيْهِ الْجَنَّةَ وَمَاْوٰىهُ
النَّارُ ۗ وَمَا لِلظّٰلِمِيْنَ مِنْ اَنْصَارٍ ﴿٧٢﴾
لَقَدْ كَفَرَ الَّذِيْنَ قَالُوْٓا اِنَّ اللّٰهَ ثَالِثُ
ثَلٰثَةٍ ۘ وَمَا مِنْ اِلٰهٍ اِلَّآ اِلٰهٌ وَّاحِدٌ ۗ

Messiah, son of Mary. The Messiah (himself) said: O Children of Israel, worship Allah, my Lord and Your Lord. Lo! whoso ascribeth partners unto Allah, for him Allah hath forbidden Paradise. His abode is the Fire.

For evil–doers there will be no helpers.

They surely disbelieve who say: Lo! Allah is the third of three; when there is no God save the One God. If they desist not from so saying, a painful doom will fall on those of them who disbelieve.

5:72–73

3. The Messiah, son of Mary, was no other than a messenger, messengers (the like of whom) had passed away before him. And his mother was a saintly woman. And they both used to eat (earthly) food. See how We make the revelations clear for them, and see how they are turned away!

5:75

RELATIONS OF MUSLIMS WITH NON–MUSLIMS

1. O ye who believe! Take not for intimates others than your own folk, who would spare no pains to ruin you; they love to hamper you. Hatred is revealed by (the utterance of) their mouths, but that which their breasts hide is greater. We have made plain for you the revelations if ye will understand.

Lo! ye are those who love them though they love you not, and ye believe in all the Scriptures. When they fall in with you they say:

وَ إِنْ لَّمْ يَنْتَهُوْا عَمَّا يَقُوْلُوْنَ لَيَمَسَّنَّ
الَّذِيْنَ كَفَرُوْا مِنْهُمْ عَذَابٌ اَلِيْمٌ ۝٧٣

3. مَا الْمَسِيْحُ ابْنُ مَرْيَمَ اِلَّا رَسُوْلٌ ۚ
قَدْ خَلَتْ مِنْ قَبْلِهِ الرُّسُلُ ۗ وَ اُمُّهٗ
صِدِّيْقَةٌ ۗ كَانَا يَاْكُلٰنِ الطَّعَامَ ۗ
اُنْظُرْ كَيْفَ نُبَيِّنُ لَهُمُ الْاٰيٰتِ ثُمَّ
انْظُرْ اَنّٰى يُؤْفَكُوْنَ ۝٧٥

○

1. يٰاَيُّهَا الَّذِيْنَ اٰمَنُوْا لَا تَتَّخِذُوْا بِطَانَةً
مِّنْ دُوْنِكُمْ لَا يَاْلُوْنَكُمْ خَبَالًا ۗ وَدُّوْا مَا
عَنِتُّمْ ۚ قَدْ بَدَتِ الْبَغْضَآءُ مِنْ اَفْوَاهِهِمْ ۚ
وَ مَا تُخْفِيْ صُدُوْرُهُمْ اَكْبَرُ ۚ قَدْ بَيَّنَّا
لَكُمُ الْاٰيٰتِ اِنْ كُنْتُمْ تَعْقِلُوْنَ ○

هٰاَنْتُمْ اُولَآءِ تُحِبُّوْنَهُمْ وَلَا يُحِبُّوْنَكُمْ
وَ تُؤْمِنُوْنَ بِالْكِتٰبِ كُلِّهٖ ۚ وَ اِذَا لَقُوْكُمْ
قَالُوْٓا اٰمَنَّا ۖ وَاِذَا خَلَوْا عَضُّوْا عَلَيْكُمُ
الْاَنَامِلَ مِنَ الْغَيْظِ ۗ قُلْ مُوْتُوْا بِغَيْظِكُمْ ۗ
اِنَّ اللّٰهَ عَلِيْمٌۢ بِذَاتِ الصُّدُوْرِ ○

We believe; but when they go apart they bite their finger-tips at you, for rage. Say: Perish in your rage! Lo! Allah is Aware of what is hidden in (your) breasts.

3:118–119

REFUTATION OF TRINITY
See also: MONOTHEISM.

2. Revile not those unto whom they pray beside Allah lest they wrongfully revile Allah through ignorance. Thus unto every nation have We made their deed seem fair. Then unto their Lord is their return, and He will tell them what they used to do.

6:108

3. Keep to forgiveness (O Muhammad), and enjoin kindness, and turn away from the ignorant.

7:199

4. And if they incline to peace, incline thou also to it, and trust in Allah. Lo! He even He, is the Hearer, the Knower.

8:61

5. And if anyone of the idolaters seeketh thy protection (O Muhammad), then protect him so that he may hear the word of Allah, and afterward convey him to his place of safety. That is because they are a folk who know not.

How can there be a treaty with Allah and with His messenger for the idolaters save those with whom ye made a treaty at the Inviolable Place of Worship? So long as they are true to you, be true to them. Lo! Allah loveth those who keep their duty.

9:6–7

2. وَلَا تَسُبُّوا الَّذِينَ يَدْعُونَ مِن دُونِ اللَّهِ فَيَسُبُّوا اللَّهَ عَدْوًا بِغَيْرِ عِلْمٍ كَذَٰلِكَ زَيَّنَّا لِكُلِّ أُمَّةٍ عَمَلَهُمْ ثُمَّ إِلَىٰ رَبِّهِم مَّرْجِعُهُمْ فَيُنَبِّئُهُم بِمَا كَانُوا يَعْمَلُونَ

3. خُذِ الْعَفْوَ وَأْمُرْ بِالْعُرْفِ وَأَعْرِضْ عَنِ الْجَاهِلِينَ

4. وَإِن جَنَحُوا لِلسَّلْمِ فَاجْنَحْ لَهَا وَتَوَكَّلْ عَلَى اللَّهِ إِنَّهُ هُوَ السَّمِيعُ الْعَلِيمُ

5. وَإِنْ أَحَدٌ مِّنَ الْمُشْرِكِينَ اسْتَجَارَكَ فَأَجِرْهُ حَتَّىٰ يَسْمَعَ كَلَامَ اللَّهِ ثُمَّ أَبْلِغْهُ مَأْمَنَهُ ذَٰلِكَ بِأَنَّهُمْ قَوْمٌ لَّا يَعْلَمُونَ

كَيْفَ يَكُونُ لِلْمُشْرِكِينَ عَهْدٌ عِندَ اللَّهِ وَعِندَ رَسُولِهِ إِلَّا الَّذِينَ عَاهَدتُّمْ عِندَ الْمَسْجِدِ الْحَرَامِ فَمَا اسْتَقَامُوا لَكُمْ فَاسْتَقِيمُوا لَهُمْ إِنَّ اللَّهَ يُحِبُّ الْمُتَّقِينَ

6. فَأَعْرِضْ عَن مَّن تَوَلَّىٰ عَن ذِكْرِنَا وَلَمْ يُرِدْ إِلَّا الْحَيَاةَ الدُّنْيَا

6. Then withdraw (O Muhammad) from him who fleeth from Our remembrance and desireth but the life of the world.

53:29

See also: , Covenant, Muslim Nation.

RELATIVES

1. It is prescribed for you, when one of you approacheth death, if he leave wealth, that he bequeath unto parents and near relatives in kindness. (This is) a duty for all those who ward off (evil).
2:180

2. They ask thee, (O Muhammad), what they shall spend. Say: That which ye spend for good (must go) to parents and near kindred and orphans and the needy and the wayfarer.
2:215

3. And when kinsfolk and orphans and the needy are present at the division (of the heritage), bestow on them therefrom and speak kindly unto them.
4:8

4. Lo! Allah enjoineth justice and kindness, and giving to kinsfolk, and forbiddeth lewdness and abomination and wickedness. He exhorteth you in order that ye may take heed.
16:90

5. And let not those who possess dignity and ease among you swear not to give to the near of kin and to the needy, and to fugitives for the cause of Allah. Let them forgive and show indulgence. Yearn ye not that Allah may forgive you? Allah is Forgiving, Merciful.
24:22

1. كُتِبَ عَلَيْكُمْ إِذَا حَضَرَ أَحَدَكُمُ الْمَوْتُ إِن تَرَكَ خَيْرًا الْوَصِيَّةُ
لِلْوَالِدَيْنِ وَالْأَقْرَبِينَ بِالْمَعْرُوفِ ۖ حَقًّا عَلَى الْمُتَّقِينَ ﴿١٨٠﴾

2. يَسْأَلُونَكَ مَاذَا يُنفِقُونَ ۖ قُلْ مَا أَنفَقْتُم
مِّنْ خَيْرٍ فَلِلْوَالِدَيْنِ وَالْأَقْرَبِينَ وَالْيَتَامَىٰ
وَالْمَسَاكِينِ وَابْنِ السَّبِيلِ ۗ

3. وَإِذَا حَضَرَ الْقِسْمَةَ أُولُو الْقُرْبَىٰ وَالْيَتَامَىٰ
وَالْمَسَاكِينُ فَارْزُقُوهُم مِّنْهُ وَقُولُوا
لَهُمْ قَوْلًا مَّعْرُوفًا ﴿٨﴾

4. إِنَّ اللَّهَ يَأْمُرُ بِالْعَدْلِ وَالْإِحْسَانِ وَإِيتَاءِ ذِي
الْقُرْبَىٰ وَيَنْهَىٰ عَنِ الْفَحْشَاءِ وَالْمُنكَرِ وَالْبَغْيِ ۚ
يَعِظُكُمْ لَعَلَّكُمْ تَذَكَّرُونَ ﴿٩٠﴾

5. وَلَا يَأْتَلِ أُولُو الْفَضْلِ مِنكُمْ وَالسَّعَةِ
أَن يُؤْتُوا أُولِي الْقُرْبَىٰ وَالْمَسَاكِينَ
وَالْمُهَاجِرِينَ فِي سَبِيلِ اللَّهِ ۖ وَلْيَعْفُوا
وَلْيَصْفَحُوا ۗ أَلَا تُحِبُّونَ أَن يَغْفِرَ
اللَّهُ لَكُمْ ۗ وَاللَّهُ غَفُورٌ رَّحِيمٌ ﴿٢٢﴾

Ref: 2:177; 9:113; 33:6.

See also: Family and its Rights, Obligations Towards Relatives.

RELIGION

1. And who forsaketh the religion of Abraham save him who befooleth himself? Verily We chose him in the world, and lo! in the Hereafter he is among the righteous.

When his Lord said unto him: Surrender! he said: I have surrendered to the Lord of the Worlds.

The same did Abraham enjoin upon his sons, and also Jacob, (saying): O my sons! Lo! Allah hath chosen for you the (true) religion; therefore die not save as men who have surrendered (unto Him).

2:130–132

2. And they will not cease from fighting against you till they have made you renegades from your religion, if they can. And whoso becometh a renegade and dieth in his disbelief such are they whose works have fallen both in the world and the Hereafter. Such are rightful owners of the Fire: they will abide therein.

2:217

3. There is no compulsion in religion. The right direction is henceforth distinct from error. And he who rejecteth false deities and believeth in Allah hath grasped a firm handhold which will never break. Allah is Hearer, Knower.

2:256

4. Lo! religion with Allah

1. وَمَنْ يَّرْغَبُ عَنْ مِّلَّةِ اِبْرٰهٖمَ اِلَّا مَنْ سَفِهَ
نَفْسَهٗ ؕ وَلَقَدِ اصْطَفَيْنٰهُ فِي الدُّنْيَا ۚ وَاِنَّهٗ
فِي الْاٰخِرَةِ لَمِنَ الصّٰلِحِيْنَ ﴿١٣٠﴾
اِذْ قَالَ لَهٗ رَبُّهٗٓ اَسْلِمْ ۙ قَالَ اَسْلَمْتُ لِرَبِّ الْعٰلَمِيْنَ ﴿١٣١﴾
وَوَصّٰى بِهَآ اِبْرٰهٖمُ بَنِيْهِ وَيَعْقُوْبُ ؕ يٰبَنِيَّ اِنَّ
اللّٰهَ اصْطَفٰى لَكُمُ الدِّيْنَ فَلَا تَمُوْتُنَّ اِلَّا
وَاَنْتُمْ مُّسْلِمُوْنَ ﴿١٣٢﴾

2. وَلَا يَزَالُوْنَ يُقَاتِلُوْنَكُمْ حَتّٰى يَرُدُّوْكُمْ عَنْ
دِيْنِكُمْ اِنِ اسْتَطَاعُوْا ؕ وَمَنْ يَّرْتَدِدْ
مِنْكُمْ عَنْ دِيْنِهٖ فَيَمُتْ وَهُوَ كَافِرٌ
فَاُولٰٓئِكَ حَبِطَتْ اَعْمَالُهُمْ فِي الدُّنْيَا
وَالْاٰخِرَةِ ۚ وَاُولٰٓئِكَ اَصْحٰبُ النَّارِ ۚ هُمْ
فِيْهَا خٰلِدُوْنَ ﴿٢١٧﴾

3. لَآ اِكْرَاهَ فِي الدِّيْنِ ۙ قَدْ تَّبَيَّنَ الرُّشْدُ مِنَ
الْغَيِّ ۚ فَمَنْ يَّكْفُرْ بِالطَّاغُوْتِ وَيُؤْمِنْۢ بِاللّٰهِ
فَقَدِ اسْتَمْسَكَ بِالْعُرْوَةِ الْوُثْقٰى ۗ لَا انْفِصَامَ
لَهَا ۗ وَاللّٰهُ سَمِيْعٌ عَلِيْمٌ ﴿٢٥٦﴾

4. اِنَّ الدِّيْنَ عِنْدَ اللّٰهِ الْاِسْلَامُ ۗ وَمَا
اخْتَلَفَ الَّذِيْنَ اُوْتُوا الْكِتٰبَ اِلَّا مِنْۢ بَعْدِ
مَا جَآءَهُمُ الْعِلْمُ بَغْيًۢا بَيْنَهُمْ ۗ وَمَنْ يَّكْفُرْ
بِاٰيٰتِ اللّٰهِ فَاِنَّ اللّٰهَ سَرِيْعُ الْحِسَابِ ﴿١٩﴾

(is) the Surrender (to His Will and Guidance). Those who (formerly) received the Scripture differed only after knowledge came unto them, through transgression among themselves. Whoso disbelieveth the revelations of Allah (will find that) lo! Allah is swift at reckoning.

3:19

5. Seek they other than the religion of Allah, when unto Him submitteth whosoever is in the heavens and the earth, willingly, or unwillingly, and unto Him they will be returned.

3:83

6. Who is better in religion than he who surrendereth his purpose to Allah while doing good (to men) and followeth the tradition of Abraham, the upright? Allah (Himself) chose Abraham for friend.

4:125

7. This day have I perfected your religion for you and completed My favour unto you, and have chosen for you as religion AL-ISLAM.

5:3

8. O ye who believe! Whoso of you becometh a renegade from his religion, (know that in his stead) Allah will bring a people whom He loveth and who love Him, humble toward believers, stern toward disbelievers, striving in the way of Allah, and fearing not the blame of any blamer. Such is the grace of Allah which He giveth unto whom He will. Allah is All-Embracing, All-Knowing.

5:54

9. O ye who believe! Choose not for friends such of those who received the Scripture before you, and of the disbelievers, as make a jest and sport of your religion.

5. أَفَغَيْرَ دِينِ اللّٰهِ يَبْغُونَ وَلَهٗٓ أَسْلَمَ
مَنْ فِي السَّمٰوٰتِ وَالْأَرْضِ طَوْعًا وَّ
كَرْهًا وَّإِلَيْهِ يُرْجَعُونَ ۝

6. وَمَنْ أَحْسَنُ دِينًا مِّمَّنْ أَسْلَمَ وَجْهَهٗ
لِلّٰهِ وَهُوَ مُحْسِنٌ وَّاتَّبَعَ مِلَّةَ إِبْرٰهِيمَ
حَنِيفًا ۗ وَاتَّخَذَ اللّٰهُ إِبْرٰهِيمَ خَلِيلًا ۝

7. اَلْيَوْمَ أَكْمَلْتُ لَكُمْ دِينَكُمْ وَأَتْمَمْتُ
عَلَيْكُمْ نِعْمَتِي وَرَضِيتُ لَكُمُ الْإِسْلَامَ
دِينًا ۚ

8. يٰٓأَيُّهَا الَّذِينَ اٰمَنُوا مَنْ يَّرْتَدَّ مِنْكُمْ
عَنْ دِينِهٖ فَسَوْفَ يَأْتِي اللّٰهُ بِقَوْمٍ
يُّحِبُّهُمْ وَيُحِبُّونَهٗٓ ۙ أَذِلَّةٍ عَلَى
الْمُؤْمِنِينَ أَعِزَّةٍ عَلَى الْكٰفِرِينَ ۫
يُجَاهِدُونَ فِي سَبِيلِ اللّٰهِ وَلَا يَخَافُونَ
لَوْمَةَ لَآئِمٍ ۚ ذٰلِكَ فَضْلُ اللّٰهِ يُؤْتِيهِ
مَنْ يَّشَآءُ ۚ وَاللّٰهُ وَاسِعٌ عَلِيمٌ ۝

9. يٰٓأَيُّهَا الَّذِينَ اٰمَنُوا لَا تَتَّخِذُوا الَّذِينَ
اتَّخَذُوا دِينَكُمْ هُزُوًا وَّلَعِبًا مِّنَ الَّذِينَ
أُوتُوا الْكِتٰبَ مِنْ قَبْلِكُمْ وَالْكُفَّارَ
أَوْلِيَآءَ ۚ وَاتَّقُوا اللّٰهَ إِنْ كُنْتُمْ مُّؤْمِنِينَ ۝

10. إِنَّ الَّذِينَ فَرَّقُوا دِينَهُمْ وَكَانُوا شِيَعًا
لَّسْتَ مِنْهُمْ فِي شَيْءٍ ۚ إِنَّمَآ أَمْرُهُمْ إِلَى
اللّٰهِ ثُمَّ يُنَبِّئُهُمْ بِمَا كَانُوا يَفْعَلُونَ ۝

But keep your duty to Allah if ye are true believers.

5:57

10. Lo! As for those who sunder their religion and become schismatics, no concern at all hast thou with them. Their case will go to Allah, Who then will tell them what they used to do.

6:159

11. Who took their religion for a sport and pastime, and whom the life of the world beguiled. So this Day We have forgotten them even as they forgot the meeting of this Day and as they used to deny Our tokens.

7:51

12. And fight them until persecution is no more, and religion is all for Allah. But if they cease, then lo! Allah is Seer of what they do.

8:39

13. But if they repent and establish worship and pay the poor–due, then are they your brethren in religion. We detail Our revelations for a people who have knowledge.

And if they break their pledges after their treaty (hath been made with you) and assail your religion, then fight the heads of disbelief–Lo! they have no binding oaths–in order that they may desist.

9:11–12

14. He it is Who hath sent His messenger with the guid–ance and the Religion of Truth, that He may cause it to prevail over all religions, however much the idolaters may be averse.

9:33

15. And the believers should not all go out to fight. Of every troop of them, a party only should go forth, that they (who are left behind)

11. الَّذِينَ اتَّخَذُوا دِينَهُمْ لَهْوًا وَلَعِبًا وَ
غَرَّتْهُمُ الْحَيَاةُ الدُّنْيَا فَالْيَوْمَ نَنْسَاهُمْ
كَمَا نَسُوا لِقَاءَ يَوْمِهِمْ هَٰذَا وَمَا
كَانُوا بِآيَاتِنَا يَجْحَدُونَ

12. وَقَاتِلُوهُمْ حَتَّىٰ لَا تَكُونَ فِتْنَةٌ وَيَكُونَ
الدِّينُ كُلُّهُ لِلَّهِ فَإِنِ انْتَهَوْا فَإِنَّ اللَّهَ
بِمَا يَعْمَلُونَ بَصِيرٌ

13. فَإِنْ تَابُوا وَأَقَامُوا الصَّلَاةَ وَآتَوُا الزَّكَاةَ فَإِخْوَانُكُمْ
فِي الدِّينِ وَنُفَصِّلُ الْآيَاتِ لِقَوْمٍ يَعْلَمُونَ
وَإِنْ نَكَثُوا أَيْمَانَهُمْ مِنْ بَعْدِ عَهْدِهِمْ وَطَعَنُوا فِي
دِينِكُمْ فَقَاتِلُوا أَئِمَّةَ الْكُفْرِ إِنَّهُمْ لَا أَيْمَانَ لَهُمْ
لَعَلَّهُمْ يَنْتَهُونَ

14. هُوَ الَّذِي أَرْسَلَ رَسُولَهُ بِالْهُدَىٰ وَ
دِينِ الْحَقِّ لِيُظْهِرَهُ عَلَى الدِّينِ كُلِّهِ
وَلَوْ كَرِهَ الْمُشْرِكُونَ

15. وَمَا كَانَ الْمُؤْمِنُونَ لِيَنْفِرُوا كَافَّةً فَلَوْلَا
نَفَرَ مِنْ كُلِّ فِرْقَةٍ مِنْهُمْ طَائِفَةٌ لِيَتَفَقَّهُوا
فِي الدِّينِ وَلِيُنْذِرُوا قَوْمَهُمْ إِذَا رَجَعُوا
إِلَيْهِمْ لَعَلَّهُمْ يَحْذَرُونَ

16. قُلْ يَا أَيُّهَا النَّاسُ إِنْ كُنْتُمْ فِي شَكٍّ
مِنْ دِينِي فَلَا أَعْبُدُ الَّذِينَ تَعْبُدُونَ

may gain sound knowledge in religion, and that they may warn their folk when they return to them, so that they may beware.

9:122

16. Say (O Muhmmad): O mankind! If ye are in doubt of my religion, then (know that) I worship not

those whom ye worship instead of Allah, but I worship Allah Who causeth you to die, and I have been commanded to be of the believers.

And, (O Muhammad), set thy purpose resolutely for religion, as a man by nature upright, and be not of those who ascribe partners (to Allah).

10:104–105

17. Those whom ye worship beside Him are but names which ye have named, ye and your fathers. Allah hath revealed no sanction for them. The decision rests with Allah only, Who hath commanded you that ye worship none save Him. This is the Right religion, but most men know not.

12:40

18. And strive for Allah with the endeavour which is His right. He hath chosen you and hath not laid upon you in religion any hardship; the faith of your father Abraham (is yours). He hath named you Muslims of old time and in this (Scripture), that the messenger may be a witness against you, and that ye may be witnesses against mankind. So establish worship, pay the poor–due, and hold fast to Allah. He is your Protecting Friend. A blessed Patron and a blessed Helper!

22:78

مِنْ دُوْنِ اللّٰهِ وَلٰكِنْ اَعْبُدُ اللّٰهَ الَّذِيْ
يَتَوَفّٰىكُمْ ۖ وَاُمِرْتُ اَنْ اَكُوْنَ مِنَ الْمُؤْمِنِيْنَ ﴿١٠٤﴾
وَاَنْ اَقِمْ وَجْهَكَ لِلدِّيْنِ حَنِيْفًا ۚ وَلَا
تَكُوْنَنَّ مِنَ الْمُشْرِكِيْنَ ﴿١٠٥﴾

17. مَا تَعْبُدُوْنَ مِنْ دُوْنِهٖۤ اِلَّاۤ اَسْمَآءً
سَمَّيْتُمُوْهَاۤ اَنْتُمْ وَاٰبَآؤُكُمْ مَّاۤ اَنْزَلَ اللّٰهُ
بِهَا مِنْ سُلْطٰنٍ ۗ اِنِ الْحُكْمُ اِلَّا لِلّٰهِ ۗ اَمَرَ
اَلَّا تَعْبُدُوْۤا اِلَّاۤ اِيَّاهُ ۗ ذٰلِكَ الدِّيْنُ الْقَيِّمُ
وَلٰكِنَّ اَكْثَرَ النَّاسِ لَا يَعْلَمُوْنَ ﴿٤٠﴾

18. وَجَاهِدُوْا فِي اللّٰهِ حَقَّ جِهَادِهٖ ۗ هُوَ
اجْتَبٰىكُمْ وَمَا جَعَلَ عَلَيْكُمْ فِي الدِّيْنِ
مِنْ حَرَجٍ ۗ مِلَّةَ اَبِيْكُمْ اِبْرٰهِيْمَ ۗ
هُوَ سَمّٰىكُمُ الْمُسْلِمِيْنَ ۙ مِنْ قَبْلُ وَفِيْ
هٰذَا لِيَكُوْنَ الرَّسُوْلُ شَهِيْدًا عَلَيْكُمْ
وَتَكُوْنُوْا شُهَدَآءَ عَلَى النَّاسِ ۖ
فَاَقِيْمُوا الصَّلٰوةَ وَاٰتُوا الزَّكٰوةَ
وَاعْتَصِمُوْا بِاللّٰهِ ۗ هُوَ مَوْلٰىكُمْ ۚ فَنِعْمَ
الْمَوْلٰى وَنِعْمَ النَّصِيْرُ ﴿٧٨﴾

19. فَاَقِمْ وَجْهَكَ لِلدِّيْنِ حَنِيْفًا ۗ فِطْرَتَ
اللّٰهِ الَّتِيْ فَطَرَ النَّاسَ عَلَيْهَا ۗ لَا
تَبْدِيْلَ لِخَلْقِ اللّٰهِ ۗ ذٰلِكَ الدِّيْنُ
الْقَيِّمُ ۙ وَلٰكِنَّ اَكْثَرَ النَّاسِ لَا يَعْلَمُوْنَ ﴿٣٠﴾

19. So set thy purpose (O Muhammad) for religion as a man by nature upright—the nature (framed) of Allah, in which He hath created man. There is no altering (the laws of) Allah's creation. That is the right religion, but most

men know not—

Turning unto Him (only); and be careful of your duty unto Him, and establish worship, and be not of those who ascribe partners (unto Him);

Of those who split up their religion and became schismatics, each sect exulting in its tenets.

30:30–32

20. He hath ordained for you that religion which He commended unto Noah, and that which We inspire in thee (Muhammad), and that which We commended unto Abraham and Moses and Jesus, saying: Establish the religion, and be not divided therein. Dreadful for the idolaters is that unto which thou callest them. Allah chooseth for Himself whom He will, and guideth unto Himself him who turneth (toward Him).

42:13

21. Allah forbiddeth you not those who warred not against you on account of religion and drove you not out from your homes, that ye should show them kindness and deal justly with them. Lo! Allah loveth the just dealers.

Allah forbiddeth you only those who warred against you on account of religion and have driven you out from

مُنِيبِينَ إِلَيْهِ وَاتَّقُوهُ وَأَقِيمُوا الصَّلٰوةَ
وَلَا تَكُونُوا مِنَ الْمُشْرِكِينَ ﴿٣١﴾
مِنَ الَّذِينَ فَرَّقُوا دِينَهُمْ وَكَانُوا
شِيَعًا كُلُّ حِزْبٍ بِمَا لَدَيْهِمْ فَرِحُونَ ﴿٣٢﴾

20. شَرَعَ لَكُمْ مِنَ الدِّينِ مَا وَصّٰى بِهِ
نُوحًا وَالَّذِي أَوْحَيْنَا إِلَيْكَ وَمَا
وَصَّيْنَا بِهِ إِبْرٰهِيمَ وَمُوسٰى وَعِيسٰى
أَنْ أَقِيمُوا الدِّينَ وَلَا تَتَفَرَّقُوا فِيهِ
كَبُرَ عَلَى الْمُشْرِكِينَ مَا تَدْعُوهُمْ إِلَيْهِ
اللَّهُ يَجْتَبِي إِلَيْهِ مَنْ يَشَاءُ وَيَهْدِي
إِلَيْهِ مَنْ يُنِيبُ ﴿١٣﴾

21. لَا يَنْهٰكُمُ اللَّهُ عَنِ الَّذِينَ لَمْ يُقٰتِلُوكُمْ
فِي الدِّينِ وَلَمْ يُخْرِجُوكُمْ مِنْ دِيٰرِكُمْ
أَنْ تَبَرُّوهُمْ وَتُقْسِطُوا إِلَيْهِمْ إِنَّ
اللَّهَ يُحِبُّ الْمُقْسِطِينَ ﴿٨﴾

إِنَّمَا يَنْهٰكُمُ اللَّهُ عَنِ الَّذِينَ قٰتَلُوكُمْ فِي الدِّينِ
وَأَخْرَجُوكُمْ مِنْ دِيٰرِكُمْ وَظٰهَرُوا عَلٰى
إِخْرَاجِكُمْ أَنْ تَوَلَّوْهُمْ وَمَنْ يَتَوَلَّهُمْ
فَأُولٰئِكَ هُمُ الظّٰلِمُونَ ﴿٩﴾

○

your homes and helped to drive you out, that ye make friends of them. Whosoever maketh friends of them—(All) such are wrongdoers.

60:8–9

Ref: 2:120, 135; 3:95; 4:146, 171; 5:77; 6:138, 162; 7:29, 88–89; 8:49, 72; 9:36; 10:22; 12:37–38; 14:13; 16:52, 123; 18:20; 24:2, 25, 55; 29:65; 31:32; 33:5; 38:7; 39:2–3, 11, 14; 40:14, 26, 65; 42:8–9, 21; 48:28; 61:9; 98:4–5. **See also:** No compulsion in Religion, Religious Prejudice, Sectarianism.

RELIGIOUS PREJUDICE

1. Is it ever so that when there cometh unto you a messenger (from Allah) with that which ye yourselves desire not, ye grow arrogant, and some ye disbelieve and some ye slay?

And they say: Our hearts are hardened. Nay, but Allah hath cursed them for their unbelief. Little is that which they believe.

2:87–88

2. Neither those who disbelieve among the People of the Scripture nor the idolaters love that there should be sent down unto you any good thing from your Lord. But Allah chooseth for His mercy whom He will, and Allah is of Infinite Bounty.

2:105

3. Many of the People of the Scripture long to make you disbelievers after your belief, through envy on their own account, after the truth hath become manifest unto them. Forgive and be indulgent (toward them) until Allah give command. Lo! Allah is Able to do all things.

2:109

4. And they say: None entereth Paradise unless he be a Jew or a Christian. These are their own desires. Say: Bring your proof (of what ye state) if ye are truthful.

2:111

1. أَفَكُلَّمَا جَآءَكُمْ رَسُولٌۢ بِمَا لَا تَهْوَىٰٓ أَنفُسُكُمُ
ٱسْتَكْبَرْتُمْ فَفَرِيقًا كَذَّبْتُمْ وَفَرِيقًا
تَقْتُلُونَ ﴿٨٧﴾

وَقَالُوا قُلُوبُنَا غُلْفٌۢ بَل لَّعَنَهُمُ ٱللَّهُ بِكُفْرِهِمْ
فَقَلِيلًا مَّا يُؤْمِنُونَ ﴿٨٨﴾

2. مَّا يَوَدُّ ٱلَّذِينَ كَفَرُوا مِنْ أَهْلِ ٱلْكِتَٰبِ وَ
لَا ٱلْمُشْرِكِينَ أَن يُنَزَّلَ عَلَيْكُم مِّنْ خَيْرٍ
مِّن رَّبِّكُمْ وَٱللَّهُ يَخْتَصُّ بِرَحْمَتِهِۦ مَن
يَشَآءُ وَٱللَّهُ ذُو ٱلْفَضْلِ ٱلْعَظِيمِ ﴿١٠٥﴾

3. وَدَّ كَثِيرٌ مِّنْ أَهْلِ ٱلْكِتَٰبِ لَوْ يَرُدُّونَكُم مِّنۢ
بَعْدِ إِيمَٰنِكُمْ كُفَّارًا حَسَدًا مِّنْ عِندِ أَنفُسِهِم مِّنۢ
بَعْدِ مَا تَبَيَّنَ لَهُمُ ٱلْحَقُّ فَٱعْفُوا وَٱصْفَحُوا حَتَّىٰ
يَأْتِيَ ٱللَّهُ بِأَمْرِهِۦٓ إِنَّ ٱللَّهَ عَلَىٰ كُلِّ شَىْءٍ قَدِيرٌ ﴿١٠٩﴾

4. وَقَالُوا لَن يَدْخُلَ ٱلْجَنَّةَ إِلَّا مَن كَانَ هُودًا
أَوْ نَصَٰرَىٰ تِلْكَ أَمَانِيُّهُمْ قُلْ هَاتُوا بُرْهَٰنَكُمْ
إِن كُنتُمْ صَٰدِقِينَ ﴿١١١﴾

5. وَقَالَتِ ٱلْيَهُودُ لَيْسَتِ ٱلنَّصَٰرَىٰ عَلَىٰ شَىْءٍ
وَقَالَتِ ٱلنَّصَٰرَىٰ لَيْسَتِ ٱلْيَهُودُ عَلَىٰ شَىْءٍ
وَهُمْ يَتْلُونَ ٱلْكِتَٰبَ كَذَٰلِكَ قَالَ ٱلَّذِينَ لَا
يَعْلَمُونَ مِثْلَ قَوْلِهِمْ فَٱللَّهُ يَحْكُمُ بَيْنَهُمْ
يَوْمَ ٱلْقِيَٰمَةِ فِيمَا كَانُوا فِيهِ يَخْتَلِفُونَ ﴿١١٣﴾

5. And the Jews say the Christians follow nothing (true), and the Christians say the Jews follow nothing (true); yet both are readers of the Scripture. Even thus speak those who know not. Allah will judge between them on the Day of Resurrection concerning that wherein they differ.

2:113

6. And a party of the People of the Scripture say: Believe in that which hath been revealed, unto those who believe at the opening of the day, and disbelieve at the end thereof, in order that they may return;

And believe not save in one who followeth your religion—Say (O Muhammad): Lo! the guidance is Allah's Guidance — that any one is given the like of that which was given unto you or that they may argue with you in the presence of their Lord. Say (O Muhammad): Lo! the bounty is in Allah's hand. He bestoweth it on whom He will. Allah is All—Embracing, All—Knowing.

He selecteth for His mercy whom He will. Allah is of Infinite Bounty.

3:72—74

6. وَقَالَتْ طَّائِفَةٌ مِّنْ أَهْلِ الْكِتٰبِ اٰمِنُوْا
بِالَّذِيْٓ أُنْزِلَ عَلَى الَّذِيْنَ اٰمَنُوْا وَجْهَ
النَّهَارِ وَاكْفُرُوْٓا اٰخِرَهٗ لَعَلَّهُمْ يَرْجِعُوْنَ ۝

وَلَا تُؤْمِنُوْٓا اِلَّا لِمَنْ تَبِعَ دِيْنَكُمْ ۗ قُلْ اِنَّ
الْهُدٰى هُدَى اللّٰهِ ۙ اَنْ يُّؤْتٰٓى اَحَدٌ مِّثْلَ
مَآ اُوْتِيْتُمْ اَوْ يُحَآجُّوْكُمْ عِنْدَ رَبِّكُمْ ۗ قُلْ
اِنَّ الْفَضْلَ بِيَدِ اللّٰهِ ۚ يُؤْتِيْهِ مَنْ يَّشَآءُ ۗ
وَاللّٰهُ وَاسِعٌ عَلِيْمٌ ۝

يَّخْتَصُّ بِرَحْمَتِهٖ مَنْ يَّشَآءُ ۗ وَاللّٰهُ
ذُو الْفَضْلِ الْعَظِيْمِ ۝

7. Hast thou not seen those unto whom a portion of the Scripture hath been given, how they believe in idols and false deities and how they say of those (idolaters) who disbelieve: "These are more rightly guided than those who believe?"

4:51

7. اَلَمْ تَرَ اِلَى الَّذِيْنَ اُوْتُوْا نَصِيْبًا مِّنَ الْكِتٰبِ
يُؤْمِنُوْنَ بِالْجِبْتِ وَالطَّاغُوْتِ وَيَقُوْلُوْنَ
لِلَّذِيْنَ كَفَرُوْا هٰٓؤُلَآءِ اَهْدٰى مِنَ
الَّذِيْنَ اٰمَنُوْا سَبِيْلًا ۝

Ref: 2:10, 13, 75,—76, 89—90, 142, 146; 5:71; 63:7; 64:6.

See also: **No Compulsion in Religion, Sectarianism.**

REMEMBRANCE OF ALLAH

1. Therefore remember Me, I will remember you. Give thanks to Me, and reject not Me.

2:152

2. Such as remember Allah, standing, sitting, and reclining, and consider the creation of the heavens and the earth, (and say): Our Lord! Thou createdst not this in vain. Glory be to Thee! Preserve us from doom of Fire!

3:191

3. And do thou (O Muhammad) remember thy Lord within thyself humbly and with awe, below thy breath, at morn and evening. And be thou not of the neglectful.

7:205

4. Who have believed and whose hearts have rest in the remembrance of Allah. Verily in the remembrance of Allah do hearts find rest!

13:28

5. Recite that which hath been inspired in thee of the Scripture, and establish worship. Lo! worship preserveth from lewdness and iniquity, and verily remembrance of Allah is more important. And Allah knoweth what ye do.

29:45

6. O ye who believe! Remember Allah with much remembrance,

1. فَاذْكُرُونِيٓ أَذْكُرْكُمْ وَاشْكُرُوا لِي وَلَا تَكْفُرُونِ ﴿١٥٢﴾

2. الَّذِينَ يَذْكُرُونَ اللَّهَ قِيَامًا وَقُعُودًا وَعَلَىٰ
جُنُوبِهِمْ وَيَتَفَكَّرُونَ فِي خَلْقِ السَّمٰوٰتِ
وَالْأَرْضِ رَبَّنَا مَا خَلَقْتَ هٰذَا بَاطِلًا
سُبْحٰنَكَ فَقِنَا عَذَابَ النَّارِ ○

3. وَاذْكُر رَّبَّكَ فِي نَفْسِكَ تَضَرُّعًا وَخِيفَةً
وَدُونَ الْجَهْرِ مِنَ الْقَوْلِ بِالْغُدُوِّ
وَالْآصَالِ وَلَا تَكُن مِّنَ الْغٰفِلِينَ ﴿٢٠٥﴾

4. الَّذِينَ اٰمَنُوا وَتَطْمَئِنُّ قُلُوبُهُم بِذِكْرِ
اللَّهِ أَلَا بِذِكْرِ اللَّهِ تَطْمَئِنُّ الْقُلُوبُ ﴿٢٨﴾

5. اُتْلُ مَآ أُوحِيَ إِلَيْكَ مِنَ الْكِتٰبِ
وَأَقِمِ الصَّلٰوةَ إِنَّ الصَّلٰوةَ تَنْهٰى عَنِ
الْفَحْشَآءِ وَالْمُنكَرِ وَلَذِكْرُ اللَّهِ أَكْبَرُ
وَاللَّهُ يَعْلَمُ مَا تَصْنَعُونَ ﴿٤٥﴾

6. يٰٓأَيُّهَا الَّذِينَ اٰمَنُوا اذْكُرُوا اللَّهَ ذِكْرًا
كَثِيرًا ﴿٤١﴾

وَسَبِّحُوهُ بُكْرَةً وَأَصِيلًا ﴿٤٢﴾

7. أَلَمْ يَأْنِ لِلَّذِينَ اٰمَنُوٓا أَن تَخْشَعَ
قُلُوبُهُمْ لِذِكْرِ اللَّهِ وَمَا نَزَلَ مِنَ
الْحَقِّ وَلَا يَكُونُوا كَالَّذِينَ أُوتُوا

And glorify Him early and late.

33:41–42

7. Is not the time ripe for the hearts of those who believe to submit to Allah's reminder and to the truth which is revealed, that they become not as those who received the Scripture of old

but the term was prolonged for them and so their hearts were hardened, and many of them are evil–livers.

57:16

8. O ye who believe! When the call is heard for the prayer of the day of congregation, haste unto the remembrance of Allah and leave your trading. That is better for you if ye did but know.

And when the prayer is ended, then disperse in the land and seek of Allah's bounty, and remember Allah much, that ye may be successful.

62:9–10

9. O ye who believe! Let not your wealth nor your children distract you from remembrance of Allah. Those who do so, they are the losers.

63:9

10. Remember the name of thy Lord at morn and evening.

And worship Him (a portion) of the night. And glorify Him through the livelong night.

76:25–26

11. He is successful who groweth,

And remembereth the name of his Lord, so prayeth.

87:14–15

الْكِتٰبَ مِنْ قَبْلُ فَطَالَ عَلَيْهِمُ
الْاَمَدُ فَقَسَتْ قُلُوْبُهُمْ ؕ وَكَثِيْرٌ
مِّنْهُمْ فٰسِقُوْنَ ﴿۱۶﴾

8. يٰۤاَيُّهَا الَّذِيْنَ اٰمَنُوْۤا اِذَا نُوْدِىَ
لِلصَّلٰوةِ مِنْ يَّوْمِ الْجُمُعَةِ فَاسْعَوْا
اِلٰى ذِكْرِ اللّٰهِ وَذَرُوا الْبَيْعَ ؕ ذٰلِكُمْ
خَيْرٌ لَّكُمْ اِنْ كُنْتُمْ تَعْلَمُوْنَ ﴿۹﴾
فَاِذَا قُضِيَتِ الصَّلٰوةُ فَانْتَشِرُوْا
فِى الْاَرْضِ وَابْتَغُوْا مِنْ فَضْلِ اللّٰهِ
وَاذْكُرُوا اللّٰهَ كَثِيْرًا لَّعَلَّكُمْ تُفْلِحُوْنَ ﴿۱۰﴾

9. يٰۤاَيُّهَا الَّذِيْنَ اٰمَنُوْا لَا تُلْهِكُمْ اَمْوَالُكُمْ
وَلَاۤ اَوْلَادُكُمْ عَنْ ذِكْرِ اللّٰهِ ۚ وَمَنْ
يَّفْعَلْ ذٰلِكَ فَاُولٰۤئِكَ هُمُ الْخٰسِرُوْنَ ﴿۹﴾

10. وَاذْكُرِ اسْمَ رَبِّكَ بُكْرَةً وَّاَصِيْلًا ﴿۲۵﴾ۚ
وَمِنَ الَّيْلِ فَاسْجُدْ لَهٗ وَسَبِّحْهُ
لَيْلًا طَوِيْلًا ﴿۲۶﴾

11. قَدْ اَفْلَحَ مَنْ تَزَكّٰى ﴿۱۴﴾ۙ
وَذَكَرَ اسْمَ رَبِّهٖ فَصَلّٰى ﴿۱۵﴾ؕ

O

Ref: 2:203; 4:103; 18:24; 26:227; 33:21, 35; 73:8.

See also: Glorification of Allah, Praise to Allah, Purification.

REPENTANCE

1. But Satan caused them to deflect therefrom and expelled them from the (happy) state in which they were; and We said: Fall down, one of you a foe unto the other! There shall be for you on earth a habitation and provision for a time.

Then Adam received from his Lord words (of revelation), and He relented toward him. Lo! He is the Relenting, the Merciful.

2:36–37

2. Lo; those who hide the proofs and the guidance which We revealed, after We had made it clear in the Scripture; such are accursed of Allah and accursed of those who have the power to curse:

Except those who repent and amend and make manifest (the truth). These it is toward whom I relent. I am the Relenting, the Merciful.

2:159–160

3. Truly Allah loveth those who turn unto Him, and loveth those who have a care for cleanness.

2:222

4. Forgiveness is only incumbent on Allah toward those who do evil in ignorance (and) then turn quickly (in repentance) to Allah. These are they toward whom Allah relenteth. Allah is ever Knower, Wise.

The forgiveness is not for those who do ill deeds until, when death attendeth upon one of them, he saith: Lo! I repent now; nor yet for those who die while they are disbelievers. For such We have prepared a painful doom.

4:17–18

1. فأزلهما الشيطن عنها فأخرجهما مما كانا
فيه وقلنا اهبطوا بعضكم لبعض عدو ولكم
في الأرض مستقر ومتاع إلى حين ﴿٣٦﴾

فتلقى ادم من ربه كلمت فتاب عليه
إنه هو التواب الرحيم ﴿٣٧﴾

2. إن الذين يكتمون ما أنزلنا من البينت
والهدى من بعد ما بينه للناس في
الكتب أولئك يلعنهم الله ويلعنهم اللعنون ﴿١٥٩﴾

إلا الذين تابوا وأصلحوا وبينوا فأولئك
أتوب عليهم وأنا التواب الرحيم ﴿١٦٠﴾

3. إن الله يحب التوابين ويحب المتطهرين ﴿٢٢٢﴾

4. إنما التوبة على الله للذين يعملون
السوء بجهالة ثم يتوبون من قريب
فأولئك يتوب الله عليهم وكان
الله عليما حكيما ﴿١٧﴾

وليست التوبة للذين يعملون السيات
حتى إذا حضر أحدهم الموت قال
إني تبت الان ولا الذين يموتون
وهم كفار أولئك أعتدنا لهم
عذابا أليما ﴿١٨﴾

5. But whoso repenteth after his wrongdoing and amendeth, lo! Allah will relent toward him. Lo! Allah is Forgiving, Merciful.

5:39

6. And when those who believe in Our revelations come unto thee, say: Peace be unto you! Your Lord hath prescribed for Himself mercy, that whoso of you doeth evil through ignorance and repenteth afterward thereof and doeth right (for him) Lo! He is Forgiving, Merciful.

6:54

7. But those who do ill deeds and afterward repent and believe—lo! for them, afterward, Allah is Forgiving, Merciful.

7:153

8. Know they not that Allah is He Who accepteth repentance from His bondmen and taketh the alms, and that Allah is He Who is the Relenting, the Merciful.

9:104

9. Then lo! thy Lord— for those who do evil in ignorance and afterward repent and amned — lo! (for them) thy Lord is afterward indeed Forgiving, Merciful.

16:119

10. And lo! verily I am Forgiving toward him who repenteth and believeth and doth good, and afterward walketh aright.

20:82

5. فَمَنْ تَابَ مِنْ بَعْدِ ظُلْمِهٖ وَ اَصْلَحَ
فَاِنَّ اللّٰهَ يَتُوْبُ عَلَيْهِ ؕ اِنَّ اللّٰهَ غَفُوْرٌ رَّحِيْمٌ ﴿۳۹﴾

6. وَ اِذَا جَآءَكَ الَّذِيْنَ يُؤْمِنُوْنَ بِاٰيٰتِنَا فَقُلْ
سَلٰمٌ عَلَيْكُمْ كَتَبَ رَبُّكُمْ عَلٰى نَفْسِهِ
الرَّحْمَةَ ۙ اَنَّهٗ مَنْ عَمِلَ مِنْكُمْ سُوْٓءًۢا
بِجَهَالَةٍ ثُمَّ تَابَ مِنْ بَعْدِهٖ وَ اَصْلَحَ
فَاَنَّهٗ غَفُوْرٌ رَّحِيْمٌ ﴿۵۴﴾

7. وَ الَّذِيْنَ عَمِلُوا السَّيِّاٰتِ ثُمَّ تَابُوْا مِنْۢ
بَعْدِهَا وَ اٰمَنُوْٓا ۫ اِنَّ رَبَّكَ مِنْۢ
بَعْدِهَا لَغَفُوْرٌ رَّحِيْمٌ ﴿۱۵۳﴾

8. اَلَمْ يَعْلَمُوْٓا اَنَّ اللّٰهَ هُوَ يَقْبَلُ التَّوْبَةَ
عَنْ عِبَادِهٖ وَ يَاْخُذُ الصَّدَقٰتِ وَ اَنَّ اللّٰهَ
هُوَ التَّوَّابُ الرَّحِيْمُ ﴿۱۰۴﴾

9. ثُمَّ اِنَّ رَبَّكَ لِلَّذِيْنَ عَمِلُوا السُّوْٓءَ بِجَهَالَةٍ
ثُمَّ تَابُوْا مِنْۢ بَعْدِ ذٰلِكَ وَ اَصْلَحُوْٓا ۙ اِنَّ
رَبَّكَ مِنْۢ بَعْدِهَا لَغَفُوْرٌ رَّحِيْمٌ ﴿۱۱۹﴾

10. وَ اِنِّيْ لَغَفَّارٌ لِّمَنْ تَابَ وَ اٰمَنَ وَ عَمِلَ
صَالِحًا ثُمَّ اهْتَدٰى ﴿۸۲﴾

11. فَاعْلَمْ اَنَّهٗ لَآ اِلٰهَ اِلَّا اللّٰهُ وَ اسْتَغْفِرْ
لِذَنْۢبِكَ وَ لِلْمُؤْمِنِيْنَ وَ الْمُؤْمِنٰتِ ؕ
وَ اللّٰهُ يَعْلَمُ مُتَقَلَّبَكُمْ وَ مَثْوٰىكُمْ ﴿۱۹﴾

11. So know (O Muhammad) that there is no God save Allah, and ask forgiveness for thy sin and for believing men and believing women. Allah knoweth (both) your place of turmoil and your place of rest.

47:19

12. O ye who believe! Turn unto Allah in sincere repentance! It may be that your

Lord will remit from you your evil deeds and bring you into Gardens underneath which rivers flow, on the day when Allah will not abase the Prophet and those who believe with him. Their light will run before them and on their right hands: they will say: Our Lord! Perfect our light for us, and forgive us! Lo! Thou art Able to do all things.

66:8

13. Then hymn the praises of thy Lord, and seek forgiveness of Him. Lo! He is ever ready to show mercy.

110:3

12. يَاَيُّهَا الَّذِيْنَ اٰمَنُوْا تُوْبُوْٓا اِلَى اللّٰهِ
تَوْبَةً نَّصُوْحًا ؕ عَسٰى رَبُّكُمْ اَنْ
يُّكَفِّرَ عَنْكُمْ سَيِّاٰتِكُمْ وَيُدْخِلَكُمْ
جَنّٰتٍ تَجْرِىْ مِنْ تَحْتِهَا الْاَنْهٰرُ ۙ
يَوْمَ لَا يُخْزِى اللّٰهُ النَّبِىَّ وَالَّذِيْنَ
اٰمَنُوْا مَعَهٗ ۚ نُوْرُهُمْ يَسْعٰى بَيْنَ
اَيْدِيْهِمْ وَبِاَيْمَانِهِمْ يَقُوْلُوْنَ
رَبَّنَآ اَتْمِمْ لَنَا نُوْرَنَا وَاغْفِرْ لَنَا ۚ
اِنَّكَ عَلٰى كُلِّ شَىْءٍ قَدِيْرٌ ۝

13. فَسَبِّحْ بِحَمْدِ رَبِّكَ وَاسْتَغْفِرْهُ ؕ
اِنَّهٗ كَانَ تَوَّابًا ۝

Ref: 2:54, 128, 279; 3:89–90, 133, 136; 4:26–27, 31, 106, 145–146; 5:34, 71; 7:143; 8:33, 38; 9:3, 5, 11, 15, 27, 74, 102, 106, 126; 11:3, 52, 61, 90, 112; 13:30; 17:25; 19:59–60; 20:122; 24:4–5, 10, 31; 25:68–71; 28:67; 33:24, 73; 39:54; 40:3, 7, 55; 42:25–26; 46:15; 49:11–12; 51:18; 58:13; 66:4; 71:10; 85:10.

RESPITE OF ALLAH

1. Wait they, indeed, for nothing less than that the angels should come unto them, or thy Lord should come, or there should come one of the portents from thy Lord? On the Day when one of the portents from thy Lord cometh, its belief availeth naught a soul which theretofore believed not, nor in its belief earned good (by works). Say: Wait ye! Lo! We (too) are waiting.

6:158

2. Say: Can ye await for us aught save one of two good things (death or victory in Allah's way)? while we await for you that Allah will afflict you with a doom from Him or at our hands. Await then! Lo! We are awaiting with you.

9:52

3. If Allah were to hasten on for men the ill (that they have earned) as they would hasten on the good, their respite would already have expired. But We suffer those who look not for the meeting with Us to wander blindly on in their contumacy.

10:11

4. Mankind were but one community; then they differed; and had it not been for a word that had already gone forth from thy Lord, it had been judged between them in respect of that wherein they differ.

And they will say: If only a portent were sent down

1. هَلْ يَنْظُرُونَ إِلَّآ أَنْ تَأْتِيَهُمُ الْمَلٰٓئِكَةُ
أَوْ يَأْتِيَ رَبُّكَ أَوْ يَأْتِيَ بَعْضُ اٰيٰتِ رَبِّكَ ؕ
يَوْمَ يَأْتِي بَعْضُ اٰيٰتِ رَبِّكَ لَا يَنْفَعُ
نَفْسًا إِيْمَانُهَا لَمْ تَكُنْ اٰمَنَتْ مِنْ قَبْلُ
أَوْ كَسَبَتْ فِيْٓ إِيْمَانِهَا خَيْرًا ؕ قُلِ انْتَظِرُوْٓا
إِنَّا مُنْتَظِرُوْنَ ۝

2. قُلْ هَلْ تَرَبَّصُوْنَ بِنَآ إِلَّآ إِحْدَى
الْحُسْنَيَيْنِ ؕ وَنَحْنُ نَتَرَبَّصُ بِكُمْ
أَنْ يُّصِيْبَكُمُ اللّٰهُ بِعَذَابٍ مِّنْ عِنْدِهٖٓ
أَوْ بِأَيْدِيْنَا ۖ فَتَرَبَّصُوْٓا إِنَّا مَعَكُمْ مُّتَرَبِّصُوْنَ ۝٥٢

3. وَلَوْ يُعَجِّلُ اللّٰهُ لِلنَّاسِ الشَّرَّ اسْتِعْجَالَهُمْ
بِالْخَيْرِ لَقُضِيَ إِلَيْهِمْ أَجَلُهُمْ ؕ فَنَذَرُ
الَّذِيْنَ لَا يَرْجُوْنَ لِقَآءَنَا فِيْ
طُغْيَانِهِمْ يَعْمَهُوْنَ ۝١١

4. وَمَا كَانَ النَّاسُ إِلَّآ أُمَّةً وَّاحِدَةً
فَاخْتَلَفُوْا ؕ وَلَوْلَا كَلِمَةٌ سَبَقَتْ مِنْ
رَّبِّكَ لَقُضِيَ بَيْنَهُمْ فِيْمَا فِيْهِ يَخْتَلِفُوْنَ ۝١٩
وَيَقُوْلُوْنَ لَوْلَآ أُنْزِلَ عَلَيْهِ اٰيَةٌ مِّنْ رَّبِّهٖ ۚ فَقُلْ إِنَّمَا
الْغَيْبُ لِلّٰهِ فَانْتَظِرُوْا ۚ إِنِّيْ مَعَكُمْ مِّنَ الْمُنْتَظِرِيْنَ ۝٢٠

5. وَلَوْ أَنَّآ أَهْلَكْنٰهُمْ بِعَذَابٍ مِّنْ قَبْلِهٖ لَقَالُوْا
رَبَّنَا لَوْلَآ أَرْسَلْتَ إِلَيْنَا رَسُوْلًا فَنَتَّبِعَ
اٰيٰتِكَ مِنْ قَبْلِ أَنْ نَّذِلَّ وَنَخْزٰى ۝١٣٤
قُلْ كُلٌّ مُّتَرَبِّصٌ فَتَرَبَّصُوْا ۚ فَسَتَعْلَمُوْنَ

upon him from his Lord! Then say (O Muhammad): The Unseen belongeth to Allah. So wait! Lo! I am waiting with you.

10:19–20

5. And if We had destroyed them with some punishment before it, they would assuredly have said; Our Lord! If only

Thou hadst sent unto us a messenger, so that we might have followed Thy revelations before we were (thus) humbled and disgraced!

Say: Each is awaiting; so await ye! Ye will come to know who are the owners of the path of equity, and who is right.

20:134–135

من أصحب الصراط السوي و من اهتدى ﴿١٣٥﴾

6. And they say: When cometh this victory (of yours) if ye are truthful?

Say (unto them): On the day of the victory the faith of those who disbelieve (and who then will believe) will not avail them, neither will they be reprieved.

So withdraw from them (O Muhammad), and await (the event). Lo! they (also) are awaiting (it).

32:28–30

6. و يقولون متى هذا الفتح إن كنتم صدقين ﴿٢٨﴾

قل يوم الفتح لا ينفع الذين كفروا إيمانهم و لا هم ينظرون ﴿٢٩﴾

فأعرض عنهم و انتظر إنهم منتظرون ﴿٣٠﴾

7. Await they aught save the Hour, that it should come upon them unawares? And the beginnings thereof have already come. But how, when it hath come upon them, can they take their warning?

47:18

7. فهل ينظرون إلا الساعة أن تأتيهم بغتة فقد جاء أشراطها فأنى لهم إذا جاءتهم ذكرىهم ﴿١٨﴾

O

Ref. 2:210 6:135; 7:51; 10:102; 16:33; 19:75; 23:54-56; 35:43; 36:49-50; 38:15; 43:66; 44:59: 52:31.

See also: Ways of Allah.

RESPONSIBILITY FOR ACTIONS

1. Whoso committeth sin committeth it only against himself. Allah is ever Knower, Wise.

And whoso committeth a delinquency or crime, then throweth (the blame) thereof upon the innocent, hath burdened himself with falsehood and a flagrant crime.

4:111–112

2. O ye who believe! Ye have charge of your own souls. He who erreth cannot injure you if ye are rightly guided. Unto Allah ye will all return; and then He will inform you of what ye used to do.

5:105

3. Lo! Allah wrongeth not mankind in aught; but mankind wrong themselves.

10:44

4. Say: O mankind! Now hath the Truth from your Lord come unto you. So whosoever is guided, is guided only for (the good of) his soul, and whosoever erreth, erreth only against it. And I am not a warder over you.

10:108

5. Whosoever goeth right, it is only for (the good of) his own soul that he goeth right, and whosoever erreth, erreth only to its hurt. No laden soul can bear another's load.

1. وَمَن يَكْسِبْ إِثْمًا فَإِنَّمَا يَكْسِبُهُ عَلَىٰ نَفْسِهِ ۚ وَ
كَانَ اللَّهُ عَلِيمًا حَكِيمًا

وَمَن يَكْسِبْ خَطِيئَةً أَوْ إِثْمًا ثُمَّ يَرْمِ
بِهِ بَرِيئًا فَقَدِ احْتَمَلَ بُهْتَانًا وَإِثْمًا مُّبِينًا

2. يَا أَيُّهَا الَّذِينَ آمَنُوا عَلَيْكُمْ أَنفُسَكُمْ ۖ لَا
يَضُرُّكُم مَّن ضَلَّ إِذَا اهْتَدَيْتُمْ ۚ إِلَى
اللَّهِ مَرْجِعُكُمْ جَمِيعًا فَيُنَبِّئُكُم بِمَا
كُنتُمْ تَعْمَلُونَ

3. إِنَّ اللَّهَ لَا يَظْلِمُ النَّاسَ شَيْئًا وَلَٰكِنَّ
النَّاسَ أَنفُسَهُمْ يَظْلِمُونَ

4. قُلْ يَا أَيُّهَا النَّاسُ قَدْ جَاءَكُمُ الْحَقُّ
مِن رَّبِّكُمْ ۖ فَمَنِ اهْتَدَىٰ فَإِنَّمَا
يَهْتَدِي لِنَفْسِهِ ۖ وَمَن ضَلَّ فَإِنَّمَا يَضِلُّ
عَلَيْهَا ۖ وَمَا أَنَا عَلَيْكُم بِوَكِيلٍ

5. مَّنِ اهْتَدَىٰ فَإِنَّمَا يَهْتَدِي لِنَفْسِهِ ۖ
وَمَن ضَلَّ فَإِنَّمَا يَضِلُّ عَلَيْهَا ۚ وَلَا
تَزِرُ وَازِرَةٌ وِزْرَ أُخْرَىٰ ۗ وَمَا كُنَّا
مُعَذِّبِينَ حَتَّىٰ نَبْعَثَ رَسُولًا

6. قُلْ كُلٌّ يَعْمَلُ عَلَىٰ شَاكِلَتِهِ فَرَبُّكُمْ
أَعْلَمُ بِمَنْ هُوَ أَهْدَىٰ سَبِيلًا

We never punish until We have sent a messenger.

17:15

6. Say: Each one doth according to his rule of conduct, and thy Lord is Best Aware of him whose way is right.

17:84

7. Thy Lord is the Forgiver, Full of Mercy. If He took them to task (now) for what they earn, He would hasten on the doom for them; but theirs is an appointed term from which they will find no escape.

18:58

7. وَرَبُّكَ الْغَفُورُ ذُو الرَّحْمَةِ ۖ لَوْ
يُؤَاخِذُهُمْ بِمَا كَسَبُوا لَعَجَّلَ لَهُمُ
الْعَذَابَ ۚ بَلْ لَهُمْ مَوْعِدٌ لَنْ يَجِدُوا
مِنْ دُونِهِ مَوْئِلًا ﴿٥٨﴾

8. And We task not any soul beyond its scope, and with Us is a Record which speaketh the truth, and they will not be wronged.

23:62

8. وَلَا نُكَلِّفُ نَفْسًا إِلَّا وُسْعَهَا ۖ وَ
لَدَيْنَا كِتَابٌ يَنْطِقُ بِالْحَقِّ ۚ وَهُمْ
لَا يُظْلَمُونَ ﴿٦٢﴾

9. And whosoever striveth, striveth only for himself, for lo! Allah is altogether Independent of (His) creatures.

29:6

9. وَمَنْ جَاهَدَ فَإِنَّمَا يُجَاهِدُ لِنَفْسِهِ ۚ
إِنَّ اللَّهَ لَغَنِيٌّ عَنِ الْعَالَمِينَ ﴿٦﴾

10. And no burdened soul can bear another's burden and if one heavy laden crieth for (help with) his load, naught of it will be lifted even though he (unto whom he crieth) be of kin.

35:18

10. وَلَا تَزِرُ وَازِرَةٌ وِزْرَ أُخْرَىٰ ۚ وَإِنْ
تَدْعُ مُثْقَلَةٌ إِلَىٰ حِمْلِهَا لَا يُحْمَلْ مِنْهُ
شَيْءٌ وَلَوْ كَانَ ذَا قُرْبَىٰ ۗ

11. Whoso doth right it is for his soul, and whoso doth wrong it is against it. And thy Lord is not at all a tyrant to His slaves.

41:46

11. مَنْ عَمِلَ صَالِحًا فَلِنَفْسِهِ ۖ وَمَنْ
أَسَاءَ فَعَلَيْهَا ۗ وَمَا رَبُّكَ بِظَلَّامٍ لِلْعَبِيدِ ﴿٤٦﴾

○

Ref: 11:101; 13:11; 42:20; 45:15; 46:19; 53:31; 67:1-2; 74:38; 90:10; 91:7-10; 92:12,13.

REVEALED BOOKS

1. Lo! We did reveal the Torah, wherein is guidance and a light, by which the Prophets who surrendered (unto Allah) judged the Jews, and the rabbis and the priests (judged) by such of Allah's Scripture as they were bidden to observe, and thereunto were they witnesses. So fear not mankind, but fear Me. And barter not My revelations for a little gain. Whoso judgeth not by that which Allah hath revealed; such are disbelievers.

5:44

2. Let the People of the Gospel judge by that which Allah hath revealed therein. Whoso judgeth not by that which Allah hath revealed, such are evil-livers.

And unto thee have We revealed the Scripture with the truth, confirming whatever Scripture was before it, and a watcher over it. So judge between them by that which Allah hath revealed, and follow not their desires away from the truth which hath come unto thee. For each We have appointed a divine law and a traced-out way. Had Allah willed He could have made you one community. But that He may try you by that which He hath given you (He hath made you as ye are). So vie one with another in good works. Unto Allah ye will all return, and He wil then inform you of that wherein ye differ.

So judge between them by that which Allah hath revealed, and follow not their desires, but beware of them lest they seduce thee from some part of that which Allah hath revealed unto thee.

1. إِنَّآ أَنزَلْنَا ٱلتَّوْرَىٰةَ فِيهَا هُدًى وَنُورٌ
يَحْكُمُ بِهَا ٱلنَّبِيُّونَ ٱلَّذِينَ أَسْلَمُوا
لِلَّذِينَ هَادُوا وَٱلرَّبَّـٰنِيُّونَ وَٱلْأَحْبَارُ
بِمَا ٱسْتُحْفِظُوا مِن كِتَـٰبِ ٱللَّهِ وَكَانُوا
عَلَيْهِ شُهَدَآءَ ۚ فَلَا تَخْشَوُا ٱلنَّاسَ
وَٱخْشَوْنِ وَلَا تَشْتَرُوا بِـَٔايَـٰتِى ثَمَنًا
قَلِيلًا ۚ وَمَن لَّمْ يَحْكُم بِمَآ أَنزَلَ
ٱللَّهُ فَأُولَـٰٓئِكَ هُمُ ٱلْكَـٰفِرُونَ ﴿٤٤﴾

2. وَلْيَحْكُمْ أَهْلُ ٱلْإِنجِيلِ بِمَآ أَنزَلَ
ٱللَّهُ فِيهِ ۚ وَمَن لَّمْ يَحْكُم بِمَآ أَنزَلَ
ٱللَّهُ فَأُولَـٰٓئِكَ هُمُ ٱلْفَـٰسِقُونَ ﴿٤٧﴾

وَأَنزَلْنَآ إِلَيْكَ ٱلْكِتَـٰبَ بِٱلْحَقِّ مُصَدِّقًا
لِّمَا بَيْنَ يَدَيْهِ مِنَ ٱلْكِتَـٰبِ وَمُهَيْمِنًا
عَلَيْهِ ۖ فَٱحْكُم بَيْنَهُم بِمَآ أَنزَلَ ٱللَّهُ ۖ وَلَا
تَتَّبِعْ أَهْوَآءَهُمْ عَمَّا جَآءَكَ مِنَ ٱلْحَقِّ ۚ
لِكُلٍّ جَعَلْنَا مِنكُمْ شِرْعَةً وَمِنْهَاجًا ۚ
وَلَوْ شَآءَ ٱللَّهُ لَجَعَلَكُمْ أُمَّةً وَٰحِدَةً
وَلَـٰكِن لِّيَبْلُوَكُمْ فِى مَآ ءَاتَىٰكُمْ ۖ فَٱسْتَبِقُوا
ٱلْخَيْرَٰتِ ۚ إِلَى ٱللَّهِ مَرْجِعُكُمْ جَمِيعًا
فَيُنَبِّئُكُم بِمَا كُنتُمْ فِيهِ تَخْتَلِفُونَ ﴿٤٨﴾

وَأَنِ ٱحْكُم بَيْنَهُم بِمَآ أَنزَلَ ٱللَّهُ وَلَا
تَتَّبِعْ أَهْوَآءَهُمْ وَٱحْذَرْهُمْ أَن يَفْتِنُوكَ
عَنۢ بَعْضِ مَآ أَنزَلَ ٱللَّهُ إِلَيْكَ ۖ فَإِن

And if they turn away, then know that Allah's Will is to smite them for some sin of theirs. Lo! many of mankind are evil-livers.

5:47–49

3. Lo! Allah hath bought from the believers their lives and their wealth because the Garden will be theirs; they shall fight in the way of Allah and shall slay and be slain. It is a promise which is binding on Him in the Torah and the Gospel and the Qur'ān. Who fulfilleth His Covenant better than Allah? Rejoice then in your bargain that ye have made, for that is the Supreme triumph.

9:111

4. And verily We have written in the Scripture, after the Reminder: My righteous slaves will inherit the earth:

21:105

5. Lo! This is the former scrolls:

The Books of Ibraham and Moses.

87:18–19

تَوَلَّوْا فَاعْلَمْ اَنَّمَا يُرِيْدُ اللّٰهُ اَنْ يُّصِيْبَهُمْ
بِبَعْضِ ذُنُوْبِهِمْ ۭ وَاِنَّ كَثِيْرًا مِّنَ
النَّاسِ لَفٰسِقُوْنَ ﴿٤٩﴾

3 اِنَّ اللّٰهَ اشْتَرٰى مِنَ الْمُؤْمِنِيْنَ اَنْفُسَهُمْ
وَاَمْوَالَهُمْ بِاَنَّ لَهُمُ الْجَنَّةَ ۭ يُقَاتِلُوْنَ
فِيْ سَبِيْلِ اللّٰهِ فَيَقْتُلُوْنَ وَيُقْتَلُوْنَ ۣ وَعْدًا
عَلَيْهِ حَقًّا فِي التَّوْرٰىةِ وَالْاِنْجِيْلِ وَ
الْقُرْاٰنِ ۭ وَمَنْ اَوْفٰى بِعَهْدِهٖ مِنَ اللّٰهِ
فَاسْتَبْشِرُوْا بِبَيْعِكُمُ الَّذِيْ بَايَعْتُمْ بِهٖ ۭ
وَذٰلِكَ هُوَ الْفَوْزُ الْعَظِيْمُ ﴿١١١﴾

4. وَلَقَدْ كَتَبْنَا فِي الزَّبُوْرِ مِنْۢ بَعْدِ
الذِّكْرِ اَنَّ الْاَرْضَ يَرِثُهَا عِبَادِيَ
الصّٰلِحُوْنَ ﴿١٠٥﴾

5. اِنَّ هٰذَا لَفِي الصُّحُفِ الْاُوْلٰى ﴿١٨﴾
صُحُفِ اِبْرٰهِيْمَ وَمُوْسٰى ﴿١٩﴾

○

See also: Bible, Pslams of David, Qur'ān, Torah.

REVELATION

1. Lo! We inspire thee as We inspired Noah and the prophets after him.

4:163

2. And We sent not (as Our messengers) before thee other than men whom We inspired—Ask the followers of the Remembrance if ye know not!

16:43

3. And it was not (vouchsafed) to any mortal that Allah should speak to him unless (it be) by revelation or from behind a veil, or (that) He sendeth a messenger to reveal what He will by His leave. Lo! He is Exalted, Wise.

And thus have We inspired in thee (Muhammad) a Spirit of Our command. Thou knewest not what the Scripture was, nor what the Faith. But We have made it a light whereby We guide whom We will of Our bondmen. And lo! thou verily dost guide unto a right path:

The path of Allah, unto Whom belongeth whatsoever is in the heaven and whatsoever is in the earth. Do not all things reach Allah at last?

42:51–53

4. Say: I am no new thing among the messengers (of Allah), nor know I what will be done with me or with you.

1. إِنَّا أَوْحَيْنَا إِلَيْكَ كَمَا أَوْحَيْنَا إِلَىٰ نُوحٍ
وَالنَّبِيِّينَ مِن بَعْدِهِ

2. وَمَا أَرْسَلْنَا مِن قَبْلِكَ إِلَّا رِجَالًا نُّوحِي
إِلَيْهِمْ فَاسْأَلُوا أَهْلَ الذِّكْرِ إِن
كُنتُمْ لَا تَعْلَمُونَ

3. وَمَا كَانَ لِبَشَرٍ أَن يُكَلِّمَهُ اللَّهُ إِلَّا
وَحْيًا أَوْ مِن وَرَاءِ حِجَابٍ أَوْ يُرْسِلَ
رَسُولًا فَيُوحِيَ بِإِذْنِهِ مَا يَشَاءُ إِنَّهُ
عَلِيٌّ حَكِيمٌ
وَكَذَٰلِكَ أَوْحَيْنَا إِلَيْكَ رُوحًا مِّنْ
أَمْرِنَا مَا كُنتَ تَدْرِي مَا الْكِتَابُ
وَلَا الْإِيمَانُ وَلَٰكِن جَعَلْنَاهُ نُورًا
نَّهْدِي بِهِ مَن نَّشَاءُ مِنْ عِبَادِنَا وَ
إِنَّكَ لَتَهْدِي إِلَىٰ صِرَاطٍ مُّسْتَقِيمٍ

صِرَاطِ اللَّهِ الَّذِي لَهُ مَا فِي السَّمَاوَاتِ
وَمَا فِي الْأَرْضِ أَلَا إِلَى اللَّهِ
تَصِيرُ الْأُمُورُ

4. قُلْ مَا كُنتُ بِدْعًا مِّنَ الرُّسُلِ
وَمَا أَدْرِي مَا يُفْعَلُ بِي وَلَا بِكُمْ
إِنْ أَتَّبِعُ إِلَّا مَا يُوحَىٰ إِلَيَّ وَمَا أَنَا
إِلَّا نَذِيرٌ مُّبِينٌ

5. وَالنَّجْمِ إِذَا هَوَىٰ
مَا ضَلَّ صَاحِبُكُمْ وَمَا غَوَىٰ

I do but follow that which is inspired in me, and I am but a plain warner.

46:9

5. By the Star when it setteth,

Your comrade erreth not, nor is deceived;

Nor doth he speak of (his own) desire.

It is naught save an inspiration that is inspired,

Which one of mighty powers hath taught him.

53:1–5

6. Stir not thy tongue herewith to hasten it.

Lo! upon Us (resteth) the putting together thereof and the reading thereof.

And when We read it, follow thou the reading

Then lo! upon Us (resteth) the explanation thereof.

75:16–19

REVENGE

1. The forbidden month for the forbidden month, and forbidden things in retaliation. And one who attacketh you, attack him in like manner as he attacked you. Observe your duty to Allah, and know that Allah is with those who ward off (evil).

2:194

2. That (is so). And whoso hath retaliated with the like of that which he was made to suffer and then hath (again) been wronged, Allah will succour him. Lo! Allah verily is Mild, Forgiving.

22:60

وَمَا يَنطِقُ عَنِ الْهَوَىٰ ﴿٣﴾
إِنْ هُوَ إِلَّا وَحْيٌ يُوحَىٰ ﴿٤﴾
عَلَّمَهُ شَدِيدُ الْقُوَىٰ ﴿٥﴾

6. لَا تُحَرِّكْ بِهِ لِسَانَكَ لِتَعْجَلَ بِهِ ﴿١٦﴾
إِنَّ عَلَيْنَا جَمْعَهُ وَقُرْآنَهُ ﴿١٧﴾
فَإِذَا قَرَأْنَاهُ فَاتَّبِعْ قُرْآنَهُ ﴿١٨﴾
ثُمَّ إِنَّ عَلَيْنَا بَيَانَهُ ﴿١٩﴾

1. الشَّهْرُ الْحَرَامُ بِالشَّهْرِ الْحَرَامِ وَالْحُرُمَاتُ
قِصَاصٌ فَمَنِ اعْتَدَىٰ عَلَيْكُمْ فَاعْتَدُوا
عَلَيْهِ بِمِثْلِ مَا اعْتَدَىٰ عَلَيْكُمْ وَاتَّقُوا
اللَّهَ وَاعْلَمُوا أَنَّ اللَّهَ مَعَ الْمُتَّقِينَ ﴿١٩٤﴾

2. ذَٰلِكَ وَمَنْ عَاقَبَ بِمِثْلِ مَا عُوقِبَ
بِهِ ثُمَّ بُغِيَ عَلَيْهِ لَيَنصُرَنَّهُ اللَّهُ إِنَّ
اللَّهَ لَعَفُوٌّ غَفُورٌ ﴿٦٠﴾

REVELATION

See also: Holy Spirit, Office of Apostleship, Office of Prophethood.

REVENGE

Ref: 2:178; 5:33, 95. **See also:** Forgiveness .

REVERENCE FOR MESSENGER OF ALLAH (PBUH)

1. They only are the true believers who believe in Allah and His messenger and, when they are with him on some common errand, go not away until they have asked leave of him. Lo! those who ask leave of thee, those are they who believe in Allah and His messenger. So, if they ask thy leave for some affair of theirs, give leave to whom thou wilt of them, and ask for them forgiveness of Allah. Lo! Allah is Forgiving, Merciful.

Make not the calling of the messenger among you as your calling one of another. Allah knoweth those of you who steal away, hiding them-selves. And let those who conspire to evade orders beware lest grief or painful punishment befall them.

24:62–63

2. Lo! Allah and His angels shower blessings on the Prophet. O ye who believe! Ask blessings on him and salute him with a worthy salutation.

Lo! those who malign Allah and His messenger, Allah hath cursed them in the world and the Hereafter, and hath prepared for them the doom of the disdained.

33:56–57

3. O ye who believe! Be

1. إِنَّمَا الْمُؤْمِنُونَ الَّذِينَ آمَنُوا بِاللَّهِ
وَرَسُولِهِ وَإِذَا كَانُوا مَعَهُ عَلَىٰ أَمْرٍ
جَامِعٍ لَمْ يَذْهَبُوا حَتَّىٰ يَسْتَأْذِنُوهُ ۚ إِنَّ
الَّذِينَ يَسْتَأْذِنُونَكَ أُولَٰئِكَ الَّذِينَ
يُؤْمِنُونَ بِاللَّهِ وَرَسُولِهِ ۚ فَإِذَا اسْتَأْذَنُوكَ
لِبَعْضِ شَأْنِهِمْ فَأْذَنْ لِمَنْ شِئْتَ مِنْهُمْ
وَاسْتَغْفِرْ لَهُمُ اللَّهَ ۚ إِنَّ اللَّهَ غَفُورٌ رَحِيمٌ ﴿٦٢﴾

لَا تَجْعَلُوا دُعَاءَ الرَّسُولِ بَيْنَكُمْ كَدُعَاءِ
بَعْضِكُمْ بَعْضًا ۚ قَدْ يَعْلَمُ اللَّهُ الَّذِينَ
يَتَسَلَّلُونَ مِنْكُمْ لِوَاذًا ۚ فَلْيَحْذَرِ الَّذِينَ
يُخَالِفُونَ عَنْ أَمْرِهِ أَنْ تُصِيبَهُمْ فِتْنَةٌ
أَوْ يُصِيبَهُمْ عَذَابٌ أَلِيمٌ ﴿٦٣﴾

2. إِنَّ اللَّهَ وَمَلَائِكَتَهُ يُصَلُّونَ عَلَى النَّبِيِّ ۚ
يَا أَيُّهَا الَّذِينَ آمَنُوا صَلُّوا عَلَيْهِ
وَسَلِّمُوا تَسْلِيمًا ﴿٥٦﴾

إِنَّ الَّذِينَ يُؤْذُونَ اللَّهَ وَرَسُولَهُ
لَعَنَهُمُ اللَّهُ فِي الدُّنْيَا وَالْآخِرَةِ وَأَعَدَّ
لَهُمْ عَذَابًا مُهِينًا ﴿٥٧﴾

3. يَا أَيُّهَا الَّذِينَ آمَنُوا لَا تُقَدِّمُوا بَيْنَ
يَدَيِ اللَّهِ وَرَسُولِهِ ۖ وَاتَّقُوا اللَّهَ ۚ إِنَّ
اللَّهَ سَمِيعٌ عَلِيمٌ ﴿١﴾

يَا أَيُّهَا الَّذِينَ آمَنُوا لَا تَرْفَعُوا أَصْوَاتَكُمْ
فَوْقَ صَوْتِ النَّبِيِّ وَلَا تَجْهَرُوا لَهُ

not forward in the presence of Allah and His messenger, and keep your duty to Allah. Lo! Allah is Hearer, Knower.

O ye who believe! Lift not up your voices above the voice of the Prophet, nor shout when speaking to him as ye shout one to another, lest your works be rendered vain while ye perceive not.

Lo! they who subdue their voices in the presence of the messenger of Allah, those are they whose hearts Allah hath proven unto righteousness. Theirs will be forgiveness and immense reward.

Lo! those who call thee from behind the private apartments, most of them have no sense.

49:1–4

4. O ye who believe! When ye hold conference with the messenger, offer an alms before your conference. That is better and purer for you. But if ye cannot find (the wherewithal) then lo! Allah is Forgiving, Merciful.

58:12

بِالْقَوْلِ كَجَهْرِ بَعْضِكُمْ لِبَعْضٍ أَنْ
تَحْبَطَ أَعْمَالُكُمْ وَأَنْتُمْ لَا تَشْعُرُونَ ﴿٢﴾

إِنَّ الَّذِينَ يَغُضُّونَ أَصْوَاتَهُمْ عِنْدَ
رَسُولِ اللّٰهِ أُولٰٓئِكَ الَّذِينَ امْتَحَنَ
اللّٰهُ قُلُوبَهُمْ لِلتَّقْوٰى ۚ لَهُمْ مَغْفِرَةٌ
وَأَجْرٌ عَظِيمٌ ﴿٣﴾

إِنَّ الَّذِينَ يُنَادُونَكَ مِنْ وَرَاءِ
الْحُجُرٰتِ أَكْثَرُهُمْ لَا يَعْقِلُونَ ﴿٤﴾

4. يٰٓأَيُّهَا الَّذِينَ اٰمَنُوٓا إِذَا نَاجَيْتُمُ
الرَّسُولَ فَقَدِّمُوا بَيْنَ يَدَيْ نَجْوٰىكُمْ
صَدَقَةً ۚ ذٰلِكَ خَيْرٌ لَكُمْ وَأَطْهَرُ ۚ
فَإِنْ لَمْ تَجِدُوا فَإِنَّ اللّٰهَ غَفُورٌ رَحِيمٌ ﴿١٢﴾

Ref: 8:24; 9:61; 33:53. See also: *Sirah*

REVOLUTION

1. These are (only) the vicissitudes which We cause to follow one another for mankind, to the end that Allah may know those who believe and may choose wit–nessess from among you; and Allah loveth not wrong–doers.

And that Allah may prove those who believe and may blight the disbelievers.

3:140–141

2. Thy Lord is the Absolute, the Lord of Mercy. If He will, He can remove you and can cause what He will to follow after you, even as He raised you from the seed of other folk.

6:133

3. Lo! Allah changeth not the condition of a folk until they (first) change that which is in their hearts; and if Allah willeth misfortune for a folk there is none that can repel it, nor have they a defender beside Him.

13:11

1. وَتِلْكَ الْأَيَّامُ نُدَاوِلُهَا بَيْنَ النَّاسِ ۚ
وَلِيَعْلَمَ اللَّهُ الَّذِينَ آمَنُوا وَيَتَّخِذَ مِنكُمْ
شُهَدَاءَ ۗ وَاللَّهُ لَا يُحِبُّ الظَّالِمِينَ ۝
وَلِيُمَحِّصَ اللَّهُ الَّذِينَ آمَنُوا وَيَمْحَقَ
الْكَافِرِينَ ۝

2. وَرَبُّكَ الْغَنِيُّ ذُو الرَّحْمَةِ ۚ إِن يَشَأْ يُذْهِبْكُمْ
وَيَسْتَخْلِفْ مِن بَعْدِكُم مَّا يَشَاءُ كَمَا
أَنشَأَكُم مِّن ذُرِّيَّةِ قَوْمٍ آخَرِينَ ۝

3. إِنَّ اللَّهَ لَا يُغَيِّرُ مَا بِقَوْمٍ حَتَّىٰ يُغَيِّرُوا
مَا بِأَنفُسِهِمْ ۗ وَإِذَا أَرَادَ اللَّهُ بِقَوْمٍ
سُوءًا فَلَا مَرَدَّ لَهُ ۚ وَمَا لَهُم مِّن دُونِهِ
مِن وَالٍ ۝

REWARD

1. And give glad tidings (O Muhammad) unto those who believe and do good works; that theirs are Gardens underneath which rivers flow; as often as they are regaled with food of the fruit thereof, they say: This is what was given us aforetime; and it is given to them in resemblance. There for them are pure companions; there for ever they abide.

2:25

2. Whoso bringeth a good deed will receive tenfold the like thereof, while whoso bringeth an ill deed will be awarded but the like thereof; and they will not be wronged.

6:160

3. Whosoever doth right, whether male or female, and is a believer, him verily We shall quicken with good life, and We shall pay them a recompense in proportion to the best of what they used to do.

16:97

4. But whoso cometh unto Him a believer, having done good works for such are the high stations;

Gardens of Eden underneath which rivers flow, wherein they will abide for ever. That is the reward of him who groweth.

20:75–76

5 Those who believe and do good works, them verily We shall house in lofty dwellings of the Garden underneath which rivers flow. There they will dwell secure. How sweet the guerdon of the toilers,

Who persevere, and put their trust in their Lord!

29:58–59

1. وَبَشِّرِ الَّذِينَ آمَنُوا وَعَمِلُوا الصَّالِحَاتِ أَنَّ لَهُمْ
جَنَّاتٍ تَجْرِي مِنْ تَحْتِهَا الْأَنْهَارُ ۖ كُلَّمَا رُزِقُوا
مِنْهَا مِنْ ثَمَرَةٍ رِزْقًا ۙ قَالُوا هَٰذَا الَّذِي
رُزِقْنَا مِنْ قَبْلُ ۖ وَأُتُوا بِهِ مُتَشَابِهًا ۖ وَلَهُمْ
فِيهَا أَزْوَاجٌ مُطَهَّرَةٌ ۖ وَهُمْ فِيهَا خَالِدُونَ ﴿٢٥﴾

2. مَنْ جَاءَ بِالْحَسَنَةِ فَلَهُ عَشْرُ أَمْثَالِهَا ۖ وَ
مَنْ جَاءَ بِالسَّيِّئَةِ فَلَا يُجْزَىٰ إِلَّا مِثْلَهَا
وَهُمْ لَا يُظْلَمُونَ ○

3. مَنْ عَمِلَ صَالِحًا مِنْ ذَكَرٍ أَوْ أُنْثَىٰ وَهُوَ مُؤْمِنٌ
فَلَنُحْيِيَنَّهُ حَيَاةً طَيِّبَةً ۖ وَلَنَجْزِيَنَّهُمْ أَجْرَهُمْ
بِأَحْسَنِ مَا كَانُوا يَعْمَلُونَ ﴿٩٧﴾

4. وَمَنْ يَأْتِهِ مُؤْمِنًا قَدْ عَمِلَ الصَّالِحَاتِ
فَأُولَٰئِكَ لَهُمُ الدَّرَجَاتُ الْعُلَىٰ ﴿٧٥﴾

جَنَّاتُ عَدْنٍ تَجْرِي مِنْ تَحْتِهَا الْأَنْهَارُ
خَالِدِينَ فِيهَا ۚ وَذَٰلِكَ جَزَاءُ مَنْ تَزَكَّىٰ ﴿٧٦﴾

5. وَالَّذِينَ آمَنُوا وَعَمِلُوا الصَّالِحَاتِ
لَنُبَوِّئَنَّهُمْ مِنَ الْجَنَّةِ غُرَفًا تَجْرِي
مِنْ تَحْتِهَا الْأَنْهَارُ خَالِدِينَ فِيهَا ۚ
نِعْمَ أَجْرُ الْعَامِلِينَ ﴿٥٨﴾

الَّذِينَ صَبَرُوا وَعَلَىٰ رَبِّهِمْ يَتَوَكَّلُونَ ﴿٥٩﴾

6. And it is not your wealth nor your children that will bring you near unto Us, but he who believeth and doth good (he draweth near). As for such, theirs will be twofold reward for what they did, and they will dwell secure in lofty halls.

And as for those who strive against Our revelations, challenging, they will be brought to the doom.
34:37–38

6. وَمَآ أَمْوَالُكُمْ وَلَآ أَوْلَادُكُم بِالَّتِي
تُقَرِّبُكُمْ عِندَنَا زُلْفَىٰٓ إِلَّا مَنْ ءَامَنَ
وَعَمِلَ صَالِحًا فَأُولَٰٓئِكَ لَهُمْ جَزَآءُ
الضِّعْفِ بِمَا عَمِلُوا وَهُمْ فِي الْغُرُفَاتِ
ءَامِنُونَ ﴿٣٧﴾
وَالَّذِينَ يَسْعَوْنَ فِيٓ ءَايَاتِنَا مُعَاجِزِينَ
أُولَٰٓئِكَ فِي الْعَذَابِ مُحْضَرُونَ ﴿٣٨﴾

7. Whoso doth right, whether male or female, and is a believer, (all) such will enter the Garden, where they will be nourished without stint.
40:40

7. وَمَنْ عَمِلَ صَالِحًا مِّن ذَكَرٍ أَوْ
أُنثَىٰ وَهُوَ مُؤْمِنٌ فَأُولَٰٓئِكَ يَدْخُلُونَ
الْجَنَّةَ يُرْزَقُونَ فِيهَا بِغَيْرِ
حِسَابٍ ﴿٤٠﴾

8. O ye who believe! Be mindful of your duty to Allah and put faith in His messenger. He will give you twofold of His mercy and will appoint for you a light wherein ye shall walk, and will forgive you. Allah is Forgiving, Merciful:
57:28

8. يَٰٓأَيُّهَا الَّذِينَ ءَامَنُوا اتَّقُوا اللَّهَ وَءَامِنُوا
بِرَسُولِهِۦ يُؤْتِكُمْ كِفْلَيْنِ مِن رَّحْمَتِهِۦ
وَيَجْعَل لَّكُمْ نُورًا تَمْشُونَ بِهِۦ وَيَغْفِرْ
لَكُمْ ۚ وَاللَّهُ غَفُورٌ رَّحِيمٌ ﴿٢٨﴾

9. (And) lo! those who believe and do good works are the best of created beings.

Their reward is with their Lord: Gardens of Eden underneath which rivers flow, wherein they dwell for ever. Allah hath pleasure in them and they have pleasure in Him. This is (in store) for him who feareth his Lord.
98:7–8

9. إِنَّ الَّذِينَ ءَامَنُوا وَعَمِلُوا الصَّٰلِحَٰتِ
أُولَٰٓئِكَ هُمْ خَيْرُ الْبَرِيَّةِ ﴿٧﴾
جَزَآؤُهُمْ عِندَ رَبِّهِمْ جَنَّٰتُ عَدْنٍ
تَجْرِي مِن تَحْتِهَا الْأَنْهَٰرُ خَٰلِدِينَ
فِيهَآ أَبَدًا ۖ رَّضِيَ اللَّهُ عَنْهُمْ وَرَضُوا
عَنْهُ ۚ ذَٰلِكَ لِمَنْ خَشِيَ رَبَّهُۥ ﴿٨﴾

Ref: 27:89–90; 29:53–54; 32:19–21; 42–22,40; 57:11,18–19; 64:17.
See aslo: Sin, Recompense.

RIGHTS OF PARENTS

1. Thy Lord hath decreed that ye worship none save Him, and (that ye show) kindness to parents. If one of them or both of them attain to old age with thee, say not "Fie" unto them nor repulse them, but speak unto them a gracious word.

And lower unto them the wing of submission through mercy, and say: My Lord! Have mercy on them both as they did care for me when I was little!

17:23–24

2. And We have enjoined upon man concerning his parents—His mother beareth him in weakness upon weakness and his weaning is in two years—Give thanks unto Me and unto thy parents. Unto Me is the journeying.

But if they strive with thee to make thee ascribe unto Me as partner that of which thou hast no knowledge, then obey them not. Consort with them in the world kindly, and follow the path of him who repenteth unto Me. Then unto Me will be your return, and I shall tell you what ye used to do.

31:14–15

3. And We have commended unto man kindness toward parents. His mother beareth him with reluctance, and bringeth him forth with reluctance, and the bearing of him and the weaning of him

1. وَقَضَىٰ رَبُّكَ أَلَّا تَعْبُدُوا إِلَّا إِيَّاهُ وَ
بِالْوَالِدَيْنِ إِحْسَانًا ۚ إِمَّا يَبْلُغَنَّ عِندَكَ
الْكِبَرَ أَحَدُهُمَا أَوْ كِلَاهُمَا فَلَا تَقُل لَّهُمَا
أُفٍّ وَلَا تَنْهَرْهُمَا وَقُل لَّهُمَا قَوْلًا كَرِيمًا ۝
وَاخْفِضْ لَهُمَا جَنَاحَ الذُّلِّ مِنَ الرَّحْمَةِ
وَقُل رَّبِّ ارْحَمْهُمَا كَمَا رَبَّيَانِي صَغِيرًا ۝

2. وَوَصَّيْنَا الْإِنسَانَ بِوَالِدَيْهِ حَمَلَتْهُ
أُمُّهُ وَهْنًا عَلَىٰ وَهْنٍ وَفِصَالُهُ فِي
عَامَيْنِ أَنِ اشْكُرْ لِي وَلِوَالِدَيْكَ
إِلَيَّ الْمَصِيرُ ۝

وَإِن جَاهَدَاكَ عَلَىٰ أَن تُشْرِكَ بِي مَا
لَيْسَ لَكَ بِهِ عِلْمٌ فَلَا تُطِعْهُمَا وَ
صَاحِبْهُمَا فِي الدُّنْيَا مَعْرُوفًا ۖ وَاتَّبِعْ
سَبِيلَ مَنْ أَنَابَ إِلَيَّ ۚ ثُمَّ إِلَيَّ مَرْجِعُكُمْ
فَأُنَبِّئُكُم بِمَا كُنتُمْ تَعْمَلُونَ ۝

3. وَوَصَّيْنَا الْإِنسَانَ بِوَالِدَيْهِ إِحْسَانًا ۖ
حَمَلَتْهُ أُمُّهُ كُرْهًا وَوَضَعَتْهُ كُرْهًا ۖ
وَحَمْلُهُ وَفِصَالُهُ ثَلَاثُونَ شَهْرًا ۚ حَتَّىٰ
إِذَا بَلَغَ أَشُدَّهُ وَبَلَغَ أَرْبَعِينَ سَنَةً
قَالَ رَبِّ أَوْزِعْنِي أَنْ أَشْكُرَ نِعْمَتَكَ
الَّتِي أَنْعَمْتَ عَلَيَّ وَعَلَىٰ وَالِدَيَّ وَأَنْ
أَعْمَلَ صَالِحًا تَرْضَاهُ وَأَصْلِحْ لِي
فِي ذُرِّيَّتِي ۖ إِنِّي تُبْتُ إِلَيْكَ وَإِنِّي

is thirty months, till, when he attaineth full strength and reacheth forty years, he saith: My Lord! Arouse me that I may give thanks for the favour wherewith Thou hast favoured me and my parents, and that I may do right acceptable unto Thee. And be gracious unto me in the matter of my seed. Lo! I have turned unto Thee repentant, and lo!

I am of those who surrender (unto Thee).

Those are they from whom We accept the best of what they do, and overlook their evil deeds. (They are) among the owners of the Garden. This is the true promise which they were promised (in the world).

And whoso saith unto his parents: Fie upon you both! Do ye threaten me that I shall be brought forth (again) when generations before me have passed away? And they twain cry unto Allah for help (and say): Woe unto thee! Believe! Lo! the promise of Allah is true. But he saith: This is naught save fables of the men of old!

Such are those on whom the Word concerning nations of the *jinn* and mankind which have passed away before them hath effect. Lo! they are the losers.

46:15–18

مِنَ الْمُسْلِمِينَ ۝
أُولَٰئِكَ الَّذِينَ نَتَقَبَّلُ عَنْهُمْ أَحْسَنَ
مَا عَمِلُوا وَنَتَجَاوَزُ عَنْ سَيِّئَاتِهِمْ
فِي أَصْحَابِ الْجَنَّةِ ۖ وَعْدَ الصِّدْقِ
الَّذِي كَانُوا يُوعَدُونَ ۝
وَالَّذِي قَالَ لِوَالِدَيْهِ أُفٍّ لَكُمَا
أَتَعِدَانِنِي أَنْ أُخْرَجَ وَقَدْ خَلَتِ
الْقُرُونُ مِنْ قَبْلِي وَهُمَا يَسْتَغِيثَانِ
اللَّهَ وَيْلَكَ آمِنْ إِنَّ وَعْدَ اللَّهِ حَقٌّ
فَيَقُولُ مَا هَٰذَا إِلَّا أَسَاطِيرُ الْأَوَّلِينَ ۝
أُولَٰئِكَ الَّذِينَ حَقَّ عَلَيْهِمُ الْقَوْلُ فِي
أُمَمٍ قَدْ خَلَتْ مِنْ قَبْلِهِمْ مِنَ الْجِنِّ
وَالْإِنْسِ ۖ إِنَّهُمْ كَانُوا خَاسِرِينَ ۝

○

Ref: 29:8.

RISE AND FALL OF NATIONS

1. That is because Allah never changeth the grace He hath bestowed on any people until they first change that which is in their hearts, and (that is) because Allah is Hearer, Knower.

8:53

2. Lo! Allah changeth not the condition of a folk until they (first) change that which is in their hearts; and if Allah willeth misfortune for a folk there is none that can repel it, nor have they a defender beside Him.

13:11

3. And how many a community have We destroyed that was thankless for its means of livelihood! And yonder are their dwellings, which have not been inhabited after them save a little. And We, even We, were the inheritors.

28:58

4. Have they not travelled in the land and seen the nature of the consequence for those who were before them? They were stronger than these in power, and they dug the earth and built upon it more than these have built. Messengers of their own came unto them with clear proofs (of Allah's Sovereignty). Surely Allah wronged them not, but they did wrong themselves.

Then evil was the consequence to those who dealt in evil, because they denied the revelations of Allah and made a mock of them.

30:9–10

1. ذَٰلِكَ بِأَنَّ اللَّهَ لَمْ يَكُ مُغَيِّرًا نِّعْمَةً
أَنْعَمَهَا عَلَىٰ قَوْمٍ حَتَّىٰ يُغَيِّرُوا مَا بِأَنفُسِهِمْ
وَأَنَّ اللَّهَ سَمِيعٌ عَلِيمٌ

2. إِنَّ اللَّهَ لَا يُغَيِّرُ مَا بِقَوْمٍ حَتَّىٰ يُغَيِّرُوا مَا
بِأَنفُسِهِمْ ۗ وَإِذَا أَرَادَ اللَّهُ بِقَوْمٍ سُوءًا
فَلَا مَرَدَّ لَهُ ۚ وَمَا لَهُم مِّن دُونِهِ مِن وَالٍ

3. وَكَمْ أَهْلَكْنَا مِن قَرْيَةٍ بَطِرَتْ
مَعِيشَتَهَا ۖ فَتِلْكَ مَسَاكِنُهُمْ لَمْ
تُسْكَن مِّن بَعْدِهِمْ إِلَّا قَلِيلًا ۖ وَ
كُنَّا نَحْنُ الْوَارِثِينَ

4. أَوَلَمْ يَسِيرُوا فِي الْأَرْضِ فَيَنظُرُوا
كَيْفَ كَانَ عَاقِبَةُ الَّذِينَ مِن قَبْلِهِمْ ۚ
كَانُوا أَشَدَّ مِنْهُمْ قُوَّةً وَأَثَارُوا الْأَرْضَ
وَعَمَرُوهَا أَكْثَرَ مِمَّا عَمَرُوهَا وَجَاءَتْهُمْ
رُسُلُهُم بِالْبَيِّنَاتِ ۖ فَمَا كَانَ اللَّهُ
لِيَظْلِمَهُمْ وَلَٰكِن كَانُوا أَنفُسَهُمْ يَظْلِمُونَ
ثُمَّ كَانَ عَاقِبَةَ الَّذِينَ أَسَاءُوا السُّوأَىٰ
أَن كَذَّبُوا بِآيَاتِ اللَّهِ وَكَانُوا
بِهَا يَسْتَهْزِئُونَ

5. أَفَلَمْ يَسِيرُوا فِي الْأَرْضِ فَيَنظُرُوا
كَيْفَ كَانَ عَاقِبَةُ الَّذِينَ مِن
قَبْلِهِمْ ۚ كَانُوا أَكْثَرَ مِنْهُمْ وَأَشَدَّ
قُوَّةً وَآثَارًا فِي الْأَرْضِ فَمَا أَغْنَىٰ
عَنْهُم مَّا كَانُوا يَكْسِبُونَ

5. Have they not travelled in the land to see the nature of the consequence for those before them? They were more numerous than these, and mightier in power and (in the) traces (which they left behind them) in the earth. But all that they used to earn availed them not.

40:82

See also: Revolution.

RIVERS AND SEAS

1. And when Moses asked for water for his people, We said: Smite with thy staff the rock. And there gushed out therefrom twelve springs (so that) each tribe knew their drinking–place. Eat and drink of that which Allah hath provided, and do not act corruptly, making mischief in the earth.

2:60

2. Then, even after that, your hearts were hardened and became as rocks, or worse than rocks, for hardness. For indeed there are rocks from out which rivers gush, and indeed there are rocks which split asunder so that water floweth from them. And indeed there are rocks which fall down for the fear of Allah. Allah is not unaware of what ye do.

2:74

3. And He it is Who spread out the earth and placed therein firm hills and flowing streams, and of all fruits He placed therein two spouses (male and female). He covereth the night with the day. Lo! herein verily are portents for people who take thought.

13:3

4. And He it is Who hath constrained the sea to be of service that ye eat fresh meat from thence, and bring forth from thence ornaments which ye wear. And thou seest the

1. وَإِذِ اسْتَسْقَىٰ مُوسَىٰ لِقَوْمِهِ فَقُلْنَا اضْرِبْ
بِعَصَاكَ الْحَجَرَ فَانْفَجَرَتْ مِنْهُ اثْنَتَا
عَشْرَةَ عَيْنًا قَدْ عَلِمَ كُلُّ أُنَاسٍ مَشْرَبَهُمْ
كُلُوا وَاشْرَبُوا مِنْ رِزْقِ اللَّهِ وَلَا تَعْثَوْا
فِي الْأَرْضِ مُفْسِدِينَ ﴿٦٠﴾

2. ثُمَّ قَسَتْ قُلُوبُكُمْ مِنْ بَعْدِ ذَٰلِكَ فَهِيَ
كَالْحِجَارَةِ أَوْ أَشَدُّ قَسْوَةً وَإِنَّ مِنَ الْحِجَارَةِ
لَمَا يَتَفَجَّرُ مِنْهُ الْأَنْهَارُ وَإِنَّ مِنْهَا لَمَا يَشَّقَّقُ
فَيَخْرُجُ مِنْهُ الْمَاءُ وَإِنَّ مِنْهَا لَمَا يَهْبِطُ مِنْ
خَشْيَةِ اللَّهِ وَمَا اللَّهُ بِغَافِلٍ عَمَّا تَعْمَلُونَ ﴿٧٤﴾

3. وَهُوَ الَّذِي مَدَّ الْأَرْضَ وَجَعَلَ فِيهَا
رَوَاسِيَ وَأَنْهَارًا وَمِنْ كُلِّ الثَّمَرَاتِ
جَعَلَ فِيهَا زَوْجَيْنِ اثْنَيْنِ يُغْشِي اللَّيْلَ
النَّهَارَ إِنَّ فِي ذَٰلِكَ لَآيَاتٍ لِقَوْمٍ
يَتَفَكَّرُونَ ﴿٣﴾

4. وَهُوَ الَّذِي سَخَّرَ الْبَحْرَ لِتَأْكُلُوا مِنْهُ
لَحْمًا طَرِيًّا وَتَسْتَخْرِجُوا مِنْهُ حِلْيَةً
تَلْبَسُونَهَا وَتَرَى الْفُلْكَ مَوَاخِرَ فِيهِ
وَلِتَبْتَغُوا مِنْ فَضْلِهِ وَلَعَلَّكُمْ تَشْكُرُونَ ﴿١٤﴾

5. وَهُوَ الَّذِي مَرَجَ الْبَحْرَيْنِ هَٰذَا عَذْبٌ
فُرَاتٌ وَهَٰذَا مِلْحٌ أُجَاجٌ وَجَعَلَ
بَيْنَهُمَا بَرْزَخًا وَحِجْرًا مَحْجُورًا ﴿٥٣﴾

ships ploughing it that ye (mankind) may seek of His bounty, and that haply ye may give thanks.

16:14

5. And He it is Who hath given independence to the two seas (though they meet); one palatable, sweet, and the other

saltish, bitter; and hath set a bar and a forbidding ban between them.

25:53

6. And two seas are not alike: this, fresh, sweet, good to drink, this (other) bitter, salt. And from them both ye eat fresh meat and derive the ornament that ye wear. And thou seest the ship cleaving them with its prow that ye may seek of His bounty, and that haply ye may give thanks.

35:12

7. He hath loosed the two seas. They meet.

There is a barrier between them. They encroach not (one upon the other).

Which is it, of the favours of your Lord, that ye deny?

There cometh forth from both of them the pearl and coralstone.

Which is it, of the favours of your Lord, that ye deny?

His are the ships displayed upon the seas, like banners.

Which is it, of the favours of your Lord, that ye deny?

55:19—25

6. وَمَا يَسْتَوِي الْبَحْرٰنِ ۖ هٰذَا عَذْبٌ
فُرَاتٌ سَآئِغٌ شَرَابُهٗ وَ هٰذَا مِلْحٌ
اُجَاجٌ ؕ وَ مِنْ كُلٍّ تَاْكُلُوْنَ لَحْمًا
طَرِيًّا وَّ تَسْتَخْرِجُوْنَ حِلْيَةً تَلْبَسُوْنَهَا ۚ
وَ تَرَى الْفُلْكَ فِيْهِ مَوَاخِرَ لِتَبْتَغُوْا
مِنْ فَضْلِهٖ وَ لَعَلَّكُمْ تَشْكُرُوْنَ ﴿۱۲﴾

7. مَرَجَ الْبَحْرَيْنِ يَلْتَقِيٰنِ ﴿۱۹﴾
بَيْنَهُمَا بَرْزَخٌ لَّا يَبْغِيٰنِ ﴿۲۰﴾
فَبِاَيِّ اٰلَآءِ رَبِّكُمَا تُكَذِّبٰنِ ﴿۲۱﴾
يَخْرُجُ مِنْهُمَا اللُّؤْلُؤُ وَ الْمَرْجَانُ ﴿۲۲﴾
فَبِاَيِّ اٰلَآءِ رَبِّكُمَا تُكَذِّبٰنِ ﴿۲۳﴾
وَلَهُ الْجَوَارِ الْمُنْشَئٰتُ فِي الْبَحْرِ
كَالْاَعْلَامِ ﴿۲۴﴾
فَبِاَيِّ اٰلَآءِ رَبِّكُمَا تُكَذِّبٰنِ ﴿۲۵﴾

○

Ref: 7: 135–136; 20: 39, 77; 27: 63; 28: 40; 42: 32; 44: 24; 55: 50.

RUMOURS

1. And if any tidings, whether of safety or fear, come unto them, they noise it abroad, whereas if they had referred it to the messenger and such of them as are in authority, those among them who are able to think out the matter would have known it. If it had not been for the grace of Allah upon you and His Mercy ye would have followed Satan, save a few (of you).

4:83

2. O ye who believe! If an evil—liver bring you tidings, verify it, lest ye smite some folk in ignorance and afterward repent of what ye did.

49:6

1. وَإِذَا جَآءَهُمْ أَمْرٌ مِّنَ الْأَمْنِ أَوِ الْخَوْفِ
أَذَاعُوا بِهِۦ ۖ وَلَوْ رَدُّوهُ إِلَى الرَّسُولِ وَإِلَىٰٓ
أُولِى الْأَمْرِ مِنْهُمْ لَعَلِمَهُ الَّذِينَ يَسْتَنۢبِطُونَهُۥ
مِنْهُمْ ۗ وَلَوْلَا فَضْلُ اللَّهِ عَلَيْكُمْ وَرَحْمَتُهُۥ
لَاتَّبَعْتُمُ الشَّيْطَٰنَ إِلَّا قَلِيلًا ۝

2. يَٰٓأَيُّهَا الَّذِينَ ءَامَنُوٓا إِن جَآءَكُمْ فَاسِقٌۢ بِنَبَإٍ
فَتَبَيَّنُوٓا أَن تُصِيبُوا قَوْمًۢا بِجَهَٰلَةٍ فَتُصْبِحُوا
عَلَىٰ مَا فَعَلْتُمْ نَٰدِمِينَ ۝٦

SABEANS

1. Lo! those who believe (in that which is revealed unto thee, Muhammad), and those who are Jews, and Christians, and Sabaeans – whoever believeth in Allah and the Last Day and doth right—surely their reward is with their Lord, and there shall no fear come upon them neither shall they grieve.

2:62

1. ان الذين امنوا والذين هادوا والنصرى
والصبئين من امن بالله واليوم الاخر
وعمل صالحا فلهم اجرهم عند ربهم
ولا خوف عليهم ولا هم يحزنون ﴿٦٢﴾

SABBATH

1. And ye know of those of you who broke the *Sabbath* how We said unto them: Be ye apes, despised and hated!

And We made it an example to their own and to succeeding generations, and an admonition to the God-fearing.

2:65–66

1. ولقد علمتم الذين اعتدوا منكم في السبت
فقلنا لهم كونوا قردة خسئين ﴿٦٥﴾
فجعلنها نكالا لما بين يديها وما خلفها
وموعظة للمتقين ﴿٦٦﴾

2. Ask them (O Muhammad) of the township that was by the sea, how they did break the *Sabbath*, how their big fish came unto them visibly upon their *Sabbath* day and on a day when they did not keep *Sabbath* came they not unto them. Thus did We try them for that they were evil–livers.

And when a community among them said: Why preach ye to a folk whom Allah is about to destroy and punish with an awful doom, they said: In order to be free from guilt before your Lord, and that haply they may ward off (evil).

And when they forgot that whereof they had been reminded, We rescued those who forbade wrong, and visited those who did wrong with dreadful punishment because they were evil–livers.

So when they took pride in that which they had been forbidden, We said unto them: Be ye apes, despised and loathed!

7:163–166

2. وسئلهم عن القرية التي كانت حاضرة
البحر اذ يعدون في السبت اذ تاتيهم
حيتانهم يوم سبتهم شرعا ويوم لا
يسبتون لا تاتيهم كذلك نبلوهم
بما كانوا يفسقون ﴿١٦٣﴾
واذ قالت امة منهم لم تعظون قوما الله
مهلكهم او معذبهم عذابا شديدا قالوا
معذرة الى ربكم ولعلهم يتقون ﴿١٦٤﴾
فلما نسوا ما ذكروا به انجينا الذين
ينهون عن السوء واخذنا الذين ظلموا
بعذاب بئيس بما كانوا يفسقون ﴿١٦٥﴾
فلما عتوا عن ما نهوا عنه قلنا لهم كونوا
قردة خسئين ﴿١٦٦﴾

SABAEAN
See also: Jews and Christians, People of the Book.

SACRIFICE

1. Perform the pilgrimage and the visit (to Makkah) for Allah. And if ye are prevented, then send such gifts as can be obtained with ease, and shave not your heads until the gifts have reached their destination. And whoever among you is sick or hath an ailment of the head must pay a ransom of fasting or alms-giving or offering. And if ye are in safety, then whosoever contenteth himself with the Visit for the Pilgrimage (shall give) such gifts as can be had with ease. And whosoever cannot find (such gifts), then a fast of three days while on the pilgrimage, and of seven when ye have returned; that is, ten in all. That is for him whose folk are not present at the Inviolable Place of Worship. Observe your duty to Allah, and know that Allah is severe in punishment.

2:196

1. وَأَتِمُّوا الْحَجَّ وَالْعُمْرَةَ لِلّٰهِ فَإِنْ أُحْصِرْتُمْ
فَمَا اسْتَيْسَرَ مِنَ الْهَدْيِ وَلَا تَحْلِقُوا
رُءُوسَكُمْ حَتّٰى يَبْلُغَ الْهَدْيُ مَحِلَّهُ
فَمَنْ كَانَ مِنْكُمْ مَرِيضًا أَوْ بِهِ أَذًى مِنْ
رَأْسِهِ فَفِدْيَةٌ مِنْ صِيَامٍ أَوْ صَدَقَةٍ
أَوْ نُسُكٍ فَإِذَا أَمِنْتُمْ فَمَنْ تَمَتَّعَ بِالْعُمْرَةِ
إِلَى الْحَجِّ فَمَا اسْتَيْسَرَ مِنَ الْهَدْيِ فَمَنْ
لَمْ يَجِدْ فَصِيَامُ ثَلٰثَةِ أَيَّامٍ فِي الْحَجِّ وَ
سَبْعَةٍ إِذَا رَجَعْتُمْ تِلْكَ عَشَرَةٌ كَامِلَةٌ
ذٰلِكَ لِمَنْ لَمْ يَكُنْ أَهْلُهُ حَاضِرِي الْمَسْجِدِ
الْحَرَامِ وَاتَّقُوا اللّٰهَ وَاعْلَمُوا أَنَّ اللّٰهَ
شَدِيدُ الْعِقَابِ ﴿١٩٦﴾

2. O ye who believe! Profane not Allah's monuments nor the Sacred Month nor the offerings nor the garlands, nor those repairing to the Sacred House, seeking the grace and pleasure of Allah.

5:2

2. يٰأَيُّهَا الَّذِينَ اٰمَنُوا لَا تُحِلُّوا شَعَآئِرَ اللّٰهِ
وَلَا الشَّهْرَ الْحَرَامَ وَلَا الْهَدْيَ وَلَا
الْقَلَآئِدَ وَلَآ اٰمِّينَ الْبَيْتَ الْحَرَامَ
يَبْتَغُونَ فَضْلًا مِنْ رَبِّهِمْ وَرِضْوٰنًا

3. And the camels! We have appointed them among the ceremonies of Allah. Therein ye have much good. So mention the name of Allah over them when they are drawn up in lines. Then when their flanks fall (dead), eat thereof and feed the beggar and the suppliant. Thus have We made them subject unto you, that haply ye may give thanks.

Their flesh and their blood reach not Allah, but the devotion from you reacheth Him. Thus have We made

3. وَالْبُدْنَ جَعَلْنٰهَا لَكُمْ مِنْ شَعَآئِرِ اللّٰهِ
لَكُمْ فِيهَا خَيْرٌ فَاذْكُرُوا اسْمَ اللّٰهِ
عَلَيْهَا صَوَآفَّ فَإِذَا وَجَبَتْ جُنُوبُهَا
فَكُلُوا مِنْهَا وَأَطْعِمُوا الْقَانِعَ وَالْمُعْتَرَّ
كَذٰلِكَ سَخَّرْنٰهَا لَكُمْ لَعَلَّكُمْ تَشْكُرُونَ ﴿٣٦﴾
لَنْ يَنَالَ اللّٰهَ لُحُومُهَا وَلَا دِمَآؤُهَا
وَلٰكِنْ يَنَالُهُ التَّقْوٰى مِنْكُمْ كَذٰلِكَ

them subject unto you that ye may magnify Allah that He hath guided you. And give good tidings (O Muhammad) to the good.

22:36–37

4. So pray unto thy Lord, and sacrifice.

108:2

SAINTS

1. Lo! verily the friends of Allah are (those) on whom fear (cometh) not, nor do they grieve:

Those who believe and keep their duty (to Allah),

Theirs are good tidings in the life of the world and in the Hereafter—There is no changing the Words of Allah—that is the Supreme Triumph.

10:62–64

2. Say (O Muhammad): O ye who are Jews! If ye claim that ye are favoured of Allah apart from (all) mankind, then long for death if ye are truth-ful!

But they will never long for it because of all that their own hands have sent before, and Allah is Aware of evil-doers.

62:6–7

سَخَّرَهَا لَكُمْ لِتُكَبِّرُوا اللّٰهَ عَلٰى مَا
هَدٰىكُمْ ۗ وَبَشِّرِ الْمُحْسِنِيْنَ ۝

4. فَصَلِّ لِرَبِّكَ وَانْحَرْ ۝

○

1. اَلَآ اِنَّ اَوْلِيَآءَ اللّٰهِ لَا خَوْفٌ عَلَيْهِمْ
وَلَا هُمْ يَحْزَنُوْنَ ۝
اَلَّذِيْنَ اٰمَنُوْا وَكَانُوْا يَتَّقُوْنَ ۝
لَهُمُ الْبُشْرٰى فِي الْحَيٰوةِ الدُّنْيَا وَفِي
الْاٰخِرَةِ ۗ لَا تَبْدِيْلَ لِكَلِمٰتِ اللّٰهِ ۗ
ذٰلِكَ هُوَ الْفَوْزُ الْعَظِيْمُ ۝

2. قُلْ يٰٓاَيُّهَا الَّذِيْنَ هَادُوْٓا اِنْ زَعَمْتُمْ
اَنَّكُمْ اَوْلِيَآءُ لِلّٰهِ مِنْ دُوْنِ النَّاسِ
فَتَمَنَّوُا الْمَوْتَ اِنْ كُنْتُمْ صٰدِقِيْنَ ۝
وَلَا يَتَمَنَّوْنَهٗٓ اَبَدًا ۢبِمَا قَدَّمَتْ
اَيْدِيْهِمْ ۗ وَاللّٰهُ عَلِيْمٌ ۢبِالظّٰلِمِيْنَ ۝

○

SACRIFICE
Ref: 3:183; 5:27,97; 46:28; 48:25.
See also: *Hajj* and *'Umrah*.
SAINTS
See also: Love for Allah.

SALAT

1. Establish worship, pay the poor—due, and bow your heads with those who bow (in worship).

2:43

2. O ye who believe! Seek help in steadfastness and prayer. Lo! Allah is with the steadfast.

2:153

3. Be guardians of your prayers, and of the midmost prayer, and stand up with devotion to Allah.

And if ye go in fear, then (pray) standing or on horseback. And when ye are again in safety, remember Allah as He hath taught you that which (heretofore) ye knew not.

2:238–239

4. Lo! those who believe and do good works and establish worship and pay the poor—due, their reward is with their Lord and there shall no fear come upon them neither shall they grieve.

2:277

5. O ye who believe! Draw not near unto prayer when ye are drunken, till ye know that which ye utter, nor when ye are polluted, save when journeying upon the road till ye have bathed.

4:43

6. And when ye go forth in the land, it is no sin for you to

1. واقيموا الصلوة واتوا الزكوة واركعوا
مع الركعين (٤٣)

2. يايها الذين امنوا استعينوا بالصبر و
الصلوة ان الله مع الصبرين (١٥٣)

3. حفظوا على الصلوت والصلوة الوسطى
وقوموا لله قنتين (٢٣٨)

فان خفتم فرجالا او ركبانا فاذا
امنتم فاذكروا الله كما علمكم ما لم
تكونوا تعلمون (٢٣٩)

4. ان الذين امنوا وعملوا الصلحت و
اقاموا الصلوة واتوا الزكوة لهم اجرهم
عند ربهم ولا خوف عليهم ولا
هم يحزنون (٢٧٧)

5. يايها الذين امنوا لا تقربوا الصلوة وانتم سكرى
حتى تعلموا ما تقولون ولا جنبا الا عابري سبيل
حتى تغتسلوا

6. واذا ضربتم في الارض فليس عليكم
جناح ان تقصروا من الصلوة ان خفتم
ان يفتنكم الذين كفروا ان الكفرين
كانوا لكم عدوا مبينا (١٠١)

curtail (your) worship if ye fear that those who disbelieve may attack you. In truth the disbelievers are an open enemy to you.

And when thou (O Muhammad) art among them and arrangest (their) worship for them, let only a party of them stand with thee (to worship) and let them take their arms. Then when they have performed their prostrations let them fall to the rear and let another party come that hath not worshipped and let them worship with thee, and let them take their precaution and their arms. Those who disbelieve long for you to neglect your arms and your baggage that they may attack you once for all. It is no sin for you to lay aside your arms, if rain impedeth you or ye are sick. But take your precaution. Lo! Allah prepareth for the disbelievers shameful punishment.

When ye have performed the act of worship, remember Allah, standing, sitting and reclining. And when ye are in safety, observe proper worship. Worship at fixed hours hath been enjoined on the believers.

4:101–103

7. O ye who believe! When ye rise up for prayer, wash your faces, and your hands up to the elbows, and lightly rub your heads and (wash) your feet up to the ankles. And if ye are unclean, purify yourselves. And if ye are sick or on a journey, or one of you cometh from the closet, or ye have had contact with women,

وَإِذَا كُنتَ فِيهِمْ فَأَقَمْتَ لَهُمُ الصَّلَوٰةَ فَلْتَقُمْ
طَآئِفَةٌ مِّنْهُم مَّعَكَ وَلْيَأْخُذُوٓا أَسْلِحَتَهُمْ
فَإِذَا سَجَدُوا فَلْيَكُونُوا مِن وَرَآئِكُمْ وَلْتَأْتِ
طَآئِفَةٌ أُخْرَىٰ لَمْ يُصَلُّوا فَلْيُصَلُّوا مَعَكَ وَلْيَأْخُذُوا
حِذْرَهُمْ وَأَسْلِحَتَهُمْ وَدَّ الَّذِينَ كَفَرُوا
لَوْ تَغْفُلُونَ عَنْ أَسْلِحَتِكُمْ وَأَمْتِعَتِكُمْ
فَيَمِيلُونَ عَلَيْكُم مَّيْلَةً وَاحِدَةً وَلَا جُنَاحَ
عَلَيْكُمْ إِن كَانَ بِكُمْ أَذًى مِّن مَّطَرٍ أَوْ
كُنتُم مَّرْضَىٰٓ أَن تَضَعُوٓا أَسْلِحَتَكُمْ وَخُذُوا
حِذْرَكُمْ إِنَّ اللَّهَ أَعَدَّ لِلْكَٰفِرِينَ عَذَابًا مُّهِينًا ١٠٢
فَإِذَا قَضَيْتُمُ الصَّلَوٰةَ فَاذْكُرُوا اللَّهَ قِيَٰمًا
وَقُعُودًا وَعَلَىٰ جُنُوبِكُمْ فَإِذَا اطْمَأْنَنتُمْ
فَأَقِيمُوا الصَّلَوٰةَ إِنَّ الصَّلَوٰةَ كَانَتْ
عَلَى الْمُؤْمِنِينَ كِتَٰبًا مَّوْقُوتًا ١٠٣

7. يَٰٓأَيُّهَا الَّذِينَ ءَامَنُوٓا إِذَا قُمْتُمْ إِلَى الصَّلَوٰةِ فَاغْسِلُوا
وُجُوهَكُمْ وَأَيْدِيَكُمْ إِلَى الْمَرَافِقِ وَامْسَحُوا بِرُءُوسِكُمْ وَ
أَرْجُلَكُمْ إِلَى الْكَعْبَيْنِ وَإِن كُنتُمْ جُنُبًا فَاطَّهَّرُوا وَ
إِن كُنتُم مَّرْضَىٰٓ أَوْ عَلَىٰ سَفَرٍ أَوْ جَآءَ أَحَدٌ مِّنكُم مِّنَ
الْغَآئِطِ أَوْ لَٰمَسْتُمُ النِّسَآءَ فَلَمْ تَجِدُوا مَآءً فَتَيَمَّمُوا
صَعِيدًا طَيِّبًا فَامْسَحُوا بِوُجُوهِكُمْ وَأَيْدِيكُم مِّنْهُ
مَا يُرِيدُ اللَّهُ لِيَجْعَلَ عَلَيْكُم مِّنْ حَرَجٍ وَلَٰكِن يُرِيدُ
لِيُطَهِّرَكُمْ وَلِيُتِمَّ نِعْمَتَهُ عَلَيْكُمْ لَعَلَّكُمْ تَشْكُرُونَ ٦

and ye find not water, then go to clean, high ground and rub your faces and your hands with some of it. Allah would not place a burden on you, but He would purify you and would perfect His grace upon you, that ye may give thanks.

5:6

8. Say: Lo! my worship and my sacrifice and my living and my dying are for Allah, Lord of the Worlds:

6:162

9. And the believers, men and women, are protecting friends one of another; they enjoin the right and forbid the wrong, and they establish worship and they pay the poor-due, and they obey Allah and His messenger. As for these Allah will have mercy on them. Lo! Allah is Mighty, Wise.

9:71

10. Establish woship at the two ends of the day and in some watches of the night. Lo! good deeds annul ill deeds. This is a reminder for the mindful.

11:114

11. Tell My bondmen who believe to establish worship and spend of that which We have given them, secretly and publicly, before a day cometh wherein there will be neither traffick nor befriending.

14:31

12. Establish worship at the going down of the sun until the dark of night, and (the recital of) the Qur'an at dawn.

8. قُلْ إِنَّ صَلَاتِي وَنُسُكِي وَمَحْيَايَ وَ
مَمَاتِي لِلَّهِ رَبِّ الْعٰلَمِينَ

9. وَالْمُؤْمِنُونَ وَالْمُؤْمِنٰتُ بَعْضُهُمْ أَوْلِيَاءُ
بَعْضٍ يَأْمُرُونَ بِالْمَعْرُوفِ وَيَنْهَوْنَ عَنِ
الْمُنْكَرِ وَيُقِيمُونَ الصَّلٰوةَ وَيُؤْتُونَ الزَّكٰوةَ
وَيُطِيعُونَ اللّٰهَ وَرَسُولَهُ أُولٰئِكَ سَيَرْحَمُهُمُ
اللّٰهُ إِنَّ اللّٰهَ عَزِيزٌ حَكِيمٌ

10. وَأَقِمِ الصَّلٰوةَ طَرَفَيِ النَّهَارِ وَزُلَفًا
مِنَ الَّيْلِ إِنَّ الْحَسَنٰتِ يُذْهِبْنَ
السَّيِّاٰتِ ذٰلِكَ ذِكْرٰى لِلذّٰكِرِينَ

11. قُلْ لِعِبَادِيَ الَّذِينَ اٰمَنُوا يُقِيمُوا الصَّلٰوةَ
وَيُنْفِقُوا مِمَّا رَزَقْنٰهُمْ سِرًّا وَعَلَانِيَةً
مِنْ قَبْلِ أَنْ يَأْتِيَ يَوْمٌ لَا بَيْعٌ فِيهِ
وَلَا خِلٰلٌ

12. أَقِمِ الصَّلٰوةَ لِدُلُوكِ الشَّمْسِ إِلٰى غَسَقِ
الَّيْلِ وَقُرْاٰنَ الْفَجْرِ إِنَّ قُرْاٰنَ الْفَجْرِ
كَانَ مَشْهُودًا
وَمِنَ الَّيْلِ فَتَهَجَّدْ بِهِ نَافِلَةً لَكَ
عَسٰى أَنْ يَبْعَثَكَ رَبُّكَ مَقَامًا مَحْمُودًا

Lo! (the recital of) the Qur'an at dawn is ever witnessed.

And some part of the night awake for it, a largess for thee. It may be that thy Lord will raise thee to a praised estate.

17:78–79

13. وَلَا تَجْهَرْ بِصَلَاتِكَ وَلَا تُخَافِتْ بِهَا
وَابْتَغِ بَيْنَ ذَٰلِكَ سَبِيلًا

14. وَأْمُرْ أَهْلَكَ بِالصَّلَاةِ وَاصْطَبِرْ عَلَيْهَا ۖ
لَا نَسْأَلُكَ رِزْقًا ۖ نَحْنُ نَرْزُقُكَ ۗ
وَالْعَاقِبَةُ لِلتَّقْوَىٰ

15. وَأَقِيمُوا الصَّلَاةَ وَآتُوا الزَّكَاةَ
وَأَطِيعُوا الرَّسُولَ لَعَلَّكُمْ تُرْحَمُونَ

16. اتْلُ مَا أُوحِيَ إِلَيْكَ مِنَ الْكِتَابِ
وَأَقِمِ الصَّلَاةَ ۖ إِنَّ الصَّلَاةَ تَنْهَىٰ عَنِ
الْفَحْشَاءِ وَالْمُنكَرِ ۗ وَلَذِكْرُ اللَّهِ أَكْبَرُ ۗ
وَاللَّهُ يَعْلَمُ مَا تَصْنَعُونَ

17. الَّذِينَ يُقِيمُونَ الصَّلَاةَ وَيُؤْتُونَ
الزَّكَاةَ وَهُم بِالْآخِرَةِ هُمْ يُوقِنُونَ
أُولَٰئِكَ عَلَىٰ هُدًى مِّن رَّبِّهِمْ ۖ وَأُولَٰئِكَ
هُمُ الْمُفْلِحُونَ

18. إِنَّ الَّذِينَ يَتْلُونَ كِتَابَ اللَّهِ وَأَقَامُوا الصَّلَاةَ وَ
أَنفَقُوا مِمَّا رَزَقْنَاهُمْ سِرًّا وَعَلَانِيَةً يَرْجُونَ تِجَارَةً
لَّن تَبُورَ
لِيُوَفِّيَهُمْ أُجُورَهُمْ وَيَزِيدَهُم مِّن فَضْلِهِ ۚ إِنَّهُ
غَفُورٌ شَكُورٌ

13. And thou (Muhammad), be not loud voiced in thy worship nor yet silent there-in, but follow a way between.
17:110

14. And enjoin upon thy people worship and be con-stant therein. We ask not of thee a provision: We provide for thee. And the sequel is for righteousness.
20:132

15. Establish worship and pay the poor-due and obey the messenger, that haply ye may find mercy.
24:56

16. Recite that which hath been inspired in thee of the Scripture, and establish wor-ship. Lo! worship preserveth from lewdness and iniquity, and verily remembrance of Allah is more important. And Allah knoweth what ye do.
29:45

17. Those who establish worship and pay the poor-due and have sure faith in the Hereafter.

Such have guidance from their Lord. Such are the successful.
31:4–5

18. Lo! those who read the Scripture of Allah, and esta-blish worship, and spend of that which We have bestowed on them secretly and openly, they look forward to imperi-shable gain.

That He will pay them their wages and increase them of His grace. Lo! He is For–

giving, Responsive.

35:29–30

19. O ye who believe! When the call is heard for the prayer of the day of congregation, haste unto the remembrance of Allah and leave your trading. That is better for you if ye did but know.

And when the prayer is ended, then disperse in the land and seek of Allah's bounty, and remember Allah much, that ye may be successful.

62:9–10

20. Lo! thy Lord knoweth how thou keepest vigil sometimes nearly two–third of the night, or (sometimes) half or a third thereof, as do a party of those with thee. Allah measureth the night and the day. He knoweth that ye count it not, and turneth unto you in mercy. Recite, then, of the Qur'ān that which is easy for you. He knoweth that there are sick folk among you, while others travel in the land in search of Allah's bounty, and others (still) are fighting for the cause of Allah. So recite of it that which is easy (for you), and establish worship and pay the poor–due, and (so) lend unto Allah a goodly loan. Whatsoever good ye send before you for your souls, ye will find it with Allah, better and greater in the re–

19. يٰۤاَيُّهَا الَّذِيْنَ اٰمَنُوْۤا اِذَا نُوْدِيَ لِلصَّلٰوةِ مِنْ يَّوْمِ
الْجُمُعَةِ فَاسْعَوْا اِلٰى ذِكْرِ اللّٰهِ وَذَرُوا الْبَيْعَ ذٰلِكُمْ
خَيْرٌ لَّكُمْ اِنْ كُنْتُمْ تَعْلَمُوْنَ ۝٩
فَاِذَا قُضِيَتِ الصَّلٰوةُ فَانْتَشِرُوْا فِي الْاَرْضِ
وَابْتَغُوْا مِنْ فَضْلِ اللّٰهِ وَاذْكُرُوا اللّٰهَ كَثِيْرًا
لَّعَلَّكُمْ تُفْلِحُوْنَ ۝١٠

20. اِنَّ رَبَّكَ يَعْلَمُ اَنَّكَ تَقُوْمُ اَدْنٰى
مِنْ ثُلُثَيِ الَّيْلِ وَنِصْفَهٗ وَثُلُثَهٗ
وَطَآئِفَةٌ مِّنَ الَّذِيْنَ مَعَكَ ؕ وَاللّٰهُ
يُقَدِّرُ الَّيْلَ وَالنَّهَارَ ؕ عَلِمَ اَنْ لَّنْ
تُحْصُوْهُ فَتَابَ عَلَيْكُمْ فَاقْرَءُوْا
مَا تَيَسَّرَ مِنَ الْقُرْاٰنِ ؕ عَلِمَ اَنْ
سَيَكُوْنُ مِنْكُمْ مَّرْضٰى ۙ وَاٰخَرُوْنَ
يَضْرِبُوْنَ فِي الْاَرْضِ يَبْتَغُوْنَ مِنْ
فَضْلِ اللّٰهِ ۙ وَاٰخَرُوْنَ يُقَاتِلُوْنَ فِيْ
سَبِيْلِ اللّٰهِ ۖ فَاقْرَءُوْا مَا تَيَسَّرَ مِنْهُ ۙ
وَاَقِيْمُوا الصَّلٰوةَ وَاٰتُوا الزَّكٰوةَ
وَاَقْرِضُوا اللّٰهَ قَرْضًا حَسَنًا ؕ وَمَا
تُقَدِّمُوْا لِاَنْفُسِكُمْ مِّنْ خَيْرٍ تَجِدُوْهُ
عِنْدَ اللّٰهِ هُوَ خَيْرًا وَّاَعْظَمَ اَجْرًا ؕ
وَاسْتَغْفِرُوا اللّٰهَ ؕ اِنَّ اللّٰهَ غَفُوْرٌ رَّحِيْمٌ ۝٢٠

compense. And seek forgiveness of Allah. Lo! Allah is Forgiving, Merciful.

73:20

21. Remember the name of thy Lord at morn and evening.

And worship Him (a portion) of the night. And

glorify Him through the live–long night.

76:25–26

22. He is successful who groweth,
And remembereth the name of his Lord, so prayeth.

87:14–15

23. Ah, woe unto worship–pers
Who are heedless of their prayer:
Who would be seen (at worship)
Yet refuse small kind-nesses!

107:4–7

21. وَاذْكُرِ اسْمَ رَبِّكَ بُكْرَةً وَأَصِيلًا ﴿٢٥﴾
وَمِنَ اللَّيْلِ فَاسْجُدْ لَهُ وَسَبِّحْهُ
لَيْلًا طَوِيلًا ﴿٢٦﴾

22. قَدْ أَفْلَحَ مَنْ تَزَكَّىٰ ﴿١٤﴾
وَذَكَرَ اسْمَ رَبِّهِ فَصَلَّىٰ ﴿١٥﴾

23. فَوَيْلٌ لِلْمُصَلِّينَ ﴿٤﴾
الَّذِينَ هُمْ عَنْ صَلَاتِهِمْ سَاهُونَ ﴿٥﴾
الَّذِينَ هُمْ يُرَاءُونَ ﴿٦﴾
وَيَمْنَعُونَ الْمَاعُونَ ﴿٧﴾

Ref: 2:3,45,110,117; 4:77,162; 5:58; 6:72,92; 7:170; 8:2-3; 9:11,54; 14:37, 40 20:14,130; 22:34-35,41,78; 23:1-2,9; 24:37; 25:64; 27:3; 30:31; 35:18; 42:38; 70:22-23; 73:2-4,6-7; 74:42-43; 75:31; 96:9-10; 98:5; 108:2.

See also: **Call for Prayer, Friday Congregation,** ***Tahajjud. Tayammum, Wadhu.***

SALUTATION

1. Lo! Allah and His angels shower blessings on the Prophet. O ye who believe! Ask blessings on him and salute him with a worthy salutation.

33:56

SALVATION

1. And Allah inviteth unto the Garden, and unto forgiveness by His grace, and expoundeth thus His revelations to mankind that haply they may remember.

2:221

2. The devil promiseth you destitution and enjoineth on you lewdness. But Allah promiseth you forgiveness from Himself with bounty.

2:268

3. Allah hath promised those who believe and do good works: Theirs will be forgiveness and immense reward.

5:9

4. Lo! they who subdue their voices in the presence of the messenger of Allah, those are they whose hearts Allah hath proven unto righteousness. Theirs will be forgiveness and immense reward.

49:3

5. Lo! thy Lord is of vast mercy.

53:32

6. Race one with another for forgiveness from your Lord and a Garden whereof the breadth is as the breadth of the heavens and the earth, which is in store for those who believe in Allah and His messengers. Such is the bounty of Allah, which He bestoweth upon whom He will.

57:21

1. إِنَّ اللهَ وَمَلٰٓئِكَتَهُ يُصَلُّوْنَ عَلَى النَّبِيِّ
يٰٓاَيُّهَا الَّذِيْنَ اٰمَنُوْا صَلُّوْا عَلَيْهِ
وَسَلِّمُوْا تَسْلِيْمًا ۝

○

1. وَاللهُ يَدْعُوْٓا اِلَى الْجَنَّةِ وَالْمَغْفِرَةِ بِاِذْنِهٖ وَيُبَيِّنُ
اٰيٰتِهٖ لِلنَّاسِ لَعَلَّهُمْ يَتَذَكَّرُوْنَ ۝

2. اَلشَّيْطٰنُ يَعِدُكُمُ الْفَقْرَ وَيَاْمُرُكُمْ
بِالْفَحْشَآءِ وَاللهُ يَعِدُكُمْ مَّغْفِرَةً مِّنْهُ
وَفَضْلًا

3. وَعَدَ اللهُ الَّذِيْنَ اٰمَنُوْا وَعَمِلُوا الصّٰلِحٰتِ لَهُمْ
مَّغْفِرَةٌ وَّاَجْرٌ عَظِيْمٌ ۝

4. اِنَّ الَّذِيْنَ يَغُضُّوْنَ اَصْوَاتَهُمْ عِنْدَ
رَسُوْلِ اللهِ اُولٰٓئِكَ الَّذِيْنَ امْتَحَنَ
اللهُ قُلُوْبَهُمْ لِلتَّقْوٰى لَهُمْ مَّغْفِرَةٌ
وَّاَجْرٌ عَظِيْمٌ ۝

5. اِنَّ رَبَّكَ وَاسِعُ الْمَغْفِرَةِ

6. سَابِقُوْٓا اِلٰى مَغْفِرَةٍ مِّنْ رَّبِّكُمْ وَجَنَّةٍ
عَرْضُهَا كَعَرْضِ السَّمَآءِ وَالْاَرْضِ
اُعِدَّتْ لِلَّذِيْنَ اٰمَنُوْا بِاللهِ وَرُسُلِهٖ
ذٰلِكَ فَضْلُ اللهِ يُؤْتِيْهِ مَنْ يَّشَآءُ

SALVATION

Ref: 2:175; 3:133,136,157; 4:96; 8:4,74; 11:11; 13:6; 22:50; 24:26; 33:35; 34:4; 35:7; 36:11, 41:43; 47:15; 48:29; 57:20; 74:56.

See also: Mercy

SANCTITY OF OATH

1. And make not Allah, by your oaths, a hindrance to your being righteous and observing your duty unto Him and making peace among mankind. Allah is Hearer, Knower.

Allah will not take you to task for that which is unintentional in your oaths. But He will take you to task for that which your hearts have garnered. Allah is Forgiving, Clement.

2:224–225

2. Allah will not take you to task for that which is unintentional in your oaths, but He will take you to task for the oaths which ye swear in earnest. The expiation thereof is the feeding of ten of the needy with the average of that wherewith ye feed your own folk, or the clothing of them, or the liberation of a slave, and for him who findeth not (the wherewithal to do so) then a three days' fast. This is the expiation of your oaths when ye have sworn; and keep your oaths. Thus Allah expoundeth unto you His revelations in order that ye may give thanks.

5:89

3. And if they break their pledges after their treaty (hath been made with you) and assail your religion, then fight the heads of disbelief—Lo! they have no binding oaths—in order that they may desist.

1. وَلَا تَجْعَلُوا اللَّهَ عُرْضَةً لِأَيْمَانِكُمْ أَنْ تَبَرُّوا
وَتَتَّقُوا وَتُصْلِحُوا بَيْنَ النَّاسِ ۗ وَاللَّهُ سَمِيعٌ عَلِيمٌ ﴿٢٢٤﴾

لَا يُؤَاخِذُكُمُ اللَّهُ بِاللَّغْوِ فِي أَيْمَانِكُمْ وَلَٰكِنْ
يُؤَاخِذُكُمْ بِمَا كَسَبَتْ قُلُوبُكُمْ ۗ وَاللَّهُ غَفُورٌ حَلِيمٌ ﴿٢٢٥﴾

2. لَا يُؤَاخِذُكُمُ اللَّهُ بِاللَّغْوِ فِي أَيْمَانِكُمْ
وَلَٰكِنْ يُؤَاخِذُكُمْ بِمَا عَقَّدْتُمُ الْأَيْمَانَ ۖ
فَكَفَّارَتُهُ إِطْعَامُ عَشَرَةِ مَسَاكِينَ مِنْ
أَوْسَطِ مَا تُطْعِمُونَ أَهْلِيكُمْ أَوْ كِسْوَتُهُمْ
أَوْ تَحْرِيرُ رَقَبَةٍ ۖ فَمَنْ لَمْ يَجِدْ فَصِيَامُ
ثَلَاثَةِ أَيَّامٍ ۚ ذَٰلِكَ كَفَّارَةُ أَيْمَانِكُمْ إِذَا
حَلَفْتُمْ ۚ وَاحْفَظُوا أَيْمَانَكُمْ ۚ كَذَٰلِكَ يُبَيِّنُ
اللَّهُ لَكُمْ آيَاتِهِ لَعَلَّكُمْ تَشْكُرُونَ ﴿٨٩﴾

3. وَإِنْ نَكَثُوا أَيْمَانَهُمْ مِنْ بَعْدِ عَهْدِهِمْ
وَطَعَنُوا فِي دِينِكُمْ فَقَاتِلُوا أَئِمَّةَ الْكُفْرِ ۙ
إِنَّهُمْ لَا أَيْمَانَ لَهُمْ لَعَلَّهُمْ يَنْتَهُونَ ﴿١٢﴾

أَلَا تُقَاتِلُونَ قَوْمًا نَكَثُوا أَيْمَانَهُمْ وَهَمُّوا
بِإِخْرَاجِ الرَّسُولِ وَهُمْ بَدَءُوكُمْ أَوَّلَ مَرَّةٍ ۚ
أَتَخْشَوْنَهُمْ ۚ فَاللَّهُ أَحَقُّ أَنْ تَخْشَوْهُ
إِنْ كُنْتُمْ مُؤْمِنِينَ ﴿١٣﴾

Will ye not fight a folk who broke their solemn pledges, and purposed to drive out the messenger and did attack you first? What! Fear ye them? Now Allah hath more right that ye should fear Him, if ye are believers.

9:12–13

4. Fulfil the covenant of Allah when ye have covenanted, and break not your oaths after the asseveration of them, and after ye have made Allah surety over you. Lo! Allah knoweth what ye do.

And be not like unto her who unravelleth the thread, after she hath made it strong, to thin filaments, making your oaths a deceit between you because of a nation being more numerous than (another) nation. Allah only trieth you thereby, and He verily will explain to you on the Day of Resurrection that wherein ye differed.

Had Allah willed He could have made you (all) one nation, but He sendeth whom He will astray and guideth whom He will, and ye will indeed be asked of what ye used to do.

Make not your oaths a deceit between you, lest a foot should slip after being firmly planted and ye should taste evil forasmuch as ye debarred (men) from the way of Allah, and yours should be an awful doom.

16:91–94

5. Allah hath made lawful for you (Muslims) absolution from your oaths (of such a kind), and Allah is your Protector. He is the Knower,

4. وَأَوْفُوا بِعَهْدِ اللَّهِ إِذَا عَاهَدْتُمْ وَلَا
تَنْقُضُوا الْأَيْمَانَ بَعْدَ تَوْكِيدِهَا وَقَدْ
جَعَلْتُمُ اللَّهَ عَلَيْكُمْ كَفِيلًا ۚ إِنَّ اللَّهَ
يَعْلَمُ مَا تَفْعَلُونَ ﴿٩١﴾
وَلَا تَكُونُوا كَالَّتِي نَقَضَتْ غَزْلَهَا مِنْ
بَعْدِ قُوَّةٍ أَنْكَاثًا تَتَّخِذُونَ أَيْمَانَكُمْ
دَخَلًا بَيْنَكُمْ أَنْ تَكُونَ أُمَّةٌ هِيَ
أَرْبَىٰ مِنْ أُمَّةٍ ۚ إِنَّمَا يَبْلُوكُمُ اللَّهُ
بِهِ ۚ وَلَيُبَيِّنَنَّ لَكُمْ يَوْمَ الْقِيَامَةِ مَا
كُنْتُمْ فِيهِ تَخْتَلِفُونَ ﴿٩٢﴾

وَلَوْ شَاءَ اللَّهُ لَجَعَلَكُمْ أُمَّةً وَاحِدَةً
وَلَٰكِنْ يُضِلُّ مَنْ يَشَاءُ وَيَهْدِي مَنْ
يَشَاءُ ۚ وَلَتُسْأَلُنَّ عَمَّا كُنْتُمْ تَعْمَلُونَ ﴿٩٣﴾

وَلَا تَتَّخِذُوا أَيْمَانَكُمْ دَخَلًا بَيْنَكُمْ
فَتَزِلَّ قَدَمٌ بَعْدَ ثُبُوتِهَا وَتَذُوقُوا
السُّوءَ بِمَا صَدَدْتُمْ عَنْ سَبِيلِ اللَّهِ ۖ
وَلَكُمْ عَذَابٌ عَظِيمٌ ﴿٩٤﴾

5. قَدْ فَرَضَ اللَّهُ لَكُمْ تَحِلَّةَ أَيْمَانِكُمْ ۚ
وَاللَّهُ مَوْلَاكُمْ ۖ وَهُوَ الْعَلِيمُ الْحَكِيمُ ﴿٢﴾
6. وَلَا تُطِعْ كُلَّ حَلَّافٍ مَهِينٍ ﴿١٠﴾

the Wise.

66:2

6. Neither obey thou each feeble oath-monger,

68:10

Ref: 3:77: 5:53.92; 6:109; 16:38: 24:53.

SATAN

1. O ye who believe! Come, all of you, into submission (unto Him); and follow not the footsteps of the devil. Lo! he is an open enemy for you.
2:208

2. The devil promiseth you destitution and enjoineth on you lewdness. But Allah pro– miseth you forgiveness from Himself with bounty. Allah is All – Embracing, All-Knowing.
2:268

3. And (also) those who spend their wealth in order to be seen of men, and believe not in Allah nor the Last Day. Whoso taketh Satan for a comrade, a bad comrade hath he.
4:38

4. Those who believe do battle for the cause of Allah, and those who disbelieve do battle for the cause of idols. So fight the minions of the devil. Lo! the devil's strategy is ever weak,
4:76

5. O ye who believe! Strong drink and games of chance and idols and divining arrows are only an infamy of Satan's handiwork. Leave it aside in order that ye may succeed.

Satan seeketh only to cast among you enmity and

1. يا أيها الذين آمنوا ادخلوا في السلم كافة
ولا تتبعوا خطوات الشيطن إنه لكم
عدو مبين ﴿٢٠٨﴾

2. الشيطن يعدكم الفقر ويأمركم
بالفحشاء والله يعدكم مغفرة منه
وفضلا والله واسع عليم ﴿٢٦٨﴾

3 والذين ينفقون أموالهم رئاء الناس
ولا يؤمنون بالله ولا باليوم الآخر
ومن يكن الشيطن له قرينا فساء قرينا ﴿٣٨﴾

4. الذين آمنوا يقاتلون في سبيل الله
والذين كفروا يقاتلون في سبيل
الطاغوت فقاتلوا أولياء الشيطن إن
كيد الشيطن كان ضعيفا ﴿٧٦﴾

5. يا أيها الذين آمنوا إنما الخمر والميسر والأنصاب
والأزلام رجس من عمل الشيطن فاجتنبوه
لعلكم تفلحون ﴿٩٠﴾
إنما يريد الشيطن أن يوقع بينكم العداوة
والبغضاء في الخمر والميسر ويصدكم عن
ذكر الله وعن الصلوة فهل أنتم منتهون ﴿٩١﴾

6. فلولا إذ جاءهم بأسنا تضرعوا ولكن
قست قلوبهم وزين لهم الشيطن ما

hatred by means of strong drink and games of chance, and to turn you from remem-- brance of Allah and from (His) worship. Will ye then have done?
5:90–91

6. If only, when our disaster came on them, they had been humble! But their hearts were hardened and the devil made all that they used to do seem fair unto them!

6:43

7. Lo! the devils do inspire their minions to dispute with you. But if ye obey them, ye will be in truth as idolaters

6:121

8. And when thou recitest the Qur'ān, seek refuge in Allah from Satan, the outcast.

Lo! he hath no power over those who believe and put trust in their Lord.

His power is only over those who make a friend of him, and those who ascribe partners unto Him (Allah).

16:98–100

9. Lo! the squanderers were ever brothers of the devils, and the devil was ever an ingrate to his Lord.

17:27

10. And when We said unto the angels: Fall down prostrate before Adam and they fell prostrate all save Iblis, he said: Shall I fall prostrate before that which Thou hast created of clay?

He said: Seest Thou this (creature) whom Thou hast honoured above me, if Thou

كَانُوْا يَعْمَلُوْنَ ﴿٤٣﴾

7. وَاِنَّ الشَّيٰطِيْنَ لَيُوْحُوْنَ اِلٰٓى اَوْلِيٰٓـِٕهِمْ
لِيُجَادِلُوْكُمْ ۚ وَاِنْ اَطَعْتُمُوْهُمْ اِنَّكُمْ
لَمُشْرِكُوْنَ ﴿١٢١﴾

8. فَاِذَا قَرَاْتَ الْقُرْاٰنَ فَاسْتَعِذْ بِاللّٰهِ
مِنَ الشَّيْطٰنِ الرَّجِيْمِ ﴿٩٨﴾
اِنَّهٗ لَيْسَ لَهٗ سُلْطٰنٌ عَلَى الَّذِيْنَ اٰمَنُوْا
وَعَلٰى رَبِّهِمْ يَتَوَكَّلُوْنَ ﴿٩٩﴾
اِنَّمَا سُلْطٰنُهٗ عَلَى الَّذِيْنَ يَتَوَلَّوْنَهٗ
وَالَّذِيْنَ هُمْ بِهٖ مُشْرِكُوْنَ ﴿١٠٠﴾

9. اِنَّ الْمُبَذِّرِيْنَ كَانُوْٓا اِخْوَانَ الشَّيٰطِيْنِ ۭ
وَكَانَ الشَّيْطٰنُ لِرَبِّهٖ كَفُوْرًا ﴿٢٧﴾

10. وَاِذْ قُلْنَا لِلْمَلٰٓىِٕكَةِ اسْجُدُوْا لِاٰدَمَ فَسَجَدُوْٓا
اِلَّآ اِبْلِيْسَ ۭ قَالَ ءَاَسْجُدُ لِمَنْ
خَلَقْتَ طِيْنًا ﴿٦١﴾
قَالَ اَرَءَيْتَكَ هٰذَا الَّذِيْ كَرَّمْتَ عَلَيَّ ۡ
لَىِٕنْ اَخَّرْتَنِ اِلٰى يَوْمِ الْقِيٰمَةِ لَاَحْتَنِكَنَّ
ذُرِّيَّتَهٗٓ اِلَّا قَلِيْلًا ﴿٦٢﴾
قَالَ اذْهَبْ فَمَنْ تَبِعَكَ مِنْهُمْ فَاِنَّ
جَهَنَّمَ جَزَاۗؤُكُمْ جَزَاۗءً مَّوْفُوْرًا ﴿٦٣﴾
وَاسْتَفْزِزْ مَنِ اسْتَطَعْتَ مِنْهُمْ بِصَوْتِكَ

give me grace until the Day of Resurrection I verily will seize his seed, save but a few.

He said: Go, and whosoever of them followeth thee—lo! hell will be your payment, ample payment.

And excite any of them whom thou canst with thy voice, and urge thy horse and foot against them, and be a partner in their wealth and children, and promise them. Satan promiseth them only to deceive.

Lo! My (faithful) bondmen—over them thou hast no power, and thy Lord sufficeth as (their) guardian.

17:61–65

11. Lo! the devil is an enemy for you, so treat him as an enemy. He only summoneth his faction to be owners of the flaming Fire.

35:6

12. When thy Lord said unto the angels: Lo! I am about to creat a mortal out of mire,

And when I have fashioned him and breathed into him of My Spirit, then fall down before him prostrate.

The angels fell down, prostrate every one,

Saving Iblis; he was scornful and became one of the disbelievers.

He said: O Iblis! What hindereth thee from falling prostrate before that which I have created with My hands. Art thou too proud or art thou of the high exalted?

He said: I am better than him. Thou createdst me of fire, whilst him Thou didst create of clay.

He said: Go forth from

وَاَجْلِبْ عَلَيْهِمْ بِخَيْلِكَ وَرَجِلِكَ وَشَارِكْهُمْ
فِى الْاَمْوَالِ وَالْاَوْلَادِ وَعِدْهُمْ ۭ وَمَا
يَعِدُهُمُ الشَّيْطٰنُ اِلَّا غُرُوْرًا ﴿٦٤﴾
اِنَّ عِبَادِىْ لَيْسَ لَكَ عَلَيْهِمْ سُلْطٰنٌ ۭ
وَكَفٰى بِرَبِّكَ وَكِيْلًا ﴿٦٥﴾

11. اِنَّ الشَّيْطٰنَ لَكُمْ عَدُوٌّ فَاتَّخِذُوْهُ
عَدُوًّا ۭ اِنَّمَا يَدْعُوْا حِزْبَهٗ لِيَكُوْنُوْا
مِنْ اَصْحٰبِ السَّعِيْرِ ۭ ﴿٦﴾

12. اِذْ قَالَ رَبُّكَ لِلْمَلٰٓئِكَةِ اِنِّىْ خَالِقٌۢ
بَشَرًا مِّنْ طِيْنٍ ﴿٧١﴾
فَاِذَا سَوَّيْتُهٗ وَنَفَخْتُ فِيْهِ مِنْ
رُّوْحِىْ فَقَعُوْا لَهٗ سٰجِدِيْنَ ﴿٧٢﴾
فَسَجَدَ الْمَلٰٓئِكَةُ كُلُّهُمْ اَجْمَعُوْنَ ﴿٧٣﴾
اِلَّآ اِبْلِيْسَ ۭ اِسْتَكْبَرَ وَكَانَ
مِنَ الْكٰفِرِيْنَ ﴿٧٤﴾
قَالَ يٰٓاِبْلِيْسُ مَا مَنَعَكَ اَنْ تَسْجُدَ
لِمَا خَلَقْتُ بِيَدَىَّ ۭ اَسْتَكْبَرْتَ
اَمْ كُنْتَ مِنَ الْعَالِيْنَ ﴿٧٥﴾
قَالَ اَنَا خَيْرٌ مِّنْهُ ۭ خَلَقْتَنِىْ مِنْ
نَّارٍ وَّخَلَقْتَهٗ مِنْ طِيْنٍ ﴿٧٦﴾
قَالَ فَاخْرُجْ مِنْهَا فَاِنَّكَ رَجِيْمٌ ﴿٧٧﴾
وَّاِنَّ عَلَيْكَ لَعْنَتِىْٓ اِلٰى يَوْمِ الدِّيْنِ ﴿٧٨﴾
قَالَ رَبِّ فَاَنْظِرْنِىْٓ اِلٰى يَوْمِ يُبْعَثُوْنَ ﴿٧٩﴾
قَالَ فَاِنَّكَ مِنَ الْمُنْظَرِيْنَ ﴿٨٠﴾

hence, tor lo! thou art outcast,

And lo! My curse is on thee till the Day of Judgment.

He said: My Lord! Reprieve me till the Day when they are raised.

He said: Lo! thou art of those reprieved.

Until the Day of the time appointed.	إِلَىٰ يَوْمِ الْوَقْتِ الْمَعْلُومِ ۝٨١
He said: Then, by Thy might, I surely will beguile them every one,	قَالَ فَبِعِزَّتِكَ لَأُغْوِيَنَّهُمْ أَجْمَعِينَ ۝٨٢
Save Thy single-minded slaves among them.	إِلَّا عِبَادَكَ مِنْهُمُ الْمُخْلَصِينَ ۝٨٣
He said: The Truth is, and the Truth I speak,	قَالَ فَالْحَقُّ وَالْحَقَّ أَقُولُ ۝٨٤
That I shall fill hell with thee and with such of them as follow thee, together. 38:71–85	لَأَمْلَأَنَّ جَهَنَّمَ مِنكَ وَمِمَّن تَبِعَكَ مِنْهُمْ أَجْمَعِينَ ۝٨٥
13. And he whose sight is dim to the remembrance of the Beneficent, We assign unto him a devil who becometh his comrade; 43:36	13. وَمَن يَعْشُ عَن ذِكْرِ الرَّحْمَٰنِ نُقَيِّضْ لَهُ شَيْطَانًا فَهُوَ لَهُ قَرِينٌ ۝٣٦
14. The devil hath engrossed them and so hath caused them to forget remembrance of Allah. They are the devil's party. Lo! is it not the devil's party who will be the losers? 58:19	14. اسْتَحْوَذَ عَلَيْهِمُ الشَّيْطَانُ فَأَنسَاهُمْ ذِكْرَ اللَّهِ ۚ أُولَٰئِكَ حِزْبُ الشَّيْطَانِ ۚ أَلَا إِنَّ حِزْبَ الشَّيْطَانِ هُمُ الْخَاسِرُونَ ۝١٩

○

Ref: 2:14,36,102,168–169,275; 3:155; 4:177,119–120; 6:68,112,121,142; 7:11–27,30,175,200–201; 8:11,48; 14:22; 15:17,30–32; 17:27,53; 18:50; 19:44–45,83; 20:116–124; 21:82; 22:3,52–53; 23:97; 24:21; 25:29; 26:95–97,210,221; 27:24; 29:38; 31:21; 34:20; 35:6; 36:60; 37:7; 38:37,41; 41:36; 43:62; 47:25; 59:16; 67:5; 81:25.

SCROLL OF ACTIONS

1. And every man's augury have We fastened to his own neck, and We shall bring forth for him on the Day of Resurrection a book which he will find wide open.

(And it will be said unto him): Read thy book. Thy soul sufficeth as reckoner against thee this day.

17:13–14

2. Then, as for him who is given his record in his right hand, he will say: Take, read my book!

Surely I knew that I should have to meet my reckoning.

Then he will be in a blissful state.

In a high Garden

Whereof the clusters are in easy reach.

(And it will be said unto those therein): Eat and drink at ease for that which ye sent on before you in past days.

But as for him who is given his record in his left hand, he will say: Oh, would that I had not been given my book!

And knew not what my reckoning is!

Oh, would that it had been death!

My wealth hath not availed me,

My power hath gone from me.

69:19–29

3. Lo! there are above you guardians,

1. وَكُلَّ إِنسَانٍ أَلْزَمْنَاهُ طَائِرَهُ فِي عُنُقِهِ
وَنُخْرِجُ لَهُ يَوْمَ الْقِيَامَةِ كِتَابًا يَلْقَاهُ مَنشُورًا ﴿١٣﴾
اقْرَأْ كِتَابَكَ كَفَىٰ بِنَفْسِكَ الْيَوْمَ
عَلَيْكَ حَسِيبًا ﴿١٤﴾

2. فَأَمَّا مَنْ أُوتِيَ كِتَابَهُ بِيَمِينِهِ فَيَقُولُ
هَاؤُمُ اقْرَءُوا كِتَابِيَهْ ﴿١٩﴾
إِنِّي ظَنَنتُ أَنِّي مُلَاقٍ حِسَابِيَهْ ﴿٢٠﴾
فَهُوَ فِي عِيشَةٍ رَّاضِيَةٍ ﴿٢١﴾
فِي جَنَّةٍ عَالِيَةٍ ﴿٢٢﴾
قُطُوفُهَا دَانِيَةٌ ﴿٢٣﴾
كُلُوا وَاشْرَبُوا هَنِيئًا بِمَا أَسْلَفْتُمْ
فِي الْأَيَّامِ الْخَالِيَةِ ﴿٢٤﴾
وَأَمَّا مَنْ أُوتِيَ كِتَابَهُ بِشِمَالِهِ فَيَقُولُ
يَا لَيْتَنِي لَمْ أُوتَ كِتَابِيَهْ ﴿٢٥﴾
وَلَمْ أَدْرِ مَا حِسَابِيَهْ ﴿٢٦﴾
يَا لَيْتَهَا كَانَتِ الْقَاضِيَةَ ﴿٢٧﴾
مَا أَغْنَىٰ عَنِّي مَالِيَهْ ﴿٢٨﴾
هَلَكَ عَنِّي سُلْطَانِيَهْ ﴿٢٩﴾

3. وَإِنَّ عَلَيْكُمْ لَحَافِظِينَ ﴿١٠﴾
كِرَامًا كَاتِبِينَ ﴿١١﴾
يَعْلَمُونَ مَا تَفْعَلُونَ ﴿١٢﴾

4. فَأَمَّا مَنْ أُوتِيَ كِتَابَهُ بِيَمِينِهِ ﴿٧﴾
فَسَوْفَ يُحَاسَبُ حِسَابًا يَسِيرًا ﴿٨﴾
وَيَنقَلِبُ إِلَىٰ أَهْلِهِ مَسْرُورًا ﴿٩﴾

Generous and recording,

Who know (all) that ye do.

82:10–12

4. Then whoso is given his account in his right hand,

He truly will receive an easy reckoning

And will return unto his folk in joy.

But whoso is given his account behind his back,

He surely will invoke destruction

And be thrown to scorching fire.

84:7–12

5. That day mankind will issue forth in scattered groups to be shown their deeds.

And whoso doth good an atom's weight will see it then,

And whoso doth ill an atom's weight will see it then.

99:6–8

SECTARIANISM

1. And be ye not as those who separated and disputed after the clear proofs had come unto them. For such there is an awful doom

3:105

2. Lo! As for those who sunder their religion and become schismatics, no concern at all hast thou with them. Their case will go to Allah, Who then will tell them what they used to do.

6:159

3. So set thy purpose (O Muhammad) for religion as a man by nature upright — the nature (framed) of Allah, in which He hath created man. There is no altering (the laws of) Allah's creation. That is the right religion, but most men know not—

وَأَمَّا مَنْ أُوتِيَ كِتَابَهُ وَرَاءَ ظَهْرِهِ ۝
فَسَوْفَ يَدْعُوا ثُبُورًا ۝
وَيَصْلَىٰ سَعِيرًا ۝

5. يَوْمَئِذٍ يَصْدُرُ النَّاسُ أَشْتَاتًا
لِّيُرَوْا أَعْمَالَهُمْ ۝
فَمَن يَعْمَلْ مِثْقَالَ ذَرَّةٍ خَيْرًا
يَرَهُ ۝
وَمَن يَعْمَلْ مِثْقَالَ ذَرَّةٍ شَرًّا يَرَهُ ۝

○

1. وَلَا تَكُونُوا كَالَّذِينَ تَفَرَّقُوا وَاخْتَلَفُوا
مِن بَعْدِ مَا جَاءَهُمُ الْبَيِّنَاتُ ۚ وَأُولَٰئِكَ
لَهُمْ عَذَابٌ عَظِيمٌ ۝

2. إِنَّ الَّذِينَ فَرَّقُوا دِينَهُمْ وَكَانُوا شِيَعًا
لَّسْتَ مِنْهُمْ فِي شَيْءٍ ۚ إِنَّمَا أَمْرُهُمْ إِلَى
اللَّهِ ثُمَّ يُنَبِّئُهُم بِمَا كَانُوا يَفْعَلُونَ ۝

3. فَأَقِمْ وَجْهَكَ لِلدِّينِ حَنِيفًا ۚ فِطْرَتَ اللَّهِ الَّتِي فَطَرَ
النَّاسَ عَلَيْهَا ۚ لَا تَبْدِيلَ لِخَلْقِ اللَّهِ ۚ ذَٰلِكَ الدِّينُ
الْقَيِّمُ وَلَٰكِنَّ أَكْثَرَ النَّاسِ لَا يَعْلَمُونَ ۝
مُنِيبِينَ إِلَيْهِ وَاتَّقُوهُ وَأَقِيمُوا الصَّلَاةَ
وَلَا تَكُونُوا مِنَ الْمُشْرِكِينَ ۝
مِنَ الَّذِينَ فَرَّقُوا دِينَهُمْ وَكَانُوا
شِيَعًا ۖ كُلُّ حِزْبٍ بِمَا لَدَيْهِمْ فَرِحُونَ ۝

Turning unto Him (only); and be careful of your duty unto Him, and establish worship, and be not of those who ascribe partners (unto Him);

Of those who split up their religion and became schismatics, each sect exulting in its tenets.

30:30–32

SCROLL OF ACTIONS

Ref: 17:71; 75:13; 83:7-9, 18-21.

See also: Recording Angels, Weighing of Deeds.

4. He hath ordained for you that religion which He commended unto Noah, and that which We inspire in thee (Muhammad), and that which We commended unto Abraham and Moses and Jesus, saying: Establish the religion, and be not divided therein. Dreadful for the idolaters is that unto which thou callest them. Allah chooseth for Himself whom He will, and guideth unto Himself him who turneth (toward Him).

42:13

4. شَرَعَ لَكُمْ مِّنَ الدِّيْنِ مَا وَصّٰى بِهٖ
نُوْحًا وَّ الَّذِيْٓ اَوْحَيْنَآ اِلَيْكَ وَمَا
وَصَّيْنَا بِهٖٓ اِبْرٰهِيْمَ وَمُوْسٰى وَعِيْسٰٓى
اَنْ اَقِيْمُوا الدِّيْنَ وَلَا تَتَفَرَّقُوْا فِيْهِ
كَبُرَ عَلَى الْمُشْرِكِيْنَ مَا تَدْعُوْهُمْ اِلَيْهِ
اَللّٰهُ يَجْتَبِيْٓ اِلَيْهِ مَنْ يَّشَآءُ وَيَهْدِيْٓ
اِلَيْهِ مَنْ يُّنِيْبُ ﴿١٣﴾

SELF-PURIFICATION

1. Hast thou not seen those who praise themselves for purity? Nay, Allah purifieth whom He will, and they will not be wronged even the hair upon a date–stone.

4:49

1. اَلَمْ تَرَ اِلَى الَّذِيْنَ يُزَكُّوْنَ اَنْفُسَهُمْ بَلِ
اللّٰهُ يُزَكِّيْ مَنْ يَّشَآءُ وَلَا يُظْلَمُوْنَ فَتِيْلًا ﴿٤٩﴾

2. Thou warnest only those who fear their Lord in secret, and have established worship. He who groweth (in goodness), groweth only for himself, (he cannot by his merit redeem others). Unto Allah is the journeying.

35:18

2. اِنَّمَا تُنْذِرُ الَّذِيْنَ يَخْشَوْنَ رَبَّهُمْ
بِالْغَيْبِ وَاَقَامُوا الصَّلٰوةَ وَمَنْ تَزَكّٰى
فَاِنَّمَا يَتَزَكّٰى لِنَفْسِهٖ وَاِلَى اللّٰهِ
الْمَصِيْرُ ﴿١٨﴾

3. He it is Who hath sent among the unlettered ones a messenger of their own, to recite unto them His revelations and to make them grow, and to teach them the Scripture and Wisdom, though heretofore they were indeed in error manifest,

62:2

3. هُوَ الَّذِيْ بَعَثَ فِي الْاُمِّيّٖنَ رَسُوْلًا
مِّنْهُمْ يَتْلُوْا عَلَيْهِمْ اٰيٰتِهٖ وَيُزَكِّيْهِمْ
وَيُعَلِّمُهُمُ الْكِتٰبَ وَالْحِكْمَةَ وَاِنْ
كَانُوْا مِنْ قَبْلُ لَفِيْ ضَلٰلٍ مُّبِيْنٍ ﴿٢﴾

SECTARIANISM

See also: Religious Prejudice.

4. And a soul and Him Who perfected it
And inspired it (with conscience of) what is wrong for it and (what is) right for it.
He is indeed successful who causeth it to grow,
And he is indeed a failure ho stunteth it.
91:7–10

SELF—RESTRAINT

1. I do not exculpate myself. Lo! the (human) soul enjoineth unto evil, save that whereon my Lord hath mercy, Lo! my Lord is Forgiving, Merciful.
12:53

2. Nay, I swear by the Day of Resurrection;
Nay, I swear by the accusing soul (that this Scripture is true).
75:1–2

3. But ah! thou soul at peace!
Return unto thy Lord, content in His good pleasure!
89:27–28

4. And a soul and Him Who perfected it
And inspired it (with conscience of) what is wrong for it and (what is) right for it.
He is indeed successful

4 وَنَفْسٍ وَّمَا سَوّٰىهَا ۝
فَأَلْهَمَهَا فُجُوْرَهَا وَتَقْوٰىهَا ۝
قَدْ أَفْلَحَ مَنْ زَكّٰىهَا ۝
وَقَدْ خَابَ مَنْ دَسّٰىهَا ۝

1. وَمَآ أُبَرِّئُ نَفْسِيْ ۚ إِنَّ النَّفْسَ لَأَمَّارَةٌ
بِالسُّوْٓءِ إِلَّا مَا رَحِمَ رَبِّيْ ۚ إِنَّ رَبِّيْ
غَفُوْرٌ رَّحِيْمٌ ۝

2. لَآ أُقْسِمُ بِيَوْمِ الْقِيٰمَةِ ۝
وَلَآ أُقْسِمُ بِالنَّفْسِ اللَّوَّامَةِ ۝

3. يٰٓأَيَّتُهَا النَّفْسُ الْمُطْمَئِنَّةُ ۝
ارْجِعِيْٓ إِلٰى رَبِّكِ رَاضِيَةً مَّرْضِيَّةً ۝

4. وَنَفْسٍ وَّمَا سَوّٰىهَا ۝
فَأَلْهَمَهَا فُجُوْرَهَا وَتَقْوٰىهَا ۝
قَدْ أَفْلَحَ مَنْ زَكّٰىهَا ۝
وَقَدْ خَابَ مَنْ دَسّٰىهَا ۝

who causeth it to grow,
And he is indeed a failure who stunteth it.
91:7–10

SELF-PURIFICATION
See also: Remembrance of Allah.

SELLING FAITH

1. These are they who pur–chase error at the price of guidance, so their commerce doth not prosper, neither are they guided.

2:16

2. Therefore woe be unto those who write the Scrip–ture with their hands and then say, "This is from Allah," that they may purchase a small gain therewith! Woe unto them for that their hands have written, and woe unto them for that they earn thereby!

2:79

3. Lo! those who hide aught of the Scripture which Allah hath revealed, and purchase a small gain therewith, they eat into their bellies nothing else than fire. Allah will not speak to them on the Day of Re–surrection, nor will He make them grow. Theirs will be a painful doom.

Those are they who pur–chase error at the price of guidance, and torment at the price of pardon. How con–stant are they in their strife to reach the Fire!

2:174–175

4. Lo! those who purchase a small gain at the cost of Allah's covenant and their oaths, they have no portion in the Hereafter. Allah will neither speak to them nor look upon them on the Day of Resurrection, nor will He make them grow. Theirs will be a painful doom.

3:77

1. اُولٰٓئِكَ الَّذِيْنَ اشْتَرَوُا الضَّلٰلَةَ بِالْهُدٰى فَمَا
رَبِحَتْ تِّجَارَتُهُمْ وَمَا كَانُوْا مُهْتَدِيْنَ ﴿١٦﴾

2. فَوَيْلٌ لِّلَّذِيْنَ يَكْتُبُوْنَ الْكِتٰبَ بِاَيْدِيْهِمْ ثُمَّ
يَقُوْلُوْنَ هٰذَا مِنْ عِنْدِ اللّٰهِ لِيَشْتَرُوْا بِهٖ ثَمَنًا
قَلِيْلًا فَوَيْلٌ لَّهُمْ مِّمَّا كَتَبَتْ اَيْدِيْهِمْ
وَوَيْلٌ لَّهُمْ مِّمَّا يَكْسِبُوْنَ ﴿٧٩﴾

3. اِنَّ الَّذِيْنَ يَكْتُمُوْنَ مَآ اَنْزَلَ اللّٰهُ مِنَ
الْكِتٰبِ وَيَشْتَرُوْنَ بِهٖ ثَمَنًا قَلِيْلًا اُولٰٓئِكَ
مَا يَاْكُلُوْنَ فِيْ بُطُوْنِهِمْ اِلَّا النَّارَ وَلَا يُكَلِّمُهُمُ
اللّٰهُ يَوْمَ الْقِيٰمَةِ وَلَا يُزَكِّيْهِمْ وَلَهُمْ عَذَابٌ اَلِيْمٌ ﴿١٧٤﴾

اُولٰٓئِكَ الَّذِيْنَ اشْتَرَوُا الضَّلٰلَةَ بِالْهُدٰى
وَالْعَذَابَ بِالْمَغْفِرَةِ فَمَآ اَصْبَرَهُمْ عَلَى النَّارِ ﴿١٧٥﴾

4. اِنَّ الَّذِيْنَ يَشْتَرُوْنَ بِعَهْدِ اللّٰهِ وَاَيْمَانِهِمْ
ثَمَنًا قَلِيْلًا اُولٰٓئِكَ لَا خَلَاقَ لَهُمْ فِي
الْاٰخِرَةِ وَلَا يُكَلِّمُهُمُ اللّٰهُ وَلَا يَنْظُرُ اِلَيْهِمْ
يَوْمَ الْقِيٰمَةِ وَلَا يُزَكِّيْهِمْ وَلَهُمْ عَذَابٌ اَلِيْمٌ ۝

5. وَاِذْ اَخَذَ اللّٰهُ مِيْثَاقَ الَّذِيْنَ اُوْتُوا الْكِتٰبَ
لَتُبَيِّنُنَّهٗ لِلنَّاسِ وَلَا تَكْتُمُوْنَهٗ فَنَبَذُوْهُ
وَرَآءَ ظُهُوْرِهِمْ وَاشْتَرَوْا بِهٖ ثَمَنًا قَلِيْلًا
فَبِئْسَ مَا يَشْتَرُوْنَ ۝

5. And (remember) when Allah laid a charge on those who had received the Scrip-ture (He said): Ye are to ex-pound it to mankind and not to hide it. But they flung it behind their backs and bought thereby a little gain. Verily evil is that which they have gained thereby.

3:187

Ref: 2:41,86; 3:199; 4:44; 5:44; 9:9; 16:95.

SENILITY

1. And Allah createth you, then causeth you to die, and among you is he who is brought back to the most abject stage of life, so that he knoweth nothing after (having had) knowledge. Lo! Allah is Knower, Powerful.
16:70

2. He whom We bring unto old age, We reverse him in creation (making him go back to weakness after strength). Have ye then no sense?
36:68

3. He it is Who created you from dust, then from a drop (of seed) then from a clot, then bringeth you forth as a child, then (ordaineth) that ye attain full strength and afterward that ye become old men—though some among you die before—and that ye reach an appointed term, that haply ye may understand.
40:67

1. وَاللّٰهُ خَلَقَكُمْ ثُمَّ يَتَوَفّٰىكُمْ ۙ وَمِنْكُمْ مَّنْ يُّرَدُّ اِلٰٓى اَرْذَلِ الْعُمُرِ لِكَیْ لَا يَعْلَمَ بَعْدَ عِلْمٍ شَيْئًا ؕ اِنَّ اللّٰهَ عَلِيْمٌ قَدِيْرٌ ۝

2. وَمَنْ نُّعَمِّرْهُ نُنَكِّسْهُ فِی الْخَلْقِ ؕ اَفَلَا يَعْقِلُوْنَ ۝

3. هُوَ الَّذِیْ خَلَقَكُمْ مِّنْ تُرَابٍ ثُمَّ مِنْ نُّطْفَةٍ ثُمَّ مِنْ عَلَقَةٍ ثُمَّ يُخْرِجُكُمْ طِفْلًا ثُمَّ لِتَبْلُغُوْٓا اَشُدَّكُمْ ثُمَّ لِتَكُوْنُوْا شُيُوْخًا ۚ وَمِنْكُمْ مَّنْ يُّتَوَفّٰى مِنْ قَبْلُ وَلِتَبْلُغُوْٓا اَجَلًا مُّسَمًّى وَّلَعَلَّكُمْ تَعْقِلُوْنَ ۝

Ref: 2:166; 9:91; 11:72; 12:78; 17:75; 19:4; 28:23; 30:54; 35:11; 73:17.

SEVEN SLEEPERS

1. Or deemest thou that the People of the Cave and the Inscription are a wonder among Our portents?

When the young men fled for refuge to the Cave and said: Our Lord! Give us mercy from Thy presence, and shape for us right conduct in our plight:

Then We sealed up their hearing in the Cave for a number of years:

And afterward We raised them up that We might know which of, the two parties would best calculate the time that they had tarried.

We narrate unto thee their story with truth. Lo! They were young men who believed in their Lord, and We increased them in guidance.

And We made firm their hearts when they stood forth and said: Our Lord is the Lord of the heavens and the earth. We cry unto no god beside Him, for then should we utter an enormity.

These, our people, have chosen (other) gods beside Him though they bring no clear warrant (vouchsafed) to them. And who doth greater wrong than he who inventeth a lie concerning Allah?

And when ye withdraw from them and that which they worship except Allah, then seek refuge in the Cave; your Lord will spread for you of His mercy and will prepare for you a pillow in your plight.

1. أم حسبت أن أصحب الكهف
والرقيم كانوا من ءايتنا عجبا ﴿٩﴾
إذ أوى الفتية إلى الكهف فقالوا ربنا ءاتنا من
لدنك رحمة وهيئ لنا من أمرنا رشدا ﴿١٠﴾
فضربنا على ءاذانهم في الكهف
سنين عددا ﴿١١﴾
ثم بعثنهم لنعلم أي الحزبين
أحصى لما لبثوا أمدا ﴿١٢﴾
نحن نقص عليك نبأهم بالحق
إنهم فتية ءامنوا بربهم وزدنهم هدى ﴿١٣﴾
وربطنا على قلوبهم إذ قاموا فقالوا
ربنا رب السموت والأرض لن ندعوا
من دونه إلها لقد قلنا إذا شططا ﴿١٤﴾
هؤلاء قومنا اتخذوا من دونه ءالهة
لولا يأتون عليهم بسلطن بين فمن
أظلم ممن افترى على الله كذبا ﴿١٥﴾
وإذ اعتزلتموهم وما يعبدون إلا الله
فأوا إلى الكهف ينشر لكم ربكم من
رحمته ويهيئ لكم من أمركم مرفقا ﴿١٦﴾
وترى الشمس إذا طلعت تزور عن
كهفهم ذات اليمين وإذا غربت
تقرضهم ذات الشمال وهم في فجوة

And thou mightest have seen the sun when it rose move away from their cave to the right, and when it set go past them on the left, and they were in the cleft thereof. That was (one) of the portents of Allah. He whom Allah guideth, he indeed is led aright, and he whom He sendeth astray, for him thou wilt not find a guiding friend.

مِّنْهُ ۚ ذٰلِكَ مِنْ اٰيٰتِ اللّٰهِ ۗ مَنْ يَّهْدِ
اللّٰهُ فَهُوَ الْمُهْتَدِ ۚ وَمَنْ يُّضْلِلْ فَلَنْ تَجِدَ
لَهٗ وَلِيًّا مُّرْشِدًا ﴿١٧﴾
وَتَحْسَبُهُمْ اَيْقَاظًا وَّهُمْ رُقُوْدٌ ۖ وَّ
نُقَلِّبُهُمْ ذَاتَ الْيَمِيْنِ وَذَاتَ الشِّمَالِ ۖ
وَكَلْبُهُمْ بَاسِطٌ ذِرَاعَيْهِ بِالْوَصِيْدِ ۚ
لَوِ اطَّلَعْتَ عَلَيْهِمْ لَوَلَّيْتَ مِنْهُمْ فِرَارًا
وَّلَمُلِئْتَ مِنْهُمْ رُعْبًا ﴿١٨﴾
وَكَذٰلِكَ بَعَثْنٰهُمْ لِيَتَسَآءَلُوْا بَيْنَهُمْ ۚ قَالَ
قَآئِلٌ مِّنْهُمْ كَمْ لَبِثْتُمْ ۚ قَالُوْا لَبِثْنَا يَوْمًا
اَوْ بَعْضَ يَوْمٍ ۚ قَالُوْا رَبُّكُمْ اَعْلَمُ بِمَا لَبِثْتُمْ
فَابْعَثُوْٓا اَحَدَكُمْ بِوَرِقِكُمْ هٰذِهٖٓ اِلَى الْمَدِيْنَةِ
فَلْيَنْظُرْ اَيُّهَآ اَزْكٰى طَعَامًا فَلْيَاْتِكُمْ
بِرِزْقٍ مِّنْهُ وَلْيَتَلَطَّفْ وَلَا يُشْعِرَنَّ
بِكُمْ اَحَدًا ﴿١٩﴾
اِنَّهُمْ اِنْ يَّظْهَرُوْا عَلَيْكُمْ يَرْجُمُوْكُمْ
اَوْ يُعِيْدُوْكُمْ فِيْ مِلَّتِهِمْ وَلَنْ
تُفْلِحُوْٓا اِذًا اَبَدًا ﴿٢٠﴾
وَكَذٰلِكَ اَعْثَرْنَا عَلَيْهِمْ لِيَعْلَمُوْٓا اَنَّ
وَعْدَ اللّٰهِ حَقٌّ وَّاَنَّ السَّاعَةَ لَا رَيْبَ
فِيْهَا ۚ اِذْ يَتَنَازَعُوْنَ بَيْنَهُمْ اَمْرَهُمْ
فَقَالُوا ابْنُوْا عَلَيْهِمْ بُنْيَانًا ۚ رَبُّهُمْ
اَعْلَمُ بِهِمْ ۚ قَالَ الَّذِيْنَ غَلَبُوْا عَلٰٓى
اَمْرِهِمْ لَنَتَّخِذَنَّ عَلَيْهِمْ مَّسْجِدًا ﴿٢١﴾
سَيَقُوْلُوْنَ ثَلٰثَةٌ رَّابِعُهُمْ كَلْبُهُمْ ۚ وَ

And thou wouldst have deemed them waking though they were asleep, and We caused them to turn over to the right and the left, and their dog stretching out his paws on the threshold. If thou hadst observed them closely thou hadst assuredly turned away from them in flight, and hadst been filled with awe of them.

And in like manner We awakened them that they might question one another. A speaker from among them said: How long have ye tarried? They said: We have tarried a day or some part of a day, (others) said: Your Lord best knoweth what ye have tarried. Now send one of you with this your silver coin unto the city, and let him see what food is purest there and bring you a supply thereof. Let him be courteous and let no man know of you.

For they, if they should come to know of you, will stone you or turn you back to their religion; then ye will never prosper.

And in like manner We disclosed them (to the people of the city) that they might know that the promise of Allah is true, and that, as for the Hour, there is no doubt concerning it. When (the people of the city) disputed of their case among themselves, they said: Build over them a building; their Lord knoweth best concerning them. Those who won their point said: We verily shall build a place of worship over them.

(Some) will say: They were three, their dog the fourth, and (some) say: Five, their dog the sixth, guessing at random; and (some) say: Seven, and their dog the eighth. Say (O Muhammad): My Lord is Best Aware of their number. None knoweth them save a few. So contend not concerning them except with an outward contending, and ask not any of them to pronounce concerning them.

And say not of anything: Lo! I shall do that tomorrow,

Except if Allah will. And remember thy Lord when thou forgettest, and say: It may be that my Lord guideth me unto a nearer way of truth than this.

And (it is said) they tarried in their Cave three hundred years and add nine.

Say: Allah is Best Aware how long they tarried. His is the Invisible of the heavens and the earth. How clear of sight is He and keen of hearing! They have no protecting friend beside Him, and He maketh none to share in His government.

18:9–26

يَقُولُونَ خَمْسَةٌ سَادِسُهُمْ كَلْبُهُمْ رَجْمًا
بِالْغَيْبِ وَيَقُولُونَ سَبْعَةٌ وَّثَامِنُهُمْ
كَلْبُهُمْ قُلْ رَّبِّيْ أَعْلَمُ بِعِدَّتِهِمْ مَّا
يَعْلَمُهُمْ إِلَّا قَلِيلٌ فَلَا تُمَارِ فِيهِمْ
إِلَّا مِرَاءً ظَاهِرًا وَّلَا تَسْتَفْتِ فِيهِمْ
مِّنْهُمْ أَحَدًا ﴿٢٢﴾
وَلَا تَقُولَنَّ لِشَايْءٍ إِنِّيْ فَاعِلٌ ذٰلِكَ غَدًا ﴿٢٣﴾
إِلَّا أَنْ يَّشَاءَ اللّٰهُ وَاذْكُرْ رَّبَّكَ إِذَا نَسِيْتَ
وَقُلْ عَسٰى أَنْ يَّهْدِيَنِ رَبِّيْ لِأَقْرَبَ
مِنْ هٰذَا رَشَدًا ﴿٢٤﴾
وَلَبِثُوْا فِيْ كَهْفِهِمْ ثَلٰثَ مِائَةٍ سِنِيْنَ
وَازْدَادُوْا تِسْعًا ﴿٢٥﴾
قُلِ اللّٰهُ أَعْلَمُ بِمَا لَبِثُوْا لَهٗ غَيْبُ
السَّمٰوٰتِ وَالْأَرْضِ أَبْصِرْ بِهٖ وَأَسْمِعْ
مَا لَهُمْ مِّنْ دُوْنِهٖ مِنْ وَّلِيٍّ وَّلَا يُشْرِكُ
فِيْ حُكْمِهٖٓ أَحَدًا ﴿٢٦﴾

SHADOW

1. And unto Allah falleth prostrate whosoever is in the heavens and the earth, willingly or unwilling, as do their shadows in the morning and the evening hours.

13:15

2. Have they not observed all things that Allah hath created, how their shadows incline to the right and to the left, making prostration unto Allah, and they are lowly?

16:48

3. Hast thou not seen how thy Lord hath spread the shade—And if He willed He could have made it still—then We have made the sun its pilot;

Then We withdraw it unto Us, a gradual withdrawal.

25:45–46

1. وَلِلَّهِ يَسْجُدُ مَن فِي السَّمٰوٰتِ وَالْأَرْضِ
طَوْعًا وَكَرْهًا وَظِلٰلُهُم بِالْغُدُوِّ وَالْآصَالِ

2. أَوَلَمْ يَرَوْا إِلَىٰ مَا خَلَقَ اللَّهُ مِن شَيْءٍ
يَتَفَيَّؤُا ظِلٰلُهُ عَنِ الْيَمِينِ وَالشَّمَائِلِ
سُجَّدًا لِّلَّهِ وَهُمْ دٰخِرُونَ

3. أَلَمْ تَرَ إِلَىٰ رَبِّكَ كَيْفَ مَدَّ الظِّلَّ
وَلَوْ شَاءَ لَجَعَلَهُ سَاكِنًا ثُمَّ جَعَلْنَا
الشَّمْسَ عَلَيْهِ دَلِيلًا
ثُمَّ قَبَضْنٰهُ إِلَيْنَا قَبْضًا يَسِيرًا

Ref: 16:81.

SHARI'AH

1. And unto thee have We revealed the Scripture with the truth, confirming whatever Scripture was before it, and a watcher over it. So judge between them by that which Allah hath revealed, and follow not their desires away from the truth which hath come unto thee. For each We have appointed a divine law and a traced-out way. Had Allah willed He could have made you one community. But that He may try you by that which He hath given you (He hath made you as ye are). So vie one with another in good works. Unto Allah ye will all return, and He will then inform you of that wherein ye differ.

5·48

2. He hath ordained for you that religion which He commended unto Noah, and that which We inspire in thee (Muhammad), and that which We commended unto Abraham and Moses and Jesus, saying: Establish the religion and be not divided therein.

42:13

3. Or have they partners (of Allah) who have made lawful for them in religion that which Allah allowed not? and but for a decisive Word (gone forth already), it would have been judged between them. Lo! for wrong-doers is a painful doom.

42:21

1. وَأَنزَلْنَا إِلَيْكَ الْكِتَابَ بِالْحَقِّ مُصَدِّقًا لِّمَا بَيْنَ
يَدَيْهِ مِنَ الْكِتَابِ وَمُهَيْمِنًا عَلَيْهِ فَاحْكُم بَيْنَهُم بِمَا
أَنزَلَ اللَّهُ وَلَا تَتَّبِعْ أَهْوَاءَهُمْ عَمَّا جَاءَكَ مِنَ الْحَقِّ
لِكُلٍّ جَعَلْنَا مِنكُمْ شِرْعَةً وَمِنْهَاجًا وَلَوْ شَاءَ اللَّهُ
لَجَعَلَكُمْ أُمَّةً وَاحِدَةً وَلَٰكِن لِّيَبْلُوَكُمْ فِي مَا آتَاكُمْ
فَاسْتَبِقُوا الْخَيْرَاتِ إِلَى اللَّهِ مَرْجِعُكُمْ جَمِيعًا فَيُنَبِّئُكُم
بِمَا كُنتُمْ فِيهِ تَخْتَلِفُونَ ﴿٤٨﴾

2. شَرَعَ لَكُم مِّنَ الدِّينِ مَا وَصَّىٰ بِهِ
نُوحًا وَالَّذِي أَوْحَيْنَا إِلَيْكَ وَمَا
وَصَّيْنَا بِهِ إِبْرَاهِيمَ وَمُوسَىٰ وَعِيسَىٰ
أَنْ أَقِيمُوا الدِّينَ وَلَا تَتَفَرَّقُوا فِيهِ

3. أَمْ لَهُمْ شُرَكَاءُ شَرَعُوا لَهُم مِّنَ
الدِّينِ مَا لَمْ يَأْذَن بِهِ اللَّهُ وَلَوْ
لَا كَلِمَةُ الْفَصْلِ لَقُضِيَ بَيْنَهُمْ وَإِنَّ
الظَّالِمِينَ لَهُمْ عَذَابٌ أَلِيمٌ ﴿٢١﴾

4. ثُمَّ جَعَلْنَاكَ عَلَىٰ شَرِيعَةٍ مِّنَ الْأَمْرِ
فَاتَّبِعْهَا وَلَا تَتَّبِعْ أَهْوَاءَ الَّذِينَ
لَا يَعْلَمُونَ ﴿١٨﴾

O

4. And now have We set thee (O Muhammad) on a clear road of (Our) commandment; so follow it, and follow not the whims of those who know not.

45:18

SHOOTING STAR

1. And verily in the heaven We have set mansions of the stars, and We have beautified it for beholders.

And We have guarded it from every outcast devil,

Save him who stealeth the hearing, and then doth a clear flame pursue.

15:16–18

2. Lo! We have adorned the lowest heaven with an ornament, the planets;

With security from every froward devil.

They cannot listen to the Highest Chiefs for they are pelted from every side,

Outcast and theirs is a perpetual torment;

Save him who snatcheth a fragment, and there pursueth him a piercing flame.

37:6–10

3. And (the Jinn who had listened to the Qur'ân said): We had sought the heaven but had found it filled with strong warders and meteors.

And we used to sit on places (high) therein to listen. But he who listened now findeth a flame in wait for him.

72:8–9

1. وَلَقَدْ جَعَلْنَا فِي السَّمَآءِ بُرُوجًا وَّزَيَّنّٰهَا لِلنّٰظِرِيْنَ ﴿١٦﴾
وَحَفِظْنٰهَا مِنْ كُلِّ شَيْطٰنٍ رَّجِيْمٍ ﴿١٧﴾
اِلَّا مَنِ اسْتَرَقَ السَّمْعَ فَاَتْبَعَهٗ
شِهَابٌ مُّبِيْنٌ ﴿١٨﴾

2. اِنَّا زَيَّنَّا السَّمَآءَ الدُّنْيَا بِزِيْنَةِ ٍالْكَوَاكِبِ ﴿٦﴾
وَحِفْظًا مِّنْ كُلِّ شَيْطٰنٍ مَّارِدٍ ﴿٧﴾
لَا يَسَّمَّعُوْنَ اِلَى الْمَلَاِ الْاَعْلٰى وَيُقْذَفُوْنَ مِنْ
كُلِّ جَانِبٍ ﴿٨﴾
دُحُوْرًا وَّلَهُمْ عَذَابٌ وَّاصِبٌ ﴿٩﴾
اِلَّا مَنْ خَطِفَ الْخَطْفَةَ فَاَتْبَعَهٗ شِهَابٌ
ثَاقِبٌ ﴿١٠﴾

3. وَّاَنَّا لَمَسْنَا السَّمَآءَ فَوَجَدْنٰهَا مُلِئَتْ
حَرَسًا شَدِيْدًا وَّشُهُبًا ﴿٨﴾
وَّاَنَّا كُنَّا نَقْعُدُ مِنْهَا مَقَاعِدَ لِلسَّمْعِ
فَمَنْ يَّسْتَمِعِ الْاٰنَ يَجِدْ لَهٗ
شِهَابًا رَّصَدًا ﴿٩﴾

SIBGHAH

1. (We take our) colour from Allah, and who is better than Allah at colouring? We are His worshippers.

2:138

1. صِبْغَةَ اللّٰهِ ۚ وَمَنْ اَحْسَنُ مِنَ اللّٰهِ صِبْغَةً ۫
وَّنَحْنُ لَهٗ عٰبِدُوْنَ ﴿١٣٨﴾

SIGNS OF ALLAH

1. Lo! in the creation of the heavens and the earth, and the difference of night and day, and the ships which run upon the sea with that which is of use to men, and the water which Allah sendeth down from the sky, thereby reviving the earth after its death, and dispersing all kinds of beasts therein, and (in) the ordinance of the winds, and the clouds obedient between heaven and earth: are signs (of Allah's Sovereignty) for people who have sense.

2:164

2. Is it not a guidance for them (to know) how many a generation We destroyed before them, amid whose dwellings they walk? Lo! therein verily are signs for men of thought.

20:128

3. Hast thou not seen how Allah wafteth the clouds, then gathereth them, then maketh them layers, and thou seest the rains come forth from between them; He sendeth down from the heaven mountains wherein is hail, and smiteth therewith whom He will, and averteth it from whom He will. The flashing of His lightning all but snatcheth away the sight.

Allah causeth the revolution of the day and the night.

1. إِنَّ فِي خَلْقِ السَّمٰوٰتِ وَالْأَرْضِ وَاخْتِلَافِ الَّيْلِ
وَالنَّهَارِ وَالْفُلْكِ الَّتِي تَجْرِي فِي الْبَحْرِ بِمَا يَنفَعُ
النَّاسَ وَمَآ أَنزَلَ اللّٰهُ مِنَ السَّمَآءِ مِن مَّآءٍ فَأَحْيَا
بِهِ الْأَرْضَ بَعْدَ مَوْتِهَا وَبَثَّ فِيهَا مِن كُلِّ دَآبَّةٍ
وَتَصْرِيفِ الرِّيٰحِ وَالسَّحَابِ الْمُسَخَّرِ بَيْنَ السَّمَآءِ
وَالْأَرْضِ لَاٰيٰتٍ لِّقَوْمٍ يَعْقِلُونَ ﴿١٦٤﴾

2. أَفَلَمْ يَهْدِ لَهُمْ كَمْ أَهْلَكْنَا قَبْلَهُم مِّنَ
الْقُرُونِ يَمْشُونَ فِي مَسٰكِنِهِمْ إِنَّ فِي
ذٰلِكَ لَاٰيٰتٍ لِّأُولِي النُّهٰى ﴿١٢٨﴾

3. أَلَمْ تَرَ أَنَّ اللّٰهَ يُزْجِي سَحَابًا ثُمَّ يُؤَلِّفُ
بَيْنَهُ ثُمَّ يَجْعَلُهُ رُكَامًا فَتَرَى الْوَدْقَ
يَخْرُجُ مِنْ خِلٰلِهِ وَيُنَزِّلُ مِنَ السَّمَآءِ
مِن جِبَالٍ فِيهَا مِن بَرَدٍ فَيُصِيبُ بِهِ
مَن يَشَآءُ وَيَصْرِفُهُ عَن مَّن يَشَآءُ
يَكَادُ سَنَا بَرْقِهِ يَذْهَبُ بِالْأَبْصٰرِ ﴿٤٣﴾
يُقَلِّبُ اللّٰهُ الَّيْلَ وَالنَّهَارَ إِنَّ فِي ذٰلِكَ
لَعِبْرَةً لِّأُولِي الْأَبْصٰرِ ﴿٤٤﴾

وَاللّٰهُ خَلَقَ كُلَّ دَآبَّةٍ مِّن مَّآءٍ
فَمِنْهُم مَّن يَمْشِي عَلٰى بَطْنِهِ وَمِنْهُم
مَّن يَمْشِي عَلٰى رِجْلَيْنِ وَمِنْهُم مَّن
يَمْشِي عَلٰى أَرْبَعٍ يَخْلُقُ اللّٰهُ مَا يَشَآءُ
إِنَّ اللّٰهَ عَلٰى كُلِّ شَيْءٍ قَدِيرٌ ﴿٤٥﴾

Lo! herein is indeed a lesson for those who see.

Allah hath created every animal of water. Of them is (a kind) that goeth upon its belly and (a kind) that goeth upon two legs and (a kind) that goeth upon four. Allah createth what He will. Lo! Allah is Able to do all things.

24:43–45

4. Have they not seen the earth, how much of every fruitful kind We make to grow therein?

Lo! herein is indeed a portent; yet most of them are not believers.

26:7–8

5. Those who disbelieve in the revelations of Allah and in (their) meeting with Him, such have no hope of My mercy. For such there is a painful doom.

29:23

6. Have they not pondered upon themselves? Allah created not the heavens and the earth, and that which is between them, save with truth and for a destined end. But truly, many of mankind are disbelievers in the meeting with their Lord.

30:8

7. And of His signs is this: He created you of dust, and behold you human beings, ranging widely!

And of His signs is this: He created for you helpmates from yourselves that ye might find rest in them,and He ordained between you love and mercy. Lo, herein indeed are portents for folk who reflect.

And of His signs is the creation of the heavens and the earth, and the difference of your languages and colours.

4. أَوَلَمْ يَرَوْا إِلَى الْأَرْضِ كَمْ أَنْبَتْنَا
فِيهَا مِنْ كُلِّ زَوْجٍ كَرِيمٍ ﴿٧﴾
إِنَّ فِي ذَٰلِكَ لَآيَةً ۖ وَمَا كَانَ
أَكْثَرُهُمْ مُؤْمِنِينَ ﴿٨﴾

5. وَالَّذِينَ كَفَرُوا بِآيَاتِ اللَّهِ وَلِقَائِهِ أُولَٰئِكَ يَئِسُوا
مِنْ رَحْمَتِي وَأُولَٰئِكَ لَهُمْ عَذَابٌ أَلِيمٌ ﴿٢٣﴾

6. أَوَلَمْ يَتَفَكَّرُوا فِي أَنْفُسِهِمْ ۗ مَا خَلَقَ
اللَّهُ السَّمَاوَاتِ وَالْأَرْضَ وَمَا بَيْنَهُمَا
إِلَّا بِالْحَقِّ وَأَجَلٍ مُسَمًّى ۗ وَإِنَّ
كَثِيرًا مِنَ النَّاسِ بِلِقَاءِ رَبِّهِمْ لَكَافِرُونَ ﴿٨﴾

7. وَمِنْ آيَاتِهِ أَنْ خَلَقَكُمْ مِنْ تُرَابٍ
ثُمَّ إِذَا أَنْتُمْ بَشَرٌ تَنْتَشِرُونَ ﴿٢٠﴾
وَمِنْ آيَاتِهِ أَنْ خَلَقَ لَكُمْ مِنْ أَنْفُسِكُمْ
أَزْوَاجًا لِتَسْكُنُوا إِلَيْهَا وَجَعَلَ بَيْنَكُمْ
مَوَدَّةً وَرَحْمَةً ۚ إِنَّ فِي ذَٰلِكَ لَآيَاتٍ
لِقَوْمٍ يَتَفَكَّرُونَ ﴿٢١﴾
وَمِنْ آيَاتِهِ خَلْقُ السَّمَاوَاتِ وَالْأَرْضِ
وَاخْتِلَافُ أَلْسِنَتِكُمْ وَأَلْوَانِكُمْ ۚ إِنَّ
فِي ذَٰلِكَ لَآيَاتٍ لِلْعَالِمِينَ ﴿٢٢﴾
وَمِنْ آيَاتِهِ مَنَامُكُمْ بِاللَّيْلِ وَالنَّهَارِ
وَابْتِغَاؤُكُمْ مِنْ فَضْلِهِ ۚ إِنَّ فِي ذَٰلِكَ
لَآيَاتٍ لِقَوْمٍ يَسْمَعُونَ ﴿٢٣﴾
وَمِنْ آيَاتِهِ يُرِيكُمُ الْبَرْقَ خَوْفًا وَ

Lo! herein indeed are portents for men of knowledge.

And of His signs is your slumber by night and by day, and your seeking of His bounty. Lo! herein indeed are portents for folk who heed.

And of His signs is this: He showeth you the lightning

for a fear and for a hope, and sendeth down water from the sky, and thereby quickeneth the earth after her death. Lo! herein indeed are protents for folk who understand.

And of His signs is this: The heavens and the earth stand fast by His command, and afterward, when He calleth you, lo! from the earth ye will emerge.

30:20–25

8. And of His signs is this: He sendeth herald winds to make you taste His mercy, and that the ships may sail at His command, and that ye may seek His favour, and that haply ye may be thankful.

30:46

9. We shall show them Our portents on the horizons and within themselves until it will be manifest unto them that it is the Truth. Doth not thy Lord suffice, since He is Witness over all things?

41:53

طَمَعًا وَّيُنَزِّلُ مِنَ السَّمَآءِ مَآءً فَيُحْيِ
بِهِ الْأَرْضَ بَعْدَ مَوْتِهَا ۗ إِنَّ فِي
ذَٰلِكَ لَآيَاتٍ لِّقَوْمٍ يَعْقِلُونَ ﴿٢٤﴾
وَمِنْ آيَاتِهِ أَن تَقُومَ السَّمَآءُ وَ
الْأَرْضُ بِأَمْرِهِ ۚ ثُمَّ إِذَا دَعَاكُمْ دَعْوَةً
مِّنَ الْأَرْضِ ۖ إِذَا أَنتُمْ تَخْرُجُونَ ﴿٢٥﴾

8. وَمِنْ آيَاتِهِ أَن يُرْسِلَ الرِّيَاحَ
مُبَشِّرَاتٍ وَلِيُذِيقَكُم مِّن رَّحْمَتِهِ
وَلِتَجْرِيَ الْفُلْكُ بِأَمْرِهِ وَلِتَبْتَغُوا
مِن فَضْلِهِ وَلَعَلَّكُمْ تَشْكُرُونَ ﴿٤٦﴾

9. سَنُرِيهِمْ آيَاتِنَا فِي الْآفَاقِ وَفِي أَنفُسِهِمْ
حَتَّىٰ يَتَبَيَّنَ لَهُمْ أَنَّهُ الْحَقُّ ۗ أَوَلَمْ
يَكْفِ بِرَبِّكَ أَنَّهُ عَلَىٰ كُلِّ شَيْءٍ شَهِيدٌ ﴿٥٣﴾

○

Ref: 3:190; 10:101; 12:105; 17:12,59; 28:72–73; 29:19–20,44; 30:9,37; 31:20,29; 34:9; 36:37,41,46,77,81; 40:81; 41:39; 42:29; 45:3–5; 50:6–11, 37; 51:20–22; 67:19; 71:15; 75:7–10; 77:20–23; 78:6–16; 79:27–33; 88:17–20; 90:8–10.

See also: Monuments of Allah.

SILLY TALK

1. O ye who believe! Ask not of things which, if they were made known unto you, would trouble you, but if ye ask of them when the Qur'ān is being revealed, they will be made known unto you. Allah pardoneth this, for Allah is Forgiving, Clement.

A folk before you asked (for such disclosures) and then disbelieved therein.

5:101–102

2. Successful indeed are the believers,

Who are humble in their prayers,

And who shun vain conversation,

23:1–3

3. The (faithful) slaves of the Beneficent are they who walk upon the earth modestly, and when the foolish ones address them answer: Peace!

25:63

4. And those who will not witness vanity, but when they pass near senseless play, pass by with dignity.

25:72

5. And when they hear vanity they withdraw from it and say: Unto us our works and unto you your works. Peace be unto you! We desire not the ignorant.

28:55

1. يٰٓأَيُّهَا الَّذِينَ ءَامَنُوا لَا تَسْـَٔلُوا عَنْ أَشْيَآءَ
إِن تُبْدَ لَكُمْ تَسُؤْكُمْ وَإِن تَسْـَٔلُوا عَنْهَا
حِينَ يُنَزَّلُ الْقُرْءَانُ تُبْدَ لَكُمْ عَفَا اللَّهُ
عَنْهَا وَاللَّهُ غَفُورٌ حَلِيمٌ ﴿١٠١﴾
قَدْ سَأَلَهَا قَوْمٌ مِّن قَبْلِكُمْ ثُمَّ أَصْبَحُوا
بِهَا كَٰفِرِينَ ﴿١٠٢﴾

2. قَدْ أَفْلَحَ الْمُؤْمِنُونَ ﴿١﴾
الَّذِينَ هُمْ فِي صَلَاتِهِمْ خَٰشِعُونَ ﴿٢﴾
وَالَّذِينَ هُمْ عَنِ اللَّغْوِ مُعْرِضُونَ ﴿٣﴾

3. وَعِبَادُ الرَّحْمَٰنِ الَّذِينَ يَمْشُونَ عَلَى
الْأَرْضِ هَوْنًا وَإِذَا خَاطَبَهُمُ الْجَٰهِلُونَ
قَالُوا سَلَٰمًا ﴿٦٣﴾

4. وَالَّذِينَ لَا يَشْهَدُونَ الزُّورَ وَإِذَا
مَرُّوا بِاللَّغْوِ مَرُّوا كِرَامًا ﴿٧٢﴾

5. وَإِذَا سَمِعُوا اللَّغْوَ أَعْرَضُوا عَنْهُ وَ
قَالُوا لَنَا أَعْمَٰلُنَا وَلَكُمْ أَعْمَٰلُكُمْ
سَلَٰمٌ عَلَيْكُمْ لَا نَبْتَغِي الْجَٰهِلِينَ ﴿٥٥﴾

○

SIN

1. If ye avoid the great (things) which ye are forbidden, We will remit from you your evil deeds and make you enter at a noble gate.

4:31

2. Forsake the outwardness of sin and the inwardness thereof. Lo! those who garner sin will be awarded that which they have earned.

6:120

3. And unto Allah belongeth whatsoever is in the heavens and whatsoever is in the earth, that He may reward those who do evil with that which they have done, and reward those who do good with goodness.

Those who avoid enormities of sin and abominations, save the unwilled offences—(for them) lo! thy Lord is of vast mercy. He is Best Aware of you (from the time) when He created you from the earth, and when ye were hidden in the bellies of your mothers. Therefor ascribe not purity unto yourselves. He is Best Aware of him who wardeth off (evil).

53:31–32

1. إِنْ تَجْتَنِبُوا كَبَآئِرَ مَا تُنْهَوْنَ عَنْهُ نُكَفِّرْ عَنْكُمْ سَيِّاٰتِكُمْ وَنُدْخِلْكُمْ مُّدْخَلًا كَرِيمًا ﴿٣١﴾

2. وَذَرُوا ظَاهِرَ الْإِثْمِ وَبَاطِنَهُ ۚ إِنَّ الَّذِينَ يَكْسِبُونَ الْإِثْمَ سَيُجْزَوْنَ بِمَا كَانُوا يَقْتَرِفُونَ ○

3. وَلِلّٰهِ مَا فِي السَّمٰوٰتِ وَمَا فِي الْأَرْضِ لِيَجْزِيَ الَّذِينَ أَسَآءُوا بِمَا عَمِلُوا وَيَجْزِيَ الَّذِينَ أَحْسَنُوا بِالْحُسْنٰى ﴿٣١﴾

الَّذِينَ يَجْتَنِبُونَ كَبٰٓئِرَ الْإِثْمِ وَالْفَوَاحِشَ إِلَّا اللَّمَمَ ۚ إِنَّ رَبَّكَ وَاسِعُ الْمَغْفِرَةِ ۚ هُوَ أَعْلَمُ بِكُمْ إِذْ أَنْشَأَكُمْ مِّنَ الْأَرْضِ وَإِذْ أَنْتُمْ أَجِنَّةٌ فِي بُطُونِ أُمَّهٰتِكُمْ ۖ فَلَا تُزَكُّوا أَنْفُسَكُمْ ۚ هُوَ أَعْلَمُ بِمَنِ اتَّقٰى ﴿٣٢﴾

○

See also: Recompense.

SIRAH

1. It was by the mercy of Allah that thou wast lenient with them (O Muhammad), for if thou hadst been stern and fierce of heart they would have dispersed from round about thee. So pardon them and ask forgiveness for them and consult with them upon the conduct of affairs. And when thou art resolved, then put thy trust in Allah. Lo! Allah loveth those who put their trust (in Him).

3:159

2. O people of the Scripture! Now hath Our messenger come unto you, expounding unto you much of that which ye used to hide in the Scripture, and forgiving much. Now hath come unto you light from Allah and a plain Scripture:

Whereby Allah guideth him who seeketh His good pleasure unto paths of peace, He bringeth them out of darkness unto light by His decree, and guideth them unto a straight path.

5:15–16

3. We know well how their talk grieveth thee, though in truth they deny not thee (Muhammad), but evil–doers flout the revelations of Allah.

6:33

4. If ye help him not, still Allah helped him when those who disbelieve drove him forth, the second of two; when they two were in the cave, when he said unto his comrade: Grieve not. Lo! Allah is with us. Then Allah caused His peace of reassurance to descend upon him and supported him with hosts ye cannot see, and made the word of those who disbelieved the nethermost, while Allah's Word it was that became the uppermost. Allah is Mighty, Wise.

9:40

1. فَبِمَا رَحْمَةٍ مِّنَ اللَّهِ لِنتَ لَهُمْ ۖ وَلَوْ كُنتَ فَظًّا
غَلِيظَ الْقَلْبِ لَانفَضُّوا مِنْ حَوْلِكَ ۖ فَاعْفُ عَنْهُمْ
وَاسْتَغْفِرْ لَهُمْ وَشَاوِرْهُمْ فِي الْأَمْرِ ۖ فَإِذَا عَزَمْتَ
فَتَوَكَّلْ عَلَى اللَّهِ ۚ إِنَّ اللَّهَ يُحِبُّ
الْمُتَوَكِّلِينَ ﴿١٥٩﴾

2. يَا أَهْلَ الْكِتَابِ قَدْ جَاءَكُمْ رَسُولُنَا
يُبَيِّنُ لَكُمْ كَثِيرًا مِّمَّا كُنتُمْ تُخْفُونَ
مِنَ الْكِتَابِ وَيَعْفُو عَن كَثِيرٍ ۚ قَدْ جَاءَكُم
مِّنَ اللَّهِ نُورٌ وَكِتَابٌ مُّبِينٌ ﴿١٥﴾

يَهْدِي بِهِ اللَّهُ مَنِ اتَّبَعَ رِضْوَانَهُ
سُبُلَ السَّلَامِ وَيُخْرِجُهُم مِّنَ الظُّلُمَاتِ
إِلَى النُّورِ بِإِذْنِهِ وَيَهْدِيهِمْ إِلَىٰ
صِرَاطٍ مُّسْتَقِيمٍ ﴿١٦﴾

3. قَدْ نَعْلَمُ إِنَّهُ لَيَحْزُنُكَ الَّذِي يَقُولُونَ
فَإِنَّهُمْ لَا يُكَذِّبُونَكَ وَلَٰكِنَّ الظَّالِمِينَ
بِآيَاتِ اللَّهِ يَجْحَدُونَ ﴿٣٣﴾

4. إِلَّا تَنصُرُوهُ فَقَدْ نَصَرَهُ اللَّهُ إِذْ أَخْرَجَهُ
الَّذِينَ كَفَرُوا ثَانِيَ اثْنَيْنِ إِذْ هُمَا فِي الْغَارِ
إِذْ يَقُولُ لِصَاحِبِهِ لَا تَحْزَنْ إِنَّ اللَّهَ مَعَنَا ۖ
فَأَنزَلَ اللَّهُ سَكِينَتَهُ عَلَيْهِ وَأَيَّدَهُ بِجُنُودٍ
لَّمْ تَرَوْهَا وَجَعَلَ كَلِمَةَ الَّذِينَ كَفَرُوا
السُّفْلَىٰ ۗ وَكَلِمَةُ اللَّهِ هِيَ الْعُلْيَا ۗ وَاللَّهُ
عَزِيزٌ حَكِيمٌ ﴿٤٠﴾

5. And of them are those who vex the Prophet and say: He is only a hearer. Say: A hearer of good for you, who believeth in Allah and is true to the believers, and a mercy for such of you as believe. Those who vex the messenger of Allah, for them there is a painful doom.

9:61

6. There hath come unto you a messenger, (one) of yourselves, unto whom aught that ye are overburdened is grievous full of concern for you, for the believers full of pity, merciful.

9:128

7. And though thou try much, most men will not believe.

Thou askest them no fee for it. It is naught else than a reminder unto the peoples.

12:103–104

8. Yet it may be, if they believe not in this statement, that thou (Muhammad) wilt torment thy soul with grief over their footsteps.

18:6

5. وَمِنْهُمُ الَّذِيْنَ يُؤْذُوْنَ النَّبِيَّ وَيَقُوْلُوْنَ
هُوَ اُذُنٌ ؕ قُلْ اُذُنُ خَيْرٍ لَّكُمْ يُؤْمِنُ
بِاللّٰهِ وَيُؤْمِنُ لِلْمُؤْمِنِيْنَ وَرَحْمَةٌ لِّلَّذِيْنَ
اٰمَنُوْا مِنْكُمْ ؕ وَالَّذِيْنَ يُؤْذُوْنَ رَسُوْلَ
اللّٰهِ لَهُمْ عَذَابٌ اَلِيْمٌ ﴿٦١﴾

6. لَقَدْ جَآءَكُمْ رَسُوْلٌ مِّنْ اَنْفُسِكُمْ عَزِيْزٌ
عَلَيْهِ مَا عَنِتُّمْ حَرِيْصٌ عَلَيْكُمْ
بِالْمُؤْمِنِيْنَ رَءُوْفٌ رَّحِيْمٌ ﴿١٢٨﴾

7. وَمَآ اَكْثَرُ النَّاسِ وَلَوْ حَرَصْتَ بِمُؤْمِنِيْنَ ﴿١٠٣﴾
وَمَا تَسْـَٔلُهُمْ عَلَيْهِ مِنْ اَجْرٍ ؕ اِنْ هُوَ
اِلَّا ذِكْرٌ لِّلْعٰلَمِيْنَ ﴿١٠٤﴾

8. فَلَعَلَّكَ بَاخِعٌ نَّفْسَكَ عَلٰٓى اٰثَارِهِمْ
اِنْ لَّمْ يُؤْمِنُوْا بِهٰذَا الْحَدِيْثِ اَسَفًا ﴿٦﴾

9. يٰٓاَيُّهَا الَّذِيْنَ اٰمَنُوْا لَا تَدْخُلُوْا بُيُوْتَ
النَّبِيِّ اِلَّآ اَنْ يُّؤْذَنَ لَكُمْ اِلٰى طَعَامٍ
غَيْرَ نٰظِرِيْنَ اِنٰىهُ ۙ وَلٰكِنْ اِذَا دُعِيْتُمْ
فَادْخُلُوْا فَاِذَا طَعِمْتُمْ فَانْتَشِرُوْا وَلَا
مُسْتَاْنِسِيْنَ لِحَدِيْثٍ ؕ اِنَّ ذٰلِكُمْ كَانَ
يُؤْذِى النَّبِيَّ فَيَسْتَحْيٖ مِنْكُمْ ۫ وَاللّٰهُ
لَا يَسْتَحْيٖ مِنَ الْحَقِّ ؕ وَاِذَا سَاَلْتُمُوْهُنَّ

9. O ye who believe! Enter not the dwellings of the Prophet for a meal without waiting for the proper time, unless permission be granted you. But if ye are invited, enter, and, when your meal is ended, then dispers. Linger not for conversation. Lo! that would cause annoy–ance to the Prophet, and he would be shy of (asking) you (to go); but Allah is not shy of the truth. And when ye ask of them (the wives of the Prophet) anything, ask it

of them from behind a curtain. That is purer for your hearts and for their hearts. And it is not for you to cause annoyance to the messenger of Allah, nor that ye should ever marry his wives after him. Lo! that in Allah's sight would be an enormity.

33:53

10. Muhammad is the messenger of Allah. And those with him are hard against the disbelievers and merciful among themselves. Thou (O Muhammad) seest them bowing and falling prostrate (in worship), seeking bounty from Allah and (His) acceptance. The mark of them is on their foreheads from traces of prostration. Such is their likeness in the Torah and their likeness in the Gospel—like as sown corn that sendeth forth its shoot and strengtheneth it and riseth firm upon its stalk, delighting the sowers—that He may enrage the disbelievers with (the sight of) them. Allah hath promised, unto such of them as believe and do good works, forgiveness and immense reward.

48:29

مَتَاعًا فَسْـَٔلُوْهُنَّ مِنْ وَّرَاۤءِ حِجَابٍ ۭ
ذٰلِكُمْ اَطْهَرُ لِقُلُوْبِكُمْ وَقُلُوْبِهِنَّ ۭ وَمَا
كَانَ لَكُمْ اَنْ تُؤْذُوْا رَسُوْلَ اللّٰهِ وَلَآ
اَنْ تَنْكِحُوْٓا اَزْوَاجَهٗ مِنْۢ بَعْدِهٖٓ اَبَدًا ۭ
اِنَّ ذٰلِكُمْ كَانَ عِنْدَ اللّٰهِ عَظِيْمًا ﴿۵۳﴾
10. مُحَمَّدٌ رَّسُوْلُ اللّٰهِ ۭ وَالَّذِيْنَ مَعَهٗٓ اَشِدَّاۤءُ عَلَى
الْكُفَّارِ رُحَمَاۤءُ بَيْنَهُمْ تَرٰىهُمْ رُكَّعًا سُجَّدًا يَّبْتَغُوْنَ
فَضْلًا مِّنَ اللّٰهِ وَرِضْوَانًا ۡ سِيْمَاهُمْ فِيْ وُجُوْهِهِمْ
مِّنْ اَثَرِ السُّجُوْدِ ۭ ذٰلِكَ مَثَلُهُمْ فِي التَّوْرٰىةِ
وَمَثَلُهُمْ فِي الْاِنْجِيْلِ ۾ كَزَرْعٍ اَخْرَجَ شَطْــَٔهٗ
فَاٰزَرَهٗ فَاسْتَغْلَظَ فَاسْتَوٰى عَلٰي سُوْقِهٖ يُعْجِبُ
الزُّرَّاعَ لِيَغِيْظَ بِهِمُ الْكُفَّارَ ۭ وَعَدَ اللّٰهُ الَّذِيْنَ
اٰمَنُوْا وَعَمِلُوا الصّٰلِحٰتِ مِنْهُمْ مَّغْفِرَةً
وَّاَجْرًا عَظِيْمًا ﴿۲۹﴾
11. وَالنَّجْمِ اِذَا هَوٰى ۙ﴿۱﴾
مَا ضَلَّ صَاحِبُكُمْ وَمَا غَوٰى ﴿۲﴾
وَمَا يَنْطِقُ عَنِ الْهَوٰى ﴿۳﴾
اِنْ هُوَ اِلَّا وَحْيٌ يُّوْحٰى ﴿۴﴾
عَلَّمَهٗ شَدِيْدُ الْقُوٰى ﴿۵﴾
ذُوْ مِرَّةٍ ۭ فَاسْتَوٰى ﴿۶﴾
وَهُوَ بِالْاُفُقِ الْاَعْلٰى ﴿۷﴾
ثُمَّ دَنَا فَتَدَلّٰى ﴿۸﴾
فَكَانَ قَابَ قَوْسَيْنِ اَوْ اَدْنٰى ﴿۹﴾
فَاَوْحٰٓى اِلٰى عَبْدِهٖ مَآ اَوْحٰى ﴿۱۰﴾

11. By the Star when it setteth,

Your comrade erreth not, nor is deceived;

Nor doth he speak of his own desire.

It is naught save an inspiration that is inspired,

Which one of mighty powers hath taught him,

One vigorous; and he grew clear to view

When he was on the uppermost horizon.

Then he drew nigh and came down

Till he was (distant) two bows length or even nearer,

And He revealed unto His slave that which He revealed.

The heart lied not (in seeing) what it saw.

Will ye then dispute with him concerning what he seeth?

And verily he saw him yet another time

By the lote-tree of the utmost boundary,

Nigh unto which is the Garden of Abode.

When that which shroudeth did enshroud the lote-tree,

The eye turned not aside nor yet was overbold.

Verily he saw one of the greater revelations of his Lord.

53: 1–18

12. By the pen and that which they write (therewith),

Thou art not, for thy Lord's favour unto thee, a madman.

And lo! thine verily will be a reward unfailing.

And lo! thou art of a tremendous nature.

68: 1–4

13. O thou wrapped up in thy raiment!

Keep vigil the night long, save a little–

A half thereof, or abate a little thereof

Or add (a little) thereto and chant the Qur'ān in measure.

For We shall charge thee with a word of weight.

Lo! the vigil of the night is (a time) when impression is more keen and speech more certain.

Lo! thou hast by day a chain of business.

So remember the name of thy Lord and devote thyself with a complete devotion–

73: 1–8

مَا كَذَبَ الْفُؤَادُ مَا رَأَىٰ
أَفَتُمَارُونَهُ عَلَىٰ مَا يَرَىٰ
وَلَقَدْ رَآهُ نَزْلَةً أُخْرَىٰ
عِندَ سِدْرَةِ الْمُنتَهَىٰ
عِندَهَا جَنَّةُ الْمَأْوَىٰ
إِذْ يَغْشَى السِّدْرَةَ مَا يَغْشَىٰ
مَا زَاغَ الْبَصَرُ وَمَا طَغَىٰ
لَقَدْ رَأَىٰ مِنْ آيَاتِ رَبِّهِ الْكُبْرَىٰ
12. وَالْقَلَمِ وَمَا يَسْطُرُونَ
مَا أَنتَ بِنِعْمَةِ رَبِّكَ بِمَجْنُونٍ
وَإِنَّ لَكَ لَأَجْرًا غَيْرَ مَمْنُونٍ
وَإِنَّكَ لَعَلَىٰ خُلُقٍ عَظِيمٍ
13. يَا أَيُّهَا الْمُزَّمِّلُ
قُمِ اللَّيْلَ إِلَّا قَلِيلًا
نِّصْفَهُ أَوِ انقُصْ مِنْهُ قَلِيلًا
أَوْ زِدْ عَلَيْهِ وَرَتِّلِ الْقُرْآنَ
تَرْتِيلًا
إِنَّا سَنُلْقِي عَلَيْكَ قَوْلًا ثَقِيلًا
إِنَّ نَاشِئَةَ اللَّيْلِ هِيَ أَشَدُّ وَطْئًا
وَأَقْوَمُ قِيلًا
إِنَّ لَكَ فِي النَّهَارِ سَبْحًا طَوِيلًا
وَاذْكُرِ اسْمَ رَبِّكَ وَتَبَتَّلْ إِلَيْهِ
تَبْتِيلًا
14. وَالضُّحَىٰ
وَاللَّيْلِ إِذَا سَجَىٰ
مَا وَدَّعَكَ رَبُّكَ وَمَا قَلَىٰ

14. By the morning hours

And by the night when it is stillest,

Thy Lord hath not for–

saken thee nor doth He hate thee.

And verily the latter portion will be better for thee than the former,

And verily thy Lord will give unto thee so that thou wilt be content.

Did He not find thee an orphan and protect (thee)?

Did He not find thee wandering and direct (thee)?

Did He not find thee destitute and enrich (thee)?

Therefor the orphan oppress not,

Therefor the beggar drive not away.

93: 1–10

15. Have We not caused thy bosom to dilate.

And eased thee of the burden

Which weighed down thy back;

And exalted thy fame?

But lo! with hardship goeth ease,

Lo! with hardship goeth ease;

So when thou art relieved, still toil

And strive to please thy Lord.

94: 1–8

16. Lo! We have given thee Abundance;

So pray unto thy Lord, and sacrifice.

وَلَلْآخِرَةُ خَيْرٌ لَّكَ مِنَ الْأُولَىٰ ﴿٤﴾
وَلَسَوْفَ يُعْطِيكَ رَبُّكَ فَتَرْضَىٰ ﴿٥﴾
أَلَمْ يَجِدْكَ يَتِيمًا فَآوَىٰ ﴿٦﴾
وَوَجَدَكَ ضَالًّا فَهَدَىٰ ﴿٧﴾
وَوَجَدَكَ عَائِلًا فَأَغْنَىٰ ﴿٨﴾
فَأَمَّا الْيَتِيمَ فَلَا تَقْهَرْ ﴿٩﴾
وَأَمَّا السَّائِلَ فَلَا تَنْهَرْ ﴿١٠﴾
15. أَلَمْ نَشْرَحْ لَكَ صَدْرَكَ ﴿١﴾
وَوَضَعْنَا عَنكَ وِزْرَكَ ﴿٢﴾
الَّذِي أَنقَضَ ظَهْرَكَ ﴿٣﴾
وَرَفَعْنَا لَكَ ذِكْرَكَ ﴿٤﴾
فَإِنَّ مَعَ الْعُسْرِ يُسْرًا ﴿٥﴾
إِنَّ مَعَ الْعُسْرِ يُسْرًا ﴿٦﴾
فَإِذَا فَرَغْتَ فَانصَبْ ﴿٧﴾
وَإِلَىٰ رَبِّكَ فَارْغَب ﴿٨﴾
16. إِنَّا أَعْطَيْنَاكَ الْكَوْثَرَ ﴿١﴾
فَصَلِّ لِرَبِّكَ وَانْحَرْ ﴿٢﴾
إِنَّ شَانِئَكَ هُوَ الْأَبْتَرُ ﴿٣﴾

Lo! it is thy insulter (and not thou) who is without posterity.

108: 1–3

See also: Finality of Prophethood, Manners of Holy Prophet (PBUH), Miracles of Prophet Muhammad (PBUH), Office of Apostleship, Office of Prophethood, Reverence for Messenger of Allah, Salutation.

SKY

1. He it is Who created for you all that is in the earth. Then turned He to the heaven, and fashioned it as seven heavens. And He is Knower of all things.

2:29

2. Allah it is Who raised up the heavens without visible supports, then mounted the Throne, and compelled the sun and the moon to be of service, each runneth unto an appointed term; He ordereth the course; He detaileth the revelations, that haply ye may be certain of the meeting with your Lord.

13:2

3. And verily in the heaven We have set mansions of the stars, and We have beautified it for beholders.

And We have guarded it from every outcast devil,

Save him who stealeth the hearing, and then doth a clear flame pursue.

15:16–18

4. The seven heavens and the earth and all that is therein praise Him, and there is not a thing but hymneth His praise; but ye understand not their praise. Lo! He is ever Clement, Forgiving.

17:44

5. Hast thou not seen how Allah hath made all that is

1. هُوَ الَّذِي خَلَقَ لَكُم مَّا فِي الْأَرْضِ جَمِيعًا
ثُمَّ اسْتَوَىٰ إِلَى السَّمَاءِ فَسَوَّاهُنَّ سَبْعَ
سَمَاوَاتٍ ۚ وَهُوَ بِكُلِّ شَيْءٍ عَلِيمٌ ﴿٢٩﴾

2. اللَّهُ الَّذِي رَفَعَ السَّمَاوَاتِ بِغَيْرِ عَمَدٍ تَرَوْنَهَا ۖ ثُمَّ
اسْتَوَىٰ عَلَى الْعَرْشِ ۖ وَسَخَّرَ الشَّمْسَ وَالْقَمَرَ ۖ كُلٌّ
يَجْرِي لِأَجَلٍ مُّسَمًّى ۚ يُدَبِّرُ الْأَمْرَ يُفَصِّلُ الْآيَاتِ
لَعَلَّكُم بِلِقَاءِ رَبِّكُمْ تُوقِنُونَ ﴿٢﴾

3. وَلَقَدْ جَعَلْنَا فِي السَّمَاءِ بُرُوجًا وَزَيَّنَّاهَا لِلنَّاظِرِينَ ﴿١٦﴾
وَحَفِظْنَاهَا مِن كُلِّ شَيْطَانٍ رَّجِيمٍ ﴿١٧﴾
إِلَّا مَنِ اسْتَرَقَ السَّمْعَ فَأَتْبَعَهُ
شِهَابٌ مُّبِينٌ ﴿١٨﴾

4. تُسَبِّحُ لَهُ السَّمَاوَاتُ السَّبْعُ وَالْأَرْضُ
وَمَن فِيهِنَّ ۚ وَإِن مِّن شَيْءٍ إِلَّا يُسَبِّحُ
بِحَمْدِهِ وَلَٰكِن لَّا تَفْقَهُونَ تَسْبِيحَهُمْ ۗ
إِنَّهُ كَانَ حَلِيمًا غَفُورًا ﴿٤٤﴾

5. أَلَمْ تَرَ أَنَّ اللَّهَ سَخَّرَ لَكُم مَّا فِي
الْأَرْضِ وَالْفُلْكَ تَجْرِي فِي الْبَحْرِ
بِأَمْرِهِ وَيُمْسِكُ السَّمَاءَ أَن تَقَعَ
عَلَى الْأَرْضِ إِلَّا بِإِذْنِهِ ۗ إِنَّ اللَّهَ
بِالنَّاسِ لَرَءُوفٌ رَّحِيمٌ ﴿٦٥﴾

in the earth subservient unto you? And the ship runneth upon the sea by His command, and He holdeth back the heaven from falling on the earth unless by His leave. Lo! Allah is, for mankind, Full of Pity, Merciful.

22:65

6. And of His signs is this: The heavens and the earth stand fast by His Command, and afterward, when He calleth you, lo! from the earth ye will emerge.

Unto Him belongeth whosoever is in the heavens and in the earth. All are obedient unto Him.

30:25–26

7. And they esteem not Allah as He hath the right to be esteemed, when the whole earth is His handful on the Day of Resurrection, and the heavens are rolled in His right hand. Glorified is He and High Exalted from all that they ascribe as partner (unto Him).

39:67

8. And when the heaven splitteth asunder and becometh rosy like red hide—

55:37

9. Who hath created seven heavens in harmony. Thou (Muhammad) canst see no fault in the Beneficent One's creation; then look again: Canst thou see any rifts?

Then look again and yet again, thy sight will return unto thee weakened and made dim.

And verily We have beautified the world's heaven with lamps, and We have made them missiles for the devils, and for them We have prepared doom of flame.

67:3–5

6. وَمِنْ اٰيٰتِهٖٓ اَنْ تَقُوْمَ السَّمَآءُ وَ
الْاَرْضُ بِاَمْرِهٖ ؕ ثُمَّ اِذَا دَعَاكُمْ دَعْوَةً ۖ
مِّنَ الْاَرْضِ ۖ اِذَآ اَنْتُمْ تَخْرُجُوْنَ ﴿٢٥﴾
وَلَهٗ مَنْ فِى السَّمٰوٰتِ وَالْاَرْضِ ؕ
كُلٌّ لَّهٗ قٰنِتُوْنَ ﴿٢٦﴾

7. وَمَا قَدَرُوا اللّٰهَ حَقَّ قَدْرِهٖ ۖ وَ
الْاَرْضُ جَمِيْعًا قَبْضَتُهٗ يَوْمَ الْقِيٰمَةِ
وَالسَّمٰوٰتُ مَطْوِيّٰتٌۢ بِيَمِيْنِهٖ ؕ سُبْحٰنَهٗ
وَتَعٰلٰى عَمَّا يُشْرِكُوْنَ ﴿٦٧﴾

8. فَاِذَا انْشَقَّتِ السَّمَآءُ فَكَانَتْ
وَرْدَةً كَالدِّهَانِ ﴿٣٧﴾

9. الَّذِىْ خَلَقَ سَبْعَ سَمٰوٰتٍ طِبَاقًا ؕ مَا
تَرٰى فِىْ خَلْقِ الرَّحْمٰنِ مِنْ تَفٰوُتٍ ؕ
فَارْجِعِ الْبَصَرَ ۙ هَلْ تَرٰى مِنْ فُطُوْرٍ ﴿٣﴾
ثُمَّ ارْجِعِ الْبَصَرَ كَرَّتَيْنِ يَنْقَلِبْ
اِلَيْكَ الْبَصَرُ خَاسِئًا وَّهُوَ حَسِيْرٌ ﴿٤﴾
وَلَقَدْ زَيَّنَّا السَّمَآءَ الدُّنْيَا بِمَصَابِيْحَ
وَجَعَلْنٰهَا رُجُوْمًا لِّلشَّيٰطِيْنِ وَاَعْتَدْنَا
لَهُمْ عَذَابَ السَّعِيْرِ ﴿٥﴾

Ref: 2:19,22,29,59,144,164; 7:162; 9:36; 10:24,61; 14:32,38; 25:25; 29:22,34; 41:11; 44:10,29; 52:9; 70:8; 73:18; 77:9; 78:12,19; 81:11; 84:1–2.

See also: Creation of Universe, Earth, Subjugation of Universe.

SLANDER

1. Whoso committeth sin committeth it only against himself. Allah is ever Knower, Wise.

And whoso committeth a delinquency or crime, then throweth (the blame) thereof upon the innocent, hath burdened himself with falsehood and a flagrant crime.

4:111–112

2. And those who accuse honourable women but bring not four witnesses, scourge them (with) eighty stripes and never (afterward) accept their testimony—They indeed are evil-doers.

24:4

3. As for those who accuse their wives but have no witnesses except themselves; let the testimony of one of them be four testimonies, swearing by Allah that he is of those who speak the truth.

24:6

4. Lo! they who spread the slander are a gang among you. Deem it not a bad thing for you; nay, it is good for you. Unto every man of them (will be paid) that which he hath earned of the sin; and as for him among them who had the greater share therein, his will be an awful doom.

Why did not the believers, men and women, when

1. وَمَن يَكْسِبْ إِثْمًا فَإِنَّمَا يَكْسِبُهُ عَلَىٰ
نَفْسِهِ ۚ وَكَانَ اللَّهُ عَلِيمًا حَكِيمًا ﴿١١١﴾
وَمَن يَكْسِبْ خَطِيئَةً أَوْ إِثْمًا ثُمَّ يَرْمِ
بِهِ بَرِيئًا فَقَدِ احْتَمَلَ بُهْتَانًا وَإِثْمًا مُّبِينًا ﴿١١٢﴾

2. وَالَّذِينَ يَرْمُونَ الْمُحْصَنَاتِ ثُمَّ لَمْ يَأْتُوا بِأَرْبَعَةِ
شُهَدَاءَ فَاجْلِدُوهُمْ ثَمَانِينَ جَلْدَةً وَلَا
تَقْبَلُوا لَهُمْ شَهَادَةً أَبَدًا ۚ وَأُولَٰئِكَ هُمُ
الْفَاسِقُونَ ﴿٤﴾

3. وَالَّذِينَ يَرْمُونَ أَزْوَاجَهُمْ وَلَمْ يَكُن
لَّهُمْ شُهَدَاءُ إِلَّا أَنفُسُهُمْ فَشَهَادَةُ
أَحَدِهِمْ أَرْبَعُ شَهَادَاتٍ بِاللَّهِ ۙ إِنَّهُ
لَمِنَ الصَّادِقِينَ ﴿٦﴾

4. إِنَّ الَّذِينَ جَاءُوا بِالْإِفْكِ عُصْبَةٌ مِّنكُمْ ۚ لَا
تَحْسَبُوهُ شَرًّا لَّكُم ۖ بَلْ هُوَ خَيْرٌ لَّكُمْ ۚ لِكُلِّ امْرِئٍ
مِّنْهُم مَّا اكْتَسَبَ مِنَ الْإِثْمِ ۚ وَالَّذِي تَوَلَّىٰ كِبْرَهُ
مِنْهُمْ لَهُ عَذَابٌ عَظِيمٌ ﴿١١﴾
لَّوْلَا إِذْ سَمِعْتُمُوهُ ظَنَّ الْمُؤْمِنُونَ
وَالْمُؤْمِنَاتُ بِأَنفُسِهِمْ خَيْرًا وَقَالُوا
هَٰذَا إِفْكٌ مُّبِينٌ ﴿١٢﴾

5. إِنَّ الَّذِينَ يَرْمُونَ الْمُحْصَنَاتِ الْغَافِلَاتِ الْمُؤْمِنَاتِ
لُعِنُوا فِي الدُّنْيَا وَالْآخِرَةِ وَلَهُمْ عَذَابٌ
عَظِيمٌ ﴿٢٣﴾

ye heard it, think good of their own folk, and say: It is a manifest untruth?

24:11–12

5. Lo! as for those who traduce virtuous, believing women (who are) careless,

cursed are they in the world and the Hereafter. Theirs will be an awful doom.

24:23

6. And those who malign believing men and believing women undeservedly, they bear the guilt of slander and manifest sin.

33:58

7. O Prophet! If the believing women come unto thee, taking oath of allegiance unto thee that they will ascribe nothing as partner unto Allah, and will neither steal nor commit adultery nor kill their children, nor produce any lie that they have devised between their hands and feet, nor disobey thee in what is right, then accept their allegiance and ask Allah to forgive them.

60:12

6. وَالَّذِيْنَ يُؤْذُوْنَ الْمُؤْمِنِيْنَ وَالْمُؤْمِنٰتِ
بِغَيْرِ مَا اكْتَسَبُوْا فَقَدِ احْتَمَلُوْا
بُهْتَانًا وَّاِثْمًا مُّبِيْنًا ﴿۵۸﴾

7. يٰٓاَيُّهَا النَّبِيُّ اِذَا جَآءَكَ الْمُؤْمِنٰتُ
يُبَايِعْنَكَ عَلٰٓى اَنْ لَّا يُشْرِكْنَ بِاللّٰهِ
شَيْـًٔا وَّلَا يَسْرِقْنَ وَلَا يَزْنِيْنَ
وَلَا يَقْتُلْنَ اَوْلَادَهُنَّ وَلَا يَاْتِيْنَ
بِبُهْتَانٍ يَّفْتَرِيْنَهٗ بَيْنَ اَيْدِيْهِنَّ
وَاَرْجُلِهِنَّ وَلَا يَعْصِيْنَكَ فِيْ
مَعْرُوْفٍ فَبَايِعْهُنَّ وَاسْتَغْفِرْ لَهُنَّ
اللّٰهَ

Ref: 2:145; 5:48,77; 6:56,120,151; 30:29; 42:15; 47:16; 54:3.
See also: *Ifk.*

SLAUGHTER

1. Eat of that over which the name of Allah hath been mentioned, if ye are believers in His revelations.

How should ye not eat of that over which the name of Allah hath been mentioned, when He hath explained unto you that which is forbidden unto you, unless ye are compelled thereto. But lo! many are led astray by their own lusts through ignorance. Lo! thy Lord, He is Best Aware of the transgressors.

6:118–119

2. And eat not of that whereon Allah's name hath not been mentioned,

6:122

SLAVERY

1. It is not for a believer to kill a believer unless (it be) by mistake, He who hath killed a believer by mistake must set free a believing slave and pay the blood–money to the family of the slain, unless they remit it as a charity. If he (the victim) be of a people hostile unto you, and he is a believer, then (the penance) is to set free a believing slave. And if he cometh of a folk between whom and you there is a covenant, then the blood–money must be paid unto his folk and (also) a believing slave must be set free. And whoso hath not the where–withal must fast two conse–cutive months. A penance

1. فَكُلُوا مِمَّا ذُكِرَ اسْمُ اللَّهِ عَلَيْهِ إِنْ
كُنْتُمْ بِآيَاتِهِ مُؤْمِنِينَ ○
وَمَا لَكُمْ أَلَّا تَأْكُلُوا مِمَّا ذُكِرَ اسْمُ اللَّهِ
عَلَيْهِ وَقَدْ فَصَّلَ لَكُمْ مَا حَرَّمَ عَلَيْكُمْ إِلَّا
مَا اضْطُرِرْتُمْ إِلَيْهِ وَإِنَّ كَثِيرًا لَيُضِلُّونَ
بِأَهْوَائِهِمْ بِغَيْرِ عِلْمٍ إِنَّ رَبَّكَ هُوَ
أَعْلَمُ بِالْمُعْتَدِينَ ○

2. وَلَا تَأْكُلُوا مِمَّا لَمْ يُذْكَرِ اسْمُ اللَّهِ
عَلَيْهِ

○

1. وَمَا كَانَ لِمُؤْمِنٍ أَنْ يَقْتُلَ مُؤْمِنًا إِلَّا خَطَأً وَمَنْ
قَتَلَ مُؤْمِنًا خَطَأً فَتَحْرِيرُ رَقَبَةٍ مُؤْمِنَةٍ وَدِيَةٌ مُسَلَّمَةٌ
إِلَىٰ أَهْلِهِ إِلَّا أَنْ يَصَّدَّقُوا فَإِنْ كَانَ مِنْ قَوْمٍ عَدُوٍّ
لَكُمْ وَهُوَ مُؤْمِنٌ فَتَحْرِيرُ رَقَبَةٍ مُؤْمِنَةٍ وَإِنْ كَانَ
مِنْ قَوْمٍ بَيْنَكُمْ وَبَيْنَهُمْ مِيثَاقٌ فَدِيَةٌ مُسَلَّمَةٌ
إِلَىٰ أَهْلِهِ وَتَحْرِيرُ رَقَبَةٍ مُؤْمِنَةٍ فَمَنْ لَمْ يَجِدْ
فَصِيَامُ شَهْرَيْنِ مُتَتَابِعَيْنِ تَوْبَةً مِنَ اللَّهِ وَكَانَ
اللَّهُ عَلِيمًا حَكِيمًا ﴿٩٢﴾

2. إِنَّمَا الصَّدَقَاتُ لِلْفُقَرَاءِ وَالْمَسَاكِينِ وَالْعَامِلِينَ عَلَيْهَا
وَالْمُؤَلَّفَةِ قُلُوبُهُمْ وَفِي الرِّقَابِ وَالْغَارِمِينَ وَفِي
سَبِيلِ اللَّهِ وَابْنِ السَّبِيلِ فَرِيضَةً مِنَ اللَّهِ
وَاللَّهُ عَلِيمٌ حَكِيمٌ ﴿٦٠﴾

from Allah. Allah is Knower, Wise.

4:92

2. The alms are only for the poor and the needy, and those who collect them, and those whose hearts are to be reconciled, and to free the captives and the debtors, and for the cause of Allah,

and (for) the wayfarers; a duty imposed by Allah. Allah is Knower, Wise.

9:60

3. And such of your slaves as seek a writing (of emancipation), write it for them if ye are aware of aught of good in them, and bestow upon them of the wealth of Allah which He hath bestowed upon you. Force not your slave-girls to whoredom that ye may seek enjoyment of the life of the world, if they would preserve their chastity. And if one force them, then (unto them), after their compulsion, lo! Allah will be Forgiving, Merciful.

24:33

4. Those who put away their wives (by saying they are as their mothers) and after-ward would go back on that which they have said, (the penalty) in that case (is) the freeing of a slave before they touch one another. Unto this ye are exhorted; and Allah is Informed of what ye do.

58:3

3. وَالَّذِيْنَ يَبْتَغُوْنَ الْكِتٰبَ مِمَّا مَلَكَتْ اَيْمَانُكُمْ فَكَاتِبُوْ
هُمْ اِنْ عَلِمْتُمْ فِيْهِمْ خَيْرًا ۖ وَّ اٰتُوْهُمْ مِّنْ مَّالِ
اللّٰهِ الَّذِيْٓ اٰتٰىكُمْ ۭ وَلَا تُكْرِهُوْا فَتَيٰتِكُمْ عَلَى الْبِغَاۗءِ
اِنْ اَرَدْنَ تَحَصُّنًا لِّتَبْتَغُوْا عَرَضَ الْحَيٰوةِ الدُّنْيَا ۭ وَ
مَنْ يُّكْرِهْهُّنَّ فَاِنَّ اللّٰهَ مِنْۢ بَعْدِ اِكْرَاهِهِنَّ غَفُوْرٌ
رَّحِيْمٌ ۝٣٣

4. وَالَّذِيْنَ يُظٰهِرُوْنَ مِنْ نِّسَاۗىِٕهِمْ ثُمَّ
يَعُوْدُوْنَ لِمَا قَالُوْا فَتَحْرِيْرُ رَقَبَةٍ
مِّنْ قَبْلِ اَنْ يَّتَمَاۗسَّا ۭ ذٰلِكُمْ تُوْعَظُوْنَ
بِهٖ ۭ وَاللّٰهُ بِمَا تَعْمَلُوْنَ خَبِيْرٌ ۝٣

SLUMBER

1. And He it is Who maketh night a covering for you, and sleep repose, and maketh day a resurrection.

25:47

2. And of His signs is your slumber by night and by day, and your seeking of His bounty. Lo! herein indeed are portents for folk who heed.

30:23

3. And have appointed your sleep for repose,

And have appointed the night as a cloak,

And have appointed the day for livelihood.

78:9–11

SOCIAL ORDER

1. And covet not the thing in which Allah hath made some of you excel others. Unto men a fortune from that which they have earned, and unto women a fortune from that which they have earned. (Envy not one another) but ask Allah of His bounty. Lo! Allah is ever Knower of all things.

4:32

2. Men are in charge of women, because Allah hath made the one of them to excel the other, and because they spend of their property (for the support of women).

4:34

1. وَهُوَ الَّذِي جَعَلَ لَكُمُ الَّيْلَ لِبَاسًا
وَالنَّوْمَ سُبَاتًا وَجَعَلَ النَّهَارَ نُشُورًا ﴿٤٧﴾

2. وَمِنْ ءَايَٰتِهِ مَنَامُكُم بِالَّيْلِ وَالنَّهَارِ
وَابْتِغَاؤُكُم مِّن فَضْلِهِ إِنَّ فِي ذَٰلِكَ
لَآيَٰتٍ لِّقَوْمٍ يَسْمَعُونَ ﴿٢٣﴾

3. وَجَعَلْنَا نَوْمَكُمْ سُبَاتًا ﴿٩﴾
وَجَعَلْنَا الَّيْلَ لِبَاسًا ﴿١٠﴾
وَجَعَلْنَا النَّهَارَ مَعَاشًا ﴿١١﴾

1. وَلَا تَتَمَنَّوْا مَا فَضَّلَ اللَّهُ بِهِ بَعْضَكُمْ عَلَىٰ بَعْضٍ
لِّلرِّجَالِ نَصِيبٌ مِّمَّا اكْتَسَبُوا وَلِلنِّسَاءِ نَصِيبٌ مِّمَّا
اكْتَسَبْنَ وَسْئَلُوا اللَّهَ مِن فَضْلِهِ إِنَّ اللَّهَ كَانَ
بِكُلِّ شَيْءٍ عَلِيمًا ﴿٣٢﴾

2. الرِّجَالُ قَوَّٰمُونَ عَلَى النِّسَاءِ بِمَا فَضَّلَ
اللَّهُ بَعْضَهُمْ عَلَىٰ بَعْضٍ وَبِمَا أَنفَقُوا مِنْ
أَمْوَٰلِهِمْ

3. لَا يَسْتَوِي الْقَٰعِدُونَ مِنَ الْمُؤْمِنِينَ غَيْرُ
أُولِي الضَّرَرِ وَالْمُجَٰهِدُونَ فِي سَبِيلِ
اللَّهِ بِأَمْوَٰلِهِمْ وَأَنفُسِهِمْ فَضَّلَ اللَّهُ
الْمُجَٰهِدِينَ بِأَمْوَٰلِهِمْ وَأَنفُسِهِمْ عَلَى
الْقَٰعِدِينَ دَرَجَةً وَكُلًّا وَعَدَ اللَّهُ
الْحُسْنَىٰ وَفَضَّلَ اللَّهُ الْمُجَٰهِدِينَ عَلَى
الْقَٰعِدِينَ أَجْرًا عَظِيمًا ﴿٩٥﴾

3. Those of the believers who sit still, other than those who have a (disabling) hurt, are not on an equality with those who strive in the way of Allah with their wealth and lives. Allah hath conferred on those who strive with their wealth and lives a rank above the sedentary.

Unto each Allah hath promised good, but He hath bestowed on those who strive a great reward above the sedentary;

4:95

4. He it is Who hath placed you as viceroys of the earth and hath exalted some of you in rank above others, that He may try you by (the test of) that which He hath given you. Lo! Thy Lord is swift in prosecution, and lo! He is Forgiving, Merciful.

6:165

5. And Allah hath favoured some of you above others in provision. Now those who are more favoured will by no means hand over their provision to those (slaves) whom their right hands possess, so that they may be equal with them in respect thereof. Is it then the grace of Allah that they deny?

16:71

6. Is it they who apportion thy Lord's mercy? We have apportioned among them their livelihood in the life of the world, and raised some of them above others in rank that some of them may take labour from others; and the mercy of the Lord is better than (the wealth) that they amass.

43:32

4. وَهُوَ الَّذِي جَعَلَكُمْ خَلَائِفَ الْأَرْضِ وَرَفَعَ
بَعْضَكُمْ فَوْقَ بَعْضٍ دَرَجَاتٍ لِيَبْلُوَكُمْ
فِي مَا آتَاكُمْ ۗ إِنَّ رَبَّكَ سَرِيعُ الْعِقَابِ
وَإِنَّهُ لَغَفُورٌ رَحِيمٌ ۝

5. وَاللَّهُ فَضَّلَ بَعْضَكُمْ عَلَىٰ بَعْضٍ فِي الرِّزْقِ ۚ
فَمَا الَّذِينَ فُضِّلُوا بِرَادِّي رِزْقِهِمْ عَلَىٰ
مَا مَلَكَتْ أَيْمَانُهُمْ فَهُمْ فِيهِ سَوَاءٌ ۚ
أَفَبِنِعْمَةِ اللَّهِ يَجْحَدُونَ ۝

6. أَهُمْ يَقْسِمُونَ رَحْمَتَ رَبِّكَ ۚ نَحْنُ
قَسَمْنَا بَيْنَهُمْ مَعِيشَتَهُمْ فِي الْحَيَاةِ
الدُّنْيَا ۚ وَرَفَعْنَا بَعْضَهُمْ فَوْقَ بَعْضٍ
دَرَجَاتٍ لِيَتَّخِذَ بَعْضُهُمْ بَعْضًا سُخْرِيًّا ۗ
وَرَحْمَتُ رَبِّكَ خَيْرٌ مِمَّا يَجْمَعُونَ ۝

○

Ref: 2:228; 6:132; 9:20; 12:76; 17:21; 46:19; 57:10.

SULICITING DIVINE HELP

1. Praise be to Allah, Lord of the Worlds,
The Beneficent, the Merciful.
Owner of the Day of Judgment,
Thee (alone) we worship; Thee (alone) we ask for help.
1:1–4

2. Seek help in patience and prayer; and truly it is hard save for the humble-minded,
Who know that they will have to meet their Lord, and that unto Him they are returning.
2:45–46

3. O ye who believe! Seek help in steadfastness and prayer. Lo! Allah is with the steadfast.
2:153

1. اَلْحَمْدُ لِلّٰهِ رَبِّ الْعٰلَمِيْنَ ۙ
الرَّحْمٰنِ الرَّحِيْمِ ۙ
مٰلِكِ يَوْمِ الدِّيْنِ ۙ
اِيَّاكَ نَعْبُدُ وَاِيَّاكَ نَسْتَعِيْنُ ۙ

2. وَاسْتَعِيْنُوْا بِالصَّبْرِ وَالصَّلٰوةِ ؕ وَاِنَّهَا لَكَبِيْرَةٌ
اِلَّا عَلَى الْخٰشِعِيْنَ ۙ﴿۴۵﴾
الَّذِيْنَ يَظُنُّوْنَ اَنَّهُمْ مُّلٰقُوْا رَبِّهِمْ وَاَنَّهُمْ
اِلَيْهِ رٰجِعُوْنَ ﴿۴۶﴾

3. يٰۤاَيُّهَا الَّذِيْنَ اٰمَنُوا اسْتَعِيْنُوْا بِالصَّبْرِ وَ
الصَّلٰوةِ ؕ اِنَّ اللّٰهَ مَعَ الصّٰبِرِيْنَ ﴿۱۵۳﴾

SORCERY

1. And follow that which the devils falsely related against the kingdom of Solomon. Solomon disbelieved not; but the devils disbelieved, teaching mankind magic and that which was revealed to the two angels in Babel, Hārût and Mārût. Nor did they (the two angels) teach it to anyone till they had said: We are only a temptation, therefore disbelieve not (in the guidance of Allah). And from these two (angels) people learn that by which they cause division between man and wife; but they injure thereby no–one save by Allah's leave. And they learn that which harmeth them and profiteth them not. And surely they do know that he who trafficketh therein will have no (happy) portion in the Hereafter; and surely evil is the price for which they sell their souls, if they but knew.

2:102

2. And Pharaoh said: Bring every cunning wizard unto me.

And when the wizards came, Moses said unto them: Cast your cast!

And when they had cast, Moses said: That which ye have brought is magic. Lo! Allah will make it vain.
Lo! Allah upholdeth not the work of mischief–makers:

10:79–81

3. Throw that which is in thy right hand! It will eat up

1. وَاتَّبَعُوا مَا تَتْلُوا الشَّيٰطِيْنُ عَلٰى مُلْكِ سُلَيْمٰنَ
وَمَا كَفَرَ سُلَيْمٰنُ وَلٰكِنَّ الشَّيٰطِيْنَ كَفَرُوْا
يُعَلِّمُوْنَ النَّاسَ السِّحْرَ وَمَآ اُنْزِلَ عَلَى
الْمَلَكَيْنِ بِبَابِلَ هَارُوْتَ وَمَارُوْتَ وَمَا
يُعَلِّمٰنِ مِنْ اَحَدٍ حَتّٰى يَقُوْلَآ اِنَّمَا نَحْنُ
فِتْنَةٌ فَلَا تَكْفُرْ فَيَتَعَلَّمُوْنَ مِنْهُمَا مَا يُفَرِّقُوْنَ
بِهٖ بَيْنَ الْمَرْءِ وَزَوْجِهٖ وَمَا هُمْ بِضَآرِّيْنَ
بِهٖ مِنْ اَحَدٍ اِلَّا بِاِذْنِ اللّٰهِ وَيَتَعَلَّمُوْنَ مَا
يَضُرُّهُمْ وَلَا يَنْفَعُهُمْ وَلَقَدْ عَلِمُوْا لَمَنِ
اشْتَرٰىهُ مَا لَهٗ فِي الْاٰخِرَةِ مِنْ خَلَاقٍ وَ
لَبِئْسَ مَا شَرَوْا بِهٖٓ اَنْفُسَهُمْ لَوْ كَانُوْا يَعْلَمُوْنَ ﴿١٠٢﴾

2. وَقَالَ فِرْعَوْنُ ائْتُوْنِيْ بِكُلِّ سٰحِرٍ عَلِيْمٍ ﴿٧٩﴾
فَلَمَّا جَآءَ السَّحَرَةُ قَالَ لَهُمْ مُّوْسٰٓى اَلْقُوْا
مَآ اَنْتُمْ مُّلْقُوْنَ ﴿٨٠﴾

فَلَمَّآ اَلْقَوْا قَالَ مُوْسٰى مَا جِئْتُمْ بِهِ السِّحْرُ
اِنَّ اللّٰهَ سَيُبْطِلُهٗ اِنَّ اللّٰهَ لَا يُصْلِحُ
عَمَلَ الْمُفْسِدِيْنَ ﴿٨١﴾

3. وَاَلْقِ مَا فِيْ يَمِيْنِكَ تَلْقَفْ مَا صَنَعُوْا
اِنَّمَا صَنَعُوْا كَيْدُ سٰحِرٍ وَلَا يُفْلِحُ
السّٰحِرُ حَيْثُ اَتٰى ﴿٦٩﴾

4. قُلْ اَعُوْذُ بِرَبِّ الْفَلَقِ ﴿١﴾
مِنْ شَرِّ مَا خَلَقَ ﴿٢﴾

that which they have made. Lo! that which they have made is but a wizard's artifice, and a wizard shall not be successful to whatever point (of skill) he may attain.

20:69

4. Say: I seek refuge in the Lord of Daybreak,

From the evil of that which He created,

From the evil of the

darkness when it is intense,
And from the evil of malignant witchcraft,
And from the evil of the envier when he envieth.
113:1–5

SOVEREIGNTY OF ALLAH

1. Unto Allah belongeth whatsoever is in the heavens and whatsoever is in the earth; and unto Allah all things are returned.
3:109

2. Say: I am (relying) on clear proof from my Lord, while ye deny Him. I have not that for which ye are impatient. The decision is for Allah only. He telleth the truth and He is the Best of Deciders.
6:57

3. Then are they restored unto Allah, their Lord, the Just. Surely His is the Judgment. And He is the most swift of reckoners.
6:62

4. Had it been possible for a Lecture to cause the mountains to move, or the earth to be torn asunder, or the dead to speak, (this Qur'ān would have done so). Nay, but Allah's is the whole command.
13:31

5. We (angels) come not down save by commandment of thy Lord. Unto Him belongeth all that is before us and all that is behind us and all that is between those two, and thy Lord was never

وَمِنْ شَرِّ غَاسِقٍ إِذَا وَقَبَ ﴿٣﴾
وَمِنْ شَرِّ النَّفّٰثٰتِ فِي الْعُقَدِ ﴿٤﴾
وَمِنْ شَرِّ حَاسِدٍ إِذَا حَسَدَ ﴿٥﴾

1. وَلِلّٰهِ مَا فِي السَّمٰوٰتِ وَمَا فِي الْأَرْضِ ۚ
وَإِلَى اللّٰهِ تُرْجَعُ الْأُمُورُ ﴿١٠٩﴾

2. قُلْ إِنِّي عَلٰى بَيِّنَةٍ مِّنْ رَّبِّي وَكَذَّبْتُمْ
بِهِ ۚ مَا عِنْدِي مَا تَسْتَعْجِلُونَ بِهِ ۚ إِنِ
الْحُكْمُ إِلَّا لِلّٰهِ ۖ يَقُصُّ الْحَقَّ وَهُوَ
خَيْرُ الْفٰصِلِينَ ﴿٥٧﴾

3. ثُمَّ رُدُّوا إِلَى اللّٰهِ مَوْلٰهُمُ الْحَقِّ ۚ أَلَا
لَهُ الْحُكْمُ وَهُوَ أَسْرَعُ الْحٰسِبِينَ ﴿٦٢﴾

4. وَلَوْ أَنَّ قُرْاٰنًا سُيِّرَتْ بِهِ الْجِبَالُ
أَوْ قُطِّعَتْ بِهِ الْأَرْضُ أَوْ كُلِّمَ بِهِ
الْمَوْتٰى ۗ بَلْ لِّلّٰهِ الْأَمْرُ جَمِيعًا ۗ

5. وَمَا نَتَنَزَّلُ إِلَّا بِأَمْرِ رَبِّكَ ۚ لَهُ مَا
بَيْنَ أَيْدِينَا وَمَا خَلْفَنَا وَمَا بَيْنَ
ذٰلِكَ ۚ وَمَا كَانَ رَبُّكَ نَسِيًّا ﴿٦٤﴾

6. وَرَبُّكَ يَخْلُقُ مَا يَشَاءُ وَيَخْتَارُ ۗ مَا
كَانَ لَهُمُ الْخِيَرَةُ ۚ سُبْحٰنَ اللّٰهِ وَتَعٰلٰى
عَمَّا يُشْرِكُونَ ﴿٦٨﴾

forgetful.
19:64

6. Thy Lord bringeth to pass what He willeth and chooseth. They have never any choice. Glorified be Allah and Exalted above all that they associate (with Him)!
28:68

SORCERY

See also: Exorcism.

7. Allah's is the command in the former case and in the latter–

30:4

7. لِلّٰهِ الْاَمْرُ مِنْ قَبْلُ وَمِنْ بَعْدُ

8. Say: O Allah! Creator of the heavens and the earth! Knower of the Invisible and the Visible Thou wilt judge between Thy slaves concerning that wherein they used to differ.

39:46

8. قُلِ اللّٰهُمَّ فَاطِرَ السَّمٰوٰتِ وَالْاَرْضِ
عٰلِمَ الْغَيْبِ وَالشَّهَادَةِ اَنْتَ تَحْكُمُ
بَيْنَ عِبَادِكَ فِيْ مَا كَانُوْا فِيْهِ يَخْتَلِفُوْنَ (40)

9. And in whatsoever ye differ, the verdict therein belongeth to Allah. Such is my Lord, in Whom I put my trust, and unto Whom I turn.

42:10

9. وَمَا اخْتَلَفْتُمْ فِيْهِ مِنْ شَيْءٍ فَحُكْمُهٗ
اِلَى اللّٰهِ ذٰلِكُمُ اللّٰهُ رَبِّيْ عَلَيْهِ تَوَكَّلْتُ
وَاِلَيْهِ اُنِيْبُ (10)

○

Ref: 1:3; 2:113,210; 3:128–129,154; 5:1; 8:47; 11:123; 16:91,124; 22:17, 69,76; 27:78; 28:70,88; 32:25; 82:19.

See also: Authority, Signs of Allah.

SPIRIT

1. O People of Scripture! Do not exaggerate in your religion nor utter aught concerning Allah save the truth. The Messiah Jesus son of Mary, was only a messenger of Allah, and His Word which He conveyed unto Mary, and a spirit from Him. So believe in Allah and His messengers,

4:171

2. And (remember) when thy Lord said unto the angels: Lo! I am creating a mortal out of potter's clay of black mud altered.

So, when I have made him and have breathed into him of My Spirit do ye fall down, prostrating yourselves unto him.

15:28–29

3. They will ask thee concerning the Spirit. Say: The Spirit is by command of my Lord, and of knowledge ye have been vouchsafed but little.

17:85

4. And make mention of Mary in the Scripture, when she had withdrawn from her people to a chamber looking East,

And had chosen seclusion from them. Then We sent unto her Our spirit and it assumed for her the likenss of a perfect man.

19:16–17

1. يٰۤاَهۡلَ الۡكِتٰبِ لَا تَغۡلُوۡا فِىۡ دِيۡنِكُمۡ وَلَا
تَقُوۡلُوۡا عَلَى اللّٰهِ اِلَّا الۡحَقَّؕ اِنَّمَا الۡمَسِيۡحُ
عِيۡسَى ابۡنُ مَرۡيَمَ رَسُوۡلُ اللّٰهِ وَكَلِمَتُهٗۚ
اَلۡقٰهَاۤ اِلٰى مَرۡيَمَ وَرُوۡحٌ مِّنۡهُ فَاٰمِنُوۡا
بِاللّٰهِ وَرُسُلِهٖ

2. وَاِذۡ قَالَ رَبُّكَ لِلۡمَلٰۤئِكَةِ اِنِّىۡ خَالِقٌۢ
بَشَرًا مِّنۡ صَلۡصَالٍ مِّنۡ حَمَاٍ مَّسۡنُوۡنٍ ﴿۲۸﴾
فَاِذَا سَوَّيۡتُهٗ وَنَفَخۡتُ فِيۡهِ مِنۡ رُّوۡحِىۡ
فَقَعُوۡا لَهٗ سٰجِدِيۡنَ ﴿۲۹﴾

3. وَيَسۡـئَلُوۡنَكَ عَنِ الرُّوۡحِؕ قُلِ الرُّوۡحُ مِنۡ
اَمۡرِ رَبِّىۡ وَمَاۤ اُوۡتِيۡتُمۡ مِّنَ الۡعِلۡمِ
اِلَّا قَلِيۡلًا ﴿۸۵﴾

4. وَاذۡكُرۡ فِى الۡكِتٰبِ مَرۡيَمَۘ اِذِ انْتَبَذَتۡ
مِنۡ اَهۡلِهَا مَكَانًا شَرۡقِيًّا ﴿۱۶﴾
فَاتَّخَذَتۡ مِنۡ دُوۡنِهِمۡ حِجَابًا فَاَرۡسَلۡنَاۤ
اِلَيۡهَا رُوۡحَنَا فَتَمَثَّلَ لَهَا بَشَرًا سَوِيًّا ﴿۱۷﴾

5. وَمَرۡيَمَ ابۡنَتَ عِمۡرٰنَ الَّتِىۡۤ اَحۡصَنَتۡ
فَرۡجَهَا فَنَفَخۡنَا فِيۡهِ مِنۡ رُّوۡحِنَا
وَصَدَّقَتۡ بِكَلِمٰتِ رَبِّهَا وَكُتُبِهٖ
وَكَانَتۡ مِنَ الۡقٰنِتِيۡنَ ﴿۱۲﴾

5. And Mary, daughter of 'Imrān, whose body was chaste, therefor We breathed therein something of Our Spirit. And she put faith in the words of her Lord and His Scriptures, and was of the obedient.

66:12

6. On the day when the angels and the Spirit stand arrayed, they speak not, saving him whom the Beneficent alloweth and who speaketh right.

That is the True Day. So whoso will should seek recourse unto his Lord.

78:38–39

6. يَوْمَ يَقُومُ الرُّوحُ وَالْمَلٰٓئِكَةُ صَفًّاۜ لَّا يَتَكَلَّمُونَ اِلَّا مَنْ اَذِنَ لَهُ الرَّحْمٰنُ وَقَالَ صَوَابًا۝ ذٰلِكَ الْيَوْمُ الْحَقُّۚ فَمَنْ شَآءَ اتَّخَذَ اِلٰى رَبِّهٖ مَاٰبًا۝

SPLITING OF MOON

1. The hour drew nigh and the moon was rent in twain.

And if they behold a portent they turn away and say: Prolonged illusion.

They denied (the Truth) and followed their own lusts. Yet everything will come to a decision.

54:1–3

1. اِقْتَرَبَتِ السَّاعَةُ وَانْشَقَّ الْقَمَرُ۝ وَاِنْ يَّرَوْا اٰيَةً يُّعْرِضُوْا وَيَقُوْلُوْا سِحْرٌ مُّسْتَمِرٌّ۝ وَكَذَّبُوْا وَاتَّبَعُوْٓا اَهْوَآءَهُمْ وَكُلُّ اَمْرٍ مُّسْتَقِرٌّ۝

O

SPIRIT

Ref: 16:2; 32:9; 38:72; 40:15; 58:22.

STARS

1. And He it is Who hath set for you the stars that ye may guide your course by them amid the darkness of the land and the sea. We have detailed Our revelations for a people who have knowledge.

6:97

2. And He hath cast into the earth firm hills that it quake not with you, and streams and roads that ye may find a way.

And landmarks (too), and by the star they find a way.

16:15–16

3. Hast thou not seen that unto Allah payeth adoration whosoever is in the heavens and whosoever is in the earth, and the sun, and the moon, and the stars, and the hills, and the trees, and the beasts, and many of mankind.

22:18

4. Nay, I swear by the places of the stars—

And lo! that verily is a tremendous oath, if ye but knew—

56:75–76

5. By the heaven and the Morning Star

1. وَهُوَ الَّذِىْ جَعَلَ لَكُمُ النُّجُوْمَ لِتَهْتَدُوْا
بِهَا فِىْ ظُلُمٰتِ الْبَرِّ وَالْبَحْرِ قَدْ فَصَّلْنَا
الْاٰيٰتِ لِقَوْمٍ يَّعْلَمُوْنَ ○

2. وَاَلْقٰى فِى الْاَرْضِ رَوَاسِىَ اَنْ تَمِيْدَ
بِكُمْ وَاَنْهٰرًا وَّسُبُلًا لَّعَلَّكُمْ تَهْتَدُوْنَ ۝١٥
وَعَلٰمٰتٍ وَبِالنَّجْمِ هُمْ يَهْتَدُوْنَ ۝١٦

3. اَلَمْ تَرَ اَنَّ اللّٰهَ يَسْجُدُ لَهٗ مَنْ فِى
السَّمٰوٰتِ وَمَنْ فِى الْاَرْضِ وَالشَّمْسُ
وَالْقَمَرُ وَالنُّجُوْمُ وَالْجِبَالُ وَالشَّجَرُ
وَالدَّوَآبُّ وَكَثِيْرٌ مِّنَ النَّاسِ

4. فَلَآ اُقْسِمُ بِمَوٰقِعِ النُّجُوْمِ ۝٧٥
وَاِنَّهٗ لَقَسَمٌ لَّوْ تَعْلَمُوْنَ عَظِيْمٌ ۝٧٦

5. وَالسَّمَآءِ وَالطَّارِقِ ۝١
وَمَآ اَدْرٰىكَ مَا الطَّارِقُ ۝٢
النَّجْمُ الثَّاقِبُ ۝٣
اِنْ كُلُّ نَفْسٍ لَّمَّا عَلَيْهَا حَافِظٌ ۝٤

○

—Ah, what will tell thee what the Morning Star, is!

—The piercing Star!

No human soul but hath a guardian over it.

86:1–4

See also: Astronomy, Creation of Universe, Shooting Star, Subjugation of Universe.

STEADFASTNESS

1. O ye who believe! Endure, outdo all others in endurance, be ready, and observe your duty to Allah, in order that ye may succeed.

3:200

2. So tread thou the straight path as thou art commanded, and those who turn (unto Allah) with thee, and transgress not. Lo! He is Seer of what ye do.

11:112

3. Lo! those who say: Our Lord is Allah, and afterward are upright, the angels descend upon them, saying: Fear not nor grieve, but hear good tidings of the Paradise which ye are promised.

We are your protecting friends in the life of the world and in the Hereafter. There ye will have (all) that your souls desire, and there ye will have (all) for which ye pray.

A gift of welcome from One Forgiving, the Merciful.

41:30–32

4. So hold thou fast to that which is inspired in thee. Lo! thou art on a right path.

43:43

5. Lo! those who say: Our Lord is Allah, and thereafter walk aright, there shall no fear come upon them neither shall they grieve.

Such are rightful owners of the Garden, immortal therein, as a reward for what they used to do.

46:13–14

6. So wait patiently (O Muhammad) for thy Lord's decree, for surely thou art in Our sight; and hymn the praise of thy Lord when thou uprisest,

52:48

1. يَا أَيُّهَا الَّذِينَ آمَنُوا اصْبِرُوا وَصَابِرُوا
وَرَابِطُوا وَاتَّقُوا اللَّهَ لَعَلَّكُمْ تُفْلِحُونَ ﴿٢٠٠﴾

2. فَاسْتَقِمْ كَمَا أُمِرْتَ وَمَنْ تَابَ مَعَكَ
وَلَا تَطْغَوْا ۚ إِنَّهُ بِمَا تَعْمَلُونَ بَصِيرٌ ﴿١١٢﴾

3. إِنَّ الَّذِينَ قَالُوا رَبُّنَا اللَّهُ ثُمَّ اسْتَقَامُوا
تَتَنَزَّلُ عَلَيْهِمُ الْمَلَائِكَةُ أَلَّا تَخَافُوا
وَلَا تَحْزَنُوا وَأَبْشِرُوا بِالْجَنَّةِ الَّتِي
كُنْتُمْ تُوعَدُونَ ﴿٣٠﴾
نَحْنُ أَوْلِيَاؤُكُمْ فِي الْحَيَاةِ الدُّنْيَا وَ
فِي الْآخِرَةِ ۖ وَلَكُمْ فِيهَا مَا تَشْتَهِي أَنْفُسُكُمْ
وَلَكُمْ فِيهَا مَا تَدَّعُونَ ﴿٣١﴾
نُزُلًا مِنْ غَفُورٍ رَحِيمٍ ﴿٣٢﴾

4. فَاسْتَمْسِكْ بِالَّذِي أُوحِيَ إِلَيْكَ ۖ إِنَّكَ
عَلَىٰ صِرَاطٍ مُسْتَقِيمٍ ﴿٤٣﴾

5. إِنَّ الَّذِينَ قَالُوا رَبُّنَا اللَّهُ ثُمَّ
اسْتَقَامُوا فَلَا خَوْفٌ عَلَيْهِمْ
وَلَا هُمْ يَحْزَنُونَ ﴿١٣﴾
أُولَٰئِكَ أَصْحَابُ الْجَنَّةِ خَالِدِينَ فِيهَا
جَزَاءً بِمَا كَانُوا يَعْمَلُونَ ﴿١٤﴾

6. وَاصْبِرْ لِحُكْمِ رَبِّكَ فَإِنَّكَ بِأَعْيُنِنَا
وَسَبِّحْ بِحَمْدِ رَبِّكَ حِينَ تَقُومُ ﴿٤٨﴾

Ref: 3:100–101,103; 4:175; 9:8; 10:89; 41:6; 42:15; 43:43; 44:59; 46:35; 68:48; 70:5; 72:16; 73:10–11; 81; 28:29.

See also: Perseverance.

STERILITY

1. A mention of the mercy of thy Lord unto His servant, Zachariah.

When he cried unto his Lord a cry in secret,

Saying. My Lord! Lo! The bones of me wax feable and my head is shining with grey hair, and I have never been unblest in prayer to Thee, my Lord.

Lo! I fear my kinsfolk after me, since my wife is barren. Oh, give me from Thy presence a successor!

Who shall inherit of me and inherit (also) of the house of Jacob. And make him, my Lord, acceptable (unto Thee).

(It was said unto him): O Zachariah! Lo! We bring thee tidings of a son whose name is John, We have given the same name to none before (him).

He said: My Lord! How can I have a son when my wife is barren and I have reached infirm old age?

He said: so (it will be) Thy Lord saith: it is easy for Me, even as I created thee before, when thou wast naught.

19:2–9

2. Unto Allah belongeth the Sovereignty of the heavens and the earth. He createth what He will. He bestoweth female (offspring) upon whom He will, and bestoweth male (offspring) upon whom He will;

Or He mingleth them, males and femlaes, and He maketh barren whom He will. Lo! He is Knower, Powerful.

42:49–50

1. ذِكْرُ رَحْمَتِ رَبِّكَ عَبْدَهُ زَكَرِيَّا ﴿٢﴾
اِذْ نَادٰى رَبَّهٗ نِدَآءً خَفِيًّا ﴿٣﴾
قَالَ رَبِّ اِنِّيْ وَهَنَ الْعَظْمُ مِنِّيْ وَ
اشْتَعَلَ الرَّاْسُ شَيْبًا وَّ لَمْ اَكُنْ
بِدُعَآئِكَ رَبِّ شَقِيًّا ﴿٤﴾
وَ اِنِّيْ خِفْتُ الْمَوَالِيَ مِنْ وَّرَآءِيْ وَكَانَتِ
امْرَاَتِيْ عَاقِرًا فَهَبْ لِيْ مِنْ لَّدُنْكَ وَلِيًّا ﴿٥﴾
يَّرِثُنِيْ وَيَرِثُ مِنْ اٰلِ يَعْقُوْبَ وَاجْعَلْهُ
رَبِّ رَضِيًّا ﴿٦﴾
يٰزَكَرِيَّآ اِنَّا نُبَشِّرُكَ بِغُلٰمِ اسْمُهٗ يَحْيٰى
لَمْ نَجْعَلْ لَّهٗ مِنْ قَبْلُ سَمِيًّا ﴿٧﴾
قَالَ رَبِّ اَنّٰى يَكُوْنُ لِيْ غُلٰمٌ وَّ كَانَتِ
امْرَاَتِيْ عَاقِرًا وَّ قَدْ بَلَغْتُ مِنَ
الْكِبَرِ عِتِيًّا ﴿٨﴾
قَالَ كَذٰلِكَ قَالَ رَبُّكَ هُوَ عَلَيَّ هَيِّنٌ
وَّ قَدْ خَلَقْتُكَ مِنْ قَبْلُ وَلَمْ تَكُ شَيْـًٔا ﴿٩﴾

2. لِلّٰهِ مُلْكُ السَّمٰوٰتِ وَ الْاَرْضِ يَخْلُقُ
مَا يَشَآءُ يَهَبُ لِمَنْ يَّشَآءُ اِنَاثًا
وَّ يَهَبُ لِمَنْ يَّشَآءُ الذُّكُوْرَ ﴿٤٩﴾
اَوْ يُزَوِّجُهُمْ ذُكْرَانًا وَّ اِنَاثًا وَ
يَجْعَلُ مَنْ يَّشَآءُ عَقِيْمًا اِنَّهٗ
عَلِيْمٌ قَدِيْرٌ ﴿٥٠﴾

STRAIGHT PATH

1. Thee (alone) we wor–shop: Thee (alone) we ask for help.

Show us the straight path,

The path of those whom Thou hast favoured; Not (the path) of those who earn Thine anger nor of those who go astray,

1:5–7

2. Allah guideth whom He will unto a straight path.

2:213

3. Lo! Allah is my Lord and your Lord, so worship Him. That is the straight path.

3:51

4. He who holdeth fast to Allah, he indeed is guided unto a right path.

3:101

5. Lo! I have put my trust in Allah, my Lord and your Lord. Not an animal but He doth grasp it by the forelock! Lo! my Lord is on the straight path.

11:56

6. Lo! Allah verily is guid–ing those who believe unto a right path.

22:54

7. By the wise Qur'ān,

1. اِيَّاكَ نَعْبُدُ وَاِيَّاكَ نَسْتَعِيْنُ ۝
اِهْدِنَا الصِّرَاطَ الْمُسْتَقِيْمَ ۝
صِرَاطَ الَّذِيْنَ اَنْعَمْتَ عَلَيْهِمْ غَيْرِ
الْمَغْضُوْبِ عَلَيْهِمْ وَلَا الضَّآلِّيْنَ ۝

2. وَاللّٰهُ يَهْدِيْ مَنْ يَّشَآءُ اِلٰى صِرَاطٍ مُّسْتَقِيْمٍ (٢١٣)

3. اِنَّ اللّٰهَ رَبِّيْ وَرَبُّكُمْ فَاعْبُدُوْهُ هٰذَا صِرَاطٌ مُّسْتَقِيْمٌ (٥١)

4. وَمَنْ يَّعْتَصِمْ بِاللّٰهِ فَقَدْ هُدِيَ اِلٰى صِرَاطٍ
مُّسْتَقِيْمٍ ۝

5. اِنِّيْ تَوَكَّلْتُ عَلَى اللّٰهِ رَبِّيْ وَرَبِّكُمْ مَا
مِنْ دَآبَّةٍ اِلَّا هُوَ اٰخِذٌ بِنَاصِيَتِهَا اِنَّ
رَبِّيْ عَلٰى صِرَاطٍ مُّسْتَقِيْمٍ (٥٦)

6. وَاِنَّ اللّٰهَ لَهَادِ الَّذِيْنَ اٰمَنُوْٓا اِلٰى
صِرَاطٍ مُّسْتَقِيْمٍ (٥٤)

7. وَالْقُرْاٰنِ الْحَكِيْمِ (٢)
اِنَّكَ لَمِنَ الْمُرْسَلِيْنَ (٣)
عَلٰى صِرَاطٍ مُّسْتَقِيْمٍ (٤)

8. اِنَّكَ لَتَهْدِيْٓ اِلٰى صِرَاطٍ مُّسْتَقِيْمٍ (٥٢)

○

Lo! thou art of those sent

On a straight path,

36:2–4

8. And lo! thou verily dost guide unto a right path:

42:52

SUBJUGATION OF UNIVERSE

1. Allah is He Who created the heavens and the earth, and causeth water to descend from the sky, thereby producing fruits as food for you, and maketh the ships to be of service unto you, that they may run upon the sea at His command, and hath made of service unto you the rivers;

And maketh the sun and the moon constant in their courses, to be of service unto you, and hath made of service unto you, the night and the day.

And He giveth you of all ye ask of Him, and if ye would count the bounty of Allah ye cannot reckon it. Lo! man is verily a wong-doer, an ingrate.

14:32–34

2. Hast thou not seen how Allah hath made all that is in the earth subservient unto you? And the ship runneth upon the sea by His command, and He holdeth back the heaven from falling on the earth unless by His leave. Lo! Allah is, for mankind, Full of Pity, Merciful.

22:65

3. See ye not how Allah hath made serviceable unto you whatsoever is in heavens and whatsoever is in the earth and hath loaded you with His favours both without and within? Yet of mankind is he who disputeth concerning Allah without knowledge or guidance or a Scripture giving light.

31:20

1. الله الذى خلق السموت و الارض
و انزل من السماء ماء فاخرج به
من الثمرت رزقا لكم و سخر لكم
الفلك لتجرى فى البحر بامره و سخر
لكم الانهر ﴿٣٢﴾
و سخر لكم الشمس و القمر دائبين
و سخر لكم اليل و النهار ﴿٣٣﴾
و اتكم من كل ما سالتموه و ان
تعدوا نعمت الله لا تحصوها ان الانسان
لظلوم كفار ﴿٣٤﴾

2. الم تر ان الله سخر لكم ما فى
الارض و الفلك تجرى فى البحر
بامره و يمسك السماء ان تقع
على الارض الا باذنه ان الله
بالناس لرءوف رحيم ﴿٦٥﴾

3. الم تروا ان الله سخر لكم ما
فى السموت و ما فى الارض و اسبغ
عليكم نعمه ظاهرة و باطنة و من
الناس من يجادل فى الله بغير علم
و لا هدى و لا كتب منير ﴿٢٠﴾

4. الله الذى سخر لكم البحر لتجرى
الفلك فيه بامره و لتبتغوا من
فضله و لعلكم تشكرون ﴿١٢﴾
و سخر لكم ما فى السموت و ما فى

4. Allah it is Who hath made the sea of service unto you that the ships may run thereon by His command, and that ye may seek of His bounty, and that haply ye may be thankful;

And hath made of service unto you whatsoever is in the heavens and whatsoever is in the earth; it is all from Him. Lo! herein verily are portents for people who reflect.

45:12–13

SUBMISSION TO ALLAH AND HIS MESSENGER (PBUH)

1. Say: Obey Allah and the messenger. But if they turn away, lo! Allah loveth not the disbelievers (in His guidance).

3:32

2. Whoso obeyeth Allah and His messenger, He will make him enter Gardens underneath which rivers flow, where such will dwell forever. That will be great success.

And whoso disobeyeth Allah and His messenger and transgresseth His limits, He will make him enter Fire, where such will dwell for ever; his will be a shameful doom.

4:13–14

3. O ye who believe! Obey Allah, and obey the messenger and those of you who are in authority; and if ye have a dispute concerning any matter, refer it to Allah and the messenger if ye are (in truth) believers in Allah and the Last Day. That is better and more seemly in the end.

4:59

4. Whoso obeyeth Allah and the messenger, they are with those unto whom Allah hath shown favour, of the Prophets and the saints and the martyrs and the righteous. The best of company are they!

4:69

الْأَرْضِ جَمِيعًا مِّنْهُ ۚ إِنَّ فِي ذَٰلِكَ
لَآيَاتٍ لِّقَوْمٍ يَتَفَكَّرُونَ ﴿١٣﴾

1. قُلْ أَطِيعُوا اللَّهَ وَالرَّسُولَ ۖ فَإِن تَوَلَّوْا
فَإِنَّ اللَّهَ لَا يُحِبُّ الْكَافِرِينَ ○

2. وَمَن يُطِعِ اللَّهَ وَرَسُولَهُ يُدْخِلْهُ جَنَّاتٍ
تَجْرِي مِن تَحْتِهَا الْأَنْهَارُ خَالِدِينَ فِيهَا ۚ
وَذَٰلِكَ الْفَوْزُ الْعَظِيمُ ﴿١٣﴾

وَمَن يَعْصِ اللَّهَ وَرَسُولَهُ وَيَتَعَدَّ
حُدُودَهُ يُدْخِلْهُ نَارًا خَالِدًا فِيهَا
وَلَهُ عَذَابٌ مُّهِينٌ ﴿١٤﴾

3. يَا أَيُّهَا الَّذِينَ آمَنُوا أَطِيعُوا اللَّهَ وَأَطِيعُوا
الرَّسُولَ وَأُولِي الْأَمْرِ مِنكُمْ ۖ فَإِن
تَنَازَعْتُمْ فِي شَيْءٍ فَرُدُّوهُ إِلَى اللَّهِ وَالرَّسُولِ
إِن كُنتُمْ تُؤْمِنُونَ بِاللَّهِ وَالْيَوْمِ الْآخِرِ ۚ
ذَٰلِكَ خَيْرٌ وَأَحْسَنُ تَأْوِيلًا ﴿٥٩﴾

4. وَمَن يُطِعِ اللَّهَ وَالرَّسُولَ فَأُولَٰئِكَ مَعَ
الَّذِينَ أَنْعَمَ اللَّهُ عَلَيْهِم مِّنَ النَّبِيِّينَ
وَالصِّدِّيقِينَ وَالشُّهَدَاءِ وَالصَّالِحِينَ ۚ
وَحَسُنَ أُولَٰئِكَ رَفِيقًا ﴿٦٩﴾

5. وَأَطِيعُوا اللَّهَ وَأَطِيعُوا الرَّسُولَ وَاحْذَرُوا ۚ
فَإِن تَوَلَّيْتُمْ فَاعْلَمُوا أَنَّمَا عَلَىٰ رَسُولِنَا
الْبَلَاغُ الْمُبِينُ ﴿٩٢﴾

5. Obey Allah and obey the messenger, and beware! But if ye turn away, then know that the duty of Our messenger is only plain conveyance (of the message).

5:92

SUBJUGATION OF UNIVERSE
Ref: 16:10,18.
See also: Earth, Moon, Sky, Stars, Sun.

6. Say: Obey Allah and obey the messenger. But if ye turn away, then (it is) for him (to do) only that wherewith he hath been charged, and for you (to do) only that wherewith ye have been charged. If ye obey him, ye will go aright. But the messenger hath no other charge than to convey (the message), plainly.

24:54

.6 قُلْ أَطِيعُوا اللَّهَ وَأَطِيعُوا الرَّسُولَ فَإِن تَوَلَّوْا فَإِنَّمَا عَلَيْهِ مَا حُمِّلَ وَعَلَيْكُم مَّا حُمِّلْتُمْ وَإِن تُطِيعُوهُ تَهْتَدُوا وَمَا عَلَى الرَّسُولِ إِلَّا الْبَلَاغُ الْمُبِينُ ﴿٥٤﴾

7. O ye who believe! Be not forward in the presence of Allah and His messenger, and keep your duty to Allah. Lo! Allah is Hearer, Knower.

49:1

.7 يَا أَيُّهَا الَّذِينَ آمَنُوا لَا تُقَدِّمُوا بَيْنَ يَدَيِ اللَّهِ وَرَسُولِهِ وَاتَّقُوا اللَّهَ إِنَّ اللَّهَ سَمِيعٌ عَلِيمٌ ﴿١﴾

SUBSISTENCE

1 Beautified is the life of the world for those who disbelieve; they make a jest of the believers. But those who keep their duty to Allah will be above them on the Day of Resurrection. Allah giveth without stint to whom He will.

2:212

.1 زُيِّنَ لِلَّذِينَ كَفَرُوا الْحَيَاةُ الدُّنْيَا وَيَسْخَرُونَ مِنَ الَّذِينَ آمَنُوا وَالَّذِينَ اتَّقَوْا فَوْقَهُمْ يَوْمَ الْقِيَامَةِ وَاللَّهُ يَرْزُقُ مَن يَشَاءُ بِغَيْرِ حِسَابٍ ﴿٢١٢﴾

2. Eat of that which Allah hath bestowed on you as food lawful and good, and keep your duty to Allah in Whom ye are believers.

5:88

.2 وَكُلُوا مِمَّا رَزَقَكُمُ اللَّهُ حَلَالًا طَيِّبًا وَاتَّقُوا اللَّهَ الَّذِي أَنتُم بِهِ مُؤْمِنُونَ ﴿٨٨﴾

3. And there is not a beast in the earth but the sustenance thereof dependeth on Allah. He knoweth its habitation and its repository. All is in a clear Record.

11:6

.3 وَمَا مِن دَابَّةٍ فِي الْأَرْضِ إِلَّا عَلَى اللَّهِ رِزْقُهَا وَيَعْلَمُ مُسْتَقَرَّهَا وَمُسْتَوْدَعَهَا كُلٌّ فِي كِتَابٍ مُّبِينٍ ﴿٦﴾

SUBMISSION TO ALLH AND HIS MESSENGER (PBUH).
Ref: 3:132; 4:64; 8:1,20.46; 9:71; 24:47–48; 47:33; 48:17; 58:13; 64:12.
See also: **Disobedience to Allah and His Messenger (PBUH), Love ror Allah.**

4. And Allah hath favoured some of you above others in provision. Now those who are more favoured will by no means hand over their provision to those (slaves) whom their right hands possess, so that they may be equal with them in respect thereof. Is it then the grace of Allah that they deny?

16:71

5. And how many animal there is that beareth not its own provision! Allah provideth for it and for you. He is the Hearer, the Knower.

29:60

6. Say: Lo! my Lord enlargeth the provision for whom He will of His bondmen, and narroweth (it) for him. And whatsoever ye spend (for good) He replaceth it. And He is the Best of Providers.

34:39

7. And if Allah were to enlarge the provision for His slaves they would surely rebel in the earth, but He sendeth down by measure as He willeth. Lo! He is Informed, a Seer of His bondmen.

42:27

8. And whosoever keepeth his duty to Allah, Allah will appoint a way out for him,

And will provide for him from (a quarter) whence he hath no expectation. And whosoever putteth his trust in Allah, He will suffice him. Lo! Allah bringeth His command to pass. Allah hath set a measure for all things.

65:2–3

.4 وَاللَّهُ فَضَّلَ بَعْضَكُمْ عَلَىٰ بَعْضٍ فِي الرِّزْقِ
فَمَا الَّذِينَ فُضِّلُوا بِرَادِّي رِزْقِهِمْ عَلَىٰ
مَا مَلَكَتْ أَيْمَانُهُمْ فَهُمْ فِيهِ سَوَاءٌ
أَفَبِنِعْمَةِ اللَّهِ يَجْحَدُونَ ﴿٧١﴾

.5 وَكَأَيِّن مِّن دَابَّةٍ لَّا تَحْمِلُ رِزْقَهَا
اللَّهُ يَرْزُقُهَا وَإِيَّاكُمْ وَهُوَ السَّمِيعُ الْعَلِيمُ ﴿٦٠﴾

.6 قُلْ إِنَّ رَبِّي يَبْسُطُ الرِّزْقَ لِمَن
يَشَاءُ مِنْ عِبَادِهِ وَيَقْدِرُ لَهُ وَمَا
أَنفَقْتُم مِّن شَيْءٍ فَهُوَ يُخْلِفُهُ وَهُوَ
خَيْرُ الرَّازِقِينَ ﴿٣٩﴾

.7 وَلَوْ بَسَطَ اللَّهُ الرِّزْقَ لِعِبَادِهِ لَبَغَوْا
فِي الْأَرْضِ وَلَٰكِن يُنَزِّلُ بِقَدَرٍ مَّا
يَشَاءُ إِنَّهُ بِعِبَادِهِ خَبِيرٌ بَصِيرٌ ﴿٢٧﴾

.8 وَمَن يَتَّقِ اللَّهَ يَجْعَل لَّهُ مَخْرَجًا ﴿٢﴾
وَيَرْزُقْهُ مِنْ حَيْثُ لَا يَحْتَسِبُ
وَمَن يَتَوَكَّلْ عَلَى اللَّهِ فَهُوَ حَسْبُهُ
إِنَّ اللَّهَ بَالِغُ أَمْرِهِ قَدْ جَعَلَ
اللَّهُ لِكُلِّ شَيْءٍ قَدْرًا ﴿٣﴾

See also: Want and Plenty.

SUCCESSFUL

1. O, ye who believe! Bow down and prostrate yourselves, and worship your Lord, and do good, that haply ye may prosper.

22:77

2. Successful indeed are the believers,

Who are humble in their prayers,

And who shun vain conversation,

And who are payers of the poor-due;

And who guard their modesty—

Save from their wives or the (slaves) that their right hands possess, for then they are not blameworthy.

But whoso craveth beyond that, such are transgressors—

And who are shepherds of their pledge and their covenant,

And who pay heed to their prayers.

These are the heirs,

Who will inherit Paradise. There they will abide.

23:1–11

3. O ye who believe! Guard your duty to Allah, and speak words straight to the point;

He will adjust your works for you and will forgive you your sins. Whosoever obeyeth Allah and His messenger, he verily hath gained a signal victory.

33:70–71

1. يَٰٓأَيُّهَا ٱلَّذِينَ ءَامَنُوا ٱرْكَعُوا وَٱسْجُدُوا
وَٱعْبُدُوا رَبَّكُمْ وَٱفْعَلُوا ٱلْخَيْرَ
لَعَلَّكُمْ تُفْلِحُونَ ۩ ٧٧

2. قَدْ أَفْلَحَ ٱلْمُؤْمِنُونَ ١
ٱلَّذِينَ هُمْ فِى صَلَاتِهِمْ خَٰشِعُونَ ٢
وَٱلَّذِينَ هُمْ عَنِ ٱللَّغْوِ مُعْرِضُونَ ٣
وَٱلَّذِينَ هُمْ لِلزَّكَوٰةِ فَٰعِلُونَ ٤
وَٱلَّذِينَ هُمْ لِفُرُوجِهِمْ حَٰفِظُونَ ٥
إِلَّا عَلَىٰٓ أَزْوَٰجِهِمْ أَوْ مَا مَلَكَتْ أَيْمَٰنُهُمْ
فَإِنَّهُمْ غَيْرُ مَلُومِينَ ٦
فَمَنِ ٱبْتَغَىٰ وَرَآءَ ذَٰلِكَ فَأُولَٰٓئِكَ
هُمُ ٱلْعَادُونَ ٧
وَٱلَّذِينَ هُمْ لِأَمَٰنَٰتِهِمْ وَعَهْدِهِمْ رَٰعُونَ ٨
وَٱلَّذِينَ هُمْ عَلَىٰ صَلَوَٰتِهِمْ يُحَافِظُونَ ٩
أُولَٰٓئِكَ هُمُ ٱلْوَٰرِثُونَ ١٠
ٱلَّذِينَ يَرِثُونَ ٱلْفِرْدَوْسَ هُمْ
فِيهَا خَٰلِدُونَ ١١

3. يَٰٓأَيُّهَا ٱلَّذِينَ ءَامَنُوا ٱتَّقُوا ٱللَّهَ وَقُولُوا
قَوْلًا سَدِيدًا ٧٠
يُصْلِحْ لَكُمْ أَعْمَٰلَكُمْ وَيَغْفِرْ لَكُمْ
ذُنُوبَكُمْ وَمَن يُطِعِ ٱللَّهَ وَرَسُولَهُۥ
فَقَدْ فَازَ فَوْزًا عَظِيمًا ٧١

4. And when the prayer is ended, then disperse in the land and seek of Allah's bounty, and remember Allah much, that ye may be successful.

62:10

4. فَإِذَا قُضِيَتِ الصَّلَوٰةُ فَانْتَشِرُوْا
فِي الْأَرْضِ وَابْتَغُوْا مِنْ فَضْلِ اللّٰهِ
وَاذْكُرُوا اللّٰهَ كَثِيْرًا لَّعَلَّكُمْ تُفْلِحُوْنَ ﴿١٠﴾

5. Lo! those who believe and do good works, theirs will be Gardens underneath which rivers flow. That is the Great Success.

85:11

5. إِنَّ الَّذِيْنَ اٰمَنُوْا وَعَمِلُوا الصّٰلِحٰتِ
لَهُمْ جَنّٰتٌ تَجْرِيْ مِنْ تَحْتِهَا الْأَنْهٰرُ
ذٰلِكَ الْفَوْزُ الْكَبِيْرُ ﴿١١﴾

SUICIDE

1. And kill not yourselves. Lo! Allah is ever Merciful unto you:

4:29

1. وَلَا تَقْتُلُوْٓا أَنْفُسَكُمْ إِنَّ اللّٰهَ كَانَ بِكُمْ رَحِيْمًا ﴿٢٩﴾

SUN

1. Lo! your Lord is Allah Who created the heavens and the earth in six Days, then mounted He the Throne. He covereth the night with day, which is in haste to follow it, and hath made the sun and the moon and the stars subservient by His command. His verily is all creation and commandment. Blessed be Allah, the Lord of the Worlds!

7:54

1. إِنَّ رَبَّكُمُ اللّٰهُ الَّذِيْ خَلَقَ السَّمٰوٰتِ وَ
الْأَرْضَ فِيْ سِتَّةِ أَيَّامٍ ثُمَّ اسْتَوٰى عَلَى
الْعَرْشِ يُغْشِي الَّيْلَ النَّهَارَ يَطْلُبُهٗ
حَثِيْثًا وَّالشَّمْسَ وَالْقَمَرَ وَالنُّجُوْمَ
مُسَخَّرٰتٍ بِأَمْرِهٖ أَلَا لَهُ الْخَلْقُ وَالْأَمْرُ
تَبٰرَكَ اللّٰهُ رَبُّ الْعٰلَمِيْنَ ﴿٥٤﴾

SUCCESSFUL

Ref: 2:5,22,189; 3:185; 4:13; 5:101,119; 6:16,135; 9:21,72,88-89,100,112; 37:60; 45:30; 48:5; 61:12; 64:9; 92:1-7.

See also: Qualities of Faithful and Pious.

2. He it is Who appointed the sun a splendour and the moon a light, and measured for her stages, that ye might know the number of the years, and the reckoning. Allah created not (all) that save in truth. He detaileth the revelations for people who have knowledge.

10:5

3. Allah it is Who raised up the heavens without visible supports, then mounted the Throne, and compelled the sun and the moon to be of service, each runneth unto an appointed term: He ordereth the course: He detaileth the revelations, that haply ye may be certain of the meeting with your Lord.

13:2

4. Hast thou not seen that unto Allah payeth adoration whosoever is in the heavens and whosoever is in the earth, and the sun, and the moon, and the stars, and the hills, and the trees, and the beasts, and many of mankind.

22:18

5. It is not for the sun to overtake the moon, nor doth the night outstrip the day. They float each in an orbit.

36:40

2. هُوَ الَّذِي جَعَلَ الشَّمْسَ ضِيَاءً وَالْقَمَرَ نُورًا وَّ
قَدَّرَهُ مَنَازِلَ لِتَعْلَمُوا عَدَدَ السِّنِينَ وَالْحِسَابَ ۚ مَا
خَلَقَ اللَّهُ ذَٰلِكَ إِلَّا بِالْحَقِّ ۚ يُفَصِّلُ الْآيَاتِ لِقَوْمٍ
يَعْلَمُونَ ۝

3. اللَّهُ الَّذِي رَفَعَ السَّمَاوَاتِ بِغَيْرِ عَمَدٍ
تَرَوْنَهَا ۖ ثُمَّ اسْتَوَىٰ عَلَى الْعَرْشِ ۖ وَسَخَّرَ
الشَّمْسَ وَالْقَمَرَ ۖ كُلٌّ يَجْرِي لِأَجَلٍ
مُسَمًّى ۚ يُدَبِّرُ الْأَمْرَ يُفَصِّلُ الْآيَاتِ
لَعَلَّكُمْ بِلِقَاءِ رَبِّكُمْ تُوقِنُونَ ۝

4. أَلَمْ تَرَ أَنَّ اللَّهَ يَسْجُدُ لَهُ مَنْ فِي
السَّمَاوَاتِ وَمَنْ فِي الْأَرْضِ وَالشَّمْسُ
وَالْقَمَرُ وَالنُّجُومُ وَالْجِبَالُ وَالشَّجَرُ
وَالدَّوَابُّ وَكَثِيرٌ مِنَ النَّاسِ ۖ

5. لَا الشَّمْسُ يَنْبَغِي لَهَا أَنْ تُدْرِكَ
الْقَمَرَ وَلَا اللَّيْلُ سَابِقُ النَّهَارِ ۚ
وَكُلٌّ فِي فَلَكٍ يَسْبَحُونَ ۝

Ref: 71:15–16.

See also: Astronomy, Subjugation of Universe, Universe.

SUPERSTITIONS OF PAGANS

1. They ask thee, (O Muhammad), of new moons. Say: They are fixed seasons for mankind and for the pilgrimage. It is not righte-ousness that ye go to houses by the backs thereof (as do the idolaters at certain seasons), but the righteous man is he who wardeth off (evil). So go to houses by the gates thereof, and observe your duty to Allah, that ye may be successful.

2:189

2. They invoke in His stead only females, they pray to none else than Satan, a rebel.

Whom Allah cursed, and he said: Surely I will take of Thy bondmen an appoint-ed portion,

And surely I will lead them astray, and surely I will arouse desires in them, and surely I will command them and they will cut the cattle's ears, and surely I will comm-and them and they will change Allah's creation. Who-so chooseth Satan for a patron instead of Allah is verily a loser and his loss is mani-fest.

He promiseth them and stirreth up desires in them, and Satan promiseth them only to beguile.

4:117–120

3. Allah hath not appointed anything in the nature of a *Bāhirah* or a *Sa'ibah* or a

1. يَسْـَٔلُونَكَ عَنِ الْأَهِلَّةِ ۖ قُلْ هِيَ مَوَاقِيتُ لِلنَّاسِ
وَالْحَجِّ ۗ وَلَيْسَ الْبِرُّ بِأَن تَأْتُوا الْبُيُوتَ مِن ظُهُورِهَا
وَلَٰكِنَّ الْبِرَّ مَنِ اتَّقَىٰ ۗ وَأْتُوا الْبُيُوتَ مِنْ أَبْوَابِهَا ۚ
وَاتَّقُوا اللَّهَ لَعَلَّكُمْ تُفْلِحُونَ ﴿١٨٩﴾

2. إِن يَدْعُونَ مِن دُونِهِ إِلَّا إِنَاثًا وَإِن
يَدْعُونَ إِلَّا شَيْطَانًا مَّرِيدًا ﴿١١٧﴾
لَّعَنَهُ اللَّهُ ۘ وَقَالَ لَأَتَّخِذَنَّ مِنْ عِبَادِكَ
نَصِيبًا مَّفْرُوضًا ﴿١١٨﴾
وَلَأُضِلَّنَّهُمْ وَلَأُمَنِّيَنَّهُمْ وَلَآمُرَنَّهُمْ
فَلَيُبَتِّكُنَّ آذَانَ الْأَنْعَامِ وَلَآمُرَنَّهُمْ فَلَيُغَيِّرُنَّ
خَلْقَ اللَّهِ ۚ وَمَن يَتَّخِذِ الشَّيْطَانَ وَلِيًّا مِّن
دُونِ اللَّهِ فَقَدْ خَسِرَ خُسْرَانًا مُّبِينًا ﴿١١٩﴾
يَعِدُهُمْ وَيُمَنِّيهِمْ ۖ وَمَا يَعِدُهُمُ
الشَّيْطَانُ إِلَّا غُرُورًا ﴿١٢٠﴾

3. مَا جَعَلَ اللَّهُ مِن بَحِيرَةٍ وَلَا سَائِبَةٍ
وَلَا وَصِيلَةٍ وَلَا حَامٍ ۙ وَلَٰكِنَّ الَّذِينَ
كَفَرُوا يَفْتَرُونَ عَلَى اللَّهِ الْكَذِبَ ۖ وَ
أَكْثَرُهُمْ لَا يَعْقِلُونَ ﴿١٠٣﴾
وَإِذَا قِيلَ لَهُمْ تَعَالَوْا إِلَىٰ مَا أَنزَلَ اللَّهُ
وَإِلَى الرَّسُولِ قَالُوا حَسْبُنَا مَا وَجَدْنَا
عَلَيْهِ آبَاءَنَا ۚ أَوَلَوْ كَانَ آبَاؤُهُمْ
لَا يَعْلَمُونَ شَيْئًا وَلَا يَهْتَدُونَ ﴿١٠٤﴾

Wasilah or a *Hāmi*, but those who disbelieve invent a lie against Allah. Most of them have no sense.

And when it is said unto them: Come unto that which Allah hath revealed and unto the messenger, they say: Enough for us is that wherein we found our fathers.

What! Even though their fathers had no knowledge whatsoever, and no guidance?

5:103–104

4. They assign unto Allah, of the crops and cattle which He created, a portion, and they say: "This is Allah's"—in their make believe—"and this is for (His) partners in regard to us." Thus that which (they assign) unto His partners in them reacheth not Allah and that which (they assign) unto Allah goeth to their (so-called) partners. Evil is their ordinance.

Thus have their (so-called) partners (of Allah) made the killing of their children to seem fair unto many of the idolaters, that they may ruin them and make their faith obscure for them. Had Allah willed (it otherwise), they had not done so. So leave them alone with their devices.

And they say: Such cattle and crops are forbidden. No one is to eat of them save whom we will—in their make-believe—cattle whose backs are forbidden, cattle over which they mention not the name of Allah. (All that is) a lie against Him. He will repay them for that which they invent.

And they say: That which is in the bellies of such cattle is reserved for our males and is forbidden to our wives; but if it be born dead, then they (all) may be partakers thereof. He will reward them for their attribution (of such

4. وَجَعَلُوا لِلّٰهِ مِمَّا ذَرَاَ مِنَ الْحَرْثِ وَالْاَنْعَامِ
نَصِيبًا فَقَالُوا هٰذَا لِلّٰهِ بِزَعْمِهِمْ وَهٰذَا
لِشُرَكَآئِنَا ۚ فَمَا كَانَ لِشُرَكَآئِهِمْ فَلَا يَصِلُ
اِلَى اللّٰهِ ۚ وَمَا كَانَ لِلّٰهِ فَهُوَ يَصِلُ اِلٰى
شُرَكَآئِهِمْ ؕ سَآءَ مَا يَحْكُمُوْنَ ○

وَكَذٰلِكَ زَيَّنَ لِكَثِيْرٍ مِّنَ الْمُشْرِكِيْنَ
قَتْلَ اَوْلَادِهِمْ شُرَكَآؤُهُمْ لِيُرْدُوْهُمْ
وَلِيَلْبِسُوْا عَلَيْهِمْ دِيْنَهُمْ ؕ وَلَوْ شَآءَ اللّٰهُ مَا
فَعَلُوْهُ فَذَرْهُمْ وَمَا يَفْتَرُوْنَ ○

وَقَالُوْا هٰذِهٖٓ اَنْعَامٌ وَّحَرْثٌ حِجْرٌ ۖ لَّا
يَطْعَمُهَآ اِلَّا مَنْ نَّشَآءُ بِزَعْمِهِمْ وَاَنْعَامٌ
حُرِّمَتْ ظُهُوْرُهَا وَاَنْعَامٌ لَّا يَذْكُرُوْنَ
اسْمَ اللّٰهِ عَلَيْهَا افْتِرَآءً عَلَيْهِ ؕ سَيَجْزِيْهِمْ
بِمَا كَانُوْا يَفْتَرُوْنَ ○

وَقَالُوْا مَا فِيْ بُطُوْنِ هٰذِهِ الْاَنْعَامِ خَالِصَةٌ
لِّذُكُوْرِنَا وَمُحَرَّمٌ عَلٰٓى اَزْوَاجِنَا ۚ وَاِنْ
يَّكُنْ مَّيْتَةً فَهُمْ فِيْهِ شُرَكَآءُ ؕ سَيَجْزِيْهِمْ
وَصْفَهُمْ ؕ اِنَّهٗ حَكِيْمٌ عَلِيْمٌ ○

قَدْ خَسِرَ الَّذِيْنَ قَتَلُوْٓا اَوْلَادَهُمْ سَفَهًا
بِغَيْرِ عِلْمٍ وَّحَرَّمُوْا مَا رَزَقَهُمُ اللّٰهُ افْتِرَآءً
عَلَى اللّٰهِ ؕ قَدْ ضَلُّوْا وَمَا كَانُوْا مُهْتَدِيْنَ ○

○

ordinances unto Him). Lo, He is Wise, Aware.

They are losers who besottedly have slain their children without knowledge, and have forbidden that which Allah bestowed upon them, inventing a lie against Allah. They indeed have gone astray and are not guided.

6:136–140

See also: Refutation of Polytheism.

SUSPICION

1. If thou obeyedst most of those on earth they would mislead thee far from Allah's way. They follow naught but an opinion, and they do but guess.

6:116

2. They who are idolaters will say: Had Allah willed, we had not ascribed (unto Him) partners neither had our fathers, nor had we forbidden aught. Thus did those who were before them give the lie (to Allah's messengers) till they tasted of the fear of Us. Say: Have ye any knowledge that ye can adduce for us? Lo! ye follow naught but an opinion. Lo! ye do but guess.

6:148

3. Most of them follow naught but conjecture. Assuredly conjecture can by no means take the place of truth Lo! Allah is Aware of what they do.

10:36

4. O ye who believe! Shun much suspicion; for lo! some suspicion is a crime. And spy not, neither backbite one another. Would one of you love to eat the flesh of his dead brother? Ye abhor that

1. وَاِنْ تُطِعْ اَكْثَرَ مَنْ فِي الْاَرْضِ يُضِلُّوْكَ
عَنْ سَبِيْلِ اللّٰهِ ؕ اِنْ يَّتَّبِعُوْنَ اِلَّا الظَّنَّ
وَاِنْ هُمْ اِلَّا يَخْرُصُوْنَ ○

2. سَيَقُوْلُ الَّذِيْنَ اَشْرَكُوْا لَوْ شَآءَ اللّٰهُ مَآ
اَشْرَكْنَا وَلَآ اٰبَآؤُنَا وَلَا حَرَّمْنَا مِنْ شَيْءٍ ؕ
كَذٰلِكَ كَذَّبَ الَّذِيْنَ مِنْ قَبْلِهِمْ حَتّٰى
ذَاقُوْا بَاْسَنَا ؕ قُلْ هَلْ عِنْدَكُمْ مِّنْ عِلْمٍ
فَتُخْرِجُوْهُ لَنَا ؕ اِنْ تَتَّبِعُوْنَ اِلَّا الظَّنَّ وَ
اِنْ اَنْتُمْ اِلَّا تَخْرُصُوْنَ ○

3. وَمَا يَتَّبِعُ اَكْثَرُهُمْ اِلَّا ظَنًّا ؕ اِنَّ
الظَّنَّ لَا يُغْنِيْ مِنَ الْحَقِّ شَيْـًٔا ؕ اِنَّ
اللّٰهَ عَلِيْمٌۢ بِمَا يَفْعَلُوْنَ (٣٦)

4. يٰۤاَيُّهَا الَّذِيْنَ اٰمَنُوا اجْتَنِبُوْا كَثِيْرًا مِّنَ الظَّنِّ اِنَّ
بَعْضَ الظَّنِّ اِثْمٌ وَّلَا تَجَسَّسُوْا وَلَا يَغْتَبْ
بَّعْضُكُمْ بَعْضًا ؕ اَيُحِبُّ اَحَدُكُمْ اَنْ يَّاْكُلَ لَحْمَ
اَخِيْهِ مَيْتًا فَكَرِهْتُمُوْهُ ؕ وَاتَّقُوا اللّٰهَ ؕ اِنَّ اللّٰهَ
تَوَّابٌ رَّحِيْمٌ (١٢)

○

Ref: 10:66; 53:23, 27–28.

TAGHÛT

1. There is no compulsion in religion. The right direction is henceforth distinct from error. And he who rejecteth false deities and believeth in Allah hath grasped a firm handhold which will never break. Allah is Hearer, Knower.

Allah is the Protecting Friend of those who believe. He bringeth them out of darkness into light. As for those who disbelieve, their patrons are false deities. They bring them out of light into darkness. Such are rightful owners of the Fire. They will abide therein.

2:256–257

2. Hast thou not seen those unto whom a portion of the Scripture hath been given, how they believe in idols and false deities and how they say of those (idolaters) who disbelieve: "These are more rightly guided than those who believe?"

4:51

3. Hast thou not seen those who pretend that they believe in that which is revealed unto thee and that which was revealed before thee, how they would go for judgement (in their disputes) to false deities when they have been ordered to abjure them? Satan would mislead them far astray.

4:60

1. لَآ اِكْرَاهَ فِي الدِّيْنِ قَدْ تَّبَيَّنَ الرُّشْدُ مِنَ
الْغَيِّ فَمَنْ يَّكْفُرْ بِالطَّاغُوْتِ وَيُؤْمِنْ بِاللّٰهِ
فَقَدِ اسْتَمْسَكَ بِالْعُرْوَةِ الْوُثْقٰى لَا انْفِصَامَ
لَهَا وَاللّٰهُ سَمِيْعٌ عَلِيْمٌ ﴿٢٥٦﴾
اَللّٰهُ وَلِيُّ الَّذِيْنَ اٰمَنُوْا يُخْرِجُهُمْ مِّنَ
الظُّلُمٰتِ اِلَى النُّوْرِ وَالَّذِيْنَ كَفَرُوْٓا اَوْلِيٰٓـُٔهُمُ
الطَّاغُوْتُ يُخْرِجُوْنَهُمْ مِّنَ النُّوْرِ اِلَى الظُّلُمٰتِ
اُولٰٓئِكَ اَصْحٰبُ النَّارِ هُمْ فِيْهَا خٰلِدُوْنَ ﴿٢٥٧﴾

2. اَلَمْ تَرَ اِلَى الَّذِيْنَ اُوْتُوْا نَصِيْبًا مِّنَ الْكِتٰبِ
يُؤْمِنُوْنَ بِالْجِبْتِ وَالطَّاغُوْتِ وَيَقُوْلُوْنَ
لِلَّذِيْنَ كَفَرُوْا هٰٓؤُلَآءِ اَهْدٰى مِنَ
الَّذِيْنَ اٰمَنُوْا سَبِيْلًا ﴿٥١﴾

3. اَلَمْ تَرَ اِلَى الَّذِيْنَ يَزْعُمُوْنَ اَنَّهُمْ اٰمَنُوْا بِمَآ
اُنْزِلَ اِلَيْكَ وَمَآ اُنْزِلَ مِنْ قَبْلِكَ يُرِيْدُوْنَ
اَنْ يَّتَحَاكَمُوْٓا اِلَى الطَّاغُوْتِ وَقَدْ اُمِرُوْٓا
اَنْ يَّكْفُرُوْا بِهٖ وَيُرِيْدُ الشَّيْطٰنُ اَنْ
يُّضِلَّهُمْ ضَلٰلًا بَعِيْدًا ﴿٦٠﴾

4. اَلَّذِيْنَ اٰمَنُوْا يُقَاتِلُوْنَ فِيْ سَبِيْلِ اللّٰهِ
وَالَّذِيْنَ كَفَرُوْا يُقَاتِلُوْنَ فِيْ سَبِيْلِ
الطَّاغُوْتِ فَقَاتِلُوْٓا اَوْلِيَآءَ الشَّيْطٰنِ اِنَّ
كَيْدَ الشَّيْطٰنِ كَانَ ضَعِيْفًا ﴿٧٦﴾

4. Those who believe do battle for the cause of Allah; and those who disbelieve do battle for the cause of idols. So fight the minions of the devil. Lo! the devil's strategy

is ever weak.

4:76

5. Say: Shall I tell thee of a worse (case) than theirs for retribution with Allah? (Worse is the case of him) whom Allah hath cursed, him on whom His wrath hath fallen and of whose sort Allah hath turned some to apes and swine, and who serveth idols. Such are in worse plight and further astray from the plain road.

5:60

6. And those who put away false gods lest they should worship them and turn to Allah in repentance, for them there are glad tidings. Therefor give good tidings (O Muhammad) to My bondmen,

39:17

5. قُلْ هَلْ أُنَبِّئُكُمْ بِشَرٍّ مِّنْ ذٰلِكَ مَثُوْبَةً
عِنْدَ اللّٰهِ ۭ مَنْ لَّعَنَهُ اللّٰهُ وَغَضِبَ عَلَيْهِ
وَجَعَلَ مِنْهُمُ الْقِرَدَةَ وَالْخَنَازِيْرَ وَعَبَدَ
الطَّاغُوْتَ ۭ اُولٰۗىِٕكَ شَرٌّ مَّكَانًا وَّاَضَلُّ
عَنْ سَوَاۗءِ السَّبِيْلِ ﴿٦٠﴾

6. وَالَّذِيْنَ اجْتَنَبُوا الطَّاغُوْتَ اَنْ يَّعْبُدُوْهَا
وَاَنَابُوْٓا اِلَى اللّٰهِ لَهُمُ الْبُشْرٰى ۚ فَبَشِّرْ عِبَادِ ﴿١٧﴾

Rev: 16:36. **See also:** Idols.

TAHAJJUD

1. Establish worship at the going down of the sun until the dark of night, and (the recital of) the Qur'ān at dawn. Lo! (the recital of) the Qur'ān at dawn is ever witnessed.

And some part of the night awake for it, a largess for thee. It may be that thy Lord will raise thee to a praised estate.

17:78–79

2. O thou wrapped up in thy raiment!

Keep vigil the night long, save a little–

A half thereof, or abate a little thereof

Or add (a little) thereto-and chant the Qur'ān in measure.

For We shall charge thee with a word of weight.

Lo! the vigil of the night is (a time) when impression is more keen and speech more certain.

Lo! thou hast by day a chain of business.

So remember the name of thy Lord and devote thy-self with a complete devotion.

73:1–8

3. Lo! thy Lord knoweth how thou keepest vigil some-times nearly two–thirds of the night, or (sometimes) half or a third thereof, as do a party of those with thee. Allah

1. اَقِمِ الصَّلٰوةَ لِدُلُوْكِ الشَّمْسِ اِلٰى غَسَقِ
الَّيْلِ وَقُرْاٰنَ الْفَجْرِ اِنَّ قُرْاٰنَ الْفَجْرِ
كَانَ مَشْهُوْدًا ﴿٧٨﴾
وَمِنَ الَّيْلِ فَتَهَجَّدْ بِهٖ نَافِلَةً لَّكَ
عَسٰٓى اَنْ يَّبْعَثَكَ رَبُّكَ مَقَامًا مَّحْمُوْدًا ﴿٧٩﴾

2. يٰٓاَيُّهَا الْمُزَّمِّلُ ﴿١﴾
قُمِ الَّيْلَ اِلَّا قَلِيْلًا ﴿٢﴾
نِّصْفَهٗٓ اَوِ انْقُصْ مِنْهُ قَلِيْلًا ﴿٣﴾
اَوْ زِدْ عَلَيْهِ وَرَتِّلِ الْقُرْاٰنَ
تَرْتِيْلًا ﴿٤﴾
اِنَّا سَنُلْقِيْ عَلَيْكَ قَوْلًا ثَقِيْلًا ﴿٥﴾
اِنَّ نَاشِئَةَ الَّيْلِ هِيَ اَشَدُّ وَطْاً
وَّاَقْوَمُ قِيْلًا ﴿٦﴾
اِنَّ لَكَ فِي النَّهَارِ سَبْحًا طَوِيْلًا ﴿٧﴾
وَاذْكُرِ اسْمَ رَبِّكَ وَتَبَتَّلْ اِلَيْهِ
تَبْتِيْلًا ﴿٨﴾

3. اِنَّ رَبَّكَ يَعْلَمُ اَنَّكَ تَقُوْمُ اَدْنٰى
مِنْ ثُلُثَيِ الَّيْلِ وَنِصْفَهٗ وَثُلُثَهٗ
وَطَآئِفَةٌ مِّنَ الَّذِيْنَ مَعَكَ وَاللّٰهُ
يُقَدِّرُ الَّيْلَ وَالنَّهَارَ عَلِمَ اَنْ لَّنْ
تُحْصُوْهُ فَتَابَ عَلَيْكُمْ فَاقْرَءُوْا
مَا تَيَسَّرَ مِنَ الْقُرْاٰنِ

measureth the night and the day. He knoweth that ye count it not, and turneth unto you in mercy. Recite, then, of the Qur'ān that which is easy for you.

73:20

TALÛT

1. أَلَمْ تَرَ إِلَى الْمَلَإِ مِنْ بَنِي إِسْرَاءِيلَ مِنْ
بَعْدِ مُوسَىٰ إِذْ قَالُوا لِنَبِيٍّ لَهُمُ ابْعَثْ لَنَا
مَلِكًا نُقَاتِلْ فِي سَبِيلِ اللَّهِ ۖ قَالَ هَلْ
عَسَيْتُمْ إِنْ كُتِبَ عَلَيْكُمُ الْقِتَالُ أَلَّا
تُقَاتِلُوا ۖ قَالُوا وَمَا لَنَا أَلَّا نُقَاتِلَ فِي
سَبِيلِ اللَّهِ وَقَدْ أُخْرِجْنَا مِنْ دِيَارِنَا وَ
أَبْنَائِنَا ۖ فَلَمَّا كُتِبَ عَلَيْهِمُ الْقِتَالُ تَوَلَّوْا
إِلَّا قَلِيلًا مِنْهُمْ ۗ وَاللَّهُ عَلِيمٌ بِالظَّالِمِينَ ﴿٢٤٦﴾
وَقَالَ لَهُمْ نَبِيُّهُمْ إِنَّ اللَّهَ قَدْ بَعَثَ لَكُمْ
طَالُوتَ مَلِكًا ۚ قَالُوا أَنَّىٰ يَكُونُ لَهُ الْمُلْكُ
عَلَيْنَا وَنَحْنُ أَحَقُّ بِالْمُلْكِ مِنْهُ وَلَمْ
يُؤْتَ سَعَةً مِنَ الْمَالِ ۚ قَالَ إِنَّ اللَّهَ
اصْطَفَاهُ عَلَيْكُمْ وَزَادَهُ بَسْطَةً فِي الْعِلْمِ
وَالْجِسْمِ ۖ وَاللَّهُ يُؤْتِي مُلْكَهُ مَنْ يَشَاءُ ۚ
وَاللَّهُ وَاسِعٌ عَلِيمٌ ﴿٢٤٧﴾
وَقَالَ لَهُمْ نَبِيُّهُمْ إِنَّ آيَةَ مُلْكِهِ أَنْ يَأْتِيَكُمُ
التَّابُوتُ فِيهِ سَكِينَةٌ مِنْ رَبِّكُمْ وَبَقِيَّةٌ
مِمَّا تَرَكَ آلُ مُوسَىٰ وَآلُ هَارُونَ تَحْمِلُهُ
الْمَلَائِكَةُ ۚ إِنَّ فِي ذَٰلِكَ لَآيَةً لَكُمْ إِنْ
كُنْتُمْ مُؤْمِنِينَ ﴿٢٤٨﴾
فَلَمَّا فَصَلَ طَالُوتُ بِالْجُنُودِ قَالَ إِنَّ اللَّهَ
مُبْتَلِيكُمْ بِنَهَرٍ فَمَنْ شَرِبَ مِنْهُ فَلَيْسَ
مِنِّي وَمَنْ لَمْ يَطْعَمْهُ فَإِنَّهُ مِنِّي إِلَّا مَنِ
اغْتَرَفَ غُرْفَةً بِيَدِهِ ۚ فَشَرِبُوا مِنْهُ إِلَّا

1. Bethink thee of the leaders of the Children of Israel after Moses, how they said unto a Prophet whom they had: Set up for us a king and we will fight in Allah's way. He said: Would ye then refrain from fighting if fighting were prescribed for you? They said: Why should we not fight in Allah's way when we have been driven from our dwellings with our children? Yet, when fighting was prescribed for them, they turned away, all save a few of them. Allah is Aware of evil—doers.

Their Prophet said unto them: Lo! Allah hath raised up Saul to be a king for you. They said: How can he have kingdom over us when we are more deserving of the kingdom than he is, since he hath not been given wealth enough? He said: Lo! Allah hath chosen him above you, and hath increased him abundantly in wisdom and stature. Allah bestoweth His Sovereignty on whom He will. Allah is All—Embracing, All—Knowing.

And their Prophet said unto them: Lo! the token of his kingdom is that there shall come unto you the ark wherein is peace of reassurance from your Lord, and a remnant of that which the house of Moses and the house of Aaron left behind, the angels bearing it. Lo! herein shall be a token for you if (in truth) ye are believers.

And when Saul set out with the army, he said: Lo! Allah will try you by (the ordeal of) a river. Whosoever therefore drinketh thereof he is not of me, and whosoever tasteth it not he is of me, save him who taketh (thereof) in the hollow of his hand. But they drank thereof, all save a few of them. And after he had crossed (the river), he and those who believed with him, they said: We have no power this day against Goliath and his hosts. But those who knew that they would meet their Lord exclaimed: How many a little company hath overcome a mighty host by Allah's leave! Allah is with the steadfast.

And when they went into the field against Goliath and his hosts they said: Our Lord! Bestow on us endurance, make our foothold sure, and give us help against the disbelieving folk.

So they routed them by Allah's leave and David slew Goliath; and Allah gave him the kingdom and wisdom, and taught him of that which He willeth. And if Allah had not repelled some men by others the earth would have been corrupted. But Allah is a Lord of Kindness to (His) creatures.

2:246–251

قَلِيلًا مِّنْهُمْ ۚ فَلَمَّا جَاوَزَهُ هُوَ وَالَّذِينَ آمَنُوا
مَعَهُ قَالُوا لَا طَاقَةَ لَنَا الْيَوْمَ بِجَالُوتَ وَ
جُنُودِهِ ۚ قَالَ الَّذِينَ يَظُنُّونَ أَنَّهُم مُّلَاقُوا
اللَّهِ كَم مِّن فِئَةٍ قَلِيلَةٍ غَلَبَتْ فِئَةً
كَثِيرَةً بِإِذْنِ اللَّهِ ۗ وَاللَّهُ مَعَ الصَّابِرِينَ ﴿٢٤٩﴾
وَلَمَّا بَرَزُوا لِجَالُوتَ وَجُنُودِهِ قَالُوا رَبَّنَا
أَفْرِغْ عَلَيْنَا صَبْرًا وَثَبِّتْ أَقْدَامَنَا وَ
انصُرْنَا عَلَى الْقَوْمِ الْكَافِرِينَ ﴿٢٥٠﴾
فَهَزَمُوهُم بِإِذْنِ اللَّهِ وَقَتَلَ دَاوُودُ جَالُوتَ
وَآتَاهُ اللَّهُ الْمُلْكَ وَالْحِكْمَةَ وَعَلَّمَهُ مِمَّا
يَشَاءُ ۗ وَلَوْلَا دَفْعُ اللَّهِ النَّاسَ بَعْضَهُم
بِبَعْضٍ لَّفَسَدَتِ الْأَرْضُ وَلَٰكِنَّ اللَّهَ
ذُو فَضْلٍ عَلَى الْعَالَمِينَ ﴿٢٥١﴾

TAYAMMUM

1. وَإِن كُنتُم مَّرْضَىٰ أَوْ عَلَىٰ سَفَرٍ أَوْ جَاءَ أَحَدٌ
مِّنكُم مِّنَ الْغَائِطِ أَوْ لَامَسْتُمُ النِّسَاءَ فَلَمْ
تَجِدُوا مَاءً فَتَيَمَّمُوا صَعِيدًا طَيِّبًا
فَامْسَحُوا بِوُجُوهِكُمْ وَأَيْدِيكُم مِّنْهُ ۚ
مَا يُرِيدُ اللَّهُ لِيَجْعَلَ عَلَيْكُم مِّنْ حَرَجٍ
وَلَٰكِن يُرِيدُ لِيُطَهِّرَكُمْ وَلِيُتِمَّ نِعْمَتَهُ
عَلَيْكُمْ لَعَلَّكُمْ تَشْكُرُونَ ﴿٦﴾

1. And if ye are sick or on a journey, or one of you cometh from the closet, or ye have had contact with women, and ye find not water, then go to clean, high ground and rub your faces and your hands with some of it. Allah would not place a burden on you, but He would purify you and would perfect His grace upon you, that ye may give thanks.

5:6

TAYAMMUM
See also: *Wadhu.*

THANKSGIVING

1. Remember Me, I will remember you. Give thanks to Me, and reject not Me.

2:152

2. What concern hath Allah for your punishment if ye are thankful (for His mercies) and believe (in Him)? Allah was ever Responsive, Aware.

4:147

3. And when your Lord proclaimed: If ye give thanks, I will give you more; but if ye are thankless, lo! My punishment is dire.

14:7

4. So eat of the lawful and good food which Allah hath provided for you, and thank the bounty of your Lord if it is Him ye serve.

16:114

5. Whosoever giveth thanks he only giveth thanks for (the good of) his own soul: and whosoever is ungrateful (is ungrateful only to his own soul's hurt). For lo! my Lord is Absolute in independence, Bountiful.

27:40

6. If ye are thankless, yet Allah is Independent of you, though He is not pleased with thanklessness for His bond—men; and if ye are thankful He is pleased therewith for you. No laden soul will bear another's load. Then unto your Lord is your return; and He will tell you what ye used to do. Lo! He knoweth what is in the breasts (of men).

39:7

1. فَاذْكُرُونِي أَذْكُرْكُمْ وَاشْكُرُوا لِي وَلَا تَكْفُرُونِ ﴿١٥٢﴾

2. مَا يَفْعَلُ اللَّهُ بِعَذَابِكُمْ إِنْ شَكَرْتُمْ
وَآمَنْتُمْ ۚ وَكَانَ اللَّهُ شَاكِرًا عَلِيمًا ﴿١٤٧﴾

3. وَإِذْ تَأَذَّنَ رَبُّكُمْ لَئِنْ شَكَرْتُمْ لَأَزِيدَنَّكُمْ
وَلَئِنْ كَفَرْتُمْ إِنَّ عَذَابِي لَشَدِيدٌ ﴿٧﴾

4. فَكُلُوا مِمَّا رَزَقَكُمُ اللَّهُ حَلَالًا طَيِّبًا
وَاشْكُرُوا نِعْمَتَ اللَّهِ إِنْ كُنْتُمْ
إِيَّاهُ تَعْبُدُونَ ﴿١١٤﴾

5. وَمَنْ شَكَرَ فَإِنَّمَا يَشْكُرُ لِنَفْسِهِ ۖ
وَمَنْ كَفَرَ فَإِنَّ رَبِّي غَنِيٌّ كَرِيمٌ ﴿٤٠﴾

6. إِنْ تَكْفُرُوا فَإِنَّ اللَّهَ غَنِيٌّ عَنْكُمْ ۖ وَلَا
يَرْضَىٰ لِعِبَادِهِ الْكُفْرَ ۖ وَإِنْ تَشْكُرُوا
يَرْضَهُ لَكُمْ ۗ وَلَا تَزِرُ وَازِرَةٌ وِزْرَ
أُخْرَىٰ ۗ ثُمَّ إِلَىٰ رَبِّكُمْ مَرْجِعُكُمْ فَيُنَبِّئُكُمْ
بِمَا كُنْتُمْ تَعْمَلُونَ ۚ إِنَّهُ عَلِيمٌ
بِذَاتِ الصُّدُورِ ﴿٧﴾

Ref: 3:145; 31:12. **See also: Ingratitude.**

THEFT

1. As for the thief, both male and female, cut off their hands. It is the reward of their own deeds, an exemplary punishment from Allah. Allah is Mighty, Wise.

But whoso repenteth after his wrongdoing and amendeth, lo! Allah will relent toward him. Lo! Allah is Forgiving, Merciful.

5:38–39

1. وَالسَّارِقُ وَالسَّارِقَةُ فَاقْطَعُوْٓا اَيْدِيَهُمَا
جَزَآءً بِمَا كَسَبَا نَكَالًا مِّنَ اللّٰهِ ۭ وَاللّٰهُ
عَزِيْزٌ حَكِيْمٌ ﴿۳۸﴾

فَمَنْ تَابَ مِنْۢ بَعْدِ ظُلْمِهٖ وَاَصْلَحَ
فَاِنَّ اللّٰهَ يَتُوْبُ عَلَيْهِ ۭ اِنَّ اللّٰهَ غَفُوْرٌ رَّحِيْمٌ ﴿۳۹﴾

2. O Prophet! If the believing women come unto thee, taking oath of allegiance unto thee that they will ascribe nothing as partner unto Allah, and will neither steal nor commit adultery nor kill their children, nor produce any lie that they have devised between their hands and feet, nor disobey thee in what is right, then accept their allegiance and ask Allah to forgive them. Lo! Allah is Forgiving, Merciful.

60:12

2. يٰٓاَيُّهَا النَّبِيُّ اِذَا جَآءَكَ الْمُؤْمِنٰتُ
يُبَايِعْنَكَ عَلٰٓي اَنْ لَّا يُشْرِكْنَ بِاللّٰهِ
شَيْـــًٔا وَّلَا يَسْرِقْنَ وَلَا يَزْنِيْنَ
وَلَا يَقْتُلْنَ اَوْلَادَهُنَّ وَلَا يَاْتِيْنَ
بِبُهْتَانٍ يَّفْتَرِيْنَهٗ بَيْنَ اَيْدِيْهِنَّ
وَاَرْجُلِهِنَّ وَلَا يَعْصِيْنَكَ فِيْ
مَعْرُوْفٍ فَبَايِعْهُنَّ وَاسْتَغْفِرْ لَهُنَّ
اللّٰهَ ۭ اِنَّ اللّٰهَ غَفُوْرٌ رَّحِيْمٌ ﴿۱۲﴾

○

See also: *Hudud*

THINGS SWORN BY ALLAH

1. By the wise Qur'ān,
Lo! thou art of those sent

36:2–3

2. By those who set the ranks in battle order
And those who drive away (the wicked) with reproof
And those who read (the Word) for a reminder,
Lo! thy Lord is surely One;

37:1–4

3. By the renowned Qur'ān,
Nay, but those who disbelieve are in false pride and schism.

38:2-3

4. By the Scripture which maketh plain:
Lo! We have appointed it a Lecture in Arabic that haply ye may understand.

43:2–3

5. By the Glorious Qur'ān,

50:1

6. By those that winnow with a winnowing,
And those that bear the burden (of the rain),
And those that glide with ease (upon the sea),
And those who distribute (blessings) by command,
Lo! that wherewith ye are threatened is indeed true,
And lo! the judgement will indeed befall,
By the heaven full of path:
Lo! ye, forsooth, are of various opinions (concerning the truth).

51:1–8

7. And by the Lord of the heavens and the earth, it is the truth even as (it is true) that ye speak.

51:23

1. وَالْقُرْاٰنِ الْحَكِيْمِ ۝
إِنَّكَ لَمِنَ الْمُرْسَلِيْنَ ۝
2. وَالصّٰٓفّٰتِ صَفًّا ۝
فَالزّٰجِرٰتِ زَجْرًا ۝
فَالتّٰلِيٰتِ ذِكْرًا ۝
إِنَّ إِلٰهَكُمْ لَوَاحِدٌ ۝
3. وَالْقُرْاٰنِ ذِي الذِّكْرِ ۝
بَلِ الَّذِيْنَ كَفَرُوْا فِيْ عِزَّةٍ وَّشِقَاقٍ ۝
4. وَالْكِتٰبِ الْمُبِيْنِ ۝
إِنَّا جَعَلْنٰهُ قُرْءٰنًا عَرَبِيًّا لَّعَلَّكُمْ
تَعْقِلُوْنَ ۝
5. وَالْقُرْاٰنِ الْمَجِيْدِ ۝
6. وَالذّٰرِيٰتِ ذَرْوًا ۝
فَالْحٰمِلٰتِ وِقْرًا ۝
فَالْجٰرِيٰتِ يُسْرًا ۝
فَالْمُقَسِّمٰتِ أَمْرًا ۝
إِنَّمَا تُوْعَدُوْنَ لَصَادِقٌ ۝
وَّإِنَّ الدِّيْنَ لَوَاقِعٌ ۝
وَالسَّمَآءِ ذَاتِ الْحُبُكِ ۝
إِنَّكُمْ لَفِيْ قَوْلٍ مُّخْتَلِفٍ ۝
7. فَوَرَبِّ السَّمَآءِ وَالْأَرْضِ إِنَّهُ لَحَقٌّ
مِّثْلَ مَآ أَنَّكُمْ تَنْطِقُوْنَ ۝

8. By the Mount,
And a Scripture inscribed
On fine parchment unrolled,
And the House frequented,
And the roof exalted,
And the sea kept filled,
Lo! the doom of thy Lord will surely come to pass;
52:1–7

9. By the Star when it setteth,
Your comrade erreth not, nor is deceived;
Nor doth he speak of (his own) desire.
53:1–3

10. Nay, I swear by the places of the stars –
And lo! that verily is a tremendous oath, if ye but knew –
That (this is indeed) a noble Qur'ān).
56:75–77

11. By the pen and that which they write (therewith),
Thou art not, for thy Lord's favour unto thee, a madman.
And lo! thine verily will be a reward unfailing.
68:1–3

12. But, nay! I swear by all that ye see
And all that ye see not.
That it is indeed the speech of an illustrious messenger.
69:38–40

13. But nay! I swear by the Lord of the rising–

8. وَالطُّوْرِ ۝١
وَكِتٰبٍ مَّسْطُوْرٍ ۝٢
فِيْ رَقٍّ مَّنْشُوْرٍ ۝٣
وَالْبَيْتِ الْمَعْمُوْرِ ۝٤
وَالسَّقْفِ الْمَرْفُوْعِ ۝٥
وَالْبَحْرِ الْمَسْجُوْرِ ۝٦
اِنَّ عَذَابَ رَبِّكَ لَوَاقِعٌ ۝٧
9. وَالنَّجْمِ اِذَا هَوٰى ۝١
مَا ضَلَّ صَاحِبُكُمْ وَمَا غَوٰى ۝٢
وَمَا يَنْطِقُ عَنِ الْهَوٰى ۝٣
10. فَلَآ اُقْسِمُ بِمَوٰقِعِ النُّجُوْمِ ۝٧٥
وَاِنَّهٗ لَقَسَمٌ لَّوْ تَعْلَمُوْنَ عَظِيْمٌ ۝٧٦
اِنَّهٗ لَقُرْاٰنٌ كَرِيْمٌ ۝٧٧
11. وَالْقَلَمِ وَمَا يَسْطُرُوْنَ ۝١
مَآ اَنْتَ بِنِعْمَةِ رَبِّكَ بِمَجْنُوْنٍ ۝٢
وَاِنَّ لَكَ لَاَجْرًا غَيْرَ مَمْنُوْنٍ ۝٣
12. فَلَآ اُقْسِمُ بِمَا تُبْصِرُوْنَ ۝٣٨
وَمَا لَا تُبْصِرُوْنَ ۝٣٩
اِنَّهٗ لَقَوْلُ رَسُوْلٍ كَرِيْمٍ ۝٤٠
13. فَلَآ اُقْسِمُ بِرَبِّ الْمَشٰرِقِ وَالْمَغٰرِبِ
اِنَّا لَقٰدِرُوْنَ ۝٤٠
عَلٰٓى اَنْ نُّبَدِّلَ خَيْرًا مِّنْهُمْ وَمَا نَحْنُ
بِمَسْبُوْقِيْنَ ۝٤١
14. كَلَّا وَالْقَمَرِ ۝٣٢
وَالَّيْلِ اِذْ اَدْبَرَ ۝٣٣

places and the setting–places of the planets that We verily are Able
To replace them by (others) better than them. And We are not to be outrun.
70:40–41

14. Nay, by the Moon
And the night when it withdraweth
And the dawn when it shineth forth

Lo! this is one of the greatest (portents)

As a warning unto men,

74:32–36

15. Nay, I swear by the Day of Resurrection;

Nay, I swear by the accusing soul (that this Scrip–ture is true).

Thinketh man that We shall not assemble his bones?

Yea, verily We are Able to restore his very fingures;

75:1–4

16. By the emissary winds, (sent) one after another

By the raging hurricanes,

By those which cause earth's vegetation to revive;

By those who winnow with a winnowing,

By those who bring down the Reminder,

To excuse or to warn,

Surely that which ye are promised will befall.

77:1–7

17. By those who drag forth to destruction,

By the meteors rushing,

By the lone stars floating,

By the angels hastening,

And those who govern the event,

On the day when the first trumpet resoundeth

And the second followe–th it,

On that day hearts beat painfully

وَالصُّبْحِ إِذَآ أَسْفَرَ (٣٤)
إِنَّهَا لَإِحْدَى الْكُبَرِ (٣٥)
نَذِيرًا لِّلْبَشَرِ (٣٦)
15. لَآ أُقْسِمُ بِيَوْمِ الْقِيٰمَةِ (١)
وَلَآ أُقْسِمُ بِالنَّفْسِ اللَّوَّامَةِ (٢)
أَيَحْسَبُ الْإِنسٰنُ أَلَّن نَّجْمَعَ عِظَامَهُۥ (٣)
بَلَىٰ قٰدِرِينَ عَلَىٰٓ أَن نُّسَوِّىَ بَنَانَهُۥ (٤)
16. وَالْمُرْسَلٰتِ عُرْفًا (١)
فَالْعٰصِفٰتِ عَصْفًا (٢)
وَالنّٰشِرٰتِ نَشْرًا (٣)
فَالْفٰرِقٰتِ فَرْقًا (٤)
فَالْمُلْقِيٰتِ ذِكْرًا (٥)
عُذْرًا أَوْ نُذْرًا (٦)
إِنَّمَا تُوعَدُونَ لَوٰقِعٌ (٧)
17. وَالنّٰزِعٰتِ غَرْقًا (١)
وَالنّٰشِطٰتِ نَشْطًا (٢)
وَالسّٰبِحٰتِ سَبْحًا (٣)
فَالسّٰبِقٰتِ سَبْقًا (٤)
فَالْمُدَبِّرٰتِ أَمْرًا (٥)
يَوْمَ تَرْجُفُ الرَّاجِفَةُ (٦)
تَتْبَعُهَا الرَّادِفَةُ (٧)
قُلُوبٌ يَوْمَئِذٍ وَاجِفَةٌ (٨)
أَبْصٰرُهَا خٰشِعَةٌ (٩)
18. فَلَآ أُقْسِمُ بِالْخُنَّسِ (١٥)

While eyes are downcast.

79:1–9

18. Oh, but I call to witness the planets,

The stars which rise and set,

And the close of night,
And the breath of morning
That this is in truth the word of an honoured messenger.

81:15–19

19. Oh, I swear by the afterglow of sunset,
And by the night and all that it enshroudeth,
And by the moon when she is at the full,
That ye shall journey on from plane to plane.

84:16–19

20. By the heaven, holding mansions of the stars,
And by the Promised Day.
And by the witness and that whereunto he beareth testimony,
(Self-) destroyed were the owners of the ditch
Of the fuel-fed fire,
When they sat by it,

85:1–6

21. By the heaven and the Morning Star
—Ah, what will tell thee what the Morning Star is!
—The piercing Star!
No human soul but hath a guardian over it.

86:1–4

22. By the heaven which giveth the returning rain,
And the earth which splitteth (with the growth of trees and plants)
Lo! this (Qur'ān) is a conclusive word,
It is no pleasantry.

86:11–14

23. By the Dawn
And ten nights,
And the Even and the Odd.

الْجَوَارِ الْكُنَّسِ ﴿١٦﴾
وَاللَّيْلِ إِذَا عَسْعَسَ ﴿١٧﴾
وَالصُّبْحِ إِذَا تَنَفَّسَ ﴿١٨﴾
إِنَّهُ لَقَوْلُ رَسُولٍ كَرِيمٍ ﴿١٩﴾
19. فَلَا أُقْسِمُ بِالشَّفَقِ ﴿١٦﴾
وَاللَّيْلِ وَمَا وَسَقَ ﴿١٧﴾
وَالْقَمَرِ إِذَا اتَّسَقَ ﴿١٨﴾
لَتَرْكَبُنَّ طَبَقًا عَنْ طَبَقٍ ﴿١٩﴾
20. وَالسَّمَاءِ ذَاتِ الْبُرُوجِ ﴿١﴾
وَالْيَوْمِ الْمَوْعُودِ ﴿٢﴾
وَشَاهِدٍ وَمَشْهُودٍ ﴿٣﴾
قُتِلَ أَصْحَابُ الْأُخْدُودِ ﴿٤﴾
النَّارِ ذَاتِ الْوَقُودِ ﴿٥﴾
إِذْ هُمْ عَلَيْهَا قُعُودٌ ﴿٦﴾
21. وَالسَّمَاءِ وَالطَّارِقِ ﴿١﴾
وَمَا أَدْرَاكَ مَا الطَّارِقُ ﴿٢﴾
النَّجْمُ الثَّاقِبُ ﴿٣﴾
إِنْ كُلُّ نَفْسٍ لَمَّا عَلَيْهَا حَافِظٌ ﴿٤﴾
22. وَالسَّمَاءِ ذَاتِ الرَّجْعِ ﴿١١﴾
وَالْأَرْضِ ذَاتِ الصَّدْعِ ﴿١٢﴾
إِنَّهُ لَقَوْلٌ فَصْلٌ ﴿١٣﴾
وَمَا هُوَ بِالْهَزْلِ ﴿١٤﴾
23. وَالْفَجْرِ ﴿١﴾
وَلَيَالٍ عَشْرٍ ﴿٢﴾
وَالشَّفْعِ وَالْوَتْرِ ﴿٣﴾

وَالَّيْلِ إِذَا يَسْرِ ﴿٤﴾
هَلْ فِي ذَٰلِكَ قَسَمٌ لِّذِي حِجْرٍ ﴿٥﴾

24. لَا أُقْسِمُ بِهَٰذَا الْبَلَدِ ﴿١﴾
وَأَنتَ حِلٌّ بِهَٰذَا الْبَلَدِ ﴿٢﴾
وَوَالِدٍ وَمَا وَلَدَ ﴿٣﴾
لَقَدْ خَلَقْنَا الْإِنسَانَ فِي كَبَدٍ ﴿٤﴾

25. وَالشَّمْسِ وَضُحَاهَا ﴿١﴾
وَالْقَمَرِ إِذَا تَلَاهَا ﴿٢﴾
وَالنَّهَارِ إِذَا جَلَّاهَا ﴿٣﴾
وَاللَّيْلِ إِذَا يَغْشَاهَا ﴿٤﴾
وَالسَّمَاءِ وَمَا بَنَاهَا ﴿٥﴾
وَالْأَرْضِ وَمَا طَحَاهَا ﴿٦﴾
وَنَفْسٍ وَمَا سَوَّاهَا ﴿٧﴾
فَأَلْهَمَهَا فُجُورَهَا وَتَقْوَاهَا ﴿٨﴾
قَدْ أَفْلَحَ مَن زَكَّاهَا ﴿٩﴾
وَقَدْ خَابَ مَن دَسَّاهَا ﴿١٠﴾

26. وَاللَّيْلِ إِذَا يَغْشَىٰ ﴿١﴾
وَالنَّهَارِ إِذَا تَجَلَّىٰ ﴿٢﴾
وَمَا خَلَقَ الذَّكَرَ وَالْأُنثَىٰ ﴿٣﴾
إِنَّ سَعْيَكُمْ لَشَتَّىٰ ﴿٤﴾

27. وَالضُّحَىٰ ﴿١﴾
وَاللَّيْلِ إِذَا سَجَىٰ ﴿٢﴾
مَا وَدَّعَكَ رَبُّكَ وَمَا قَلَىٰ ﴿٣﴾

And the night when it departeth,

There surely is an oath for thinking man.

89:1–5

24. Nay, I′ swear by this city–

And thou art an in-dweller of this city

And the begetter and that which he begat,

We verily have created man in an atmosphere.

90:1–4

25. By the sun and his brightness,

And the moon when she followeth him,

And the day when it revealeth him,

And the night when it enshroudeth him,

And the heaven and Him Who built it,

And the earth and Him Who spread it,

And a soul and Him Who perfected it

And inspired it (with conscience of) what is wrong for it and (what is) right for it.

He is indeed successful who causeth it to grow,

And he is indeed a failure who stunteth it.

91:1–10

26. By the night enshrouding
And the day resplendent
And Him Who hath created male and female,
Lo! your effort is dispersed (toward divers ends).

92:1–4

27. By the morning hours

And by the night when it is stillest,

Thy Lord hath not forsaken thee nor doth He hate thee.

93:1–3

28. By the fig and the olive,
By Mount Sinai,
And by this land made safe;
Surely We created man of the best stature.
95:1–4

29. By the snorting coursers,
Striking sparks of fire
And scouring to the raid at dawn,
Then, therewith, with their trail of dust,
Cleaving, as one, the centre (of the foe),
Lo! man is an ingrate unto his Lord.
100:1–6

30. By the declining day,
Lo! man is in a state of loss.
103:1–2

28. وَالتِّيْنِ وَالزَّيْتُوْنِ ۝
وَطُوْرِ سِيْنِيْنَ ۝
وَهٰذَا الْبَلَدِ الْاَمِيْنِ ۝
لَقَدْ خَلَقْنَا الْاِنْسَانَ فِيْٓ اَحْسَنِ تَقْوِيْمٍ ۝

29. وَالْعٰدِيٰتِ ضَبْحًا ۝
فَالْمُوْرِيٰتِ قَدْحًا ۝
فَالْمُغِيْرٰتِ صُبْحًا ۝
فَاَثَرْنَ بِهٖ نَقْعًا ۝
فَوَسَطْنَ بِهٖ جَمْعًا ۝
اِنَّ الْاِنْسَانَ لِرَبِّهٖ لَكَنُوْدٌ ۝

30. وَالْعَصْرِ ۝
اِنَّ الْاِنْسَانَ لَفِيْ خُسْرٍ ۝

Ref: 44:2–6

THIS LIFE AND HEREAFTER

1. Beautified for mankind is love of the joys (that come) from women and offspring, and stored-up heaps of gold and silver, and horses branded (with their marks), and cattle and land. That is comfort of the life of the world. Allah! With Him is a more excellent abode.

Say: Shall I inform you of something better than that? For those who keep from evil, with their Lord, are Gardens underneath which rivers flow wherein they will abide, and pure companions, and contentment from Allah. Allah is Seer of His bondmen.

3:14–15

2. O ye who believe! What aileth you that when it is said unto you: Go forth in the way of Allah, ye are bowed down to the ground with heaviness? Take ye pleasure in the life of the world rather than in the Hereafter? The comfort of the life of the world is but little than in the Hereafter.

9:38

3. Whoso desireth the life of the world and its pomp, We shall repay them their deeds herein, and therein they will not be wronged.

Those are they for whom is naught in the Hereafter save the Fire. (All) that

1. زُيِّنَ لِلنَّاسِ حُبُّ الشَّهَوٰتِ مِنَ النِّسَآءِ
وَالْبَنِيْنَ وَالْقَنَاطِيْرِ الْمُقَنْطَرَةِ مِنَ
الذَّهَبِ وَالْفِضَّةِ وَالْخَيْلِ الْمُسَوَّمَةِ
وَالْاَنْعَامِ وَالْحَرْثِ ؕ ذٰلِكَ مَتَاعُ
الْحَيٰوةِ الدُّنْيَا ۚ وَاللّٰهُ عِنْدَهٗ حُسْنُ الْمَاٰبِ ۝
قُلْ اَؤُنَبِّئُكُمْ بِخَيْرٍ مِّنْ ذٰلِكُمْ ؕ لِلَّذِيْنَ
اتَّقَوْا عِنْدَ رَبِّهِمْ جَنّٰتٌ تَجْرِيْ مِنْ تَحْتِهَا
الْاَنْهٰرُ خٰلِدِيْنَ فِيْهَا وَاَزْوَاجٌ مُّطَهَّرَةٌ وَّ
رِضْوَانٌ مِّنَ اللّٰهِ ؕ وَاللّٰهُ بَصِيْرٌۢ بِالْعِبَادِ ۝

2. يٰۤاَيُّهَا الَّذِيْنَ اٰمَنُوْا مَا لَكُمْ اِذَا قِيْلَ لَكُمُ
انْفِرُوْا فِيْ سَبِيْلِ اللّٰهِ اثَّاقَلْتُمْ اِلَى الْاَرْضِ ؕ
اَرَضِيْتُمْ بِالْحَيٰوةِ الدُّنْيَا مِنَ الْاٰخِرَةِ ۚ
فَمَا مَتَاعُ الْحَيٰوةِ الدُّنْيَا فِي الْاٰخِرَةِ
اِلَّا قَلِيْلٌ ۝٣٨

3. مَنْ كَانَ يُرِيْدُ الْحَيٰوةَ الدُّنْيَا وَزِيْنَتَهَا
نُوَفِّ اِلَيْهِمْ اَعْمَالَهُمْ فِيْهَا وَهُمْ
فِيْهَا لَا يُبْخَسُوْنَ ۝١٥
اُولٰٓئِكَ الَّذِيْنَ لَيْسَ لَهُمْ فِي الْاٰخِرَةِ
اِلَّا النَّارُ ۖ وَحَبِطَ مَا صَنَعُوْا فِيْهَا
وَبٰطِلٌ مَّا كَانُوْا يَعْمَلُوْنَ ۝١٦

4. اَللّٰهُ يَبْسُطُ الرِّزْقَ لِمَنْ يَّشَآءُ وَيَقْدِرُ ؕ
وَفَرِحُوْا بِالْحَيٰوةِ الدُّنْيَا ؕ وَمَا الْحَيٰوةُ

they contrive here is vain and (all) that they are wont to do is fruitless.

11:15–16

4. Allah enlargeth livelihood for whom He will, and straiteneth (it for whom He will); and they rejoice in the life of the

world, whereas the life of the world is but brief comfort as compared with the Hereafter.

13:26

5. Whoso desireth that (life) which hasteneth away, We hasten for him therein what We will for whom We please. And afterward We have appointed for him hell; he will endure the heat thereof, condemned, rejected.

And whoso desireth the Hereafter and striveth for it with the effort necessary, being a believer, for such, their effort findeth favour (with their Lord)

Each do We supply both these and those, from the bounty of thy Lord. And the bounty of thy Lord can never be walled up.

See how We prefer one above another, and verily the Hereafter will be greater in degrees and greater in preferment.

17:18–21

6. Wealth and children are an ornament of life of the world. But the good deeds which endure are better in thy Lord's sight for reward, and better in respect of hope.

18:46

7. And whatsoever ye have been given is a comfort of the life of the world and an ornament thereof; and that which Allah hath is better and more lasting. Have ye then no sense?

28:60

الدُّنْيَا فِي الْآخِرَةِ إِلَّا مَتَاعٌ ﴿٢٦﴾

5. مَنْ كَانَ يُرِيدُ الْعَاجِلَةَ عَجَّلْنَا لَهُ
فِيهَا مَا نَشَاءُ لِمَنْ نُرِيدُ ثُمَّ جَعَلْنَا
لَهُ جَهَنَّمَ يَصْلَاهَا مَذْمُومًا مَدْحُورًا ﴿١٨﴾
وَمَنْ أَرَادَ الْآخِرَةَ وَسَعَىٰ لَهَا سَعْيَهَا وَ
هُوَ مُؤْمِنٌ فَأُولَٰئِكَ كَانَ سَعْيُهُمْ مَشْكُورًا ﴿١٩﴾
كُلًّا نُمِدُّ هَٰؤُلَاءِ وَهَٰؤُلَاءِ مِنْ عَطَاءِ
رَبِّكَ وَمَا كَانَ عَطَاءُ رَبِّكَ مَحْظُورًا ﴿٢٠﴾
انْظُرْ كَيْفَ فَضَّلْنَا بَعْضَهُمْ عَلَىٰ بَعْضٍ
وَلَلْآخِرَةُ أَكْبَرُ دَرَجَاتٍ وَأَكْبَرُ تَفْضِيلًا ﴿٢١﴾

6. الْمَالُ وَالْبَنُونَ زِينَةُ الْحَيَاةِ الدُّنْيَا
وَالْبَاقِيَاتُ الصَّالِحَاتُ خَيْرٌ عِنْدَ رَبِّكَ
ثَوَابًا وَخَيْرٌ أَمَلًا ﴿٤٦﴾

7. وَمَا أُوتِيتُمْ مِنْ شَيْءٍ فَمَتَاعُ الْحَيَاةِ
الدُّنْيَا وَزِينَتُهَا وَمَا عِنْدَ اللَّهِ خَيْرٌ
وَأَبْقَىٰ أَفَلَا تَعْقِلُونَ ﴿٦٠﴾

8. وَمَا هَٰذِهِ الْحَيَاةُ الدُّنْيَا إِلَّا لَهْوٌ وَ
لَعِبٌ وَإِنَّ الدَّارَ الْآخِرَةَ لَهِيَ
الْحَيَوَانُ لَوْ كَانُوا يَعْلَمُونَ ﴿٦٤﴾

9. أَهُمْ يَقْسِمُونَ رَحْمَتَ رَبِّكَ نَحْنُ
قَسَمْنَا بَيْنَهُمْ مَعِيشَتَهُمْ فِي الْحَيَاةِ
الدُّنْيَا وَرَفَعْنَا بَعْضَهُمْ فَوْقَ بَعْضٍ

8. This life of the world is but a pastime and a game. Lo! the home of the Hereafter —that is Life, if they but knew.

29:64

9. Is it they who apportion thy Lord's mercy? We have apportioned among them their livelihood

in the life of the world, and raised some of them above others in rank that some of them may take labour from others; and the mercy of thy Lord is better than (the wealth) that they amass.

And were it not that mankind would have become one community, We might well have appointed for those who disbelieve in the Beneficent, roofs of silver for their houses and stairs (of silver) whereby to mount,

And for their houses doors (of silver) and couches of silver whereon to recline,

And ornaments of gold. Yet all that would have been but a provision of the life of the world. And the Hereafter with your Lord would have been for those who keep from evil.

43:32–35

10. Know that the life of this world is only play, and idle talk, and pageantry, and boasting among you, and rivalry in respect of wealth and children as the likeness of vegetation after rain, whereof the growth is pleasing to the husbandman, but afterward it drieth up and thou seest it turning yellow, then it becometh straw. And in the Hereafter there is grievous punishment, and (also) forgiveness from Allah and His good pleasure, whereas the life of the world is but

دَرَجٰتٍ لِّيَتَّخِذَ بَعْضُهُمْ بَعْضًا سُخْرِيًّا
وَرَحْمَتُ رَبِّكَ خَيْرٌ مِّمَّا يَجْمَعُوْنَ ۝
وَلَوْلَآ اَنْ يَّكُوْنَ النَّاسُ اُمَّةً وَّاحِدَةً
لَّجَعَلْنَا لِمَنْ يَّكْفُرُ بِالرَّحْمٰنِ لِبُيُوْتِهِمْ
سُقُفًا مِّنْ فِضَّةٍ وَّمَعَارِجَ عَلَيْهَا
يَظْهَرُوْنَ ۝
وَلِبُيُوْتِهِمْ اَبْوَابًا وَّسُرُرًا عَلَيْهَا يَتَّكِـُٔوْنَ ۝
وَزُخْرُفًا ؕ وَاِنْ كُلُّ ذٰلِكَ لَمَّا مَتَاعُ
الْحَيٰوةِ الدُّنْيَا ؕ وَالْاٰخِرَةُ عِنْدَ رَبِّكَ
لِلْمُتَّقِيْنَ ۝

10. اِعْلَمُوْٓا اَنَّمَا الْحَيٰوةُ الدُّنْيَا لَعِبٌ وَّلَهْوٌ وَّزِيْنَةٌ وَّ
تَفَاخُرٌۢ بَيْنَكُمْ وَتَكَاثُرٌ فِى الْاَمْوَالِ وَالْاَوْلَادِ ؕ كَمَثَلِ
غَيْثٍ اَعْجَبَ الْكُفَّارَ نَبَاتُهٗ ثُمَّ يَهِيْجُ فَتَرٰىهُ
مُصْفَرًّا ثُمَّ يَكُوْنُ حُطَامًا ؕ وَفِى الْاٰخِرَةِ عَذَابٌ
شَدِيْدٌ ۙ وَّمَغْفِرَةٌ مِّنَ اللّٰهِ وَرِضْوَانٌ ؕ وَمَا الْحَيٰوةُ
الدُّنْيَآ اِلَّا مَتَاعُ الْغُرُوْرِ ۝

11. بَلْ تُؤْثِرُوْنَ الْحَيٰوةَ الدُّنْيَا ۝
وَالْاٰخِرَةُ خَيْرٌ وَّاَبْقٰى ۝

matter of illusion.

57:20

11. But ye prefer the life of the world

Although the Hereafter is better and more lasting.

87:16–17

Ref: 2:86,94,130,200,217,220; 3:22,56,145,152; 4:74,77,134; 5:33; 6:32, 92,113; 7:147,156,169; 8:67; 9:38,69,74; 10:64; 12:101; 109; 13:34; 14:3; 14:27; 16:22,30,41,60; 17:72; 22:15; 24:14,19,23; 29:27; 30:7; 33:57; 39:26; 40:39; 41:31; 42:20,36; 47:36; 53:25; 59:3; 93:4; 75:20-21; 76:27.

THRONE OF ALLAH

1. Lo! your Lord is Allah Who created the heavens and the earth in six Days, then He established Himself upon the Throne, directing all things. There is no intercessor (with Him). save after His permission. That is Allah, your Lord, so worship Him. Oh, will ye not remind?

10:3

2. And He it is Who created the heavens and the earth in six Days— and His Throne was upon the water—that He might try you, which of you is best in conduct.

11:7

3. Say: Who is Lord of the seven heavens, and Lord of the Tremendous Throne?

They will say: Unto Allah (all that belongeth). Say: Will ye not then keep duty (unto Him)?

23:86–87

4. Now Allah be Exalted, the True King! There is no God save Him, the Lord of the Throne of Grace.

23:116

1. إِنَّ رَبَّكُمُ اللّٰهُ الَّذِي خَلَقَ السَّمٰوٰتِ
وَالْأَرْضَ فِي سِتَّةِ أَيَّامٍ ثُمَّ اسْتَوٰى
عَلَى الْعَرْشِ يُدَبِّرُ الْأَمْرَ مَا مِنْ شَفِيعٍ
إِلَّا مِنْ بَعْدِ إِذْنِهِ ذٰلِكُمُ اللّٰهُ رَبُّكُمْ
فَاعْبُدُوهُ أَفَلَا تَذَكَّرُونَ ۝٣

2. وَهُوَ الَّذِي خَلَقَ السَّمٰوٰتِ وَالْأَرْضَ فِي
سِتَّةِ أَيَّامٍ وَكَانَ عَرْشُهُ عَلَى الْمَاءِ
لِيَبْلُوَكُمْ أَيُّكُمْ أَحْسَنُ عَمَلًا

3. قُلْ مَنْ رَبُّ السَّمٰوٰتِ السَّبْعِ وَ
رَبُّ الْعَرْشِ الْعَظِيمِ ۝٨٦
سَيَقُولُونَ لِلّٰهِ قُلْ أَفَلَا تَتَّقُونَ ۝٨٧

4. فَتَعٰلَى اللّٰهُ الْمَلِكُ الْحَقُّ لَا إِلٰهَ إِلَّا هُوَ
رَبُّ الْعَرْشِ الْكَرِيمِ ۝

5. وَتَرَى الْمَلٰٓئِكَةَ حَآفِّينَ مِنْ حَوْلِ
الْعَرْشِ يُسَبِّحُونَ بِحَمْدِ رَبِّهِمْ
وَقُضِيَ بَيْنَهُمْ بِالْحَقِّ وَقِيلَ الْحَمْدُ
لِلّٰهِ رَبِّ الْعٰلَمِينَ ۝٧٥

6. الَّذِينَ يَحْمِلُونَ الْعَرْشَ وَمَنْ حَوْلَهُ يُسَبِّحُونَ بِحَمْدِ
رَبِّهِمْ وَيُؤْمِنُونَ بِهِ وَيَسْتَغْفِرُونَ لِلَّذِينَ اٰمَنُوا

7. فَيَوْمَئِذٍ وَقَعَتِ الْوَاقِعَةُ ۝١٥
وَانْشَقَّتِ السَّمَآءُ فَهِيَ يَوْمَئِذٍ وَاهِيَةٌ ۝١٦

5. And thou (O Muhammad) seest the angels thronging round the Throne, hymning the praises of their Lord. And they are judged aright. And it is said: Praise be to Allah, the Lord of the Worlds!

39:75

6. Those who bear the Throne, and all who are round about it, hymn the praises of their Lord and believe in Him and ask forgiveness for those who believe

40:7

7. Then, on that day, will the Event befall.

And the heaven will split asunder, for that day it will be frail.

And the angels will be on the sides thereof, and eight will uphold the Throne of their Lord that day, above them.

On that day ye will be exposed; not a secret of you will be hidden.

69:15–18

وَّ الْمَلَكُ عَلٰٓى اَرْجَآئِهَا ۭ وَيَحْمِلُ
عَرْشَ رَبِّكَ فَوْقَهُمْ يَوْمَئِذٍ ثَمٰنِيَةٌ ۝١٧

يَوْمَئِذٍ تُعْرَضُوْنَ لَا تَخْفٰى مِنْكُمْ خَافِيَةٌ ۝١٨

8. And He is the Forgiving, the Loving,

Lord of the Throne of Glory,

Doer of what He will.

85:14–16

8. وَهُوَ الْغَفُوْرُ الْوَدُوْدُ ۝١٤

ذُو الْعَرْشِ الْمَجِيْدُ ۝١٥

فَعَّالٌ لِّمَا يُرِيْدُ ۝١٦

○

Ref: 7:54; 9:129; 13:2; 20:5; 25:58–59; 32:4; 40:15; 43:82; 57:4; 81:19–20.

TORAH

1. He hath revealed unto thee (Muhammad) the Scripture with truth, confirming that which was (revealed) before it, even as He revealed the Torah and the Gospel.

3:3

2. And We caused Jesus, son of Mary, to follow in their footsteps, confirming that which was (revealed) before him in the Torah and We bestowed on him the Gospel wherein is guidance and a light confirming that which was (revealed) before it in the Torah—a guidance and an admonition unto those who ward off (evil).

5:46

3. Say: O People of the Scripture! Ye have naught (of guidance) till ye observe the Torah and the Gospel and that which was revealed unto you from your Lord.

5:68

4. Say (unto the Jews who speak thus): Who revealed the Book which Moses brought, a light and guidance for mankind, which ye have put on parchments which ye show, but ye hide much (thereof), and by which ye were taught that which ye knew not yourselves nor (did) your fathers (know it)? Say: Allah. Then leave them to their play of cavilling.

6:91

1. نَزَّلَ عَلَيْكَ الْكِتٰبَ بِالْحَقِّ مُصَدِّقًا لِّمَا
بَيْنَ يَدَيْهِ وَاَنْزَلَ التَّوْرٰىةَ وَالْاِنْجِيْلَ ۝

2. وَقَفَّيْنَا عَلٰٓى اٰثَارِهِمْ بِعِيْسَى ابْنِ
مَرْيَمَ مُصَدِّقًا لِّمَا بَيْنَ يَدَيْهِ مِنَ
التَّوْرٰىةِ ۪ وَاٰتَيْنٰهُ الْاِنْجِيْلَ فِيْهِ
هُدًى وَّنُوْرٌ ۙ وَّمُصَدِّقًا لِّمَا بَيْنَ
يَدَيْهِ مِنَ التَّوْرٰىةِ وَهُدًى وَّ
مَوْعِظَةً لِّلْمُتَّقِيْنَ ۝

3. قُلْ يٰٓاَهْلَ الْكِتٰبِ لَسْتُمْ عَلٰى شَيْءٍ
حَتّٰى تُقِيْمُوا التَّوْرٰىةَ وَالْاِنْجِيْلَ وَمَآ
اُنْزِلَ اِلَيْكُمْ مِّنْ رَّبِّكُمْ

4. قُلْ مَنْ اَنْزَلَ الْكِتٰبَ الَّذِيْ جَآءَ بِهٖ مُوْسٰى
نُوْرًا وَّهُدًى لِّلنَّاسِ تَجْعَلُوْنَهٗ قَرَاطِيْسَ
تُبْدُوْنَهَا وَتُخْفُوْنَ كَثِيْرًا ۚ وَعُلِّمْتُمْ مَّا لَمْ
تَعْلَمُوْٓا اَنْتُمْ وَلَآ اٰبَآؤُكُمْ ۭ قُلِ اللّٰهُ ۙ
ثُمَّ ذَرْهُمْ فِيْ خَوْضِهِمْ يَلْعَبُوْنَ ۝

5. مُحَمَّدٌ رَّسُوْلُ اللّٰهِ ۭ وَالَّذِيْنَ مَعَهٗٓ
اَشِدَّآءُ عَلَى الْكُفَّارِ رُحَمَآءُ بَيْنَهُمْ
تَرٰىهُمْ رُكَّعًا سُجَّدًا يَّبْتَغُوْنَ فَضْلًا
مِّنَ اللّٰهِ وَرِضْوَانًا ۡ سِيْمَاهُمْ فِيْ
وُجُوْهِهِمْ مِّنْ اَثَرِ السُّجُوْدِ ۭ ذٰلِكَ
مَثَلُهُمْ فِي التَّوْرٰىةِ ڔ وَمَثَلُهُمْ فِي
الْاِنْجِيْلِ ڔ كَزَرْعٍ اَخْرَجَ شَطْـَٔهٗ

5. Muhammad is the messenger of Allah. And those with him are hard against the disbelievers and merciful among themselves. Thou (O Muhammad) seest them bowing and falling prostrate (in worship), seeking bounty from Allah and (His) acceptance. The mark of them is on their foreheads from traces of prostration. Such is

their likeness in the Torah and their likeness in the Gospel—like as sown corn that sendeth forth its shoot and strengtheneth it and riseth firm upon its stalk, delighting the sowers—that He may enrage the disbelievers with (the sight of) them. Allah hath promised, unto such of them as believe and do good works, forgiveness and immense reward.

48:29

TOURING

1. Systems have passed away before you. Do but travel in the land and see the nature of the consequence for those who did deny (the messengers).

3:137

2. Say (O Muhammad, to the disbelievers): Travel in the land, and see the nature of the consequence for those who were before you! Most of them were idolaters.

30:42

فَآزَرَهُ فَاسْتَغْلَظَ فَاسْتَوَىٰ عَلَىٰ
سُوقِهِ يُعْجِبُ الزُّرَّاعَ لِيَغِيظَ بِهِمُ
الْكُفَّارَ ۗ وَعَدَ اللَّهُ الَّذِينَ آمَنُوا
وَعَمِلُوا الصَّالِحَاتِ مِنْهُم مَّغْفِرَةً
وَأَجْرًا عَظِيمًا

○

1. قَدْ خَلَتْ مِن قَبْلِكُمْ سُنَنٌ فَسِيرُوا
فِي الْأَرْضِ فَانظُرُوا كَيْفَ كَانَ
عَاقِبَةُ الْمُكَذِّبِينَ

2. قُلْ سِيرُوا فِي الْأَرْضِ فَانظُرُوا كَيْفَ
كَانَ عَاقِبَةُ الَّذِينَ مِن قَبْلُ ۚ
كَانَ أَكْثَرُهُم مُّشْرِكِينَ

○

TORAH

Ref: 2:53; 3:50; 5:110; 6:154; 11:110; 17:2; 21:48; 32:23; 40:53; 41:45; 46:12; 53:36. See also: Revealed Books.

TRADE AND COMMERCE

1. It is no sin for you that ye seek the bounty of your Lord (by trading).
2:198

2. Be not averse to writing down (the contract) whether it be small or great, with (record of) the term thereof. That is more equitable in the sight of Allah and more sure for testimony, and the best way of avoiding doubt between you; save only in the case when it is actual merchandise which ye transfer among yourselves from hand to hand. In that case it is no sin for you if ye write it not. And have witnesses when ye sell one to another.
2:282

3. O ye who believe! Squander not your wealth among yourselves in vanity, except it be a trade by mutual consent, and kill not one another. Lo! Allah is ever Merciful unto you:
4:29

4. Say: If your fathers, and your sons, and your brethren, and your wives, and your tribe, and the wealth ye have acquired, and merchandise for which ye fear that there will be no sale, and dwellings ye desire are dearer to you than Allah and His messenger and striving in His way: then wait till Allah bringeth His command to pass. Allah guideth not wrongdoing folk.
9:24

5. Lo! those who read the Scripture of Allah, and establish worship, and spend of that which We have bestowed on them secretly and openly, they look forward to imperishable gain.

1. لَيْسَ عَلَيْكُمْ جُنَاحٌ أَن تَبْتَغُوا فَضْلًا مِّن رَّبِّكُمْ
2. وَلَا تَسْأَمُوا أَن تَكْتُبُوهُ صَغِيرًا أَوْ كَبِيرًا إِلَىٰ
أَجَلِهِ ذَٰلِكُمْ أَقْسَطُ عِندَ اللَّهِ وَأَقْوَمُ لِلشَّهَادَةِ
وَأَدْنَىٰ أَلَّا تَرْتَابُوا إِلَّا أَن تَكُونَ تِجَارَةً
حَاضِرَةً تُدِيرُونَهَا بَيْنَكُمْ فَلَيْسَ عَلَيْكُمْ
جُنَاحٌ أَلَّا تَكْتُبُوهَا وَأَشْهِدُوا إِذَا تَبَايَعْتُمْ
3. يَا أَيُّهَا الَّذِينَ آمَنُوا لَا تَأْكُلُوا أَمْوَالَكُم
بَيْنَكُم بِالْبَاطِلِ إِلَّا أَن تَكُونَ تِجَارَةً
عَن تَرَاضٍ مِّنكُمْ وَلَا تَقْتُلُوا أَنفُسَكُمْ
إِنَّ اللَّهَ كَانَ بِكُمْ رَحِيمًا ۝
4. قُلْ إِن كَانَ آبَاؤُكُمْ وَأَبْنَاؤُكُمْ وَإِخْوَانُكُمْ
وَأَزْوَاجُكُمْ وَعَشِيرَتُكُمْ وَأَمْوَالٌ اقْتَرَفْتُمُوهَا
وَتِجَارَةٌ تَخْشَوْنَ كَسَادَهَا وَمَسَاكِنُ تَرْضَوْنَهَا
أَحَبَّ إِلَيْكُم مِّنَ اللَّهِ وَرَسُولِهِ وَجِهَادٍ فِي
سَبِيلِهِ فَتَرَبَّصُوا حَتَّىٰ يَأْتِيَ اللَّهُ بِأَمْرِهِ
وَاللَّهُ لَا يَهْدِي الْقَوْمَ الْفَاسِقِينَ ۝
5. إِنَّ الَّذِينَ يَتْلُونَ كِتَابَ اللَّهِ وَأَقَامُوا
الصَّلَاةَ وَأَنفَقُوا مِمَّا رَزَقْنَاهُمْ سِرًّا وَ
عَلَانِيَةً يَرْجُونَ تِجَارَةً لَّن تَبُورَ ۝
لِيُوَفِّيَهُمْ أُجُورَهُمْ وَيَزِيدَهُمْ مِّن
فَضْلِهِ إِنَّهُ غَفُورٌ شَكُورٌ ۝

That He will pay them their wages and increase them of His grace. Lo! He is Forgiving, Responsive.

35:29–30

6. O ye who believe! Shall I show you a commerce that will save you from a painful doom?

Ye should believe in Allah and His messenger, and should strive for the cause of Allah with your wealth and your lives. That is better for you, if ye did but know:

61:10–11

7. O Ye who believe! When the call is heard for the prayer of the day of congregation, haste unto remembrance of Allah and leave your trading. That is better for you if ye did but know.

And when the prayer is ended, then disperse in the land and seek of Allah's bounty, and remember Allah much, that ye may be successful.

But when they spy some merchandise or pastime they break away to it and leave thee standing. Say: That which Allah hath is better than pastime and than merchandise, and Allah is the Best of providers.

62:9–11

6. يَا أَيُّهَا الَّذِينَ آمَنُوا هَلْ أَدُلُّكُمْ عَلَىٰ
تِجَارَةٍ تُنجِيكُم مِّنْ عَذَابٍ أَلِيمٍ ﴿١٠﴾
تُؤْمِنُونَ بِاللَّهِ وَرَسُولِهِ وَتُجَاهِدُونَ
فِي سَبِيلِ اللَّهِ بِأَمْوَالِكُمْ وَأَنفُسِكُمْ ۚ
ذَٰلِكُمْ خَيْرٌ لَّكُمْ إِن كُنتُمْ تَعْلَمُونَ ﴿١١﴾

7. يَا أَيُّهَا الَّذِينَ آمَنُوا إِذَا نُودِيَ
لِلصَّلَاةِ مِن يَوْمِ الْجُمُعَةِ فَاسْعَوْا
إِلَىٰ ذِكْرِ اللَّهِ وَذَرُوا الْبَيْعَ ۚ ذَٰلِكُمْ
خَيْرٌ لَّكُمْ إِن كُنتُمْ تَعْلَمُونَ ﴿٩﴾
فَإِذَا قُضِيَتِ الصَّلَاةُ فَانتَشِرُوا
فِي الْأَرْضِ وَابْتَغُوا مِن فَضْلِ اللَّهِ
وَاذْكُرُوا اللَّهَ كَثِيرًا لَّعَلَّكُمْ تُفْلِحُونَ ﴿١٠﴾
وَإِذَا رَأَوْا تِجَارَةً أَوْ لَهْوًا انفَضُّوا
إِلَيْهَا وَتَرَكُوكَ قَائِمًا ۚ قُلْ مَا عِندَ
اللَّهِ خَيْرٌ مِّنَ اللَّهْوِ وَمِنَ التِّجَارَةِ ۚ
وَاللَّهُ خَيْرُ الرَّازِقِينَ ﴿١١﴾

Ref: 2:16. 254: 14:31; 24:37.

See also: Marketing, Usury, Weights and Measures.

TRADITIONS OF HOLY PROPHET (PBUH)

1. Allah verily hath shown grace to the believers by sending unto them a messenger of their own who reciteth unto them His revelations, and causeth them to grow, and teacheth them the Scripture and wisdom, although before (he came to them) they were in flagrant error.

3:164

2. O ye who believe! Obey Allah and His messenger, and turn not away from him when ye hear (him speak).

8:20

3. Verily in the messenger of Allah ye have a good example for him who looketh unto Allah and the Last Day, and remembereth Allah much.

33:21

4. And whatsoever the messenger giveth you, take it. And whatsoever he forbiddeth, abstain (from it). And keep your duty to Allah. Lo! Allah is stern in reprisal.

59:7

1. لَقَدْ مَنَّ اللّٰهُ عَلَى الْمُؤْمِنِيْنَ اِذْ بَعَثَ
فِيْهِمْ رَسُوْلًا مِّنْ اَنْفُسِهِمْ يَتْلُوْا عَلَيْهِمْ
اٰيٰتِهٖ وَيُزَكِّيْهِمْ وَيُعَلِّمُهُمُ الْكِتٰبَ
وَالْحِكْمَةَ ۚ وَاِنْ كَانُوْا مِنْ قَبْلُ
لَفِيْ ضَلٰلٍ مُّبِيْنٍ ○

2. يٰۤاَيُّهَا الَّذِيْنَ اٰمَنُوْۤا اَطِيْعُوا اللّٰهَ وَرَسُوْلَهٗ
وَلَا تَوَلَّوْا عَنْهُ وَاَنْتُمْ تَسْمَعُوْنَ ۝

3. لَقَدْ كَانَ لَكُمْ فِيْ رَسُوْلِ اللّٰهِ اُسْوَةٌ
حَسَنَةٌ لِّمَنْ كَانَ يَرْجُوا اللّٰهَ وَالْيَوْمَ
الْاٰخِرَ وَذَكَرَ اللّٰهَ كَثِيْرًا ۝

4. وَمَاۤ اٰتٰىكُمُ الرَّسُوْلُ فَخُذُوْهُ ۚ وَمَا
نَهٰىكُمْ عَنْهُ فَانْتَهُوْا ۚ وَاتَّقُوا اللّٰهَ ۗ اِنَّ
اللّٰهَ شَدِيْدُ الْعِقَابِ ۝

TRANSGRESSION

1. Lo! Allah disdaineth not to coin the similitude even of a gnat. Those who believe know that it is the truth from their Lord; but those who disbelieve say, What doth Allah wish (to teach) by such a similitude? He misleadeth many thereby, and He guideth many thereby; and He misleadeth thereby only miscreants;

Those who break the covenant of Allah after ratifying it, and sever that which Allah ordered to be joined, and (who) make mischief in the earth: Those are they who are the losers.

2:26—27

2. Verily We have revealed unto thee clear tokens, and only miscreants will disbelieve in them.

2:99

3. The pilgrimage is (in) the well-known months, and whoever is minded to perform the pilgrimage therein (let him remember that) there is (to be) no lewdness nor abuse nor angry conversation on the pilgrimage.

2:197

4. And have witnesses when ye sell one to another, and let no harm be done to scribe or witness. If ye do (harm to them) lo! it is a sin in you. Observe your duty to Allah.

2:282

1. إِنَّ اللَّهَ لَا يَسْتَحْيِي أَنْ يَضْرِبَ مَثَلًا مَا بَعُوضَةً
فَمَا فَوْقَهَا فَأَمَّا الَّذِينَ آمَنُوا فَيَعْلَمُونَ أَنَّهُ
الْحَقُّ مِنْ رَبِّهِمْ وَأَمَّا الَّذِينَ كَفَرُوا فَيَقُولُونَ
مَاذَا أَرَادَ اللَّهُ بِهَٰذَا مَثَلًا يُضِلُّ بِهِ كَثِيرًا وَ
يَهْدِي بِهِ كَثِيرًا وَمَا يُضِلُّ بِهِ إِلَّا الْفَاسِقِينَ ﴿٢٦﴾
الَّذِينَ يَنْقُضُونَ عَهْدَ اللَّهِ مِنْ بَعْدِ مِيثَاقِهِ
وَيَقْطَعُونَ مَا أَمَرَ اللَّهُ بِهِ أَنْ يُوصَلَ وَيُفْسِدُونَ
فِي الْأَرْضِ أُولَٰئِكَ هُمُ الْخَاسِرُونَ ﴿٢٧﴾

2. وَلَقَدْ أَنْزَلْنَا إِلَيْكَ آيَاتٍ بَيِّنَاتٍ وَمَا يَكْفُرُ
بِهَا إِلَّا الْفَاسِقُونَ ﴿٩٩﴾

3. الْحَجُّ أَشْهُرٌ مَعْلُومَاتٌ فَمَنْ فَرَضَ فِيهِنَّ الْحَجَّ
فَلَا رَفَثَ وَلَا فُسُوقَ وَلَا جِدَالَ فِي الْحَجِّ

4. أَشْهِدُوا إِذَا تَبَايَعْتُمْ وَلَا يُضَارَّ كَاتِبٌ وَلَا
شَهِيدٌ وَإِنْ تَفْعَلُوا فَإِنَّهُ فُسُوقٌ
بِكُمْ وَاتَّقُوا اللَّهَ

5. وَلَوْ آمَنَ أَهْلُ الْكِتَابِ لَكَانَ خَيْرًا لَهُمْ مِنْهُمُ
الْمُؤْمِنُونَ وَأَكْثَرُهُمُ الْفَاسِقُونَ ○

6. حُرِّمَتْ عَلَيْكُمُ الْمَيْتَةُ وَالدَّمُ وَلَحْمُ
الْخِنْزِيرِ وَمَا أُهِلَّ لِغَيْرِ اللَّهِ بِهِ وَالْمُنْخَنِقَةُ
وَالْمَوْقُوذَةُ وَالْمُتَرَدِّيَةُ وَالنَّطِيحَةُ
وَمَا أَكَلَ السَّبُعُ إِلَّا مَا ذَكَّيْتُمْ

5. And if the People of the Scripture had believed it had been better for them. Some of them are believers; but most of them are evil-livers.

3:110

6. Forbidden unto you (for food) are carrion and blood and swine-flesh, and that which hath been dedicated unto any

other than Allah, and the dead through beating, and the strangled, and the dead through falling from a height, and that which hath been killed by (the goring of) horns, and the devoured of wild beasts, saving that which ye make lawful (by the death-stroke), and that which hath been immolated unto idols. And (forbidden is it) that ye swear by the divining arrows. This is an abomination.

5:3

7. Whoso judgeth not by that which Allah hath revealed, such are evil-livers.

5:47

8. Allah guideth not the froward folk.

5:108

9. Forsake the outwardness of sin and the inwardness thereof. Lo! those who garner sin will be awarded that which they have earned.

And eat not of that whereon Allah's name hath not been mentioned, for lo! it is abomination.

6:120–121

10. The hypocrites, both men and women proceed one from another. They enjoin the wrong and they forbid the right and they withhold their hands (from spending for the cause of Allah). They forget Allah, so He hath forgotten them. Lo! the hypocrites, they are the transgressors.

9:67

11. And (remember) when

وَمَا ذُبِحَ عَلَى النُّصُبِ وَاَنْ تَسْتَقْسِمُوْا
بِالْاَزْلَامِ ذٰلِكُمْ فِسْقٌ

7. وَمَنْ لَّمْ يَحْكُمْ بِمَآ اَنْزَلَ اللّٰهُ
فَاُولٰٓئِكَ هُمُ الْفٰسِقُوْنَ ۝

8. وَاللّٰهُ لَا يَهْدِى الْقَوْمَ الْفٰسِقِيْنَ ۝

9. وَذَرُوْا ظَاهِرَ الْاِثْمِ وَبَاطِنَهٗ ۚ اِنَّ الَّذِيْنَ
يَكْسِبُوْنَ الْاِثْمَ سَيُجْزَوْنَ بِمَا كَانُوْا
يَقْتَرِفُوْنَ ۝
وَلَا تَأْكُلُوْا مِمَّا لَمْ يُذْكَرِ اسْمُ اللّٰهِ
عَلَيْهِ وَاِنَّهٗ لَفِسْقٌ

10. اَلْمُنٰفِقُوْنَ وَالْمُنٰفِقٰتُ بَعْضُهُمْ مِّنْ بَعْضٍ
يَاْمُرُوْنَ بِالْمُنْكَرِ وَيَنْهَوْنَ عَنِ الْمَعْرُوْفِ
وَيَقْبِضُوْنَ اَيْدِيَهُمْ ۚ نَسُوا اللّٰهَ فَنَسِيَهُمْ
اِنَّ الْمُنٰفِقِيْنَ هُمُ الْفٰسِقُوْنَ ۝

11. وَاِذْ قُلْنَا لِلْمَلٰٓئِكَةِ اسْجُدُوْا لِاٰدَمَ فَسَجَدُوْٓا اِلَّآ اِبْلِيْسَ
كَانَ مِنَ الْجِنِّ فَفَسَقَ عَنْ اَمْرِ رَبِّهٖ ۗ اَفَتَتَّخِذُوْنَهٗ
وَذُرِّيَّتَهٗٓ اَوْلِيَآءَ مِنْ دُوْنِيْ وَهُمْ لَكُمْ عَدُوٌّ ۚ بِئْسَ
لِلظّٰلِمِيْنَ بَدَلًا ۝

12. وَالَّذِيْنَ يَرْمُوْنَ الْمُحْصَنٰتِ ثُمَّ لَمْ
يَاْتُوْا بِاَرْبَعَةِ شُهَدَآءَ فَاجْلِدُوْهُمْ

We said unto the angels: Fall prostrate before Adam, and they fell prostrate, all save Iblis. He was of the jinn, so he rebelled against his Lord's command. Will ye choose him and his seed for your protecting friends instead of Me, when they are an enemy unto you? Calamitous is the exchange for evil-doers!

18:50

12. And those who accuse honourable women but bring not four witnesses, scourge them (with) eighty stripes and never (afterward) accept their testimony—They indeed are evildoers—.

24:4

13. Is he who is a believer like unto him who is an evil-liver? They are not alike.

But as for those who believe and do good works, for them are the Gardens of Retreat—a welcome (in reward) for what they used to do.

And as for those who do evil, their retreat is the Fire. Whenever they desire to issue forth from thence, they are brought back thither. Unto them it is said: Taste the torment of the Fire which ye used to deny.

32:18–20

14. Then have patience (O Muhammad) even as the stout of heart among the messengers (of old) had patience, and seek not to hasten on the doom for them. On the Day when they see that which they are promised (it will seem to them) as though they had tarried but an hour of daylight. A clear message. Shall any be destroyed save evil-living folk?

46:35

ثَمٰنِيْنَ جَلْدَةً وَّلَا تَقْبَلُوْا لَهُمْ
شَهَادَةً اَبَدًا ۚ وَاُولٰٓئِكَ هُمُ الْفٰسِقُوْنَ ﴿٤﴾

13. اَفَمَنْ كَانَ مُؤْمِنًا كَمَنْ كَانَ فَاسِقًا ۚ
لَا يَسْتَوٗنَ ﴿١٨﴾
اَمَّا الَّذِيْنَ اٰمَنُوْا وَعَمِلُوا الصّٰلِحٰتِ
فَلَهُمْ جَنّٰتُ الْمَاْوٰى ۡ نُزُلًا بِمَا كَانُوْا
يَعْمَلُوْنَ ﴿١٩﴾
وَاَمَّا الَّذِيْنَ فَسَقُوْا فَمَاْوٰىهُمُ النَّارُ ۚ
كُلَّمَآ اَرَادُوْٓا اَنْ يَّخْرُجُوْا مِنْهَآ اُعِيْدُوْا
فِيْهَا وَقِيْلَ لَهُمْ ذُوْقُوْا عَذَابَ النَّارِ
الَّذِيْ كُنْتُمْ بِهٖ تُكَذِّبُوْنَ ﴿٢٠﴾

14. فَاصْبِرْ كَمَا صَبَرَ اُولُوا الْعَزْمِ مِنَ
الرُّسُلِ وَلَا تَسْتَعْجِلْ لَّهُمْ ۚ كَاَنَّهُمْ
يَوْمَ يَرَوْنَ مَا يُوْعَدُوْنَ ۙ لَمْ يَلْبَثُوْٓا
اِلَّا سَاعَةً مِّنْ نَّهَارٍ ۚ بَلٰغٌ ۚ فَهَلْ
يُهْلَكُ اِلَّا الْقَوْمُ الْفٰسِقُوْنَ ﴿٣٥﴾

15. يٰٓاَيُّهَا الَّذِيْنَ اٰمَنُوْٓا اِنْ جَآءَكُمْ
فَاسِقٌۢ بِنَبَاٍ فَتَبَيَّنُوْٓا اَنْ تُصِيْبُوْا
قَوْمًا ۢ بِجَهَالَةٍ فَتُصْبِحُوْا عَلٰى مَا
فَعَلْتُمْ نٰدِمِيْنَ ﴿٦﴾

15. O ye who believe! If an evil-liver bring you tidings, verify it, lest ye smite some folk in ignorance and afterward repent of what ye did.

49:6

Ref: 59:19. See also: Wicked.

TRAVELLING

1. (Fast) a certain number of days; and (for) him who is sick among you, or on a journey, (the same) number of other days;
2:184

2. If ye be on a journey and cannot find a scribe, then a pledge in hand (shall suffice). And if one of you entrusteth to another let him who is trusted deliver up that which is entrusted to him (according to the pact between them) and let him observe his duty to Allah his Lord. Hide not testimony. He who hideth it, verily his heart is sinful. Allah is Aware of what ye do.
2:283

3. O ye who believe! Draw not near unto prayer when ye are drunken, till ye know that which ye utter, nor when ye are polluted, save when journeying upon the road till ye have bathed. And if ye be ill, or on a journey, or one of you cometh from the closet, or ye have touched women, and ye find not water, then go to high clean soil and rub your faces and your hands (therewith). Lo! Allah is Benign, Forgiving.
4:43

1. أَيَّامًا مَّعْدُودَاتٍ ۚ فَمَن كَانَ مِنكُم مَّرِيضًا
أَوْ عَلَىٰ سَفَرٍ فَعِدَّةٌ مِّنْ أَيَّامٍ أُخَرَ

2. وَإِن كُنتُمْ عَلَىٰ سَفَرٍ وَلَمْ تَجِدُوا كَاتِبًا فَرِهَانٌ
مَّقْبُوضَةٌ ۖ فَإِنْ أَمِنَ بَعْضُكُم بَعْضًا فَلْيُؤَدِّ الَّذِي
اؤْتُمِنَ أَمَانَتَهُ وَلْيَتَّقِ اللَّهَ رَبَّهُ ۗ وَلَا تَكْتُمُوا
الشَّهَادَةَ ۚ وَمَن يَكْتُمْهَا فَإِنَّهُ آثِمٌ قَلْبُهُ ۗ وَاللَّهُ بِمَا
تَعْمَلُونَ عَلِيمٌ ﴿٢٨٣﴾

3. يَا أَيُّهَا الَّذِينَ آمَنُوا لَا تَقْرَبُوا الصَّلَاةَ
وَأَنتُمْ سُكَارَىٰ حَتَّىٰ تَعْلَمُوا مَا تَقُولُونَ
وَلَا جُنُبًا إِلَّا عَابِرِي سَبِيلٍ حَتَّىٰ
تَغْتَسِلُوا ۚ وَإِن كُنتُم مَّرْضَىٰ أَوْ عَلَىٰ
سَفَرٍ أَوْ جَاءَ أَحَدٌ مِّنكُم مِّنَ الْغَائِطِ
أَوْ لَامَسْتُمُ النِّسَاءَ فَلَمْ تَجِدُوا مَاءً
فَتَيَمَّمُوا صَعِيدًا طَيِّبًا فَامْسَحُوا بِوُجُوهِكُمْ
وَأَيْدِيكُمْ ۗ إِنَّ اللَّهَ كَانَ عَفُوًّا غَفُورًا ﴿٤٣﴾

See also: Way-farer.

TREES

1. He it is Who sendeth down water from the sky, whence ye have drink, and whence are trees on which ye send your beasts to pasture.

Therewith He causeth crops to grow for you, and the olive and the date-palm and grapes and all kinds of fruit. Lo! herein is indeed a portent for people who reflect.

16:10–11

2. Is not He (best) Who created the heavens and the earth, and sendeth down for you water from the sky wherewith We cause to spring forth joyous orchards, whose trees it never hath been yours to cause to grow. Is there any God beside Allah? Nay, but they are folk who ascribe equals (unto Him)!

27:60

3. Have ye observed the fire which ye strike out;

Was it ye who made the tree thereof to grow, or were We the Grower?

We, even We, appointed it a memorial and a comfort for the dwellers in the wilderness.

Therefor (O Muhammad), praise the name of thy Lord, the Tremendous.

56:71–74

1. هُوَ الَّذِيْٓ اَنْزَلَ مِنَ السَّمَاۗءِ مَاۗءً لَّكُمْ
مِّنْهُ شَرَابٌ وَّمِنْهُ شَجَرٌ فِيْهِ تُسِيْمُوْنَ ۝
يُنْۢبِتُ لَكُمْ بِهِ الزَّرْعَ وَالزَّيْتُوْنَ
وَالنَّخِيْلَ وَالْاَعْنَابَ وَمِنْ كُلِّ الثَّمَرٰتِ
اِنَّ فِيْ ذٰلِكَ لَاٰيَةً لِّقَوْمٍ يَّتَفَكَّرُوْنَ ۝

2. اَمَّنْ خَلَقَ السَّمٰوٰتِ وَالْاَرْضَ وَ
اَنْزَلَ لَكُمْ مِّنَ السَّمَاۗءِ مَاۗءً فَاَنْۢبَتْنَا بِهٖ
حَدَاۗىِٕقَ ذَاتَ بَهْجَةٍ مَا كَانَ لَكُمْ
اَنْ تُنْۢبِتُوْا شَجَرَهَا ءَاِلٰهٌ مَّعَ اللّٰهِ
بَلْ هُمْ قَوْمٌ يَّعْدِلُوْنَ ۝

3 اَفَرَءَيْتُمُ النَّارَ الَّتِيْ تُوْرُوْنَ ۝
ءَاَنْتُمْ اَنْشَاْتُمْ شَجَرَتَهَآ اَمْ نَحْنُ
الْمُنْشِــُٔوْنَ ۝
نَحْنُ جَعَلْنٰهَا تَذْكِرَةً وَّمَتَاعًا لِّلْمُقْوِيْنَ ۝
فَسَبِّحْ بِاسْمِ رَبِّكَ الْعَظِيْمِ ۝

Ref: 16:68; 22:18; 36:80; 55:6.

TRIALS AND TRIBULATIONS

1. And surely We shall try you with something of fear and hunger, and loss of wealth and lives and crops; but give glad tidings to the steadfast.

Who say, when a misfortune striketh them: Lo! we are Allah's and lo! unto Him we are returning.

Such are they on whom are blessings from their Lord, and mercy. Such are the rightly guided.

2:155–157

2. · Or think ye that ye will enter Paradise while yet there hath not come unto you the like of (that which came to) those who passed away before you? Affliction and adversity befell them, they were shaken as with earthquake, till the messenger (of Allalı) and those who believed along with him said: When cometh Allah's help? Now surely Allah's help is nigh.

2:214

3. Assuredly ye will be tried in your property and in your persons, and ye will hear much wrong from those who were given the Scripture before you, and from the idolators. But if ye persevere and ward off (evil), then that is of the steadfast heart of things.

3:186

1. ولنبلونكم بشيء من الخوف والجوع
ونقص من الأموال والأنفس والثمرات
وبشر الصابرين ﴿١٥٥﴾
الذين إذا أصابتهم مصيبة قالوا إنا
لله وإنا إليه راجعون ﴿١٥٦﴾
أولئك عليهم صلوات من ربهم ورحمة
وأولئك هم المهتدون ﴿١٥٧﴾

2. أم حسبتم أن تدخلوا الجنة ولما يأتكم
مثل الذين خلوا من قبلكم مستهم
البأساء والضراء وزلزلوا حتى يقول
الرسول والذين آمنوا معه متى نصر
الله ألا إن نصر الله قريب ﴿٢١٤﴾

3. لتبلون في أموالكم وأنفسكم ولتسمعن
من الذين أوتوا الكتاب من قبلكم ومن
الذين أشركوا أذى كثيرا وإن تصبروا
وتتقوا فإن ذلك من عزم الأمور ○

4. ومن يرد الله فتنته فلن تملك له من الله
شيئا أولئك الذين لم يرد الله أن يطهر
قلوبهم لهم في الدنيا خزي ولهم
في الآخرة عذاب عظيم ﴿٤١﴾

○

4. He whom Allah doometh unto sin, thou (by thine efforts) wilt avail him naught against Allah. Those are they for whom the Will of Allah is that He cleanse not their hear s. Theirs in the world will be ignominy, and in the Hereafter an awful doom;

5:41

5. يَا أَيُّهَا الَّذِينَ آمَنُوا لَيَبْلُوَنَّكُمُ اللَّهُ بِشَيْءٍ
مِنَ الصَّيْدِ تَنَالُهُ أَيْدِيكُمْ وَرِمَاحُكُمْ
لِيَعْلَمَ اللَّهُ مَنْ يَخَافُهُ بِالْغَيْبِ ۚ فَمَنِ
اعْتَدَىٰ بَعْدَ ذَٰلِكَ فَلَهُ عَذَابٌ أَلِيمٌ ﴿٩٤﴾

6. وَلَقَدْ أَرْسَلْنَا إِلَىٰ أُمَمٍ مِنْ قَبْلِكَ
فَأَخَذْنَاهُمْ بِالْبَأْسَاءِ وَالضَّرَّاءِ
لَعَلَّهُمْ يَتَضَرَّعُونَ ﴿٤٢﴾
فَلَوْلَا إِذْ جَاءَهُمْ بَأْسُنَا تَضَرَّعُوا وَلَٰكِنْ
قَسَتْ قُلُوبُهُمْ وَزَيَّنَ لَهُمُ الشَّيْطَانُ مَا
كَانُوا يَعْمَلُونَ ﴿٤٣﴾

7. وَهُوَ الَّذِي جَعَلَكُمْ خَلَائِفَ الْأَرْضِ وَرَفَعَ
بَعْضَكُمْ فَوْقَ بَعْضٍ دَرَجَاتٍ لِيَبْلُوَكُمْ
فِي مَا آتَاكُمْ ۗ إِنَّ رَبَّكَ سَرِيعُ الْعِقَابِ
وَإِنَّهُ لَغَفُورٌ رَحِيمٌ

8. وَاعْلَمُوا أَنَّمَا أَمْوَالُكُمْ وَأَوْلَادُكُمْ فِتْنَةٌ
وَأَنَّ اللَّهَ عِنْدَهُ أَجْرٌ عَظِيمٌ ﴿٢٨﴾

9. أَوَلَا يَرَوْنَ أَنَّهُمْ يُفْتَنُونَ فِي كُلِّ عَامٍ مَرَّةً أَوْ
مَرَّتَيْنِ ثُمَّ لَا يَتُوبُونَ وَلَا هُمْ يَذَّكَّرُونَ ﴿١٢٦﴾

10. فَقَالُوا عَلَى اللَّهِ تَوَكَّلْنَا رَبَّنَا لَا تَجْعَلْنَا
فِتْنَةً لِلْقَوْمِ الظَّالِمِينَ ﴿٨٥﴾

5. O ye who believe! Allah will surely try you somewhat (in the matter) of the game which ye take with your hands and your spears, that Allah may know him who feareth Him in secret. Whoso transgresseth after this, for him there is a painful doom.

5:94

6. We have sent already unto peoples that were before thee, and We visited them with tribulation and adversity, in order that they might grow humble.

If only, when Our disaster came on them, they had been humble! But their hearts were hardened and the devil made all that they used to do seem fair unto them!

6:42–43

7. He it is Who hath placed you as viceroys of the earth and hath exalted some of you in rank above others, that He may try you by (the test of) that which He hath given you. Lo! Thy Lord is swift in prosecution, and lo! He is Forgiving, Merciful.

6:165

8. And know that your possessions and your children are a test, and that with Allah is immense reward.

8:28

9. See they not that they are tested once or twice in every year? Still they turn not in repentance, neither pay they heed.

9:126

10. They said: In Allah we put trust. Our Lord! Oh, make us not a lure for the

wrongdoing folk!

And, of Thy mercy, save us from the folk that disbelieve.

10:85–86

11. Lo! We have placed all that is in the earth as an ornament thereof that We may try them: which of them is best in conduct.

18:7

12. And strain not thine eyes toward that which We cause some wedded pairs among them to enjoy the flower of the life of the world, that We may try them thereby. The provision of thy Lord is better and more lasting.

20:131

13. Every soul must taste of death, and We try you with evil and with good, for ordeal. And unto Us ye will be returned.

21:35

14. And among mankind is he who worshippeth Allah upon a narrow marge so that if good befalleth him he is content therewith, but if a trial befalleth him, he falleth away utterly. He loseth both the world and the Hearafter. That is the sheer loss.

22:11

15. Do men imagine that they will be left (at ease) because they say, We believe,

وَنَجِّنَا بِرَحْمَتِكَ مِنَ الْقَوْمِ الْكٰفِرِيْنَ ﴿٨٦﴾

11. اِنَّا جَعَلْنَا مَا عَلَى الْاَرْضِ زِيْنَةً لَّهَا
لِنَبْلُوَهُمْ اَيُّهُمْ اَحْسَنُ عَمَلًا ﴿٧﴾

12. وَلَا تَمُدَّنَّ عَيْنَيْكَ اِلٰى مَا مَتَّعْنَا بِهٖۤ
اَزْوَاجًا مِّنْهُمْ زَهْرَةَ الْحَيٰوةِ الدُّنْيَا ۙ۬
لِنَفْتِنَهُمْ فِيْهِ ؕ وَرِزْقُ رَبِّكَ خَيْرٌ وَّاَبْقٰى ﴿١٣١﴾

13. كُلُّ نَفْسٍ ذَآئِقَةُ الْمَوْتِ ؕ وَنَبْلُوْكُمْ بِالشَّرِّ وَالْخَيْرِ
فِتْنَةً ؕ وَاِلَيْنَا تُرْجَعُوْنَ ﴿٣٥﴾

14. وَمِنَ النَّاسِ مَنْ يَّعْبُدُ اللّٰهَ عَلٰى
حَرْفٍ ۚ فَاِنْ اَصَابَهٗ خَيْرُ ۨ اطْمَاَنَّ
بِهٖ ۚ وَاِنْ اَصَابَتْهُ فِتْنَةُ ۨ انْقَلَبَ
عَلٰى وَجْهِهٖ ۚ خَسِرَ الدُّنْيَا وَالْاٰخِرَةَ ؕ
ذٰلِكَ هُوَ الْخُسْرَانُ الْمُبِيْنُ ﴿١١﴾

15. اَحَسِبَ النَّاسُ اَنْ يُّتْرَكُوْۤا اَنْ
يَّقُوْلُوْۤا اٰمَنَّا وَهُمْ لَا يُفْتَنُوْنَ ﴿٢﴾
وَلَقَدْ فَتَنَّا الَّذِيْنَ مِنْ قَبْلِهِمْ
فَلَيَعْلَمَنَّ اللّٰهُ الَّذِيْنَ صَدَقُوْا
وَلَيَعْلَمَنَّ الْكٰذِبِيْنَ ﴿٣﴾

16. فَاِذَا مَسَّ الْاِنْسَانَ ضُرٌّ دَعَانَا ۫
ثُمَّ اِذَا خَوَّلْنٰهُ نِعْمَةً مِّنَّا ۙ قَالَ
اِنَّمَاۤ اُوْتِيْتُهٗ عَلٰى عِلْمٍ ؕ بَلْ هِيَ فِتْنَةٌ

and will not be tested with affliction?

Lo! We tested those who were before you. Thus Allah knoweth those who are sincere, and knoweth those who feign.

29:2–3

16. Now when hurt toucheth a man he crieth unto Us, and afterward when We have granted him a boon from Us, he saith: Only by force of knowledge I obtained it. Nay, but it is a test. But most of them know not.

Those before them said it, yet (all) that they had earned availed them not;

But the evils that they earned smote them; and such of these as do wrong, the evils that they earn will smite them; they cannot escape.

39:49–51

17. Blessed is He in Whose hand is the Sovereignty, and He is Able to do all things:

Who hath created life and death that He may try you, which of you is best in conduct; and He is the Mighty, the Forgiving,

Who hath created seven heavens in harmony.

67:1–3

18. As for man, whenever his Lord trieth him by honouring him, and is gracious unto him, he saith: My Lord honoureth me.

But whenever He trieth him by straitening his means of life, he saith: My Lord despiseth me.

89:15–16

وَلٰكِنَّ اَكْثَرَهُمْ لَا يَعْلَمُوْنَ ﴿٤٩﴾
قَدْ قَالَهَا الَّذِيْنَ مِنْ قَبْلِهِمْ فَمَآ
اَغْنٰى عَنْهُمْ مَّا كَانُوْا يَكْسِبُوْنَ ﴿٥٠﴾
فَاَصَابَهُمْ سَيِّاٰتُ مَا كَسَبُوْا ۭ وَالَّذِيْنَ
ظَلَمُوْا مِنْ هٰٓؤُلَاۗءِ سَيُصِيْبُهُمْ سَيِّاٰتُ
مَا كَسَبُوْا ۙ وَمَا هُمْ بِمُعْجِزِيْنَ ﴿٥١﴾

17. تَبٰرَكَ الَّذِيْ بِيَدِهِ الْمُلْكُ ۡ وَهُوَ عَلٰي كُلِّ شَيْءٍ
قَدِيْرُ ۙ ﴿١﴾
الَّذِيْ خَلَقَ الْمَوْتَ وَالْحَيٰوةَ لِيَبْلُوَكُمْ اَيُّكُمْ
اَحْسَنُ عَمَلًا ۭ وَهُوَ الْعَزِيْزُ الْغَفُوْرُ ۙ ﴿٢﴾
الَّذِيْ خَلَقَ سَبْعَ سَمٰوٰتٍ طِبَاقًا ۭ

18. فَاَمَّا الْاِنْسَانُ اِذَا مَا ابْتَلٰىهُ رَبُّهٗ
فَاَكْرَمَهٗ وَنَعَّمَهٗ ڏ فَيَقُوْلُ رَبِّيْٓ اَكْرَمَنِ ﴿١٥﴾ ۭ
وَاَمَّآ اِذَا مَا ابْتَلٰىهُ فَقَدَرَ عَلَيْهِ
رِزْقَهٗ ڏ فَيَقُوْلُ رَبِّيْٓ اَهَانَنِ ﴿١٦﴾ ۚ

○

Ref: 2:49,102,124,216; 3:7,140,152,154,178–179; 4:6,90,102; 5:48,71; 6:23, 53; 7:27,155,163,168; 8:17,39,72; 9:16,47,49,55; 10:21,30,83; 11:17; 14:6; 16:92,110; 17:60,73; 20:40,85,90; 21:111; 22:53; 23:30; 24:63; 25:20; 27:40, 47; 29:10; 33:11,14; 37:63,106,162; 38:24,34; 44:17,33; 47:4,31; 51:13–14; 54:27; 57:14; 60:5; 64:15; 68:6,17; 72:16–17; 74:31; 85:10; 86:9.

TRUMPET OF ISRAFIL

1. The Day when the Trumpet is blown. On that Day We assemble the guilty white-eyed (with terror).

20:102

2. And when the trumpet is blown there will be no kinship among them that day, nor will they ask of one another.

23:101

3. And (remind them of) the Day when the Trumpet will be blown, and all who are in the heavens and the earth will start in fear, save him whom Allah willeth. And all come unto Him, humbled.

27:87

4. And the Trumpet is blown and lo! from the graves they hie unto their Lord,

Crying: Woe upon us! Who hath raised us from our place of sleep? This is that which the Beneficent did promise, and the messengers spoke truth:

It is but one Shout, and behold them brought together before Us!

36:51–53

5. And the trumpet is blown, and all who are in the earth, swoon away, save him whom Allah willeth. Then it is blown a second time, and behold them standing waiting!

39:68

6. And when the trumpet shall sound one blast

1. يَوْمَ يُنْفَخُ فِي الصُّوْرِ وَ نَحْشُرُ
الْمُجْرِمِيْنَ يَوْمَئِذٍ زُرْقًا ﴿١٠٢﴾

2. فَإِذَا نُفِخَ فِي الصُّوْرِ فَلَآ أَنْسَابَ
بَيْنَهُمْ يَوْمَئِذٍ وَّلَا يَتَسَآءَلُوْنَ ﴿١٠١﴾

3. وَيَوْمَ يُنْفَخُ فِي الصُّوْرِ فَفَزِعَ مَنْ
فِي السَّمٰوٰتِ وَمَنْ فِي الْأَرْضِ إِلَّا مَنْ
شَآءَ اللّٰهُ ۚ وَكُلٌّ أَتَوْهُ دٰخِرِيْنَ ﴿٨٧﴾

4. وَنُفِخَ فِي الصُّوْرِ فَإِذَا هُمْ مِّنَ الْأَجْدَاثِ
إِلٰى رَبِّهِمْ يَنْسِلُوْنَ ﴿٥١﴾
قَالُوْا يٰوَيْلَنَا مَنْۢ بَعَثَنَا مِنْ مَّرْقَدِنَا ۜ
هٰذَا مَا وَعَدَ الرَّحْمٰنُ وَ صَدَقَ
الْمُرْسَلُوْنَ ﴿٥٢﴾
إِنْ كَانَتْ إِلَّا صَيْحَةً وَّاحِدَةً فَإِذَا
هُمْ جَمِيْعٌ لَّدَيْنَا مُحْضَرُوْنَ ﴿٥٣﴾

5. وَ نُفِخَ فِي الصُّوْرِ فَصَعِقَ مَنْ فِي
السَّمٰوٰتِ وَمَنْ فِي الْأَرْضِ إِلَّا مَنْ
شَآءَ اللّٰهُ ۖ ثُمَّ نُفِخَ فِيْهِ أُخْرٰى
فَإِذَا هُمْ قِيَامٌ يَّنْظُرُوْنَ ﴿٦٨﴾

6. فَإِذَا نُفِخَ فِي الصُّوْرِ نَفْخَةٌ وَّاحِدَةٌ ﴿١٣﴾
وَّحُمِلَتِ الْأَرْضُ وَ الْجِبَالُ فَدُكَّتَا
دَكَّةً وَّاحِدَةً ﴿١٤﴾
فَيَوْمَئِذٍ وَّقَعَتِ الْوَاقِعَةُ ﴿١٥﴾

7. يَوْمَ يُنْفَخُ فِي الصُّوْرِ فَتَأْتُوْنَ أَفْوَاجًا ﴿١٨﴾

And the earth with the mountains shall be lifted up and crushed with one crash,

Then, on that day, will the Event befall.

69:13–15

7. A day when the trumpet is blown and ye come in multitudes,

78:18

Ref: 6:73; 18:99; 37:19; 50:20; 79:6–8; 80:33–42.

See also: Description of Doomsday.

TRUST

1. If ye be on a journey and cannot find a scribe, then a pledge in hand (shall suffice). And if one of you entrusteth to another let him who is trusted deliver up that which is entrusted to him (according to the pact between them) and let him observe his duty to Allah, his Lord. Hide not testimony. He who hideth it, verily his heart is sinful. Allah is Aware of what ye do.

2:283

2. Among the People of the Scripture there is he who, if thou trust him with a weight of treasure, will return it to thee. And among them there is he who, if thou trust him with a piece of gold will not return it to thee unless thou keep standing over him. That is because they say: We have no duty to the Gentiles. They speak a lie concerning Allah knowingly.

3:75

3. Lo! Allah commandeth you that ye restore deposits to their owners, and, if ye judge between mankind, that ye judge justly. Lo! comely is this which Allah admonisheth you. Lo! Allah is ever Hearer, Seer.

4:58

1. وَاِنْ كُنْتُمْ عَلٰى سَفَرٍ وَّلَمْ تَجِدُوْا كَاتِبًا
فَرِهٰنٌ مَّقْبُوْضَةٌ ؕ فَاِنْ اَمِنَ بَعْضُكُمْ
بَعْضًا فَلْيُؤَدِّ الَّذِى اؤْتُمِنَ اَمَانَتَهٗ وَلْيَتَّقِ
اللّٰهَ رَبَّهٗ ؕ وَلَا تَكْتُمُوا الشَّهَادَةَ ؕ وَمَنْ
يَّكْتُمْهَا فَاِنَّهٗۤ اٰثِمٌ قَلْبُهٗ ؕ وَاللّٰهُ بِمَا
تَعْمَلُوْنَ عَلِيْمٌ ۝٢٨٣

2. وَمِنْ اَهْلِ الْكِتٰبِ مَنْ اِنْ تَاْمَنْهُ
بِقِنْطَارٍ يُّؤَدِّهٖۤ اِلَيْكَ ۚ وَمِنْهُمْ مَّنْ اِنْ
تَاْمَنْهُ بِدِيْنَارٍ لَّا يُؤَدِّهٖۤ اِلَيْكَ اِلَّا مَا
دُمْتَ عَلَيْهِ قَآئِمًا ؕ ذٰلِكَ بِاَنَّهُمْ قَالُوْا
لَيْسَ عَلَيْنَا فِى الْاُمِّيّٖنَ سَبِيْلٌ ۚ وَيَقُوْلُوْنَ
عَلَى اللّٰهِ الْكَذِبَ وَهُمْ يَعْلَمُوْنَ ۝

3. اِنَّ اللّٰهَ يَاْمُرُكُمْ اَنْ تُؤَدُّوا الْاَمٰنٰتِ اِلٰٓى
اَهْلِهَا ۙ وَاِذَا حَكَمْتُمْ بَيْنَ النَّاسِ اَنْ
تَحْكُمُوْا بِالْعَدْلِ ؕ اِنَّ اللّٰهَ نِعِمَّا يَعِظُكُمْ
بِهٖ ؕ اِنَّ اللّٰهَ كَانَ سَمِيْعًۢا بَصِيْرًا ۝٥٨

۝

Ref: 70:32. **See also:** Breach of Trust.

TRUST IN ALLAH

1. In Allah let believers put their trust.

3:122

2. And when thou art resolved, then put thy trust in Allah. Lo! Allah loveth those who put their trust (in Him).

3:159

3. Those unto whom men said: Lo! the people have gathered against you, therefor fear them. But (the threat of danger) increased the faith of them and they cried: Allah is sufficient for us! Most Excellent is He in Whom we trust!

3:173

4. And Allah is sufficient as Defender.

4:171

5. Whoso putteth his trust in Allah (will find that) lo! Allah is Mighty, Wise.

8:49

6. And if they incline to peace, incline thou also to it, and trust in Allah. Lo: He even He, is the Hearer, the Knower. 8:61

7. And Allah's is the Invisible of the heavens and the earth and unto Him the whole matter will be returned. So worship Him and put thy trust in Him. Lo! thy Lord is not unaware of what ye (mortals) do.

11:123

.1 وَعَلَى اللهِ فَلْيَتَوَكَّلِ الْمُؤْمِنُونَ ○

.2 فَإِذَا عَزَمْتَ فَتَوَكَّلْ عَلَى اللهِ ۚ إِنَّ اللهَ
يُحِبُّ الْمُتَوَكِّلِينَ ○

.3 الَّذِينَ قَالَ لَهُمُ النَّاسُ إِنَّ النَّاسَ
قَدْ جَمَعُوا لَكُمْ فَاخْشَوْهُمْ فَزَادَهُمْ
إِيمَانًا ۖ وَقَالُوا حَسْبُنَا اللهُ وَنِعْمَ الْوَكِيلُ ○

.4 وَكَفَىٰ بِاللهِ وَكِيلًا

.5 وَمَن يَتَوَكَّلْ عَلَى اللهِ فَإِنَّ اللهَ عَزِيزٌ
حَكِيمٌ

.6 وَإِن جَنَحُوا لِلسَّلْمِ فَاجْنَحْ لَهَا وَتَوَكَّلْ
عَلَى اللهِ ۚ إِنَّهُ هُوَ السَّمِيعُ الْعَلِيمُ

.7 وَلِلَّهِ غَيْبُ السَّمَاوَاتِ وَالْأَرْضِ وَإِلَيْهِ
يُرْجَعُ الْأَمْرُ كُلُّهُ فَاعْبُدْهُ وَتَوَكَّلْ
عَلَيْهِ ۚ وَمَا رَبُّكَ بِغَافِلٍ عَمَّا تَعْمَلُونَ

.8 وَتَوَكَّلْ عَلَى الْحَيِّ الَّذِي لَا يَمُوتُ وَسَبِّحْ
بِحَمْدِهِ ۚ وَكَفَىٰ بِهِ بِذُنُوبِ
عِبَادِهِ خَبِيرًا

.9 وَمَن يَتَوَكَّلْ عَلَى اللهِ فَهُوَ حَسْبُهُ

8. And trust thou in the Living One Who dieth not, and hymn His praise. He sufficeth as the Knower of His bondmen's sins:

25:58

9. And whosoever putteth his trust in Allah, He will suffice him.

65:3

Ref: 4:81; 5:11; 8:2; 9:51,129; 10:71; 13:30; 14:11–12; 16:42; 26:217; 27:79; 33:3; 39:38; 42:36; 58:10; 64:13; 67:29; 73:9.

TRUTH

1. Allah saith: This is a day in which their truthfulness profiteth the truthful, for theirs are Gardens underneath which rivers flow, wherein they are secure for ever, Allah taking pleasure in them and they in Him. That is the great triumph.

5:119

1. قَالَ اللّٰهُ هٰذَا يَوْمُ يَنْفَعُ الصّٰدِقِيْنَ
صِدْقُهُمْ ؕ لَهُمْ جَنّٰتٌ تَجْرِيْ مِنْ تَحْتِهَا
الْاَنْهٰرُ خٰلِدِيْنَ فِيْهَآ اَبَدًا ؕ رَضِيَ اللّٰهُ
عَنْهُمْ وَرَضُوْا عَنْهُ ؕ ذٰلِكَ الْفَوْزُ الْعَظِيْمُ ﴿١١٩﴾

2. O ye who believe! Be careful of your duty to Allah, and be with the truthful.

9:119

2. يٰٓاَيُّهَا الَّذِيْنَ اٰمَنُوا اتَّقُوا اللّٰهَ وَكُوْنُوْا
مَعَ الصّٰدِقِيْنَ ﴿١١٩﴾

3. Of the believers are men who are true to that which they covenanted with Allah. Some of them have paid their vow by death (in battle), and some of them still are waiting; and they have not altered in the least;

That Allah may reward the true men for their truth, and punish the hypocrites if He will, or relent toward them (if He will). Lo! Allah is Forgiving, Merciful.

33:23–24

3. مِنَ الْمُؤْمِنِيْنَ رِجَالٌ صَدَقُوْا مَا
عَاهَدُوا اللّٰهَ عَلَيْهِ ۚ فَمِنْهُمْ مَّنْ قَضٰى
نَحْبَهٗ وَمِنْهُمْ مَّنْ يَّنْتَظِرُ ۖ وَمَا
بَدَّلُوْا تَبْدِيْلًا ﴿٢٣﴾
لِيَجْزِيَ اللّٰهُ الصّٰدِقِيْنَ بِصِدْقِهِمْ
وَيُعَذِّبَ الْمُنٰفِقِيْنَ اِنْ شَآءَ اَوْ يَتُوْبَ
عَلَيْهِمْ ؕ اِنَّ اللّٰهَ كَانَ غَفُوْرًا رَّحِيْمًا ﴿٢٤﴾

4. Lo! men who surrender unto Allah, and women who surrender, and men who believe and women who believe, and men who obey and women who obey, and men who speak the truth and women who speak the truth, and men who persevere (in righteousness) and women who persevere, and men who are humble and women who are humble, and men who give alms and women who give alms, and men who fast and women who fast, and men who guard their modesty and women who guard (their modesty), and men who remember Allah much and women who remember—Allah hath prepared for them forgiveness and a vast reward.

33:35

4. اِنَّ الْمُسْلِمِيْنَ وَالْمُسْلِمٰتِ وَالْمُؤْمِنِيْنَ
وَالْمُؤْمِنٰتِ وَالْقٰنِتِيْنَ وَالْقٰنِتٰتِ وَ
الصّٰدِقِيْنَ وَالصّٰدِقٰتِ وَالصّٰبِرِيْنَ
وَالصّٰبِرٰتِ وَالْخٰشِعِيْنَ وَالْخٰشِعٰتِ وَ
الْمُتَصَدِّقِيْنَ وَالْمُتَصَدِّقٰتِ وَالصَّآئِمِيْنَ
وَالصّٰٓئِمٰتِ وَالْحٰفِظِيْنَ فُرُوْجَهُمْ
وَالْحٰفِظٰتِ وَالذّٰكِرِيْنَ اللّٰهَ كَثِيْرًا
وَّالذّٰكِرٰتِ ۙ اَعَدَّ اللّٰهُ لَهُمْ مَّغْفِرَةً
وَّاَجْرًا عَظِيْمًا ﴿٣٥﴾

5. And whoso bringeth the truth and believeth therein—Such are the dutiful.

They shall have what they will of their Lord's bounty. That is the reward of the good:

That Allah will remit from them the worst of what they did, and will pay them for reward the best they used to do.

39:33–35

5. وَالَّذِىْ جَآءَ بِالصِّدْقِ وَصَدَّقَ بِهٖٓ اُولٰٓئِكَ هُمُ الْمُتَّقُوْنَ ﴿٣٣﴾

لَهُمْ مَّا يَشَآءُوْنَ عِنْدَ رَبِّهِمْ ۭ ذٰلِكَ جَزٰۗؤُا الْمُحْسِنِيْنَ ﴿٣٤﴾

لِيُكَفِّرَ اللّٰهُ عَنْهُمْ اَسْوَاَ الَّذِىْ عَمِلُوْا وَيَجْزِيَهُمْ اَجْرَهُمْ بِاَحْسَنِ الَّذِىْ كَانُوْا يَعْمَلُوْنَ ﴿٣٥﴾

See also: Falsehood.

TRUTH AND FALSEHOOD

1. Confound not truth with falsehood, nor knowingly conceal the truth.

2:42

2. O ye who believe! Squander not your wealth among yourselves in vanity, except it be a trade by mutual consent, and kill not one another. Lo! Allah is ever Merciful unto you:

4:29

3. O mankind! The messenger hath come unto you with the truth from your Lord. Therefor believe; (it is) better for you. But if ye disbelieve, still, lo! unto Allah belongeth whatsoever is in the heavens and the earth. Allah is ever Knower, Wise.

4:170

4. And of those whom We created there is a nation who guide /ith the Truth and establish justice therewith.

7:181

5. He it is Who hath sent His messenger with the guidance and the Religion of Truth, that He may cause it to prevail over all religions, however much the idolaters may be averse.

9:33

6. Such then is Allah, your rightful Lord. After the Truth

1. وَلَا تَلْبِسُوا الْحَقَّ بِالْبَاطِلِ وَتَكْتُمُوا الْحَقَّ
وَأَنْتُمْ تَعْلَمُونَ ﴿٤٢﴾

2. يَاأَيُّهَا الَّذِينَ آمَنُوا لَا تَأْكُلُوا أَمْوَالَكُمْ
بَيْنَكُمْ بِالْبَاطِلِ إِلَّا أَنْ تَكُونَ تِجَارَةً
عَنْ تَرَاضٍ مِنْكُمْ وَلَا تَقْتُلُوا أَنْفُسَكُمْ
إِنَّ اللَّهَ كَانَ بِكُمْ رَحِيمًا ﴿٢٩﴾

3. يَاأَيُّهَا النَّاسُ قَدْ جَاءَكُمُ الرَّسُولُ بِالْحَقِّ
مِنْ رَبِّكُمْ فَآمِنُوا خَيْرًا لَكُمْ وَإِنْ تَكْفُرُوا
فَإِنَّ لِلَّهِ مَا فِي السَّمَاوَاتِ وَالْأَرْضِ وَ
كَانَ اللَّهُ عَلِيمًا حَكِيمًا ﴿١٧٠﴾

4. وَمِمَّنْ خَلَقْنَا أُمَّةٌ يَهْدُونَ بِالْحَقِّ وَ
بِهِ يَعْدِلُونَ ﴿١٨١﴾

5. هُوَ الَّذِي أَرْسَلَ رَسُولَهُ بِالْهُدَىٰ وَ
دِينِ الْحَقِّ لِيُظْهِرَهُ عَلَى الدِّينِ كُلِّهِ
وَلَوْ كَرِهَ الْمُشْرِكُونَ ﴿٣٣﴾

6. فَذَٰلِكُمُ اللَّهُ رَبُّكُمُ الْحَقُّ فَمَاذَا بَعْدَ الْحَقِّ إِلَّا
الضَّلَالُ فَأَنَّىٰ تُصْرَفُونَ ﴿٣٢﴾

7. قُلْ هَلْ مِنْ شُرَكَائِكُمْ مَنْ يَهْدِي
إِلَى الْحَقِّ قُلِ اللَّهُ يَهْدِي لِلْحَقِّ أَفَمَنْ
يَهْدِي إِلَى الْحَقِّ أَحَقُّ أَنْ يُتَّبَعَ أَمَّنْ لَا
يَهِدِّي إِلَّا أَنْ يُهْدَىٰ فَمَا لَكُمْ
كَيْفَ تَحْكُمُونَ ﴿٣٥﴾

what is there saving error? How then are ye turned away!

10:32

7. Say: Is there of your pai ners (whom ye ascribe unto Allah) one that leadeth to the Truth? Say: Allah

leadeth to the Truth. Is He Who leadeth to the Truth more deserving that He should be followed, or he who findeth not the way unless he (himself) be guided. What aileth you? How judge ye?

Most of them follow naught but conjecture. Assuredly conjecture can by no means take the place of truth Lo! Allah is Aware of what they do.

10:35:36

8. He sendeth down water from the sky, so that valleys flow according to their measure, and the flood beareth (on its surface) swelling foam—from that which they smelt in the fire in order to make ornaments and tools riseth a foam like unto it—thus Allah coineth (the similitude of) the true and the false. Then, as for the foam, it passeth away as scum upon the banks, while, as for that which is of use to mankind, it remaineth in the earth. Thus Allah coineth the similitudes.

13:17

9. And say: Truth hath come and falsehood hath vanished away. Lo! falsehood is ever bound to vanish.

17:81

10. We send not the messengers save as bearers of good news and warners. Those who disbelieve contend with falsehood in order to refute

وَمَا يَتَّبِعُ أَكْثَرُهُمْ إِلَّا ظَنًّا ۚ إِنَّ
الظَّنَّ لَا يُغْنِي مِنَ الْحَقِّ شَيْئًا ۚ إِنَّ
اللَّهَ عَلِيمٌ بِمَا يَفْعَلُونَ ﴿٣٦﴾

8. أَنْزَلَ مِنَ السَّمَاءِ مَاءً فَسَالَتْ أَوْدِيَةٌ
بِقَدَرِهَا فَاحْتَمَلَ السَّيْلُ زَبَدًا رَابِيًا ۚ
وَمِمَّا يُوقِدُونَ عَلَيْهِ فِي النَّارِ ابْتِغَاءَ
حِلْيَةٍ أَوْ مَتَاعٍ زَبَدٌ مِثْلُهُ ۚ كَذَٰلِكَ
يَضْرِبُ اللَّهُ الْحَقَّ وَالْبَاطِلَ ۚ
فَأَمَّا الزَّبَدُ فَيَذْهَبُ جُفَاءً ۖ وَأَمَّا مَا
يَنْفَعُ النَّاسَ فَيَمْكُثُ فِي الْأَرْضِ ۚ
كَذَٰلِكَ يَضْرِبُ اللَّهُ الْأَمْثَالَ ﴿١٧﴾

9. وَقُلْ جَاءَ الْحَقُّ وَزَهَقَ الْبَاطِلُ ۚ إِنَّ
الْبَاطِلَ كَانَ زَهُوقًا ﴿٨١﴾

10. وَمَا نُرْسِلُ الْمُرْسَلِينَ إِلَّا مُبَشِّرِينَ
وَمُنْذِرِينَ ۚ وَيُجَادِلُ الَّذِينَ كَفَرُوا
بِالْبَاطِلِ لِيُدْحِضُوا بِهِ الْحَقَّ ۖ وَاتَّخَذُوا
آيَاتِي وَمَا أُنْذِرُوا هُزُوًا ﴿٥٦﴾

11. لَوْ أَرَدْنَا أَنْ نَتَّخِذَ لَهْوًا لَاتَّخَذْنَاهُ
مِنْ لَدُنَّا ۖ إِنْ كُنَّا فَاعِلِينَ ﴿١٧﴾
بَلْ نَقْذِفُ بِالْحَقِّ عَلَى الْبَاطِلِ
فَيَدْمَغُهُ فَإِذَا هُوَ زَاهِقٌ ۚ وَلَكُمُ
الْوَيْلُ مِمَّا تَصِفُونَ ﴿١٨﴾

the Truth thereby. And they take Our revelations and that wherewith they are threatened as a jest.

18:56

11. If We had wished to find a pastime, We could have found it in Our presence—if We ever did.

Nay, but We hurl the true against the false and it doth break its head and lo! it vanisheth. And yours will be woe for that which ye ascribe (unto Him).

21:17–18

12. That is because Allah, He is the True, and that whereon they call instead of Him, is the False, and because Allah, He is the High, the Great.

22:62

13. And those who believe in vanity and disbelieve in Allah, they it is who are the losers.

29:52

14. That (is so) because Allah, He is the True, and that which they invoke beside Him is the False, and because Allah, He is the Sublime, the Great.

31:30

15. Say: Lo! my Lord hurleth the truth. (He is) the Knower of Things Hidden.

Say: The Truth hath come, and falsehood showeth not its face and will not return.

34:48-49

16. And Allah will wipe out the lie and will vindicate the truth by His Words. Lo! He is Aware of what is hidden in the breasts (of men).

42:24

17. And those who believe and do good works and believe in that which is revealed unto Muhammad— and it is the truth from their Lord— He riddeth them of their ill-deeds and improveth their state.

That is because those who disbelieve follow falsehood and because those who believe follow the truth from their Lord. Thus Allah coineth their similitudes for mankind.

47:2–3

12. ذٰلِكَ بِاَنَّ اللّٰهَ هُوَ الْحَقُّ وَ اَنَّ مَا
يَدْعُوْنَ مِنْ دُوْنِهٖ هُوَ الْبَاطِلُ وَ
اَنَّ اللّٰهَ هُوَ الْعَلِيُّ الْكَبِيْرُ ﴿٦٢﴾

13. وَالَّذِيْنَ اٰمَنُوْا بِالْبَاطِلِ وَكَفَرُوْا بِاللّٰهِ
اُولٰٓئِكَ هُمُ الْخٰسِرُوْنَ ﴿٥٢﴾

14. ذٰلِكَ بِاَنَّ اللّٰهَ هُوَ الْحَقُّ وَاَنَّ مَا
يَدْعُوْنَ مِنْ دُوْنِهِ الْبَاطِلُ وَاَنَّ
اللّٰهَ هُوَ الْعَلِيُّ الْكَبِيْرُ ﴿٣٠﴾

15. قُلْ اِنَّ رَبِّيْ يَقْذِفُ بِالْحَقِّ عَلَّامُ
الْغُيُوْبِ ﴿٤٨﴾
قُلْ جَآءَ الْحَقُّ وَ مَا يُبْدِئُ الْبَاطِلُ
وَ مَا يُعِيْدُ ﴿٤٩﴾

16. وَيَمْحُ اللّٰهُ الْبَاطِلَ وَيُحِقُّ الْحَقَّ بِكَلِمٰتِهٖ
اِنَّهٗ عَلِيْمٌ بِذَاتِ الصُّدُوْرِ ﴿٢٤﴾

17. وَ الَّذِيْنَ اٰمَنُوْا وَ عَمِلُوا الصّٰلِحٰتِ
وَ اٰمَنُوْا بِمَا نُزِّلَ عَلٰى مُحَمَّدٍ وَّهُوَ
الْحَقُّ مِنْ رَّبِّهِمْ كَفَّرَ عَنْهُمْ
سَيِّاٰتِهِمْ وَ اَصْلَحَ بَالَهُمْ ﴿٢﴾
ذٰلِكَ بِاَنَّ الَّذِيْنَ كَفَرُوا اتَّبَعُوا
الْبَاطِلَ وَ اَنَّ الَّذِيْنَ اٰمَنُوا اتَّبَعُوا
الْحَقَّ مِنْ رَّبِّهِمْ كَذٰلِكَ يَضْرِبُ
اللّٰهُ لِلنَّاسِ اَمْثَالَهُمْ ﴿٣﴾

See also: Concealing Truth.

UMMA

1. Thus We have appointed you a middle nation, that ye may be witnesses against mankind, and that the messenger may be a witness against you,

2:143

2. Mankind were one community, and Allah sent (unto them) prophets as bearers of good tidings and as warners, and revealed therewith the Scripture with the truth that it might judge between mankind concerning that wherein they differed. And only those unto whom (the Scripture) was given differed concerning it, after clear proofs had come unto them, through hatred one of another. And Allah by His Will guided those who believe unto the truth of that concerning which they differed. Allah guideth whom He will unto a straight path.

2:213

3. And there may spring from you a nation who invite to goodness, and enjoin right conduct and forbid indecency. Such are they who are successful.

3:104

4. Ye are the best community that hath been raised up for mankind. Ye enjoin right conduct and forbid indecency; and ye believe in Allah. And if the People of the Scripture had believed it had been better for them.

1. وَكَذٰلِكَ جَعَلْنٰكُمْ اُمَّةً وَّسَطًا لِّتَكُوْنُوْا شُهَدَآءَ
عَلَى النَّاسِ وَيَكُوْنَ الرَّسُوْلُ عَلَيْكُمْ شَهِيْدًا ؕ

2. كَانَ النَّاسُ اُمَّةً وَّاحِدَةً فَبَعَثَ اللّٰهُ
النَّبِيّٖنَ مُبَشِّرِيْنَ وَمُنْذِرِيْنَ وَاَنْزَلَ
مَعَهُمُ الْكِتٰبَ بِالْحَقِّ لِيَحْكُمَ بَيْنَ النَّاسِ
فِيْمَا اخْتَلَفُوْا فِيْهِ ؕ وَمَا اخْتَلَفَ فِيْهِ اِلَّا
الَّذِيْنَ اُوْتُوْهُ مِنْ بَعْدِ مَا جَآءَتْهُمُ الْبَيِّنٰتُ
بَغْيًا بَيْنَهُمْ ۚ فَهَدَى اللّٰهُ الَّذِيْنَ اٰمَنُوْا لِمَا
اخْتَلَفُوْا فِيْهِ مِنَ الْحَقِّ بِاِذْنِهٖ ؕ وَاللّٰهُ
يَهْدِيْ مَنْ يَّشَآءُ اِلٰى صِرَاطٍ مُّسْتَقِيْمٍ ۝٢١٣

3. وَلْتَكُنْ مِّنْكُمْ اُمَّةٌ يَّدْعُوْنَ اِلَى الْخَيْرِ
وَيَاْمُرُوْنَ بِالْمَعْرُوْفِ وَيَنْهَوْنَ عَنِ
الْمُنْكَرِ ؕ وَاُولٰٓئِكَ هُمُ الْمُفْلِحُوْنَ ۝

4. كُنْتُمْ خَيْرَ اُمَّةٍ اُخْرِجَتْ لِلنَّاسِ تَاْمُرُوْنَ
بِالْمَعْرُوْفِ وَتَنْهَوْنَ عَنِ الْمُنْكَرِ وَتُؤْمِنُوْنَ
بِاللّٰهِ ؕ وَلَوْ اٰمَنَ اَهْلُ الْكِتٰبِ لَكَانَ خَيْرًا لَّهُمْ ؕ
مِنْهُمُ الْمُؤْمِنُوْنَ وَاَكْثَرُهُمُ الْفٰسِقُوْنَ ۝

5. وَلَوْ شَآءَ اللّٰهُ لَجَعَلَكُمْ اُمَّةً وَّاحِدَةً
وَّلٰكِنْ لِّيَبْلُوَكُمْ فِيْ مَآ اٰتٰىكُمْ فَاسْتَبِقُوا
الْخَيْرٰتِ ؕ اِلَى اللّٰهِ مَرْجِعُكُمْ جَمِيْعًا
فَيُنَبِّئُكُمْ بِمَا كُنْتُمْ فِيْهِ تَخْتَلِفُوْنَ ۝٤٨

Some of them are believers; but most of them are evil-livers.

3:110

5. Had Allah willed He could have made you one community. But that He may try you by that which He hath given you (He hath made you as ye are). So vie one with another in good works. Unto Allah ye will all return

and He will then inform you of that wherein ye differ.

5:48

6. If they had observed the Torah and the Gospel and that which was revealed unto them from their Lord, they would surely have been nourished from above them and from beneath their feet. Among them there are people who are moderate, but many of them are of evil conduct.

5:66

7. Revile not those unto whom they pray beside Allah lest they wrongfully revile Allah through ignorance. Thus unto every nation have We made their deed seem fair. Then unto their Lord is their return, and He will tell them what they used to do.

6:108

8. And every nation hath its term, and when its term cometh, they cannot put it off an hour nor yet advance (it).

7:34

9. And for every nation there is a messenger. And when their messenger cometh (on the Day of Judgement) it will be judged between them fairly, and they will not be wronged.

10:47

10. Lo! Abraham was a nation obedient to Allah, by nature upright, and he was not of

6. وَلَوْ أَنَّهُمْ أَقَامُوا التَّوْرَاةَ وَالْإِنجِيلَ
وَمَا أُنزِلَ إِلَيْهِم مِّن رَّبِّهِمْ لَأَكَلُوا
مِن فَوْقِهِمْ وَمِن تَحْتِ أَرْجُلِهِم ۚ
مِّنْهُمْ أُمَّةٌ مُّقْتَصِدَةٌ ۖ وَكَثِيرٌ مِّنْهُمْ
سَاءَ مَا يَعْمَلُونَ ﴿٦٦﴾

7. وَلَا تَسُبُّوا الَّذِينَ يَدْعُونَ مِن دُونِ اللَّهِ
فَيَسُبُّوا اللَّهَ عَدْوًا بِغَيْرِ عِلْمٍ ۗ كَذَٰلِكَ
زَيَّنَّا لِكُلِّ أُمَّةٍ عَمَلَهُمْ ثُمَّ إِلَىٰ رَبِّهِم
مَّرْجِعُهُمْ فَيُنَبِّئُهُم بِمَا كَانُوا يَعْمَلُونَ ﴿١٠٨﴾

8. وَلِكُلِّ أُمَّةٍ أَجَلٌ ۖ فَإِذَا جَاءَ أَجَلُهُمْ
لَا يَسْتَأْخِرُونَ سَاعَةً ۖ وَلَا يَسْتَقْدِمُونَ ﴿٣٤﴾

9. وَلِكُلِّ أُمَّةٍ رَّسُولٌ ۖ فَإِذَا جَاءَ
رَسُولُهُمْ قُضِيَ بَيْنَهُم بِالْقِسْطِ وَهُمْ
لَا يُظْلَمُونَ ﴿٤٧﴾

10. إِنَّ إِبْرَاهِيمَ كَانَ أُمَّةً قَانِتًا لِّلَّهِ حَنِيفًا
وَلَمْ يَكُ مِنَ الْمُشْرِكِينَ ﴿١٢٠﴾
شَاكِرًا لِّأَنْعُمِهِ ۚ اجْتَبَاهُ وَهَدَاهُ إِلَىٰ
صِرَاطٍ مُّسْتَقِيمٍ ﴿١٢١﴾

11. إِنَّ هَٰذِهِ أُمَّتُكُمْ أُمَّةً وَاحِدَةً
وَأَنَا رَبُّكُمْ فَاعْبُدُونِ ﴿٩٢﴾

the idolaters;

Thankful for His bounties: He chose him and He guided him unto a straight path.

16:120–121

11. Lo! this, your religion, is one religion, and I am your Lord, so worship Me.

And they have broken their religion (into fragments) among them, (yet) all are returning unto Us.

21:92–93

وَتَقَطَّعُوْٓا اَمْرَهُمْ بَيْنَهُمْ ۭ كُلٌّ
اِلَيْنَا رٰجِعُوْنَ ﴿٩٣﴾

12. And for every nation have We appointed a ritual, that they may mention the name of Allah over the beast of cattle that He hath given them for food, and your God is One God, therefore surrender unto Him.

22:34

12. وَلِكُلِّ اُمَّةٍ جَعَلْنَا مَنْسَكًا لِّيَذْكُرُوا
اسْمَ اللّٰهِ عَلٰي مَا رَزَقَهُمْ مِّنْۢ بَهِيْمَةِ
الْاَنْعَامِ ۭ فَاِلٰـهُكُمْ اِلٰهٌ وَّاحِدٌ فَلَهٗٓ
اَسْلِمُوْا ۭ

13. And (remind them of) the Day when We shall gather out of every nation a host of those who denied Our revelations, and they will be set in array;

Till, when they come (before their Lord), He will say: Did ye deny My revelations when ye could not compass them in knowledge, or what was it that ye did?

27:83–84

13. وَيَوْمَ نَحْشُرُ مِنْ كُلِّ اُمَّةٍ فَوْجًا
مِّمَّنْ يُّكَذِّبُ بِاٰيٰتِنَا فَهُمْ يُوْزَعُوْنَ ﴿٨٣﴾
حَتّٰٓى اِذَا جَاۗءُوْ قَالَ اَكَذَّبْتُمْ بِاٰيٰتِيْ
وَلَمْ تُحِيْطُوْا بِهَا عِلْمًا اَمَّا ذَا
كُنْتُمْ تَعْمَلُوْنَ ﴿٨٤﴾

14. And there is not a nation but a warner hath passed among them.

35:24

14. وَاِنْ مِّنْ اُمَّةٍ اِلَّا خَلَا فِيْهَا نَذِيْرٌ ﴿٢٤﴾

Ref: 2:128,141; 3:113; 4:41; 7:38,159,164,181; 10: 19,49; 11:118; 12:45; 13:30; 15:5; 16:36,84,89; 22:67; 23:43–44,52; 28:75; 35:24; 40:5; 43: 22–23,33; 45:28.

UNDERSTANDING

1. And whatsoever good ye do Allah knoweth it. So make provision for yourselves (hereafter); for the best provision is to ward off evil. Therefore keep your duty unto Me, O men of understanding.

2:197

2. He giveth wisdom unto whom He will, and he unto whom wisdom is given, he truly hath received abundant good. But none remember except men of understanding.

2:269

3. Lo! in the creation of the heavens and the earth and (in) the difference of night and day are tokens (of His Sovereignty) for men of understanding.

3:190

4. And in the Earth are neighbouring tracts, vineyards and ploughed lands, and date-palms, like and unlike, which are watered with one water. And We have made some of them to excel others in fruit: Lo! herein verily are portents for people who have sense.

13:4

5. Are those who know equal with those who know not? But only men of understanding will pay heed.

39:9

1. وَمَا تَفْعَلُوا مِنْ خَيْرٍ يَعْلَمْهُ اللَّهُ
وَتَزَوَّدُوا فَإِنَّ خَيْرَ الزَّادِ التَّقْوَىٰ وَاتَّقُونِ
يَا أُولِي الْأَلْبَابِ ١٩٧

2. يُؤْتِي الْحِكْمَةَ مَنْ يَشَاءُ وَمَنْ يُؤْتَ
الْحِكْمَةَ فَقَدْ أُوتِيَ خَيْرًا كَثِيرًا وَمَا
يَذَّكَّرُ إِلَّا أُولُو الْأَلْبَابِ ٢٦٩

3. إِنَّ فِي خَلْقِ السَّمَاوَاتِ وَالْأَرْضِ وَاخْتِلَافِ
اللَّيْلِ وَالنَّهَارِ لَآيَاتٍ لِأُولِي الْأَلْبَابِ

4. وَفِي الْأَرْضِ قِطَعٌ مُتَجَاوِرَاتٌ وَجَنَّاتٌ
مِنْ أَعْنَابٍ وَزَرْعٌ وَنَخِيلٌ صِنْوَانٌ
وَغَيْرُ صِنْوَانٍ يُسْقَىٰ بِمَاءٍ وَاحِدٍ
وَنُفَضِّلُ بَعْضَهَا عَلَىٰ بَعْضٍ فِي الْأُكُلِ
إِنَّ فِي ذَٰلِكَ لَآيَاتٍ لِقَوْمٍ يَعْقِلُونَ ٤

5. هَلْ يَسْتَوِي الَّذِينَ يَعْلَمُونَ
وَالَّذِينَ لَا يَعْلَمُونَ إِنَّمَا يَتَذَكَّرُ
أُولُو الْأَلْبَابِ ٩

UNITY

1. Mankind were one community, and Allah sent (unto them) prophets as bearers of good tidings and as warners, and revealed therewith the Scripture with the truth that it might judge between mankind concerning that wherein they differed. And only those unto whom (the Scripture) was given differed concerning it, after clear proofs had come unto them, through hatred one of another. And Allah by His Will guided those who believe unto the truth of that concerning which they differed. Allah guideth whom He will unto a straight path.

2:213

2. Lo! religion with Allah (is) The Surrender (to His Will and Guidance) Those who (formerly) received the Scripture differed only after knowledge came unto them, through transgression among themselves. Whoso disbelieveth the revelations of Allah (will find that) lo! Allah is swift at reckoning.

3:19

3. And hold fast, all of you together, to the cable of Allah, and do not separate. And remember Allah's favour unto you: how ye were enemies and He made friendship between your hearts so that ye became as brothers by His grace; and (how) ye were upon the brink of an abyss of fire,

1. كَانَ النَّاسُ أُمَّةً وَّاحِدَةً فَبَعَثَ اللّٰهُ
النَّبِيّٖنَ مُبَشِّرِيْنَ وَمُنْذِرِيْنَ وَاَنْزَلَ
مَعَهُمُ الْكِتٰبَ بِالْحَقِّ لِيَحْكُمَ بَيْنَ النَّاسِ
فِيْمَا اخْتَلَفُوْا فِيْهِ وَمَا اخْتَلَفَ فِيْهِ اِلَّا
الَّذِيْنَ اُوْتُوْهُ مِنْۢ بَعْدِ مَا جَآءَتْهُمُ الْبَيِّنٰتُ
بَغْيًاۢ بَيْنَهُمْ فَهَدَى اللّٰهُ الَّذِيْنَ اٰمَنُوْا لِمَا
اخْتَلَفُوْا فِيْهِ مِنَ الْحَقِّ بِاِذْنِهٖ وَاللّٰهُ
يَهْدِيْ مَنْ يَّشَآءُ اِلٰى صِرَاطٍ مُّسْتَقِيْمٍ ﴿٢١٣﴾

2. اِنَّ الدِّيْنَ عِنْدَ اللّٰهِ الْاِسْلَامُ وَمَا
اخْتَلَفَ الَّذِيْنَ اُوْتُوا الْكِتٰبَ اِلَّا مِنْۢ بَعْدِ
مَا جَآءَهُمُ الْعِلْمُ بَغْيًاۢ بَيْنَهُمْ وَمَنْ يَّكْفُرْ
بِاٰيٰتِ اللّٰهِ فَاِنَّ اللّٰهَ سَرِيْعُ الْحِسَابِ ○

3. وَاعْتَصِمُوْا بِحَبْلِ اللّٰهِ جَمِيْعًا وَّلَا تَفَرَّقُوْا
وَاذْكُرُوْا نِعْمَتَ اللّٰهِ عَلَيْكُمْ اِذْ كُنْتُمْ اَعْدَآءً
فَاَلَّفَ بَيْنَ قُلُوْبِكُمْ فَاَصْبَحْتُمْ بِنِعْمَتِهٖۤ
اِخْوَانًا وَكُنْتُمْ عَلٰى شَفَا حُفْرَةٍ مِّنَ
النَّارِ فَاَنْقَذَكُمْ مِّنْهَا كَذٰلِكَ يُبَيِّنُ اللّٰهُ
لَكُمْ اٰيٰتِهٖ لَعَلَّكُمْ تَهْتَدُوْنَ ○

4. وَاَنَّ هٰذَا صِرَاطِيْ مُسْتَقِيْمًا فَاتَّبِعُوْهُ وَلَا تَتَّبِعُوا
السُّبُلَ فَتَفَرَّقَ بِكُمْ عَنْ سَبِيْلِهٖ ذٰلِكُمْ وَصّٰكُمْ بِهٖ
لَعَلَّكُمْ تَتَّقُوْنَ ﴿١٥٣﴾

and He did save you from it. Thus Allah maketh clear His revelations unto you, that haply ye may be guided.

3:103

4. This is My straight path, so follow it. Follow not other ways, lest ye be parted from His way. This hath He ordained for you, that ye may ward off (evil).

6:153

5. Lo! As for those who sunder their religion and become schismatics, no concern at all hast thou with them. Their case will go to Allah, Who then will tell them what they used to do.

6:159

6. And as for those who chose a place of worship out of opposition and disbelief, and in order to cause dissent among the believers, and as an outpost for those who warred against Allah and His messenger aforetime, they will surely swear: We purposed naught save good. Allah beareth witness that they verily are liars.

9:107

5. إِنَّ الَّذِينَ فَرَّقُوا دِينَهُمْ وَكَانُوا شِيَعًا
لَّسْتَ مِنْهُمْ فِي شَيْءٍ ۚ إِنَّمَا أَمْرُهُمْ إِلَى
اللَّهِ ثُمَّ يُنَبِّئُهُم بِمَا كَانُوا يَفْعَلُونَ

6. وَالَّذِينَ اتَّخَذُوا مَسْجِدًا ضِرَارًا وَ
كُفْرًا وَتَفْرِيقًا بَيْنَ الْمُؤْمِنِينَ وَإِرْصَادًا
لِّمَنْ حَارَبَ اللَّهَ وَرَسُولَهُ مِن قَبْلُ ۚ
وَلَيَحْلِفُنَّ إِنْ أَرَدْنَا إِلَّا الْحُسْنَىٰ ۖ وَ
اللَّهُ يَشْهَدُ إِنَّهُمْ لَكَاذِبُونَ

7. وَمَا كَانَ النَّاسُ إِلَّا أُمَّةً وَاحِدَةً
فَاخْتَلَفُوا ۚ وَلَوْلَا كَلِمَةٌ سَبَقَتْ مِن
رَّبِّكَ لَقُضِيَ بَيْنَهُمْ فِيمَا فِيهِ يَخْتَلِفُونَ

8. شَرَعَ لَكُم مِّنَ الدِّينِ مَا وَصَّىٰ بِهِ
نُوحًا وَالَّذِي أَوْحَيْنَا إِلَيْكَ وَمَا
وَصَّيْنَا بِهِ إِبْرَاهِيمَ وَمُوسَىٰ وَعِيسَىٰ
أَنْ أَقِيمُوا الدِّينَ وَلَا تَتَفَرَّقُوا فِيهِ ۚ
كَبُرَ عَلَى الْمُشْرِكِينَ مَا تَدْعُوهُمْ إِلَيْهِ ۚ
اللَّهُ يَجْتَبِي إِلَيْهِ مَن يَشَاءُ وَيَهْدِي
إِلَيْهِ مَن يُنِيبُ

9. وَإِن طَائِفَتَانِ مِنَ الْمُؤْمِنِينَ اقْتَتَلُوا
فَأَصْلِحُوا بَيْنَهُمَا ۖ فَإِن بَغَتْ إِحْدَاهُمَا
عَلَى الْأُخْرَىٰ فَقَاتِلُوا الَّتِي تَبْغِي حَتَّىٰ

7. Mankind were but one community; then they differed; and had it not been for a word that had already gone forth from thy Lord, it had been judged between them in respect of that wherein they differ.

10:19

8. He hath ordained for you that religion which He commended unto Noah, and that which We inspire in thee (Muhammad), and that which We commended unto Abraham and Moses and Jesus, saying: Establish

the religion, and be not divided therein. Dreadful for the idolaters is that unto which thou callest them. Allah chooseth for Himself whom He will, and guideth unto Himself· him who turneth (toward Him).

42:13

9. And if two parties of believers fall to fighting, then make peace between them. And if one party of them doth wrong to the other, fight ye that which doth wrong till it return unto the ordinance of Allah; then if it return, make peace between them justly, and act equitably. Lo! Allah loveth the equitable.

The believers are naught else than brothers. Therefore make peace between your brethren and observe your duty to Allah that haply ye may obtain mercy.

49:9–10

10. Nor were the People of the Scripture divided until after the clear proof came unto them.

98:4

تَفِيْٓءَ اِلٰٓى اَمْرِ اللّٰهِ ۚ فَاِنْ فَآءَتْ
فَاَصْلِحُوْا بَيْنَهُمَا بِالْعَدْلِ وَ اَقْسِطُوْا ؕ
اِنَّ اللّٰهَ يُحِبُّ الْمُقْسِطِيْنَ ۝٩
اِنَّمَا الْمُؤْمِنُوْنَ اِخْوَةٌ فَاَصْلِحُوْا بَيْنَ
اَخَوَيْكُمْ وَ اتَّقُوا اللّٰهَ لَعَلَّكُمْ تُرْحَمُوْنَ ۝١٠

10. وَ مَا تَفَرَّقَ الَّذِيْنَ اُوْتُوا الْكِتٰبَ اِلَّا
مِنْۢ بَعْدِ مَا جَآءَتْهُمُ الْبَيِّنَةُ ۝٤

Ref: 2:176; 3:105; 19:36–37; 39:3; 41:45; 42:10,14; 43:63–65; 45:17;
See also: Fraternity.

UNIVERSE

1. Lo! in the creation of the heavens and the earth, and the difference of night and day, and the ships which run upon the sea with that which is of use to men, and the water which Allah sendeth down from the sky, thereby reviving the earth after its death, and dispersing all kinds of beasts therein, and (in) the ordinance of the winds, and the clouds obedient between heaven and earth: are signs (of Allah's Sovereignty) for people who have sense.

2:164

2. There is not an animal in the earth, nor a flying creature flying on two wings, but they are peoples like unto you. We have neglected nothing in the Book (of Our decrees). Then unto their Lord they will be gathered.

6:38

3. Lo! your Lord is Allah Who created the heavens and the earth in six Days, then He established Himself upon the Throne, directing all things. There is no intercessor (with Him) save after His permission. That is Allah, your Lord, so worship Him. Oh, will ye not remind?

10:3

4. He it is Who appointed the sun a splendour and the moon a light, and measured for her stages, that ye might know the number of the years, and the reckoning. Allah created not (all) that save in truth. He detaileth the revelations for people who have knowledge.

Lo! in the difference of

1. إِنَّ فِي خَلْقِ السَّمٰوٰتِ وَالْأَرْضِ وَاخْتِلَافِ
اللَّيْلِ وَالنَّهَارِ وَالْفُلْكِ الَّتِي تَجْرِي فِي
الْبَحْرِ بِمَا يَنْفَعُ النَّاسَ وَمَا أَنْزَلَ اللّٰهُ
مِنَ السَّمَاءِ مِنْ مَاءٍ فَأَحْيَا بِهِ الْأَرْضَ
بَعْدَ مَوْتِهَا وَبَثَّ فِيهَا مِنْ كُلِّ دَابَّةٍ
وَتَصْرِيفِ الرِّيٰحِ وَالسَّحَابِ الْمُسَخَّرِ بَيْنَ
السَّمَاءِ وَالْأَرْضِ لَآيٰتٍ لِقَوْمٍ يَعْقِلُونَ ﴿١٦٤﴾

2. وَمَا مِنْ دَابَّةٍ فِي الْأَرْضِ وَلَا طٰئِرٍ
يَطِيرُ بِجَنَاحَيْهِ إِلَّا أُمَمٌ أَمْثَالُكُمْ
مَا فَرَّطْنَا فِي الْكِتٰبِ مِنْ شَيْءٍ ثُمَّ
إِلَىٰ رَبِّهِمْ يُحْشَرُونَ ﴿٣٨﴾

3. إِنَّ رَبَّكُمُ اللّٰهُ الَّذِي خَلَقَ السَّمٰوٰتِ
وَالْأَرْضَ فِي سِتَّةِ أَيَّامٍ ثُمَّ اسْتَوٰى
عَلَى الْعَرْشِ يُدَبِّرُ الْأَمْرَ مَا مِنْ شَفِيعٍ
إِلَّا مِنْ بَعْدِ إِذْنِهِ ذٰلِكُمُ اللّٰهُ رَبُّكُمْ
فَاعْبُدُوهُ أَفَلَا تَذَكَّرُونَ ﴿٣﴾

4. هُوَ الَّذِي جَعَلَ الشَّمْسَ ضِيَاءً وَالْقَمَرَ
نُورًا وَقَدَّرَهُ مَنَازِلَ لِتَعْلَمُوا عَدَدَ
السِّنِينَ وَالْحِسَابَ مَا خَلَقَ اللّٰهُ ذٰلِكَ
إِلَّا بِالْحَقِّ يُفَصِّلُ الْآيٰتِ لِقَوْمٍ يَعْلَمُونَ ﴿٥﴾

إِنَّ فِي اخْتِلَافِ اللَّيْلِ وَالنَّهَارِ وَمَا خَلَقَ
اللّٰهُ فِي السَّمٰوٰتِ وَالْأَرْضِ لَآيٰتٍ
لِقَوْمٍ يَتَّقُونَ ﴿٦﴾

day and night and all that Allah hath created in the heavens and the earth are portents, verily, for folk who ward off (evil).

10:5–6

5. The seven heavens and the earth and all that is therein praise Him, and there is not a thing but hymneth His praise; but ye understand not their praise. Lo! He is ever Clement, Forgiving.

17:44

6. Say (O Muhammad, unto the idolaters): Disbelieve ye verily in Him Who created the earth in two Days, and ascribe ye unto Him rivals? He (and none else) is the Lord of the Worlds.

He placed therein firm hills rising above it, and blessed it and measured therein its sustenance in four Days, alike for (all) who ask.

Then turned He to the heaven when it was smoke, and said unto it and unto the earth: Come both of you, willingly or loth. They said: We come, obedient.

Then He ordained them seven heavens in two Days and inspired in each heaven its mandate; and We decked the nether heaven with lamps, and rendered it inviolable. That is the measuring of the Mighty, the Knower.

41:9–12

5. تُسَبِّحُ لَهُ السَّمٰوٰتُ السَّبْعُ وَالْاَرْضُ وَمَنْ فِيْهِنَّ
وَاِنْ مِّنْ شَيْءٍ اِلَّا يُسَبِّحُ بِحَمْدِهٖ وَلٰكِنْ لَّا تَفْقَهُوْنَ
تَسْبِيْحَهُمْ ۗ اِنَّهٗ كَانَ حَلِيْمًا غَفُوْرًا ﴿٤٤﴾

6. قُلْ اَئِنَّكُمْ لَتَكْفُرُوْنَ بِالَّذِيْ خَلَقَ الْاَرْضَ فِيْ
يَوْمَيْنِ وَتَجْعَلُوْنَ لَهٗٓ اَنْدَادًا ۗ ذٰلِكَ رَبُّ الْعٰلَمِيْنَ ﴿٩﴾
وَجَعَلَ فِيْهَا رَوَاسِيَ مِنْ فَوْقِهَا وَبٰرَكَ فِيْهَا
وَقَدَّرَ فِيْهَآ اَقْوَاتَهَا فِيْٓ اَرْبَعَةِ اَيَّامٍ ۭ سَوَاۗءً
لِّلسَّاۗىِٕلِيْنَ ﴿١٠﴾
ثُمَّ اسْتَوٰٓى اِلَى السَّمَاۗءِ وَهِيَ دُخَانٌ فَقَالَ لَهَا
وَلِلْاَرْضِ ائْتِيَا طَوْعًا اَوْ كَرْهًا ۭ قَالَتَآ اَتَيْنَا
طَاۗىِٕعِيْنَ ﴿١١﴾
فَقَضٰىهُنَّ سَبْعَ سَمٰوٰتٍ فِيْ يَوْمَيْنِ وَاَوْحٰى
فِيْ كُلِّ سَمَاۗءٍ اَمْرَهَا ۭ وَزَيَّنَّا السَّمَاۗءَ الدُّنْيَا
بِمَصَابِيْحَ ڰ وَحِفْظًا ۭ ذٰلِكَ تَقْدِيْرُ الْعَزِيْزِ
الْعَلِيْمِ ﴿١٢﴾

7. تَبٰرَكَ الَّذِيْ بِيَدِهِ الْمُلْكُ ۡ وَهُوَ عَلٰي
كُلِّ شَيْءٍ قَدِيْرُۨ ﴿١﴾
الَّذِيْ خَلَقَ الْمَوْتَ وَالْحَيٰوةَ لِيَبْلُوَكُمْ
اَيُّكُمْ اَحْسَنُ عَمَلًا ۭ وَهُوَ الْعَزِيْزُ الْغَفُوْرُ ﴿٢﴾
الَّذِيْ خَلَقَ سَبْعَ سَمٰوٰتٍ طِبَاقًا ۭ مَا
تَرٰى فِيْ خَلْقِ الرَّحْمٰنِ مِنْ تَفٰوُتٍ ۭ

7. Blessed is He in Whose hand is the Sovereignty, and He is Able to do all things:

Who hath created life and death that He may try you, which of you is best in conduct;

and He is the Mighty, the Forgiving,

Who hath created seven heavens in harmony. Thou (Muhammad) canst see no fault in the Beneficent One's creation; then look again: Canst thou see any rifts?

Then look again and yet again, thy sight will return unto thee weakened and made dim.

And verily We have beautified the world's heaven with lamps, and We have made them missiles for the devils, and for them We have prepared the doom of flame.

67:1–5

'USHR

1. O ye who believe! Spend of the good things which ye have earned, and of that which We bring forth from the earth for you,

2:267

2. He it is Who produceth gardens trellised and untrellised, and the date-palm, and crops of divers flavour, and the olive and the pomegranate, like and unlike. Eat ye of the fruit thereof when it fruiteth, and pay the due thereof upon the harvest day, and be not

فَارْجِعِ الْبَصَرَ هَلْ تَرٰى مِنْ فُطُوْرٍ ۝
ثُمَّ ارْجِعِ الْبَصَرَ كَرَّتَيْنِ يَنْقَلِبْ
اِلَيْكَ الْبَصَرُ خَاسِئًا وَّ هُوَ حَسِيْرٌ ۝
وَلَقَدْ زَيَّنَّا السَّمَآءَ الدُّنْيَا بِمَصَابِيْحَ
وَجَعَلْنٰهَا رُجُوْمًا لِّلشَّيٰطِيْنِ وَاَعْتَدْنَا
لَهُمْ عَذَابَ السَّعِيْرِ ۝

○

1. يٰاَيُّهَا الَّذِيْنَ اٰمَنُوْٓا اَنْفِقُوْا مِنْ طَيِّبٰتِ
مَا كَسَبْتُمْ وَمِمَّآ اَخْرَجْنَا لَكُمْ مِّنَ
الْاَرْضِ

2. وَهُوَ الَّذِيْٓ اَنْشَاَ جَنّٰتٍ مَّعْرُوْشٰتٍ وَّغَيْرَ
مَعْرُوْشٰتٍ وَّ النَّخْلَ وَالزَّرْعَ مُخْتَلِفًا
اُكُلُهٗ وَالزَّيْتُوْنَ وَالرُّمَّانَ مُتَشَابِهًا وَّغَيْرَ
مُتَشَابِهٍ كُلُوْا مِنْ ثَمَرِهٖٓ اِذَآ اَثْمَرَ وَ
اٰتُوْا حَقَّهٗ يَوْمَ حَصَادِهٖ وَلَا تُسْرِفُوْا
اِنَّهٗ لَا يُحِبُّ الْمُسْرِفِيْنَ ۝

○

prodigal. Lo! Allah loveth not the prodigals.

6: 141

UNIVERSE

Ref: 2: 22,29,30; 3: 90; 4: 126; 23: 17,19,86; 65: 12; 71: 14.

See also: Astronomy, Creation of Universe, Earth, Moon, Mountains, Rivers and Seas, Sky, Stars, Sun.

USURY

1. Those who swallow usury cannot rise up save as he ariseth whom the devil hath prostrated by (his) touch. That is because they say: Trade is just like usury; whereas Allah permitteth trading and forbiddeth usury. He unto whom an admonition from his Lord cometh and (he) refraineth (in obedience thereto) he shall keep (the profits of) that which is past, and his affair (henceforth) is with Allah. As for him who returneth (to usury) —Such are rightful owners of the Fire. They will abide therein.

Allah hath blighted usury and made almsgiving fruitful. Allah loveth not the impious and guilty.

2:275–276

2. O ye who believe! Observe your duty to Allah, and give up what remaineth (due to you) from usury, if ye are (in truth) believers.

And if ye do not, then be warned of war (against you) from Allah and His messenger. And if ye repent, then ye have your principal (without interest). Wrong not, and ye shall not be wronged.

2:278–279

3. O ye who believe. Devour not usury, doubling and quadrupling (the sum lent). Observe your duty to Allah, that ye may be successful.

3:130

1. اَلَّذِيْنَ يَاْكُلُوْنَ الرِّبٰوا لَا يَقُوْمُوْنَ اِلَّا كَمَا
يَقُوْمُ الَّذِيْ يَتَخَبَّطُهُ الشَّيْطٰنُ مِنَ الْمَسِّ
ذٰلِكَ بِاَنَّهُمْ قَالُوْٓا اِنَّمَا الْبَيْعُ مِثْلُ الرِّبٰوا
وَاَحَلَّ اللّٰهُ الْبَيْعَ وَحَرَّمَ الرِّبٰوا فَمَنْ
جَآءَهٗ مَوْعِظَةٌ مِّنْ رَّبِّهٖ فَانْتَهٰى فَلَهٗ
مَا سَلَفَ وَاَمْرُهٗٓ اِلَى اللّٰهِ وَمَنْ عَادَ فَاُولٰٓئِكَ
اَصْحٰبُ النَّارِ هُمْ فِيْهَا خٰلِدُوْنَ ۝

يَمْحَقُ اللّٰهُ الرِّبٰوا وَيُرْبِي الصَّدَقٰتِ وَاللّٰهُ
لَا يُحِبُّ كُلَّ كَفَّارٍ اَثِيْمٍ ۝

2. يٰٓاَيُّهَا الَّذِيْنَ اٰمَنُوا اتَّقُوا اللّٰهَ وَذَرُوْا مَا
بَقِيَ مِنَ الرِّبٰوٓا اِنْ كُنْتُمْ مُّؤْمِنِيْنَ ۝

فَاِنْ لَّمْ تَفْعَلُوْا فَاْذَنُوْا بِحَرْبٍ مِّنَ اللّٰهِ
وَرَسُوْلِهٖ وَاِنْ تُبْتُمْ فَلَكُمْ رُءُوْسُ
اَمْوَالِكُمْ لَا تَظْلِمُوْنَ وَلَا تُظْلَمُوْنَ ۝

3. يٰٓاَيُّهَا الَّذِيْنَ اٰمَنُوْا لَا تَاْكُلُوا الرِّبٰوٓا
اَضْعَافًا مُّضٰعَفَةً وَاتَّقُوا اللّٰهَ لَعَلَّكُمْ تُفْلِحُوْنَ ۝

4. وَمَآ اٰتَيْتُمْ مِّنْ رِّبًا لِّيَرْبُوَا۟ فِيْٓ اَمْوَالِ
النَّاسِ فَلَا يَرْبُوْا عِنْدَ اللّٰهِ وَمَآ
اٰتَيْتُمْ مِّنْ زَكٰوةٍ تُرِيْدُوْنَ وَجْهَ
اللّٰهِ فَاُولٰٓئِكَ هُمُ الْمُضْعِفُوْنَ ۝

4. That which ye give in usury in order that it may increase on (other) people's property hath no increase with Allah; but that which ye give in charity, seeking Allah's Countenance, hath increase manifold.

30:39

VAIN LITERATURE

1. Seccessful indeed are the believers,

Who are humble in their prayers,

And who shun vain conversation,

23: 1–3

2. And of mankind is he who payeth for mere pastime of discourse, that he may mislead from Allah's way without knowledge and maketh it the butt of mockery. For such there is a shameful doom.

31:6

1. قَدْ اَفْلَحَ الْمُؤْمِنُوْنَ ۝١
الَّذِيْنَ هُمْ فِيْ صَلَاتِهِمْ خٰشِعُوْنَ ۝٢
وَالَّذِيْنَ هُمْ عَنِ اللَّغْوِ مُعْرِضُوْنَ ۝٣

2. وَمِنَ النَّاسِ مَنْ يَّشْتَرِيْ لَهْوَ
الْحَدِيْثِ لِيُضِلَّ عَنْ سَبِيْلِ اللّٰهِ بِغَيْرِ
عِلْمٍ ۖ وَّيَتَّخِذَهَا هُزُوًا ۭ اُولٰۗىِٕكَ
لَهُمْ عَذَابٌ مُّهِيْنٌ ۝٦

VANITY

1. And the Jews will not be pleased with thee, nor will the Christians, till thou follow their creed. Say: Lo! the guidance of Allah (Himself) is Guidance. And if thou shouldst follow their desires after the knowledge which hath come unto thee, then wouldst thou have from Allah no protecting friend nor helper.

2:120

2. And Allah would turn to you in mercy; but those who follow vain desires would have you go tremendously astray.

4:27

3. O ye who believe! Be ye staunch in justice, witnesses for Allah, even though it be against yourselves or (your) parents or (your) kindred, whether (the case be of) a rich man or a poor man, for Allah is nearer unto both (than ye are). So follow not passion lest ye lapse (from truth) and if ye lapse or fall away, then lo! Allah is ever Informed of what ye do.

4:135

4. Now there hath succeeded them a later generation who have ruined worship and have followed lusts. But they will meet deception,

19:59

5. And if the Truth had followed their desires, verily the heavens and the earth

1. وَلَن تَرْضَىٰ عَنكَ الْيَهُودُ وَلَا النَّصَارَىٰ حَتَّىٰ تَتَّبِعَ
مِلَّتَهُمْ قُلْ إِنَّ هُدَى اللَّهِ هُوَ الْهُدَىٰ وَلَئِنِ
اتَّبَعْتَ أَهْوَاءَهُم بَعْدَ الَّذِي جَاءَكَ مِنَ
الْعِلْمِ مَا لَكَ مِنَ اللَّهِ مِن وَلِيٍّ وَلَا نَصِيرٍ ﴿١٢٠﴾

2. وَاللَّهُ يُرِيدُ أَن يَتُوبَ عَلَيْكُمْ وَيُرِيدُ الَّذِينَ
يَتَّبِعُونَ الشَّهَوَاتِ أَن تَمِيلُوا مَيْلًا عَظِيمًا ﴿٢٧﴾

3. يَا أَيُّهَا الَّذِينَ آمَنُوا كُونُوا قَوَّامِينَ بِالْقِسْطِ
شُهَدَاءَ لِلَّهِ وَلَوْ عَلَىٰ أَنفُسِكُمْ أَوِ الْوَالِدَيْنِ
وَالْأَقْرَبِينَ إِن يَكُنْ غَنِيًّا أَوْ فَقِيرًا
فَاللَّهُ أَوْلَىٰ بِهِمَا فَلَا تَتَّبِعُوا الْهَوَىٰ أَن
تَعْدِلُوا وَإِن تَلْوُوا أَوْ تُعْرِضُوا فَإِنَّ اللَّهَ
كَانَ بِمَا تَعْمَلُونَ خَبِيرًا ﴿١٣٥﴾

4. فَخَلَفَ مِن بَعْدِهِمْ خَلْفٌ أَضَاعُوا
الصَّلَاةَ وَاتَّبَعُوا الشَّهَوَاتِ فَسَوْفَ
يَلْقَوْنَ غَيًّا ﴿٥٩﴾

5. وَلَوِ اتَّبَعَ الْحَقُّ أَهْوَاءَهُمْ لَفَسَدَتِ
السَّمَاوَاتُ وَالْأَرْضُ وَمَن فِيهِنَّ
بَلْ أَتَيْنَاهُم بِذِكْرِهِمْ فَهُمْ عَن
ذِكْرِهِم مُّعْرِضُونَ ﴿٧١﴾

6. أَرَأَيْتَ مَنِ اتَّخَذَ إِلَٰهَهُ هَوَاهُ
أَفَأَنتَ تَكُونُ عَلَيْهِ وَكِيلًا ﴿٤٣﴾

and whosoever is therein had been corrupted. Nay, We have brought them their Reminder, but from their Reminder they now turn away.

23:71

6. Hast thou seen him who chooseth for his god his own lust? Wouldst thou then be guardian over him?

Or deemest thou that most of them hear or understand? They are but as the cattle—nay, but they are farther astray!

25:43–44

7. Say (unto them, O Muhammad): Then bring a Scripture from the presence of Allah that giveth clearer guidance than these two (that) I may follow it, if ye are truthful.

And if they answer thee not, then know that what they follow is their lusts. And who goeth farther astray than he who followeth his lust without guidance from Allah? Lo! Allah guideth not wrongdoing folk.

28:49–50

8. Nay, but those who do wrong follow their own lusts without knowledge. Who is able to guide him whom Allah hath sent astray? For such there are no helpers.

30:29

9. (And it was said unto him): O David, Lo! We have set thee as a viceroy in the earth; therefor judge aright between mankind, and follow not desire that it beguile thee from the way of Allah. Lo! those who wander from the way of Allah have an awful doom, forasmuch as they forgot the Day of Reckoning.

38:26

أَمْ تَحْسَبُ أَنَّ أَكْثَرَهُمْ يَسْمَعُونَ
أَوْ يَعْقِلُونَ ۚ إِنْ هُمْ إِلَّا كَالْأَنْعَامِ
بَلْ هُمْ أَضَلُّ سَبِيلًا ﴿٤٤﴾

7. قُلْ فَأْتُوا بِكِتَابٍ مِنْ عِنْدِ اللَّهِ هُوَ
أَهْدَىٰ مِنْهُمَا أَتَّبِعْهُ إِنْ كُنْتُمْ صَادِقِينَ ﴿٤٩﴾
فَإِنْ لَمْ يَسْتَجِيبُوا لَكَ فَاعْلَمْ أَنَّمَا
يَتَّبِعُونَ أَهْوَاءَهُمْ ۚ وَمَنْ أَضَلُّ
مِمَّنِ اتَّبَعَ هَوَاهُ بِغَيْرِ هُدًى
مِنَ اللَّهِ ۚ إِنَّ اللَّهَ لَا يَهْدِي
الْقَوْمَ الظَّالِمِينَ ﴿٥٠﴾

8. بَلِ اتَّبَعَ الَّذِينَ ظَلَمُوا أَهْوَاءَهُمْ
بِغَيْرِ عِلْمٍ ۖ فَمَنْ يَهْدِي مَنْ أَضَلَّ
اللَّهُ ۖ وَمَا لَهُمْ مِنْ نَاصِرِينَ ﴿٢٩﴾

9. يَا دَاوُودُ إِنَّا جَعَلْنَاكَ خَلِيفَةً فِي الْأَرْضِ
فَاحْكُمْ بَيْنَ النَّاسِ بِالْحَقِّ وَلَا تَتَّبِعِ
الْهَوَىٰ فَيُضِلَّكَ عَنْ سَبِيلِ اللَّهِ ۚ إِنَّ
الَّذِينَ يَضِلُّونَ عَنْ سَبِيلِ اللَّهِ لَهُمْ
عَذَابٌ شَدِيدٌ بِمَا نَسُوا يَوْمَ الْحِسَابِ ﴿٢٦﴾

Ref: 2:145; 3:14; 5:48,77; 6:56,119,151; 30:29; 42:15; 47:16; 54:3.

VEIL

1. Tell the believing men to lower their gaze and be modest. That is purer for them. Lo! Allah is Aware of what they do.

And tell the believing women to lower their gaze and be modest, and to display of their adornment only that which is apparent, and to draw their veils over their bosoms, and not to reveal their adornment save to their own husbands or fathers or husbands' fathers, or their sons or their husbands' sons, or their brothers, or their brothers' sons or sisters' sons, or their women, or their slaves, or male attendants who lack vigour, or children who know naught of women's nakedness. And let them not stamp their feet so as to reveal what they hide of their adornment. And turn unto Allah together, O believers, in order that ye may succeed.

24:30–31

2. O ye wives of the Prophet! Ye are not like any other women. If ye keep your duty (to Allah), then be not soft of speech, lest he in whose heart is a disease aspire (to you), but utter customary speech.

And stay in your houses.

1. قُلْ لِّلْمُؤْمِنِيْنَ يَغُضُّوْا مِنْ اَبْصَارِهِمْ
وَيَحْفَظُوْا فُرُوْجَهُمْ ذٰلِكَ اَزْكٰى لَهُمْ
اِنَّ اللّٰهَ خَبِيْرٌ بِمَا يَصْنَعُوْنَ ۝
وَقُلْ لِّلْمُؤْمِنٰتِ يَغْضُضْنَ مِنْ اَبْصَارِهِنَّ
وَيَحْفَظْنَ فُرُوْجَهُنَّ وَلَا يُبْدِيْنَ
زِيْنَتَهُنَّ اِلَّا مَا ظَهَرَ مِنْهَا وَلْيَضْرِبْنَ
بِخُمُرِهِنَّ عَلٰى جُيُوْبِهِنَّ وَلَا يُبْدِيْنَ
زِيْنَتَهُنَّ اِلَّا لِبُعُوْلَتِهِنَّ اَوْ اٰبَآئِهِنَّ اَوْ اٰبَآءِ
بُعُوْلَتِهِنَّ اَوْ اَبْنَآئِهِنَّ اَوْ اَبْنَآءِ بُعُوْلَتِهِنَّ
اَوْ اِخْوَانِهِنَّ اَوْ بَنِيْٓ اِخْوَانِهِنَّ اَوْ بَنِيْٓ
اَخَوٰتِهِنَّ اَوْ نِسَآئِهِنَّ اَوْ مَا مَلَكَتْ
اَيْمَانُهُنَّ اَوِ التّٰبِعِيْنَ غَيْرِ اُولِي الْاِرْبَةِ
مِنَ الرِّجَالِ اَوِ الطِّفْلِ الَّذِيْنَ لَمْ
يَظْهَرُوْا عَلٰى عَوْرٰتِ النِّسَآءِ وَلَا يَضْرِبْنَ
بِاَرْجُلِهِنَّ لِيُعْلَمَ مَا يُخْفِيْنَ مِنْ زِيْنَتِهِنَّ
وَتُوْبُوْٓا اِلَى اللّٰهِ جَمِيْعًا اَيُّهَ الْمُؤْمِنُوْنَ
لَعَلَّكُمْ تُفْلِحُوْنَ ۝

2. يٰنِسَآءَ النَّبِيِّ لَسْتُنَّ كَاَحَدٍ مِّنَ
النِّسَآءِ اِنِ اتَّقَيْتُنَّ فَلَا تَخْضَعْنَ
بِالْقَوْلِ فَيَطْمَعَ الَّذِيْ فِيْ قَلْبِهٖ
مَرَضٌ وَّقُلْنَ قَوْلًا مَّعْرُوْفًا ۝
وَقَرْنَ فِيْ بُيُوْتِكُنَّ وَلَا تَبَرَّجْنَ
تَبَرُّجَ الْجَاهِلِيَّةِ الْاُوْلٰى وَاَقِمْنَ الصَّلٰوةَ
وَاٰتِيْنَ الزَّكٰوةَ وَاَطِعْنَ اللّٰهَ وَرَسُوْلَهٗ

Bedizen not yourselves with the bedizenment of the Time of Ignorance. Be regular in prayer, and pay the poor–due, and obey

Allah and His messenger. Allah's wish is but to remove uncleanness far from you, O Folk of the Household, and cleanse you with a thorough cleansing.

33:32–33

إِنَّمَا يُرِيدُ اللَّهُ لِيُذْهِبَ عَنكُمُ
الرِّجْسَ أَهْلَ الْبَيْتِ وَيُطَهِّرَكُمْ تَطْهِيرًا ﴿٣٣﴾

3. And when ye ask of them (the wives of the Proph–et) anything, ask it of them from behind a curtain. That is purer for your hearts and for their hearts.

33:53

3. وَإِذَا سَأَلْتُمُوهُنَّ مَتَاعًا فَسْـَٔلُوهُنَّ مِن
وَرَآءِ حِجَابٍ ۚ ذَٰلِكُمْ أَطْهَرُ لِقُلُوبِكُمْ
وَقُلُوبِهِنَّ ۚ

4. O Prophet! Tell thy wives and thy daughters and the women of the believers to draw their cloaks close round them (when they go abroad). That will be better, so that they may be recognised and not annoyed. Allah is ever Forgiving, Merciful.

33:59

4. يَٰٓأَيُّهَا النَّبِيُّ قُل لِّأَزْوَٰجِكَ وَبَنَاتِكَ
وَنِسَآءِ الْمُؤْمِنِينَ يُدْنِينَ عَلَيْهِنَّ
مِن جَلَٰبِيبِهِنَّ ۚ ذَٰلِكَ أَدْنَىٰٓ أَن
يُعْرَفْنَ فَلَا يُؤْذَيْنَ ۗ وَكَانَ اللَّهُ
غَفُورًا رَّحِيمًا ﴿٥٩﴾

VILE AND GOOD

1. يَاأَيُّهَا الَّذِينَ آمَنُوا أَنفِقُوا مِن طَيِّبَاتِ
مَا كَسَبْتُمْ وَمِمَّا أَخْرَجْنَا لَكُم مِّنَ
الْأَرْضِ وَلَا تَيَمَّمُوا الْخَبِيثَ مِنْهُ
تُنفِقُونَ وَلَسْتُم بِآخِذِيهِ إِلَّا أَن
تُغْمِضُوا فِيهِ وَاعْلَمُوا أَنَّ اللَّهَ غَنِيٌّ حَمِيدٌ ۝

2. مَا كَانَ اللَّهُ لِيَذَرَ الْمُؤْمِنِينَ عَلَىٰ مَا أَنتُمْ
عَلَيْهِ حَتَّىٰ يَمِيزَ الْخَبِيثَ مِنَ الطَّيِّبِ وَمَا
كَانَ اللَّهُ لِيُطْلِعَكُمْ عَلَى الْغَيْبِ وَلَٰكِنَّ اللَّهَ
يَجْتَبِي مِن رُّسُلِهِ مَن يَشَاءُ فَآمِنُوا بِاللَّهِ
وَرُسُلِهِ وَإِن تُؤْمِنُوا وَتَتَّقُوا فَلَكُمْ أَجْرٌ عَظِيمٌ ۝

3. وَآتُوا الْيَتَامَىٰ أَمْوَالَهُمْ وَلَا تَتَبَدَّلُوا
الْخَبِيثَ بِالطَّيِّبِ وَلَا تَأْكُلُوا أَمْوَالَهُمْ
إِلَىٰ أَمْوَالِكُمْ إِنَّهُ كَانَ حُوبًا كَبِيرًا ۝

4. قُل لَّا يَسْتَوِي الْخَبِيثُ وَالطَّيِّبُ وَلَوْ
أَعْجَبَكَ كَثْرَةُ الْخَبِيثِ فَاتَّقُوا اللَّهَ يَا أُولِي
الْأَلْبَابِ لَعَلَّكُمْ تُفْلِحُونَ ۝

5. الْخَبِيثَاتُ لِلْخَبِيثِينَ وَالْخَبِيثُونَ
لِلْخَبِيثَاتِ وَالطَّيِّبَاتُ لِلطَّيِّبِينَ وَ
الطَّيِّبُونَ لِلطَّيِّبَاتِ أُولَٰئِكَ مُبَرَّءُونَ
مِمَّا يَقُولُونَ لَهُم مَّغْفِرَةٌ وَرِزْقٌ
كَرِيمٌ ۝

1. O ye who believe! Spend of the good things which ye have earned, and of that which We bring forth from the earth for you, and seek not the bad (with intent) to spend thereof (in charity) when ye would not take it for yourselves save with disdain; and know that Allah is Absolute, Owner of Praise.

2:267

2. It is not (the purpose) of Allah to leave you in your present state till He shall separate the wicked from the good. And it is not (the purpose of) Allah to let you know the unseen. But Allah chooseth of His messengers whom He will, (to receive knowledge thereof). So believe in Allah and His messengers. If ye believe and ward off (evil), yours will be a vast reward.

3:179

3. Give unto orphans their wealth. Exchange not the good for the bad (in your management thereof) nor absorb their wealth into your own wealth. Lo! that would be a great sin.

4:2

4. Say: The evil and the good are not alike even though the plenty of the evil attract thee. So be mindful of your duty to Allah, O men of understanding, that ye may succeed.

5:100

5. Vile women are for vile men, and vile men for vile women. Good women are for good men, and good men for good women; such are innocent of that which peopel say: For them is pardon and bountiful provision.

24:26

VIRTUE

1. Enjoin ye righteousness upon mankind while ye yourselves forget (to practise it)? And ye are readers of the Scripture! Have ye then no sense?

2:44

2. And each one hath a goal toward which he turneth; so vie with one another in good works. Wheresoever ye may be, Allah will bring you all together. Lo! Allah is Able to do all things.

2:148

3. It is not righteousness that ye turn your faces to the East and the West; but righteous is he who believeth in Allah and the Last Day and the angels and the Scripture and the Prophets; and giveth his wealth, for love of Him, to kinsfolk and to orphans and the needy and the wayfarer and to those who ask, and to set slaves free; and observeth proper worship and payeth the poor-due. And those who keep their treaty when they make one, and the patient in tribulation and adversity and time of stress. Such are they who are sincere. Such are the God-fearing.

2:177

4. It is not righteousness that ye go to houses by the backs thereof (as do the idolaters at certain seasons), but the righteous man is he who wardeth off (evil). So go to houses by the gates thereof,

1. أَتَأْمُرُونَ النَّاسَ بِالْبِرِّ وَتَنْسَوْنَ أَنْفُسَكُمْ
وَأَنْتُمْ تَتْلُونَ الْكِتٰبَ ۚ أَفَلَا تَعْقِلُونَ ﴿٤٤﴾

2. وَلِكُلٍّ وِّجْهَةٌ هُوَ مُوَلِّيهَا فَاسْتَبِقُوا الْخَيْرٰتِ ۚ
أَيْنَ مَا تَكُونُوا يَأْتِ بِكُمُ اللّٰهُ جَمِيعًا ۚ
إِنَّ اللّٰهَ عَلٰى كُلِّ شَيْءٍ قَدِيرٌ ﴿١٤٨﴾

3. لَيْسَ الْبِرَّ أَنْ تُوَلُّوا وُجُوهَكُمْ قِبَلَ الْمَشْرِقِ
وَالْمَغْرِبِ وَلٰكِنَّ الْبِرَّ مَنْ اٰمَنَ بِاللّٰهِ وَالْيَوْمِ
الْاٰخِرِ وَالْمَلٰٓئِكَةِ وَالْكِتٰبِ وَالنَّبِيّٖنَ ۚ وَاٰتَى
الْمَالَ عَلٰى حُبِّهٖ ذَوِي الْقُرْبٰى وَالْيَتٰمٰى وَ
الْمَسٰكِينَ وَابْنَ السَّبِيلِ ۙ وَالسَّآئِلِينَ وَفِي
الرِّقَابِ ۚ وَأَقَامَ الصَّلٰوةَ وَاٰتَى الزَّكٰوةَ ۚ وَ
الْمُوفُونَ بِعَهْدِهِمْ إِذَا عٰهَدُوا ۚ وَالصّٰبِرِينَ
فِي الْبَأْسَآءِ وَالضَّرَّآءِ وَحِينَ الْبَأْسِ ۗ أُولٰٓئِكَ
الَّذِينَ صَدَقُوا ۖ وَأُولٰٓئِكَ هُمُ الْمُتَّقُونَ ﴿١٧٧﴾

4. وَلَيْسَ الْبِرُّ بِأَنْ تَأْتُوا الْبُيُوتَ مِنْ
ظُهُورِهَا وَلٰكِنَّ الْبِرَّ مَنِ اتَّقٰى ۚ وَأْتُوا الْبُيُوتَ
مِنْ أَبْوَابِهَا ۖ وَاتَّقُوا اللّٰهَ لَعَلَّكُمْ
تُفْلِحُونَ ﴿١٨٩﴾

5. لَنْ تَنَالُوا الْبِرَّ حَتّٰى تُنْفِقُوا مِمَّا تُحِبُّونَ ۚ
وَمَا تُنْفِقُوا مِنْ شَيْءٍ فَإِنَّ اللّٰهَ بِهٖ عَلِيمٌ ○

and observe your duty to Allah, that ye may be successful.

2:189

5. Ye will not attain unto piety until ye spend of that which ye love. And whatsoever ye spend, Allah is Aware thereof.

3:92

6. Those who spend (of that which Allah hath given them) in ease and in adversity, those who control their wrath and are forgiving toward mankind; Allah loveth the good.

3:134

7. And serve Allah: And ascribe no thing as partner unto Him. (Show) kindness unto parents, and unto near kindred, and orphans, and the needy, and unto the neighbour who is of kin (unto you) and the neighbour who is not of kin, and the fellow-traveller and the wayfarer and (the slaves) whom your right hands possess. Lo! Allah loveth not such as are proud and boastful.

4:36

8. And help ye one another unto righteousness and pious duty. Help not one another unto sin and transgression, but keep your duty to Allah. Lo! Allah is severe in punishment.

5:2

9. For those who do good in this world there is a good (reward) and the home of the Hereafter will be better. Pleasant indeed will be the home of those who ward off (evil).

16:30

10. Lo! Allah enjoineth justice and kindness, and giving to kinsfolk, and forbiddeth

6. الَّذِينَ يُنفِقُونَ فِي السَّرَّاءِ وَالضَّرَّاءِ
وَالْكَاظِمِينَ الْغَيْظَ وَالْعَافِينَ عَنِ النَّاسِ
وَاللَّهُ يُحِبُّ الْمُحْسِنِينَ

7. وَاعْبُدُوا اللَّهَ وَلَا تُشْرِكُوا بِهِ شَيْئًا
وَبِالْوَالِدَيْنِ إِحْسَانًا وَبِذِي الْقُرْبَىٰ
وَالْيَتَامَىٰ وَالْمَسَاكِينِ وَالْجَارِ ذِي الْقُرْبَىٰ
وَالْجَارِ الْجُنُبِ وَالصَّاحِبِ بِالْجَنبِ
وَابْنِ السَّبِيلِ وَمَا مَلَكَتْ أَيْمَانُكُمْ إِنَّ
اللَّهَ لَا يُحِبُّ مَن كَانَ مُخْتَالًا فَخُورًا

8. وَتَعَاوَنُوا عَلَى الْبِرِّ وَالتَّقْوَىٰ وَلَا تَعَاوَنُوا
عَلَى الْإِثْمِ وَالْعُدْوَانِ وَاتَّقُوا اللَّهَ إِنَّ اللَّهَ
شَدِيدُ الْعِقَابِ

9. لِّلَّذِينَ أَحْسَنُوا فِي هَٰذِهِ الدُّنْيَا حَسَنَةٌ
وَلَدَارُ الْآخِرَةِ خَيْرٌ وَلَنِعْمَ دَارُ
الْمُتَّقِينَ

10. إِنَّ اللَّهَ يَأْمُرُ بِالْعَدْلِ وَالْإِحْسَانِ
وَإِيتَاءِ ذِي الْقُرْبَىٰ وَيَنْهَىٰ عَنِ
الْفَحْشَاءِ وَالْمُنكَرِ وَالْبَغْيِ يَعِظُكُمْ
لَعَلَّكُمْ تَذَكَّرُونَ

11. وَلَا تَسْتَوِي الْحَسَنَةُ وَلَا السَّيِّئَةُ ادْفَعْ بِالَّتِي

lewdness and abomination and wickedness. He exhorteth you in order that ye may take heed.

16:90

11. The good deed and the evil deed are not alike. Repel the evil deed with one which is better, then lo! he, between

whom and thee there was enmity (will become) as though he was a bosom friend.

But none is granted it save those who are steadfast, and none is granted it save the owner of great happiness.

41:34–35

هِيَ أَحْسَنُ فَإِذَا الَّذِي بَيْنَكَ وَبَيْنَهُ عَدَاوَةٌ كَأَنَّهُ وَلِيٌّ حَمِيمٌ ۝ وَمَا يُلَقَّاهَا إِلَّا الَّذِينَ صَبَرُوا وَمَا يُلَقَّاهَا إِلَّا ذُو حَظٍّ عَظِيمٍ ۝

12. Whoso doth right it is for his soul, and whoso doth wrong it is against it. And thy Lord is not at all a tyrant to His slaves.

41:46

12. مَنْ عَمِلَ صَالِحًا فَلِنَفْسِهِ وَمَنْ أَسَاءَ فَعَلَيْهَا وَمَا رَبُّكَ بِظَلَّامٍ لِلْعَبِيدِ ۝

○

Ref: 2:83,195,261–263; 3:115; 4:114; 7:58; 10:26; 20:112; 23:96; 28:54; 58:9; 98:7–8.

VOW

1. Whatever alms ye spend or vow ye vow, lo! Allah knoweth it. Wrong–doers have no helpers.

2:270

2. And proclaim unto mankind the Pilgrimage. They will come unto thee on foot and on every lean camel; they will come from every deep ravine:

That they may witness things that are of benefit to them, and mention the name of Allah on appointed days over the beast of cattle that He hath bestowed upon them. Then eat thereof and feed therewith the poor, unfortunate.

Then let them make an end of their unkemptness and pay their vows and go around the ancient House.

22:27–29

3. Lo! the righteous shall drink of a cup whereof the mixture is of Kafûr;

A spring wherefrom the slaves of Allah drink, making it gush forth abundantly,

(Because) they perform the vow and fear a day whereof the evil is wide–spreading,

76:5–7

1. وَمَا أَنْفَقْتُمْ مِنْ نَفَقَةٍ أَوْ نَذَرْتُمْ مِنْ
نَذْرٍ فَإِنَّ اللَّهَ يَعْلَمُهُ ۗ وَمَا لِلظَّالِمِينَ
مِنْ أَنْصَارٍ ﴿٢٧٠﴾

2. وَأَذِّنْ فِي النَّاسِ بِالْحَجِّ يَأْتُوكَ رِجَالًا
وَعَلَىٰ كُلِّ ضَامِرٍ يَأْتِينَ مِنْ كُلِّ
فَجٍّ عَمِيقٍ ﴿٢٧﴾

لِيَشْهَدُوا مَنَافِعَ لَهُمْ وَيَذْكُرُوا
اسْمَ اللَّهِ فِي أَيَّامٍ مَعْلُومَاتٍ عَلَىٰ مَا
رَزَقَهُمْ مِنْ بَهِيمَةِ الْأَنْعَامِ ۖ فَكُلُوا
مِنْهَا وَأَطْعِمُوا الْبَائِسَ الْفَقِيرَ ﴿٢٨﴾

ثُمَّ لْيَقْضُوا تَفَثَهُمْ وَلْيُوفُوا نُذُورَهُمْ
وَلْيَطَّوَّفُوا بِالْبَيْتِ الْعَتِيقِ ﴿٢٩﴾

3. إِنَّ الْأَبْرَارَ يَشْرَبُونَ مِنْ كَأْسٍ
كَانَ مِزَاجُهَا كَافُورًا ﴿٥﴾
عَيْنًا يَشْرَبُ بِهَا عِبَادُ اللَّهِ يُفَجِّرُونَهَا
تَفْجِيرًا ﴿٦﴾
يُوفُونَ بِالنَّذْرِ وَيَخَافُونَ يَوْمًا
كَانَ شَرُّهُ مُسْتَطِيرًا ﴿٧﴾

Ref: 2:196

WADHU

1. O ye who believe! When ye rise up for prayer, wash your faces, and your hands up to the elbows, and lightly rub your heads and (wash) your feet up to the ankles.

5:6

WANT AND PLENTY

1. Allah desireth for you ease; He desireth not hardship for you.

2:185

2. But he who turneth away from remembrance of Me, his will be a narrow life, and I shall bring him blind to the assembly on the Day of Resurrection.

He will say: My Lord! Wherefor hast Thou gathered me (hither) blind, when I was wont to see?

He will say: So (it must be). Our revelations came unto thee but thou didst forget them. In like manner thou art forgotten this Day!

20:124–126

3. Let him who hath abundance spend of his abundance, and he whose provision is measured, let him spend of that which Allah hath given him. Allah asketh naught of any soul save that which He hath given it. Allah will

1. يَاأَيُّهَا الَّذِينَ آمَنُوا إِذَا قُمْتُمْ إِلَى الصَّلٰوةِ
فَاغْسِلُوا وُجُوهَكُمْ وَأَيْدِيَكُمْ إِلَى الْمَرَافِقِ
وَامْسَحُوا بِرُءُوسِكُمْ وَأَرْجُلَكُمْ إِلَى
الْكَعْبَيْنِ

○

1. يُرِيدُ اللّٰهُ بِكُمُ الْيُسْرَ وَلَا يُرِيدُ بِكُمُ الْعُسْرَ

2. وَمَنْ أَعْرَضَ عَنْ ذِكْرِي فَإِنَّ لَهُ مَعِيشَةً
ضَنْكًا وَنَحْشُرُهُ يَوْمَ الْقِيٰمَةِ أَعْمٰى ۝
قَالَ رَبِّ لِمَ حَشَرْتَنِي أَعْمٰى وَقَدْ
كُنْتُ بَصِيرًا ۝
قَالَ كَذٰلِكَ أَتَتْكَ آيٰتُنَا فَنَسِيتَهَا
وَكَذٰلِكَ الْيَوْمَ تُنْسٰى ۝

3. لِيُنْفِقْ ذُو سَعَةٍ مِنْ سَعَتِهِ وَمَنْ قُدِرَ عَلَيْهِ رِزْقُهُ
فَلْيُنْفِقْ مِمَّا آتٰهُ اللّٰهُ لَا يُكَلِّفُ اللّٰهُ نَفْسًا إِلَّا مَا
آتٰهَا سَيَجْعَلُ اللّٰهُ بَعْدَ عُسْرٍ يُسْرًا ۝

4. فَإِنَّ مَعَ الْعُسْرِ يُسْرًا ۝
إِنَّ مَعَ الْعُسْرِ يُسْرًا ۝

vouchsafe, after hardship, ease.

65:7

4. But lo! with hardship goeth ease,

Lo! with hardship goeth ease

94:5–6

WADHU

See also: *Tayammum*

WAR—BOOTY

1. O ye who believe! When ye go forth (to fight) in the way of Allah, be careful to discriminate, and say not unto one who offereth you peace: "Thou art not a be–liever," seeking the chance profits of this life (so that ye may despoil him). With Allah are plenteous spoils. Even thus (as he now is) were ye before; but Allah hath since then been gracious unto you. Therefore take care to discriminate. Allah is ever Informed of what ye do.

4:94

2. They ask thee (O Muha–mmad) of the spoils of war. Say: The spoils of war be–long to Allah and the messenger, so keep your duty to Allah, and adjust the matter of your difference, and obey Allah and His messenger, if ye are (true) believers.

8:1

3. And know that whatever ye take as spoils of war, lo! a fifth thereof is for Allah, and for the messenger and for the kinsman (who hath need) and orphans and the needy and the wayfarer, if ye believe in Allah and that which We revealed unto Our slave on the Day of Discri–mination, the day when the two armies met. And Allah is Able to do all things.

8:41

1. يَا أَيُّهَا الَّذِينَ آمَنُوا إِذَا ضَرَبْتُمْ فِي
سَبِيلِ اللَّهِ فَتَبَيَّنُوا وَلَا تَقُولُوا لِمَنْ
أَلْقَىٰ إِلَيْكُمُ السَّلَامَ لَسْتَ مُؤْمِنًا تَبْتَغُونَ
عَرَضَ الْحَيَاةِ الدُّنْيَا فَعِنْدَ اللَّهِ مَغَانِمُ
كَثِيرَةٌ كَذَٰلِكَ كُنْتُمْ مِنْ قَبْلُ فَمَنَّ اللَّهُ
عَلَيْكُمْ فَتَبَيَّنُوا إِنَّ اللَّهَ كَانَ بِمَا
تَعْمَلُونَ خَبِيرًا ﴿٩٤﴾

2. يَسْأَلُونَكَ عَنِ الْأَنْفَالِ قُلِ الْأَنْفَالُ
لِلَّهِ وَالرَّسُولِ فَاتَّقُوا اللَّهَ وَأَصْلِحُوا ذَاتَ
بَيْنِكُمْ وَأَطِيعُوا اللَّهَ وَرَسُولَهُ إِنْ
كُنْتُمْ مُؤْمِنِينَ ﴿١﴾

3. وَاعْلَمُوا أَنَّمَا غَنِمْتُمْ مِنْ شَيْءٍ فَأَنَّ لِلَّهِ
خُمُسَهُ وَلِلرَّسُولِ وَلِذِي الْقُرْبَىٰ وَالْيَتَامَىٰ
وَالْمَسَاكِينِ وَابْنِ السَّبِيلِ إِنْ كُنْتُمْ آمَنْتُمْ
بِاللَّهِ وَمَا أَنْزَلْنَا عَلَىٰ عَبْدِنَا يَوْمَ الْفُرْقَانِ
يَوْمَ الْتَقَى الْجَمْعَانِ وَاللَّهُ عَلَىٰ كُلِّ شَيْءٍ قَدِيرٌ ﴿٤١﴾

4. فَكُلُوا مِمَّا غَنِمْتُمْ حَلَالًا طَيِّبًا وَاتَّقُوا
اللَّهَ إِنَّ اللَّهَ غَفُورٌ رَحِيمٌ ﴿٦٩﴾

5. سَيَقُولُ الْمُخَلَّفُونَ إِذَا انْطَلَقْتُمْ إِلَىٰ
مَغَانِمَ لِتَأْخُذُوهَا ذَرُونَا نَتَّبِعْكُمْ
يُرِيدُونَ أَنْ يُبَدِّلُوا كَلَامَ اللَّهِ

4. Now enjoy what ye have won, as lawful and good, and keep your duty to Allah. Lo! Allah is Forgiving, Merciful.

8:69

5. Those who were left behind will say, when ye set forth to capture booty:

Let us go with you. They fain would change the verdict of Allah. Say (unto them, O Muhammad): Ye shall not go with us. Thus hath Allah said beforehand. Then they will say: Ye are envious of us. Nay, but they understand not, save a little.

48:15

WARNING

1. And warn them of the Day of anguish when the case hath been decided. Now they are in a state of carelessness, and they believe not.

19:39

2. O mankind! Fear your Lord. Lo! the earthquake of the Hour (of Doom) is a tremendous thing.

On the day when ye behold it, every nursing mother will forget her nursling and every pregnant one will be delivered of her burden, and thou (Muhammad) wilt see mankind as drunken, yet they will not be drunken, but the Doom of Allah will be strong (upon them)

22:1–2

O mankind! Keep your duty to your Lord and fear a Day when the parent will not be able to avail the child in aught, nor the child to avail the parent. Lo! Allah's promise is the very truth. Let not the life of the world beguile you, nor let the deceiver

قُلْ لَّنْ تَتَّبِعُوْنَا كَذٰلِكُمْ قَالَ اللّٰهُ
مِنْ قَبْلُ ۚ فَسَيَقُوْلُوْنَ بَلْ تَحْسُدُوْنَنَا ۚ
بَلْ كَانُوْا لَا يَفْقَهُوْنَ اِلَّا قَلِيْلًا ۝

○

1. وَاَنْذِرْهُمْ يَوْمَ الْحَسْرَةِ اِذْ قُضِيَ
الْاَمْرُ ۘ وَهُمْ فِيْ غَفْلَةٍ وَّهُمْ لَا يُؤْمِنُوْنَ ۝

2. يٰۤاَيُّهَا النَّاسُ اتَّقُوْا رَبَّكُمْ ۚ اِنَّ
زَلْزَلَةَ السَّاعَةِ شَيْءٌ عَظِيْمٌ ۝
يَوْمَ تَرَوْنَهَا تَذْهَلُ كُلُّ مُرْضِعَةٍ
عَمَّاۤ اَرْضَعَتْ وَتَضَعُ كُلُّ ذَاتِ حَمْلٍ
حَمْلَهَا وَتَرَى النَّاسَ سُكٰرٰى وَمَا
هُمْ بِسُكٰرٰى وَلٰكِنَّ عَذَابَ اللّٰهِ
شَدِيْدٌ ۝

3. يٰۤاَيُّهَا النَّاسُ اتَّقُوْا رَبَّكُمْ وَاخْشَوْا يَوْمًا
لَّا يَجْزِيْ وَالِدٌ عَنْ وَّلَدِهٖ ۡ وَلَا مَوْلُوْدٌ
هُوَ جَازٍ عَنْ وَّالِدِهٖ شَيْـًٔا ۭ اِنَّ وَعْدَ
اللّٰهِ حَقٌّ فَلَا تَغُرَّنَّكُمُ الْحَيٰوةُ الدُّنْيَا ۥ
وَلَا يَغُرَّنَّكُمْ بِاللّٰهِ الْغَرُوْرُ ۝

4. وَمَاۤ اَرْسَلْنَا فِيْ قَرْيَةٍ مِّنْ نَّذِيْرٍ
اِلَّا قَالَ مُتْرَفُوْهَاۤ ۙ اِنَّا بِمَاۤ اُرْسِلْتُمْ
بِهٖ كٰفِرُوْنَ ۝

beguile you in regard to Allah.

31:33

4. And We sent not unto any township a warner, but its pampered ones declared: Lo! we are disbelievers in that wherewith ye have been sent.

34:34

WAR-BOOTY See also: *Jihad*

WARNING

Ref: 2:6,119,213; 5:21; 6:19,92; 7:2; 9:122; 10:2; 14:44; 16:2; 17:105; 18:2,4; 19:98; 22:49; 25:1; 26:214; 28:46; 36:10–11; 74:1–2; 102:6. See also: Glad Tidings

WATER

1. Who hath appointed the earth a resting–place for you, and the sky a canopy; and causeth water to pour down from the sky, thereby producing fruits as food for you. And do not set up rivals to Allah when ye know (better).

2:22

2. He it is Who sendeth down water from the sky, and therewith We bring forth buds of every kind: We bring forth the green blade from which We bring forth the thick–clustered grain; and from the date–palm, from the pollen thereof, spring pendant bunches; and (We bring forth) gardens of grapes, and the olive and the pomegranate, alike and unlike. Look upon the fruit thereof, when they bear fruit, and upon its ripening. Lo! herein verily are portents for a people who believe.

6:99

3. The similitude of the life of the world is only as water which We send down from the sky, then the earth's growth of that which men and cattle eat mingleth with it till, when the earth hath taken on her ornaments and is embellished, and her people deem that they are masters of her, Our commandment cometh by night or by day and We make it as reaped corn as if it had not flourished yesterday. Thus do We expound the revelations for people who reflect.

10:24

4. And in the Earth are neighbouring tracts, vineyards and ploughed lands, and date–palms, like and unlike, which are watered with one water. And We have made some of them to excel others in fruit. Lo! herein verily are portents for people who have sense.

13:4

1. الَّذِي جَعَلَ لَكُمُ الْأَرْضَ فِرَاشًا وَالسَّمَاءَ
بِنَاءً وَأَنْزَلَ مِنَ السَّمَاءِ مَاءً فَأَخْرَجَ بِهِ
مِنَ الثَّمَرَاتِ رِزْقًا لَكُمْ فَلَا تَجْعَلُوا
لِلَّهِ أَنْدَادًا وَأَنْتُمْ تَعْلَمُونَ ﴿٢٢﴾

2. وَهُوَ الَّذِي أَنْزَلَ مِنَ السَّمَاءِ مَاءً فَأَخْرَجْنَا
بِهِ نَبَاتَ كُلِّ شَيْءٍ فَأَخْرَجْنَا مِنْهُ خَضِرًا
نُخْرِجُ مِنْهُ حَبًّا مُتَرَاكِبًا وَمِنَ النَّخْلِ
مِنْ طَلْعِهَا قِنْوَانٌ دَانِيَةٌ وَجَنَّاتٍ مِنْ
أَعْنَابٍ وَالزَّيْتُونَ وَالرُّمَّانَ مُشْتَبِهًا
وَغَيْرَ مُتَشَابِهٍ انْظُرُوا إِلَى ثَمَرِهِ إِذَا أَثْمَرَ
وَيَنْعِهِ إِنَّ فِي ذَٰلِكُمْ لَآيَاتٍ لِقَوْمٍ يُؤْمِنُونَ ○

3. إِنَّمَا مَثَلُ الْحَيَاةِ الدُّنْيَا كَمَاءٍ أَنْزَلْنَاهُ
مِنَ السَّمَاءِ فَاخْتَلَطَ بِهِ نَبَاتُ الْأَرْضِ
مِمَّا يَأْكُلُ النَّاسُ وَالْأَنْعَامُ حَتَّىٰ
إِذَا أَخَذَتِ الْأَرْضُ زُخْرُفَهَا وَازَّيَّنَتْ
وَظَنَّ أَهْلُهَا أَنَّهُمْ قَادِرُونَ عَلَيْهَا أَتَاهَا
أَمْرُنَا لَيْلًا أَوْ نَهَارًا فَجَعَلْنَاهَا حَصِيدًا
كَأَنْ لَمْ تَغْنَ بِالْأَمْسِ كَذَٰلِكَ نُفَصِّلُ
الْآيَاتِ لِقَوْمٍ يَتَفَكَّرُونَ ﴿٢٤﴾

4. وَفِي الْأَرْضِ قِطَعٌ مُتَجَاوِرَاتٌ وَجَنَّاتٌ
مِنْ أَعْنَابٍ وَزَرْعٌ وَنَخِيلٌ صِنْوَانٌ
وَغَيْرُ صِنْوَانٍ يُسْقَىٰ بِمَاءٍ وَاحِدٍ

5. Allah is He Who created the heavens and the earth, and causeth water to descend from the sky, thereby producing fruits as food for you, and maketh the ships to be of service unto you, that they may run upon the sea at His command, and hath made of service unto you the rivers:

14:32

6. He it is Who sendeth down water from the sky, whence ye have drink, and whence are trees on which ye send your beasts to pasture. Therewith He causeth crops to grow for you, and the olive and the date–palm and grapes and all kinds of fruit. Lo! herein is indeed a portent for people who reflect.

16:10–11

7. And We made every living thing of water. Will they not then believe?

21:30

8. Allah hath created every animal of water. Of them is (a kind) that goeth upon its belly and (a kind) that goeth upon two legs and (a kind) that goeth upon four. Allah createth what He will. Lo! Allah is Able to do all things.

24:45

9. Have they not seen how

وَنُفَضِّلُ بَعْضَهَا عَلٰى بَعْضٍ فِي الْأُكُلِ ۚ
إِنَّ فِي ذٰلِكَ لَاٰيٰتٍ لِّقَوْمٍ يَّعْقِلُوْنَ ④

5. اَللّٰهُ الَّذِيْ خَلَقَ السَّمٰوٰتِ وَالْاَرْضَ
وَاَنْزَلَ مِنَ السَّمَآءِ مَآءً فَاَخْرَجَ بِهٖ
مِنَ الثَّمَرٰتِ رِزْقًا لَّكُمْ ۚ وَسَخَّرَ لَكُمُ
الْفُلْكَ لِتَجْرِيَ فِي الْبَحْرِ بِاَمْرِهٖ ۚ وَسَخَّرَ
لَكُمُ الْاَنْهٰرَ ㉜

6. هُوَ الَّذِيْٓ اَنْزَلَ مِنَ السَّمَآءِ مَآءً لَّكُمْ
مِّنْهُ شَرَابٌ وَّمِنْهُ شَجَرٌ فِيْهِ تُسِيْمُوْنَ ⑩
يُنْۢبِتُ لَكُمْ بِهِ الزَّرْعَ وَالزَّيْتُوْنَ
وَالنَّخِيْلَ وَالْاَعْنَابَ وَمِنْ كُلِّ الثَّمَرٰتِ ۗ
اِنَّ فِيْ ذٰلِكَ لَاٰيَةً لِّقَوْمٍ يَّتَفَكَّرُوْنَ ⑪

7. وَجَعَلْنَا مِنَ الْمَآءِ كُلَّ شَيْءٍ حَيٍّ ۗ
اَفَلَا يُؤْمِنُوْنَ ㉚

8. وَاللّٰهُ خَلَقَ كُلَّ دَآبَّةٍ مِّنْ مَّآءٍ ۚ
فَمِنْهُمْ مَّنْ يَّمْشِيْ عَلٰى بَطْنِهٖ ۚ وَمِنْهُمْ
مَّنْ يَّمْشِيْ عَلٰى رِجْلَيْنِ ۚ وَمِنْهُمْ مَّنْ
يَّمْشِيْ عَلٰٓى اَرْبَعٍ ۗ يَخْلُقُ اللّٰهُ مَا يَشَآءُ ۗ
اِنَّ اللّٰهَ عَلٰى كُلِّ شَيْءٍ قَدِيْرٌ ㊺

9. اَوَلَمْ يَرَوْا اَنَّا نَسُوْقُ الْمَآءَ اِلَى
الْاَرْضِ الْجُرُزِ فَنُخْرِجُ بِهٖ زَرْعًا

We lead the water to the barren land and therewith bring forth crops whereof their cattle eat, and they themselves? Will they not then see?

32:27

10. Have ye observed the water which ye drink?

Is it ye who shed it from the raincloud, or are We the Shedder?

If We willed We verily could make it bitter, Why, then, give ye no thanks?

56:68–70

WAYFARER

1. They ask thee, (O Muhammad), what they shall spend. Say: That which ye spend for good (must go) to parents and near kindred and orphans and the needy and the wayfarer. And whatsoever good ye do, lo! Allah is Aware of it.

2:215

2. Give the kinsman his due, and the needy, and the wayfarer, and squander not (thy wealth) in wantonness.

17:26

3. That which Allah giveth as spoil unto His messenger from the people of the townships, it is for Allah and His messenger and for the near of kin and the orphans and the needy and the wayfarer, that it become not a commodity between the rich among you. And whatsoever the messenger giveth you, take it. And whatsoever he forbiddeth, abstain (from it). And keep your duty to Allah. Lo! Allah is stern in reprisal.

59:7

تَأْكُلُ مِنْهُ أَنْعَامُهُمْ وَأَنْفُسُهُمْ
أَفَلَا يُبْصِرُونَ ﴿٢٧﴾

10. أَفَرَءَيْتُمُ الْمَاءَ الَّذِي تَشْرَبُونَ ﴿٦٨﴾
ءَأَنْتُمْ أَنْزَلْتُمُوهُ مِنَ الْمُزْنِ أَمْ
نَحْنُ الْمُنْزِلُونَ ﴿٦٩﴾
لَوْ نَشَاءُ جَعَلْنَاهُ أُجَاجًا فَلَوْلَا
تَشْكُرُونَ ﴿٧٠﴾

1. يَسْأَلُونَكَ مَاذَا يُنْفِقُونَ ۖ قُلْ مَا أَنْفَقْتُمْ
مِنْ خَيْرٍ فَلِلْوَالِدَيْنِ وَالْأَقْرَبِينَ وَالْيَتَامَىٰ
وَالْمَسَاكِينِ وَابْنِ السَّبِيلِ ۗ وَمَا تَفْعَلُوا
مِنْ خَيْرٍ فَإِنَّ اللَّهَ بِهِ عَلِيمٌ ﴿٢١٥﴾

2. وَآتِ ذَا الْقُرْبَىٰ حَقَّهُ وَالْمِسْكِينَ وَابْنَ
السَّبِيلِ وَلَا تُبَذِّرْ تَبْذِيرًا ﴿٢٦﴾

3. مَا أَفَاءَ اللَّهُ عَلَىٰ رَسُولِهِ مِنْ أَهْلِ
الْقُرَىٰ فَلِلَّهِ وَلِلرَّسُولِ وَلِذِي الْقُرْبَىٰ
وَالْيَتَامَىٰ وَالْمَسَاكِينِ وَابْنِ السَّبِيلِ
كَيْ لَا يَكُونَ دُولَةً بَيْنَ الْأَغْنِيَاءِ
مِنْكُمْ ۚ وَمَا آتَاكُمُ الرَّسُولُ فَخُذُوهُ
وَمَا نَهَاكُمْ عَنْهُ فَانْتَهُوا ۚ وَاتَّقُوا اللَّهَ
إِنَّ اللَّهَ شَدِيدُ الْعِقَابِ ﴿٧﴾

WATER
Ref: 2:74; 5:6; 7:57; 15:22; 16:65; 18:29,45; 20:53; 22:5,63; 23:18; 27:60; 29:63; 30:24; 31:10; 32:8; 35:27; 39:21; 41:39; 47:15; 50:9; 54:11–12,28; 56:31; 67:30; 72:16; 77:27; 78:14; 79:31; 80:25.

WAYFARER
Ref: 4:36; 8:41; 9:60; 30:38. **See also:** Journey.

WAYS OF ALLAH

1. And they indeed wished to scare thee from the land that they might drive thee forth from thence, and then they would have stayed (there) but a little after thee?

(Such was Our) method in the case of those whom We sent before thee (O mankind), and thou wilt not find for Our method aught of power to change.

17:76–77

2. There is no reproach for the Prophet in that which Allah maketh his due. That was Allah's way with those who passed away of old— and the commandment of Allah is certain destiny—

Who delivered the message of Allah and feared Him, and feared none save Allah. Allah keepeth good account.

33:38–39

3. Then, when they saw Our doom, they said: We believe in Allah only and reject (all) that we used to associate (with Him).

But their faith could not avail them when they saw Our doom. This is Allah's law which hath ever taken course for his bondmen. And then the disbelievers will be ruined.

40:84–85

4. And if those who dis–

1. وَإِنْ كَادُوا لَيَسْتَفِزُّونَكَ مِنَ الْأَرْضِ
لِيُخْرِجُوكَ مِنْهَا وَإِذًا لَا يَلْبَثُونَ خِلٰفَكَ
إِلَّا قَلِيلًا ﴿٧٦﴾
سُنَّةَ مَنْ قَدْ أَرْسَلْنَا قَبْلَكَ مِنْ
رُسُلِنَا وَلَا تَجِدُ لِسُنَّتِنَا تَحْوِيلًا ﴿٧٧﴾

2. مَا كَانَ عَلَى النَّبِيِّ مِنْ حَرَجٍ فِيمَا
فَرَضَ اللَّهُ لَهُ سُنَّةَ اللَّهِ فِي الَّذِينَ
خَلَوْا مِنْ قَبْلُ وَكَانَ أَمْرُ اللَّهِ
قَدَرًا مَقْدُورًا ﴿٣٨﴾
الَّذِينَ يُبَلِّغُونَ رِسٰلٰتِ اللَّهِ وَيَخْشَوْنَهُ
وَلَا يَخْشَوْنَ أَحَدًا إِلَّا اللَّهَ وَكَفٰى
بِاللَّهِ حَسِيبًا ﴿٣٩﴾

3. فَلَمَّا رَأَوْا بَأْسَنَا قَالُوا آمَنَّا بِاللَّهِ
وَحْدَهُ وَكَفَرْنَا بِمَا كُنَّا بِهِ مُشْرِكِينَ ﴿٨٤﴾
فَلَمْ يَكُ يَنْفَعُهُمْ إِيمَانُهُمْ لَمَّا رَأَوْا
بَأْسَنَا سُنَّتَ اللَّهِ الَّتِي قَدْ خَلَتْ
فِي عِبَادِهِ وَخَسِرَ هُنَالِكَ الْكٰفِرُونَ ﴿٨٥﴾

4. وَلَوْ قٰتَلَكُمُ الَّذِينَ كَفَرُوا لَوَلَّوُا الْأَدْبَارَ
ثُمَّ لَا يَجِدُونَ وَلِيًّا وَلَا نَصِيرًا ﴿٢٢﴾
سُنَّةَ اللَّهِ الَّتِي قَدْ خَلَتْ مِنْ قَبْلُ
وَلَنْ تَجِدَ لِسُنَّةِ اللَّهِ تَبْدِيلًا ﴿٢٣﴾

believe join battle with you they will take to flight, and afterward they will find no protecting friend nor helper.

It is the law of Allah which hath taken course aforetime. Thou wilt not find for the law of Allah aught of power to change.

48:22–23

Ref: 33:62; 35:43.

WEIGHING OF DEEDS

1. The weighing on that day is the true (weighing). As for those whose scale is heavy, they are the successful.

And as for those whose scale is light: those are they who lose their souls because they disbelieved Our revelations.

7:8–9

2. Then those whose scales are heavy, they are the successful.

And those whose scales are light are those who lose their souls, in hell abiding.

The fire burneth their faces, and they are glum therein.

23:102–104

3. Then, as for him whose scales are heavy (with good works),

He will live a pleasant life.

But as for him whose scales are light,

The Bereft and Hungry One will be his mother.

Ah, what will convey unto thee what she is!—

Raging Fire!

101:6–11

1. وَالْوَزْنُ يَوْمَئِذٍ الْحَقُّ ۚ فَمَن ثَقُلَتْ
مَوَازِينُهُ فَأُولَٰئِكَ هُمُ الْمُفْلِحُونَ ﴿٨﴾
وَمَنْ خَفَّتْ مَوَازِينُهُ فَأُولَٰئِكَ الَّذِينَ
خَسِرُوا أَنفُسَهُم بِمَا كَانُوا بِآيَاتِنَا يَظْلِمُونَ ﴿٩﴾

2. فَمَن ثَقُلَتْ مَوَازِينُهُ فَأُولَٰئِكَ
هُمُ الْمُفْلِحُونَ ﴿١٠٢﴾
وَمَنْ خَفَّتْ مَوَازِينُهُ فَأُولَٰئِكَ الَّذِينَ
خَسِرُوا أَنفُسَهُمْ فِي جَهَنَّمَ خَالِدُونَ ﴿١٠٣﴾
تَلْفَحُ وُجُوهَهُمُ النَّارُ وَهُمْ فِيهَا كَالِحُونَ ﴿١٠٤﴾

3. فَأَمَّا مَن ثَقُلَتْ مَوَازِينُهُ ﴿٦﴾
فَهُوَ فِي عِيشَةٍ رَّاضِيَةٍ ﴿٧﴾
وَأَمَّا مَنْ خَفَّتْ مَوَازِينُهُ ﴿٨﴾
فَأُمُّهُ هَاوِيَةٌ ﴿٩﴾
وَمَا أَدْرَاكَ مَا هِيَهْ ﴿١٠﴾
نَارٌ حَامِيَةٌ ﴿١١﴾

Ref: 21:47.

WEIGHTS AND MEASURES

1. And unto Midian (We sent) their brother Shuéyb. He said: O my people! Serve Allah. Ye have no other God save Him! And give not short measure and short weight. Lo! I see you well-to-do, and lo! I fear for you the doom of a besetting Day.

O my people! Give full measure and full weight in justice, and wrong not people in respect of their goods. And do not evil in the earth, causing corruption.

That which Allah leaveth with you is better for you if ye are believers; and I am not a keeper over you.

11:84–86

2. Fill the measure when ye measure, and weigh with a right balance; that is meet, and better in the end.

17:35

3. And the sky He hath uplifted; and He hath set the measure.

That ye exceed not the measure,

But observe the measure strictly, nor fall short thereof.

55:7–9

4. Woe unto the defrauders:

Those who when they take the measure from mankind demand it full,

But if they measure unto them or weigh for them, they cause them loss.

Do such (men) not consider that they will be raised again

Unto an Awful Day,

The day when (all) mankind stand before the Lord of the Worlds?

83:1–6

1. وَإِلَىٰ مَدْيَنَ أَخَاهُمْ شُعَيْبًا ۚ قَالَ
يَٰقَوْمِ اعْبُدُوا اللَّهَ مَا لَكُم مِّنْ إِلَٰهٍ
غَيْرُهُ ۖ وَلَا تَنقُصُوا الْمِكْيَالَ وَالْمِيزَانَ
إِنِّي أَرَاكُم بِخَيْرٍ وَإِنِّي أَخَافُ عَلَيْكُمْ
عَذَابَ يَوْمٍ مُّحِيطٍ ﴿٨٤﴾
وَيَٰقَوْمِ أَوْفُوا الْمِكْيَالَ وَالْمِيزَانَ بِالْقِسْطِ
وَلَا تَبْخَسُوا النَّاسَ أَشْيَاءَهُمْ وَلَا
تَعْثَوْا فِي الْأَرْضِ مُفْسِدِينَ ﴿٨٥﴾
بَقِيَّتُ اللَّهِ خَيْرٌ لَّكُمْ إِن كُنتُم مُّؤْمِنِينَ ۚ
وَمَا أَنَا عَلَيْكُم بِحَفِيظٍ ﴿٨٦﴾

2. وَأَوْفُوا الْكَيْلَ إِذَا كِلْتُمْ وَزِنُوا بِالْقِسْطَاسِ
الْمُسْتَقِيمِ ۚ ذَٰلِكَ خَيْرٌ وَأَحْسَنُ تَأْوِيلًا ﴿٣٥﴾

3. وَالسَّمَاءَ رَفَعَهَا وَوَضَعَ الْمِيزَانَ ﴿٧﴾
أَلَّا تَطْغَوْا فِي الْمِيزَانِ ﴿٨﴾
وَأَقِيمُوا الْوَزْنَ بِالْقِسْطِ وَلَا تُخْسِرُوا
الْمِيزَانَ ﴿٩﴾

4. وَيْلٌ لِّلْمُطَفِّفِينَ ﴿١﴾
الَّذِينَ إِذَا اكْتَالُوا عَلَى النَّاسِ
يَسْتَوْفُونَ ﴿٢﴾
وَإِذَا كَالُوهُمْ أَو وَّزَنُوهُمْ يُخْسِرُونَ ﴿٣﴾
أَلَا يَظُنُّ أُولَٰئِكَ أَنَّهُم مَّبْعُوثُونَ ﴿٤﴾
لِيَوْمٍ عَظِيمٍ ﴿٥﴾
يَوْمَ يَقُومُ النَّاسُ لِرَبِّ الْعَالَمِينَ ﴿٦﴾

Ref: 7:85.

WHISPERING

1. There is no good in much of their secret conferences save (in) him who enjoineth almsgiving and kindness and peace-making among the people. Whoso doeth that seeking the good pleasure of Allah, We shall bestow on him a vast reward.

4:114

2. O ye who believe! When ye conspire together, conspire not together for crime and wrongdoing and disobedience toward the messenger, but conspire together for righteousness and piety, and keep your duty toward Allah, unto Whom ye will be gathered.

Lo! Conspiracy is only of the devil, that he may vex those who believe; but he can harm them not at all unless by Allah's leave. In Allah let believers put their trust.

58:9–10

3. O ye who believe! When ye hold conference with the messenger, offer an alms before your conference. That is better and purer for you. But if ye cannot find (the wherewithal) then lo! Allah is Forgiving, Merciful.

Fear ye to offer alms before your conference? Then, when ye do it not and Allah hath forgiven you, establish worship and pay the poor-due and obey Allah and His messenger. And Allah is Aware of what ye do.

58:12–13

1. لَا خَيْرَ فِي كَثِيرٍ مِّن نَّجْوَاهُمْ إِلَّا مَنْ أَمَرَ بِصَدَقَةٍ
أَوْ مَعْرُوفٍ أَوْ إِصْلَاحٍ بَيْنَ النَّاسِ وَمَن يَفْعَلْ
ذَٰلِكَ ابْتِغَاءَ مَرْضَاتِ اللَّهِ فَسَوْفَ نُؤْتِيهِ
أَجْرًا عَظِيمًا ﴿١١٤﴾

2. يَا أَيُّهَا الَّذِينَ آمَنُوا إِذَا تَنَاجَيْتُمْ فَلَا
تَتَنَاجَوْا بِالْإِثْمِ وَالْعُدْوَانِ وَمَعْصِيَتِ
الرَّسُولِ وَتَنَاجَوْا بِالْبِرِّ وَالتَّقْوَىٰ
وَاتَّقُوا اللَّهَ الَّذِي إِلَيْهِ تُحْشَرُونَ ﴿٩﴾
إِنَّمَا النَّجْوَىٰ مِنَ الشَّيْطَانِ لِيَحْزُنَ الَّذِينَ
آمَنُوا وَلَيْسَ بِضَارِّهِمْ شَيْئًا إِلَّا بِإِذْنِ
اللَّهِ وَعَلَى اللَّهِ فَلْيَتَوَكَّلِ الْمُؤْمِنُونَ ﴿١٠﴾

3. يَا أَيُّهَا الَّذِينَ آمَنُوا إِذَا نَاجَيْتُمُ
الرَّسُولَ فَقَدِّمُوا بَيْنَ يَدَيْ نَجْوَاكُمْ
صَدَقَةً ذَٰلِكَ خَيْرٌ لَّكُمْ وَأَطْهَرُ
فَإِن لَّمْ تَجِدُوا فَإِنَّ اللَّهَ غَفُورٌ رَّحِيمٌ ﴿١٢﴾
أَأَشْفَقْتُمْ أَن تُقَدِّمُوا بَيْنَ يَدَيْ
نَجْوَاكُمْ صَدَقَاتٍ فَإِذْ لَمْ تَفْعَلُوا
وَتَابَ اللَّهُ عَلَيْكُمْ فَأَقِيمُوا الصَّلَاةَ
وَآتُوا الزَّكَاةَ وَأَطِيعُوا اللَّهَ وَرَسُولَهُ
وَاللَّهُ خَبِيرٌ بِمَا تَعْمَلُونَ ﴿١٣﴾

WICKED

1. Shall We treat those who believe and do good works as those who spread corruption in the earth; or shall We treat the pious as the wicked?

38:28

2. Lo! the righteous verily will be in delight.

And lo! the wicked verily will be in hell;

They will burn therein on the Day of Judgement,

And will not be absent thence.

Ah, what will convey unto thee what the Day of Judgement is!

Again, what will convey unto thee what the Day of Judgement is!

A day on which no soul hath power at all for any (other) soul. The (absolute) command on that day is Allah's.

82:13–19

3. Nay but the record of the vile is in *Sijjin*—

Ah! what will convey unto thee what *Sijjin* is!—

A written record.

Woe unto the repudiators on that day!

Those who deny the

1. أَمْ نَجْعَلُ الَّذِينَ آمَنُوا وَعَمِلُوا الصَّالِحَاتِ كَالْمُفْسِدِينَ
فِي الْأَرْضِ أَمْ نَجْعَلُ الْمُتَّقِينَ كَالْفُجَّارِ ٢٨

2. إِنَّ الْأَبْرَارَ لَفِي نَعِيمٍ ١٣
وَإِنَّ الْفُجَّارَ لَفِي جَحِيمٍ ١٤
يَصْلَوْنَهَا يَوْمَ الدِّينِ ١٥
وَمَا هُمْ عَنْهَا بِغَائِبِينَ ١٦
وَمَا أَدْرَاكَ مَا يَوْمُ الدِّينِ ١٧
ثُمَّ مَا أَدْرَاكَ مَا يَوْمُ الدِّينِ ١٨
يَوْمَ لَا تَمْلِكُ نَفْسٌ لِنَفْسٍ شَيْئًا
وَالْأَمْرُ يَوْمَئِذٍ لِلَّهِ ١٩

3. كَلَّا إِنَّ كِتَابَ الْفُجَّارِ لَفِي سِجِّينٍ ٧
وَمَا أَدْرَاكَ مَا سِجِّينٌ ٨
كِتَابٌ مَرْقُومٌ ٩
وَيْلٌ يَوْمَئِذٍ لِلْمُكَذِّبِينَ ١٠
الَّذِينَ يُكَذِّبُونَ بِيَوْمِ الدِّينِ ١١

Day of Judgement
83:7–11

See also: Transgression, Vile and Good

WILL

1. It is prescribed for you, when death approacheth one of you if he leave wealth that he bequeath unto parents and near relatives in kindness. (This is) a duty for all those who ward off (evil).

And whoso changeth (the will) after he hath heard it—the sin thereof is only upon those who change it. Lo! Allah is Hearer, Knower.

But he who feareth from a testator some unjust or sinful clause, and maketh peace between the parties, (it shall be) no sin for him. Lo! Allah is Forgiving, Merciful.

2:180–182

2. (In the case of) those of you who are about to die and leave behind them wives, they should bequeath unto their wives a provision for the year without turning them out, but if they go out (of their own accord) there is no sin for you in that which they do of themselves within their rights. Allah is Mighty, Wise.

2:240

3. O ye who believe! Let there be witnesses between you when death draweth nigh unto one of you, at the time of bequest—two witnesses, just men from among you, or two others from another tribe in case ye are compaign-

1. كُتِبَ عَلَيْكُمْ إِذَا حَضَرَ أَحَدَكُمُ الْمَوْتُ
إِنْ تَرَكَ خَيْرًا ۖۚ الْوَصِيَّةُ لِلْوَالِدَيْنِ وَالْأَقْرَبِينَ
بِالْمَعْرُوفِ ۚ حَقًّا عَلَى الْمُتَّقِينَ ﴿١٨٠﴾

فَمَنْ بَدَّلَهُ بَعْدَ مَا سَمِعَهُ فَإِنَّمَا إِثْمُهُ
عَلَى الَّذِينَ يُبَدِّلُونَهُ ۚ إِنَّ اللَّهَ سَمِيعٌ عَلِيمٌ ﴿١٨١﴾

فَمَنْ خَافَ مِنْ مُوصٍ جَنَفًا أَوْ إِثْمًا فَأَصْلَحَ
بَيْنَهُمْ فَلَا إِثْمَ عَلَيْهِ ۚ إِنَّ اللَّهَ غَفُورٌ رَحِيمٌ ﴿١٨٢﴾

2. وَالَّذِينَ يُتَوَفَّوْنَ مِنْكُمْ وَيَذَرُونَ
أَزْوَاجًا ۖۚ وَصِيَّةً لِأَزْوَاجِهِمْ مَتَاعًا إِلَى
الْحَوْلِ غَيْرَ إِخْرَاجٍ ۚ فَإِنْ خَرَجْنَ فَلَا
جُنَاحَ عَلَيْكُمْ فِي مَا فَعَلْنَ فِي أَنْفُسِهِنَّ
مِنْ مَعْرُوفٍ ۗ وَاللَّهُ عَزِيزٌ حَكِيمٌ ﴿٢٤٠﴾

3. يَا أَيُّهَا الَّذِينَ آمَنُوا شَهَادَةُ بَيْنِكُمْ إِذَا
حَضَرَ أَحَدَكُمُ الْمَوْتُ حِينَ الْوَصِيَّةِ
اثْنَانِ ذَوَا عَدْلٍ مِنْكُمْ أَوْ آخَرَانِ مِنْ
غَيْرِكُمْ إِنْ أَنْتُمْ ضَرَبْتُمْ فِي الْأَرْضِ
فَأَصَابَتْكُمْ مُصِيبَةُ الْمَوْتِ ۚ تَحْبِسُونَهُمَا
مِنْ بَعْدِ الصَّلَاةِ فَيُقْسِمَانِ بِاللَّهِ إِنِ
ارْتَبْتُمْ لَا نَشْتَرِي بِهِ ثَمَنًا وَلَوْ كَانَ ذَا
قُرْبَىٰ ۙ وَلَا نَكْتُمُ شَهَادَةَ اللَّهِ إِنَّا إِذًا
لَمِنَ الْآثِمِينَ ﴿١٠٦﴾

ing in the land and the calamity of death befall you. Ye shall empanel them both after the prayer, and, if ye doubt, they shall be made to swear by Allah (saying): We will not take a bribe, even though it were (on behalf of) a near kinsman nor will we hide the testimony of Allah, for then indeed we should be of the sinful.

But then, if it is after–wards ascertained that both of them merit (the suspicion of) sin, let two others take their place of those nearly con–cerned, and let them swear by Allah, (saying): Verily our testimony is truer than their testimony and we have not transgressed (the bounds of duty), for then indeed we should be of the evil–doers.

Thus it is more likely that they will bear true witness or fear that after their oaths the oaths (of others) will be taken. So be mindful of your duty (to Allah) and hearken. Allah guideth not the froward folk,

5:106–108

فَإِنْ عُثِرَ عَلَىٰٓ أَنَّهُمَا اسْتَحَقَّآ إِثْمًا فَـَٔاخَرٰنِ
يَقُومٰنِ مَقَامَهُمَا مِنَ الَّذِينَ اسْتَحَقَّ
عَلَيْهِمُ الْأَوْلَيٰنِ فَيُقْسِمٰنِ بِاللَّهِ لَشَهٰدَتُنَآ
أَحَقُّ مِنْ شَهٰدَتِهِمَا وَمَا اعْتَدَيْنَآ إِنَّآ
إِذًا لَّمِنَ الظّٰلِمِينَ ﴿١٠٧﴾
ذٰلِكَ أَدْنَىٰٓ أَنْ يَأْتُوا بِالشَّهٰدَةِ عَلَىٰ وَجْهِهَآ
أَوْ يَخَافُوٓا أَنْ تُرَدَّ أَيْمٰنٌۢ بَعْدَ أَيْمٰنِهِمْ ۗ وَاتَّقُوا
اللَّهَ وَاسْمَعُوا ۗ وَاللَّهُ لَا يَهْدِى الْقَوْمَ
الْفٰسِقِينَ ﴿١٠٨﴾

WINDS

1. And He it is Who sendeth the winds as tidings heralding His mercy, till, when they bear a cloud heavy (with rain), We lead it to a dead land, and then cause water to descend thereon and thereby bring forth fruits of every kind. Thus bring We forth the dead. Haply ye may remember.

7:57

2. He it is Who maketh you to go on the land and the sea till, when ye are in the ships and they sail with them with a fair breeze and they are glad therein, a storm-wind reacheth them and the wave cometh unto them from every side and they deem that they are overwhelmed therein; (then) they cry unto Allah, making their faith pure for Him only: If Thou deliver us from this, we truly will be of the thankful.

10:22

3. And We send the winds fertilising, and cause water to descend from the sky, and give it you to drink. It is not ye who are the holders of the store thereof.

15:22

4. And He it is Who sendeth the winds, glad tidings heralding His mercy, and We send down purifying water from the sky.

25:48

1. وَهُوَ الَّذِىۡ يُرۡسِلُ الرِّيٰحَ بُشۡرًاۢ بَيۡنَ
يَدَىۡ رَحۡمَتِهٖ ؕ حَتّٰۤى اِذَاۤ اَقَلَّتۡ سَحَابًا ثِقَالًا
سُقۡنٰهُ لِبَلَدٍ مَّيِّتٍ فَاَنۡزَلۡنَا بِهِ الۡمَآءَ
فَاَخۡرَجۡنَا بِهٖ مِنۡ كُلِّ الثَّمَرٰتِ ؕ كَذٰلِكَ
نُخۡرِجُ الۡمَوۡتٰى لَعَلَّكُمۡ تَذَكَّرُوۡنَ ﴿٥٧﴾

2. هُوَ الَّذِىۡ يُسَيِّرُكُمۡ فِى الۡبَرِّ وَالۡبَحۡرِ ؕ حَتّٰۤى
اِذَا كُنۡتُمۡ فِى الۡفُلۡكِ ۚ وَجَرَيۡنَ بِهِمۡ بِرِيۡحٍ
طَيِّبَةٍ وَّفَرِحُوۡا بِهَا جَآءَتۡهَا رِيۡحٌ عَاصِفٌ
وَّجَآءَهُمُ الۡمَوۡجُ مِنۡ كُلِّ مَكَانٍ وَّظَنُّوۡۤا
اَنَّهُمۡ اُحِيۡطَ بِهِمۡ ۙ دَعَوُا اللّٰهَ مُخۡلِصِيۡنَ
لَهُ الدِّيۡنَ ۚ لَئِنۡ اَنۡجَيۡتَنَا مِنۡ هٰذِهٖ
لَنَكُوۡنَنَّ مِنَ الشّٰكِرِيۡنَ ﴿٢٢﴾

3. وَاَرۡسَلۡنَا الرِّيٰحَ لَوَاقِحَ فَاَنۡزَلۡنَا مِنَ
السَّمَآءِ مَآءً فَاَسۡقَيۡنٰكُمُوۡهُ ۚ وَمَاۤ اَنۡتُمۡ
لَهٗ بِخٰزِنِيۡنَ ﴿٢٢﴾

4. وَهُوَ الَّذِىۡۤ اَرۡسَلَ الرِّيٰحَ بُشۡرًاۢ
بَيۡنَ يَدَىۡ رَحۡمَتِهٖ ۚ وَاَنۡزَلۡنَا مِنَ
السَّمَآءِ مَآءً طَهُوۡرًا ۙ ﴿٤٨﴾

5. وَمِنۡ اٰيٰتِهٖۤ اَنۡ يُّرۡسِلَ الرِّيٰحَ
مُبَشِّرٰتٍ وَّلِيُذِيۡقَكُمۡ مِّنۡ رَّحۡمَتِهٖ
وَلِتَجۡرِىَ الۡفُلۡكُ بِاَمۡرِهٖ وَلِتَبۡتَغُوۡا
مِنۡ فَضۡلِهٖ وَلَعَلَّكُمۡ تَشۡكُرُوۡنَ ﴿٤٦﴾

5. And of His signs is this: He sendeth herald winds to make you taste His mercy, and that the ships may sail at His command, and that ye may seek His favour and that haply ye may be thankful.

30:46

6. O ye who believe! Remember Allah's favour unto you when there came against you hosts, and We sent against them a great wind and hosts ye could not see. And Allah is ever Seer of what ye do.

33:9

7. And Allah it is Who sendeth the winds and they raise a cloud; then We lead it unto a dead land and revive therewith the earth after its death. (Such is the Resurrection).

35:9

8. And of His portents are the ships, like banners on the sea;

If He will He calmeth the wind so that they keep still upon its surface—Lo! herein verily are signs for every steadfast grateful (Heart):—

42:32–33

9. And as for 'Aâd, they were destroyed by a fierce roaring wind,

Which He imposed on them for seven long nights and eight long days so that thou mightest have seen men lying overthrown, as they were hollow trunks of palm-trees.

Canst thou (O Muhammad) see any remnant of them?

69:6–8

6. يٰٓاَيُّهَا الَّذِيْنَ اٰمَنُوا اذْكُرُوْا نِعْمَةَ اللّٰهِ
عَلَيْكُمْ اِذْ جَآءَتْكُمْ جُنُوْدٌ فَاَرْسَلْنَا
عَلَيْهِمْ رِيْحًا وَّجُنُوْدًا لَّمْ تَرَوْهَا ۚ وَ
كَانَ اللّٰهُ بِمَا تَعْمَلُوْنَ بَصِيْرًا ۝٩

7. وَاللّٰهُ الَّذِيْٓ اَرْسَلَ الرِّيٰحَ فَتُثِيْرُ
سَحَابًا فَسُقْنٰهُ اِلٰى بَلَدٍ مَّيِّتٍ فَاَحْيَيْنَا
بِهِ الْاَرْضَ بَعْدَ مَوْتِهَا ۚ كَذٰلِكَ النُّشُوْرُ ۝٩

8. وَمِنْ اٰيٰتِهِ الْجَوَارِ فِي الْبَحْرِ كَالْاَعْلَامِ ۝٣٢
اِنْ يَّشَاْ يُسْكِنِ الرِّيْحَ فَيَظْلَلْنَ رَوَاكِدَ
عَلٰى ظَهْرِهٖ ۚ اِنَّ فِيْ ذٰلِكَ لَاٰيٰتٍ لِّكُلِّ
صَبَّارٍ شَكُوْرٍ ۝٣٣

9. وَاَمَّا عَادٌ فَاُهْلِكُوْا بِرِيْحٍ صَرْصَرٍ
عَاتِيَةٍ ۝٦
سَخَّرَهَا عَلَيْهِمْ سَبْعَ لَيَالٍ وَّثَمٰنِيَةَ
اَيَّامٍ ۙ حُسُوْمًا ۙ فَتَرَى الْقَوْمَ فِيْهَا
صَرْعٰى ۙ كَاَنَّهُمْ اَعْجَازُ نَخْلٍ خَاوِيَةٍ ۝٧
فَهَلْ تَرٰى لَهُمْ مِّنْ بَاقِيَةٍ ۝٨

○

Ref: 3:117; 14:18; 18:46; 21:81; 22:31; 27:63; 30:48,51; 34:12; 38:37; 45:5; 46:24–25; 54:19–20.

WINE

1. They question thee about strong drink and games of chance. Say: In both is great sin, and (some) utility for men; but the sin of them is greater than their usefulness.

2:219

2. O ye who believe! Strong drink and games of chance and idols and divining arrows are only an infamy of Satan's handiwork. Leave it aside in order that ye may succeed.

Satan seeketh only to cast among you enmity and hatred by means of strong drink and games of chance, and to turn you from remembrance of Allah and from (His) worship. Will ye then have done?

5:90–91

1. يَسْـَٔلُونَكَ عَنِ الْخَمْرِ وَالْمَيْسِرِ ۖ قُلْ
فِيهِمَآ إِثْمٌ كَبِيرٌ وَمَنَٰفِعُ لِلنَّاسِ وَإِثْمُهُمَآ
أَكْبَرُ مِن نَّفْعِهِمَا ۗ

2. يَٰٓأَيُّهَا الَّذِينَ ءَامَنُوٓا إِنَّمَا الْخَمْرُ وَالْمَيْسِرُ
وَالْأَنصَابُ وَالْأَزْلَٰمُ رِجْسٌ مِّنْ عَمَلِ
الشَّيْطَٰنِ فَاجْتَنِبُوهُ لَعَلَّكُمْ تُفْلِحُونَ ۝٩٠
إِنَّمَا يُرِيدُ الشَّيْطَٰنُ أَن يُوقِعَ بَيْنَكُمُ الْعَدَٰوَةَ
وَالْبَغْضَآءَ فِي الْخَمْرِ وَالْمَيْسِرِ وَيَصُدَّكُمْ
عَن ذِكْرِ اللَّهِ وَعَنِ الصَّلَوٰةِ ۖ فَهَلْ
أَنتُم مُّنتَهُونَ ۝٩١

See also: Intoxication

WISDOM

1. وَاذْكُرُوْا نِعْمَتَ اللّٰهِ عَلَيْكُمْ وَمَآ اَنْزَلَ
عَلَيْكُمْ مِّنَ الْكِتٰبِ وَالْحِكْمَةِ يَعِظُكُمْ
بِهٖ ۗ وَاتَّقُوا اللّٰهَ وَاعْلَمُوْٓا اَنَّ اللّٰهَ بِكُلِّ
شَيْءٍ عَلِيْمٌ ﴿٢٣١﴾

2. يُّؤْتِي الْحِكْمَةَ مَنْ يَّشَآءُ ۚ وَمَنْ يُّؤْتَ الْحِكْمَةَ فَقَدْ
اُوْتِيَ خَيْرًا كَثِيْرًا ۗ وَمَا يَذَّكَّرُ اِلَّآ اُولُوا الْاَلْبَابِ ﴿٢٦٩﴾

3. لَقَدْ مَنَّ اللّٰهُ عَلَى الْمُؤْمِنِيْنَ اِذْ بَعَثَ
فِيْهِمْ رَسُوْلًا مِّنْ اَنْفُسِهِمْ يَتْلُوْا عَلَيْهِمْ
اٰيٰتِهٖ وَيُزَكِّيْهِمْ وَيُعَلِّمُهُمُ الْكِتٰبَ
وَالْحِكْمَةَ ۚ وَاِنْ كَانُوْا مِنْ قَبْلُ
لَفِيْ ضَلٰلٍ مُّبِيْنٍ ﴿١٦٤﴾

4. وَاَنْزَلَ اللّٰهُ عَلَيْكَ الْكِتٰبَ وَالْحِكْمَةَ
وَعَلَّمَكَ مَا لَمْ تَكُنْ تَعْلَمُ ۗ وَكَانَ
فَضْلُ اللّٰهِ عَلَيْكَ عَظِيْمًا ﴿١١٣﴾

5. اُدْعُ اِلٰى سَبِيْلِ رَبِّكَ بِالْحِكْمَةِ وَالْمَوْعِظَةِ
الْحَسَنَةِ وَجَادِلْهُمْ بِالَّتِيْ هِيَ اَحْسَنُ ۗ اِنَّ
رَبَّكَ هُوَ اَعْلَمُ بِمَنْ ضَلَّ عَنْ سَبِيْلِهٖ
وَهُوَ اَعْلَمُ بِالْمُهْتَدِيْنَ ﴿١٢٥﴾

6. وَاذْكُرْنَ مَا يُتْلٰى فِيْ بُيُوْتِكُنَّ مِنْ
اٰيٰتِ اللّٰهِ وَالْحِكْمَةِ ۗ اِنَّ اللّٰهَ كَانَ
لَطِيْفًا خَبِيْرًا ﴿٣٤﴾

1. And remember Allah's grace upon you and that which He hath revealed unto you of the Scripture and of wisdom, whereby He doth exhort you. Observe your duty to Allah and know that Allah is Aware of all things.

2:231

2. He giveth wisdom unto whom He will, and he unto whom wisdom is given, he truly hath received abundant good. But none remember except men of understanding.

2:269

3. Allah verily hath shown grace to the believers by sending unto them a messenger of their own who reciteth unto them His revelations, and causeth them to grow, and teacheth them the Scripture and wisdom; although before (he came to them) they were in flagrant error.

3:164

4. Allah revealeth unto thee the Scripture and wisdom, and teacheth thee that which thou knewest not. The grace of Allah toward thee hath been infinite.

4:113

5. Call unto the way of thy Lord with wisdom and fair exhortation, and reason with them in the better way. Lo! thy Lord is Best Aware of him who strayeth from His way, and He is Best Aware of those who go aright.

16:125

6. And bear in mind that which is recited in your houses of the revelations of Allah and wisdom. Lo! Allah is Subtile, Aware.

33:34

Ref: 31:12; 38:20; 54:5.

See also: Knowledge, Jurisprudence.

WOMEN

1. Your women are a tilth for you (to cultivate) so go to your tilth as ye will, and send (good deeds) before you for your souls, and fear Allah, and know that ye will (one day) meet Him. Give glad tidings to believers, (O Muhammad).

2:223

2. And call to witness, from among your men, two witnesses. And if two men be not (at hand) then a man and two women, of such as ye approve as witnesses, so that if the one erreth (through forgetfulness) the other will remember.

2:282

3. And their Lord hath heard them (and He saith): Lo! I suffer not the work of any worker, male or female, to be lost. Ye proceed one from another.

3:195

4. O mankind! Be careful of your duty to your Lord Who created you from a single soul and from it created its mate and from them twain hath spread abroad a multitude of men and women. Be careful of your duty toward Allah in Whom ye claim (your rights) of one another, and toward the wombs (that bore you). Lo! Allah hath been a Watcher over you.

4:1

5. Men are in charge of

1. نِسَآؤُكُمْ حَرْثٌ لَّكُمْ فَأْتُوا حَرْثَكُمْ أَنَّىٰ
شِئْتُمْ وَقَدِّمُوا لِأَنفُسِكُمْ ۚ وَاتَّقُوا اللَّهَ
وَاعْلَمُوا أَنَّكُم مُّلَاقُوهُ ۗ وَبَشِّرِ الْمُؤْمِنِينَ ﴿٢٢٣﴾

2. وَاسْتَشْهِدُوا شَهِيدَيْنِ مِن رِّجَالِكُمْ ۖ فَإِن لَّمْ يَكُونَا
رَجُلَيْنِ فَرَجُلٌ وَامْرَأَتَانِ مِمَّن تَرْضَوْنَ مِنَ الشُّهَدَاءِ
أَن تَضِلَّ إِحْدَاهُمَا فَتُذَكِّرَ إِحْدَاهُمَا الْأُخْرَىٰ

3. فَاسْتَجَابَ لَهُمْ رَبُّهُمْ أَنِّي لَا أُضِيعُ عَمَلَ عَامِلٍ
مِّنكُم مِّن ذَكَرٍ أَوْ أُنثَىٰ ۖ بَعْضُكُم مِّن بَعْضٍ ۖ

4. يَا أَيُّهَا النَّاسُ اتَّقُوا رَبَّكُمُ الَّذِي
خَلَقَكُم مِّن نَّفْسٍ وَاحِدَةٍ وَخَلَقَ مِنْهَا
زَوْجَهَا وَبَثَّ مِنْهُمَا رِجَالًا كَثِيرًا وَنِسَاءً ۚ
وَاتَّقُوا اللَّهَ الَّذِي تَسَاءَلُونَ بِهِ وَالْأَرْحَامَ ۚ
إِنَّ اللَّهَ كَانَ عَلَيْكُمْ رَقِيبًا ﴿١﴾

5. الرِّجَالُ قَوَّامُونَ عَلَى النِّسَاءِ بِمَا فَضَّلَ
اللَّهُ بَعْضَهُمْ عَلَىٰ بَعْضٍ وَبِمَا أَنفَقُوا مِنْ
أَمْوَالِهِمْ ۚ فَالصَّالِحَاتُ قَانِتَاتٌ حَافِظَاتٌ لِّلْغَيْبِ
بِمَا حَفِظَ اللَّهُ ۚ وَاللَّاتِي تَخَافُونَ نُشُوزَهُنَّ
فَعِظُوهُنَّ وَاهْجُرُوهُنَّ فِي الْمَضَاجِعِ
وَاضْرِبُوهُنَّ ۖ فَإِنْ أَطَعْنَكُمْ فَلَا تَبْغُوا
عَلَيْهِنَّ سَبِيلًا ۗ إِنَّ اللَّهَ كَانَ
عَلِيًّا كَبِيرًا ﴿٣٤﴾

6. وَإِنِ امْرَأَةٌ خَافَتْ مِن بَعْلِهَا نُشُوزًا أَوْ إِعْرَاضًا
فَلَا جُنَاحَ عَلَيْهِمَا أَن يُصْلِحَا بَيْنَهُمَا صُلْحًا ۚ وَالصُّلْحُ

women, because Allah hath made the one of them to excel the other, and because they spend of their property (for the support of women). So good women are the obedient, guarding in secret that which Allah hath guarded. As for those from whom ye fear rebellion, admonish them and banish them to beds apart, and scourge them.

Then if they obey you, seek not a way against them. Lo! Allah is ever High, Exalted, Great.

4:34

6. If a woman feareth ill–treatment from her husband, or desertion, it is no sin for them twain if they make terms of peace between themselves. Peace is better. But greed hath been made present in the minds (of men). If ye do good and keep from evil, lo! Allah is ever Informed of what ye do.

Ye will not be able to deal equally between (your) wives, however much ye wish (to do so). But turn not altogether away (from one), leaving her as in suspense. If ye do good and keep from evil, lo! Allah is ever Forgiving, Merciful.

4:128–129

7. Allah promiseth to the believers, men and women, Gardens underneath which rivers flow, wherein they will abide–blessed dwellings in Gardens of Eden. And – greater (far)! – acceptance from Allah. That is the Supreme triumph.

9:72

8. Whosoever doeth right, whether male or female, and is a believer, him verily We shall quicken with good life, and We shall pay them a recompense in proportion to the best of what they used to do.

16:97

خَيْرٌ وَأُحْضِرَتِ الْأَنْفُسُ الشُّحَّ وَإِنْ تُحْسِنُوا وَ
تَتَّقُوا فَإِنَّ اللَّهَ كَانَ بِمَا تَعْمَلُونَ خَبِيرًا ۝
وَلَنْ تَسْتَطِيعُوا أَنْ تَعْدِلُوا بَيْنَ النِّسَاءِ
وَلَوْ حَرَصْتُمْ فَلَا تَمِيلُوا كُلَّ الْمَيْلِ
فَتَذَرُوهَا كَالْمُعَلَّقَةِ وَإِنْ تُصْلِحُوا وَتَتَّقُوا
فَإِنَّ اللَّهَ كَانَ غَفُورًا رَحِيمًا ۝

7. وَعَدَ اللَّهُ الْمُؤْمِنِينَ وَالْمُؤْمِنَاتِ جَنَّاتٍ
تَجْرِي مِنْ تَحْتِهَا الْأَنْهَارُ خَالِدِينَ فِيهَا
وَمَسَاكِنَ طَيِّبَةً فِي جَنَّاتِ عَدْنٍ وَرِضْوَانٌ
مِنَ اللَّهِ أَكْبَرُ ذَٰلِكَ هُوَ الْفَوْزُ الْعَظِيمُ ۝

8. مَنْ عَمِلَ صَالِحًا مِنْ ذَكَرٍ أَوْ أُنْثَىٰ
وَهُوَ مُؤْمِنٌ فَلَنُحْيِيَنَّهُ حَيَاةً طَيِّبَةً
وَلَنَجْزِيَنَّهُمْ أَجْرَهُمْ بِأَحْسَنِ مَا
كَانُوا يَعْمَلُونَ ۝

9. وَمِنْ آيَاتِهِ أَنْ خَلَقَ لَكُمْ مِنْ أَنْفُسِكُمْ
أَزْوَاجًا لِتَسْكُنُوا إِلَيْهَا وَجَعَلَ بَيْنَكُمْ
مَوَدَّةً وَرَحْمَةً إِنَّ فِي ذَٰلِكَ لَآيَاتٍ
لِقَوْمٍ يَتَفَكَّرُونَ ۝

10. وَيُعَذِّبَ الْمُنَافِقِينَ وَالْمُنَافِقَاتِ وَ
الْمُشْرِكِينَ وَالْمُشْرِكَاتِ الظَّانِّينَ
بِاللَّهِ ظَنَّ السَّوْءِ عَلَيْهِمْ دَائِرَةُ السَّوْءِ
وَغَضِبَ اللَّهُ عَلَيْهِمْ وَلَعَنَهُمْ وَأَعَدَّ
لَهُمْ جَهَنَّمَ وَسَاءَتْ مَصِيرًا ۝

9. And of His signs is this: He created for you helpmates from yourselves that ye might find rest in them, and He ordained between you love and mercy. Lo, herein indeed are portents for folk who reflect.

30:21

10. And may punish the hypocritical men and the hypocritical women, and the idolatrous men and the idolatrous women, who think an evil thought concerning Allah. For them is the evil turn of fortune, and Allah is wroth against them and hath cursed them, and hath made ready for them hell, a hapless journey's end.

48:6

WOMEN OF PROHIBITED DEGREE

1. Wed not idolatresses till they believe; for lo! a believing bondwoman is better than an idolatress though she please you; and give not your daughters in marriage to idolaters till they believe, for lo! a believing slave is better than an idolater though he please you. These invite unto the Fire, and Allah inviteth unto the Garden, and unto forgiveness by His grace, and expoundeth thus His revelations to mankind that haply they may remember.

2:221

2. And marry not those women whom your fathers married, except what hath already happened (of that nature) in the past. Lo! it was ever lewdness and abomination, and an evil way.

Forbidden unto you are your mothers, and your daughters, and your sisters, and your father's sisters, and your mother's sisters, and your brother's daughters

1. وَلَا تَنْكِحُوا الْمُشْرِكٰتِ حَتّٰى يُؤْمِنَّ ؕ وَلَاَمَةٌ
مُّؤْمِنَةٌ خَيْرٌ مِّنْ مُّشْرِكَةٍ وَّلَوْ اَعْجَبَتْكُمْ ۚ
وَلَا تُنْكِحُوا الْمُشْرِكِيْنَ حَتّٰى يُؤْمِنُوْا ؕ وَلَعَبْدٌ
مُّؤْمِنٌ خَيْرٌ مِّنْ مُّشْرِكٍ وَّلَوْ اَعْجَبَكُمْ ؕ اُولٰٓئِكَ
يَدْعُوْنَ اِلَى النَّارِ ۖۚ وَاللّٰهُ يَدْعُوْٓا اِلَى الْجَنَّةِ
وَالْمَغْفِرَةِ بِاِذْنِهٖ ۚ وَيُبَيِّنُ اٰيٰتِهٖ لِلنَّاسِ
لَعَلَّهُمْ يَتَذَكَّرُوْنَ ﴿۲۲۱﴾

2. وَلَا تَنْكِحُوْا مَا نَكَحَ اٰبَآؤُكُمْ مِّنَ النِّسَآءِ اِلَّا
مَا قَدْ سَلَفَ ؕ اِنَّهٗ كَانَ فَاحِشَةً
وَّمَقْتًا ؕ وَسَآءَ سَبِيْلًا ﴿۲۲﴾
حُرِّمَتْ عَلَيْكُمْ اُمَّهٰتُكُمْ وَبَنٰتُكُمْ وَاَخَوٰتُكُمْ
وَعَمّٰتُكُمْ وَخٰلٰتُكُمْ وَبَنٰتُ الْاَخِ وَبَنٰتُ
الْاُخْتِ وَاُمَّهٰتُكُمُ الّٰتِیْٓ اَرْضَعْنَكُمْ وَاَخَوٰتُكُمْ
مِّنَ الرَّضَاعَةِ وَاُمَّهٰتُ نِسَآئِكُمْ وَرَبَآئِبُكُمُ
الّٰتِیْ فِیْ حُجُوْرِكُمْ مِّنْ نِّسَآئِكُمُ الّٰتِیْ
دَخَلْتُمْ بِهِنَّ ؗ فَاِنْ لَّمْ تَكُوْنُوْا دَخَلْتُمْ
بِهِنَّ فَلَا جُنَاحَ عَلَيْكُمْ ؗ وَحَلَآئِلُ
اَبْنَآئِكُمُ الَّذِيْنَ مِنْ اَصْلَابِكُمْ ۙ وَاَنْ
تَجْمَعُوْا بَيْنَ الْاُخْتَيْنِ اِلَّا مَا قَدْ سَلَفَ ؕ
اِنَّ اللّٰهَ كَانَ غَفُوْرًا رَّحِيْمًا ﴿۲۳﴾
وَّالْمُحْصَنٰتُ مِنَ النِّسَآءِ اِلَّا مَا مَلَكَتْ
اَيْمَانُكُمْ ۚ كِتٰبَ اللّٰهِ عَلَيْكُمْ ۚ

3 اَلزَّانِيَةُ وَالزَّانِیْ فَاجْلِدُوْا كُلَّ

and your sister's daughters, and your foster-mothers, and your foster-sisters, and your mothers-in-law, and your step-daughters who are under your protection (born) of your women unto whom ye have gone in—but if ye have not gone in unto them, then it is no sin for you (to marry their daughters)— and the wives of your sons who (spring) from your own loins. And (it is forbidden unto you) that ye should have two sisters together, except what hath already happened (of that nature) in the past. Lo! Allah is ever Forgiving, Merciful.

And all married women (are forbidden) unto you save those (captives) whom your right hands possess. It is a decree of Allah for you.

4:22–24

3. The adulterer and the adulteress, scourge ye each one of them (with) a hundred stripes, and let not pity for the twain withhold you from obedience to Allah, if ye believe in Allah and the Last Day. And let a party of believers witness their punishment.

24:2

WOMEN PERMISSIBLE TO MARRY

1. This day are (all) good things made lawful for you. The food of those who have received the Scripture is lawful for you, and your food is lawful for them. And so are the virtuous women of the believers and the virtuous women of those who received the Scripture before you (lawful for you) when ye give them their marriage portions and live with them in honour, not in fornication, nor taking them as secret concubines. Whoso denieth the faith, his work is vain and he will be among the losers in the Hereafter.

5:5

وَاحِدٍ مِّنْهُمَا مِائَةَ جَلْدَةٍ ۖ وَّلَا
تَأْخُذْكُمْ بِهِمَا رَأْفَةٌ فِي دِينِ اللَّهِ
إِنْ كُنْتُمْ تُؤْمِنُونَ بِاللَّهِ وَالْيَوْمِ
الْآخِرِ ۖ وَلْيَشْهَدْ عَذَابَهُمَا طَائِفَةٌ
مِّنَ الْمُؤْمِنِينَ ﴿٢﴾

1. الْيَوْمَ أُحِلَّ لَكُمُ الطَّيِّبَاتُ ۖ وَطَعَامُ الَّذِينَ أُوتُوا
الْكِتَابَ حِلٌّ لَّكُمْ وَطَعَامُكُمْ حِلٌّ لَّهُمْ ۖ وَالْمُحْصَنَاتُ
مِنَ الْمُؤْمِنَاتِ وَالْمُحْصَنَاتُ مِنَ الَّذِينَ أُوتُوا
الْكِتَابَ مِنْ قَبْلِكُمْ إِذَا آتَيْتُمُوهُنَّ أُجُورَهُنَّ
مُحْصِنِينَ غَيْرَ مُسَافِحِينَ وَلَا مُتَّخِذِي أَخْدَانٍ ۗ
وَمَنْ يَكْفُرْ بِالْإِيمَانِ فَقَدْ حَبِطَ عَمَلُهُ وَهُوَ
فِي الْآخِرَةِ مِنَ الْخَاسِرِينَ ﴿٥﴾

WOMEN PERMISSIBLE TO MARRY

See also: Women of Prohibited Degree.

WORLDLY LIFE

1. Naught is the life of the world save a pastime and a sport. Better far is the abode of the Hereafter for those who keep their duty (to Allah). Have ye, then no sense?

6:32

2. The similitude of the life of the world is only as water which We send down from the sky, then the earth's growth of that which men and cattle eat mingleth with it till, when the earth hath taken on her ornaments and is embellished, and her people deem that they are masters of her, Our commandment cometh by night or by day and We make it as reaped corn as if it had not flourished yesterday. Thus do We expound the revelations for people who reflect.

10:24

3. Whoso desireth the life of the world and its pomp, We shall repay them their deeds herein, and therein they will not be wronged.

Those are they for whom is naught in the Hereafter save the Fire. (All) that they contrive here is vain and (all) that they are wont to do is fruitless.

11:15–16

4. And coin for them the similitude of the life of the world as water which We send down from the sky, and the vegetation of the earth mingleth with it and then becometh dry twigs that the winds scatter. Allah is Able to do all things.

18:46

1. وَمَا الْحَيٰوةُ الدُّنْيَآ اِلَّا لَعِبٌ وَّلَهْوٌ ۗ وَلَلدَّارُ
الْاٰخِرَةُ خَيْرٌ لِّلَّذِيْنَ يَتَّقُوْنَ ۗ اَفَلَا تَعْقِلُوْنَ ﴿٣٢﴾

2. اِنَّمَا مَثَلُ الْحَيٰوةِ الدُّنْيَا كَمَآءٍ اَنْزَلْنٰهُ
مِنَ السَّمَآءِ فَاخْتَلَطَ بِهٖ نَبَاتُ الْاَرْضِ
مِمَّا يَاْكُلُ النَّاسُ وَالْاَنْعَامُ ۗ حَتّٰٓى
اِذَآ اَخَذَتِ الْاَرْضُ زُخْرُفَهَا وَازَّيَّنَتْ
وَظَنَّ اَهْلُهَآ اَنَّهُمْ قٰدِرُوْنَ عَلَيْهَآ ۙ اَتٰىهَآ
اَمْرُنَا لَيْلًا اَوْ نَهَارًا فَجَعَلْنٰهَا حَصِيْدًا
كَاَنْ لَّمْ تَغْنَ بِالْاَمْسِ ۗ كَذٰلِكَ نُفَصِّلُ
الْاٰيٰتِ لِقَوْمٍ يَّتَفَكَّرُوْنَ ﴿٢٤﴾

3. مَنْ كَانَ يُرِيْدُ الْحَيٰوةَ الدُّنْيَا وَزِيْنَتَهَا
نُوَفِّ اِلَيْهِمْ اَعْمَالَهُمْ فِيْهَا وَهُمْ
فِيْهَا لَا يُبْخَسُوْنَ ﴿١٥﴾
اُولٰٓئِكَ الَّذِيْنَ لَيْسَ لَهُمْ فِي الْاٰخِرَةِ
اِلَّا النَّارُ ۖ وَحَبِطَ مَا صَنَعُوْا فِيْهَا
وَبٰطِلٌ مَّا كَانُوْا يَعْمَلُوْنَ ﴿١٦﴾

4. وَاضْرِبْ لَهُمْ مَّثَلَ الْحَيٰوةِ الدُّنْيَا كَمَآءٍ
اَنْزَلْنٰهُ مِنَ السَّمَآءِ فَاخْتَلَطَ بِهٖ نَبَاتُ
الْاَرْضِ فَاَصْبَحَ هَشِيْمًا تَذْرُوْهُ الرِّيٰحُ ۗ
وَكَانَ اللّٰهُ عَلٰى كُلِّ شَيْءٍ مُّقْتَدِرًا ﴿٤٥﴾

5. وَمَا هٰذِهِ الْحَيٰوةُ الدُّنْيَآ اِلَّا لَهْوٌ وَّ
لَعِبٌ ۗ وَاِنَّ الدَّارَ الْاٰخِرَةَ لَهِيَ

5. This life of the world is but a pastime and a game. Lo! the home of the Hereafter—that is Life, if they but knew.

29:64

6. Know that the life of this world is only play, and idle talk, and pageantry, and boasting among you, and rivalry in respect of wealth and children as the likeness of vegetation after rain, whereof the growth is pleasing to the husbandman, but afterward it drieth up and thou seest it turning yellow, then it becometh straw. And in the Hereafter there is grievous punishment, and (also) forgiveness from Allah and His good pleasure, whereas the life of the world is but matter of illusion.

57:20

7. And Allah hath caused you to grow as a growth from the earth,

And afterward He maketh you return thereto, and He will bring you forth again, a (new) forthbringing.

71:17–18

الْحَيَوَانُ لَوْ كَانُوْا يَعْلَمُوْنَ ﴿٦٤﴾

6. اِعْلَمُوْٓا اَنَّمَا الْحَيٰوةُ الدُّنْيَا لَعِبٌ وَّ
لَهْوٌ وَّزِيْنَةٌ وَّتَفَاخُرٌۢ بَيْنَكُمْ وَ
تَكَاثُرٌ فِي الْاَمْوَالِ وَالْاَوْلَادِ كَمَثَلِ
غَيْثٍ اَعْجَبَ الْكُفَّارَ نَبَاتُهٗ ثُمَّ يَهِيْجُ
فَتَرٰىهُ مُصْفَرًّا ثُمَّ يَكُوْنُ حُطَامًا
وَفِي الْاٰخِرَةِ عَذَابٌ شَدِيْدٌ وَّمَغْفِرَةٌ
مِّنَ اللّٰهِ وَرِضْوَانٌ وَمَا الْحَيٰوةُ
الدُّنْيَآ اِلَّا مَتَاعُ الْغُرُوْرِ ۝

7. وَاللّٰهُ اَنْۢبَتَكُمْ مِّنَ الْاَرْضِ نَبَاتًا ﴿١٧﴾
ثُمَّ يُعِيْدُكُمْ فِيْهَا وَيُخْرِجُكُمْ اِخْرَاجًا ﴿١٨﴾

YOUTH

1. يٰۤاَيُّهَا النَّاسُ اِنْ كُنْتُمْ فِيْ رَيْبٍ مِّنَ
الْبَعْثِ فَاِنَّا خَلَقْنٰكُمْ مِّنْ تُرَابٍ ثُمَّ
مِنْ نُّطْفَةٍ ثُمَّ مِنْ عَلَقَةٍ ثُمَّ مِنْ
مُّضْغَةٍ مُّخَلَّقَةٍ وَّغَيْرِ مُخَلَّقَةٍ
لِّنُبَيِّنَ لَكُمْ ؕ وَنُقِرُّ فِي الْاَرْحَامِ مَا
نَشَآءُ اِلٰۤى اَجَلٍ مُّسَمًّى ثُمَّ نُخْرِجُكُمْ
طِفْلًا ثُمَّ لِتَبْلُغُوْۤا اَشُدَّكُمْ ۚ وَمِنْكُمْ
مَّنْ يُّتَوَفّٰى وَمِنْكُمْ مَّنْ يُّرَدُّ اِلٰۤى اَرْذَلِ
الْعُمُرِ لِكَيْلَا يَعْلَمَ مِنْۢ بَعْدِ عِلْمٍ شَيْـًٔا ؕ

1. O mankind! If ye are in doubt concerning the Resurrection, then lo! We have created you from dust, then from a drop of seed, then from a clot, then from a little lump of flesh shapely and shapeless, that We may make (it) clear for you. And We cause what We will to remain in the wombs for an appointed time, and afterward We bring you forth as infants, then (give you growth) that ye attain your full strength. And among you there is he who dieth (young), and among you there is he who is brought back to the most abject time of life, so that, after knowledge, he knoweth naught.

22:5

2. وَوَصَّيْنَا الْاِنْسَانَ بِوَالِدَيْهِ اِحْسٰنًا ؕ
حَمَلَتْهُ اُمُّهٗ كُرْهًا وَّوَضَعَتْهُ كُرْهًا ؕ
وَحَمْلُهٗ وَفِصٰلُهٗ ثَلٰثُوْنَ شَهْرًا ؕ حَتّٰۤى
اِذَا بَلَغَ اَشُدَّهٗ وَبَلَغَ اَرْبَعِيْنَ سَنَةً ۙ
قَالَ رَبِّ اَوْزِعْنِيْۤ اَنْ اَشْكُرَ نِعْمَتَكَ
الَّتِيْۤ اَنْعَمْتَ عَلَيَّ وَعَلٰى وَالِدَيَّ وَاَنْ
اَعْمَلَ صَالِحًا تَرْضٰىهُ وَاَصْلِحْ لِيْ
فِيْ ذُرِّيَّتِيْ ؕ اِنِّيْ تُبْتُ اِلَيْكَ وَاِنِّيْ
مِنَ الْمُسْلِمِيْنَ ۝١٥

2. And We have commended unto man kindness toward parents. His mother beareth him with reluctance, and bringeth him forth with reluctance, and the bearing of him and the weaning of him is thirty months, till, when he attaineth full strength and reacheth forty years, he saith: My Lord! Arouse me that I may give thanks for the favour wherewith Thou hast favoured me and my parents, and that I may do right acceptable unto Thee. And be gracious unto me in the matter of my seed. Lo! I have turned unto Thee repentant, and lo! I am of those who surrender (unto Thee).

46:15

Ref: 6:152; 17:34; 18:82; 40:67

ZAKAT

1. وأقيموا الصلوة وآتوا الزكوة ۚ وما تقدموا
لأنفسكم من خير تجدوه عند الله ۗ
إن الله بما تعملون بصير ﴿١١٠﴾

2. إن الذين آمنوا وعملوا الصلحت و
أقاموا الصلوة وآتوا الزكوة لهم أجرهم
عند ربهم ۚ ولا خوف عليهم ولا
هم يحزنون ﴿٢٧٧﴾

3. ورحمتي وسعت كل شيء ۚ فسأكتبها
للذين يتقون ويؤتون الزكوة والذين
هم بآيتنا يؤمنون ﴿١٥٦﴾

4. إنما يعمر مسجد الله من آمن بالله واليوم الآخر
وأقام الصلوة وآتى الزكوة ولم يخش إلا الله فعسى
أولئك أن يكونوا من المهتدين ﴿١٨﴾

5. إنما الصدقت للفقراء والمسكين
والعملين عليها والمؤلفة قلوبهم
وفي الرقاب والغرمين وفي سبيل
الله وابن السبيل ۖ فريضة من الله ۗ
والله عليم حكيم ﴿٦٠﴾

6. الذين إن مكنهم في الأرض
أقاموا الصلوة وآتوا الزكوة وأمروا
بالمعروف ونهوا عن المنكر ۗ
ولله عاقبة الأمور ﴿٤١﴾

1. Establish worship, and pay the poor–due and whatever of good ye send before (you) for your souls, ye will find it with Allah. Lo! Allah is Seer of what ye do.

2:110

2. Lo! those who believe and do good works and establish worship and pay the poor–due, their reward is with their Lord and there shall no fear come upon them neither shall they grieve.

2:277

3. And My mercy embraceth all things, therefore I shall ordain it for those who ward off (evil) and pay the poor-due, and those who believe in Our revelations.

7:156

4. He only shall tend Allah's sanctuaries who believeth in Allah and the Last Day and observeth proper worship and payeth the poor–due and feareth none save Allah. For such (only) is it possible that they can be of the rightly guided.

9:18

5. The alms are only for the poor and the needy, and those who collect them, and those whose hearts are to be reconciled, and to free the captives and the debtors, and for the cause of Allah, and (for) the wayfarer; a duty imposed by Allah. Allah is Knower, Wise.

9:60

6. Those who, if We give them power in the land, establish worship and pay the poor–due and enjoin kindness and forbid iniquity.

22:41

7. Successful indeed are the believers,
Who are humble in their prayers,
And who shun vain conversation,
And who are payers of the poor–due;
23:1–4

8. Establish worship and pay the poor–due and obey the messenger, that haply ye may find mercy.
24:56

9. That which ye give in usury in order that it may increase on (other) people's property hath no increase with Allah; but that which ye give in charity, seeking Allah's Countenance hath increase manifold.
30:39

10. And establish worship and pay the poor–due, and (so) lend unto Allah a goodly loan. Whatsoever good ye send before you for your souls, ye will find it with Allah, better and greater in the recompense. And seek forgiveness of Allah. Lo! Allah is Forgiving, Merciful.
73 : 20

7. قَدْ أَفْلَحَ الْمُؤْمِنُونَ ①
الَّذِينَ هُمْ فِي صَلَاتِهِمْ خَاشِعُونَ ②
وَالَّذِينَ هُمْ عَنِ اللَّغْوِ مُعْرِضُونَ ③
وَالَّذِينَ هُمْ لِلزَّكَوٰةِ فَاعِلُونَ ④

8. وَأَقِيمُوا الصَّلَوٰةَ وَآتُوا الزَّكَوٰةَ
وَأَطِيعُوا الرَّسُولَ لَعَلَّكُمْ تُرْحَمُونَ ٥٦

9. وَمَا آتَيْتُمْ مِنْ رِبًا لِيَرْبُوَا فِي أَمْوَالِ
النَّاسِ فَلَا يَرْبُوا عِنْدَ اللَّهِ وَمَا
آتَيْتُمْ مِنْ زَكَوٰةٍ تُرِيدُونَ وَجْهَ
اللَّهِ فَأُولَٰئِكَ هُمُ الْمُضْعِفُونَ ٣٩

10. وَأَقِيمُوا الصَّلَوٰةَ وَآتُوا الزَّكَوٰةَ
وَأَقْرِضُوا اللَّهَ قَرْضًا حَسَنًا وَمَا
تُقَدِّمُوا لِأَنْفُسِكُمْ مِنْ خَيْرٍ تَجِدُوهُ
عِنْدَ اللَّهِ هُوَ خَيْرًا وَأَعْظَمَ أَجْرًا
وَاسْتَغْفِرُوا اللَّهَ إِنَّ اللَّهَ غَفُورٌ رَحِيمٌ ٢٠

Ref: 2:43,83,110,177,277; 4:77,162; 5:12,55; 7:156; 9:5,11,18,71; 19:31,55; 21:73; 22:41,78; 23:4; 24:56; 27:3; 30:39; 31:4; 33:33; 41:7; 58:13; 73:20; 98:5. **See also: Alms, Charity**

ZAQQUM

1. Is this better as a welcome, or the tree of Zaqqûm?
Lo! We have appointed it a torment for wrongdoers.
Lo! it is a tree that springeth in the heart of hell,
Its crop is as it were the heads of devils!
And lo! they verily must eat thereof, and fill (their) bellies therewith.
37:62–66

1. أَذٰلِكَ خَيْرٌ نُّزُلًا اَمْ شَجَرَةُ الزَّقُّوْمِ ﴿٦٢﴾
اِنَّا جَعَلْنٰهَا فِتْنَةً لِّلظّٰلِمِيْنَ ﴿٦٣﴾
اِنَّهَا شَجَرَةٌ تَخْرُجُ فِيْٓ اَصْلِ الْجَحِيْمِ ﴿٦٤﴾
طَلْعُهَا كَاَنَّهٗ رُءُوْسُ الشَّيٰطِيْنِ ﴿٦٥﴾
فَاِنَّهُمْ لَاٰكِلُوْنَ مِنْهَا فَمَالِـُٔوْنَ
مِنْهَا الْبُطُوْنَ ﴿٦٦﴾

2. Lo! the tree of Zaquûm.
The food of the sinner!
Like molten brass, it seetheth in their bellies.
As the seething of boiling water.
44:43–46

2. اِنَّ شَجَرَتَ الزَّقُّوْمِ ﴿٤٣﴾
طَعَامُ الْاَثِيْمِ ﴿٤٤﴾
كَالْمُهْلِ ۚ يَغْلِيْ فِي الْبُطُوْنِ ﴿٤٥﴾
كَغَلْيِ الْحَمِيْمِ ﴿٤٦﴾

3. Then lo! ye, the erring, the deniers,
Ye verily will eat of a tree called Zaqqûm
And will fill your bellies therewith;
And thereon ye will drink of boiling water,
Drinking even as the camel drinketh.
This will be their welcome on the Day of Judgement.
56:51–56

3. ثُمَّ اِنَّكُمْ اَيُّهَا الضَّاۤلُّوْنَ الْمُكَذِّبُوْنَ ﴿٥١﴾
لَاٰكِلُوْنَ مِنْ شَجَرٍ مِّنْ زَقُّوْمٍ ﴿٥٢﴾
فَمَالِـُٔوْنَ مِنْهَا الْبُطُوْنَ ﴿٥٣﴾
فَشٰرِبُوْنَ عَلَيْهِ مِنَ الْحَمِيْمِ ﴿٥٤﴾
فَشٰرِبُوْنَ شُرْبَ الْهِيْمِ ﴿٥٥﴾
هٰذَا نُزُلُهُمْ يَوْمَ الدِّيْنِ ﴿٥٦﴾

ZIHAR

1. Such of you as put away your wives (by saying they are as their mothers)—They are not their mothers; none are their mothers except those who gave them birth—they indeed utter an ill word and a lie. And lo! Allah is Forgiving, Merciful.

Those who put away their wives (by saying they are as their mothers) and afterward would go back on that which they have said, (the penalty) in that case (is) the freeing of a slave before they touch one another. Unto this ye are exhorted; and Allah is Informed of what ye do.

And he who findeth not (the wherewithal), let him fast for two successive months before they touch one another; and for him who is unable to do so (the penance is) the feeding of sixty needy ones. This, that ye may put trust in Allah and His messenger. Such are the limits (imposed by Allah); and for disbelievers is a painful doom.

58:2–4

1. الَّذِينَ يُظَٰهِرُونَ مِنكُم مِّن نِّسَآئِهِم
مَّا هُنَّ أُمَّهَٰتِهِمْ ۖ إِنْ أُمَّهَٰتُهُمْ إِلَّا الَّٰٓـِٔي
وَلَدْنَهُمْ ۚ وَإِنَّهُمْ لَيَقُولُونَ مُنكَرًا
مِّنَ الْقَوْلِ وَزُورًا ۚ وَإِنَّ اللَّهَ
لَعَفُوٌّ غَفُورٌ ﴿٢﴾
وَالَّذِينَ يُظَٰهِرُونَ مِن نِّسَآئِهِمْ ثُمَّ
يَعُودُونَ لِمَا قَالُوا فَتَحْرِيرُ رَقَبَةٍ
مِّن قَبْلِ أَن يَتَمَآسَّا ۚ ذَٰلِكُمْ تُوعَظُونَ
بِهِۦ ۚ وَاللَّهُ بِمَا تَعْمَلُونَ خَبِيرٌ ﴿٣﴾
فَمَن لَّمْ يَجِدْ فَصِيَامُ شَهْرَيْنِ
مُتَتَابِعَيْنِ مِن قَبْلِ أَن يَتَمَآسَّا ۖ
فَمَن لَّمْ يَسْتَطِعْ فَإِطْعَامُ سِتِّينَ
مِسْكِينًا ۚ ذَٰلِكَ لِتُؤْمِنُوا بِاللَّهِ وَ
رَسُولِهِۦ ۚ وَتِلْكَ حُدُودُ اللَّهِ ۗ وَ
لِلْكَٰفِرِينَ عَذَابٌ أَلِيمٌ ﴿٤﴾

O

Ref: 33:4

ZODICAL SIGNS

1. And verily in the heaven We have set mansions of the stars, and We have beautified it for beholders.
15:16

2. Blessed be He Who hath placed in the heaven mansions of the stars, and hath placed therein a great lamp and a moon giving light!
25:61

3. By the heaven, holding mansions of the stars,
85:1

1. وَلَقَدْ جَعَلْنَا فِي السَّمَاءِ بُرُوجًا وَ
زَيَّنّٰهَا لِلنّٰظِرِيْنَ ﴿١٦﴾

2. تَبٰرَكَ الَّذِيْ جَعَلَ فِي السَّمَآءِ بُرُوْجًا
وَّجَعَلَ فِيْهَا سِرٰجًا وَّقَمَرًا مُّنِيْرًا ﴿٦١﴾

3. وَالسَّمَآءِ ذَاتِ الْبُرُوْجِ ﴿١﴾

See also: Astronomy.

S.No. of Surah	Arabic Name of Surah	English Name as Translated by Muhammad Marmaduke Pickthall	English Name as Translated by Abdullah Yousaf Ali
1.	اَلْفَاتِحَة	The Opening	The Opening Chapter
2.	اَلْبَقَرَة	The Cow	The Heifer
3.	اٰلِ عِمْرٰن	The Family of Imran	The Family of Imran
4.	اَلنِّسَآء	Women	The Women
5.	اَلْمَآئِدَة	The Table Spread	The Table Spread
6.	اَلْاَنْعَام	Cattle	Cattle
7.	اَلْاَعْرَاف	The Heights	The Heights
8.	اَلْاَنْفَال	Spoils of War	The Spoils of War
9.	اَلتَّوْبَة	Repentance	Repentance or Immunity
10.	يُوْنُس	Jonah	Jonah
11.	هُوْد	Hud	Hud
12.	يُوْسُف	Joseph	Joseph
13.	اَلرَّعْد	The Thunder	Thunder
14.	اِبْرٰهِيْم	Abraham	Abraham
15.	اَلْحِجْر	Al-Hijr	The Rocky Tract
16.	اَلنَّحْل	The Bee	The Bee
17.	بَنِيْٓ اِسْرَآءِيْل	The Children of Israel	The Children of Israel
18.	اَلْكَهْف	The Cave	The Cave
19.	مَرْيَم	Mary	Mary
20.	طٰهٰ	Ta Ha	Ta Ha
21.	اَلْاَنْبِيَاء	The Prophets	The Prophets
22.	اَلْحَجّ	The Pilgrimage	The Pilgrimage

23.	المؤمنون	The Believers	The Believers
24.	النور	Light	Light
25.	الفرقان	The Criterion	The Criterion
26.	الشعراء	The Poets	The Poets
27.	النمل	The Ant	The Ants
28.	القصص	The Story	The Narration
29.	العنكبوت	The Spider	The Spider
30.	الروم	The Romans	The Roman Empire
31.	لقمن	Luqman	Luqman (The Wise)
32.	السجدة	The Prostration	Adoration
33.	الأحزاب	The Clans	The Confederates
34.	سبا	Saba	The City of Saba
35.	فاطر	The Angels	The Originator of Creation or The Angels
36.	يس	Ya Sin	Ya-Sin
37.	الصفت	Those Who Set the Ranks	Those Ranged in Ranks
38.	ص	Sad	Sad
39.	الزمر	The Troops	The Crowds
40.	المؤمن	The Believer	The Believer
41.	حم السجدة	Fussilat	Ha-Mim Sajda
42.	الشورى	Counsel	Consultation
43.	الزخرف	Ornaments of Gold	Gold Adornments
44.	الدخان	Smoke	Smoke or Mist
45.	الجاثية	Crouching	Bowing the Knee
46.	الأحقاف	The Wind-Curved Sandhills	Winding Sand-tracts
47.	محمد	Muhammad	Muhammad

48.	اَلْفَتْح	Victory	Victory
49.	اَلْحُجُرٰت	The Private Apartments	The Inner Apartments
50.	قٓ	Qaf	Qaf
51.	اَلذّٰرِيٰت	The Winnowing Winds	The Winds that Scatter
52.	اَلطُّوْر	The Mount	The Mount
53.	اَلنَّجْم	The Star	The Star
54.	اَلْقَمَر	The Moon	The Moon
55.	اَلرَّحْمٰن	The Beneficent	Most Gracious
56.	اَلْوَاقِعَة	The Event	The Inevitable Event
57.	اَلْحَدِيْد	Iron	Iron
58.	اَلْمُجَادَلَة	She That Disputeth	The Women who Pleads
59.	اَلْحَشْر	Exile	The Gathering or Banishment
60.	اَلْمُمْتَحِنَة	She that is to be Examined	The Woman to be Examined
61.	اَلصَّفّ	The Ranks	Battle Array
62.	اَلْجُمُعَة	The Congregation	The Assembly (Friday) Prayer
63.	اَلْمُنٰفِقُوْن	The Hypocrites	The Hypocrites
64.	اَلتَّغَابُن	Mutual Disillusion	Mutual Loss and Gain
65.	اَلطَّلَاق	Divorce	Divorce
66.	اَلتَّحْرِيْم	Banning	Holding (something) to be Forbidden
67.	اَلْمُلْك	The Sovereignty	Dominion
68.	اَلْقَلَم	The Pen	The Pen
69.	اَلْحَاقَّة	The Reality	The Sure Reality

70.	اَلْمَعَارِج	The Ascending Stairways	The Ways of Ascent
71.	نُوح	Noah	Noah
72.	اَلْجِنّ	The Jinn	The Spirits
73.	اَلْمُزَّمِّل	The Enshrouded One	Folded in Garments
74.	اَلْمُدَّثِّر	The Cloaked One	One Wrapped Up
75.	اَلْقِيٰمَة	The Rising of the Dead	The Resurrection
76.	اَلدَّهْر	Time or Man	Time or Man
77.	اَلْمُرْسَلٰت	The Emissaries	Those Sent Forth
78.	اَلنَّبَا	The Tidings	The (Great) News
79.	اَلنّٰزِعٰت	Those Who Drag Forth	Those Who Tear Out
80.	عَبَسَ	He Frowned	He Frowned
81.	اَلتَّكْوِير	The Overthrowing	The Folding Up
82.	اَلْاِنْفِطَار	The Cleaning	The Cleaving Asunder
83.	اَلْمُطَفِّفِين	Defrauding	Dealing in Fraud
84.	اَلْاِنْشِقَاق	The Sundering	The Rending Asunder
85.	اَلْبُرُوج	The Mansions of the Stars	The Zodiacal Signs
86.	اَلطَّارِق	The Morning Star	The Night-Visitant
87.	اَلْاَعْلٰى	The Most High	The Most High
88.	اَلْغَاشِيَة	The Overwhelming	The Overwhelming Event
89.	اَلْفَجْر	The Dawn	The Break of Day
90.	اَلْبَلَد	The City	The City
91.	اَلشَّمْس	The Sun	The Sun
92.	اَللَّيْل	The Night	The Night

93.	اَلضُّحٰى	The Morning Hours	The Glorious Morning Light
94.	اَلْاِنْشِرَاح	Solace	The Expansion
95.	اَلتِّيْن	The Fig	The Fig
96.	اَلْعَلَق	The Clot	Read or Proclaim
97.	اَلْقَدْر	Power	The Night of Power (or Honour)
98.	اَلْبَيِّنَة	The Clear Proof	The Clear Evidence
99.	اَلزِّلْزَال	The Earthquake	The Convulsion
100.	اَلْعٰدِيٰت	The Coursers	Those that Run
101.	اَلْقَارِعَة	The Clamity	The Day of Noise and Clamour
102.	اَلتَّكَاثُر	Rivalry in Worldly Increase	Piling up
103.	اَلْعَصْر	The Declining Day	Time through the Ages
104.	اَلْهُمَزَة	The Traducer	The Scandal-monger
105.	اَلْفِيل	The Elephant	The Elephant
106.	قُرَيْش	Winter or Qureysh	The Quraish
107.	اَلْمَاعُوْن	Small Kindnesses	Neighbourly Needs
108.	اَلْكَوْثَر	Abundance	Abundance
109.	اَلْكٰفِرُوْن	The Disbelievers	Those who reject Faith
110.	اَلنَّصْر	Succour	Help
111.	اَللَّهَب	Palm Fibre	The (Father of) Flame
112.	اَلْاِخْلَاص	The Unity	Purity (of Faith)
113.	اَلْفَلَق	The Daybreak	The Dawn
114.	اَلنَّاس	Mankind	Mankind

سرٹیفکیٹ

مضامینِ قرآنِ حکیم میں درج جملہ قرآنی آیات کو میں نے حرف بہ حرف پورے غور و خوض اور نظرِ عمیق سے دیکھا ہے اور میں تصدیق کرتا ہوں کہ اِن میں کتابت، اعراب، صحتِ لفظی اور خوشخطی کو باحسن طریق ملحوظ رکھا گیا ہے۔ اور تمام آیاتِ کریمہ ہر قسم کی اغلاط سے مبرّا ہیں۔

فجزاھم اللہ احسن الجزاء

محمد یونس

حافظ محمد یونس
سینئر پروف ریڈر۔ حکومتِ پاکستان
خطیب جامع مسجد الفرقان۔ سٹلائٹ ٹاؤن۔ راولپنڈی